SOCIOLOGY

TEXAS

SOCIOLOGY

Richard Cheever Wallace
University of Michigan
Wendy Drew Wallace
Spring Arbor College

SECOND EDITION

ALLYN and BACON
BOSTON · LONDON · SYDNEY · TORONTO

Library of Congress Cataloging-in-Publication Data

Wallace, Richard Cheever, 1945–
Sociology.

Bibliography: p.
Includes index.
1. Sociology. I. Wallace, Wendy Drew, 1945–
II. Title.
HM51.W145 1989 301 88-24933
ISBN 0-205-11746-5

Printed in the United States of America

10 9 8 7 6 5 4 3 2 1 93 92 91 90 89

Photo Credits: p. ii (left)—The Michigan Daily; (top right)—AP/Wide World Photos; (middle right)—Jeffry W. Myers/FPG International; (bottom right)—UPI/Bettmann Newsphotos; p. iii—the author; p. v—the author; p. vi—Esther A. Gerling/FPG International; p. vii—David S. Strickler/The Picture Cube; p. viii—the author; p. ix—the author; p. x—the author; p. xi—the author; p. xii—AP/Wide World Photos; p. xiii—the author; p. xiv—the author; p. xv—the author; p. xvi—the author; p. xvii—the author; p. xviii—the author; p. xix—the author; p. xxi—the author; p. xxii—the author. All text photos are credited in the captions.

CONTENTS

PART
2 SOCIAL PATTERNS 29

CHAPTER 2
CULTURE 30

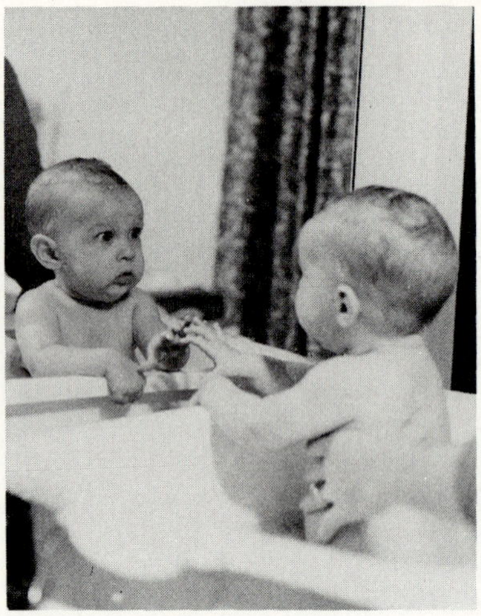

CHAPTER 5 GROUPS AND ORGANIZATIONS 104

CHAPTER 6
DEVIANCE AND SOCIAL CONTROL 132

CHAPTER 7 COLLECTIVE BEHAVIOR AND SOCIAL MOVEMENTS 162

CHAPTER 10

CHAPTER 11
GENDER ROLE INEQUALITIES 278

PART 5 SOCIAL INSTITUTIONS 301

CHAPTER 12 AGING IN INDUSTRIAL SOCIETY 301

CHAPTER *13*
MARRIAGE AND THE FAMILY

CHAPTER 14 RELIGION

CHAPTER 15

WORK AND THE ECONOMY 390

CHAPTER 17 EDUCATION 458

CHAPTER 18 POPULATION AND THE ENVIRONMENT 486

CHAPTER 19 SOCIAL CHANGE: URBANIZATION AND MODERNIZATION 520

PREFACE

In this, the second edition of **Sociology,** you will find the same qualities and features that readers admired in the first edition, as well as new subjects, new theories, new findings, and new features.

The book is designed for both learning and enjoyment. We draw vivid examples relevant to today's reader, leave out jargon, introduce technical terms only where they serve a purpose, and demonstrate the significance of the questions we raise to our social lives. We have included relevant materials, organized them logically, and discussed them clearly. But we want to go further than this: we want to arouse curiosity about social behavior. Toward this goal, we ask many questions in the text, some of which are answered and some of which are left to future researchers and theorists to answer.

Special Features of the Text

Our book has several unique features that work toward the goal of enjoyable education. **How's Your Sociological Intuition?** appears at the beginning of each chapter. It arouses interest, previews some of the issues of the chapter, and demonstrates that sociology is much more than just common sense. **When You Have Finished Studying This Chapter, You Should Know** then previews the major goals of each chapter and introduces the concepts to the students.

Close-Ups on Research and **Theory** introduce specific works of well-known sociologists and give the reader a closer view of original theory and research than normally found in an introductory text. The scholarly works are carefully edited to allow the reader to learn a significant theory or major research finding in each chapter. These Close-Ups are selected from the best works in sociology, some contemporary and some classics, and from all orientations.

The **Close-Up on Theory** first presents the theorist's personal and professional background and the setting for the work. The issue addressed is usually stated in the theorist's words, as are most concepts and propositions. We discuss the central ideas and the implications of the theory, and suggest questions that evaluate, apply, or extend the theory within the reader's own experience.

The format of the **Close-Up on Research** differs to reflect a research orientation. Again we often quote the researchers regarding their purpose, hypotheses, and methodology, and discuss the approach and its implications. The reader thus learns, through example and in some detail, how sociologists test and develop theories.

The **Close-Ups** offer a unique opportunity for introductory students to encounter primary research and theory at a level they can understand and in a way that facilitates the building of sociological skills. They are intended to make sociology real and exciting by showing how sociologists actually approach important sociological issues in **each** chapter of the book **as well as** in the separate research and theory sections of Chapter 1.

In order to give the reader an even clearer image of the work sociologists are presently doing, we introduce a new and unique feature: **Sociologists at Work.** Each chapter includes an interview in which a contemporary sociologist talks about his or her current work. This feature highlights the cutting edge of the discipline by reporting—in the sociologists' own words—on work that is often yet to appear in print!

Readability. The book is clear and interesting. Our examples, while often dramatic, are always memorable and stay close to the common experience so that readers will appreciate the relevance of the theory and research that carries them beyond a commonsense level of understanding of their social lives.

Substance. We deliver an exceptional amount of real sociology, especially theory and research, through the unique Close-Up on Theory and Close-Up on Research features.

Integrated Text and Supplements. To accompany the main text, we have **ourselves** written the *Study Guide, Instructor's Manual,* and *Test Items.* The *Study Guide* contains supplementary material, practice exercises, and practice tests. A major feature of the *Study Guide* is the Review Map, which visually portrays for the student the major questions, key theories, and key research studies presented to address the questions. This visual outline is a unique, highly effective method to grasp the core material.

Our *Instructor's Manual* is designed to aid our colleagues in adapting this text to their individual course. In it, we have drawn upon our accumulated years of teaching introductory sociology to present lecture outlines, demonstration ideas, and vivid examples that should help instructors make the subject come alive in their classrooms. We both enjoy teaching, and we transmit our enthusiasm for both the subject and the students through this *Manual.*

Our *Test Items* contains over 2,000 questions, nearly a thousand of which are totally new. Questions retained from the earlier edition have been re-designed and revised to match the modifications introduced in the new edition. Each test item has been referenced to the appropriate passage in this new edition.

SQ3R: A Time Tested Learning Technique

About forty years ago, a teacher named Francis Robinson designed a study system to help his students remember what they read. He titled it SQ3R, for the five basic steps in the study: Survey, Question, Read, Recite, and Review.

Robinson's research showed that students remembered better if they skimmed over and summarized the headings of the assignment and read the final or summary paragraphs before they read the text itself. This he termed Surveying.

The second step, Questioning, consists of changing all the major points or headings into questions in order to provide an orientation to the material. These questions become guides to what is important to watch for while reading. Next, Reading should be done to find the appropriate material with which to answer the questions posed by the reader.

Robinson's students remembered much better when they used these three steps, but they still forgot about 80 percent of the material within two weeks. After experimenting with techniques to expand their retention, he added Recite and Review. When these steps were added, they forgot only 20 percent of the material after two weeks.

Recitation is used after an answer to a question has been found. The students should recite the answer *aloud,* fixing it both orally and with their eyes for greater learning.

For best results, Reviewing should occur immediately after a reading assignment is finished. Within the next 24 hours, a second review should occur, and within 48 hours, a third. If a student knows he or she has memory difficulties, the reviews of previously learned material should continue throughout the semester.

Both this text and the *Student's Guide* have been designed to aid students in using the SQ3R method of study. In the text, Chapter Openers highlight the major questions we address. Section Headings echo these questions to facilitate reading and understanding. Study Questions at the end of each chapter help the student recite and review the material. In the *Student Guide* additional aids help to ensure that the student will master and retain the subject matter.

Robinson's SQ3R system has withstood the test of time by being useful to many students. We are confident that our readers will find it useful in the study of sociology.

New in the Second Edition

We have added much new and valuable material including new topics, up-to-the-minute research findings, recent theories, and a unique feature that appears in each chapter.

New Topics. We have added **two totally new chapters** in areas of growing interest to students and professionals: **Aging in Industrial Society** (Chapter 12) and **Work and the Economy** (Chapter 15). We have also introduced discussions of recent social developments including teen suicide imitation, America in an age of decline, mass murder, AIDS as hysteria, contemporary Marxism, social class and stress, homeless Americans, elder abuse, children of alcoholics, new religious movements, democracy in the workplace, sexism in the classroom, and public reaction to nuclear power.

Recent Research Developments and New Theories. The past four years have produced much good and relevant research and theory in sociology. We have reviewed the literature and updated our text with over 600 new citations.

Unique Feature: Sociologists at Work. Each chapter contains a **Sociologist at Work** feature in which a contemporary sociologist discusses their current work in interviews with the authors.

We are enthusiastic about the total learning package we have produced, using the suggestions and enthusiasm of our colleagues who reviewed the project at various stages. We can expect much social change in our lifetime. Our ability to survive and thrive in this rapidly changing scene depends largely on our ability to understand these changing social patterns, which we shape and which shape us. We are not just individuals: we are part of a family, a team, an ethnic group, a religion, a society. Not only are we affected by these groups, but also we affect them. We hope this text serves you well in this endeavor, and we welcome your reactions to it.

Acknowledgments

Certainly, without the support, guidance, and love of many people, we never would have finished this book. The advice of the many conscientious teachers who reviewed our manuscript was invaluable to the entire process. We want to specially thank the following people:

Steven Stack, Auburn University; William Finlay, University of Iowa; Charles Harper, Creighton University; Barbara Stenross, The University of North Carolina at Chapel Hill; Paul Schervish, Boston College; Gary Kiger, Utah State University; Leonard Beeghley, University of Florida; Steven Green, North Adams State College; Jeanne S. Hurlbert, Louisiana State University; David Ward, Washington State University; Nancy Hooyman, University of Washington; Terry Rodenberg, Central Missouri State; Steven Ciafullo, Central Missouri State; Steven Ainley, Holy Cross College; Claire Renzetti, St. Joseph's University.

Series editor Karen Hanson and developmental editor Alicia Reilly gave generously of their time and made many valuable suggestions for this second edition. We are also indebted to editors Al Levitt and Allen Workman, who contributed greatly to the project in the first edition.

We would also like to thank some of our friends, family, and colleagues: Carey Wallace, Mark Wallace, W. Donald Wallace, Esther Wallace, Jean Drew, Richard E. Drew, Marilyn Grasse-Brubaker, Clifford Brubaker, JoAnn and Larry Whiting, Robert J. Ackerman, Wendell Bell, Albert J. Reiss, Jr., Jerome K. Myers, Marvin Harris, Alfred McClung Lee, Elizabeth Briant Lee, Carl F. H. Henry, O. Wayne Rollins, Lucy Bredeson-Smith, Kathy Cromer, Brenda Franklin, Jennifer White, Susan Fitton, Laura Harrell, Stephen Colditz, Marianna Sklikas, Jim Ridenour, Doris Ridenour, Sharon Prescott, Larry Prescott, John Andrews, Jr., Susan Shapiro, Melvin Boozer, Mark Wasylyshyn, Kenneth R. Tucci, Joseph L. Jensen, Ethel Jensen, Daisy Newman, Herbert Joachim Schmidt, Debra Slee, and the staff at the Barry College Library, Hillsdale College Library, and the Yale University Library.

PART 1

The Sociological Approach

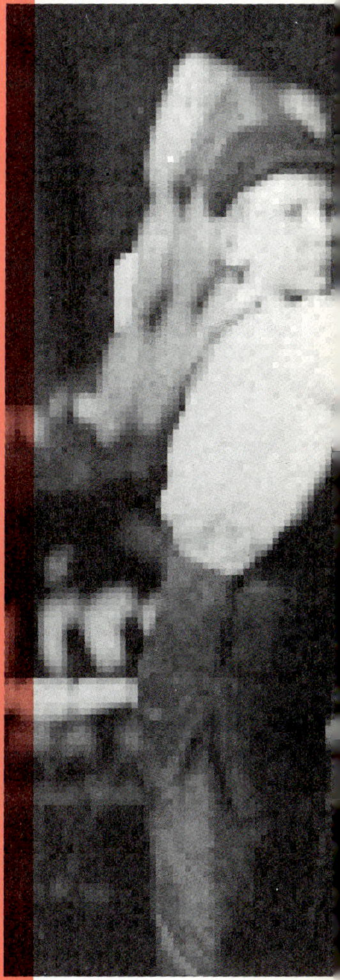

CHAPTER 1

SOCIOLOGY: ORIGINS, PERSPECTIVES, and TECHNIQUES

- How Is Sociology a Discipline with a Special Approach?
- How Did Sociology Develop?
- What Are the Three Major Theoretical Perspectives?
- How Is Sociological Theory Constructed?
- Close-Up on Theory: Max Weber on Protestantism as a Cause of Capitalism
- What Are the Basic Tenets of Sociological Research?
- Close-Up on Research: Emile Durkheim on Suicide and Society
- Sociologists at Work: Reece McGee Discusses Sociology's Benefits for Today's Student

How's Your Sociological Intuition?

1. Which of these topics do sociologists address?

a. Why people commit suicide
b. The effects of peer pressure on a person's judgment
c. The origins of capitalism
d. All of the above

2. The factor found to be most strongly linked to the success of social protest movements in the U.S. was whether the movement:

a. used violence or not
b. had a single goal rather than several
c. was bureaucratically organized
d. had a centralized power structure

3. What do you think most professional sociologists do most often?

a. Pure research in universities and research institutions
b. Applied sociology for government and industry
c. Teaching at universities and colleges
d. Social work

4. How do sociologists test their theories about social behavior?

a. Through public opinion surveys
b. Through experiments
c. By analyzing existing documents
d. All of the above ways

Answers

1. d. In this chapter we encounter discussion of all three topics, and we learn that whereas sociology encompasses a vast range of behavior, it approaches the topics from a special sociological perspective.
2. b. As we see later in the chapter, sociology as an organized discipline is a recent historical development.
3. c. Sociologists engage in many activities including research and applied sociology, but their most common activity is teaching in colleges and universities.
4. d. Sociologists test their theories in all these ways. As we see later in this chapter, they also make direct observations of human behavior in everyday settings as a way to test theories and get ideas for new theories.

WHEN YOU HAVE FINISHED STUDYING THIS CHAPTER, YOU SHOULD KNOW:

- The varieties of activities sociologists engage in
- The sorts of questions sociologists address
- What is special about the way sociologists approach topics
- What theories, concepts, and propositions are and how they are used
- How sociologists test their theories with observations
- The history of the development of sociology
- The places of Comte, Spencer, Marx, Weber, and Durkheim in the development of sociology
- The contributions of Parsons, Coser, Mills, Collins, Wright, Mead, Cooley, and Goffman to the development of these theories
- The basic concepts of structural-functionalism, the conflict approach, and symbolic interactionism
- What the scientific method is and how it can be applied to the study of sociology
- The advantages and disadvantages of the survey method, document study, observational study, and experimental research in the study of sociology
- The uses and limits of sociology
- What the ethical issues in the study of sociology are

"Peter, you want a ride to the party at Talbot's?"

"Sure," Peter agrees, figuring once there he won't have to spend much time with Harry, or with Tom, the front-seat passenger.

Peter has not met Michelle and Lois until they also climb into the back seat of Harry's five-year-old Cutlass. As Harry crosses the double yellow line to pass a stationwagon, Peter wonders whether Harry's bad driving is because he's been drinking or because he is merely a bad driver. At any rate Peter is glad they're now only four blocks from the party.

A familiar aroma fills the car as Harry exhales loudly and says:

"What d'ya say we take a short ride in the country?"

Tom takes the joint from Harry. "OK by me!"

Peter looks at Michelle who rolls her eyes in resignation.

"Why not?"

Peter is annoyed. He wants to get to the party, but he keeps still.

The back roads dip and wind through rolling hills. Finding a straightaway, Harry steps down on the accelerator, Peter turns toward Lois. She's pretty, and even more so as she smiles when their eyes meet.

Suddenly they both lurch forward as Harry hits the brakes and downshifts. The car skids sideways into a sharp left curve, leaves the pavement, and violently rolls over twice before landing upright.

Peter's face hurts as though it's been hit by a giant fist. He feels his nose and lips bleeding. He can't breathe, but he recognizes from having played football that he's just had the breath knocked out of him. To his left Michelle cries aloud. Lois' head rests in his lap. He senses immediately that she's dead. Outside someone is trying to get the doors open, but Peter and his companions are trapped inside for half an hour until a wrecker arrives to pry them loose.

How Is Sociology a Discipline with a Special Approach?

POWERFUL INVISIBLE FORCES

To what extent are people the pawns of groups, and how much of our social behavior is rooted in our genetic makeup? How do groups pressure individuals to go against their best judgment? Do groups or individuals make more responsible decisions? In this book we explore all these questions and more, using the theories and methods of sociology. ***Sociology** is the science that studies society and human behavior.*

Peter is trapped in the car by obvious physical forces, but even before the wreck he was caught in a social trap constructed of powerful but invisible social forces. Perhaps because it is unflattering to think of ourselves as socially manipulated, we often, in our common sensible thought, ignore, deny, or underestimate the extent to which we are moved by social forces. Had we asked Peter or Lois if they were "trapped" in the car before the wreck, they would almost certainly deny it. Who can be trapped by an innocent "Anyone mind if we go for a ride in the country?" Yet neither disagreed or said "Why not?" Both Peter and Lois, in fact, got into the car to go to a party, not to smoke pot or be in a wreck, and had they pried themselves loose from the social forces ensnaring them they would never have encountered the physical forces that broke Lois' neck. In this case, the social forces involved peer pressure to conform to the politeness norms of society and play the role of polite guest in the car by not complaining to the host-driver.

Laboratory experiments demonstrate that people readily violate their own best judgment, either through the urging of an authority figure or under the influence

Bravado has a strange way of showing up when groups are watching. Would there be as much incentive for a stunt like this if the other boys were not watching? Sociologists study how groups influence our behavior. (*Photo courtesy the author*)

of peer pressure. After such an experiment the subject frequently denies or underestimates the influence of the authority figure, as though the subject is unaware of the social forces deliberately unleashed upon him or her by the experimenter. The metal structure of the car within which Peter and the others were trapped is directly observable and undeniable. The social structure that trapped Peter and Lois is equally as powerful in its consequences, yet dangerous and interesting because it is harder to observe and easier to deny.

One of the great challenges in solving social riddles is that quite often the subject matter is literally invisible. No one directly observes or "sees" group pressures authority, prestige, or a society. We *can* observe their consequences. We must, then, form images of these concepts through what C. Wright Mills has called a "sociological imagination." Mills (1959) describes a social scene of broader scope, but the message is the same:

> When wars happen, an insurance salesman becomes a rocket launcher; a store clerk, a radar man; a wife lives alone; a child grows up without a father. Neither the life of an individual nor the history of a society can be understood without understanding both.
>
> The sociological imagination enables its possessor to understand the larger scene in terms of its meaning for the inner life and the external career of a variety of individuals.
>
> The key to the sociological imagination is the ability to see how the sweep of history relates to individual lives at one point in time. The science of sociology, at its best, can make this connection and give us not only a knowledge of society but also a greater understanding of ourselves (pp. 3–5).

The sociological approach takes into account that a person's social environment influences the way that person views the world. Sociologists try to suspend this influence and to view their own and other societies as an outsider might. In doing this they become more aware that social forces influence personal experiences and interpretations, and they begin to understand just how this process works.

The study of sociology leads to a better understanding of the way groups interact. Understanding social structure may help people avoid and solve social problems and to fulfill opportunities in their social lives. Sociology may also be useful at the personal level, because much human social behavior takes place in relatively intimate, face-to-face settings where sociological understanding of social dynamics can be applied to an advantage.

FOCUS ON SOCIAL PATTERNS

Where do societal rules come from, and how do they work? Which types of social arrangements make people happiest, and which arrangements are most productive and enduring?

In general terms sociologists want to understand *what goes on in and between groups of people.* How is conflict acted out when one group in a society gains most of the power and wealth?

Sociologists also study important *social differences* such as those between rich and poor, young and old, and males and females. What can magazine advertisements tell us about how women are treated in American society? How probable is it that someone from a poor background will accomplish the American Dream?

Sociologists study the large complex *social institutions:* the family, religion, education, government, and the economy. How does the educational institution perpetuate the stratification system and work against change? What is the future for the American family?

Finally, sociologists apply their knowledge in these areas to the topic of *social change*. What are the basic population trends in the United States? What does rapid urbanization mean to society as a whole?

Sociologists are keenly aware of the impact our social world has on us. This is the basis for their interest in these social patterns.

PREFERENCE FOR SOCIAL EXPLANATIONS

Sociologists have a strong preference for finding social explanations to questions about social behavior. This stems from a fundamental belief that social groups—such as societies, corporations, schools, and families—have a reality of their own kind, which is not the simple product of individual characteristics. In other words, just as the human body cannot be understood by considering only the individual cells that compose it, most sociologists believe that groups cannot be understood by looking only at the individual people who compose them.

This belief can be traced to Emile Durkheim's classic work, *The Rules of the Sociological Method* (1895). Durkheim (1858–1917) called group characteristics—such as cohesiveness, rigidity, homicide rates, and suicide rates—"social facts." He implored sociologists always to "explain a social fact with a social fact. (p. 45)"

Durkheim believed people have a tendency to ignore social circumstances and to attribute behavior to innate individual traits or to free will. He thought that sociologists should overcome this tendency and explain social behavior with social theories. For example, people often explain a suicide with statements like "Oscar was crazy from the day I met him" or "Sheila decided life was not worth living, so she jumped off the Bay Bridge." In contrast, Durkheim studied suicide rates of populations as social facts. He found that social factors do influence suicide rates. (We feature Durkheim's research on suicide as a "Close-Up on Research" later in this chapter.)

Most sociologists still strive to explain a social fact with a social fact. By this we do not mean that we consider human beings to be pawns of their culture. Rather, when we seek to explain the rising crime rate, we generally are not content with an explanation that a rise in crime is due to an increased number of "criminal personalities." Instead, we seek to discover the social factors that bring about crime, such as increasing disparity between the social resources of the poor and the rich.

When sociologists discuss the rising divorce rate, we are not satisfied with a theory that suggests there is more divorce because more people lack the desire to make marriages work. Rather, we look for social conditions that make marriages break apart, such as changes in divorce laws or increased economic independence for women. Similarly, in considering civil disorders the sociologists might look at the process of the power base labeling as "deviant" those whose opinions are not mainstream.

In other words, human behavior is not determined solely by social factors. One of the major insights to be gained from the study of sociology is that many social circumstances can be different if individuals in a society choose to make them different. As George Bernard Shaw suggested, Some men see things as they are and say "Why?" while others see things as they have never been and say "Why not?"

THE CHALLENGE AND ETHICAL BASE OF SOCIOLOGY

In many ways sociology presents a unique set of challenges. One challenge is that our subjects have human rights, including the rights to life, freedom, privacy, dignity, private property, and physical and emotional well-being. These rights limit what we as social scientists can do with our subjects. We cannot peer in on our subjects at will, neither can we subject them to studies that might harm them. Because social scientists have occasionally performed research later viewed as harmful, most research conducted today on human subjects must first be reviewed by committees, and potentially harmful research is usually prohibited regardless of how valuable might be the knowledge gained. Ethical standards for research are set and enforced by various governmental agencies, universities, and the American Sociological Association, the major professional organization of sociologists.

Laud Humphreys' research on homosexuals, as reported in *The Tearoom Trade* (1970, 1975), aroused controversy which raised concerns over rights of human subjects. Humphreys posed as a lookout, alerting homosexuals of approaching police or juveniles at a public bathroom, or "tearoom". When the homosexuals left, he recorded their license plate numbers. Over a year later, he used this information to find the participants and to enter their homes, asking for survey research data. In this way, he was able to fairly accurately describe the social characteristics of those who participate in impersonal homosexual activity.

Humphreys' work was praised for its thoroughness at the same time that his methods were severely criticized. By keeping the records that he did, he put his subjects in danger of being discovered and criticized by the community or even arrested. By deceiving his subjects twice as to his real identity, he encouraged a jaundiced view of social science research in general. In the second edition of his book, Humphreys admitted that his methods were indeed faulty and that he should have identified himself honestly when he entered the homes of his subjects.

The Tearoom Trade typifies the many ethical issues raised by sociological research. Sociologists must constantly trade off their interest in knowing about social phenomenon with their subjects' rights to privacy and dignity and with the truth. Although official standards have been written, many cases require that individual researchers make ethical decisions themselves.

Another challenge to those involved in the social sciences is dealing with subjects who can tell us about themselves and their world. This is a blessing and a curse. Our subjects can give us important information, but they are fallible. They may distort information to please us, to place themselves in a favorable light, or because they inaccurately remember the past. We need to consider carefully when we can rely on reports from our subjects.

A major theme of this text is that human beings and their world are remarkably flexible. Each group and individual is unique, and human beings have great freedom to determine and alter their own behaviors. As we progress through this text we encounter some important and distinct patterns in our social lives, but we do not encounter hard-and-fast laws of human social behavior. Human social behavior is shaped by social structure, but it is not determined by it.

How Did Sociology Develop?

The rise of sociology can be traced to the social, political, and intellectual upheaval surrounding the Industrial Revolution of the nineteenth century. The political and social world was in a state of flux. Previously ensconced in the estate system, societies were beginning to emphasize indiviudal human rights and the idea of freedom. The motto of the French Revolution, "Liberty, Fraternity, and Equality," gained preeminence far beyond the borders of its own nation.

Technology was burgeoning and beginning to create the Industrial Revolution. The growth of industry brought about concentrations of people in cities, and for the first time significant numbers depended on something other than agriculture for their living. The massing together of people in cities and the adjustments that they had to make in leaving agriculture for industry created tremendous social changes.

Scientific through was just beginning to develop from its roots in metaphysics and theology. The fact that science was being applied to the physical world naturally spawned the idea that its particular strengths might be focused on the social world as well.

FROM THREE ROOTS TO THREE BRANCHES

Out of this nineteenth-century chaos came some of the most brilliant social thinkers of any generation. Three branches of sociology began to grow from roots in three interest groups: social activities; a new breed of scientists dedicated to applying the scientific approach to society; and philosophers interested in humanity's social nature.

FROM INTELLECTUAL ACTIVISM TO THE CONFLICT APPROACH. Intellectual activists, concerned with the dramatic and rapid social changes taking place in nineteenth century Europe and seeking a means to a better society, established what has come to be known as the ***conflict perspective,*** *which stresses social inequality and conflict between the dominant group and the masses.* The conflict approach was developed in an effort to understand and control the course of social change in Europe during the mid 1800s—as we have just described, a time of great institutional and political turmoil.

We banned child labor like this during the industrial revolution. Besides changing how we worked, the industrial revolution altered our thinking about what should and should not be allowed to happen in society. (*Lewis Hine/ The Bettmann Archive*)

Karl Marx (1818–1883) was the first major proponent of the conflict perspective. Marx believed people are basically good and resort to evil measures only when they lack one of the essentials of life: food, shelter, or nurturing (Marx, 1867). Marx suggested that inequality between social classes—providing scarcity for some and plenty for others—causes conflict between groups of people. Whereas many disadvantaged accept their inferior position, some appraise the situation and attempt to achieve balance by taking from those who have plenty. Marx believed that society must change in order to fulfill the needs of all people (Marx, 1848). Marx studied society in order to develop a further understanding of it, which could then be used to change it. With Friederich Engels, he authored *The Communist Manifesto* (1848), the seminal work of communism.

Near the middle of the twentieth century, **C. Wright Mills,** a professor of sociology at Columbia University, effectively promoted a general conflict perspective. Whereas Marx had founded a political theory of conflict, Mills focused on social class differences and introduced the concept of the *power elite,* a tiny minority of government, military, and business figures believed to control the United States (Mills, 1956).

The number of sociologists favoring the conflict perspective has risen considerably since Mills' death in the late 1950s. For example, **Randall Collins** has developed a formal theory of conflict applicable to all levels of society. He has also analyzed the American educational system, showing that it tends to promote the interests of the wealthy over those less well off.

The conflict perspective is especially suited to the study of social class. For instance, the work of **Erik Olin Wright** discusses working conditions as influenced by a worker's social relations. One interesting observation that Wright makes is that some blue-collar workers—for instance, self-employed carpenters—actually have greater control over when and where they work than white-collar workers, who are tied to an office schedule.

Contemporary conflict theory uses Marxist thought as a base from which to build but expands from it. Though today's conflict theorists value Marx's insights and seek to analyze social life from this general perspective, few accept the necessity of violent revolution for social progress (Wright and Martin, 1987; Wright 1984, Wright 1983).

FROM SCIENTIFIC REVOLUTION TO STRUCTURAL FUNCTIONALISM. The scientific revolution of the late nineteenth century propelled early sociologists toward the development of a second perspective: structural-functionalism. The ***structural-functional perspective*** *views social patterns as serving to stabilize and maintain groups and their members.* The scientific, or positivistic, approach held that sociologists could study society scientifically, using the same methods that chemists and biologists use to study the elements and life. The idea was first promoted (1915) by **Auguste Comte** (1798–1857), the French scholar who gave sociology its name. Others, including **Herbert Spencer** (1820–1903), developed the idea that society was an organic whole that could be studied much like the human body (Spencer, 1898). They held that the structures of society, such as the family, the state, and the economy, served special functions and evolved through interaction between the society and its environment.

Emile Durkheim, the French sociologist we mentioned before, promoted sociology as a science and structural-functionalism as a perspective. Durkheim believed social groups have a reality of their own, and his study of suicide rates (1897) holds the distinction of being the first scientific study of human social behavior. Durkheim also believed that social structures arise to fill functions for society and its members—for instance, that one of religion's major functions was to help hold society together.

Talcott Parsons (1902–1979), longtime chairman of sociology at Harvard, continued Durkheim's tradition into the twentieth century. Parsons was interested in studying the sets of rules and norms by which a society is governed. His book, *The Structure of Social Action* (1931), introduced the variant of the perspective known as structural-functionalism. Parsons developed the idea that society could be viewed as a system, which would naturally conform to certain imperatives. Simply stated, the social system must (1) adapt to changes in its environment, (2) pursue its goals, (3) integrate itself with other systems, and (4) maintain order within itself. Parsons held that the human personality, the human biological organism, and the culture could also be viewed as systems. He believed that the cultural system governs the social system, that the social system in turn governs the personality system, and that the personality system governs the biological system. All these systems can be analyzed as having functional structures.

Kingsley Davis, one of Parsons' students and a major contemporary proponent of the structural-functionalist perspective, analyzes wealth and poverty from this viewpoint. We explore his thought further in the chapters on stratification and mobility and social class in the United States. Davis is an internationally recognized expert on population, and we consider his explanation of worldwide urbanization in the chapter on urbanization and social change (Davis, 1940, 1951, 1955, 1976; Davis and Moore 1945).

FROM PHILOSOPHY TO SYMBOLIC INTERACTIONISM. Philosophers helped launch the third major perspective in sociology: symbolic interactionism. Philosopher and sociologist **George Herbert Mead** (1863–1931) focused on how we use symbols, including language, and how our use of symbols influences our social development and social life (Mead, 1934). A ***symbol*** *is a word, gesture, or sign that conveys meaning.* ***Symbolic interactionism*** *is a sociological perspective that sees symbols as central to understanding social patterns and a person's sense of self.*

Mead believed a person develops self-awareness and *personality* or *self* only by interacting with other people through symbols. Our use of symbols distinguishes us from the rest of the animal kingdom and enables a person to be aware of his or her self as distinct from the social world. This self-awareness, combined with our ability to communicate symbolically, allows us to reflect on ourselves and our social world so we can discuss and change our social arrangements.

Early in its life a child begins to recognize itself as a unique person through the use of symbols, specifically the words "I," "me," as well as the child's name. As he or she learns to speak, the child begins to master the art of interacting through symbols. Even very young children become quite adept at using these word symbols to describe others and their selves. Later, as Mead observes, they learn to take their places in society through games that rely heavily on symbols. Most grade school children can master a role like "playing second base," but this is because they have learned to reason symbolically and to place their selves in different roles. They are able to equate "me" with "second baseman" or "shortstop." As symbolic-interactionists have emphasized, not all names and roles are as neutral as "Kathy," "Stephen," or "shortstop." Children also learn to symbolically represent themselves and others in categories like "pest," "princess," or perhaps even "pervert."

In the early twentieth century **W. I. Thomas** (1863–1947) extended Mead's ideas and applied them to everyday settings (1918; 1923; 1937). Thomas theorizes that people define or construct their social reality. For example, the fact that we define alcohol as a legal intoxicant, whereas we define marijuana as an illegal one, means the difference between freedom and prison for some people. Our definitions become real because they are real in their consequences, and we thus construct our social reality. Some sociologists summarize Thomas' thought in the so-called Thomas' Theorem: He who defines a situation controls it.

In recent times **Erving Goffman** has served as a major spokesperson for the symbolic interaction perspective. Goffman's **dramaturgical approach** describes how people present themselves in everyday life in order to manage the impression they give to others. In writing about the many small dramas he observes in everyday life, Goffman suggests that people have two types of social interaction: onstage behavior, which is easily shared with the outside world, and backstage behavior, which is shared with a chosen few after developing an intimate relationship. This division applies both to actions and to the physical placement of interactions—for example, some guests are never invited past the living room, whereas others may freely roam the entire house.

Goffman also suggests that people develop a "studied nonobservance" of interactions that could be embarrassing. For example, if your companion's stomach growls during a movie, neither of you will mention it. Children learn by observation of adult behavior that they are to avoid certain topics. We look more closely at Goffman's work when we consider his analysis of team action in hospital operating rooms in the chapter on culture and his analysis of symbols in advertising in the chapter on gender and age inequality. (Goffman, 1956, 1961a, 1961b, 1963, 1966, 1967, 1977).

Each of these perspectives continues as a tradition

today, and many sociologists are more inclined toward one than the others. Often sociologists draw from two or more of the perspectives, and sometimes their work is not directly part of any one. The perspectives serve as starting points for analysis and help us to present the rich and varied field of sociology.

Each perspective makes its own assumptions about society, raises its own questions, and employs its own concepts. In the next section we summarize these perspectives.

What Are the Three Major Theoretical Perspectives?

CONFLICT THEORY

Conflict theory assumes that the dominant process in society is conflict and that society divides into two groups, the masses and a small elite who exploit them. The questions frequently raised from this perspective include: How do current social arrangements and ideas benefit the elites? How do the elites exercise their power to exploit the masses? How can the masses be aroused to overthrow a corrupt social order? Major concepts of this perspective are conflict, power, exploitation, elites, and masses.

STRUCTURAL-FUNCTIONAL THEORY

Structural-functional theory assumes that order is dominant in society and that social arrangements arise and persist because they serve society and its members well. For instance, if we consider schools from this perspective we would ask: What are their functions? That is, what do schools do to help the society and its members survive and remain stable? Our schools have several obvious functions, such as teaching important skills and passing on important values and attitudes.

We would then go on to ask: Do schools have some hidden or latent functions, such as serving as babysitters in a society where both parents often work outside the home? Are schools in some ways dysfunctional (not functional)? One answer might be that they fail the especially talented or those in need of remedial programs. Finally: Are there alternative structures, and how functional are they? Whether we consider the school or some other social structure, such as religion or politics, we will generally rely heavily on the concepts of function, dysfunction, and structure.

SYMBOLIC INTERACTION THEORY

The symbolic interaction perspective assumes that the important action in society takes place around the use of symbols. Symbols channel our thoughts and thereby define what is socially comprehensible and incomprehensible. Often practitioners of this approach focus on interaction among individuals, in contrast to the other perspectives, which tend to look more abstractly at institutional arrangements. Symbolic interactionists raise questions like: How does our use of symbols and language influence the way we interact? How do we learn to accept our roles in life and to define who we are? Specifically, symbolic interactionists consider how our use of language influences the way we react to others. For instance, how would labeling someone a "high school dropout" influence our reaction to that person and influence the way the person acts and views himself or herself? Major concepts of this perspective are symbols, social interaction, labels, role, and self.

APPLYING THE PERSPECTIVES

We can better understand these three perspectives by seeing how they explain an important feature of our society—the presence of wealth and poverty. Each of the three theoretical perspectives offers insights into the processes by which some become and remain financially better off than others. We will briefly state each perspective's position and illustrate it with the life experiences of actual people.

From the structural-functionalist approach, differences in wealth, as well as other social structures, persist because they are functional. That is, they contribute to the stability and persistence of society. Structural-functionalists suggest that having some people be well off while others are not provides incentives for people to work in ways that are socially significant. High income and wealth are viewed as rewards for doing work that is especially important and requires special training or skills.

For Mark to have a net worth of $4 million while most of his former high school classmates have managed to save less than $100,000 is seen as functional. Why? Because through his business of buying, restoring, and renting homes to low-income tenants, Mark provides a valued function to society. Mark's work provides homes for people at higher quality and lower price than they would otherwise find—work clearly important to society—and his income and wealth can be viewed as rewards in an incentive system that motivates people to do work of social value. This same principle, that society rewards significant work, also

Unstable? Sociologists study groups and their properties. They have long noted that a three-person group is inherently unstable. (*Photo courtesy the author*)

applies to Leslie, an obstetrician. Lives depend on how well she does her work. Her high income rewards her efforts, intelligence, and training. This generous income provides an incentive to others to pursue similar options. On the other hand, while Charlie's work as a junior high school band director is also significant to society, his contribution is less important and requires less talent, training, and effort than Leslie's or Mark's. Thus, his income and wealth are substantially lower than theirs.

From the structural-functionalist perspective differences in income and wealth provide important incentives for people to apply themselves in the ways that are most beneficial to society. High income is the reward for being brilliant, highly trained, or willing to take business risks that will ultimately benefit the investor and the public.

The conflict perspective explains wealth and poverty in a very different way. Those who advance this perspective point out that often people at the top and bottom do little to deserve or earn their positions—people are born into two fundamental classes, the haves and the have-nots, that struggle against each other. The smaller class of wealthy people use their power and wealth to assure their children a place at the top, and to extract labor, at unfair wages, from those below. Proponents of this perspective call our attention to people like Hugh, the son of the richest man in his state. Hugh's wealth far exceeds that of Mark, the real estate investor. In fact, Hugh's father has deposited sums to Hugh's two-year-old son's trust fund that already exceed the common person's lifetime earnings! Hugh exemplifies what conflict theorists would call a member of the ruling or upper class. From the time he was born he was given the experiences and resources to follow his father as a major owner of industry. Hugh lived in a mansion, ate the finest foods, and attended the best schools money could buy. Because his father sat on the board of directors of a major Ivy League university, Hugh's acceptance into an elite university and the attendant contacts this affords was assured.

Advocates of the conflict perspective would suggest that we contrast Hugh's experiences with those of Billie, the daughter of a migrant worker. Born on the ground outside her dad's pickup truck, she helped deliver and raise her younger siblings. At an age when Hugh entered an elite prep school, Billie was just learning what a light switch on the wall was—she simply had no experience with wall switches because, in the migrant workers' dormitories, lights were centrally turned off by the manager. Billie's dad, who "sometimes grew tired of doing the rich man's work," would occasionally leave the orange groves and head for what he hoped was better opportunity. He never really found it, so when there was little or no money left he often set Billie to selling "flowers" made of weeds and tissue paper. On one of these excursions Billie discovered something so marvelous that the words still excite her: a public library. At age 6 she found it to be first place she was welcome to enter that was clean and quiet. Billie eventually managed to earn an advanced degree in the social sciences, but society has not rewarded her talents, training, and effort with anything approaching wealth.

From the conflict perspective, wealth represents

part of a long-standing pattern of inequality, passed down from generation to generation. Proponents of this view reject the structural-functionalist notion that wealth provides a socially beneficial incentive system. Conflict theorists would argue that structural-functionalism fails to come to grips with the fact that many of the wealthy, like Hugh, do not earn their wealth, and many of the worthy, like Billie, never get it. Wealth, according to theorists of the conflict perspective, rests on ownership. Thus, Mark, the landlord, has found one of the few paths into true wealth. As employees, Billie the professor, Charlie the band director, and even Leslie the obstetrician, will never achieve the wealth and attendant power with which Hugh was born. Mark the landlord might, but a conflict theorist would quickly point out that his fortune rests in part on others' misfortunes. Mark grows progressively wealthier renting housing to those who are too poor to own the houses in which they live. Wealth, seen from the conflict perspective, comes from ownership. Ownership of land, factories, or shares of stock provides the means to even more wealth. To the wealthy comes the power to require others, who own little or nothing, to work in ways that make the rich richer and the poor poorer or only slightly better off.

Whereas the structural-functionalists and conflict theorists usually focus on major social features such as classes or society as a whole, the symbolic interactionists look primarily at what goes on between individuals. Symbolic interactionists study how we use symbols to create impressions and how these symbols and impressions shape our selves. How does this view improve our understanding of differences in wealth? The approach speaks most clearly to why the wealthy stay wealthy. Wealth places an individual in the position of giving and receiving many messages that establish and reinforce his or her self esteem. Hugh, the industrialist's son, had little reason to doubt his importance and worth. From a young age his possessions and training gave him the ability to impress people. Conversely, Billie, the migrant worker's daughter, was left wondering how she might get to be a "real person," one who lived in her own house and grew up in a particular town. Like Hugh and Billie, we tend to gauge our worth and that of others according to the social assets we have. If we have more than others, we are inclined to think we must be better than they are. If we have less, perhaps we are inclined to believe that we are not as good. In short, our possessions symbolize our worth.

Wealthy people more easily control the impressions they give, and thus they are able to reinforce their superior status and others' subordinate status. Wayne, a near-billionaire owner of various businesses, wears a custom-tailored suit, drives his Rolls Royce to work, and parks indoors in his reserved parking space. He works in a private paneled office with a large desk, sofa, and easy chairs, a conference table large enough for eight, large potted plants, a model of one of his several Lear Jets, and original sculptures. His private secretary takes his calls, greets his visitors, and regulates when others may see him. Ken, a plumber, parks his used Plymouth near the work site, and toils in coveralls at an outdoor construction site where anyone can observe his work habits. The difference in symbols, such as clothes and cars, combined with differences in ability to control others' observation of their work, give Wayne an enormous advantage in creating the impression that he is worthy of his $100 million per year whereas Ken's efforts are worth only $60,000.

The symbolic interactionist points to the ability of highly placed individuals to impress those of lower status. At the same time, the higher placed individual is better able to hide his or her behavior. Thus, being rich allows one to send impressions of superiority that are often reflected back. As symbolic interactionists observe, our sense of self is largely formed by accumulated impressions. Should it surprise us then that both the wealthy and those who are not frequently feel they got what they deserved, despite their actual talent, training, and effort?

The three perspectives focus our attention on different aspects of the same reality. They can serve as starting points for analyzing social settings. In another sense they are grand theories, attempting to explain all of social behavior in very general terms. In this regard the conflict perspective, with its claim that conflict and change are the central dynamics of society, clearly contradicts the structural-functional perspective, which holds that harmony and stability are the dominant social processes. The fact that all three perspectives survive suggests that no single grand theory has a monopoly on the truth and that all three have considerable utility and validity. These perspectives can serve as bases from which we can build theories of narrower scope.

FOCUS ON SPECIAL FEATURES: SOCIOLOGISTS AT WORK

A special feature of this text is the "Sociologists at Work" section in each chapter. Here you meet sociologists from each of these theoretical schools and learn about what they are currently studying, from the social structure of "Dungeons and Dragons" games to how and why cooperative industries can be successful. As you read about their work, the theoretical ideas of the three basic sociological perspectives will become more real to you.

How Is Sociological Theory Constructed?

Often our goals in studying society are rather specific. Instead of seeking answers to very general issues or questions like: What is the nature of society and social action? we seek answers to questions like: Why are there so many violent outbreaks in our society? Why are the relations between races sometimes peaceful and other times hostile? How do we select our mates? And why has the percentage of women increased in the workplace? As we progress through this book we encounter theories that address questions such as these.

A ***sociological theory*** *is a general explanation of a social phenomenon.* A ***theoretical issue*** *is a question we seek to answer with a theory.* For instance, Paul Harrison, a contemporary British sociologist, has developed a theory to address the theoretical issue: Why do some nations remain poor as others become wealthy? In this theoretical issue, nations, wealth, and poverty are examples of concepts. ***Concepts*** *are categories of behavior, events, or characteristics that are considered similar for the sake of theory construction.* We lump together countries like India and Bangladesh and assume they are enough alike that we can make a general theoretical statement about "poor nations." For instance, Harrison advances the proposition that poor nations are more likely to have been colonialized in early times.

Theories are built from ***propositions*** that *are statements that explain one concept in terms of another.* Often a theorist will say that one concept is the cause of another. Harrison, for instance, uses the concept of previous colonialization as a cause of national poverty. However, sometimes the proposition involves some other relationship than cause, as in Neil Smelser's theory about riots, in which Smelser identifies six concepts that are necessary for but not a cause of a riot. However, propositions usually involve casual statements. Theories often include several propositions. As we see in Chapter 15, "Work and the Economy," Harrison's theory involves propositions that link poverty to other concepts, such as climate and technology.

FOCUS ON SPECIAL FEATURES: CLOSE-UP ON THEORY

We encounter many theories as we explore our social world through sociology. Each chapter of this book contains a "Close-Up on Theory" that highlights the work of an important sociologist who addresses a central issue of the discipline. They begin with background on the theorist and the setting, and then specify the issue that the theorist addressed, the major concepts of the theory, and the central propositions that serve to answer the issue raised. Each "Close-Up" contains core passsages in the theorist's own words. In the "Interpretation" section we comment on the place of the work in sociology, often calling the readers' attention to the particular perspective from which the theorist operates. Following each "Close-Up" are discussion questions to help you reflect upon, evaluate, and apply the theory. Our "Close-Ups" usually focus on recent works, but because this chapter deals with the origins of sociology, we introduce the feature with a classic by one of the early masters of sociology, Max Weber.

Weber's genius involved being able to deal with sweeping issues like capitalism and Protestantism at the social level while incorporating the subjective meanings these phenomena have to the individuals involved. Some sociologists, such as Emile Durkheim, whose work we feature in the "Close-Up on Research" in this chapter, excelled in statistical analysis and insisted that sociologists stick to considering group phenomena. Weber dealt more with ideas whereas Durkheim dealt more with data, though each used both data and ideas. Unlike Durkheim, Weber suggested that sociologists employ *Verstehen*. This German word refers to the subjective meaning of something, in this case Protestantism. By empathizing with those in the role of a Protestant, Weber could better understand the tensions that led Protestants to act in ways that led towards capitalism. Through *Verstehen* he realized that a religion that preached that individuals were preordained to go to heaven (members of the elect) or hell (members of the damned) would leave people in a state of tension over their status. Though they could not "work their way into heaven," Protestants might understandably grasp at success in the world of work as indication of their elect status. This, combined with their emphasis on frugality, produced surplus resources that they reinvested in their work as capital.

What Are the Basic Tenets of Sociological Research?

Sociological research uses either a deductive or an inductive model. ***Deductive research*** *begins with a general idea that the scientist wishes to test.* The researcher then gathers facts to test his general idea. Conversely, ***inductive research*** *begins with specific facts for which the researcher seeks a general explanation.*

FOUR MAJOR SOCIOLOGICAL RESEARCH METHODS

Sociologists use a variety of ***research methods***, *systematic techniques for gathering and analyzing facts about theories.* The following section gives an overview and examples of the four most common research methods used in sociology today: the survey, study of existing sources, the observational study, and the experiment. Sections called "Close-Up on Research" that appear throughout the book feature these methods.

THE SURVEY METHOD. Have white people in the Southern United States become less prejudiced against blacks since the late 1950s? To answer this question we might rely on hunches or on our informal observations. We could also turn to scientific research techniques to test the idea that prejudice is on the decline in the South, such as that of the Gallup Organization, founded by George Gallup, a pioneer in public opinion research.

In a scientific research poll, researchers contact a **sample**, or a *part of a population that represents the entire population*. A seemingly small sample of 2,000 cases can accurately reflect the opinion of a large population like that of the United States (about 165,000,000 people aged 21 or older), when the sample is drawn in such a way that each member of the population has an equal chance of being selected. The Gallup Organization conducts many of its polls in person, although researchers increasingly rely on telephone interviews.

One measure of prejudice would be how people respond to an item carried on Gallup polls for several years: "Would you object to your child attending a school with a few black children?" The proportion of white people in southern states saying they would object to their children attending a school with a few black children has plummeted from 73 percent in 1957 to 6 percent in 1980. Public opinion has shifted more rapidly and completely on this issue than virtually any other yet studied (Gallup, 1980).

Public opinion pollster Daniel Yankelovich's work illustrates one of the most common research methods employed in sociology: the survey. *A **survey** is a research method in which a sample of a population is asked to respond to questions.* There are two major types of surveys: interviews and questionnaires. *An **interview** is a means of gathering information in which one person asks another questions, either in person or by telephone. A **questionnaire** is a means of gathering information by having the respondent fill in answers to printed questions.*

Mailed questionnaires have some advantage over interviews, including saving money and time; convenience to the respondent, who can reply at will; greater assurance that the respondent will remain anonymous, that the question is not rephrased by the interviewer,

CLOSE-UP on • *THEORY* •

Max Weber on Protestantism as a Cause of Capitalism

The Theorist and the Setting

Industrialization has transformed our social world from one comprised of farmers to one made up of factory and office workers. Almost no aspect of social life, including the family, religion, politics, and the economy, has been left unchanged by this revolution. But why did a world that for centuries led a traditional life centered around farming suddenly change so drastically?

The German scholar Max Weber (1864–1920) was a key figure in the development of sociology as a discipline. His analysis of the major dynamics of society and social change provides the foundation for much of the sociological theory and research of our time. Weber wrote on a wide variety of topics, including the nature and growth of bureaucracy, religion, and the economy. He studied the roots of the Industrial Revolution, which was sweeping through the world in his day, and believed a new form of capitalism, backed by a capitalist spirit or mentality, was at the root of the revolution. Weber first published these ideas in 1904 as "The Protestant Ethic and the Spirit of Capitalism." In 1920 he revised the book, and in 1930 Talcott Parsons, an American sociologist at Harvard, translated the work into English.

The Theorist's Goal

In "The Protestant Ethic and the Spirit of Capitalism" Weber tries to explain how the capitalism of Western Europe and the United States became so strong that it transformed the world. An astute student of history, Weber knew capitalism had existed in many other cultures, particularly India and China, but nowhere had it transformed the societies as it did in the West. Why? Weber believed the answer resided in religious ideas, and pursued the question: What is "the influence of certain religious ideas on the development of an economic spirit, or the ethos of an economic system" (Weber, 1904, p. 27)?

Concepts and Propositions

Let us first consider what Weber means by *capitalism*. "We will define a capitalistic economic action as one which rests on the expectation of profit by the utilization of opportunities for exchange, that is on (formally) peaceful chances for profit" (p. 17).

In rather stilted prose Weber is talking of what we today might call a "bottom line" mentality. "Everything is done in terms of balances: at the beginning of the enterprise an initial balance, before every individual decision a calculation to ascertain its probable profitableness, and at the end a final balance to ascertain how much profit has been made" (p. 18).

Weber saw capitalism as emanating from the *spirit of capitalism,* a sense that making a profit was morally right—in fact, so right that it became "a duty of the individual toward the increase of his capital" (p. 51).

Benjamin Franklin embodied this spirit of capitalism. Consider Franklin's urgings as quoted by Weber: "He that idly loses five shillings' worth of time, loses five shillings, and might as prudently throw five shillings into the sea. He that loses five shillings, not only loses that sum, but all the advantage that might be made by turning it in dealing, which by the time that a young man becomes old, will amount to a considerable sum of money" (p. 50).

Weber establishes a link between the ethic of the Protestant Reformation and this spirit of capitalism. This is quite a feat, because Protestants of the Reformation era had no intention of establishing worldly capitalism. In Weber's words: "The religious circles which today most enthusiastically celebrate that great achievement of the Reformation are by no means friendly to capitalism in any sense. And Luther himself would, without doubt, have sharply repudiated any connection with a point of view like that of Franklin" (p. 82).

To understand how Weber could believe that Protestants "accidentally" caused capitalism, we need to consider how people looked at their world before and after the Reformation. We need to focus especially on what religion taught about work, making money, and spending it.

Before the Reformation traditional religious belief held that worldly work was of little significance and accumulation of wealth was wrong. According to Weber, the Roman Catholic Church taught that

> . . . one may attain salvation in any walk of life on the short pilgrimage of life. There is no use in laying weight on the form of occupation. The pursuit of material gain beyond personal needs must thus appear as a symptom of lack of grace, and since it can apparently only be attained at the expense of others, directly reprehensible (p. 84).

Two major changes came with Protestantism, or, more precisely, the Calvinist form of Protestantism. First was the belief that each person is predestined either for heaven or hell at birth. The outward signs of being among "the elect" were great works flowing from one's spirituality. Although one could not earn the way into heaven, one had to clearly demonstrate godliness to believe one was among the elect. Demonstrating godliness translated into being successful in an earthly station or calling.

Another major Protestant belief was in living frugally. Many denominations that arose after the Reformation rejected displays of worldly wealth. Weber, therefore, defines the two core components of the "Protestant ethic" as a drive to worldly success to prove one's "elect" status, combined with frugal life-style.

Weber suggests that, though no one intended it, the combination of diligence and frugality leads inevitably to the accumulation of wealth. Thus the Protestant ethic provided fertile ground for the spirit embodied so clearly by Benjamin Franklin. This spirit was useful in the development of capitalism, which was in turn a driving force in industrializing the world.

Weber's central idea, then, can be summed up:

Proposition: Capitalism is a social pattern arising from the pursuit of profit created by the internal tensions of Calvinism.

Interpretation

Along with this brief introduction to Weber's thought we need to add some qualifications. Weber did not believe Protestantism was the only cause of capitalism. He was well aware that Karl Marx believed that ideas did not cause material world changes so much as that changes in the material world led to new ideas. In his introduction Weber states his hope that his "study may form a contribution to the understanding of the manner in which ideas become effective forces in history" (p. 90). In his closing paragraph, Weber states that history and culture are influenced by spiritual and material forces. Yet

> the modern man is in general . . . unable to give religious ideas a significance for culture and national character which they deserve. But it is . . . not my aim to substitute for a one-sided materialistic, an equally one-sided spiritualistic, causal interpretation of culture and of history. Each is equally possible . . . (p. 183).

Weber's work laid the foundations of interactionism as it is broadly conceived. We can see similarity between this work and contemporary symbolic-interactionist work, which stresses symbolically learned and communicated beliefs as a means of understanding people's behavior.

Weber's theory calls our attention to the importance of ideas, especially religious ideas, in understanding major institutions like the economy.

Questions

1. Is the "spirit of capitalism" still an accepted value in Western culture? How are economic and religious ideas linked in an important way today?
2. What governs our present ideas about how hard one should work and what we should do with our money?
3. Is Weber's theory persuasive to you? Why, or why not?

SOURCE Max Weber. 1904. *The Protestant Ethic and the Spirit of Capitalism.* Translated from the German by Talcott Parsons. New York: Charles Scribner's Sons, 1958.

and that the respondent is not biased by the interviewer; availability of time for the respondent to consult other sources before responding; and ease of access to people who are widely separated geographically (Kenneth Bailey, 1978). However, questionnaires lack the flexibility of interviews; they generally have lower response rates because it is easier for the recipient not to respond, and they measure verbal behavior only, without allowing the researcher to make observations. Furthermore, mailed questionnaires enable the respondent to skip questions.

ANALYSIS OF EXISTING SOURCES. Does watching televised reports of actual suicides or documentary programs about suicide encourage teen-age suicides? David Phillips and his colleagues analyzed the daily fluctuations of suicide rates for some 12,585 teen-age suicides. Using information from the Vanderbilt Television News Archive and the CBS News Index, they identified the timing of suicide news stories and compared suicide rates before and following that publicity (Phillips, 1982; Phillips & Carstensen, 1986).

Phillips' study represents a second major research technique: the analysis of existing sources, which is also sometimes called *content* or *documents analysis*. The ***analysis of existing sources*** *is a research technique in which the researcher uses existing documents that were created for some other purpose.* In this case Phillips relied on general data from the National Center for Health Statistics, together with indexed information about news stories.

Does suicide publicity cause increased suicide? Even after Phillips anticipated and controlled for six other possible explanations, the answer came back a clear yes. Suicide rates rise distinctly after television news or documentaries feature suicide.

Whereas Phillips relied on government data banks and new indexes, other sociologists using this technique have turned to newspapers, records kept by organizations about their members, personal letters, textbooks, recordings, and many other sources of existing data. Sometimes sociologists analyze textbooks or television shows to discover how they deal with a particular topic such as gender roles or drinking. In fact, *most* sociological research is based on existing datasets.

Analysis of existing sources allows access to data about otherwise unavailable subjects, such as deceased persons. It also involves nonreactive data, in which responses are not influenced by the wording of a question or the particular traits of the interviewer. Document studies also allow us to consider behavior over long periods of time, and they often involve considerable spontaneity by the subject. Document studies can produce remarkable quality at low cost.

These studies also have drawbacks. Documents are usually produced for a specific purpose, and the truth may have been distorted to serve that purpose. For instance, because many taxpayers understate their income on tax forms, Internal Revenue Service figures generally underestimate income. Also, some documents the researcher wants may be missing, incomplete, restricted, or unavailable.

THE OBSERVATIONAL STUDY. In the popular but controversial board game "Dungeons & Dragons," players verbally enact characters who explore territories and engage in battles. Often played at regular meeting times, games may go on for months or years. Although devotees of the game love it, outsiders have claimed that the game sometimes gets out of hand, leading to actual rather than verbal violence, or that the game leads participants into the occult world. What is really going on when people gather to play the game "Dungeons & Dragons"? Critics have linked this popular game to various forms of undesirable behavior. Gary Fine spent months directly observing people playing the "Dungeons & Dragons" game. Did horrible things happen? Though Fine did not attempt to trace the consequences the game had in the outside lives of the players, he did get a very close look at who plays the game and how. Among his observations: Mostly males play "Dungeons & Dragons," and through this game these players often verbalize rape fantasies. From his research Fine can describe the common behavior in this setting. He also offers evidence that many males who probably would not rape have verbalized fantasies about rape with other males. *In an* ***observational study*** *the researcher actually witnesses social behavior in its natural setting or laboratory. In* ***participant observation*** *the researcher takes part in the activity being studied;* for instance, sport parachuting or enacting the role of a patient in a mental hospital. *In* ***unobtrusive observation*** *the researcher acts as an observer, but not as a participant, in the activity being studied;* for instance, riding in a police car to observe police or criminal behavior.

The great advantage of the observational study is that the research is accomplished by directly observing subjects' behavior, as opposed to a survey or an analysis of existing sources in which the researcher must rely on others' observations and reports. Observational techniques are also greatly superior to either the survey or the document study in providing information about nonverbal behavior. Observation also allows the researcher to observe the subject in a natural setting, and provides for study of the subject over time rather than at one point, as a survey usually does. However, the observing researcher has no control over what happens and might have difficulty putting the observations into systematic form in order to draw conclusions. Also, the number of subjects the researcher can observe is small, and there are often severe problems gaining entry to a natural setting. Many potential subjects—for example,

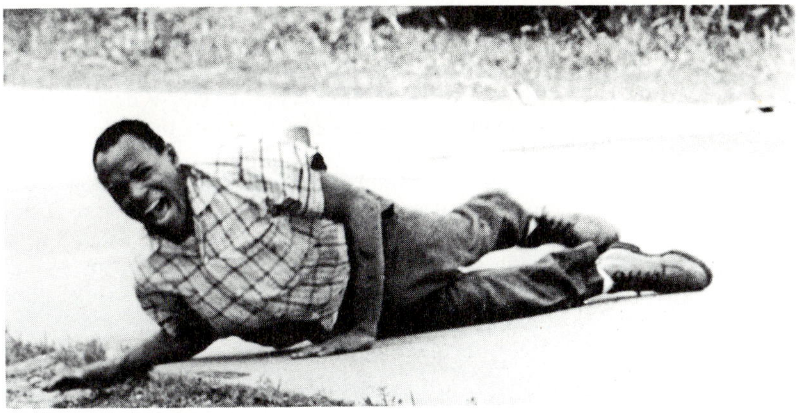

Have whites in the southern United States become less prejudiced against blacks than in the past decades? In the 1960s black and white civil rights demonstrators were often beaten, sometimes shot, and occasionally killed. Here a shotgun-toting white dentist hiding in the bushes opens fire on James Meredith as he leads a peaceful freedom march. Fortunately, survey research indicates a rapid drop in prejudice following the civil rights movement, and scenes like this are much less frequent. *(AP/Wide World Photos)*

the very wealthy and the very deviant—do not want to be subjects for the benefit of social science research.

THE EXPERIMENT. As social creatures we tend to assess one another's status and respond accordingly. For instance, one may conjecture that those who are highly educated are wiser and therefore be more easily swayed by their opinions. Similarly one might discount what some people have to say just because they are old, female, or belong to an ethnic minority.

Barry Markovsky, LeRoy Smith, and Joseph Berger devised an experiment to test whether people can be trained not to consider status in group decision making (1984). Experiments represent the fourth major sociological research method. *An **experiment** is a research design in which the researcher exposes a group of subjects to a treatment and observes its effect, usually in comparison to a similar control group that did not receive the treatment.*

In this case, young white males were recruited as subjects and told they were participating in two separate studies. Subjects were led to believe they were making decisions with some partners who were younger and less educated and other partners who were older and more educated. Later the subject was given information indicating the person of higher status was not very competent at the task at hand. Under these circumstance our young subjects paid less heed to the judgment of these "older and wiser" partners. But what would happen when they found themselves in a different setting, with different tasks, and different partners—would they return to being swayed by the other person's general status? Not nearly as much as they first were. Or, in other words, these subjects were rather easily trained to look past status in assessing another person's competence in decision making. The advantages of the experiment technique are considerable. Experiments can demonstrate clearly that a variable has a particular effect on the subject group. The researcher can retain maximum control over the circumstances of the research and at least in principle can provide for studying changes over time.

However, of the four major techniques described in this section, the experiment is probably the least frequently employed by sociologists, as experiments also have disadvantages. First, they are very expensive. The case of conducting experiments often makes it difficult to include a large number of observations and thus may limit the validity of the experiment. Second, sometimes the experiment or the experimenter may have an effect on the subjects that is difficult to sort out from the treatment. In the classic Hawthorne study, factory worker productivity increased when the lights were turned up, leading to the preliminary conclusion that lighting was linked to productivity (Roethlisberger and Dickson, 1939). Productivity increased again when the lights were lowered, suggesting that the subjects were probably responding to being observed in the process of the experiment rather than to the treatment—in this case, a change in lighting.

Another disadvantage of experiments is that the experimental environment is often artificial. For instance, we discover some interesting patterns in studying decision making in a laboratory setting, but our subjects might display different behavior in the face of real decisions. One way to avoid the problem of artificiality is to conduct field experiments in a real setting. *A **field experiment** is one in which the effect of a treatment is studied in a real rather than a simulated setting.* Peter Rossi, a former president of the American Sociological Association, is one sociololgist to employ this approach. Rossi and colleagues studied the effect of paying support money to newly released prisoners until they could locate work and found that under certain conditions this lessened the likelihood that the former prisoner would return to prison (Rossi, Berk & Lenihan, 1980).

No single research method is best for all problems. We must use our best judgment to decide which technique is most appropriate in a particular setting and for the issue being researched.

FOCUS ON SPECIAL FEATURES: CLOSE-UP ON RESEARCH

Gaining a strong grasp on research techniques in sociology is a bit like learning to understand a complicated sport like football. One can get started by reading about it or by listening to a discussion, but one needs to watch or play in many games before having a full understanding. Similarly, one gains only a superficial understanding of research techniques through a discussion of them, even when there are clear and interesting examples. A feature parallel to the "Close-Up on Theory" can help the reader develop a deeper understanding of, and appreciation for, the four research methods.

In each chapter of this book we pay special attention to a particularly important contribution to sociology in the form of a "Close-Up on Research." In so doing we are teaching additional lessons in methodology as we present a major sociological work and its findings. We can see in considerable detail how the best minds in the field use the four research method tech-

CLOSE-UP on • *RESEARCH* •

Emile Durkheim on Suicide and Society

The Researcher and the Setting

French scholar and sociological pioneer Emile Durkheim's classic work, *The Rules of Sociological Method* (1895), serves even today as a major statement of how sociologists should construct theory and conduct research. As one of the first scholars to regard himself a sociologist, Durkheim sought to establish sociology as a useful scientific discipline. As he stated, "The progress of a science is proven by the progress toward solution of the problems it treats. It is said to be advancing when laws hitherto unknown are discovered, or when at least new facts are acquired, modifying the formulation of these problems even though not furnishing the final solution" (Durkheim, 1895).

Suicide might seem a peculiar starting place for one trying to establish sociology as a significant discipline, especially because on the surface it seems to be a very individual rather than a social act. But Durkheim saw several reasons to pursue the topic. First, he recognized suicide as a major and growing social problem, one which persists into our present era. Second, he was convinced that suicide has social origins, and once we understand these we can effect remedies that will lower suicide rates. Third, Durkheim saw the topic as leading to insights and even to laws about human social behavior. In Durkheim's words:

> Few subjects are more clearly defined, . . . Real laws are discoverable which demonstrate the possibility of sociology, . . . (and) there will emerge from our study some suggestions concerning the causes of the general contemporary maladjustment being undergone by European societies and concerning remedies which may relieve it (1897, pp. 36–37).

The Researcher's Goal

Durkheim attempts to validate his theory that suicide rates are the consequence of social circumstances.

The Theory and Concepts

Durkheim theorized that social circumstances can explain suicide. He distinguished three major types of suicide depending on the social factors involved:

1. ***Egoistic suicide*** *results from a lack of integration of the individual into society*. For instance, single adults not integrated into a marriage or family would be more suicide-prone than married adults.
2. ***Altruistic suicide*** *involves an individual taking his or her own life because of higher commandments*. Durkheim provided an example in the form of religiously motivated suicidal sacrifices in earlier times in Japan, China, and India.
3. ***Anomic suicide*** *results from a lack of regulation of the individual by society*. Durkheim theorized that people need society to help regulate their lives, and when the collective order is disturbed, so is the regulation mechanism. People who kill themselves in times of economic crisis may be anomic suicides.

Research Design

Durkheim used the evaluation of existing sources technique described earlier. He gathered data on suicides from official statistical publications of various nations; for example, the Tenth Census of the United States' *Report on the Mortality and Vital Statistics of the United States,* 11th part (1880) provided his information about United States suicides.

He then compared suicide rates for populations that his theory predicted would be relatively high or low for egoistic, altruistic, and anomic suicide. For each of the three suicide types, he selected groups or eras that allowed comparisons. Because egoistic suicide results from insufficient integration of the individual into society, Durkheim believed single (never married) adults would have more tendency to commit suicide than married adults. He therefore compared the rates of singles to those of married persons. Durkheim believed that in times of national *political* crisis, people tend to pull together, becoming more socially integrated. He therefore studied suicide rates during such crises, predicting they would be lower than those of the same group during normal periods.

Durkheim offered examples of altruistic suicide in the less technologically developed countries; but he also predicted that such altruistic behavior would be more likely evidenced by military personnel, who are selected and trained to risk their lives for society, than it would be for civilians. To test the idea, he compared military and civilian suicide rates.

Anomic suicide results from breakdown or failure of the rules that guide our lives. Durkheim believed that national *economic* crises create a weakening of norms (societal rules). When a person loses a job or a fortune, he or she loses social direction as well. So Durkheim compared suicide rates during economic crises to those in normal times. Similarly, he believed that divorce destroys part of the social structure guiding a person's life, and that marriage regulates a man's life even more than it does a woman's. He therefore predicted higher suicide rates for divorced people in general and even higher rates for divorced men.

Findings

Durkheim found substantial support for his theory as tested. The original work, which contained scores of tables with detailed explanations, is briefly summarized in Table 1.1. Durkheim found, for instance, that married persons are relatively immune to suicide, with rates less than half those of single persons. Rates of suicide are demonstrably higher during economic crises and lower during political ones. Military suicides are much more common than civilian ones. Also, Durkheim documents higher suicide rates for divorced people versus married people, and he finds divorced men have a higher rate of suicide than do divorced women.

Implications

Durkheim demonstrated clearly that social factors influence even so seemingly personal an act as suicide. He was able to demonstrate apparent egoistic suicide among the unmarried. His suggestion that a political crisis draws society together, reducing the rate of egoistic suicide, was confirmed by a comparison of suicide rates during and after political crises. He also documented the existence of altruistic suicide in the form of religious self-sacrifice. He interpreted a higher military suicide rate as an example of tendency toward altruistic suicide. Finally, he demonstrated that those he would expect to evidence high levels of anomie—divorced persons, particularly divorced males, who he claimed were more regu-

TABLE 1.1 Summary of Durkheim's Findings on Suicide

Theoretical Factor (Type of Suicide)	Research Groups or Situations Compared	Theoretical Suicide Risk	Observed Suicides
Egoistic	Married	Lower	74/10,000
	Single	Higher	130/10,000
	People living through a national *political* crisis	Lower	4,157 (France at war 1870)
	People living in a normal period	Higher	5,114 (France at peace 1869)
Altruistic	Military personnel	Higher	680/1,000,000 } U.S. 1870–84
	Civilians	Lower	80/1,000,000 } U.S. 1870–84
Anomic	People living through a national *economic* crisis	Higher	7,213 France 1882
	People living in a normal period	Lower	6,741 France 1881
	Those married	Lower	218 } Württemberg 1873–1892
	Those divorced	Higher	796 } Württemberg 1873–1892
	Divorced men	Higher	1,875 } Prussia 1887–89
	Divorced women	Lower	290 } Prussia 1887–89

lated by marriage than females—did in fact have higher suicide rates.

So Durkheim found evidence that a person's involvement of lack of involvement in society affects the probability of suicide. He also showed that the state of society influences the suicide rate.

Durkheim believed the high rates of suicide in Europe during his own era to be egoistic suicide resulting from a "poverty of morals." This he believed came about from a loss of community as society became more centralized. In a rather complicated argument, he proposed that governments promote economic or occupational decentralization to heighten communal life without weakening national unity. Thus, the first major scientific study in sociology led both to confirmation of an important theory and to a recommended remedy for a social problem.

Questions

1. How can we use Durkheim's findings to improve our social world?
2. Do you see any places in which error may have crept into Durkheim's study? Where? What remedies might you suggest?
3. Could one of the other four major forms of research methods be used to investigate this topic? If so, which one? If not, why would you eliminate the other methods?

niques introduced before to address nearly a score of interesting and important issues.

The "Close-Up on Research" features allow study of individual pieces of research, bringing research to life rather than merely summarizing it. Most of the research highlighted is contemporary, but this opening chapter introduces a classic that many sociologists regard as the first example of scientific research in the field: Emile Durkheim's study of suicide.

DURKHEIM REVISITED

Since its publication in 1897, Durkheim's *Suicide* has received tremendous attention and had enormous impact. The work was instrumental in creating Durkheim's status as a major scholar, and he was, perhaps more than any other individual, the founder of modern academic sociology. Still, by contemporary standards, the classic closely examined has significant flaws (Stack, 1983a; Stack, 1983b; Stark, Doyle & Rushing, 1983).

Survey research. Modern survey research involves thousands of interviews which are often conducted by phone. This woman is interviewing subjects for the Survey Research Center at the Institute for Social Research, University of Michigan. (*Photo courtesy the author*)

Whitney Pope (1976) devotes an entire book to evaluating *Suicide*. He concludes that there is tremendous ambiguity among Durkheim's central concepts and that in their entirety his data fail to confirm his theory. Yet even Pope recognizes that "in terms of both its influence and its continuing relevance as a model for integrating theory and data, *Suicide* remains a monument (p. 204). Though *Suicide* may have lost the battle, it has been instrumental in winning the war.

SOCIOLOGY AND SCIENCE

Science is one of humanity's most powerful social inventions. Application of science to the fields of biology, physics, and chemistry has resulted in dramatic increases in our mastery over the physical world. Social scientists apply the methods of science to humanity itself in the disciplines of psychology, economics, political science, anthropology, and sociology.

The logic of science rests on two central assumptions. First, in employing science we assume that natural laws govern the subject matter so that nature repeats itself. Second, we assume that we can discern natural laws through careful observation of events that are similar and that we can then classify the observed events into categories for the sake of analysis.

The institutionalized practice of science within a community of scholars rests on their maintaining certain attitudes. The first is ***detachment***, *or the ability of*

TABLE 1.2 Summary of Terms Commonly Used in Sociological Research

Term	Definition	Example
HYPOTHESIS	A conditional statement about the relationships between two or more variables.	Employed students will earn lower grades.
VARIABLE	A characteristic that can change depending on conditions. An **INDEPENDENT VARIABLE,** when altered, causes changes in a second characteristic, called the **DEPENDENT VARIABLE**.	Grades are the dependent variable, whereas working is the independent variable.
OPERATIONAL DEFINITION	A definition that states an abstract concept in concrete terms in order that it might be measured.	We could operationalize grades as the student's overall grade point average for the period we study, and operationalize work various ways, such as the number of paid hours of employment outside the home.
POPULATION	The entire set of people a researcher studies.	We might consider all United States students within an age bracket of 14–22 years as the population we would study.
SAMPLE	A part of a population that represents the entire population.	Because 20,000,000 students might be more than we need, we could take a sample of them, targeting a group such as those in a certain high school.
RANDOM SAMPLE	A sample that is chosen in such a way that every person in the population had an equal chance of being chosen.	Because our high school is probably not "typical," we could better represent the population with a sample of 2,000 students in which all students have an equal chance to be selected.
CORRELATION	A relationship between two variables in which one changes with the other, but one does not cause the other.	Aha! We have found that students who work have lower grades. Now we consider a rival hypothesis: Perhaps students with lower grades are more likely to work. A correlation does not tell us which "caused" which.
CONTROL GROUP	Experimental subjects who are not exposed to the independent variable, and can be used as a comparison group to the subjects who are introduced to it.	Ideally, we would be most sure of our results if we could assign students from our sample to work or not work. We could then call the employed group our experimental group and the nonemployed group our control group.
CONTROLS	Characterstrics that are held constant in order to exclude factors that might influence the subject's reactions in the experiment.	Without conducting an experiment, we can exert control statistically. We'll measure grades before the study begins. Then we can compare the effects of student employment on those with high grades or those with low grades. In this way we can rule out the rival hypothesis.
REPLICATION	Repeating a piece of research in order to determine whether the findings will be consistent with the first research.	Once we're done, somone may want to repeat the study to verify it or see if our results hold true for a different sample or population.

These are terms which you will encounter frequently in this text and others that concern themselves with research. Refer back to this chart if their meaning is not clear to you as they are used in "Close-Ups" and elsewhere. We illustrate them by applying them to an ongoing research question:
What are the consequences of students working while they are in school?

Hurting his grades? Research techniques can be used to answer questions such as, "What happens when teens work?" Some studies show that teen work interferes with school, extracurriculars, and contributes to certain types of delinquency such as liquor offenses. (*Photo courtesy the author*)

the scientist to set aside cherished beliefs so that new ideas can be given the chance to be tested. The second attitude is one of ***skepticism***, *in which the scientist endeavors to test even ideas that are widely accepted as truth.* Without these attitudes a researcher can miss important concepts or can fail to note implications in the data that could lead to new insights and theories.

Science also depends on adherence to important core values. The first is scrupulous honesty, so that one scholar can trust another's work. The second is a spirit of cooperation, which allows a free exchange of data and research findings.

Our culture is so strongly oriented toward education and science that many people are familiar with the *scientific method*, a deductive model, whose basic steps are summarized as follows:

1. Observation of an event or events in the world that stimulate thinking.
2. Definition or classification of the terms and events being considered.
3. Formulation of the research issue, or hypothesis—a careful phrasing of the question to be answered.
4. Generation of a theory or proposition—a general statement that serves as a potential answer to the research question.
5. Creation of research design—a means to test whether the theory or proposition is valid.
6. Collection of data—working through the research design to make the necessary observations.
7. Analysis of data—organizing the findings to bear on the theory.
8. Conclusions—estimating the merits of the theory.

In order to show causality—that one event occurs due to another event—three requirements must be filled. The events must occur *in time order* and be *correlated* or occurring consistently with each other. Finally, the relationship must be *nonspurious*, or not due to an unusual circumstance outside of the researched variable.

This is an idealization of the scientific method. Scientists tend to follow such a procedure, but they often move back and forth between steps. For instance, when collecting data, one might have an insight that could serve as a new proposition to answer the research issue. Similarly, in drawing conclusions one often becomes aware of new research issues.

Many research projects are guided by the scientific approach, but some sociologists conduct research primarily to provide detailed description of social behavior or to gain insights which may lead to better understanding and to new theories. Other sociologists, specializing in theory, engage in little or no organized research. They apply reason and logic to their own and others' observations and theories to arrive at new theories. Most sociologists conduct research, and most research falls into the four major categories described in the following subsection.

VALUES IN SOCIOLOGY

Sociologists such as Max Weber who come from a *value-free orientation*, believe sociologists should not let their own political views influence their theories and research. They argue that the realm of facts (like "74 percent of the wealth is held by 20 percent of the population") is totally separate from the realm of values (like "the poor *should* have more money").

Proponents of value-free sociology generally argue that knowledge is neutral and that it is the scientist's task to develop theories and facts but not to use them to promote personally desired change. This argument is based on two assumptions. The first is that the scientist's special knowledge of the social world does not bring with it any special right to dictate the future of that world. The second assumption is that in making a value judgment publicly a scientist may undermine public trust in that science as an impartial process.

Within sociology a counterargument is made, which might be called the *value-committed* approach or the *humanist* rebuttal. Social scientists such as Karl Marx, for instance, argue that value neutrality is either naive or a convenient rationalization of the fact that one is working for the "establishment" or the elite. They suggest that even the value-free position is not neutral, because it values neutrality over partisanship and honesty over dishonesty. Taken to its extreme, value neutrality would mean value irrelevance.

Humanists and conflict theorists like Howard Becker (1967) and Alfred McLung Lee (1978) raise such questions in their writings as "Whose side are you on?" and "Sociology for whom?" They point out that values influence even the most neutral work, because they influence decisions as to which questions are worth pursuing and which organizations are to sponsor research. Becker and Lee suggest that most research is funded by, directed by, and disproportionately available to the powerful elites. They advocate that more sociological research be created to benefit the ordinary person and be available to society at large.

Sociologists at Work •

REECE McGEE
DISCUSSES SOCIOLOGY'S BENEFITS FOR TODAY'S STUDENT
Head, Department of Sociology and Anthropology
Purdue University

Reece McGee, Head of the Sociology and Anthropology Department at Purdue University, is known for his commitment to quality undergraduate teaching as a primary focus of academic sociologists. Never content to rest on his many years of teaching experience, McGee is always seeking new methods and examples for teaching sociological concepts. Here he answers our questions by sharing with us some of his underlying assumptions about the importance of sociology to today's students:

Why Do You Believe It Is Important to Study Sociology?

Sociology is good for students in two important ways: 1. it informs them about a significant aspect of their world; and 2. knowing more about the world permits them to better control their own lives in it. The world we live in is an unstable and dangerous place. People lose their jobs, go hungry, are persecuted, and are even killed. The more we learn about how this world works, the more we will be able to adjust our own behavior to survive in it and contribute to its growth. That seems to me to be a compelling reason to try to learn about it.

How Is the Study of Sociology Uniquely Qualified to Help Us Control Our Lives in the World?

There are a variety of disciplines, called "social sciences," that study one aspect or another of this social world, which, by the way, probably has much greater impact on us than does the physical. But sociology asks questions, and therefore finds answers, about that social world that no one else asks or finds. The central subject matter of sociology is the human group, or more generally, human social arrangements. Despite our beliefs about our "individualism," we are in many ways the product of our interactions with other people in groups. On the first day of my own introductory classes, I have my students do a simple exercise to demonstrate this fact. I ask students to take a sheet of scratch paper, and, in about 45 seconds, write down as many answers as they can to the question Who are you? Then I ask if anyone has any answer that is not in fact a statement of membership in some human group or category. I, for example, answering that question, might say, "I am a male, an American citizen, an ex-soldier, a husband, a father, a teacher," and so on . . . *each and every one of which is a statement of group membership!* Typically, well over 95 percent of all the responses given in my huge classes also fall into that category.

I think this suggests the significance of groups to us: we define our *selves*—our most intimate and important possession—in terms of group memberships. Thus it is important to understand groups and other social arrangements such as social institutions and classes in order to better understand what happens to us in the world and to offer us a greater degree of control over it. By understanding sociology we come to understand ourselves better and the "reality" we live in.

How Does Understanding Affect What You Teach Your Students?

Most of my students are freshmen and sophomores of conventional college age. Most are American-born, and most have little experience beyond their home towns, high schools, and families with the society and the world in which they live. I try to choose readings, movies, and lecture materials for them that will illuminate aspects of the world other than those they are familiar with, or explore things they *are* familiar with in ways that will encourage them to pause and think about what they have hitherto taken for granted. Only by becoming aware of the social influences upon our own lives can we actually *decide*, have the freedom to choose, whether or not we should abide by them—and that, to me, is what sociology is all about. ●

Conclusion

We all start out as amateur sociologists. Students generally have a wealth of knowledge and ideas about social behavior before they take their first sociology course. In a sense we all create and apply social theories whether we think of our ideas that way or not.

Professional sociologists combine experiences, ideas, and intuition with the special tools of the trade, such as technical concepts, theories, research designs, and statistical analysis to extend scientifically our knowledge of the social world. As you begin to master the sociological approach, you will sharpen your intuition, discard your mistaken impressions, capitalize on your own experiences by looking at them from new perspectives, and benefit from the best thinking and research of thousands of professional sociologists who have devoted their careers to a better understanding of human behavior.

REVIEW

Summary Questions

1. What is sociology?
2. What is special about the way sociologists approach topics?
3. What sort of questions do sociologists address?
4. What are theories, concepts, and propositions, and how are they used?
5. How did the discipline of sociology develop?
6. What is the place of Marx, Comte, Spencer, Durkheim, Mead, and Weber in the development of sociology?
7. What are the basic concepts of structural-functionalism, the conflict approach, and symbolic-interactionism?
8. What are the contributions of Mills, Collins, Parsons, Davis, Thomas, and Goffman to the development of these theories?
9. What is the scientific method, and how can it be applied to the study of sociology?
10. What are the advantages and disadvantages of the survey method, analysis of existing sources, observational study, and experimental research in the study of sociology?
11. What are some of the challenges and ethical issues in the study of sociology?

Summary Answers

1. Sociology is the science that studies society and human behavior.
2. The subject matter of sociology is quite often invisible, or not directly observable. However, sociologists can observe the consequences of such social characteristictics as group pressure, authority, prestige, and culture. They then form images of these concepts using what C. Wright Mills has called the "sociological imagination," taking into account the influence of social environment, and trying to suspend this influence in order to view their own society as an outsider might.
3. Sociologists want to understand: (a) what goes on in and between groups of people; (b) what are the social differences we observe; (c) what is happening in social institutions; and (d) why and how social change is occurring.
4. A sociological issue is a question we seek to answer with a theory or general explanation of a social phenomenon. A concept is a category of behavior, events, or characteristics that are considered similar for the sake of theory construction. A proposition is a statement that explains one concept by means of another. For example, if we seek to discover why racial groups sometimes live in harmony and sometimes do not (the sociological issue), we may use the concept of racial harmony to describe the differing ways of relating. We would define certain behaviors as indicating harmony exists (operational definition). We would then state our theory in propositions; for example: Different racial groups will live in harmony in situations where enough work exists for all groups to earn a decent living.
5. Sociology developed in the midst of the social and intellectual upheaval surrounding the Industrial Revolution of the nineteenth century. Three branches of sociology grew from roots in three interest groups: social activists, a new breed of scientists dedicated to applying the scientific approach to society, and philosophers interested in humanity's social nature.
6. Karl Marx was the first major proponent of the conflict perspective. He believed that inequality between classes causes conflict between groups of people, and that society must change in order to fulfill the needs of all the people.

   Auguste Comte was the French scientist who gave sociology its name, and promoted the scientific study of society. Herbert Spencer extended his work, developing the idea that society was an organic whole that could be studied much like the human body—the beginnings of structural-functionalism. Emile Durkheim also promoted sociology as a science and structural-functionalism as a perspective, with his emphasis on social facts explaining other social facts—for example, in his classic study, *Suicide*.

George Herbert Mead focused on how we use symbols, including language, and how our use of symbols influences our social development and social life—the beginnings of symbolic-interactionism.

Max Weber's analysis of the major dynamics of society and social change provides the foundations for much of the sociological theory and research of our time. His study, "The Protestant Ethic and the Spirit of Capitalism," was an important study of the roots of the Industrial Revolution, which was sweeping the world in his day.

7. Structural-functionalism assumes that order is dominant in society and that social arrangements arise and persist because they serve society and its members well.

The conflict approach assumes the dominant process in society is conflict and that society divides into two groups, the masses and a small elite who exploit them.

The symbolic-interaction perspective assumes that the important action in society takes place around the use of symbols that channel our thoughts and thereby define what is socially comprehensible and incomprehensible. Practitioners of this approach often focus on interaction among individuals, in contrast to the other perspectives, which tend to look more at social institutions.

8. C. Wright Mills effectively promoted a general conflict perspective in the United States, focusing on social class differences and introducing the concept of the power elite, a tiny minority of government, military, and business figures believed to control the United States.

Randall Collins is one of the most articulate voices today from that perspective, and he developed a formal theory of conflict applicable to all levels of society, especially analyzing the inequalities in the American educational system.

Talcott Parsons extended Durkheim's tradition into the twentieth century, developing the idea that society could be viewed as a system that must (a) adapt to changes in its environment, (b) pursue its goals, (c) integrate itself with other systems, and (d) maintain order within itself, much like a biological organism.

Kingsley Davis is a major contemporary proponent of this structural-functional persepective, and he analyzes wealth and poverty from this viewpoint.

W. I. Thomas extended Mead's ideas, theorizing that people define or construct their own social reality and that their definitions become real because they are real in their consequences.

Erving Goffman has served as a major contemporary spokesperson for the symbolic interaction perspective, and he describes how people present themselves in everyday life in order to manage the impression they give to others.

9. The scientific method involves eight basic steps:

- **a.** Observation of an event that stimulates thinking
- **b.** Defining or classifying the terms or events being considered
- **c.** Formulating the research issue, or hypothesis
- **d.** Generating a theory or proposition—a general statement that serves as a potential answer to the research question
- **e.** Creating a research design in order to test whether the theory or proposition is valid
- **f.** Collecting data—working through the research design to make observations
- **g.** Analyzing the data
- **h.** Making conclusions and evaluating the theory

10. A survey is a research method in which a representative sample of a population is asked to respond to questions. In principle, every member of the population has an equal chance of being selected, so the survey should give an accurate representation of the views of a population. However, people may try to answer questions as they think the survey interviewer wants them to, biasing the results of the research.

Analysis of existing sources is a research technique in which the researcher uses existing documents that were created for some other purpose. This research generally costs much less than the survey, allows access to otherwise unavailable subjects and to data over long periods of time, and involves data that is not influenced by the interviewer. Documents used, however, may be biased toward their original purpose and thus distort the true picture the researcher is trying to find.

In an observational study, the researcher actually witnesses social behavior in its natural setting, either as a participant or an unobtrusive observer. The advantage of this study is that research is accomplished by directly observing subjects' behavior, thus permitting access to nonverbal as well as verbal behavior. Observation also allows for study over a time rather than at one point. However, the researcher has no control over what happens and may have difficulty making order out of his or her observations in order to draw conclusions. Further, the number of subjects a researcher can observe is small, and there are often severe problems in gaining entry to a natural setting.

An experiment is a research design in which the researcher exposes a group of subjects to a treatment and observes its effect, usually in comparison to a similar control group that did not receive the treatment. Experiments can demonstrate clearly that a variable has a particular effect on the subject group, because the researcher retains maximum control over the circumstances of the research. However, experiments are very expensive. Sometimes an aspect of the experiment, other than the "treatment," is the real cause of the experiment's outcome, but this goes unnoticed, and the artificiality of many experimental settings makes generalizing to natural settings risky.

11. Sociology faces the challenge of working with human beings and their social groupings, because people have rights that limit what we can do with them while we are studying them. Sociological subjects can give us important information, but their information can be distorted. Sociologists must decide whether their own views will influence their research and theory development, either believing that knowledge is neutral (value-free sociology) or that value neutrality is either naive or a rationalization for the fact that one is working for the elite (humanist sociology), because most sociological research is funded by and disproportionately available to powerful elites.

Glossary

altruistic suicide when an individual takes his or her own life because of higher commandments

analysis of existing sources a research technique in which the researcher uses existing documents that were created for some other purpose

anomic suicide suicide that results from a lack of regulation of the individual by society

concept a category of behaviors, events, or characteristics that are considered similar for the sake of theory construction

conflict perspective the theoretical position that assumes that conflict is the dominant process in society, that social arrangements represent the dominance of a powerful establishment over the masses, and that once the masses become aware of their plight, they will overthrow the prevailing order and establish a more just world

control group experimental subjects who are not exposed to the independent variable, and can be used as a comparison group to the subjects who are introduced to it

controls characteristics that are held constant in order to exclude factors that might influence the subject's reactions in the experiment

correlation a relationship between two variables in which one changes with the other, but one does not cause the other

detachment the ability of the scientist to set aside cherished beliefs so that new ideas can be given the chance to be tested

egoistic suicide suicide that results from a lack of integration of the individual into society

experiment a research design in which the researcher exposes a group of subjects to a treatment and observes its effect, usually in comparison to a similar control group that did not receive the treatment

field experiment a type of experiment in which the effect of a treatment is studied in a real rather than a simulated setting

hypothesis a conditional statement about the relationships between two or more variables

interview a means of gathering information in which one person asks another questions, either in person or by telephone

observational study a research method in which the researcher actually witnesses social behavior in its natural setting

operational definition a definition that states an abstract concept in concrete terms in order that it might be measured

participant observation a type of observational study in which the researcher takes part in the activity being studied

population the entire set of people a researcher studies

proposition a statement that explains one concept by means of another

questionnaire a research device that gathers information by having the respondent fill in answers to printed questions

random sample a sample that is chosen in such a way that every person in the population had an equal chance of being chosen

research methods systematic techniques for gathering and analyzing facts about theories

sample a part of a population that represents the entire population

replication repeating a piece of research in order to

determine whether the findings will be consistent with the first research

skepticism the attitude in which the scientist endeavors to test even ideas that are widely accepted as truth

sociological theory a general explanation of a social phenomenon

sociology the science that studies society and human behavior

structural-functional perspective thc theoretical position that views social patterns as serving to stabilize and maintain groups and their members

survey a research method in which a sample of a population is asked to respond to questions

symbol a word, gesture, or sign that conveys meaning

symbolic interactionism a sociological perspective that sees symbols as central to understanding social patterns and a person's sense of self

theoretical issue a question we seek to answer with a theory

theory a set of logical statements, or propositions, of relationships among several concepts

unobtrusive observation a type of observational study in which the researcher acts as an observer, but not as a participant, in the activity being studied

variable a characteristic that can change depending on conditions

Suggested Readings

Collins, Randall. 1982. *Sociological Insights: An Introduction to Nonobvious Sociology*. New York: Oxford University Press.

An interesting piece of sociology that refutes the often-quoted myth that sociology is "just common sense."

Goffman, Erving. 1959. *The Presentation of Self in Everyday Life*. Garden City, N.Y.: Doubleday/Anchor.

This is a classic analysis of social interaction from the point of view of life as drama, written in Goffman's entertaining and provocative style.

Lee, Alfred McClung. 1986. *Sociology for Whom*? New York: Oxford University Press.

In this book, Lee suggests that sociologists should be responsible for upholding the highest ethical standards in their work, rather than trying to serve the various "publics" they are in contact with, from publishers to politicians. As past president of the American Sociological Association and founder of the Association for Humanistic Sociology, Lee's opinion on such matters has weight in the sociological community.

Mills, C. Wright. 1967. *The Sociological Imagination*. New York: Oxford University Press.

A well-written exposition of the conflict viewpoint of society. Mills draws upon his vast knowledge and experience to make the book a useful resource for sociologists of all persuasions.

Reynolds, P. D. 1982. *Ethics and Social Science Research*. Englewood Cliffs, N.J.: Prentice–Hall.

Reynolds discusses the problems social science researchers have in dealing ethically with the lives of human beings.

Whyte, William F. 1981. *Street Corner Society, Third Edition*. Chicago: University of Chicago Press.

In this updated version of a classic description of participant observation research, Whyte adds an Appendix in which he discusses the difficulties and rewards of this research method.

PART 2

Social Patterns

CHAPTER 2

CULTURE

- What Is Culture?
- What Are Values and Norms?
- Close-Up on Theory: William Graham Sumner on the Mores Can Make Anything Right
- What Are the Symbolic Elements of Culture?
- Why Do Cultures Differ?
- What Are the Basic Variations Within a Culture?
- How Can Cultures Be Compared?
- How Can We Examine the Culture of the United States?
- Close-Up on Research: Daniel Yankelovich on Changes in the American Culture
- Sociologists at Work: Gary Alan Fine Observes Dungeons and Dragons Subcultures

How's Your Sociological Intuition?

1. Which of the attitudes below differ from culture to culture?
   a. Standards of morality
   b. Standards of beauty
   c. Beliefs about what is true
   d. All of the above
2. Which behavior has been socially acceptable in an actual culture?
   a. Church-sponsored prostitution
   b. Punishing a criminal by having a public official violate the criminal's wife
   c. Child sacrifice
   d. All of the above
3. In virtually all cultures:
   a. Men fight with their fists rather than their feet
   b. Homosexuality is punished
   c. People tend to stand the same distance apart while talking
   d. None of the above

Answers

1. d. Although we believe we "know" what is beautiful and what is not, every culture holds different standards about morality, beauty, and truth. We will see dramatic examples of this fact in our opening section, "What Is Culture?"
2. d. Cultures can have such different ideas about morality that a behavior considered criminal in one culture is accepted as normal in another. We will discuss this more fully in our "Close-Up on Theory: Sumner: The Mores Can Make Anything Right."
3. d. Although we may think of fighting with our feet as ridiculous, in Brazil it is the accepted practice. Similarly, in some cultures homosexuality is thought of as just another normal sexual variation. As we will discover in the section about symbolic elements of culture, even the distance between you and a person with whom you are talking is culturally determined.

WHEN YOU HAVE FINISHED STUDYING THIS CHAPTER, YOU SHOULD KNOW:

- What sociologists mean by culture
- The importance of norms
- How values underlie norms
- How norms vary between cultures
- The difference between folkways and mores
- What the symbolic elements of culture are
- The importance of language in transmitting culture
- How we communicate through "silent language"
- How language affects thought and culture
- Five explanations for cultural differences: the functional, the ecological, the evolutionary, the conflict, and the symbolic interactionist
- Variations within a culture: subcultures, countercultures
- How cultural universalism and cultural relativism differ
- How ethnocentrism affects one's viewpoint
- Why culture shock occurs
- How the value patterns of democracies compare
- What major changes have occurred in the American value system during the past three decades

Beauty Salon to Offer Facial Laceration Services

Daniel's of Hollywood announced today that they now offer facial laceration services to their clients. Gabriealla Stafford, noted model, will be among the first to receive this novel beauty treatment which involves the cutting and tearing of facial skin to leave permanently "beautiful" scar tissue. Fashion consultants are predicting widespread adoption of this radically new approach to total fashion grooming.

Father Offers Daughter for Execution Following Her "Adulterous" Relations

A Tucson, Arizona, man paid private detectives to track down his daughter and her fiance and then turned them over to authorities of a religious order, who put them to death. Despite protests and pleas for protection, the couple was unable to escape a well-financed professional dragnet that located them in their hideaway in a remote region of Oregon. The father, Curtis Johnson, said he now "has peace in his soul knowing God's will has been done in righting the wrongs" committed by his daughter. The couple had been married for over a year, but they were known by friends, and eventually by family, to have lived together for several months before their marriage. This, according to Johnson, is a vile offense to God, punishable by death.

These stories may sound like items from a sensationalistic newspaper, but each actually describes a "normal" behavior in its own cultural setting. Many South American, African, Australian, North American, European, and Asian peoples have practiced facial laceration as means of beautification. Indeed, numerically speaking, ours may be in a minority of societies that do not practice this craft.

The story of the execution of the "adulterous" couple may remind you of a news story from the Middle East, where even in recent time fornication is such a serious offense that it is technically punishable by death. Press reports of the late 1970s described the shooting of an Arabian princess, Mashall bint Abdul Aziz, 23, and the beheading of her lover after their conviction by an Islamic court for adultery. Other similar incidents have passed with much less press attention. In one case a prince drowned one of his daughters in a swimming pool when he learned that she had slept with a man before her marriage (*Time*, February 13, 1978, p. 46) Whereas contemporary Americans do not literally execute for adultery, we may "execute" people's careers for the act; for instance, TV evangelist Jim Bakker and presidential hopeful Gary Hart.

In their original settings, these behaviors are routine and based in reality. Scarred faces *are* pretty to members of some African tribes. Muslims are still morally outraged by those who defile the marriage bed. Indeed, in the native contexts, it would be *not* scarring one's face and *not* avenging extramarital sex that would be newsworthy! These rather incredible facts are explained by a fundamental sociological principle: Societies create their own realities through culture.

What Is Culture?

Many people associate *culture* with the fine arts, such as opera and ballet, but to social scientists it has a different meaning. ***Culture** includes the values, norms, language, tools, and other shared products of society that provide a plan for social life* and are passed on from generation to generation.

In sociological terms, culture defines reality by defining beauty, morality, and truth. We learn what is beautiful and ugly, what is right and wrong, and what

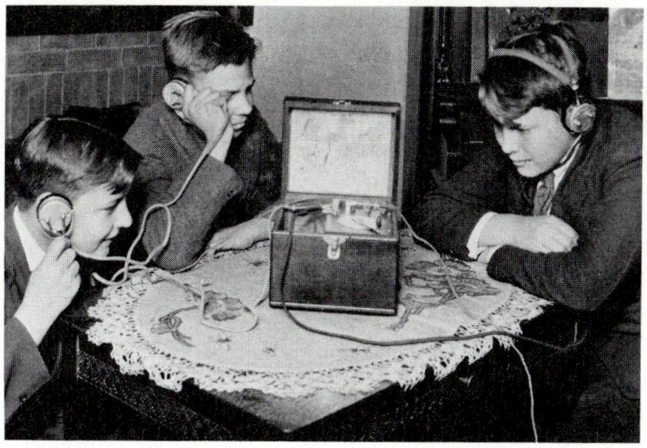

Artifacts may bring us together or isolate us. We act out our culture, which is influenced by our inventions or technology. The boys huddled around an early crystal radio are brought together (at least physically) while the person with a "Walkman" is isolated (sometimes even dangerously) from social interaction by the crystal radio's great grandchild. (*The Bettmann Archive*)

is true and false from our society. It is easy to believe that fashions like Guess? jeans or shaved heads are social creations. It is not too difficult to view others' beliefs as socially created, even when they involve bizarre acts like scarring faces in the name of beauty or executing people who fornicate.

It is perhaps most difficult to realize that some of our own most deeply felt beliefs are also culturally defined. Yet because beliefs differ from one culture to another we can see that such ideas are often social creations rather than ultimate truths. Culture involves intangibles such as democracy, religion, or the rules governing football, and it involves tangible objects such as plows, gasoline engines, television, and computers. These material products of society are called ***artifacts***. In our next chapter, "Society," we explore the impact of tools on social patterns and ideas. Throughout the text we also see how ideas affect society.

The study of culture forms a large part of the subject matter of sociology. Sociologists are interested in such issues as how rules and values are developed, how they affect social behavior, and how they are transmitted throughout the society.

What Are Values and Norms?

Due to illness, you missed an exam. The professor arranges a make-up time, and you meet at the appointed hour. The professor gives you the exam and your directions and after a few minutes tells you that you will be left on your own to finish. You need a good grade, and you feel moderately well prepared. Will you look at your notes to be certain of an A, or will you rely on your own knowledge?

The chances are strong that you will remain honest, even without fear of being caught, not out of loyalty to the professor but out of loyalty to the values and norms your society has passed on to you. ***Values*** *are shared ideas about what is right and wrong, good and bad, desirable and undesirable.* Values are general concepts, whereas ***norms*** *are shared rules or guidelines for behavior in specific situations.* The *norm* that says we do not cheat on an exam is based on the positive *value* our culture calls honesty. That value, which you may never have considered consciously, underlies your everyday behavior.

You agree with other members of your society that certain values are important, and that your behavior should be guided by them. In fact, as William Gamson suggests, "Every social situation is built upon a working consensus among its participants" (Gamson, Fireman, Rytina, 1982, p. 111). If this were not true, we would all be paralyzed in the face of the decisions we are asked to make every day.

We share a common value of responsibility. As we walk into a building we trust the architects were careful in planning the structure and the workers followed the plans diligently. We assume, implicitly of course, that if they did not, the building inspector was responsible and ordered corrections. As our society becomes more complicated, we are forced to trust more individuals and organizations. Some sociologists are studying how these trust relationships are formed and what social controls will come into play to regulate this process (Shapiro, 1987).

These values are transmitted to individual society members by other members, and they remain fairly stable over time. Robin Williams, a sociologist who specializes in studying values and culture compares the transmission of values through personal attachments between people to the transmission of physical traits through genetic processes. To him, values are like the information encoded on the RNA molecules, which are transmitted or carried by personal attachments much as DNA is the carrier of RNA information. Carrying this analogy further, Williams suggests that societies remember their past, including their values. For example, a society which has recently won a violent conflict may continue for some time to place a positive value on physical might. As Williams puts it, "*Successful* bloody societies tend to glorify bloodiness" (Williams, 1983).

The culture of the United States, for example, places value on life, liberty, equality, and the individual pursuit of happiness. Many socialist societies, in contrast, tend to rate economic equality above other values, such as liberty of personal movement, that we might rank high. Similarly, whereas Western societies tend to stress material well-being, traditional societies of the Far East emphasize spiritual well-being instead.

These values reflect the basic beliefs of their societies. For example, when people commonly believed that mental illness was a symptom of being possessed by demons or the result of immoral behavior, societies tended to punish those who were mentally ill. Today, most Western cultures believe that "crazy people" are, in fact, ill, and deserve the best medical treatment we can give them. Whereas our ancestors might have seen hallucinating as "wicked," we view it as a symptom of disease. When we learned about the origins of hallucinations, we altered the value we placed on being in touch with reality. This change in beliefs also caused us to change our value on punishing those who hallucinate: we no longer punish this behavior, because we do not see it as evil. The change in our basic beliefs has affected our values and, in turn, our conception of the reality of treatment for mental illness (Robin Williams, 1983).

Every society develops norms, often derived from or tested against its values. For instance, the United States Constitution is regarded as a key statement of the American value system, and a new law may be tested against the Constitution to determine its legality. ***Laws*** *are norms that are formally enacted or stated.* A law usually carries defined punishment for its violation.

Norms may be formal and stated or informal and unstated. Sometimes norms other than laws are stated, as when parents tell children not to interrupt their elders. Sometimes norms are unstated, as when a child learns masculine and feminine behavior patterns from people he or she observes.

The norms that carry the most extreme penalties are taboos. ***Taboos*** *are rules that prohibit certain behavior and carry severe punishment for violators.* For example, American culture—and most other cultures—has a strong taboo against incest, or sexual contact between brother and sister or between parent and child. A parent who has sexually abused his child is almost universally scorned because of this taboo.

Norms usually carry sanctions. *A* ***sanction*** *is a reward for behavior that conforms to a norm or punishment for behavior that violates a norm.* In addition to formal norms such as laws, informal norms can also carry sanctions; in fact, most sanctions are informal. For example, if a man is late meeting a friend for a date, he may receive an icy stare or a sarcastic remark, though no formal statement of these consequences exists. Formal sanctions are spelled out more explicitly. For example, receiving a varsity letter for outstanding service in a school sport is a sanction that supports the norm of participation in sports.

Some of the most important norms of a society are parts of institutions. ***Institutions*** *are organized sets of norms, values, statuses, and roles that are centered around a basic need of society.* (We will discuss the concepts of status and role in Chapter 3, "Society.") For example, the family is an almost universal social institution that provides for raising children, among other activities. People grow up with strong beliefs about how the family should raise children, but they rarely think of themselves as guided by specific rules (norms). These rules do exist, however, in the form of beliefs such as "families should live together," "parents should control young children's activities," "family members should help each other when in trouble," or "families should share their resources according to a plan laid down by the parents." The concept of social institutions will be discussed more fully in the next chapter and in Part 5, which features the five basic institutions of most societies: the family, religion, the state, the economic system, and education.

NORMS THAT VARY BETWEEN CULTURES. Some norms are nearly universal, like the incest taboo, but many are specific to one society or to one group in a society. For example, Arab women are expected to cover themselves at all times, and even well-educated, "modern" Arab women follow this norm. In contrast, American women are often encouraged by advertisements to dress in a manner that reveals their bodies and is considered "sexy" by others in the society.

Some central African tribes consider obesity beautiful, and at puberty a girl is separated from others, fed sweet and fatty foods, allowed little activity, and rubbed with oils. During this period a girl is taught what her womanly duties are to be, and when sufficiently fat, she parades around the village to her proud bridegroom (Benedict, 1934). In the United States, the high incidence of anorexia nervosa, which involves teenage girls starving themselves to death, reflects the opposite norm—slimness at all costs. These examples show that variation among norms of different cultures may be virtually endless.

CLOSE-UP on • *THEORY* •

William Graham Sumner on the Mores Can Make Anything Right

The Theorist and the Setting

Folkways is one of the classic works in sociology and is fascinating even eighty years after its publication in 1906. William Graham Sumner wrote it as a diversion from writing an introductory sociology textbook, similar to this one, in 1899. He became so engrossed in the topic of mores and folkways that he decided to write a book solely about them instead of the text.

One of the founders of sociology in the United States, Sumner came to the discipline from an earlier career as an Episcopal minister. He preferred to call sociology "the science of society," because he "detested with fury most of the work done under the name of sociology, most of its tendencies, and nearly all those who taught it" (Sumner, p. viii). This was perhaps because many early sociologists wrote from a philosophical perspective, which Sumner considered a sham.

Sumner was the first sociologist to address in depth the topic of norms. He identified two types of norms: folkways and mores (pronounced MORE-ays). ***Folkways** are norms that prescribe ordinary ways of behaving in everyday social situations*. A person who violates a folkway may be thought peculiar or inconsiderate. ***Mores** are more powerful norms that are considered vital to the society's well-being*. Generally, a person who violates social mores will be judged either immoral or insane—a much more severe judgment than that imposed for violating a folkway. For example, in the United States stealing violates social mores and is harshly punished. Letting a door slam in someone's face violates a folkway.

The Theorist's Goal

In *Folkways* Sumner attempts to answer the question: What, if any, limits exist upon a society's ability to define a behavior as right?

Concepts and Propositions

Sumner's central proposition is simple:

Proposition: Mores can make anything right and prevent condemnation of anything (p. 521).

Sumner defines *mores* as "the ways of doing things which are current in a society to satisfy human needs and desires together with the faiths, notions, codes, and standards of well living which inhere in those ways, having a genetic connection with them" (p. 520). Sumner's lengthy definition refers to the accepted and practiced norms of a community, which define right and wrong. For instance, our law against murder and our imprisoning of murderers define murder as morally wrong. Murder violates our mores.

Sumner's operational definition of the term *right* is "behavior which is socially accepted and correct" (p. 520). Note that *right* in this context means "socially accepted" rather than right according to a universal ethical standard. In contrast, Sumner uses the term *rational* to define ultimate moral truth: "morally correct in a way which goes beyond reference to one's culture" (p. 532). Sumner's basic thesis is that there appears to be no limit to the ability of mores to justify or make right even the most extreme behavior, which might be condemned if judged by rational, or ultimate, standards.

To illustrate and support this proposition, Sumner cites behaviors accepted as proper in other times or in other cultures but which seem outrageous by rational standards. Among these are the "horrors of the medieval dungeons . . . dark, damp, cold, and infested by vermin, rats, snakes" (p. 524). He also cites a law from the same period that provided that if a criminal had no property to be taken, his wife should be violated by a public official as a penalty for his wrongdoing. Sumner discusses the rules of warfare of the same period: "If two parties got into a controversy about such a question as whether Christ and his apostles lived by beggary, they understood that the victorious party in the controversy would burn the defeated party. That was the rule of the game, and they went into it on that understanding" (p. 524). Other examples include church-sponsored prostitution and child sacrifice, both widely accepted by people whose cultural mores defined these acts as right.

Interestingly, Sumner stops short of saying that moral values are totally linked to a culture's mores. Rather, he suggests that individuals can rise above society's mores and make judgments that are morally superior to them: "It cannot be doubted that, at any time, all ethical judgments are made through the atmosphere of the mores of the time. It is they which tell us what is right. It is only by high mental discipline that we can be trained to rise above that atmosphere and form rational judgments on current cases" (p. 432).

In other words, with effort people can train themselves to think not only in terms of the mores of their culture, but to think rationally also, in terms of an ultimate good and evil. For example, although owning slaves was an accepted norm in upperclass United States' society in the early 1800s, many people believed that owning another person was morally, rationally wrong and publicly denounced the practice. Sumner would see this as a rational judgment made by rising above the mores of the time, which sanctioned slavery. It is important to note, however, that the pressures that guide us toward being members of a group may also inhibit our clear rethinking of our group's mores in this way.

Sumner also saw culture as oppressive to the young of the society. His second basic thesis was that culture coerces and restricts the young of the group. For the purposes of explicating a long and complicated theory, however, we have considered only one proposition in this Close-Up.

Interpretation

If Sumner is right, one can expect to see virtually any behavior defined as morally correct in some social settings. However, Sumner implies that a moral person need not blindly follow the prevailing definitions of right and wrong, because it is possible for a person to rise above cultural definitions. This suggests that individuals are responsible for judging the morality of their conduct beyond justifying their acts as one's society sanctions.

Questions

1. What are some examples of behavior once accepted as morally right but now defined as wrong?
2. What are some behaviors socially defined by us as morally right that would violate the mores of another culture?
3. How might one rise above cultural definitions to determine what is right and wrong on a rational, or universal, scale?
4. Is there an inconsistency between claiming that mores can make any behavior socially acceptable and simultaneously claiming that individuals can rise above their cultural mores?

SOURCE William Graham Sumner. 1906. *Folkways: A Study of the Sociological Importance of Usages, Manners, Customs, Mores, and Morals*. New York: Dover, 1959 reprint.

What Are the Symbolic Elements of Culture?

*A **symbol** is that which represents something else.* A symbol may represent something concrete or something abstract—a concept or an idea. Thus, the skull and crossbones is a symbol for poison, the Statue of Liberty represents freedom, and words, our most versatile symbols, take on an almost infinite array of meanings. Symbols are socially important because norms and values are transmitted within a culture or to other cultures through symbols.

Much of human communication is through symbols such as gestures, signs, stance, style of clothing, and hairstyle. We all knew by the way our mother looked at us when we came home late, for example, if she was angry or relieved and if we were therefore in trouble or not. A mother's gestures and expressions are symbols through which we learn our family's norms from a very young age.

Although symbols are used primarily to help convey meanings, they can also instill meaning into experiences or events. Symbols not only provide focus and direction for a society, but also sustain personal emotional experiences. When ideas and values surrounding an emotion become embodied in a symbol, they retain their force and remain in the minds of the people more easily. The flag, for instance, is such an emotionally laden symbol of national values to citizens of the country it represents.

LANGUAGE

Language is a profoundly important set of symbols. Written and spoken words represent objects or ideas. Among all animals, only humans communicate through language to indicate complex concepts like feelings, space, and time. The ability to arrange verbal symbols in new patterns, instead of repeating only what they have heard, is generally accepted as an ability that separates humans from other species of animals. Some biologists believe humans' power to reason through language replaces the protection of claws, teeth, speed, or strength. People use symbols to think and talk their way out of difficulties instead of fighting their way out, and this thinking helps them survive.

THE SAPIR–WHORF HYPOTHESIS

Most social scientists see a strong connection between a society's language and the rest of its culture. Clyde Kluckhohn wrote that "every language is also a special way of looking at the world and interpreting experiences" (1964, p. 124).

This concept was studied and debated by two early researchers at Yale University, Edward Sapir and his student Benjamin Whorf. Their theory of "linguistic relativity," the Sapir–Whorf hypothesis, is no longer fully accepted, but it continues to raise important issues. After studying the structure of many different languages, Sapir and Whorf came to believe that all higher levels of thinking depend on language, and the structure of a people's language influences how they understand the world (Whorf, 1956). In other words, language is not merely a means of communicating; it also influences what ideas can be communicated.

The Sapir–Whorf hypothesis can be illustrated by examining how the English language and the Hopi language speak about time. English uses three tenses: past, present, and future. For the Hopi Indian, time is on a continuum, with yesterday being simply part of the preparation for today, and tomorrow being an extension of today, including today, yesterday, and all time. To the Hopi, time is not a motion but a "getting later" of everything that has ever been done. Hopi verb forms indicate only whether a statement is a report of an event, an expectation of an event, or a generalization about events (Whorf, in Carroll, 1956).

Because speakers of English must constantly choose a tense to speak in, they are constantly aware of time. This may help explain our preoccupation with diaries, time systems, histories, calendars, and clocks. The Hopi take time as it comes and do not try to tie it to artificial systems of accounting. Neither do they record dates of events that have happened, because by definition those events are part of today.

The words people use to name things in their environment also say much about what is important in their culture. The Hopi have one noun that stands for everything that flies except birds. For instance, they call a mosquito and an airplane by the same name.

English speakers may believe their language is "better" because it distinguishes different objects that fly. English, on the other hand, has only one word for snow, while the Inuit Eskimo have over twenty words to describe it, distinguishing falling snow from slushy snow, snow on the ground, snow packed hard like ice, wind-driven flying snow, and so on. Snow is an important concept in the Inuit culture, and they might be astonished by the English-speaker's ignorance of its many forms.

To go one step further, snow was almost never seen by the Aztecs. Their language expresses this fact in that it has a single word to represent cold, ice, and snow (Whorf, in Carroll, 1956). Clearly, the language of a society reflects what is important to that society. But our ability to communicate and reason is culturally limited by limitations of our particular language.

Various observers, including George Orwell in his classic *1984* have noted the tendency of governments, especially oppressive ones, to seek to control perceptions of reality by controlling the vocabulary. For instance, the citizens in Orwell's novel were to refer to their leader as "Big Brother." This kept them from simply referring to him as the dictator he was. Here in the United States the "Department of Defense" is now the official name of the agency once called, perhaps more accurately, the "War Department." Thus each time we refer to this branch of government we associate it with positive perceptions of defending the innocent rather than making war on the same. Similarly, that reprehensible behavior called a "numbers racket," when private citizens do it, is called a "lottery" when the government does it. To paraphrase Kluckhohn: the language of our goverment agencies demonstrates their special way of looking at the world and interpreting experience.

NONVERBAL SYMBOLS

Much of human communication is still nonverbal, as in the case of certain hand gestures that have extremely negative or insulting meanings. Such gestures, of course, vary from culture to culture. For example, a group of American prisoners of war were asked by their North Vietnamese captors to pose for a photograph to be sent to the United States as evidence of the prisoners' good spirits in captivity. The picture was accompanied by letters praising the North Vietnamese. The GIs posed with smiling faces, but each of them was also demonstrating the familiar American hand-sign signifying contempt. The Vietnamese, unfamiliar with the symbolic meaning of the gesture, ignored it completely. In this case, the symbolic hand gesture easily outweighed the hundreds of words sent with the picture.

Edward T. Hall, an anthropologist, expanded on the Sapir–Whorf hypothesis by studying nonverbal rather than verbal communication. Hall's thesis is that perceptions of space and time are closely tied to culture and can be identified by studying the culture's "silent language," or nonverbal space and time messages (1959, 1983).

For example, when Arabs from the Middle East are being friendly, they stand very close to each other. In the United States, in contrast, people stand far enough apart to avoid offending others by their breath or other body odors or invading another's space. This illustrates cultural differences in ***social distance****, or the distance at which it is comfortable to relate to someone else*. The distance people tolerate will change depending on what type of interaction is taking place; for instance, you can feel comfortable when a friend is talking to you from only fifteen inches away (intimate distance), but a stranger talking to you at that distance will probably cause you to feel uncomfortable. Try talking to a friend while standing very close, perhaps ten or twelve inches away. If the friend is from the United States, he or she will almost certainly back away, because cultural conditioning in this country requires more space than that to be comfortable.

This social distance is an important concept when training exchange students with organizations such as the American Field Service. American students are taught what distance is considered appropriate in the country where they will be living, and they practice feeling comfortable at that distance. If not taught this, the Americans may unconsciously back away from people in the countries they visit, which may be taken by their hosts as a sign of unfriendliness.

Perceptions of time also vary from culture to culture. For example, in the United States, business appointments may be made weeks in advance, and it is considered impolite to invite people to dinner on short notice. This is different from, for instance, the Middle Eastern attitude toward time, which "places everything beyond a week into a single category of 'future' " (Hall, 1959). This and Hall's other examples suggest that nonverbal communication both helps form an individual's ideas about life and reflects a culture's dominant values and norms.

Why Do Cultures Differ?

Because we so often follow culturally prescribed rules, we can learn a lot about social behavior by studying culture. Cultures differ in their definitions of what is beautiful and ugly, right and wrong, and true and false, as well as in the tools they develop with which to work.

Why do cultures differ? This is a very broad question. We will begin to sketch the answers here and fill in the details as we proceed through the book.

THE FUNCTIONAL APPROACH

As we saw in Chapter 1, the *functional approach explains the presence of a particular cultural trait by considering how effectively it works with other elements of the existing culture to maintain the society.* A *functional* ***cultural trait*** *has a positive consequence for the society.* This theory recognizes that a particular innovation will probably not be adopted into the culture unless it fits well with the existing culture and contributes to the well-being of the society. The innovation may be introduced through invention, discovery, or ***diffusion****, the process in which one society adopts a cultural trait from another society's culture.* (Linton, 1936).

Sociologists of the functional school believe that culture maintains societies in two important ways. First, culture provides for continuing social order by handing down prescribed ways of behaving in specific situations, such as who controls land, who is responsible for caring for the young or the old, what obligations are owed to God and to government, which side of the road to drive on, and what to wear to a wedding. Second, culture is a social inheritance, distinct from a biological inheritance; culture allows people to benefit from the achievements of previous generations. Culture promotes the survival of a society by providing the knowledge and technology necessary to ensure the sustenance and protection of its members. In other words, culture allows each society to build upon discoveries of the past. In this way, the culture of societies tends to perpetuate differences between them.

The functionalists' emphasis on the need to integrate new traits with the old can help explain various new adaptations. For instance, many developing societies are stressing their environment with overpopulation, but they have not adopted available birth control techniques because the culture continues to value large families. Conversely, modern birth control techniques have been more readily adopted in industrialized societies where the culture places value on small families.

THE ECOLOGICAL APPROACH. The ***ecological approach*** *examines the way societies adapt culture to their physical environment in order to survive*, and as such can be seen as a special case of the functional approach. This point of view focuses on how the society adapts patterns that are functional with regard to the physical surroundings.

The ecological approach often helps explain cultural differences that from other points of view seem irrational. Many people from Western cultures are puzzled at the Hindu belief that cows are sacred and not to be used for food. Why does such a cultural trait survive in a country like India where malnutrition is rampant? First, the assumption that the cow is never eaten is incorrect, because non-Hindus from lower social strata will eat the meat after a cow dies naturally. Also, cows serve several important functions for Hindus, of whom many are small farm operators. Cows produce manure for fertilizer and fuel. Oxen are used for plowing. Moreover, the cattle subsist on otherwise useless scrub vegetation. Thus, leading ecological theorist Marvin Harris concludes from his study of this Indian custom that what appears to be an irrational cultural trait can be seen after closer examination as functional to the society (Harris, 1974).

Artifacts provide a clear example of adaptation to the environment. ***Artifacts***, the material products of society, include the diverse set of human inventions ranging from important developments like the wheel, plow, steam engine, and computer to less significant products like jewelry and Barbie dolls. The development of snowshoes in the sub-Arctic cultures, outrigger canoes in Polynesia, and agricultural terraces by the Inca allows societies to inhabit territories that pose unusual problems of survival (Caneiro, 1968).

The ecological view may be used to explain social relationships as well as material culture. For example, seasonal activities brought changes in the authority structure of the Plains Indian culture:

> During most of the year . . . the band chief had little authority, and the socioceremonial life of

the band was simple. For the summer buffalo hunt, however, the bands came together and assumed a form of tribal organization that was distinctly more complex. Band chiefs, previously without superiors, now formed themselves into a council from which a paramount tribal chief was selected. The tribal chief wielded considerably greater authority than he had as band chief; it was now his responsibility to coordinate and direct the activities of the tribe as a whole.

Men's associations, inactive during most the year, re-formed when the bands came together. . . . One of these men's societies was designated by the tribal chief to serve as a police force charged with punishing violations of the strict rules that prevailed during the buffalo hunt, as well as with preserving order during the march and on the occasion of the sun dance. . . . All the features—the council, the tribal chief, the men's societies, the police force, the sun dance organization—lapsed when the tribe broke up into its constituent units in the autumn. (Carneiro, 1968, p. 555)

The Plains Indians hunted buffalo together out of necessity. The task was so large it required a group effort. As a result, the social structure of the tribe became much more complex during the summer months when buffalo hunting was an important activity.

Even differences in religious beliefs may be related to the physical environment. Societies that exist in extremely adverse climates often have elaborate religions in part to account for life's many hardships. Societies in benign climates, like the Pacific Islands, often have a much less elaborate religion.

The ecological niche of a culture may also influence the personalities of its members. For instance, some nomadic peoples develop restlessness after the band has spent more than a few weeks in one place,

High technology? Though primitive by our standards, societies that have introduced the technology of domesticating and herding animals represent a step forward from those that only hunt and gather. Sociocultural evolution refers to the process of increasingly complex social change caused by the introduction of new technology. (*Esther A. Gerling/FPG International*)

even when food is plentiful. Carneiro explains this phenomenon:

> By being mentally adapted to [their] normal ecological conditions, the individuals in a culture are always ready, and even eager, to make what is ordinarily the most appropriate response. The matter may be put this way: a sociocultural system works best when it makes people *want* to do what they *have* to do. (1968, p. 553)

THE EVOLUTIONARY APPROACH. Another major explanation of cultural patterns is *the* ***evolutionary approach****, which views culture as developing through a series of stages toward forms that are increasingly well suited to the environment.* As such it can be seen as a subcategory of the functionalist approach, while also being related to conflict theory. For instance, societies seem to proceed through various major stages according to societies' means of obtaining food. Very simple societies, called hunting and gathering societies, gather wild fruits and vegetables, catch fish, and hunt game. When cultivation of plants is discovered, the culture adjusts to incorporate it. Often the next major discovery is that animals can be gathered into herds and controlled as a food supply. Eventually, according to the evolutionary approach, increasingly sophisticated means of food production lead the societies to fixed, agriculture-based settlements, then into forms of industrialization.

This evolution does not proceed in a direct line at one speed. A society may skip some stages altogether, and, whereas some change rapidly, others seem to stay at one stage indefinitely. The evolutionary approach explains cultural differences as responses to major shifts in how the society produces food and other goods and services. Societies innovate, adapt to their environment, and select ideas from the practices of other cultures they encounter. Depending on physical and cultural circumstances, a particular trait may or may not become part of the culture.

Gerhard and Jean Lenski termed this process ***sociocultural evolution***, referring to *the process of increasingly complex social change because of the introduction of new technology* (1982). As we discuss more completely in the next chapter, this change tends to be more rapid the more "advanced" the society becomes. Chapter 3 also discusses the ways in which societies may be categorized into types according to how most people work. For instance, in an industrial society most people work in a factory setting, whereas in an agrarian society most of the population works in agriculture. By classifying societies this way we shall see that societies, in a very rough sense, seem to evolve or develop from a very primitive and simple form, in which people hunt wild game and gather natural vegetation for food, through various stages on to complex industrial forms. As societies change from one stage to another, their cultures change too. Throughout this book we devote a good deal of attention to explaining cultural patterns and why they change.

The origins of cultural change are discussed at greater length in Part 5 as we study social institutions such as the family (Chapter 13) and religion (Chapter 14), government (Chapter 16), education (Chapter 17), and social change and urbanization (Chapter 19).

THE CONFLICT APPROACH

Sociologists working from the conflict perspective assume that conflict, competition, and change are the dominant process in society. Hence social arrangements such as cultural definitions about who should do which work and how much they should be paid are viewed as the result of power struggles. Marx said that the history of all hitherto existing societies was a history of class conflict, a struggle between the owners, who control the tools of production (capitalists), and the workers (the proletariat). Marx argued that in virtually all societies culture is created and imposed on the masses by the ruling class (1867).

Whereas functionalists emphasize how cultural traits harmonize with the overall goals of the society, conflict theorists point out that prevailing definitions of truth, justice, and beauty may serve the elites at the expense of the masses. One need only to consider recent history to recognize that cultural issues have often been determined through violent conflict. The United States not only pioneered democracy, it established it by being victorious in the Revolutionary War. Similarly, the People's Republic of China was established after a massive revolution. Clearly the versions of political justice and historical truth taught in the United States and the People's Republic of China are quite different as the result of the outcome of power struggles between those in power and those not.

Conflict theorists remind us that much social change develops through conflict between groups. For example, breakthroughs in civil rights were accomplished through the nonviolent protests of the sixties, both in the South and North. Similarly, without the mobilization of such organizations as NOW fighting against injustices that women have suffered and continue to suffer merely because of their gender, positive change in the area of women's rights would either not have occurred or would have been very long in coming. Although both women and blacks are still "second-rate citizens" in many ways, changes in the way present-day culture receives them are due primarily to the conflicts of the past. (Chambliss, 1973; R. Collins, 1974; Kerbo, 1983).

As we try to understand differences in culture, we should consider how a particular cultural feature relates to the society at large (the functionalist approach) and what its relation is to the elites (the conflict approach). For instance, in discussing why vast differences in wealth are considered acceptable in our society, we might ask: Is this for the benefit of society or for the benefit of those who are wealthy?

THE SYMBOLIC INTERACTIONIST APPROACH

In small groups and large, people create their own cultural symbols. Gary Alan Fine studied the culture of Little League teams to watch this process in action (Fine, 1987). He argues that in order for an element to take its place in the culture of a human group, it must meet five criteria. First, it must be part of the known culture and be able to be understood by all its members. Second, the usable elements of the culture cannot be taboo. Third, the element must serve a function to the culture. Although Fine sees structural functionalism as fairly well discounted on a societal level, he does be-

TABLE 2.1 Differing Explanations of Cultural Variation

Functional	If a cultural variation has a positive consequence for society, it will be adopted and contribute to the well-being of society.
Ecological (A type of functional approach)	Societies adapt culture to their physical environment in order to survive.
Evolutionary	Culture develops through a series of stages toward forms that are increasingly well suited to the environment, based on changes in the tools or technology of the culture.
Conflict	Prevailing definitions of beauty, truth, and justice may serve the elites at the expense of the masses, with culture being created and imposed on the masses by the ruling class.
Symbolic interactionist	The importance of symbols in understanding culture and the social behavior it creates suggests that symbols are the major agent for transmitting and shaping culture.

Safe! And if this contributes to winning the game, the team will be more likely to adopt an innovation such as the wrist bands that this runner introduced into his team culture. (*AP/Wide World Photos*)

lieve that in the small group the things that persevere are those which are seen as useful. Fourth, the cultural element should be appropriate in terms of status hierarchy, so that honored people in the group will receive certain symbolic group rewards. Fine's fifth principle is that an element must be triggered by circumstance to be accepted as part of the culture.

If the Little League team captain wore a new wristband at a winning game, the trigger to its inclusion in the culture of that team would be winning the game. Because the boys are familiar with the wearing of athletic wristbands, it is not a taboo element in their culture. Its use might promote positive feelings about belonging to the team, and if it was worn by a person of power in the group, the chances are great that more wristbands will be worn after that winning game, especially by the more prestigious players.

Through this process, satisfying the five criteria, elements of the small-group interaction that occurs in groups of kids playing ball together can become a part of the culture of Little League. The culture will change gradually over time, as new elements are introduced and either meet or fail to meet the criteria. This same process occurs in all the groups to which we belong, to a greater or lesser extent, depending on the purpose and longevity of the group.

Thus, in symbolic interactionist terms, we are all creating our own cultures. Symbols are not only one of the elements of culture, they are a major agent for transmitting and shaping culture. The symbolic interactionist approach highlights the importance of symbols in understanding culture and the social behavior it shapes. As we seek to understand culture and society, the symbolic-interactionist approach sensitizes us to symbols, words, ideas, and their power.

What Are the Basic Variations Within a Culture?

We have been speaking of a culture as if it were a single, integrated social stucture. Obviously, this is rarely true. Walking down any major city street brings us into contact with dozens of groups, all with some distinct cultural traits. Two of the most common variations within a culture are subcultures and countercultures.

SUBCULTURES

Large, complex societies often contain smaller social groups with some distinctive cultural features not shared with the dominant culture. *A **subculture** is the culture of a subgroup of society which adopts norms that set them apart from the dominant group.*

Many subcultures thrive in the United States. For instance, some cities have a Chinatown, a community of Asian-Americans who take part in the general culture but also have distinctive cultural patterns in language, food, child-rearing customs, and philosophy. Members of the Jewish faith constitute another subcultural group in the United States, though this would make them part of the dominant group in Israel. On the other hand, although physicians share norms distinct from those of many other occupations, they do not constitute a subculture, because their normative system is known to the rest of society and is integrated into the general culture.

Many sociologists have suggested that there is a subculture of youth in our society (Becker, 1964; Eisenstadt, 1956; Riesman et al., 1961; Coleman, 1961). This idea does not simply mean that youths have different behavior patterns from adults. A youth subculture consists of interests, speech patterns, and aesthetic tastes that are generally known *only* among young people. The subculture is formed because those who are in the category of youth have a distinct set of norms and values that replaces those prescribed by the dominant culture during that period of time in which they are in that category.

Other subcultures abound in American society today. Anyone who has ever moved from the country to the city, or from the North to the South can testify to strong differences between these regions in value structures and behaviors, from what is considered good manners to what kinds of churches people attend.

Americans disagree about many important, emotionally laden issues. Gay activists and antihomosexuals square off in elections. Pro-life and pro-choice groups meet in what have sometimes been violent clashes. Groups that urge our schools to get "back to basics" are countered by those that encourage more "enrichment and creativity" for our young people. It has been said that once you get beyond values regarding good health, honesty, having a happy family, and such topics, Americans do not actually share many values. Instead, we disagree about most things! The many subcultures in the United States create a vibrant diversity in its culture.

COUNTERCULTURES

*A **counterculture** is a subculture whose norms and values are not just different from but in conflict with those of the dominant culture.* For example, the Amish, a conservative Protestant community of people living primarily in southeastern Pennsylvania, believe in preserving a strict, traditional way of life based on farming and close family and church ties. The Amish do not use motor-driven equipment like tractors and automobiles be-

The Amish rejection of relatively high-tech automobiles in favor of lower-tech horses and buggies, or in this case simple bicycle carts is a countercultural pattern. They represent a subculture whose norms and values are not just different from but in conflict with those of the dominant culture. (*The Picture Cube*)

cause they believe that such use will ultimately weaken their community by encouraging Amish to become too worldly and taking the focus of their energies off of devotion to God and right living. Because their fundamental values conflict with the dominant culture's emphasis on technological advances, the Amish have virtually isolated themselves from the rest of American society and have come to constitute a countercultural group.

Some countercultural groups seek to change the dominant culture to conform to their normative system, leading to radical conflict. In the 1960s a countercultural group called the Weathermen were dedicated to bringing about the overthrow of the United States political and economic institutions. The anti-Nazi Underground, which worked for the overthrow of the Nazi regime in Europe during World War II, could also have been viewed as a counterculture of the dominant culture of Nazi Germany.

Milton Yinger, the sociologist who first defined the concept of counterculture, suggests that subcultures will appear "as a result of mobility or an extension of communication that brings groups of different cultural backgrounds into membership in the same society, followed by physical or social isolation of both that prevents full assimilation." Countercultures, on the other hand, arise "under conditions of deprivation and frustration of major values, and where value confusion and weak social controls exist, contracultural norms will appear" (Yinger, 1960, p. 635).

Yinger applied his theory to Afro-Americans and predicted a movement from a black subculture toward a black counterculture, a trend that in fact occurred with the Black Power movement of the 1960s. Yinger forecast the emergence of radical organizations such as the Black Panthers nearly a decade before they became prominent. This is a good example of being able to predict events in the real world by applying sociological theory.

How Can Cultures Be Compared?

In view of the tremendous variation between and within cultures, sociologists have long discussed the question of whether any aspects of human cultures can be described as ***cultural universals****, or cultural traits common to all human societies.* George Murdock created the first list of supposed cultural universals. He included such items as sports, cooking, dance, family, incest taboos, religion, and attempts to control the weather (Murdock, 1945). Modern anthropologists have found that many aspects of culture that seem necessary to most Western societies, like government or belief in a single god, are missing from other cultures. Norms that now appear to be universal include rules excluding sexual relations with close relatives, rules defining an individual's privacy, and cultural distinctions between males and females. In short there are relatively few cultural universals, and each culture is unique.

Cultural relativism *is the doctrine that suggests each culture should be studied only in relation to itself, and not judged by an external culture's standards or by a universal standard.* The cultural relativist believes all value systems are equal, although they may be different. Many social scientists try to adopt this stance in order to guard against judging other cultures from the viewpoint of their own culture. Others suggest that universals, or absolutes for all societies, do exist and should be studied (Cantril, 1963; W. Moore, 1966; Bell and Mau, 1971).

ETHNOCENTRISM

The cultural relativist is trying to avoid ethnocentrism in doing social science research. ***Ethnocentrism*** *is the tendency to use one's own cultural values in evaluating the beliefs and customs of other cultures with different values.* Most people comfortably believe they are "right" about moral issues and that people from cultures with different value structures are "wrong." It seldom occurs to most people that those from other cultures believe just as strongly in the correctness of their ways.

Ethnocentrism may be useful to a society in that it bonds members together in believing in one set of norms and values. It can be stifling, however, and can lead to a society's isolation from or conflict with people from other cultures. Learning about other ways of life and studying foreign languages and cultures help to minimize the stifling effects of ethnocentrism.

CULTURE SHOCK

Culture shock *is the disorientation and emotional distress which may occur when people encounter a culture very different from their own.* Imagine visiting a beach in Sweden and finding that instead of having sexually segregated beach houses, Scandinavians change their clothes—as discreetly as possible—on the beach. Americans usually find this embarrassing, as most of us are raised to believe that exposing our bodies in public is immoral.

The more different the new culture's language, customs, and norms, the more likely the traveler is to experience culture shock. American Peace Corps personnel often have difficulty accepting cultural eating and living habits where they are sent, as well as mores on such subjects as sexual behavior, reaction to death, raising children, and working styles. This occurs despite training efforts designed to minimize ethnocentrism among Peace Corps volunteers.

To some extent, culture shock and ethnocentrism may be inevitable in interactions between cultures. For societies to remain stable, they must convince their members that their values and norms are worthy. Thus, a member of any culture will inevitably approach members of other cultures with a pre-set cultural outlook. As communication between people from different cultures increases, however, the ability of people to accept other cultural patterns should grow also.

How Can We Examine the Culture of the United States?

The United States is a heterogeneous nation of many subcultures formed along lines of race, ancestral nationality, religion, age, and other similarities. Some subcultures are related to the primary activity of the people in the group, such as the subculture of college students, which embraces some aspects of the language and value systems of the dominant culture and other aspects that set college students apart from that culture. Other groupings are related to situational variables, such as the subculture of an ethnic neighborhood.

American subcultures are integrated into the main culture in varying degrees. In order to continue as separate subcultures, groups must to some extent be eth-

Weird? Sacreligious? Pagan? Does the draping of money over a religious statue seem strange or even offensive? To residents of the North End of Boston this custom is normal. When we use our own cultural values in evaluating the beliefs and customs of other cultures that have different values, we are being ethnocentric. *(AP/ Wide World Photos)*

nocentric. In other words, if Italian-American family members do not present the culture of Italy to their children in a positive way, the children may disregard it in favor of the dominant American culture. The fact that these families do educate their children in the traditions and values of the ancestral country indicates that they feel this is of potential importance to their children. Subcultures serve useful functions for their members, such as providing a sense of community for immigrants. The members of a subculture are ethnocentric enough to want to preserve the precious elements of their original culture while embracing many aspects of the dominant culture.

VALUE PATTERNS OF DEMOCRACIES

Other sociologists describe the core values of the United States in comparison to those of other cultures. Seymour Martin Lipset provides an interesting analysis of four English-speaking democracies: Australia, Canada, England, and the United States (Lipset, 1963). He finds that the United States, compared to the others, is more egalitarian, more achievement oriented (likely to treat people in a certain manner based on their abilities and accomplishments rather than on the basis of their inherited social position), more universalistic (likely to apply a universal standard of judgment rather than responding to personal relationships), and more specific (inclined to relate to a specific aspect of another person rather than to many aspects).

Lipset concludes that these qualities are functional for stable democracies like the United States. The emphasis on achievement allows upper classes to accept upward movement by people in lower classes without feeling morally offended, since all persons are expected to try to improve their position. The emphases on egalitarianism, universal standards, and specificity in personal relations mean that persons can expect fair treatment on their own merits, which allows lower-class persons to change social positions without needing to become revolutionary. We might note the functionalist tone of this argument, which interprets the American culture as useful in explaining why the United States has been such a successful democracy.

From the conflict perspective one would view these cultural traits differently. Conflict theorists view some "cultural values" as ideas promoted by the wealthy elites to hide their exploitation of ordinary people.

For example, Lipset sees emphasis on specificity as positive. Conflict theorists would point out, however, that specificity could allow elites to evaluate only one attribute of a person, while ignoring the rest of the person. Thus, modern businesses may ask for business behaviors from their executives and workers that may be harmful to their personal lives and to their health, such as extensive traveling and social drinking.

Conflict interpretations can also be made concerning other qualities Lipset describes. Most cultural traits can be intepreted in more than one way, partly because a cultural trait may have both positive and negative consequences and partly because different observers begin with different assumptions.

AMERICAN VALUES

To help us understand American culture, many social scientists have offered lists of major cultural value patterns (Coleman, 1961; Henslin, 1975; Robin Williams, 1970). In terms of what Americans really value, however, information from current polls of what they think is important may be of more interest. For years the Gallup Poll has been asking people what the most important aspects of their lives are, and the answers have been remarkably consistent. Americans value (1) good health, and (2) a happy marriage/family situation above all other things (Gallup, 1987). Although attitudes toward specific questions concerning the family have changed, the importance of the family in establishing a happy life remains unchanged, as we will explore further in the following "Close-Up on Research."

CLOSE-UP on • *RESEARCH* •

Daniel Yankelovich on Changes in the American Culture

The Researcher and the Setting

As Robin Williams points out, the culture of the United States is active and is currently undergoing great changes in norms and values. These changes have been studied by Daniel Yankelovich, who reports his findings in the interesting book *New Rules* (1981).

Yankelovich, former professor of psychology at New York University and the New School for Social Research, is now president of the social research firm of Yankelovich, Skelly, and White, Inc., one of the best known public opinion polling agencies in the nation. Research findings of the Yankelovich firm are often reported in the national media.

Yankelovich's interests span the boundaries of sociology and psychology; thus, he can be described as a social psychologist. The topic here is sociological because Yankelovich continues the analysis of the United States culture previously begun by Myrdal, Williams, and others.

The Researcher's Goal

Yankelovich addresses three central issues: (1) How is the culture of the United States changing? (2) How are Americans reacting to the changing culture? (3) Where is this leading our society? We focus on the first issue: how norms and values in the culture of the United States are changing.

Theory and Concepts

Because Yankelovich is trying to describe change rather than explain it, he does not use an explicit theory. He does, however, organize the research around the concepts of culture and cultural revolution: "Tomorrow is being shaped by a cultural revolution that is transforming the rules of American life and moving us into wholly unchartered territory." He goes on to define this cultural revolution: "A genuine cultural revolution, then, is one that makes a decisive break with the shared meanings of the past, particularly those that relate to the deepest questions of the purpose and nature of human life" (Yankelovich, 1981, p. 36).

Yankelovich relies on the survey method to document the cultural revolution and chart its course. He conducted some survey research especially for *New Rules*, but he also analyzes existing sources of information gathered by other researchers, including the Gallup Opinion Index, the National Opinion Research Center of the University of Chicago, the Institute for Social Research of the University of Michigan, the Roper Organization, and the Harris Survey.

How does one measure cultural change by the survey method? Yankelovich attempts to measure norms and values, and changes in them, by asking representative samples of the public about their beliefs. For instance, the United States has long been regarded as a nation with a strong work ethic. To estimate this value's strength Yankelovich observes how many people agree with statements such as "Hard work pays off" and "Work is the center of my life." Yankelovich finds dramatic indication that this important value in our culture is shifting rapidly. Fifty-seven percent of the population in 1969 agreed that "Hard work pays off." By 1976 the number agreeing dropped to 42 percent. Similarly, 34 percent of Americans in 1970 agreed with the statement, "Work is the center of my life," whereas only 14 percent agreed in 1978.

Findings

As indicated above, one of Yankelovich's major findings is that the value we place on work is declining slightly. It would be a mistake, however, to assume these findings mean that many people are about to quit working. In 1976 the vast majority of citizens also agreed with the statement, "I would go on working for pay even if I didn't have to." This suggests that work is still important to Americans although it is no longer of *central* importance.

Yankelovich also reports growing distrust of government:

Issue	Responses	
	1966	**1977**
1. The people running the country don't care what happens to people like me.	26%	68%
	1958	**1978**
2. You can trust the government in Washington to do what is right.	55%	28%

Many changes were found in the cultural definitions of marriage and family, as summarized below:

Issue	Positive Responses	
	1950	**1970s**
1. Those who prefer to remain single have something wrong with them.	80%	25%
	1945	**1980**
2. Four or more children is the ideal number for a family to have.	48%	16%
	1970	**1980**
3. Both sexes have the responsibility to care for small children.	33%	54%
	1971	**1980**
4. It is all right for husbands and wives to have separate vacations.	34%	51%
	1937	**1980**
5. I would vote for a qualified woman for President.	32%	76%
	1938	**1978**
6. Women should not work if their husbands can support them.	75%	24%

Implications

Yankelovich's findings are provocative. Major values such as those concerning work, sex, marriage, parenthood, gender roles, and government have changed dramatically. The changes have taken years, yet they are rapid in comparison with the lifespan of a society or even the lifespan of an individual member of the society. Yankelovich presents considerable evidence to back the idea that we are living in the middle of a cultural revolution.

Yankelovich has continued to study changes in values during the 1980s. His research suggests that the central theme of the sixties and seventies was to find a place in life for the expressive side of the self, in reaction to the fifties' patterns of obligations and rigid roles. In the 1980s, Yankelovich suggests "Americans are sorting it all out" and will come to a stable blending of the two patterns.

This blending will presume limits that the 1970s did not admit to. In that decade, says Yankelovich, Americans supposed that affluence would be universal and that we would have no limits on our growth and potential. In the 1980s, the reality is accepted that we may not be able to meet every need or have every conceivable experience, but that we can be happy within those limits anyway.

Along with this blending within limits, Americans are redefining success as involving inner qualities as well as outer symbols, realizing that pleasure does not have be sensual, and being concerned with creating close bonds with other people, both within and outside our families. Yankelovich sees Americans as modulating their desires and demands in such areas as politics, family patterns, and in their personal lives. He believes that we will see less drug abuse among the young, for example, as people seek for and find guidance and limits to their behavior.

Questions

1. How valid is the evidence presented by Yankelovich? Are there weaknesses in the survey approach? Has Yankelovich overlooked other information or possibilities?
2. What might be causing the apparent changes in culture described in this Close-Up?
3. What future changes in our culture might we expect? Do these changes seem to be irreversible? Why or why not?
4. Do you see the changes that Yankelovich speaks of in your life and the lives of those close to you? What blending of ideas and redefinitions have you or those you know made?

SOURCES Keene, Karlyn. 1984. "American Values: Change and Stability: Conversation with Daniel Yankelovich," *Public Opinion* 6: December/January 2–8. Daniel Yankelovich. 1981. *New Rules.* New York: Random House.

Sociologists at Work •

GARY ALAN FINE
OBSERVES DUNGEONS AND DRAGONS SUBCULTURES
University of Minnesota
Minneapolis, Minnesota

Gary Alan Fine is a symbolic interactionist who researches various social phenomena, from tracking urban legends like the Kentucky Fried Rat (1980) to identifying the culture of Little League baseball teams (1987). Fine works primarily through participant observation ethnography, becoming a part of life of the groups he studies. The excellent writing that has come out of his experiences proves that loving one's work helps one to work well.

Here Gary talks about the popular game "Dungeons & Dragons."

Why Did You Choose "Dungeons & Dragons (D&D)" to Study Culture?

(D&D) is an excellent setting for studying culture, interaction, and social structure because the players are involved in creating a whole universe or culture of their own, complete with social structure. I spent eighteen months with these groups and looked at the way that our culture is reflected in the culture that they produce in the game as well as at the thought frames of the group, based in part on Goffman's frame analysis.

What Were Your Observations?

One of the things that is immediately notable is the fact that D&D players create an almost entirely male world. Ninety-five percent of the players are male.

Why Should That Be?

First, there's the fact that the fantasies in which the games are generally based are male fantasies. They are fantasies of space ships, science fiction, and knights in shining armor. The roles for women in this medieval fantasy include the princess and the mother but no dominant, active, adventuresome roles.

The second element is the recruitment process. The games grow out of war games and science fiction, which basically reflect the male social world. Males recruit their friends and build up from that base. It is a subcultural phenomenon.

A third element is that the whole game is part of male bonding. You have this image from Lionel Tiger, *Men in Groups*. They are buddies with each other. Part of the "buddyness" is the ability to talk about sex in the kind of rough and tumble way that men sometimes do. If it is an all-male group, they can say sexist, offensive things in this play context. They can have fantasy rapes. That's disturbing, but there is this membrane around it. Men who are not rapists themselves have rape fantasies.

This is certainly not a new claim, but it is empirically documented here. Feminists say that the culture is shot through with rape fantasies, but they don't have the data. Here is the data to present: examples of people talking about forcible sexual encounters in a generic way that men talk about women, "I'll grab her and pull her towards me and she will melt with passion." I think that some of that is healthy, but some is harmful to the point of being semipornographic.

How Does Frame Analysis Help Your Understanding of D&D?

These players are operating on several different frameworks simultaneously. The primary framework is that mundane environment that is "reality": the level that is present when the game is being played. The boys are the *boys*, and they talk about all the things that boys do. At the same time, they are also *players* in the game, and there are rules for playing. Simultaneously, they are also *characters* in the game. So I can be Gary Fine, Gary

Fine the player who takes the game seriously, or I can be Sir Ralph the Rash. I can talk as Sir Ralph, roleplaying, and other people can talk to me as their characters.

These different frameworks provide different levels of disclaiming reality. I, Gary Fine, know some things that Sir Ralph does not know. That is, I know how to shoot a gun, but if this is a medieval game, *he* doesn't. I know a whole number of things that might help me in this game, for example various kinds of poisons. On the other hand, Sir Ralph knows things that I do not. That's strange when you think about it, because he is just a character. But he knows, for instance, what their world looks like because he's really in it. It would be unfair for the referee of the game, for instance, to say to me that Sir Ralph just walked into a wall. I couldn't see the wall, because it was imaginary. But presumably Sir Ralph, who was in the situation, would see the wall and avoid it! So I would complain bitterly if the referee said something like, "He walked over a cliff." The culture of this game, like all worlds of culture, depends on the structure of the game, the relationships among the participants, and the content of their talk and action. ●

Conclusion

The study of culture is basic to the study of society. A society's norms and values are the basic integrative factors that are passed through the culture. Determining the differences and similarities among cultures and among norms within a culture and learning to observe our own culture from an objective point of view can be useful both to the student of sociology and to the average citizen. Only by observing such patterns carefully can we determine which cultural elements are still functional to our society and which will be or should be replaced by new norms and values.

Summary Questions

1. How do sociologists define culture?
2. What do functionalists see as the functions of culture?
3. What are norms, and why are they important?
4. How do values underlie norms?
5. How do norms vary between cultures?
6. What are the symbolic elements of culture?
7. What is the importance of language in transmitting culture?
8. How do cultures vary?
9. How do the functional, ecological, evolutionary, conflict, and symbolic interactionist approaches explain cultural variation?
10. How do subcultures and countercultures differ from the dominant culture?
11. How do cultural universalism and cultural relativism differ?
12. How does ethnocentrism affect one's viewpoint?
13. How do the values of the people of the United States compare with those of other democracies?
14. What major changes have occurred in the American value system during the past three decades?

Summary Answers

1. Culture is the values, norms, language, tools, and other shared products of society that provide a plan for social life.
2. Functionalists suggest that culture provides for continuing social order, by handing down prescribed ways of behaving in specific situations, and allows people to benefit from the achievements of previous generations.
3. Norms are shared rules or guidelines for behavior in specific situations. The strongest norms are taboos, or rules that prohibit certain behavior and carry severe punishment for violators. Norms carry sanctions, or rewards for behavior, that conform to a norm and punishment for behavior that violates a norm. Institutions are organized sets of norms, values, statuses, and roles that are centered on the basic needs of society. The five basic institutions of most societies are: the family, religion, the state, the economic system, and education.
4. Values are shared ideas about what is right and wrong, good and bad, desirable and undesirable. Values are the general concepts on which our specific norms are built.
5. Many norms are specific to one society or to one group in a society, for example, most college students in the United States share a norm against turning in a fellow student for cheating.
6. A symbol is that which represents something else. Norms and values are often transmitted within a culture or to other cultures through symbolic elements such as language, gesture, stance, style of clothing, hairstyle, social distance, time use, or symbolic representation such as flags.
7. Most social scientists see a strong connection between a society's language and the rest of its culture, with the language reflecting what is important to that society to its new members and those outside of the culture. Our "silent language," or nonverbal space and time messages, are also tied to our culture.
8. Cultures differ in the degree of complexity (whether they are focused around kinship or institutions) and the pace of change. In simple societies, kinship organizes people's lives around families and relatives. Such societies might change rather slowly compared to modern postindustrial society.
9. The functional approach suggests that a functional cultural trait has a positive consequence for the society, and will probably not be adopted unless it fits well with the existing culture and contributes to the well-being of the society.

   The ecological approach shows how societies adapt culture to their physical environment in order to survive, thus making it a subform of the functional approach.

The evolutionary approach views culture as developing through a series of stages toward forms that are increasingly well suited to the environment, based on changes in the culture's basic tools or technology.

The conflict approach points out that prevailing definitions of beauty, justice, and truth may serve the elites at the expense of the masses, with culture being created and imposed on the masses by the ruling class.

The symbolic interactionist approach highlights the importance of symbols in understanding culture and the social behavior it shapes, suggesting that symbols are the major agent for transmitting and shaping culture.

10. A subculture is the culture of a subgroup of society that adopts norms that set them apart from the dominant group; for instance, persons who live in a Chinatown but are integrated into the life of the city as a whole. A counterculture is a subculture whose norms and values are not just different from but in conflict with those of the dominant culture; for example, the Amish who believe that using machines will encourage their members to become too worldly and divert the focus of their energies from devotion to God. Milton Yinger suggests that countercultures arise when deprivation and frustration of major values occur with value confusion and weak social controls.

11. Some sociologists believe that cultural universals, or traits common to all human societies, exist. Others suggest that each culture should be studied only in relation to itself and not be judged by an external culture's standards or by a universal standard, a stance known as cultural relativism.

12. Ethnocentrism is the tendency to use one's own cultural values in evaluating the beliefs and customs of other cultures with different values. It can be useful to a society in that it bonds members together, but can also lead to conflict with people from other cultures.

13. Compared to other democracies, the United States is more egalitarian, more likely to treat people in a certain manner based on their abilities and accomplishments rather than on the basis of their inherited position (achievement oriented), more likely to apply a universal standard of judgment rather than responding to personal relationships (universalistic), and more inclined to relate to a specific aspect of another person rather than to many aspects (specific).

14. Daniel Yankelovich has found that the value we place on work is declining, that cultural values have changed to allow singleness, that smaller families are being valued, that the majority of Americans feel both sexes have the responsibility to care for small children, that premarital sex is more accepted, that women are becoming more independent of men, and that as a culture we are growing more distrustful of government. Yankelovich feels that Americans are beginning to accept the reality that they can be happy within limits, redefining success as involving inner qualities as well as outer symbols, deemphasizing sensual pleasure, and concentrating on forming close bonds with other people.

artifacts the material products of a society

counterculture a subculture whose norms and values are in conflict with those of the dominant culture

cultural relativism the doctrine that suggests each culture should be studied only in relation to itself, not judged by an external culture's standards or by a universal standard

cultural universals cultural traits common to all human societies

culture the values, norms, language, tools, and other shared products of society that provide a plan for social life and are passed on from generation to generation

culture shock the disorientation and emotion people feel when encountering a culture very different from their own

diffusion the borrowing of cultural traits from other cultures

ecological approach the theory of cultural development that examines the way societies adapt culture to their physical environment in order to survive

ethnocentrism the tendency to use one's own cultural values in evaluating the beliefs and customs of other cultures with different values

evolutionary approach the theory of cultural development that views culture as developing through a series of stages toward forms that are increasingly well suited to the society's environment

folkways ordinary ways of behaving in everyday social situations

functional approach the theory of cultural development that explains the presence of a cultural trait by considering how effectively it works with other elements of the existing culture to maintain the society

functional cultural trait one which has a positive consequence for the society

institutions organized sets of norms, values, statuses, and roles that are centered around a basic need of society

kinship a social plan that organizes people's lives around families and relatives

laws norms that have been formally enacted or stated

mores powerful norms that are considered vital to the society's well-being

norms shared rules or guidelines for behavior in specific social situations

sanction a reward for behavior that conforms to a norm or punishment for behavior that violates a norm

social distance the distance at which it is comfortable to relate to someone else

sociocultural evolution the process of increasingly complex social change as a result of the introduction of new technology

subculture a subgroup of society that has some norms and values different from the dominant society while sharing many other aspects of the larger society's culture

symbol that which represents something else in a meaningful way

taboos rules that prohibit certain behavior and carry severe punishment for violators

values shared ideas about what is right and wrong, good and bad, desirable and undesirable

Suggested Readings

Hall, Edward T. 1984. *The Dance of Life: The Other Dimensions of Time*. New York: Anchor Books.

Hall fascinates the reader with examples of how differing definitions of time between cultures can create misunderstandings between their members.

Harris, Marvin. 1974. *Cows, Pigs, Wars, and Witches: The Riddles of Culture*. New York: Random House.

A description of culturally accepted practices that might be labeled strange by outsiders but that have definite functions within their own culture.

Roszak, Theodore. 1969. *The Making of a Counter-Culture: Reflections on the Technocratic Society and Its Youthful Opposition*. Garden City, N.Y.: Doubleday.

An interesting study of the creation of a youth counterculture in the 1960s.

Slater, Philip. 1976. *The Pursuit of Loneliness* (revised edition). Boston, Mass.: Beacon Press.

Slater's analysis of American culture, in which he suggests that Americans actually foster the loneliness and isolation that plagues our present society.

Yankelovich, Daniel. 1981. *New Rules: Searching for Self-Fulfillment in a World Turned Upside Down*. New York: Random House.

Yankelovich uses his public opinion firm's data to describe changes in American values over the past two decades and to suggest possible alternatives for the future.

Yinger, J. Milton. 1982. *Countercultures*. New York: Free Press.

Yinger presents a comprehensive overview of counterculture behavior, critiqued from a sociological viewpoint.

CHAPTER

3

SOCIETY

How's Your Sociological Intuition?

1. Societies differ from other groups because:

- **a.** Their members are born into rather than joining it
- **b.** They are identified with a territory
- **c.** They have a unique set of beliefs and rules
- **d.** They are self-sufficient

2. Which invention distinguishes best between different types of societies?

- **a.** The plow
- **b.** The wheel
- **c.** Language
- **d.** Fire

3. Cities first arise as features of a society when the society:

- **a.** learns to hunt game
- **b.** discovers how to herd animals
- **c.** learns to grow plants from seed
- **d.** produces a reliable food surplus

4. Who most often deviates from their role behavior?

- **a.** The chief surgeon
- **b.** An intern
- **c.** The assisting surgeon
- **d.** A scrub nurse

Answers

1. d. In principle, a society is a self-sufficient social system. Other groups, such as families, schools, or corporations are clearly dependent on outside groups for their survival.

2. a. The plow is a key invention which makes agriculture, a new type of society, possible.

3. d. Because city dwellers do not produce their own food, cities only arise after the society develops considerable surplus food, the means of transporting it to cities, and the ability to store it long enough to support the urban population.

4. a. Erving Goffman noted in his research in surgical operating rooms that the chief surgeon most frequently steps out of a formal role, often to reduce the anxiety of the team to ensure that the surgery is successful.

When You Have Finished Studying This Chapter, You Should Know:

- What society, social structure, and institutions are
- How role and status interact
- Two ways in which status is conferred
- What a status intervention is and how it might affect the workings of a group
- The differences between role strain and role conflict
- Erving Goffman's explanation of why people reject their roles
- How subsistence adaptation and technology help in the process of sorting types of societies
- Important social distinctions between: hunting and gathering societies; herding societies; horticultural societies; agricultural societies; industrial societies
- What postindustrial societies are and what distinguishes them from industrial societies
- How Wendell Bell approaches the study of future social worlds
- Several major differences between modern and premodern societies
- The five features of Daniel Bell's predicted post-industrial society
- How Blumberg explains America's economic decline and what he predicts
- The essential nature of the basic social processes: conflict; coercion; exploitation; competition; cooperation
- What Bellah's idea of the "good society" is
- How the conflict and functional perspectives view social processes

> No man is an island, entire unto himself. Every man is a piece of the continent, a part of the main. Every man's loss is my loss, every man's gain is mine. Ask not for whom the bell tolls, it tolls for thee.
>
> *John Donne*

John Donne's well known quotation inspired the title for a film classic *No Man Is an Island*, and one of Hemingway's best known novels *For Whom the Bell Tolls*. It also poetically expresses a fundamental sociological truth—none of us stands alone. We are all part of a society whose fate we share. When one dies, we are all diminished.

But if society can be compared to an island, what a strange and marvelous island it is. We might liken these social islands to coral reefs that are comprised of the shells of dead organisms who once lived there. These social islands are comprised of living human beings who create, share, and are governed by their cultural plans. Our islands are far more complicated than coral reefs, and indeed we are part of a social body more diverse than even the human body.

Judging from the 5,000 or so distinct languages within our human family, we can deduce that humanity once divided into some 5,000 different "islands" or societies. How are we to begin to understand such a diversity of things as complicated as societies? Yet, dare we ignore the task of better understanding these lumbering social giants with whom our lives are so intertwined?

What Are Societies?

Viewed from space, our world is a beautiful blue-green sphere with distinct continents. On a conventional geographic globe, political groupings known as nations divide the continents. For the sociologist, boundaries between societies provide one of the most important ways of distinguishing people on earth. In principle, a ***society*** *is a self-sufficient group of people who live in a common territory and transmit their unique language and culture to those who are born or accepted into the group.* In practice, societies have become increasingly interdependent so that some are no longer truly self-sufficient.

Over the centuries, political powers have arisen that sought to unite separate societies into political groupings known as nations. Nations are not the same as societies; a society can be only one small part of a large nation. Thus, the United States contains remnants of dozens of Native American societies, and the Soviet Union includes scores of earlier societies. China actually encompasses more than 100 traditional societies. A society can also span the political boundaries of more than one nation. Korea, Germany, and Vietnam are all examples of societies that have been politically divided.

Despite the importance of modern nations, societies remain highly significant units, largely because people may feel a greater sense of belonging within their society than within their nation. People often fear and distrust those from another society, even when they are all members of the same nation. For instance, the struggle between Israel and the Palestine Liberation Organization is intersocietal rather than international, because Palestine is technically not a nation, and some

Palestinians are even Israeli citizens. In the United States during World War II, Americans of Japanese ancestry were forced into concentration camps even as some of their sons fought in the United States armed forces.

In this chapter, we begin to unravel some social mysteries by considering these immensely important groups—societies. Through studying the societies' various forms and exploring their structures, we move toward a better understanding of other people's societies, our own society, and the massive social changes taking place today in the nations and societies of the world.

What Are the Elements of Social Structure?

How long could we live without a society? A society is like a complicated life-support system, except that it is made up of the beings it supports. The term ***social structure*** *refers to the enduring patterns of social behavior, including statuses, roles, norms, and institutions, which constitute relatively stable relations in society.*

Considerable overlap exists between culture and social structure. The culture provides a general plan for society and the social structure encompasses the actual patterns of behavior, which often comply with the plan but sometimes do not. For example, some sociologists think the Japanese are out-competing the United States in business for cultural reasons: They are raised to be loyal to the group, including the company. Others think they are out-competing Americans for social-structural reasons: They have a system of permanent employment in the big companies, and better management techniques. Although culture and social structure are closely linked, they are separate entities.

INSTITUTIONS

Every person belongs to a society, and, in principle, every society is a whole unto itself, capable of sustaining itself and its individual members. Yet societies differ enormously from each other and over time. Some of this difference can be accounted for by studying the differences in the institutions of the societies.

An ***institution*** *is a complex set of norms, values, statuses, and roles that are centered around a basic need of a society.* Institutions such as the family, religion, the economy, and education are major components of society. Institutions create the form within which societies grow and prosper.

All societies have recognizable institutions, from the universally found families and religious groups, to economic and political institutions that are generally found only in more highly developed societies. The most complex societies may develop new institutions to meet their needs, such as science and formal education. We will consider several major institutions in depth in Part 5 of this book, "Social Institutions."

STATUS AND ROLE

Sociologists have developed the concepts of status and role in order to more clearly describe social structure. *A* ***status*** *is a position in a particular social pattern. A* ***role*** *includes the behavior which goes with, but is distinct from, the status.*

In a family, for instance, the status of parent differs from the status of child. Although they are all adult statuses, the status of aunt or uncle also differs from that of mother or father. An individual can simultaneously occupy multiple statuses; for instance, mother, lawyer, and neighbor.

Role refers to the behavior that goes with but is distinct from the status. Thus, the status of father has taken on more of a nurturing role toward children during the past decade, as the status of mother now includes more roles than it did previously. Status differences between parent and child have remained relatively constant. Status and role are separate but related phenomena.

Members of society teach us the roles that correspond to our statuses and the rights and responsibilities they carry with them. For example, fraternities and sororities have various status positions, including rushee, pledge, member, and alumni. Roles are important aspects of social structure because they standardize behavior and make it predictable. Without knowing a person at all, we can engage in simple or complex interactions by knowing their role in the interactions. The new fraternity or sorority pledge learns the different rights and responsibilities of pledges and those of members in order to act appropriately toward individuals in each status group: being friendly to fellow pledges, subservient to full members, and respectful to alumni. Whether in New York City or in Pocatello, Idaho, we expect similar treatment from a waitress at a fast-food restaurant.

Roles also sometimes depersonalize or even dehumanize human interaction. People behaving according to the requirements of a social role often set aside personal feelings. For example, a police officer endeavors not to let his personal feelings about an offender affect his decision to arrest or not. A striking experiment illustrates how status and role can lead to outright dehumanization of behavior. Philip Zimbardo set up a mock prison and randomly assigned student volunteers to the status of guard and prisoner. The subjects too readily took to their arbitrarily assigned roles. The "guards" began to take pleasure in the exercise of power and cruelty, and the "prisoners" become passive, thinking only of escape, survival, and hatred of the guards. The experiment was discontinued after only six days when the majority of the students were no longer able to differentiate clearly between role playing and self (Zimbardo, 1972).

We are so accustomed to performing our roles in ways society expects that it may be difficult to realize how much our actions and feelings are influenced by the status positions we hold. Generally, however, roles, statuses, and norms, as the building blocks of society, organize human behavior so it can be highly complicated and still proceed smoothly.

ASCRIBED AND ACHIEVED STATUS

We usually receive our status in one of two ways: through ascription or achievement. *An* ***ascribed status*** *is one that is conferred independent of the individual's effort or abilities,* such as on the basis of kinship, race, sex, skin color, or age. In contrast, *an* ***achieved status*** *is one that is at least partly attained through effort or performance.*

For example, the ascribed status of king was often conferred upon the first-born son of the previous king. Children of royal parents automatically become roy-

CLOSE-UP on • *RESEARCH* •

Barry Markovsky, LeRoy F. Smith, and Joseph Berger on How to Eliminate Status Disadvantages

The Researchers and the Setting

Researchers find that when persons with a high-status characteristic such as a Ph.D. enter a group: (1) they are given more opportunity to talk, (2) they talk more and offer more opinions and suggestions, (3) they receive more approval and agreement, and (4) they are less likely to give in when they disagree. Interestingly, this effect holds *even when the high status characteristic is irrelevant to the decision or task at hand!*

Thus in a town meeting to discuss transportation, the local doctor's opinion may carry more weight than his knowledge justifies, because of his high status in medicine. Similarly, in a discussion about farm subsidies featured in the day's news, the graduate student resident advisor eating with a group of freshmen will likely monopolize the conversation unless someone reveals that some freshmen have equal or superior knowledge.

Scientists have learned how to reduce or eliminate the effects of status characteristics like gender, race, age, or academic achievement. When someone *attempts to diminish the influence of an undesirable status characteristic,* this is called a ***status intervention***. In the laboratory, a researcher might present evidence such as test scores to show that the person of high general status has less-than-average ability in the task at hand. In our examples, a status intervention might involve revealing that others in attendance at the town meeting have knowledge and training in transportation that exceed that of the physician. In the case of the graduate student "expert," one might profess to be especially interested in the opinions of the freshmen who grew up on farms, rather than that of the graduate student who has read about the issue in the newspaper.

The Researchers' Goal

As early as the 1970s researchers found they could achieve certain effects through status interventions. For instance, in a group whose task was to match geometric patterns, a common status intervention would be to reveal scores on pattern-matching tasks, which indicate that the high-status Ph.D. has normal or below-normal ability at this task compared to the freshmen in the group.,

Before Barry Markovsky, LeRoy Smith, and Joseph Berger began their work, it had been understood that: (1) outside status characteristics influence group decision making even when they reflect no real ability in the task at hand, (2) one can intervene to neutralize these irrelevant status effects, and (3) the intervention will carry over to encounters with new high-status people.

These researchers set out to find whether a status intervention would transfer to new tasks as well as new groups. Their question was: Once a high status, like a graduate degree in English, has been shown to be irrelevant to discerning geometric shapes, will group members pay less respect to the high status in some other task, such as judging shades of color?

Theory and Concepts

Markovsky, Smith, and Berger theorized that the altered status will carry on. In their words: "An actor who expected to do well on the last task will, upon completion of that task, expect to do well on the current task" (p. 375).

Research Design

Markovsky, Smith, and Berger borrowed their design from Berger's earlier research. They report:

> In this study we were interested in determining whether expectations developed for an initial partner in a first group task would transfer to a second partner in a second group's task. Therefore our design consists of two consecutive standard experiment situations. . . . Subjects were white, male students, age 18–21, and were paid volunteers recruited from junior colleges. . . . We distinguish between two types of status characteristics. *Specific* status characteristics differentiate actors in terms of particular abilities such as mathematical or artistic skill. *Diffuse* status characteristics involve much more general, overarching types of performance expectations. Characteristics such as gender, race, occupation, and physical appearance have been shown to operate in this way (pp. 375–376).

The researchers told the subjects that they were participating in two separate studies, and that they were being asked to participate in both for the sake of convenience. Subjects were introduced to fictitious partners by watching a videotape. The experiment involved four conditions. In condition 1, the subject "met" a junior high school seventh grader. This would give the subject relatively high diffuse status in comparison to the seventh grader's lower diffuse status. Under condition 2, subjects "met" a fourth-year graudate student, which gave the subject relatively low status. In both conditions 1 and 2, no information was given besides the diffuse status.

The researchers created specific status by giving a Meaning Insight Test. In condition 3, the subjects were led to believe they had high diffuse status by being paired with the junior high schooler. But the subjects were also told they had scored poorly on this test (6 correct out of 25), whereas their younger partner had scored very well (22 correct out of 25). Under condition 4, the subjects were led to believe they had relatively low diffuse status by being paired with the fourth-year graduate student. Here, however, subjects were informed they had a superior score (22 correct out of 25), whereas the graduate student did poorly (6 correct out of 25). Although the subjects really took a test, the researchers fabricated fictitious scores to serve their purposes.

Once the researchers had given the subjects information about their partners, they arranged for the partners to make joint decisions about the contrast differences of slides. Subjects were told their partner was in a different room, but the experimenter actually provided the partner's "opinions." The subjects were led to believe that the partner frequently disagreed. This gave the researchers maximum chance to find the conditions under which the subject would stay with his original choice. Sticking with their decisions indicated high influence in the decision making; going along with the partner indicated low influence.

After the subjects performed the contrast task, they were taken to another room to participate in a "different study," and the researchers observed the subjects to determine if the newly established status expectations would be carried along. Here each subject was introduced to a new experimenter, a new partner, and a new task. The new partner happened to have the same status as the first partner, but no mention was made of the first task and no information was provided on anyone's ability in the second task. The theory predicts that the subject will transfer his status expectations from the first to the second partner.

Findings

The various conditions allowed the researchers to test their assumptions. Data confirmed that the subjects were more assertive under condition 1 (when paired with the seventh grader) and less assertive under condition 2 (when paired with the graduate student). The results from conditions 3 and 4 confirmed that the effect of this diffuse status could be reduced through a status intervention, in this case, scores on a test.

The major finding was that subjects did carry their status expectation on from the first partner to the second and from the first task to the second. For instance, when the subjects thought they had been paired with a graduate student who was incompetent on one task, they held to their own judgments more strongly than those subjects who had been told the partner was a graduate student but were not offered information on test scores. But they *also* carried this tendency toward assertiveness on to the second partner and the second task.

Implications

This theory and the research that supports it offer hope in day-to-day settings where people of diffuse status often receive advantages or disadvantages. It suggests that people with low-status characteristics, such as children, the elderly, people in humble jobs, women, and minorities can be helped to be assertive in their own realm by learning that people of higher status do not necessarily know more about everything. The research also suggests that once this point is made in a particular setting, the low-status person will carry the effect over to new settings.

Questions

1. Give some examples in which diffuse status characteristics affect peoples' influence.
2. In what ways is this laboratory research strong and weak? For instance, how realistic is it?
3. How might a teacher use these findings to help offset unfair advantages of whites and males?

SOURCE Barry Markovsky, LeRoy Smith, and Joseph Berger. June, 1984. "Do Status Interventions Persist?" *American Sociological Review*, 49:373–382.

alty. Before the American War Between the States, or Civil War, the status of slave was ascribed. Children of enslaved parents automatically became slaves. In modern times, the status of citizen is ascribed to those born in a particular nation or those born to citizens of that nation.

An achieved status, in contrast, is attained during the individual's lifetime. Senior class valedictorian, President of the United States, and Olympic Gold Medal Winner are all statuses achieved through personal effort and demonstrated merit.

In practice, we will see that very important social statuses like our social class identity may involve a blending of ascription and achievement. For instance the high social standing of physicians may result partly from their achievements in medical school, but these may be based to some degree on ascribed factors such as their birth into an upper middle-class family that prized and could afford an enriched private school education.

Our culture values achievement over ascription. Yet often people are ascribed a low status that follows them from setting to setting in spite of their abilities, effort, or performance. For instance, if you have the status characteristics of child, old person, black, or female, some people tend to hold you in lower regard than if your characteristics are adult, young, white, or male. Conversely, people may be ascribed a high status in spite of their ability or effort, simply by being born wealthy. Some status characteristics, like a medical degree or a doctorate, involve both achievement and ascription. Professors have to *achieve* their Ph.D. degrees, but, once earned, members of society tend to *ascribe* them an "expert" status that often goes beyond the bounds of their discipline. In Part 4: Social Inequality, we explore status in depth and consider how occupations, racial and ethnic characteristics, gender, and age are used to categorize people in higher or lower positions.

Sometimes such categorization may be justifiable; often it is not. In the following "Close-Up on Research" we see how social scientists seek to study and control our tendency to judge people by their status characteristics.

ROLE CONFLICT AND ROLE STRAIN

Role conflict *occurs when two of an individual's roles call for different behaviors*. For example, the role of son or daughter may require a person to attend a family event at the same time that the role of student requires studying for final examinations. A person attempting to fulfill the requirements of both roles is caught in a situation of role conflict.

Similarly, a father may be caught in role conflict when his boss wants him to work overtime on the night of his son's baseball game. In his role as good worker, the overtime would be gladly accepted. In his role as father, however, he should support his son at the game. Again, role conflict exists.

When a single role contains conflicting expectations, the person is caught in role strain. ***Role strain*** *exists when one role requires two conflicting courses of action*. For example, a business manager is responsible for keeping costs as low as possible to maximize profits,

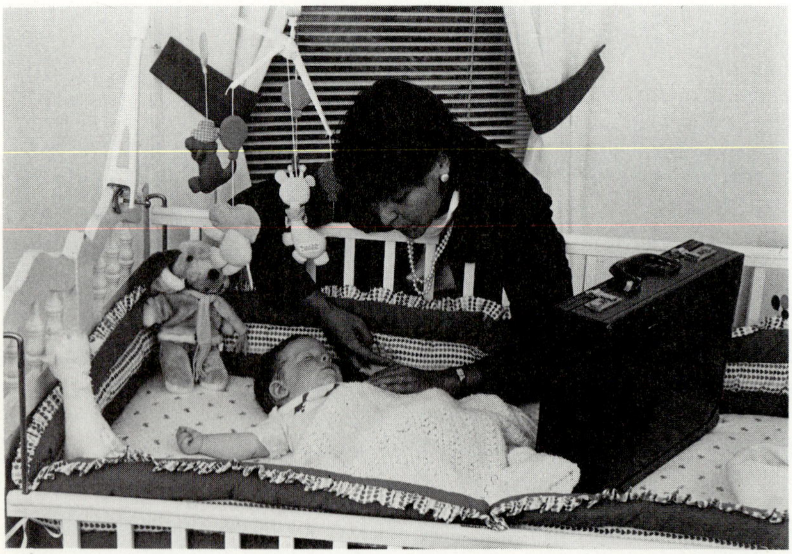

Role conflict? What happens if the baby wakes up and cries at the moment one is due to leave for work? Couples arrive at various means of coping with sometimes conflicting demands of the roles of parent and worker. (© *Jeffry W. Myers/FPG International*)

and for seeing that employees are paid adequately. Balancing these two responsibilities sometimes creates a situation of role strain for the manager. Teachers may also experience role strain when they try to speak to their students' needs at the same time that they are required to evaluate them in terms of a letter grade. Role conflict, then, stems from having two opposing roles, whereas role strain stems from two opposing requirements of a single role.

ROLE DISTANCING

The study of how persons interact in accordance with their social roles has been carried out primarily by the symbolic interactionists. Much human interaction occurs in familiar social roles, such as physician, parent, priest, or police officer. Symbolic interactionist Erving Goffman developed sociological explanations for these everyday social interactions (1971). Goffman noticed that people often seek to put a distance between their roles and themselves. He introduced the term ***role distance*** to describe *the situation in which people act as if they are not fully involved in their roles.* For instance, he observed that when children who might be considered too old to ride a merry-go-round do so, they often have a "careful, bemused look on their face . . . implying, 'This is not the real me' " (p. 118).

Goffman suggests that when role distancing occurs, it is frequently done by leaders acting for the benefit of the group. He observed that surgeons and interns engage in role distancing before, during, and after surgery. For example, the surgeon might joke about something during an operation in order to reduce tension at a critical moment.

Role distancing is appropriately used only by those of superior status, however. Subordinates should expect to be punished for role distancing, unless it is seen by the leader as in the best interest of the group. Thus, a nurse trying to make a joke during surgery would probably be reprimanded. The symbolic interactionist perspective is especially well-suited for providing such interesting sociological insights.

The structure of societies depends on the closely related concepts of status and role. They help us organize our societies by forming the basis of most of our enduring behavior patterns, or social structure.

What Are the Basic Types of Societies?

Through science, we have come to better understand and often control matter, living things, and even diseases. The key to success in science has often been to simplify the subject matter by dividing and conquering. The scientist creates a few useful categories into which many things are divided. Thus a major advance in chemistry came when we realized that the millions of compounds actually comprised only 100 or so basic elements.

We can understand much about society and the differences between societies by categorizing them by type and then focusing on the similarities within, and differences between, types. By dividing the roughly 5,000 societies of the world into six types, we can much better understand the mysteries of cultural differences.

One very useful way to classify societies is according to their most common form of work. In all societies people work for their livelihood. For instance, we might contrast agrarian societies, where most people work at agriculture, with industrial societies, where most people work in manufacturing. Broadly speaking, there are a relatively small number of solutions to the question of how a society can support itself. By focusing on the dominant form of work in the society, we can identify six types of society.

Because work is done for the sake of survival or subsistence, we could also view these six types as sorting according to subsistence adaptation. ***Subsistence adaptation*** is the technical term that describes *the society's strategy for producing the goods and services necessary for survival.* Because work and tools are so closely related, when we sort by type of work, we are also sorting according to technology. ***Technology*** refers to *tools, machines, or other means by which the society or group works.* So this set of six types simultaneously classifies societies according to the most common form of work, the subsistence adaptation, and the technology.

HUNTING AND GATHERING SOCIETIES

In the economically simplest of societies, ***hunting and gathering***, *people live by hunting wild animals and by gathering food as it grows naturally* in the form of fruits, nuts, and vegetables. They use primitive weapons like spears to hunt for game. Hunting and gathering societies are by necessity nomadic, since they must move to follow game and natural food supplies. Such societies are extremely small by modern standards, with sometimes as few as a dozen members. They are dominated by kinship relationships and have virtually no political and economic institutions in the modern sense of these terms. (Lenski and Lenski, 1987).

Some hunters and gatherers constantly face extinction in a struggle against adverse environments. Among the Itibamute Eskimos who range over arctic ice floes in search of fish and game, a family's fate rests in the hands of the father, who must find and catch the game, build the house, and maintain the family dogsled and kayak.

In an adverse environment, with limited technology, sharing is the norm, serving as a form of "social insurance" to guarantee access to food for the group as a whole. The hunter who shares his walrus today is assured of having someone share with him when his catch is not good. Here close cooperation becomes a technological resource itself, with a minimum hierarchy and leadership only for specific activities needing coordination at specific times. Each member of such a society has a broad range of productive and social skills, with relatively little specialization. At the same time, most members must command a complex knowledge of the plants, animals, environmental conditions, and signs of change in the environment. Though the hunting and gathering lifestyle seems alien to us, it has been the most common form of society for most of history.

In such societies, the social structure is relatively simple. Often men do the hunting, and women do the gathering. Because virtually everyone participates in the major work of hunting and gathering food, there are few roles and only minor differences in status. Where there are status distinctions, such as leader or chief, they are almost always achieved through demonstrated ability, for instance, as a hunter. The small number of norms and roles leave little likelihood of role strain (Lee, 1979).

HERDING SOCIETIES

Another common form of society is *the **herding, or pastoral, society**, which relies on the domestication of animals into herds as a major means of support*. The addition of this core technology enhances the security and productivity of the society. Herding is never practiced as a sole means of support, but is linked with either hunting and gathering or a more advanced technology.

Herding societies are usually adapted to heavy grasslands, mountains, deserts, or other land that would not readily support crops. Like hunters and gatherers, herders are nomadic because of their seasonal need to find sufficient grazing areas for their herds. Herding societies may have hundreds or even thousands of members, due to their technological "invention" of the domesticated animal that can be used for human food.

The Bakhtiari of western Iran, for example, number between 50,000 and 150,000. They herd goats and sheep in the Zagros mountains, moving their flocks twice yearly (Salzman, 1967). Before the cold weather reaches the mountains, they travel to the warmer plains near the Iraqian border. In spring these pastures dry up for lack of water, and the Bakhtiari return to the mountain valleys, which are again habitable. In order to make this trip, they divide into five groups of about 10,000 people and 50,000 animals each. The trip is treacherous, and many animals are lost crossing mountains and rivers. The best routes are known, and this knowledge is passed from generation to generation.

The Bakhtiari live in black tents of goat-hair cloth, which is woven by the women. The tents are sparsely furnished with rugs, goatskin containers, copper utensils, and clay jugs; they retain heat and repel water during the winter, and keep out the heat during the summer. This and their portability show the tents as excellent adaptations to the herding life: serving the needs of the people and using the products of their herd.

The introduction of herding as a technology brings several social changes. Pastoral societies place a higher value on their temporary territories than do hunting and gathering societies, and disputes with other herding societies sometimes result in warfare. Herding societies may also relate to neighboring herders in peaceful ways such as through trade (Lenski and Lenski, 1987).

The major development in social structure here involves status. A herd is obvious property, which can be inherited, opening the way for clear status distinctions. Because owners of large herds can have higher status, with herding comes greater status differences and more ascription of status: Because the roles of hunters and gatherers remain and the new roles of shepherd, goatherd, and so on are added, there is a diversity of roles and more norms as well.

HORTICULTURAL SOCIETIES

In a horticultural society, people have made the elementary discovery that plants can be grown from seeds. *A **horticultural society** produces its food through cultivation of the soil with hand tools*. Whereas herding is common in areas with poor soil, horticulture is more common as a means of subsistence in regions with fertile soil. Horticultural settlements are more permanent than those of herding societies, but the soil usually becomes exhausted within three to five years and the people must find new fertile ground.

The Gururumba tribe in New Guinea is a good example of horticultural adaptation (Newman, 1965). Each village has many plots containing the gardens of several families within one fence. A family's prestige is partially based on the neatness and productivity of its gardens. Crops are planted sequentially so they will be ready for harvesting throughout the year.

Typical of horticultural societies, the Gururumba society is based on a complex system of gift exchange. Men give each other large gifts, primarily of food, and

Gardening with sticks. Horticultural societies, like the Gurmuba in New Guinea, produce food through cultivating the soil with hand tools rather than with the animal- or machine-drawn plows employed by societies that are more socio-culturally advanced. *(Julie O'Neil/ The Picture Cube)*

thereby accumulate a number of people who owe them debts. The more a man gives away, the greater prestige he has, which is why most men set aside one garden to grow food for gifts.

Closely related to this is their custom of keeping pigs, which are raised primarily as gifts rather than for food. Every five to seven years a huge feast is held in which hundreds of pigs are killed, cooked, and distributed. Old debts are thereby absolved and new ones are established toward the clan that gives the feast. This also ensures that the pigs will never become so numerous that their feeding will take important nourishment from the people.

As with herding, the introduction of horticulture brings social change. Better food production techniques allow larger surpluses and larger societies, so the prospects of personal wealth and differences in social position arise. Warfare to protect wealth and property may be more common, and developed trades, crafts, and political institutions begin to emerge.

The social structure of horticultural societies is more complex than hunting and gathering societies and new technology brings new roles and strains. Of special importance is the introduction of the garden land as private property, which opens the way for obvious status differences, either ascribed through inheritance or gained by achievement. Private property also opens the way for role conflict between the lessening role of "cooperative life member" and the new role of "independent gardener" who is seeking as big a private garden as possible.

AGRICULTURAL SOCIETIES

Agricultural societies *employ animal-drawn plows to cultivate the land.* Although the plow may seem a rather humble object, its invention 6,000 years ago enabled people to make a great leap forward in food production. The plow brings up nutrients from deeper soil than the hoe, and rids crops of weeds, which use nutrients.

Combining irrigation techniques with the use of the plow increased productivity even in drought and made the increased yields more reliable. It also made it possible to work land that had previously been useless for food production. This increased production and ability to renew the soil allowed the development of some of the first permanent settlements.

These inventions also introduced new social forms. First, increased productivity in the fields allowed more people to work in trades other than food production. The plow itself was usually made by a full-time specialist, for instance. Because these activities could most easily be accomplished in concentrated populations, cities and associated social structures began to emerge.

Second, the complex irrigation systems were attended by a group of men who specialized in managing them. This group sometimes became the governing body and elite social class of a society. Agricultural societies developed hierarchies in which wealth was much less equally shared, and a few people became very wealthy while most were still relatively poor. Political institutions linked to the earlier kinship structures frequently came to power, usually in the form of monarchies. Land became increasingly valuable, and wars over territory became more frequent.

Many of these characteristics can be seen in the ancient Babylonian empire, which was based on agriculture. Its government became complex. Its great trade, based on the surpluses produced through plowing and irrigation, led to the growth of inns and other services for travelers. The family changed greatly. The common custom in horticultural societies of one man marrying two or more women gradually disappeared, perhaps because with the plow one household could cultivate an increased area without increasing the number of women in the household to dig the fields with their sticks.

Land, the primary source of wealth, was individually owned and could be inherited. This created major differences between social strata: there were now those who owned land and those who worked on the land or in another specialized industry which supported the landowners in some way. The peasant workers were often poorly fed and grew stunted due to their meager diets (Braudel, 1981).

Agricultural societies were able to support people whose sole purpose was to provide creative ideas to the culture. Poets, writers, historians, painters, and scientists were encouraged to spend their days cultivating wisdom and beauty rather than fields.

The transition to agriculture revolutionized the social structure (M. Harris, 1986). Status differences between wealthy landowners and the typical worker were vast—rigid inequality grew, with the most important positions ascribed rather than achieved. Entirely new institutions also emerged, often including a monarchial state, a religious priesthood, cities, and bureaucracies. Elaborate sets of norms were developed around the new technology and institutions, and, of course, people defined many new roles associated with these additional institutions.

INDUSTRIAL SOCIETIES

In ***industrial societies****, the largest portion of the labor force is involved in mechanized production of goods and services.* Fuel-powered machines free increasing numbers of people from agricultural tasks. Occupations become increasingly specialized. For instance, in food production new occupations develop in processing, transporting, distributing, and selling food. Similarly, most homes are no longer built by their owners but by teams of specialized workers.

Partly because of this specialization in occupations, grown children have been more likely to leave the community in which their parents live. The institution of the family becomes less important as center for work and caretaker of the young and old. Government, business, schools, medicine, and science take over some of the functions once served by the family and community and become much more important as institutions. Bureaucratic procedures dominate business, government, religion, and education.

The high levels of productivity of industrial societies further stimulate population growth, with increasing numbers living in cities and metropolitan areas. The enormous productivity also seems to promote ever-increasing needs and widening social differences. Automobiles, large wardrobes, carpeting, television, and property-protecting devices like insurance all become "necessities." Extreme poverty and affluence often exist in the midst of the plenty gathered from increased productivity.

The social structure diversifies even more than with less-industrial societies. Vast numbers of new roles emerge around new technologies. More institutions develop, including formal education and science, and they are more elaborate. Status differences are vast and involve thousands of occupational roles. Both ascription and achievement influence a person's adult

Does he run the machine or does the machine run him? Mechanized production of goods and services characterizes the industrial society. Critics suggest that even the humans become mechanized. (© *Ellis Herwig/The Picture Cube*)

status. The number of norms grow to such a proportion that no individual can know them all. Lawyers, as members of a special occupation schooled in volumes of norms called laws, devote their lives to interpreting legal matters.

POSTINDUSTRIAL SOCIETY

The United States, Japan, and other highly industrialized countries are rapidly approaching what some sociologists term a postindustrial society (D. Bell, 1973). *In a* ***postindustrial society****, increasingly sophisticated, virtually automatic machines take over much unskilled work, and the majority of the labor force becomes employed in service occupations*, such as managers, clerks, salespeople, physicians, or entertainers. Daniel Bell states that a postindustrial society has five main features: (1) the majority of the labor force is involved in services rather than agriculture or manufacturing; (2) the professional and technical class is growing twice as fast as the average labor force; (3) theoretical problem solving replaces trial-and-error problem solving; (4) technology must be planned to avoid possible negative side-effects; and (5) new intellectual technologies arise to help society reach rational decisions in complex and uncertain situations (D. Bell, 1973).

The postindustrial society is still emerging as a concept and as a social form. The social structure is even more diverse than industrial society, and includes more norms, statuses, and roles. Especially in the areas of family and work, we see much role strain, for instance in the dual-career family. Because most of society's members have multiple roles, the incidence of role conflict increases. Both ascription and achievement continue to be important in attaining status. Postindustrial society presents the most challenging of all social structures to understand.

BEYOND

Postindustrial society is based on sophisticated technology that allows most people to work in service occupations. It is ethnocentric to believe that it represents the final stage or type of society. In fact, the choice of the term *postindustrial* is unfortunate, as it fails to define the subsistence adaptation. Perhaps it is better to call this form a *service society* or an *information-based society*.

Another major shift in the way work is done will probably cause more changes in the structure of society. Some futurologists have suggested, for instance, that a new generation of "smart" machines may replace many of the people working in relatively routine service occupations such as clerks, security guards, and taxi drivers. If this occurs, more workers will be available for the creative occupations, like artist, architect, and scientist. Such a change could also produce a period of high unemployment like that experienced in the United States in the late 1970s and early 1980s.

Another major technological advance might also mean that people will work less and have more leisure time. As in the past, a major change in the way society produces its goods and services can be expected to have a strong impact on social institutions like the family, religion, government, and education.

Although technology is a major determinant of social change, many sociologists point out the importance of social values such as belief in the work ethic or dedication to democracy or communism, as factors that also shape society. Wendell Bell and James Mau, for instance, argue that hopes and fears about the future will strongly influence the shape of social change (Bell and Mau, 1971). We all share the responsibility of being aware of both social and technological changes that may affect our society's future.

We learn several things from studying different types of societies. Historically, most societies are not like ours. Human beings have spent most of their time on this planet as hunters and gatherers. Yet the societies of the world seem rapidly headed toward agriculture, industrialization, and forms beyond these.

We know that differences in subsistence adaptation are related to major differences in social structure, and we see that social structure is currently adapting to a postindustrial, or service and information, mode. This helps explain why we see rapid social change all around us. Throughout this text, we will consider in more depth the changing features of our society, and in the closing chapter, "Social Change: Urbanization and Modernization," will return to the general questions of what propels social change.

Striking differences exist between modern societies and the pre-modern societies that preceded them, some of which still exist in various regions of the world. Sociologists and anthropologists have attempted to clarify the differences in the quality of social life by distinguishing between the two extremes.

Many view the transformation to modern societies that takes place through industrialization as a transformation in the basic nature of societies. Emile Durkheim suggested that differences exist in the basic social forces that bind these types of societies (1893). According to Durkheim, pre-modern societies are held together by ***mechanical solidarity****, bonds of common activities and values*. Durkheim suggested that members of pre-modern societies feel the commonality of their situation and pull together because they share common values and care about each other.

Modern societies, in contrast, are held together by ***organic solidarity***, *bonds based on interdependence*. In other words, members of a modern society realize at some level that they will not survive as easily or as well without cooperating. They work together as a business proposition rather than as part of an emotional bonding process. Ferdinand Tönnies used the labels *Gemeinschaft* (*community*) and *Gesellschaft* (*association*) to describe similar differences (1887). Robert Redfield draws a distinction between *folk* and *urban* societies (Redfield, 1941).

The modern industrial societies these theorists discuss experience many social situations differently from pre-modern societies. Modern societies have (1) more complexity in occupational structure, (2) more formal relationships, (3) more reliance on nonfamily institutions, and (4) less reliance on custom to regulate behavior.

Perhaps the most significant difference is the degree of complexity in occupational systems. The occupational structure of modern societies, with thousands of intricately related occupations, is far more complex than that of hunting and gathering societies, in which men hunt and women gather fruit and raise children.

Durkheim referred to this specialization found in modern societies as the *division of labor*. Consider, for example, a few of the occupations involved in flying people from city to city: skycap, ticket agent, flight attendant, pilot, navigator, air traffic controller, and baggage claim clerk. This complex structure represents a technological advance in organizing people that is similar in form and scale to the technological advances achieved in machines of the modern world.

One important consequence of division of labor is that, as people begin to function like cogs in an elaborate social mechanism, they may relate to one another as objects rather than as whole persons. In simple societies, social relations generally involve people who have known one another for their lifetime. Relations are personal, and individual emotions and needs are considered.

Social contact in a modern society, on the other hand, is often between relative strangers who have little or no emotional involvement with each other. Most modern people would be little affected if many service occupations were occupied by robots. Conversely, workers in most service positions do not particularly care who their clients are personally, because no real emotional attachment exists in this kind of relationship. Modern people may be treated as living material to be processed, in much the same way that raw material is treated in factories. This attitude is what Durkheim, Tönnies, and Redfield characterize as the modern form of social bond: formal rather than informal, distant rather than close. In sociological terms, modern societies are characterized much more by secondary

CLOSE-UP on • *THEORY* •

Paul Blumberg on America in an Age of Decline

The Theorist and the Setting

Professor of Sociology Paul Blumberg holds posts at Queens College and the Graduate Center of the City University of New York. Blumberg writes to both his academic colleagues and the public at large, with his work appearing in *The Nations*, *The New Republic*, *Dissent*, *Midstream*, and *The American Quarterly*.

As Blumberg observes: "The America we have always known is disappearing before our eyes. . . . (The) crisis of the American economy and the associated weakening of American power around the world" are transforming the entire society (p. xi).

The Theorist's Goal

Blumberg claims that this crisis has had its greatest impact on our class structure. Once a society of increasing affluence and growing equality, the United States now faces stagnating living standards and growing inequality. Blumberg seeks to discover the causes and consequences of this "crisis in American capitalism" (p. xii).

Concepts and Propositions

Blumberg begins by sketching the extent of America's economic problems. Following World War II, from 1947 to 1965, real spendable income rose by 36 percent. In 1965 it leveled off and has not risen since. Even with the rapid rise in number of women in the work force and increasing numbers of youths working, family income has failed to grow since the early 1970s.

Over the same time period the United States' economic position compared to other nations has eroded. American military personnel and their families lived luxuriously while stationed abroad in the 1960s, but as other nations' economies have become strong, the value of U.S. dollars has shrunk abroad. The wife of one black GI recently said that trying to live on military pay in Germany was "like living in the ghetto, only worse."

Though the United States exported twice the manufactured products it imported in 1958, by 1978 it imported more than it exported. From 1966 to 1977 the amount of steel, clothing, and textiles imported increased fourfold, and the number of televisions, phonographs, and recording equipment increased sevenfold. In that same time period, the United States increased by ten times the dollar amount of shoes imported.

Proposition 1: A "permanent war economy" contributes to the crisis of American capitalism.

The concept of a permanent war economy refers to the fact that the United States military investment rivals that spent during wartime. "A tank can neither be used to increase production nor be purchased and used by consumers to enhance their standard of living" (p. 144). For every dollar the United States invests in domestic production, it spends 33 cents on the military. In comparison, West Germany spends 13 cents and Japan only 2 cents (p. 143). Furthermore, engineers who are building rockets and war equipment are not designing better stereos—in this way the United States has lost the stereo industry and others as well to Japan.

Proposition 2: The rapid international diffusion of technology contributes to the economic crisis.

The concept of rapid international diffusion of technology refers to nations adapting technology from one another. Often the Japanese have excelled in copying and advancing technology. The Japanese steel industry adopted the high-efficiency basic oxygen furnace, perhaps the most important advance in steelmaking in the twentieth century, long before the United States did. Complacent U.S. steel company owners, who had grown accustomed to government shelter and support, failed to adopt this and other state-of-the-art technology, and partly as a result they have lost much of the world market for steel. Other nations moved so far and rapidly ahead, steel plant closings became commonplace in the late nineteen seventies (p. 119). Often the United States' industrialists have facilitated this diffusion by moving production facilities to other countries.

Proposition 3: The crisis threatens cherished beliefs in "classlessness" (or equal opportunity).

During the burst of affluence from the mid-nineteen forties to the mid-sixties, the U.S. culture emphasized achievement and increased income for all. Many experts believed the United States was becoming more equal. But the current economic crisis is obviously bringing more growth for the wealthy than for the less wealthy. As the gap between rich and poor widens and grows more obvious, we are less able to believe in a land of equal opportunity for all.

During this period when overall income fails to grow and industry is being lost, the sale of luxury cars like Cadillacs and Lincolns is increasing and that of ordinary cars like Chevrolets and Fords is declining. The housing industry produces and sells increasingly expensive houses to the wealthy while the production and sale of modest homes falls. The proportion of Americans able to afford the median-priced home has fallen from 47 percent in 1970 to 27 percent in just six years.

Proposition 4: The crisis threatens to bring social conflict at home and abroad.

Conflict could break out between union and nonunion labor as it did in Great Britain in the late 1970s, for example (p. 219). But conflict could also develop along racial, sexual, educational, or even generational lines, as people become aware of economic privileges and penalties of these status positions.

Proposition 5: This tendency toward domestic conflict and international belligerence may be offset by the stabilizing influences of increasing democracy and civility in American life.

The past few decades have brought increasing tolerance of minorities and harmony between ethnic groups. Blumberg sees as hopeful the signs that religious tolerance and tolerance toward homosexuality, for example, have increased. These factors may offset a tendency toward violent conflict, but they are unlikely to help close the widening economic gap.

Interpretation

Blumberg offers a stark image of the future in the United States and a clear explanation of how it came to these circumstances. He also suggests where it may be headed.

Blumberg writes from the conflict perspective, and as he admits in his book, research as well as theorizing in this area has been strongly colored by political viewpoints. Even sociologists sometimes allow their value perspectives to influence their analytical judgment. In this case Blumberg documents much of what he says about the state of the United States. He also cites examples of the factors he claims cause and are caused by the economic crisis. Future research will help to determine whether these factors are causally related the way he has proposed.

Questions

1. What sort of research might best be used to test these propositions?
2. What, if anything, has Blumberg omitted? What other factors might contribute to our economic situation? What other consequences might result?
3. If Blumberg is generally right, what does this imply about what we should do? Why?

SOURCE Paul Blumberg. 1980. *Inequality in an Age of Decline.* New York: Oxford University Press.

than primary group relationships. (Chapter 5, "Groups and Organizations," discusses more fully the division of labor and its social consequences.)

The simplest pre-modern societies are organized around the kinship institution we think of as the family, including parents, children, and others, which carries out economic, politcal, religious, and educational tasks. Modern societies, on the other extreme of the continuum, not only have division of labor among individuals, but also an entirely different level of organization among the institutions of society. The relatively separate institutions of modern society, including family, religion, government, and the economy, divide those tasks accordingly.

Finally, in pre-modern societies behavior is controlled by custom through the traditional rules of the community. Modern societies attempt to control behavior through more institutionalized means, like written contracts and laws with specific penalties and procedures for dealing with offenders. In rural Brazil, an apprehended thief is immediately given a firm beating by the witnesses to the crime. In the United States most witnesses would not pursue a thief themselves, but would call the police. If the police catch the thief, the prosecutor's office could bring charges and might obtain a conviction, which could result in a prison sentence. Again relationships are more formalized in the modern world.

The terms *pre-modern* and *modern* have been used to facilitate discussion. It is important to note, however, that societies actually exist on a continuum from pre-modern to modern rather than as purely one or the other. Furthermore, no modern society is modern throughout its territory. Social relations in some areas are more *Gemeinschaft* than *Gesellschaft*, more folk than urban, and more characterized by mechanical than organic solidarity. In the United States, for example, parts of Appalachia and other rural areas are characterized by pre-modern social relations. Generally, however, as societies move toward the modern end of the spectrum they experience increasing division of labor, fewer primary relations, greater reliance on nonfamily institutions, and less reliance on custom to regulate behavior.

What Are the Basic Social Processes?

Many of the sciences are divided into two branches, one dealing with the *static*, or structural, elements and one dealing with the *dynamic*, or active, elements. Most sociological concepts developed thus far describe the static or structural aspects of society. This section deals with the dynamic aspects: the fundamental social processes. The question addressed is: What are the elementary ways members of society can act toward one another?

CONFLICT

***Conflict** is the process in which the parties struggle against one another for a commonly prized object* (Nisbet, 1970). Wars, feuds, and fights are examples of conflict. Karl Marx believed that a conflict-free state of society is possible, but only intensified conflict between the classes would bring about his advance (Marx and Engels, 1970 translation). Most modern conflict theorists, including Seymour Melman (1974) and Paul Blumberg (1980), build their theories on Marx's insights about the central importance of class conflict. These classes struggle over who will control the productive resources and reap the wealth of the society. Some sociologists, including Ralf Dahrendorf (1959), see such conflict as an inevitable component of modern complex societies. Lewis Coser (1956) argues further that conflict may even be a beneficial process in that it may bring about desirable social change or unite a group against a common enemy.

COERCION AND EXPLOITATION

***Coercion** is a process of being forced to act against one's will.* Similar to coercion is ***exploitation**, a process in which one is deprived of things that one rightfully is due.* Some examples of coercion and exploitation seem obvious. Slavery involves definite and clear coercion, and slave labor seems obviously exploitative.

Sometimes, however, coercion and exploitation are harder to discern. For example, during periods of war the United States institutes a draft. Some people volunteer for military service, and others are drafted into it against their will. The volunteers are not necessarily coerced into the military, but some of the involuntary draftees are. The difference is one of attitude rather than behavior. Coercion involves more than being commanded to do something; it is being commanded to do something one does not want to do.

The nation of South Africa provides an unfortunately clear example of both coercion and exploitation. Most South Africans are black, but the nation is dominated by an elite minority of whites. Blacks must request permission from the state before they can visit another city. Industry is controlled by whites, and blacks work for wages that most people would see as exploitative. When blacks have protested this arrangement, they have typically been harassed or jailed.

Though this arrangement of extreme inequality has persisted for decades, in the last ten to fifteen years it has come to widespread attention. In the middle

1970s, students at many U.S. universities began to protest against their schools' ownership of stock in businesses profiting from this coercion and exploitation. In the past five years many major U.S. corporations once operating in South Africa have left. There is an important point here: exploitation is both a matter of physical circumstance and socially influenced expectations. Change is slowly coming to South Africa, not so much because the oppression was growing worse, but because people's acceptance of it has declined.

Similarly coercion is a matter of forceful threats that go against one's will. If blacks once accepted inferior treatment, but later became less willing to take this treatment, coercion increases—not because the treatment has changed, but because blacks have changed their minds about what is tolerable.

Ideas about coercion and exploitation depend on socially shared definitions of what is fair and what people will or will not do voluntarily. Wars are fought for freedom from coercion and revolutions are staged to end exploitation, but these social processes are defined as much by social expectations as material circumstances.

They can't both win! When two or more parties seek a goal not available to them all, we have competition. (© *Mike Valeri/FPG International*)

COMPETITION

Much social interaction involves the familiar process of **competition**, *the process in which two or more parties seek a goal that is not available to them all.* Most sports and games involve competition. Only one driver wins the Indianapolis 500, there is only one heavyweight champion in the world at a given time, and only one person wins the World Championship Monopoly Contest each year.

Competition is often seen as useful by people in a capitalist system. Theoretically, the competition between businesses for sales to consumers coupled with the competition between applicants for jobs and schooling assures that the best products come to market and that they are produced with maximum efficiency by the best qualified people.

COOPERATION

Cooperation *is a social process in which the parties involved act jointly to bring about mutual benefit.* Most people would define cooperation as the most pleasant of these social processes.

Robert Nisbet defined four types of cooperation (1970). *Spontaneous cooperation* occurs when there is no explicitly prescribed pattern of behavior, and people simply act to help each other. Several drivers stopping to help push a car out of a snowdrift exhibit spontaneous cooperation.

Traditional cooperation is part of the culture. For example, politeness dictates that people clean up after themselves in public parks so that those who come after can enjoy a clean area.

Directed cooperation requires a leader or person of authority directing a group effort so that a mutually desired end is achieved. NASA projects involve elaborate degrees of directed cooperation, perhaps epitomized by the Apollo mission to reach the moon.

Contractual cooperation involves formally specifying the parties' obligations. Modern industrial production of all of the parts of an automobile is achieved through contractual cooperation between major automotive firms, like General Motors, and other firms that provide specialized items like electrical switches or rubber gaskets. This cooperation often literally involves a contract between the automotive firm and the vendor.

Most societies depend on cooperation as their basic social process. Cooperation allows members of a society to accomplish things they could not do as individuals. So we can see that cooperation is necessary for the survival of most groups.

What Is the "Good" Society and How Does It Work?

Robert Bellah, well-known in the field of the sociology of religion, points out that the underlying question in

Many hands make light work. Building a barn would be impossible without cooperation. Here barn-raising, common in rural communities in the nineteenth century and still practiced by the Amish, exemplifies what Nisbet termed traditional cooperation. (*David S. Strickler/The Picture Cube*)

many of the works of Machiavelli, Hobbes, Weber, and other early social philosophers was often "What is the 'good' society?" (1981). Max Weber believed his work to be "scientific" because it was based on truth rather than values. However, Bellah sees in it a constant battle between Weber's natural desire to see love displayed between people and his belief that human behavior is largely determined by the search for power.

Bellah suggests that sociologists are beginning to realize that they do have ethical aims in their research and theory, and that at the bottom of much social science today are these same value questions. One example of this is Kai Erikson's work, *Everything in Its Path: Destruction of Community in the Buffalo Creek Flood* (1978). In this work, Erikson describes the social results of a collapsed dam that dumped 132 million gallons of water and coal waste into Buffalo Creek, West Virginia, killing 125 people and destroying the homes of 4,000 others.

Erikson describes the community spirit, or communality, that existed in Buffalo Creek before the flood as

> a constant readiness to look after one's neighbors—or, rather, to know without being asked what needs to be done. . . . A community of the sort we are talking about here derives from and depends on an almost perfect democracy of the spirit, where people are not only assumed to be equal in status but virtually identical in temperament and outlook. . . . Much of the agony experienced in Buffalo Creek is related to the fact that the Hollow is now without much in the way of nourishing community life (p. 153).

The loss of loved ones, homes, and jobs due to the flood caused a breakup of the community sense in Buffalo Creek. Many people had to move away, some temporarily and some permanently. No longer could the people experience the sense of extended caring that had existed previously. Erikson makes a clear value judgment about this situation. He, like the subjects of his study, values this social support system. He sees the communality as depending on a strong sense of democracy, which was a positive source of strength for the Buffalo Creek people. He states that many of the traumatic symptoms that the people showed in his research can be directly attributed to the loss of this sense of community rather than to the loss of physical goods or individual family members. This distinction makes the Buffalo Creek case a landmark one: It marks the first time in U.S. judicial history that people were awarded money for the destruction of their sense of community rather than for physical goods or loss of persons.

Bellah suggests that more sociologists are needed who, like Erikson, acknowledge their ethical bias and share it with society. Such social scientists would be

While the flooding here seems to be promoting a sense of community cooperation, a devastating flood like that at Buffalo Creek destroys homes, lives, and even the community spirit. So real was the loss of community at Buffalo Creek that for the first time in judicial history, the court awarded money for the destruction of community separate from that awarded for loss of property and lives. *(UPI/Bettmann Newsphotos)*

trained to look at the workings of society as well as be willing to state what they see as good and bad about the patterns they see. Only then will we have a total picture that might allow us to make the best decisions concerning our society's future.

We do not conduct our personal lives without value judgments. Perhaps, as Bellah proposes, it is time to realize that we make the same kinds of judgments on a community level. As you think about the basic social processes, for instance, keep in mind the ethical questions you face as a member of your own society. For instance: Should cooperation be the strongest value in society? If so, how might you individually or we as a society foster cooperation?

How Do the Functional and Conflict Perspectives View Society?

The functional perspective sees societies as serving the function of nurturing and protecting human babies in a group setting, thus assuring the survival of the species. Structural-functionalists argue that the society must provide for the maintenance of its members, perpetuate itself through reproduction or recruitment, and socialize new members, transmitting to them the rules and beliefs of the society. In this way, lessons learned through past experience of the group are not lost. They suggest also that society must be flexible enough to change when conditions change and compete successfully with other groups for needed resources. Functionalists think of society as being composed of institutions and their smaller building blocks—statuses, roles, and norms. This approach suggests that the society that builds these institutions and fills these needs for its members will flourish.

Structural-functionalists assume that cooperation is part of the nature of society and look for ways that the structure functions to maintain society. In the case of social structure, they see institutions such as religion and the family as stable clusters of roles, statuses, and beliefs that arise through consensus to keep society stable and surviving.

Sociologists at Work •

WENDELL BELL
CREATES SOCIOLOGICALLY REALISTIC FUTURE SCENARIOS
Yale University
New Haven, Connecticut

Wendell Bell's enthusiasm and vigor continue to infect his students as they have done throughout his 35-year teaching career. Bell received the first Ph.D. in Sociology ever granted by UCLA in 1952, doing social-area analysis and developing, with Eshref Shevky, what later became known as the Shevky–Bell social-area typology. Since then, he has studied group membership in relationship to anomie, urban sociology, the emergence of new nations, and future thinking. Several common threads run between these areas; among them are inequality and social justice, social change, and action in relationship to future thinking. Here he speaks with us about his latest work, *The Foundations of the Futures Field: An Introduction* (1988).

What Was the Purpose of This Research?
For two decades now, I have tried to generalize the principles of future thinking, attempting to create a sociology in the future conditional tense rather than a sociology in the past tense, which we have now. As early as 1971, I co-edited the volume *The Sociology of the Future*, one step in the process of trying to change the focus of our discipline. One of the purposes of my new book is to futurize the social sciences so that the future is more fully taken into account, not just as an afterthought, but as a focus of one's entire work.

What Is Futuristics?
Futuristics focuses on trying to invent or discover, examine and evaluate, and propose possible, probable, and preferable futures. Our modern conception of time is no longer merely a circular one of an endless repetition of the same past. Instead, we are moving linearly, progressively, and irreversibly through time, out of the past toward the future. Furturists seek to help people realize what all of the possibilities before them really are and to enunciate and clarify their goals and values so that they know which ones they should try to bring into being. I am trying to help people realize that there are many more real possibilities for the future than they are now taking into account.

Futures research is, in some sense, a combination of a science and a system of ethics. It is very much an action science oriented toward decision making that creates the action to bring particular futures into being and to prevent others from occurring. There are no future facts, and the future is not determined until it occurs.

What Is the Goal of the Futures Field?
Rather than aiming to predict the future, futurists try to increase human responsibility for the present, and human control over it, by explicating and exploring the alternative futures and making the results available to people, in order to increase their effectiveness in creating the world they desire.

Some futurists contend that we are entering an era of discovery like nothing before in human history. The new age may become an Age of Misinformation, depending on who controls access to the new technology and to the information, or misinformation, that goes into the data banks. Manipulation, rather than enlightenment of people, is a possible outcome. An elite may arise with exclusive access to the new technologies and information systems, whereas the mass may be limited to what is broadcasted for them to receive.

In the course of human development, as societies have been increasing in scale, equality and social justice have become, perhaps second only to survival itself, the top moral imperative of our time. Each new development in society brings the potential for the emergence of new inequalities and injustices as well as for the achievement of greater equality. For instance, as new means to increase human potential develop, who will control them? Will the people who are already rich and powerful end up even more rich and powerful relative to others? These questions must be addressed in order for equality and social justice to grow as society grows.

Futurists tend to share the underlying vision that the fate of humanity depends largely on what humans do, and what they do depends largely on their images of the future. My commitment is to arouse an interest in an awareness of the future, make the future problematic in peoples' mind, help them create more options for themselves, and to discover the futures people want and how to achieve them. •

Conflict sociologists emphasize the central place of social class structure in understanding society. For example, the private ownership of productive property, such as land, mines, ships, or factories, divided society into two opposing classes: the wealthy and those who must work for the wealthy because they do not own productive property. The elites in the wealthy class become even more powerful because of their wealth, while those who lack ownership become relatively powerless. The powerful wealthy class is able to influence what will and will not be allowed in society, so the prevailing culture and social structure will be largely shaped by them for their benefit and will attempt to justify what is good for the elites rather than to determine what may be in the best interests of the entire society.

In conflict theory, the building blocks of society would be classes, with special attention being drawn to the upper class and its politically active subgrouping, the power elite. They would see competition and conflict rather than cooperation as the basic social processes, and point out ways in which institutions such as religion and the family might use coercion and exploitation to harm the individual and keep the lower classes from rising. Conflict theorists believe that it is in this conflict between classes that social structure is formed. If the society fails, conflict theorists might hypothesize the cause as inadequate attempts to equalize conditions between the classes and thus use the potential of all members of the society.

We can highlight their differences by applying the theories to the sociological issue: How are we to explain the prevalence and persistence of poverty in the United States? In a nation of great wealth and pride in equality, why must 30 million people, most of them working full time, try to subsist on poverty incomes?

From the functional perspective, poverty is regrettable but is part of a productive system that benefits society. The functionalist would focus on the overall productivity of one economy as a system, and see differences in income, including poverty and affluence, as a strong incentive system motivating people toward positions, like doctors and lawyers, that require special skills, training, and education. Similarly, the fact that people must work to obtain income ensures that they will work, and work well, even in mundane and menial positions.

From the conflict perspective, however, poverty is due to exploitation, backed by thinly veiled coercion. Though no one is explicitly forced to work for poverty wages, the wealthy have created and maintained a system that benefits them and virtually assures that poor people will take such work in preference to having even less money or having their families starve. Because the poor have little power, they are unable to change the system to be more equitable to all members of the society. Conflict between these classes is, therefore, inevitable.

It is not surprising that the functional and conflict perspectives lead us to radically different conclusions, because they proceed from radically different assumptions. Nevertheless, both are capable of rendering valid insights into society, for each can reveal patterns that might be invisible from the opposite viewpoint.

Conclusion

The concepts and ideas we have encountered here will serve us as we move through the study of social behavior. We have learned the importance of technology in setting opportunities and constraints on human societies. We have also developed concepts such as role, status, institution, conflict, coercion, exploitation, competition, and cooperation, which will help us to describe and understand our social life.

REVIEW

Summary Questions

1. How do subsistence adaptation and technology help in the process of sorting societies?
2. What are the elements of social structure?
3. What are two ways in which status is conferred?
4. What is a status intervention, and how might it affect a group?
5. What are postindustrial societies and how are they distinguished from industrial societies?
6. What are the major differences between modern and pre-modern societies?
7. What does Bellah suggest about defining the "good" society?
8. What is the essential nature of the basic social processes?
9. How do conflict and functionalist theories view social processes?

Summary Answers

1. We can identify six types of societies by focusing on the dominant form of work in a society, or subsistence adaptation. In hunting and gathering societies, people live by hunting wild animals using primitive weapons and gathering food as it grows naturally. Herding, or pastoral, societies often arise in areas with poor soil, and rely on the domestication of animals into herds as a major means of support, linked with either hunting and gathering or other technology. The semipermanent

horticultural society produces its food through cultivation of the soil with hand tools, and is more common in areas with fertile soil, which is exhausted within three to five years. Agricultural societies employ animal-drawn plows to cultivate the land, and often combine this with irrigation to increase productivity. In industrial societies, the largest portion of the labor force is involved in mechanized production of goods and services.

2. Social structure is the enduring patterns of social behavior, including statuses, roles, norms, and institutions that constitute relatively stable relations in society. A status is a position in a particular social pattern. A role includes the behavior that goes with, but is distinct from, the status.
3. Status is either conferred independently of the individual's efforts or abilities (ascribed) or attained through effort or performance (achieved).
4. A status intervention is an attempt to diminish the influence of an undesirable status characteristic. Research shows that groups will discount the input of persons with low-status characteristics and be overly positive toward the input of persons with high-status characteristics, even if the status has nothing to do with the task of the group at the time. People of low status can be taught to be assertive in their own realm by learning that people of higher status do not necessarily know more about everything.
5. In a postindustrial society, increasingly sophisticated, virtually automatic machines take over much unskilled work, and the majority of the labor force becomes employed in service occupations. Government becomes more involved in realms that were previously dominated by the other institutions of society: family, religion, education, and the economy. This form of society might be thought of as a service society or an information-based society.
6. According to Durkheim, pre-modern societies are held together by mechanical solidarity, or bonds of common activities and values, as opposed to modern societies that are held together by organic solidarity, or bonds based on interdependence. Tönnies used the labels *Gemeinschaft*, or community, and *Gesellschaft*, or association, to describe similar differences. Modern societies have more complexity in occupational structure, more formal relationships, more reliance on nonfamily insititutions, and less reliance on custom to regulate behavior.
7. Robert Bellah suggests that much of early scholarly work addressed this question and that social scientists of today must address it as well, with their ethical biases plainly acknowledged rather than from a "value-free" stance. One example of this type of work is Kai Erikson's study of the social results of a collapsed dam that destroyed Buffalo Creek, West Virginia. Erikson described the loss of sense of community in the town as being a disaster in itself, and was instrumental in winning an award of money for the people of Buffalo Creek based on this premise.
8. Conflict is the process in which the parties struggle against one another for a commonly prized object—for example, wars and feuds. Coercion is a process of being forced to act against one's will, as in slavery. Similar to coercion is exploitation, a process in which one is deprived of things that one rightfully is due—for instance, when migrant workers are not paid their full wage due to inability to function well in the English language and cheating occurs on the part of the produce company. Competition involves two or more parties seeking a goal that is not available to them all—for instance, getting a contract to build a bank. Cooperation is a social process in which the parties involved act jointly to bring about mutual benefit, either as a result of traditional values, direction of an authority figure, or a contract.
9. Structural-functionalists assume that cooperation is part of the nature of society, and they look for ways in which the structure functions to maintain society. Conflict theorists assume that conflict is intrinsic to society and examine society for signs of conflict, coercion, and exploitation.

Glossary

achieved status status attained by an individual at least partly through effort or performance

agricultural society one characterized by use of the animal-drawn plow for cultivation of the land

ascribed status status conferred by society independent of an individual's effort or abilities

coercion being forced to act against one's will

competition the social process in which two or more parties seek a goal that is not available to them all

conflict the social process in which two or more parties struggle against one another for a commonly prized objective

cooperation the social process in which the parties involved act jointly to bring about some mutual benefit; the four types are spontaneous cooperation, traditional cooperation, directed cooperation, and contractual cooperation

exploitation the social process in which one is deprived of things that one is rightfully due

Gemeinschaft community

Gesellschaft association

herding society one in which people rely on the domestication of animals into herds as a major means of support

horticultural society a society that produces its food through cultivation of the soil with hand tools

hunting and gathering society one in which people live by hunting wild animals and by gathering plants as they grow naturally

industrial society one in which the largest portion of the labor force is involved in mechanized production of goods and services

institution a complex set of norms, values, statuses, and roles that are centered around a basic need of a society

mechanical solidarity social bonds based on common activities and values

organic solidarity social bonds based on interdependence

postindustrial society one in which increasingly sophisticated, virtually automatic machines do much unskilled work, and the majority of people are employed in service occupations

role the behavior that goes with, but is distinct from, the status

role conflict when two of an individual's roles call for different behaviors

role distance the situation in which people act as if they are not fully involved in their roles

role strain when one role requires two conflicting courses of action

social structure the fundamental, enduring patterns of actual behavior in a society

society a self-sufficient group of people who live in a common territory and transmit their unique language and culture to those who are born or accepted into the group

status a position in a group or society

subsistence adaptation the society's strategy for producing the goods and services necessary for survival

status intervention an attempt by a person to diminish the influence of an undesirable status characteristic

technology the tools, machines, or other means by which the society or group works

Suggested Readings

Bell, Wendell. 1988. *The Foundations of Futuristics: An Introduction to Futures Research*. New York: Random House.

An attempt to create a sociology in the future conditional tense, focusing on optimal directions for the future.

Dahrendorf, Ralf. 1959. *Class and Class Conflict in Industrial Societies*. Stanford: Stanford University Press.

A useful description of the basic social processes from the conflict theorists' point of view.

Erikson, Kai T. 1976. *Everything in Its Path: Destruction of Community in the Buffalo Creek Flood.* New York: Simon and Schuster.

Erikson's firsthand account of the social destruction that followed the physical destruction of a small mining community and the landmark court rulings that came out of the disaster.

Janowitz, Morris. 1978. *The Last Half.* Chicago: University of Chicago Press.

A theoretical work on how the social structure of the United States has changed in modern times.

Kephart, William M. 1982. *Extraordinary Groups: The Sociology of Unconventional Life-Styles*, 2nd ed. New York: St. Martin's Press.

A lively account of the daily lives of some societies within the United States today, including Amish, Shakers, Mormons, Gypsies, and Hutterites.

Lenski, Gerhard and Jean Lenski. 1987. *Human Societies*. 5th ed. New York: McGraw-Hill.

An interesting analysis of the differences between the various types of socieites, from primitive to industrial.

Skolnick, Jerome H. and Elliott Curie. 1985. *Crisis in American Institutions*, 6th ed. Boston: Little, Brown and Co.

Skolnick and Curie show the interrelationship between the failure of our various social institutions and today's social problems.

Williams, Robin M. Jr. 1970. *American Society: A Sociological Interpretation*, 3rd ed. New York: Alfred A. Knopf.

A scholarly analysis of American culture that stimulates examination of one's own cultural roots.

PART 3

Living in Groups

CHAPTER 4

SOCIALIZATION

How's Your Sociological Intuition?

1. The idea that human social behavior is largely genetically inherited is:
   - **a.** Widely accepted by sociologists
   - **b.** Widely rejected by sociologists
   - **c.** Widely accepted by sociobiologists
   - **d.** Not a proper question to be raised in sociology
2. Experiments demonstrate that the best way to teach a particular behavior is:
   - **a.** Severe punishment for each mistake
   - **b.** Intermittent reward for success
   - **c.** Regular reward for each success
   - **d.** Reward or punishment administered by women because they innately know more about teaching
3. When parents smoke cigarettes, the likelihood that the children will smoke is:
   - **a.** Greatly increased
   - **b.** Significantly increased
   - **c.** Not affected
   - **d.** Reduced
4. Evidence indicates that human beings deprived of normal sustained loving interaction during infancy:
   - **a.** Are likely to have difficulty establishing intimate relations later in life
   - **b.** Can be normal adults if they are loved enough later
   - **c.** Will be superior corporate executives
   - **d.** Will be more loving adults, because they are more aware of what it is like not to be loved

Answers

1. b. Sociologists have a strong bias toward the social influences on social behavior. However, recent theorists and researchers are challenging this view, as you will discover in the chapter section, "How Does Genetics Influence Social Development?"
2. b. B. F. Skinner's experiments regarding conditioning of behavior have raised significant questions for sociologists, as we discuss in our section on conditioning.
3. b. Children learn healthy and unhealthy habits from adults. In this case, parents' smoking increases the likelihood of children's smoking to a significant degree, as we see later in the chapter.
4. a. Love in infancy is crucial to building a person's ability to sustain intimate relationships later, as you will learn in the subsection, "Environmental Deprivation Syndrome."

WHEN YOU HAVE FINISHED STUDYING THIS CHAPTER, YOU SHOULD KNOW:

- How the self is social
- The effects of environmental deprivation on an individual
- What Charles Horton Cooley meant by "looking-glass self"
- George Herbert Mead's explanation of how people take the "role of the other"
- How Erving Goffman explained impression management
- Erik Erikson's eight stages of personality development
- Jean Piaget's four stages of intellectual development
- Lawrence Kohlberg's six stages of moral development
- Carol Gilligan's theory of differences in moral development of men and women
- How socialization continues in adulthood
- How jobs can actually help shape personalities
- What the basic agents of socialization or domination are and how they affect individuals
- What resocialization is and how people are resocialized
- The varying effects of nature and nurture on individual development
- What sociobiology is and why it is controversial
- Three modes of socialization
- Who the Children Without Childhood are
- Three characteristics of the socialization process
- Why socialization is important to society

It is just about noon, and we are not quite an hour into the surgery. The dramatic moment arrives: the surgeon lifts our newborn baby from its mother's womb. "It's a boy!" I exclaim. We now know his name will be Mark rather than the name we had picked if "it" had been a girl. Thus begins a process of biological and social growth. A short ten years later, Mark speaks fluent English, rides a bike, plays soccer and the violin, and can spell and do long division. He is also well aware of the holidays and traditions of his culture and the intricate web of social norms governing his life. He knows how to act in school, on the playground, at the dinner table, and in our place of worship. He would identify himself as an American and a Christian.

This process of social and biological development will continue. He has yet to learn how to act on a date, how to behave at a party, how to operate a voting machine, or how to drive a car. Some day he will learn the skills and norms of an occupation and will come to think of himself as "a veterinarian" or "a scientist." He will probably learn to be a husband and a father. Learning will likely continue into old age: learning how to regard himself as a retired person, a senior citizen, perhaps eventually as a nursing home resident.

What a different set of things Mark would need to have learned if he had been a different person born into different social circumstances: a king in the time of Moses, a peasant girl in medieval Europe, a daughter of a farmer during the American Revolution, the son of a party official in the Soviet Union. As human beings we learn so easily that much of what we learn seems natural, almost instinctual. We have to remember that we once had to *learn* to ride a bike, speak English, read, write, and act like a male or female.

This chapter presents the process of ***socialization,*** *or transmitting socially appropriate beliefs and behavior patterns to an individual and making possible the development of a self, or personality.* In studying socialization you will learn how we come to see ourselves as a reflection of our social world and how we learn what we need to know to live in our particular society.

What Is the Social Nature of Self-Image?

Suppose a baby girl was misidentified in the hospital and sent home with people not her biological parents. If the misplaced child were the biological daughter of a welfare recipient but had been sent home with a millionaire, the switch would make a great difference in the child's future, the social setting she would enter, and the socialization she would receive.

A real example is found in parts of traditional India, where one class of people was regarded as so low its members were "unseeable." They could not come outside during the day and had to work at night to avoid being seen. Conversely, many European monarchs were selected because they were descendants of monarchs. In both settings children were socialized into perceiving their own natural identity as either an unseeable or as an heir to the throne. Often they were told their unusual status was the will of God, and they were unlikely to challenge that assumption.

Few Americans see themselves as either unseeable or born to rule. But Americans are just as likely as future kings and queens to become what they are told they will be. If you parents treat you as if you are stupid, you will probably think of yourself as stupid. We accept the definitions of ourselves that we are taught by our families and other members of society.

ENVIRONMENTAL DEPRIVATION SYNDROME

What happens when the process of positive self-development through social contact is denied a child?

Infants who are denied intimate social contact—such as being held and fondled by their parents or others—may suffer from *retardation of social and physical growth,* termed **environmental deprivation syndrome.** Thus, a child who is deprived of the affectionate contact that is normally part of socialization can be physically and emotionally impaired for life.

The first study to address this issue was conducted by Rene Spitz in 1945. Spitz compared infants raised in a orphanage with infants raised by their own parents with comparable nutritional and physical care. However, in the orphanage Spitz studied, the infants had virtually no social interaction except at feedings and when clothes and beds were changed. The institutionalized children had lower IQ scores and were more aggressive and more easily distracted than children raised by their parents. They also showed less initiative and lacked emotional warmth. Since publication of the findings of these and other similar experiments, orphanages and foster-care facilities changed their policies to fill their charges' social and emotional as well as physical needs.

Sometimes environmental deprivation occurs when both parents are alive but choose not to care for their child. Kingsley Davis was the first social scientist to intensively study a socially isolated child (1940). More recently, sociologists studied Genie, described as a "modern-day wild child," who had been shut in a room by herself, strapped to a potty chair, forbidden to make noise, never spoken to, and fed poorly from age 20 months to age 13 (Curtiss, 1977). Although therapists worked diligently with Genie to develop basic language and social skills, she was never able to learn enough to leave the institution and enter society.

Becky Holmes was eight years old when she was found by the police, but she weighed only 24 pounds and was 32 inches tall, about the size of an average 2-year-old (M. Carter, 1979). Becky had been kept in a closet, hidden from view by a screen, and had been given no social contact. She was placed in foster care, given much nurturing and made great strides. She doubled her weight, learned to walk, began to eat normally, was toilet-trained, and developed a vocabulary of several hundred words. However, it is likely that Becky will be intellectually and physically retarded for the rest of her life due to the deprivation she experienced during her first eight years.

Love, or intimate social contact as sociologists refer to it, is necessary for normal social development. Without it a child may experience environmental deprivation syndrome. (© *Patricia Reynolds/ The Picture Cube*)

These cases are not as rare as one would wish. Many children who had received little or no socialization have been discovered since Davis' work in the 1940s. Because of situations like these, sociologists have been interested in the effects on children of lack of early socialization and in remedial socialization techniques. Socialization has diverse and important consequences for individuals and for society. It provides the individual with social identity and makes possible the creation of a "self" that is social.

COOLEY'S LOOKING-GLASS SELF

Charles Horton Cooley was one of the first sociologists to study socialization and the sense of self (1902). Cooley was curious about how human beings come to think of themselves as an "I" or "me." He was also concerned about what *kind* of person one comes to think of himself or herself as being. When Cooley's 2-year-old daughter referred to her nose as "my nose," Cooley was puzzled. How did this little girl know it was appropriate to call her nose "my nose," because "my" is a word that takes on different meanings when different people use it? Furthermore, no one had ever referred to her nose as "my nose."

"Is that what I look like?" A mirror, or looking glass as it was called in Cooley's time, provides a reflection of our physical image. Cooley argues that other people provide a reflection of us that becomes part of our self-image. If others respond to us as noble, we come to see ourselves as noble, but if others react to us as foolish, we are likely to feel and act foolish. This process of defining ourself as we are seen by others is what Cooley called the looking-glass self. (*Photo courtesy the author*)

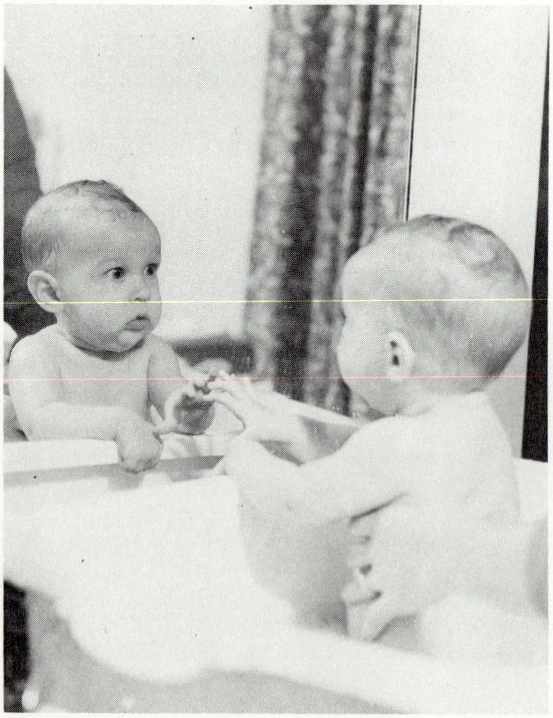

Cooley eventually decided that people come to think of themselves as an "I" through a combination of biological and social processes. He believed that even a newborn infant has a consciousness, as well as desires or needs that he called *acquisitiveness.* From the beginning children experience desires and needs. As they grow, they see other people expressing similar desires and needs by saying "mine" or "me" or "I want." The children learn that "mine" is associated with things a person either possesses or wants to possess.

Cooley argues that objects a person labels as "mine" are those that society defines as his or hers. A person's ***self,*** *or personality, consists of the thoughts, emotions, and actions a person sees as integral to his or her sense of identity.* People see themselves as being the way they are, in part, because others reflect their selves to them. People look to the mirror to see what they look like physically and look to other people to see what they are like as persons. Cooley called this phenomenon the ***looking-glass self,*** *or the image of self reflected by others.* A person

> is continually imagining how he appears . . . ; if thought judicious he looks as if he were, if accused of dishonesty he appears guilty, and so on. In short, a sensitive man, in the presence of an impressive personality, tends to become, for the time, his interpretation of what the other thinks he is (Cooley, 1902, p. 207).

The looking-glass self develops when an individual imagines how he or she looks to others, imagines their response, and responds to that by creating a sense of self modified by their reaction.

This process may sound superficial or hypocritical, but Cooley felt the concept of the looking-glass self encouraged personal growth because it requires people at least momentarily to accept another's impressions. In other words, basing one's sense of self on the reflections of others may be an expanding process rather than a stifling one.

MEAD'S ROLE OF THE OTHER

George Herbert Mead was an early social psychologist who studied the interaction between society and the individual. Mead was especially concerned with how society and the *human qualities of mind* (roughly meaning "intelligence") and *self* (roughly meaning "self-awareness") originate. As we learned in Chapter 1, "Sociology, Origins, Perspectives, and Techniques," Mead was a major figure in founding the theoretical perspective we call symbolic interactionism. His lectures at the University of Chicago were published as a book, *Mind, Self, and Society* (1934), a classic in sociology as well as social psychology.

The Self Is Made of "I" and "Me." Mead defined the self as "that which can be an object to itself" (1934). He believed that the self had two parts, which he called the *I* and the *me.*

The "I" is the conscious, spontaneous, and creative part of the self, the part that experiences pleasure, pain, and spontaneous impulses. Whereas the "I" is inborn, the "me" arises from social interaction. The "me" is other people's definition of who one is. It includes the internal controls taught by society. The "I" accounts for what people want to do, and the "me" accounts for what people feel they should do. For example, a person might think, "*I* would like to sleep around a lot, but I don't want people to think of *me* as promiscuous." The *me* makes people aware of how they appear to others and how they fit into a social setting.

With Cooley, Mead believed the self arises only through social interaction. Every individual must develop a self. Because the "I" is inborn, the developmental process is one of establishing the "me." This development proceeds through three basic stages.

In Stage 1 an infant is all "I." He or she is impulsive and knows nothing of the social environment or the internalized controls of the "me," which will allow it to enter social life as an active participant.

The "me" begins to develop through play, in Stage 2. A very young child may enjoy playing alone with a ball. This requires no "me." As the child becomes more aware of a social environment, he or she may learn about baseball and pretend to play baseball like an older sibling. When this playing merely involves throwing the ball or hitting it with a bat, the child is in Mead's terms *taking the role of the other,* the "other" being the sibling.

Mead coined the term ***significant other*** *to describe persons with whom an individual has intimate and long-term contact.* To Mead, childhood socialization largely depends on these significant others. In other words, new members of society become what society wants them to become because they strive to please significant others who are already members of that society and follow its norms. This is one way of describing socialization.

The "me" fully develops as the child learns to *respond to the generalized other* in Stage 3. This means the child takes into account the broader social community—beyond the significant others. In our baseball example, the child must not just learn one role but must be able to understand all the positions on the team and their relationships to one another. Baseball is only one of many complex games that help children acquire a "me." As children develop "me" through play and other social interactions, they learn to function in complex social structures.

This self-awareness makes it possible for people to position themselves within larger social units, becoming, for instance, a bagger in a supermarket, a violinist in an orchestra, or a goalie on the soccer team. Other animals cannot be trained to act out roles in this way because they are not able to develop the "me," the quality of knowing what is expected in complex social settings.

Mead and others believe individual self-consciousness is necessary for organized human society to exist. In one sense, society is like a machine, and when individuals interact, they do so as parts of the machine. Only through abstract reasoning do people see themselves as objects that can be a part of a larger social unit, like a club, a baseball team, an orchestra, a retail corporation, or indeed an entire nation.

GOFFMAN'S IMPRESSION MANAGEMENT

Cooley and Mead emphasized our tendency to *receive* impressions about ourselves from others. More recently contemporary symbolic interactionists like Erving Goffman have explored the way we manage the impressions we *give* others about ourselves. ***Impression management*** *refers to . . . the ways in which in daily activity we alter ourselves to fit the audience we are addressing* (Goffman, 1959). Children may learn at a young age, for example, to clown for Daddy and to be sweet for Mommy.

Goffman explains both our intimate and our public behaviors in terms of what we are socially taught rather than what Sigmund Freud would term our unconscious motives. Goffman describes our actions as if we were indeed in a play on a stage. Only those in our intimate social group are invited to the backstage areas of our homes, for instance—our bedrooms or kitchens. Less intimate callers are confined to the front stage areas such as our living room, dining room, or den. Goffman's terminology has led to labeling his approach *dramaturgical.*

Impression management allows you to present only that aspect of yourself that you think will be best accepted by the persons with whom you are currently interacting. For instance, when entertaining their employer for dinner, your parents will probably instruct you about appropriate language and behavior during the meal. Similarly, a fourth grader may use "ain't"

TABLE 4.1 A Comparison of Three Developmental Theories

	Piaget's Intellectual Stages	Erikson's Personality Stages	Kohlberg's Moral Stages (all male subjects)	Gilligan's Moral Stages
Age 1	(1) Sensory-motor (learning that our body is separate from the environment)	(1) Basic trust versus mistrust (develop ability to trust that others are sensitive to our needs)	(1) Moral decisions based on fear of punishment	(1) Moral decisions based on fear of punishment
2		(2) Autonomy versus shame and doubt (develop ability to make choices for ourselves)		
3			(2) The idea of rewards is taken into account	(2) The idea of rewards is taken into account
4	(2) Preoperational (learning to communicate through symbols)	(3) Initiative versus guilt (develop ability to initiate activities on our own)	(3) Immediate punishments and rewards not necessary	(3) Immediate punishments and rewards not necessary
7	(3) Concrete operations (learn to think in physical terms)	(4) Industry versus inferiority (develop the ability to reason and play by rules)	(4) Strict adherence to rules	(4) Strict adherence to rules
12		(5) Identity versus role confusion (develop the ability to combine our knowledge of ourselves into a coherent sense of self)	(5) Recognition that conventional rules may come into conflict with a higher sense of right and wrong (not achieved by all)	(5) Recognition that conventional rules may come into conflict with a higher sense of right and wrong
16	(4) Formal operations (learn to manipulate abstract systems of thought such as math and logic)			
18		(6) Intimacy versus isolation (develop ability to risk developing an intimate relationship)	(6) Universal principles of justice, human rights, and human dignity guide decisions (not achieved by all)	(6) The principle of protecting relationships and people (the care approach) guides decisions of women, whereas the principle of valuing individual rights guides decisions of men
25		(7) Generativity versus stagnation (develop the ability to become concerned with the outside world)		
65		(8) Ego integrity versus despair (develop the ability to be satisfied with our lives)		

and "gross!" on the playground to gain the attention of other children, even though the child's actual vocabulary is at a much higher level.

Thinking of the socialization process as Mead and Cooley present it leads naturally to such observations as Goffman and other symbolic interactionists offer. If the "me" develops by responding to the generalized other rather than through some inner psychological process, it is natural to assume that this process is made up of thousands of small, everyday responses. These fascinating interactions are the primary material studied by symbolic interactionists and others.

What Are the Developmental Theories of Socialization?

Developmental theories of socialization observe how a person progresses through social stages from infancy to adulthood. **Erik Erikson** (1964), for example, presented an eight-stage theory of personality development (see Table 4.1). Erikson's classic work suggests that each stage is brought on by a physiological change or by a new social position, and each poses a fresh challenge to the individual. People tend to pass through the stages in order, and each stage may be positively resolved or unresolved. Resolving the stage's crisis adds a new dimension to one's personality. Erikson's work in the developmental field emphasizes the close interaction between the social environment and personality.

Jean Piaget also portrays development as a cumulative process (Piaget and Inhelder, 1969). Piaget's theory suggests that people pass through four major intellectual stages, from the first two years of life to adolescence. Like Erikson, Piaget believes that social contact is necessary for advancing through the stages, and that the content varies from culture to culture.

Lawrence Kohlberg attempts to show how abrupt shifts in an individual's moral perspective may occur developmentally. Kohlberg's six-stage model of moral development is structured such that people cannot skip a stage, nor can they understand a higher level of thinking if they are more than one stage away from it (1981).

According to Kohlberg, people progress from stages 1 and 2, in which a child obeys to avoid punishment or gain rewards, to Stage 6, in which an adult adopts "universal principles of justice, . . . the reciprocity and equality of human rights, and . . . respect for the dignity of human beings as individual persons" (Kohlberg and Gilligan, 1971, p. 1068). Kohlberg suggests that about one-half of Americans never leave Stage 4, the "law and order" stage.

Kohlberg's research was done entirely with males, from the assumption that females rarely reached his defined highest moral plane. One of his associates, **Carol Gilligan,** questioned this assumption and hypothesized instead that women may have different criteria by which they make moral decisions (Gilligan, 1982). Gilligan suggests that women define moral problems as problems in protecting relationships and people, what she terms the "care approach." In contrast, men are taught to compete with one another and "get ahead" in the world, which causes them to value an individual's rights—the "justice approach."

Gilligan agrees that women more often try to find a compromise position in Kohlberg's stated moral dilemmas. She suggests, however, that this is the result of their socialization toward valuing social attachments over strict justice rather than because they are inferior to men in making moral decisions. This important question is certain to be the center of more research; for example, that of Nona Lyons seems to confirm Gilligan's suggestions (Lyons, 1983).

These developmental theories are compared in Table 4.1. Notice that during each stage the interaction between the environment and the individual determines the amount and direction of change.

What Are the Life Cycle Theories of Socialization?

Although much socialization takes place in childhood, many researchers believe significant socialization experiences continue after childhood (Clausen, 1972; Inkeles and Smith, 1974). Much attention has been focused on adult socialization, and sociologists have growing interest in such areas as life stages (Neugarten, 1968), life crises (Dannefer, 1984), and aging (Hareven, 1982).

As an individual's life situation changes, his or her role changes. The changes, say, from wife to mother to working woman to widow, create a need in each instance for socialization in new roles to take place. People must learn different socially appropriate behaviors for each new situation (Lopata, 1973).

Socialization in adulthood is more concerned with learning overt norms and behaviors than is the socialization of childhood, which is concerned primarily with regulating antisocial behavior. The primary study areas of adult socialization are the changes surrounding marriage, parenthood, and learning an occupation. Marriage and parenthood present challenges mainly for young adults. Most people have only an image of their parents' marriages from which to pattern their own marriages, and they use this image to devise satisfactory marriage roles for themselves and their spouses. This role-taking becomes more complicated when a couple has a child and emerges as a family. The responsibility for nurturing and providing for the physical needs of a child and the added difficulties a couple may have in

CLOSE-UP on • *RESEARCH* •

Melvin L. Kohn and Carmi Schooler on How Jobs Shape Personalities

The Researchers and the Setting

Melvin L. Kohn is chief and Carmi Schooler a senior investigator in the Laboratory of Socio-Environmental Studies at the National Institute of Mental Health. They research as a full-time activity, and their articles and books focus on how social settings, such as our jobs or our parents' jobs, influence our personalities.

The Researcher's Goal

In this study Kohn and Schooler expand their earlier investigation into the ways our work shapes our personalities. Previously they had established that engaging in complex work socializes us toward more intellectual flexibility. For instance, a telephone installer faces more complex problems than an assembly-line worker, and this will tend to increase the telephone installer's ability to handle new (or contrasting) ideas and situations.

Here Kohn and Schooler turn their attention to the effects different jobs have on two different personality traits: our willingness to take initiative and our sense of distress. Does the assembly-line worker become less willing to take initiative and then begin to have a negative attitude about life because he works in relatively oppressive working conditions? Will the telephone installer develop more willingness to lead and an increasingly positive sense of self-confidence? Kohn and Schooler are also concerned about how the personality traits shaped by one job influence the individual's chance of finding better work. Will people who have worked as telephone installers be left better equipped to become supervisors or start businesses of their own? In Kohn and Schooler's words: "In this paper we assess the effects of men's working conditions on their personalities and the effects of their personalities on their working conditions" (1982, p. 1257).

The Theory and Concepts

The researchers' theory relates to a central proposition of this chapter—the idea that some personality traits are learned through socialization. The technical name for the theory they use here is the *learning-generalization model.* This theory suggests that what we learn in one setting is generalized to, or used in, other settings. For instance, if we learn to feel self confident at work, we may carry this into our family and friendships. Within this general theory, Kohn and Schooler are working with some hypotheses. *A* ***hypothesis*** (the plural is hypotheses) *is a proposition that logically falls within a broader theory.* For instance, here the theory could be considered to be: *Work conditions influence personality.* The hypotheses within the theory are that: (1) *the complexity of the job leads the worker toward flexibility in handling ideas and* (2) *a worker's position in the bureaucracy shapes his level of self-confidence.*

Research Design

Kohn and Schooler test their ideas by analyzing data from a 1964 survey of 3,101 men who were chosen as a representative sample of all men employed in civilian occupations in the United States. In 1974 about one-fourth of those who were still under 65 years of age were interviewed again. *Data gathered on the same subjects over a time period is called* ***longitudinal.*** Longitudinal studies allow researchers to observe cause and effect better than data gathered at the same point in time. Suppose Kohn and Schooler only gathered data at one time—they might be able to show that people in complex jobs are more intellectually flexible, but they would not know whether the jobs made people flexible or whether flexible people sought complex jobs. By watching the subjects over a time period, the researchers can see whether a person in a particular job became *more* flexible, more distressed, and so forth. This sheds light on whether the job causes the personality trait, or whether the personality trait causes the person to take (or get) the job.

How did the researchers measure these job features and personality traits? The subjects were interviewed and asked a wide variety of questions about their work and their feelings about their work, the world, and themselves. The subjects were also asked to perform certain exercises designed to reveal intellectual abilities. Consider some traits of interest to us:

> Closeness of supervision is measured by a worker's own appraisals of his freedom to disagree with his supervisor, how closely he is supervised, the extent to which his supervisor tells him what to do instead of discussing it with him, and the importance in his job of doing what one is told to do. . . . In our surveys, intellectual flexibility is evidenced by performance in handling cognitive problems that require weighing both sides of an economic or social issue, in differentiating figure from ground in complex color designs, and in drawing a recognizably human figure whose parts fit together in a meaningful whole. . . . In order to measure whether the subject was self-directed, the researchers considered how the subjects responded to questions which measured self-confidence and self deprecation. . . . The signs of oppressive work conditions which the researchers asked about included: lack of job protection, dirty work, close supervision, and a low position in the supervisory hierarchy. Finally, they measured distress by asking questions designed to gauge the subjects' anxiety, lack of self-confidence, and distrust (pp. 1261-1272).

Findings

The experiences of these subjects supports both of the hypotheses Kohn and Schooler sought to test. A statistical analysis demonstrates that the structural demands of the job affect personality, supporting the learning-generalization model. Self-directed work leads to flexibility of ideas and being self-directed with regard to yourself and society; oppressive working conditions lead to less flexibility and distress. Personality also affects an individual's place in the job structure and in the system of social stratification. Both having flexible ideas and being self-directed may lead to workers having more responsible, self-directed jobs.

Implications

Because we devote so much time to our work, these findings have striking implications. Our choice of where to work will likely have an effect on our personality, including our sense of self-confidence and our intellectual functioning. These in turn will play a role in determining the quality of work we can later obtain. We should be careful, then, to consider the quality of the work we pursue, which may in the long run be of greater concern than the initial rate of pay. This would be especially true for early work experiences.

Those in a position to control another's work should remain alert to the consequences the work has on the worker's personality. For instance, by changing how closely a manager supervises, we may be able to enrich the jobs of those being supervised. Industries must consider not just the immediate efficiency of work arrangements, but their long-term consequence. Both the workers and the corporation lose in the long range if they breed intellectual dullness and emotional distress.

Questions

1. What jobs can you think of that would illustrate Kohn and Schooler's findings?
2. What might be done to offset the negative effects of certain types of work, such as assembly-line work?
3. Consider two of the most common occupations: secretary and clerk. What kind of effect might these jobs have on personality? How might women in these positions feel, and how would that affect their future job choice?

SOURCE Melvin L. Kohn and Carmi Schooler. 1982. "Job Conditions and Personality: A Longitudinal Assessment of Their Reciprocal Effects." *American Journal of Sociology*, vol. 87, no. 6, pp. 1257–1286.

choosing a parenting style present adults with new opportunities for growth.

Individuals are also socialized into their work roles. Most people have not yet held a steady job when they leave school. Managing a new occupational role creates not only a sense of excitement and promise but also sometimes a burdensome sense of responsibility. Most people learn to accept their occupational role and soon adjust to the expectations of the new social system of their workplace. The following "Close-Up on Research" describes how socialization to a work role can actually shape an adult worker's personality.

LEVINSON'S SEASONS OF A MAN'S LIFE

The four developmental theories discussed before view growth from a psychological perspective, something that emanates from within a person as he or she grows older and proceeds through natural stages. Little sociological research has been done to substantiate the proposals of Erikson, Piaget, Kohlberg, and Gilligan.

In contrast, the developmental life cycle theory of Daniel Levinson began with an intensive research study of the lives of forty men, aged 35 to 45, in four occupations (1978). Given biographical data from interviews, Levinson projects a view of the life cycle as shown in Figure 4.1.

Transitions from one stage of life to another are of crucial importance. During the early adult transition a person starts to move into the adult world, to modify or terminate existing relationships, and to reappraise and modify his or her sense of self. This sets the stage for the mid-life transition when the life structure next comes into question. At this time a person raises questions such as, "Where am I now? Of what value is my life to society, to other persons, and especially to myself?"

Because a person derives much of his or her sense of self from an occupation, the career is a primary factor in the mid-life transition. Questioning career goals can lead to questioning in other areas, such as, "How can I become more independent, more manly or womanly, and accomplish more of what I most want? Can my relationships with my loved ones grow to accept my new goals?" During this transition, paying attention to previously neglected parts of the self can stimulate personal growth.

The issues faced during this transition are described by Levinson as polarities, and he characterizes them as follows. The *young–old polarity* asks, "What positive qualities are there in aging—for example, can wisdom become an important value for me?" The *destructive–creative polarity* asks, "How can I deal with my new realization that my tragedies and failures are, to a large extent, the result of my own tragic flaws?" The

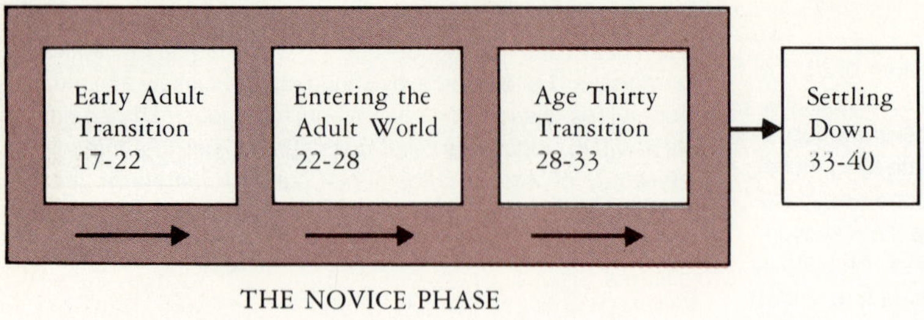

FIGURE 4.1 Levinson's View of the Life Cycle. SOURCE After Levinson, 1978.

masculine–feminine polarity asks, "Must I exercise control over others and be recognized as a person of strong will to be masculine (or to be feminine)? Must I devote myself to my occupation in a highly impersonal way?" The *attachment–separateness polarity* asks, "How can I find a better balance between the needs of the self and the needs of my group? How can I reduce my involvement in the external world and become less tyrannized by my ambitions, dependencies, and passions, so that I can be involved with other individuals and perform my social roles in a more responsible way than ever before? How can I become more separate and yet more loving?"

Levinson's research convinced him that a person's ability to handle the mid-life transition depends on his development through the Novice Phase (ages 17–33). During these years, Levinson claims, people form their personality base by meeting four distinct challenges: (1) developing an ideal or goal to strive for, (2) forming a mentor relationship with an older person who acts as an example, (3) finding an occupation that will allow them to use their interests and abilities, and (4) beginning intimate relationships, usually with a wife and children. If these challenges are met, Levinson theorizes, the individuals will have little trouble settling down during the mid-life years.

It is important to note that, unlike the other developmental theorists, Levinson did not begin his research with a theory but developed his concepts of stages and transitions after examining the research data. This marks a shift in developmental work from a theory base to a research-based development of theory.

What Are the Agents of Socialization or Domination?

Socialization agents *are the persons or devices that act to carry out the process of socialization.* The major socialization agents of twentieth-century United States are the family, peer groups and other personally known role models, schools, day care, and television. What these agents have in common is that they affect the individual through all stages of development, although one agent or another may be dominant at a particular age. For example, the family carries out most of a person's initial socialization, an influence that is never completely erased. Later one's peer group gains in importance. A particular role model outside the family, such as a teacher, may also be a strong influence. As we see from Levinson's work on mid-life crisis, such role models or mentors are especially important to young adults. A person may be resocialized into a new set of values at any age. The process of socialization is lifelong.

Conflict theorists point out that these same agents can be thought of as agents of domination. For example, families marked by domineering parents face a greatly increased chance of teen suicide. Similarly, a teacher could systematically destroy a child's creativity or self-confidence using negative feedback daily. A peer group can as easily influence young people toward drug use as toward giving their all to the school basketball team. And the effects of television, in most educated minds, are primarily negative. As in all elements of our social life, the same elements can be used to positive or negative ends.

THE FAMILY

Those close to a child during the early years are primarily responsible for the child's socialization. This can include parents, grandparents, other relatives, babysitters, or neighbors. In the United States mothers have the major responsibility for raising young children.

Several trends begun by industrialization have led to mothers' assuming most of the responsibility for socialization. Modern industrial society is characterized by a family structure containing a father who is away from the home for most of the young children's waking hours for five days of a week, in contrast to agrarian society, where the father is working in the fields near his children for six days a week (D. Lynn, 1974). Mothers also used to be aided by grandparents who lived with or very near to the family. The *extended family*, as this is called, existed for centuries before the Industrial Revolution changed lifestyles so drastically only a century ago. The smaller family size of an industrialized society means fewer older brothers and sisters to help teach and be examples to young children. Increasing numbers of children are being raised in single-parent homes. From 1970 to 1985 the families with children under 18 that were headed by a single adult nearly doubled from 11.2 percent to 22.2 percent (U.S. Bureau of the Census, 1986, p. 48).

The scene has changed drastically from the agrarian era when a family largely worked together from birth to death, and, naturally, children were socialized in all four modes by parents, grandparents, and other family members as they grew up. The trends begun by industrialization meant mothers became increasingly important socialization agents.

In modern societies a family's relative wealth strongly influences the time spent by parents with children. For example, in the late 1800s and early 1900s virtually all poor people worked long hours: father, mother, and children over age 7. In wealthier families, mothers were generally in charge of household affairs and available to their children most of the time, and fathers were present in the evenings. After passage of child labor laws, the poor children who had been working were put in school. The idea that mothers should be home with their small children became more prevalent, and the economy became more productive, so that by 1950 only about 12 percent of mothers of children under age 6 worked outside the home, again, primarily the poor.

Then a reversal occurred. By 1975, the number of working mothers had increased to 37 percent, and by 1987 to 61 percent (U.S. Bureau of Census, 1987, p. 383). Relative wealth plays a part; parents with more education and higher income are often able to arrange their working hours such that they can still spend time with their children. Working-class parents are more likely to be locked into a shift schedule that does not allow much contact with children except on weekends. In both cases, this trend tends to reduce the influence of the mother as a socializing agent and increases the influence of others, including fathers and other relatives, as well as babysitters or day-care centers.

PEER GROUPS AND NONFAMILY ROLE MODELS

As a child grows up, the influence of people outside the family as socialization agents becomes more important. A child may emulate an older friend or neighbor. A teacher or coach may exert a strong socialization influence. By the teen years cliques or peer groups help define or redefine personality. Sometimes a girlfriend or boyfriend has a major socialization influence. Long-term studies indicate that the influence of peer groups on such decisions as clothing styles has increased in today's society (Bronfrenbrenner, 1970; Singer and Singer, 1983). However, children eventually move toward parental values on issues of larger importance such as religion and career choice (Troll and Bengston, 1983).

The peer group is an important socialization agent. From peers we learn what is appropriate group behavior in various settings. A ten-year old's birthday party, for instance, is a time for clowning. *(Photo courtesy the author)*

TELEVISION

Television is a relatively new but very influential socialization agent in the United States. American families now watch an average of 49 hours of television per week (U.S. Bureau of Census, 1984), and its effect can be seen on both adults and children. Young people typically spend more time watching television than any other activity except sleeping (Anderson and Lorch, 1983). When one researcher asked children ages 4 to 6, "Which do you like better, TV or Daddy?", 44 percent preferred TV (Mankiewicz and Swerdlow, 1978).

When television was introduced in the 1940s, people hoped it would improve society. However, the fact that it is watched so much has led to unexpected problems. One of these is that TV watching stimulates primarily the right half of the brain, which controls emotional responses rather than analytical thinking. The rapidly changing images on television have a numbing effect on viewers, and produce brain waves similar to those during daydreaming, gradually shortening the attention span of long-term viewers. Eventually, viewers

The American addiction to television shows itself in consumption patterns. Here a family of modest means in respect to their housing has spent several thousand dollars for a TV satellite dish in order to get all of their favorite programs. (*Photo courtesy the author*)

have great difficulty in concentrating on analytical problems such as mathematics or phonetics. This short attention span is widespread in United States' schoolchildren and a constant barrier to their learning.

Equally as damaging to the institution of education is the passive attitude fostered by children's spending hours in a receiving mode, not being asked to interact or use their own creativity. Eventually, these children are handicapped in their abilities to think creatively or offer input into discussions. They are simply not used to *giving* information, ideas, or other feedback, because they spend most of their hours *receiving* from their television sets.

Disturbing evidence also exists that television has contributed to violent and aggressive behavior in society. Studies have shown that children learn about violence from watching violent shows, and poorly adjusted children may imitate the violent behavior they see (Carter and Strickland, 1975; National Institute of Mental Health, 1982). As prime-time television increasingly displays explicit sex and violence, our young people are taught through role modeling that these are normally accepted behaviors in the adult world.

Another concern has been the extent to which television is used by parents of preschoolers as a babysitter (Bane, 1976). Not only does this practice expose young children to the dangers just discussed, it also robs them of the social interactions with their parents and siblings that are so vital to developing a positive sense of self.

Important as the television is, its importance is usually less than that of the family and peer group. Contact with family and peers is sustained, intimate, and intensely responsive, whereas contact with television figures is intermittent, superficial, and one-way.

DAY CARE

The U.S. Census Bureau reported in 1983 that for the first time over one-half of all mothers with children under the age of 6 were working outside the home for pay. Fifteen percent of these children, and 66 percent of those between ages 3 and 5, spend their days in day-care facilities. By contrast, only 20 percent of such mothers were employed in 1960, and most of their children were cared for in private homes or by relatives and friends (Kamerman, 1983).

What accounts for such a rapid increase in the number of women who choose to work both inside and outside the home while their children are young? A major factor is the rising divorce rate, which has doubled the number of single-parent families in the past decade (R. Watson et al., 1984). These women are forced to either work for pay or subsist on welfare until their children are older; most choose to work. Another factor is the availability of job opportunites for women. More jobs, more interesting jobs, and often more lucrative jobs are available now than were available in 1960. Finally, Americans growing up in the 1940s and 1950s were raised in an era of "good living." These children are now adults and want the same standard of living their parents have. In order to accomplish this, at today's prices and wages, couples often need two incomes.

Thus, day-care centers are assuming some traditional functions of the family, including much of the socialization of young children (Kamerman, 1983). What are the effects of this situation on the children and families involved? The experts do not agree.

On the positive side, children in day care may be intellectually and socially advanced, and more assertive than their home-raised counterparts. Children who spend time in day care may also learn to separate from their parents more easily (Collins, 1984). Research shows that children of working women who use day care learn to view the world with fewer gender stereotypes and have a higher regard for the place of women in society (Hoffman, 1974), thus encouraging in future generations of women a greater sense of competence. Furthermore, day care is much preferable for children raised by women who feel frustrated in the home and would rather be working (White, 1980).

On the negative side, other research finds that young children may need a primary caregiver who spends time and energy on them individually, rather than in a group setting (White, Bronfenbrenner, and Bruner, 1981; Brazelton and Elkind, 1984). Psychologists have long suggested that this bonding will produce an emotionally stable person with a positive sense of self (Magnet, 1983). As Burton White, director of Boston's Center for Parent Education, states it, "A child needs large doses of custom made love" (1984). Because poor pay and long hours cause rapid turnover, day care is rarely able to provide this continuity of care (Magnet, 1983). T. Berry Brazelton, called the "Dr. Spock of the Eighties," shares concern that research thus far has focused on cognitive outcomes of day care and wants long-term research done on more subtle effects—for instance, on personality and adjustment (1984). Jerome Bruner, well-respected researcher on child development, cautions parents on emphasizing academic growth only in evaluating day care, saying, "What you want is a human being, a *mensch,* not a genius" (1981).

The most common criticisms of day-care centers focus on lack of proper supervision and challenge (Elkind, 1984). The child–teacher ratio varies greatly from state to state, and some centers have too many students to be properly guided, leading to situations in which children are injured by other children or simply are poorly cared for. Further, kids may be so tightly regimented, due to large groups, that they are not allowed to simply explore their world, which child development expert David Elkind says is "very necessary" for development at later stages (1984). Although rare, the recent flurry of cases in which children have been sexually abused in day-care settings also speaks to difficulties inherent in supervising large groups. Obviously problems such as these will occur in some day care, but certainly not in the majority of facilities. Most research concludes *that the effects of day care on children depend on the quality* of the *particular* day-care setting (Blusiewicz, 1984; Kagan, 1978).

How will day care affect the family? Perry Mendel, head of the largest day-care firm, Kinder-Care Learning Centers, says, "Guilt is the one reason we've been so successful" (Mendel, 1984). Working parents struggle with the feeling that group care may not be as good for their children as home care might be. Furthermore, the average two-parent family with an income of $24,000 pays 26 percent of that to care for two small children (R. Watson, 1984). Parents, saddled with all the normal household tasks to accomplish "after work," bear guilt for not having enough "quality time" to spend with their youngsters and lose a significant financial bite from their "extra income." Certainly the situation is not ideal, but for some, the dependability of a large, nationally recognized organization like Kinder-Care is worth the price.

What will be the effects on society of a generation raised in day care? Again, opinions vary. Edward Zigler, Sterling Professor of Psychology at Yale University, suggests that the assertiveness, which is bred in a group-care setting, may lead to aggressiveness in later childhood and adulthood. He agrees with Brazelton that current research is simply not good enough to determine whether this will be a serious problem (Zigler, 1984). Burton White states that the increased use of day care by parents who are working to maintain an affluent lifestyle rather than for basic needs of the family could create a future generation even more tied to things than to relationships (White, 1984). Other researchers believe that it is impossible to make any predictions about the future effect on society (Clarke–Stewart, 1984).

In spite of day care's drawbacks, it serves a need, and Americans are clamoring for more (Roper Organization, 1980). In 1982, over 200,000 women had to refuse work because of problems in arranging for care of their preschool children, and 1.7 million women decided not to look for work because they knew that child care was not available for them (O'Connell and Rogers, 1983).

At the same time that women who had previously not worked are entering the work force, many other women and men who had been working are leaving the workplace when their children are young, either because of a lack of adequate day care in their area or because they want only one full-time job in the family at a time (Cosell, 1985; A. Fisher, 1986; Garey, 1986). Rather than reflecting a bias toward one or another side of the issue, however, these parents seem to simply have decided that their lives and those of their families are more enjoyable when they are not both employed outside the home—they are freer from guilt, have more energy when not working two jobs, and feel less stressed when they are not coordinating two work schedules with children's lives. Other parents have begun to demand such changes as flex-time schedules so that they can more easily coordinate the demands of work and family.

Whether or not day care will grow, become refined, be federally subsidized, or affect the future atmosphere of our society will depend on millions of such independent decisions. In the long run, it will not be researchers or policymakers but families who will determine the future of day care in the United States.

SCHOOLS

Schools are very important socialization agents. A child's experience in school affects and is affected by his self image. Schools teach not only cognitive material, but a hidden curriculum as well. In school, children learn to be socially acceptable members of groups, through such rituals as standing in line for the drinking

Resocialized to kill. Few of us have been taught to kill, but military training teaches new ways of thinking and acting. Such resocialization takes place in a total institution, the military, organized so that the trainee is isolated from the outside world, brought under a formalized routine, and subjected to a bureaucratic staff. (© *Orlando/Globe Photos*)

fountain and raising their hands to ask questions. These and other ways in which schools socialize young people will be discussed at length in Chapter 17, "Education."

What Is Resocialization?

Resocialization *occurs when an individual is socialized to adopt a system of beliefs different from those he or she was first socialized into.* Modern society demonstrates many attempts to resocialize individuals. For example, military training resocializes people from civilian beliefs and behaviors to military ones. Medical schools resocialize students to beliefs and behaviors found among physicians. Alcoholics Anonymous attempts to rehabilitate problem drinkers by resocializing them.

TOTAL INSTITUTIONS

Much resocialization occurs in ***total institutions,*** *or organizations that are relatively closed off from the outside world and that follow a formalized life routine under the control of a bureaucratic staff.* Erving Goffman (1961a) suggests that total institutions have in common a pattern of development that is designed to resocialize the individuals who enter them and that total institutions are by nature coercive—even if one has joined voluntarily, the contact is maintained through coercion by the organization.

When people become part of a total institution, mortification begins, during which people leave behind all of the physical and emotional possessions of the outside world. They are given new clothes, new equipment, and perhaps a new name or number as well, in an effort to eradicate the individual's previous sense of self. As part of the second step in resocialization, they are required to perform rituals and to respond quickly to commands given by the staff. They are further mortified by being under constant surveillance with absolutely no privacy. Their movements are programmed by the authorities, and they are not required or invited to think for themselves about anything. This process promotes a dependency on the total institution and begins the development of a new identity, based on the institution's goals. The result is a new member who is suited for the goals of the institution.

RESOCIALIZATION IN THE TOTAL INSTITUTION OF JONESTOWN

In November of 1978 in Jonestown, Guayana, 911 followers of Jim Jones drank Kool-Aid laced with cyanide at his command in order to escape the mercenaries Jones had told them were hiding in the jungle ready to attack and torture them. From a layperson's point of view, it was a horror show. From a sociologist's perspective, it was a social phenomenon that should be studied in order to prevent future horrors. Two well-respected sociologists, Rose Laub Coser and Lewis Coser, approached the study of Jonestown as a "perverse utopia" that had developed into a total institution (1979).

The Cosers point out that when a "utopia" becomes regulated by a central authority rather than by the people themselves, the organization becomes what they term a "greedy institution," anxious not only for its followers' material goods, but for their total allegiance.

Jonestown displays many of the characteristics of classic utopias turned to destructive purposes. By design, it was physically isolated, being 150 miles from any other people. Secrecy was encouraged. Children were taught to lie in school, and converts left the United States for Guayana without contacting relatives.

This isolation was exacerbated by the fact that the members gave Jones their houses, cars, bank accounts,

Total institutions, such as Jim Jones' commune, command total surrender from their followers. Here Jones' body lies stacked among those of his followers whom he led in a mass homicide/suicide. *(UPI/Bettmann Newsphotos)*

cash, even their passports, when they arrived at Jonestown. This total commitment, in combination with their isolation from former friends and family members, made it difficult for members to even consider returning to their previous lives. It set the stage for making Jonestown a "total institution," following a formalized life under strict control of the central staff.

The next stage in creating the kind of blind obedience Jones required was *to revamp the personal and moral values of the members through physical and mental humiliations*—what Goffman termed *mortification.* Almost daily people were called to the front of the group to be accused of dishonesty, sexual misbehavior, and other sins and to be cursed by their friends and family until they accepted Jones' authority without reservation. Through this process the Jonestown people became dependent upon their central authority for all direction, thought only in the present, and were unable to establish relationships.

Jones sought to prevent members of the commune from becoming bonded to each other in any way. Marriages were ended and rearranged by Jones. He directed members of the commune to stop having sexual relations, while he bragged to outsiders about the fact that he had frequent and numerous sexual encounters with both men and women; as he said, "to assure their loyalty to him." The Cosers point out that such concurrent promiscuous and celibate behaviors break up and prevent stable dyads.

From a sociological viewpoint, Jonestown was doomed because individual emotional energies

> cannot simply be "channeled" for the common or not-so-common good. Arbitrary and unpredictable interference with them leads to their being damaged at best and destroyed at worst. When people are cut off from emotional bonds with their fellows they have no psychic energies left that can be mobilized even in situations of extreme peril (p. 162).

Jones' major goal was to destroy the normal social relationships in his group. When he did this, "devouring" his members by "reducing them to human pulp," he made it impossible for them to relate to each other and rise up against this horrible evil. They all felt, as one survivor stated, "dead inside." As "dead" persons, they had no ability to make decisions.

The Cosers close their analysis by pointing out that although Jones' followers were from all social classes and all psychological and spiritual backgrounds, they came to this group because United States' society of the 1970s had "failed to provide satisfactory bonds, meaningful community, and fraternal solidarities" (p. 163). The Cosers' discussion should stimulate in us greater respect for the need of human beings to develop personal attachments and should encourage us to live in a manner that encourages the growth of such attachments, rather than in ways that create barriers to relationships, such as overindividualizing or bowing completely to a central authority.

How Does Genetics Influence Social Development?

As we have discussed, much social development depends on the interaction of the individual with his or her social environment. Babies are not identical at birth, however, and their behavior will also be influenced by their genetic makeup.

Innate characteristics can have limiting or facilitating social impact on a person's life. Perhaps one child's genes have given her an especially lithe body. If her parents value athletics, they may nurture this ability and make her feel special and worthwhile because of this talent. On the other hand, they may feel ashamed of her success in a traditionally male area and discourage her, making her feel like a misfit. Similarly, a small baby, who will never grow taller than 5 feet 2 inches, will not be a college basketball center, no matter how much society encourages him or her.

INSTINCTS AND DRIVES

Fewer than 100 years ago many psychologists believed people largely behaved according to ***instincts,*** *complex behavior patterns that are genetically transmitted.* For example, all Baltimore orioles instinctively build the same type of hanging nest, which is distinct from the nest of any other bird. A spider can spin the complex web pattern of its parents even when it has never seen a web and has had no contact with its mother since birth.

It is easy to observe hereditary behaviors in other animals, but do such patterns exist in human beings? Most modern social scientists agree that some human behavior patterns are guided by **drives,** *inborn forces that motivate organisms to seek water, food, self-preservation, sex, and nurturing.* However, biological drives in human beings are general rather than specific, as lower animals' instincts tend to be. People share no specific mating dance. They satisfy their sex drive in a remarkable variety of ways. Unlike the wolf, they do not instinctively circle and stamp upon the spot where they intend to lie down. In other words, human heredity builds in each of us general drives and sets limits on our capacities. It has not been proved, however, that heredity dictates *any* specific or complex behavior in humans. Instead, genes set our potential. Our culture and environment (including diet) affect whether that potential is realized.

THE INTERACTION OF NATURE AND NURTURE

The problem of separating genetic effects (nature) from socialization and other environmental effects (nurture) in a person's development is a very complicated one. One reason for the difficulty is that socialization is a complex process that takes place over many years. It is often difficult to establish with certainty that a particular characteristic is the result of socialization. Alcoholism, for instance, may occur in succeeding generations of the same family. Does this mean the children of alcoholic parents may inherit an addiction to alcohol, or does it mean the children become socialized to abuse alcohol because they follow their parents' model? Research shows that a genetic predisposition toward alcoholism increases the chances of becoming an alcoholic if the social environment encourages that behavior, but no one is genetically predestined to be an alcoholic any more than someone without alcoholic relatives is immune from becoming an alcoholic.

Another difficulty in the nature–nurture debate is that the field of genetics has identified only a tiny portion of the characteristics that may be transmitted through human genes. It is obvious that much development is socially stimulated, as shown in case studies like that of Becky Holmes, the child who was kept in the closet. At the same time, until scientists can account for the effects of unexplained genes, it is premature to say unequivocally that human social characteristics are not inherited.

IMPLICATIONS OF GENETIC EXPLANATIONS

What makes the nature versus nurture question so important is that human behavior is often attributed to a person's "nature," implying that the behavior is genetically based and unchangeable. Much of the nature–nurture debate has centered around sex-role socialization, as we shall discuss more fully in Chapter 11, "Gender Role Inequalities." For example, it is often claimed that women "instinctively" know about childrearing and men do not. Similarly, many people believe that blacks have "natural" rhythm and a flair for athletics. Some criminals have been called "born killers."

The implication is important. If specific behavior is innate, there is no point in trying to change it; only women should raise children, and all blacks should be jazz musicians or play basketball. Furthermore, rehabilitation of criminals would be a waste of money. No evidence shows, however, that child-rearing, playing basketball, or homicide is behavior that is genetically transmitted.

It is important to stress that no current scientific evidence indicates that any individual or group is born

CLOSE-UP on • *THEORY* •

Edward Wilson on Sociobiology

The Theorist and the Setting

Claims that social behavior and intelligence are genetically inherited have been controversial among social scientists, as we saw in the cases of research by Jensen and by Burt. Another scientist who has stirred up public controversy is Harvard University's zoologist Edward O. Wilson, who introduced the concept ***sociobiology***, or *the "systematic study of the biological basis of social behavior in every kind of organism"* (Wilson, 1978, p. 222). When he proposed the theory in 1975, Wilson's ideas were praised on the front page of *The New York Times*. However, when he attempted to address the annual meeting of the American Association for the Advancement of Science that year, protestors stormed the platform chanting slogans against racism, sexism, and fascism.

Wilson created this furor by proposing a startling change in the social scientific attitude toward the study of human beings. Social scientists have long believed that human social behavior is not determined by heredity, as is evidently true of other social animals such as ants, bees, birds, and even other primates. Wilson asserts that human social behavior, too, is regulated by forces like those he believes control social behavior in nonhuman species. To support his thesis, he attempts to merge three disciplines: ***ethology***, *the study of social behavior in animals;* ***genetics,*** *the study of inherited traits*; and ***sociology,*** *the study of human social behavior*.

In 1975 Wilson stated that he was "increasingly impressed with the functional similarities between invertebrate and vertebrate society" (p. 4). Later, he expanded and clarified his theory, specifically focusing on human behavior (Wilson, 1978).

The Theorist's Goal

A basic issue addressed by Wilson is: How is human social behavior shaped by evolutionary forces acting through genetic mechanisms? His central thesis is clear: "Human social behavior rests on a genetic foundation" (1978, p. 32). Although he leaves the idea of social behavior undefined, his context suggests that it includes aggression, sex roles, altruism, and religion.

Concepts and Propositions

The idea of a genetic foundation is the application of *natural selection* to social behavior. First proposed by Charles Darwin, natural selection asserts that the better an individual's chance for survival, the more likely he or she will pass characteristics on to the following generation. Thus, an individual with characteristics that are favorable in a given environment will pass on those genes to future generations of the species and the characteristics will spread and persist.

Natural selection has usually been applied to physical traits, for example, skin color. Because dark skin is more resistant to certain diseases such as skin cancer, it is better suited for areas and lifestyles where people are exposed to lots of sunshine. According to the theory, in a sunny, hot environment where the population has varying shades of skin, those with dark skin will have a better chance to survive and reproduce, thus passing on larger proportions of genes for dark skin in future generations.

Wilson extends this argument to social behavior.

Proposition: Some social behavior is genetically based and shaped by an evolutionary process of natural selection.

According to Wilson, the aggressive pattern of warfare may evolve as a human trait because it brings direct and tangible benefits for individuals exhibiting that quality. He cites a tribe of headhunters from Brazil, the Mundurucu. This hunting and gathering tribe regularly engaged in predawn attacks on enemy villages, setting huts on fire, chasing inhabitants into the open, and beheading as many as possible. Wilson suggests that when "competitors were decimated by murderous attacks, the Mundurucu share of the forest yield was correspondingly increased" (1978, p. 113). Thus warfare increased the likelihood of survival of members of the Mundurucu tribe and their "aggressive" genes. Wilson similarly argues that conventional sex roles, altruism, and religion persist because they contribute to the survival and reproduction of individuals or their near kin.

Although Wilson asserts that social behavior and genes are linked, he does not claim that *all* human behavior is genetically influenced. "Human social evolution is obviously more cultural then genetic" (1978, p. 153). Wilson also does not claim that genes determine behavior. "Rather than specifying a single trait, human genes prescribe the capacity to develop a certain array of traits" (1978, p. 56).

Interpretation

Although Wilson is not a sociologist, we have presented his ideas because they address a fundamental question raised in this chapter: How do people acquire their social behavior?

Certain groups denounce Wilson's theories because they feel that to accept the idea that some people are born with certain traits may lead to pessimism about the possibilities of change for human beings. For example, blacks are disproportionately overrepresented in the population of those arrested for crimes in the United States. One might use sociobiological arguments to blame this on the genetic nature of black people and even to argue for limiting the fertility of blacks. Most theorists, however, believe that the history of deprivation and oppression of blacks in the United States more accurately explains the statistics, and they believe that Wilson's theory furthers racism.

As another example, Wilson suggests that women are naturally more "intimately sociable and less physically venturesome" (1978, p. 129). Feminists fear this can be used as an argument for not trying to change women's politically and economically oppressed position in society.

Interestingly, Wilson sees himself more as a liberator than an oppressor, for he believes that by recognizing the source of some traits as genetic, we may proceed to alter human nature through biological means. Suppose we want to create a society of highly altruistic people ("saints," as Wilson irreverently calls them). We could try to teach people to be considerate of others through psychological conditioning. Or, if we follow Wilson's theory of sociobiology, we could engage in selective breeding, encouraging especially considerate people to reproduce more frequently, and discouraging selfish people from reproducing at all.

Little experimental evidence exists to shed light on the relative strengths of genetic and cultural influences on human social behavior. Sociobiology is still a largely untested theory.

Questions

1. How might Wilson explain an act of apparent heroism, such as throwing one's body over a grenade to save the lives of one's fellow soldiers? What would be a cultural explanation of the same act?
2. Using Wilson's ideas, how might we eliminate human warfare? What practical obstacles might we encounter?
3. Are Wilson's arguments racist? Why? Are his arguments sexist? Why?

SOURCES Edward O. Wilson. 1975. *Sociobiology: The New Synthesis*. Cambridge: Harvard University Press. Edward O. Wilson. 1978. *On Human Nature*. Cambridge: Harvard University Press.

naturally to fit any social role. From slave traders to Hitler, people have abused genetic explanations of behavior by asserting that any socially inconvenient group was born to fill the role of subordinate for instance as slave. This abuse, as well as the uncertainty of knowing whether any purely genetic components exist, prompts many social scientists to deny any claims of nature theories as they arise. Therefore, the theories of scientists who emphasize the influence of genetics, such as Arthur Jensen and Edward Wilson, create a stormy atmosphere in the field.

Arthur Jensen (1969) argues that about 80 percent of individual differences in IQ are determined genetically. He bases his conclusion on studies of identical twins who, he found, are likely to have very similar IQ scores, even when the twins were adopted and raised in separate families. In studying other adopted children, Jensen found IQ scores to be more strongly associated with a child's biological mother than with his or her adopted parents.

The question of how strongly intelligence is influenced by heredity is more complicated than Jensen's studies could resolve. We still do not know how individual intelligence arises. Those, like Jensen, who have suggested that intelligence is mostly nature are attacked by those who feel such ideas may be used to justify racism and other forms of prejudice and exploitation. The work of Thomas Sowell and others is important in this debate, and will be discussed fully in Chapter 10, "Race and Ethnic Relations."

It is difficult to design effective scientific studies to resolve this controversy because separating biological influences from social influences involves separating children from their natural parents. To further complicate matters, doubt has been cast on some of this research by an apparent scandal. Sir Cyril Burt was a highly honored English psychologist who shared with Jensen his data on the intelligence of identical twins separated at birth. After Burt's death his biographer published a report stating his reluctant conclusion that Burt falsified data before sending his findings to Jensen (Dorfman, 1978). Jensen defended Burt (1978), but others continued the investigation and severely damaged Burt's credibility (Hearnshaw, 1979; Hartley and Rooum, 1983).

Amid the claims, counterclaims, and methodological complexities of this issue, we can only conclude that this important and controversial question requires much more research before it can be finally resolved. We do know that both inherited and social factors interact in one's growth from infancy to adulthood, and in human beings the influence of socialization seems to play the leading role in determining personality and behavior.

What Are the Three Modes of Socialization?

Socialization takes place in many ways. The process goes on throughout our lives, and is often conducted in private. Sometimes it is quiet. A daughter watches carefully as her father demonstrates how to tie a trout fly. A son closely observes the way his mother stakes tomatoes in the garden. The child in the back seat notes the way his angry parent vents emotions by driving recklessly.

Sometimes the socialization process is not so quiet. The parent screams, "You'll grow up to be just like your good-for-nothing father!" A principal spanks a wayward student in front of the class.

At times socialization is touchingly tender. A mother smiles lovingly at the thoughtful child who brings her flowers during a time of grief. A sister is overheard bragging about the car her brother has rebuilt.

Sometimes socialization is harsh. The rest of the team shuns one member after a Little League game in which he missed catching an easy fly ball and cost them the victory.

Socialization is obviously not one unified process but a set of processes. Socialization occurs through: (1) explicit instruction, (2) conditioning and innovation, and (3) role modeling. In practice, these modes are usually blended, but it is useful to discuss them individually.

EXPLICIT INSTRUCTION

In ***explicit instruction*** *the socializer deliberately shows or tells the person how to behave or what to believe.* A parent teaches a child how to make popcorn. A grandparent tells a child that members of a different racial group are dirty and not to be trusted.

Only a small portion of socialization occurs through explicit instruction, partly because it is time consuming. People are usually so preoccupied with other concerns that they do not try deliberately to show someone else how to do something.

Another reason that explicit socialization is not the dominant mode is that the rest of the environment may be hostile to the messages sent this way. For example, schools often fail in their attempts to turn young people away from illicit drug use because these students are more powerfully influenced by informal socialization from their peers than by explicit instruction from their teachers.

CONDITIONING

B. F. Skinner developed a major theory of human behavior based on the idea that behavior patterns are shaped by conditioning (1971). ***Conditioning*** *is the means of establishing a behavior pattern by repeatedly associating a reward or punishment with the behavior.* All social environments have prevailing norms that are followed by most members of the group and are encouraged by rewards and discouraged by punishment. A reward is often called *positive reinforcement*, and punishment is called *negative reinforcement*.

Skinner actually succeeded in teaching pigeons to play table tennis using conditioning techniques. He used no explicit instruction but simply rewarded desirable behavior—behavior that approximated hitting the Ping-Pong ball—as it occurred. Food was the positive reinforcement.

One of Skinner's most important findings is that reward is a stronger reinforcer than punishment. Skinner also found that behavior conditioned by intermittent reward persists, or lasts, longer than behavior conditioned by constant reward.

Skinner tries to explain much of human behavior through conditioning. His theory assumes the existence of *random initial behavior, basic human drives*, and *physical limitations*. Skinner had to wait for his pigeons to exhibit random behavior, such as unintentionally perching near the end of the table, or pecking at the Ping-Pong ball. When a bird performed such a behavior, Skinner rewarded it and thus "taught" the bird to perform the behavior. Basic drives, such as the need for food and water, cannot be significantly altered by conditioning. Conditioning also cannot generate behavior patterns beyond physical limitations; no set of rewards can enable a person to broad-jump 50 yards.

Conditioning works best where both the behavior and the reinforcements are simple. Most human behavior is not simple, however. Skinner's positive reinforcement is also useful only in certain situations, because what rewards one person may be punishment to another. For an outstanding sales record one month, a sales manager might give an employee two opera tickets in seats next to the sales manager and her husband. Depending on the employee's attitude toward opera and toward the manager as leisure-time company, this bonus could cause the employee to want to do equally well the next month or to avoid the "prize" again.

One complex form of socialization is innovation. ***Innovation*** *occurs when a person acquires a behavior pat-*

Just like mama—A young girl re-enacts the role patterns her mother undoubtedly modeled. Role modeling proves most effective when the subject likes the role model. (© *Harold S. Summers/The Picture Cube*)

tern through experimentation. A child tries out behavior by standing on the dining-room table, writing on walls, and shouting "no!" when mother tells her to do something. Depending on the responses to these behaviors, the child will repeat them or not. Trial and error is also the way a child learns to walk. In this case, the laws of physics responds to the child's experiments—falling down is the child's negative reinforcement, and getting somewhere is the child's reward.

Adults, too, can be socialized through innovation. A man experiments with a new style of clothes; if he gets compliments, he adopts the style. An idea occurs to an athlete for a new maneuver; if it works, he incorporates it into the set of plays the team uses. Through college courses a student learns the meaning of some new words and uses them in conversation; if people are impressed, the student keeps using them. If the new vocabulary brings disdainful looks or snide comments, the student will probably drop it.

ROLE MODELING

"Do as I say, not as I do." Despite this instruction, children often model their behavior after parents or after significant others in their lives. ***Role modeling*** *refers to one person's behavior serving as a pattern for another person's behavior.* Children learn many things through role modeling, including how to speak. First they mimic basic sounds, then they practice intonation patterns, and finally they form words older people use. Through observation and practice children come to understand and speak an entire language.

Through role modeling children also learn which emotions to suppress and how to express those the social environment condones. For instance, a boy is socialized not to cry, in part by the fact that he seldom sees his father or other men cry. Girls are socialized into helping roles by seeing their mothers and other adult women in such roles.

Drinking and smoking habits are strongly influenced by family modeling. A recent survey concludes that the children of alcoholic parents are twice as likely to become alcoholics as the children of nonalcoholic parents (Hindman, 1976). Similarly, teenagers with parents who smoke are 40 percent more likely to smoke than those with parents who do not. Teenagers with an older sibling who smokes are 115 percent more likely to smoke than those without an older sibling who smokes (Ashton and Stepney, 1982).

Peers also serve as role models. For example, a 6-year-old boy showed no interest in swimming in the family's new pool, despite his parents' coaxing. He said matter-of-factly, "I don't want to go swimming in the pool; I could drown." When his 3-year-old cousin jumped in the pool and demonstrated her recently acquired swimming ability, the 6-year-old quickly mustered his courage and also jumped in. Here a peer served as the role model.

Albert Bandura (1977) suggests that some behavior has elements of both conditioning and role modeling. He points out that much social learning has no immediate reinforcement. A pre-school child can learn much about working in a kitchen by watching a parent prepare meals, although the child is not immediately able to use the information and is not rewarded then for learning it.

People may even learn from watching others receive reinforcement. For instance, when children were shown an adult receiving praise for beating a large plastic doll, most of the children later beat and yelled at the same doll, even though they did not know they were being observed and they received no praise themselves (Bandura, Ross, and Ross, 1961). Bandura labels this phenomenon *vicarious reinforcement*, a combination of conditioned reinforcement and vicarious learning (*vicarious* means "substitute").

CHILDREN WITHOUT CHILDHOOD

The National Lampoon did a special children's issue a few years ago, in which they described the typical child of a generation ago as having in his pocket a "knife, compass, 36 cents, marble, rabbit's foot." With these treasures, on a Saturday morning, he would "climb around a construction site, jump off a garage roof onto an old sofa, have a crabapple war, and mow the lawn." Today's youth, in contrast, carries "hash pipe, Pop Rocks, condom, $20, 'ludes, Merits, . . . sleeps late, watches TV, has a tennis lesson, goes to the mall to buy albums and a new screen for Bong, plays electronic World War II, and gets high" (National Lampoon, 1979).

Sociologist Marie Win investigated children of today and concludes in her book, *Children Without Childhood* (1983), that children today are different. As the Lampoon article suggests, children have lost their innocence as our society changed its conception of childhood. Winn recognizes that childhood of yesteryear was not totally happy, nor free of jealousy, shame, or anger. It was, however, a time of innocence and a conscious protection of that innocence by adults:

> It was the secure certainty that he was a child, and that adults were adults, and that in spite of the wretchedness he might glimpse in their world he could still remain, in his different state, untouched by it. This is the essence of adult protectiveness: transmitting to children the sense that they are separate and special and under the adults' careful supervision.

Today, Winn explains, the "Age of Protection has ended," and the "Age of Preparation has set in," the natural result of several social factors working together: changes in women's roles, the breakdown of the conventional two-parent family, the sexual revolution, the drug epidemic, the spread of psychoanalytic thinking, and the proliferation of television.

During what Winn terms the "Golden Age of Childhood," mothers were primarily working at home and closely aligned with their children's lives. Women were thought of as vulnerable creatures, as were the children for whom they cared. As women became more emotionally and economically independent from men, they perhaps encouraged more independence in their children as well. Both mothers and fathers learned to value their own needs and began to be involved in many more activities outside of the family than had been the previous generation's parents.

This trend was encouraged by the breakdown of many family structures. The economic pressures on women and their children after divorce may have encouraged the children to become more adultlike of necessity, taking more responsibility for their own care and that of their siblings, as well as for household chores. Parents who have suffered hurts may decide to make their children "tough" by exposing them to everything they can at an early age, in order to immunize them from the same hurts when they grow up.

Added to these trends is the presence of television, which brings into the child's realm the violence, futility, misery, and injustice that previous generations of children had been shielded from. Today's children often act in an adult manner, imitating behavior they see on television. These children, however, have no more coping mechanisms than had their counterparts of the last generation; when they find they cannot han-

OT DEZILAICOS ERA EW
DAER YLLACITAMOTUA
MORF LAIRETAM DETNIRP
.THGIR OT TFEL

FIGURE 4.2 Example of the socialization process. Try starting at the top right and reading to the left.

dle the stresses they are exposed to so early, they often turn to drugs, alcohol, or promiscuous sexual behavior to fill the emotional gap. The fact that both parents are at work a good portion of the day often leaves children less supervised and more able to experiment in these areas. As the children grow to adulthood, their problems become more prominent in society.

Coupled with these social trends is a new emphasis on Freudian parenting. Previous generations had relied upon their own parents as role models. Now experts warn that parents must be careful about what they say and do in order to raise nonneurotic adults, and some urge that children be treated as equals rather than as subordinates. As a result of often conflicting and unclear advice, parents have become unsure of their parenting abilities.

Winn realizes that the social trends that produced these adultlike children, especially changes in family patterns and the dominance of television in socialization, cannot be reversed. However, she makes several suggestions for the future: First, she suggests that parents, rather than divorcing, might readjust their goals for marriage in cases where their marriage does not fill all their expectations; second, that adults once again assert their authority over children, recognizing that children must be treated with respect but not as equals. Finally, Winn hopes that parents will rededicate themselves to creating a childhood period of nurture and support that will allow their children to form strong positive self-concepts and become responsible adults.

What Are Three Characteristics of the Socialization Process?

Now that we have examined the basic nature of socialization, including its social and biological components, we will turn to the study of some recurring processes and patterns that occur as a person is socialized. Society accomplishes the feat of turning babies into social beings through the socialization process. This process transmits customs, knowledge, and skills that (1) tend to be general rather than specific, (2) call forth almost automatic behaviors and responses, and (3) persist through time.

GENERALIZED NATURE

People are usually socialized to accept generalized or abstract behavior patterns rather than specific ones. For instance, in traditional settings boys are taught to be "masculine" and girls are taught to be "feminine," although the definitions of these concepts change over time and between cultures. In the 1970s the definition of "feminine" in the United States began to include careers, whereas in the 1950s women were taught to exclude careers from their lives in the interest of maintaining their homes.

The concepts of masculinity and femininity, career, and home are general or abstract, as opposed to specific. They do not refer directly to specific behavior or people. Yet these abstractions shape our behavior, and allegiance to these ideas helps bond us to our social group.

AUTOMATIC REACTIONS

Socialized thought and behavior patterns become so automatic that people often forget they are using them. After people learn to read, for example, they see words as wholes rather than as sets of letters to be sounded out or decoded. Musicians translated printed notes and proper fingerings into music that is performed much too quickly to be thought through "consciously." People meet someone they know and automatically say, "Hi, how are you?" without consciously considering their words.

PERSISTENCE

Socialized patterns also persist over time. You would have a difficult time copying this paragraph quickly without dotting any i's or crossing any t's, because your training in correct writing would persist. It is difficult to change a speech accent learned in childhood. Similarly, it may be hard to change one's emotional habits. Some psychologists claim that people even have *learned* favorite emotions (Berne, 1972). Faced with a situation, one person gets angry and blames others, whereas another feels guilty and blames himself or herself. Familiar behaviors and beliefs tend to feel right, although they are not always pleasant. Such patterns are not changed easily.

Sociologists at Work •

LOIS LEE
RESCUES CHILDREN FROM PROSTITUTION
Children of the Night
Hollywood, California

Lois Lee encountered the problem of child prostitution while doing research for her graduate degree in sociology. In 1981, she chose to use her sociological training to develop a resocialization program for such children that has proven remarkably successful.

What Is the Basic Thrust of Your Work?
I work primarily with children ages 11 to 17 who are involved in prostitution and pornography. We provide them with a 24-hour crisis line, an intake center for more extensive counseling services, and a program that provides services right on the streets. We help them to obtain anything from birth certificates to picture IDs, social security cards, placement in drug programs, public assistance, jobs, foster homes, clothing, and food—whatever they need to get off the street.

How Do These Young Kids Get Involved in Prostitution?
Over 80 percent of them have been sexually molested as children. They tend to be the kids who were never detected or reported as victims of child abuse. In most situations the abuse goes on and on, and at the age of anywhere from 11 to 13, kids will say, "I'm not going to put up with this anymore," and they leave. Typically they run away to the nearest urban area; here on the West Coast, it tends to be Hollywood Boulevard.

Usually they have not planned to run away, so they don't have much money or clothing with them. They may call around for help, but no centralized agency will come and take a kid off the street and provide him or her with food and shelter.

What happens is that they find someone who says, "You can come and stay at my house." That person can be anything from a pedophile (someone who likes to have sex with kids), to a street pornographer who takes nude pictures of kids, to a professional pimp, to another boy or girl on the street. In these situations they are often sexually exploited again, whether they are raped or abused, or someone gives them drugs to lower their inhibitions. They are told they have to provide sexual favors or have no place to stay.

Eventually, some of the girls will meet a professional pimp who will sweet-talk them and provide them with whatever gap there is in their development. A pimp, unlike other street people, will not try to have sex with her. This becomes a very powerful game, because for the first time in her life, she finds someone who wants to just like her without having sex with her. The pimp will introduce her to prostitution by fabricating an immediate crisis. He may tell her he was dealing drugs to buy her nice things, someone stole the drugs, and the Mafia is out to kill him unless he comes up with $5,000 in three days. Then he asks her to turn tricks for him, just so he doesn't get killed.

Once she has begun to prostitute herself, the pimp will begin to resocialize her, saying things like "You are just a whore; nobody cares about you; nobody can help you except me." A pimp makes the girls think he is omnipotent and knows everything they are doing at all times. So, rescuing these kids in their natural environment and showing them that you can handle issues like cops is very important.

How Do You Reach the Girls?
We pass out cards to all kinds of kids on the streets, and we have stickers on pay phones with our crisis number. They may call in times of crisis: Maybe they have a close call with a trick or a pimp, maybe they need medical attention, maybe they almost OD'd, maybe they just want to get away from the pimp. We will keep the kid on the phone, and have a cab come out and

pick her up. If the pimp is nearby, we may have to call certain friends on the police force. They will go out and pretend to arrest her and take her back to the station before they bring her to the center, because if the pimp knows she has called the police, he will kill her. The girls are impressed that we are able to finesse dealing with the police.

When they come in, we begin to change their image of themselves by suggesting positive alternatives to their present situation. For example, we tell them, "You need a birth certificate. We will pay for it and have it mailed here. Then you can get a social security card to set up a bank account or get a job or receive Medicaid if you get sick."

How Well Does Your Program Work?
Our definition of success means the girls are not dependent on any kind of criminal activity. In our yearly follow-ups, we find that 80 percent of our kids have succeeded in staying off the streets, fewer than 2 percent are in jail, and the rest are back on the streets. Once they have legitimate credentials, and are headed toward some kind of nonstreet life, they have a very high chance of never being involved in this kind of trap again. •

Why Is Socialization Important to Society?

In spite of the many factors that encourage us to become like members of one group, occasionally someone rises above these standards and becomes what we term a *genius:* someone with special skill or talent in a certain area. Sociologist Robert Nisbet (1982) has recently re-addressed the question of where genius comes from and offers a somewhat new hypothesis. Nisbet's idea is that genius is not purely biological or individually learned, but that the conditions within a society at a particular time may be conducive to creating genius within an individual. In other words, the *milieu,* or *social setting,* provides crucial experiences that foster the growth of genius.

Nisbet believes that the history of a social group contributes tradition, convention, and memory to the creation of genius. The genius uses these aspects of the social setting as a starting point or base from which to grow. Nisbet believes that society as a whole can stimulate or stifle genius growth. For instance, when Puritan England stopped the production of works of religious art, it became more difficult for artistic genius to flourish in that time and location.

The traditional struggle between those who believe intelligence is *inborn* and those who argue it is *made* has often focused on the family. Nisbet argues that the larger society also has an effect on this process that should no longer be ignored. If this is true, the intellectual environment of the society becomes important to protect as a natural resource, because it nurtures the geniuses we count on to carry forward our society.

This makes it clear why the study of socialization can be vital in the life of the society as a whole. At the personal level, knowing about the effects of various socialization agents could cause you to change your social and personal habits in order to stimulate certain types of growth in yourself or your family. As a member of society, knowing how various socialization agents foster certain behaviors in society should help you to evaluate proposed changes in society. As Nisbet suggests, socialization involves us collectively as well as individually.

Conclusion

Socialization is a process. We can trace and isolate elements of socialization, and in it we can look for patterns. In the end, however, we cannot predict how any particular individual personality will form. This is partly because one socialization agent seldom gains total control over an individual and partly because different agents may have vastly different effects on the person being socialized.

Conflicting messages from several socialization agents may be confusing and even frustrating. Parents may tell a child shoplifting is wrong, but other neighborhood children may perceive it as courageous. Where contradictions exist, the individual must make a choice. Thus, we sometimes find a "good" kid from a "good" home being bailed out of jail on a Saturday night to his parents' horror. Such a situation can be a matter of one socializing agent winning over another, or the individual choosing between conflicting socialization influences.

REVIEW

Summary Questions

1. How does socialization shape a person's self-image?
2. What does Cooley mean by "looking-glass self"?
3. How does Mead explain people "taking the role of the other"?
4. What is Goffman's contribution to the idea of the social self?
5. What are the effects of environmental deprivation on an individual?
6. What are the varying effects of nature and nurture on individual development?
7. What is sociobiology and why is it controversial?
8. What are three modes of socialization?
9. What are three characteristics of the socialization process?
10. Who are the Children Without Childhood about whom Winn writes?
11. What are the basic agents of socialization or domination?
12. What are some of the effects of the massive increase in day care in the United Sates today?
13. What are the basic theses of Erikson, Piaget, Kohlberg, and Gilligan?
14. How does socialization continue in adulthood?
15. How might our jobs actually shape our personalities?
16. In what ways is socialization important to society as a whole?

Summary Answers

1. To some extent, we accept the definitions of ourselves that we are taught by our families and other members of our society.
2. Cooley decided that a person comes to think of himself or herself as an "I" through a combination of biological and social processes. The "looking-glass self" is the image of self that a person sees reflected by others.
3. Mead believes people take the role of the other by progressing through three stages. In Stage 1, the infant is all "I." The "me" begins to develop through play in Stage 2, and fully develops as the child learns to respond to the generalized other in Stage 3, taking into account the broader social community. Significant others, or persons with whom an individual has intimate and long-term contact, facilitate this process. This self-awareness makes it possible for people to position themselves within larger social units.
4. Goffman points out that the socialization process continues into adulthood. He discusses, for instance, impression management, or how in daily activity we alter ourselves to fit the audience we are addressing, a process made up of thousands of small, everyday social responses.
5. As can be seen in the cases of Becky and Genie, children who are denied intimate social contact may suffer from retardation of social and physical growth, which is termed *environmental deprivation syndrome,* and may remain physically and emotionally impaired for life.
6. Although some human behavior patterns are guided by drives, or inborn forces that motivate organisms to seek water, food, self-preservation, sex, and nurturing, these drives are general rather than specific, as in lower animal forms. No current scientific evidence indicates that any individual or group is born naturally to fit any social role. Instead, our genetic make-up sets our potential, but our culture and environment, including diet, affect whether that potential will be realized.
7. Sociobiology, introduced by Edward Wilson, is the systematic study of the biological basis of social behavior in every kind of organism. Wilson believes that human social behavior rests on a genetic foundation. His ideas have created controversy because they could conceivably be used to promote racist and sexist policies.
8. Socialization occurs through explicit instruction, conditioning and innovation, and role modeling. In practice, these modes are usually blended.
9. The socialization process tends to be general rather than specific, calls forth automatic behaviors and responses, and persists through time.
10. Children without childhood are children of today who are given adultlike responsibilities at an early age because of several social factors: changes in women's roles, the breakdown of the two-parent family, the sexual revolution, the drug epidemic, the spread of psychoanalytic thinking, and the proliferation and abuse of television.
11. The family, peer groups, television, day care, and schools are today's basic agents of socialization (the persons or devices that carry out the process of socialization). Conflict theorists point out that these same agents can be thought of as agents of domination, because they may use their position to perpetuate an unequal power situation and to dominate the one being socialized.
12. Over one-fourth of the children in the United States between the ages of 3 and 5 spend their days in a day-care center. This situation is largely due to the increasing divorce rate, which forces women into the work world, and the rise in the material expectations of the young family, which encourages two-paycheck families. The experts do not agree about the effects. Day-care children tend to be more advanced intellectually and socially, more assertive, and less sexist in their attitudes as adults. Some researchers, however, feel that young children need one primary caregiver in order to develop into emotionally stable persons with a positive sense of self. The assertiveness that may be positive in such a child may also turn to aggressiveness in later childhood and adulthood.
13. Erikson presented an eight stage theory of personality development in which each stage may be positively resolved or unresolved. He stressed the close interaction between the social environment and personality.

    Piaget suggests that everyone passes through four major intellectual stages: Sensory-motor, preoperational, concrete operations, and formal operations. He believes that social contact is necessary for advancing through the stages.

    Kohlberg: Moral decisions based on fear of punishment, idea of rewards taken into account, immediate punishments and rewards not necessary, strict adherence to rules, recognition that conventional rules may come into conflict with a higher sense of right and wrong, and universal principles of justice, human rights, and human dignity guide decisions.

    Gilligan: When women reach the upper stages of moral development their decisions are guided by the principle of protecting relationships and people (the care principle) rather than by the principle of individual rights that guides men's decisions.

14. Socialization in adulthood is more concerned with learning overt norms and behaviors than is the socialization of childhood, which is concerned primarily with regulating antisocial behavior. Levinson's work suggests that successfully completing the transitions between our life stages is of crucial importance in leading a fulfilling life. Resocialization may occur in adulthood when an individual commits himself or herself to a new goal or enters a total institution.

15. Kohn's and Schooler's research suggests that our work affects our personalities in a variety of ways. For instance, engaging in complex work socializes us toward more intellectual flexibility. Self-directed work leads to flexibility of ideas, whereas oppressive working conditions lead to less flexibility and more distress, as measured by anxiety, lack of self-confidence, and distrust.

16. Society as a whole may encourage or discourage the development of individual characteristics. A genius can grow in a social group more easily if the intellectual atmosphere of the group nurtures genius. Nisbet urges that we protect our social setting to provide experiences that foster the growth of genius in our society.

Glossary

conditioning the means of establishing a behavior pattern by repeatedly associating a reward or punishment with the behavior

drives inborn forces that motivate organisms to seek water, food, self-preservation, sexual gratification, and nurturing of their young

environmental deprivation syndrome retardation of a child's social and physical growth due to lack of intimate contact in infancy

ethology the study of social behavior in animals

explicit instruction a form of socialization in which the socializing agent deliberately shows or tells the person how to behave or what to believe

genetics the study of inherited traits

hypothesis a proposition that logically falls within a broader theory

impression management Erving Goffman's concept that in daily activity an individual alters his or her self to fit the audience

innovation a form of socialization in which a person acquires a behavior pattern through experimentation

instincts complex behavior patterns that are genetically transmitted

longitudinal data data gathered on the same subjects over a time period

looking-glass self Charles Horton Cooley's concept that one's self-image is reflected by others

milieu social setting

mortification revamping the personal and moral values of group members through physical and mental humiliations

resocialization the process that occurs when an individual is socialized to adopt a system of beliefs different than those into which he or she was first socialized

role modeling a form of socialization in which one person's behavior serves as a pattern for another person's behavior

self the thoughts, emotions, and actions a person sees as integral to his or her sense of identity (also can be called personality)

significant others persons with whom an individual has intimate and long-term contact

socialization the process of transmitting a society's beliefs and behavior patterns to an individual and making possible an individual's development of a self, or personality

socialization or domination agents persons or devices that act to carry out the process of socialization

sociobiology systematic study of the biological basis of social behavior in every kind of organism

total institutions organizations that are relatively closed off from the outside world and that follow a formalized life routine under the control of a bureaucratic staff

Suggested Readings

Howard S. Becker, et al., 1961. *Boys in White.* Chicago: University of Chicago Press.

An extremely interesting look at the resocialization process during a medical school education.

Peter Rose, (ed.). 1979. *Socialization and the Life Cycle.* New York: St. Martin's Press.

A well-organized reader containing both classic and new pieces regarding socialization as a lifelong process.

Michael Rutter. 1980. *Changing Youth in a Changing Society: Pattern of Adolescent Development and Disorder.* Cambridge: Harvard University Press.

Rutter focuses on the social and psychological problems of today's adolescents in relation to changes in society.

Marie Winn. 1983. *Children Without Childhood.* New York: Pantheon Books.

An interesting analysis of the trends of the Sixties and Seventies that led to "unchildlike children and unprotecting adults" and to a redefinition of childhood in the Eighties.

CHAPTER

5

GROUPS and ORGANIZATIONS

- What Is a Group?
- How Is Social Support an Important Factor in the Quality and Length of Life?
- What Are Small Groups?
- How Do Groups Influence Individuals?
- Close-Up on Research: Solomon Asch on Group Pressure
- How Is Group Decision-Making Different from Individual Decision-Making?
- What Is a Formal or Complex Organization?
- What Are the Characteristics of Bureaucracy?
- What Are the Functions and Dysfunctions of Bureaucracy?
- Close-Up on Theory: Robert Merton on How Bureaucracy Affects Personality
- How Does Worker Input Affect Bureaucratic Structures?
- Sociologists at Work: Merlin Pope Counsels Ethnically Diverse Firms on Productivity

How's Your Sociological Intuition?

1. The social support that we give and receive in families and other groups has a positive effect on:
   - **a.** Our satisfaction with life
   - **b.** Our health and well-being
   - **c.** Our ability to handle stress
   - **d.** All of the above
2. Solomon Asch devised an experiment in which college students were asked to pick, from a set of three lines, the line that was the same length as a fourth line. The students erred in fewer than 1 percent of the cases when they performed this task in private. When making the selection in a group of seven other subjects, who had all been secretly instructed to select the same wrong answer, the students erred in:
   - **a.** 1% of the cases
   - **b.** 5% of the cases
   - **c.** 33% of the cases
   - **d.** 97% of the cases
3. Laboratory experiments with small groups indicate that when faced with a dilemma:
   - **a.** Individuals make riskier decisions when acting alone than when acting in groups
   - **b.** Groups make riskier decisions than the individual members would make acting alone
   - **c.** A group environment has no measurable effect on the amount of risk people take
   - **d.** Individuals make less risky decisions the second time they face the same problem regardless of whether they first encountered the problem in a group or alone
4. If we are seeking to influence an individual by using unanimous peer pressure, which size of majority is most effective?
   - **a.** Two against one
   - **b.** Four against one
   - **c.** Eight against one
   - **d.** Fifteen against one

Answers

1. d. Social support has all these positive effects as recent research by James House and others demonstrates.
2. c. As we indicate in the "Close-Up on Research," peer pressure is quite strong, but we will also learn that it affects some individuals more than others.
3. b. That's right, and we might keep this in mind the next time someone suggests setting up a committee rather than appointing an individual.
4. b. The effectiveness of peer pressure actually begins to diminish as the size of the pressuring group gets beyond four persons.

When You Have Finished Studying This Chapter, You Should Know:

- What a group is
- How groups are different from individuals
- The difference between primary and secondary groups
- How important social support is to the quality and length of life
- How small groups differ in structure, leadership, size, and membership
- How leaders emerge within groups
- How groups influence individual perception and behavior
- How group decision-making is different from individual decision-making
- What a formal organization is
- The stages in the development of bureaucracy
- The six characteristics of Max Weber's ideal bureaucracy
- The functions and dysfunctions of modern bureaucracy
- How bureaucracy affects personality
- How the Peter Principle works
- What recent research indicates about worker involvement in corporate decision-making
- How sociologists work to change organizations

A pretty girl is standing across the library table from Dave. "Hi," she says. "Looks like you could use a study break."

For the past couple of weeks Dave has been living with the sick feeling that he is flunking out of college and only a miracle on the finals will prevent it.

"I sure could."

"Well, come on! My friends are having a party."

This is a new approach. Usually it's Dave trying to pick up the girl. But why not? There's almost no hope of passing history, and Dave has been wondering why he's in college anyhow.

The party is fun. Nancy's friends are a bit squeaky clean, but they are really interested in him. He receives more compliments than he can remember, and they seem to understand his situation—there must be more to life than college courses and exams.

Dave is unaware of it, but he has been "love bombed." The seemingly chance meeting in the library is a well-rehearsed recruitment routine, practiced repeatedly by Nancy's religious cult, a worldwide organization with thousands of members and millions of dollars in assets. The party was actually held "in his honor" after he was spotted as a promising prospect.

Dave does flunk out, but his newfound friends provide him with companionship, direction, a place to live, and a routine. His day is regimented with early rising, meditation, lectures, housekeeping, fund raising, and recruiting. Increasingly Dave is expected to make public commitments to the "Church" and to shed his old degenerate identity in favor of a new reformed one. Within two months he has decided that the Omnibus Church, led by its charismatic Reverend Luna Sola, has the answers to all the important questions. He has sold his belongings and surrendered his money to the Church. He has learned to accept Reverend Sola's interpretation of the scriptures as the ultimate authority and has found a place in this growing organization.

Dave has become unwittingly involved in a group that takes the form of a total institution, like those discussed in the previous chapter. This group elicits tremendous devotion from its members by escalating the commitments it seeks from them, instituting rigid regimens, carefully scrutinizing members' behavior, and applying intense peer pressure.

Groups are clearly capable of changing our moods, swaying our judgment, reshaping our deepest beliefs, and allowing us to accomplish things we could never do as individuals. We have chosen a very unusual group to dramatize our point, because through extreme examples we see clearly the dynamics that often go unnoticed in our everyday groups.

In this chapter we consider several types of groups, from face-to-face intimate ones to lumbering, impersonal bureaucracies. We discuss how groups influence individual judgment and personality. We also evaluate several proposals for improving the very large formal organizations that dominate business, education, religion, and politics today.

Groups can help you perform superhuman feats, distort your judgment, change your moods, or reshape your personality. Unlikely as it may sound, scientific evidence indicates that human groups can do all these things—and more.

Groups are highly influential social entities that can have various effects on individuals. Each of us has an intuitive idea of what a group is; we often eat our meals with a group, the President meets with a group of advisers, the people in a dormitory, apartment, fraternity, or sorority are a group. Because groups are so common and because they constitute the major unit of study in sociology, it may seem logical to think that sociologists have agreed on exactly what a group is.

What Is a Group?

Instead of agreeing, experts have introduced several different definitions of groups. In fact, it is possible that no other sociological term has received as many different definitions. Some experts' definitions are based on the structure of groups, others on group interaction, and still others on motivation or the group members' perception of themselves. Our definition attempts to represent mainstream thought on the topic:

*A **group** is a set of people recurrently interacting according to shared patterns and expectations about each other's behavior.*

AGGREGATES AND CATEGORIES

The people standing in a college cafeteria line for dinner are not a group but an aggregate. *An **aggregate** is a set of people who happen to be in one area.* Some of them may be interacting with each other, but they do not constitute a group. They do not act as a unit, even though most or even all of these individuals may act in orderly and predictable ways. The norms they follow, such as not cutting in line, are part of a custom that does not originate with this one set of people. Aggregates are thus not groups, because their members do not act as a unit in a structured way with shared expectations.

Another set of people that is not a group is a category. *A **category** is a set of people who share a common characteristic.* All college students who have attended private schools, for instance, form a category but not a group nor an aggregate. Groups, as we said, involve persons interacting in a structured way. Therefore, the people who get together to play bridge are a group, but the set of people who know how to play bridge is a category. They have a characteristic in common, but they do not interact together.

Aggregates and categories are likely places for groups to develop. For example, if some of the people in the cafeteria line were to agree among themselves to stage a demonstration protesting the low quality and high price of the food, they would then have become a group. They would have interacted in a structured way with shared expectations.

GROUP ROLES AND NORMS

In order for an aggregate or category to become a group, its members must perform different roles and follow group norms in support of some common purpose. Even groups that do not appear to have norms and roles do have them.

This group of young Suzuki students has learned the norms that are specific to the role of violinist, including how to stand in rest position. Even at their young ages, they perform them admirably. (*Photo courtesy the author*)

Consider the hypothetical cafeteria protestors: Suppose their demonstration involves a series of acts of sabotage against the food service authorities. Perhaps they all agree the first night to "spill" their beverages on the tables and chairs. On the second night they chant "better food or else" and show the authorities they are serious by inverting their plates as they leave. The third night the group's "prank mastermind" suggests they all "accidentally" break a dish, but another group member, who has acted as an informal leader, turns the idea aside as too extreme. Instead, they decide to take all the silverware from the dining hall and hold it for a "ransom" of better food. They also agree the plan will remain secret and, if caught, no person will identify the others involved. The initial aggregate has developed norms, such as secrecy and loyalty, and roles, including leader, prank inventor, and follower. They are now a functioning group.

PRIMARY AND SECONDARY GROUP RELATIONSHIPS

In 1909 the American sociologist Charles Horton Cooley coined a term that became the cornerstone of the sociology of groups: the *primary group* (Cooley, 1909).

*A **primary group** is a relatively small, enduring group characterized by intimacy.* Primary groups are small groups by definition, because large groups cannot sustain intimate relationships.

A healthy group activity? Besides the sunshine these women are enjoying, they provide each other with social support which promotes human health and well-being in several ways. (© *Sarah Putnam/The Picture Cube*)

Cooley used this term to discuss the family and the play group: groups that were responsible for the early socialization of the child before the advent of day care, public school, and television. He believed these primary groups are the original source of our moral norms and are our reinforcers and stabilizers while we are adults (Cooley, 1909).

In preindustrial societies, people are most likely to relate by means of primary groups. Most villages are small, and many village members are relatives. The people of a village depend on each other for food, for help in raising children, and for support in emotionally trying times. The people live, work, and play together.

The term *primary group* has recently been extended to include those groups of close friends and associates from whom we receive nurturing and support. Some social scientists even consider certain political groups to be primary groups.

Most social contacts in modern industrialized societies, however, are with *secondary groups,* which are outside the circle of one's family and friends. ***A secondary group** is a social group characterized by impersonal and often transitory interaction.* Secondary groups have less cohesiveness, more formality, and offer less support than primary groups, and feature less intensity, less frequent interaction, a shorter duration, and have lower priority among their members than primary groups, which are most important to individuals.

Groups of people who share a common workplace, neighborhood groups, and religious groups are examples of secondary groups. Most Americans, for example, work with one group of people, worship with another group, and live in a neighborhood with still another. They have less overall contact with members of their family and close friends than members of less industrialized societies, and they often reserve visits with primary group members for weekends and evenings.

Primary groups often involve a wide range of activities which people engage in as ends in themselves. A family for instance may eat together, work together, play together, celebrate and mourn together. Secondary groups usually involve a much narrower range of activities, and the participants often see these as a means to some other end. Groups found working together in factories, construction sites, stores, or offices better fit the description of secondary groups.

Groups are not necessarily primary or secondary but may be on a continuum ranging from very primary, such as the family, to very secondary, such as large bureaucracies. Such groups as fraternities, religious groups, and self-help groups, for instance, combine characteristics of both primary and secondary groups, being based on intimacy but grounded in formality as well. Even the most formal of secondary groups such as the military often will be found to contain highly intimate primary groups, such as combat units, living within them.

Our society's emphasis on secondary rather than on primary relationships is partly due to the fact that modern society encourages working long hours and moving away from family and close friends for career advancement, especially for middle-class professionals. Many researchers have studied the impact of our limited contact with primary groups. We address the topic further in Chapter 19, "Social Change: Urbanization and Modernization."

How Is Social Support an Important Factor in the Quality and Length of Life?

The social support we gain from relationships in groups promotes human health and well-being in several ways. Indeed, as Durkheim's pioneering study of suicide showed, social support can be a matter of life and death (1897). Researcher James House has further advanced the study of social supports in recent surveys of the American public. House and his colleagues gathered information about marriage, contacts with friends, church and other organization memberships, as well as health status (1980). They found that people with better social support systems have longer and happier lives. Providing such social support in the workplace and elsewhere promotes health and well-being by creating an atmosphere in which the social group tries to eliminate conditions that might produce stress or other health problems. When stress or other health hazards already exist, social support can reduce or eliminate their effects and even stimulate people toward positive health practices like good diet and exercise.

House identifies several interesting implications. For instance, increasing social supports in the workplace should decrease job stress or buffer its adverse health effects. Where the work limits interaction among the workers, support of supervisors becomes especially important. Supportive family relationships can decrease stress, even in severe situations such as layoffs from work.

As a society we have cause for concern. Americans have fewer significant informal social relationships and supports than twenty-five years ago, although they also indicate they would prefer more. Though respondents indicated they long for more such supports, American adults are more likely to live alone and less likely to marry, join voluntary organizations, and visit informally with others than twenty-five years ago. Our primary group life is decreasing, which confirms Alvin Toffler's prediction two decades ago in *Future Shock* (1970). There he observed that we live in a society in which our rapidly changing social patterns, including high rates of mobility and family dissolution, challenge our ability to maintain important social supports.

House's research suggests that women are more able to offer social support than men. They tend to be more empathetic, warm, open, and socio-emotionally skilled. Because more women are working full-time and raising children alone after divorce, however, they might be less able to provide social support to others. With growing willingness on the part of many males to nurture these traits in themselves, social support might increasingly come from that quarter.

House invites sociologists to explore how changing patterns of social relationships in our society relate to the experience of social support and the quality and length of life in the United States. Given the adverse consequences of lack of social supports, improving our social support systems is important to us as individuals and as a society (House, 1987; Kessler, House, and Turner, 1987; LaRocco, House, and French, 1980).

What Are the Dynamics of Small Groups?

As we see later in this chapter, secondary groups in the form of bureaucracies may grow to enormous size in modern societies. Modern nations themselves are examples of these "megagroups" that may include hundreds of millions of members. A group, then, may range from an intimate parent-child or marriage relationship of just two people to a secondary group of 4 billion people who share this planet. Human beings are not islands unto themselves, neither are we simply cogs in an enormous social machine. No doubt our lives are touched and in some ways governed by the megagroups of which we are a part—our nation of 250 million, a corporation of 25 million employees, a national labor union, or a religious organization with millions of members. But most of us act in the context of relatively small groups.

Even within the megagroups of millions of people, the routine social interaction occurs largely in what sociologists have come rather loosely to call small groups. A ***small group*** *is a collection of people who meet more or less regularly in face-to-face interaction, who possess a common identity or exclusiveness of purpose, and who share a set of standards governing their activities* (Crosbie, 1975). Most social interaction takes place in these face-to-face groups of a few people, the people who work the counter at our particular McDonald's, the other people in our office, those in our car pool, our next-door neighbors, and our family. A substantial number of sociologists devote their efforts to studying social interaction in small groups. They assume small groups share some important and fundamental similarities in spite of obvious but perhaps relatively superficial differences.

The small group is distinguished from other kinds of groups by the group dynamics that occur rather than by the number of group members. ***Group dynamics*** *are the patterns of interaction of group members.* Most research in the field of small groups has been research in group dynamics.

Cartwright and Zander suggest that four basic assumptions are held by most researchers in the field of small-group dynamics (1967).

1. *Groups are inevitable and are found everywhere.* We find groups in all eras, in all social strata from the abjectly poor to the very wealthy, around the globe, and from the most primitive to the most sophisticated societies. The fact that almost all human activity takes place in a group context suggests that groups are virtually inevitable.
2. *Groups mobilize powerful forces that produce effects of utmost importance to individuals.* As we have seen

in the chapter on socialization, a person's identity is formed to a great extent by the groups he or she belongs to. Consider the difference it makes to be socialized as a peasant rather than as a noble. Belonging to a group can be a prized possession, as in the case of being a member of an elite group such as Phi Beta Kappa, the United States Senate, or an Olympic team. Belonging to a group can also be an oppressive burden, as often happens in cases of ethnic or political antagonism. To have been Jewish in Nazi Germany, to be black in South Africa, or to be a political dissident in the Soviet Union is to experience the awesome negative power that can be generated by a group.

3. *Groups may produce good and bad.* In many ways the human race's finest achievements and our greatest catastrophes have been attained through groups. Groups have brought us the greatest musical performances, the most exciting sports, the most productive economies in the history of the human race, and our greatest technological advances. On the other hand, the Nazi death camps, the Jonestown mass suicides and murders, and two world wars required the coordination of group action to make them happen.
4. *Group performance can be enhanced through research into group dynamics.* Group dynamicists believe the more we learn about group dynamics the better able we will be to control groups and to harness the power developed and exercised by groups. Theorists and researchers study fundamental issues about groups, including how groups influence members to conform to the group's standards, how decisions made in group settings differ from those made by individuals, how formal structure develops in groups, and what types of leadership provide best results (Cartwright and Zander, 1967).

The study of small-group dynamics was accelerated by George Homans's classic work, *The Human Group* (1950). Shortly after its publication came studies of paid volunteers who engaged in small-group interactions surrounding a research task (Bales, 1953; Hare, 1964). Since then, the structure of small groups, group leadership, the importance of size for the functioning of the group, and the characteristics of those who seek group membership have all been topics of research, both in the laboratory setting and in the real world.

GROUP STRUCTURE

Whenever several people come together for the first time they exhibit differences in handling the activity at hand, whether meeting for a few beers after the game or planning a formal dinner for visiting dignitaries. ***Group structure*** *defines both what positions group members will fill and what the pattern of relationships among the various positions will be.* This structure is generally thought to help groups achieve their goals (Shaw and Gilchrist, 1966).

In many small groups there is both a formal structure and an informal one. ***Formal structure*** *is public and explicit.* ***Informal structure*** *is private and implicit.* Thus, the official manager may give orders to everyone else in the company, but everyone knows that much of the real power belongs to the administrative assistant

In order to perform well, members of this band have had to learn the appropriate roles and statuses of their various positions. Together the group has its own social structure. (*Photo courtesy the author*)

who checks all income and expenditures and who can help or hold up business at will. Similarly, although no one really wants to give a going-away party for an unpopular staff member, if the office organizer plans one, most people show up.

Social scientists have determined that many factors affect a person's place in a group's social structure. The status system within a group serves to limit how "high" or "low" a position one will attain. Communication is affected by the status hierarchy, with some information being withheld at both the top and bottom. This means those low in the group hide their mistakes, whereas the group's authorities have access to information, such as salaries, they do not share with those of lower status. Whether a member conforms or does not conform to group norms also affects that member's place in the structure.

The structure a group develops also depends on the inner needs of group members. A group with members who have a high need for security may tend to develop with a hierarchical structure, whereas a group with members who have a high need for esteem may develop a more egalitarian structure.

Thus, group structure influences the way group members relate to each other, and the structure, in turn, is influenced by the way group members relate to each other. This interrelationship makes a challenging and fascinating subject to study.

GROUP LEADERSHIP

The nature of a group's structure usually depends a great deal on its central member—a leader, a scapegoat, an idol, or some other important person. This is true of both formal and informal groups. Group members tend to take positions revolving around this central figure. Because of the pivotal role the leader plays in determining group structure, it has been the most frequently studied aspect of group behavior.

R. F. Bales (1953) studied the emergence of a group leader over a series of four meetings of a new group. He discovered that the member who was "best liked" in the first session was also cited as having the "best ideas" and "guidance." Over the course of the later meetings, however, the roles of "best liked" and "best ideas" diverged. In fact, when all four meetings were summarized, it appeared that the member who was full of "guidance" and "best ideas" (and who was therefore the activity leader) was also often the most *disliked* person in the group. The "most liked" ended up second or third in terms of ideas and guidance. Bales also found that if one person was obviously capable of being both the activity leader ("best ideas" and "guidance") and the emotional leader ("best liked"), he or she would usually choose to be the emotional leader and let someone else be the activity leader.

The major variable affecting the selection of leader is the rate of group participation. Members who have the highest rate of group participation are most often chosen to be leaders (Crosbie, 1975). Certain other traits also seem linked with a higher probability of becoming a leader; these include intelligence, enthusiasm, dominance, self-confidence, and egalitarianism (Hare, 1976).

LEADERSHIP STYLES. Once leaders emerge, they must choose whether to rule in an authoritarian or a democratic manner. Authoritarian leadership has been found more suited to accomplishing tasks and is useful in situations in which time is an important factor. For example, during evacuation procedures it is useful for one knowledgeable person to give orders and for the rest to follow the orders carefully.

Democratic leadership has been found useful when there is time to involve the entire group in a decision. Such involvement encourages members to give their best to the group process by sharing their ideas freely and to support the action decided upon, because they will feel part of the decision. Suppose the head of the English Department wants to replace the textbook used for freshman English for fifteen years. He or she will find the transition more acceptable to the rest of the English faculty if all have a chance to suggest and discuss new texts before a final decision is made.

Knowing the differences between these two styles of leadership and their varying uses can help us to make decisions in our own group memberships more wisely. Research has shown that a person whose leadership style is effective in one situation may be totally ineffective in the other. Chemers, for instance, predicts that nondirective, democratic leaders are more effective in groups facing moderately favorable conditions, whereas authoritarian, directive leaders are more effective when conditions are either highly favorable or highly unfavorable (1974). Testing seems to corroborate this hypothesis (Chemers et al., 1975; Fodor, 1978). Thus, if you know you work best as a democratic leader and the group time limit requires an authoritarian leadership, you might do well to pass by the opportunity to be the leader of that particular group.

The style of leadership most often chosen in groups within a society in some ways reflects the culture of that society. For example, in the United States, where there is a strong emphasis on democratic principles, many students feel they should have an opportunity to influence the administration of their college. In countries where deomocracy is not so highly valued, there are many colleges where decisions are always made by faculty and staff, and no student feels injured at not

Impossible? Groups routinely do things that would be impossible for an individual. Here a cheerleading team tosses a member ten feet into the air and safely returns her to firm ground. (*Photo courtesy the author*)

being consulted. The boundaries between the ruling group of the university and the student group are clearly defined and do not cause difficulty for either group. Here again leadership modes are influenced by our culture.

THE IMPORTANCE OF GROUP SIZE

Almost a century ago a German sociologist named Georg Simmel was the first to study the effect of group size on the sort of interaction that takes place in groups (1902; English translation, 1950). Not until about one-half century later did sociologists begin to perform laboratory experiments to further investigate the nature of small groups.

The number of persons in a group may determine the total potential of participation in the group, the ways a leader will be chosen, how the members feel about the group, whether agreement will be reached easily or with difficulty, and what resources are available to solve the group's problems. As group size increases, the knowledge and abilities potentially available to the group also increase. Larger groups also potentially allow members to meet more people; paradoxically, they also tend to allow members to remain more anonymous (Shaw, 1981).

As a group increases in size, the amount of time available for each individual member's participation decreases. As the group gets even larger, more members participate less and a small group of central persons emerges. Finally, the members who speak in discussions or who communicate in writing begin to address the group as a whole rather than individuals of the group (Bales et al., 1951). Not surprisingly, a leader is more likely to emerge in a large group than a small one (Hemphill, 1950). Perhaps this is because as groups grow the informal ways of planning and communicating that work in small groups are not so satisfactory.

As groups become large, they also are likely to develop explicit or formal structures that are increasingly elaborate. Rules are formalized in a charter and perhaps in a policy manual. Roles become distinct and clearly specialized as labor is divided among the participants. Multiple layers of leadership evolve. The group may establish important ties with other groups and organizations. As we see later, such highly structured groups may be better able to withstand turmoil, especially the crisis that can occur when the founder or key leader of a social movement dies. We will explore this aspect of the development of groups in more depth in the chapters on collective behavior and social movements (Chapter 7), religion (Chapter 14), and the economic and political institutions (Chapters 15 and 16).

Despite our culture's tendency toward large groups, individual group members are more satisfied with smaller groups, and smaller groups are more cohesive, tending toward primary rather than secondary relationships (Slater, 1970). Studies have found that large organizations usually suffer more from absenteeism and personnel turnover than do smaller organizations, which have more affectional ties. College students also indicate that they are more satisfied with smaller work groups.

A group often needs to reach consensus on an issue in order to go ahead with its work. ***Consensus*** *is agreement without dissension.* For example, a college homecoming committee needs first to agree on a theme before suggesting activities. As one might expect, studies have shown that consensus is easier to achieve in small groups (Hare, 1976).

EVEN AND ODD NUMBERS IN GROUPS. In groups having more than two members, there are strong differences between even-numbered and odd-numbered groups. In even-numbered groups division into two equal parts is possible, and disagreement and conflict prevail. In groups of odd numbers where a majority and minority opinion are more probable, there tends to be more agreement and open-minded discussion. People seem to size up their chances of being in the majority and act accordingly; in an even-numbered group members hold to their opinions more emphatically.

TRIADS. As anyone who grew up in a family of three children can testify, *a* ***triad,*** *or three-person group,* is also a special odd-numbered group.

Simmel noted that triads are unstable largely because of their tendency toward conflict in which two members side with each other against a third. This of course threatens the existence of the triad since the third may chose to leave rather than fight. Simmel also referred to the tertius gaudens, (literally the third who enjoys). Often a third party may be drawn into a dispute in a dyad as a mediator or an arbitrator. This third party, the tertius gaudens, can play an important role in helping to resolve the conflict in the dyad. In this case an important triad may be formed. But the third party may also use the power to their own ends by siding with one contestant against the other. As Simmel pointed out, the same dynamics which apply to small groups of individuals may apply to a small number of parties such as nations or other groups (1902, translated 1950).

The triad has been a favorite topic of social scientists. Theodore Caplow devoted an entire book to the cry from the back seat of a station wagon, *Two Against One* (1969). He describes all the various power coalitions possible in a group of three.

The ***dyad,*** *or two-person group,* is potentially the most intimate of groups. One theory gaining acceptance among couple counselors is that the potential for intimacy in the dyad is so great that it may be threatening. Consequently, members of a dyad frequently try to convert them to triads (triangulating), thus diluting the intensity of the intimacy (M. Bowen, 1978). For example, a mother may talk to her daughter about her son's career plans rather than approach her son directly. If the mother discussed the subject with the son instead, whether they agreed or disagreed about his choice, they would be closer in terms of understanding each other's wishes and beliefs. This closeness, although consciously sought by most people, may also be a threat to independence and self-sufficiency.

How Do Groups Influence Individuals?

People allow groups to influence their behavior; they routinely do things with a group that they would be embarrassed or afraid to do by themselves. The group seems to think something is a good idea, and everyone goes along.

Groups also influence their members' attitudes about themselves. People sometimes even join groups that specialize in fostering individual growth through group influence.

GROUP CONFORMITY

Groups generally reward members who conform to their norms. That is, they will accept and offer friendship to those who deal with issues the way the group does. The need to be accepted by the groups we belong to may even affect our perceptions of physical reality.

An individual will be more likely to conform to group opinion: (1) when the object being judged is ambiguous, (2) when his or her opinion will be stated publicly, (3) when the majority expressing the opinion is a large one, or (4) when the group is especially close-knit (Hare, 1976). The extent of human conformity to group norms has been clearly shown in several classic studies that address the issue of the effects of group norms on individual judgments.

A series of studies by Solomon Asch, for example, suggests that group opinion strongly influences indi-

Reference group. These young men measure their worth in in terms of how they compare to other members of their neighborhood group. (*Photo courtesy the author*)

vidual behavior and judgment. In these studies, individuals were induced to misjudge the length of lines (Asch, 1951). (See the "Close-Up on Research" for a fuller description of how this operated.) Although it may seem unlikely that what people see with their own eyes can be distorted by social relationships, this study and replications of it support this social fact.

George Homans views conformity to the group's ideas as an example of his *exchange theory,* which states that people try to maximize rewards and minimize costs in social transactions, much as they do in economic ones. Homans states that people will conform to a group's expectation if the cost of not conforming to that expectation is high and the rewards for conforming are high, or if any other combination of rewards and costs will yield a "profit." According to Homans's theory, people will not conform if the costs of conforming exceed the profits from conforming. For example, if a group of acquaintances asks you to stop at a restaurant with them after a meeting, but you know your family is expecting you for dinner, you will probably go home. The cost of your family's being angry would outweigh the reward of having a meal with some pleasant people whom you might never see again (Homans, 1974).

Another theorist suggests that *pressure toward group conformity,* or *deindividuation,* is closely linked to one's self-awareness (Diener, 1980). In order to direct our behavior according to our own standards rather than the group standard, and thus to resist group conformity, we must be aware of our own feelings, attitudes, and behaviors. When we feel submerged in a large group that has strong feelings of group unity and a focus on external goals, our feelings of self-awareness are reduced and we may be deindividuated.

When deindividuated, a person (1) shows reduced ability to regulate his or her behavior, (2) becomes less able to do long-term planning, (3) shows less concern about the opinions of others, and (4) tends toward impulsive, uninhibited behavior. These characteristics are implicit in the phrase "being swept along by the crowd," which describes the behavior of persons who have acted in a group as they would not have acted alone, as most of us have done at one time or another. Diener's theory shows clearly that groups can reduce restraint against impulsive behavior and can alter the feelings and thoughts of their members. This important topic will be continued in the section, "How Is Group Decision-Making Different from Individual Decision-Making?"

Conformity to group pressure can have an overall positive effect in some cases. For example, in a controversial study by Stanley Milgram (1964), subjects were asked to give what they thought were increasingly strong electric shocks to a victim who gave "wrong" answers, while the victim screamed and begged them to stop. When each was in the experimental situation alone, most subjects did as they were told by the experimenter and administered shocks they thought were real. However, later each subject was grouped with two of the experimenter's confederates who refused to shock the victim when the indicator went from "slight shock" to "danger: severe shock." In this group situation only four out of forty subjects continued to administer shocks to the victim. Apparently, having the group's permission *not* to conform to the experimenter's wishes helped a subject disobey the authority figure (the experimenter) and follow his or her own best judgment. If would seem, then, that the good or evil of group conformity must be evaluated in terms of the situation.

CLOSE-UP on • *RESEARCH* •

Solomon Asch on Group Pressure

The Researcher and the Setting

Social scientists as well as the public were shocked at the Nazis' success in the 1930s and 1940s in organizing large groups of people to engage systematically and routinely in atrocities against Jews and other groups. In the aftermath of the war many social scientists turned their attention to questions like, "What kind of people would do such a thing?" (Adorno, et al., 1950) Others, like Solomon Asch, asked how social circumstances might lead people to abandon their own best judgment. In a now-classic social psychology article Asch (1951) summarizes his findings about the effects of group pressure on individual judgment.

The Researcher's Goal

According to Asch, "Our immediate object was to study the social and personal conditions that induce individuals to resist or to yield to group pressures when the latter are perceived to be contrary to fact." For Asch this issue is central to the understanding of public opinion and propaganda. He criticizes "the current approach": "This mode of thinking has almost exclusively stressed the slavish submission of individuals to group forces, has neglected to inquire into their possibilities for independence and for productive relations with the human environment, and has virtually denied the capacity of men under certain conditions to rise above group passion and prejudice."

Theory and Concepts

Asch's work is an example of experimental research that is not guided by a specific systematic theory. "Today we do not possess an adequate theory of these central psycho-social processes. Empirical investigation has been predominantly controlled by general propositions concerning group influence which have as a rule been assumed but not tested." In other words, the experiments have been guided by intuition and common assumptions of how group pressure works.

Research Design

Asch devised an ingenious experiment that placed a male college student in a dilemma in which he was forced to choose between going against his own judgment or contradicting the unanimous judgment of eight peers. To create this situation, Asch used *confederates, persons who were previously told by the experimenter what to do or say.*

The subject and each confederate were given two sets of white cards (see Figure 5.1). One had a single black line on it. The other card had a set of three lines, each a different length. One of these three lines was the same length as the single line on the other card, and the other two lines were visibly longer or shorter. The experimenter first asked each confederate and then the subject to say which of the three lines matched the single line. In eighteen different trials, the confederates unanimously picked the wrong answer twelve times. (In a control group without confederates, each subject simply wrote down his judgments so that the experimenter could find out how many errors were made without group pressure.)

In this original version of the experiment there were two major variables. First, the amount of discrepancy between the true answer and the one the group unanimously reported as correct ranged from ¾ inch to 1¾ inch. Second, a different subject was used for each run of the experiment. In subsequent versions Asch also varied the number of confederates in each group from one to fifteen, and he considered the effect of nonunanimous majorities by using two subjects per session instead of one.

Findings

In the original version of the experiment, Asch found that 74 percent of the fifty subjects made errors either by agreeing with the group or by picking the line intermediate between the correct one and the one given by the group. However, subjects varied widely in their tendency to go along with a mistaken judgment. The average (mean) number of errors was 3.84 out of 12, or about 32 percent. Group pressure appeared to cause nearly all errors, because subjects in the control group who were not subjected to group pressure erred in only .6 percent of the judgments. Asch also found that the larger the error by the group, the less likely the subject was to be influenced by it.

When Asch varied the size of the groups, he found the subjects were most inclined to be swayed to a group error when a majority of four confederates unanimously reported wrong errors. When the group size was increased from four to fifteen confederates, the effect was slightly weakened, but when the group size was decreased from four to one, the subject was dramatically less likely to conform.

To summarize, Asch found that male college students would bias their judgment of factual material in 32 percent of the cases when seven others unanimously voiced the same inaccurate judgment. Individuals differed considerably in their willingness to go against their own judgment. In general, the influence of the group was strongest when there were four others who held a unanimous opinion. The greater the discrepancy between the group opinion and the truth, the less likely a subject was to go along with the group, and when someone else also gave correct responses, the subject was much more likely to respond accurately.

Implications

Asch's research illustrates the experimental approach in a laboratory setting and allows us to see the strength and weak-

FIGURE 5.1 What is the letter of the line segment in the right box that is the same length as the line segment in the left box? This is a typical example of the task Asch's subjects faced.

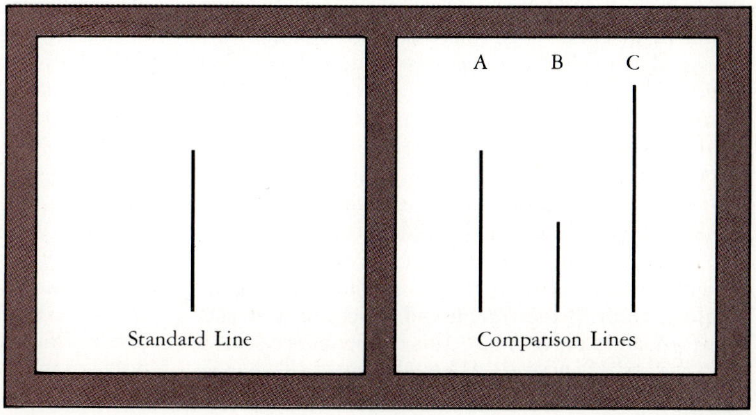

nesses of this approach. Experiments allow the researcher great control over many of the variables of interest. Asch was able to create a situation that would be difficult to observe naturally and to vary the amount of discrepancy between the "true" answer and the group opinion, the size of the group, and the strength of the majority opinion.

Among the weaknesses of the approach are that Asch's setting is contrived, his subjects were not a natural group but a set of strangers, and the task was a trivial one. From this research we cannot tell whether this effect would be as strong or stronger among people who know each other or how the subjects would respond if the judgment involved higher stakes or a moral rather than a factual decision. Yet, in spite of these shortcomings, his research suggests that group pressure may have strong influence over some individuals in certain settings.

Questions

1. How might Asch's research be modified to answer other questions about group pressure on individuals?
2. Where might Asch's findings be of significance to non-scientists?
3. Are Asch's findings more useful to people with good purposes or people with evil purposes? Why?

SOURCE Solomon E. Asch. 1951. Effects of group pressure upon the modification and distortion of judgments. In H. Guetzko (ed.), *Groups, Leadership, and Men.* Pittsburgh: Carnegie Press.

How Is Group Decision-Making Different from Individual Decision-Making?

From the number of committees in all aspects of our culture, one would think that conclusive proof exists that decision-making is more effective in a group setting. A look at the research shows, however, that although group decisions are *different* from individual decisions, they are not necessarily *better* than individual decisions.

The classic study of how groups make decisions suggested that groups generally move through four stages in making decisions (Bales and Strodtbeck, 1951). First, members *orient* themselves to each other and to the problem, collect information, and analyze the facts. Second, they begin to *evaluate* the various alternatives. In the third, or *control,* stage, members express negative and positive emotions and make a decision. In the final stage, more positive emotions are expressed in an effort to re-achieve group *solidarity* after a decision has been made by the majority against the minority. All of this seems logical today, because we are more attuned to our interactions within groups, but this research was revolutionary in its time.

More recent studies suggest that group decision-making, compared to individual decision-making, is a slow process. Groups have been tested against individuals on everything from simple recall to a complex planning problem and were found to be slower in each case (Fox and Lorge, 1962). This deliberateness, however, has its advantages. Although slower, it appears group decisions are more accurate in both simple and complex solutions (J. Davis and Restle, 1963).

THE RISKY SHIFT

People in a group may be willing to make decisions involving greater risk than they would alone. In one study twelve "life dilemma" problems were presented first to individuals and later to a group (Stoner, 1965). Most often the groups agreed on a solution that was more risky than the answer individuals in the group had decided upon alone. M. A. Wallach, N. Kogan, and D. J. Bem (1962) believed Stoner's results could have come about because he used industrial management students as subjects. To test this hypothesis, they replicated his study using liberal arts undergraduates. Again, there was a significant shift toward risk in the group decisions as compared to individual decisions. Sociologists use *risky shift* to describe the increase in willingness to make risky decisions found when individuals act as groups rather than independently.

Robert Brown has endeavored to explain the shift toward taking risks that groups appear to exhibit by pointing out that in the United States there is a positive cultural value attached to taking moderate risks (R. Brown, 1965). Americans tend to believe in striking out on their own, but they rely on others to help them set reasonable boundaries. Therefore, in these studies, it may be that the subjects listen to other group members during group discussion for clues to how the others feel and decide on a riskier alternative than they would individually. People may become brave when they hear other people talk as if they were brave.

GROUPTHINK

One of the most interesting studies of how groups make decisions is Irving Janis's work on the phenomenon of *groupthink,* or "the mode of thinking that persons engage in when concurrence seeking becomes so dominant in a cohesive group that it tends to override realistic appraisal of alternative courses of action" (Janis, 1971). Janis believes that groupthink is epidemic in the United States' governmental structure. He fears this may lead to poor decisions, judged in terms of reality rather than in terms of making the group members happy with each other. He uses President John Kennedy's decision to attempt to invade Cuba's Bay of Pigs, President Lyndon Johnson's escalation of the war in Vietnam, and Kimmel's failure to prepare for a Japanese attack on Pearl Harbor as examples of this phenomenon.

Janis outlines eight characteristics of groupthink:

1. An illusion of invulnerability.
2. Collective construction of rationales for actions.
3. Unquestioning belief in the inherent morality of the group, leading to ignoring the moral consequences of the group's behavior.
4. Stereotyped views of the leaders of other, opposing groups.
5. Use of pressure toward any individual who expresses doubts about the group's shared illusions or policies.
6. Avoiding deviance from the group consensus.
7. Illusion of unanimity within the group concerning all judgments by the group.
8. Acting as "mindguards" to protect the leader and other members from adverse information from the outside that could alter the group's decisions.

Later, Janis systematically studied situations in which he felt American presidents and their advisors made *good* decisions together. He found that the groupthink phenomenon does not occur when the leader takes precautions against it; for instance, by being receptive to the opinions of everyone in the group, by asking for advice outside of the group, and by specifically asking group members to troubleshoot certain options the group is considering (Janis, 1982).

If groupthink is indeed prevalent in high levels of our government groups, it can lead to making decisions out of loyalty to the group norm rather than from thoughtful consideration of the facts. That Janis's work has been highly publicized may help deter groups from acting in the groupthink mode. Leaders who follow his advice for avoiding groupthink, coupled with awareness of the ill effect of pressure to support a group's consensus, may cause group members to consider their motives and decisions more carefully.

What Is a Formal or Complex Organization?

Thus far we have discussed small groups, which approximate the characteristics of Cooley's primary groups, including relatively frequent and intense interactions and relatively lengthy relationships that require high degrees of allegiance. Such small, informal groups are common to all societies. In modern societies we find small groups in families, among circles of friends, and in neighborhoods, dormitories, and work settings.

However, modern industrial societies also contain a radically different type of group not found in simpler societies—the formal or complex organizations. *A **formal organization** is a group deliberately constructed to achieve specific objectives through explicitly defined roles and specified rules.* This group form is a major departure from the primary and kinship groups of earlier societies, and it comes closer to Cooley's idea of a secondary group. In comparison to primary groups, formal organizations normally involve less frequent and intense interactions and shorter relationships that command less allegiance.

The emergence of formal organizations is one of the most dramatic and important developments in our social history. Formal organizations are prominent features of modern societies and in many cases are a dominant influence in the culture. Most people in modern societies associate with one formal organization for education (school), another for religion (church or synagogue), another for work (business corporation), and still another for public matters (government or government agency). In fact, most of us were born and will die in a formal organization, the hospital.

Amitai Etzioni, well known for his work in this area, has shown the importance of three basic types of formal organizations: voluntary, coercive, and utilitarian (1961). ***Voluntary associations*** *are specialized formal organizations whose members join and leave of their own will but not necessarily without resistance.* Such organizations as amateur sports teams, hobby clubs, and fraternal or charitable organizations are voluntary associations. As organizations, voluntary associations are relatively informal; they exercise minor influence over their membership, rely on voluntary participation and contributions, and often have no explicit policies. ***Coercive organizations*** *are organizations that people are forced* *to join.* Prisons, public schools, and the nonvolunteer armed forces are coercive organizations. The most common type of organization is utilitarian. *People join **utilitarian organizations** for practical reasons, but they do so voluntarily.* For instance, most people "join" a business in order to make money.

What Are the Characteristics of Bureaucracy?

Many formal organizations also are bureaucracies. ***Bureaucracies** are large-scale, formal organizations that are highly differentiated and organized through elaborate policies and procedures in a hierarchy of authority.* The United States government is an example of a bureaucracy whose rules and regulations literally fill volumes.

Max Weber (1946) studied bureaucracies in settings as diverse as ancient Egypt, the Roman Empire, the Roman Catholic Church, China in the time of Shih Huang-ti (259–210 B.C.), and large modern capitalist enterprises. Weber saw the development of bureaucracy as part of the increasing rationalization of society. ***Rationality** refers to the deliberate calculation of the most efficient means to achieve a particular end.* Weber observed that societies tend to replace traditional patterns that are based on long standing, sometimes inefficient, practices with rational ones. For example, in traditional societies the monarch's eldest son often inherits his father's position even though he may not be the most qualified person. Modern states, which apply more rationality, are more likely to employ elections and thereby bestow power through a rational legal process. Besides this trend toward rationality, Weber named three other conditions necessary for the rise of bureaucracy: a money economy, a steady income to the bureaucracy, such as through taxation, and a large population base.

Weber also created a scientific definition of bureaucracy, which carefully outlines the important characteristics of this kind of organization. Weber's description is what sociologists call an *ideal type,* which in this case means "the idea of the bureaucratic organization in its essence or conceptual form." An ideal type gives a picture of what a bureaucracy (or any phenomenon) would look like if all of the characteristics were present in their essential form.

Weber describes what he believes to be the central characteristics of bureaucracy. No actual organization conforms perfectly to his description, any more than any society conforms perfectly to its culture. Weber's characteristics are only *approximated* by bureaucracies. Also, the term *ideal type* does *not* imply that bureaucracy is the "best" style of human relations.

Weber believed that government civil service agencies are among the clearest examples of bureaucracies. Today so much of our life has become bureaucratic that we can use the restaurant industry as a livelier illustration of Weber's characteristics of bureaucracy. We shall compare what we encounter in today's "fast-food" hamburger restaurant to what we would have found in a small "mom and pop" food stand of the late ninteenth century. We will let Louis' Lunch of New Haven, Connecticut, represent the nonbureaucratic, or primary, group mode. Louis' has been operated by the same family for three generations and seems to be a living example of what the business was like nearly a century ago. The proprietor claims, quite plausibly, that his grandfather was the inventor of the modern hamburger. (Louis' makes an excellent site for a field study of this issue for those who find themselves in New Haven.) For the contrasting example, any of several nationally marketed hamburger chains clearly exhibit Weber's six characteristics of bureaucracy.

FIXED DIVISION OF LABOR

Bureaucracies are characterized by a division of the task at hand into "fixed and official jurisdictional areas which are generally ordered by rules . . . or administrative regulations" (Weber, 1946).

In the fast-food setting the division of labor is distinct and specialized. At the counter we meet a clerk who takes orders, collects money, and fills an order by placing food from supply areas on a tray or in a bag. Backstage are other specialists: cooks preparing burgers, cooks preparing fries, and other workers filling the drink orders or wrapping sandwiches. In the dining area cleaning specialists remove debris and wipe tables.

Although Louis' Lunch is remarkably carefully organized, we do not encounter such a highly specialized division of labor. The husband and wife owners alternate and mix the above roles so that the customer often orders directly from the cook who wraps and serves the fare, refusing payment until after the food has been eaten at its peak of flavor. At clean-up time it is again the owners who take the responsibility.

When Weber described the "fixed division of labor" he meant that the work of the organization is divided into jobs with clearly defined duties. Typically the jobs are not designed with a particular person in mind; instead of the job fitting the person, the person is to fit the job. The positions might involve some authority, but the power they carry would be clearly limited. Rather than being the sort of position that could be passed on to the next generation, people are appointed to these official positions on the basis of technical competence. They are typically reimbursed through a salary with an opportunity for career advancement through a lifelong career.

HIERARCHY OF OFFICES. The second characteristic of bureaucracies is a hierarchy of offices. In a bureaucracy each position is nested in a vertical authority structure so that there is a "supervision of the lower offices by the higher ones" (Weber, 1946).

Amid the hustle and bustle of the fast-food restaurant wanders an individual without obvious purpose: the manager. Occasionally he or she gives orders or lends a hand where things are not moving according to plan. This person has authority over the others, and one may also know or sense that the manager is serving as the agent of the owner-operator who, in turn, is one element in a large hidden bureaucracy organized to provide hamburgers by the billion. We see only part of the base of this vast social mountain, and somewhere at its peak are executives whose decisions touch the lives of tens of thousands of employees.

At Louis' the hierarchy doesn't stretch so high, nor can we even see one. Maybe the husband part of this team has more authority over the wife than vice versa, but that is not obvious nor does the authority ever reach the point of one dictating to the other hours of work, tasks, or terms of employment.

The hierarchy of offices Weber mentions involves a chain of command running up (or down) through a series of positions. In a large firm this might extend upward from worker to department manager, through division manager, on to the vice-president, the president, and the board of directors. These positions constitute a hierarchy of authority, which is a distinct characteristic of the firm independent of the people who fill the offices at a particular time.

WRITTEN DOCUMENTS

Another significant aspect of bureaucratic organization is written documentation, or red tape.

The fast-food industry's documents are largely hidden from the customer except for a receipt that documents the date, time of sale, foods purchased, and prices. The employee may punch out or fill in a time card. At higher levels of authority the trickle of paperwork becomes a stream of financial accounting, food and container orders, and reports such as those from specialists who travel through the network of restaurants noting how friendly the clerks acted and other observations.

Undoubtedly Louis' must create some written documents, but many of these are to satisfy the purposes of outside bureaucracies such as the Internal Revenue Service. Here the cook keeps track of the orders mentally and trusts customers to report accurately what food they consumed when they pay after eating. Orders for supplies are phoned in to local suppliers. No written accounts of hours worked or friendly greetings extended is made or needed.

When Weber said bureaucracy is characterized by written documents he meant that bureaucracies routinely rely on communication by letters and memorandums, extensive forms and record keeping, and often governance through printed policy manuals and statements.

MANAGEMENT BY TRAINED EXPERTS

Weber recognized the logic of having officially *trained* experts manage the affairs of the bureaucracy. Viewed from inside a vast hamburger empire it seems to make sense that business school graduates can bring the public a better burger at a lower price than the seeming amateurs with a tiny operation in New Haven. The point is that bureaucracies are commonly inhabited by a new type of worker who has been *specially educated* in the art of directing other people's activities.

OFFICIAL WORK AS THE PRIMARY ACTIVITY

The fifth important characteristic of a bureaucracy is that management, which Weber called "official work," is the primary occupation of the executive, and it is not part of the activities of all workers. These full-time managers, or executives, are common in large corporations, including national restaurant chains, and in government agencies, schools, and religious organizations.

One might have a hard time convincing the folks at Louis' that they could really benefit from the services of a full-time executive. Weber points out, however, that bureaucracies typically employ officials whose full-time work is administration. Thus administration becomes a full-time occupation.

MANAGEMENT BY RULES

Weber's sixth characteristic of bureaucracy is management through set rules, rather than through orders that may change from case to case. Hence the common bureaucratic excuse, "I'm sorry, but I don't *make* the rules, I just *enforce* them."

The customer may not see the rules in print at the local fast-food palace, but the fact that if you've seen one Burger King you've seen them all testifies that somewhere, someone has made up a rule book. Rules dictate what employees wear, how customers are greeted, how many ounces of fries makes a giant order of fries, and so forth.

Overspecialization? In Charlie Chaplin's "Modern Times" work has become so highly specialized that it drives Charlie nuts. He becomes so obsessed with tightening the two nuts on every part that goes by that when he is accidentally sucked into the machinery he continues to tighten bolts rather than to seek escape. (*The Museum of Modern Art/Film Stills Archives*)

An observant student of social life would note that there are rules at Louis' as well. The distinction between a bureaucracy and a primary group is that a bureaucracy's rules are usually more impersonal, more pervasive, and more specific. In a primary group setting such as Louis' there is more room for management through leadership. The rules can be adjusted for the person or the situation, and they can be left loosely drawn. In a bureaucracy with thousands of clerks, it may be imperative to define clearly all important procedures. Not all managers may have the ability to lead effectively in a flexible style. Having a thick rule book may be an attractive alternative to trusting that enough effective leaders can be found to manage all operations of the bureaucracy.

When Weber points to management by rules he identifies one of the most prominent features of bureaucracies. The bureaucracy operates according to officially enacted rules. These rules may govern the terms of employment and dismissal, the duties of various officials and their powers, and the day-to-day work routines. Generally, these rules are not easily changed even by the people who administer them.

Weber demonstrates that bureaucracy differs greatly from earlier ways of organizing groups, but is this new way better or worse? Of course, contrasting "old" and "new" styles of organizing a hamburger restaurant probably reveals our somewhat romantic bias for the good old days. Weber himself was no fan of bureaucracy, although he devoted much of his life to studying it. Weber saw bureaucracy more as an inevitable development rather than as a step toward Utopia. His statement written more than half a century ago still seems current and realistically ominous:

> Imagine the consequences of that comprehensive bureaucratization and rationalization which already today we see approaching. Already now . . . in all economic enterprises run on modern lines, rational calculation is manifest at every stage. By it, the performance of each individual worker is mathematically measured, each man becomes a little cog in the machine and aware of this, his one preoccupation is whether he can become a bigger cog. . . . It is apparent that today we are proceeding towards an evolution which resembles [the ancient kingdom of Egypt] in every detail, except that it is built on other foundations, on technically more perfect, more rationalized, and therefore much more mechanized foundations. The problem which besets us now is not: how can this evolution be changed?—for that is impossible, but: what will come of it? (Weber, quoted in Bendix, 1961)

Weber recognizes the paradoxical nature of the bureaucratic creation. On the one hand, bureaucracy promises to free us of our materialistic burdens; on the other hand, it enslaves our very personalities toward its impersonal ends. In the next section we discuss some of the advantages and disadvantages that bureaucracy has to offer society and the individual. In the "Close-Up on Theory" for this chapter, Robert Merton amplifies Emile Durkheim's idea that bureaucracy may have undesirable effects on the human personality.

THE PETER PRINCIPLE

One tongue-in-cheek theory, the Peter Principle, has come to be used by sociologists in discussing organizations because it so clearly articulates some basic principles of bureaucracy. The Peter Principle states that "in a hierarchy, every employee tends to rise to his or her level of incompetence" (Peter and Hull, 1969). Because bureaucracy is based upon a hierarchical system of power distribution, the principle suggests that bureaucratic structure itself may lead to the destruction of the bureaucracy.

Lawrence Peter and Raymond Hull observed that people who do good work at one level in a bureaucracy are likely to be promoted to the next level. This process will continue until the person does *not* do good work and can no longer be promoted. Unfortunately, however, this leaves many people working at one level higher than their level of competence.

Several social scientists have discussed the Peter Principle and its ramifications. Blau and Meyer (1971) extend it by suggesting that if people have reached their level of incompetence and feel insecure about their performance, they may make the problem worse by concentrating on rules and regulations instead of on perfecting their work on the task at hand. Attention to rules keeps such people from worrying about whether or not they can actually do the work, but it will probably reduce the quality of their work even more, because they now have even less time and energy for getting it done.

What Are the Functions and Dysfunctions of Bureaucracy?

Bureaucratic organization is *functional* in some ways, meaning it contributes to the survival and maintenance of society and its members. Dividing labor, organizing it in a rational way, and institutionalizing it through sets of rules are all methods designed to accomplish tasks efficiently. A list of the major functions of bureaucracy would include the following:

1. Bureaucracy functions to allow a society to accomplish very large and complicated tasks, such as taking the population census, tracking crime rates, and collecting taxes. Very complex tasks cannot usually be accomplished without a high degree of organization. The Apollo project, for example, could not have succeeded in putting men on the moon without a highly structured and rational organization.
2. Bureaucracy often provides an efficient means of performing repetitive tasks. For example, large agricultural corporations that employ mass production techniques and bureaucratic organization can produce food at lower prices than can a small farm.
3. Bureaucracy also functions to create and maintain order in society. Governments, schools, and churches provide clear rules and social controls to induce "good" behavior and discourage "bad" behavior. This facilitates the routine functioning of society and provides at least some meaning, direction, and security for the individual.

But bureaucracy can also be dysfunctional. Whereas bureaucracy in some ways leads to order (or the appearance of order), it also can facilitate large-scale conflict, such as that between unions and management, between political parties, and among nations. Also, as Weber was well aware, bureaucracy can be a limiting force on the individual's freedom. Some of the dysfunctions of bureaucracy include:

1. Fixed rules generally work well, but they may be inappropriate or even harmful. For example, a hospital's insistence tht entering patients fill out the appropriate forms before care is rendered may occasionally endanger a patient's health. Once rules are established, the reasons for them are sometimes forgotten, and they can become an end in themselves rather than simply the means to an end. (See the "Close-Up on Theory.")
2. The hierarchy of authority can slow the upward communication of bad news. Subordinates may try to hide information that might reflect badly on them from their superiors, and this makes effective management difficult. For instance, when a teacher discovers students cheating, he or she may be reluctant to tell the supervisor for fear the supervisor could think the teacher had done a poor job of preparing or administering exams.
3. Authority relationships tend to promote antagonism between superiors and subordinates (Dahrendorf, 1959). This antagonism often becomes institutionalized within a bureaucratic structure. Labor unions, for example, may be a direct offshoot of bureaucratic commercial organization.

4. Bureaucratic organizations tend to perpetuate themselves even after they have served their original purpose. The classic example is the National Foundation for Infantile Paralysis (the March of Dimes), which successfully sought the elimination of polio and had to find other reasons to exist after a vaccine for polio was developed.
5. In bureaucracies that provide services, such as welfare departments, hospitals, and schools, it is difficult to measure efficiency. There is a strong tendency for bureaucratic organization to grow dysfunctionally, for various managers to attempt to build "empires" by hiring more and more employees.
6. As an organization grows and its bureaucratic structure mechanizes human relations, people often begin to feel like cogs in a machine rather than persons. The bureaucratic division of labor may be functional from the viewpoint of society's material needs, but it may be dysfunctional to individuals who feel a need for meaningful work.
7. Dividing labor among different people will inevitably increase the importance of some of the people. Thus a corporation president's work is considered exciting and important; the president's opinion counts the most; and the president's salary, office, and prestige are the largest in the organization. At the same time, the importance of people at the bottom of the organizational chart is reduced. Formal organizations can make society materially better off, but at the expense of creating a greater gulf between those at the top and those at the bottom.
8. In the hands of those who would exploit their fellow human beings, bureaucracy may be an awesome tool, as Nazi death camps illustrate.

In the "Close-Up on Theory" below, Robert Merton elaborates on how bureaucracy promotes a personality shift toward narrow-mindedness and rigid thinking.

CLOSE-UP on • *THEORY* •

Robert Merton on How Bureaucracy Affects Personality

The Theorist and the Setting

Several early sociologists, including the pioneering German sociologist, Max Weber, wrote extensively about bureaucracy, including both its advantages for society and its potentially dehumanizing qualities. Here a mid–twentieth century sociologist, Robert K. Merton, theorizes about the effects of bureaucracy on personality.

The Theorist's Goal

Merton is concerned with explaining how bureaucracy emphasizes certain personality traits, and how these traits contribute to bureaucratic inefficiency.

Concepts and Propositions

Using Weber's definition, Merton describes the following characteristics of bureaucracy: (1) a clear-cut division of labor, (2) a set of rules for control, (3) the assignment of people to positions through impersonal means such as examination, (4) a hierarchy of salaried experts, and (5) governance by clearly defined rules that eliminate the need for specific instructions in each case.

Although Merton refers to "personality," in the title of this essay, he actually addresses certain personality traits or attitudes, including rigid conformity to the rules, timidness toward authority, and a domineering posture toward subordinates.

Merton's theory of bureaucracy and personality can be summarized in five propositions:

Proposition 1: "An effective bureaucracy demands reliability of response and strict devotion to regulations" (Merton, 1957, p. 198).

Proposition 2: "Such devotion to the rules leads to their transformation into absolutes: they are no longer conceived as relative to a set of purposes" (p. 199).

Proposition 3: "This [exaggerated concern for following the rules] interferes with ready adaptation under special conditions not clearly envisioned by those who drew up the general rules" (p. 200).

Proposition 4: "The impersonal treatment of affairs which are at times of great personal significance to the client, gives rise to the charge of 'arrogance' and 'haughtiness' of the bureaucrat" (p. 202).

Proposition 5: "The bureaucrat acts as a representative of the power and prestige of the entire structure. . . . This often leads to an actually or apparently domineering attitude" (p. 203).

To further clarify Merton's theory, let's apply these propositions about bureaucracy to education. Bureaucracy was introduced in education during the nineteenth century in order to facilitate educating the masses. Before that time, education was largely a matter of tutoring the children of the elite, and lessons were adapted to each student. In the bureaucratic public schools, the same lesson had to be taught simultaneously and repeatedly to scores of students; the students adapted to the lesson.

As Proposition 1 predicts, rules were considered necessary to achieve the goal of mass education. Students were required to come to each session and to arrive on time. They sat quietly and followed directions for a prescribed lesson. Teachers were expected to be impartial. They governed the class by clear rules and evaluated progress impersonally through such devices as written examinations. Teachers were responsible for disciplining students and were, in turn, subject to the rules and regulations of their department heads, principals, and school boards.

Adaptation of the masses and concentration on rules are still considered necessary in public schools. In Merton's words, "If the bureaucracy is to operate successfully, it must attain a high degree of reliability of behavior [and] an unusual degree of conformity with prescribed patterns of action" (p. 199).

As Proposition 2 suggests, the focus often becomes order for its own sake. It is easier to observe order than learning, so teachers may be rewarded for quiet classes even if little learning goes on. Similarly, teachers may be penalized for disorderly classes even if a great deal of learning takes place.

In the same manner, students may be encouraged to memorize presented material rather than to develop skills in creating ideas and finding facts, because the multiple-choice exam is a common tool in bureaucratic educations. Test scores become the goal even if the tests do not measure meaningful learning (p. 200).

A rigid bureaucracy cannot adapt to unusual situations, as Merton said in Proposition 3. In bureaucratic schools, especially talented students such as Thomas Edison may be viewed as behavior problems, because their methods of learning do not conform to the rules. Students who have not made normal progress are often promoted with their age group in the interest of avoiding disruptions in the classroom. This rigid adherence to rules is counterproductive to the major goal of education in two ways. Misplaced students are frustrated by lessons beyond their grasp, and students who have little hope of success may create diversions and disturbances for others.

It is difficult for the teacher (or bureaucrat) to take into account all students' (or clients') personal concerns. A teacher who is brusque in answering a question, who doesn't call on a student whose hand is raised, or who is insensitive to a student comment can be mislabeled as arrogant. Having authority over a group can also contribute to real arrogance over time, which is what Merton warns of in Proposition 4.

Although a teacher is in one sense just another person, he or she is in another sense the representative of the entire school system. The teacher, as Merton points out in Proposition 5, can invoke the power, authority, and resources of the school system in dealing with what is seen as misbehavior. In this situation it is easy for the teacher to seem or actually to become domineering.

To summarize, Merton argues that bureaucracies tend to get entangled in their own rules, partly due to the strong incentives they create to conform to these rules. This tends to reinforce timid and rigid attitudes among members of a bureaucracy. Furthermore, the built-in emphasis on depersonalization tends to make bureaucrats act as if they were cold and arrogant, even when they are not. Finally, the fact that each individual bureaucrat represents the authority of the entire bureaucracy makes it easy for them to appear domineering or actually to become domineering.

Table 5.1 illustrates Merton's theory. Note that bureaucracy affects personality in a way that is eventually detrimental to the bureaucracy. If bureaucracy does have this effect, one possibility is that it may eventually self-destruct.

Interpretation

Merton's theory is similar to structural functionalism, although he focuses on the dysfunctions rather than the functions of bureaucracy. As with most theories, Merton does not attempt to state how strong these effects are or to conclude whether the dysfunctions of bureaucracy outweigh its functions. One

TABLE 5.1 Merton's Theory Regarding Bureaucracy and Personality

Bureaucratic Characteristics	Personality Traits	Outcomes
Explicit rules with strong incentives to conform	Rigid and timid attitudes	Inflexibility and inefficiency
Impersonal treatment	Actual or perceived "coldness"	Conflict and dissatisfied clients
Each bureaucrat representing the bureaucracy to the public	Actual or perceived domineering attitude	Conflict and dissatisfied clients

could predict the eventual collapse of a bureaucracy, because the theory suggests it will eventually become rigid and inefficient and will be attacked by dissatisfied clients. One might also use Merton's theory to change bureaucracies so their benefits are maximized as their liabilities are minimized. The next section develops this idea. Because the world is becoming increasingly bureaucratic, Merton's theory is as relevant today as when it was introduced in 1957.

Questions

1. What is in the future for bureaucracies? Why?
2. Merton has concentrated on personality traits—such as rigidity, timidity, arrogance, and dominance—which are displayed within the bureaucratic setting. Would you expect the bureaucrat to take these *outside* the bureaucracy to family, friends, and religious groups? Why or why not?
3. Suppose we found research evidence showing that persons working in bureaucracies have more rigid personalities than those who do not. How could you establish whether (a) the bureaucracy made them more rigid or (b) a bureaucracy attracts rigid employees?

SOURCE Robert K. Merton, 1957. "Bureaucratic Structure and Personality." Chapter 5 of *Social Theory and Social Structure*, Glencoe, Ill.: Free Press.

How Does Worker Input Affect Bureaucratic Structures?

In its classical form bureaucratic authority is a one-way street with subordinates taking orders from superiors. Newer forms of bureaucracy try to remedy some of the dysfunctions built into this rigid model. Recently businesspeople have begun to suggest that more worker input may be good not only for morale but for business.

UP THE ORGANIZATION

Robert T. Townsend is a thoroughly successful businessman. He explains his success by contrasting the old system of managerial thought, called Theory X, with how he thinks the business world works best in the twentieth century, called Theory Y. Many of Townsend's suggestions, which may seem radical to traditional businesspeople, are now being supported by research.

The presence of fewer supervisors and more worker integration into the decision-making of a business may increase productivity (Dickson, 1975). Workers may be more satisfied with their jobs, and presumably do them better and more efficiently, when they have some control over their work situation (Tannenbaum et al., 1974). In addition, a study of hierarchical power arrangements like those generally seen in bureaucratic organizations found that workers closest to the top of the hierarchy had the greatest motivation to work hard for the organization (Tannenbaum et al., 1974). In Townsend's words (1970, pp. 137–142):

> Until the last forty or fifty years the average churchgoer, soldier, and factory worker was uneducated and dependent on orders from above. And authority carried considerable weight because disobedience brought the death penalty or its equivalent.
>
> From the behavior of people in these early industrial organizations we arrived at the following assumptions on which all modern organizations are still operating: (Theory X)
>
> 1. People hate work.
> 2. They have to be driven and threatened with punishment to get them to work toward organization objectives.
> 3. They like security, aren't ambitious, want to be told what to do, dislike responsibility.
>
> You don't think we are operating on these assumptions? Consider:
>
> 1. Office hours nine to five for everybody except the fattest cats at the top. Just a giant cheap timeclock. (Are we buying brains or hours?)
> 2. Unilateral promotions. For more money and a bigger title I'm expected to jump at the chance of moving my family to New York City. I run away from the friends and a lifestyle in Denver that have made me and my family happy and effective. (Organization comes first; individuals must sacrifice themselves to its demands.)
> 3. Hundreds of millions of dollars are spent annually "communicating" with employees. The message always boils down to: "Work hard, obey orders. We'll take care of you." (That message is obsolete by fifty years and wasn't very promising then.)
>
> The result of our outmoded organizations is that we're still acting as if people were uneducated peasants. Much of the work done today would be more suitable for young children or mental defectives.

And look at the rewards we're offering our people today: higher wages, medical benefits, vacations, pensions, profit sharing, bowling and baseball teams. *Not one can be enjoyed on the job.* You've got to leave work, get sick, or retire first. No wonder people aren't having fun on the job.

So what are the valid assumptions for present-day circumstances?: (Theory Y)

1. People *don't* hate work. It's as natural as rest or play.
2. They don't *have* to be forced or threatened. If they commit themselves to mutual objectives, they'll drive themselves more effectively than you can drive them.
3. But they'll commit themselves only to the extent they can see ways of satisfying their ego needs ("Gee, I'm terrific. Aren't I? Yes, you are"), and their development needs ("Gee, I'm better than I was last year").

When I took over in 1962, after thirteen years Avis had never made a profit. Three years later the company had grown internally (not by acquisitions) from $30 million sales to $75 million sales, and had made successive annual profits of $1 million, $3 million, and $5 million. If I had anything to do with this, I ascribe it all to my application of Theory Y. . . .

When I became head of Avis, I was assured that no one at headquarters was any good, and that my first job was to start recruiting a whole new team. Three years later, Hal Geneen, the President of ITT (which had just acquired Avis), after meeting everybody and listening to them in action for a day, said, "I've never seen such depth of management; why I've already spotted three chief executive officers!" You guessed it. Same people. I'd brought in only two new people, a lawyer and an accountant. . . .

Get to know your people. What they do well, what they enjoy doing, what their weaknesses and strengths are, and what they want and need to get from their job. And then try to create an organization around your people, not jam your people into those organization-chart rectangles. The only excuse for organization is to maximize the chance that each one, working with others, will get what he needs for growth in his job. You can't motivate people. That door is locked from the inside. You *can* create a climate in which most of your people will motivate themselves to help the company reach its objectives. Like it or not, the only practical act is to adopt Theory Y and get going.

Ethnic diversity. Sociologists like Merlin Pope study how best to manage work organizations which are becoming increasingly ethnically diverse. (*Photo courtesy the author*)

THEORY Z

A glimpse at Figure 5.2 will quickly explain why Americans might be interested in studying Japanese business practices. For, as the chart indicates, the Japanese have been winning the "productivity race" for nearly thirty years. Unfortunately, growth in productivity for the U.S. worker has been the lowest of the industrialized nations represented on the chart.

The fact that Japanese industry is fast outpacing other industrialized nations has focused attention on its management techniques. William G. Ouchi studied Japanese techniques and formulated "Theory Z." This theory contains basic principles intrinsic to Japanese culture but that Ouchi feels are capable of being transplanted, with modifications, to the United States (Ouchi, 1982). Ouchi feels that "Z organizations" can improve worker productivity, quality, and job satisfaction. Ouchi contrasts several characteristics of Japanese and American organizations in Table 5.2.

Ouchi describes these conditions as inherent in each country's cultural traditions and stemming from a variety of historical and social situations. Because of this, for instance, Japanese managers have difficulty managing Americans: "All the Japanese here have had problems managing the Americans. The Japanese ex-

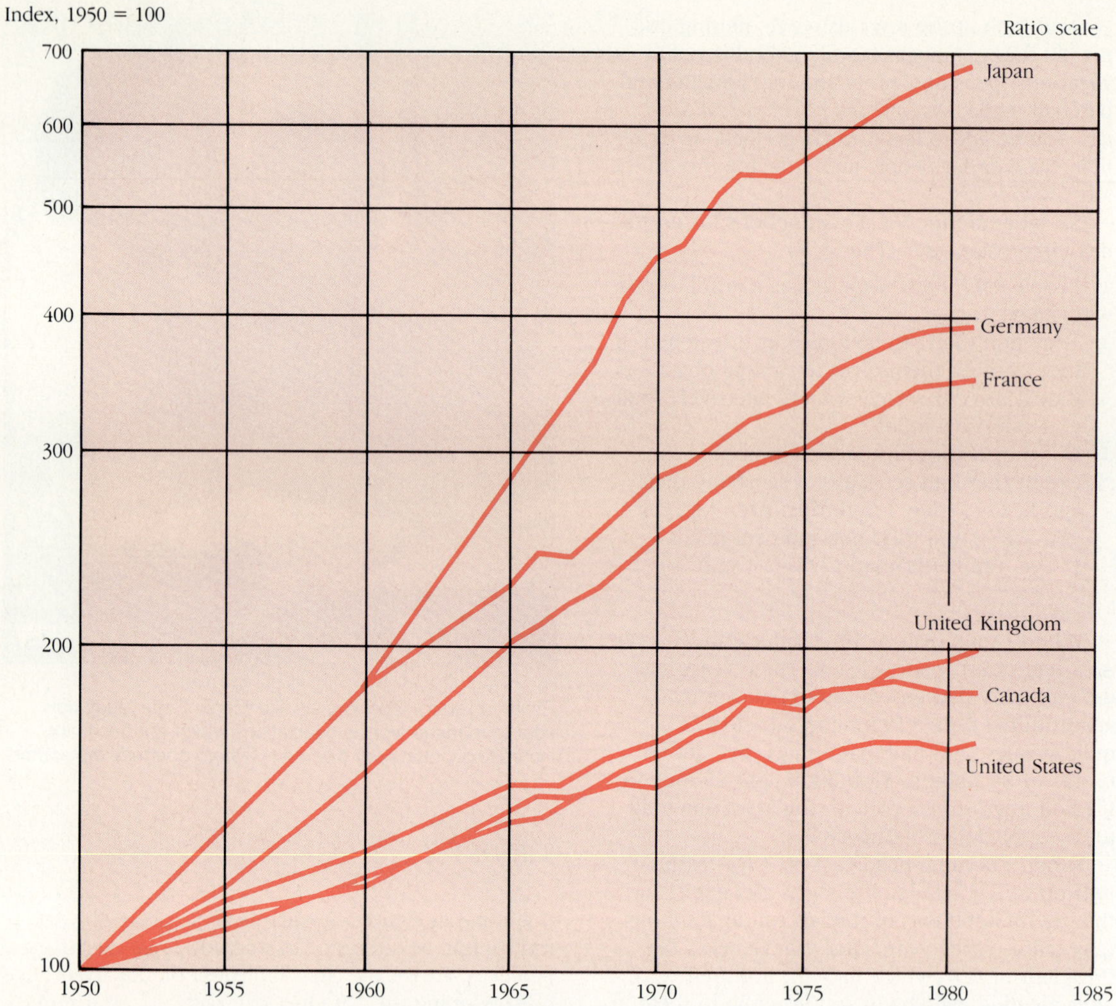

FIGURE 5.2 Growth in Worker Productivity. Using 1950 as a base of comparison, the productivity of the average laborer has increased more rapidly in Japan than these other industrialized nations. Gains have been smallest in the United States. (Productivity here is measured by dividing the gross national product by the number of employees.) (SOURCE Bureau of Labor Statistics)

pect their subordinates to think, but the American attitude is 'You tell me what to do and I'll do it—but it's your responsibility' " (R. Johnson and Ouchi, 1974, p. 19).

Ouchi does not see these differences affecting only the marketplace. They also appear in the administration of the federal bureaucracy, which most of us have tackled at one time or another (Ouchi, 1982, pp. 92–93):

> In a sense the federal bureaucracy is a microcosm of our society. Here our values of equality of opportunity for all people are crystallized. . . . What this means is that the government must promulgate a series of bureaucratic rules that should ordinarily prevent, insofar as humanly possible, the application of capricious or unfair standards that will harm women and ethnic minorities. . . . They cannot leave any rule ambiguous . . . since that leaves open the possibility of the manager arriving at a discriminatory interpretation. . . . Thus the bureaucratic rules are not only explicit and inflexible, but also constraining and impersonal. . . . The price we pay, of course, is in inefficiency, inflexibility, indolence, and impersonality. All too often

TABLE 5.2 Characteristics of Business Organizations in Japan and the United States (after Ouchi, 1982)

Japanese	American
Lifetime employment	Short-term employment
Slow evaluation and promotion	Rapid evaluation and promotion
Nonspecialized career paths	Specialized career paths
Implicit control mechanisms	Explicit control mechanisms
Collective decision-making	Individual decision-making
Collective responsibility	Individual responsibility
Wholistic concern and collective values	Preference for the concept of the individual self
Homogeneous cultural and philosophic background of organization members	Heterogeneous cultural backgrounds and philosophies of organization members
Bottom-up innovative path	Top-down innovative path

a federal bureau will fail to do that which makes sence because common sense does not fit the rules. All too often bureaucrats, trained not to allow personal values to intrude on decisions, will treat us, their customers, in an unfeeling manner. All too often the machinery of government will respond slowly and inefficiently with poor coordination between agencies, because they have learned not to trust one another, not to rely on subtlety, not to develop intimacy.

Despite these basic differences, Ouchi feels that American managers can adapt to Theory Z if they wish to increase productivity in their organizations. He sees this as a process of learning to emphasize all the "Seven S's."

The Seven S's (from Pascale and Athos, 1981) are:

1. *Strategy*. Plan a course of action that leads to the allocation of scarce resources, over time, to reach identified goals.
2. *Structure*. How the organizational chart would be characterized (functional, decentralized, and the like).
3. *Systems*. Proceduralized reports and routinized processes such as meeting formats.
4. *Staff*. "Demographic" description of important personnel categories within the firm.
5. *Style*. How key managers behave in achieving the organization's goals and the cultural style of the organization.
6. *Skills*. Distinctive capabilities of key personnel or the firm as a whole.
7. *Superordinate goals*. The significant meanings of guiding concepts that an organization transmits to its members.

Ouchi feels American companies tend to favor the first three items on the list: strategy, structure, and systems and to neglect the remaining four, thereby inhibiting morale, development, and growth. For example, Japanese industry often uses "quality circles," or small groups of workers and managers within one department who meet regularly to share ideas about increasing productivity and improving working conditions. The use of such techniques is growing in the United States, and in some cases has reduced personnel problems and increased productivity.

Ouchi recognizes several weaknesses of Type Z organizations. Specifically, they experience some loss of professionalism, because they rely on employees who are more generalized in their abilities. They could become racist and sexist, in keeping with their idea of developing a homogeneous organizational culture and shared value orientation. Finally, adopting Type Z organization is a long-term process, requiring full commitment by all people involved.

Many managers are choosing to work with the weaknesses of a Type Z organization in an attempt to increase their productivity and to remain competitive. The fact that Japanese companies now own over 500 plants in the United States and employ over 73,000 workers will increase American familiarity with Japanese methods (*Wilson Quarterly*, Winter, 1984). Early studies show mixed results in applying these techniques to American businesses, but the topic is certain to be one of continuing importance in the study of the organizational structure of bureaucracies.

Sociologists at Work

MERLIN POPE
COUNSELS ETHNICALLY DIVERSE FIRMS ON PRODUCTIVITY
Pope and Associates
Cincinnati, Ohio

Merlin Pope, a Yale-trained sociologist, applies his sociological skills to improving relations in the workplace between people of diverse social backgrounds and ethnic groups, and between men and women. Pope and Associates, launched fourteen years ago, helps many organizations, including Proctor and Gamble, Bristol Myers, Citibank, and General Motors raise their productivity by improving the relations between people from different backgrounds.

How Did You Decide to Use Your Sociology in the Business World?

I see an incredible opportunity in industry to use some of the same skills I was taught as a sociologist in an applied setting. I learned to observe patterns of behavior, to discern them, to look at relationships, and to understand what variables impact and cause things to happen. Those are the same skills that one needs to develop planned change in an organization. My interest is in the area of diversity.

What Is Your Specific Focus?

We are trying to move companies beyond what I call the traditional notions of affirmative action. [Affirmative action refers to federal laws designed to assure that firms seek to remedy the effects of past discrimination by actively seeking to include members of minority groups.] Unfortunately some organizations have done affirmative action from the point of special treatment for women and minorities, whereas what these groups really need is true equal opportunity.

Consider working in an industrial setting today as running track. Let's say that you and I are going to participate in a race in which I've got hurdles and you do not. Some people would suggest giving me a head start to compensate for the hurdles. When you do that you undermine my credibility, because when I don't come across the line at the same time you do, people say, "Merlin, you had a head start." You also undermine my development, because I have been denied the same experiences you had that are necessary for greater organizational responsibilities, and you generate resentment. We will never know who is the faster runner until we remove the hurdles through cooperation and collaboration on the things we are doing. Good affirmative action has got to be based on actively creating true equal opportunity, that is, removing the barriers, and holding people accountable for interacting cooperatively together, rather than giving some a head start.

Removing structural barriers is critically important. Most organizations have moved women and minorities up the organization vertically, without paying much attention to horizontal integration. You must lay the groundwork in terms of horizontal integration by functions to achieve true vertical integration. Most organizations are laid out in concentric circles, from the most central functions, such as finance, sales, and advertising, to the most peripheral functions, such as personnel. If you were to map women and minorities across those functions, you would find that they are around the periphery. People at the top of the organization come from the core, not the edge of the circle. You never really get good vertical integration of an organization until you lay groundwork through horizontal integration across functions.

What Are the Challenges in Your Work?

This whole issue of diversity is very subtle. It is sometimes as simple as: you and I are not comfortable interacting together, so we get out of interactions as soon as possible. But I end up losing your years of experience in how to make something happen in a corporation, so I don't get the same level of informal training that someone might get who has fewer barriers than myself.

The times when I have grown the most personally have been those times when I had professors or managers who patted me on the back when I deserved it but figuratively kicked me in the behind when I needed it. Typically the second component is missing in these difficult interfaces, because you do not have the relationship to allow it to happen. As soon as you start that, I will ask the question, "How much of this is due to prejudice?" and you will ask, "How's Merlin going to take this?" I try to train executives, managers, and first-line supervisors to build relationships that remove those barriers across difficult interfaces.

So, integration must occur at three levels for change to happen: (1) provide the right concepts to the right groups in the right sequence, (2) have some kind of vehicle to institutionalize those concepts into behavior, and (3) remove the structural barriers to both horizontal and vertical integration.

MANAGING ORGANIZATIONAL CHANGE

We live in a world of rapid social change. Our business organizations, especially, need to adapt rapidly and successfully to changes that pose both opportunities and threats. Frequently American firms are challenged by competition from products made in other nations; the automotive industry is a key example.

But other changes are challenging these organizations—the dynamic nature of high technology. In earlier times, a manufacturer of office equipment might spend years developing a product that would be on the market for decades. The IBM Selectric typewriter provides an example. Introduced in the 1960s, it maintained a dominant position in the market for over two decades. Now high technology firms sometimes must develop a new product in months with the awareness that it may become relatively obsolete in a matter of a few years. In the personal-computer realm, IBM's original entry, the PC, has been "upstaged," first by IBM's own PC-XT, and now by the IBM PC–AT, all within five years.

Government deregulation of major industries like telecommunications, air travel, and banking has jolted many companies that once enjoyed comfortable dominant positions in stable markets. In the early 1980s many banks suddenly found themselves competing with large firms like Sears Roebuck, which jumped into the financial-services industry following that industry's deregulation. Faced with sudden competition and volatile markets, some firms thrive, and some do not survive.

Sociologist Rosabeth Kantor (1983) has studied the organizations that have done especially fine jobs in dealing with the challenge of change. She calls them "change masters." Based on her research with scores of organizations, she has developed a profile of the "progressive" versus the average firm. Kantor learned some important lessons that she shares both with students and as a consultant to businesses.

Kantor began to recognize patterns of success and failure. She found that firms, like societies, have cultures—rules, often unwritten, that guide behavior within the firm, as well as attitudes and beliefs that support the rules. Among the troubled firms the culture typically discourages innovations, especially from those among the ranks of ordinary workers. In contrast Kantor found a culture of pride, a climate of success, and incentives for innovating in growing firms. In these firms even low-level employees were involved in innovation and change.

Kantor believes that many American firms have developed some of the dysfunctions of bureaucracy, including an overreliance on doing things "the way we always have," and placing too much of the responsibility on the people at the top of the authority ladder. She argues that companies need to develop a spirit of enterprise throughout their corporate cultures that will carry them a long way toward handling change and improving their productivity.

Conclusion

The study of groups and organizations is central to the field of sociology. How people interact in groups and what effects groups have on their members is important in understanding human social life. Because formal organizations have grown in members and influence, the study of this group form is also basic to the study of modern societies.

REVIEW

Summary Questions

1. What is a group?
2. What is the difference between primary and secondary groups?
3. How important is social support to the quality and length of life?
4. How do small groups differ in structure, leadership, size, and membership?
5. How do leaders emerge within groups?
6. How do groups influence individual perception and behavior?
7. How is group decision-making different from individual decision-making?
8. What is a formal organization?
9. What are the stages in the development of bureaucracy?
10. What are the six characteristics of Weber's ideal bureaucracy?
11. What are the functions and dysfunctions of modern bureaucracy?
12. How does the Peter Principle work?
13. What does recent research indicate about worker involvement in corporate decision-making?

REVIEW

Summary Answers

1. A group is a set of people recurrently interacting in a structured way according to shared expectations about each other's behavior.
2. A primary group is based on intimate, face-to-face interaction, whereas a secondary group is less cohesive, more formal, and less supportive of members.
3. Social support has been found to significantly increase an individual's satisfaction with life, promote the health and well-being of individuals, and reduce the effects of stress in a person's life. People who have supportive primary-group relationships also live longer. Over the past twenty-five years the average American has experienced a decrease of such support.
4. A small group is a collection of people who meet more or less regularly in face-to-face interaction, who possess a common identity or exclusiveness of purpose, and who share a set of standards governing their activities. Their structure can be formal—that is, public and explicit—or informal—private and implicit—depending on the needs of the group members. The nature of a group's structure often depends on its central person. As groups grow, they are likely to develop formal structures that are increasingly elaborate. Even-numbered groups are more characterized by disagreement and conflict than odd-numbered groups.
5. Members who have the highest rate of group participation are most often chosen to be leaders. Other traits associated with leadership are intelligence, enthusiasm, dominance, self-confidence, and egalitarianism. Democratic leadership is most useful when there is sufficient time to involve the entire group in decisions.
6. Groups generally reward members who conform to their norms. Group opinion strongly influences individual behavior and judgment toward that of the group. Homans' exchange theory states that people try to maximize rewards and minimize costs in social transactions, and will conform to the group under these conditions. Deindividuation occurs when a person feels submerged in a large group that has strong feelings of group unity and focuses on external goals. The lack of self-awareness that results may cause pressure toward group conformity.
7. Group decision-making is much slower than individual, but group decisions tend to be more accurate. People in a group are sometimes willing to make decisions involving greater risk than they would alone. Groups first orient themselves, evaluate, control the expression of negative and positive reactions, and then achieve solidarity in making a decision. In some cases, groups seek concurrence so strongly that groupthink occurs, creating a situation in which alternatives are not viewed realistically but only in terms of making the group members happy with each other. This can be combatted by the leader being receptive to the opinions of everyone, by asking for outside advice on the issue, and by assigning group members to troubleshoot suggested options.
8. A formal organization is a group deliberately constructed to achieve specific objectives through explicitly defined roles and specified rules. Modern societies are characterized by the growth of such organizations and the reduction of primary groups.
9. Three conditions are necessary for the rise of bureaucracy: a money economy, a steady income to the bureaucracy, and a large population base.
10. Bureaucracies are large-scale, formal organizations that are highly differentiated and organized through elaborate policies and procedures in a hierarchy of authority. They are characterized by fixed division of labor, hierarchy of offices, written documents, management by trained experts, official work as the primary activity, and management by rules.
11. Bureaucracy allows a society to accomplish large and complicated tasks, provides an efficient means for repetitive tasks, and creates order in society. It also facilitates large-scale conflict by sometimes creating inappropriate or harmful rules, slowing upward communication of bad news, promoting antagonism between superiors and subordinates, perpetuating itself after it has served its purpose, growing beyond a size that is efficient, creating a situation in which workers feel dehumanized, creating a gulf between those at the top and those at the bottom, and becoming a tool for exploitation. Robert Merton suggests that working in a bureaucracy for extended periods tends to entangle workers in rules, reinforcing timid and rigid attitudes among them.
12. The Peter Principle states that in a hierarchy competent employees tend to be promoted until they reach a level at which they are not competent to do the work, and then they remain there. Because they then feel insecure about their shoddy work, they begin to concentrate on rules and regulations, reducing the quality of their work even more.
13. Robert Townsend says that we must make new assumptions about workers if our businesses are to be productive, including workers and appreciating them for their work. Theory Z, by which the

Japanese industries are run, assumes that if workers are given more responsibility, they will be more productive. Rosabeth Kantor finds that organizations that thrive in the midst of a quickly changing market are those that develop a culture of pride, a climate of success, and incentives for innovation, even at the lowest level.

Glossary

aggregate a set of people who happen to be together in one area

bureaucracy a large-scale, formal organization which is highly differentiated and organized through elaborate policies and procedures in a hierarchy of authority

category a set of people with a common characteristic

coercive organizations organizations people are forced to join

confederates persons who are told by an experimenter what to say when an experimental subject is present

consensus agreement without dissension

deindividuation pressure toward group conformity

dyad a two-person group

formal or complex organizations human groups which have been deliberately constructed to achieve specific objectives through explicitly defined roles and specified rules

group a set of people recurrently interacting according to shared patterns and expectations about each other's behavior

group dynamics the patterns of interaction of group members

group structure defines both what positions the group members will fill and what the pattern of relationships between the various positions will be. **Formal structure** is public and explicit; **informal structure** is private and implicit.

primary group a relatively small, enduring, group characterized by intimacy

rationality the deliberate calculation of the most efficient means to achieve a particular end

secondary group a social group characterized by impersonal and often transitory interaction

small group a collection of people who meet more or less regularly in face-to-face interaction, who possess a common identity or exclusiveness of purpose, and who share a set of standards governing their activities

triad a three-person group

utilitarian organizations organizations which individuals join freely but for practical purposes

voluntary associations specialized formal organizations whose members join and leave at will

Suggested Readings

Peter M. Blau. 1973. *The Dynamics of Bureaucracy: A Study of Interpersonal Relations in Two Government Agencies. Rev. ed.* Chicago: University of Chicago Press.

A discussion of bureaucracy by perhaps the best-known contemporary theorist of bureaucracy.

Rosabeth Moss Kanter. 1983. *The Change Masters.* New York: Simon and Schuster.

An excellent analysis of what makes organizations grow through change and outside challenges.

William Ouchi. 1981. *Theory Z: How American Business Can Meet the Japanese Challenge.* Reading, Mass: Addison-Wesley.

A well-written and interesting summary of the differences between Japanese and American business styles.

Charles Perrow. 1986. *Complex Organizations. (3d ed.)* New York: Random House.

An excellent overview of the topic of formal organizations.

Marvin Shaw. 1981. *Group Dynamics. (3d. ed.)* New York: McGraw-Hill.

The classic summary of the research and theory in the field of small-group dynamics and structure.

CHAPTER 6

DEVIANCE and SOCIAL CONTROL

How's Your Sociological Intuition?

1. For every 100 serious property crimes known to the police in the United States, how many people will go to prison?
   - a. 63
   - b. 44
   - c. 19
   - d. fewer than 1
2. Which group of people will continue to think of a recovered mental patient as insane?
   - a. High-income with much education
   - b. Medium-income people with moderate education
   - c. Low-income people with little education
   - d. All of the above groups react similarly to former mental patients
3. When healthy people were experimentally institutionalized in mental hospitals, researchers found that:
   - a. The mental health professionals consistently spotted the healthy people
   - b. The mental health professionals consistently treated the healthy people as if they were insane
   - c. Healthy people could tolerate the mental hospital atmosphere for less than a day when they were treated as if they were patients
   - d. The patients treated the healthy people as if they were insane
4. Which is the strongest deterrent to shoplifting?
   - a. Family and friends condemning shoplifting
   - b. Severe legal penalties
   - c. High chance of being apprehended by the law
   - d. Public condemnation of shoplifting

Answers

1. d. You will read about why the percentage is this low in the subsection, "How Do Prisons Function?"
2. c. Those of lower class background are slower to assign or remove the label of insanity.
3. b. See our account of Rosenhan's fascinating and controversial experiment in the subsection, "Professional Definitions of Mental Illness."
4. a. The "Close-Up on Research" features Robert Kraut's study that shows that one's family's and friends' attitudes are strong influences on shoplifting.

WHEN YOU HAVE FINISHED STUDYING THIS CHAPTER, YOU SHOULD KNOW:

- What sociologists mean by deviance and social control and when social controls influence behavior
- How the social control or anomie theories, cultural transmission theories, and functionalist theories explain deviance as norm violation
- How symbolic interactionist and conflict theories explain deviance as a definitional process
- How mental illness is defined by professionals and by society
- How the mentally ill are treated
- How people learn the mentally ill role
- How society defines crime
- How crime rates are changing
- Who criminals are and how they are treated by society
- What factors help explain shoplifting
- The characteristics of mass murderers
- What distinguishes white collar crime and how it might be deterred
- How prisons function as social control
- Whether capital punishment is an effective deterrent

"He French-kissed me, when he kissed me goodnight."

The daughter is understandably tense as she reveals to the family counselor her father's recent behavior. This previously sexually abusive father had seemed to be making excellent progress. The counselor studies the father's face, but rather than registering guilt, he looks confused. This man was raised by a father who quite openly engaged his daughters in sexual activity. The counselor realizes that the girl's father was making a sincere effort *not* to be sexually abusive. He meant the gesture to be warm and loving. He had successfully learned from his father that to love his daughter was to engage in sexual activity with her. He had been taught to draw any line in affectionate displays with a daughter. Once he understands that the French kiss is not acceptable, though a hug and a kiss on the cheek or even lips may be, the problem does not recur.

The young criminology professor invites a convicted check forger to class to give a first-hand account of his experiences. In his dealings with the professor, Howard behaves honorably. The class session goes well, and several of the students who find Howard to be very interesting arrange to consult later with him on papers they are writing. The following week the professor is alarmed to learn from three students, two female and one male, that Howard made explicit sexual advances towards them.

In the seventh game of the World Series, Kirk Gibson hits a home run with men on base. The Tigers have a commanding lead, the game comes to a quick end, and Detroit fans in and outside the stadium go wild. Some swarm the field trying to get to the players. Others in search of souvenirs literally rip up the field, tossing pieces of sod to those still in the stands. Some members of the mob destroy much of the press box. Fans outside dance atop busses as they make their way through traffic and try to overturn a bus carrying the Michigan Marching Band, which has performed at the game.

What Are Deviance and Social Control?

These rather dramatic instances of misconduct help us to see the natural tie between social control and deviance. ***Social control*** is *the means by which members of a society attempt to induce each other to comply with the society's norms.* Social controls include silent controls, subtle, almost invisible forms of social pressure, and official rules and penalties that may be applied after all else fails. ***Deviance*** is *behavior that violates the norms of the social group in which the behavior occurs.*

In each of these examples, a social control has failed in a way that helps to explain the deviant act. The father who French-kissed his daughter represents a failure to internalize the standards of conventional society. In the case of the forger, someone acts appropriately in the presence of informal external controls, but strays in their absence. Finally, the disruptive fans at the stadium took advantage of the fact that they could overwhelm the ability of the formal control agents, the police and security personnel, to keep their deviant tendencies in check.

Social controls and deviance go hand in hand. Where there is some tendency toward deviance, we can expect people to develop social controls. This explains the presence of chaperons at dances, security guards near valuable properties, and police forces in society. Conversely, where there is a breakdown or absence of social controls, we might expect deviance, as in our opening examples.

Definitions of deviance also vary from group to group. For example, members of mainstream twentieth century American society would define passing bad checks, having long conversations with the devil, getting married to someone of the same sex, or using heroin as deviance. These same behaviors, however, may be accepted in *another* group. Deviance is relative. Because norms change from group to group, from culture

What is deviant in one group is normative behavior in another. This businessman in Bermuda regularly rides his motor bike to work wearing Bermuda shorts, appropriate behavior for his small and hot island working environment, but deviant for a businessman in the United States. (*Photo courtesy the author*)

to culture, and from one era to another, deviance is defined differently in different groups. The drug subculture, for instance, assumes members use heroin. The criminal subculture assumes members pass bad checks. In the gay community a homosexual marriage is not considered odd. And talking with the devil is positively sanctioned by Satan worshipers.

Each society teaches that its norms are the most valid standards of conduct. Often the claim is made that social norms are "natural law" or that they were handed down from a god. Yet different societies have radically different definitions of what is normal and what is deviant. For example, incest is almost universally considered immoral, yet societies disagree on which relatives are too close to marry or to have sex with. Social scientists have found few universal standards of conduct shared by all societies.

How Can Deviance Be Seen as Norm Violation?

Many of the earlier theories of deviance simply took the norms for granted and set about to explain violations of these norms. In this subsection we consider some classical and contemporary explanations of deviance that grow from this perspective.

SOCIAL CONTROL OR ANOMIE THEORIES

Learning why individuals conform to norms may shed light on why other individuals deviate from the norms. Control theory argues that deviance is largely a matter of failed social controls. Emile Durkheim, Travis Hirschi, and Robert Merton base their theories of deviance on the idea of social control.

Emile Durkheim, the pioneering French sociologist, was the first to look systematically for explanations of deviance in terms of failed social controls. In his classic study of suicide rates (1897), he introduced the term ***anomie*** to mean *an absence of clear norms for a society or an individual.* Anomie exists in a social setting when the norms governing behavior have always been weak or have suddenly become weakened. Members of a society can experience anomie during times of social upheaval—for instance, during economic advances and declines.

Durkheim claimed that anomic suicide, which "results from man's activity lacking regulation and his consequent sufferings" (p. 258), was a major suicide type. He suggested that norms were regulated by society through social bonds between the individual and social groups.

Durkheim gathered and analyzed data on suicide to confirm his theory. Among other findings, he discovered that suicide was about four times as common among divorced people as among married people, and that suicide rates were higher than average during times of unusual economic prosperity or of economic crisis.

Robert Merton's social theory concerning the genesis of deviance, one of the most widely known, extends Durkheim's concept of anomie to include situations in which norms are in apparent conflict (Merton, 1968). Merton believes there is often a strain between the norms that define socially appropriate goals and the norms that specify socially appropriate means for attaining these goals.

A good boy gone bad? Merton's theory of anomie suggests that some deviance arises when poor people who are blocked from legitimate goals like purchasing consumer goods, seek them instead through illegitimate means like shoplifting. (*The Picture Cube*)

For example, most college students want to get good grades. They assume if they work hard, come to class, study the text, and do the library research required, they will get good grades and gain the respect of other students. Some students, however, do all these things and still fail exams. This puts them in a situation of strain with their campus society's goals and may lead them to find other means to attain goals they want to reach.

TABLE 6.1 Merton's Five Ways of Adapting to Socially Approved Goals

Adaptation	Accepts Socially Approved Goals	Accepts Socially Approved Norms
Innovation	Yes	No
Ritualism	No	Yes
Retreatism	No	No
Rebellion	No—works toward new goals	No—works toward new norms
Conformity	Yes	Yes

SOURCE Adapted with permission of The Free Press, a Division of Macmillan, Inc. from SOCIAL THEORY AND SOCIAL STRUCTURE, Enlarged 1968 Edition, by Robert K. Merton. Copyright © 1968, 1967 by Robert K. Merton.

Merton suggests there are five basic adaptions to the combination of culturally approved goals and means, some of which shown strain and some of which do not (see Table 6.1): (1) ***innovation*** *involves trying to attain the goals by deviant means,* for example, by cheating on exams; (2) ***ritualism*** *involves following the norms even when you don't think they will help you reach the goals*—for example, studying hard even when you expect to fail; (3) ***retreatism*** *involves deciding that neither the goals nor the norms are worthy of your attempts*—for example, students who drink themselves off campus within one semester; (4) ***rebellion*** *is an adaptation that creates new norms and goals*—for example, the campus radical who decides that what is really important is changing the administration's attitude about some issue at the expense of his or her studies; and (5) ***conformity*** *involves agreement with the norms and goals of society and working within them to achieve what degree of success you can*—for example, a student who hires a tutor, discusses problems with the instructor, and always works for high grades.

Merton sees the imbalance between cultural goals and inequalities as producing anomie. He theorizes that people from lower classes often resent the discrepancy between the goals of society and their means of attaining those goals. They feel unable to get a good education, a good job, and a step up the ladder as easily as those in upper and middle classes. Their sense of lacking control over their future leads to anomie, and they may turn to other methods of achieving their goals, methods that deviate from social norms. Whereas the rest of society sees their adaptive behavior as criminal, poorer people may see this behavior as reaching the approved goals of society in the only way available. Official arrest and apprehension statistics bear out the idea that lower class people are arrested more often than middle-class people, although the reasons for this are unclear. (See "Who Are the Criminals?" later in this chapter.)

Merton's theory is useful sociologically because it concentrates on social causes of deviance rather than on the deviants themselves. However, Merton's ideas are more readily applicable to criminal deviance than they are to other forms of deviance, because they focus on social system and class-group advantages rather than on other categories.

Recently three researchers at the University of Alberta have produced findings consistent with Merton's ideas. Harvey Krahn, Timothy Hartnagel, and John Gartrell (1986) considered data on homicide rates from sixty-five countries in comparison to other features of those societies. They found that homicide rates tend to be higher in countries that had a combination of considerable income inequality and a high emphasis on democratic values. Such societies could be expected to produce large numbers of people who want to be equal (the democratic value) at the same time that they contain many people who are relatively poor (high degree of inequality).

Travis Hirschi, a contemporary proponent of control theory, elaborates on Durkheim's theme by introducing four components of the bond between the individual and a group (1969). The major aspect of this bond is ***commitment,*** *the degree to which a person has a "stake in conforming."* "A person who rejects and is rejected by a group is likely to have a low commitment to the group. This weakened bond lessens the group's social control over the individual and increases the likelihood of deviance from that group's norms" (p. 161).

Hirschi studied deviance in relation to social control among a large number of California youths. He measured the strength of social control, or commitment, by asking his subjects about their ties to parents and peers. Where ties were reported as not strong, social control was regarded as not strong. Confirming Hirschi's original hypothesis, youths who reported having weak social bonds with their primary groups also were more socially deviant in general.

EVALUATION. Control theories, which explain deviance in terms of problems with social controls, offer a partial explanation of deviance. They are appealing because they correspond with our conventional wisdom that clear rules backed by swift, certain, and strong punishment will deter misbehavior. When the norms are weak or missing, or when they put people into a bind, we can expect some people to act deviantly. But even under these circumstances not everyone deviates, and we often find people who behave in deviant ways even when the social controls appear to be normal. As we shall see in the next section, other important theories can help explain deviance.

CULTURAL TRANSMISSION THEORIES

Edwin H. Sutherland suggests that deviance is a natural outgrowth of a person's ***differential associations,*** or *differential contacts during socialization.* Because different groups define right and wrong differently, people socialized in a group develop the group's distinct ideas about right and wrong. In short, Sutherland's theory states criminal or deviant behavior is learned as appropriate behavior from associating with those who define the deviant behavior as appropriate (Sutherland, 1978). For example, the French-kissing father had learned his behavior from *his* father, who defined it as appropriate.

Sutherland suggests that five things predispose a person to adopt deviant behavior: (1) intimate contact with a deviant person, (2) contact at a young age, (3) frequent contact, (4) long periods spent with a deviant person, and (5) a large number of contacts with a deviant individual. In other words, the more the social environment encourages contact with deviant behavior, the more likely the child is to learn deviant behavior.

We can see a clear illustration of Sutherland's ideas (along with some of Merton's) in the autobiography of John Allen (1977), a mugger, pimp, dope pusher, armed robber, and killer. (See "How It Feels to Be a Criminal: The Story of John Allen.") Allen asserts that his criminal career was almost inevitable because most of the people he knew as a child were criminals, from friends and neighbors to other family members.

Allen's goal was a "good life," but he couldn't afford it and hadn't the education or job to get it. He also associated primarily with criminals and was socialized in a criminal subculture that regarded what he did as acceptable behavior for a young man. By his own admission, and not in keeping with the usual experience of ex-convicts, Allen was offered good jobs and other help every time he came out of prison, yet he chose to continue his previous behavior—whatever the primary motivation for his criminal behavior, he was compelled by his early socialization to continue it.

HOW IT FEELS TO BE A CRIMINAL: THE STORY OF JOHN ALLEN

"It seems to me that the kind of neighborhood you come up in may make all the difference in which way you go and where you end up. There was a lot of people in my neighborhood, in the southwest part of Washington, D.C., that didn't do much work and there was a lot of people who did, but the majority didn't. Hustling was their thing: numbers running, bootlegging, selling narcotics, selling stolen goods, prostitution. There's so many things that go on—it's a whole system that operates inside itself.

In our neighborhood, the kids ran wild, and the adults were wild. It would be nothing for us to be on the front steps playing hide-and-seek and all of a sudden you hear bang, bang, bang, and people are shooting at each other in the street.

I learned a lot of things at Junior Village—mostly more bad than good. Kids from all over town were sent there. It was a tough little place; it was a place where you fought almost every day because everybody was trying to be tougher than the next person. Before I got to the place, I knew all about it—what you supposed to do, how you supposed to act. So you just walk right in and fight, two or three times a day, and then you'd wake up the next morning and fight some more.

I also learned how to shoot craps pretty good, and I learned the right way to go about housebreaking, the right way to get away from the truant officers, the right way to steal from the Safeway. I learned how to hot-wire cars right there in the place—on the superintendent's car. And I learned about drop pockets. You make a small tear in the lining of your coat, big enough for whatever you want to put in there, then you steal cigarettes. You take a couple of packs at a time and put it in there and shake it all down.

Very few people that go into a juvenile joint come out with the feeling that 'I'm not going back.' They know they're going to end up back in a place like Junior Village, because they know the things that got them there in the first place, and they aren't going to stop doing them.

I had quite a few jobs—all kinds . . . but they never lasted no long period of time. I worked two or three days, then quit. Most of the time it's my own fault. I can't say, well, I had a record, so everybody was down on me. . . . Ninety percent of the time it was me. I really was the actual cause of losing a job, or I just quit or did something purposely to get fired. But the only reason I ever took a job was to please my parole officer.

Of course now everybody go about it a different way. Some dudes figure they'll work their way out. I say, 'Well, I'll rob my way out.'

I know how to steal. I know how to be hard on broads. I know how to stick somebody up better than anything. I know how to take a small amount of narcotics and eventually work it way up and make me some money. Fencing property or credit cards, I know how to do all that. But society says all that's wrong. I feel like it's survival, making the dollar. I don't have nothing against a guy that makes a dollar. Whatever his bag is, that's his bag."

SOURCE John Allen. 1977. *Assault with a Deadly Weapon: The Autobiography of a Street Criminal.* Dianne Kelly and Philip Heyman, eds. New York: Pantheon, pp. 1–92.

However, Sutherland's doubts have not diminished interest in the theory. Even in the present, research evidence is confirming much of what he theorized to be true. A team of researchers (Tittle, Burke, & Jackson, 1986) recently clarified Sutherland's sometimes ambiguous propositions and explored the issues through a survey of nearly 2,000 subjects, 15 years of age or older, from Iowa, New Jersey, and Oregon. The survey contained questions about the subjects' contact with people who engage in various types of criminal conduct. It also asked subjects to indicate the likelihood that they would engage in varieties of criminal conduct if a strong need or desire arose. In the researchers' words: "Despite some important anomalies, our findings support the major theme of Sutherland's thinking. Association with criminal definitions does seem to be a generator of crime, and it appears to exercise its influence indirectly through its effect on a learned symbolic construct—motivation to engage in criminal behavior" (Tittle, Burke, & Jackson, 1986, p. 429).

Closely related to differential association theory, ***cultural transmission theory*** *stresses that deviant behav-*

ior may be part of a subculture that can be transmitted indefinitely through socialization. For example, in a now-classic study, Shaw and McKay (1929) tabulated neighborhood crime rates in Chicago for twenty years. They found that although different ethnic groups moved in and out of the study areas, the crime rate of each area remained stable. They interpreted this as confirmation that a subculture of crime existed in some neighborhoods and not in others. This subculture was transmitted from group to group, and although the groups changed in ethnic background, the culture that transmitted the deviant behavior persisted.

Judith and Peter Blau (1982) have examined the experience of the 125 largest American metropolitan areas for evidence bearing on this cultural transmission theory. On the surface the case seems to be strong. Within the South and among blacks, criminal violence rates are distinctly higher than in the country as a whole. However, when the Blaus took into account economic inequality, they found that the violence rates were primarily due to the relatively low economic status of Southerners and blacks. That is, when they compared the violent crime rate of Southerners and blacks to that of other groups of the same economic status, they found little or no difference in crime rates. The Blaus suggest that the relative inequality of wealth in the United States leads to despair in the poor, who see themselves as victims in an unjust system. Thus, the interaction between poverty and culture produces higher crime rates. Differences in economic status appear to be the root cause of the crime, with culture being at most an agent in the transmission of crime.

EVALUATION. Differential association and cultural transmission theories explain the process by which much deviant behavior is transmitted through the subcultures. These theories build from the central idea developed in the socialization chapter: much human behavior is learned from those close to us. Differential association and cultural transmission extend socialization theory to explain deviant as well as normal behavior. Sociologists have tended to apply these theories of deviance to youth and criminal behavior, but they may also help to explain broader ranges of behavior. For instance, an adult entering a firm where fraudulent practices are part of the corporate culture may experience strong social pressure to conform to those deviant norms.

However, these theories do not explain why the deviance arose in the subculture in the first place, or why the behavior was defined as deviant by the dominant culture. They also do not address the obvious fact that some people who are in close contact with such a deviant subculture fail to adopt its standards and do not become deviant.

WHAT IS THE FUNCTIONALIST THEORY OF DEVIANCE?

Much of what we do every day depends on trusting others: walking across the street in confidence that drivers are able to control their cars and will not kill us; buying meat on the assumption that the weight label on the package is correct; sending our children to school believing they will not be beaten while there. If individuals had to think about the reliability of all the social institutions they now take for granted, their lives would be much more difficult. So we can see that deviance has some undesirable consequences for society. When too much deviance exists, a lowered level of trust and interdependence among individuals results. When standards of behavior are agreed upon and followed, a more progressive, active society results.

Deviance also makes people less willing to conform to some norms. For instance, if the butcher systematically cheats customers, they may begin to do the same to the butcher. If dishonesty in paying income taxes becomes rampant, many who had previously paid honestly may follow suit.

Finally, deviance can use up society's resources in control efforts. Spending valuable time, energy, and money on controlling gambling, for example, means that the society has less of these resources for activities that would increase general welfare and happiness.

Deviance may also be useful to society, in that defining deviance necessarily means defining normality. Durkheim was the first sociologist to point out that limits and norms for living are developed to some degree from watching what is *not* tolerated by other members of society (Durkheim, 1895a). Learning what is deviant, therefore, is an essential part of the socialization process.

This can be seen in the ***medicalization of deviance,*** *the process through which deviant behavior previously socially defined becomes defined by the medical community.* For example, fifty years ago inebriated citizens were routinely rounded up and placed in jail on Saturday nights. They were charged with various crimes, from public drunkenness to drunk and disorderly conduct, and often given fines or jail terms. Today, habitual drunkenness is given the medical diagnosis of "alcohol abuse," and the "offender" becomes a "patient" referred to a "treatment program" rather than a criminal sent for punishment. The behavior has been redefined. Although habitually drinking too much is still considered abnormal by most of society, it is now treated rather than punished.

We are also socialized to avoid society's punishments for deviants—ostracism, denial of privileges, and loss of friendship. Seeing the consequences that face the deviant can be strong reason to follow the norms of society more closely. Being "normal" is an attractive option when one sees how "abnormal" people are treated.

Deviance also enhances feelings of unity within a society. When all members agree upon norms and sanctions for violators of the norms, it produces a feeling of solidarity—of a joint stake in the status quo—and of willingness to defend that status quo against deviants who challenge it.

The possibility of deviance also allows individuals to vent anger at society without totally dropping out of it. Occasional low-level deviance (like drunkenness) is usually tolerated as a means of "blowing off steam."

Deviance sometimes creates worthwhile change in society. Societies may eventually adopt behaviors they had previously scorned. For example, eighty years ago many women felt that they should have the right to vote. These suffragettes were generally scorned for their views. Polite society dropped them, husbands forbade their wives to join the movement, and some marriages broke up when the women disobeyed. The women's suffrage movement gradually gained supporters, however, and as it grew it became more socially acceptable. Today women have the right to vote due to efforts of these "deviant" women.

EVALUATION. Functional theory provides only an outline of how deviance contributes to stability in social structure, rather than representing a complete system of thought about deviance. Although deviance may be seen as useful to society, conflict theorists remind us that deviance may more often be useful to those who dominate a given society at a given time.

How Can Deviance Be Seen as a Definitional Process?

Although those theorists we have just discussed take for granted the existence of the norms and try to explain deviance in terms of norm violation, symbolic interactionists and conflict theorists question who creates the norms and why. These two perspectives focus on deviance as definitional rather than a matter of rule-breaking.

LABELING THEORY: THE SYMBOLIC INTERACTIONIST APPROACH

Growing from the symbolic interactionist approach, labeling theory began to emerge as an important body of deviance theory about three decades ago through the writing of Edwin M. Lemert (1951). Other labeling theorists of importance are Howard Becker (1963), John Kitsuse (1962), Erving Goffman (1963), and Kai Erikson (1962). The introduction of *labeling theory* marked a significant change in focus, from concentration on nature and origins of deviant behavior to concentration on the reactions of others to deviance, including why some people are labeled deviant and some are not.

SANCTIONS AND LABELING. Labeling theorists focus on the sanctioning and labeling of deviance rather than on deviance itself, because they see society's reactions as more important than the individual's deviance. They attempt to explain the group and its social control agents' reactions to deviant behavior, dealing with such issues as what determines which offenders will be negatively sanctioned, whom authorities will label deviant, and the effect on a person of being labeled deviant. Labeling theorists study the question of *which* offenders will be punished rather than which individuals are likely to break the law, and which people will be treated as insane rather than which ones act insane.

Instead of attempting to explain where rule-breaking behavior originates, labeling theorists assume that deviant behavior is common but that it is only occasionally labeled deviant. For example, they point out one youth's behavior is regarded as mischievous while another's similar behavior is labeled delinquent, or that one adult's behavior is regarded as eccentric while another's similar behavior is labeled mentally ill. Howard Becker explains that deviance is a "consequence of the application by others of rules and sanctions to an 'offender.' The deviant is one to whom the label has successfully been applied; deviant behavior is behavior that people label" (Becker, 1963, p. 9). Because their definition focuses on rule enforcement rather than on rule breaking, labeling theorists do not address the issue of why people break the rules initially.

Symbolic interactionists reserve the term ***deviant*** to mean *one who is characterized as a violator of a norm.* The distinction between engaging in deviance and being socially regarded as deviant is important for two reasons.

First, some people routinely commit deviant acts but are able to avoid being called deviants. For example, many people have cheated on more than one occasion, but neither they nor other members of society see them as immoral. Similarly, engaging in sex for favors does not always lead to the label of "prostitute."

Second, and contrarily, some people are labeled deviant even when they exhibit only a little abnormal behavior. People who have once been in prison or in a mental hospital often continue to be treated as exconvicts or as mental patients for the rest of their lives, although their behavior after release may look normal to an impartial observer.

Engaging in deviant behavior does not automatically lead to a deviant reputation or self-image. The explanations of *deviance as a behavior* and of *coming to have a deviant label* are quite different, as are the consequences of the processes for the individuals. Symbolic interactionist sociologists, therefore, are careful to use the terms precisely.

PRIMARY AND SECONDARY DEVIANCE AND DEVIANT CAREERS. Labeling theorists describe the process by which an individual becomes socially regarded as deviant as a progression from initial rule-breaking behavior to the individual's gaining a reputation and a self-image that is essentially deviant. The stages in this progression are called primary deviance, secondary deviance, and deviant career.

Primary deviance *is behavior that violates the norms of society but which is transitory and may be unnoticed by others in the society.* A pre–teen-age girl who experiments sexually with a girlfriend violates the norm that says it is inappropriate for girls to interact sexually. The sex play is probably an experiment that will not be repeated, and her deviant behavior (primary deviance) will be forgotten.

Secondary deviance *is deviance that comes as a response to society's reaction to primary deviance.* If the girl's parents were to discover her playing with her girlfriend, they might berate her for being a bad person in what Harold Garfinkel has named a "degradation ceremony" (Garfinkel, 1956). The girl might then begin to think of herself not as someone who was naturally curious but rather as someone who is deviant. She may then adopt new behaviors that reflect her idea of what is expected of her as a deviant. She could make new friends at school, adopt new forms of dress, and use new language. This secondary deviance results from her parents' applying the deviant label to her, rather than from her initial curiosity.

When secondary deviance becomes a life-style, the deviant person begins living what is termed a ***deviant career.*** For example, a person who becomes publicly known as a homosexual may take on this identity as a *master status.* A ***master status*** *affects one's overall standing in the community.* For instance, known homosexuals used to be barred from certain professions like teaching or military service. Becker describes public reaction to a person who pursues a deviant career as follows (Becker, 1963, pp. 33–34): "The question is raised: 'What kind of person would break such an important rule?' And the answer is given: 'One who is different from the rest of us, who cannot or will not act as a moral human being and therefore might break other important rules.' "

Another example of this process can be found in labeling mental illness or retardation. Once a person has been labeled mentally ill, the label tends to stick, regardless of whether it later appears to be untrue. The resulting secondary deviance often means that a person who has been mislabeled originally may, in the end, actually need treatment. More than once, for example, children thought to have been retarded have been discovered not to be. After years of being treated as if they *were* retarded, living with other children who were retarded, and never being expected to act normally (by showing responsibility in caring for themselves or taking initiative on a project they care about, for example), these children have great difficulty entering the normal world. Their social habits, dress, manner of speaking, world outlook, and attitudes all say to the outside world that they are retarded. Escaping the label usually requires years of work.

EVAULATION. Labeling theory helps explain differences in societal reaction and secondary deviance. In so doing, labeling theorists expose the fact that sanctioning past deviant behavior may contribute to future deviance. Conversely, other deviance theories tend to overlook the differences and consequences of sanctioning. Labeling theory explains some of what these other theories miss, but it does not explain all aspects of deviance. Most important, it fails to explain fully why individuals commit their first deviant acts.

CONFLICT THEORY

The conflict theory of deviance is based on a Marxist interpretation of society. Conflict theorists trace the origin of deviant behavior to class conflict between the powerful and wealthy group and the weak and exploited (Quinney, 1970; Chambliss and Seidman, 1982; Greenberg, 1981). They see laws as written in the interest of the wealthy and powerful and enforced upon the exploited masses by government, the agent of the wealthy. Nonconflict theorists tend to assume that law represents the consensus of the population and exists for the benefit of all of society.

In the conflict perspective, criminals are viewed as reasonable individuals forced by circumstances to break laws in order to regain some of what has been taken from them or denied to them by an exploitative system. This resembles Merton's anomie theory, which also portrays deviance as an attempt to reach a goal that is blocked by social norms. Unlike Merton, however, conflict theorists condemn the social order that tends to keep some people poor and others rich.

Conflict theorists claim that within our criminal justice system, not only are poor people more motivated to act in deviant ways (such as stealing), they are also likely to be caught. When caught, they are more likely to be severely punished than persons of higher socioeconomic status who are caught stealing or shoplifting. Conflict theorists point out that police patrols are concentrated in poor neighborhoods; poor people cannot afford high-priced lawyers; upper class criminals are more able to shield themselves from detection, and so on. Also, when the wealthy do violate the law and are discovered, they are more likely to be given clemency by police, prosecutors, jurors, and the courts, because they appear to be more respectable than lower class offenders. (See "White-Collar Crime" later in this chapter.) Conflict theorists suggest that less powerful individuals are more likely to have their behavior labeled deviant than powerful individuals. For example, a prolonged pattern of misbehavior may cause a lower class youth to be labeled and punished as a delinquent, whereas the same pattern in an upper class youth may be regarded as a stage of adolescent rebellion. The first child may be sent to jail while the second escapes with a few visits to a psychiatrist. Chambliss found gang behavior described as "sowing wild oats" when committed by upper middle-class boys and as disruptive to community life when committed by lower class boys (Chambliss, 1973).

In these cases, similar deviance from the norm was defined differently because of traits of the individuals who were deviant. This can be seen clearly in the case of corporation executives who embezzle money from their companies. They are rarely put in prison and are sometimes not even arrested, if the money is returned. If a lesser-ranked employee of that same corporation were discovered stealing money from the cash register, however, the police would probably be called and criminal proceedings begun.

EVALUATION. Conflict sociologists often support their views by pointing out that prison populations are disproportionately filled with the poor and racial minorities and by arguing that this demonstrates that the system is organized for the benefit of the wealthy.

One recent research study supports the conflict perspective. If deviance is a reaction of economically exploited people, we might expect that in hard economic times such exploitation would become more acute, and crime and other forms of deviance would increase. Catalano, Dooley, and Jackson found that when the economy takes a turn downward, admissions to mental hospitals rise, though they point out that this is clearly but one of serveral factors explaining changing rates of admissions (Catalano, Dooley, and Jackson, 1985).

How Can Mental Illness Be Seen as Deviance?

One group widely viewed as deviant by sociologists and the general population is those persons who have been labeled mentally ill at some point in their lives. It is difficult to outlive the label of mentally ill once it has been applied to you. Sociologists are interested in the process of determining who is mentally ill, in evaluating standards of mental illness that are accepted by today's practitioners, and in studying how the mentally ill are treated by society.

PROFESSIONAL DEFINITIONS OF MENTAL ILLNESS

Medical definitions of most kinds of mental illness exist, most of them carefully delineated by the American Psychiatric Association (APA) in a 1980 publication called *Diagnostic and Statistical Manual of Mental Disorders (DSM)*. These definitions range from "317: mild mental retardation" (significantly subaverage general intellectual functioning) through "297.0: paranoia" (persistent persecutory delusions). Concern is growing, however, both inside the psychiatric community and elsewhere, about the accuracy of the standard definitions of mental illness and the effects of such definitions on therapeutic treatment.

One of the factors in this concern is that every few years the APA revises the *DSM*, resulting in vehement arguments about new definitions. The most recent revision defines tobacco dependence as a substance-use disorder, and redefines homosexuality as an atypical gender-identity disorder, a label which is less condemning of the behavior than those previously in use. The uproar these and other changes created indicates that practitioners do not always agree on exactly what constitutes mental illness.

For example, Erving Goffman's famous study of mental institutions *Asylums* (1963), discussed the process of *discrediting* of patients by staff members. Discrediting is accomplished by including in the patient's case record only those incidents that contribute to the definition of the patient as mentally ill. The overall quality of the person's life and interactions is ignored, as is information that shows the patient coping well in his or her life situation. This tendency reaffirms the patient's diagnosis and strengthens the practitioner's feeling about the treatment's viabilty. We all undoubtedly exhibit some negative behaviors at various points in our lives, and Goffman suggests that if a list of them were put together without other information, most people might be labeled insane.

SOCIAL DEFINITIONS OF MENTAL ILLNESS

The dominant group in society helps to define mental health, independent of the psychiatrists who write the definitions in the *DSM*. Thomas Scheff thinks that mental illness may be more usefully considered a social status than labeled a disease (1964, 1984). Scheff believes that the symptoms of mental illness are vaguely defined and widely distributed and that the definition of behavior as symptomatic of mental illness is usually dependent on social rather than medical variables. He points out that the mental-status exam, which is often given to determine whether a person is in contact with the real world and is functioning at a "normal" level of competence, has never been tested on the general population. This exam might well be unable to distinguish a mentally ill person from one with a mentally "normal" level of competence. Scheff quotes one physician, who was consulted professionally by a court to decide upon commitments, as saying "The petition cases are pretty automatic. If the patient's own family wants to get rid of him, you know there is something wrong" (Scheff, 1964, p. 410). In other words, Scheff believes if the people you live with define your behavior as nonstandard, you are likely to be sent to an institution and treated as mentally ill.

Thomas Szasz shocked the mental health community by suggesting that mental illness does not exist (1974, 1986). Rather, Szasz says, people we have lumped into the category "mentally ill" can be divided into two groups: people with neurological disease (less than 10 percent of the total) and people with problems in living, any of who may or may not be treatable. The recent trend toward self-help programs and lay therapists reflects a swing toward this point of view. Szasz agrees with labeling theorists that mental illness might not exist if it were not labeled as such.

HOW ARE THE MENTALLY ILL TREATED?

Those labeled mentally ill are treated not only as deviants but as frightening ones. Because so few people understand the origins of mental illness, most are afraid to associate with people defined as mentally ill. In many hospitals, patients are stripped of power and treated as objects (Rosenhan, 1973). Outside the hospital, they are feared and avoided by those who could help them re-establish their definition of self as normal rather than deviant. Ex-patients often face the awkward situation of being accepted by individuals who would reject them if their background of mental illness were kown (Goffman, 1963). The process is obviously self-defeating; denied normal social relations, the patients tend to become more abnormal.

In his review of the scientific literature on the topic, Bernard Gallagher (1980) found that people with lower income and education are more likely to be treated for socially disruptive emotional disorders. Several studies indicate that the psychiatric disorders of schizophrenia—which involves loss of contact with reality, hearing voices, and seeing visions—and manic depressive illness—which involves radical mood swings from euphoria to deep depression—are more prevalent among those with lower social status. This appears to be partly the result of greater life stress and less coping ability of those in these categories. We discuss this further in Chapter 9: "Social Class in the United States." Gallagher also found that the mentally ill receive varying treatment according to their social status. People of high status, with higher amounts of education and income, were more likely to receive psychotherapeutic counseling for their disorder, whereas those of lower status were more likely to receive only medicine or custodial in-patient care.

Women and minorities are also treated differently by the mental health community. Blacks have higher mental hospitalization rates than whites, and women have higher rates than men (Dohrenwend, 1982).

The study of mental illness as deviance is a fledging discipline. It is obvious that some people, because of chemical imbalance, neurological disturbance, or social and psychological background and circumstances, need the trained assistance of mental health practitioners. What is yet to be learned is how to distinguish these people accurately, and how to help them after successful treatment to see themselves as normal again.

How Can Crime Be Seen as Deviance?

Over the past several decades the public has routinely ranked crime as one of the five greatest problems facing our nation. A large number of sociologists devote their studies to crime and deviance. Crime, by its nature, is a specific sort of deviance, and the general theories of deviance we have been discussing help to guide research about crime. Conversely, research studies help sociologists test and refine their theories of deviance.

As we consider crime as a major type of deviance, we learn how sociologists seek to better understand crime by keeping accurate measurements and studying the characteristic "criminals." In this section, we focus on specific types of crime, such as shoplifting, white-collar crime, or mass murder. Sociologists also study how society reacts to crime, particularly by focusing on the criminal-justice system, prisons, and capital punishment.

WHAT IS CRIME?

Julian Parker is a convicted check forger who has often turned small amounts of his time into large sums of

CLOSE-UP on • *THEORY* •

Thomas Scheff on the Mentally Ill Role

The Theorist and the Setting

With the rise of modern medicine, people who would earlier have been regarded as crazy or insane have come to be called mentally ill, a term that attributes a person's behavior to a mental or neurological disease or disorder.

In 1960 the psychiatrist Thomas Szasz wrote an essay entitled "The Myth of Mental Illness," in which he described mental illnesses such as hysteria and schizophrenia as the "impersonation" of sick persons by those whose "real" problems are "problems of living" (1961). Earlier, sociologists Erving Goffman (1956) and Harold Garfinkel (1956) had pointed out that serious deviance, which could be labeled crime and mental illness, is often overlooked. When the deviance is officially treated, they suggested, it is exaggerated, and the deviant's reputation is defamed. Thomas Scheff builds a theory from these earlier works that comes to the radical conclusion that most mentally ill people have been taught their unusual role.

The Theorist's Goal

Scheff's theory addresses two questions: What are the beliefs and practices that constitute the social institution of insanity? and How do they figure in the development of mental disorder? (Scheff, 1963, p. 437).

Concepts and Propositions

Examples help to define Scheff's central concept of ***residual deviance,*** Scheff's label for *"diverse kinds of deviation for which our society provides no explicit label, and which, therefore, sometimes lead to the labeling of the violator as mentally ill"* (p. 439). Scheff points out that some norms are explicit and violating them constitutes a specific category of deviance. For example, violating a criminal statute is a crime, whereas violating etiquette is rude. But many of society's norms, such as ideas about what is real, decent, or within the realm of possibility, are not written down. Violating a nonexplicit norm does not automatically lead to a particular label, even though breaking one makes a person seem strange, bizarre, or frightening. To claim to have seen a deceased relative, to have a child by your brother, or to make plans to leave earth on a UFO is to violate shared norms about reality, decency, and the realm of possibility.

In our culture such behavior may lead to a label of mentally ill.

Scheff states his theory in nine propositions:

Proposition 1: "Residual deviance arises from fundamentally diverse sources" (p. 439).

Sources include physiological origins, such as genetic or biochemical disorders; differences in upbringing; external stress, such as that encountered in combat; and personal acts of innovation and defiance.

Proposition 2: "Relative to the rate of treated mental illness, the rate of unrecorded residual deviance is extremely high" (p. 440).

Public health studies have identified relatively widespread symptoms of mental illness and suggest that "for every treated patient we should expect to find fourteen untreated cases in the 'community' " (p. 441). Some symptoms may go untreated because they are not very serious, but these studies indicate that only one of two of the most severe psychotic disorders receives medical attention (p. 441).

Proposition 3: "Most residual deviance is 'denied' and transitory" (p. 441).

Building on the above observations and propositions, Scheff explains why only a few people get labeled insane when the residual deviance is so common.

Proposition 4: In modern culture "stereotyped imagery of mental disorder is learned in early childhood" (p. 445).

Even small children learn that some people are "crazy" and are therefore to be feared.

Proposition 5: "The stereotypes of insanity are continually reaffirmed, inadvertently, in ordinary social interaction" (p. 445).

Mass media often perpetuate a distorted image of mental illness by mentioning that a rapist or murderer is a former mental patient. In contrast, research studies indicate that mental patients, as a group, are less violent than members of the general population. The cultural stereotypes are reaffirmed when they come up in conversation, as "Are you crazy?" or "It was a madhouse."

Proposition 6: "In the crisis occurring when a primary deviant is publicly labeled, the deviant is highly suggestible and may accept the proffered role of the insane as the only alternate" (p. 449).

For instance, a formerly respected high school teacher whose affair with a 14-year-old student becomes public knowledge may find accepting a label of mentally ill preferable to facing a charge of statutory rape. The community may also prefer this interpretation.

Proposition 7: "Labeled deviants may be rewarded for playing the stereotyped deviant role" (p. 449).

Once a label is placed, it tends to seem accurate to observers. "Patients who manage to find evidence of 'illness' in their past and present behavior, confirming the medical and societal diagnosis, receive benefits" (p. 449). Specifically, the staff of a mental institution will treat such patients as sick people who are cooperating for the sake of their recovery.

Proposition 8: "Labeled deviants are punished when they attempt to return to conventional roles" (p. 449).

A former mental patient is unlikely to be welcomed back to his previous job even after release from treatment.

Proposition 9: "Among residual deviants, labeling is the single most important cause of careers of residual deviance" (p. 451).

"For a person who has acquired an image of himself as lacking the ability to control his own actions, the process of self-control is likely to break down under stress. Such a person may feel that he has reached his 'breaking point' under circumstances that would be endured by a person with a 'normal' self-conception" (p. 451).

Interpretation

Scheff intended his theory to be a guide for future research, but he also introduced some facts that make the propositions seem more plausible. He shows that the stereotype of mental illness is largely a distortion of the actual behavior. As he observes, the relatively new concept of being mentally ill is not natural but was created by modern societies. Other cultures make different interpretations of residual deviance. For example, what we regard as delusions are viewed in some cultures as religious experiences.

Also, public health researchers have consistently found that many more people report symptoms of mental illness than receive treatment. Based on a mixture of facts, observations, and intuition, Scheff builds an argument for his conclusion that being labeled deviant is the primary reason that an episode of residual deviance turns into a career as a mental patient.

Scheff's theory clearly implies that care should be exercised in placing, accepting, and reacting to the label of mental illness. Scheff's work has already had some impact in this area. Over the past two decades, psychiatry has moved toward treating people in community settings rather than state hospitals, partly due to a concern about the stigma attached to having been an institutionalized mental patient.

Scheff's theory is a social-psychological one, because it in part explains psychological states with the social concepts of labels and roles. The theory is also a good example of the symbolic interaction approach, which historically has considered the impact of language and social interaction on one's self-concept.

Questions

1. What are the indications that someone is "really" mentally ill? If your answer is that you do not know, what would make you suspect that someone might be mentally ill?
2. When someone is "really" mentally ill, what evidence suggests this is an illness? Do germs cause mental illness? Can a person be driven crazy?
3. Do you believe that labeling is the single most important cause of careers of residual deviance or "mental illness"? Why or why not? What would it take to change your mind?

SOURCE Thomas J. Scheff. 1963. "The role of the mentally ill and the dynamics of mental disorder: A research framework," *Sociometry*, 26 (December), pp. 436–453. Used by permission of the American Sociological Association and the author.

cash by passing bad checks. On a good day Parker might make several thousand dollars for a few hours' work. Julian once complained that many people have committed the "crime" for which he spent time in prison—even you, if you have written a check when you had insufficient funds to cover it, intending to make a deposit before the check cleared. What makes it a crime for Julian Parker to write bad checks, when many of us can avoid prosecution simply by covering the bounced check? Would Parker's crime disappear if he offered to make good his bogus checks?

Of course we "know" we are not criminals, whereas we also "know" that Julian is. Confusion on this fact illustrates the difficulty in defining crime. Clear definitions are needed if we are to measure crime in order to chart trends and to test competing explanations of crime. Because crime is difficult to measure once defined, the best crime statistics are but estimates. However, some estimates are more valid than others.

We consider three approaches to defining and measuring crime: (1) legal definitions of crime, (2) official police reports, and (3) victimization surveys.

THE LEGAL APPROACH. The task of defining crime is deceptively simple, as we can see from the check forger who says he is doing no worse than anyone else

The state trooper represents formal social controls in our society. Although we teach our children that "policemen are your friends," most of us fear seeing the flashing red lights in our rearview mirror that often indicate we have broken one of our society's formally sanctioned norms, or laws. (*Photo courtesy the author*)

who bounces a check. Although the law appears to forbid certain behaviors, it also allows for motivation and circumstances. All bad checks are not equal. You do intend to cover your checks, whereas Julian does not.

Crime *is behavior that violates criminal law.* Legally, a crime is what a court decides is a crime, but this definition is too narrow for most research purposes. Only a court can judge evidence, weigh motives and reasoning, and decide that the defendant is guilty of a crime. But many criminal acts never result in a trial, let alone a conviction. If we want to understand crime, we will usually be more interested in reported acts of crime rather than only in crimes that result in a conviction.

POLICE REPORTS. Police departments and the FBI use a different working definition of crime than do the courts. The FBI's Uniform Crime Report is based on local police reports of crime. Local police reports include direct observation of crimes by police and, more frequently, reports of crimes from citizens. Although some of these reports involve incidents courts may later decide were accidents or justifiable actions, police reports probably provide a more reasonable estimate of actual crime than do court reports. However, even these official statistics underestimate substantially the actual incidence of crime at any given time.

VICTIMIZATION SURVEYS. Sociologists have attempted to approximate the "real" crime rate more closely by surveying samples of the population and asking whether they have been victims of particular crimes during the period of study. These victimization surveys produce crime rates nearly twice as high as those measured by police reports.

The National Opinion Research Center (NORC), for example, found in its 1965 survey of 10,000 households that there were 42.5 forcible rapes per 100,000 people per year, as compared to the 11.6 reported in the FBI's Uniform Crime Report. Similarly, FBI measurement of the robbery rate was 94 per 100,000 per year, whereas the NORC figure was 296.6 (Ennis, 1967).

Recently the Law Enforcement Assistance Administration (LEAA) sponsored the largest social survey ever conducted. Their figures indicate 2.1 times more rapes, 2.3 times more robberies, and 2.7 times more burglaries as reported by the FBI. FBI figures exceed those of the victimization survey only in the case of homicide (where the victim is unlikely to be available for interviews with criminologists!) and auto theft, which is usually officially reported because the victim can be reimbursed for the loss by an insurance company.

Why do so many crimes go unreported? Thirty-four percent of those not reporting crimes to police did not report because they lacked proof or believed nothing could be done. Twenty-eight percent did not regard the crime as serious enough to report. Other victims said they were afraid, embarrassed, or they found reporting the crime inconvenient (Reid, 1976).

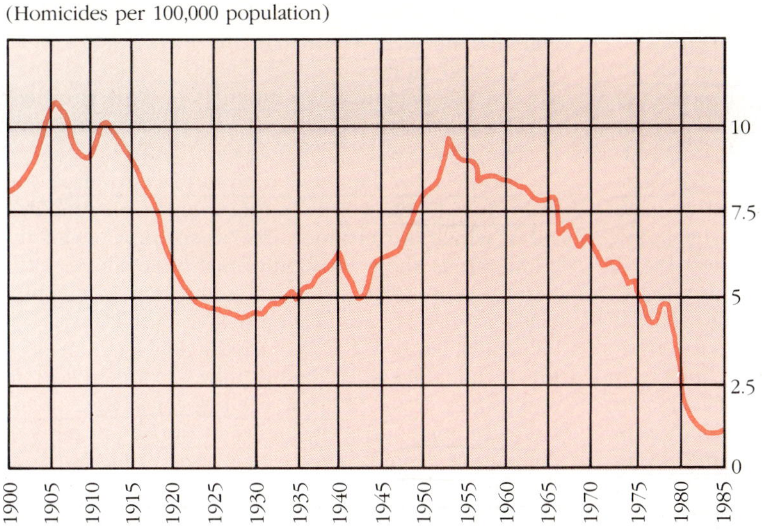

FIGURE 6.1 U.S. Homicide Rate, 1900–1985. SOURCE National Center for Health Statistics. *Vital Statistics of the United States* and U.S. Department of Justice's *Crime in the United States.*

The fact that we find we need several ways to define and measure crime points up a major feature of the concept. As labeling theorists point out, the concept of crime is socially defined, not natural, and the word *criminal* is a prime example of a label. In our culture the label is one that is applied and removed with great difficulty. Statistics show that the number of reported crimes is much greater than the number of convictions. This suggests that many people who could be labeled criminal are not. Conversely, once the label has been applied, it may become a master status having great influence over how one is regarded and acts, far after the debt to society has been repaid. Consider, for instance, how your estimation of a person would change by the revelation that he or she bore the label ex-convict.

Crime is socially defined in a very real sense. As a society we decide first what behaviors will be defined as criminal and second who will be officially labeled as such. We begin by considering some basic statistics about trends in crime and characteristics of those convicted of crimes. But as we look behind these statistics, we see that our definition of what crime is and how individuals come to be treated as criminals determines to a large degree what these trends and patterns are.

CHANGES AND DIFFERENCES IN THE UNITED STATES CRIME RATES

Using the various crime indices we can measure how crime increases or decreases, and compare regions to one another. The FBI Crime Index, which is probably the most often cited, has a peculiarity we should consider. The Index includes eight crimes: murder, forcible rape, robbery, aggravated assault, burglary, larceny-theft, motor vehicle theft, and arson. However, all of these crimes are counted equally. The most common of these Index crimes is larceny-theft, which means the unlawful taking of another's property. Shoplifting of items worth more than a certain value (like $100) is larceny. Because all offenses are lumped together to form this Crime Index, shoplifting is counted as heavily as premeditated murder. Furthermore, because crimes against property, such as larceny and burglary, are much more common than crimes of violence against persons, such as murder, assault, and rape, the Index is more sensitive to changes in these property offenses than to changes in violent crimes.

How have crime rates changed over time in the United States? In the past two decades the public has grown increasingly fearful of crime. This fear is, in part, due to actual dramatic increases in crime rates from the period 1960 to 1974. It is also due to the media attention crime has commanded. Suppose we consider the homicide rate. As we can see from Figure 6.1, the reported homicide rate at the turn of the century was about one-tenth of our present rate. From 1905 to 1935 the rate soared, and for the next two decades it declined to about half the mid-1930s high. In the 1960s the homicide rate began to rise rapidly until the middle 1970s when it surpassed the previous high reached in the middle 1930s. After a brief reversal, the rate rose to an all-time high in 1980, from which it has dropped about 20 percent during the early 1980s.

Why do crime rates like that for homicide change? Several major factors need to be considered. During this century the reliability of reporting procedures has improved. Presently some 15,000 individual police departments supply data to the FBI. Early reporting was less reliable, so early rates may have been underestimated. Another major factor is simply the age distribution of the population. Murders, as well as many other crimes, are more often committed by young males in the 16–21 age bracket. After World War II the United States experienced very high birth rates. As this "baby boom" generation grew, schools were expanded for the increasing number of students. When those students reached ages 18–24, the bracket in which crime is most common, the crime rate increased, and prisons were expanded to accommodate them. Thus the baby boom helps to explain the homicide rate rising in the late 1960s and early 1970s. Now that those born during the baby boom have grown older, they have passed through the high-crime age bracket, and we see a reduction in crime rates.

Our ability to measure and analyze crime is relatively primitive. Some things are clear. Crime is more common in urban areas than in suburban and rural areas. Beginning in the middle 1970s, the population of urban areas in the United States stopped growing and began shrinking, which could cause crime rates to diminish. We also know that arrest rates for most crimes are higher for blacks than whites. This probably relates more closely to the conditions blacks typically live in—poverty, bad housing, poor schooling, broken homes—and with prejudice within the criminal justice system, than with race in itself.

Criminologist James Alan Fox (1978) developed a computer model to forecast crime rates. He input previous crime rates, size of police force, and three major predicting variables: (1) percent of the population that is nonwhite and age 14–17, (2) percent of the population that is nonwhite and age 18–21; and (3) the consumer price index. Using this model Fox made some remarkably accurate predictions: He predicted a 1980 crime rate for urban areas of between 735.9 and 752.4 crimes per 100,000 population—the actual figure was 745.9. Fox's model predicted the decline in violent crime in the early 1980s to a new low in 1992, to about 20 percent below the current level. Much of this decline has and will occur because of lowered birthrates for both blacks and whites from a postwar high of 3.8 children per woman to 1.8 in 1976, the lowest recorded level in U.S. history.

Not all the experts expect this decline. Lawrence E. Cohen, a sociologist from Indiana University, believes that crime will continue to increase because greater opportunities exist for criminals to engage in criminal conduct. According to Cohen, the vast increase in lightweight items suitable for theft, including radios, televisions, stereos, and video cassette recorders, and the influx of women in the work force, which leaves more homes empty for longer periods of time, as well as enabling fewer mothers to supervise their youth, may also contribute to increases in crime (Cohen, 1981).

Crime rates vary widely from place to place and from time to time. This is true even in metropolitan areas, where, for instance, the New York City violent-crime rate is about forty times that of St. Cloud, Minnesota. Why are crime rates so different in different places? Again we are dealing with a complicated set of behaviors, but based on statistical analysis we can identify certain factors as being linked to differences in crime rates. Rates of crime are higher in larger population centers, and even higher in the denser parts of population centers. As we have seen, crime rates are typically higher for populations that are disproportionately young, nonwhite, and male. Crime is also more prevalent in areas where the population is increasing than in areas where the population is decreasing or stable.

Crime rates also vary as we change our definitions of crime. Public drunkenness, once the most common crime in the United States, was largely "decriminalized" in the 1970s. Abortion was once a felony offense; it no longer is. On the other hand, some behaviors such as drunk driving are being added to the list of criminal offenses.

WHO ARE THE CRIMINALS?

A ***criminal*** *is someone who has become publicly associated with commission of a crime or crimes*. Several studies indicate that if the term "criminal" referred to anyone who ever exhibited criminal behavior, almost everyone in society could be called a criminal. Wallerstein and Wyle (1947) surveyed 1,678 New Yorkers and found that 91 percent admitted breaking at least one law for which they could have been fined or imprisoned. Other studies indicate law-breaking is common and that only a fraction of it comes to the attention of authorities.

If so many people break the law, why are so few punished? The answers to this difficult question lie partly in deviance patterns and partly in the organization of the criminal-processing institutions of our society. It is comfortable to think that police succeed in catching the most frequent and worst offenders—the "real" criminals—and that many of those who self-reported criminal behavior to sociologists are only infrequent offenders of minor laws. But it is also possible that many professional criminals never get caught and that the law is structured to find and label only a particular segment of the "criminal" population—perhaps only those who can be more easily caught. Little is

TABLE 6.2 Proportion of Arrests by Gender

	Serious Violent Crime (%)	Serious Property Crime (%)
Males	89.0	77.6
Females	10.4	22.4

SOURCE FBI, *Uniform Crime Reports*, 1986

As can be seen clearly from these figures, those arrested for serious crimes are overwhelmingly males.

known about people who commit crimes and escape. Sociological studies of criminals are usually studies of apprehended offenders.

Who are these apprehended individuals, and why do they find themselves in custody whereas others who violate the criminal law do not? Because criminal acts involve a diverse set of behaviors, it is impossible to generalize about the "typical offender." Yet there are some similarities among individuals who are processed as criminals or criminal suspects.

For instance, as Table 6.2 indicates, the population of arrests is overwhelmingly male. Of those arrested for serious crimes in 1985, 83 percent were male, and for less serious offenses 85 percent were male (FBI, 1985). It has been pointed out, however, that female participation in crime is growing slightly, especially in larceny (Adler & Adler, 1979; Conklin, 1986).

What do these statistics imply about the validity of the various theories of deviance? We do well to evaluate and extend our theories by considering data, but we need to be careful in the case of official crime statistics. Often these statistics involve those who were arrested, convicted, or imprisoned rather than the whole population of offenders, many of whom are never even arrested. Also, in the case of arrest data we are dealing with some people who will later be found innocent of the crime of which they were accused. Although the population of arrestees may be similar to the population of offenders, it may also be a systematically different one. For instance, if police are more likely to arrest black offenders than white offenders, the profiles of arrestees will be a distorted image of the profile of offenders in general. In short, criminal justice statistics depend on two factors: (1) who commits crimes, and (2) who is processed or set free by the system. With this caution in mind, we now consider what we might be able to learn about the various theories from arrest data.

The profile of the typical arrestee can be viewed as supporting various theories of deviance. The fact that males are overrepresented in the criminal population may support differential association theory, since males tend to associate primarily with other males.

The high crime rates for those in the 15–24-year-old age bracket can be interpreted as supporting social control theories (see Table 6.3). People in this age bracket often lack the stabilizing influence of a family, being "between" families—having left parents but not yet having married. They may also lack the social control afforded by schools. Similarly, many youths have not yet found full-time employment, which would provide a measure of social control. Young persons are also more capable than older ones of committing crimes like burglary.

The fact that blacks and American Indians are highly overrepresented in crime statistics can be viewed as support for the conflict interpretation. (See Table 6.4.) It seems plausible that oppressed minorities are more likely to be reported, arrested, prosecuted, and imprisoned than their more influential counterparts in the dominant group. Also, minority crimes may be more easily detected that those of the white-collar criminal from the dominant white culture.

Two other ethnic groups, the Chinese and Japanese, have lower crime rates than whites. One could use cultural transmission theory or social control theories to explain this finding. These groups might have strong internal social control mechanisms that prohibit criminal behavior more effectively than other groups do. Also, as we will see in Chapter 9, those of Japanese

TABLE 6.3 Arrest Distribution of Criminal Activity for Those in Different Age Groups

	Ages 15–24	Ages 25–34	Ages 35–44	Ages 45–54
Serious violent crime rate	45.1	31.1	12.2	4.3
Serious property crime rate	50.7	26.4	11.1	3.1

SOURCE FBI, *Uniform Crime Reports, 1986;* and U.S. Census Bureau, *Crime in the United States, 1986,* Table 33, Total Arrests Distributed by Age, 1985, pp. 174–175.

The official criminal is likely to be an individual under 25, an age category that accounts for half the arrests for all crime. Official figures clearly show that those arrested in 1985 for serious crime were disproportionately young.

TABLE 6.4 Arrest Percentages for Those of Different Racial Groups

	Serious Violent Crime Rate	Serious Property Crime Rate
White	51.5	67.7
Black	47.1	30.3
Native American	.8	1.1
Asian or Pacific Islander	.6	.9

SOURCE FBI, *Uniform Crime Reports, 1986,* and U.S. Census Bureau, *Crime in the United States, 1986,* Table 38, Total Arrests, Distributed by Race.

Blacks and American Indians (Native Americans) were arrested for serious property and violent crimes in a much higher proportion than whites. Blacks account for almost half the arrests for violent crime and 30 percent of the arrests for property crime, although they comprise only 12 percent of the population. The proportion of arrested Asians in 1986 is much smaller than that of whites. It is important to note that these statistics report *arrests;* legally, a person is not regarded as a criminal unless convicted.

and Chinese heritage in the United States are less economically disadvantaged than are blacks and American Indians.

Crime, like deviance in general, is not simply a matter of violation of norms, but the result of behavior on the part of individuals and reactions on the part of others. We must be careful not to misinterpret reactions and actions. Blacks, for instance, show up disproportionately as offenders, but this is in part due to the fact that they are more likely to be prosecuted, and more likely to receive harsh penalties. As we see in a later section, when we consider blacks and whites guilty of the same crime—homicide—blacks are five times more likely to receive the death sentence. The profile of the "typical" offender may reveal as much about how society reacts to crime as it does about those who become labeled offenders.

A combination of theories is usually needed to explain comprehensively the interactions of deviance and social control. One way to test which theories are most valid is to compare predictions of each theory to actual observations. This is, of course, the heart of the research process. In the following Close-Up on Research, Robert Kraut's study of shoplifting helps test two theories of

CLOSE-UP on • *RESEARCH* •

Robert Kraut on Shoplifting and Deviance Theory

The Researcher and the Setting

Robert Kraut is interested in shoplifting for its practical importance. In addition, "it is a promising area for examining theories of deviance" (Kraut, 1976, p. 358). Much of earlier research in deviance deals either with official records of criminals or with experiments of an artificial nature.

The Researcher's Goal

Through this research Kraut attempts to identify the factors that "might influence a shopper's decision to steal" and to study the effects of apprehension on the shoplifter's self-concept and his or her perception of the risks involved in shoplifting (p. 358).

Theories and Concepts

The deterrence model and the labeling model of deviance guide Kraut's research. Deterrence theory is based on formal and informal external social controls, and suggests that deviance increases as the perceived risk of punishment decreases. Labeling theory states that an actor is more likely to perform an action when it is consistent with his or her self-concept.

Kraut's findings help us to evaluate these models in terms of how well they describe the circumstances of real deviance.

Research Design

Kraut uses the survey technique. He sent 1,500 questionnaires to a random sample of University of Pennsylvania students who lived in campus housing. An advantage of this approach, in contrast to using official records, is that it provides information about deviants who have not been apprehended. The questionnaire contained 149 precoded questions and could be completed in one-half hour. It sought information about the subjects' shoplifting experiences, how much risk they perceived in shoplifting, their self-image, the image they had of a typical shoplifter, their friends' attitudes toward shoplifting, and whether they had been apprehended for shoplifting. If the subject had been apprehended, he or she was asked about the authorities' reaction as well as that of family and friends. Of the 606 students who returned the questionnaire, 372, or 61 percent, reported they had shoplifted, and 60 students, or 16 percent, had been caught at least once.

Findings

The research findings seem to be consistent with the deterrence model. "As deterrence theory would predict, respondents who shoplifted most saw the least risk associated with shoplifting" (p. 360). Also, "the more [that] respondents shoplifted, the more they described themselves as invulnerable to apprehension, compared to others who steal. They were also more likely to predict that 'nothing serious would happen' if caught" (pp. 361–362). Finally, respondents who shoplifted more often believed that other people approved of shoplifting, and the relationship between frequency of shoplifting and this belief was significantly stronger when subjects described "people who were important to them" (p. 362). Shoplifters were more likely to have friends who shoplifted and to make high estimates of the proportion of college students who shoplift.

Kraut's findings also support labeling theory. Kraut measured the discrepancy between the shoplifter's self-description and description of a typical shoplifter. Respondents who shoplifted more described themselves and typical shoplifters in similar terms. This held true for both apprehended and unapprehended shoplifters. Apprehended shoplifters describe a typical shoplifter as more fearful than unapprehended shoplifters woiuld describe him or her.

Self-concept was found to be important in another way. Those who did not steal were likely to attribute their nonstealing to their own honesty, but shoplifters did not attribute their stealing to their own dishonesty. The three most important reasons given by shoplifters for shoplifting were "their desire not to pay for an item, their desire of the item, and the small risk of apprehension they saw" (p. 363).

Implications

We find several implications in this research. First, deterrence appears to be important in preventing shoplifting. "On every measure included in the questionnaire to assess perception of risk, those who shoplifted more estimated less risk" (p. 365). For this crime the approval or disapproval of friends and relatives was a stronger influence than either official sanctions or public disapproval. Second, self-concept appears to correlate positively with behavior. "When respondents explained why they hadn't stolen the last time they bought an item in a store, the two most important reasons they gave were their own honesty and their belief that shoplifting was unacceptable behavior" (p. 365).

Of course we could make other interpretations of these findings. For instance, Kraut reports that those who shoplifted more estimated less risk. Following deterrence theory he reasons that those who shoplifted less did so because they estimated a higher risk of sanction. Perhaps instead the experience of not being caught leads to lower perceptions of the chances of being caught. Also, Kraut reports that approval or disapproval of friends and relatives was a stronger influence than either official sanctions or public disapproval. This seems to directly support differential association theory, though Kraut does not raise this point in the article.

As Kraut indicates, these results are suggestive rather than definitive. There are several shortcomings in this work. Perhaps the most important is that the students used are not representative of the general public. Also, about 60 percent of those sent the questionnaire failed to respond at all, which raises the possibility that those who did are not even typical University of Pennsylvania students. In spite of these weaknesses, the research gives some preliminary indications about an interesting and important form of deviance and tends to substantiate two major theories of deviance being used by social scientists.

Questions

1. How well would you expect Kraut's results to apply to other forms of deviance, such as use of illegal drugs, burglary, or robbery? Why?
2. Kraut reports that nearly two-thirds of the respondents admitted shoplifting (372 out of 606). Who do you think would be more likely to respond to his questionnaire, a shoplifter or nonshoplifter? Why? How would this affect the accuracy of Kraut's estimate of the prevalence of shoplifting?
3. How might we apply Kraut's findings (a) to protect shops? and (b) to reduce the likelihood our children will shoplift?

SOURCE Robert E. Kraut. February 1976. "Deterrent and definitional influences on shoplifting." *Social Problems* 23 pp. 358–367.

deviance: labeling theory and a form of social control theory we call deterrence theory. ***Deterrence theory*** *claims that deviance increases as the perceived risk of sanction decreases.*

WHITE-COLLAR CRIME

Ken sits at his desk in New York, having just completed a half-hour conversation with his mother in San Francisco on the company phone. He remembers the article his wife wanted him to copy, walks over to the copy machine, and runs it through. He has a speech to give this weekend at his church, which he picks up, typed, from his secretary. Glancing at his watch he decides there's not enough time to start a new project, so he heads for home half an hour early.

His boss, Mike, is wrapping up details on the expense account for his recent business trip. Somehow

Much of the business done in the United States is based on trust. The transactions of this member of the New York Stock Exchange, for instance, are completely verbal, with the buyers and sellers simply making notes on their own pads as to how many shares of what they agreed to buy or sell. When trust is violated, as in the instance of the stock exchange inside information scandal, reverberations are felt throughout the business community. (*Photo courtesy the author*)

he used up the $300 cash advance and must now show where it went. For that one special dinner he did overspend the limit the company normally pays, but he can solve that by claiming he had a client along with him, which is almost true, because he did visit a client that afternoon. Then there are the drinks he is not allowed to charge off to the company. Mike decides to claim them as "cab fare" and reports several fictitious cab rides.

Over the course of a year Ken and Mike may easily each take a $1,000 advantage of their employer, yet neither of them sees himself as a criminal. Admittedly, their crimes are not as calculated as those of Fred, who works at a bank in Baltimore. Fred is an obsessive gambler who has found an ingenious way to use his computer skills to "borrow" thousands of dollars from dormant savings accounts.

In a corporate suite in Seattle, Louise and John have just traded "secrets" that will enable both of them to invest more profitably in the stock market the next day. They do not see this as illegal, but rather as a friendly gesture toward a colleague.

Edwin Sutherland (1949) coined the term "white-collar crime" to describe certain criminal offenses that differ in significant ways from violent crimes and the usual crimes against property. ***White-collar crime*** *is crime committed by a person of responsibility and high social status in the course of his or her occupation.* Some common white-collar offenses are embezzlement, misrepresentation in advertising, patent or copyright infringement, and tax fraud.

Sutherland researched for ten years before he published his book *White-Collar Crime*, which documented crimes he had discovered by America's seventy largest private companies and fifteen public utility corporations (1949). His publisher refused to allow names in the book, for fear of lawsuits. Thirty years later Americans began to believe that white-collar crime is more serious and deserving of longer prison sentences than many forms of common crime, and Sutherland's book was published uncut (Braithwaite, 1985).

WHAT DISTINGUISHES WHITE-COLLAR CRIME? White-collar crime differs from more conventional crime in several important ways. Frequently the victims remain unaware they have been victimized. Buyers may not know prices have been fixed, the government may not discover that a corporation has filed a fraudulent tax return, and a company does not realize it has financed the new Mercedes of an executive.

Frequently, also, the offender does not view himself or herself as a criminal. Lee Iacocca said employees of Chrysler Corporation were "stupid" for having systematically reset the odometers of hundreds of used cars so the cars could be fraudulently sold as new. This behavior is a criminal offense in many states, but probably the individuals involved do not see themselves as criminals. Certainly Iacocca never said we should prosecute these employees for their crime, though he did publicly apologize, and Chrysler Corporation made compensatory payments. To the surprise of many members of Congress, Oliver North seemed to be able to convince the public and even some of his political opponents that his participation in the raising of secret

One hundred million dollar man. As the old folksong goes, some rob you with a six-gun and some with a fountain pen. White collar criminal Ivan Boesky paid $100 million in fines and served a jail sentence for securities laws violations that allowed him to cheat fellow investors out of millions. *(AP/Wide World Photos)*

funds to sell weapons to Iran was not a crime but a patriotic duty. Whether it is stealing from one's employer, like Ken in the opening example, or the higher stake crimes of corporate and political fraud, white-collar crime often seems less criminal than other types of crime.

Clinard and Quinney (1973) have proposed that white-collar crime be divided into occupational and corporate crime. They define *occupational crime* as offenses committed by individuals themselves in the course of their occupations, and the offenses of employees against their employers, including blue-collar crimes, and *corporate crime* as the offenses committed by corporate officials for the corporation, and offenses of the corporation itself. Many researchers think that this distinction must be made for further progress in the study of white-collar crime, with concentration on corporate crime (Braithwaite, 1985). Because occupational crime is so varied, it is difficult to study. But much corporate crime has a common base, which could be identified and studied with positive results for society as a whole.

The qualities that make white-collar crime different from street crime also make white-collar crime more difficult for social scientists to measure: Little money is spent to apprehend white-collar criminals; the realm in which they operate is away from police patrols; and their crimes may be difficult to detect in any event. Also, most police arrests for any crime result from a complaint from a victim, and victims of white-collar crime are often unaware of their victimization (Reiss, 1971).

EXPLANATIONS OF WHITE-COLLAR CRIME. One central idea of labeling theory is that higher status people are more able to control what is labeled as deviance, so they are better able to avoid this label. This seems to be the case with white-collar crime. The offender seldom regards himself or herself as criminal and often succeeds in convincing others that the offense is not serious. Thus we find apparent paradoxes—embezzler of $60,000 goes home on probation, but a person who steals a $6,000 car goes to prison.

Those who take the conflict-theory perspective would argue what white-collar crime serves as an illustration supporting their point of view. They see the legal system as a tool the elites used to exploit and manipulate the powerless. Naturally, the elites rarely use this weapon on themselves. When caught, they are able to use their status, power, and money to bluff, bully, and bribe their way out of sanctions provided by law. Whereas conflict theorists would agree with labeling theorists that high-status offenders manipulate the labeling process, they go farther to suggest that this is part of a systematic application of power to exploit those of low status.

Some theories of deviance more easily explain white-collar crime. Theories that explain crime in terms of the offender's poverty, exploitation, or anomie do not readily apply, because the offenders are of "high status." Sutherland believed that differential association could explain white-collar crime because workers might learn criminal behavior from other workers on the way up the ladder. Another explanation stresses the importance of opportunity for white-collar crime. For example, executives must be in a position to set prices before they can commit the crime of price-fixing.

THE LEGAL RESPONSE. In the past, citizens and law-enforcement agencies have not always acknowledged such activities as price-fixing as crimes. White-collar crimes usually involve more money than conventional property crimes. The average computer crime involves $25,000, and the average bank robbery, $2,500. The embezzlement of $21.3 million from Wells Fargo National Bank in San Francisco in 1980 caused losses totaling more than half of all bank robberies in the United States that year (Ball, 1982). Most of this crime has gone unpunished or lightly punished (Sutherland, 1983). One reason for this is that it is more difficult to prove the guilt of white-collar suspects, and they are more able to defend themselves by hiring teams of lawyers (Levi, 1981).

An example of law enforcement attitudes is found in the case of David Begelman. While president of Columbia Pictures, he forged actor Cliff Robertson's signature on a $10,000 check and embezzled a total of $60,000. Begelman was charged with felony grand theft but sentenced only to three years' probation. Begelman spent a year on probation during which he made a film on the dangers of the drug, angel dust. Then the judge reduced his conviction from a felony to a misdemeanor and ended his probation (Egan, 1982).

The situation in some areas of public corruption is dire. One study found that members of the New York State legislature in the 1970s had four times as great a chance of having criminal records as the ordinary New York voter (Katz, 1980).

Even when white-collar offenses are detected, they are more likely to be handled by an administrative agency like the IRS than by legal institutions, and offenders are less likely to receive a criminal sentence. Sutherland found that only 9 percent of the cases he studied ever entered criminal courts (Sutherland 1949), although this percentage is growing as public sentiment against white-collar crime grows stronger. The research of Meier and Short (1984) shows that citizens now view white-collar crime as serious and think they are more likely to be victims of it than victims of street crime. Furthermore, most citizens are now clamoring for punishment of white-collar criminals (Cullen et al., 1983; 1982).

DETERRING WHITE-COLLAR CRIME Chambliss points out that white-collar criminals should be very deterrable compared to other criminals, because they do not see crime as their way of life, and they commit their crimes for the money rather than as a way of expressing their feelings about life (Chambliss, 1967). They also have many of the outer rewards of society, which they could lose if their crime was detected, unlike many street criminals who have little to lose in terms of prestige, power, and material goods (Holland, 1982; Fisse and Braithwaite, 1983). Several researchers believe that rehabilitation and incapacitation, which are not generally effective with street criminals, are much more useful with white-collar criminals (Braithwaite and Geis, 1982). All these observations suggest that the threat and application of strong sanctions might be an effective policy against white-collar crime.

More resources and energy applied by punishing agencies may not be the only or best answer to control this sort of crime, however. One prominent expert in the field believes that prevention is much more effective than punishment in white-collar crime. He suggests that in order to reduce such crimes, governments should give bargaining clout to regulatory agencies and force top management of companies to back internal compliance groups. This would award corporations responsibility for policing their own ranks (Braithwaite, 1984, 1985).

In the next section we describe how criminals are processed through the American criminal justice system today. As we shall see, there is ample opportunity for both the white-collar criminal and other offenders to leave the system unchanged.

THE SOCIAL CONTROL OF CRIME

Suspected criminal offenders are "processed" through a complicated and cumbersome bureaucracy that the public and government expect to serve both as an instrument of justice and as an effective means of social control. Authorities at each level of the bureaucracy have discretionary judgment to free the suspect or pass him or her on to the next level. The police decide whether or not to arrest a suspect. The magistrate decides the suspect can be released on bail. The prosecutor determines the charge and may try the individual or not. Courts may find the accused innocent or guilty. The judge renders a short, long, or suspended sentence. The warden selects the type of prison or jail setting, and the parole board decides for or against early release.

As we imply in "How's Your Sociological Intuition?" and show in Table 6.5, the connection between committing a crime and going to prison is far from automatic. On the surface it might appear there is almost no chance of going to prison for committing even a serious property crime in the United States. The fact is that roughly half of all crimes go unreported, and

TABLE 6.5 Legal Actions Against Crime in the United States

For every 100 serious property crimes known to the police:
18 are "cleared by arrest"
17 people are charged
5 are found guilty
For every 100 serious violent crimes known to the police:
47 are "cleared by arrest"
38 people are charged
10 people are found guilty as charged
2 people are found guilty of a lesser charge
For every 100 serious violent or property crimes known to the police:
.88 people, less than 1 percent, go to prison

SOURCE Based on data from FBI, *Uniform Crime Reports*, 1986.

only 26 percent of crimes reported to police result in an arrest. Of those who are charged, a relatively small proportion are found guilty. Nearly a third of those arrested are under 18, and they are charged with juvenile delinquency rather than with committing a crime, as they would be if they were adults. Thus some of what Table 6.5 considers to be crimes are redefined by the system as delinquency. These and other factors account for the fact that a relatively small proportion of crimes results in prison sentences.

HOW DO PRISONS FUNCTION?

For thousands of years, prisons were used as holding places for accused persons who had not yet been tried. Once their guilt had been determined, the accused were generally either tortured, beaten, or executed. Ancient governments never considered the expensive option of holding prisoners for long periods of time as punishment.

William Penn, Quaker founder of a new way of life in Pennsylvania, first began the practice of incarceration instead of extermination as part of his "holy experiment." The idea that there is "that of God in every man" prohibits Quakers from taking any life. Instead, they ordered convicted criminals to work at hard labor in order to pay back those they had wronged and support themselves at the same time. When this system was found wanting, the Quakers modified it with the building of the first penitentiary, from the idea that prisoners should be isolated and silent in order to learn to be penitent, or sorry for their sins. Their cells were small and their lives simple. Prisoners still worked, but did so in silence and went back to their isolation when the day was done.

In the 1940s, labor unions began to resent the goods and services being provided at low cost by state and federal prisoners, and forced most work programs to shut down. This led to new problems: prisoner boredom and free time to cause trouble. It also severely increased the cost of imprisonment, which had previously been at least somewhat self-sustaining. In 1986 most states paid an average of $20,000 per year to keep each prisoner locked up.

REHABILITATION. During the 1950s and 1960s, a reform movement swept the prison systems, with social workers and psychologists endeavoring to "cure" criminals of their tendencies toward crime by intervening psychologically and trying to change the environment in which they lived. Although the basic ideal was praiseworthy, the program appears to have failed. The recidivism rate, or percentage of prisoners who are readmitted, is still 60 percent.

It is generally accepted that prisons do *not* often rehabilitate offenders. Approximately 61 percent of those currently in federal prisons or reformatories have previous records of incarceration. Almost half of these would still have been in prison at the time of their second arrest if they had served their full first sentence, and 60 percent of them reenter prison within three years of leaving it (Greenfield, 1985). Considering the inability of legal institutions to detect crime and put an offender in prison, it is unlikely that many of the remaining 40 percent were rehabilitated; perhaps they were simply luckier in their renewed careers.

SCHOOLS FOR CRIME. In fact, a common argument is that prisons and jails are really "schools for crime," in which relatively inexperienced offenders learn new criminal techniques and deviant values. In prison, the argument goes, a person can learn anything from safecracking and forgery to murder (Goldfarb, 1974). One critic (Wicker, 1975) suggests:

> Precisely at the point where the first offender has been apprehended, tried and placed in the custody of society . . . he ought to be treated, trained, redirected, and sent back to a useful place in society. . . . [He] is instead cast into squalid and terrifying confinement among hardened criminals, . . . trained (if at all) in the most menial or useless kind of work, in many cases treated little better than an animal and effectively separated from any glimpse of decency or beauty or hope in life (p. 5).

On the other hand, few first offenders go to prison; those sent to prison have already learned to commit crime. Prison inmates may learn new techniques and values, but their presence in prison probably indicates they have a well-established criminal life-style. A typical newcomer to prison has been arrested several times and often has been previously convicted and given a suspended sentence. Research generally indicates that modern prisons do not have a rehabilitative effect, nor do they create criminals.

DO PRISONS DETER CRIME? If prisons do not rehabilitate, do they help control crime by existing as a deterrent to those who might be tempted to behave unlawfully? Do they at least prevent the crime rate from rising even faster by keeping the serious and frequent offender behind bars?

Some people believe punishment deters people from committing crimes, because it serves as a negative incentive to engage in criminal behavior. Although several studies show that crime rates are lower where punishment is more severe, that could be due to more cases pending than the prosecutors can handle. Under these conditions prosecutors are more likely to *plea bargain*—ask for a reduced charge—if the defendant agrees to plead guilty to the lesser charge. This reduces the prosecutor's work, because no preparation for a trial is needed—the prosecutor might have had to drop other cases because witnesses forgot details or failed to appear when the case dragged on. Criminal sanctions are also lessened to compensate for crowded court time and crowded prisons. Thus, although we know crime and punishment are related inversely (one drops when the other rises), more research is needed to determine whether this is due to a deterrence effect, to overload, or to both.

In the 1970s and 1980s, many states began get-tough campaigns, in which they began to imprison many more criminals than previously. This led to massive overcrowding of prison facilities and to overtaxed prison officials and guards. Prisons have doubled their population since 1970, and 1 out of every 500 Americans is now in prison or jail (U.S. Bureau of the Census, 1988). As a result, most prison systems are returning to a custodial role in prison care, abandoning the idea that they might rehabilitate prisoners.

Unfortunately, because so few criminals are actually caught and imprisoned, even this massive campaign has brought little relief of crime in the streets. Researchers estimate that tripling the state and federal prison population would reduce serious crime by only 20 percent (Currie, 1982). Because we catch and sentence only a small percentage of criminals, and those we do catch tend to return to prison, we can assume that those who are "better" at crime will continue to plague the rest of society, almost regardless of penalties and programs.

Recent studies suggest that imprisonment may not even prevent further violence. Many violent offenders who are arrested have no previous offenses on their records, and only 10 to 40 percent of violent offenders are ever apprehended (Currie, 1982).

One alternative given serious consideration is to determine which criminals are most dangerous, sentence them to longer periods of time, and reduce the terms of other offenders. Called *selective incapacitation*, this idea was proposed by Peter Greenwood, researcher at Rand Corporation (G. Moore, 1983). As early as the 1930s, Sheldon and Eleanor Glueck studied the characteristics of male delinquents in an attempt to separate them into those who would become "prolifically criminal" and those who would not (Glueck & Glueck, in Moore, 1983). Marvin Wolfgang of the University of Pennsylvania studied the criminal records of young men in Philadelphia over a period of thirty years and discovered that about 6 percent of them had been responsible for more than 50 percent of the crimes committed by the group as a whole, including having committed almost all of the serious crimes (Wolfgang, in Moore, 1983). Obviously there are inherent problems in trying to identify the "bad" criminals, but more research will probably be done toward this goal, because it has the potential of reducing crime significantly while reducing prison overcrowding.

It is possible to make certain general statements about the American criminal justice system. Most offenses that could result in someone's going to prison do not. People in prison are in general neither rehabilitated nor made significantly worse offenders by the experience. Stricter law enforcement in terms of stiffer sentences does not seem to deter criminal behavior. Some crime is prevented by keeping offenders in custody, although tripling our prison population would reduce crime by only 20 percent.

AN EYE FOR AN EYE: THE DEATH PENALTY DEBATE

Another result of the new attitude toward crime and rehabilitation is an upswing in the number of states with death-penalty provisions and the number of persons being condemned to death. In the period 1965–1967, for instance, only ten persons, or about three per year, were executed for murder. By 1984, this had risen to twenty-one. More people are now awaiting execution than at any other time in history. Among the roughly 1,600 people awaiting capital punishment in 1985, blacks were statistically overrepresented by a factor of 5.4 (U.S. Bureau of Census, 1986: Wicker, 1985).

In 1967, the Supreme Court ruled that most state capital-punishment laws were unconstitutional because they favored certain groups over others and were not specific enough in defining the crimes for which capital punishment was to be meted out. Since that time, many states have reworked their laws under new guidelines. Other states continue to substitute life imprisonment for death. Critics of the death penalty had hoped that the Court would declare it to be "cruel and unusual punishment," and thereby prohibited by the Fourth Amendment, but in 1972 that line of attack was struck down by the *Furman vs. Georgia* decision. Nevertheless, during that period, from 1967 to 1977, no executions took place.

Those who favor the reinstatement of the death penalty in states of the United States do so from various perspectives. Some, like governmental officials of yesterday, think that society wastes money supporting such people for any length of time. Others feel that it is right and just for society to take a life in payment for a life, and that the death penalty strengthens the moral norms of the society.

Capital punishment is opposed for many reasons. Quakers, Mennonites, and other religious groups oppose it on the grounds that no human being has the right to take the life of another under any circumstance. Other opponents often point to the fact that mistakes can be made in sentencing. For instance, Senator Howard Metzenbaum has documented forty-eight cases of Americans sentenced to death and later found to be innocent of the crime of which they were accused (Harper's Magazine, 1984).

Social activists have opposed the death penalty on the ground that it is negatively selective toward minorities. (See Figure 6.2) For every crime category, nonwhites are more likely to be arrested than whites and will serve longer sentences than whites convicted of the same crime (Blumstein, 1982). Blacks are 5.3 times more likely to be executed than whites, and the murder of a white is more likely to produce a death sentence than the murder of a black (Garfinkel, 1949; Gross and Mauro, 1984; Kleck, 1981; Greenhouse, 1983; U.S. Bureau of Census, 1986).

Some opponents maintain that the death penalty creates an atmosphere in the society that "might makes right," and actually increases the chance of homicides by adding to the general brutality evident in the culture (Bowers & Pierce, 1980; Bonn, 1984; Forst, 1983). The fact that underprivileged groups more often are executed than others may in fact feed this lack of concern for the human life.

The chief criticism of capital punishment, however, is that it does not serve to deter crime. Much of the earlier research, and some contemporary research, finds little or no lasting effect of capital punishment on occurrence of homicide, the major crime for which people are executed (Forst, 1983; *Crime and Delinquency,* 1980; D. King, 1978; W. Bailey, 1980; Tyler and Weber, 1982). This seems consistent with the fact that most murders, perhaps upwards of 80 percent, are crimes of passion rather than planned acts (Geerken and Gove, 1977). These murderers seem less likely to be deterred by the threat of a death penalty because they are committing their crime when angry or otherwise out of control, or drunk or under the influence of other drugs, and not likely to think through the consequences of their actions.

The research of economist Isaac Ehrlich (1975) used new statistical techniques to show that a negative correlation exists between capital punishment and executions. He concluded, in fact, that every execution in the United States from 1933 to 1969 prevented eight murders. In replicating Ehrlich's studies with his techniques, some researchers had similar results (Yunker, 1982), whereas others dismissed his work as the result of improper use of statistical techniques (McGahey, 1980). The research of David Phillips also supports the hypothesis that executions deter homicide (Phillips, 1980). The effect that Phillips discovered lasted only two weeks after the execution, however.

Steven Stack studied the impact of publicity on deterrence. He found that there are, on the average, thirty fewer homicides in months with publicized executions; in contrast, months with nonpublicized ex-

FIGURE 6.2 Breakdown by race of the 1,274 inmates who had been sentenced to die in the United States as of 1983. SOURCE Legal Defense Fund (Greenwood, 1983).

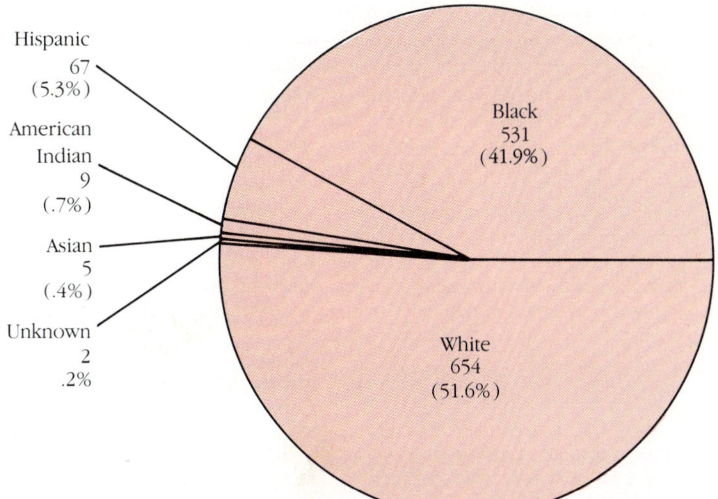

Sociologists at Work •

JAMES FOX
DEVELOPS SOCIOLOGICAL PROFILES OF THE MASS MURDERER
Northeastern University
Boston, Massachusetts

Jamie Fox has been studying mass murders with his colleague, Jack Levin, for eight years. Fox and Levin undertook the first systematic study to explore whether the common journalistic image of mass murderers is valid; are they crazed loners who feel an irresistible compulsion to kill and start shooting people at random?

What Are You Finding in Terms of an Actual Sociological Profile of a Mass Murderer?
In studying hundreds of cases of mass murder, we generally find that the mass murderer is not crazy at all. He tends to be bitter, angry, hostile. He tends to kill for jealousy or revenge, and he usually kills people he knows. Forty percent of mass murderers' victims are family members.

First, we discover that the mass killer is someone who has had years of experience with frustration, failure, and disappointments. He has had a difficult time at home, at work, in school, and in the military. His ability to cope with those disappointments is wearing thin.

Second, he has very weak forms of external controls. He doesn't have close peers, friends or co-workers who would ordinarily help him out in the roughest times.

Third, he has familiarity and training with firearms—usually through the military or law enforcement or just target shooting. He is very comfortable using a gun, and often uses guns to resolve problems in his life.

Finally, there is some precipitating event—that proverbial straw that breaks the camel's back. It is usually unemployment or divorce. We find these characteristics and conditions in almost all mass murderers, but not everybody who fits this profile will kill.

Tell Us More About the Use of Firearms
I don't want to blame mass murder just on firearms. However, it is very difficult to commit a mass murder with any other weapon. Seventy-five percent of mass murders are committed with firearms. You can't kill twenty-one people with a knife. The other 25 percent are a mixture of fire, bombings, and a few strangulations. But the firearm is the most effective means of mass destruction, particularly for the family member who is killing the entire clan. The gun distances him from his victims. It would be psychologically very difficult to kill his loved ones with his hands.

Can You Comment on What Seems To Be the Recency of This Social Behavior?
Nineteen sixty-six marks the onset of an age of mass murder in this country when Richard Speck killed eight nurses in Chicago. In that summer, Charles Whitman climbed the tower at the University of Texas the day after he murdered his mother and his wife and killed fourteen students.

Since that time the incidence of mass murder and the numbers killed in each murder have been steadily rising. They called Speck's crime the crime of the century, but it pales in comparison to the twenty-one killed at a McDonald's restaurant, the sixteen in Arkansas, the fourteen in a post office in Oklahoma.

It is a horrible statement that the game of *Trivial Pursuit* has the names of three mass murders in it. When I ask my students to list five mass murderers and five vice-presidents, they have no trouble with the murderers, but can't do the vice-presidents. You become famous by committing mass murder!

Why Is Mass Murder on the Increase?
Like any social trend, the increase has more than one cause. But one of the most important factors is that in modern American society, the traditional forms of social control—family, community, and church—are much weaker than they used to be. Many more people in society now, when they feel desperate or alone, don't have those support systems that were much stronger in this country thirty years ago. Sociologists refer to this situation as anomie.

A second important factor is the greater availability of firearms today. Fifty percent of Americans now own a handgun, and firearms are uniquely suited to mass murders. Cases of mass murder in other countries are few and far between. Mass murder is an American phenomenon in some part because we own so many more firearms in this country than in other western nations.

What Will the Trends Be in the Future?
It is difficult to predict. The homicide rate has been declining since 1981, and will continue to decrease because of the fact that the baby boom young people grew up and outgrew their crime-prone ages. However, mass murderers are a lot older than the usual killer—in their 30s and 40s as opposed to being between 18 and 24. The future incidence will depend on social factors such as trends that counteract anomie, gun availability, and demographics. •

ecutions exhibit no change in the homicide rate. Most earlier work had lumped little-publicized executions (which constitute over 90 percent of all executions in 1950–1980) together with publicized executions. Stack singled out publicized executions (Stack, 1987); if the public is unaware of executions, they can have little deterrent effect.

One alternative to the death penalty is life imprisonment. At $20,000 per year, incarceration for life is a burden on the public, but those so sentenced represent only about 3 percent of the total prison population (Bruck, 1983). However, under the present system, almost all of those condemned to die go through a lengthy and extremely costly set of appeal procedures to have the sentence commuted to life imprisonment (Nakell, 1978). A 1982 study of New York State cases concluded that the cost to taxpayers of such appeals could reach $1.8 million—more than twice the amount of imprisoning the offender for life (Bruck, 1983). In the long run, the government might save money by simply giving a life sentence initially and avoiding the appeals process.

Conclusion

Deviance represents not only violation of norms, but also the definition of the norms in the first place and the often selective enforcement of them later. As the examples of mental illness and crime show us, this is an area of considerable complexity in which several theories may be needed to better understand what is happening.

REVIEW

Summary Questions

1. What do sociologists mean by social control, and when do social controls influence behavior?
2. How do the various theories explain deviance?
3. How might anomie create a climate for deviance?
4. What is the difference between deviance and deviants?
5. How are the mentally ill treated?
6. How does society define crime?
7. Who are the criminals, and how are they treated by society?
8. What distinguishes white-collar crime, and how might it be deterred?
9. How do prisons function as social controls?
10. How effective is capital punishment as a deterrent to deviant behavior?

Summary Answers

1. Social control is the means by which members of a society attempt to induce each other to comply with the society's norms. Social controls influence behavior constantly, because they are internalized and come into play every time a person has a deviant impulse.
2. Social-control theory argues that deviance is largely a matter of failed social controls. Merton believes that the strain between the norms that define socially appropriate goals and the norms that specify socially appropriate means for attaining these goals creates an atmosphere in which deviance will appear. Travis Hirschi says that persons with a weakened bond to their social group are likely to become deviant.

   Differential association and cultural transmission theories propose that deviance is a natural outgrowth of a person's contacts during socialization and can be a part of a subculture that can be transmitted indefinitely.

   Conflict theory traces the origin of criminal behavior to class conflict between the powerful and the weak and sees criminals as reasonable individuals forced by circumstance to break laws in order to regain some of what has been taken from them or denied to them by an exploitative system.

   Functionalist theory proposes that deviance enhances feelings of unity within a society and helps define and redefine the norms.

   Labeling theory concentrates on the reactions of others to deviance, and studies which offenders are likely to be punished rather than which are likely to commit deviant acts.

   Deterrence theory suggests that deviance

increases as the perceived risk of being punished decreases and that people are more likely to be deviant if they think of themselves as deviant.

3. Durkheim believed that an absence of clear norms for a society or an individual might create a social setting in which deviance will occur.
4. Deviance is behavior that violates the norms of the social group in which the behavior occurs, whereas a deviant is one who is characterized as a violator of a norm. Engaging in deviant behavior does not automatically lead to a deviant reputation or self-image.
5. The mentally ill not only are treated as deviants but are feared. The fact that society treats them in this way increases their chances of being deviant in the future. The labeling of the mentally ill decreases their chances of future employment and of normal social relationships.
6. Crime is behavior that violates criminal law. It can be defined through laws, through official police reports of crimes, or through victimization surveys of persons who have been involved in crime but perhaps not involved with the police department.
7. A criminal is someone who has become publicly associated with commission of a crime. In the United States, the typical offender is a lower class male between 15 and 24 years old.
8. White-collar crime is crime committed by a person of responsibility and high social status in the course of his or her occupation. It differs from conventional crime in that the victims may be unaware of the crime and the offender may not view himself as a criminal. Deterrence of white-collar crime by regulatory agencies and internalized controls in organizations appears to be most promising.
9. Prisons do not often rehabilitate offenders; in fact they have been labeled "schools for crime." Because so few street criminals are actually caught and imprisoned, even massive campaigns to send them to prison have failed to relieve street crime. The idea of selective incapacitation, or finding those criminals who are most dangerous and sentencing them to longer sentences, appears to hold hope for the future.
10. The deterrent effect of capital punishment on the murder rate in the United States is short-lived, lasting a few weeks at most. Because murder is most often a crime of passion rather than a crime that is thought through, the deterrence of a punishment will probably never be large. An alternative is mandatory life imprisonment with no chance of appeal.

Glossary

anomie the absence of clear norms for a society or an individual

commitment the degree to which a person has a stake in conforming

conformity agreement with the norms and goals of society and working within them to achieve what degree of success one can

crime behavior that violates criminal law

criminal a person who has become publicly associated with commission of a crime or crimes

cultural transmission theory the theory that stresses that deviant behavior is part of a subculture that can be transmitted indefinitely through socialization

deterrence theory the theory that claims that deviance increases as a perceived risk of sanction decreases

deviance behavior that violates the norms of the social group in which the behavior occurs

deviant one who is characterized as a violator of a norm

deviant career when secondary deviance becomes a life-style

differential associations different contacts with socialization agents

innovation trying to attain society's goals by deviant means

master status a status that affects one's overall standing in the community

medicalization of deviance the process through which deviant behavior previously socially defined becomes defined by the medical community

primary deviance behavior that violates the norms of society but is transitory and may be unnoticed by others in the society

rebellion an adaptation that creates new norms or goals

residual deviance diverse kinds of deviation for which our society provides no explicit label and that sometimes lead to the labeling of the violator as mentally ill

ritualism trying to attain society's goals by following the norms even when unconvinced that they lead toward the goals

retreatism deciding that neither society's goals nor norms are worthy of the attempts to reach them

secondary deviance deviance that comes as a response to society's reaction to primary deviance

social control the means by which members of a society attempt to induce each other to comply with its norms

white-collar crime crime committed by persons of responsibility and high social status in the course of their occupation

Suggested Readings

Howard Becker, (ed.). 1964. *The Other Side: Perspectives on Deviance.* New York: Free Press.

Becker's classic explication of the interactionist view, especially strong in the area of secondary deviance.

Edwin Lemert, (ed.). 1972. *Human Deviance: Social Problems and Social Control.* 2d ed. Englewood Cliffs, N.J.: Prentice-Hall.

These writers clearly state their theories as to how deviance arises from the social control system itself.

Jeremiah Lowney, Robert Winslow, and Virginia Winslow. 1981. *Deviant Reality: Alternative World Views.* 2d ed. Boston: Allyn and Bacon.

Fascinating, first-hand accounts of what it is to be deviant in today's society.

Charles Silberman. 1980. *Criminal Violence, Criminal Justice.* New York: Vintage Press.

An interesting analysis of the causes and results of crime in the United States, focused on the criminal justice system itself.

David Simon, and Stanley Eitzen. 1986. *Elite Deviance.* 2d ed. Boston: Allyn and Bacon.

A well-done study of the field of corporate and occupational deviance.

CHAPTER

7

COLLECTIVE BEHAVIOR and SOCIAL MOVEMENTS

How's Your Sociological Intuition?

1. The suicide death of a popular teenage television actress receives prominent attention in the mass media. Based on research findings we could reasonably expect:

- **a.** A measurable rise in teenage suicide
- **b.** No detectable rise in teenage suicide
- **c.** A measurable decline in teenage suicide
- **d.** No one has yet conducted such research

2. Information passed by rumor tends to become:

- **a.** Distorted through loss of information
- **b.** Distorted through addition of information
- **c.** Distorted through focusing on particular details
- **d.** All of the above

3. The urban riots of the 1960s in the United States:

- **a.** Were the work of a small riff-raff element
- **b.** Had widespread support among black residents of cities
- **c.** Were protests against the Vietnam War
- **d.** Could not happen again

4. Scholars have tried to explain the unusual behavior of crowds in terms of:

- **a.** The irrational influence of a crowd on an individual
- **b.** The organized nature of crowds
- **c.** The unusual types of people a crowd attracts
- **d.** All of the above

Answers

1. a. The "imitative" effect of mass-media suicide coverage has been reported in several research studies, including one recently published in the *New England Journal of Medicine.*

2. d. This has been demonstrated in experiments and can make an interesting classroom demonstration.

3. b. Although many commentators blamed the riots on a small minority of agitators, scientific surveys established widespread support by black city dwellers.

4. d. We will look at some of these theories in our section on crowd behavior.

WHEN YOU HAVE FINISHED STUDYING THIS CHAPTER, YOU SHOULD KNOW:

- The differences between collective behavior and social movements
- Four types of crowd behavior
- What contagion and convergence theories say about crowd behavior
- How norms emerge in crowd interaction
- The elements of Richard Berk's rational decision theory
- How Neil Smelser explains collective behavior
- How Smelser's theory can be applied to preventing crowd disasters
- What diffuse crowd or mass behavior is
- Why we believe in rumors and how they affect our actions
- What the social meaning of urban legends is
- How hysteria and panic affect us
- What the AIDS hysteria is about
- The differences between fashions and fads
- The major influences on public opinion
- How the mass media influences other social phenomena
- How suicide can be triggered by television
- The stages in the life of a social movement
- Four types of social movements
- How social movements begin and grow
- How the two branches of the women's liberation movement began
- How social movements become "professionalized"

In Cleveland, a member of a racist group murders two blacks and a white he mistakenly thought was Jewish. In San Francisco skinheads throw a teenage boy through a plate-glass window for trying to stop them from pasting up anti-Semitic posters. The National Council of Churches issues a report that such violence has reached "epidemic proportions," in the United States. In the 1980s, racism motivated at least 121 murders, 302 assaults, and 301 cross burnings. In the Council's words: "Bigoted violence has become the critical criminal-justice issue of the late 1980s" (Leo, 1988).

The evening news and newspapers carry a story of a teenage suicide. During the week following the story, researchers will be able to measure a significant rise in the teenage suicide rate, especially among females (Phillips and Carstensen, 1986).

In Arcadia, Florida, Cliff Ray's neighbors did not want their children to attend school with his three sons, who are hemophiliacs with AIDS antibodies. Although the disease is not transmitted through casual contact, the neighbors boycotted classes and sent death threats to the Rays. Finally, someone set the house afire, destroying it and driving the Rays away. Fortunately for the Rays, their new neighbors in Sarasota did not succumb to similar mass hysteria. (*New York Times,* 1987a; 1987b)

These three recent events exemplify our general topic for this chapter: collective behavior. Here we will be exploring new movements, such as militant racism, mass behavior—the imitative effect of suicide publicity, and hysteria, such as that sometimes associated with AIDS.

What Are Collective Behavior and Social Movements?

Most social situations are governed by clearly defined norms. People know that on the first day of class they should arrive on time, bring a notebook, and smile at the professor. They understand that on a first date they greet their partner with a smile, not a passionate kiss.

Occasionally people are thrown into situations that do not have clearly defined rules. For example, imagine a fire is discovered in a large hotel at night. Some people panic, others coolly lead their friends and family outside. People who usually rely on clothes to hide their figures arrive in any bit of cloth.

This new collective of people huddling together in the darkness will form its rules as the situation demands. *A **collectivity** is a set of people who share common values and interests.* Old norms must be relaxed and new ones made up by the group to fit the situation. For instance, if blankets become available, the group will decide, often through a vocal leader, how they will be distributed. This is collective behavior.

***Collective behavior** describes the actions, thoughts, and feelings of a relatively temporary and unstructured group of people.* Collective behavior can be separated into two categories: crowd behavior and diffuse crowd, or mass, behavior.

*A **crowd** is a set of people who are physically close together and share a common concern. **Diffuse crowd,** or **mass, behavior** involves action by people with common concerns who may or may not have met each other.*

Crowds generally have a short lifespan and remain unstructured, sometimes participating in mobs and

Groups often perform collectively in ways that the individual members would not. "The Wave" going around football or baseball stadiums illustrates this phenomenon. (*Photo courtesy the author*)

riots. A diffuse crowd can participate together in such activities as forming public opinion, responding to rumors, hysteria and panic, and creating or continuing fashions and fads. In both forms of collective behavior participants come together without clear goals or norms, and they are acted upon by few external social controls. This characteristic separates collective behavior from group activities of people in formally defined organizations, like schools or businesses.

*A **social movement** is a large, ongoing group of people engaged in organized behavior designed to bring about or resist change in society.* Social movements are closely related to collective behavior; in fact, some sociologists define social movements as one type of collective behavior. Others feel they are a separate entity. Most social movements are more organized and more stable than other sorts of collective behavior, although the categories overlap at their extremities. It is probably most helpful for the beginning student to think of collective behavior and social movements as closely related but separate phenomena.

How Are Crowds Collective Behavior?

The essence of crowd behavior is that it is irrational rather than planned. Four distinct types of crowds have been named: casual, conventional, expressive, and acting crowds (Blumer, 1951).

The crowd around two cars that collided is a casual crowd. The people are there only to watch the action; they have no leaders or agreed-upon purpose; and they disperse as soon as the action is over without ever interacting with each other. *The **casual crowd** gathers around a specific event, and its members have little interaction with one another.*

An audience of stockholders at an annual meeting is a conventional crowd. They come together for the ceremony and follow conventional norms while there. It is accepted, for instance, that no one will yell obscenities at the chair even if he or she feels like doing that. *A **conventional crowd** gathers for a socially sanctioned purpose.*

*An **expressive crowd,** on the other hand, gathers specifically for the purpose of letting out emotions.* A campus end-of-term party is a modern example of an expressive crowd. Students gather to vent accumulated frustrations and to express delight at having finished another term of college. People who have spent weeks studying and writing papers late at night, putting off fun in order to do well in their studies, suddenly let out their emotions in a burst of energy, dancing and drinking until they are exhausted. Behavior that would be considered socially unacceptable at any other time is not only accepted at this party but encouraged by the free and somewhat wild atmosphere. Still, the crowd is not a rational gathering, and it has no stated leaders or agenda.

*The **acting crowd** focuses on a specific action or goal.* The members are generally angry at some force or person outside of the group and want to act against it. Lynchings have been carried out by crowds who were incensed at some wrongdoing. *Mobs* and *rioters* are acting crowds.

Ralph Turner and Lewis Killian (1972) have added another type of crowd to Blumer's classifications: the solidaristic crowd. *A* ***solidaristic crowd*** *forms a network of supportive relationships that form a unity within the crowd.* The crowd attending a Fourth of July parade would be considered solidaristic. The Fourth of July paraders encourage each other in their almost religious feelings about their country and form a short-lived collective for that purpose only.

EXPLAINING CROWD BEHAVIOR

The behavior of crowds differs from that of organized groups or individuals. Many theories have been suggested to explain these differences. Among the best known are LeBon's contagion theory, convergence theory, emergent-norms theory, and the rational-calculus model.

LEBON'S THEORY. One of the first interpretations of why crowd behavior differs from that of individuals or organized groups was the "contagion" theory proposed by Gustave LeBon (1895). LeBon suggested that a "collective mind" forms in a crowd and that this form of thought takes over the individual minds of crowd members and causes them to act alike. LeBon believed that individuals become susceptible to "suggestion" in crowds, as they melt into the group and become anonymous. Because nobody seems to notice what anyone says or does in a crowd, one's personal beliefs seem less important. The collective belief is formed from the "contagious growth of a belief that is suggested and spread throughout the crowd," much as we now believe disease is spread. If you have ever unexpectedly found yourself on your feet, yelling, while watching a sports event, you should be able to relate to the idea of "contagion."

CONVERGENCE THEORY. Convergence theory builds on LeBon's ideas by suggesting that crowd members do not really lose their individuality in a group but act from their unconscious selves. We have all heard someone say that "they didn't know what got into them" at a party, a football game, a family gathering, or the like. Convergence theorists would say that nothing "got into" them. Instead, a part of them that is rarely expressed got out of them!

EMERGENT-NORMS THEORY. Perhaps the most accepted theory today is the emergent-norms theory of Turner and Killian (1972). Emergent-norms theory concentrates not on what is happening psychologically within the crowd member, but rather on what happens among members. Turner and Killian believe that contagion and convergence do not fully explain crowd interaction. They suggest that as people interact in a crowd they form new norms for that specific crowd and that, as the norms emerge, the crowd pressures its members to conform to them.

Turner and Killian, unlike LeBon, do not think all members of a crowd begin to think and act alike. They believe there are many dissenters from the opinions most vocally expressed in the crowd, but because the social pressure to conform is great, dissenters do not object to what they feel is the majority opinion. In this type of situation, a loud minority could actually sway the behavior of the group. According to this theory, crowds *are* guided by norms, just as other groups in society are, but the norms are devised as the crowd goes along, rather than assumed from the beginning as they are in most social situations.

Different norms might emerge from relatively similar situations. Consider how workers in several companies might respond to news that the United States has just been struck by twelve nuclear missiles. In one company the norm might emerge to seek immediate shelter. In another the workers might decide the appropriate thing to do is to evacuate to presumably safer areas. A third company's norm might emerge to try to make it back to one's family in order to share the crisis with the people one loves. Emergent-norm theory stresses that collectives rather than individuals will tend to define appropriate behavior by developing new or emergent norms.

BERK'S RATIONAL CALCULUS MODEL. Richard Berk (1974) takes a new approach to the problem of how crowds decide on a course of action. Instead of emphasizing crowd irrationality, as LeBon and the convergence theorists do, he suggests that members of a crowd are actually seeking information they can use to make a rational decision. Berk believes that crowd members: (1) seek information from each other, (2) use the information they obtain to predict occurrences, (3) consider their options, (4) rank order the probable outcomes of the various actions, and (5) decide on an action that will give them the most reward for the least cost.

CONFLICT THEORY. From the conflict-theory perspective, crowd behavior may be seen as part of the broader class struggle between an oppressed people and their oppressors. Collective behavior overlaps political and economic processes; rioting, for example, sometimes serves as an important political activity. Because collective behavior in the form of social movements and riots may be part of a revolutionary movement, we discuss this aspect of the subject in more depth in Chapters 15 and 16, focusing on politically and economically motivated collective behavior in the form of challenge groups.

SMELSER'S THEORY APPLIED TO CROWDS. Neil Smelser (1963) has developed a general theory of collective behavior that addresses crowds as well as other forms of collective behavior, such as social movements and panics. We highlight Smelser's work in "Close-Up on Research." Although we have applied his theory to the issue of crowd violence, keep in mind that it should also be useful in explaining diffuse crowds or mass behavior, our topics following the Close-Up.

CLOSE-UP on • *THEORY* •

Neil Smelser's Theory of Collective Behavior

The Theorist and the Setting

Smelser's theory of collective behavior is reminiscent of the structural-functional "systems" theory. This is not surprising, as Smelser was a student of Talcott Parsons, a major founder of structural functionalism, which portrays social life as the mechanistic functioning of a social system. Smelser's theory departs from earlier explanations of crowd behavior that focused on the effect of the crowd on individuals.

The Theorist's Goal

The issues Smelser addresses are: "Why do collective episodes occur *where* they do, *when* they do, and *in the ways* they do?" (Smelser, 1962, p. 1; italics added.)

Concepts and Propositions

Smelser uses ***collective behavior*** to mean *"mobilization on the basis of a belief which redefines social action"* (p. 8). That is, collective behavior involves new behavior patterns, such as crazes, riots, and revolution, which result from new ideas about the origins of social problems.

Proposition: The following six determinants are necessary and sufficient for a collective episode to occur, and they will also determine the type of episode.

Notice that Smelser links the determinants to collective behavior with the adjectives "necessary" and "sufficient." That is, if all are present, collective behavior occurs; but if one is missing it will not. A list of Smelser's concepts with abbreviated versions of his definitions follows:

Structural conduciveness: The degree to which structural characteristics permit or encourage episodes of collective behavior (p. 15).

Structural strain: "An impairment of the relations among and consequently inadequate functioning of the components of action" (p. 47).

Growth and spread of a generalized belief: "Those beliefs that activate people for participation in episodes of collective behavior" (p. 80). "A generalized belief identifies the source of the strain, attributes certain characteristics to this source, and specifies certain responses to the strain as possible or appropriate" (p. 16).

Precipitating factors: An event that "confirms the existence, sharpens the definition, or exaggerates the effect of . . . conditions of conduciveness, strain, and generalized aggression" (p. 249).

Mobilization of participants for action: The process of "bringing the affected group into action" (p. 17).

The operation of social control: "Those counterdeterminants which prevent, interrupt, deflect, or inhibit the accumulation of the determinants just reviewed" (p. 17).

Application

Sociologist Jerry M. Lewis witnessed the shootings at Kent State University. We paraphrase his application of Smelser's theory to that historic display of collective behavior to illustrate Smelser's ideas.

The Kent State Commons, a traditional meeting place for rallies and a busy crosswalk area, provided the necessary *structurally conducive* setting for collective behavior. That Monday, May 4, 1970 the Ohio National Guard was guarding the partially burned ROTC building at the Commons, which had been set afire following antiwar demonstrations the previous Saturday night. The governor had summoned the Guard on Sunday, ordering them to "protect property and lives." But by Monday he gave them responsibility for "breaking up any assembly on campus whether it was peaceful or violent" (Lewis, 1972, p. 89).

The university opened for classes on Monday, and many students felt they had a right to assemble at the Commons for a noon rally that had been announced the previous Friday. They saw the troops as an intrusion interfering with normal campus life. *Structural strain* existed between the student's expectations and the Guard's order not to permit assembly.

At noon a crowd began to gather. Many students were confused about whether a rally would be legal. Of the assembled 2,000 students, most were curious onlookers who resented the Guard's presence. A *generalized belief grew and spread* that the Guard was wrong to be on the student Commons. An active core of the crowd sought to punish the Guard, and feelings of omnipotence began to develop in the crowd.

A tennis match? At the May 4, 1970, Kent State incident, members of the crowd simply lobbed the tear-gas cannisters back at the guard in what one student described as a "tennis match." The situation deteriorated. The Guardsmen shot at the crowd, killing four students and injuring nine others. (*UPI/Bettmann Newsphotos*)

Lewis suggests there were two major *precipitating factors:* (1) the call for the Monday rally first put out at the Friday rally, and (2) the decision of the Guard to make a stand in front of the burned ROTC building (1972, p. 93).

The mobilization for action was not coordinated by any identifiable leadership. Some students rang the victory bell, which attracted attention, and others began chanting: "One, two, three, four, stop, your, fucking, war" and "Pigs off campus, pigs off campus."

The Guard's attempt at *social control* of the hostile outburst was largely ineffective and probably contributed to the outburst's growth. They did not move in to arrest members of the active core, who remained around the bell, but waited until the crowd had become large before trying to disperse it with tear gas. This tactic proved to be ineffective. Members of the crowd simply lobbed the tear-gas canisters back at the Guard, who in turn threw them back into the crowd in what one student described as a "tennis match." As the Guard moved in to disperse the crowd, they drove a group of students to the nearby practice football field, unintentionally leaving themselves surrounded by other students. Some students began pelting the Guard with clods of dirt and rocks. Most simply watched or yelled taunts.

The situation deteriorated. As one student observed, "They couldn't pursue and they couldn't contain. The students started gaining the upper hand for the first time, and they knew it" (Lewis, 1972, p. 93). The Guard marched in formation to the top of Taylor Hall Hill. At least sixteen Guardsmen "knelt and formed a skirmish line, pointing their M1 rifles at the students in the parking lot" (Lewis, 1972, p. 93). Many students, feeling a sense of victory and omnipotence, began yelling, "Shoot, shoot, shoot." The Guardsmen shot, killing four students and wounding nine others.

Within hours the news spread around the nation and

around the world. Virtually everywhere people sought an explanation for why heavily armed soldiers would open fire on unarmed college students who were their fellow citizens.

Implications

Semlser's theory represents one distinguished sociologist's attempt to explain events, like that at Kent State, which sometimes seem beyond belief and explanation. If the theory is valid, it should help to explain, predict, plan, or prevent collective behavior. As stated, this theory is like a recipe: When all ingredients are present, Smelser tells us to expect collective behavior. Should any ingredient be left out, collective behavior should not occur.

Questions

1. Would you agree that the six determinants were all necessary to development of this "hostile outburst"? Would you agree that, taken together, the six are sufficient to make the outcome inevitable?
2. What are the strengths and weaknesses of this theory?
3. What steps could be taken to move collective-behavior theory and research closer to the goal of being able to predict collective behavior?

SOURCES Jerry M. Lewis. 1972. "A study of the Kent State incident using Smelser's theory of collective behavior," *Sociological Inquiry*, 42(2), pp. 87–96. Neil J. Smelser. 1962. *Theory of Collective Behavior.* New York: Free Press.

What Is Diffuse Crowd or Mass Behavior?

Because Smelser's theory deals with collective behavior in general, it provides a good transition from our discussion of crowds to our next topic, the second type of collective behavior: diffuse crowd or mass behavior. Crowds require close physical contact, but ***diffuse crowd,*** *or* ***mass, behavior*** *involves action by people with common concerns who may or may not have met each other*. For example, when hundreds of men buy turtleneck sweaters and sports jackets and wear them instead of suits and ties, they are participating in a mass behavior known as a fashion trend. The basic forms of diffuse crowd behavior are rumor transmission, hysteria and panic, fashions and fads, and public opinion.

RUMORS

One aspect of public opinion that has lately become a focus of attention is the transmission of ***rumors,*** *information that travels from person to person, usually by word of mouth*. It has been suggested that rumors have been important in several national incidents, including the riots of the 1960s.

The mass media play a dual role in the transmission of rumor in this country. First, they may be able to stop a rumor by reporting the facts, but they also may be the source of the rumor if a story is reported without corroborating the facts. When a news source later retracts its statements, most people do not believe the second report. The seeds of doubt planted by rumors are difficult to uproot.

In the classic study on the transmission of rumors, Gordon Allport and Leo Postman (1947) found that a rumor gets simplified as it is passed on, a process they labeled "leveling." The second process they describe was the "sharpening" of certain details that are retained in the transmission of the rumor and elaborated upon. Allport and Postman believe that unsubstantiated rumors surrounding a single event were often a causal factor in riots. There is some indication that rumor-control centers, such as were set up during the 1960s riots and staffed by people whom the public trusted, can be useful in dispelling rumors (Rosenthal, 1971). Because rumors have been a prime source of information in small towns, and more Americans are moving to such towns today, the transmission of rumors may become of increasing interest. One of the authors recalls vividly her first small-town experience when, upon being introduced to a "stranger" she was greeted with, "How's your son? I heard he was sick."

Tamotsu Shibutani (1966) suggests that we transmit and believe rumors in order to have some reality to agree on. In other words, people do not like to live with ambiguity, and a half-truth they can agree on is easier to accept than several undecided possibilities. "Rumor is a substitute for news" (Shibutani, 1966, p. 62). In today's world of so many uncertainties, it is possible that this function of rumor will be heightened.

URBAN LEGENDS

Legends are universally part of the folklore of various cultures. Such tales as "Cinderella," for instance, are known in over 700 variants, each reflecting elements of different cultures. There are, for instance, Cinderellas who are vengeful and those who are forgiving, those who are sly and those who are naive, those who are useful and those who are helpless. Folklorists have spent much time determining why certain elements are retained in various cultures.

Recently the phenomena of modern American folk narratives has been a topic of study for symbolic interactionists. These are stories that most people have been told as a "true" story that happened to someone else, most often to a relative of a friend. They are realistic stories concerning recent events, often with an ironic or supernatural twist. Because of their portrayal, listeners often assume they are true. Jan Brunvand describes the process:

> The storytellers assume that the true facts of each case lie just one or two informants back down the line with a reliable witness, or in a news-media report. The mass media themselves participate in the dissemination and apparent validation of urban legends, just as they sometimes do with rumor and gossip, adding to their plausibility. (Brunvand, 1985, p. xi–xii)

Investigators have tried to determine why these stories are told, in an effort to learn more about the culture that tells them. One that has been studied extensively is "The Boyfriend's Death," in which a young couple are parked under a tree on a deserted road. When the girl decides it is time to go home, they try to start the car, but it won't start. The boy decides to walk to the nearest phone for help, and wants to go alone; he can walk faster than she can, because she has on high-heeled shoes and a dress. The girl locks herself inside the car to wait. The boyfriend does not come back for a long time, and soon the girl starts hearing a scratching sound on the roof of the car. When daylight arrives, a police car pulls up and officers help her out of the car. When she looks up, her boyfriend is hanging from the tree, his feet scraping against the roof of the car.

Brunvand suggests that legends such as this will survive if they contain a strong basic story appeal, have a foundation in actual belief, and contain a meaningful message or "moral." This story obviously contains a warning to young couples not to park on deserted roads and thereby get into trouble of whatever kind. On a symbolic level, it suggests that a young female is vulnerable in the "outside world" and helpless against evil. Only the authority figure of the police (presumably male) or her boyfriend can save her (Brunvand, 1985, pp. 10–13).

Another widely circulated urban legend concerns soft drinks and decomposed matter. The most common of these has two women as its victims, again showing the vulnerability of women to evil forces. The women are served soft drinks in bottles, and discover halfway through that one of the bottles contains a dead mouse. The "victim" faints or is sick in some other way and is rushed for medical treatment. Later the soft drink company is sued for damages, both physical and psychological.

One investigator searched legal documents for evidence that any such incident had occurred, and found a total of forty-five cases in which mice were actually found in soft-drink bottles from 1914 to 1976, with the 1950s having the largest number of cases (Fine, 1979). In this case, then, the myth grew out of fact. In the actual cases, however, most of the victims were male. The researcher suggests that this story spread and was embellished because it tells of a dramatic, horrifying experience and because it expresses real fears about the industrialization of America and our vulnerability to large-scale production methods. The moral is obvious: Don't trust big food companies to always give you safe food.

A more recent food-related legend has been traced to over 115 beginnings by Fine (1980) who labels it the "Kentucky Fried Rat" story. In this legend, a woman has nothing prepared for supper one night and resorts to buying fast-food chicken for her and her husband. As they eat it in the darkened car, she says to her husband, "My chicken tastes funny." She continues to complain about it, until her husband says, "Let me see it." They turned on the car light and discovered that the wife was eating a floured and fried rat. She went into shock, was hospitalized, and later died. The husband is said to be suing the chicken company for thousands of dollars. Fine suggests that the symbolic significance of this story begins with the lack of dinner. The moral: Women must make sure to take seriously their role as dinner preparer for the family or they will be rewarded for their lack of attention to cooking with illness and/or death. The underlying message, of course, is, again, don't trust a large corporation to produce safe food.

Urban legends are an excellent example of another way in which people in modern societies symbolically communicate to each other their anxieties about social issues. We share these stories that happened to "someone" "a few months ago" and teach lessons to one another in a dramatic, memorable form about living in this fast-changing society.

HYSTERIA AND PANIC

Rumors are a key factor in the development of hysteria and panic. ***Hysteria*** *is a generalized anxiety about some unknown situation.* People reacting with hysteria see generalized, evil traits in an ambiguous situation.

One of the most interesting cases of hysteria that has been studied is referred to as the June Bug Episode (Kerckhoff and Back, 1968). A textile mill was closed because ten women and one man reported nausea and body rash. One of them attributed the symptoms to having been bitten by a bug at the plant. A new load of cloth had arrived from England, and the rumor spread that it harbored a mysterious bug that caused sickness.

The mill managers sprayed with insecticide and reopened, but more workers fell ill and were sent to the hospital for treatment and observation. Experts were sent to determine the cause and found no unusual insects and no diagnosable illness in workers who had reported being ill, including the original eleven. The authorities declared the June Bug nonexistent and the sickness psychosomatic, and the rate of sickness dropped to zero almost immediately. Researchers concluded that most of the people had become ill due to acute anxiety about the epidemic itself.

When people react by running away from a feared object, panic occurs. ***Panic** is an attempt to flee from an imagined or real threat.*

A famous example of panic behavior is the reaction to Orson Welles' 1939 radio broadcast of H. G. Wells' novel *War of the Worlds.* Thousands of people were convinced that Martians had landed in New Jersey and were taking over the country. People panicked, overrunning roads going west with cars. Their fear and anxiety produced panic action.

AIDS: HYSTERIA IN THE EIGHTIES

As the account of the death threats, arson, and banishment of three young children with AIDS antibodies at the beginning of this chapter demonstrates, AIDS has stimulated considerable hysteria recently in the United States. Here we consider the real and imagined threat of AIDS, and the development of hysteria within the public, surrounding this virus.

Acquired Immune Deficiency Syndrome (AIDS) appeared first in epidemic proportions in Zaire and other African countries, probably as a mutant of a virus that affects the green monkey population of that area. Public health officials believe that it was later carried to Haiti and from there transmitted to the United States by tourists or Haitian immigrants. The disease has spread so rapidly in the United States that although it first appeared here in 1975, it has killed 15,000 Americans and infected another 1.5 million with a lesser form of the disease (AIDS-related complex) or with the virus, which can incubate for as long as seven years (Kantrowitz, 1986).

The alarming spread of the disease and its certain-death outcome have combined to create an atmosphere in the United States conducive to the growth of hysteria concerning the disease. A leading British newspaper suggested in 1985 that perhaps "the real plague is panic!" (*London Guardian,* Feb. 19, 1985). When AIDS was first diagnosed in this country, in 1981, the media shied away from reporting it, seeing it as a story about gays that they couldn't sell to their editors or the general public (Altman, 1986). That at first it affected primarily the gay community was the reason for the medical community's slow response to AIDS. The general public did not see it as the threat that, for instance, cancer or heart disease was.

Some people believe that AIDS represents a divine punishment for homosexual behavior; a 1985 Gallup poll found that 20 percent of the population would classify AIDS as a "judgment from God." Campus graffiti announced that AIDS stands for "America's Ideal Death Sentence" (*Newsweek on Campus,* May, 1984). After three Australian babies died from blood contaminated by AIDS virus, a right-wing Australian party labeled it the "wrath-of-God disease," and the Anglican Dean of Sydney said that the gay community there had blood on its hands. There were even calls to indict the homosexuals who had donated the blood, if they could be found, for manslaughter (Altman, 1986).

By 1985 scientists realized that AIDS was spreading into the general populace through blood banks and blood transfusions, or by way of persons who engaged in both homosexual and heterosexual sex, or by sex involving intravenous drug users, or by exchanges of hypodermic syringes by drug users. At this time more funds became available and communities began to focus attention on the understanding and prevention of AIDS.

Even though medical information clearly indicates that AIDS cannot be transmitted except by direct interchange of body fluids, most notably blood and semen, fear in the general public has caused people to demand irrational measures in the treatment of AIDS victims. The fear of AIDS grew to hysteric proportions: people have demanded that children with AIDS be banned from schools and that homosexuals be barred from jobs in which they have direct contact with people. One writer describes being pulled over for a traffic violation and being asked by the policeman before he turned over his driver's license, "You don't have AIDS or any of those weird things, do you?" Some police were issued special gloves and masks to wear in case they had contact with homosexuals who might have AIDS (Altman, 1986).

Social and political measures have been suggested to stop the spread of AIDS. Quarantining "recalcitrant" homosexuals, or those who refuse to stop engaging in frequent and casual sexual contact, has been suggested. Renewing anti-sodomy laws, in order to be able to prosecute those who might spread the disease through sexual contact, has been suggested. Blood-testing of all food-handlers or all public employees has been put forth as a possibility. Residents of San Francisco, home to a large gay population, proposed that the bathhouses where homosexual behavior occurs be closed as public-health hazards.

What social effects has the AIDS hysteria produced? Most noticeably, the homosexual community has closed ranks, producing greater stability in relationships and monumental support for those already afflicted with the disease. Dr. Mervyn Silverman, head of the San Francisco Health Department, calls it "the most dramatic change in behavior of any group in society that I have seen in my career in public health" *San Francisco Chronicle,* July, 1984 p. 4-24).

The use of condoms has been strongly supported by the gay and straight communities, as one way to prevent transmission of the disease (Bruno, 1985). This has led to a corresponding reduction since 1985 in the number of other sexually transmitted diseases (STDs), presumably because they also are not passed from person to person through condoms (L. Edwards, 1985).

Fads are sometimes revived as "nostalgia." For instance, poodle skirts, bobby socks, Keds, and pony tails were first popular in the 1950s, and are being worn again in the 1980s. (*Photo courtesy the author*)

The use of condoms, however, is not a sure protection against any of the sexually transmitted diseases.

Education of the population has reduced the hysteria somewhat and promises to help in the reduction of the numbers affected. Surgeon General C. Everett Koop has suggested that children at the lowest grade possible be told of the dangers of sexual behavior and drug use that could lead to their contracting AIDS (Kantrowitz, 1986). The National Institute of Justice studied the problem of transmission in jails and prisons and advocates education of our inmate population (Hammett, 1986). The American College Health Association is writing a series of recommendations and guidelines for its members in dealing with what they now see as "a major concern on college campuses" (Bruno, 1985).

As a by-product of the hysteria, the sexual behavior of both homosexuals and heterosexuals is also becoming "safer," both in terms of choosing partners and in techniques (L. Edwards, 1985). More people are choosing not to be sexually active. As Washington University junior Phil Ebeling put it, "You don't get sick if you don't get sacked" (Bruno, 1985). Well-respected futurist, Edward Cornish, believes that the epidemic will usher in what he terms The Age of New Restraint. In this Age, romantic love will make a comeback, marriages will be less likely to break up due to extramarital affairs, pornography will become less acceptable in polite society, traditional religious practices may revive, and people will spend more time at home, both to avoid contagion and temptation and to enjoy their newly committed relationships (Cornish, 1986).

Though no one can be sure what the future implications might be, the links between this disease and the social reactions to it are unmistakable. Social historian Jeffrey Weeks notes that the type of hysteria seen surrounding AIDS is seen often when societies are in flux, floundering in their attempts to create a new social order (Weeks, 1985). If his hypothesis is correct, the social changes that have come about as a result of the AIDS hysteria may indeed usher in an end to the sexual revolution and be the harbinger of more traditional sexual values including emphasis on sex being confined to a monogamous marriage.

FADS AND FASHIONS

Collective behavior also involves the realm of fashion and fads. Both represent transitory norms dealing with what currently is held to be "in" or "out." Although both fads and fashions involve popular behavior, they also differ considerably. A ***fashion*** *is a currently valued style of appearance or behavior.* Fashion involves a variation on a routine social theme. In clothing, for instance, the length of skirts, the width of lapels and ties, the "in" colors and textures vary from season to season. We can appropriately discuss fashions in architecture, automobiles, hairstyles, kitchen decor, food, or even life-styles and political views.

For example, thirty-five years ago, denim was used exclusively in work clothes. Schools restricted the wearing of denim, and most adults would not appear outside their yards in it. Gradually, people began wearing blue jeans for other occasions, and today many professors wear denim to class; blue jeans and T-shirts, in fact, have been called the "college uniform." Even dressy outfits are now sometimes made of denim, and casual slacks are made of satin or velvet, something reserved for formal wear in the 1950s. But this transition was a slow one, and women who cared to be in fashion did not make a change from one fabric or style too quickly.

*A **fad** is a popular but short-lived form of conduct.* Fashions are, by their nature, components of relatively predictable trends, shifting gradually along a rather determinable scale. Men's very short hairstyles of the early 1950s gave way to the longer hair of the 1960s and have since gradually returned to a more moderate length. Presuming we will have hair, fashion can dictate length, and thus we know in advance it can only be long, moderate, or short. Similarly, skirts can go up or down, ties and lapels become wider and narrower, and often these changes happen gradually rather than abruptly.

Fads, in contrast, burst on the scene as an innovation, often to fade nearly totally out of existence almost as quickly. Whereas fashion represents the current way of doing what we routinely do, fads often represent doing something almost totally novel and often frivolous. The public's fascination for Rubik's Cubes dissipated as fast as their interest in hula hoops and in streaking had earlier. Diamond-shaped "Baby on Board" signs in rear windows of automobiles spawned a deluge of cutesy "Mother-in-Law in Trunk" imitation signs that have now virtually disappeared. The public's short-lived but widespread fascination with CB radios also represents a fad. Even the great home computer "revolution" of the 1980s had fadlike qualities. Many machines that had been bought to organize the recipes in the kitchen, keep the family budget on track, entertain the kids, teach math, build vocabulary, and process words, now sit in closets processing mostly dust.

How do sociologists explain fashions and fads? In traditional societies, people tend to revere the way they and their ancestors have always done things. The concept of fashion has no meaning in a society where there is little or no change. Both represent some degree of innovation, which is prized by people in modern societies who do not want to be old-fashioned. A major reason that fashions are prominent in modern societies is that they represent enormous profits to producers. When the consumer can be convinced to discard functional clothing because it is no longer in style, the clothing industry benefits. Marx suggested that capitalists would search the world for new markets and create artificial demand where there had been none. Designer jeans that sell for nearly $100 and are made for a fraction of that cost are a capitalist's dream.

PUBLIC OPINION

*A **public** is an unorganized diffuse crowd with opinions on an issue of current interest.* Every issue has a different number of people in its public. For instance, relatively few people bother to write their senators about the fact that certain foods contain Red Dye Number 40, a possible carcinogen. However, the public who responded to the federal government's attempt to ban liquor sales during Prohibition was vast, vocal, and powerful enough to eventually repeal the Amendment.

***Public opinion** consists of the views of the members of a public on a certain issue.* Public opinion constantly changes. For example, no President of the United States has ever held steady favor in the eyes of his public. Public opinion regarding television programs, fashion trends, upcoming elections, or tax issues rarely remains static for an extended period.

Public opinion generally becomes known through the reporting of public opinion polls, such as the Gallup or Harris polls. Because public opinion changes so rapidly, however, it has been suggested that public opinion polls may not actually report the trends in the society, as opinion pollers claim, but only how *some* people feel about *one* issue at *one* particular moment in time (Blumer, 1948). Another criticism of public opinion polls is that instead of simply reporting opinion, they may help to form the opinion and the behavior that may accompany it. For instance, hearing that many others feel living in an inner city is so dangerous they are trying to move to the suburbs may influence previously nonfearful city-dwellers to consider moving. Even though their area is secure, the idea that "everyone else" feels it is dangerous may cause people to reconsider their situation.

It is obviously not only difficult to define public opinion, but also to decide how it formed. Both these areas are now being studied extensively by social scientists.

INFLUENCES ON PUBLIC OPINION. Opinons are influenced in two major ways, often at the same time: (1) by friends, or ***reference groups****—those collectives to which we belong and relate,* and (2) by members of *that group whose judgment is considered important***—opinion leaders**.

For instance, if football games are the dominant campus Saturday afternoon activity, most students will probably go to them with little thought about alternate activities. Similarly, most middle-class teens aim to go on to school after high school, even though they may have no specific educational goal beyond "getting a good job." Our reference groups, specifically our group of significant others (in Mead's term (1934)), influence us in these decisions, sometimes without our consciously knowing it. Conversely, we often reject the opinions of people who have different backgrounds than ours with little thought of the possibility that they may be right.

Opinion leaders, on the other hand, may reinforce or question our opinions more or less consciously. When a person we trust and respect speaks for one side of an issue, we tend to want to believe that opinion and mold ours to match.

Celebrities are obvious examples of opinion leaders. Hence we frequently see them enlisted to lead public opinion in a variety of areas ranging from a positive opinion of lite beer and live aid to a negative opinion of drugs. Such efforts apply the sociology of public opinion to very specific issues often with notable results.

THE MASS MEDIA

The national media have an important role in the formation of public opinion. The public forms many opinions based on information from newspapers, magazines, television, and radio. This makes the media's role very important, because directors and editors decide what is reported and from what bias it comes. It has been shown that violent crime rates rise when more violent crimes are reported and shown in bloody detail in magazines and news programs. We have yet to determine whether the coverage causes more violence or simply reports it.

The media have also been cited as a catalyst in some types of social explosions, such as riots (Knopf, 1975). The managerial staff at CBS, apparently responding to what they believe to be good evidence that the media can prolong or encourage rioting, entered this warning into their 1976 codes and standards manual (Griffith, 1977):

> If, in your judgment, your presence is clearly inspiring, continuing or intensifying a dangerous, or potentially dangerous, disturbance, cap your cameras and conceal your microphones regardless of what other news organizations may do. . . . Avoid coverage of (1) self-designated "leaders" if they appear to represent only themselves or (2) any individuals or groups who are clearly "performing."

The media often has a positive function in shaping collective behavior. Rumors can be squelched by informative programming, for instance. Public-service messages, such as those warning against drunk-driving and drugs, have demonstrable positive results as well.

One problem specific to television is the immediacy of the programming. With the new cameras, reporters can be included in news programming live from the scene of an event. Their vantage point is only that: a vantage point. "Live" broadcasts can leave out important aspects of the scene. People who watch the event as it happens, however, have already formed their opinions about its nature. Previously, when reporters made films that were transferred to a studio and edited before airing, all aspects of the action could be considered. Some newscasters think their earlier reporting was more realistic because they were able to go through this process of filtering and verifying information before delivering it to the public.

IMITATION

Two depressed teenagers on a Saturday night date decide to write notes to their parents describing their hopeless feelings. Then they pull into the garage and close the door, leaving the motor running. In the morning, the girl's parents find them dead. The story hits the evening papers and is on everyone's mind for days. A week later, this scene is repeated in another garage in the same city. The second couple might have been imitating the behavior in order to receive the attention the first suicides did, might have poor impulse control and have felt depressed that night, might have been drunk and therefore not thinking clearly, or simply wanted so much to be "in" that they were willing to die to prove their loyalty to their group.

Such imitative suicides have sometimes resulted in several groups of suicides over a period of a few weeks or months in a specific area. Although killing yourself would never become a generally accepted "fad," teenage suicides of this sort do have some of the aspects of fad behavior, in that the outbreaks are short-lived and accepted only by one part of the population. Called "cluster suicides," the phenomenon of teenagers following each other to death has been alarming society and spurring research in the area of teen suicide (Strother, 1986). It is even possible that the short-lived "fad" of suiciding is contributing to the growing "fashion" of teenage suicide.

Suicide is now the second most common cause of death among 15- to 24-year-olds. Between 1970 and 1987, the suicide rate for this group rose 40 percent

Fashions tend to be trendy in that they evolve in discernible patterns. Women in the United States, for instance, have followed a fashion trend from earrings to pierced earrings to multiple pierced earrings. (*Photo courtesy the author*)

(*New York Times*, Feb. 22, 1987). Approximately 1,000 adolescents attempt suicide every day, and 6,500 of them will succeed in 1987 (Steele, 1985). By far the largest group of these "successful" suicides are white males (G. Bracey, 1985).

Explanations for the rise in suicides have included increasing breakdowns of families, drug use, and decreasing job and educational opportunities. In addition the ready availability of guns is a factor. Whereas in 1970 most girls used pills to try to kill themselves, today they use guns, which are much more likely to complete the task.

Many suicidal people are depressed. Others are addicted to alcohol or drugs and have poor impulse control. Still others are habitually antisocial, often in trouble in school, with their families, and with the law. A large group tends toward perfectionism, being rigid in their expectations of themselves and others and isolated from social groups (Holden, 1986). As Durkheim demonstrated, people are more likely to commit suicide when they live in a state of confusion about norms, a condition that we call anomie. (See Chapter 1.)

One of the practical applications of social science research in this area has been the development of a list of warning signals of possible suicidal behavior. By asking the families and friends of those who have committed suicide about the deceased's recent behavior, social psychologists have determined that the following signals should be taken seriously:

1. Change in social interactions, either becoming more isolated or more outgoing
2. Change in sleeping and eating habits
3. Beginning or increase in taking drugs or alcohol
4. Any reference in conversation to dying
5. Any loss: a relationship, a goal, physical illness or disability, divorce, failure to achieve what was expected
6. Inconsistency in behavior or mood
7. "Putting-life-in-order" behaviors, such as giving away special things
8. Attitude of not caring about things that were previously important
9. Expression of feeling powerless or unable to control life
10. Expression of feeling useless and unable to contribute to those around them

(Holden, 1986; Steele, 1985)

Although all of these signals have been found in the presuicidal behavior of teens, they are not all present in every case. Because research has shown them to often predate a suicide, however, the existence of one or more of these symptoms should be cause for those who are close to a potential suicide to show concern, ask pertinent questions, and bring in professional help as soon as possible.

Social scientists are now trying to determine to what degree the rise in teenage suicide is imitative. Researchers are concerned that sensational or romanticized media attention of a youth suicide may cause additional suicides. The research of David Phillips, which is highlighted in the following "Close-Up on Research" speaks clearly to this problem.

CLOSE-UP on • *RESEARCH* •

David Phillips and Lundie Carstensen on Whether Television News Stories about Suicide Trigger Teenage Suicides

The Researcher and the Setting

Does watching televised reports of actual suicides or documentary programs about suicide encourage teenage suicides? In the past, David Phillips (1977) and Kenneth Bollen and Phillips (1981) have shown that front-page metropolitan newspaper stories of actual suicides are directly linked to increased suicides, as well as to traffic accidents that researchers assume are sometimes disguised suicides. More recently, Phillips has turned his attention to the effects of televised coverage of suicide and its effects (1982; Phillips & Carstensen, 1986).

The Researcher's Goal

Phillips sought to determine whether "clustering of teenage suicides occurs nationally and is statistically significant" (1986, p. 685).

Theory and Concepts

Phillips is examining a general theory that can be stated: Media violence causes audience violence. The concepts of media violence and audience violence are very general. Phillips seeks to better understand when and to what degree the general theory is true. In this research (1986), he tests a specific branch of the theory. The relatively specific—and therefore more easily tested—components of a theory are called *hypotheses.* Phillips' hypothesis is that "television news or feature stories about suicides trigger additional suicides, perhaps because of imitation" (p. 685).

Research Design

Phillips and Carstensen analyzed "the daily fluctuations of a total of 12,585 suicides among American teenagers before and after news or feature stories about suicides televised from 1973 to 1979" (p. 685). They set four criteria for the stories whose effects they would study: (1) they used only stories that appeared on the three major television news progams, to ensure broad coverage; (2) they eliminated "mixed" stories about someone who suicided after killing others, and group suicides; (3) they treated stories about suicides that occurred within seven days of each other as one story, because the effect of a suicide is observable from zero to seven days after the event; and (4) they excluded all stories whose observation period overlapped with a national holiday, because holidays are also times during which suicide fluctuates.

Daily suicide data was obtained by the National Center for Health Statistics, and the subjects of the television news stories were obtained from the Vanderbilt Television News Archive and the CBS News Index.

Phillips and Carstensen were careful to correct for other factors that might affect daily suicide rates, including day of the week, month of the year, yearly trends, and holidays. They then used a regression-analysis statistical technique to generate estimates of the number of suicides that could be expected to occur during the observation period following the news stories, and compared these numbers with the number of actual suicides observed.

Findings

Phillips and Carstensen found that "the national rate of suicide among teenagers rises significantly just after television news or feature stories about suicide," supporting the idea of "clusters" of teenage suicides, especially for female teenagers; that "the more publicity a news story receives, the greater is the increase in teenage suicides"; and that "news stories providing general information about suicide are just as dangerous as specific stories" (p. 689).

The researchers statistically eliminated six other possible explanations for their findings, including that prior conditions might produce a wave of suicides of which the publicized suicide is merely one example, that the stories might precipitate a suicide that would have occurred soon anyway, that authorities might classify ambiguous deaths as suicides more often after a suicide story, that the publicized suicide triggers grief rather than imitation and the grief causes the suicides, that stories occur at the times of year when suicide rates are high, and that the significant level was statistically inflated due to the time-series regression-analysis technique.

Implications

Phillips and Carstensen hope that further research into this phenomenon with a larger sample of news stories will occur. They also hope that their findings may cause educators, policymakers, and journalists to "consider ways of reducing public exposure to stories, both general and specific, about suicide" (p. 689).

Questions

1. Are you convinced that televised stories about suicides actually create "cluster" suicides among teenagers? Why or why not?
2. What other interpretations of these data can be made?
3. If Phillips and Carstensen's findings are shown to be true in more expanded studies, how serious a problem do you believe it to be, and how should it be addressed?

SOURCES David P. Phillips and Lundie Carstensen. 1986. "Clustering of teenage suicides after television news stories about suicide." *New England Journal of Medicine* 315, (11): pp. 685–689. K. A. Bollen and David Phillips. 1981. Suicidal motor vehicle fatalities in Detroit: A replication." *American Journal of Sociology* 87, pp. 404–412. David Phillips. 1977. "Motor vehicle fatalities increase just after publicized suicide stories." *Science* 1196: pp. 1464–1465. David Phillips. 1982. "The impact of fictional television stories on U.S. adult fatalities: New evidence on the effect of mass media on violence." *American Journal of Sociology* 87 (4): pp. 1340–1359.

What Is the Life of a Social Movement?

A social movement is a large ongoing group of people engaged in organized behavior designed to bring about or resist change in society. For example, thousands of people shaken by the Three Mile Island nuclear accident participated in a social movement dedicated to forcing the United States to rethink its nuclear energy policies. Since the 1960s civil rights movement, social movements have become a major feature on the American social scene. We have seen a long progression of "movements," including the peace movement, the women's movement, gay liberation, gray liberation, and handicapped liberation movements.

Social movements as forms of collective behavior often begin when unrelated people come to believe in something and decide to put some of their time and energy behind that belief. Herbert Blumer (1951) did much of the early theoretical work in the field, focusing on interactions among members of such movements.

Blumer suggests that in the *preliminary stage* of a social movement, society shows a restless concern over an issue on which people are divided. In the *popular stage* the movement begins to rally around a figure

Jerry Falwell's attempt to create a Moral Majority movement was not aided by recent charges of immorality on the part of other celebrity television preachers. (© Cynthia Johnson/Gamma Liaison)

(charismatic leader) who speaks of reform, revolution, resistance, or expression of self in such a way that people relate to the leader and begin to feel hopeful that their questions have answers. In the third stage the participants *organize formally,* choose organizational leaders, formulate policies which they agree upon, and decide where to begin change. The group often abandons its charismatic leaders at this stage in favor of leaders whom they think can accomplish their goals rather than simply articulate their feelings.

If successful, a social movement destroys itself in its last stage of development, when it becomes an *institution* (Spector and Kitsuse, 1973). At this point it is no longer collective behavior because it is organized, follows accepted norms of society, and had replaced its emotional base with the assumption that change will take time. In fact, politicians often quiet a vocal minority by making their leader a member of a politician's staff in some capacity. Lulled into thinking something real might happen because their representative is in an important position, the social movement dissipates and loses strength, having been coopted by the majority.

WHAT ARE THE TYPES OF SOCIAL MOVEMENTS?

When we are trying to understand things as complicated as social movements, it is useful to be able to classify them into types. We saw in Chapter 3, "Society," the utility of such a classification scheme in learning to understand societies by considering six basic types. Sociologists have been busy creating typologies of social movements. John Wilson (1973) reports on three different means of classifying social movements, those of Turner and Killian (1957), Aberle (1966), and Smelser (1963). We introduce a simple typology of social movements that classifies them according to what they are trying to achieve.

Resistance movements *are formed to resist a change that is already occurring in society.* For example, antiabortion advocates are trying to repeal laws that permit legalized abortions for most women, in the belief that abortions are detrimental to society.

Reform movements operate on the opposite principle. *Reformers endeavor to change elements of the system as it currently stands.* Reformers generally accept the system as viable, but believe thaat some basic changes would make it more equitable to all members. Environmentalists and antipollution groups today are involved in reform movements.

Revolutionary movements *deny that the system will ever work.* Revolutionary movements advocate replacing the entire existing structure. The American colonists who fought for independence from England were such thinkers.

Expressive movements *concentrate on change among their members and their immediate social contacts.* Members of an expressive movement might form a community, expecting that their quality of life will be significantly affected by the way community members treat each other. Religious communities such as the Children of God, whose purpose is to seek a better life together through inner change rather than through political or social change, are expressive social movements.

How Do Social Movements Begin and Grow?

DAVIES AND SMELSER: STRAIN THEORY

Much of the early thinking on social movements focused on socially induced strains. The basic idea was that people whose lives are made painful in society will be more likely to form social movements to change their social situation. One variant of this theory focuses on ***absolute deprivation****—the situation in which some people lack an important social resource,* such as adequate food, clothing, and shelter. Marx believed that industrialization would leave the working class so absolutely deprived that they would rise up in revolution. In the closing of the *Manifesto of the Communist Party,* he urged, "Workers of the World Unite—You have nothing to lose but your chains!" More recent theorists have pointed to a related form of social strain called ***relative deprivation****—the situation in which some people have a much greater share of the resources than others.* Welfare recipients in the United States are quite poor relative to the average standard of living here, but even they receive much more than the poor in some parts of the world, such as India or Bangladesh, where absolute deprivation results in widespread starvation. Yet, this relative deprivation of United States' poor has led to a welfare rights movement, from which was formed the Welfare Rights Organization.

Social strain also involves people's perception of their situation. The French scholar Alexis de Tocqueville believed that leaders who promised reform risked revolution, for, if they raised the people's hopes and therefore their expectations, but then failed to deliver improved living conditions, the people might rise against them.

Neil Smelser recognized the importance of social strain in collective-behavior settings. As we discuss in the "Close-Up on Theory" he believes social strain is a necessary condition for collective behavior. His theory is a general explanation of collective behavior that can be applied to social movements as well as other forms of collective behavior, such as mass hysteria and riots.

McCARTHY AND ZALD: RESOURCE MOBILIZATION

An especially interesting and enlightening approach is that introduced by John McCarthy and Mayer Zald, called *resource mobilization theory* (1977). McCarthy and Zald point out that the traditional approach to understanding social movements has assumed that social movements and their organizations arise, grow, or decline based on the frustrations or grievances of a collectivity. Thus, from this "traditional" perspective, we would set out to explain the black civil rights movement or the women's movement in terms of how frustrated and exploited blacks and women are or were. Furthermore, the traditional view has seen social-movement leaders in a bargaining position with authorities, and the environment has been portrayed as a force influencing the movement.

McCarthy and Zald call our attention to other aspects of social movements. First, they point to the importance of supporters, whom they call *conscience constituents*, who may provide money and other resources but do not benefit directly from the movement. The black civil rights movement, for instance, had important white supporters. Second, McCarthy and Zald point out that besides direct bargaining with authorities, social movement leaders have other important strategic tasks, including mobilizing supporters and changing public opinion from hostility toward neutrality or even support. Third, McCarthy and Zald say that the movement is not simply influenced by its social environment, but that it uses that environment, including the media, preexisting social networks, and existing institutional centers, to achieve its own ends. A successful movement manipulates the environment perhaps more than it is manipulated by the environment. In this section we consider Jo Freeman's study of the women's movement, and we see how it used existing social networks to develop important resources and influence.

McCarthy and Zald build some predictions from their assumptions about social movements. They predict that as the discretionary resources of a society grow, so will the amount of resources available to social movements. They also point out that the movement organizations rely heavily on the amount of resources available to the conscience constituents, supporters who agree with the goals of the movement but would not benefit directly. For instance, in the "Save the Whales" movement, it is whale-lovers and not the whales who put up the resources for the campaign! We need, then, to watch carefully for the level of support from such conscience supporters, whether the movement is pro-whale, pro-civil rights, pro-choice, or pro-something else. McCarthy and Zald point out that social-movement organizations that rely on the support of isolated constituents are in a precarious position; because those who are the beneficiaries of the movement are often isolated, the support of conscience supporters is very important. Successful movements are more likely to focus on a relatively narrow goal, develop a large stable income, and develop a professional staff. These professionalized social-movement organizations then actually use the beneficiaries of the movement as tools to gain their ends. For instance, the Hunger Commission is such a professional social-movement organization. The staff are professionals, and as professionals are neither poor nor hungry, but they use poor and hungry people strategically to achieve their purposes—for instance, as witnesses before legislative panels, and as demonstrators (McCarthy and Zald, 1977).

MAUSS AND GUSFIELD: THE SOCIAL CONSTRUCTION OF SOCIAL PROBLEMS

Armand Mauss (1975) also challenges the traditional or commonsensible view of social movements. Although many people, including some social scientists, would hold that social movements grow out of social problems, Mauss contends that it is often the other way around! Various existing interest groups may become "champions" of social causes, defining particular behaviors as problems and amassing popular support and resources to deal with them. This perspective provides an interesting interpretation of the Prohibition Era. Gusfield (1963) argues that the crusade against alcohol was led by religious groups, who represented a minority of the population, but were for a while able to build enough support to pass a Constitutional Amendment. Reversal of that Amendment seems to indicate a lack of lasting widespread support for the proposal. So whereas alcohol abuse is, was, and most likely will be with us, this "problem" along with its aborted "solution" seem to have had more to do with the dynamics of a powerful interest group than with changing levels of alcohol abuse. Similarly, the crime problem that received relatively little public concern in the 1950s was a convenient plank in the conservative politician's platform in the late 1960s. Mauss suggests this illustrates how interest groups champion a cause and create a social problem in the public's mind independent of the actual size of the problem in terms of people and pain involved.

KLANDERMANS AND OLSON: RATIONAL COST–BENEFIT ANALYSIS

Recently, Bert Klandermans has suggested that resource mobilization theorists may have over-reacted in abandoning the traditional approach of considering frustrations and grievances. He suggests that we can best explain participation by examining the perceived costs and benefits of participation as viewed by potential participants (1984). This position resembles that of Mancur Olson (1977), who created a mathematical model of collective behavior based largely on assumptions common in the realm of economics. Olson assumes people weigh both cost and benefits of participation. This assumption leads to an interesting phenomenon we have not yet discussed. Whereas McCarthy and Zald point out the importance of the conscience supporters who participate without benefiting, Olson points to the free-rider who benefits without participating.

Examples of such free-riders would include those United States residents who "benefited" from the successful efforts of antinuclear power groups, without paying the "costs" of having protested with them.

Olson's theory is especially good at explaining why people who would benefit from the success of a social movement often do not participate. Put simply, people consider the costs and benefits of participation. Faced with a situation in which one might benefit from reforms, at the same time that participation might mean threats or loss of a job, people may be acting rationally not to participate. Especially in the case where someone else is already fighting the battle, it may make sense, at least in economic terms to "let George do it."

Walsh and Warland recently tested Olson's theory on the collective behavior which followed the nation's most serious nuclear radiation mishap which occurred at Three Mile Island (1983). Because of radiation leaks from Unit 2 at Three Mile Island, some 150,000 people were evacuated. Following their return a social movement began in an attempt to achieve two goals: shutting down the other reactor, Unit 1, and monitoring the cleanup of Unit 2. Though all nearby residents were potential beneficiaries of these goals, a relative minority participated. Most people were, in Olson's term, free-riders.

The question Walsh and Warland set out to answer was whether Olson was also right that the free-riding resulted from a rational calculation of costs and benefits of participating, or whether it had to do with the ability of the social-movement organization to mobilize resources. After analyzing data from an extensive survey that they conducted, Walsh and Warland concluded that both perspectives are needed to explain the free-riding. People often mentioned their sizing up of costs and benefits, but Walsh and Warland also found that some did not participate who otherwise might have, because the social-movement organization did not get them information that would have won their support. Walsh and Warland conclude: "Any attempt to explain social-movement organization involvement without including both structural and social-psychological variables is unrealistic and misleading" (Walsh and Warland, 1983, p. 779).

FREEMAN: NETWORK THEORY

Jo Freeman derived three propositions to explain the origin of the women's movement in particular and the processes by which social movements are "constructed" in general (Freeman, 1974). First, Freeman states, every social movement must have "preexisting communications network" within the social base of a movement. Furthermore, this network must be composed of like-minded people. Once this network is in place, a strained situation and at least one precipitating event must occur that will make use of the network to begin to organize the affected people into some collective action.

Freeman explains the emergence of two distinct branches of the women's movement. The "older" branch grew within a network of women who had come together to form State Commissions on the Status of Women. The female members of these State Commissions began a series of three annual Conferences of Commissions on the Status of Women in 1963. They constituted a cooptable communications network, one in which many women who might be interested in beginning a social movement concerning women's rights were already linked.

The precipitating crisis was a "refusal by conference officials to bring to the floor a proposed resolution that urged the Equal Employment Opportunities Commission to give equal enforcement to the sex provision of Title VII as was given to the race provision." When the resolution was vetoed, the women who had pushed for its passage broke off from the main group and formed an "action organization," labeled the National Organization for Women (NOW). Its founder is Betty Friedan. Before the day was over NOW had twenty-eight members, and by 1974 there were 8,000. NOW and the other organizations involved in the older branch focused on drawing media attention to women's issues and lobbying for support of legal change.

The "younger" branch of the movement is less organized and works more toward making women aware of their exploitation under the current system, a bias that reflects its origins as well. During the 1960s many college-age people participated in "youth" and "freedom" movements, which protested militarism and exploitation of the poor and of ethnic minorities. Some members of this "radical" community were young women who cherished ideals of equality. They thus formed a communications network that was readily cooptable by women's movement organizers. The callous disregard for women's rights by males in movements advocating racial, ethnic, and economic equality became the precipitant for this consciousness-raising branch. For instance, at the 1967 National Conference for New Politics a women's caucus "met for days but was told its resolution wasn't significant enough to merit floor discussion." The rejected women later formed the first independent women's group in the country. Soon, other groups focusing largely on consciousness-raising were formed throughout the country.

Freeman's research clarifies the emergence of a major social movement and the emergence of social movements in general. She points out that those seeking to explain or start a movement should look for existing communications networks and precipitating events.

The women's movement continues today, although, like many social movements, it has become largely institutionalized. Throughout the 1970s and 1980s, the movement raised public awareness of women's issues. Much inequality persists, but prejudice and discrimination against women have declined, and women have increasingly been accepted into previously all-male realms. The nation came close to ratifying an Equal Rights Amendment that would have made formal the equal legal rights of women in the United States. That in 1984 a woman was a major-party candidate for the U.S. Vice-Presidency is one more indication of the change in women's status for which this movement works. We look more closely at these issues in Chapter 11, "Gender Role and Inequalities."

How Can We See Social Movements in Historical Perspective?

Social movements have played an important role in the history of our country. People tend to think of society as it exists as the natural order. Only when members of a social movement bring to our attention an injustice, a dangerous situation, or a misuse of our communal resources do we begin to think that life could be different. For example, for years it was assumed that children would begin to work at the age of 8 or 9. Child labor supported many mines and factories in the United States during the nineteenth century. Only when a few people became outraged at the idea were child labor laws passed and all children sent to school instead of work. This caused a radical change in our idea of what constitutes a "normal childhood."

A more recent example can be found in the withdrawal of the United States from the Vietnam War. In the early 1960s most Americans assumed our participation in the war must be necessary or our government would not be fighting there. By the time our troops withdrew, however, most citizens did *not* support our presence in Indochina and pressured the government to abandon its efforts there.

The antiwar movement began with a handful of people who learned the facts and spent their time and energy educating friends and associates about the United States' role in Vietnam. Many college professors and students were involved in the movement, and teach-ins—extended simultaneous lectures on the war—were held on college campuses across the country. At some schools students boycotted classes until the administration allowed free discussion of the issue or declared itself against American military participation in the conflict. Eventually, the general public became aware of the nature of the war and most were convinced of the virtual impossibility of "winning" it. It was this public that pressured politicians to speak and legislate against it. Our troops were pulled out, and the antiwar movement ended before it became an institution. However, many peace groups, such as the American Friends Service Committee, became nationally known due to their participation in this social movement. These same groups are now trying to raise public consciousness concerning United States' involvement in Central American wars.

Social movements are becoming more "professionalized" (McCarthy and Zald, 1973), and many social movements today have leaders whose primary function is to organize and to obtain funds and support for a movement. This, of course, may change the nature of a movement, transforming it from a broad-based effort to a highly centralized organization run by professionals. Whether this trend in social movements will continue is a matter for future study.

Conclusion

As social movements emerge, grow, and mature, they affect the course of our personal and social lives. The processes of collective behavior and social movements help democracy in the United States remain viable, because they offer the ordinary citizen an opportunity to express views and change the system.

Sociologists at Work

JERRY M. LEWIS
ADVISES AUTHORITIES ON CROWD AND RIOT CONTROL

Kent State University
Kent, Ohio

Jerry M. Lewis has received every possible teaching award from students and faculty at Kent State University and a Ford Foundation Award for Teaching, as well. Lewis also studies riots and other instances of crowd behavior in settings as diverse as rock concerts and soccer games.

How Did You Get Interested in Crowd Problems?

When I was in graduate school at the University of Illinois, I took a class in social movements with Joe Gusfield. He got me turned on to the subject. Early on, my research was on crowds associated with the black protest movement. After 1968, I began to focus on student crowds, particularly at Kent State. Then, in 1970, I was an eyewitness to the May 4 tragedy there. That really still affects my work directly. I did various studies with colleagues on the long-term impact of May 4, and then, in 1975, I developed a course and wrote a book on May 4 and its aftermath.

What Are You Working on Now?

As a result of my interest in Kent State and all the things that I saw going wrong, particularly crowd control, I became interested in nonlethal crowd control. At the same time I became interested in sports crowds and the violence that went on in sports crowds that nobody seemed to get excited about.

The other side of my research looks at the crowd tragedy. One international event I am working on right now is the study of the Heysel riots that took place in Brussels, Belgium. The reason the riot is so important, beyond the tragedy of thirty-nine deaths, is that it has significantly altered European soccer, in terms of attitudes toward crowds and particularly attitudes toward the English. Indeed, I think the Heysel riot will probably be the most talked about riot in the next ten years. It is certainly almost as well-known internationally as the Kent State May 4 riot.

What Went Wrong at Heysel?

Several things happened at Heysel. The Belgian police didn't liaison with the Liverpool police to get a real picture of the number of fans that were coming over. Liverpool had a good reputation, but they underestimated the number of fans coming over. The second thing is that the Liverpool fans were placed next to the Italian fans. Typically they segregate the fans at opposite ends of the playing field. A lot of people got black-market tickets, which put the English and the Italian fans right next to each other. The third breakdown was the distribution of police. Typically, in an English stadium the police will be inside the stadium, but most of the Belgian social control forces were *outside* the stadium directing people into the stadium where all the trouble was occurring. The fourth problem of social control was that it was difficult to get access to the crowd. It was almost a case study of how to handle a crowd improperly.

How Do You Set Out to Understand a Riot?

I have developed a protocol for working with Smelser's model. I focus on one riot and try to look at all dimensions of it. One of the things that we need to teach our students is to be better observers, to really look at the social world. The approach I take using the case-history approach and Smelser's model allows an in-depth look at rare but important events.

What Benefits Come from Your Studies?

There are a variety of applications of my work. The first is to instill understanding in students who are later going to be policymakers, officials, and roles like these. The second application is working with the media. I have done a lot of interviews with media about crowds, not only tragic crowds but typical crowds. The third area I have worked with is training auditorium managers, marshals, and other social-control officials. I try to move them away from stereotypic thinking about the crowds—that the crowds are all crazy, that they are all one man (kind of like a big blob). In fact, I like to point out that they are highly differentiated systems. And so, in a sense, what I do with students, the media, and the police is all the same thing—trying to knock down stereotypes about very emotional things that we call crowds.

Once we recognize that crowds are highly differentiated, we can take Smelser's model to show how to diffuse or prevent something like the Heysel riot. We still have a lot of problems with sports crowds in America. However, a small group of people *are* doing crowd research. Our colleagues, the media, and social-control agencies are paying attention to what we have to say. I think that is the positive side of it, that people are realizing that collective behavior is as scientific as any other subdiscipline in sociology.

Summary Questions

1. What are the differences between collective behavior and social movements?
2. What are the four types of crowd behavior?
3. What do contagion and convergence theories say about crowd behavior?
4. How do norms emerge in crowd interaction?
5. What are the elements of Richard Berk's rational-decision theory?
6. When are crowds likely to use violence?
7. How does Neil Smelser explain collective behavior?
8. Under what circumstances does a diffuse crowd form?
9. Why do we believe in rumors and how do they affect our actions?
10. What is the social meaning of urban legends?
11. How do hysteria and panic affect us?
12. What is the AIDS hysteria about?
13. What is the difference between fashions and fads?
14. What are the major influences on public opinion?
15. How does the mass media influence other social phenomena?
16. What is the relationship between television and suicide?
17. What are the stages in the life of a social movement?
18. What are four types of social movements?
19. How do social movements begin and grow?
20. How did the two branches of the women's movement begin?
21. How do social movements become "professionalized"?

Summary Answers

1. Collective behavior describes the actions, thoughts, and feelings of a relatively temporary and unstructured group of people. In contrast, a social movement is a large, ongoing group of people engaged in organized behavior designed to bring about or resist change in society.
2. The casual crowd gathers around a specific event, and its members have little interaction with one another. A conventional crowd gathers for a socially sanctioned purpose. An expressive crowd gathers specifically for the purpose of letting out emotions. An acting crowd focuses on a specific action or goal.
3. LeBon's contagion theory is that a collective mind forms in a crowd which takes over the individual minds of crowd members and causes them to act alike. Convergence theory builds on this by suggesting that crowd members do not really lose their individuality in a group but act from their unconscious selves.
4. Turner and Killian say that as people interact in a crowd they form new norms for that specific crowd, and, as the norms emerge, the crowd pressures its members to conform to them.
5. Instead of emphasizing crowd irrationality, as LeBon and the convergence theorists do, Berk believes that members of a crowd are actually seeking information they can use to make a rational decision. He believes that crowd members seek information from each other, use it to predict occurrences, consider their options, rank order the probable outcomes of the actions, and decide on an action that will give them the most reward for the least cost.
6. Crowds are more likely to use violence—rioting, for example—when they feel they are being oppressed and wish to overthrow their oppressors.
7. Smelser says six determinants are necessary and sufficient for a collective episode to occur. They are (a) structural conduciveness; (b) structural strain; (c) growth and spread of a generalized belief; (d) precipitating factors; (e) mobilization of participants for action; and (f) the operation of social control.
8. Diffuse crowd, or mass, behavior involves action by people with common concerns who may or may not have met each other.
9. Rumors are information that travels from person to person, usually by word of mouth. As they spread, rumors become leveled, or simplified, and sharpened, or focused, on certain details. Rumors may be a causal factor in riots. It has been suggested that they are often a substitute for news.
10. Urban legends have a strong basic story appeal, a foundation in actual belief, and a meaningful message or moral. They are an excellent example of a way that people in modern societies symbolically communicate to each other their anxieties about social issues in a fast-changing environment.
11. Hysteria—generalized anxiety about some unknown situation—and panic—an attempt to flee from an imagined or real threat—often create behavior changes in individuals, from illness caused by an imagined bug to flight out of town in response to an imagined invasion from Mars.
12. The alarming spread of AIDS and its certain prognosis have combined to create an atmosphere in the United States conducive to the growth of hys-

teria concerning the disease. For example, police officers have been wearing rubber gloves when arresting suspects for fear of contracting AIDS unknowingly. Education of the population is reducing the hysteria somewhat and promises to help in the reduction of the numbers affected.

13. Fashions and fads are changing styles currently accepted by a part of the population, but which are not considered a permanent part of the culture. Fashions change more gradually than fads.

14. A public is an unorganized diffuse crowd with opinions on an issue of current interest. Public opinion is influenced in two major ways: by friends, or reference groups, and by members of that group whose judgment is considered important—opinion leaders.

15. The national media strongly influence the formation of public opinion. They may also be a catalyst in social explosions such as riots. The fact that programming is now immediate leads to less sorting of what is important and what is not and may actually distort reality for the viewer.

16. David Phillips and Lundie Carstensen determined that in the specific case of teenage suicide, media violence causes audience violence. They found that television news or feature stories about suicides triggered additional teenage suicides, perhaps because of imitation.

17. In the preliminary stage, society shows a restless concern over an issue on which people are divided. In the popular stage, the movement begins to rally around a charismatic leader who speaks for reform, revolution, resistance, or expression of self in such a way that people relate to the leader and begin to feel hopeful that their questions have answers. In the third stage, participants organize formally, formulate policies, and decide where to begin change. In the last stage, it destroys itself as a movement and becomes an institution, with all the organized and accepted norms of society.

18. Resistance movements are formed to resist a change that is already occurring in society. Reform movements endeavor to change elements of the system as it currently stands. Revolutionary movements deny that the system will ever work, and seek to replace it. Expressive movements concentrate on change among their members and their immediate social contacts.

19. McCarthy and Zald's resource-mobilization theory suggests that the success of social movements depends on their ability to gain support, especially from influential people, called conscience constituents, who contribute money and other resources but do not benefit directly from the movement. They note that in order to be successful, social movements manipulate the environment, focus on a specific goal, and develop a large stable income and professional staff.

Mauss goes a step further and suggests that the interest groups may in fact "create" social problems rather than the problems creating interest groups.

Klandermans suggests that we can best explain social-movement participation by examining the costs and benefits. When the benefits of participating in a movement outweigh the costs, the person will participate.

Olson points out that social movements support many free-riders, who benefit from the movement without participating in it. Walsh and Warland use elements of both perspectives to describe the collective behavior that followed the nuclear radiation mishap at Three Mile Island, in which they discovered that most people were free-riders.

20. The "older" branch grew within a network of women who had come together to form State Commissions on the Status of Women. They eventually formed NOW, which focuses on drawing media attention to women's issues and lobbying for support of legal change. The "younger" branch grew out of the "youth" and "freedom" movements of the 1960s and was nurtured by the oppression women in these movements felt from the male leaders of the groups. They focus largely on raising the consciousness of women to their oppression by men.

21. It has been suggested that many social movements today have leaders whose primary function is to organize and obtain funds and support for a movement, thus making it a highly centralized organization run by professionals.

Glossary

absolute deprivation the situation in which some people lack an important social resource

acting crowd one that gathers to focus on a specific action or goal

casual crowd one that gathers around a specific event but its members have little interaction with one another

collectivity a set of people who share common values and interests

collective behavior the actions, thoughts, and feelings of a relatively temporary and unstructured group of people

conventional crowd one that gathers for a socially sanctioned purpose

crowd a set of people who are physically close together and share a common concern

diffuse crowd a group of people who are separated by time or space barriers but who share a common concern; their behavior can also be termed **mass behavior**

expressive crowd one that gathers specifically for the purpose of letting out emotions

expressive movements social movements that concentrate on change among their members and their immediate social contacts

fad a popular but short-lived form of conduct

fashion a currently valued style of appearance or behavior

hysteria a generalized anxiety about some unknown situation

mob a crowd that is emotionally aroused and is about to undertake violent action

opinion leaders those members of our reference groups who endeavor to change our minds

panic an attempt to flee from an imagined or real threat

public an unorganized diffuse crowd with opinions on an issue of current interest

public opinion the views of the members of a public on a certain issue

reference groups those collectives to which we belong and relate

reform movements social movements that are trying to change elements of the system as it currently stands

relative deprivation the situation in which some people have a much greater share of the resources than others

resistance movements social movements formed to resist a change that is already occurring in society

revolutionary movements social movements formed to overthrow the entire existing structure and replace it

riot a violent and destructive public disturbance

rumors information that travels from person to person, usually by word of mouth

social movement a large, ongoing group of people engaged in organized behavior designed to bring about or resist change in society

solidaristic crowd one that gathers to form a network of supportive relationships that form a unity within the crowd

Suggested Readings

Myra Marx Ferree and Beth B. Hess. 1985. *Controversy and Coalition: The New Feminist Movement*. Boston: Twayne Press.

An excellent analytic view of the women's movement from the 1960s through the 1980s.

Jo Freeman (ed.). 1983. *Social Movements of the Sixties and Seventies*. New York: Longman Press.

An interesting look at the development of the social movements that helped shaped the 1980s.

Frederick Koenig. 1985. *Rumor in the Marketplace: The Social Psychology of Commercial Hearsay*. Dover, Mass: Auburn House.

Koenig discusses the various rumors that have affected American business, how they started and what their consequences were for the corporations involved.

Jerry D. Rose. 1982. *Outbreaks: The Sociology of Collective Behavior*. New York: Free Press.

Rose analyzes collective behavior from the standpoint of etiology, membership, process, and outcome.

PART 4

Social Inequality

CHAPTER 8

SOCIAL STRATIFICATION and MOBILITY

- What Is Stratification?
- What Are the Dimensions of Stratification?
- How Did Stratification Change in the Great Transition?
- Why Are Societies Stratified?
- Close-Up on Theory: Karl Marx and Friedrich Engels on the Final Class Struggle
- Close-Up on Research: Gerhard Lenski on Whether Marxism Works or Not
- What Explains Social Mobility?
- Sociologists at Work: Robert Robinson Explores How Families Face Class Issues

How's Your Sociological Intuition?

1. Which type of society usually has the most inequality of wealth, prestige, and power?
   - **a.** a hunting and gathering society
   - **b.** a horticultural society
   - **c.** an agricultural society
   - **d.** an industrial society
2. In which of these nations is the income most equally divided?
   - **a.** West Germany
   - **b.** France
   - **c.** United States
   - **d.** United Kingdom
3. In West Germany, a person in the top fifth of the income distribution earns as much as six people in the lowest fifth. In France, the ratio of income for those in the top fifth to those in the lowest is 24:1. What would this ratio be in the United States?
   - **a.** 1:5
   - **b.** 1:10
   - **c.** 1:25
   - **d.** 1:50
4. In which of the following societies would an individual be most likely to move between social levels?
   - **a.** United States
   - **b.** Norway
   - **c.** Japan
   - **d.** West Germany

Answers

1. c. Social inequality is most extreme in agricultural societies because they are productive yet easily dominated by a small corps of elite. In the "Close-Up on Theory" Gerhard Lenski discusses subsistence adaptation as one of the factors influencing social inequality.
2. a. West Germany has the most equal distribution of income among the industrialized nations. We compare income distribution in the section, "Characteristics of Stratification."
3. b. The United States is in the midrange regarding income inequality, as we see when we discuss income inequality in this chapter.
4. b. Norway scores highest on what sociologists call circulation mobility, an indicator of how many people change their social rank. We consider this topic in the section, "Social Mobility."

When You Have Finished Studying This Chapter, You Should Know:

- What *social stratification* and *class* mean
- The major forms of stratification
- How stratification structures differ in equality and openness
- Weber's three dimensions of stratification
- How stratification changed with the great transition
- In what regard some stratification is inevitable
- What the functionalists and conflict theorists believe to be the reasons for stratification
- The basic premises of the evolutionary interpretation of stratification
- How supporting beliefs are symbolically important to a stratification system
- What social mobility is
- How structural mobility differs from circulation mobility
- Why some societies have more mobility than others

On the first night of his visit to Northern Brazil, Tim sat outside drinking beer with friends of his host, Juan. The next morning, Juan receives a phone call and tells Tim about it.

"Remember Sergio, the guy with the motorcycle you met last night?"

"Sure," Tim responds.

"Well, after he left here, he was killed. A car hit him from behind on his motorcycle."

"Oh no!"

"Yeah."

"You don't seem very broken up about it."

"I'm not. I suppose you could say he had it coming."

"What are you talking about?"

"Well, he used to like to run people down with his car."

"He what?!"

"He ran people over with his car—just for the hell of it."

"That's incredible! I didn't know him, but he sure didn't impress me as a murderer."

"Well, it's true. I suspect he's killed at least a dozen people. I was even with him one night when he ran down some peasant type who was just walking along the edge of the road."

"That's disgusting! Why wasn't he in prison or executed?"

"His family is very important, and the people he ran down are not."

"Well, why didn't you do anything?"

"What am I supposed to do? Our parents were friends before we were born."

"So what?"

"So it's not my place to get involved. Do you call the police every time one of your friends does some drugs or sells some?"

"That's different. This is no gray area. We're not talking about drugs, we're talking about people. There must be wives and kids out there who are all screwed up because some nut got his kicks running somebody over."

"You don't understand, and anyhow it wouldn't have done any good. His father holds one of the most influential positions in the country. Sergio was caught once and spent the night in jail, but they just dropped the case and wrote it up as though the guy walked out in front of him."

Later that week Tim attends Sergio's funeral. There he encounters many of the people he met on his first night at Juan's. The scene is typical—flowers and even an open casket. The people go through the familiar routine of offering sympathy to the family of the deceased. Informally, however, the talk more than once touches on Sergio's homicidal pastime. Some note the crude justice in how he met his death.

But when Tim inquires why someone did not turn him in, he gets similar answers. Sergio's social status protected him from serious reprisal. Although his friends were repulsed by what was happening, they did not see it as their place to get the law involved. Why do people accept such blatant injustice as occurred in this true story? Part of the answer to this question lies in the answer to some underlying sociological questions. How and why do societies distribute such rewards as power, wealth, and prestige so unequally?

In the coming chapters we will look at various forms of social inequality: social stratification based on occupation or ownership, racially or ethnically based social inequality, and social inequality linked to gender and age. We will try to help you better understand how and why positions of privilege and denigration are created and maintained. We will also try to raise your awareness of social inequality and arouse your conscience to be critical of what you see. For, like the passive witnesses of Sergio's murders, we are all in jeopardy of confusing what is with what ought to be.

We will begin by considering perhaps the most pervasive social inequality of all: that based on our occupation or place in the world of work. In Chapter 8, "Social Stratification," we consider this sort of social stratification as it appears through time and in various

Mansions are largely a phenomenon of industrialization which provides enough differences in wealth for both mansions and shacks. The agrarian era involved enormous inequality in that some people lived in castles while most lived in huts. (*Photo courtesy the author*)

cultures. In Chapter 9, "Social Class in the United States," we move on to consider economically based social inequality in our own society. In Chapter 10, "Race and Ethnic Relations," we look at how ethnicity and race are used to create positions that are often highly unequal. Later in Chapter 11, "Gender Inequality," we consider how social inequality is often based on gender. Finally, at the end of Part 3, "Social Inequality," in Chapter 12, "Inequality Based on Age" we consider how age is used to sort people into positions with great differences in social resources.

What Is Stratification?

Stratification is a characteristic of all known human societies. In the broadest sense of the word, ***stratification*** *is any systematic ranking of social positions that influences the wealth, power, and prestige of the people in those positions.* Social stratification can be based on a variety of characteristics, including one's occupation, gender, age, race, or ethnicity. Thus executives receive privileges not extended to unskilled laborers, and men are often given power not extended to women. Older persons, younger persons, and people from minority racial or ethnic groups are often afforded less than full status in a wide variety of social settings. Stratification can also refer to the hierarchy of offices within a bureaucracy or the ranking of nations within a world political-economic system.

Stratification is often used to describe the way societies rank people according to work or economic position. Thus, owners rank above workers, and professionals rank above clerks. Especially in modern societies, the distribution of wealth, prestige, and power depends greatly on one's place in the world of work. In this chapter we study this ranking by economic position.

Earlier we introduced the term *status* as a place in any social structure, such as the father of a family, the clown of a group, or president of a company (see Chapter 3, "Society"). In a discussion of stratification, *status* often takes one of two narrower meanings. Sociologists often use **status** to mean, *generally, a position in a social structure*. Depending on context, it may also mean *a position in a social stratification structure, or the amount of prestige associated with one's position in a stratification structure*. For instance, if we ask about a person's social status, we expect to get an idea of the person's rank in society. In this context "high status" may imply considerable wealth, power, and prestige. In this chapter we usually use *status* to refer to a particular place in a social stratification system that ranks people according to their productive function, such as owner, executive, professional, clerk, worker, servant, or slave.

A modern industrial society has tens of thousands of occupations, each of which can be considered a status. Sociologists generally gather positions of similar rank together and regard them as a *stratum* (the singular of *strata*). A ***stratum*** *is a level in a stratification structure at which people share similar status.*

In some societies the levels of status are obvious. The strata have explicit names and clearly defined boundaries, such as the line between slave and free person. In other societies the strata blend together so that naming them and identifying their boundaries is difficult. Scholars sometimes have difficulty agreeing on where strata begin and end in the United States. In all societies, however, people of low status are viewed as inferior and receive less wealth, prestige, and power than those of higher status.

MAJOR FORMS OF STRATIFICATION

No two societies have developed identical stratification structures. Societies with similar production modes usually have similar stratification, but ideas play an important role, and societies have considerable latitude in developing their particular form of social stratification. In the diversity of systems, sociologists have discerned five basic types (Kerbo, 1983).

PRIMITIVE COMMUNALISM. ***Primitive communalism*** *is a form of stratification characterized by a high degree of sharing and minimal social inequality.* Traditional Na-

Born into poverty. These youths live in a status of poverty, not because of what they did or deserve, but because our society is stratified and they were born into low status families. (*Photo courtesy the author*)

tive American groups often lived under primitive communalism. Food and tools are shared equally. There is no chief or official leader, though one or two individuals are acknowledged to have slightly more informal influence than the rest. Because there is virtually no social inequality, the question of how one achieves higher status is moot. With no inequality, there is no conflict between "haves" and "have nots." Indeed, there may be no evidence of violence among such groups or between them and the other tribes they occasionally meet. Some Eskimo tribes, for instance, even lack a word for human violence or warfare.

Often, in societies practicing primitive communalism, some individuals achieve elevated status as chief, respected leader, medicine man, or shaman. But the level of social inequality is very low, and the rewards associated with high status are primarily honorary. No special system of political or religious ideas supports the differences in status. It is simply a matter of custom that an especially talented hunter is awarded special status and honor. Primitive communalism is common in hunting and gathering societies, which, we recall from the chapter on society, has been the most common form of society for most of the history of our species. We may also recall that because these societies often exhaust local food resources, they tend to be nomadic. A food-production strategy with little surplus and a nomadic lifestyle that discourages the accumulation of property combine to limit the amount of wealth anyone can achieve. This in turn helps limit the degree of inequality. Societies with such equality and harmony may seem as distant as the Garden of Eden to us today, but they were typical for more than 99 percent of our 4 million years of life as a species.

SLAVERY. Only recently has humanity become civilized. The transition to agriculture, begun some 5,000 years ago, serves as a basis of civilization by providing sufficient surplus for some to leave food-procuring activity and become full-time religious or military leaders, artisans, philosophers, or other specialists. Often civilization brings with it another social innovation: slavery.

***Slavery** is a form of social stratification involving great social inequality and the ownership of some persons by others.* Slavery is common to early agrarian societies, as exemplified by the Roman Empire at its height of power. Two tiny elite orders dominated the Romans' important social, economic, and political positions. One person in 50,000 ranked as a senator, whereas one out of 1,000 belonged to the less powerful "equites." To attain senatorial status one needed property 250,000 times a laborer's wage. About half that amount was required to reach the *equite* status. The masses lived in material poverty and endured the contempt of the wealthy. They were forced to defer to the wealthy to the point of self-degradation. But even worse off than the general masses were the slaves, who numbered about a fourth of the population.

Obviously, when stratification takes the form of slavery, social inequality is extreme. Americans, familiar with slavery in our own history, tend to think of it as a permanent hereditary status. This is often not the case. In the Roman Empire, as in many slave systems, a person could be born free and become a slave as the result of military conquest. One might also "fall" into slavery by not paying debts. There was a slim possibility one could buy one's way out of slavery or one could gain freedom by doing well in the advanced system of education and thereby becoming especially useful to the upper classes.

Slavery has often been justified as being the right of the conquering nation or the obligation of the bankrupt. It is less often based on racism, though this was the major justification for slavery in the early United States. As mentioned earlier, slavery is most commonly found in the early stages of agrarianism. It is neither particularly rare nor especially common.

CASTE. The caste system leaves less opportunity to leave one's birth status than any other stratification system. ***Caste** is a form of stratification in which an individual is permanently assigned to a status based on his or her parents' status*. The term *caste* originates with the traditional stratification structure of India. China also had an extensive enduring system with castelike features. Despite extreme inequality and lack of opportunity, such systems have sometimes persisted for thousands of years with little or no overt resistance. In the traditional Indian caste system, the highest strata or caste were priests (Brahmans) and warriors (Kshatriyas). Beneath them were two other major castes. All castes were divided into hundreds of occupational subcastes (*jati*). Lower still were the outcastes, so lowly and unclean as to be unworthy of caste. Among the outcastes were the *untouchables* who were obliged to hide themselves from the view of anyone with caste status. Where this was impossible, they were required to bow with their faces to the earth.

In the caste system one can almost never move up or down, nor can one marry out of one's caste. Under these circumstances we say the status is *ascribed*. ***Ascribed status** is a status determined by one's birth*. The fact that members of the Indian higher castes were much wealthier and more powerful than those below was seen as a logical consequence of the central difference between strata: those in high castes were honorable because of their virtue, whereas those in lower castes were less honorable because they were less virtuous. The outcastes were despicable because they were presumed to be morally corrupt.

It took great power to impose such a rigid and oppressive system. The power took the form of control over people's minds, largely through religion, rather than control of their physical beings through direct application of police or military power. In the language of the chapter on deviance, the social controls were *internalized*. The key is in the Hindu religion, which taught that after death one is reincarnated (reborn), and how well one behaves in the present life determines one's caste in the next life. Acceptance of this belief was widespread and provided a powerful incentive to cooperate with the caste system. Who would want to challenge the system if this would mean being next reborn as an untouchable? Certainly not the untouchables, who were most aware of misery of their status. Probably not those of higher status, who were taught to interpret their privilege as the mark of righteousness. Furthermore, those of other strata despised and oppressed the outcastes, who had been so clearly labeled as the worst of the sinners. So strong was belief in this logic that the system persisted for some 2,000 years with no recorded incident of an outcaste rebellion.

Untouchable? In parts of India, certain low status workers were defined as untouchable, so much so that their touch, or even the touch of their shadow was regarded as defiling the one touched. (*AP/Wide World Photos*)

The caste system provides dramatic illustration of both stratification and of the power of legitimating beliefs to create a stable system amidst tremendous inequality. Yet, though impressive, these social structures are not particularly common, and they occur mostly in agrarian societies.

ESTATE. Castles, the changing of the guard at Buckingham Palace, or a royal wedding of the lovely lady to the handsome prince are the treasured mementos of a largely bygone era. These images are also remnants of an earlier form of stratification known as the *estate system*, which became common to much of Europe during the Middle Ages. Initially there were two primary strata: the nobility, a militaristic land-holding class; and their vassals, comprising peasants and serfs. Under the ***estate system***, *peasants were required by law to work land owned by their lords in return for food and protection from outside attacks.*

The estate system, instituted into law in much of Europe during the twelfth century, created three major strata: the First Estate, composed of priests; the Second Estate, composed of the nobility; and the Third Estate, composed of commoners. The estate system was backed by law and supported by the established church doctrine that kings derived their rights from God. According to some experts, inequality reached an all-time high in this form of stratification. Opportunity for advancement from the Third Estate to either higher rank was limited to the most talented few. An individual's status was almost solely determined by heredity. The estate system is a common form of stratification in agrarian societies, and it prevailed in Europe for most of the past 1,000 years.

CLASS. The familiar class system current in the United States, Canada, and most of the Western world arrived more recently—about the time of the Industrial Revolution. A ***class stratification system*** *is a form of stratification in which people are ranked into categories according to their occupation or economic status, but in which some opportunity exists for mobility between the categories based on achievement or merit.*

The estate system involves the agrarian mode, with the vast majority of people compelled to work as farm laborers on land owned by a relatively small number of lords. In contrast, the class system appears in industrial societies, with the majority of people working in a large variety of occupations. Although sociologists agree that analyzing the class system is central to understanding social behavior, they have defined *class* in several different, though similar, ways. Various definitions emphasize different aspects of stratification.

Karl Marx, for instance, used *class* to mean those who share a common position in relation to the means of production. For Marx, industrial societies tend to divide into two important classes—owners and workers. Because workers have virtually no opportunity to become owners, Marx's classes have a castelike quality (Marx, 1867).

For Max Weber, *class* refers to those who have common life chances in the marketplace, meaning those who have similar amounts of wealth or income. As did Marx, Weber focused on economic position, but he did not envision society as split into two classes. Rather, Weber's definition allows for an indefinite number of classes (Weber, 1925).

When sociologists in the middle of this century began to study class structure in specific towns, they relied heavily on how their subjects viewed the class system. W. Lloyd Warner took into account a person's reputation in the community and defines *social class* as an aggregate of individuals who are ranked about equally on a continuum from superior to inferior positions by other members of their community (Warner & Lunt, 1941). Richard Centers considers the individual's perception of his or her own social rank and defines a *class* as a psychosocial grouping that involves a feeling of membership based on common interests, attitudes, and behavior (1949).

Class can mean several specific things, but in general it *is a large set of people regarded by themselves or others as sharing similar status with regard to wealth, power, and prestige.*

In a class system, ***achieved status*** *is determined at least partly through the individual's effort.* For instance, the son of a laborer might "work his way up" to a career in a profession. As we have seen, upward mobility is much less likely in other stratification systems, like caste or estate systems, where status is more likely to be ascribed.

The class system offers more opportunity to change one's status than any other stratification system yet observed. Inequality persists, but it is less extreme than in most other systems (except for primitive communalism). The distinctions between classes are much less obvious than those between castes, partly because in a class system people change status, whereas in a caste system they generally do not. Class stratification, though relatively new, is becoming increasingly common as the world becomes more industrialized. Before we focus our attention on the workings of the class system in the United States, we will consider some important distinguishing characteristics of stratification systems in general. These will be useful in helping to describe and understand differences between stratification systems as well as changes in one stratification system over time.

CHARACTERISTICS OF STRATIFICATION

Besides categorizing a society's stratification system into one of the five types above, we can also analyze a particular stratification system, or stratification in general, by considering two important dimensions of stratification: (1) the degree of openness, or opportunity for individuals to change their status; and (2) the degree of equality, or amount of equal sharing between levels in a stratification system.

OPENNESS. ***Openness*** *is the opportunity for individuals to change their status.* In principle, a stratification system could be completely open, having no barriers to changing from one status to another. However, no such system has ever existed. A completely closed system could also theoretically exist, under which no one would ever leave his or her original status. The caste system approaches the completely closed alternative.

In traditional India, if a man washed clothes for a living, his son would also. The son could not attain a more skilled occupation, such as carpenter, regardless of how talented or motivated he was. Furthermore, the launderer's son would be forbidden to marry a carpenter's daughter, in spite of how well matched the two might otherwise be.

But India is only one of many societies to assign status permanently at birth. A slave system may be a form of caste stratification. In Colonial America, for instance, a slave remained a slave regardless of ability. The individual's talents bore no relationship to chances for advancement; a person born a slave could not advance to higher positions of society. Even half a century after the *United States Constitution* was ratified, hundreds of thousands of black people lived in the permanently assigned status of slave. In 1950, nearly a century after slavery was abolished, it was still illegal for a black person to marry a white person in Alabama.

A caste determines the social standing of each individual, and individuals rarely leave their caste. Generally a caste comprises one or more occupations. One assumes one's parents' caste for life, thus one's occupation and stature in the community and society are fixed at birth.

All men are created equal? The children in this photo were born into a relatively high status family where membership in the yacht club is taken for granted. Contrast their life experiences with the kids riding their bikes through a neighborhood of poverty in the photograph appearing on p. 192. *(Photo courtesy the author)*

For thousands of years in India and China individuals were assigned the caste of their parents, which determined their occupation, prestige, and place of residence. Marriage out of the caste was prohibited, and it was inappropriate even to consider moving out of one's caste occupationally.

Although the traditional Indian system of castes has now been banned by law, much of it still persists in fact (even as racial discrimination in the United States persists in spite of new laws). A small village of 250 people may have twenty different castes. A city of 50,000 may involve 200 castes, all known, well-defined, and adhered to despite the law (Beals, 1962).

In contrast to caste stratification, class stratification structures offer more openness, or opportunity to improve one's status, than do caste systems. Even though the class system is more open than the caste system, status is not determined solely on the basis of achievement or merit in it or any known stratification system. Even in a class system, the parents' status is a strong determinant of the child's adult status, as we see in Chapter 9, where we consider the United States as a modern class stratification system.

In the United States, as in the class systems of many other industrial societies, merit and achievement determine social status to a large degree. Heritage, however, also plays an important role. From birth to adulthood, children are generally assigned the status of their parents, enjoying the life-style and social experiences of their parents' status. So, whereas an individual's status is *permanently ascribed* in the caste system, it is *temporarily ascribed* at birth in the class system. This affords obvious advantages to children of high-status parents and disadvantages to children of low-status parents.

The person born into a family of great means, who literally inherits the family fortune, provides an obvious example of status inheritance in class systems. So does a person who is disadvantaged by being born into abject poverty. In both cases there is a strong tendency to remain at one's parents' level. In the midrange between extreme wealth and extreme poverty, status may also be partly inherited, especially through differences in opportunities. The higher status family, which can afford private schools, lessons, camps, and college, may reap significant dividends in terms of the child's adult status. On the other hand, even a highly capable person born into a lower status family may be disadvantaged by weaker schools, lower aspirations, untreated disease, or malnutrition. The percentage of poor black orphans with great musical talent who reach the status of Louis Armstrong continues to be minute. It is apparent that, although a class system is open in principle, in practice it exhibits some qualities of the more closed estate and slave systems while being more open than caste systems.

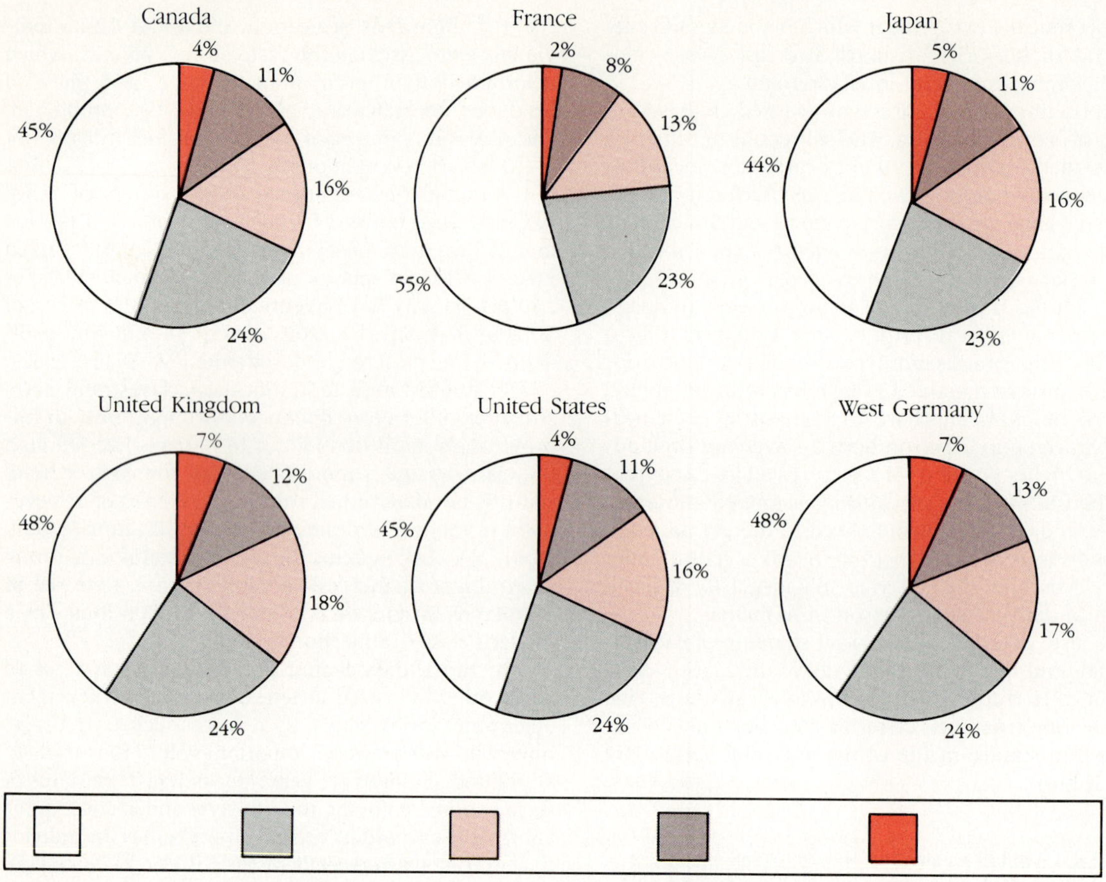

FIGURE 8.1 Comparative Equality of Income for Six Nations. SOURCE Based on data presented in Harold R. Kerbo [1983], *Social Stratification and Inequality*, New York: McGraw-Hill, p. 32. Used by permission.

EQUALITY. Stratification structures also differ in how equally they distribute wealth, power, prestige, and other social resources. Over the course of human history, hunting and gathering societies, with their primitive communal form of stratification, have typically demonstrated a very equal distribution of resources. Such societies have exhibited almost no poverty and few instances of extreme wealth. In the later stages of horticulture and agriculture, inequality develops, with a small number of immensely powerful, wealthy, and prestigious people dominating the masses, who live largely in poverty. With the arrival of industrialism, the trend seems to swing back in the direction of equality. Although some extremes of wealth and poverty still exist, a large middle class develops, which includes most of the society's population. (This chapter's "Close-Up on Theory: Gerhard Lenski on Power and Privilege," explores this connection further.) The degree of equality is the second major characteristic of stratification structures and measures how equally the society distributes its social resources. *The **degree of equality** is the degree to which the social structure approaches an equal distribution of resources.*

We can measure a society's equality in several ways. A common technique is to compare the proportion of resources controlled by different strata. For instance, in 1950 the top 5 percent of income recipients in the United States received 17.3 percent of all income. By 1980 the proportion of income received by this top 5 percent had declined to 15.3 percent. In the same period the proportion of income received by the lowest 20 percent of the population rose from 4.5 percent to nearly 5.1 percent. Relatively speaking, the rich became somewhat less well off, and the poor improved their position. During this period, therefore, the stratification structure became a bit more equal. Figure 8.1 allows us to compare income inequality for various nations. As the chart reveals, some countries (like France) have much less income equality than does the United States, whereas others (like West Germany) have more income equality.

We have considered two significant characteristics

of stratification structures—the degree of openness and the degree of equality. We discover that, whereas some stratification structures are notably more open and more equal than others, no known societies are totally open or totally equal. In fact, the totally equal society would have no stratification.

What Are the Dimensions of Stratification?

We have discussed stratification in general, as though being of high status automatically affords one large portions of wealth, power, and prestige. Yet we can readily find cases where a person has great quantities of one or two of these resources, but much less of the others. Consider the person who is a major aide to the president of the United States. In a sense he or she is only the president's servant, but as an adviser this person actually exercises influence over the president, thus achieving some of the power of the presidency, while not actually holding the office. Compared with this awesome power, the income and prestige of such a position is considerably less. Although the aide has the status of great power, the position does not offer commensurate prestige or wealth.

Consider the president of the United States, one of the most powerful people in the world. The income from that status ranks below many thousands of others, including relatively minor corporate executives and even some members of the better paid rock groups. The prestige and power associated with the presidential status far exceed the accompanying wealth. Upon leaving office, the former president will have a new status with tremendous prestige, vastly diminished power, but a pension about equal to that of the new president.

If we consider more common occupations, we note that they often bring high status with respect to one social resource, but not all resources. Local political positions, like mayor or state legislator, offer considerable power, some prestige, but little income. Some occupations, like insurance sales, offer potentially great income, little power, and such a lack of prestige that the salespeople may try to redefine themselves as "brokers," "estate planners," or even "investment counselors." Other occupations, like philosopher, historian, artist, or poet, carry high levels of prestige but offer little power or income.

Though an individual's wealth, power, and prestige levels often coincide, the frequent exceptions suggest that it is worthwhile to consider that these are three distinct resources governed by separate processes.

Max Weber, the pioneering German sociologist, first suggested there are three basic dimensions of stratification: *class*, *party*, and *status group* (Gerth and Mills, 1959). These correspond to the three important social resources: wealth, power, and prestige, respectively.

CLASS AND WEALTH OR INCOME. According to Weber, ***class*** *is a set of people with similar amounts of income or wealth.* Although we have previously used *wealth* interchangeably with *income*, we should note that technically ***income*** *refers to the rate at which one receives money*, whereas ***wealth*** *refers to the value of one's holdings*.

Class, in Weber's sense, refers to economic status, so the rich, the poor, or the "comfortably well off" can be regarded as examples of classes. (Notice that this is a more limited definition of class than the one introduced earlier for general use in this chapter.)

PARTY AND POWER. Weber uses ***party*** *to refer to a set of people with similar amounts of power.* ***Power*** *is the ability to have one's way, even against the wishes of others.* In Weber's terms *power* refers primarily to authority gained through one's office, such as that of senator or president, or through one's position in a bureaucracy, such as the secretary of state. State and local governments also bestow power to individuals.

STATUS GROUP AND PRESTIGE. Weber's third dimension of stratification is represented by a ***status group*** *or a set of people with similar social prestige.* ***Prestige*** *is the amount of positive regard members of a society have for a status.*

In the United States and most other industrial societies occupations are good examples of status groups. As a group, physicians have higher prestige than mail carriers, who in turn have higher prestige than janitors. Industrial society members generally agree on distinct prestige rankings by occupation, and these rankings influence the amount of respect paid to people in certain occupations. This may explain why the first question when people are introduced is often, "What do you do?"

Just as great wealth often coincides with great power, so prestige is often related to wealth and power. Nevertheless, wealth and prestige are distinct dimensions. This can be seen in the fact that many occupations provide considerable prestige but average income, including those of scientist, professor, and minister. Also, wealth alone is not sufficient to assure the highest levels of prestige. People with "old money," or inherited wealth, often snub those with "new" money, thought their fortunes may be of similar size. The prestige of an "old money" name such as Rockefeller may linger after the fortune is gone. Prestige, therefore, is a resource that may be allocated independently of power or wealth, leading Weber to believe status group significantly different from party or class.

Weber suggested that stratification is multidimensional in industrial societies. Three important social re-

WEBER'S TERM	THE CONTEMPORARY TERM
Class	Income and Wealth Stratum
Status Group	Prestige Stratum
Party	Power Stratum

FIGURE 8.2 Relationship between the Concepts in Max Weber's Stratification Theory and Our Contemporary Terminology

sources—wealth, power, and prestige—are ranked in three separate hierarchies creating classes, parties, and status groups. The relationship between Weber's concepts and the conventional terminology is diagrammed in Figure 8.2.

Before we move on to consider the theoretical issue of why stratification exists, we can benefit from considering how the industrial revolution has affected stratification and our thinking about it.

How Did Stratification Change in the Great Transition?

Even a casual look at world history would reveal a dramatic pattern of social change. During the past two centuries throughout the world societies have been going through a dramatic metamorphosis as they leave the agrarian mode of production and enter an industrial one. This shift shatters old social structures and opens the way for new ones in their place. One of the most important changes is the collapse of the old political and economic order and its replacement with a new one.

In agrarian societies the political order is usually a ***monarchy*** or *a system of government headed by an individual, such as a king or queen, who reigns for that person's lifetime.* The monarch is extremely powerful and the stratification system under monarchy consists principally of two classes: the monarch and his or her administration, and a very large class of commoners. Inequality is enormous with the ***nobility***, the *monarch and the monarch's administration* often holding life-and-death power over this larger class of peasants who work the fields. Usually the monarchy is dominated by a royal family, so that when the monarch dies he or she is replaced by another family member, often the first-born son. This sort of arrangement is common and apparently stable, as long as the society stays agrarian. In most cases, as the society begins to shift into industrialism, the monarchy is attacked politically and/or militarily and replaced with a new regime that promises more equality. Sometimes the central leader may not literally be called a king or queen, but will function as one—hoarding enormous wealth, not standing for election, and wielding great military power within and sometimes beyond his or her society.

The shift away from a monarchy is usually brought on by a revolution. The recent ousting of Ferdinand Marcos in the Philippines was such a political revolution. When the government of the Shah of Iran toppled, the Shah took with him some nearly $20 billion dollars, an amount greater than the income of all the people living in the ten poorest nations of the world. The recent history of the world is the history of the decline of monarchies or obvious dictatorships. A century ago there was royalty in Russia, China, Japan, Germany, Spain, Sweden, Belgium, the Netherlands, Denmark, Greece; in short, most of the world.

The transition from agriculture to industrialization brings with it the collapse of political systems, and with their collapse we often see a predictable change in the social stratification system. We will briefly sketch the nature of these changes in the next section, and in the following sections will consider how well five different perspectives on stratification deal with them.

INCREASED EQUALITY

The general pattern we see in the agrarian-to-industrial transformation, [we will call it the "great transition"] is from very obvious extreme inequality toward equality or at least less obvious inequality. The American Revolution was among the first examples of a people going through this great transition. After the American Revolution, people in the colonies were freed from the absolute rule of the King of England. The rise of political equality was immediate as democracy replaced monarchy, although a conflict theorist might observe

One woman's shoes. Agrarian societies frequently spawn extreme inequality and monarchy. These in turn often result in material excess, here represented by the shoe collection of the wife of deposed Philippine leader Ferdinand Marcos. (*Reuters/Bettmann Newsphotos*)

that working behind the scenes were, and are, extremely wealthy, powerful individuals, like those in the Rockefeller family, whose fortune might match or exceed that of earlier kings. But such inequality is less obvious, and not flaunted the way even the remnants of royalty today display their wealth and status in public spectacles like the recent royal weddings in England.

Another example of the moderating of inequality is seen in the Russian Revolution. After the overthrow of the czar in 1915, V. I. Lenin helped to establish the Soviet Union with the announced intention of creating a classless society. Most observers would acknowledge that economic inequality was greatly reduced, though on closer look great political inequality remains, with a small core of Communist Party leaders governing the society.

INCREASED MOBILITY

The great transition also involves relatively widespread and sudden mobility. With industrialization, the living standard rises dramatically. In a sense almost all members of the society experience upward mobility from their low status as peasants to the status of industrial worker. The fact that nearly everyone ends up with better housing, more clothes, and a more secure food supply may distract our attention from the persistence of extreme inequality, which we see if we look more closely.

The impression may be that the nobility and peasants have been joined in a new massive middle class. Actually, in capitalist societies a class of enormously wealthy owners of industry rests above the middle class and below it lies the extreme poverty of the unemployed and powerless. While Socialist countries may virtually eliminate the lower class in economical terms, they frequently create a small class of political elites and sizable segment of political prisoners who are politically "poor."

Another important shift is a trend of the stratification system toward more openness. The chance of a serf becoming a member of the nobility was remote. After the great transition, mobility is much more common. People born to families of modest means may rise to very high positions, as has been dramatically illustrated by Henry Ford and Ronald Reagan. Most people do not make such dramatic changes, but in the industrial era stratification structures do allow more opportunity to rise (and fall) from one's birth status than in the era of monarchs.

MORE COMPLEX OCCUPATIONAL STRUCTURES

The agrarian mode features relatively few occupations—most people work in agriculture on small farms using simple technology. In the industrial mode we see an enormous proliferation of occupations and formation of large-scale businesses. General Motors, for instance, employs some 700,000 people.

EQUALITY REPLACES INEQUALITY AS DESIRABLE, JUST, AND NATURAL

In the agrarian mode, stratification is usually portrayed as being natural, just, and desirable, whereas in the industrial mode equality is prized as natural, just, and desirable. In a monarchy, people often believe that the monarch rules through the will of God. The monarch often claims to be ruling in the best interests of all his or her subjects, who it is widely assumed were placed naturally unequal to the monarchy by God. With industrialization a democratic or socialist revolution often appears that emphasizes equality in terms of voting, opportunities, and living standards. Let us turn now to five common explanations of stratification to see how well they explain stratification in general and this great transition in particular.

Why Are Societies Stratified?

Why does inequality exist in human societies? Why are different methods employed to assign status to people? How important are ideas in these processes? What accounts for persistence and change in stratification structures? These are significant sociological, political, and moral issues. A good theory should be able to explain both the presence of stratification and changes in it. In considering each theory, evaluate it in terms of how well it can explain the change in stratification systems we earlier called the "great transition."

We will consider in turn (1) the natural-inevitability perspective, (2) the structural-functional perspective, (3) the conflict approach, (4) the evolutionary perspective, and (5) the symbolic interactionist perspective. Because of the enormous impact of the conflict approach on societies around the world, as well as on sociology, we discuss it in substantial detail. Both the Close-Up on Theory and the Close-Up on Research feature discussions of the conflict approach.

THE NATURAL-INEVITABILITY PERSPECTIVE

We begin by considering a rather informal yet popularly accepted perspective on stratification. A wide variety of people believe stratification is natural, therefore inevitable, and not something we can or should change. We refer to this perspective as the *natural-inevitability* point of view. Advocates of this perspective believe inequality originates from natural differences in people's ability. The social strata develop from these differences; the talented dominate the less talented, who become in one form or another their servants. Natural-inevitability adherents view nature as the force that assigns a person to his or her status. Inferior talent or motivation leads to inferior social rank.

Edward O. Wilson, the Harvard zoologist introduced in the chapter on socialization, has stirred interest in the biological roots of human social behavior with his controversial works *Socio-biology* (1975) and *On Human Behavior* (1978). Wilson has pointed to the fact that some social insects, such as ants and bees, work in organizations that resemble human bureaucracies. The *American Sociological Review* honored the approach of studying human behavior through animal research by publishing an article dealing with social dominance in small groups of chickens (Chase, 1980).

ASSESSING THE NATURAL-INEVITABILITY PERSPECTIVE. The weakness of the natural-inevitability approach is obvious when we apply it to the great transition. If a prevailing stratification system results from people taking their natural places in society, how can we explain the rise in equality that accompanies industrialization? During the reign of a monarchy we might be able to imagine that the king or queen and the nobility are genetically superior. But the "theory" has no ability to explain the transition. According to this perspective, some dramatic natural change, perhaps in the gene pool, would have to be invented to account for the reduction of inequality we routinely witness as societies leave the agrarian mode and enter the industrial one. Surely no one would suggest that nobility genes and serf genes were suddenly replaced by middle-class genes. Putting this perspective to the test only shows such "common sense" reasoning as bunk. We move on lesser known, more technical, and better interpretations of stratification.

THE STRUCTURAL-FUNCTIONAL PERSPECTIVE

Structural-functionalism approaches social structure with the assumption that societies tend to be stable and held together through consensus. A structural-functionalist seeks to understand social life by discovering how particular social structures function to keep society intact and stable. In this case, we would ask how stratification benefits society. We would focus on possible functions of inequality, strata, the rules governing how status is attained, and the supporting beliefs.

Various scholars have approached stratification from this perspective (Abrahamson, 1973, 1979; K. Davis & Moore, 1945; Parsons, 1937, 1964, 1970; Sumner, 1883). They have concluded that social inequality represents differences in rewards, which function as incentives to attract the best talent to society's most important tasks and to assure diligence in the world of work. Strata are seen as clusters of positions that the members of society agree are of similar importance to society.

Often the function of structures becomes clearer if we imagine what would happen after removing the structure from the social setting. Taking away the structure also removes the functions it provides, so the consequences we mentally observe are due to the loss of the structure's functions. If we remove the inequality of rewards, we remove most of the incentive to try hard. The inequality of wealth, power, and especially honor induces those at the bottom of the heap to work hard to move up, and it keeps those at the top on their toes for fear of sliding down.

ASSESSING THE STRUCTURAL-FUNCTIONAL APPROACH. The structural-functional perspective does not explain social change particularly well, because it focuses on forces that stabilize rather than change society. If we pay too much attention to explaining why the prevailing structure is functional, we risk misinterpreting what is actually happening.

Can the structural-functional perspective explain the changes in the stratification system accompanying industrialization? Yes. From the structural-functionalist perspective, agrarian societies typically had a small upper class and a massive lower class because this fit the prevailing conditions of society. Agriculture is a simple technology that requires only a small administrative class. The common person produced meagerly and received the same way. A few were granted the opportunity to rule, to be religious leaders, or to be military leaders. What of the lack of mobility? Truly exceptional people could be absorbed into the monarch's nobility. The fact that the people in high positions passed their rank on to their heirs may seem unfair, but it reduced the chance of a political struggle at the death of the monarch. In this sense the lack of mobility may have been functional by promoting the stability of the political system and thus the society.

In a sense the discoveries and inventions necessary for industrialization can be viewed as society discovering more functional arrangements. Once new means of producing fabrics for industry were developed, new social structures became more appropriate. As people stopped making fabric on looms in cottages and began to make it with machines in large factories, new stratification arrangements would become functional. Under these new conditions, an array of social classes has evolved, providing positions as unskilled laborers, skilled laborers, clerks, managers, and professionals, to the benefit of society. Furthermore, the new openness of this industrial class structure allows opportunity for people with special talents to be matched to appropriate positions, which may be functional to society and its members. Thus, the structural-functional approach is able to explain this massive structural change in terms of what is functional to society and its members.

Our access to wealth, power, and prestige depends a great deal on the status of our society in a world stratification system. This American man has social resources which far exceed the Jamaican woman, but what if they had traded places at birth? *(Photo courtesy the author)*

THE CONFLICT APPROACH

Sociologists sharply disagree about the origins and consequences of stratification. The conflict approach has had as many or more insights and adherents as the structural-functionalist perspective. The theoretical debate became especially strong during the 1950s and 1960s, as Melvin Tumin offered the conflict theorists' response to Kingsley Davis' classic statement of the structural-functionalist view (Tumin 1953, 1963).

Stratification takes on a very different appearance when viewed from the conflict perspective. Conflict theorists point out how individuals' conflicting desires for social resources result both in the creation of stratification structures and in their eventual overthrow. Elites use their superior power to take, rather than earn, an unreasonably large share of the social resources, whereas people in lower strata are coerced or deceived into producing more than they are compensated for.

The earliest conflict theorists, like Marx, believed there were only two important strata—the owners of the means of production (such as land or factories) and the workers, whose choice was substandard earnings or starvation. Later conflict theorists, like Ralf Dahrendorf (1959), describe a larger number of strata. In the more recent view, the key distinction is between those who have power and those who do not. Conflict theorists believe people are placed in strata according to what is beneficial to powerful people in the upper strata, rather than according to what is beneficial to society or is fair for its members.

Conflict theorists note that the masses are sometimes duped into believing the elites' explanation that the lower class gets less because it contributes less, and they have introduced the term *false consciousness* to describe the situation in which those in lower strata are unaware of or deny their own oppression.

Karl Marx and Friedrich Engels first advanced the conflict perspective on social stratification in the mid-nineteenth century. Their works have had profound impact academically and politically. As many as a third of the world's people now live under governments that espouse a Marxian philosophy, and because of that profound social and sociological significance we feature Marx and Engels' work in our "Close-Up on Theory." In the "Close-Up on Research" that follows it we feature Lenski's assessment of how much these ideas have actually changed the stratification systems in the societies that have adopted them.

CLOSE-UP on • *THEORY* •

Karl Marx and Friedrich Engels on the Final Class Struggle

The Theorists and the Setting

Born in 1818 in what is now Germany, to Jewish parents who had converted to Christianity, Karl Marx studied at the University of Berlin. There, through the influence of the philosophy of Hegel and Bauer, he came to believe the Bible was not a record of history but of human fantasies arising from emotional needs.

After earning a doctorate from the University at Jena, Marx became editor of a major newspaper, which the authorities eventually closed because of its radical political views. For these views Marx was later expelled from Prussia, Belgium, and France. He came to England in 1849 and there lived out his life.

Friedrich Engels and Karl Marx were lifelong friends. Engels, the son of the owner of a textile firm, converted to communism. Engels co-authored many works with Marx and edited some of Marx's major writings after Marx's death. Engels helped support Marx, who during his London years had virtually no other income.

In this Close-Up we focus on *The Manifesto of the Communist Party*, a political pamphlet written for the Communist League, a secret society in London composed largely of German handicraftsmen.

The Theoretical Issues

Marx and Engels try to explain how the different social classes have related in the past, how they relate now, and what should be done and why.

Concepts and Propositions

"The history of all hitherto existing society is the history of class struggles" (p. 335). Thus begins *The Manifesto of the Communist Party*. Here class refers to a set of people who share similar social positions in the society's economy. Examples include: "Freeman and slave, patrician and plebeian, lord and serf, guild-master and journeyman, in a word, oppressor and oppressed" (pp. 335–336).

But, in Marx's current epoch:

> Society as a whole is more and more splitting up into two great hostile camps, into two great classes directly facing each other: Bourgeoisie [pronounced boorjwah-zee] and Proletariat (p. 336). By bourgeoisie is meant the class of modern Capitalists, owners of the means of social production and employers of wage-labour. By proletariat, the class of modern wage-labourers who, having no means of production of their own, are reduced to selling their labour power in order to live (p. 335).

According to Marx and Engels, the bourgeoisie initially grew out of a middle class of small producers existing during feudal times. As production shifted from being based in the family to being based in the factory, the owners of the production facilities like factories became increasingly influential. They eventually became the capitalists of the present who have taken over control of the state from the nobility of earlier times.

But just as feudal society set the stage for its downfall through the rise of the bourgeoisie, so does the bourgeois society contain the seeds of its own destruction: ". . . a society that has conjured up such gigantic means of production and of exchange is like the sorcerer, who is no longer able to control the power of the nether world whom he has called up by his spells" (p. 340).

In creating a world in which ownership is concentrated in the hands of a few, the bourgeoisie have also created an enormous working class—the proletarians. In Marx and Engels' words:

> not only has the bourgeoisie forged the weapons that bring death to itself; it has also called into existence the men who are to wield those weapons—the modern working class (p. 340).
>
> Owing to the extensive use of machinery and to division of labour, the work of the proletarians has lost all individual character, and consequently, all charm for the workman. He becomes an appendage of the machine, and it is only the most simple, most monotonous, and most easily acquired knack that is required of him (p. 341).
>
> But with the development of industry the proletariat not only increases in number; it becomes concentrated in greater masses, its strength grows, and it feels that strength more (p. 342).

For various reasons the other classes descend into, or even voluntarily join, the proletariat. For instance:

> The lower strata of the middle class—the small tradespeople, shopkeepers, . . . the handicraftsmen and peasants—all these sink gradually into the proletariat, partly because their diminutive capital does not suffice for the scale on which Modern Industry is carried on, and is swamped in the competition with the large capitalists, partly because their specialized skill is rendered worthless by new methods of production (pp. 341–342).

One part of the ruling class can be expected to switch sides and join the proletariat. These are the intellectuals "who have raised themselves to the level of comprehending theoretically the historical movement as a whole" (p. 343). (Engels himself typifies this side-switching.)

The stage becomes set for a final class conflict.

> All previous historical movements were movements of minorities, or in the interest of minorities. The proletarian movement is the self-conscious, independent movement of the immense majority, in the interests of the immense majority. The proletariat, the lowest stratum of our present society, cannot stir, cannot raise itself up, without the whole superincumbent strata of official society being sprung into the air (p. 344).

How then should the revolution proceed? Marx and Engels offer a ten-point general plan:

> 1. Abolition of property in land and application of all rents of land to public purposes.
> 2. A heavy progressive or graduated income tax.
> 3. Abolition of all right of inheritance.
> 4. Confiscation of the property of all emigrants and rebels.
> 5. Centralization of credit in the hands of the State, by means of a nation bank with State capital and an exclusive monopoly.
> 6. Centralization of the means of communication and transport in the hands of the State.
> 7. Extension of factories and instruments of production owned by the State; the bringing into cultivation of waste-lands, and the improvement of the soil generally in accordance with a common place.
> 8. Equal liability of all to labour. Establishment of industrial armies, especially for agriculture.
> 9. Combination of agriculture with manufacturing industries; gradual abolition of the distinction between town and country, by a more equitable distribution of the population of the country.
> 10. Free education for all children in public schools, abolition of children's factory labour in its present form, combination of education with industrial production (p. 352).

When this is accomplished and "class distinctions have disappeared, and all production has been concentrated in the hands of a vast association of the whole nation, the public power will lose its political character. . . . In place of the old bourgeois society, with its classes and class antagonisms, we shall have an association in which the free development of each is the condition for the free development of all" (pp. 352–353).

Marx and Engels close *The Communist Manifesto* with a call to put their theory to practice:

> The Communists disdain to conceal their views and aims. They openly declare that their ends can be attained only by the forcible overthrow of all existing social conditions. Let the ruling classes tremble at a Communistic revolution. The proletarians have nothing to lose but their chains. They have a world to win.
>
> WORKING MEN OF ALL COUNTRIES, UNITE! (p. 362).

Implications

In 1917, about seventy-five years after Marx and Engels published *The Communist Manifesto,* Russia experienced a communist revolution. Later, Mao Tse Tung, following the writings of Marx, Engels, and other theorists, led a revolution that established communism in China, the world's most populous nation.

Although there are significant distinctions between the classic communism proposed by Marx and Engels and that of modern times, perhaps one-third of the earth's population live in nations that adhere quite closely to Marx and Engels' theory.

Questions

1. What evidence have we that would support Marx and Engels' theory of an inevitable class struggle leading to a proletariat revolution? What evidence refutes these ideas?
2. Which of Marx's ten proposals have been implemented in the United States?
3. Where are the weaknesses in this theory of class conflict?

SOURCES Karl Marx and Friedrich Engels. 1972 (originally 1848). "The Manifesto of the Communist Party," in *The Marx–Engels Reader*. Robert C. Tucker (ed.). New York: Norton and Co., pp. 335–362. Used by permission.

CLOSE-UP on • *RESEARCH* •

Gerhard Lenski on Whether or Not Marxism Works

The Researcher and the Setting

Professor Gerhard Lenski, at the University of North Carolina at Chapel Hill, has studied and taught social stratification for over three decades. His many books and articles report his theories and research.

The Researcher's Goal

Lenski seeks to assess the strengths and weaknesses of Marx's theory by considering the success and failure of the socio-political experiments undertaken by Marxist elites in Europe, Asia, Latin America, and most recently, in Africa. "These experiments attempt nothing less than a massive reorganization of entire societies and the elimination of inequality, exploitation, alienation, and social injustice" (pp. 364–365).

Theories and Concepts

Lenski tests several propositions; the first is from Marx's critics, and the others are from Marx.

Proposition 1: A communist or socialist society would have a stagnant economy because the incentives to work hard would be eliminated. [We will treat the terms *communism* and *socialism* interchangeably in the discussion.]

Proposition 2: Political inequality will be eliminated in the Marxist state, because it is grounded in economic inequality.

Proposition 3: Because alienation from labor (feeling powerless over one's work and that the work is meaningless) is a product of capitalism, it will disappear as communism replaces capitalism.

Proposition 4: Because sex inequality is a product of class conflict, elimination of the classes under socialism should eliminate class conflict and eventually eliminate sex inequality.

Proposition 5: Because capitalism set up the exploitation of those in rural areas by those in urban areas, eliminating capitalism should put an end to rural and urban inequality.

Proposition 6: Socialist societies will breed a new socialist man who will seek to live cooperatively with his fellow man rather than exploiting him.

Research Design

Lenski reviews fifty-two studies that report on conditions in socialist societies. These offer various types of data for consideration: (1) official government statistics that have become relatively plentiful in the case of Eastern Europe and the Soviet Union since the 1950s; (2) an increasing number of studies by East European sociologists; (3) data and analysis by dissidents who have left socialist regimes; (4) novels and other thinly fictionalized accounts of contemporary life in socialist countries; (5) reports from the East European and Soviet press; (6) writings of emigré sociologists who "know these societies not only from intimate firsthand experience but from their own research which they conducted prior to emigration" (p. 365); and (7) reports by knowledgeable Western visitors, both scholars and journalists. Lenski advises, "None of these sources can, or should, be accepted at face value, but taken together they provide us with much of the evidence we need . . . (p. 365).

Findings

Lenski gives Marxism mixed reviews based on these sources. "One of the most impressive successes of Marxist societies has been the demonstration that modern societies do not require the private ownership of the means of production or a free enterprise system to enjoy the fruits of rapid economic growth" (p. 369). "Marxist regimes have made possible a second important accomplishment—a substantial reduction in the degree of income inequality in their societies." Nongovernmental data from sociologists indicates the ratio of top salaries to minimum wage are as follows: U.S.S.R., 50-to-1; Poland, 35- or 40-to-1; People's Republic of China, 40-to-1; and Cuba, 7.3-to-1.

> By contrast, the corresponding ratio in the United States in recent years has been approximately 300:1, or six times the range in the Soviet Union and forty times that in Cuba (p. 370).
>
> Despite these impressive successes, there have also been important failures. . . . The first and most obvious failure of Marxist societies has been their inability to eliminate, or even substantially reduce political inequality. . . . This near monopolization of power at the top seems often to have as a corollary the creation of a stratum of political prisoners at the bottom. A second major failure . . . lies in the area of work. Marxist societies should be making substantial progress in reducing inequalities in the attractiveness of different kinds of work (371).

Yet Lenski urges us to consider this Polish sociologist's observations: . . . the workers are still hired labor. The socialist revolution does not change . . . his relation to the machine or his subordination to the foreman and the management of the factory" (Szczepanski, 125); (Lenski, p. 372).

A third failure of Marxist regimes, according to Lenski, has been their inability to overcome traditional inequalities based on gender, despite early attention to the subject by Marx and Engels. "We often hear that 70 percent of all Soviet physicians are women, but. . . . most Soviet physicians are poorly paid and their skill level is similar to that of paramedics in this country. . . . The upper echelons . . . where the rewards are the greatest, are dominated by men. . . . Ninety percent of the physicians in the Soviet Academy of Sciences are men" (Lenski, pp. 373–374).

In addition, Lenski points out that recent Soviet studies show that women's responsibilities in the home are much more time-consuming than those of men, as they are in the United States.

Lenski identifies a fourth area of significant inequality throughout Eastern Europe, that between town and country.

> "one Russian visitor to the United States commented recently that the greatest surprise for her was to see how narrow the gap in living standards between city and country is here compared to that in Russia. . . . To add insult to injury, [in the U.S.S.R.] collective farm workers were, until 1975, denied the internal passports necessary for geographical mobility, and thus were tied to the land, not unlike serfs of an earlier era . . . "(Lenski, p. 374).

Lenski mentions a fifth failure which he suggests is the most serious of all: the failure "to create 'the new socialist man.' This is critical because Marxian theory views this as a necessary precondition for the emergence of communism. Without the new man, most Marxist theorists of the past believed you could not hope to establish a truly egalitarian society.

Instead,

> absenteeism and negligence have been widespread in industry and agriculture despite (or possibly because of) improvements in working conditions that removed the element of fear of unemployment. . . . A study of teachers and teacher education in Poland reports bribes and threats directed at members of committees controlling admission to desirable schools, with these unsocialist actions coming chiefly from members of the new elite who have the resources needed to bribe or threaten. . . . Meanwhile, crime and alcoholism refuse to fade away more than half a century after the Revolution, and citizens have not yet developed the same respect for public property that they have for private" (p. 375).
>
> "Finally, I am inclined to believe that Marxism, like sociology, rests on much too naive, much too innocent, much too optimistic an assumption about human nature. Marxism, like sociology, still employs an eighteenth century view of man. Environment is everything, genetics nothing. Thus, given proper social institutions, utopia is possible. . . . Possibly, I fear this is dangerous nonsense because it leads to serious miscalculations in the formulation of public policy, and these, in turn, lead to repression as a necessaary corrective. In short, there seems to be an inevitable tension built into the very fabric of every society—a tension between the cooperative and the competitive elements in human nature. Karl Marx never really faced up to this possibility, nor have his followers who today guide the destinies of one-third of the people of this planet. As a consequence, modern Marxism is simultaneously inspiring and depressing" (p. 380).

Questions

1. Has Lenski been even-handed or is his work biased?
2. How might even the most objective scientist be misled by this type of research?
3. What other types of research might be useful in trying to assess Marx's theory of stratification?

SOURCES Gerhard Lenski. 1978. "Marxist Experiments in De-stratification: An Appraisal," *Social Forces,* 12/78, pp. 364–383. Used by permission. Jan Szczepanski. 1970. *Polish Society.* New York: Random House. Hendrick Smith. 1976. *The Russians.* New York: Quadrangle.

ASSESSING THE CONFLICT APPROACH. We have devoted a considerable amount of attention to Karl Marx's theory of stratification because of its tremendous prominence in sociology and our social world. We should recall that we are in the midst of trying to answer the questions of why stratification exists in the forms it does. Earlier we considered the natural-inevitability position and the structural-functionalist position. We have now considered Marx's theory, which is a part of the conflict approach. We will now return to our "testing grounds" to see how well this view can explain the great transition in stratification structures, and then proceed to look into the two remaining theoretical perspectives.

The contemporary conflict approach, like that of the structural-functionalists, is a composite of several scholars' ideas, but the assumptions are nearly opposite those of structural-functionalism.

Some of the differences in these viewpoints reduce to value questions dealing with what should be, rather than what is. Much of the disagreement hinges on describing fair distribution of resources. Do the elites perform vital functions for which they should be well paid, as structural-functionalists suggest? Or are the elites coercing others to accept less than they deserve, as conflict theorists would lead us to believe? Structural-functionalists seem willing to believe the prevailing order is just. Conflict theorists are convinced the lower strata deserve more.

The latent value issue here is: Who deserves what? Given the sale of an Apple computer, how much of the proceeds should go to the inventors of the components, to the inventors of the computer itself, to the owners of the firm who put up the money, to the managers, to the workers who build the machines, to the advertising copywriters, to the salespeople? These are specific versions of perennial questions.

In one sense, a perspective gives us descriptions of the subject, rather like viewing a town from Main Street or from a back alley. The choice of perspective gives us different prescriptions. Structural-functionalism is biased toward accepting the prevailing establishment, whereas the conflict perspective is reluctant to acknowledge the justice of inequality. Hence, structural-functionalism has a built-in conservatism leading toward continuation of the status quo, and the conflict viewpoint has built-in radicalism, leading toward equality and social change.

These two approaches will persist for a long time because each directs our attention to important aspects of stratification. Used wisely, the two perspectives can be valuable tools that we can apply to particular settings in pursuing better knowledge and control of stratification.

How well does the conflict approach explain the great transition in stratification structures that accompanies industrialization? This, as we have seen, is a major focus of the ideas of Marx, which are central to the perspective. From this perspective the nobles are locked in conflict with the peasant whom they exploit. By monopolizing violence and owning the land, the nobility are for a time able to extract the labor of the common man. However, the system contains the seeds of its own destruction. The exploitative nobles pressure the peasants to produce more products for less expense. In response, those who produce and market goods like fabrics find increasingly effective technologies and begin to operate on a large scale in bigger markets.

In the short run this benefits the nobility, but in the long run a new elite will arise from the producers and traders. Growing out of what had been tiny operations and small-scale trade, a new class of producers and traders arises, which will form the capitalist class. They will eventually overpower the reigning nobility as they gain increasing shares of the wealth.

As Marx suggests, this quest for ever-increasing profits drives the capitalists around the world into buying and selling and remaking the world in their image. Marx, of course, sees this as a step to the eventual final class conflict preceding classless communist societies. Marx suggests that industrialism will bring great inequality and that the working class of industrial societies will launch another round of revolutions.

Although the perspective predicts the end of monarchies, it does not anticipate the direct move from agrarian societies to communism that has occurred in societies like China or Cuba. It also has trouble explaining why highly industrialized societies like England, Japan, and the United States have not developed effective communist revolutions. The theory in its original form does not allow for the possibility of stable democracy in capitalistic societies. A century and one-half of experience has led conflict theorists to soften or reinterpret this part of the theory. But as we see, the perspective is quite capable of coming to terms with the great transition.

THE EVOLUTIONARY PERSPECTIVE

Gerhard Lenski borrows from both conflict and structural-functionalist explanations in synthesizing a view we call the *evolutionary perspective.* For fourteen years preceding publication of his book, *Power and Privilege* (1966), Lenski taught social stratification and faced the problem of organizing various stratification theories and research results for his students. He came to believe that the seemingly contradictory functional and conflict theories could be synthesized into a single unified theory.

In his work, Lenski addresses the question: Who gets what and why? He is more concerned with the causes of social stratification than with its consequences and focuses on differences in power and privilege rather than on differences in prestige. In contrast to conventional definitions, which identify stratification with social classes or strata, Lenski defines *social stratification* as "the distributive process in human societies—the process by which scarce values are distributed" (Lenski, 1966).

To explain stratification, Lenski introduces two "laws of distribution" based on his assumptions about the nature of humans and of society. The laws state:

1. People will share the product of their labors to the extent required to ensure the survival and continued productivity of others whose actions are necessary or beneficial to themselves.
2. Power will determine the distribution of nearly all of the surplus possessed by a society.

In Lenski's view, stratification systems are strongly affected by the technology available to the society. For example, hunting and gathering societies have little stratification because their primitive technology does not produce any significant surplus, and no one becomes much better off than anyone else. People share because they must cooperate to survive, and they have almost no distribution system because there is rarely a surplus.

As a society develops increasingly sophisticated technology, surplus resources grow. According to Lenski's second law, the more powerful members of society take larger shares of the resources. Thus, inequality increases as technology advances (at least to a point). Hunting and gathering societies, for example, tend to be made up of social equals. Simple horticultural societies, which use only wooden digging sticks, show noticeable amounts of institutionalized inequality, involving chiefs, a military order, and religious offices. Advanced horticultural societies that use more efficient metal hoes have more pronounced inequality. Lenski gives an example: "Even the highest ministers of state in Dahomey (an advanced horticultural society) had to grovel in the dust when in the king's presence, and throw dirt on their heads and bodies" (p. 46).

With new productive technology comes a new weapons technology. The discovery of metalworking allows the development of spears and swords as well as hoes. The combination of new weapons and new surplus provides both the means and the incentive for a dominant group to establish a strong state, which governs through a monopoly of violence. Using its power, the state levies taxes from the rest of society.

With the introduction of agriculture, using animals to draw plows, the productive efficiency and the size of the surplus again increase. This means even more wealth for those who control the state. Inequality increases because the rich are able to get even richer.

Because industrialized societies surpass agrarian ones in production, efficiency, military strength, and the power of the state, we might expect to find even more social inequality at this stage. Instead, the trend toward more inequality reverses. Lenski claims this reversal has two causes. First, a small elite cannot easily rule an industrialized society by command, because the increased complexity of industrialization makes it impossible for those in command to understand the work of all of the workers who are beneath them. The rulers must then choose between two options: They can keep their command and frequently issue inappropriate orders that might interfere with their economic growth, or they can delegate power to, and share the wealth with, some technically skilled non-elites to encourage efficiency and economic growth. The second cause: Because considerable economic growth usually accompanies industrialization, the elite may actually become more wealthy by sharing more equally with the non-elites. For example, if they control 80 percent of a $10 billion economy, the elites will have more income than if they control 95 percent of a $5 billion economy that has stopped growing due to their poor management. Figure 8.3 summarizes the relationship between technology and inequality.

Lenski's theory advances our understanding of stratification by introducing an important variable: technology. He recognizes the significance of power in determining the stratification structure, a point reminiscent of the conflict perspective. Lenski pays tribute to the structural-functional approach by recognizing that even the powerful must consider what is functional for society, and that they will sometimes share more equally knowing that a smaller share of a stronger society's resources can be better than a bigger share of a weaker society's resources.

ASSESSING THE EVOLUTIONARY PERSPECTIVE. How useful is the evolutionary perspective? It explains some aspects of stratification much better than others. It is the most global of the approaches considered here, and it deals better with general issues such as what explains different levels of inequality than it does with specific issues like why particular strata rank the way they do. However, the evolutionary perspective has little to say about how status is allocated, beyond observing that those who control the productive and destructive technologies will be the elites. It also points out that in the industrial stage the elites find it beneficial to recruit managerial talent from outside their ranks. The perspective does not address the significance of beliefs to stratification systems.

The evolutionary viewpoint excels at explaining differences in inequality over time and between cul-

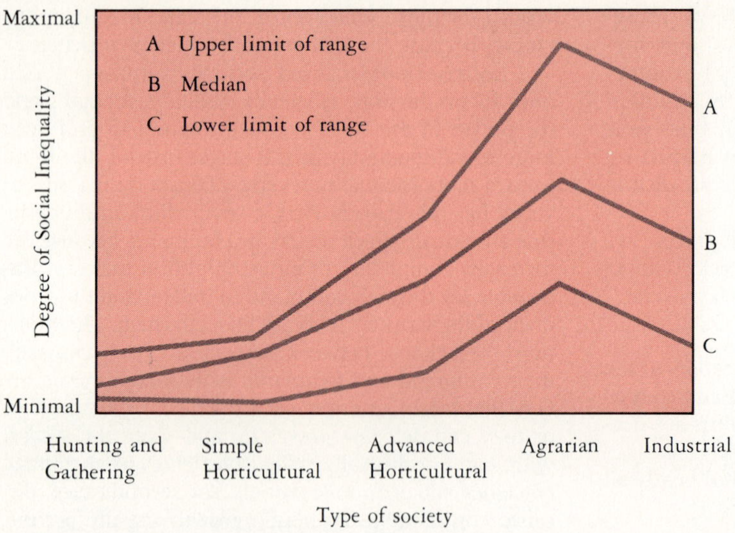

FIGURE 8.3 Lenski's Ideas about the Relationship between the Type of Society and the Degree of Social Inequality. SOURCE Adapted from Lenski, 1966, p. 437.

tures. It proposes a plausible set of hypotheses without addressing moral issues. This gives the perspective a more scientific tone than the conflict or the structural-functional perspectives, which either implicitly or explicitly address what should be. The evolutionary perspective considers descriptive issues, which helps us deal with predictive issues while avoiding prescriptive or value issues. In other words, it asks what is happening rather than what should happen, and helps us to discuss what will happen in the future.

As we see, the evolutionary theory explicitly addresses the great transition from agriculture to industrial society and more. To summarize, Lenski brings together parts of structural-functionalism and the conflict approach by suggesting people act cooperatively only so long as they must to ensure their survival and productivity. Inequality remains very high during the agrarian period because agriculture, a simple technology, lends itself to power being concentrated in a small elite class. With the advent of industrialization, the small elite are helpless to stop the occupational structure and technology from growing more complex. As a result, more experts are needed, and workers, especially skilled ones, are in a position to demand a larger share of the resources.

Lenski and others have sought to confirm his general theory and its various parts. Even though Lenski focuses largely on the role of technology, he also suggets that as the masses become more politically active economic inequality will decline. The "Close-Up on Research" tends to substantiate this connection between socialism, a dramatic form of mass participation, and reduced income inequality. Other researchers have looked even more closely at the relation between political participation, such as the right to vote and the degree to which the population exercises that right, and economic inequality. Whereas there are disagreements about how to measure these concepts, the research thus far tends further to confirm Lenski's idea of a connection between political equality and economic equality, which of course overlaps a great deal with conflict theory (Hewitt, 1977; Lenski, 1978; Stack, 1979; Weede, 1980).

The evolutionary approach does not answer all the questions but provides provocative answers to the key question: What determines the amount of inequality in a society? The next perspective, symbolic interactionism, is nearly as different from the evolutionary perspective as the conflict perspective is from structural-functionalism.

THE SYMBOLIC-INTERACTION PERSPECTIVE

No stratification system can work without having supporting beliefs. By its nature, stratification creates and sustains inequality; it inhibits some people from moving into positions they might otherwise seek.

Some method is needed to get people to accept stratification. We saw in the chapter on deviance and social control that coercive formal controls are often expensive and ineffective compared to informal controls and internalized social controls. Mammoth social resources would be needed to force stratification on people. Yet when people accept a system's supporting beliefs, they not only accept the stratification, they teach others to do the same and even serve as social control agents to punish those who do not. We now explore the perspective that emphasizes the importance of these supporting beliefs, the symbolic-interaction viewpoint first encountered in Chapter 1.

Two master premises support the symbolic-interaction perspective: (1) symbols help define the meaning of a social action; and (2) a person's self, or personality, is developed socially through symbolic interaction.

Symbolic interactionism helps us understand how symbols, words, and ideas are used to legitimate a stratification system and how we incorporate this societal structure into our inner consciousness. Legitimating ideas, expressed symbolically in the form of language, provide reasons for inequality, for the strata, for the way people are placed in the strata, and for changes (or lack of them) in the stratification system. A wide variety of ideas have justified or attacked stratification. These include religious ideas about divine monarchs or reincarnation; philosophical values of equality or freedom; and capitalist or socialist doctrine.

Supporting ideas are more than mere rules; they affect what people think of themselves—their self-evaluation. Such beliefs are implanted in people's minds through symbols. As we recall from the chapter on socialization, Charles Horton Cooley and other symbolic interactionists theorize that a person's self-concept is based largely on what others think of the person. As one modern symbolic interactionist observes, "Those who perceive that they are viewed as important by the widest audience, and particularly by others who are also viewed as important, have the highest self-evaluation" (Della Fave, 1980).

How much we think we are worth influences how much we think we deserve. But we tend to gauge our worth and that of others according to the social assets we have. If we have more than others, we are inclined to think we must be better than they are. If we have less, perhaps we are not as good. Through this circular process those who have little see themselves as unworthy and therefore not deserving of much.

Individuals with great power, prestige, and wealth can more easily control the impressions they give, thus reinforcing their superior status and others' subordinate status. The top executive, wearing custom-tailored clothes, drives a new Cadillac to work and parks in a reserved parking space. He or she works in a walnut-paneled office protected by a secretary who types the correspondence, answers the phone, and regulates when others may see the executive. The factory worker parks a used Chevrolet in the vast plant car lot and hopes to remember its location after an eight-hour shift. He or she toils in "work clothes" amidst noise and grime where workers are easily observed by anyone else in the plant. Clearly the higher status position offers more support for one's self-esteem and social esteem.

Highly placed individuals can impress those of lower status in many ways, including prominent, often symbolic, displays of their wealth, determining when and where meetings take place, and keeping subordinates waiting. At the same time, the higher placed individual is better able to hide his or her behavior from others. As others become impressed, they convey their awe to the high-status person, and he or she develops a self-image of superiority.

This embedding of the social order in the minds of individuals helps explain why so many disadvantaged people hold beliefs in seeming violation of their own self-interest. In a successful stratification system, people internalize the supporting beliefs to the degree that the beliefs help form their private assessment of themselves: a king *feels* noble, and a peasant *feels* lowly. A properly established belief system can help establish and maintain social interaction with extreme levels of inequality and rigid strata. When the legitimating process falters, the entire social structure crumbles.

ASSESSING THE SYMBOLIC INTERACTIONIST PERSPECTIVE. How well does this symbolic interactionist viewpoint help us understand the great transition from the relatively closed highly unequal systems common in agrarian societies to the more open and more equal stratification systems of industrial societies? As we noted in the "Close-Up on Theory" in Chapter 1: "Sociology: Origins, Perspectives, and Techniques," the idea of the Protestant Ethic was a highly significant force in setting the stage for the transition to industrial capitalism. In earlier times and in most agrarian societies, religion plays an important role in justifying the very obvious and extreme social inequality. If God ordains Saul or King Henry to be the reigning monarch, how is a mere mortal, especially a peasant, to disagree? Monarchs frequently engage in very conspicuous displays of their power and wealth, which would surely support the impression that they were superior, whereas the peasants' lowly circumstances could be misinterpreted as indication of their inferiority. Near the time of the great transition, we see not only an explosion of technology, but an explosion of old ideas. The Protestant challenge to the Pope's claims of infallibility, the publication of the Bible in English, and the acceptance of the Protestant work ethic set the stage for more democratic thinking and acting. Surely we would be in error to ignore the ideals contained in documents like the United States *Declaration of Independence* and the *Communist Manifesto*. Each of these is only a set of symbols, but when these symbols take on life in the minds of people, they can radically change expectations and behaviors.

The symbolic-interactionist perspective focuses our attention on the importance of the symbolic displays in maintaining the monarchical stratification systems. It also recognizes the importance of ideas that are conveyed only through symbols in the ending of an old

TABLE 8.1 Differing Explanations of Social Stratification

Structural-Functionalist	Natural Inevitability	Conflict	Evolutionary	Symbolic Interactionist
1. Societies tend to be stable and held together through consensus. **2.** Stratification is useful to society because it enhances stability. **3.** Stratification develops to fill the needs of society as a whole. **4.** Inequality is useful to society, because it induces those at the bottom to work hard to move up, and keeps those on top vigilant not to lose their position in the hierarchy.	**1.** Stratification is natural and therefore inevitable in society. **2.** Inequality exists because of natural differences in people's abilities. **3.** The order that grows from this inequality is natural and just. **4.** The system should not be changed, because that would lead to unnatural and inferior arrangements that would ultimately weaken society.	**1.** Society tends toward conflict and disorder rather than consensus and harmony. **2.** Social structure benefits the elites and oppresses the masses. **3.** Stratification occurs through conflict between different classes, with the upper classes using superior power to take a larger share of the social resources. **4.** Conflict between classes provides the driving force for society and social change.	**1.** People will share enough resources to ensure the survival of the group that is necessary for their personal survival. **2.** Power determines how the surplus of a society will be distributed. **3.** As industrialization takes over from agriculture, societies become more equal in distribution of resources.	**1.** Symbols help define meaning of social action, and a person's self develops through social interaction. **2.** We tend to gauge our self-worth by our assets. **3.** Wealthy, powerful, and prestigious people more easily control their impressions, thus supporting their superior status and others' subordinate status.

way of life. As W. I. Thomas, one of the founders of the symbolic-interactionist perspective, is credited with saying, "He who defines a situation controls it." If the ideas of a Luther, a Jefferson, or a Marx become the dominant ideas of an era, we can expect that massive changes in the social structure will bring patterns of behavior into line with the new definitions. The symbolic-interactionist perspective lends important insights into the dynamics of the industrial transformation, and thus demonstrates its ability to contribute to a better understanding of stratification.

STRATIFICATION THEORIES COMPARED

We have approached the issue of why stratification exists from different perspectives and have discovered several contributing factors. The idea of "natural," biologically established stratification systems appears untenable because it does not explain differences in stratification structures among human societies nor their sometimes rapid change. Instead, several social factors seem to operate to influence the form and stability of the stratification system. Stratification occurs because it works well for society as a whole and because it works well for elite groups who are able to manipulate social structure to their own ends. Technology and the subsistence strategy of the society also affect the stratification structure chosen by a society. Finally, supporting beliefs are necessary to maintain stratification systems.

Though some of these perspectives may prove more useful than others in a particular setting, all are useful to those who would understand and influence their social environment.

What Explains Social Mobility Rates?

Which nations offer people the most opportunity for advancement? What does it take to get ahead? Are successful people happier? These questions interest both ordinary people and sociologists. In this section we consider the topic of social mobility and research that has been directed at these questions.

Social mobility *is the movement of a person from one status to another.* Sociologists are interested in mobility from two perspectives. At the micro level they study individual mobility to discover features such as what traits are shared by those who move up or down. At the macro level sociologists lump together thousands of individuals' experiences to determine the rate of mo-

Upward bound? Some of these college graduates bet four years of their life on the idea that their college education would improve their chances of moving up the career ladder. Social science research confirms that education is one key to upward mobility. (*AP/Wide World Photos*)

bility for a society. *The **mobility rate** is the number of instances of mobility per 100 people in the population.* For instance, sociologists may measure, in two different nations, how many people per hundred rise above their fathers' status. Mobility rates are useful in comparing stratification systems.

***Intergenerational social mobility** is a change in status from that which a child began with in the parents' household to that of the child upon reaching adulthood.* ***Intragenerational social mobility** is a change in social status that occurs within a person's adult career.* The transition from one status to another usually occurs between childhood and adulthood. As people reach adulthood, they normally leave their families of origin (their parents and siblings) to form new families. The new family's status is determined largely by the occupations of its adult members. When these occupations are significantly different in status from that of the original parents, the status of the individual changes. For instance, it is the dream of many working-class people to send their children to college. The college graduate will probably enter a white-collar position and will immediately earn about as much as the parent is earning after many years of working, and the child will have a potentially much higher income and status than that of the parents.

THE MACRO PERSPECTIVE: EXPLAINING MOBILITY RATES

In some societies it is rare for people to have a social status different from their parents'. Caste in traditional India was inherited at birth and kept until death. Such a society has a relatively closed stratification system, and its social mobility rate is virtually zero, meaning no social mobility among a typical 100 people. In other societies, like the present-day United States, there is considerable mobility between classes. In noncaste societies we find varying mobility rates.

It is interesting to compare mobility rates of various nations and discuss factors that influence these rates. Many people believe the United States provides the greatest opportunity to rise above one's initial social status. If this were true, we would expect considerable mobility resulting from a relatively large number of people who exercise the opportunity to leave their birth status. Lenski (1966) compared the mobility rates of various nations by comparing the percentage of the population that crossed the boundary between manual and nonmanual labor. The United States tops the list on this measure of social mobility (see Table 8.2).

Measuring mobility across the manual–nonmanual line is not the best indicator of opportunity, however. As we see in the next section, a factor called *structural mobility* may distort the figures.

STRUCTURAL MOBILITY. One influence on the amount of mobility in a society is whether there is a change in the *relative sizes* of the classes. The size of the classes can change for various reasons, but the introduction of new technology is a major influence. If some high-status positions disappear, some individuals who would have had high-status positions are likely to locate at lower positions. Similarly, when the low positions are replaced by automation, people who once

TABLE 8.2 Comparative Mobility Across Manual–Nonmanual Class Boundary for Nine Industrial Nations

Nation	Percentage of Manual–Nonmanual upward or downward mobility
United States	34
Sweden	32
England	31
Denmark	30
Norway	30
France	29
West Germany	25
Japan	25
Italy	22

SOURCE Lenski, (1966: 411). The dates of the figures vary from the late 1950s to the early 1960s.

would have held them may find higher positions, or they may become unemployed. This mobility is imposed by changes in the system rather than by individual initiative, and we call it *structural mobility*. ***Structural mobility*** *is brought about by changes in the stratification hierarchy.*

As a society becomes more technologically advanced, many people experience upward mobility because the higher status categories get larger rather than because people have actually moved upward relative to their peers. When the United States changed from a farming society to an industrial society, the number of skilled positions increased and were filled by former farm workers. Many families changed their social status when the primary worker became a skilled worker, although the famiy did not change its position relative to other families (see Figure 8.4).

In order to determine the amount of opportunity in a society, we want to discount structural mobility and measure the amount of mobility of people actually exchanging positions, or *circulation mobility*. ***Circulation mobility*** *is the amount of mobility resulting from exchange movements within the stratification hierarchy.* Here, the movement of one person up necessarily displaces one person down.

In a study more recent than Lenski's, Lawrence Hazelrigg and Maurice Garnier (1976) presented data from which Harold Kerbo (1983) computed circulation mobility rates for fifteen industrial nations. Here we find the United States ranking fifth, with Norway ranking at the top and Belgium the lowest of those studied (see Table 8.3). This provides us with an interesting image, one more accurate than Lenski's.

Even more recently, Kazuo Yamaguchi (1987) closely analyzed the mobility rates of Great Britain, the United States, and Japan. He found that though the

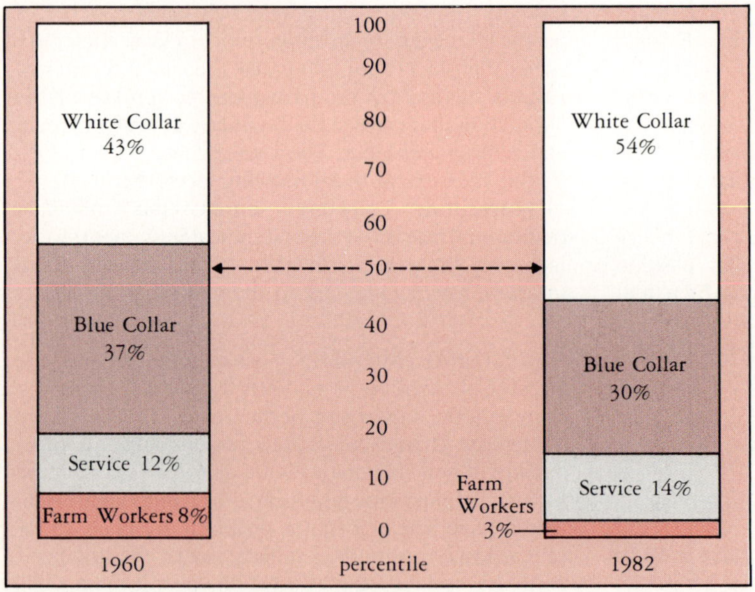

FIGURE 8.4 Changes in the Occupational Structure Generate Structural Mobility. The family at the 50th percentile was swept into the middle class when the class boundaries changed. SOURCE U.S. Bureau of the Census, 1960, 1982.

TABLE 8.3 Comparative Circulatory Mobility in Fifteen Industrial Nations

Rank	Country	Circulation Rate*
1	Norway	.415
2	Australia	.394
3	Bulgaria	.389
4	West Germany	.380
5	United States	.369
6	Japan	.365
7	Yugoslavia	.364
8	Finland	.356
9	Hungary	.337
10	Denmark	.318
11	France	.312
12	Italy	.303
13	Spain	.298
14	Sweden	.298
15	Belgium	.292

*The circulation rate is estimated by making the nations comparable with respect to the occupational distribution of origins (see Hazelrigg and Garnier 1976:501).

SOURCE Table constructed from data presented in Hazelrigg, Lawrence and Maurice Garnier. 1976. "Occupational mobility in industrial societies: a comparative analysis of differential access to occupational ranks in seventeen countries." *American Sociological Review* 41:498-511.

United States has more equality of occupational opportunity than British society, Japan exceeds even the United States in this regard. However, occupational opportunity has declined in Japan during the past twenty years. This lends some support to Treiman's (1970) and Featherman's (1975) idea that the amount of occupational opportunity among modern nations converges toward a common level.

As Yamaguchi notes, such comparisons are complicated, and we are still in the primitive stages of comparing mobility between nations. The fact that we are comparing stratification systems with differing numbers and sizes of classes makes measurement difficult and questionable. Therefore, we should remember that these mobility comparisons are estimates at best and subject to error. (Featherman et al., 1975; Treiman, 1970; Yamaguchi, 1987)

CULTURAL DEFINITIONS. A second major factor influencing mobility is how much motivation individuals show to move from one stratum to another. Many Americans strive upward, and "getting ahead" is seen as appropriate and desirable. In some cultures, such as traditional India, it is appropriate and desirable to be content with one's present social status. It is difficult, therefore, to decide if people do not move up because they do not try, or if people do not try because they cannot move up. Societies with low mobility rates often have religious beliefs that justify and legitimize staying in the same social situation.

FORMAL AND INFORMAL POLICIES. A third factor that influences mobility rates is the policy those in control have toward accepting people into higher status occupations. For example, a formal or informal policy that bars people of particular ethnic groups from certain positions will eliminate mobility in those positions. Similarly, policies that discriminate against any category of people—such as against the elderly, the young, or women—decrease the amount of mobility in the society.

Informal policy, too, can restrict mobility. A small company that does not advertise its vacancies but relies on informal word-of-mouth communication may limit mobility, because informal communication generally occurs among people of similar social status and ethnicity. If people from other status groups do not hear of vacancies, they obviously will not be able to be upwardly mobile through these jobs.

In some cases, official policy facilitates mobility. The federal government's affirmative action policy has encouraged active recruitment of people who have historically been in low-status positions. Such recruitment aims at increasing mobility. Patterns of recruitment and personnel selection may have an important influence in determining how much mobility there is in society.

Conclusion

Stratification is an important element in most human societies, especially modern ones. Most stratification systems are one of the five types we have described here. Stratification systems vary in terms of their equality and their opportunity for a person to change status. As a stratification system changes, so does the mobility within the system.

We have considered some of the major theories of why human societies have the stratification systems they do, and we have considered social mobility from the macro perspective. In the next chapter, "Social Class in the United States," we look more closely at inequality and opportunity in this country, as well as the dynamics of mobility from the micro perspective.

Sociologists at Work •

ROBERT ROBINSON
EXPLORES HOW FAMILIES FACE CLASS ISSUES

Director, Institute of Social Research
Indiana University
Bloomington, Indiana

Rob Robinson is a dynamic, young sociologist who has spent a good deal of energy in combining his dedication to teaching with his expertise and interest in research. Since earning his doctorate from Yale University in 1979, Robinson's major field of interest has been stratification and mobility. He has published extensively in the field, and his article with Jonathan Kelley, "Class as Conceived by Marx and Dahrendorf" (*ASR* 44, February 1979), has been widely read and well received.

Who Are You Working With in Your Present Research?

The research I am involved in right now is in the context of a graduate course that we call "The Sociological Research Practicum." This used to be called the "Indianapolis Area Project." Basically the idea is to combine a graduate-training exercise with a faculty-research project so that the students can get first-hand experience collecting data, and the faculty member has the help of the students in gathering data that might otherwise require special funds to collect.

What Sort of Study Are You Conducting?

What I decided to do is an historical analysis of residents of Indianapolis from 1860 to about 1930: an historical archival type of data gathering effort rather than survey-research type of project. The students in the practicum chose two samples of 500 men and women from both the 1860 census and the 1900 census of Indianapolis. For each of the 500 people in both years, we have the original census forms that the census takers filled out when they talked to these people back in 1860 and 1900. These forms detailed who was living in the household, for example spouse, children, grandparents, boarders, servants: the age and sex of everyone in the household, the wealth of people in the household, the occupation of the husband, wife, and children, where they were born and where their parents were born—so we are able to get a pretty good picture of what's going on in each of these families.

What Other Data Did You Use?

We follow people from one census to the next, every ten years. In addition we use city directories and marriage license applications, wills, cemetery records, and obituaries to flesh out the lives of these people from the little description that we had of them in each of these different sources. We decided to follow our original 500 people for 1860 and 1900, as well as their spouses, their children, and their children's spouses for the next thirty years or so after each one of those original years. In all, we followed about 4,000 people during the period. Basically, the data allow us to examine changes in the same people and families over time as we trace each family forward over time, and also to compare the post-1860 period with the post-1900 period. This gives us a developmental perspective for each family and individual over time and also a cross-temporal perspective during the post-1860 and post-1900 period.

What Are You Hoping to Learn?

The issues were chosen in part to reflect student interests, so that when the students decided that they were interested in family structure or social mobility, for example, we expanded into those areas. We are studying things like changes in family composition and size over time, and the influence of family size and birth order on children's chances for social mobility. We are especially interested in family strategies for coping with economic hardships, such as living with relatives, taking in boarders, and sending children out as servants in other families. We are also examining women's participation in the pay-labor market as it relates to the economic circumstances of their families: whether they were single, married, or widowed, how big their families were, and whether they had children employed outside the home or not. Another question we're looking at is which people decided to leave Indianapolis to seek their fortunes elsewhere, comparing persons in terms of age, class, race, and marital status.

At this point, we're about three-quarters of the way through the process of putting the data onto the computer. The analysis of all of these relationships could go on for years, but our graduate students are going to write Master's theses using these data soon. ●

Summary Questions

1. What is social stratification?
2. What is class?
3. What are the major forms of stratification?
4. How do stratification systems differ?
5. What are Weber's three dimensions of stratification?
6. What are the five basic viewpoints on why stratification exists?
7. In what regard is some stratification inevitable?
8. What are the functionalist and conflict theories as to the reasons for stratification?
9. What are the basic premises of the evolutionary perspective?
10. How are the supporting beliefs symbolically important to a stratification system?
11. What is social mobility?
12. What is structural mobility?

Summary Answers

1. Stratification is a hierarchy of positions with regard to economic production, which influences the social rewards to those in the positions.
2. Class is a large set of people regarded by themselves or others as sharing similar status with regard to wealth, power, and prestige.
3. Primitive communalism, characterized by a high degree of sharing and minimal social inequality.

   Slavery, involving great social inequality and the ownership of some persons by others.

   Caste, in which an individual is permanently assigned to a status based on his or her parents' status.

   Estate, in which peasants are required by law to work land owned by the noble class in exchange for food and protection from outside attacks.

   Class, in which people are ranked into categories according to their economic status, but in which some opportunity exists for mobility between the categories, based on achievement or merit.
4. Openness is the opportunity for individuals to change their status. Caste stratification systems are closed, whereas class stratification systems are more open.

   The degree of equality is the degree to which the social structure approaches an equal distribution of resources. Hunting and gathering societies are typically very equal, with inequality developing in later stages of agriculture and industrialization.
5. Class, or a set of people with similar amounts of income (the rate at which one receives money) and wealth (the value of one's holdings).

   Party, or a set of people with similar amounts of power.

   Status group, or a set of people with similar social prestige, or positive regard from members of a society.
6. Natural inevitability, which suggests that inequality exists because of natural differences in people's abilities, and is a just system.

   Structural-functionalist, which states that stratification is useful to society because it enhances stability and induces members of the society to work hard.

   Conflict, which suggests that stratification occurs through conflict between different classes, with the upper classes using superior power to take a larger share of the social resources.

   Evolutionary, which states that people will share enough resources to ensure the survival of the group until a surplus exists, at which time power determines how the surplus is distributed.

   Symbolic interactionist, which calls attention to the importance of symbolic displays of wealth and power that influence one's definition of self and the importance of ideas in defining social situations.
7. Inequality may emanate from natural differences in people's abilities.
8. Structural-functionalists believe that societies tend to be stable and are held together through consensus. Stratification provides an important function to society by aiding this process because it lessens conflict and provides structure.

   Conflict theorists believe that society tends toward conflict and change, and that stratification systems coerce the lower classes in order to benefit the upper classes.
9. In primitive societies, the survival of the group is paramount, and people will share their resources

to ensure that the group survives. As society develops increasingly sophisticated technology, surplus exists, and power will determine the distribution of the surplus.

10. Symbolic interactionists point out that symbols help to define the meaning of all social actions, and a person's self is developed socially through social interaction. Legitimating ideas, expressed symbolically in the form of language, provide reasons for inequality, for strata, for the ways people are placed in the strata, and for changes in the stratification system. These supporting ideas also strongly affect how people evaluate themselves within the system, influencing them to accept their position in the structure as good and right.
11. Social mobility is the movement of a person from one status to another, either between generations or within a person's adult career.
12. Structural mobility is mobility brought about by changes in the stratification hierarchy, for instance, as society becomes more technologically advanced.

Glossary

achieved status status determined at least partly through the individual's effort

ascribed status status determined by one's birth

caste a closed social stratum. Caste stratification is a system in which an individual is permanently assigned to a status based on his or her parents' status

circulation mobility the amount of mobility resulting from exchange movements within the stratification hierarchy

class a large set of people regarded by themselves or others as sharing similar status with regard to wealth, power, and prestige

class (according to Weber) a set of people with similar amounts of income or wealth

class stratification system one in which people are ranked into categories according to their occupation or economic status, but in which some opportunity exists for mobility between the categories based on achievement or merit

degree of equality the degree to which the social structure approaches an equal distribution of resources

estate a stratification system in which peasants were required by law to work land owned by their lords in return for food and protection from outside attack

income the rate at which one receives money

intergenerational social mobility a change in status from that which a child began with in the parents' household to that of the child upon reaching adulthood

intragenerational social mobility a change in social status that occurs within a person's adult career

monarchy a system of government headed by a king or queen who reigns for that person's lifetime

mobility rate the number of instances of mobility per 100 people in the population

nobility the monarch and his or her administration

openness the opportunity for individuals to change their status

party (according to Weber) a set of people with similar amounts of power

power the ability to have one's way, even against the wishes of others

prestige the amount of positive regard members of a society have for a status

primitive communalism a form of stratification characterizied by a high degree of sharing and minimal social inequality

slavery a form of social stratification involving great social inequality and the ownership of some persons by others

social mobility movement of a person or persons from one status to another

status a position in a social structure. Depending on the context, it might also mean a position in a social stratification structure, or the amount of prestige associated with one's position in a stratification structure

status group a set of people with similar social prestige

stratification any systematic ranking of social positions that influences the wealth, power, and prestige of the people in those positions

stratum a level in a stratification structure at which people share similar status

structural mobility mobility that is brought about by changes in the stratification hierarchy

wealth the value of one's holdings

Suggested Readings

B. Reinhard Bendix and Seymour Martin Lipset, (eds.). 1966. *Class, Status, and Power Social Stratification in Comparative Perspective,* 2d. ed. New York Free Press.

An excellent collection of the classic works in the area, from Weber to modern theorists.

Kingsley Davis and Wilbert Moore. 1945. "Some principles of stratification." *American Sociological Review,* 10, pp. 242–249.

The classic statement of the functionalist interpretation of stratification.

CHAPTER 9

SOCIAL CLASS in the UNITED STATES

- How Is the United States Stratified?
- What Are the Consequences of Social Stratification?
- Close-Up on Research: Ronald Kessler on Social Class and Stress
- Why Is the United States Stratified?
- Close-Up on Theory: Kingsley Davis and Wilbert E. Moore on the Function of Our Class Structure
- What Are the Causes and Consequences of Poverty?
- How Are We Responding to Poverty?
- What Is the Situation Regarding Social Mobility in the United States?
- What Are the Consequences of Mobility?
- Sociologists at Work: Peter Rossi Enumerates and Describes Chicago's Homeless

How's Your Sociological Intuition?

1. Which does social class affect?

a. life expectancy
b. lifestyle
c. attitudes toward religion and politics
d. all of the above

2. Which occupation was ranked by American respondents as having the highest prestige?

a. lawyer
b. bank teller
c. bus driver
d. farm laborer

3. If total income in the United States were to be divided equally among the populace, what would be the annual income for a family of four?

a. $11,000
b. $32,000
c. $59,000
d. $78,000

4. Social scientists seek to explain why people move up and down the social class ladder. What proportion of social mobility has been explained by today's sophisticated research designs?

a. 90 percent
b. 70 percent
c. 50 percent
d. 30 percent

Answers

1. d. Social class influences our life chances and our beliefs, as well as the amount of income, power, and social prestige we receive from others, as we see in the section "Consequences of Stratification."

2. a. Americans, like other people, have a distinct ranking of occupations that influences the prestige afforded those in the occupations. We learn about this ranking in the section, "How Is the United States Stratified?"

3. c. The majority of American families would benefit from an equal distribution of income. People generally learn to accept inequality as justified through supporting beliefs even when the people receive smaller shares of the resources, as shown in the previous chapter on social stratification and mobility.

4. d. Although we have learned a good deal about mobility, we still have a long way to go in explaining who moves up the social class ladder and why.

When You Have Finished Studying This Chapter, You Should Know:

- How income and wealth, power, and prestige are distributed in the United States
- How open the American class structure is
- What the major classes in the United States are
- How class influences our life chances, mental health, and involvement with the law
- How class influences our life-style
- Why the United States is stratified
- What the situation of the homeless in the United States is today
- Who the poor are in the United States today
- The economic and social causes and consequences of poverty
- The social characteristics and consequences of poverty
- The facts behind welfare myths
- How the government is responding to poverty
- How education affects mobility
- Some of the consequences of upward mobility

General Douglas Whitman opens the meeting: "Selective Service wants to coordinate, informally of course, with you folks at the White House and the Congress. When the President reinstates the draft later this week, we want to have it up and running quickly so we can get these men trained and in action as soon as possible. We think our best move is to resurrect the system we had operating during Vietnam, pretty much as it was. This certainly is no time for protracted philosophical debate or political snags."

David Webster, the Senate Armed Services Committee counsel, a Harvard Law School graduate, leans forward. "Sir, the present differs considerably from the 1960s in several regards. Back then, someone could avoid the draft by going to college or taking a job in engineering or teaching. We deferred people because there were shortages in areas where we now have surpluses. Today's economy can't absorb all the people the colleges are turning out. Are we going to defer college students, and, if so, how will we justify it?"

The general folds his arms and tries to mask his impatience. "Working-class men have always served loyally and effectively in the past. I see no reason to disturb the existing arrangement. We need not burden the infantry with too many book-smart college 'brains.' We'll simply say these college kids are more valuable at home."

Bob Kerman, the House Armed Services counsel, glares at the general and clears his throat. Bob spent the better part of a year wading through jungle swamps, avoiding booby traps, and trying in vain to get the South Vietnamese to defend their country against the approaching North Vietnamese. He had wanted to go to college, but no one in his family and few of his friends had gone. His stint ended early when he took a shot in the back while rescuing his men from an ambush. Though doctors initially said he'd never walk again, he did, with almost no visible sign of the injury. After the war Bob finally attended college and earned honors there and in law school.

This former second lieutenant's eyes meet the general's. "Speaking as one of those loyal and effective working-class grunts, I see no justification for depriving America's middle- and upper-class youth from the honor of serving their country. Why the hell should these kids wait out this war in college while their high school classmates are getting shot up and shipped home in body bags?"

The general looks away. His mind presents him with the unforgettable image of young men's bodies packed into heavy duty plastic bags like so much grotesque garbage. "Bob, I was in 'Nam too, and I got shot in Korea. Personally, I happen to agree with you. But realize you are speaking from your own personal point of view. The voting public won't see it that way, nor will big political donors, so it's not likely to be the way the president, the Senate, or that House committee you work for will see it."

"Well, General, we aren't sure of that," Webster interjects. "Maybe the country is ready for a moral equal liability, and maybe the lower classes won't be so cooperative this time."

"Sure, and maybe we're ready to draft women and do away with exemptions for weirdos and the blind. Let's keep this discussion reality-based! Chip, you haven't said much. Where's the White House on this?"

Sanford "Chip" Oaks, heir to one of the largest fortunes in the United States, owes his powerful White House staff position to connections, charm, and brains. "As you said, General, we need to expedite this thing. With reelection eighteen months away, the president want to minimize the damage with a tight but neat system. Of course we anticipate the conventional deferments. We also want to minimize any potential protest. Since most of the youth are going to be in the clear, single out the few you need quickly, and let the rest know they're home free. It's probably wise to focus on the 19-year-olds and hold a lottery among them.

Destined to die? Those from society's lower strata are more likely to be exposed to hazards, including being killed in times of war. (*AP Wirephoto*)

The small proportion selected will not have much chance to protest, and the others will not have much motivation.'' Oaks pauses. ''The President asked me to convey his trust in your good judgment. Of course, he'll meet with you personally to accept your plan. Let us know if you anticipate major changes.''

The meeting breaks up with Bob the person most aware that, based on their social status, several thousand unsuspecting young men soon will be destined to kill, to die, or to become handicapped during the next few years.

What is to be learned from this scenario? First, social class can be a matter of life and death. Our scenario is fictional but is based on sociological realities. Three out of every four American soldiers in the Vietnam War came from lower-middle-class or working-class families. One in four men came from families below the official poverty level. ''Ivy League college graduates were conspicuously rare in Vietnam'' (Summers, 1983).

Second, a person's views and actions are influenced by the person's social status. Kerman initially identifies with the working class because of his working-class background, but he eventually acquiesces to a plan he deplores. To do otherwise would jeopardize his high achieved status (as counsel to a congressional committee). Like the general, Kerman appears to be governed by his social status within a bureaucracy that is largely controlled by the middle and upper classes. In this chapter we will see that social class is linked to both political opinion and political power. Those near the bottom of the social ladder are underrepresented in national decision-making. These people are likely to vote less frequently than those who are well off, and they have fewer financial resources to back candidates and to lobby for programs on their own behalf.

Third, and less apparent, the war that motivated this meeting probably stems from a conflict over how society should be stratified. A major issue in the Vietnam war was whether South Vietnam was to become a country with a more equal distribution of resources. Much of the armed conflict in the world this century has involved struggles over how social resources are best distributed. Matters of class and status, then, are of vital importance.

How Is the United States Stratified?

As a democracy the United States expressly values equality and freedom, yet the society perpetuates considerable social inequality and some citizens are clearly more "free" than others. Earlier we stated that stratification systems differ in terms of their equality and openness. How equal and open is the United States?

EQUALITY IN THE UNITED STATES

INCOME AND WEALTH. We can clearly compare how equally income and wealth are distributed in the United States because we have a convenient unit, the dollar, with which to measure income and wealth. In a perfectly equal society, all members would have an equal share of income, the rate at which one receives money, and wealth, the value of one's holdings. In the previous chapter we have already seen that contemporary societies distribute income quite unequally, with some more and others less equal than is the United States.

If all income in the United States were divided equally, every family of four would receive about $59,000 (U.S. Bureau of the Census, 1986). Of course, this is not how income is distributed. Some people receive much more than others. The family at the middle of the income distribution actually receives about $26,000—around $33,000 less than an equal share. In fact, a middle-income family gets less than half of what it would receive if income were equally shared. On the other hand, those who are in the top fifth of income receive on the average a "double" share of over $120,000. This twenty percent of population receives 42 percent of the total income produced by the society. Those unfortunate enough to be in the bottom twenty percent of the income distribution receive just 5 percent of the total United States income. This amounts to one-quarter of an equal share, which translates to an income for a family of four of around $15,000.

Wealth, or property ownership, is even less equally shared. Data are scarce, but in 1983, the last year for which this information is available, we find 59 percent of the wealth is held by the wealthiest fifth of the population, whereas the poorest fifth of the population owned only 5 percent of the total wealth (S. Rose, 1986) (See Figure 9.1). The median household in the United States wealth, or net worth, is

FIGURE 9.1 Distribution of Income and Wealth in the United States. SOURCES [a]U.S. Bureau of the Census, 1984, *Income Estimate of Households 1982*, by Charles Nelson and Angela Feldman. [b]*American Profile Poster*, 1986, Stephen J. Rose, Random House, Table 30, p. 31. Used by permission.

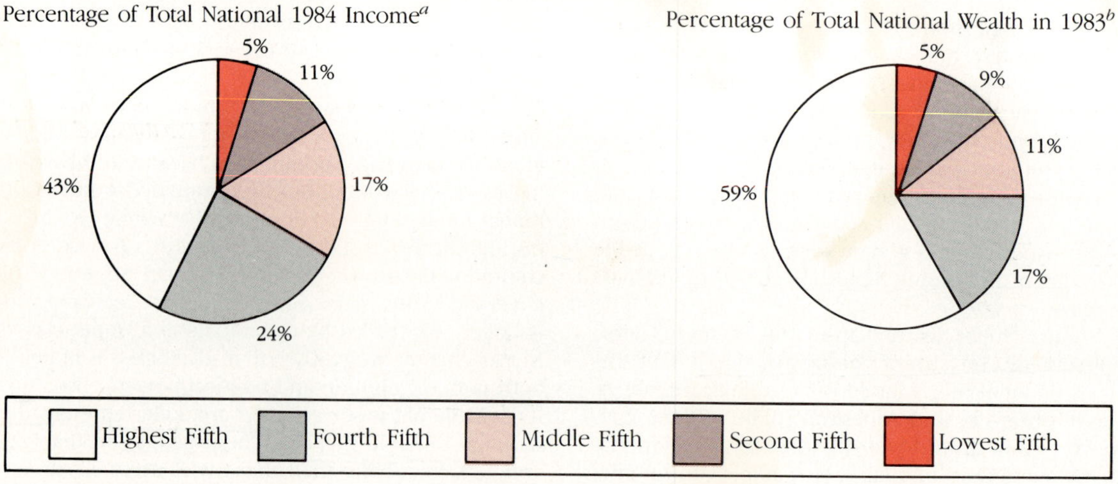

$32,667. Some 11 percent of the population has a zero or negative net worth. Yet about 1.5 percent have accumulated over a million dollars. The wealthiest man in the United States, Sam Walton, whose fortune *Forbes Magazine* estimates at $8 billion, has as much wealth as 650,000 average Americans or the 33 million poorest Americans!

In order to better envision the distribution of wealth in the United States, let's imagine five people sitting down to share a ten piece pizza. If they shared equally, each would receive two pieces. Each person represents a fifth of the population, so we have one representing the wealthiest or top fifth of the wealth distribution. Similarly, another person represents the poorest or bottom fifth of the distribution. Continuing the analogy, the "wealthy" person would "own" 5.5 pieces of the pizza, while the "poor" person would own one-half of a piece. The middle three are left to share 3.5 pieces; one has 1.7 pieces, another gets 1.1 slices, and the third has .9 of a slice. We might imagine the person with .5 of a piece of pizza glaring enviously across the table at the person with almost 6 pieces, who looks up and says, "I deserve this share because my father's grandfather worked hard and invested wisely. Too bad your ancestors were not so industrious, wise, and fortunate." Of course those with wealth rarely eat with those who are poor, and perhaps this fantasy illustrates why friendships tend to grow among social equals rather than between the haves and have nots. Of course there is a lot more to wealth than pizza.

The average American's wealth includes personal belongings, and part ownership in a car and a house, the rest of which is owed to, and therefore owned by, a bank. Those with great wealth often own lavish homes, luxurious cars, yachts, and a large parcel of real estate. They can vacation in exotic places, hire servants, eat at the finest restaurants and influence others, including politicians and corporations, with their wealth. They are also in a position to earn sizable income from their wealth. A millionaire could simply bank the money and receive $50 thousand or more a year in interest. In fairness to Mr. Walton, we might mention that the vast share of his wealth is invested in his corporation. He lives in a rather ordinary three-bedroom house and drives an old pick-up truck.

POWER. Is power more equally distributed than wealth and income? Answering this question depends on our ability to measure the inequality of power. We have a greater challenge here than in the case of wealth and income. There, the dollar provided a convenient measure, but we have no analogous unit of power.

Considerable evidences suggests that power in the United States is at least as unequally distributed as wealth or income. Marx and Engels suggested that industrial societies would split into two antagonistic classes: the extremely wealthy owners and the poor and relatively powerless workers. On the surface, it would seem this has not happened. In general the living standard has risen for the masses in the United States as the result of industrialization. But in the 1950s sociologist C. Wright Mills suggested that the United States class structure actually resembles the one Marx predicted.

For Mills, society is divided between two categories: the power elite and ordinary men. The power elite includes the chief executives of major firms, the most influential of the government leaders, and the top officers of the military establishment. This tiny class enjoys tremendous power, freedom, and luxury. "They need not merely 'meet the demands of the day and hour'; in some part, they create these demands and cause others to meet them." (Mills, 1957, p. 3) The vast majority of society falls into the class of ordinary people. They live in an everyday world, "driven by forces they can neither understand nor govern," and they work on projects not of their own design, but those created by the power elite. Thus they are "without purpose in an epoch in which they are without power " (Mills, 1957, p. 3.).

The steel industry in the United States provides a dramatic example of the two classes: the power elite and the ordinary people. In 1958, as Mills was writing of the power elite, the executives at Bethlehem Steel would have been near the top of the list. Seven out of the ten highest paid men in America were on Bethlehem's payroll. Like the capitalists Marx described, they continued to seek new markets, and they increased their steel-producing capacity. Today the world's steel mills can produce 50 percent more steel than the world needs.

But Bethlehem has lost 25 percent of its own home market to foreign competition and now is left with too many mills. The executives at Bethlehem repeatedly met demands for wage increases far in excess of those paid to laborers elsewhere in the economy. Besides high wages, the union created rules requiring more workers than were really needed for the work to do. In 1959 management tried to get the union to relax these rules, but the workers went on strike and the federal courts (also part of what Mills calls the power elite) sided with the strikers. As a result by 1982, steelworkers were making $26 per hour, which was twice the average U.S. manufacturing wage. With an oversupply of steel in the world market, and the cost of American steel high, many of Bethlehem's steel mills have closed and are rusting. Largely as a consequence of the management decisions of the power elite, 250,000 once very attractive blue-collar jobs have been lost, probably forever (Strohmeyer, 1986).

Philanthropy? John D. Rockefeller, Sr., oil multimillionaire, gives a caddy his favorite gift, a brand new dime. Rockefeller exemplifies what Mills called the power elite, members of U.S. society with enormous power related to their position in government, industry, or the military. (*UPI/Bettmann Newsphotos*)

Does a power elite actually control the United States? William Domhoff devoted nearly two decades of research to showing that it does. Domhoff focuses on a wealthy upper class of just 0.5 percent of the population. His category includes those listed in the *Social Register*, those who attended certain exclusive prep schools, or those who belong to certain exclusive social clubs. Domhoff believes this wealthy, exclusive set of people constitute a governing class in America. He shows that this tiny minority wields tremendous authority through its representation in the seats of governmental and corporate power (Domhoff, 1967; 1970; 1974; 1975; 1983).

For instance, from 1897 to 1973, 66 percent of all Cabinet members were drawn from this upper class (Freitag, 1975; Mintz, 1975). In business the upper class maintains an awesome presence. Half of all business assets in 1979 were controlled by just 201 firms. Some 3,572 top executive officers and members of boards of directors, in turn, control these 201 firms; 44 percent of these executives and directors are members of one or more upper-class clubs. Clearly upper-class people are much more likely to hold important political and economic positions than those who are not (Dye, 1979).

In *Who Rules America Now?* (1983), Domhoff strengthens the case made in his 1967 work, *Who Rules America?* Domhoff's 1967 work attracted praise from those holding to the conflict perspective but criticism from some others. In the fifteen intervening years, Domhoff has gathered more data and honed his arguments. He makes a very convincing case that a small minority of Americans, educated at a small set of elite schools and holding membership in exclusive clubs, dominates the highest positions of business and government. He has a more difficult time proving that they act together as a class, because this is much harder to demonstrate, but Domhoff has gathered strong evidence of the concentration of power as well as wealth in the hands of a few.

PRESTIGE. How equally does the United States class system distribute prestige? As is the case with power, we have no common units by which to measure the amount of respect or positive regard a society has for a particular status. Still, most of us are well aware that the prestige depends to a large degree on one's occupation. The status of physician, for instance, assures one much more respect than that of taxicab driver. Clearly not all positions in the class system command the same prestige; in other words, prestige is unequally distributed, as we have seen is the case for wealth, income, and power.

Although sociologists have not measured prestige in terms of specific units, they have carefully studied prestige rankings of various status positions, usually occupations. The general approach has been to ask a representative sample of the population to indicate their ranking of various occupations (see Table 9.1). For instance, the subject is asked, "On a scale of zero to 100, what is your own personal opinion of the general standing of being a bank teller?" After asking thousands of respondents hundreds of similar questions about various occupations, sociologists have discovered that the public in general has a quite clear image of the prestige associated with different lines of work. Several decades of research indicate that the hierarchy of occupations remains stable over time and is substantially similar among all industrialized societies sampled (National Opinion Research Center, 1983).

Thus we see that prestige, wealth, income, and power are all quite unequally distributed. Before we begin to explore why this is so, let us explore just how open the United States class system is.

TABLE 9.1 Prestige Ranking of Selected Occupations in the United States

Occupation	Prestige Score
Physicians, medical and osteopathic	82
College and university teachers	78
Lawyers	76
Dentists	74
Aeronautical and astronautical engineers	71
Clergy	69
Sociologists	66
Chiropractors	60
Schoolteachers	60
Bank tellers	50
Electricians	49
Police officers and detectives	48
Insurance agents	48
Machinists	48
Secretaries	46
Mail carriers	42
Farmers (owners and tenants)	40
Telephone operators	40
Restaurant managers	38
Plumbers and pipefitters	34
Bus drivers	32
Taxicab drivers	28
Gas station attendants	22
Waiters/Waitresses	20
Farm laborers, wage workers	18
Maids and servants, private household	18
Janitor	16
Bellhop	14
Shoeshiner	09

SOURCE: *General Social Survey, 1972–1983: Cumulative Codebook*, 1983. Chicago, National Opinion Research Center, pp. 338–349. Used by permission.

This ranking is based on the public's response to the question: "What is your own personal opinion of the general standing of being a waiter (or other occupation)?" The ranking has remained nearly constant over several decades, and occupational rankings in other industrial societies are very similar to that found in the United States.

HOW OPEN IS THE UNITED STATES?

Tom was raised in a Catholic orphanage. As a boy he dreamed of playing on the Detroit Tigers or being an architect. He enrolled in the University of Michigan, but dropped out to help his brother run an ailing pizza business. Not many people wanted to eat there, so the brothers catered to the take-out and delivery trade, which most successful pizza restaurants avoided. Tom worked hard and kept his eye out for ways to get the pizza delivered quicker and better. He developed a stronger box to keep the cheese from sticking to the lid when the pizzas were stacked in transit, and he began to use a new device to keep them hot. Domino's Pizza has grown enormously; today Tom owns the Detroit Tigers, and recently hired the architect of his choice to build his lavish central-office complex.

Perhaps the inequality we have observed is not a bad thing if the "good life" is available to all diligent entrepreneurs who, like Tom, offer highly desirable goods or services. Surely the United States has no impermeable occupational caste boundaries of the sort found in traditional India. Yet sociologists have long noted a strong tendency for those born of a particular status to remain at that status. This could be because lower status people do not have the ambition or skill to move up, or it could be because there are barriers in our class structure that are simply less obvious than those in the caste system. In this section, we discuss various descriptions of the American class structure as a means of exploring the distinctions and boundaries between groups. Later we examine the dynamics of who moves up the American class structure.

THE CONFLICT PERSPECTIVE: TWO CLASSES. As we saw in the preceding subsection on "Equality in the United States," sociologists from the conflict perspective make a strong case for the existence of a small, unacknowledged, governing elite in the United States comprising primarily very wealthy people. Though this class lacks the official titles and public recognition of the nobility of earlier times, it resembles nobility in terms of power, wealth, and the fact that the positions of its members are largely inherited. A recent analysis of the 400 wealthiest individuals in the United States indicated that only 159, less than 40 percent of the total, had made all of their own fortune. The others inherited the wealth and the status and power that accompanies it (Thurow, 1984). So the majority of people in these tremendously high positions received their status through ascription, not achievement. This demonstrates again how the power elite is more closed than open to mobility.

A FUNCTIONALIST VIEW: MULTIPLE CLASSES. Conflict theorists discuss two classes: the upper class, or owners, who exploit the lower class, or workers. Functionalists believe there are more than two classes, and that they work together for the benefit of society rather than one exploiting the other. Though different sociologists have described varying numbers of American classes, many sociologists find it useful to analyze the system in terms of five classes: an upper class, an upper-middle class, a lower-middle class, a working class, and a lower class (Rossides, 1976).

The *upper class* is distinguished by its "old" (inherited) wealth, usually millions of dollars. Income, mostly from investments, is very high. This class includes heads of corporations or very high-ranking officials in government and the military. Members of this class have often been educated at elite liberal arts colleges, including the Ivy League universities. This group is essentially identical to Mills' power elite, and it is estimated at about 1 percent of the population of the United States.

Next is the *upper-middle class* of professionals, such as physicians, lawyers, and high-level managers. Their income is high, and they are likely to have graduate school or professional training beyond their basic college education. Some 10 percent of Americans are in this class.

The *lower-middle class* are generally white-collar workers of modest rank and income. They are typically office workers and semiprofessionals, and their ranks include small business people, sales workers, and small farmers. They are likely to have some college education. This class includes about 30 percent of Americans.

Commonly called "blue-collar workers," the *working class* consists of skilled laborers—such as machinists, carpenters, and plumbers—and unskilled laborers—such as factory workers and construction laborers. They generally have had a high school education but have not attended college. Often their high school training took the form of a vocational program. This class accounts for about 40 percent of the population.

At the bottom of the class system is the *lower class*, or the poor. Their income is very low. They are often unemployed, although the number of "working poor" is increasing. They are poorly educated, and it is not uncommon for members of this class to be illiterate. Nearly 20 percent of Americans are found in the lower class.

Table 9.2 offers a comparison of the Conflict and Structural Functionalist Views of the class structure, along with estimates of the size of these classes.

THE SHRINKING MIDDLE CLASS. The term *middle class* covers a wide range of income and behavior variables, from the $65,000 income of the dentist to the $20,000 income of the individual farmer. Nevertheless, this class has long been said to be the backbone of the American economy. Thus it is with some concern that economists watch what they call the "eroding" of the middle class in the past decade.

From 1978 to 1986, the proportion of families in the middle class dropped from 52 percent to 44 percent of the population. One-third of those persons who left the middle class rose in income and entered the upper class, whereas two-thirds of them dropped into the working or lower class. The group with incomes over $47,000 grew by 2.8 percent and those with incomes under $19,000 increased by 5.2 percent (Rose, 1986).

Several reasons for this change seem possible. The first is that the great increase in divorce creates one-parent families that earn the same income but must pay almost double the costs—two rents, two utilities, and so on. This accounts for a great proportion of the rising number of women and children in poverty. Another reason is that the wages of young male workers are lower than they have been for some time. Other contributing factors include automation, postponement of retirement, foreign competition, and the declining strength of the union movement. Changes in government policy and social factors such as the slowing of the divorce epidemic will determine the future of this social class trend.

CLASS BOUNDARIES: BARRIERS TO OPENNESS. The more barriers there are between classes, the more fixed is one's status at birth—a characteristic of closed systems. Let's consider each class boundary individually.

The characteristic that separates the upper class from the upper-middle class is the former's great inherited wealth. Membership in the upper class is therefore generally by birth, and one stands little chance of being forced out. Conversely, whereas it is technically possible to earn extreme wealth, most members inherited rather than earned it. People find themselves on one side or the other because of ascription or birth rather than achievement.

What of the boundary between the upper-middle class and the lower-middle class? Here the distinguishing trait is not wealth, but occupation, and entrance into the higher occupations and professions hinges on entrance into graduate and professional schools. Although it is possible for the lower classes to be admitted to the schools that lead to upper-middle class occupations, it is still unusual and certainly not probable.

College education is often the key to escaping from the working class to the middle class. In families in which every member must give financial assistance, arranging for one child to spend the time and money to receive such an education is difficult if not impossible.

What distinguishes the working class from the lower class? This boundary, like the previous two, is

TABLE 9.2 The Conflict and Functionalist Views of Class Structure in the United States

The Conflict View

Class	Percent of Population	Characteristics
Governing class, power elite, bourgeoisie, or owners	1% or less	Top ranking officials of government, industry, and the military, and especially owners of major industrial firms.
Ordinary men, masses, or workers	99% or more	The vast majority of people in society whose means of income is their earnings and who have little control over society or their place in it.

The Functionalist View

Class	Percent of Population	Characteristics
Upper class	1%	Inherited wealth and high income
Upper-middle class	10%	Professionals with training beyond college, high income
Lower-middle class	30%	White-collar office workers and semiprofessionals with some college background
Working class	40%	Blue-collar skilled laborers with high school diplomas and moderate incomes
Lower class, or poor	20%	Often unemployed or underemployed and poorly educated

somewhat vague, but opportunity to enter the skilled-labor category is often restricted by trade unions that make it easier to follow one's parent's trade (usually, a son following his father's trade). For example, a young person might have the brains and will to become a pipefitter or a plumber, but without access to the union and apprenticeship programs of those occupations, usually through a friend or relative, that person cannot pursue those fields.

Clearly we can conceive of the United States society as stratified into five classes, and people do move between them. However, mobility between the classes is less common than remaining in the class of one's birth. In a perfectly open society, we would expect less relationship between parents' and child's status. That few people succeed in crossing the boundaries suggests the presence of significant, if sometimes subtle, barriers. In a sense, these boundaries are castelike, because their effect is to keep people at or near their birth status. Of course we do not literally have castes because this involves explicit recognition of the boundaries, moral support for them, and virtually no crossing of them.

Many social forces besides clear-cut class barriers tend to keep people in their original social class. In the next section we observe how the different classes pose considerably different opportunities, incentives, attitudes, and role models that create a strong tendency for class to be determined by birth.

What Are the Consequences of Social Stratification?

So far we have considered stratification as influencing primarily one's wealth or income, power, and prestige. Actually, stratification touches virtually every aspect of our lives, as the following case study of two real people illustrates.

Dick and Ken were born about the same time and grew up in the same Midwestern town. Both were Anglo-Saxon Protestants, and both attended the same public schools. Dick's father was a physician, and Ken's father was a plumber. Soon after his birth at the local hospital Dick was driven home in a Cadillac to a large stone house with his own bedroom. Ken was driven in the family Ford to a frame house and a bedroom shared with his brother.

As he was growing up, Dick could be found reading, playing clarinet in the high school band, swimming at the country club, or waterskiing at the lake near his parents' cottage. Ken spent his spare time racing his bike around the neighborhood, fishing in a polluted stream near his house, and skinny-dipping in the pond near the town dump.

Dick's wardrobe came from the finer department stores and specialty clothing shops, whereas Ken's clothes came from K-Mart. Dick's family ate at the finest restaurant; Ken's family seldom ate out at all. Dick's parents stressed understanding and self-acceptance. Ken's parents stressed obedience.

Schoolteachers knew Dick's father was a doctor, and they expected good performance from Dick. Teachers did not know Ken's father, the construction-site plumber, but from Ken's clothing and mannerisms they could tell that Ken was the son of a working man, and they did not expect as much of him. Dick studied hard and was in the classes for the "brighter" college-bound students. Ken never studied much and was placed in sections for the "slower" vocationally oriented students.

After high school, when the war came, Dick was insulated from the war in Southeast Asia by a college-student deferment. Ken would almost certainly have been drafted had he not chosen to enlist. After serving in the infantry, Ken came home, entered an apprenticeship, and is now a journeyman plumber. Dick went from college to medical school. He entered the Air Force as a captain and a physician, served his stint, and now practices medicine with a group of physicians.

People in Dick's community, including the politicians, afford him respect and listen when he has an opinion. When Ken talks, he is likely to be seen as one more blue-collar redneck.

Ken and Dick are examples of the differential treatment one receives according to one's class in our society. Much of the difference in their lives has nothing to do with their innate abilities, but rather with what family they were born into. Let's move on to consider a sampling of the vast array of research about how class is related to life chances, life-style, and attitudes.

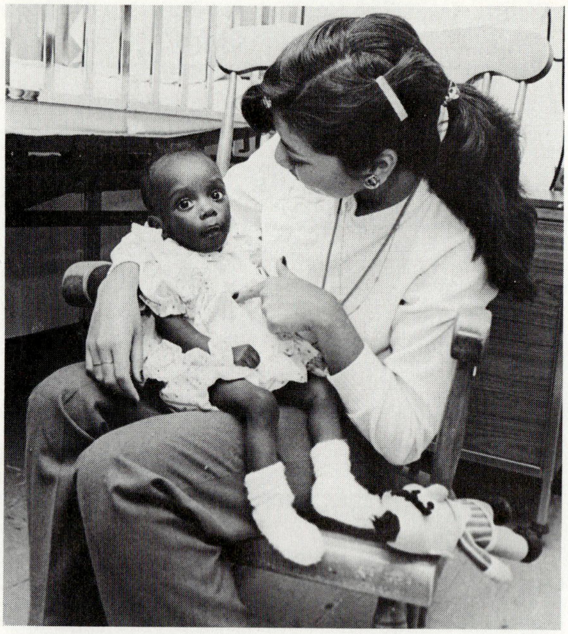

Equality and justice for all? Social class background not only influences how we live, but even whether we will survive birth and infancy. This child's chances are less than those of a child born into a higher social status. (*AP/Wide World Photos*)

LIFE CHANCES

Our social class background not only influences how we live, but even whether we will survive birth and infancy and how long we will probably live. Class partly determines the chance of being handicapped or institutionalized. In the United States and most industrialized nations, those from lower social classes have higher infant mortality rates and a greater probability of job-related deaths (Gortmaker, 1979). The lower one's social class, the higher is the proportion of family income spent on food—yet nearly half the poor are malnourished to a degree that affects physical, intellectual, and emotional development. Malnutrition may even cause a permanent handicap such as mental retardation (Winick, 1980). Social class affects one's likelihood of contracting serious illness, including heart disease, cancer, and diabetes (Luft, 1978).

SOCIAL CLASS AND MENTAL HEALTH

Along with influencing our physical health and well-being, social class affects our mental health as well. As early as the 1950s sociologists demonstrated that people in the lower social classes are more likely to experience psychological distress, including anxiety, depression, and symptoms such as headaches and digestive disorders, as well as more serious emotional disorders like schizophrenia (Hollingshead & Redlich, 1958). In our "Close-Up on Research" we look more deeply into how social class relates to emotional distress.

CLOSE-UP on • *RESEARCH* •

Ronald Kessler on Social Class and Stress

The Researcher and the Setting

For nearly half a century researchers have found that rates of psychological distress, such as anxiety or depression, are higher for those in the lower socioeconomic positions than those of higher social status in the United States. This is an example of an inverse relationship, one in which increases in one variable are linked with decreases in the other. As sociologist Ronald Kessler of the University of Michigan points out, this is one of the most firmly established relationships in the field of public health. Kessler studies an area sometimes called social-psychiatry, which looks at the relationships between social status and emotional disorders or well-being. Social-psychiatry is also studied by epidemiologists, that is, scientists who study epidemics or the relation between society and disease.

The Objective

Kessler observes that many researchers report the inverse relationship between social class and psychological distress, "There is serious conceptual confusion, though, about just what aspects of socioeconomic status are related to distress. My purpose here is to clear away this confusion through a comprehensive analysis of eight epidemiologic surveys" (p. 752).

The Theory

Because socioeconomic status takes on different meanings in different contexts, Kessler focused on the three major variables people usually employ to measure socioeconomic status: income, education, and occupational status. He theorized that the variables might individually or collectively be tied to psychological distress.

Research Design

Kessler considers data from eight earlier surveys: two that draw subjects from rural populations, two from urban populations, and four from the noninstitutionalized population (not in prisons or mental hospitals) of the United States. Psychological distress was measured by two types of *scales,* one that measured depressed mood and another that considered bodily feelings known to be linked with anxiety and depression, such as headaches, stomach problems, or sleep difficulties. A *scale is a set of questions found to be useful in measuring a concept such as social status or psychological distress.*

Kessler used three primary factors to indicate socioeconomic status. Income was measured in thousands of dollars, education in years, and occupational position on the Hollingshead scale, which classifies occupation into the following categories: (1) executives and proprietors of large concerns and major professionals (highest status); (2) managers and proprietors of medium-sized businesses and lesser professionals; (3) administrative personnel of large concerns; (4) owners of small independent businesses; (5) semiprofessionals; (6) owners of little businesses; (7) clerical and sales workers; and (8) unskilled workers (lowest status). Sometimes an eight-category census scale was used, which included the following categories: (1) professional, (2) managerial, (3) clerical, (4) sales, (5) craftsperson, (6) operative, (7) services worker, and (8) laborer.

Findings

For the general population, Kessler finds repeated confirmation of a relationship between each of the variables: education, income, and occupational status. However, the relation between education and distress is more pronounced than that of income or occupational status. We should bear in mind that all these relationships are inverse; that is, the less education, the more likely a person is to be psychologically distressed.

Kessler also examines the strength of the tie between social class and psychological distress for three subpopulations: full-time homemakers, women in the labor force, and men in the labor force. He finds the general relationship strongest for homemakers, second strongest for women in the labor force, and weakest for men in the labor force. This is a bit surprising. In Kessler's words:

> This is an unexpected order, for it shows that the relationship between SES [social status or, more specifically, Social Economic Status] and distress is strongest among homemakers, who are least closely linked to the earning and occupation stratification systems of society and thus most financially dependent on the efforts of other people. Among those most

closely tied to these systems—men in the labor force—the relationship is weakest (p. 755).

When Kessler studies which aspect of socioeconomic status is most strongly linked to distress for each of the subpopulations, he finds that among men low income is the strongest predictor of stress, for employed women less education is the strongest predictor, and for homemakers less education is far more significant than income.

Implications

For nearly as long as they have known that status and stress are inversely related, people have debated why. Is it because low status stresses out people, or is it that stressed-out people do not fare well in the competition for status, and they end up in the low-status positions? Kessler's work does not answer this question, but it clarifies what we know so that future researchers might more intelligently decide how to untangle the facts. Kessler has shown that three separate variables, which are usually considered as social status, are each individually related to stress. He also shows that the factors affect men and women differently. As Kessler says: "We are far away from having complete answers. But having the right questions is a good beginning."

Questions

1. Can you make up some fictitious biographies that would be consistent with Kessler's findings? For instance: Sally Homemaker with an eighth grade education is more depressed than Joan Homemaker, the college grad. All else being equal, why might that be so? What about Joe Highearner versus John Lowearner?
2. How might we explain that homemakers seem to be more psychologically distressed by low social status than their husbands who are the ones who have the low-status jobs?
3. There are two interpretations to the research findings that social status and psychological stress are inversely related: being in a low status may cause people psychological stress or being psychologically stressed may cause a person to achieve lower status than they otherwise might. What kind of research could be designed to find out whether low status is the cause or consequence of psychological distress?

SOURCE Ronald C. Kessler. 1982. "A Disaggregation of the Relationship Between Socioeconomic Status and Psychological Distress." *American Sociological Review*, 47 (December), pp. 752–764.

SOCIAL STATUS AND DISTRESS

More recently, R. Kessler and Cleary (1980) have studied whether low status is the cause of distress or distress the cause of low status. They discovered that much of the observed relationship between status and distress results from the fact that lower-class people are more responsive emotionally to the stresses they experience. Given the same loss of a loved one, people in the lower class are more likely than those in the middle or upper class to show distress. Unfortunately present research does not tell us whether they are born this way or become weakened through their life experiences. Perhaps the harsher environment of the lower classes leaves children relatively emotionally handicapped as adults. Or perhaps people who are born emotionally handicapped gravitate toward the lower class. Because Kessler and Cleary's research deals with adult subjects instead of following the subjects from birth through adulthood, we cannot tell. We do learn that a major portion of the relation between status and emotional distress is the result of the emotional responsiveness of lower class people.

Those from the lower classes are more likely to experience emotional distress and more likely to be treated clinically. Are there differences in the kinds and treatments of emotional disorders? A rich literature documents several decades of research in this subdiscipline called social-psychiatry. One clear finding is that those in the lower classes are more likely to have externally oriented disorders, such as schizophrenia, which may involve hallucinations and paranoid thinking. Conversely, the upper class and upper middle class account for a higher percentage of internally oriented disorders, such as neuroses that involve abnormal fears or moods.

Psychiatric patients from the different classes get different treatment. The upper- and middle-class psychiatric patients are more likely to receive psychotherapy, whereas the working- and lower-class patients are more likely to be treated only with medications or put into custodial care. Though part of this is due to the differences in the type of mental illnesses, this is not the whole story. Even when we consider patients with the same disorder, the higher-social-class patient is more likely to receive psychotherapy, partly because psychotherapists come from the upper social classes and prefer patients of their own social class.

Social class differences in parenting may partially explain the relative inability of lower-class people to handle stress, and their tendency toward externally oriented disorders. The upper and middle classes tend to emphasize inner needs in their childrearing and produce adults whose values are relatively more oriented to inner needs. Parents of working- and lower-class children tend to focus more on external behavior and produce offspring who place a relative emphasis on external behavior over internal needs. (Gallagher, 1980).

SOCIAL CLASS AND THE LAW. For quite some time it appeared that members of the lower class were both more likely to commit crimes and to be arrested, denied bail, convicted, and more severely sentenced than middle- and upper-class offenders (Doleschal & Klapmuts, 1973). More recent research sheds some light on these findings. What now appears true is that lower-class people commit crimes that do not involve the abuse of occupational power at a higher rate than middle-class people. However, middle-class people do commit crimes that involve the abuse of occupational power at rates higher than those of the lower class (Braithwaite, 1979).

Conflict theorists have long argued that the law comes down more harshly on lower-class offenders than middle- or upper-class offenders. Indeed, these discriminatory practices seemed so clearly established in the 1960s and 1970s that various reforms were introduced. Among these were measures that limited judges' discretionary power to sentence offenders. Where judges once were able to choose a sentence in a range, for instance, from two to five years, laws have been rewritten to mandate a fixed sentence so all offenders found guilty of that same crime will spend three years in prison. More recent research has produced conflicting evidence about whether sentencing is social-class biased. This may be a case where sociological research findings have contributed to improving the situation earlier researchers had found (Greenberg, 1981).

SOCIAL-CLASS SUBCULTURES AND LIFE-STYLES. Because social class influences people's beliefs, attitudes, values, and behavior patterns, we can speak of relatively distinct social-class subcultures or lifestyles. Some lifestyle differences are reflections of income differences. High social class generally means more income, which translates into nicer clothes, better food, newer cars, finer housing, more luxurious vacations, and other things money can buy.

Beyond these rather obvious material differences, higher income has more subtle advantages as well. Income affects the quality of housing one can afford and the neighborhood in which one resides. Better neighborhoods mean better schools and public services such as parks, streets, and police protection. When one can afford to buy rather than rent a home, one gains significant financial advantages from the investment and from income tax deductions.

Class also influences life-styles in ways not directly related to money. Researchers have found class differences in feelings about work, in political affiliation and participation, in community activity, and in family life, childrearing, and even speech patterns. Several studies show those with higher occupational status are more likely to be satisfied with their work (Jencks et al., 1972). Ownership of business or controlling the work of others is an especially strong indicator of probable satisfaction. For example, in a national sample of 1,569 workers, employers felt the most fulfillment in work, managers were the next most satisfied group, and workers as a group felt the least fulfillment (Kalleberg & Griffin, 1980).

Politically, the middle and upper classes are more likely to vote and become involved in political parties than are the working and lower classes. Republicans draw more heavily from the middle and upper classes, whereas Democrats attract more voters from the working and lower classes (Alford and Friedland, 1975; Levinson, 1975; Wolfinger & Rosenstone, 1980). We find the working class is more liberal than the middle class on economic issues but *less* liberal on civil liberties and issues such as programs to aid minorities (Hamilton, 1972; Lipset & Raab, 1970).

Generally, the middle class is more likely than the working class to join voluntary associations such as the PTA, the Rotary, the VFW, and garden or hobby clubs (Hyman and Wright, 1971). The working class is more likely to visit parents, grandparents, or other relatives from their extended families.

Social class is related to important family patterns. Those of higher social class are more likely to delay marriage, and their marriages are more likely to be stable (Renne, 1970). Whereas middle-class parents are likely to stress understanding, self-acceptance, and freedom with their children, working-class parents tend to focus on obedience and conformity. Some studies indicate, however, that this difference between white-collar and blue-collar families may be decreasing (Erlanger, 1974).

Even speech patterns appear to reveal a person's social-class background. Subjects in one study were often able to identify a person's social class simply by listening to recordings of people reading standard sentences (Ellis, 1967).

As we see, social class has many influences on our lives. It touches us in a material sense, but it also bears on our social patterns and our beliefs and feelings about our lives. For those who are poor, social class is not just a strong influence on life-style; as we see in the following section, it is a virtual prison.

Why Is the United States Stratified?

Why have we so much social inequality in a society that proclaimed in its *Declaration of Independence* that: "We hold these truths to be self evident, that all men were created equal and endowed by their Creator with certain inalienable rights, that among these are the right to life, liberty, and the pursuit of happiness"? Many theorists have sought to explain social inequality. In the previous chapter, "Social Stratification and Mobility," we considered general theories of stratification, and we featured Marx's work in our "Close-Up on Theory" as well as Lenski's evaluation of it in the "Close-Up on Research." We also considered four other general explanations of stratification: the natural inevitability perspective, structural-functionalism, symbolic interactionism, and Lenski's synthesis, which is known as the evolutionary approach.

THE STRUCTURAL-FUNCTIONALIST APPROACH

Now as we study class in our own society and our own era, we consider how structural-functionalists explain stratification and the criticism they have drawn from those with opposing viewpoints. In keeping with our plan to introduce an in-depth discussion of either a contemporary or a classical theory in each chapter, we move now to Kingsley Davis and Wilber Moore's classical statement of the structural-functionalist position on stratification in contemporary societies.

CLOSE-UP on • *THEORY* •

Kingsley Davis and Wilbert E. Moore on the Functions of Our Class Structure

The Theorists and the Setting

Almost exactly a century after Marx and Engels wrote *The Communist Manifesto* (1848), Kingsley Davis and Wilbert E. Moore, two sociologists at Princeton University, published "Some Purposes of Stratification," now also a classic in the sociological literature. Though these Princeton professors wrote about forty years ago, we focus on the article because it outlines some of the major arguments for the persistence of inequality, especially in class societies, and because it has become such a standard in the discussion of inequality in industrial societies.

The Theoretical Issue

The two issues Davis and Moore originally address, which have been most often discussed in the sociological literature, are: (1) Why is stratification universal? and (2) Why is prestige distributed similarly in different societies? In their words: "An effort is made to explain, in functional terms, the universal necessity which calls forth stratification in any social system. Next, an attempt is made to explain the roughly uniform distribution of prestige as between the major types of position in every society." (p. 242).

Davis and Moore's ideas counter those of Marx, and debate has continued for decades over which is more valid.

Concepts and Propositions

Davis and Moore start from the assumption that "as a functioning mechanism a society must somehow distribute its members in social positions and induce them to perform the duties of these positions" (p. 242). To this they add a second assumption:

> If the duties associated with the various positions were all equally pleasant to the human organism, all equally important to societal survival, and all equally in need of the same ability or talent, it would make no difference who got into which positions, and the problem of social placement would be greatly reduced. But actually it does make a great deal of difference who gets into which positions. . . . The rewards and their distribution become a part of the social order, and thus give rise to stratification (p. 243).

From these assumptions they arrive at the conclusion that:

Proposition 1: "If the rights and perquisites of different positions in a society must be unequal, then the society must be stratified, because that is precisely what stratification means" (p. 243).

What then explains the ranking of positions? Specifically, Davis and Moore try to explain why similar occupations get similar rewards in most societies. For instance, religious, governmental leaders and technical experts receive higher social rewards than the people in ordinary positions in virtually all the societies that have such occupations. Why?

Proposition 2: "In general, those positions convey the best reward, and hence have the highest rank, which (a) have the greatest importance for the society and (b) require the greatest training and talent" (p. 244).

Let us consider the positions of religious leader, government leader, and technical expert to better understand the Davis–Moore theory. Why in every known society do religious activities tend to be under the charge of particular persons, who thereby enjoy greater rewards than the ordinary person? According to Davis and Moore, this is because "society achieves its unity primarily through the possession by its members of certain ultimate values and ends in common" (p. 244). Yet, these values are not, according to Davis and Moore, "inherited, nor from external nature. They have evolved as part of the culture by communication and moral pressure. They must, however, appear to the members of the society to have some reality, and it is the role of religious belief and ritual to supply and reinforce this appearance of reality" (pp. 244–245). Those entrusted with religious belief deal in an area of great importance to society. Proposition 2 would therefore predict that great rewards would be given to induce people to come into these positions and carry out their responsibilities well. Furthermore, "If the supernatural world governs the destinies of men more ultimately than does the real world, its earthly representative, the person through whom one may communicate with the supernatural, must be a powerful individual" (p. 245). "It is no accident, therefore, that religious functionaries have been associated with the very highest positions of power, as in theocratic regimes. Indeed, looking at it from this point of view, one may wonder why . . . they do not get entire control over their societies" (p. 245). To explain why religious leaders rarely achieve "entire control," Davis and Moore turn to their second major explanation: the scarcity of talent. They argue that "the amount of technical competence necessary for the performance of religious duties is small" and add:

> anyone can set himself up as enjoying an intimate relation with deities, and nobody can successfully dispute him. . . . The priest can never be free from competition, since the criteria of whether or not one has genuine contact with the supernatural are never strictly clear. It is this competition that debases the priestly position below what might be expected at first glance. . . . Furthermore, unless he is protected by a professional guild, the priest's identification with the supernatural tends to preclude this acquisition of abundant worldly goods" (p. 245).

In short, because not much talent is required, there is rarely a scarcity of talent, and this tends to limit how high the rank of these positions become.

In a similar vein, Davis and Moore believe that "government plays a unique and indispensable part in society. . . . The main functions of government are, internally, the ultimate enforcement of norms, the final arbitration of conflicting interests, and the overall planning and direction of society; and externally, the handling of war and diplomacy" (pp. 245–246). Because of their importance to society, Proposition 2 predicts government officials will have high rank. Like the priests, who at first glance might seem to be in a position to claim all power, government officials are limited in power and rank by several considerations: (1) the actual holders of top positions must be few in number compared with the total population, (2) the rulers represent the interest of the groups rather than themselves and are restricted by rules designed to enforce this limitation, and (3) the holder of political office has his authority by virtue of his office. "Therefore any special knowledge, talent, or capacity he may claim is purely incidental, so that he often has to depend upon others for technical assistance" (p. 246).

Those with technical skills often receive higher-than-average positions in society, and Davis and Moore explain this:

> It is the simplest case of the rewards being so distributed as to draw talent and motivate training. . . . Modern medicine, for example, is within the mental capacity of most individuals, but a medical education is so burdensome and expensive that virtually none would undertake it if the position of the M.D. did not carry a reward commensurate with the sacrifice. . . . Why they [positions requiring great technical skill] seldom if ever receive the highest rewards is also clear: the importance of technical knowledge from a societal point of view is never so great as the integration of goals, which takes place on the religious, political, and economic levels (pp. 244 and 247).

Unlike Marx, who dwells on ownership as the most significant explanation of high rank, Davis and Moore deal with it as a side issue. They first argue that ownership of private property is "a reward for the proper management of one's finances" (p. 247). But they have to acknowledge that some inherit great wealth:

> In such a case it is difficult to prove that the position is functionally important or that the scarcity involved is anything other than extrinsic and accidental. It is for this reason, doubtless, that the institution of private property . . . becomes more subject to criticism as social development proceeds towards industrialization (p. 247).

Interpretation

The mark of a good theory is how well it can deal with explaining what actually happens and how well it can predict what will happen. Davis and Moore have touched on two clearly important factors that can be used to explain much of the differences in social rank. Perhaps you are not convinced that they have the "whole" truth. Neither are their critics, whose arguments we will consider in the next section.

Questions

1. Davis and Moore present two factors to explain the rank a position is given in society: functional importance and scarcity. Are there other factors that would help explain the rank of the positions?
2. How well does the theory explain the relative ranking of firefighter and top entertainer, bus driver and airline pilot, sanitation worker and lawyer?
3. What might Marx and Engels have to say about this theory of Davis and Moore?

SOURCE Kingsley Davis, and Wilbert E. Moore. 1946. "Some Principles of Stratification." *American Sociological Review*, 10, pp. 424–249.

THE CONFLICT PERSPECTIVE

Critics, especially those from the conflict perspective, point out that Davis and Moore have overlooked some of the ways in which stratification is dysfunctional to society. In a rebuttal to Davis and Moore, Tumin (1953) listed eight dysfunctions of stratification:

1. Stratification systems limit the possibility of discovering the full range of talent available in a society because of unequal access to appropriate motivation, channels of recruitment, and centers of training.
2. By thus limiting the range of talent considered, societies limit the growth of their productive resources.
3. Social stratification functions to give the elite the political power to gain acceptance and dominance of ideas to rationalize the establishment, whatever it may be, as logical, natural, and morally right.
4. Stratification creates an unequal distribution of self-images, and may keep individuals from achieving their true potential where a favorable self-image is required.
5. Because inequality is never fully accepted by the less privileged, stratification promotes hostility, suspicion, and distrust among the various segments of a society and thus limits more complete cooperation.
6. Because a sense of being a significant member of society often depends on one's place on the prestige ladder of the society, social stratification systems create an unequal distribution of the sense of significant membership.
7. When loyalty depends on feeling as though one is a significant member of society, stratification tends to unevenly distribute loyalty in society.
8. Because participation may depend on the sense of being a significant member of the society, stratification functions to unequally distribute the motivation to participate among the population.

Of course, beyond the debate over the functions or dysfunctions of stratification lies the fundamental disagreement between conflict theorists and structural functionalists. Here the structural functionalists suggest that stratification is necessary and desirable. As we have seen in the previous chapter, and earlier in this one, wealth and power are very unequally distributed, even in the United States, as are many other rewards and risks. From the conflict perspective this supports their theory that, far from always acting in the best interest of society, the elites often act in their own best interests at the expense of the rest of society.

In the following section we focus on a dimension of stratification that is of great social and sociological significance: poverty. Following that we move on to consider who attains high status in the United States and why.

What Are the Causes and Consequences of Poverty?

AMERICA: HOME OF THE HOMELESS

> Please pause to think about what homeless means. Home less. I am less a home. I am less, because I am without a home. I am without a home. My family is homeless. Think about emptiness, hopelessness. Think about feeling demeaned. Think about being utterly and completely rejected by your fellow members of society (Jonas, 1986).

In virtually every major city of the United States one finds homeless people—a man with two sets of clothes on, sleeping on a park bench or a woman with two shopping bags, warming herself over a heating grate.

Who are these people who are without basic shelter? Based on personal attributes and life history, they have been divided into four subgroups: street people, skid row alcoholics, the chronically mentally ill, and

The plight of the homeless has finally captured the attention of both private and governmental agencies. Between 250 and 300 thousand persons in the United States subsist on the streets. *(Photo courtesy the author)*

the situationally homeless, including those who are unemployed, transient, or recently evicted from their previous home (P. Fischer, et al 1986). Street people and "drunken bums" are the groups one "expects" to see in large cities. The mentally ill and the situationally homeless are the groups that are growing and changing the nature of homelessness in the United States.

As more mentally ill people populate the streets, the usual image of the street dweller has changed from the drunken bum to the potentially dangerous "crazy" person. How did this happen? In 1955, there were 559,000 mental patients in public hospitals. In 1980, there were 146,000. This was the result of a policy of "deinstitutionalization" that proposed to build community mental health centers all over the country, originally built with federal money and later taken over by the local catchment districts (Harrington, 1984). As President Kennedy envisioned it, "Reliance on the cold mercy of custodial isolation will be supplanted by the open warmth of community concern and capability." Instead of warehousing our mentally ill, we would care for them as outpatients, surrounding them with supportive services and integrating them as much as possible into the world again.

What happened instead was that public fear made building many of the centers impossible; not enough funds were earmarked for support services; and the hospitals released the patients anyway, with the result that many of our large cities had their streets turned into unofficial mental wards. The slow movement of the federal government in funding the centers that were being built, including President Nixon's halting the processing of grant applications in 1973 and impounding funds for the support of already existing centers, added to make the task at hand impossible (Ossorio, 1986). The end result is that today 37 percent of the homeless suffer from a diagnosable mental illness (Fischer, 1986). When calling for solutions to this problem, New York City Mayor Edward Koch said, "The city can no longer afford to have its neighborhoods used as mental wards and its police officers used as orderlies" (Harrington, 1984, p. 102).

One unsatisfactory solution is the reinstitutionalization of these people in nursing homes or "adult homes," which are often worse than the state hospitals the patients have just left. Still other patients are housed in the few SROs, or single room occupancy hotels, operated in run-down neighborhoods of the large cities. Most patients housed in such facilities are funded through Supplemental Security Income (SSI), which is a federal program, thus taking the financial burden off the states without improving the lot of the patients.

The irony of the situation is that homelessness creates more mental illness, being a stress on even well-functioning persons. As one mental health practitioner stated, "Sleeping under bridges, going without needed nutrition and health care—in a word, homelessness—is dangerous to individual and public health" (Ossorio, 1986). Because at any one time approximately 60 percent of those housed in emergency shelters are children (Barthel, 1985), one must stop to contemplate what kinds of adults are being created with our present homeless situation. One study of homeless families, for instance, showed that 50 percent of homeless children had developmental lags, anxiety, depression, learning difficulties, and other psychiatric disorders (Bassuk, et al., 1986). Seventy-one percent of the mothers in the same group had personality disorders. Certainly some percentage of these persons had emotional problems before their homeless situation, but it is indisputable that being homeless creates mental anguish.

Experts debate about exactly how many homeless persons live in the United States. Although the Department of Housing and Urban Development states that between 250,000 and 300,000 persons are without a home in the United States today, homeless advocates estimate closer to 2 million (Irwin, 1986). With shelters for the homeless reporting such figures as a 25 to 50 percent increase in one year for shelter and a 30 percent increase for emergency food assistance, it is probable that those who work with the problem daily have a more accurate knowledge of its extent (DeVries, 1986). It has even been suggested that the government figures remain low in order to send a message to the public and policymakers that the problem is not so bad that one should worry about it (Irwin, 1986).

In the "Sociologists at Work" section at the end of the chapter, we learn of Peter Rossi's novel approach to locating and counting the homeless of the United States.

WHAT IS POVERTY?

Besides the growth in homeless de-institutionalized persons, many more people are now "situationally poor." These include the "working poor," the young unemployed, and those who have been working but are often laid off from their unskilled jobs (Harrington, 1984). The link between lack of work or poorly paid work and homelessness is strong. Sociologist Peter Rossi states that the problem is not simply homelessness, but extreme poverty, particularly among people without family support systems (Rossi, in Irwin, 1986). In order to fully understand why so many persons in the land of opportunity are without basic shelter, we must evaluate the situation of poverty today.

The profession of social work began in the United States as a way of determining the difference between the "worthy" and the "unworthy" poor, so that philanthropists would not feel their money was wasted when donated to those less fortunate than themselves. Debate over the definition of poverty still rages. Survey data indicates that most Americans still believe that poverty is a result of the shortcomings of those who are poor, and are reluctant to have their tax money spent on the poor (Hess, 1983).

Economists have devised several complicated systems for determining the poverty level, partly so the government will have some method of determining who should get various forms of public assistance (Moon & Smolensky, 1977; Perlman, 1976).

In 1985 the official federal government's poverty line was income below $10,989 for a family of four living in an urban setting. This amount represents the *absolute deprivation* level, which means this *money is needed for essential health care, housing, and clothes.* In 1985, the median income for all families was $27,735. Those living in poverty, therefore, had less than 40 percent of the income of the average family. Fully 14 percent of American families in 1985 fell below the official poverty line (U.S. Bureau of the Census, 1985). The federal government's official definition of the poverty line rises with rises in the cost of living. As Figure 9.2 shows, the official minimum wage is not, nor has it been, sufficient to keep one from poverty.

Another measure of poverty is *relative deprivation, a level based on the "normal" standard of living in society rather than on deprivation of essentials.* For example, it is considered normal to own a television set and an automobile and to eat out occasionally. These are obviously not essential to maintaining life, as are shelter

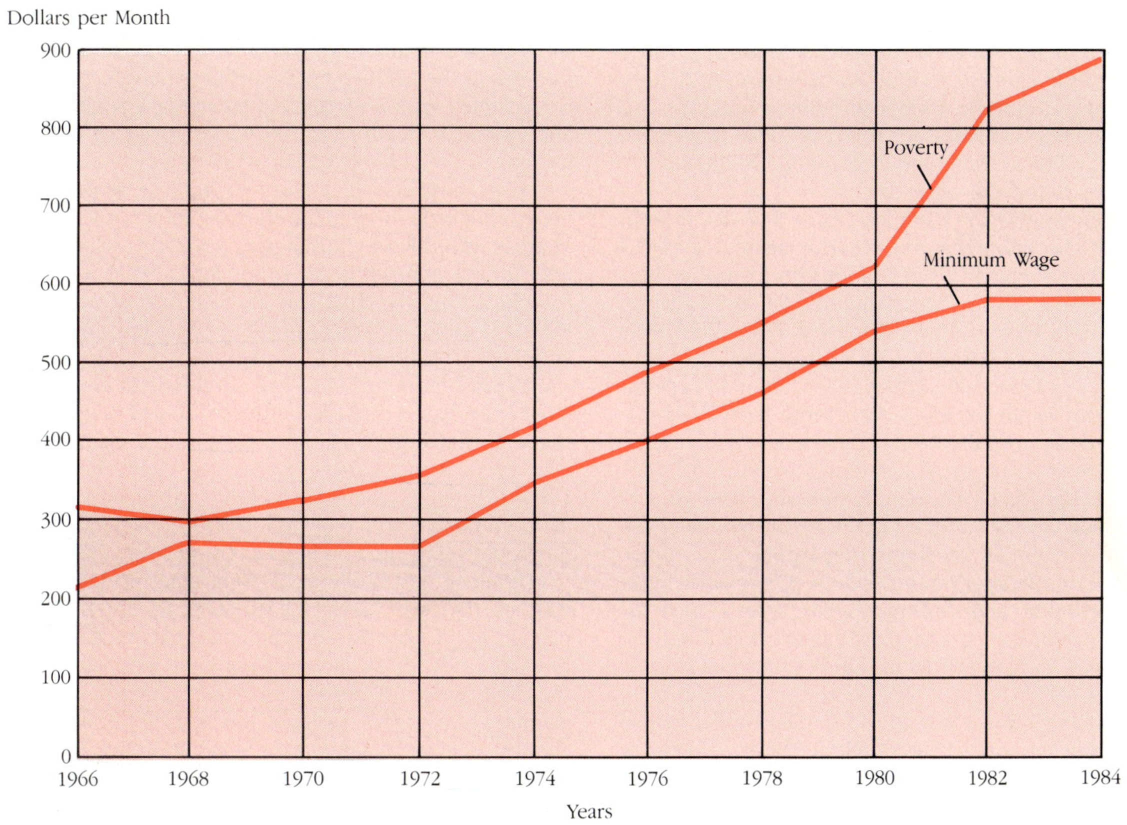

FIGURE 9.2 Monthly Income: Poverty versus Minimum Wage. This figure graphically demonstrates the rapid rise in the poverty level in dollars per month and the inability of the minimum wage to provide an escape from poverty. SOURCE *The American Profile Poster.* New York: Random House, 1986.

and basic food, but families that are unable to have these stand apart from the norm and do not participate as fully in the life of the society. In 1978, it would have required $13 billion (about as much as Americans spend on cigarettes every year) to raise all families above the official poverty level. Obviously, it would require more to raise all families to a normal standard of living.

The percentage of poor has fluctuated since the War on Poverty was declared. In 1959, 19 percent of all American families were deemed poor by the official government guidelines. This number moved downward from 1965 to 1974, and then began to rise during the 1980s, standing at 14 percent in 1986 (Hess, 1983; Pear, 1986). The incidence of poverty during this time period was greatly reduced among the elderly, Southerners, farm families, and residents of Appalachia, but was only slightly altered for whites in general and for large families (Hess, 1983). The poverty of the elderly was eased considerably by amendments to the Social Security Act of 1965 and the introduction of Medicare. These changes have reduced poverty among this group from 35 percent in 1959 to 15 percent today. During this same time period, the number of millionaires in the United States doubled, creating a situation in which 28 percent of the nation's personal wealth is held by 2.8 percent of the adult population (Internal Revenue Service, 1985).

NEAR POVERTY

Along with those who are officially defined as poor and eligible for various forms of assistance are millions more who are what is termed "near poor," with incomes just above the poverty level (*Consumer Reports,* 1987). One such family was described in a recent article. The father once earned his living in his own business installing ceramic tile, bringing home about $2,000 a month. In 1981, industry around him had a difficult time, and his business went bankrupt. He now works as a janitor in a school, and brings home $1,116 a month. His wife does not work, because their three children all have childhood diabetes and frequently require her round-the-clock care.

They receive food stamps worth $87 per month. Because the father has no medical insurance at his work, they spend $160 per month on insurance premiums. Added to this is their monthly bill for medicines and insulin, which often totals over $200. They owe over $16,000 to hospitals and doctors, and pay off a few dollars each month as they can. Their rent, utilities, food, and health expenses total more than their pay almost every month. When they need clothes, their father brings home unclaimed things from the lost-and-found at his school. This family that once took trips to places like Disneyland now has only one source of entertainment. On Friday nights, they gather $2 in change and buy one-quarter pound each of cheese puffs, pretzels, corn nuts, and sunflower seeds, spread them out on a tray for treats, and play Yahtzee together. The number of families facing this kind of financial stress is growing.

The median income for all families had dropped in the past decade, in 1984 dollars. The percentage of families with income between $20,000 and $50,000 declined from 53 percent in 1973 to 48 percent in 1984 (*Consumer Reports*, 1987). Many of these families lost enough income to place them in the working class rather than the middle class. As in the case of families who are "near poor," these former-middle-class families have been adversely affected by changes in the economic structure over which they have no control.

CONSEQUENCES OF POVERTY

The consequences of poverty are all too easy to predict. The poor have inadequate medical care, housing, educational opportunities, and protection against crime; they also face harassment from the justice system itself.

Few physicians locate offices in the poor sections of town, and most discourage the poor as patients. As a result, poor people often depend on free clinics and hospital emergency rooms for health care. Clinics are notoriously understaffed, slow, inadequately housed, and drowning in red tape required by the government and other groups that support them. A clinic patient rarely sees the same medical worker twice, so follow-up is often impossible.

Not surprisingly, the poor have higher rates of tuberculosis, physical disability and impairment, infant death, and chronic illness. The poor also lack adequate dental care, which can cause still other physical problems. Adjusting for variables in age and education of the parents, infant birth weight, order of birth, and number of the mother's previous pregnancies, poverty is associated with a 50 percent greater risk of neonatal and postnatal death than that experienced by infants not born into poverty (Gortmaker, 1979).

Poor nutrition is a chronic problem among the poor. With little money, the cheapest food must suffice. There is widespread vitamin deficiency and lack of protein among poor children (J.S. Clark, 1971). Lack of protein during the first year and one-half of a child's life may cause permanent physical and mental damage (Winick, 1976). Although malnutrition early in life causes retardation in brain-cell development and other biochemical abnormalities in the brain, recent research suggests that enriching the child's environment later *may* prevent permanent behavioral scars (Winick, 1980). The poor spend 40 percent of their income for food, compared to 11 percent for those Americans in the upper-tenth income bracket (Blumberg, 1980).

Inadequate plumbing, heating, and insulation, as well as diseased carriers such as rats, are housing plagues of the poor. It has been estimated that 4 million housing units for the poor do not have indoor plumbing, and about 18 percent of Americans live in substandard housing (Ficker and Graves, 1971). Ironically, the poor also spend a higher percentage of their income on housing than do those in the middle and upper classes.

The poor are also overrepresented in the ranks of those who are preyed upon by crime. High-crime areas are not areas where middle-class people are victimized, but areas where poor people are attacked, beaten, and robbed by other poor people. Furthermore, the poor have a greater chance of being arrested, less chance to be released without bail, and more chance of going to jail for the same crime as those who are better off (Cratsley, 1972). Recent research shows that the strongest correlate to violent crime is a socioeconomic inequality between races, which may give rise to a culture of violence (Blau & Blau, 1982). Perhaps, then, the inherent inequalities of our stratification system create the conditions for violence to grow.

Generally, the more training people have, the more money they earn and the more able they are to change jobs and locations. Very little career planning is done in American schools, in marked contrast to other countries where children are screened, selected, and channeled into appropriate training programs early so that everyone who is educated will have a worthwhile and marketable skill. Middle-class and upper-class students in the United States are given guidance by friends, family, and paid professionals in regard to career choice. Thus, in 1981, 53 percent of children from families with incomes of $25,000 or above attended college (U.S. Bureau of the Census, 1981). In contrast, a student from a poor family may actually be encouraged to drop out of school to help support brothers and sisters. Only 25 percent of children in families with incomes less than $10,000 attended any college.

Several researchers have suggested that our education system requires a more rigorous attempt to raise students' employment opportunities and earning power by "improving their abilities to communicate in words and numbers" while pointing them in some occupational direction (Perlman, 1976). Until this becomes a priority, education is another area where the poor finish last.

WHO ARE THE POOR?

RACE AND ETHNICITY. Discrimination is a definite factor in poverty. Although 66 percent of all poor people are white, blacks in America have three times the chance of becoming poor as whites do, and Hispanics have twice the chance. Because blacks and Hispanics are a more recognizable minority, discrimination against them in hiring is more probable than against other, less easily distinguishable, minorities. In 1985 the percentage of blacks living in poverty dropped slightly, from 32 to 29 percent, and the percentage of Hispanics rose from 28 to 29 percent (U.S. Bureau of the Census, 1986). In this same year, 9 percent of whites were officially classified as poor. Figure 9.3 graphically depicts the composition of the population living in poverty.

CHILDREN. The situation is especially difficult for the children of minorities. Twenty-two percent of all American children are poor, but for Hispanic children the number is 40 percent, and for black children 50 percent (U.S. Bureau of the Census, 1985). It should give all Americans pause to think that one out of every five American babies is born into a poor household, despite recent gains in battling poverty.

WOMEN. Women are twice as likely as men to be poor. In 1980, 38 percent of white families and 65 percent of black families below the poverty level were headed by women. Some of these poor women are unwed mothers raising their children alone. Although the black teenage pregnancy rate declined from 1960 to 1980, the rate of white teenagers doubled during that time period (Hess, 1983).

FIGURE 9.3 Ethnicity and Poverty, 1973–1985. SOURCE U.S. Bureau of the Census, 1986, *Statistical Abstract.*

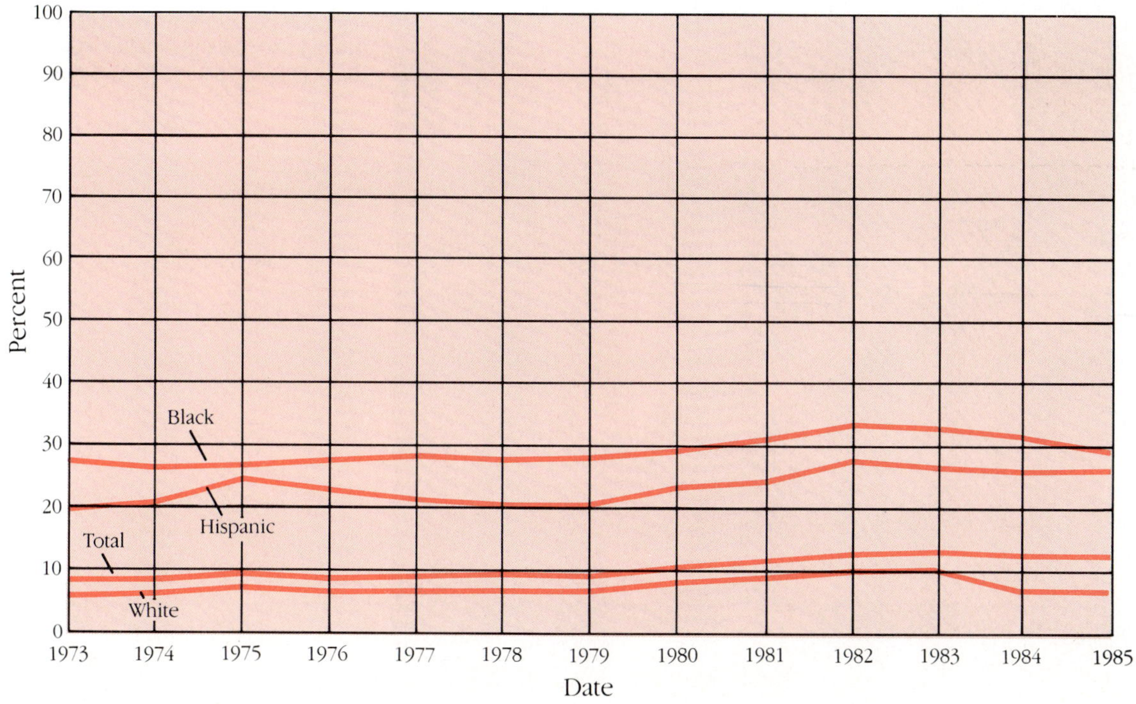

Previously married but now divorced mothers are also at risk for poverty. Only about 60 percent of mothers are awarded child support, and only half of those receive full payment, with 28 percent receiving nothing. The average amount received in any calendar year is $2,000, obviously not enough on which to raise a family. A mother with two preschool children working at minimum wage is often barely able to pay for child care and travel expenses, let alone keep her family cared for in terms of basic needs.

Displaced homemakers are divorced, deserted, or widowed women whose children are over 18, making them ineligible for Aid to Families with Dependent Children (AFDC) while they are usually too young for Social Security benefits. They often have few marketable skills or contacts in the marketplace that would allow them to find lucrative work. The combination of situations of these three groups of women has led to the finding that "the single most important predictor of economic well-being for women is marriage or a stable wage earner" (Hess, 1983, p. 29).

THE AGED. Although the percentage of aged poor has dropped, older workers who are laid off from work or forced to retire early have greater difficulty finding alternative work and may become poor. With inflation reducing the spending power of their pensions, the incomes of the elderly often do not match their needs. In 1984, 14 percent of those over 65 had incomes below the government poverty level.

WHY IS THERE POVERTY IN THE UNITED STATES?

ECONOMIC EXPLANATIONS. The causes of poverty have been debated by social theorists and philosophers for centuries. No society has ever been completely free of poverty, and it is likely that none ever will be. It has been argued that poverty is part of the natural order of things; that it purifies society (Sumner, 1883). The stratification structure itself, which tends to create inequalities of opportunity, helps ensure the continuation of poverty. Other causes include continual unemployment and discrimination.

Many of the poor are perpetually unemployed. This is often due to lack of specific training for jobs as well as to the increase in mechanization of lower-paying jobs. Furthermore, when they work the poor often have jobs that pay little and have no fringe benefits or security provisions like pension plans. This means that their working days are not as productive for themselves and their families as those of the middle class.

Unwilling to work? Robert Berry camped out overnight in Indianapolis during mid March to be first in line for a possible job. (*AP Laserphoto*)

Over 40 percent of the poor work in jobs that have no unemployment compensation, so that when they are out of work they are out of money, unlike those one step up the ladder in the working class, whose jobs are likely to be covered by compensation up to about half of their pay.

Sometimes the poor are underemployed. *Underemployment* exists *when people accept lower-skilled and lower-paying work than their abilities enable them to perform because work at their level of skill and training is unavailable.* The number of people in this group is growing, partly due to the factors Beth Hess points out: "the shift from labor-intensive to capital-intensive industries, segmented labor markets, the flight of the middle class from urban centers, banking and real estate practices, and extended life expectancy" (Hess, 1983). Approximately 40 percent of those living below the poverty line work full-time but do not earn enough to support their families. A person working forty hours a week at a minimum-wage job, for instance, would earn only $7,280 in a year. Since 1978, the number of full-time workers with income below the poverty line has doubled. Over 2 million people currently work full-time year-round and yet earn wages that are below the poverty level (*Consumer Reports,* 1987).

CULTURE OF POVERTY. Some of the consequences of poverty discussed earlier can also be seen as causes. With higher prices for poorer health care and housing, with poor nutrition and education, and with little chance for opportunities outside their subculture, the poor could easily feel that they face a hopeless task.

Some theorists suggest there is a "culture of poverty" which includes a sense of helplessness and a narrow outlook on life (Moynihan, 1968; Rainwater, 1968). According to this argument, short-term problems plague the poor, such as how to feed the family for the rest of the week when money and food are gone. These may eclipse larger issues, such as how to get into a training program that might lead to higher wages and more secure employment. Furthermore, the poor may have become discouraged by years of trying ineffectually to better themselves, thus transmitting an antiambition message to their children. The poor have limited experience outside the culture of poverty, and few contacts with those who have succeeded; this is likely to create a feeling that "nobody makes it" and it is foolish to even try. Theorists who subscribe to this view believe such ideas must be changed before there can be any real change in the status of the poor. In effect, the poor must be "reacculturated."

The idea of a culture of poverty fits into the structural-functionalist framework easily. This theory would suggest that those with more ability will naturally rise to the top of the system and receive more rewards. Conversely, those with little to offer society will sink to the bottom, and perpetuate this "culture" in their families, which will also presumably have little in the way of resources or talents to offer society.

BLAMING THE VICTIM. Lately, many sociologists are questioning these conclusions. The alternative proposal, suggested by conflict theorists, is that the shared characteristics of the poor may be a result of their poverty rather than the cause of it. It has been suggested, for example, that certain social welfare agencies and their employees have a vested interest in continuing poverty, because its existence provides them with employment (Roby, 1974). In defense of this line of thought, Seligman points out that if the money that the federal government is now spending on poverty programs was given directly to poor people instead of paid out in salaries of federal and state workers, the incomes of all the poor would be raised above the poverty line, and a surplus of $25 billion would exist (Seligman, 1984). Some conflict researchers have even suggested that the culture of poverty theory is a form of blaming the victim, rather than the perpetrator, for the crime.

In his books *Blaming the Victim* (1971) and *Equality* (1982), William Ryan says that social ills are often blamed on some defect in the person who is struggling with the social problem, rather than on the stratification system itself or the power struggles inherent in it. Ryan's ideas have been well received by many sociologists and have set off a new debate concerning social definitions. Here are some of his points:

> [Blaming the victim] is a brilliant ideology for justifying a perverse form of social action designed to change, not society, as one might expect, but rather society's victim.
>
> All of this happens so smoothly that it seems downright rational. First, identify a social problem. Second, study those affected by the problem and discover in what ways they are different from the rest of us as a consequence of deprivation and injustice. Third, define the differences as the cause of the social problem itself. Finally, of course, assign a government bureaucrat to invent a humanitarian action program to correct the differences.

How Are We Responding to Poverty?

THE WELFARE SYSTEM: MYTHS AND REALITIES

"Most people on welfare are black." "Welfare mothers have lots of children in order to 'make more money.' " "Families stay on welfare for years and generations."

"Most people on welfare *could* work if they wanted to, but they are too lazy."

The false statements above are so commonly voiced that we rightfully term them myths. Actually: Sixty-four percent of those receiving welfare payments in the United States are white. Most welfare mothers have one or two children. Most of the families who receive AFDC do so for two years or less. And finally, 60 percent of welfare recipients are children, old people, or people who have been determined by government standards to be disabled and unable to work.

The average monthly payment to a welfare family of four in 1985 was $342, ranging from $104 in Mississippi to $495 in Minnesota. This is little more than subsistence living, certainly not something people would aspire to (U.S. Bureau of the Census, 1987). Although there are noncash benefit programs along with most welfare programs, fewer than 60 percent of all poor households are enrolled in them, and most of those are involved in free lunch programs for their children and food stamps (Hess, 1983). With the average monthly food stamp benefit per person being $45, it is obvious that these programs are not financially lucrative (*Consumer Reports,* 1987).

Some states, like Massachusetts, have developed an active Employment and Training Choices Program (ET) which has helped find jobs for some 30,000 welfare recipients. Mothers who found a job through ET, however, earn an average of $15 a week more by working than by staying on welfare—a total of $8,568, still $2,000 below the official poverty line (Terry, 1986). As long as their wages are so low, the problems of poverty, the threat of homelessness, inadequate nutrition, poor medical care, low-quality education, and so on, will continue to plague these "workfare" families. Added to this low rate of pay, either for work or as assistance, is the fact that the poorest tenth of the population pays an average tax rate of 29 percent, whereas the wealthiest tenth pays 25 percent (*The New Republic,* 1985). This means that they not only earn less, they keep a smaller proportion of the little they earn.

What Is the Situation Regarding Social Mobility in the United States?

RECENT GOVERNMENT RESPONSE

Since 1981, the minimum wage has been fixed at $3.35 an hour, but inflation has brought higher living costs, leading to a wider gap between the poverty level and those who work full-time at poverty wages (see Figure 9.3).

Some observers feel that changes during the Reagan Administration have contributed to this situation. First, the greatest recession since the Depression of the 1930s occurred in 1981–1982, and greatly increased unemployment and underemployment, leading to loss of taxes. The instability of the worldwide economic picture during Reagan's time in the White House also contributed to difficulty controlling inflation and stimulating growth. The Tax Reform Act of 1981 substantially helped those in the higher income brackets and hurt those in the lower ones. For example, those in the highest income quintile received approximately 9 percent more income in 1984 than they did in 1980. During that same time period, the share of the lowest income quintile fell 8 percent (S. Rose, 1986). Thus, the average family with income greater than $50,000 reduced its tax bill by about $2,000, whereas the family with an income of $18,000 received a "tax break" of only $100.

Social maintenance programs for the poor were sharply curtailed under Reagan. Changes in eligibility criteria brought an 11 percent reduction in the number of AFDC cases, and those who are still helped by this form of welfare have lost ground, because the payments have not kept up with inflation. Thus, whereas 15 percent of children were born into poverty in the 1970s, 22 percent of all children now reside in poor households (S. Rose, 1986).

What social mechanisms keep the poor poor and the rich rich? Who makes it up the ladder of success, and why? In describing the social class system of the United States we have touched directly or indirectly on some answers to these questions. In the following subsection we direct our full attention to understanding who is likely to be socially mobile and what the consequences of social mobility are for the person who moves up or down the social ladder. In the last chapter, on stratification and mobility, we considered social mobility from the macro, or societal, level. We found that several factors, including changes in the stratification system itself, could help explain why some societies have more social mobility than others. We now move to the more personal, micro level and consider social mobility from the perspective of the individual.

THE MICRO PERSPECTIVE: EXPLAINING INDIVIDUAL MOBILITY

Who moves up? Who moves down? Who stays put? In general, how do adults get their social status? For decades sociologists have sought to explain individual social mobility in the United States. Peter Blau and Otis Duncan pioneered the research in this area with their classic: *The American Occupational Structure* (1967). Studying the actual experiences of thousands of young men, they found a person's social status to be strongly influenced by four factors: (1) how much education one receives, (2) the status of one's first occupation, (3) how much education one's father received, and (4) the status of the father's occupation.

Various researchers have followed in Blau and Duncan's footsteps. *Research* ***replication*** *occurs when investigators apply the theory and research design of an earlier study to a new set of subjects.* Several research teams, including one composed of William Sewell, Archibald Haller, and George Ohlendorf (1970) have replicated the Blau and Duncan study and added some additional factors they believed would help explain status. These included intelligence, or mental ability, and the influence of significant others, such as friends and relatives.

To test their model, Sewell, Haller, and Ohlendorf gathered data from one-third of all males who graduated from Wisconsin high schools in 1957. They diagrammed their rather complicated theory indicating with arrows where they believed the strong causal (cause–effect) relations would be. The diagram of their theory appears as Figure 9.4. The numbers that accompany the arrows in a path diagram are called *path coefficients* and are calculated from research data. A zero indicates the theorists were wrong—there was no relationship observed between the two variables. A higher path coefficient indicates a stronger relationship. This study of a path-analysis diagram showed that significant others seem to have a strong effect (.508) on level of educational aspiration. This in turn was a strong predictor (.457) of educational attainment. Educational attainment was also a strong influence (.522) on occupational attainment. The strongest relationship (.589) in the model was between mental ability and academic performance. On the other hand, some relationships were weak, such as that between the level of occupational aspiration and occupational attainment (.152).

Sewell's research confirms and extends the Blau and Duncan model, but even by their own estimates these models explain only about one-third of the process by which status is determined. This leaves a good deal of room for better theories or better ways to measure the concepts in existing theories.

One can easily get confused in the maze of statistical techniques employed by modern sociologists, but we should keep our wits about us and look critically at the ideas sociologists advance. Generally we more readily notice mistakes that are present than mistakes that involve items missing. What is missing from the Blau and Duncan or the Sewell, Haller, and Ohlendorf approaches? Later chapters will document the enormous impact of gender and race on social status. The research we have discussed here does not introudce either of these variables.

Furthermore, we may intuitively sense that the status of one's parents should have a major effect on the status of the child, yet Blau and Duncan find no data to support this. Probably the functionalist defini-

FIGURE 9.4 Path diagrams map the relationships between variables. The numbers next to the arrows are path coefficients indicating the strength of the relationship between factors. Larger numbers indicate stronger causes. Here, the strongest influence on Occupational Attainment, is seen to be Educational Attainment. SOURCE Adapted from Sewell, Haller, and Ohlendorf, 1970, p. 1023; used with permission of the American Sociological Association and the authors.

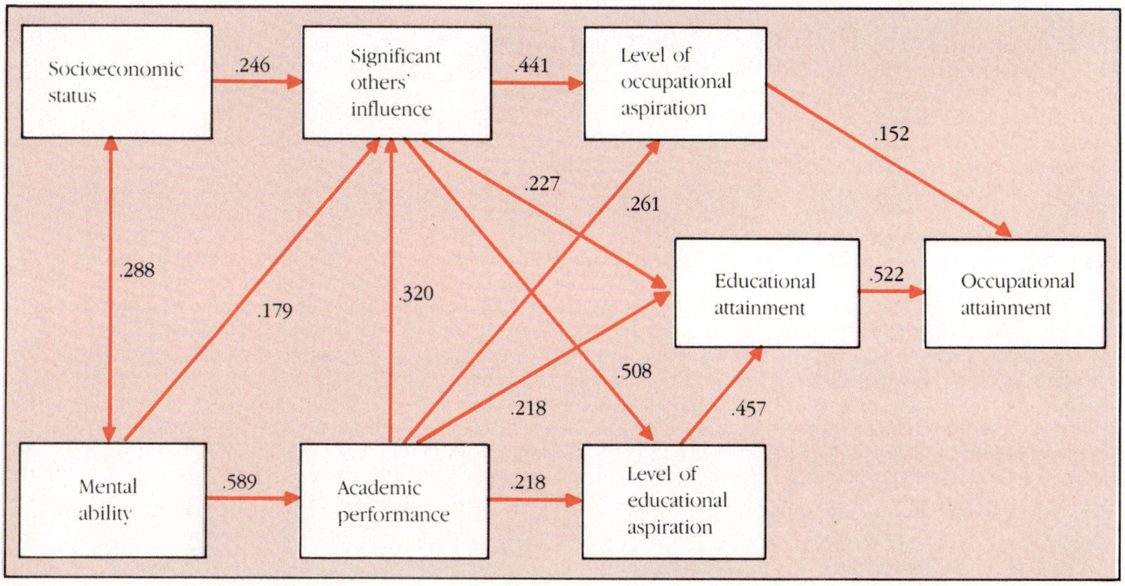

Sociologists at Work •

PETER ROSSI
ENUMERATES AND DESCRIBES CHICAGO'S HOMELESS
Director, Social and Demographic Research Institute
University of Massachusetts
Amherst, Massachusetts

Former president of the American Sociological Association Peter Rossi concentrates his energies on applying sociology to practical concerns such as prison and welfare reform. Known for his ingenuity in tackling tricky problems, Rossi here turns his attention to the homeless.

Tell Us About Some of Your Current Research.
Recently I've done a dual purpose study of homeless persons in Chicago to estimate the total number of homeless persons in Chicago and to provide a description of the social characteristics of homeless persons. Conventional sample survey technique assumes that everybody has an address or a telephone number where they can be reached. That assumption simply does not hold by definition for homeless persons, so we worked out a sampling strategy based upon non-dwelling units.

How Did You Locate These Wandering People?
The survey consisted of two parts: a sample of people who were housed in the shelters and a sample of blocks in Chicago. Interviewers accompanied by an off-duty policeman made a thorough search of all the non-dwelling-unit places on a block; alleys, garages, abandoned buildings, hallways, roofs, basements, parked cars, boxcars, park benches, viaducts, and the like. We did this between the hours of midnight and 6 A.M. so that anybody that was encountered was most likely to be a homeless person. When we met someone who was homeless, we conducted a twenty-minute interview, picking up their social characteristics, how long they've been unhomed, a short measure of the psychiatric disability, signs of unusual and bizarre thinking, as well as depression and the like.

Did You Find as Many Homeless as People Had Estimated?
We found that there were far fewer homeless persons in Chicago than the 15 to 25 thousand that advocates for the homeless had been guessing. We found less than 3,000.

I can understand how they reached those estimates, however, because there is a much larger number of persons who travel through the homeless condition during a year than you can find at any point in time. The 3,000 figure is the homeless at a point in time. If we took all persons who became homeless for an entire year, that number would be up around 10,000. More than one-third of the persons we encountered were homeless for less than two months. The average time that a person is homeless is something on the order of sixteen months.

What Is the Typical Homeless Person Like?
Three main characteristics of the homeless stand out: extreme poverty, disability, and disaffiliation. The average income for the month before the interview was $3 a day.

The second characteristic is a very large amount of disability of one kind or another. One-third have been hospitalized in a mental institution for a long period of time, more than four or five days. We found a very high incidence of disordered thinking, for instance, people would say "I hear voices." They often exhibit very serious depression, which may be, to some degree, a reaction to the depressing environment in which the homeless live. We found a very high incidence of tuberculosis and all types of communicable, respiratory diseases, some disability from old accidents, and the like. The third type of disability is substance abuse: alcoholism and drug abuse. More than 80 percent of the homeless were disabled by one of these three types of disability.

The third characteristic we found is disaffiliation. The homeless are also generally familyless: they either have rejected their families or been rejected by their families. It appears that homelessness is a condition that hits the extremely poor who have high levels of disability and extreme difficulty in getting along with other persons.

What Else Did You Find?
Another interesting thing that we found is that most of these persons were eligible for some kind of public welfare but very few of them had it, because they could not connect with the Department of Public Aid, which is three miles from where the homeless congregate. Bus fare in Chicago is 90 cents and the average amount of per capita daily cash of the homeless is less than $3. You can see that getting on a bus to get down to the public welfare, even if they knew where it was, is somewhat beyond their ability to pay. The Department of Public Aid shifted its policy and has now been sending representatives to the shelters to enroll people on public aid. General assistance in Illinois at $154 a month certainly is not enough to make anybody comfortable, but it is better than zero. ●

tion of social status, which assumes social class is adequately measured by occupation, is at fault. Occupations may not pass directly from father to son, but ownership often does, and Blau and Duncan and their followers ignore this factor. In their research, Robinson and Kelley (1979) introduce a conflict-perspective definition of class that combines Marx's idea that the most important class variable is ownership of the means of production with Ralf Dahrendorf's belief that authority over other people is the key class variable. Using ownership and authority as class variables, Robinson and Kelley find they can improve the predictive ability of the Blau and Duncan model by as much as 50 percent. This offers support for the conflict theory and helps support their claim that, at least in Britain, there are "two overlapping but distinct stratification systems, one a class system rooted in ownership of the means of production and authority, and the other a status system based on education and occupational status" (Robinson & Kelley, 1979, p. 38).

What Are the Consequences of Mobility?

There are important consequences of social mobility besides changes in prestige, power, and property (which themselves constitute social mobility). One might expect downward social mobility to be difficult for a person. Losing the respect of others and living within reduced means creates great stress.

On the other hand, one might expect upward mobility always to be a happy or gratifying experience, but for several reasons, it, too, can be difficult for a person. An upwardly mobile individual must either be resocialized to the ways of the new social stratum or be frequently at odds with these new peers. Different social classes have significantly different attitudes about important issues like politics, religion, and childrearing.

Besides having to deal with these new customs and attitudes, an upwardly mobile person often tries to live in two social worlds while remaining somewhat a stranger in both. The upwardly mobile person is not as accustomed to the norms of the higher class as those born in it. At the same time, by leaving the lower position the individual becomes somewhat estranged from those who remain there. Few upwardly mobile individuals can bring their families and friends with them up the ladder; this leaves them living in two social worlds. That this can create significant emotional distress is indicated by the fact that the socially mobile are more likely to be institutionalized for emotional disorders (Gallagher, 1980).

Of course, upward mobility is not all bad. It offers increased wealth, prestige, and power. One is able to bring one's spouse and children along. Although the upwardly mobile person may experience some discomfort in the new, higher status, their children probably will not, because they will be socialized into it. They can enjoy their elevated status, unencumbered by the ambiguity of living in different social worlds.

As we see, the area of stratification and mobility provides an especially rich demonstration of how sociologists develop new ways of thinking and proceed to test and develop these ideas through research studies.

Conclusion

Who will survive infancy? Who will die for his or her country? Who will be respected and who denigrated? As we have seen in this chapter, these are largely matters of social class. Social class influences opinions on important issues such as politics, religion, marriage, and childrearing. Social class not only determines the circumstances of our lives, it to a large degree defines who we are and even how we feel. We have also learned that the United States class system is characterized by less opportunity and more inequality and even poverty to the point of homelessness than is often acknowledged.

But we are not just the helpless pawns of an immutable social system. By understanding the nature of stratification, we increase our freedom to rise within the system and to rise above it and reshape it. Knowing the form and the dynamics of the stratification system places us in a better position to understand others and to exercise our own freedom to choose whether, and how, to change our status. By studying stratification we gain an understanding of what the system is and how it works. We can combine the knowledge and ideas we are developing with our moral inspiration to become better architects of our social environment.

Summary Questions

REVIEW

1. How are income and wealth distributed in the United States?
2. How open is the American class structure?
3. What are the major classes in the United States?
4. How does class influence our life chances?
5. How does class influence life-style?
6. What is the situation of the homeless in the United States today?
7. What is the situation of the poor in the United States today?

8. What are the economic causes of poverty?
9. What are the social causes of poverty?
10. What are the social characteristics of the poor?
11. What are the consequences of poverty?
12. What are the facts behind the myths about the welfare system that are commonly believed?
13. How does education affect mobility?
14. What are the consequences of upward mobility?

Summary Answers

1. Income and wealth are disproportionately distributed, with the highest one-fifth of the population receiving 43 percent of the income and owning 77 percent of the wealth while the lowest one-fifth earns 5 percent of the income and owns 0.2 percent of the wealth. This situation has remained fairly stable for a number of years.
2. Conflict theorists regard the United States as having two classes, the owners and the exploited workers, with little movement between them. Structural-functionalists believe that there are a number of classes, which work together for the benefit of society.
3. Upper: distinguished by "old" inherited wealth and high income, equal to 1 percent of the population

   Upper-middle: professionals with graduate training, beyond basic college, and high income—10 percent of the population

   Lower-middle: white-collar office workers and semiprofessionals with some college education—30 percent of the population

   Working class: blue-collar skilled laborers with high-school educations and moderate incomes—40 percent of the population

   Lower class, or poor: often unemployed or underemployed, and poorly educated—20 percent of the population
4. Our class influences how long we will live, because lower classes have high infant mortality, greater probability of job-related deaths, poorer nutrition, more chance of serious illness and emotional disorders, and greater chance of being in trouble with the law.
5. Income affects type and location of housing, with all the benefits and detriments involved. Higher-class persons are more likely to be satisfied with their work, more likely to vote, and more likely to join voluntary associations. They delay marriage, and their marriages are more stable. As parents they tend to stress understanding, self-acceptance, and freedom, and they visit with their extended families less often than lower classes.
6. Between 250,000 and 2 million persons are homeless in the United States today. Four subgroups of homeless persons have been identified: street people, skid row alcoholics, the chronically mental ill, and the situationally homeless, including those who are unemployed, transient, or recently evicted from their previous home. The failure of the community mental health movement accounts for the rise in the number of mentally ill persons on the streets. The facts that 60 percent of those who are homeless are children and that being homeless can be a stress that leads to mental illness should make us concerned about the future of homeless children.
7. In 1985, the official government poverty line was $10,989, and 14 percent of all Americans were classified as poor according to this guideline.
8. Poverty may be a natural part of existence in human society. Chronic unemployment greatly contributes to poverty for most of the poor. Underemployment is also a factor. Over 40 percent of the poor work full-time but earn minimum wage, which places them $3,000 below the poverty threshold. Over 2 million Americans work full-time and live below the poverty level. The median income for American families has dropped in the past decade, and many people have dropped from middle- to working- or poverty-class. Many of these "near poor" families had better-paying jobs when the economy was in better shape.
9. The stratification system that creates inequality of opportunity, unemployment, underemployment, discrimination, and the breakdown of the family all contribute to the growth of poverty. Structural-functionalists see poverty as proving that those with more ability will naturally rise to the top of the system and receive more rewards. Conflict theorists say that the shared characteristics of the poor may be the result of their poverty rather than the cause of it, and that by believing otherwise we are "blaming the victim" of a social ill.
10. Blacks have three times the chance and Hispanics twice the chance of becoming poor as do whites, although 66 percent of all poor people are white. Most poor people are children, with one out of every five American babies being born into poverty. Women are twice as likely as men to be poor, due to teenage pregnancy, divorce, desertion, and being widowed. Although the percentage of aged poor has dropped with changes in the Social Security system and the advent of Medicare, many poor people are older Americans.
11. In comparison to the rest of society, the poor have

worse health care and nutrition, inadequate housing, more chance of being preyed on by crime, less education and training.

12. Sixty-four percent of those receiving welfare payments are white. Most welfare mothers have only one or two children. Most of the families who receive AFDC do so for two years or less. Sixty percent of welfare recipients are children, old people, or those who are classified as disabled. The average monthly payment to a welfare family of four in 1981 was $282. Although workfare programs create jobs and training for welfare recipients, the workers are financially hardly better off due to the low wages paid in such jobs. Although no certain cure for poverty has been found, as a nation we are committed to increasing the chances for change for the poor.

13. Sewell and others have documented a strong relationship between educational attainment and occupational attainment. Furthermore, the influence of an individual's significant others strongly affects his or her educational aspirations, which then affect the individual's final educational attainment.

14. The upwardly mobile person may be happy and gratified at his or her new position, but moving between classes creates emotional distress from trying to live in two different classes at once.

Glossary

absolute deprivation level the amount of money needed for essential health care, housing, and clothes

lower class the bottom of the class system including the unemployed and the working poor

lower-middle class a class of white-collar workers of modest rank and income and semi-professionals

model a theory which can be expressed in mathematical terms so that it can be tested by seeing how well the predictions of the model correspond to what actually happened to the subjects of the study

relative deprivation measure of poverty based on the "normal" standard of living in society rather than on deprivation of essentials

replication research in which researchers apply the theory and research design of an earlier study to a new set of subjects

scale a set of questions found to be useful in measuring a concept

underemployment occurs when people accept lower skilled and lower paying work than their abilities enable them to perform because work at their level of skill and training is unavailable

upper class the highest class in the contemporary U.S. society, distinguished by vast fortunes which have usually been inherited

upper-middle class a class comprised largely of high income professionals such as doctors, lawyers, and high level managers

working class commonly called blue-collar workers, this class includes skilled and unskilled laborers

Suggested Readings

Paul Fussell. 1983. *Class: A Guide Through the American Status System.* New York: Summit Books.

A somewhat lighthearted look at status differences in modern-day United States.

Michael Harrington. 1984. *The New American Poverty.* New York: Penguin Books.

In this update of his poverty study of the 1960s, Harrington states that poverty has not been beaten, but is in fact worse than ever in the "greatest country in the world."

Christopher Jencks, et al. 1979. *Who Gets Ahead: The Determinants of Economic Success in America.* New York: Basic Books.

A study of social mobility that suggests that family background is still vitally important in determining success in the United States.

Charles Murray. 1984. *Losing Ground: American Social Policy, 1950–1980.* New York: Basic Books.

Murray makes a strong case for the idea that the social welfare system as we know it contributes to poverty rather than alleviating it.

Richard Sennett and Jonathan Cobb. 1973. *The Hidden Injuries of Class.* New York: Vintage Books.

A study of working-class America that suggests a strong correlation between working conditions and self-concept.

Ruth Sidel. 1986. *Women and Children Last: The Plight of Poor Women in Affluent America.* New York: Viking.

An excellent overview of the feminization of poverty in the United States, including chapters on the elderly poor woman and day care.

CHAPTER 10

RACE and ETHNIC RELATIONS

- What Is Ethnicity?
- What Is Race?
- What Is a Minority Group?
- What Is the Difference Between Prejudice and Discrimination?
- What Are the Basic Patterns of Race and Ethnic Relations?
- How Does Conflict Theory Explain Intergroup Relations?
- Close-Up Theory: Edna Bonacich's Theory of Ethnic Antagonism: The Split Labor Market
- What Are the Sources and Consequences of Prejudice and Discrimination?
- What Is Happening in the United States in Race and Ethnic Relations?
- What Is the Significance of Race?
- Close-Up on Research: Melvin Thomas and Michael Hughes on the Continuing Significance of Race and Quality of Life
- What Is Affirmative Action?
- Sociologists at Work: William Julius Wilson Identifies the Situation of Families in Poverty Areas

How's Your Sociological Intuition?

1. Which of the following statements is true about racial groups?
   - **a.** Sometimes they live in harmony, whereas in other settings they live in conflict
   - **b.** Some combinations, such as blacks and Caucasians, never get along
   - **c.** Harmony depends solely on the groups' leaders
   - **d.** Harmony has yet to happen anywhere in the world
2. In the 1980s, the black economic picture can be characterized by:
   - **a.** Gains for middle-class blacks and losses for lower-class blacks
   - **b.** Lowered unemployment for blacks
   - **c.** Continuing economic growth
   - **d.** A decrease in the number of blacks living in poverty
3. Regarding differences in incomes of racial groups in the United States, which of these statements is true?
   - **a.** Japanese Americans outearn the average American
   - **b.** Native Americans earn less than blacks
   - **c.** Blacks' income is 75 percent of the average
   - **d.** All of the above
4. In an unprecedented move, during World War II, the United States:
   - **a.** Sent German Americans home
   - **b.** Refused to allow blacks to become soldiers
   - **c.** Held Japanese Americans in "relocation centers"
   - **d.** Put all Italian Americans under FBI surveillance

Answers

1. a. This chapter explains why.
2. a. Increasingly, the black community is splitting into two groups or classes.
3. d. Income varies widely
4. c. About 120,000 Japanese Americans were kept isolated during the war.

When You Have Finished Studying This Chapter, You Should Know:

- The definitions of ethnic group, ethnicity, and race
- The concept of minority group
- The difference between prejudice and discrimination
- How prejudice relates to discrimination
- The basic patterns of race and ethnic relations, including: amalgamation; assimilation; pluralism; structured inequality; population relocation and extermination
- The conflict explanation of race and ethnic relations
- Major concepts and propositions of Bonacich's theory of ethnic antagonism
- Causes and consequences of prejudice and discrimination including socialization, stereotyping, scapegoating, self-fulfilling prophecy, authoritarian personality, and the degree of contact with minority groups
- The history and present status of American minority groups, including blacks, Hispanics, native Americans, Asian Americans, Jewish Americans, and white ethnics
- The significance of race in life chances
- What affirmative action is and what its effects have been

Our students keep journals to relate their experiences and ideas to course topics. The following account is a journal entry from a recent student:

> When I was young, I played baseball for an all-black team. We were the best team in an all-white league and had some of the best players in the league. There was a tournament for boys our age in another town, and our league was going to get an all-star team up to go and play. I was the only player from my team picked to go. This was a real puzzle to me. I couldn't understand why no other player from my team was chosen to play. I knew for sure they were good enough to play.
>
> I went to the first practice, and as I pulled up, every one just kinda stopped what they were doing and watched me walk on to the field. No one said anything; everyone just looked. Finally the coach said, "Hi Dave, welcome to the team." Practice went on, but no one talked to me. I could hardly find someone to play catch with to get loose. No one said anything to me all that day.
>
> The next day everyone met to catch rides to the out-of-town tournament. Everyone was getting into cars with their friends, but I was kinda left standing. No one wanted me to ride with them. So finally the coach told me to jump in with him. So I got in, and we went to the ball park. There were already many teams there playing. We played a few games and I played really well. We had a break, and everyone went to their cars to get picnic baskets filled with food for the players. But no one asked me to come, so I just went to the concession stand and bought a couple of hot dogs. I was just sitting by myself watching other teams play when I noticed that I was the only black person in the ball park. For some reason I lost my appetite. It came time for us to play again and we won a couple more games. Then it was time for the championship game and everyone was very tired. I was the pitcher and I didn't allow any runs, but neither did the other pitcher. It was the last inning and we had a man on second base and I was batting with two outs. All day when I batted no one said one word. But suddenly everyone was cheering for me to get a hit. I was thrilled to hear them cheer for me. So I came through with the hit to win the game. And the whole team ran out on the field and picked me up. Suddenly I had a lot of friends. I was the most valuable player in the whole tournament. After the long day of ball everyone headed back to their cars to get more things to eat and drink. Me, I was heading for the concession stand when everyone yelled, "Hey, Dave, come over here—we have pop and food." And that's when it dawned on me that they were just using me, and they didn't really like me. I turned to them and said, "No thanks," and kept walking to the concession stand (D. Johnson, 1983).

The human race seems to find itself divided into many antagonistic racial groups, and people who cross the boundaries may encounter experiences of being abused or used and feel the loneliness, anger, and alienation that Dave did.

In this chapter we explore the ideas of race, ethnicity, prejudice, and discrimination. Our goal is to understand better why racial and ethnic groups sometimes live and thrive in harmony and sometimes kill and die in discord. We examine racial and ethnic relations in various contexts, emphasizing the United States and its major ethnic groups.

What Is Ethnicity?

As Milton Gordon (1964) points out in his study of assimilation into American society, the word *ethnicity* comes from the Greek *ethnos,* which means people or nation. *An* ***ethnic group*** *thinks of itself as a people or nation, or is viewed by others as culturally different.* ***Ethnicity*** *is a sense of peoplehood or nationhood.* The members of an ethnic group feel themselves set apart from other groups by a sense of belonging together, usually due to shared customs, beliefs, language, or religion.

Ethnicity is a group of characteristics that are culturally transmitted. People think of themselves as Lithuanian because their parents and others have immersed them in the Lithuanian group and they have adopted its customs. They carry on Lithuanian traditions, teach their children Lithuanian words, and enjoy Lithuanian culture because they have been taught to do so, not because of any inherited predisposition to do so. Their sense of ethnicity is socialized.

What Is Race?

Anthropologists define a *race* as a population that has inbred for generations, producing some distinctive physical characteristics. Although this definition seems clear and concise, anthropologists have never agreed on the number of races in the world or the characteristics that distinguish them.

Look closely at any elementary school class photo, and you will see why. The characteristics that are thought to "determine" the race of the children are not clearly defined or divided. Some have dark, straight hair and fair skin, others blond, curly hair and dark eyes, and still others red hair and freckles. None of them "fits" their race type exactly.

Most anthropologists accept, with some reluctance, the division into Caucasoid (the "white" race), Negroid (the "black" race), and Mongoloid (the "yellow" race). All would agree that many genes have been exchanged among human populations, and that the concept of a "pure race" in unacceptable.

The sociological definition of race emphasizes the idea of the population thinking of itself as distinct: A ***race*** *is a population that shares visible physical characteristics from inbreeding and thinks of itself or is thought of by outsiders as distinct.* Differences in physical appearance often lead racial groups to believe they are different in other ways as well. People often claim that other "races" are temperamentally different, biologically inferior, less moral, and lacking or showing certain traits, from "musicality" to "cleanliness."

Although most differences attributed to different races are myths, they are important myths. They have been used by societies for many years to justify poor treatment of nondominant groups.

Although research shows steady progress in less prejudiced attitudes toward blacks, new policies and actions are slow in taking over in United States society. Changes in behavior follow changes in cultural beliefs, but only after the socialization of the next generation into the new belief system, one of the underlying functions of integration in the educational institution. (*Photo courtesy the author*)

Sociologists are interested in the social consequences of race, rather than the biological aspects. They use the term *race* only to locate people according to culturally defined social positions, rather than to define physical communities (P. Rose, 1974).

What Is a Minority Group?

A ***minority group*** *is one that has less power and influence than the dominant group.* To sociologists, minority refers to a difference in power and influence, rather than a difference in size. In fact, a "minority" group often forms a numerical majority, for example, women in the United States. Women outnumber men in our society, yet women have less power and influence. For example, far more men than women hold important positions in business, education, government, and politics. When a woman is appointed to an important position, this is labeled a victory for women's rights and is noteworthy, a fact that suggests the depth of the problem.

Similarly, although approximately 80 percent of the population of the Republic of South Africa is black, blacks are not allowed to vote or to hold high position and therefore have little power in the governmental structure (Hunt & Walker, 1979). Blacks must live in prescribed areas, must carry identification cards at all times, must work only at certain jobs, and must have permission to travel outside their assigned communities. Even though blacks represent a majority of the population, they have a minority of power; therefore, in sociological terms, blacks are a minority group in South Africa.

Often a society's dominant group will justify subjecting a racial or ethnic group to prejudice and discrimination by citing their distinct physical or cultural traits.

What Is the Difference Between Prejudice and Discrimination?

PREJUDICE

***Prejudice** is a judgment based on group membership or social status.* The following statements demonstrate prejudicial thinking:

"I don't expect much from Tony. You know how lazy his kind are."

"Watch out that she doesn't try to knock down your price—you know how they always do."

"Of course she dances well. You know how they all seem to have that natural sense of rhythm."

"She probably caused the accident. You know what lousy drivers women are."

"You aren't going to take his word over mine, are you? You know how forgetful old men are."

Notice that all these statements involve judging an individual on the basis of presumed knowledge about people with similar social status or group membership—not on individuals or on individual circumstances. This judging is not limited to ethnic groups, as several of the statements indicate.

DISCRIMINATION

The United States' Constitution originally provided for Congressional representation on the basis of state population, but Native Americans were not counted, and blacks were counted as three-fifths of a person. Around the turn of the twentieth century, classified newspaper advertisements frequently carried the abbreviation NJNA—No Jews Need Apply. Until the landmark civil rights case of *Brown v. the Topeka, Kansas Board of Education* (1954), blacks in many states were forced to attend separate schools. These are examples of discrimination, which differs from prejudice in that it involves actions rather than judgments. ***Discrimination** involves treating someone differently because of his or her group membership or social status.* Discrimination can also occur at the more personal level.

"I do not intend to sell my home to a black; if one inquires, I will simply tell him that I already have a buyer."

"I wouldn't consider marrying an Oriental."

HOW PREJUDICE AND DISCRIMINATION ARE RELATED

Prejudice and discrimination are closely linked, but they may exist separately. For instance, a business person might refuse to serve people of a particular minority group on the grounds that serving them would cause other customers to stay away, although he does not have prejudice against the minority group. Similarly, prejudice can exist without discrimination, if the prejudiced person is not in a position to take any action against those he or she is prejudiced against. Four variations of these qualities have been suggested (G. Simpson & Yinger, 1985):

1. There can be prejudice without discrimination.
2. There can be discrimination without prejudice.
3. Prejudice can be among the causes of discrimination.
4. Probably most frequently, prejudice and discrimination are mutually reinforcing.

Robert Merton (1976) graphically explains how prejudice and discrimination can interact in Table 10.1.

LaPiere conducted a classic study of the relationship between prejudice and discrimination in which he accompanied a Chinese couple on a trip throughout the United States (1934). During the trip, they visited over 250 hotels and restaurants and were refused service, or were openly discriminated against, at only one of these. Later, when LaPiere wrote to these establishments asking if they would serve Chinese customers, over 90 percent of the owners indicated that they would not welcome Chinese guests. Obviously, the owners were prejudiced against Chinese as a group, but when faced with them as customers, they did not usually show their prejudice by a discriminatory action.

What Are the Basic Patterns of Race and Ethnic Relations?

When groups of different ethnic origin attempt to live in the same area, they usually relate to each other using one of six basic patterns: amalgamation, assimilation, pluralism, structured inequality, population relocation,

TABLE 10.1 Four Ways in Which Prejudice and Discrimination Can Interact in Personalities

	Prejudice	No Prejudice
Discrimination	"All-around bigots"—discriminate in actions and thoughts due to their lack of belief in the values of freedom and equality	"Fair-weather liberals"—not prejudiced, but occasionally discriminate due to status and economic advantages in discrimination
No Discrimination	"Timid bigots"—do not believe in the ideals of freedom and equality, but their fear of legal and social sanctions keeps them from discriminating	"All-weather liberals"—support the ideals of freedom and equality in practice

SOURCE Robert Merton. 1976. "Discrimination and the American Creed." In *Sociological Ambivalence and Other Essays*, New York, Free Press, 189-216.

and extermination. This scheme shows the basic patterns of race and ethnic relations (Simpson & Yinger, 1985).

AMALGAMATION

Amalgamation *refers to the blending of two or more groups into a society that reflects the cultural and biological traits of the group.* A clear example of amalgamation is found in Brazil, where Portuguese and other European settlers blended their cultures with those of native Indians and former black slaves to form a distinct, new Brazilian culture. Members of Brazil's ethnic groups have often intermarried, so that past biological distinctions are no longer apparent. Thus, a new society has formed through amalgamation.

ASSIMILATION

Assimilation *refers to adoption by the minority group of the majority group culture.* There are two types of assimilation: forced and peaceful. Forced assimilation occurs when a majority group outlaws all manifestations of a minority group's culture in an effort to make them conform to the dominant culture more quickly. This occurred in czarist Russia: minorities were not allowed to speak their own languages, attend their own churches, or practice their own customs.

Peaceful assimilation occurs when the minority chooses to assume the dominant group's cultural patterns, and the majority group partakes of the minority group culture at times, as well. French immigrants to the United States, for instance, have given up their distinctive language and most other cultural traits to adopt American ways. At the same time, some Americans have enjoyed becoming "gourmet" cooks by studying French cuisine.

Sometimes newcomers have successfully claimed the role of majority group and forced an area's original inhabitants to assimilate into a new culture. Many Caribbean peoples assimilated British cultural patterns during their colonial period. Today the language, government, and educational systems have a distinctively British tone, but genetic differences between the natives and British settlers remain virtually unchanged.

PLURALISM

Pluralism *occurs when various groups actively participate in the same society while retaining distinctive identities.* In Tanzania, Africans, Europeans, and Middle Eastern peoples participate with relative equality in the public life of their society while retaining distinctive languages and customs. No group dominates the others, and all groups are allowed to participate freely in their own cultures.

STRUCTURED INEQUALITY

Structured inequality *occurs when the minority group receives inferior treatment by law* (de jure) *or by custom* (de facto). Slavery, which was legal in many parts of the United States until 1863, is an example of structured inequality supported by law. And, although racial discrimination is officially outlawed today, *de facto* segregation is still the dominant pattern of black–white relations in the United States.

Pluralism involves various groups actively participating in the same society while retaining distinctive identities. (*AP/Wide World Photos*)

POPULATION RELOCATION

Population relocation *occurs when the minority group relocates either outside the territory or in a particular part of the territory.* Population relocation can be either forced or voluntary. Sometimes relocation creates an entire new nation, as when India divided into India and Pakistan in order to create separate states for Hindu and Muslim citizens. More often, however, one group is forced to leave or decides to leave because of poor treatment in its homeland. For instance, former Uganda President Amin drove all Asians out of his country in the 1970s, even though they had lived there for several generations.

EXTERMINATION

Extermination *occurs when the majority group destroys a minority group.* The best-known example of an attempt to exterminate a population is Nazi Germany's systematic killing of an estimated six million Jews. More recently the Paraguayan government has systematically attempted to destroy the primitive Ache Indians (Arens, 1976). Often extermination attempts occur subsequent to a campaign by the majority group to convince its members that it is dangerous to allow the minority group to live in the area.

How Does Conflict Theory Explain Intergroup Relations?

Why does contact between groups sometimes end in merger and other times in slaughter? This question is important today, when contact between racial and cultural groups is becoming more frequent.

The minority and majority in intergroup relations are defined in terms of power rather than size. When conflict exists between the two groups, the group that gains the most power, wealth, and prestige becomes the majority, regardless of its size relative to the minority.

Conflict theorists see such antagonisms as inevitable between groups that must compete for limited resources in one society. Because conflict is the rule rather than the exception in relations between different race and ethnic groups, the only viable theories of intergroup relations are based on conflict theory.

Five major factors can contribute to such intergroup conflict: These are: visible differences between groups; racist ideology; competition for resources; potential for exploitation; and the minority-group response to the majority definition of the situation.

VISIBLE DIFFERENCES

Several theories can be described by the general proposition: "Similarity promotes harmony." The opposite of this would also be true: "Differences promote conflict." James Vander Zanden (1983) points to "visible differences" between groups in either physical appearance or cultural traits as necessary conditions for racism. He also believes that power differences between the groups greatly determine racism.

Prominent similarities or differences can mold relations between various minorities in the United States, suggesting that assimilation is more likely to occur where a substantial similarity exists between the groups in contact (Warner & Srole, 1945). For example, the Scots, English, and Canadians have all assimilated into the culture of the United States, whereas groups who have darker skin color, speak a language other than English, or subscribe to a non-Christian religion have had more difficulty. Using Vander Zanden's conditions, one of the reasons that the British groups assimilated easily probably is that they have similar physical and cultural backgrounds and approximately the same access to power as the Americans they joined.

RACIST IDEOLOGY

The debate about whether certain groups of people are inherently better than others has gone on at least since the time of Ancient Greece, when Aristotle taught that slavery was a natural social form because some men are rulers and some are slaves by virtue of their differing amounts of native ability to reason. *Inferior treatment on the basis of alleged inferior ability is termed* ***racism.***

For many years it was thought that primitive people could not think logically. Anthropologist Franz Boas's study, *The Mind of Primitive Man* (1965), attacked this myth by showing that the reasoning of primitive people did follow logical lines.

The modern debate in the United States began with the first standardized, objective intelligence test, developed by Alfred Binet and Theodore Simon in 1905. Results varied but were believed to indicate that "American Negroes, Indians, Italians, Portuguese, and Mexicans test definitely below the norm" (Klineberg, 1944).

Although there are differences between races in IQ scores attained on current standardized tests, the range of scores among persons *within* any ethnic or racial group is larger than the difference between the ethnic or racial group and all groups tested (Loehlin, Lindzey, and Spuhler, 1975). The debate over whether or not intelligence is linked to ethnicity has pivoted around two definitions that are not at all agreed upon: intelligence and race. No true "race" exists in today's world, and the definition of intelligence is hotly debated. Even assuming clear definitions, the further assumption that current tests can actually measure intelligence is far from proven. On the contrary, more evidence seems to point to the idea that current testing is inadequate at best and fraudulent at worst.

The strength of the ideology of racism—the belief system that justifies inferior treatment on the basis of alleged inferiority—is an important foundation for unequal and hostile intergroups relations. In South Africa, for example, the ideology of white supremacy is strong. The accepted policy of the powerful white majority is ***apartheid,*** or *strictly enforced separate facilities and privileges for blacks and whites.* Until recently, this policy was only occasionally questioned, supported as it was by the underlying belief that blacks were "naturally" inferior.

COMPETITION

Vander Zanden (1983) believes that competition for scarce economic resources is another necessary condition for discrimination. His proposition might be extended to say that the more intense the competition for scarce resources, the more severe the discrimination. European settlers of North America initially attempted to assimilate the native Americans through education and religious conversion. Later, however, when competition for western territories became intense, the white settlers resorted to forced population transfer and extermination as methods of dealing with the native American minority.

As Yetman points out, even in the most stable situations, dominant groups view minority groups as potentially threatening to their position (Yetman, 1985).

For this reason, they attempt to prevent any change in the power balance, even using violence if they feel sufficiently threatened. For example, as black Africans have become more politically aware and active, the dominant white government in South Africa has become more repressive and resistant to change.

POTENTIAL FOR EXPLOITATION

The final factor in determining which pattern of interaction will be chosen is the majority's perception of the minority's potential for exploitation. If the majority can exploit the minority economically, they will tend to work toward structured inequality (Gordon, 1964). If the majority group does not see the minority as economically exploitable, they will tend to force a population transfer or attempt extermination. For example, the early American colonists integrated Africans into American society as slaves because they perceived an economic advantage in doing so. Fierce resistance by the native Americans proved them to be unexploitable.

MINORITY GROUP RESPONSE TO THE MAJORITY DEFINITION OF THE SITUATION

Because the majority group controls most of the power and influence, it plays a large part in determining the pattern of the majority-minority relationship. However, the minority's response to the situation also influences the terms of the relationship. The minority group has three options: (1) it can accept the definition of the situation supported by the majority, (2) it can aggressively oppose that definition, or (3) it can attempt to avoid the majority.

If the minority group accepts the majority's superiority, as is often initially the case, there is a potential for integration of the groups. This usually means acceptance of inferior status for the minority, but the minority group may view this subordinate status in the society as preferable to forced migration or extermination.

The second response, aggression by the minority, is usually futile, because the majority has more power.

When the minority aggressively resists discrimination, they may be able to alter the majority group definition of the situation. (*Photo courtesy Michigan Daily*)

Furthermore, aggression is likely to make the majority reject integration and provide the impetus for expulsion or extermination. If a minority is well organized and has support from the outside, aggression may be a viable alternative for it in a struggle to realign power, but in most cases aggression does not serve the long-term interests of the minority.

The third response, avoidance, is often the choice of the minority group. Minorities often gather together in physical and social communities to provide each other with support and to insulate themselves from the hostility of majority group members. Such clusterings can also give rise to increased minority-group power.

Nathan Glazer and Daniel Patrick Moynihan (1963) believe that this has occurred in New York City. They argue that New York was never a true melting pot because of the segregation of blacks, Puerto Ricans, Jews, Italians, and Irish. Segregation led to formation of racial and ethnic power blocs, strengthening minority positions while providing reasons not to give up racial and ethnic identities.

Avoidance may also take the form of simply leaving the area occupied by the majority. When allowed, many Jews leave the Soviet Union. Native Australians (called *aborigines*) usually evacuated areas occupied by British settlers.

Isaac and Kelley (1981) believe that minority-group responses swing between the basic options. Their research shows that significant change occurs in the majority-group response to the minority immediately after an aggressive act by the minority. In the United States, for example, welfare benefits rose after the inner-city riots of the 1960s and 1970s. These increases temporarily may have led the minority group of blacks to accept the *status quo* as defined by the white majority. Conflict theorists point to this as a clear example of elites seeking to placate the oppressed people when it appears they may be headed toward full-scale revolution, which might remove the elites from their positions of power.

As is the case in most social problem areas, no single definitive explanation for ethnic and racial group relations exists. The factors we have discussed—physical and cultural differences between groups, competition for economic resources, ideology of the majority group, power differences, potential for exploitation, and minority group responses to majority initiatives—combine to allow social scientists to make some predictions about the ways majority and minority groups will relate to one another.

CLOSE-UP on • *THEORY* •

Edna Bonacich's Theory of Ethnic Antagonism: The Split Labor Market

The Theorist and the Setting

Although many theorists had attempted to explain why societies vary in degree of ethnic harmony or antagonism, Edna Bonacich was "struck by the absence of a developed theory to account for variations in ethnic antagonism" (1972, p. 548). No available theory had been able to account for the fact that some societies, such as those in Brazil, Mexico, and Hawaii, have a low degree of ethnic antagonism, whereas others, such as South Africa, Australia, and mainland United States, have a high degree of ethnic antagonism.

Bonacich believes some earlier explanations of ethnic antagonism are inaccurate. She thinks the answer does not lie in the early idea that Protestants are more antagonistic toward minorities, because Hawaii and white settlers have been predominantly Protestant. Also, she does not believe in the validity of theories that attempt to explain ethnic antagonism based on whether the dominant or subordinate group originally inhabited an area. For example, both South Africa and the American Deep South are areas of great antagonism, but they have opposite patterns of original settlement. Bonacich rejects earlier theories and synthesizes the ideas of Oliver Cox (1948) and Marvin Harris (1964) to construct her own theory.

The Theorist's Goal

Bonacich addresses the question: Why does the degree of antagonism between ethnic groups vary from setting to setting?

Concepts and Propositions

Bonacich uses the term *antagonism* to mean "all levels of intergroup conflict, including ideologies and beliefs (such as racism and prejudice), behaviors (such as discrimination, lynchings, riots), and institutions (such as laws perpetuating segregation)" (p. 548).

Proposition: "Ethnic antagonism first germinates in a labor market split along ethnic lines" (p. 549).

Bonacich defines a *split labor market* as one that contains "at least two groups of workers whose price of labor differs for the same work" (p. 549). She states:

> Business tries to pay as little as possible for labor, regardless of ethnicity, and is held in check by the resources and motives of labor groups. Since these often vary by ethnicity, it is common to find ethnically split labor markets. The price of labor business must pay is the total cost to the employer, including not only wages, but the cost of recruitment, transportation, room and board, education, health care (if the employer must bear these), and the costs of labor unrest. . . .
>
> If an expensive labor group is strong enough . . . they may be able to resist being displaced. Both exclusion (an effort . . . to prevent an ethnically different group from being part of the society) and caste (an aristocracy of labor . . . in which higher-paid labor deals with the undercutting potential of cheaper labor by excluding them from certain types of work) systems represent such victories for higher paid labor (pp. 548, 554–556).

Interpretation

Bonacich believes the struggle for jobs and income is an important cause of ethnic strife. She points out that different ethnic groups are sometimes available to do the same work at significantly different prices. For a variety of reasons—including the standard of living in the homeland—a minority group may be willing to work for less than the group already employed. This creates a threat to the wages and security of the already-employed, higher-priced group. The established, higher-paid group can then be expected to try to exclude the competing group, as was the case with Japanese and Chinese immigrants to the United States near the turn of the century. Where the established group is unable to keep the low-priced labor out completely, they will seek to exclude them from certain occupations, thereby setting up a type of caste system. This happened to a large extent in the United States—free blacks were kept in menial occupations, and professional jobs and high-status occupations were reserved for whites.

Conversely, Bonacich suggests ethnic harmony is more likely to occur where there is less competition for jobs and earnings. A lowered level of competition may occur because each group is willing to work for the same price, or because all members of one group are in the capitalist class and all members of the other group are in the laboring class. The latter situation is true in Brazil, where virtually all the Portuguese were plantation owners. There was no Portuguese working class to be threatened by competition from native labor.

In summary, Bonacich's theory states that strong competition between two different ethnic groups willing to work for significantly different prices promotes antagonism, whereas lack of such competition creates more harmonious relations between ethnic groups.

Questions

1. What implications does this theory have for American immigration policy? For instance, what might be the consequences of admitting 10 million highly motivated Mexicans who are willing to work below minimum wage?
2. How would Bonacich explain very strong antagonism between ethnic groups in one country?
3. Can Bonacich's ideas be used to prevent or lessen ethnic antagonism? If so, how?

SOURCE Edna Bonacich, 1972. "A Theory of Ethnic Antagonism: The Split Labor Market." *American Sociological Review*, vol. 37, pp. 547–559.

What Are the Sources and Consequences of Prejudice and Discrimination?

In explaining prejudice and its effects, we will focus both on individual and group influences on attitude formation. The issue to be addressed is: How can we explain individual and group differences in their tolerance toward members of minority groups? Why do some people respond to minorities with malice and others with friendship?

SOCIALIZATION

As Gorden Allport observed in his work with children (1954), discrimination is learned behavior. Attitudes are taught to children by adults and peers through direct statements ("Don't ever play with niggers!") and indirect messages ("Well, your dad really jewed him down on that deal!"). Occasionally, children learn the words for the groups they are not supposed to like before they even come to understand whom the words describe. Allport cites an example: "One little boy was agreeing with his mother, who was warning him never to play with niggers. He said, 'No, Mother, I never play with niggers. I only play with white and black children' " (1954, p. 305).

In the course of contact, intergroup patterns are established that become part of the culture, and these attitudes are then taught to the younger generation through socialization. Thus, a person's degree of tolerance or intolerance is at first usually a reflection of the culture and of socialization. Where intergroup relations are strained and unequal, prejudice and discriminatory behavior will probably exist. As the culture changes, individual attitudes change as well.

STEREOTYPE

Probably the strongest influence on prejudicial attitudes is the attitude of the culture to which one belongs. The culture defines whom to hate and why to hate them, frequently describing minority group members in terms of a stereotype. *A **stereotype** is an exaggerated belief associated with a category.* Its function is to justify or rationalize one's conduct in relation to that category. In our culture, for instance, blacks have been stereotyped as being athletic and Jews have been depicted as financially shrewd. When they believe these stereotyped views, dominant group members may treat persons from these minority groups different from members of their own group.

Recent studies of cultural change in the United States show, for instance, that although white Americans have moved toward the principle of equality from the 1950s to the 1980s, they continue to maintain prejudicial attitudes. Schuman, Steeh, and Bobo compiled data from dozens of attitude surveys from the 1940s to date (Schuman et al., 1985). They discovered steady progress in less-prejudiced answers to questions about equal job opportunity, schooling, residential choice, and intermarriage, for instance. The percentage of persons agreeing with the nonprejudiced statements rose in some cases from only 30 percent in 1942 to almost 90 percent in 1984.

At the same time that the respondents showed less prejudice, however, questions aimed at *implementing* new policies showed much less change. For instance, federal jobs for minorities programs, federal intervention in schools, and open housing policies received approximately the same number of supporting votes in 1984 as they did in 1964—between 25 and 40 percent of the population. Although their belief systems are different, people are still hesitant to put them into practice. Changes in behavior follow changes in cultural beliefs, but only after the socialization of the next generation into the new belief system.

SCAPEGOAT THEORY

The scapegoat theory of prejudice became popular in the 1940s. This theory has six basic tenets: (1) all individuals experience a variety of needs; (2) when our needs are blocked, we become frustrated; (3) frustrated individuals become angry and often feel aggressive; (4) if it is dangerous to act aggressively toward the source of the frustration, we will displace our angry impulses on someone else, a "scapegoat"; (5) we choose a weak victim; and (6) to avoid feeling guilty, we justify our behavior through rationalization.

Most of us are socialized to condemn hostile impulses toward an "innocent" victim. We, therefore, need a "reason" to hate and fear another racial or ethnic group. Racist ideology is developed to give us these reasons in spite of the facts. If we can pretend that the group we want to scapegoat is lazy, immoral, or otherwise unsavory, we feel better about treating them poorly.

Although some early studies appeared to confirm the scapegoat process, later work has contradicted it as originally written (Vander Zanden, 1983). For instance, Berkowitz discovered that highly prejudiced persons displace aggression more than nonprejudiced persons and that some groups are perceived as vulnerable because they are *already* disliked rather than because they are weaker than the aggressive group (Berkowitz, 1962). Furthermore, it appears that only certain types of frustration will actually lead to aggression and that the attitude of the culture toward aggressive behavior either stimulates or dampens the scapegoating process (Vander Zanden, 1983).

Scapegoating is a more complex process than the early theorists had imagined, and using it to describe intergroup relations must take into account other factors. Realistic social conflict, in fact, could masquerade as scapegoating. In competition for wealth, power, and prestige, aggression may breed actual counteraggression rather than displacement of frustration.

SELF-FULFILLING PROPHECY

Prejudice and discrimination are often reinforced by what Robert Merton has called the "self-fulfilling prophecy" (1968). For example, blacks in North America were initially defined by slave traders as subhuman and incapable of high achievement. This assumption became the prophecy. After 300 years of discrimination, relatively few blacks in this country have attained high positions. The original prophecy is thus fulfilled by its own consequences: whites were told that blacks were inferior and treated them as such. When few blacks consequently attained superior positions, whites used that as evidence to support the original prophecy.

Minority-group members sometimes also adopt the prophecies and definitions of the majority. Black children in the 1940s had derogatory images of themselves similar to those held about them by white children (K. Clark & Clark, 1947). The researchers conclude that the shaping of the minority group mentality under slavery had been forceful and effective. Alvin Poussaint describes the process by which blacks were made to feel inferior to whites (1974):

> The more acquiescent the slave was, the more he was rewarded within the plantation culture. . . . Those who bowed and scraped for the white boss and denied their aggressive feelings were promoted to "house nigger" and "good nigger." Thus, within this system it became a virtue for the black man to be docile and nonassertive. . . . In order to retain the most menial of jobs and keep from starving, black people quickly learned such servile responses as "yassuh, massa" (p. 50).

AUTHORITARIAN PERSONALITY

Although much prejudice and discrimination is due to group influence on individual behavior, there are some links to individual personality. A group of researchers headed by Theodore Adorno was among the first to suggest a link between an "authoritarian personality" and prejudicial attitudes (Adorno et al., 1950). A person having an *authoritarian personality* is characterized by high obedience to figures holding positions of authority. Persons who score high on scales of authoritarianism also score high on scales of prejudicial attitudes.

People who are prejudiced against one group tend to be prejudiced against others, as well (Hartley, 1946). When surveyed, many prejudiced persons even indicated prejudice against fictitious minority groups (which were mixed in with the real ones) and endorsed expulsion from the United States of such nonexistent minority groups as the Danireans, Wallonians, and Pireneans. These findings support the idea that authoritarian personality does, in fact, contribute to prejudicial thinking.

DEGREE OF CONTACT WITH MINORITY GROUPS

Another variable influencing prejudice and discrimination is the degree of contact between an individual and a minority group. This relationship is not a simple one. For example, public school integration—which is intended to equalize opportunity and lead to better race relations—sometimes exacerbates the problem by bringing out increased levels of other forms of discrimination and prejudice. One sociological study of levels of prejudice before and after integration of a southern high school indicated that prejudice had risen after a year of desegregation (E. Campbell, 1961).

Where there is strong competition between minority groups, such as for jobs, increased contact also brings increased prejudice and discrimination (Bonacich, 1972). This helps explain why lower-class whites tend to be more prejudiced against blacks than upper-class whites. Lower-class groups are more likely to compete with each other for jobs and, therefore, to treat each other as antagonists.

In terms of the impact of discrimination, however, upper classes have more power and can be more injurious to minorities than can lower-class or middle-class groups. Because upper classes to a large extent control the government, the large corporations, and the media, their attitudes and decisions affect all members of society.

When individuals from similiar social-class backgrounds but different racial or ethnic groups are not overtly competing economically, contact between them is more likely to promote mutual tolerance. Whites who have been to college, for example, show less prejudice than whites who have not (Allport, 1954).

What we know about prejudice and discrimination does not provide a quick or easy means of eradicating either of them. Both phenomena can be part of the culture or related to personality structure. We know that interacting situations may increase or decrease prejudice and discrimination. Certainly, we know that prejudiced attitudes and discriminatory behavior are ingrained in our society and are difficult to change.

What Is Happening in the United States in Race and Ethnic Relations?

THE BLACK EXPERIENCE

Although some of the first black settlers in the United States were indentured servants, most came as slaves. Before slavery was outlawed in 1863 by the *Emancipation Proclamation,* over 400,000 slaves were brought to the United States from Africa. Slaves provided cheap labor and produced more cotton for less money. Interestingly, the economic viability of slavery has since been called into question by economists who claim that Northern production without slaves was more efficient at the time than Southern production with slaves (Elkins, 1975; Fogel & Engerman, 1974).

Reconstruction after the Civil War brought blacks some political and economic gains, but soon the white population reasserted control and maintained the caste system which had existed under slavery. Most jobs available to the freed blacks were in agriculture. Often the same land they had worked as slaves they later worked as sharecroppers, renting it from whites and sharing their harvest with their white overlords. Few could make enough to buy their own land. Segregation successfully separated whites and blacks in social situations, including schools, churches, hospitals, restaurants, and trains.

In 1896 the United States Supreme Court upheld separate but equal facilities (*Plessy v. Ferguson*); in 1908 the Court held that a state could forbid even a private college from teaching whites and blacks at the same time and place (*Berea College v. Kentucky*). Whites and blacks remained fearful of each other in all sections of the United States.

DESEGREGATION. In 1941 President Roosevelt created the Fair Employment Practices Committee which added "no discrimination" clauses to government contracts, and in 1948 President Truman issued a directive calling for an end to segregation in the Armed Forces. In 1954 the Supreme Court decision ruled school segregation illegal (*Brown v. Topeka, Kansas, Board of Education*). Liberals hoped children attending school together from an early age would escape indoctrination about each other and could thus form friendships that crossed all races. Unfortunately, much bloodshed and heartache followed desegregation and busing orders in both North and South, and children who had already been socialized by school age did not readily embrace each other in friendship. Buses bombed in Michigan and children beaten in Boston testify to the fact that racial strife is not a Southern but a nationwide problem.

VOTING. In 1965 a national Voting Rights Act was passed, banning literacy tests and poll taxes as requirements for registration. Until this landmark legislation, many states stopped blacks from voting by these means. After passage, many blacks registered and voted, and this change, too, was marked by violence. The civil rights movement of the 1960s and early 1970s involved millions of people and massive demonstrations by both blacks and whites. Civil rights activists often encountered guns, attack dogs, cattle prods, and fire hoses. Violent incidents, including shooting people and bombing schools, churches, and buses, took the lives of many civil rights supporters.

BLACK POWER. In the 1960s, the Black Power movement gained a large following, inspiring blacks and frightening whites. Black Power leaders emphasized what was good and admirable about their own culture and background, in an effort to make young blacks proud to be black rather than frustrated in trying to be like whites. Conflict over goals and methods marred the movement, but growth came in many areas, again due to concentrated donations of time, energy, and money of whites and blacks from all areas of the United States.

ECONOMIC GAINS AND LOSSES

Today, there are 29 million black Americans, almost 12 percent of the population. Blacks have made economic gains. (See Figure 10.1.) Their salaries have increased substantially, even through the recession of the 1970s, but black household income was still only about 58 percent that of whites in 1986 (U.S. Bureau of Census, 1987). The number of blacks who are managers, officials, or self-employed doubled in the two decades after 1960. Black home ownership also increased between 1970 and 1980, although the increase was much larger among middle-income families (Hill, 1986).

Some of these changes have occurred because more blacks are staying in school. Twice as many blacks completed high school, went to college, and obtained white-collar jobs in 1982 as in 1960. From 1970 to 1978, when the percentage of whites attending college decreased, the percentage of blacks attending college increased by 6 percent. From 1976 to 1983, however, combined Hispanic and black college attendance fell from 35 percent to 29 percent of all high school students (Bowen, 1986). Although blacks are 12 percent of the population, they earned only 4 percent of the doctoral degrees conferred in 1983 (Moody, 1986). In contrast to the 1970s, however, a black man with a college degree can now expect to earn almost as much money as a white college graduate (Schuman et al., 1985). Although the overall racial gap in median family incomes still exists, highly educated, black husband-and-wife families have significantly narrowed the gap between themselves and similar white families (Farley, 1984). (See Figure 10.2.)

At the same time that educated blacks are making gains, the lower-class black is not better off today than twenty years ago. Only 12 percent of black workers are professionals and technicians, compared to 17 percent of whites, and 25 percent of black workers are in low-level service jobs, compared to 13 percent of whites. The proportion of black-owned firms with paid employees fell sharply from 23 percent in 1969 to 12 percent in 1982 (Hill, 1986).

Partly due to the low level of training of lower-class blacks, the black unemployment picture has consistently looked grim. In 1960 the unemployment rate was 5 percent for whites but 10 percent for blacks. In 1985, the rates were 6 percent and 14 percent, respectively, or more than twice as high for blacks as for whites (U.S. Bureau of Census, 1987). Some observers suggest that if the number of black teenagers who are out of school and looking for work were added to the unemployment figures, the rate for blacks would approach 35 percent. (See Figure 10.2.)

Since 1980, the United States has lost 2.5 million factory jobs, which are disproportionately held by black males. Because retraining for people in these jobs con-

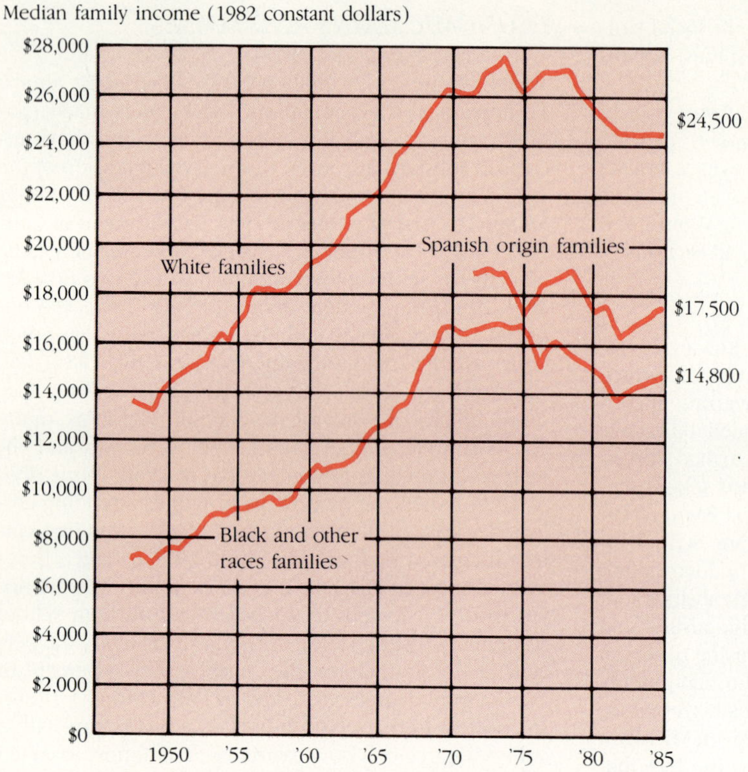

FIGURE 10.1 Median Family Income for Families of Various Ethnic Backgrounds, 1947–1982. Although the median income of black families has risen, as has that of white families, it still remains approximately 60 percent of that of white families. (SOURCE U.S. Bureau of the Census, 1983, p. 463.)

tinues to be minimal, we can expect that the unemployment situation for blacks will get worse rather than better (Swinton, 1986).

The lack of jobs for young black males may also contribute to the problem of illegitimate births in the black population. Twenty-five percent of all black births are to teenagers, and 87 percent of these mothers are unmarried. (See Figure 10.2.) John Perkins, well-respected black leader, suggests that the young black male's ego suffers from not being able to find gainful employment, and he may seek affirmation of his manhood by impregnating young black females (Perkins, 1987). John Jacob, president of the National Urban League, states that because they have no jobs, these young men don't get married or accept responsibility for the children they do produce. Thus, today the majority of black children grow up without the role model of a father who is responsible for them and who produces gainfully in the marketplace (Jacob, 1986).

These economic barriers of unemployment and low-paid employment create the situation in which three times more black Americans live below the poverty line as do white Americans (U.S. Bureau of the Census, 1987). (See Figure 10.3.) Although black poverty has declined, from 36 percent in 1983 to 34 percent in 1986, most of that decline was among the elderly and was due to increases in Social Security and Supplemental Security Income benefits (Jacob, 1986).

The changes that occurred over the Reagan administration years were primarily negative for the black community. From 1981 to 1987, the government cut its budget for job training for youth by 53 percent, its mental health budget by 26 percent, AFDC by 18 percent, and child-abuse prevention programs by 12 percent (Jacobs, 1986). Becuase blacks are three times as likely as other Americans to participate in such social service programs, these budget cuts have hit them especially hard. Although blacks experienced yearly growth in purchasing power of 2.5 percent in the decade 1970 to 1980, during the Reagan years 1980 to 1987, it fell to 0.825 percent per year (Swinton, 1986).

Reagan also launched a major effort to change federal policies on school busing and *affirmative action,* or the policy by which special consideration is given to a member of a group that has suffered discrimination in the past and is considered notable to compete for the rewards of society, such as education and jobs. The Department of Justice stopped using any pressure to use busing as a means to achieve desegregation. Reagan's administration also made cuts in aid to higher education, including the loan program that had enabled many young blacks to attend school, and did not

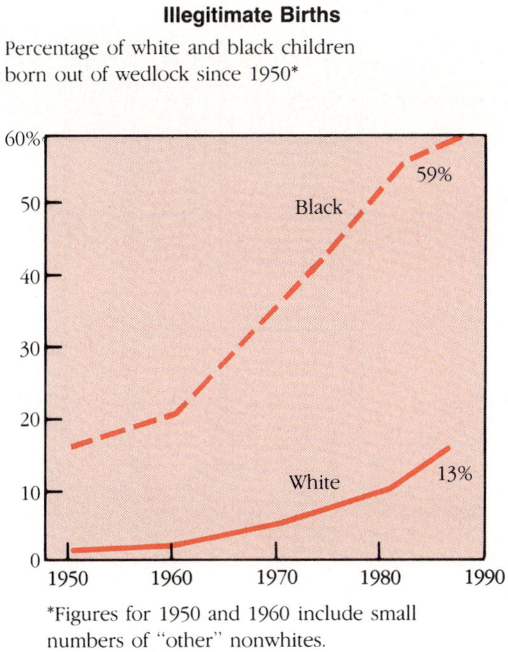

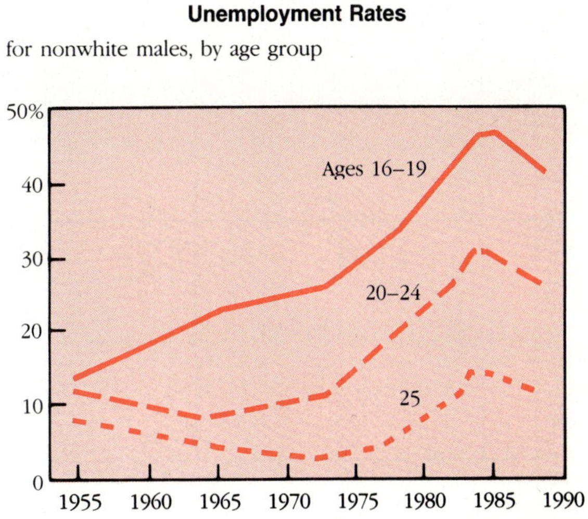

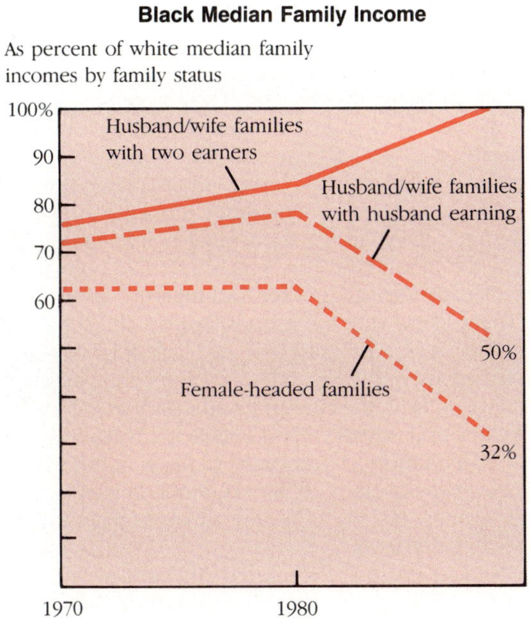

FIGURE 10.2 The combination of rising unemployment for young black males and illegitimate motherhood for young black females contributes greatly to the continuing poverty of the black underclass, which largely comprises female-headed families. (SOURCE U.S. Bureau of the Census)

positively support affirmative action (Evans, 1985; Bowen, 1985; Karmel, 1984). Together, these factors negated much of the progress that blacks made during the 1970s.

The bottom line, then, is that middle-class blacks have made gains since 1960 but lower-class blacks are not significantly better off today. The percentage of the black population with incomes below $10,000 increased from 28 percent in 1970 to 34 percent in 1984, even though the proportion with incomes over $35,000 increased slightly. Although income stagnated or declined during the Reagan years for 85 percent of the black population, income increased for the top 15 percent (Swinton, 1986).

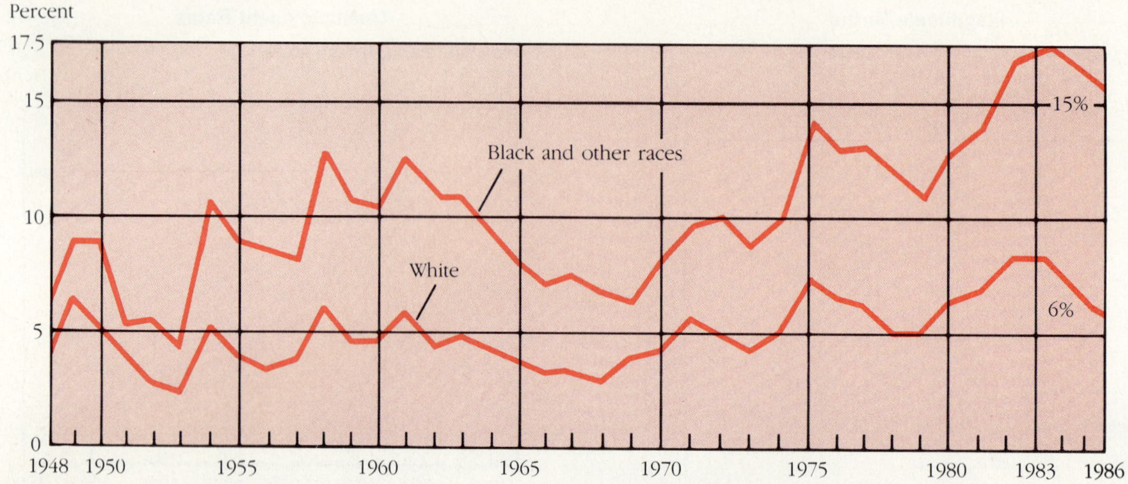

FIGURE 10.3 Comparison of Black and Other Races to White Unemployment: 1948–1986. The unemployment rates for minorities have consistently been above those for whites, including a doubling in the period 1970 to 1980. (SOURCE U.S. Bureau of the Census, *Statistical Abstract of the U.S.*, 1987, "Unemployed Workers—Summary, 1948–1985," p. 390.)

SOCIAL GAINS

Gains in black equality require social as well as economic change. Despite the declaration of former United Nations ambassador Andrew Young that the United States has "laid down the burden of race," evidence is strong that blacks are still socially excluded all over our country (McDonald, 1978).

Separate facilities for blacks and whites are now illegal, but segregation still exists. For example, although the South has about a 20 percent black population, fewer than 3 percent of those elected to office in the South are black.

Gains in this area are continuing, and blacks are winning legal and social victories. Perhaps the most dramatic change is in the number of black elected officials, which quadrupled from 1970 to 1985 (U.S. Bureau of Census, 1987, p. 240). In 1987, 6,681 blacks held public office, among them the mayors of Chicago, Philadelphia, and Los Angeles (*USA Today*, 1987). However, these legal processes are long, hard, expensive, and unlikely to produce overwhelming changes in black–white relationships quickly.

What Is the Significance of Race?

Some black social scientists, writing from a functionalist perspective, have recently put forth the proposition that race is becoming less significant in the determination of economic and social well-being. Thomas Sowell, for instance, believes that the current situation of blacks can be explained by looking at the origins of the black experience in the United States (1981a and b, 1983). Over 10 million blacks were brought to North America to be used as slaves. Their experience here, until the past forty years, was predominantly rural and southern.

Blacks began to move north into the large cities in the 1940s, in what is sometimes termed the "Great Migration." They faced a social and occupational structure in the urban North in which they had no experience or expertise. Like other "immigrant" groups before them, they were not economically viable for some time. This was especially true of black migrants, because they arrived in the cities at a time when industry was moving from the cities into suburbs that were economically and socially inaccessible to blacks. Given these extenuating circumstances, black workers remained at the bottom of the economic ladder, just as other groups facing the same circumstances might have, suggests Sowell.

William Wilson's celebrated and controversial article, "On the Declining Significance of Race," concerns the black economic experience in the United States (1980, 1984). Wilson describes three stages in the American race relations experience. Stage 1 encompasses the plantation economy. Stage 2 is characterized by industrial expansion, class conflict, and racial oppression. Stage 3, beginning in the 1960s and 1970s, is a period of progressive transition from *race* inequalities to *class* inequalities.

Wilson believes that historic rather than contem-

Can a black achieve the Presidency? Jesse Jackson tested the United States' willingness to accept a black presidential candidate in 1988. (*AP/Wide World Photos*)

porary discrimination against blacks is the basis of the difficulties of what he terms the "black underclass" today. He points out that the problems of this ghetto class today are caused by a number of economic and social problems. For example, he cites the rapid rise in the number of teenaged black mothers. The fact that 50 percent of all black births are to teenagers is an economic liability for the black community. The black youth explosion in which the number of young black adults increased by three times the number of young white adults is another of the factors that he sees as having "gone awry in the ghetto" (1984, p. 89).

Sowell suggests that the policies of affirmative action that were put into place in the 1970s may have actually hindered the progress working class blacks might have otherwise made (1983). Under pressure from government guidelines, corporations made efforts to hire black workers, but primarily in middle-class managerial positions. Their quota satisfied, they ignored the hiring of blacks in unskilled positions. Perhaps as a result, unskilled black males earned 79 percent of the income of white males before affirmative action quotas and only 69 percent after quotas. During the same time period, their educated counterparts saw their income rise from 75 percent of the income of similar whites to 98 percent (Welch, 1981). In fact, by 1980 college-educated black couples actually earned more than college-educated white couples (U. S. Bureau of the Census, 1981). Due to these twin changes, the proportion of all black income going to the top fifth of blacks increased substantially, while the percentage going to the bottom three-fifths declined (Kilson, 1981). Wilson describes the situation as a "deepening economic schism . . . developing in the black community, with the black poor falling further and further behind middle- and upper-income blacks" (p. 134).

Conflict theorists would probably counter this viewpoint, concentrating instead on the continuation of economic disparities between blacks and whites as the key variable. Whether this situation is the result of structural economic policies or of current discriminatory policies is the research question that conflict theorists Thomas and Hughes address in the following "Close-Up on Research."

CLOSE-UP on • *RESEARCH* •

Melvin Thomas and Michael Hughes on the Continuing Significance of Race and Quality of Life

The Researchers and the Setting

Over the past 25 years, legal and social changes have brought more opportunities for blacks, a decline in the expression of racist ideology, significant economic progress, especially in the middle class, and growing political power. As a result, blacks in the United States have undergone noticeable changes in their social status. As we have seen, however, these changes are not universal in the black community. Blacks are still more likely to be poor, unemployed, and uneducated than whites.

Sociologists Wilson and Sowell argue that the status improvement of some blacks, coupled with the continued poverty of others, is because race has become less important than class in determining the life chances of blacks. Thomas and Hughes, researchers at Virginia Polytechnic, propose an alternative interpretation.

The Researchers' Goals

Thomas and Hughes suggest that "if race is declining in its influence on the life chances of black Americans, this would be reflected in their reports of life satisfaction, happiness, and other measures of psychological well-being and quality of life." They examine data to determine the "mutual impact of race and socioeconomic status on psychological well-being and quality of life" (p. 830).

Theory and Concepts

The two questions studied are:

1. "Whether race has an effect on psychological well-being and quality of life that is independent of socioeconomic status; and
2. Whether or not the negative impact of race on psychological well-being and quality of life has declined in recent years" (p. 830).

Research Design

After reviewing all of the research done in this area thus far, Thomas and Hughes chose data from the General Social Survey (GSS) to test their hypotheses. This survey provides data from a representative sample of noninstitutionalized citizens every year, from 1972 to the present.

Because they have no GSS data for the twenty years prior to 1972, they rely on the findings of Bracy (1976), who showed that no overall change occurred in the relative position of blacks on happiness, and a negative change occurred in their position on life satisfaction from 1957 to 1972. They suggest, in addition, that changes in these variables that were caused by the gains blacks made in the 1960s would lag behind the actual legal changes, bringing them into the time period for which they do have data.

Thomas and Hughes used the following variables: race, year, income, education, employment status, and marital status. For each of these variables, they used the statistical techniques of regression analysis and multiple-classification analysis, techniques that allowed them to see the "actual year-by-year changes in the dependent variable" (p. 835).

Findings

The findings are very consistent across the dependent variables. For all of them, "whites experience better psychological well-being and quality of life than blacks do," regardless of social class. Furthermore, "on none of these measures of psychological well-being and quality of life has the condition of blacks improved or declined significantly relative to whites over the period 1972 to 1985" (p. 836). It is interesting to note that on the average from 1972 to 1985 the measures of psychological well-being and quality of life have declined for both whites *and* blacks.

Thomas and Hughes believe that their study "provides evidence not for the declining or inclining significance of race, but for the continuing significance of race in determining well-being." They point out that their results do not directly contradict Wilson, who argues not that racism has disappeared, but that its significance is declining. They also suggest that "some of the advantage that whites have over blacks in the probability of being in stable marriages is due to the stresses that American society puts on black as opposed to white marriages" (p. 839). Nevertheless, blacks have "lower life satisfaction, less trust in people, less general happiness, less marital happiness, more anomie, and lower self-rated physical health than whites regardless of social class, marital status, age, or year." Based on this data, they conclude that "while being black does not lead to psychopathology, it is associated with a less positive life experience than being white" (p. 839).

Implications

The researchers suggest three reasons why they could "observe continuing differences between blacks and whites in psychological well-being and life satisfaction within a context of a decline in the significance of race in American society." First, a lag of a generation or more could occur between significant social change and a difference in individual feelings. Second, the fact that changes are being made could stimulate higher aspirations in the black community. When these aspirations are not filled quickly, blacks may feel more frustrated than they did before they were looking for change. Third, the decline in the significance of race may not be large enough to change how blacks feel about their lives.

Thomas and Hughes think that perhaps the idea of a declining significance of race, or lowering of contemporary discrimination, is faulty or overrated. Farley, for instance, shows differences in earnings across age and class categories that he believes imply the persistence of discrimination (1984). If his theory is true, then discrimination is a plausible explanation for the differences that they found in this study. Wilson calls the fact that blacks and whites earn different amounts for the same work a "racial tax" (1980), and thus Thomas and Hughes can conclude from their studies of difference in psychological well-being between blacks and whites that "if there is a racial tax in American society, the cost of being black is not only economic, but psychological as well" (p. 840).

Questions

1. Given the evidence Thomas and Hughes found, evaluate Wilson's theory. What alternative explanations do you find?
2. What reasons might you find for a generation's lag between social change and change in individual psychological perceptions?
3. Given the fact that people seem so concerned today about "getting ahead" financially, were you surprised that even when they reach financial parity blacks do not enjoy life as much as whites? Why or why not?
4. What evidence do you find in your own experience for contemporary discrimination waning or still existing?

SOURCES James H. Bracy. 1976. "The Quality of Life Experience of Black People," in *The Quality of American Life: Perceptions, Evaluations, and Satisfactions*, edited by Angus Campbell, Philip Converse, and Willard Rodgers, New York: Russell Sage Foundation. Reynolds Farley. 1984. *Blacks and Whites: Narrowing the Gap?* Cambridge, MA: Harvard University Press. Melvin E. Thomas and Michael Hughes, "The Continued Significance of Race: A Study of Race, Class, and Quality of Life in America, 1972–1985." *American Sociological Review*, Vol. 51, pp 830–841. William Julius Wilson. 1980. *The Declining Significance of Race: Blacks and Changing American Institutions*, 2d ed. Chicago: University of Chicago Press.

HISPANIC AMERICANS

The fastest-growing minority in the United States are Hispanic Americans, or Americans of Spanish-speaking background. The 1980 census showed 14.6 million, or 6.4 percent of the population as Hispanic (U.S. Bureau of Census, 1982). Because Hispanics are expanding at a faster rate than any other minority group, increasing 265 percent from 1950 to 1980, they will soon displace blacks as the largest U.S. minority (C. Davis et al., 1983).

The Hispanic median family income lags behind that of non-Hispanic families, at $19,478 as opposed to $29,404 (U.S. Bureau of the Census, 1987). One reason for this may be that Hispanic-Americans hold more traditional gender role views than the rest of the population; women are reluctant to take jobs, which holds down the family income in comparison with the other two-earner families.

Hispanic families tend to be larger than those of the rest of the population: 3.83 persons instead of 3.14. Hispanics also have less education; only 50 percent finishes four years of high school and 9 percent finish college, in contrast to the non-Hispanic 77 percent and 21 percent. (U.S. Bureau of the Census, 1987). Hispanics are also more likely to be divorced or separated and live in female-headed families, and their median age is 23, seven years younger than the population as a whole (Davis et al., 1983). The Hispanic unemployment rate is 45 to 50 percent higher, and 88 percent of them live in metropolitan areas. Perhaps as a result of these factors, 29 percent of them were living below the poverty level in 1985 (U.S. Bureau of the Census, 1987, p. 444).

Hispanics are not a single group, as a casual observer might believe, but separate groupings according to their country of origin. To lump them together would be as much an oversimplification as to consider all English-speaking people to be of the same cultural background. Nevertheless, as they grow in numbers and become accustomed to life in the United States, Hispanic groups are becoming more unified and feeling more homogeneous rather than separated by their national origins (Rangel, 1984).

CHICANOS. Mexican-Americans, or Chicanos, constitute 60 percent of all Hispanics. They are concentrated in the Southwest, and many of them are descendants of the original Spanish settlers and their native American neighbors. As land became scarce, white settlers forced the Spanish-speaking farmers into New Mexico and Mexico. Many Chicanos now live and work in large cities. Some are engaged in farming today as migrant workers, doing stoop labor for low wages. César Chavez is a migrant worker who organized many of his fellow Chicano farmworkers in California and has successfully run demonstrations, such as nationwide boycotts of grapes and lettuce, to dramatize the plight of the migrant worker. His union has now signed contracts with many major growers. Chavez has been a source of pride to other Chicanos, and his influence has led to a Mexican-American political party, La Raza

Unida. Despite the gains that have been made, 29% of Chicanos still lived below the poverty line in 1985 (Womack, 1972; U.S. Bureau of the Census, 1986).

PUERTO RICANS. The United States acquired Puerto Rico during the Spanish-American War in 1898 and declared Puerto Ricans to be citizens in 1917. Due to depressed economic conditions on the island, many Puerto Ricans have come to the mainland in search of a better life. Most of the 2 million Puerto Ricans who have come here remain in New York City where they landed, and they now constitute 14 percent of that city's population (U.S. Bureau of the Census, 1982). In contrast to Chicanos, Puerto Ricans are United States citizens and can as easily migrate back and forth between their island and the mainland as others of us migrate between states for employment. Most Puerto Ricans visit their original home often and many of them retire there (J. Moore and Pachon, 1985).

Because Puerto Rican children now make up 25 percent of the enrollment, the New York City school system has had to reconsider what it must do for its new immigrants. Puerto Rican groups pushed for bilingual education, and in 1974 New York began implementing a program of teaching some classes in Spanish rather than English. Much work remains to be done to provide Puerto Rican youngsters with an education that can get them productive jobs. They face the double handicap of being new immigrants and not knowing English, the language of the dominant culture.

CUBANS. An estimated 79,000 Cubans were living in the United States, mostly in Florida, in 1959, when Fidel Castro took control of Cuba. A "second wave" of 273,000 immigrants then arrived, fleeing Castro's regime. A third group of 118,000 persons known as the Marielitos came by boat from the Cuban port of Mariel in 1980. (Moore & Pachen, 1985).

Today, 800,000 former Cuban citizens are now working and living in the United States. Those who first fled Castro tended to be educated upper-class Cubans, and they have been the most economically successful of the Hispanics in the United States. The early arrivers began businesses here that expanded so much that many of the new Cuban immigrants could be employed by those who arrived earlier (C. Bach, 1980).

Forty percent of the Hispanics in Dade County, Florida (which includes Miami), earned more than $12,000 in 1977. Sixty-five percent owned their own homes. In sharp contrast to New York City, one-third of the pupils in Dade County bilingual schools are Hispanic, and they score so well on standardized tests that 72 percent of them go to college. One result of their success is that they have edged out the county's black population for some jobs, creating anger and tension between these two minority groups.

Cesar Chavez, organizer of the first farm workers union in the United States, continues his work for this underprivileged group. In 1988 he undertook a fast to protest the use of dangerous pesticides on farm produce which threaten the lives of farm workers and the general public alike. (*Photo courtesy the author*)

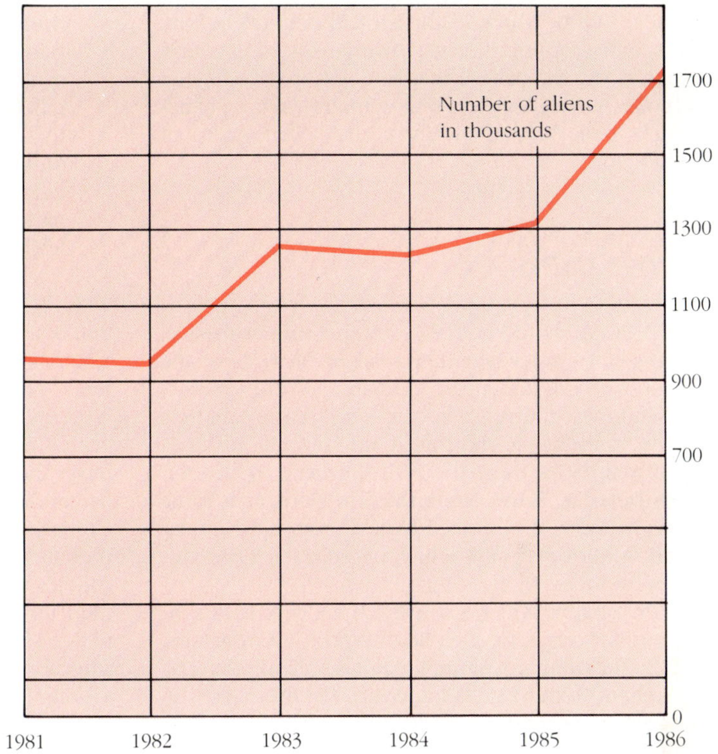

FIGURE 10.4 Apprehension of Illegal Aliens. The increase in the number of apprehended aliens from 1981 to 1986 reflects both increased numbers of would-be immigrants as well as stronger commitment by the INS to stop the flow across the borders. (SOURCE U.S. Bureau of the Census, *Statistical Abstract of the United States*, 1987 (107th ed.), Washington, D.C., 1986, p. 164.)

ILLEGAL ALIENS. The Hispanic group that is often not discussed is the estimated 9 million illegal aliens who have crossed the Mexican border in search of work. Mexico's 50 percent unemployment rate is one of the highest in the world, and its population is growing at 3.5 percent per year. Large portions of Mexico's people live in poverty. The Mexicans who come to the United States do so in an effort to make money for their starving families. The United States Immigration and Naturalization Service (INS) is also constantly rounding them up and sending them back, at twice the rate in 1986 that they had in 1981 (U.S. Bureau of the Census, 1986). (See Figure 10.4.) But the border is vast, and hundreds come into the United States every week.

Feelings about this group vary. Labor unions are firmly against the growing tide of laborers who will work for nearly any wage at any job under any conditions. The unions here have fought hard battles for good working conditions and fair pay, and they see these newcomers as a threat to those gains. However, some authorities believe the aliens are taking jobs that no one else would take, usually hard manual labor.

In October 1986, Congress passed the Immigration Reform and Control Act addressing the problem of illegal immigration, especially from Mexico. In an effort to discourage industries from drawing on cheaper alien labor, the Act provides for sanctions against employers who are found hiring undocumented aliens. It also offers legal residency status to aliens who have resided continuously in the United States since 1982. The federal government will appropriate $1 billion toward helping states provide welfare, health, and education to these new permanent residents. In addition, the Justice Department will establish a new office to investigate claims of job discrimination that might result from the new law. The INS enforcement budget will be doubled, in order to stop the illegal flow at the borders and properly enforce the employer sanctions. It is hoped that this new law will be a turning point in reducing illegal immigration (LaFranchi, 1986).

HISPANIC POWER. As a whole, Hispanics are slowly growing in influence. Many of them blame the slow progress on poor or nonexistent bilingual education. Others argue that Spanish education should not be a priority any more than a Polish education has been; in other words, other groups have survived and prospered without bilingual education, and maybe Hispanics can, too. It has also been suggested that encouraging Spanish-speaking immigrants not to learn English actually will hinder their progress in the long run.

In 1987, there were eleven Hispanic representatives to Congress (compared with sixteen black representatives), no Hispanic senators, and only one governor of Hispanic origin (Benanti, 1987; Welch &

Hibbing, 1984). Much of the present political activity of Hispanic groups is directed toward registering voters. Hispanic activists believe that true power will come at the polls, when they elect representatives who will accurately and sympathetically portray their needs in Washington.

NATIVE AMERICANS

HISTORICAL PERSPECTIVE. Many Americans feel a twinge of guilt when they read or hear about the situation of the American "Indians." White interaction with these native Americans—from early explorers to the present—is portrayed in several histories (D. Brown, 1970; Burnette, 1971; Burnette and Koster, 1974; DeLoria, 1969). From the time Europeans came to this country, they denied basic human rights of the native Americans, and many observers believe this continues today (Lurie, 1985).

Most native Americans were friendly when Europeans first came to the New World (Matthiessen, 1984). Christopher Columbus, upon meeting the Tainos Indians from El Salvador, wrote that they were "so tractable, so peaceable . . . they love their neighbors as themselves, and their discourse is ever sweet and gentle, and accompanied with a smile; and though it is true that they are naked, yet their manners are decorous and praiseworthy" (DeLoria, 1969). Similarly, the first Pilgrim settlers survived the winter because Indians of Massachusetts gave them food from their own supplies and taught them how to find wild food.

What happened to these peaceable people? Europeans took over their land and destroyed their livelihood, actions which would quickly make any group unfriendly. Indians were forced to move to prescribed territories. Eventually, whites wanted these lands, too, and took over land granted to the Indians by treaty. As General William Tecumseh Sherman said in 1890, "An Indian reservation is a tract of land set aside for the exclusive use of Indians, surrounded by thieves" (DeLoria, 1969).

The history of Indian interactions is a history of many broken agreements by the United States government. Whites were greedy for more land, gold, and minerals. When the Indians fought back, they were massacred. Captain Fred Benteen, who had saved some of Custer's men at the Battle of the Little Bighorn, was interviewed in 1879. He explained the situation (Burnette and Koster, 1974, p. 1):

> *Question:* What, in your opinion, is the cause of the Indian outbreaks which give your military men so much to do?
>
> *Answer:* For the past twelve or fifteen years, I think the Indian Bureau has been entirely responsible, and the cause has been the enormous pilfering and stealing from the Indians. . . . It is this constant robbery which goads them to outbreaks. Treat them well, and they will be all right and make good citizens. . . . We should treat the Indian as if he possessed some natural feelings.

THE INDIAN SITUATION TODAY. Today, the 800,000 native Americans are the most neglected of all American minority ethnic groups. Their unemployment rate has been about 50 percent since 1945, whereas the national average during that period has been 6 percent. Their life expectancy is about 20 years fewer than that for all Americans. Diseases such as tuberculosis, virtually nonexistent elsewhere in the United States, still claim many lives on reservations. Indians have the highest infant mortality rate in the country—twice that of blacks. Poverty is twice as common for Indians as for the general population. (Burnette, 1971; U.S. Bureau of the Census, 1983). The suicide rate for native Americans is twice the national average, and the alcoholism rate seven times. (Burnette, 1971; U.S. Bureau of the Census, 1987; Josephy, 1982).

THE AMERICAN INDIAN MOVEMENT. In 1973, the American Indian Movement (AIM) organized a takeover of reservation headquarters at Wounded Knee, South Dakota, the place where the last great massacre of Indians occurred in 1899 (Brown, 1970). The takeover was intended to dramatize that the Indian situation has not significantly altered since then. The U.S. Calvary is no longer shooting women and children, but the government is still breaking Indian treaties when it serves whites' purposes to do so. Furthermore, the Bureau of Indian Affairs continues to misrepresent Indian wishes in Washington, but the government will not disband it, despite some hope in the early 1970s for such reform. Indians were killed and wounded at this new battle of Wounded Knee, but AIM seems more firmly entrenched as a political force among Indians since the incident. The outbreak at Wounded Knee and the demonstrations following it in Washington were expressions of the anguish native Americans felt about their treatment.

Recently, Indian groups are taking a new strategy, becoming more organized and more insistent on being treated equally (DeLoria, 1981; Dorris, 1981; Nagel, 1982). Indians are beginning to demand enforcement of old treaties regarding land rights and hunting and fishing rights, for instance. Nagel has called this a period of "economic development and self-determination" (1982), which emphasizes the unique and positive aspects of the Native American culture rather than promoting assimilation into the rest of the United States or annihilation of the group completely.

An example of this new legal approach is the fight of the Navajos against eviction from their land in Arizona. Some observers believe that the land's wealth in coal and water power gave impetus to the federal government's division of the land in question between the Navajos and Hopis (T. Johnson, 1986). One expert in Indian affairs describes it as "a political and economic maneuver in which 10,000 Navajo and Hopi people will suffer from the greed and rapacity of a few politicians, lawyers, and big mining corporations" (Matthiessen, 1986). Much of the land still owned by native Americans has such mineral deposits, and the Indians are often pressured by developers who want their mineral rights (Josephy, 1982). Tribes differ on policies regarding selling their lands, and differences also exist within tribes. Nevertheless, significant victories are being won throughout the United States, and many tribes have been granted cash compensation for their loss of territory or rights (Dorris, 1981; Nagel, 1982). Perhaps by using the legal system, native Americans will eventually be granted the respect and privileges that the first settlers should have given them 200 years ago.

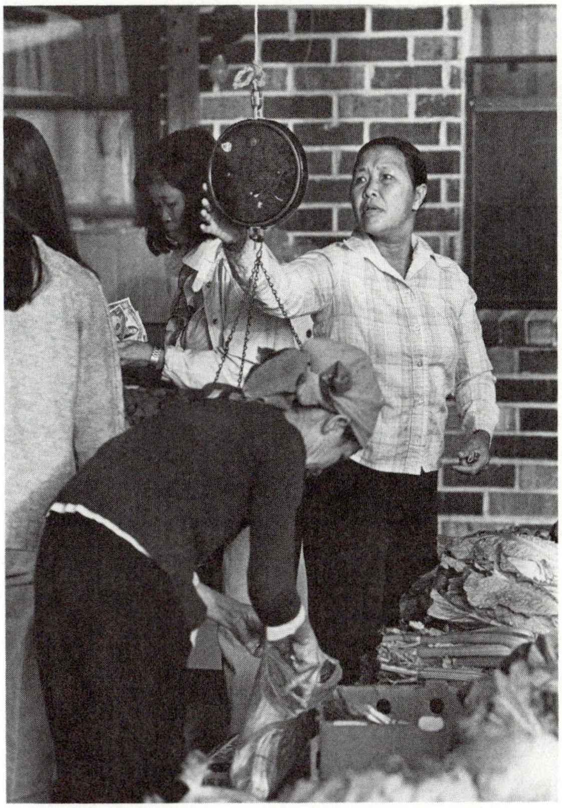

Often incoming ethnic groups, such as these Vietnamese, have started at the bottom of the social class ladder upon reaching the United States. (*UP/Bettmann Newsphotos*)

ASIAN AMERICANS: TWO DISTINCT HISTORIES

CHINESE. Although many people think of the Chinese and Japanese as similar, the two groups view themselves as quite distinct, and their lives in this country have run very different courses. The Chinese came here first, in the 1850s, mainly as laborers for the railroads being built across the country, and to dig in the newly established mines on the West Coast. They were welcomed by business owners, because they worked long hours for less pay than white laborers.

When these jobs ended and work became scarce, the white working class saw the Chinese as a threat. They dubbed them the "yellow peril," and hangings and massacres of Chinese proliferated. In 1882 Congress passed the Chinese Exclusion Act, which cut off immigration from China to the United States. This remained in force until the end of World War II.

The Chinese never assimilated easily into American society, and they still remain mostly a separate subculture. Their median income remains low. Recently, a higher percentage of Chinese Americans are finishing high school: 57.8 percent. This new emphasis on education makes their future look more promising.

JAPANESE. The Japanese came to the United States later than the Chinese, near the turn of the twentieth century. They settled primarily in Hawaii and on the West Coast. They originally worked as farmhands in the lush fields of California and Hawaii, much as the Chicanos do today. Because the Japanese particularly value education and hard work, they moved from the working class into the middle class rather rapidly compared to other immigrant groups.

In 1924 Congress stopped all Japanese immigration. In 1942 the United States government took an unprecedented action. One hundred thousand Japanese Americans on the West Coast—70 percent of whom were American citizens born and raised in the United States—were placed in "relocation centers," or internment camps where they were imprisoned until the end of the war. The government rationale for this incredible act was that Japanese Americans might collaborate with Japan, an enemy power in World War II. There was also misdirected concern that Japanese

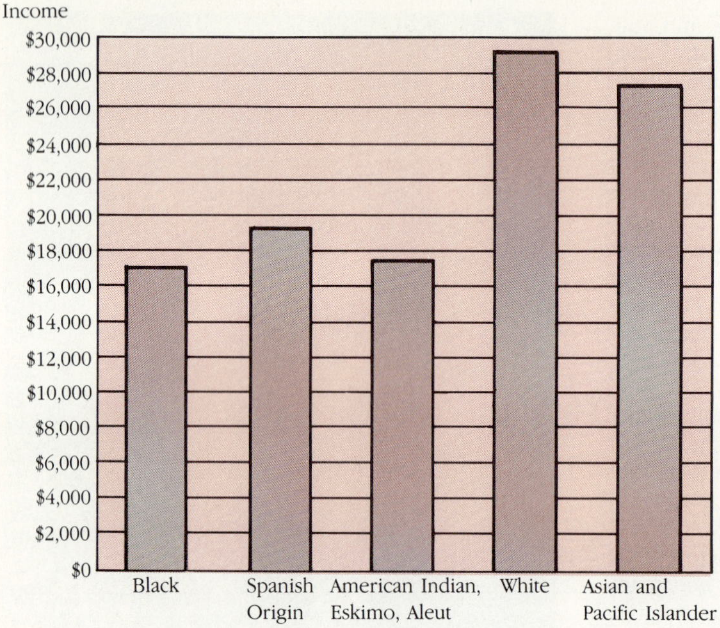

FIGURE 10.5 Median Family Income for Various Ethnic Groups in the United States: 1986. Income varies substantially between ethnic groups, with some outearning the white majority. (SOURCE U.S. Bureau of the Census, 1988, pp. 37, 427.)

Americans would become targets of white Americans' hostility.

This governmental action, clearly, had racist overtones. The United States was also at war with Germany and Italy, and, although private doubt was expressed about recent immigrants from these countries, no official collective action was taken against German Americans or Italian Americans.

The United States government, in partial apology, has recently allowed some of the interred Japanese Americans to sue for economic losses they suffered during "relocation." However, settlements are in the range of $25–35 per day in current dollars. The full impact of the experience, emotionally and economically, will probably never even be calculated, let alone repaid (Moleki, 1985).

The Japanese Americans survived this insult and hardship and are now the best educated and the most economically successful of all ethnic minorities in this country (see Figure 10.5).

JEWISH AMERICANS

Although they are not a separate race or nationality and cannot be identified by physical characteristics, American Jews generally have a strong sense of being a distinct people that can be termed ethnicity. Some believe they have been set aside as chosen people for thousands of years, and they cherish traditions and a culture just as old. Today there are 6 million Jews in the United States, more than in any other country. About 3 million of them live in and near New York City.

Like the Japanese, Jewish culture places education in high esteem. As a result, the Jewish population in the United States today is highly educated. Nationally, 23 percent of all Americans have graduated from college, but 42 percent of all Jewish Americans have a college degree (Gallup Poll, 1972). Partly due to this, their median family income is well above the national average.

Jews have had to contend with anti-Semitism, or feelings against anything Jewish, since they came to this country. Sociologists disagree as to the origins of this prejudice. Traditional Christian teachings that Jews killed Jesus may have led some to anti-Semitic behavior. Other sociologists think that anti-Semitic thought is not so much affected by Christian theology as by other negative attitudes toward Jews (Glock and Stark, 1966; Middleton, 1973). Whatever the source of the problem, the Jewish community has managed to withstand the prejudice and discrimination, and many Jews have made a place for themselves in the upper strata of American society (Heilman, 1982).

WHITE ETHNICS

Partly as a reaction to Black Power, Chicano Power, and Red Power (Indian Power), middle-class and working-class whites have been seeking their roots and becoming proud of their own ethnic heritage (Greeley and McCready, 1974). Americans whose ancestors came from Ireland, Poland, Italy, Greece, and other countries have emblazoned themselves and their cars with emblems proclaiming their dual loyalty.

When these groups first came to the United States, most wanted to assimilate easily, and they often quickly divested themselves of any trappings of the "old country." They sometimes forbade their school-age children to speak anything but English, and many stopped teaching old traditions and stories they had learned as youths. The results were not what they expected. Young people often grew up with less respect for their elders, because they had little idea of what their parents believed or where they came from.

This trend is being reversed or at least slowed today in what has been termed an "ethnic revival." Some white ethnics are relearning customs of their heritage and handing them down to the next generation with pride. They no longer consider it necessary to melt into American society. Rather, they are encouraging each other to embrace their own culture within the broader society. This important distinction could bring about a more adaptable society that can apply varied resources to its problems, rather than relying on the limited outlook and experience of its Anglo-Saxon, Protestant founders (Lieberson, 1984).

White ethnics are slowly becoming a political power as some of them begin to work together against what they see as unfair social welfare practices. They worked their way to the middle class, and they think that blacks, Hispanics, and others who want to succeed should have to work just as hard. The skin color of blacks and the accent of Hispanics set them apart from other ethnic groups in America. The question remains whether blacks' and Hispanics' historical experience is enough to warrant more help for them. White ethnics seem to be answering with a resounding "no." The issue is not yet settled for others.

What Is Affirmative Action?

The lives of the minority groups in the United States continue to be greatly affected by the prejudices of the dominant white, Anglo-Saxon Protestants. Various solutions to this situation have been suggested, from assuring such groups of a guaranteed income level to allowing the system to work out equality by itself. Perhaps the most explosive suggestion that has been implemented to some degree is the policy of ***affirmative action,*** *the policy by which special consideration is given to a member of a group that has suffered discrimination in the past and is therefore considered not as able to compete for the rewards of society, such as education and jobs.* It is based on the idea expressed by President Johnson when he announced the signing into law of Executive Order 71246: "You do not take a person who for years has been hobbled by chains and liberate him, bring him up to the starting line of a race, and then say, 'you are free to compete with all others' and still justly believe that you have been completely fair" (Johnson, 1964).

The Civil Rights Act of 1964 made it illegal to discriminate against people because of race, religion, or ethnicity. Based on this legislation, businesses and colleges that had dealings with the government were forced to evaluate past hiring and promotion practices to see if there had been *inherent discrimination,* or *institutional racism.* For instance, in some businesses no one ever considered a black person a suitable candidate for supervisor because no black person had ever been supervisor. Perhaps the law firm had no associates who were Jewish because the firm had hired friends and children of friends to fill vacancies, and none of their friends were Jewish. These acts are inherently discriminatory, although they are not meant to be directed against a particular person or group. They arise out of the comfortable *status quo,* such as the fact that most of us are friends with people who are very much like ourselves in race, ethnicity, and religion. That is what makes these practices institutional cases of discrimination rather than individual cases.

The affirmative-action approach required businesses to become more representative of the nation (or their region) as a whole. Schools were asked to compile statistics on the number of students enrolled from the various minority groups. The federal government applied pressure to recruit minority students and employees in order to counteract the fact that minorities did not apply voluntarily because doors had been previously closed to them. Although goals were set for numbers of minorities to be recruited, no specific quotas were stated and no legal penalties were imposed if goals were not met when the organizations could show good-faith attempts to achieve a balance.

The Reagan administration made changes in affirmative action that critics believe will seriously hinder the chances of advancement for minorities through this avenue. For instance, Reagan changed regulations such that companies with fewer than 250 employees and $1 million in government contracts are no longer required to submit affirmative-action plans to the government. With this ruling, 75 percent of companies that contract for federal work became exempt from affirmative action. Other regulations were also added that make it more difficult to file class-action lawsuits charging discrimination against women and minority workers (Schaefer, 1984).

Sociologists at Work •

WILLIAM JULIUS WILSON IDENTIFIES THE SITUATION OF FAMILIES IN POVERTY AREAS
University of Chicago
Chicago, Illinois

William Wilson is the Lucy Flower Distinguished Service Professor of Sociology and Public Policy and former chairman of the Department of Sociology at the University of Chicago, one of the nation's oldest and most prestigious sociology departments. Among his many books are *The Truly Disadvantaged: The Inner City, The Underclass, and Public Policy,* which was selected by the editors of the *New York Times Book Review* as one of the sixteen best books published in 1987. Professor Wilson is currently president of the Sociological Research Association and directs a $2.5 million study on poverty and family structure in the inner city, funded by a consortium of foundations including Ford, Rockefeller, Carnegie, Joyce, William T. Grant, and Spencer.

What Is Your Theoretical Base?

My work as a scientist emphasizes the importance of relating the problems of race, bias, and poverty to different historical, economic, political, and social situations. I try to identify the situational context before making any conclusions about the actual behavior that I observe and describe. I believe that failure to emphasize the situational context of group behavior leads to simplistic conclusions about why groups and individuals behave the way they do.

Can You Give Us an Example of This Situational Context?

Yes. In recent years my studies have shown that the sharp increase in the number of single-parent families in the inner cities is not due to any changes in views about the formation of families, but to the decline in employment prospects of inner-city residents, particularly young black males who have been disproportionately concentrated in industries that have recently experienced the largest number of layoffs due to economic cutbacks, plant closings, and the relocation of labor sites to the suburbs. The macro-historical data that provides the situational context we are looking for suggests that this causes a shrinking pool of marriageable men, by which I mean employed men, in these inner-city neighborhoods.

This, of course, relates to changes in the occupational structure in the city of Chicago. Take an inner-city neighborhood like Oakland, which is just north of the University of Chicago and has an unemployment rate of 60 percent. In 1950 Oakland had 70 employed males for every 100 females ages 16 and over; by 1980 that figure had decreased to 19 employed males for every 100 females. That explains why 70 percent of all the families in Oakland in 1980 were headed by women. This should not be surprising as studies have often documented the deterioration of marriage and family life following unemployment.

What Is the Thrust of Your Current Work?

Currently I am conducting a study that deals with poverty, joblessness, and family structure in the inner city. The study includes a survey of 3,000 households in low-income black, Hispanic (both Puerto Rican and Mexican-American), and white areas in the city of Chicago that have poverty rates of at least 20 percent. I also have a team of eleven research assistants who have been in the inner cities for over a year collecting what we call ethnographic data, that is to say, speaking with people in leisure conversations about family life, job experiences, and relations with spouses and friends, as well as engaging in participant observation—collecting data as they participate in groups and informal studies. Finally, a group of research assistants are collecting the data that I need to examine the social situational context in which the behavior that is described by the ethnographic research and the survey data takes place. For instance, they are looking at changes in the economic situations in the inner city of Chicago, collecting data on the state of the economy, the number of jobs that are available, the political context, class structure, and demographic changes.

What Are the Implications of Your Research Thus Far?

We are not ready to say anything definitively about the findings, but I think that research will ultimately reveal the devastating consequences of living in highly concentrated poverty areas. As soon as individuals increase their economic and social position, they leave these communities for better areas. There has been a sharp exodus in recent years of higher-income minorities from these neighborhoods, leaving behind a much more concentrated disadvantaged population.

When our researchers analyze these data, we hope to hold a series of workshops for policymakers to suggest ways to break up this social isolation and open up the opportunity structure so people can move out of these neighborhoods. What I would hope to be able to do is spell out the policymaking steps that would increase choices that these people now have so that they, too, can leave if they so desire. ●

Institutional racism still exists in the United States, and minorities may sometimes deserve to be given special consideration. If accomplished with a sense of justice, this does not need to lead to a situation of reverse discrimination (discrimination against the majority group). A reasonable goal should be to establish a society in which all members have equal access to the tools for academic and economic success, and thus an equal chance to be of use to the society.

Conclusion

Relationships between the various race and ethnic groups in the United States continue to be important in the growth and development of the nation. The ways in which we choose to resolve differences between those currently in the majority and those in minorities will determine to a great extent the commitment those groups will make to the society we all share.

Summary Questions

1. What is ethnicity, and how is it transmitted?
2. What is race, and how has it been used by societies?
3. What is a minority group?
4. What is prejudice?
5. What is discrimination?
6. What is the relationship between prejudice and discrimination?
7. What are the basic patterns of race and ethnic group relations?
8. How do conflict theorists define intergroup conflict, and what are the five major factors that might contribute to it?
9. What did the research of Edna Bonacich suggest about intergroup relations?
10. What are some of the possible sources of prejudice and discrimination?
11. What is the current situation of black Americans?
12. What are the views of prominent theorists and researchers on the continuing significance of race in the United States?
13. What is the situation of Hispanic-Americans in contemporary United States?
14. What new approaches have native Americans taken to change their economically and socially depressed state?
15. How have Asian Americans adapted to life in the United States?
16. What is the position of Jewish Americans in United States society?
17. What is the "ethnic revival"?
18. What is affirmative action, and how has it worked?

Summary Answers

1. Ethnicity is a sense of peoplehood or nationhood that is culturally transmitted.
2. A race is a population that shares visible physical characteristics from inbreeding and that thinks of itself or is thought of by outsiders as distinct. It has been used by societies to justify poor treatment of minority groups.
3. A minority group is one that has less power and influence than the dominant group.
4. Prejudice is a judgment based on group membership or social status.
5. Discrimination involves treating someone differently because of his or her group membership or social status.
6. Prejudice and discrimination can exist separately, but are most often mutually reinforcing.
7. The basic patterns of race and ethnic relations are amalgamation (blending two or more groups into a society that reflects the cultural and biological traits of the group), assimilation (the minority adopting the majority culture), pluralism (various groups actively participating in the same society while retaining distinctive identities), structured inequality (when the minority group receives inferior treatment by law or custom), population relocation (when the minority group relocates either outside the territory or in a particular part of the territory), and extermination (when the majority destroys the minority).
8. When conflict exists, as it most often does, between two groups, the group that gains the most power, wealth, and prestige becomes the majority, regardless of its size. The five major factors that contribute to such conflict are visible differences between groups, competition for resources, racist ideology (justifying inferior treatment on the basis

REVIEW

of alleged inferior ability), potential for exploitation, and the minority-group response to the majority definition of the situation.

9. Bonacich found that the struggle for jobs and income is an important cause of ethnic strife.
10. Prejudice may be formed through both individual and group influences, including socialization, rationalizing through stereotypes (an exaggerated belief associated with a category), the scapegoating process, reinforcement of a self-fulfilling prophecy, ramifications of an authoritarian personality, and degree of contact with minority groups.
11. Blacks as a group have never reached parity with whites in the United States, economically or socially. Legal gains were made in the 1960s, which led to some economic growth, an increase in the number of educated blacks, and more blacks in middle-class positions. More blacks are in political positions than ever before. As a group, however, they still lag behind. During the 1980s, the gap between the black lower class and middle class widened, with educated blacks reaching the income level of educated whites while ill-trained blacks still battled unemployment rates twice that of whites and underemployment wages in those jobs they did procure.
12. Debate rages between conservative black social scientists, who believe that race is becoming less significant in the determination of economic and social well-being, and conflict researchers, who have discovered that even blacks who have reached economic equality with whites report themselves to be less satisfied with their lives than whites.
13. Hispanic-Americans are the fastest-growing minority group in the United States. Their unemployment rate is significantly higher than whites, and their median family income lags behind also. Primarily Mexican-Americans, Puerto Ricans, and Cubans, they report growing feelings of solidarity. The Immigration Reform and Control Act is designed to stem the flow of Hispanic illegal aliens.
14. The economic and social situation of native Americans is dismal. Their poverty rate, life expectancies, suicide, alcoholism rates, and other social indicators are very negative, compared to the white population. Recently, Indian groups are taking a new strategy, by becoming more organized and more insistent on being treated equally rather than trying to assimilate into mainstream culture.
15. Asian Americans come from distinct cultural backgrounds, and as a group still remain mostly a separate subculture. Their emphasis on education leads them to be generally economically successful.
16. Jewish Americans, although not a race or nationality, have a strong sense of peoplehood that has been termed "ethnicity." Both their level of education and their median family income is well above the national average.
17. In what has been termed an "ethnic revival," some white ethnics are relearning customs of their heritage and handing them down to the next generation with pride.
18. Affirmative action is the policy by which special consideration is given to a member of a group that has suffered discrimination in the past and is therefore considered not as able to compete for the rewards of society, such as education and jobs. It was designed to counteract institutional racism, or inherent discrimination, and made some progress toward that goal in the 1970s. Several Reagan administration changes have hindered the chances of advancement for minorities through this avenue.

Glossary

affirmative action the policy by which special consideration is given to a member of a group that has suffered discrimination in the past

amalgamation the blending of two or more groups into a society that reflects the cultural and biological traits of the group

apartheid strictly enforced separate facilities and privileges for blacks and whites

assimilation the pattern of race and ethnic relations in which the minority group adopts the culture of the majority

discrimination treating someone differently because of his or her group membership or social status

ethnicity a sense of peoplehood or nationhood

ethnic group a group that thinks of itself as a people or nation or is viewed by others as culturally different

extermination the pattern of race and ethnic relations in which the majority group destroys a minority group

institutional racism discrimination inherent in an institution

minority group a group that has less power and influence than the dominant group and is therefore considered not as able to compete for the rewards of society, such as education and jobs

pluralism the pattern of race and ethnic relations in which various groups actively participate in the same society while each retains its distinctive identity

population relocation the relocation of the minority either outside the territory or in a particular part of the territory

prejudice judgment of an individual on the basis of his or her group membership or social status

race a population that shares visible physical characteristics from inbreeding and thinks of itself or is thought of by outsiders as genetically distinct

racism inferior treatment on the basis of alleged inferior ability

stereotype an exaggerated belief associated with a category

structured inequality the pattern of race and ethnic relations in which the minority group receives inferior treatment by law (*de jure*) or by custom (*de facto*)

Suggested Readings

Cary Davis, Carl Haub, and JoAnne Willette. June, 1983. "U.S. Hispanics: Changing the Face of America," *Population Bulletin*, Vol. 38, No. 3. Population Reference Bureau, Inc.: Washington, D.C.

This entire issue is devoted to the changes that have and will come about in the United States because of the high fertility and immigration of Hispanics.

Alvin M. Josephy, Jr. 1982. *Now That the Buffalo's Gone: A Study of Today's American Indians.* New York: Alfred A. Knopf.

Josephy clearly documents the injustices still being inflicted upon our native Americans. His style, alternating historical and sociological data with true stories, captures the reader's interest while informing.

Harry Kitano. 1985. *Race Relations*, 3rd ed. Englewood Cliffs, N.J.: Prentice-Hall.

Kitano's book, intended as a basic text in the field, emphasizes the interaction between the dominant group and specific minority groups as the most important factor in understanding minority behavior.

National Urban League. 1986. *The State of Black America: 1986.* New York: National Urban League.

This book documents the progress and setbacks in the black community, detailing economic, educational, and political changes that affect the black community.

George Simpson, and J. Milton Yinger. 1985. *Racial and Cultural Minorities: An Analysis of Prejudice and Discrimination*, 5th ed. New York: Plenum.

A comprehensive overview of racial and ethnic prejudice and discrimination, heavy on research and detailed enough for the serious student.

Norman Yetman. 1985. *Majority and Minority: The Dynamics of Race and Ethnicity in American Life.* 4th ed. Boston: Allyn and Bacon.

Yetman's overview and sectional commentaries, coupled with classic and contemporary work in the area, produce a fine historical and structural description of race and ethnic relations in contemporary United States culture.

CHAPTER

11

GENDER ROLE INEQUALITIES

- What Are Sex and Gender Roles?
- How Do Gender Roles Compare Cross-Culturally?
- What Are the Various Theories of the Origins of Gender Roles?
- How Are People Socialized into Gender Roles?
- Close-Up on Research: Ervin Goffman on Genderisms
- What Is the Situation in the United States Concerning Gender Roles?
- What Is the "Second Stage" of Gender Relations?
- Close-Up on Theory: Jessie Bernard on the Female World
- Sociologists at Work: Alice Rossi Investigates Femininity, Masculinity, and Family Ties

How's Your Sociological Intuition?

1. In contemporary American culture, the male is generally the sexual pursuer and the female is generally the sexual object.
   - a. This pattern is the case in every known culture.
   - b. This pattern is an exception, common only in industrial societies.
   - c. This pattern is approximately reversed in some cultures, such as that of the Trobriand Islanders.
   - d. In most cultures there is no pattern of pursuer and object.
2. Personality traits such as passivity, considerateness, and jealousy are
   - a. found to be associated with females in all cultures.
   - b. not regarded as "feminine" in all cultures.
   - c. clearly biologically linked with being a female.
   - d. pure myth; women are no different from men.
3. If we measure the status of women in terms of proportion of women in the labor force, proportion of women in high-status occupations, and proportion of women attending college, the period from 1945 to 1960 involved
   - a. growth in female status.
   - b. stability in female status.
   - c. decline in female status.
   - d. a decline followed by an increase in status.
4. In 1987 women with the same education, full-time occupation, and work experience as men would be likely to earn which percent as much as men?
   - a. 62 percent
   - b. 74 percent
   - c. 86 percent
   - d. 100 percent

Answers

1. c. Our ideas about appropriate sexual behavior relate to our notions of masculinity and femininity, which are largely social creations.
2. b. It isn't always "feminine" to be passive, considerate, and jealous, as you will discover in "Cross-Cultural Comparisons of Gender Roles."
3. c. During this period, immediately preceding the recent women's movement, women lost ground.
4. a. Women earn substantially less than men, even when they have the same qualifications.

When You Have Finished Studying This Chapter, You Should Know:

- The distinction between sex and gender roles
- How gender roles compare cross-culturally
- How functionalists and conflict theorists explain gender roles
- Who the major agents of gender socialization are, and how they transmit gender roles
- Major research findings that indicate that gender roles are largely social creations
- The specific socialization processes of molding or reinforcement, differential opportunities, role modeling, and explicit verbal instruction, and how they shape gender roles
- How schools, the mass media, and the culture in general teach and reinforce gender roles
- Structural-functional and conflict interpretations of gender roles
- What the "second stage" of gender-role relations might bring

The year was 1963. Then Wendy Drew, I graduated with high honors from high school and began studies at a prestigious large university. Although I knew no women doctors, I had decided, with the encouragement of my teachers and counselor, to become a physician. I had A's and B's in all my classes except Chemistry, in which I was struggling to keep a C. Concerned about how this would affect my admission to medical school, I went to speak to the admissions director.

He calmly told me that not only my Chemistry grade was crucial, *all* my grades must be outstanding to gain admittance. In fact, he told me that my grades must be better than those of a male with similar qualifications. You see, because I was a "girl," I was considered a risk to educate. I would probably "just" get married, raise kids, and waste the state's money by not using my training working full-time as a doctor.

Rather than face the idea of four intensive and worried years of college without time for fun, I changed my major and my career direction. I was angry and disappointed, but it never occurred to me to fight this injustice. After all, my entire world was circumscribed by similar ideas.

Fifteen years later, now Wendy Drew Wallace, I moved with my husband and our children to a very small town. Our four-year-old daughter, Carey, had been attended by a female pediatrician all her life and had visited a female midwife with me many times before and after the birth of our son. Shortly after we moved to our new home, I made an appointment for us to meet the town's only pediatrician. I told Carey only that we were meeting Dr. Herbener. Imagine the look on his face when Carey dismissed him as he walked into the room by saying, "*You* can't be the doctor; you're a man!"

The difference in her attitude and mine reflects one of the greatest social changes we have experienced in the past two decades: change in the definitions of gender roles. Most societies have two universal criteria for ascribing status within a stratification system: gender and age. These attributes may be chosen because they are immediately known at birth, "making it possible to begin the training of the individual for his potential statuses and roles at once" (Linton, 1936, pp. 115–116).

In the United States, the use of gender and age to ascribe status for years has perpetuated a system of gender role and age inequality. Ever since women have become aware of alternatives to the existing system, they have worked tirelessly for changes in the *status quo.* No longer will an admissions director casually bandy about a sexist requirement, although sexist requirements might still be in force surreptitiously. No longer would a bright woman accept his definition of the situation. No longer will most children grow to be nineteen and not have met a female physician.

We have "come a long way," but we have only made progress toward changing the situation rather than eradicating it. Women must reach parity with men

Despite continued resistance, many women are entering traditionally male professions. Female pilots are still the exception, not the rule. (*Photo courtesy the author*)

in all of the major areas of life: economic, educational, social, and personal. When these changes occur, our entire society should grow stronger, because it will be encouraging individuals to nurture their strengths, whether those lie in homemaking or open-heart surgery.

What Are Sex and Gender Roles?

***Sex** refers to the biological differences between males and females.* The genetic differences between males and females are straightforward. Each ovum (egg) the female produces has an X chromosome. Each sperm from the male carries either an X chromosome or a Y chromosome. When the ovum is fertilized with a sperm, the resulting new cell will have, then, one X from the female, and either an X or a Y from the male. Two X chromosomes produce a girl, and an X and a Y produce a boy.

When the embryo is three weeks old, some organs develop male characteristics and some develop female characteristics, due to the secretion of testosterone caused by the Y chromosome (Baker et al., 1980). Chromosome differences seem to have other physical effects. Females are less susceptible to many diseases and exhibit fewer genetically transmitted defects, such as hemophilia and colorblindness. In the United States about 106 males are born for every 100 females born, but this difference levels off, because more males die before age twenty (Baker, 1980).

Every society socializes its males and females to behavior that is considered "masculine" or "feminine" within that culture. *The term **gender** refers to culturally transmitted differences between men and women.* We learn gender-appropriate behavior through role-modeling, explicit instruction, and cultural transmission, just as we learn other social behaviors. Thus, gender refers to the social rather than biological characteristics that are related to being male or female.

How Do Gender Roles Compare Cross-Culturally?

Anthropologists have looked for links between the development of sexual divisions of labor and the assignment of gender roles (Gough, 1971; Morris, 1978). Their work suggests that sexual division of labor developed when people began to hunt for their food rather than simply to gather it. Men traveled after game, because the women were often nursing babies or taking care of young children. Evidence suggests, however, that at that time no status difference existed in their positions. Women were highly valued because they were the food gatherers. Desmond Morris (1978) explains this system and comments on its implications today:

> In our ancient past, women were absolutely at the center of society. It was the hunters, the men, who went off to the periphery. There was a division of labor: Females gathered and prepared food and reared the children. Males went off and hunted. But that division didn't mean that one sex was more important than the other. Women's Lib, I think, is becoming concerned with the wrong kinds of things. What really matters is that women should be given back their role of equal importance with men as members of society (p. 77).

The change in status of women in cultures all over the world during the past few decades clearly shows change in gender-role definition. This could be due to the fact that rigidly defined gender roles for economic and nurturing functions have outlived their usefulness. It is also possible that such roles have changed because women command more power in industrialized society than they did under former economic systems or because socialization practices have changed drastically (M. Harris, 1975).

If biology determined gender roles, every culture over time would make the same assumptions regarding the tasks of men and women. This did not happen. Instead, the world's cultures have a fascinating variety of ways to express gender.

THE HOPI INDIANS

Each Hopi Indian clan is headed by a woman and includes her brothers and sisters and all of their descendants. The mother's brother is the prime source of discipline for the children, who are given tasks according to their age and ability rather than their sex. The men and women work cooperatively in all areas, and treat each other equally. The Hopi never question the custom of a husband's living in the wife's home (Leavitt, 1970; Queen & Haberstein, 1974). All of these customs would be quite unusual in mainstream North American families.

SIMPLE CULTURES OF THE SOUTH PACIFIC

Margaret Mead's study of three tribes in the South Pacific is a landmark in cross-cultural gender-role research (Mead, 1935). Mead lived with the Arapesh, the Mundugumor, and the Tchambuli, carefully observing and minutely describing their customs and culture. She found all Arapesh people are expected to be loving, considerate, and cooperative. Both men and women tend children and are responsible for food. The Mundugumor, in sharp contrast, are usually aggressive, ruthless, and violent.

In the third tribe, the Tchambuli, the gender roles are differentiated as they are in Western culture, but the Tchambuli women are the providers and dominate the men, having an impersonal attitude toward their families. Men, in contrast, are loving toward their children, less responsible for the economic needs of the family than are women, and more emotional.

Mead concluded from her studies that culture determines what is considered "normal" behavior for a man or woman and that many of our "masculine" or "feminine" traits are "as lightly linked to sex as are the clothing, the manners, and the form of headdress that a society at a given period assigns to either sex" (Mead, 1935, p. 280).

Richard Sorenson lived among the Fore in New Guinea and observed changes in their gender roles that were obviously linked to changes in their social structure. The Fore had lived a communal life without chiefs or priests and shared all goods within the tribe. The men slashed and burned the vegetation to prepare garden sites; the women cleared weeds and grass, prepared the soil, transplanted, cultivated, and harvested (Sorenson, 1977).

The society of the Fore changed character drastically when a new road was built connecting their village with the outside world and the coffee plantations. Many of the men learned to cultivate coffee by working on the plantations and returned to the village to grow it there. Women continued their traditional tasks and took on some of the men's former tasks. In contrast to their previous tranquility and harmony, the new Fore culture came to include "many incidents of anger, withdrawal, aggressiveness, and stinginess" (p. 114). The new society included more material wealth, at the cost of more competition, less relaxation, less involvement of father in the childrearing, more emphasis on exchange, and less on sharing. In short, their world had become more "masculine" in modern Western terms, and given up its communal, benevolent roots.

Other anthropologists since Mead and Sorenson also conclude that gender differences are primarily culturally determined and change as the culture changes (D'Andrade, 1966; Rosenblatt & Cunningham, 1976). We will briefly look at gender-role definitions in several more advanced cultures.

THE ISRAELI KIBBUTZ

One of the most interesting experiments in changing gender role stereotypes was carried out in the *kibbutz*. A kibbutz is a collective farm or settlement in Israel. From its inception, the kibbutz was dedicated to the idea of equality between men and women. Women shared equally in the economic productivity of the kibbutz and were therefore not dependent on their husbands for the economic well-being. The community shared in raising the children, acquiring goods, and in household chores like cooking, laundry, and cleaning.

Gradually men and women reverted to more traditional male–female gender roles in the kibbutz (Schlesinger, 1977). Mothers spent more time with their children, and the number of family activities increased. One researcher suggests that productive work in the kibbutz was always more prestigious than service work, and women were only allowed to do productive work as long as there was a pressing need for productive workers (R. Blumberg, 1973). Another points out that although kibbutz men allowed women to take on traditional male productive roles, the men never developed a corresponding interest in traditionally female service roles. Rather, "the emphasis was on changing women's roles without any corresponding change in men's roles" (Hacker, 1975, p. 189). This lack of commitment could be the variable which caused the reversal in female and male positions.

CHINA

The People's Republic of China has experienced great change in attitudes toward gender roles, partly because its government has a high degree of control over its people. In the past, women were bought and sold, marriages were prearranged, rape was common, and women had "no rights."

In the forty years since China's Communist Revolution, the position of women in Chinese society has improved a great deal. The Marriage Law of 1950 gave women many new rights and abolished arranged marriages, the buying of wives, polygamy, the killing of female children, and child marriage. It provided procedures for divorce, for the remarriage of widows, and for females to own property.

During the Cultural Revolution under Chairman Mao, the cause of women's rights was aided through Speak-Bitterness meetings—the Chinese equivalent of consciousness-raising groups. At these meetings, women were encouraged to speak about their bitterness toward what had happened to them as women before the revolution. They released anger and found fellowship among women who felt and thought much as they did.

Today, 90 percent of Chinese women work outside their homes. They are represented in every occupation and receive equal pay for equal work. Their children are often cared for in well-run child-care centers near or in their places of work. The "aunties" who staff the centers are usually stable, loving, parent-substitutes who rarely leave their jobs. Mothers with a newborn baby may take time off from work to nurse their child. The government has declared that men and women shall share household duties like cooking and cleaning (Tavris, 1974). These changes in China seem to be useful and satisfying to the men and women there.

In spite of the gains for Chinese women, improvement is needed. New laws mandate only one child per family and strongly encourage abortion if a woman becomes pregnant a second time. Male children are still preferred by most mothers and fathers. Women are underrepresented at top levels of management, are more likely to be unemployed, and are less likely to be allowed to obtain well-paying heavy work (Yorburg, 1974).

What Are the Various Theories of the Origins of Gender Roles?

Biological differences have often been used to justify distinctions between men and women. Many formerly accepted biological arguments are now proving unfounded, and gender roles in many societies are changing rapidly. Because we can assume that our biological makeup is probably not significantly different than it was twenty years ago, we must attribute the rapid international change in gender roles to social change. Sociologists generally agree that women and men fit their gender roles largely because they are socialized to do so. However, they approach the study of gender from different assumptions.

FUNCTIONALIST THEORY

Structural-functionalists believe that men and women perform separate roles because this division is useful to society. For example, Talcott Parsons suggests the family is a social system with two major needs: getting its work done and staying in emotional order. Parsons believes men are "naturally" more "instrumental," or oriented toward getting work done, and women are "naturally" more "expressive," or oriented toward taking care of the family's socio-emotional needs (Parsons & Bales, 1955). Functionalists see the division of labor in the family system according to gender as functional to the family and to society as a whole. Though such a division may have been useful to society in the past, sociologists began to question Parsons' conclusions as they grew more attuned to issues of inequality during the 1960s. The Women's Movement sensitized Americans to the implications of neatly categorizing all economic behavior as male and all nurturing behavior as female. In the past twenty-five years more adults have sought to form relationships in which both their instrumental and expressive traits can grow to their highest potential, whether they are men or women.

CONFLICT THEORY

Conflict theory sees the almost universal inequality between the sexes in societies as an outgrowth of ***patriarchy,*** *the form of social organization in which men dominate, or rule over, women* (R. Collins, 1985; Lengermann & Wallace, 1985). Patriarchy assumes that men are superior to women. This belief is based on ***sexism,*** *or the belief that one sex is inferior and thus deserves inferior treatment*. Sexist beliefs continue to dominate our society and cause men to assume privilege and women to assume secondary status. Just as racism caused blacks and other minority groups to doubt their self-worth, so sexism may affect a women's potential by limiting her own perceived horizons.

Friedrich Engels believed women in hunting and gathering societies were generally more socially equal to men than are women in industrialized societies (Engels, 1884). When horticulture was developed and land began to be owned and hence passed down from generation to generation, men became monogamous in order to assure that children who inherited their property were their own. This forced women into a subservient role, requiring them to be faithful to one husband and dependent upon his ability to fend for the family.

The main dimensions of sexual inequality are still seen in the varying degrees of access women and men have to the power and wealth in society. Susan Chafetz writes about the many ways in which women are clearly still not as powerful as men in our society:

1. Women own fewer material goods and services.
2. They have less education.
3. They have less public and interpersonal decision-making power.
4. They hold fewer prestige-conferring roles, for instance, president of a group or organization.
5. They have fewer opportunities for enrichment and gratification.
6. They have fewer formal rights.
7. They own fewer life-sustaining necessities, for instance, property.

In addition, women must confront both societal constraints concerning proper behavior for women and fear of physical coercion (Chafetz, 1984). For instance, only women need fear being raped on a date (Loy & Stewart, 1984; E. Sweet, 1985). On all of these dimensions, men and women clearly are not yet equal in contemporary American society (Klein, 1984).

This inherently unequal system affects the men in society as well. Many writers recognize that men are

ON WOMEN

As we have already seen, the concept of "women's place" is changing drastically in our culture, and is significantly different among different cultures. These quotations illustrate these differences:

I thank thee, O Lord, that thou hast not created me a woman. (Daily Orthodox Jewish prayer for males)

In childhood a female must be subject to her father, in youth to her husband, when her husband is dead to her sons; a woman must never be independent. (*The Laws of Manus*, Hindu, from approximately 200 B.C.)

A woman is taken into man's society for the needs of generation [reproduction]; with the disappearance of woman's fecundity and beauty, she would no longer be able to associate with another man. (Thomas Aquinas, c. 1258–1264)

I never knew a tolerable woman to be fond of her own sex. (Jonathan Swift, 1710)

A man in general is better pleased when he has a good dinner than when his wife talks Greek. (Samuel Johnson, 1759)

Whatever women do they must do twice as good as men to be thought half as good. Luckily, this is not difficult. (Charlotte Whitton [mayor of Ottawa], 1963).

It would be preposterously naive to suggest that a B.A. can be made as attractive to girls as a marriage license. (Dr. Grayson Kirk [when president of Columbia University], 1969)

It occurred to me when I was thirteen and wearing white gloves and Mary Janes and going to dance school that no one should have to dance backwards all their lives (Jill Ruckelshaus, 1973).

The only thing that seems eternal and natural in motherhood is ambivalence. (Jane Lazarre [author of *The Mother Knot*], 1976).

Many people feel uncomfortable with the identity society has dealt them. They do not like being pigeonholed in a social role (breadwinner, housewife, teacher, middle-aged accountant, city dweller, student). What is new today is not the *feeling* of discomfort, but the urgency with which so many act to modify or discard the destiny prescribed for them by the old social roles. (Daniel Yankelovich, *New Rules*, 1981).

not free to develop the "feminine," or nurturing, aspects of their personalities as long as they are pressured to achieve and compete for resources (Doyle, 1983; French, 1985; Lengermann & Wallace, 1985). Men are subject to such constraints on their behavior, for instance, as being thought less masculine if they express tender emotions.

Some conflict theorists suggest that capitalism increases sexism, but studies of socialist societies reveal a strong patriarchy as well, indicating that the form of economic institution may not be the major determinant of gender role inequality (Chafetz, 1984; Swafford, 1978). The conflict perspective is based on the idea that those who control the means of production control the power, hence economic power is considered carefully in conflict analyses of gender inequality. Wealth and income enable persons to buy other kinds of power, from legal help to educational opportunities. Thus, gaining monetary parity for women must be a primary goal in reordering the sexual stratification system.

How Are People Socialized into Gender Roles?

Imagine how "feminine" a girl would be who was raised by her father and six brothers on a ranch eighty miles from the nearest town. Assume, for good measure, she had no exposure to television, magazines, newspapers, or books. Or, think about how "masculine" a boy might be who was raised by his mother on the grounds of an isolated girls' academy.

Now imagine a very different world totally void of social differences for the different genders. Families have identical expectations of sons and daughters. Children of both genders receive dolls, baseball gloves, training in how to play football, and ballet lessons. In all media, men and women act and dress in the same fashion. The language has been "cleansed" of all gender cues. Half of all secretaries are male and half of the executives are female. How much traditional "feminine" and "masculine" behavior would survive in such an environment?

We would expect these unusual socialization environments to produce some unusual variations on the masculinity–femininity theme. The imaginary scenes suggest there are many modes through which a person is taught what it is to be male or female in our culture.

Throughout our lives, we are presented with images of femininity and masculinity that help us accept these definitions while opposing any tendency to deviate from our culturally prescribed roles. The major agents of this socialization process are the family, the schools, the media, and the community.

FAMILY INFLUENCES

Parents and family are, for most people, the dominant influence in shaping gender identity. From the moment of birth, gender is an important issue. "It's a girl!" or "It's a boy!" are likely to be the first words the physician speaks upon delivery of an infant. A mother dresses her infant in blue or pink so that even strangers can detect the gender and respond appropriately—and parents take offense at someone's mistaking their cute little girl for a handsome boy. Children are given a gender label from the start, and parents treat children according to the label.

As the child grows, gender identity is established through four processes: (1) molding, or reinforcement; (2) opportunities; (3) role modeling; and (4) explicit verbal instruction.

REINFORCEMENT. One interesting experiment illustrates the *reinforcement* phenomenon. Researchers asked young mothers to play with a six-month-old infant dressed in a pink dress. Many said they could "just tell" she was a girl, others stated that "she cries more softly" than a boy. In the same study, other mothers were given a six-month-old in blue overalls. They smiled at this child less often, and offered him a doll to play with only one-third as often as they did the pink-clothed child. The interesting twist in the experiment is that all of the mothers played with the same child. Only the clothes and the name given the baby were changed (Self & Datan, 1976). Obviously, these mothers treated the same infant differently only because of the infant's supposed gender.

Although neutral bystanders cannot usually determine the sex of a diapered infant, parents have been found to describe their newborn daughters as tiny, soft, fine-featured, and delicate, and to see their newborn sons as strong, alert, and well-coordinated (Rubin et al., 1974). Parents will work harder to elicit smiling and cooing from daughters than from sons as early as age seven weeks (Moss, 1976). The "teaching" of desired feminine behavior has begun, even though no difference in actual response between boys and girls is yet noticeable (Lengermann & Wallace, 1985).

As time goes by, girls will be nurtured longer and rewarded more for dependent behavior. Boys may be given more freedom to be assertive. They are expected to break the bonds of dependence earlier than girls, and will generally be cuddled for a shorter period of their lives than girls (Baker et al. 1980; Bardwick Douvan, 1971; Bem, 1983; R. Hartley, 1966; M. Lewis, 1972).

OPPORTUNITIES. Families also provide differing opportunities for boys and girls. Although girls may sometimes wear jeans, boys do not usually wear dresses or skirts. In this way, the masculine role is more restrictive than the feminine. On the other hand, girls are less likely than boys to receive toy guns, trucks, trains, or bats and balls, and boys are unlikely to receive dolls and carriages (Hartley, 1966). Girls are more likely to be allowed access to their mother's old jewelry, dressy clothes, and high-heeled shoes. Boys are more likely to be taken along with Dad on "masculine" trips such as fishing or sports events.

An interesting study in this area reports strong sex typing regarding chores. A statewide random sample of parents of children from ages two through seven found they differentiate strongly between boys' and girls' tasks around the house. Thus, boys are expected to help Dad in the workshop and girls assist Mom in the kitchen. It is obvious that this system narrows the opportunities for children to widen their range of skills for adulthood (Hartley, 1966).

ROLE MODELING. Role modeling is a major mechanism of gender socialization. Even before they realize the sexual basis for gender labeling, children are well aware of masculine and feminine roles, and most children accept their categorization as a girl or boy (Baker et al., 1980; Sapiro, 1986). A female child usually identifies with her mother and wants to be like her, and a male child usually wants to be like his father. As a result, girls often are interested in pretty clothes, hairstyles, makeup, and cooking. They develop the passive and gentle side of their personalities, if this is what they perceive in their role models. Boys become interested in tools, cars, and sports, and they strive to be assertive and not to show their emotions. Role modeling is more effective when the child has a strong and warm relationship with the role model (Bandura, 1963).

Through watching their parents and other adults interact, children learn that gender is a basic principle in the organization of social life and that their world is patterned by it (Bem, 1983). They learn, for instance, that women avoid bad language and frequently phrase opinions in questions, whereas men state their opinions more directly and interrupt more frequently

We learn some things about being a man, such as shaving, through explicit instruction. Other more subtle lessons, such as how to relate to women, are more likely transmitted through role modeling. (*Dave Schaefer/The Picture Cube*)

(Spender, 1982). They see their fathers driving whenever both their parents are in the car and putting their arms around their mothers in a protective gesture (Walum-Richardson, 1981). They see men and older boys being rated on the basis of their aggressive abilities and women and older girls on the basis of their beauty (Banner, 1983). These implicit lessons are strong influences on the gender socialization process.

EXPLICIT VERBAL INSTRUCTION. Some of the socialization into gender roles involves *explicit verbal instruction,* that is, the child is told that certain behavior is or is not a part of the gender role: "Boys do not cry." "Girls are not supposed to let their slips or panties show." "Boys don't wear dresses." "Ladies before gentlemen." "Girls are not supposed to play rough like boys do." "Boys are stronger than girls." Verbal instruction is probably less important than opportunity differences and role modeling. Indeed, if the individual has not already begun to identify with the proper role model, then verbal instructions are likely to have little effect (Lengermann & Wallace, 1985).

SCHOOLS

In developed societies, schools are important agents of gender socialization. The school continues the teaching of appropriate gender behavior by teaching boys and girls appropriate behavior in the wider outside world. Although few teachers attempt to teach traditional roles explicitly, messages about appropriate behavior are being given in obvious ways and sometimes in less obvious ways. For example, girls most often do the "housekeeping" and "helping" chores of a classroom, while boys tend to be more defiant of their primarily female teachers, doing things like asking to go to the bathroom when they don't really need to (Best, 1983). Boys typically play competitive, tough games in larger groups and monopolize the central play areas. Girls play more verbal and imaginative games in groups of two to four (Best, 1983; Lever, 1978).

TEXTBOOKS. Within the classroom, students use textbooks to learn about the world ouside their families and classrooms. Even when textbooks do not directly address male and female role differences, they comment on gender roles through the actions of their characters and through the notable absence of female characters. Female and male characters provide models for young people who are forming self-identities. Raphaela Best calls these lessons in gender roles "the second curriculum" (1983).

Marjorie U'Ren analyzed the content of the textbooks adopted or recommended for the second through sixth grades in California (1971). She found a traditional portrayal of females as very weak. In 75 percent of the stories the main characters were males, and only 20 percent of story space was devoted to females. Stories about girls were shorter and less interesting than those about boys. Males were generally presented in adventurous activities such as discovering oil, driving race cars, playing ball, leading groups, or resolving disputes. In contrast, the girls rarely left the confines of the family or received recognition for their achievements.

Fathers were portrayed as problem solvers, builders, controllers, and creators, whereas a mother was shown as "a pleasant, hardworking, but basically uninteresting individual, [who] offers little excitement" (U'Ren, 1971, p. 221).

As U'Ren summarizes schoolbook gender differences with regard to personalities:

> The emphasis on masculine strength extends beyond physical qualities. Males of all ages are pictured as having greater mental perseverance and moral strength than females. Not only are females more often described as lazy and incapable of independent thinking or direct action, but they are also shown as giving up more easily. They collapse into tears, they betray secrets, they are more likely to act upon petty or selfish motives (p. 223).

U'Ren advocates a more balanced approach to textbook material, in order to give students a more realistic view of what it is to be a man or a woman today. She calls for "stories that inspire all people . . . to aim high and achieve their best, and an end to a textbook world where male figures outnumber and dominate, and female characters lack spirit, curiosity, and originality" (U'Ren, 1971, p. 225).

LEISURE READING. Children's leisure reading also influences their gender role assumptions. Children's literature contains stereotypic behavior that describes traditional male and female gender roles. The first major study done in this area found that prizewinning children's books contained eleven pictures of males to every one picture of a female, and one-third of the books had no female characters at all (Weitzman & Eifler, 1972). Women in the stories were all housewives, and none of the fathers helped in work around the house. In reality, 42 percent of women with children under 6 years of age and 58 percent of women with children 6 to 17 years of age were working outside the home the year the books were studied (R. Smith, 1979b). Romance novels, now popular among young teenage girls, depict women as victims of male aggression and define women only in relationship to their aggressors (Modleski, 1980; Radway, 1983). Despite some efforts to correct the balance of male and female characters, both school textbooks and children's literature continue to reinforce stereotypic gender role behavior and give a distorted picture of actual behavior in the United States today (Best, 1983; Weitzman, 1979).

COURSE SEGREGATION. Schools also channel students toward gender roles in other ways. Many courses are distinctly gender-segregated. Physical education classes have traditionally been segregated by gender, although this is changing in many parts of the country. Certain classes, such as sewing or home economics, are seldom chosen by males, and others, such as auto shop, are rarely chosen by females. For instance, although computer knowledge will be essential for tomorrow's leaders, boys far outnumber girls in high school and college computer courses (Klein, 1984). Some researchers attribute this to girls lacking confidence in their ability in such "masculine" fields; others see it as girls placating boys who want to dominate in math classes (Sherman, 1980; Tobias & Weisbrod, 1980). Furthermore, in all classes, teachers praise boys more than girls, give boys more academic help, and are more likely to accept boys' comments in classroom discussions (Sadker & Sadker, 1985). (For further discussion of this, see the "Close-Up on Research" in Chapter 17, "Education.")

In extracurricular activities, cheerleaders are usually girls, whereas the major school sports figures are usually boys. Many sports played against other schools are restricted to one sex, as wrestling, football, field hockey, and volleyball. In sports like basketball, there may be both a boys' team and a girls' team.

Title IX of the Education Amendments of 1972 prohibits any federally funded educational program or activity from discriminating on the basis of gender. This legislation has opened many programs which formerly had been closed to women (Lipman-Blumen, 1984). However, some restrictions continue as a matter of informal custom. As noted in the chapter on deviance and social control, the informal controls of custom, supported by peer pressure and informal sanctions, may be a stronger control over deviant behavior than official policies and sanctions. For these reasons, even though most male students will probably spend some of their adult lives living alone, few of them will select a home economics course in high school.

MEDIA. In addition to the influence of family and schools, most people are exposed to massive doses of television, popular music, motion pictures, magazines, and newspapers. In dealing with a category as enormous and diverse as the media, it is important to be careful about generalizing, but various analyses of segments of the media reveal consistent patterns in the portrayal of male and female roles. Although some media address factual matters, most material presented is selected for entertainment. What is transmitted, therefore, is not a realistic portrayal but an exaggerated version of social life. Gender images are often caricatures of either the audience's or the sponsor's ideal people. Thus, an audience ideal male is not just brave, he is ridiculously brave, incredibly good-looking, crafty, and lucky. The female ideal is a superwoman who is beautiful, cunning, tolerant, and properly fulfills the male's adolescent sex fantasies.

Feminine females? Women are increasingly encouraged to participate actively in sports. A few decades ago, their role was largely that of cheerleader. (*AP/Wide World Photos*)

ADVERTISING. The images of men and women that television and magazine advertisers promote are usually flattering to the intended consumer. For example, the Marlboro ads that feature men riding horses in rough weather or skillfully handling cattle aim to appeal to the virile self-image of many men who have *never* ridden a horse.

Sponsors may also portray the genders in ways that are appealing to the opposite sex. An obvious example is the use of a "classy young woman" approving the product (Goffman, 1977). The return of the miniskirted or swimsuited woman in advertising is another indicator of this trend, as is the popularity of advertisements that suggest that men might be able to "buy" a woman with diamonds or other expensive presents. Gaye Tuchman suggests that such a stereotyped portrait of women bespeaks their symbolic annihilation by the media (Tuchman, 1979).

In today's advertising, women are most often portrayed in the home instead of in an outside occupation, and men's voices are almost exclusively used as the background "voice of authority." Male actors are chosen to sell financial services and expensive household purchases such as cars, whereas women are most often in ads for food, clothes, and household cleaners (Busby, 1975; Courtney & Whipple, 1983).

The media do not transmit a unified image of male and female gender roles, but portray traditional roles, caricatured "ideal" roles, and occasionally egalitarian roles. People in American society spend a great deal of time with the media, and the media strongly influence their perceptions of gender roles. Our "Close-Up on Research" highlights Erving Goffman's analysis of the visual portrayal of gender roles in the print media.

CULTURE

The cultural environment also influences definitions of appropriate gender role behavior. The socially shared ideas of how women and men should act are transmitted in many diverse ways, including differences in language and observed interactions with the institutions of society.

LANGUAGE. The English language offers no easy way to discuss a person without revealing his or her gender. From birth, children are given names that serve

CLOSE-UP on • *RESEARCH* •

Erving Goffman on Genderisms

The Researcher and the Setting

Erving Goffman's sociological methods are rather unusual. Whereas many sociologists have adopted large-scale survey research techniques with computer-assisted data analysis, Goffman generally relies on the fieldwork method. Like most symbolic interactionists, Goffman's theories focus on the symbolic meanings of everyday interactions, in such varied settings as gambling casinos and hospital operating rooms. In this study Goffman turns his power of observation to studying the portrayal of gender roles in magazine ads.

The Researcher's Goal

A clear statement of intent can be found in the title of his article, "An Admittedly Malicious Look at How Advertising Reinforces Sexual Role Stereotypes." (Note Goffman uses the term "sexual role" in the sense we use "gender role" in this text.) Goffman sets out to explore how illustrations in advertising reinforce gender role images through the placement of models and the choice of activities in which the models engage.

Theory and Concepts

On the surface Goffman's theory appears simple: Advertising reinforces sexual role stereotypes. But, Goffman, who is often viewed as an ethnographer, goes beyond this. *Ethnographers* generally seek to describe a culture, especially the unspoken rules which define the culture. Ethnographic studies can serve two purposes. First, they help test an existing idea, such as "advertising reinforces stereotypes." Second, they help develop new ideas, such as how the ads reinforce stereotypes, and which stereotypes they convey. Thus fieldwork and ethnography often serve both to test theories and to develop theories. Theories derived from field observations or through evaluation of existing data are sometimes called *grounded theories*.

Goffman's field observations are not guided by one specific hypothesis. Instead they follow broader guidelines. In Goffman's words:

> When one looks at the presentation of gender in advertisements, attention should be directed not merely to uncovering advertisers' stereotypes concerning the differences between the sexes . . . [but] attend to how those who compose pictures can choreograph the materials available in social situations in order to achieve their end, namely, the presentation of a scene that is meaningful, whose meaning can be read at a flash (1977, p. 60).

Proposition: "Behind infinitely varied scenic configurations, one might be able to discern a single ritual idiom: behind a multitude of surface differences, a small number of structural forms" (Goffman, 1977, p. 60).

More simply stated, the wide variety of images selected for advertisements conveys important social messages about the fundamental social order.

Two of Goffman's major concepts are ritual and structural forms. *Ritual* is a culturally standardized set of actions that have symbolic significance and that are performed according to tradition. There are many gender role rituals, including "him" holding the door for "her," "him" carrying "her" books, and "him" walking on the street side of "her." Goffman cites boy–girl "wrestling" as a ritualistic form of play for which the symbolic meaning is that the male can physically dominate the female.

Structural forms are forms that appear to be different upon surface investigation, but that present a unified structure when observed in light of ritual behavior. An example of a structural form is socially prescribed female inequality, which appears in many superficially different forms. For instance, many rituals mentioned above suggest the basic theme that women are weak and dependent on men. Goffman sees this theme, or structural form, portrayed in a variety of ways in advertising. For instance the male is usually placed physically above the female in a position of symbolic superiority. These underlying themes concerning gender role stereotypes as demonstrated in advertising Goffman termed *genderisms*.

Research Design

Although this study would formally be classified as a *content analysis,* it shares many similarities with Goffman's earlier field studies. In a content analysis, the researcher uses existing communication—such as letters, newspapers, or photographs—to learn about a group. Fieldwork involves work in the real world rather than in a laboratory setting and entails approaching the subject matter with few preconceptions in an attempt to explore and to develop explanations of the subject.

Goffman seeks to find the meaning conveyed through advertising illustrations. This is particularly challenging, because meaning, by its nature, cannot be directly observed. Any particular picture, gesture, or utterance may be interpreted various ways. Yet Goffman, like other symbolic interactionists, is dedicated to further understanding how we communicate symbolically and nonverbally.

Because the study is exploratory, Goffman need not be held to all restrictions governing an experimental test of an hypothesis. By his own admission, he is not objective but is committed to the possibility that advertising reinforces stereotypes. Also, the advertising illustrations he studies are not representative of all ads. In his words, he uses illustrations "at will from newspapers and popular magazines easy to hand."

Findings

Goffman finds support for the idea that advertising reinforces gender-role stereotypes. He also elaborates on how advertising does this and what stereotypes are conveyed. He notes several patterns:

1. *Function ranking*: in photos showing men and women collaborating face-to-face in an undertaking, "the man . . . is likely to perform the executive role" (p. 61).
2. *The ritualization of subordination*: in photos showing both men and women, "men tend to be located higher than women, thus allowing elevation to be exploited as a delineative resource . . . [since] elevation seems to be employed indicatively in our society, high physical place symbolizing high social place" (p. 61).
3. *Snuggling*: women are more often shown leaning against or resting their limbs on men, the assumption being "that a woman is less likely to have sexual intent than a man, and that her use of his body is therefore less suspect than his use of hers" (p. 62).
4. *Beds and floors*: children and women are pictured on floors and beds more than men are, again placing them in a physically lower place and in a position "from which physical defense of oneself can least well be initiated . . . [thus rendering] one very dependent on the benignness of the surroundings" (p. 62).
5. *Mock assault games*: such games as "chase-and-capture" are pictured often in advertisements. In these scenes, women are shown being chased by and captured by men, while "underneath this show (is) . . . the suggestion of what he could do if he got serious about it" (p. 63).

Implications

Goffman's content analysis of advertising photographs seems to bear out his initial theory that gender role stereotypes may be reinforced in advertising, and this goes beyond blatant examples of women shown as sex objects and men shown as virile and emotionless. Advertising also indicates social position through placement of the men and women in the photos and choice of activities in which either is engaged. Although other studies are needed, the implication for those who wish to equalize the social positions of men and women is to screen advertising with these subtle variables in mind, in addition to considering obvious examples of sexist treatment.

Goffman's work here is typical of the symbolic interactionist approach in that it moves from the concrete (specific photographs) to the general (rituals and structural forms). The analysis also moves from observations of the micro level (encounters between individuals) to observations at the macro level (the role and status of male and female in society). This illustrates our suggestion in Chapter I that science need not always proceed neatly from hypothesis to testing through observation. Often observation precedes and inspires theoretical insight, which becomes the basis of future research studies.

Questions

1. The sample from which Goffman drew his examples was not representative. Do you think his findings would be upheld if a systematic search of advertising in the most popular magazines was undertaken? Why or why not?
2. It is possible that the advertisers who depict men and women in stereotypic gender roles are simply reflecting what they see in American society. If so, is this wrong? Could a change in advertising bring about a change in the social structure that would allow women a more equal place in society, or is advertising merely a reflection of society and never a molding influence?
3. A content analysis always involves some measure of subjectivity, from choosing the material to be analyzed to developing a framework in which to discuss it. Because of this subjectivity, some social scientists dismiss content analysis as "fuzzy" research. How do you react to this research method as opposed to the others you have seen thus far: the survey method and the experiment?

SOURCES Erving Goffman. August, 1977. "Genderisms: An admittedly malicious look at how advertising reinforces sexual role stereotypes." *Psychology Today*, pp. 60–63. Erving Goffman. 1979. *Gender Advertisements*. New York: Harper and Row.

as gender labels. Every time someone refers to someone else, it is either by using the person's name or by a personal pronoun (he or she) that states gender. English makes no other social difference so prominent. In virtually every discussion of a person, gender is revealed, but not age, race, ethnic background, religion, or social status. This constant reminder of who is male and who is female contributes to gender socialization, because it helps us to make associations between gender and behavior.

Another aspect of language that helps people learn their gender identity is the presence of gender-linked derogatory names, like calling a male a "sissy" or a female an "old maid." This not only describes but also condemns the person. Such name-calling teaches people what males and females should *not* be and provides strong social control over gender roles. It is interesting to note that corresponding terms are much less derogatory for males. For instance, "bachelor," the logical correlate of "old maid," does not carry the strong condemnation of the term used for women.

OBSERVED INTERACTIONS IN INSTITUTIONS. We learn much of our gender-role expectations by observing and participating in male and female behavior in society's institutions. Today's women play minor roles in the major social institutions of government, religion, economics, and education. Although women voters outnumber men, female members in religious organizations and schools is similar in proportion to that of men, and the number of women in the paid workforce is approaching that of men, few women hold leadership positions in government, religion, education, or industry. In terms of occupying powerful and prestigious positions in these institutions, women are still a minority. Male and female children observe this and assume these future roles for themselves.

In the family, women are still socially central and dominant, organizing and leading most family activities. Women usually tend the children, cook, clean or supervise cleaning, shop and arrange the social calendar. Often women successfully claim the house or major portions of it as their "turf." Thus, a wife may refer to "my kitchen" or "my living room." Attempts by children or husband to "invade" this territory with their activities may be met with indignation, such as, "Surely you do not intend to develop pictures in *my* kitchen."

In order to come to parity with men in the other institutions, women must achieve cooperation within the family that will free their energies to work elsewhere if they choose to do so (Schooler et al., 1984). Betty Friedan, in a recent assessment of the status of women in the United States, expresses her hope that we are moving to a system in which men and women "share the chores of home and children according to their abilities and needs" (Friedman, 1981). The house would be shared territory both in terms of use *and* responsibility.

Boys would be socialized to assume equal responsibility in the traditionally female-dominated family, and girls would grow to expect cooperation among all family members in household tasks. Until this occurs, women who choose to enter the paid work force, which is currently male dominated, usually are required to fill two full-time positions: one at work and one at home.

Many different agents socialize us into gender roles. Families give the earliest reinforcement for acting appropriately according to one's gender, and society continues to teach what is acceptable and what is not for men and for women. Gender roles are demonstrated and reinforced in almost every aspect of one's social life.

Women have sometimes objected to the genderisms of which Goffman wrote. (*Photo courtesy Michigan Daily*)

What Is the Situation in the United States Regarding Gender Roles?

During the World Wars, when manpower was short, womanpower was used in manual labor traditionally done by men. After World War II, however, Rosie the Riveter went back home to keep house, and women began to suffer from what Betty Friedan calls "the problem that has no name" (Friedan, 1963). In her classic book *The Feminine Mystique*, Friedan describes mothers with preschool children who use their creative energies making grocery lists and planning outings to the park rather than working in the outside world.

Women lost status steadily from the 1940s to the 1960s. Female enrollment in college dropped off, fewer women worked at any jobs, and the percentage of professional women dropped after increasing steadily from 1900 to 1940. Employers paid women less money because women "didn't have a family to support, and men did." In 1950, as today, a woman's wages were approximately 65 percent of a man's for comparable work.

Margaret Mead describes the social scene at the time:

> The 1950s built for women in the United States a world of too-narrow walls, too-early marriage, too-little productivity. Most women were confined to small, family treadmills, within which the joys of motherhood were all but smothered in a mass of repetitive household chores (1977, p. 33).

The situation worsened, and women in various parts of the country began to organize in different groups toward setting to right some of the blatant sexism they were facing. In 1966, after they were told they could take no legal action to make the United States government enforce the new Sex Discrimination in Employment Act, one group of women met in Washington and officially began the National Organization for Women (NOW). This group has since spearheaded the Women's Movement in the United States. Although the movement is noncentralized and loosely connected, the diversity of its membership has not diluted its ability to bring about many changes in gender-role definitions and behaviors of American men and women (V. Taylor, 1983).

WOMEN'S STATUS

EDUCATIONAL. The women's movement has initiated changes in educational opportunities. From 1965 to 1985 the percentage of graduate students who were female increased from 34 to 75 percent. In 1965 only 11 percent of Ph.D. recipients were female; in 1975 women received 23 percent of the Ph.D. degrees awarded; and by 1984 the percentage had risen to 50 percent (National Center for Education Statistics, 1978; U.S. Bureau of the Census, 1987).

Women are also studying new fields in college. For instance, in 1950 only 3 percent of engineering graduates were women, but by 1984, 12 percent of those receiving engineering degrees were women (U.S. Bureau of the Census, 1987). Many women are choosing more prestigious and lucrative fields of study rather than traditionally female areas like teaching and nursing.

OCCUPATIONAL. Partly due to changes in women's education levels and partly due to pressure to admit women to new fields, women's occupational status is changing also. Fifty-three percent of all women between 20 and 64 are now employed outside the home, 18 percent of them in blue-collar jobs previously closed to women (Bianchi & Spain, 1986). One poll indicates that 58 percent of working mothers would keep working even in the absence of economic necessity (Harris, 1981).

The number of female professionals is increasing, also. In 1970, 4.7 percent of lawyers and judges were women; in 1984, 37 percent of all law school graduates were women. The percentage of female medical school graduates rose from 6 percent in 1960 to 28 percent in 1984 (U.S. Bureau of Census, 1987). The proportion of female law school graduates during that same time span grew from 3 percent to 37 percent (U.S. Bureau of the Census, 1987).

Higher numbers of women in college and graduate school correlate positively with increasing numbers of women executives (Weiss et al., 1976). In 1972 only twenty women were members of boards of directors of large corporations; in 1977 there were 400 women in these positions. Between 1972 and 1983, the number of women executives more than doubled, from 1.4 million to 3.5 million (Castro, 1985).

Although the number of women in these positions has increased dramatically, the very *highest* status positions continue to be dominated by men. For instance, women are very underrepresented among *tenured* college faculty, although more women are teaching in colleges. Similarly, although many women are now executives, comparatively few of them are in the very top management group. Rosabeth Moss Kanter, well-known in the study of gender and business, suggests that organizations may be hiring "token" women in semi-influential positions while systematically keeping them out of the positions of highest influence (Kanter, 1986).

TABLE 11.1 Median Weekly Earnings of Full-Time Workers in Dollars

Occupation	Men	Women
Professional/Technical	$439	$316
Managerial/ Administrative	466	283
Salesworkers	366	190
Clerical	328	220
Craft Workers	360	239

SOURCE Nancy Rytina. April, 1982 "Earnings of Men and Women," *Monthly Labor Review*. pp. 26–29.

This table clearly indicates the disparity between men and women's income, *even when* occupational status is held constant.

FINANCIAL. Women's earnings, however, have not kept pace. In the past, industry has claimed that the discrepancy in earnings is accounted for by the fact that women have less education, often take time off from careers to raise children, and work in less lucrative areas than men. However, even when they are matched with men in similar positions, so that their wages are adjusted for differences in education, occupational status, experience on the job, and amount of time worked, women still earn only about 60 percent of the wages of their male counterparts (Bianchi & Spain, 1986; Corcoran & Duncan, 1979; Mincer & Ofek, 1982; Rytina, 1982; Tienda et al., 1987). (See Table 11.1.) Nearly 8 percent of male college graduates earn $50,000 or more, compared with 1 percent of female college graduates (Bianchi & Spain, 1986).

THE "WORKING MOTHER"

Working outside the home has benefits that go beyond the economic factors. Mothers who work outside the home report being healthier than unmarried or unemployed women (Verbrugge & Madans, 1985). When both partners agree on the wife's employment status, the marriage has the best chance to be satisfying for them (Ross et al., 1983). When the family agrees to accommodate the working mother, the marital adjustment is high and marital interaction is improved (Houseknecht & Macke, 1981; I. Simpson & England, 1981). A compilation of six national surveys found no consistent differences in patterns of life satisfaction between women who work outside the home and those who do not (Wright, 1978).

Certain circumstances, however, can create special strains on families with working mothers. When the educational, occupational, or social statuses of the husband and wife were incompatible, for example, their marriage and life satisfaction scores were significantly lowered (Hornung & McCullough, 1981). Kessler and McRae found that the mental health of working wives improved but psychological distress increases among their husbands (1982). This may reflect traditional sex role attitudes, and appears not to be related to increasing household responsibilities of the men. Research on child development and educational outcome in relationship to mother's employment has not yielded clear evidence of any consistent positive or negative effects (Bianchi & Spain, 1986; Hayes & Kamerman, 1981).

Continued occupational progress for women who work outside their homes will depend on increasing the involvement of men in household tasks. All research done shows that most working women have a full-time job to come home to at 5 P.M. (Geerken & Gove, 1983; Levitan & Belous, 1981; Nickols & Metzen, 1982). One indication of the extent of this problem is that the term "working father" is nonexistent in our culture. Only in yard work and repairs do men outdo women in household tasks. For instance, in measuring morning activities, little difference was found between husbands with employed wives and those whose wives did not work outside the home, except that husbands with employed wives were more likely to make the bed. The kitchen and child-care activities remained the province of the mother, even as she also got ready for "work." Husbands who are highly educated and employed are most likely to participate actively in housework, but as their income goes up, their chore involvement goes down (Model, 1981).

As long as women are caught in this "balancing act," they are likely to lack the energy and time needed to get ahead and learn new things about their work outside the home. This is exacerbated by the fact that when emergencies occur in the home (such as a sick child), the wife consistently takes responsibility for it, causing stress and straining her schedule.

Research indicates that if women and men shared domestic tasks equally, their pay, occupational distributions, and rates of work-force participation would be more equal (Tsuchigane & Dodge, 1974). Currently, however, few men even come close to sharing housework equally with their wives (Hedges & Barnett, 1972; Nichols & Metzen, 1982).

POWER AND WOMEN'S WORK

One reason men hesitate to do traditional female tasks is that those tasks are often seen as less valuable to society than traditional male tasks. In a Labor Department rating of occupations, work was rated on the basis of skill needed, from a high of 1 to a low of 887.

Homemakers, foster mothers, child-care attendants, nursery school teachers, and practical nurses were rated 878. In contrast, a hotel clerk (usually a male position) rated a 368. This situation is even more ironic in light of the fact that the word *economy,* a term very intimately connected to the words work and occupations, comes from the Greek *oikonomia,* meaning "management of a household or family."

This differentiation between "male" and "female" work in terms of power and prestige can be seen in the titles we give our work:

> Men who cook are chefs; women are just cooks. Men who handle finances are accountants; women are simply bookkeepers. . . . Not so long ago, when only men were secretaries and bank tellers, the jobs were training grounds for executive positions. When performed by women, those tasks are likely to be dead-end jobs (Scott, 1972, p. 57).

Although 55 percent of married women were employed outside the home in 1986, many women still work full-time as homemakers and attest to the popular new T-shirt slogan, "*Every* mother is a working mother." These homemakers fill the roles of purchasing agent, interior designer, financial consultant, cleaning person, cook, child-care worker, chauffeur, and family organizer. It has been estimated that to replace a full-time homemaker with equivalent workers in all these positions would cost approximately $35,000 per year. Society may begin to appreciate the economic and social value of homemakers, women or men.

POLITICAL GAINS FOR WOMEN

Gains for women have been made in other areas also. More women are entering government, from the local to the national level. In 1986, 15 percent of the country's mayors and city councilors were women, a threefold increase from 1976 (U.S. Bureau of the Census, 1987). The number of women state legislators also tripled from 1971 to 1981, from 300 to 900. In 1986, three women were governors, two were senators, and twenty-three were congressional representatives (Sullivan, 1986).

Although these do represent political gains for women, those in the field are quick to point out that they could be reversed. The National Women's Political Caucus is currently urging young women to become more involved politically in order that they might be ready to take over from the more experienced older women in the future. National chair Irene Natividad calls this process "replenishing the pipeline of talent" (Gardner, 1987). The group urges young women not to take for granted the gains that have been achieved, but to be continually involved in the political process, because that is most often where the power is distributed in our society.

REAL MEN DON'T SAY "I LOVE YOU"

If I wanted to, I could come up with a dozen reasons. The simple truth is, my 12-year-old son was waiting for me, and when I walked into the living room, he looked up at me and said, "I love you."

And I didn't know what to say.

Our generation has devoted a great deal of attention to getting in touch with our feelings. To verbalizing our emotions. We should know by now that our children—sons as well as daughters—need more from us than food on the table and clothes in the closet.

It's no longer enough for us to say that our fathers were Archie Bunkers who raised us to be "that way." We have done too many other things that our fathers never did. Our fathers didn't wear gold chains or designer jeans. They didn't sit in pediatricians' offices or stand in the delivery room. They didn't give baths to two-year-olds, vacuum floors, or cook desserts. None of them ever drank lite beer.

If we can adapt to all of those changes, surely we should know what to do when a 12-year-old son looks up and says, "I love you." When my son came to me that evening for his bedtime kiss—a kiss that seems to be getting briefer every night—I held on to him for an extra second. And just before he pulled away, I said in my deepest, most manly voice, "Hey, I love you, too." Maybe next time one of my kids says, "I love you," it won't take me a whole day to think of the right answer.

D. L. Stewart. September, 1985.
Redbook Magazine, p. 34.

Female body builders would once have been thought a contradiction in terms. Today, however, with growing emphasis on both genders staying physically fit, it is not unusual for a woman to work out with weights regularly. (*Photo courtesy the author*)

What Is the "Second Stage" of Gender Relations?

The changes in gender role definitions that began in the 1970s must continue until men and women are treated equally in modern society. Friedan believes that men and women are entering a second stage in their growth toward equality between the sexes (Friedan, 1981). Previously, women have fought for equality in terms of male power. Now, she asserts, women must join with men, contributing their own special qualities to building a better society, both in the family and in the business world:

> In the second stage we have to transcend that polarization between feminism and the family. We have to free ourselves from male power traps, understand the limits of women's power as a separate interest group and grasp the possibility of generating a new kind of power. . . . For the second stage . . . will put a new value on qualities once considered—and denigrated as—special to women, feminine qualities that will be liberated in men as they share experiences like child care (p. 216).

In this coming stage, as Friedan sees it, an "easy flow" would develop as "man and woman share the chores of home and children . . . according to their abilities and needs" (p. 142). This would potentially free men to pursue "self-fulfillment beyond the rat race for success and for a role in the family beyond breadwinner" (p. 142).

In the second stage, new standards will be set for running households and being successful in the working world. Currently, American men die earlier than American women and show greater signs of stress (Harrison, 1978). It has been suggested that men's stress could be significantly decreased if more women worked at well-paying work. If men shared more equally in housework and child care, perhaps women would not be as subject to depression as they are now. Furthermore, with two incomes and two retirement programs, families would be more secure.

Another promising prospect for the future is that women are again sharing their aspirations, frustrations, and desires with each other. For years, women sought for men to depend upon; as a consequence, they saw other women primarily as potential rivals for mates. This constant attention to who was better, prettier, or wittier created barriers between women. As women become less dependent on their husbands for total economic support and social identity, they should be able to see each other as potential friends. Alice Rossi, a sociologist noted for her contributions to the women's movement, notes this increase in intimate female relationships:

> What is more widespread than ever before is the realization that women may seek each other out as allies, true intimates, and friends. . . . [Previously] many people have had a conception of the marital relationship, or other intimate heterosexual relationships, as being potentially so gratifying, so all-encompassing, as to end the need for deep friendship with members of one's own sex. In fact, we believed that if you felt a need for such relationships, there was something wrong with the marriage. But all this is changing now (A. Rossi, 1972, p. 74).

Jessie Bernard, in a landmark study entitled *The Female World* (1981), thinks such trends may actually change the character of society. When women do not copy men's standards of success but form their own, the atmosphere of the business world may become less frantic and competitive. Similarly, if more men take nurturing roles in the family, cooperation and caring may become more universal as competition and fear decrease.

Bernard's theory is discussed more fully in the following "Close-Up on Theory."

CLOSE-UP on • *THEORY* •

Jessie Bernard on the Female World

The Theorist and the Setting

Jessie Bernard is professor emerita of sociology at Pennsylvania State University and has been well-respected in the field of women's studies since before such an entity existed on most college campuses. She has written more than twenty books about women's issues, including *Academic Women* and *The Future of Motherhood*. *The Female World*, which pulls together many threads from her previous research, is a natural outgrowth of her many years of study.

The Theorist's Goal

Bernard wrote *The Female World* to improve the discipline of sociology, which she believes is inadequate in its almost exclusively "male-created knowledge" (p. ix). She desires to demonstrate to women that they do have their own world, and to help them to appreciate it. "I hope such a view has a liberating effect on them by raising their self-evaluation, helping them to recognize the validity of their own experiences and the importance of their own part in the total societal structure" (p. ix).

Concepts and Propositions

Bernard outlines the history of women's societies, describing women as the probable inventors of tools such as sacks for carrying, developers of agriculture, and tamers of fire. She notes that in many different societies and times, women have formed cooperative groups. These groups can still be found in some primitive societies as they share work and play in the village squares or around the tribal fires.

Bernard's basic concept is that the character of the female is based on love, cooperation, and duty, whereas that of the male world is based on competition and striving. "Competition is the characteristic form of bonding in the male world. The fact that entities are competing for the same thing means that they belong to the same public or group. They are 'in.' Those who do not compete, conversely, are 'out' " (p. 29). This competitive spirit can be seen in both the work and the recreation of contemporary men.

In the female world bonding follows naturally with empathy and support. Thus, it does not depend upon any external input, but can grow over time and through different situations. Women's friendships are more likely to be deep and to last over distance.

This difference between the worlds has only recently been noted, and even more recently appreciated. Bernard proposes, for example, that differences in friendships of males and females are striking. "Men talk about matters of state, politics, religion. They could well learn from women real courtesy, art, wit, and inventiveness. (Women's) sex-role socialization prepares them for relating to others more intimately as contrasted with male sex-role socialization, which prepares men for one-upmanship" (p. 291).

Bernard discusses a study that found these patterns even in schoolchildren. The children were anxious to watch some chicks hatch out of their eggs. The girls in the class lined up quietly and proceeded to the chicks, while the boys wasted precious watching time in arguing over who was going to decide how to line up. Bernard wryly suggests that as this type of female cooperative interaction succeeds more in today's world, men may see that cooperation passes their ultimate test of "winning" the goal.

The language that men use to describe women reflects this one-upmanship game. Language placing women in an inferior posture is a constant reminder of the discrepancies in status between men and women. In Bernard's words: "The American-English language not only is sexually denigrating of women but is also a vehicle for asserting male superiority" (p. 377). She points out that words referring to male behavior, for instance, have connotations of power, whereas those referring to female behavior connote weakness; that is, men "yell" instead of "scream," "get angry" instead of "fret," and "growl" instead of "squeal." One of the consequences of using a language hostile and denigrating to women is that both sexes tend to see men as more authoritative than women, even when they have no evidence for that judgment.

Rather than trying to fit into the male world, however, Bernard urges women to *change* it, through political, economic, and social avenues. Women need to be more assertive in supporting their own natural strengths. Women must stop imitating men in behavior, dress, and goals. Instead, Bernard suggests, "women have to bring their own values to work with them."

In a world where the female ethos was integrated with the male's, Bernard speculates that activities might be run somewhat less efficiently, with much more emphasis on what is good for the entire society. "There would be less accent on war and dominance, greater ability to compromise, more concern about long-term solutions to problems." Such a world would direct technology more to improving the society and less to building national power and security.

Because the female world has hardly been studied, it seems less legitimate than the male world. Bernard's goal in writing this impressive historical description of the world of women is to legitimate and validate it. She hopes that women become more autonomous and self-confident through studying "their" history from a positive perspective. "Women need to stop judging everything from the male point of view. Female judgment is usually better" (p. 29). Bernard hopes that women will "change the world, making it a healthier, saner, more humane place. Women have always had the tools and the instincts to create a better society." Perhaps Jessie Bernard's work within the context of social change toward equality for the sexes will help create a more balanced world.

Interpretation

Bernard's sociological analysis relies heavily on the ideas of social structure and culture. Always drawing general conclusions from myriad specific examples, she carefully constructs social reality for the reader. Her final recommendations for integrating the female and male worlds leave the reader almost inevitably agreeing, because her method of leading has been so gentle but insistent.

Questions

1. If Jessie Bernard is correct about the differences between the male and female worlds, do you believe those worlds could ever find a common ground?
2. Give examples from your own experience of the competition–cooperation dichotomy between men and women.
3. What changes could be made in the socialization process to reduce the discrepancies between the female and male worlds?

SOURCE Jessie Bernard. 1981. *The Female World*. New York: The Free Press.

Conclusion

The changes that have evolved in the definitions of gender roles will undoubtedly suggest changes in social institutions as well. Marriages and families will continue to make many adjustments to the new roles of women. Government and economic positions will open to women, and the institutions will adapt to a new style of working as more women enter them. Education also shows changes; more men are training to teach young children, and more women receive advanced degrees in order to teach college. Much change still needs to be made in order for women to reach parity with men in all areas. Watching modifications in society in reaction to changing gender roles proves again that whenever a large group within a society gains or loses status, the society must accommodate them with other changes.

Sociologists at Work •

ALICE ROSSI
INVESTIGATES FEMININITY, MASCULINITY, AND FAMILY TIES
University of Massachusetts
Amherst, Massachusetts

Alice Rossi is the former president of both the American Sociological Association and Sociologists for Women in Society. An active feminist, she uses her sociological expertise in research while keeping her mind open to biological influences on gender traits. Here she describes her research into changes in the patterns of parent–child relationships over the lifecourse.

What Was the Goal of Your Latest Research?
Although age in its multiple meanings is the central focus of this study, one concern was to see what differences exist in parent–child relationships of the same sex or cross sex (mother/daughter, mother/son, father/daughter, father/son), and how the mother/daughter relationship differs from the father/son relationship. My main sample of respondents from the Boston area varied in age from 19 to 92, and I had their permission to contact their parents, and their children through telephone interviews. I chose a subsample of adult children and parents, trying to get as even a distribution of the four kinds of dyads of parents and children as I could get.

What Was the Focus of the Study?
I studied the multiple dimensions of the relationships from both parent's and child's point ot view. A second focus was to what extent parents and adult children show the same or different responses, and why they differ when the responses are different. On factual matters like, "How often do you telephone your mother?" I found high agreement between parents and children, but when I asked questions about the psychological qualities of the relationship, I found that parents saw much more similarity between their values and their children's values than children themselves reported. Parents had a much rosier view of the degree of closeness than children see in that relationship.

However, even as critical and central a relationship as that between parents and children changes through time. As young adults, children are separating themselves from their parents, and report less intimacy in that relationship than their parents claim exists. But when these children reach their thirties and forties, they report much closer relations with their parents. I believe this is because the young adults have grown, and established themselves with a family or a job and a place in the community. Now they are open to renegotiating the old relationship with parents that may have had some strain when they were adolescents. The adult child is a mother like her mother, or a father like his father, and that brings the generations closer together in their sense of each other and their sense of the differences between them. Not surprisingly, I found that the past colors their current relationship with their parents.

I also studied how obligation between parent and child differs from that toward other relatives or nonfamily relationships, with special emphasis on how gender affects such relationships. I found that these relationships can actually be patterned out like an onion, with the parent–child relationship at the center with the highest obligation, and lower levels of obligation with each layer out from the center.

These levels are remarkably clearly defined, with, for instance, grandparents receiving the same obligation scores as grandchildren. They are also consistent, so that even life circumstances do not make a difference. For instance, if someone you were related to had major surgery or lost his or her house as a result of fire, or some other emergency, we expected you might feel more obligation toward that person at that point in time. The reality is, however, that these variables never override their place in the wheel, which is based on how closely the people are related, coupled with gender and marital status.

I ranked these relationships to get an actual hierarchy. The persons at the top of the structure, or the persons that others report the highest

feelings of obligation toward, are widowed mothers or unmarried daughters. Notice that they're both female and unattached. Close friends ranking at a similar level to nieces, nephews, aunts, and uncles. Least obligation was felt toward ex-spouses who remarried.

What Did You Discover About These Relationships and Gender?
I derived from psychology measures of what I label dominance and expressivity, which roughly correspond to what were once called masculinity and femininity. The label "masculinity," for example, seems to refer to some biological aspect of maleness. But the actual traits that go into such an index are no more likely to be predetermined by biology than they are to be social constructions.

I discovered some interesting relationships. Sons who are high in expressivity, for instance, give more help to their parents and receive more help from their parents. The old truism that in order to get, you have to give, is true even in these primary family relationships.

What Were Your Conclusions?
My research makes it clear that most adult children and parents feel great obligations toward one another, see each other often, and help each other in a variety of ways, with their relationship being based partly on gender and expressivity. ●

Summary Questions

1. What is the difference between sex and gender?
2. What do cross-cultural comparisons of gender roles show us?
3. What are the functionalist and conflict theories of the origins of gender roles?
4. What are the major socialization agents that teach us our gender roles?
5. What are the basic modes in which the family socializes gender behavior?
6. What does research tell about school gender socialization?
7. How does the media portray the genders?
8. What cultural cues teach us appropriate gender-role behavior?
9. What is the present status of women in the United States in educational, occupational, and financial terms?
10. What is the situation of the "working mother"?
11. What is the relationship between women's work and power in society?
12. What political gains have women made?
13. What changes might occur in the "second stage" of gender relationships?
14. What is Jessie Bernard's basic concept concerning the female world?

Summary Answers

1. The term *gender* refers to culturally transmitted differences between men and women, whereas the term *sex* refers to the biological differences between males and females.
2. Culture largely determines what is considered "masculine" or "feminine." These definitions can change with social change in the culture.
3. Functionalists suggest that men perform instrumental roles and women perform expressive roles because that division is "functional" to the society. Conflict theory sees the almost universal inequality between the sexes in societies as an outgrowth of patriarchy, the form of social organization in which men dominate, or rule over, women. Patriarchy assumes that men are superior to women, based on sexism, or the belief that one sex is inferior and thus deserves inferior treatment.
4. The major gender-role socialization agents are the family, schools, the media, and the language, and observed interactions in the institutions of the culture.
5. The family socializes gender roles through reinforcement of appropriate behaviors, differential opportunities for boys and girls, role modeling of adult gender behavior, and explicit verbal instruction.
6. Girls and boys continue to be rewarded for acting in "appropriate" ways in school roles, through what has been termed the "second curriculum." Textbooks and leisure reading portray dominant roles for males. Courses are informally segregated according to sex, and teachers encourage boys more than girls.
7. The media often caricatures the genders. In advertising, few women are shown outside of the home, and any product other than household products is sold through the authoritative voice of a male. Advertising reinforces gender-role stereotypes through function ranking, ritualizing subordination, showing women leaning against or resting their limbs on men or sitting on beds and floors, and through showing mock assault games in which men are aggressive toward women.
8. The English language offers no easy way to discuss a person without revealing gender. Language also contains derogatory names for females, which reinforce accepted roles. The fact that women play minor roles in most of the institutions of society also reinforces the subordination of women.
9. Many women have been touched by the women's movement's work in education. Many more are gaining higher education and choosing more prestigious and lucrative fields. The number of women who are working continues to grow, as does the number in high-paying positions. Nevertheless, the very highest positions in all fields are still dominated by men, and women's earnings are still only about 65 percent those of men. Much change must occur before men and women are treated equally in our society.
10. Although families appear to be able to adjust to the mother working, the mothers live with a double burden. They are most often still in charge of most of the household chores and take care of emergencies as they arise. The mental health of the working mother is somewhat enhanced, but that of husbands is somewhat worse, perhaps because of gender-role expectations or perhaps strain caused by the doubled load.
11. One reason men hesitate to perform traditional female tasks is that the tasks are often seen as less valuable to society than are traditional male tasks.

As a society, we are only beginning to appreciate the economic and social value of homemakers, women or men.

12. More women are entering government, from the local to the national level.
13. In the "second stage" of gender relations, women and men must join together, contributing their own special qualities to building a better society, both in the family and in the business world. Women must seek out friendships with other women, and learn to value their own contributions to the world.
14. Bernard believes that the female world is based on love, cooperation, and duty, whereas the male world is based on competition and striving. She seeks to sensitize women to the unique contributions the female world view might make to society in order to help it to grow more cooperative and peaceful.

Glossary

gender culturally transmitted differences between men and women

patriarchy the form of social organization in which men dominate, or rule over, women

sex the biological differences between males and females

sexism the belief that one sex is inferior and thus deserves inferior treatment

Suggested Readings

Jessie Bernard. 1981. *The Female World*. New York: The Free Press.

Bernard uses her consummate skills as writer and sociologist to describe and analyze the structural and cultural aspects of the female world, as distinct from the male world. Excellent reading at all levels.

Marilyn French. 1985. *Beyond Power: On Women, Men, and Morals*. New York: Summit Books.

A critical look at the continuing phenomenon of patriarchy in relationship to modern-day feminism. French clearly describes the continuing significance of gender in today's society.

Patricia Madoo Lengermann, and Ruth Wallace. 1985. *Gender in America: Social Control and Social Change*. Englewood Cliffs, N.J.: Prentice Hall.

A fascinating overview of gender inequality from a social-control model. Lengermann and Wallace skillfully balance research and theory with anecdote to produce an easily digested scholarly work.

Karen Sacks and Dorothy Remy. 1984. *My Troubles Are Going to Have Trouble with Me*. New Brunswick, N.J.: Rutgers University Press.

An excellent collection of articles about working-class women that provide a clear picture of the world in which they live, economically, socially, and interpersonally.

PART 5

Social Institutions

CHAPTER
12

AGING in INDUSTRIAL SOCIETY

- What Is the Graying of America?
- How Do Age Roles Compare Cross-Culturally?
- What Are the Major Determinants of the Status of Different Age Groups?
- Close-Up on Theory: Matilda White Riley and John W. Riley, Jr., on Longevity and Social Structure
- What Is Ageism?
- What Myths Are Used to Justify Ageism?
- Why Does Ageism Exist? Sociological Theories of Aging
- What Is the Socio-Economic Status of the Elderly in the United States Today?
- What Is the Situation Regarding the Elderly, Work, and Retirement?
- What Are the Challenges That the Elderly Face?
- What Are the Secrets of Long Life?
- Close-Up on Research: Claire Pedrick-Cornell and Richard Gelles on Elder Abuse
- What Are Social Reactions to Death and Dying?
- Sociologists at Work: Cary Kart Researches What Wills Reveal About Families

How's Your Sociological Intuition?

1. Which of the following statements is true about older people?
   - a. Their intelligence declines with age.
   - b. Their interest in sex declines to an insignificant level.
   - c. They usually become senile.
   - d. Most of them are not happy with being older.
2. During the 1980s, the average age at retirement steadily declined, spurred by government and private pensions offering retirement benefits at ages 55 to 65. What will the situation be in the year 2010?
   - a. The average retirement age will be 55.
   - b. People will be eligible for Social Security at age 50.
   - c. People will not be eligible for Social Security until age 70.
   - d. Most people will have individual pensions and not utilize Social Security.
3. What factor has not been associated with aiding people to maintain their mental capabilities throughout old age?
   - a. Staying socially involved.
   - b. Being mentally active.
   - c. Having enough money to live comfortably.
   - d. Having a flexible personality.
4. Regarding nursing homes:
   - a. The majority of older people live in nursing homes.
   - b. Twenty-five percent of older people live in nursing homes.
   - c. Only 5 percent of older Americans live in nursing homes, and most of those are old-old and approaching death.
   - d. Nursing home care has steadily grown better.

Answers

1. None of the above. These are all myths which perpetuate ageist thinking.
2. c. New legislation makes retirement with Social Security benefits begin at age 70 by the year 2010.
3. c. Social factors appear to be important in being mentally alert.
4. c. Although most people are afraid of living in nursing homes, only 5 percent do so at any one time.

WHEN YOU HAVE FINISHED STUDYING THIS CHAPTER, YOU SHOULD KNOW:

- How the age curve of the United States has recently changed
- What ageism is and how it applies to youth and the elderly
- How functionalist, conflict, and symbolic interactionist theorists explain ageism
- How prevalent age stratification is in different cultures
- What the economic and social status of the elderly and the young is in the United States today
- Why the young and old have inferior status in our culture
- What the situation regarding the elderly and work is
- What the issues surrounding retirement are
- What the myths and realities about aging are
- What challenges the aging face, including debilitating illness, poor health care, and abuse by family members
- How increasing longevity may change societal norms in important areas such as work and medical care
- How society addresses the issues of death and dying

The Life and Death of Oliver Shay

In the winter of 1967, at age 67, Oliver Shay came down with a severe case of bacterial pneumonia, and was admitted to a hospital in a state of respiratory failure. With the widespread availability of antibiotics and new sophistication in the management of respiratory failure, Mr. Shay was just a "routine case," and was discharged in good health.

Two years passed, and Mr. Shay began to notice pressing left-sided chest pain when he exerted himself. Cardiac catheterization revealed that he had a near-total narrowing of one of the main coronary arteries, which, if allowed to progress, would likely result in death within a few years. Mr. Shay was scheduled for an elective coronary artery bypass operation, which he underwent successfully at age 73.

On the day of his 79th birthday, Mr. Shay visited his children in a neighboring suburb. When he failed to return from an upstairs bathroom, a grandson found him sprawled on the floor in his own vomit and feces, mumbling incoherently. He was rushed to the nearest hospital, where computerized tomography of his head revealed that he had suffered a cerebrovascular accident (stroke), leaving him severely paralyzed on his right side, unable to swallow, feed himself, or walk.

Two days later, a nurse found him lying in bed immobile, unresponsive, and pallid. He had no pulse and was not breathing. A cardiac-arrest emergency was announced over the hospital paging system, and within minutes, closed-chest cardiac massage was implemented by the resuscitation team, a tube was placed in his windpipe to facilitate breathing, and he was attached to a respirator. Electric defibrillation and a variety of intravenous medications followed, and within thirty minutes Mr. Shay once again had a normal heartbeat and blood pressure. Within two more weeks, impeccable nursing care and aggressive rehabilitation efforts restored Mr. Shay to a point at which he could be discharged from the hospital to a skilled-care nursing home.

After living in the nursing home for two years with essentially no improvement in his paralysis and speech disorder, Mr. Shay had a permanent cardiac pacemaker implanted. Family members began to notice that Mr. Shay at age 84 seemed even less able to care for himself than he had been previously. A neurologist advised the family that the likely diagnosis was Alzheimer's disease and that no specific treatment was possible. At age 88, Mr. Shay had blood tests that revealed a major electrolyte imbalance, and a diagnosis was made of chronic renal failure. The family requested that he be put on an artificial kidney machine. This was done, and his course remained relatively stable for the next three years, until he developed severe abdominal pain at age 91, had emergency surgery for a rupturing aortic aneurysm, and died ten days later.

The story of Mr. Shay is not at all atypical of many geriatric patients. At numerous points he experienced acute medical problems that, just a few decades earlier, would often have proved fatal. Instead, he was rescued by one medical technology after another: Antibiotics cured his pneumonia, resuscitation literally reversed his dying, a pacemaker kept his heart pumping, and an artificial kidney freed his body of impurities, much as a real kidney would do. Nevertheless, it was his chronic disabilities—his stroke and senile dementia—against which modern medicine had relatively little to offer. He was kept alive in his state of ever-decreasing functional capacity until the occurrence of his terminal catastrophe, which was itself prolonged for nearly two weeks at exorbitant cost.

The traditional view of the role of medicine holds that the physician should at all times struggle against disease and death. Only recently has an opposing view been voiced with any degree of clarity or consistency.

From Jerome L. Avorn, 1986. In *Our Aging Society: Promise and Paradox,* Alan Pifer and Lydia Bronte, eds. New York: W.W. Norton.

Grounded in either humanitarian or economic perspectives, the case is increasingly being made that, in view of our new power to keep patients alive well beyond what was once considered the point of death, we must begin to face up to the question of when additional medical care is *not* in the best interest of the patient. More attention is being devoted to the concept of the "living will," or durable power of attorney as a means of authorizing cessation of care when it is no longer meeting the stated goals or desires of the patient. Consensus is slowly growing that no good is served by prolonging the dying of a particular individual by days or weeks of intensive, often uncomfortable, and generally expensive therapies. As the practice of extending life (artificially) is widely becoming regarded as unacceptable, we must develop a more thorough understanding of the (ethical and economic) issues being raised.

Most of us fervently desire not to end our lives like Oliver Shay. Robust and useful for over seventy years, he spent over a decade totally dependent and unresponsive to his family. His life and death bring to mind major social questions about aging. What are the tradeoffs in curing our acute medical problems if we will eventually suffer from chronic disabilities? What power should other people have to decide these issues for an unable patient? How can society control the cost of medical care? How will society provide for its increasing number of elderly? What will their social, economic, and employment status be in the future? The increase in the proportion of elderly in the United States today requires that citizens in all age groups address these and related issues.

Because of the way our population has grown, the category of people including grandmothers is growing faster than grandchildren. America is graying. *(Photo courtesy the author)*

What Is the Graying of America?

The year was 1905. The median age of the U.S. population was 24 years, and the average life expectancy was 47 years. One-third of all people died before they were 5 years old, and another third before their 55th birthday. Only 4 percent of the population was over 65 (U.S. Bureau of Census, 1983, p. 47). William Osler, Johns Hopkins medical school professor, stated in his graduation address that after age 40, people "lose mental elasticity" and by age 60 have become "useless."

Osler would be tarred, feathered, and run out of town today by our increasingly old population. By 1985, 12 percent of our population was over 65, and senior citizens had begun to establish firmly the fact that they were far from useless to their society. By the year 1990, the median age will probably be 33 years and rising. As a nation the United States is "grayer" than it has ever been, and the entire population is realizing that they have a great chance of living a long time as one of America's elderly. The 75-plus category shows the fastest growth, due to advances in medical care. Fifty years ago, most people died from their first heart attack. Today, they have an excellent chance of surviving into their 80s, and suffering from other ailments, as Oliver Shay did.

What factors have caused this shift in the proportion of elderly persons in the United States? Changes in birth rates, death rates, and migration have all contributed to the growth (Kart, 1985). High birth rates after the turn of the century created large numbers of elderly in the 1970s and 1980s. The baby boom of the 1940s will continue this trend, until nearly one out of five Americans will be over 65 by the year 2040, straining the currrent retirement system considerably.

Death rates have also changed drastically. The average life expectancy in 1985 is 75 (U.S. National Center for Health Statistics, 1986). The fact that most Americans now have adequate food, clothing, housing, and medical care has increased our life expectancy considerably. Furthermore, advances in medical care have cleared the way for people to survive childhood and lengthen adulthood into their 80s and 90s. The fastest growing group of elders is the over-75 group, a seg-

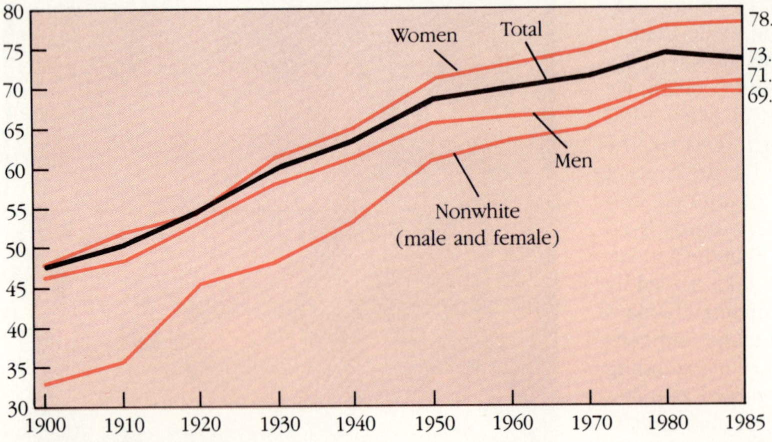

FIGURE 12.1 Rising Life Expectancy in the U.S. SOURCE U.S. Bureau of the Census, *Statistical Abstract of the United States, 1987* (107th ed.), Washington, D.C.: U.S. Government Printing Office, 1987.

ment that may reach 12 percent of the population by the year 2050 (Hallowell, 1985).

Immigration to the United States has also affected the growth of the elderly population. Most immigrants were young adults (18–25) when they arrived in the United States prior to World War I, a fact that increased the numbers of persons in that age group and has swelled the ranks of the elderly in the 1980s.

The growth in the number of elderly in America was created by changes in society, including advances in medicine, and has created many changes itself. In this chapter we will consider where the aged fit in our stratification systems, and how various societies treat those of different ages. We will also examine some of the economic, social, and health problems society must face as we grow "grayer."

How Do Age Roles Compare Cross-Culturally?

Societies differ in the amount of respect they accord to the young and old. Linton describes the status surrounding childhood in several cultures (1936, pp. 119–120):

> The importance given to the child in the family structure varies enormously from one culture to another. The status of the child among our Puritan ancestors, in which he was seen and not heard and ate at the second table, represents one extreme. At the other might be placed the status of the eldest son of a Polynesian chief. All the *mana* (supernatural powers) of the royal line converged upon such a child. He was socially superior to his own father and mother, and any attempt to discipline him would have been little short of sacrilege.

The status of older people also varies from one society to another. In some cultures old age is a time of security and freedom when one can be as active as one chooses and when the rules of conduct can be broken with little fear of reprisal. One can enjoy being called "old"—or being revered as "weak in the body"—for the young seek advice of the old. Linton points out that this custom is very practical, because the person who has lived to an old age in primitive cultures "has usually been a person of ability, and his memory constitutes a sort of reference library to which one can turn for help under all sorts of circumstances" (Linton, 1936, p. 120). Even in contemporary agrarian societies, young men seek advice and encouragement from older ones who have a reputation as good farmers. To be taken under the wing of such a mentor is a compliment, because it indicates the elder sees potential in the younger to become proficient in farming also.

One expert has suggested that the primitive societies that have been the most kind to the aged are those that have been "prosperous agricultural ones, those that also treated their children well, and those that had no written language and thus valued old members as repositories of tribal lore" (James, 1985). If a group has enough sustenance for everyone and no way to preserve legends, rituals, and production techniques other than through the memories of the elders, the aged are usually well treated.

In other cultures, the aged are required to do the work young members scorn. Some may abandon their frail elders when they become too great a burden. Glascock and Feinman uncovered twenty-six instances of killing and sixteen of abandoning the elderly in the forty-two societies that they studied (Glascock and Feinman, 1981). The Hottentots of southern Africa would leave parents too old to carry food or young children to die in the desert. The Northern Ojibwa Indians would abandon a feeble elderly person on a small island.

The relationship between how the elderly are treated and the mode of production is not at all linear, however. Some agricultural societies and some industrial societies treat the aged well, and some of both treat them poorly, according to modern standards. Research suggests that perhaps the status of the elderly drops as societies move into modernization but begins to rise again as the societies stabilize and move into the advanced stages of modernization or the postindustrial society (Palmore and Manton, 1974). As more nations go through this transition, this hypothesis will be able to be tested more thoroughly.

What Are the Major Determinants of the Status of Different Age Groups?

Age roles are often determined in part by one's own age. Everyone belongs to both an age stratum and an age cohort. An ***age stratum*** is *a group of people who are experiencing a certain stage in life at a certain time*. One's age stratum changes as one ages—from childhood through adolescence and adulthood to old age. An ***age cohort*** is *a group of people who were born during a particular period of time*. One's age cohort remains the same over time. For example, all Americans born in the 1950s have a shared heritage of the golden age of rock and roll, and they form an age cohort. They were teenagers or young adults during the Vietnam War, and were the first generation to adopt marijuana on a wide scale. Beyond recognizing the same music, this age cohort feels a sense of togetherness because they have lived through significant historical events at the same time: Watergate, Jonestown, Chernobyl, the AIDS epidemic. Age cohorts are only one factor in our society's status determination.

Societies often develop *clearly recognizable signs and ceremonies surrounding the passage of persons from one age boundary to the next*, especially from childhood to adulthood. These are called ***rites of passage***. Primitive societies have elaborate rituals boys or girls must go through to be called adults. In American society, graduation from high school or college is considered a rite of passage.

Passage from adult to older person is not so clearly marked in most societies, possibly because it is not as happily anticipated as adulthood is by children, and often involves a decline in status rather than a gain in status. It is also more difficult to tell when a person becomes "old." Many persons in their 70s appear young, while some in their 40s are already old in mind and body.

Seven major determinants of status exist in most societies: (1) property ownership, (2) strategic knowledge, (3) productivity, (4) mutual dependence, (5) tradition and religion, (6) kinship and family, and (7) community life (Rosow, 1974). Because a person must have many or all of the characteristics to be of high status, and because many of them are not available to the young and old, young and old people in the United States are often excluded from high status. For example, young persons often do not yet own property, and older people are often forced to sell theirs.

Strategic knowledge was once the province of the old, but technical knowledge of today quickly becomes obsolete. For example, one of the few remaining full-blooded Aborigines of the Gurumumba in the Northern Territories of Australia recently spent a great deal of time speaking the traditions of his people to a writer in order that they not die out completely. When his people depended on knowing where and when certain animals could be caught and certain plants should be cultivated, his knowledge and that of his contemporaries was highly valued. Today, most of the Aborigines live in the cities on the coast of Australia and earn their living in industry. The technical knowledge that they require for their current jobs will probably be useless to their children in obtaining employment in the future, just as they now consider the accumulated knowledge of their tribe, as carried down orally for years to the last "elders" of their tribe, to be useless to them.

In terms of *productivity*, the young and old are often outpaced by the middle age groups, often because of differential opportunities. Closely tied to this, the system of *mutual dependence*, in which people depended upon the group for support of all kinds, has been replaced with an emphasis on independence, affecting both the young and the old.

Tradition and religion are the backbone of simpler societies. Older people taught the young the religious beliefs that sustained the society. Today, more people seek secular supports and disregard tradition.

In traditional societies, the elderly were powerful because they knew the traditions and histories of the families and thus became the center of the *family and kinship* systems. Often this situation changes when a language is written and traditions can be preserved on paper.

Finally, *community life* was very important in the past. Families often lived within the same group for generations. Today, due to high geographic mobility, the sense of community is often lost. Elders are rarely sought out for advice but are thought of as people past their prime.

The consequences of the changes in these primary status-giving variables in industrialized societies is that older and younger people are often looked upon as of less value than those in the middle-adult category and seen as "kids" or "old folks." The elderly, in particular, are often segregated socially and may lose some of their major roles in life: provider, property owner, parent, wise person, member of the community. Rather than

Until the past few decades, Americans often cared for their older family members in the home. More recently older family members live in their own homes or in institutions. (*Jerome Wexler/FPG International*)

allowing different age groups to contribute their special talents and viewpoints to the culture, modern society has often subtly discounted the contributions of the young and the old.

Several theorists have begun to address how increased life expectancy in the United States and other industrialized nations might change the social structure in regard to the status of the elderly. Major changes can be seen in family relationships. In 1985, for example, 10 percent of the people over 65 had a child who was also over the age of 65 (J. Brody, 1985). These added years may mean more prolonged relationships within the family, both between and within generations (Uhlenberg, 1980). In addition, decreased fertility means that there are fewer family members per generation with whom to be intimate, which could lead to more intense relationships (Hagestad, 1986).

Despite gains in women's rights and increases in the number of them employed outside the home, women are still the primary caregivers for both children and aged (E. M. Brody, 1985). The lifespan extension combined with reduced fertility means that for the first time women may spend more time caring for their parents than they did raising their children (E. M. Brody, 1985A). The fact that women are living even longer than their husbands today leads to an old-old world dominated by females. Research shows that women turn more to intergenerational relationships than men, so this trend might again increase the frequency and intensity of interaction between the elderly and their grown children and grandchildren (Hagestad and Neugarten, 1985). As the Rileys suggest in our "Close-Up on Theory," these changes in the family structure will undoubtedly affect the structure of the society as a whole.

What Is Ageism?

Prejudiced attitudes and behavior toward any age groups have been termed ***ageism,*** coined by Dr. Robert N. Butler, first director of the National Institute of Aging. At the time he sarcastically defined it as "not wanting to have all those ugly old people around." Butler suggests there are three distinguishable aspects to the problem of ageism: (1) prejudicial attitudes toward the aged and the aging process, (2) discriminatory practices against the elderly, and (3) institutional practices that perpetuate stereotypes of aging and reduce opportunities for the aging to have a satisfactory life (Butler, 1980). He believes that some prejudicial attitudes are benign, or supposedly not harmful, and some are malignant. The benign ones, however, can become malignant. For example, Butler estimates that from 10 to 30 percent of all treatable mental disorders in older people are misdiagnosed as untreatable, due to the physician's benign attitude that mental impairment is "just a part of old age."

In recent years, as the proportion of elderly in the United States has grown, attempts have been made to reduce the amount of age discrimination. Congress passed the Age Discrimination in Employment Act in

CLOSE-UP on • *THEORY* •

Matilda White Riley and John W. Riley, Jr., on Longevity and Social Structure

The Theorists and the Setting

Sociologists Matilda White Riley and John Riley have turned their theoretical and research skills toward the field of aging. John is a consulting sociologist with the International Federation on Aging, and Matilda is the associate director of the National Institute on Aging. In this article, they examine the relationship between the processes of aging and changing social structures. As experts in the field of aging, they were commissioned to write this review for the Carnegie Institute-sponsored Aging Society Project in 1986.

The Theorists' Goal

The Rileys describe their goal clearly:

> This essay will touch first on the nature of longevity, which is transforming the life course of individuals. It will then describe the uneasy relation between the aging of individuals and the changes in society and imbalance that results in the current structural lag (p. 53).

Concepts and Propositions

As we have seen in this chapter, longevity is increasing at an unprecedented rate. The Rileys discuss three aspects of the interaction between this phenomena and society:

1. What are long-lived people actually capable of?
2. What roles are currently available to aging people that will use their unique capabilities?
3. What will society do with the current imbalance between the capabilities of the aged and the opportunities available to them?

The Rileys review literature that indicates strongly that longevity has many positive effects on an individual's life, and that the capacity of the elderly to participate fully and usefully in our society is high. In order for this to happen, however, the life stages that have previously been agreed upon by members of the society must be revised. They believe that this type of social change occurs most often through the process of "cohort norm formation," in which members of an age cohort react to experiences by developing common patterns of response that "crystallize into shared norms about what is appropriate, proper, or true" (p. 58).

The Rileys discuss three areas that could be affected by social change regarding the increased longevity of Americans. First, they note that the competence of older workers for productive performance has been consistently underrated since the turn of the century, when two-thirds of men over 65 and one-fourth of boys between 10 and 15 were employed full-time. Long-term societal trends in the changing boundaries of the work force have included:

> declines in agriculture and self-employment, extension of formal education, steadily increasing proportions of women in the labor force, establishment of age requirements for starting or discontinuing a job, and extension of public and private pension plans that afford alternative sources of income and often specify mandatory ages of retirement (p. 60).

The Rileys believe that as work opportunities lessen for the aged, social pressure increases to provide socially rewarding roles in retirement. Thus far, society has focused on such issues as providing long-term care for the sick and disabled elderly, who are a very small minority of older people. The research the Rileys have reviewed leads them to believe that "it is imperative that some scientific and popular attention be directed to ways of maintaining health and effective functioning among that great majority of middle-aged and older people whose potential is still high" (p. 61).

Second, the Rileys note that women live longer than men, have generally had experiences in many complex roles, and have been leaders in social innovation. Women are also statistically shown to be resilient and flexible in the face of adversity. The Rileys suggest that perhaps as future cohorts of women reach later years, they could influence other members of society to "assume greater flexibility in the phases of the life course." In other words, as the transformation in gender-role attitudes and behavior occurs in society, and as women become the dominant gender group of the growing aged population, perhaps the entire society will become more resilient, flexible, and innovative in response to the changed norms of this age cohort.

New norms are also being formed in the changing character of the dying process. At the turn of the century, many people did not live to adulthood, let alone to old age. Instead of having to deal with the problems of becoming aged, people often had to deal with living as orphans, a social category that has virtually disappeared over the past eighty years. Today, three-fourths of all deaths occur among people over age 65. Furthermore, most people in our great-grandparents' generations died rapid deaths from acute diseases that were untreatable with known medicine. In "modern" society, the process of dying is prolonged by chronic diseases and custodial medical care, sometimes beyond the point of "social death," or inability to carry on any interpersonal relationships.

New norms are being formed to address the change in the social process of death. For instance, whereas in the 1960s most doctors preferred not to tell their patients they were dying, in the 1980s most doctors are honest with patients. Because prolongation of life has become a factor, the concept of a person dying with dignity has evolved, and the Living Will, in which a person states in advance his or her wishes about terminal medical care, have become commonplace.

Interpretation

The Rileys make clear that the capacities of the elderly to contribute meaningfully to society have been highly underrated. Especially in today's world, when people are reaching old age much healthier and stronger than previous generations, we must find ways to tap the potential wisdom and strength of this group.

One way in which this process will occur is in the changing of norms through age cohorts "deciding" together to do things differently. If many wives, who are often younger than their husbands, choose to continue work after their husbands retire, for instance, it is possible that this will become an accepted social pattern. Because women consistently have been found to be innovative and flexible, the additional influence of more women in the older age brackets may contribute to these qualities in the society as a whole. Also, as the elderly live longer new social arrangements will evolve to care for them as they die.

From these observations, the Rileys conclude that (1) there is "a potential for a high degree of social control over the future shape of social structures and human lives in an aging society," and (2) "there is both urgency and risk in planning for this future." In this conclusion, they once again point out that changes in an individual's life course, and in those of any group, will bring changes in society as a whole. "Nowhere is the interdependence of human lives more apparent than in the effects of alterations in longevity itself." Thus, we do not make these decisions in an individual vacuum, but within our social context. As such, our decisions are not only a privilege, but a responsibility.

Questions

1. The Rileys speak optimistically about the possibilities of longevity influencing social structure positively. Do you agree with their optimistic stance? What changes do you see occurring in this area?
2. Although women have been identified as innovators and flexible in accepting social roles, they have also had less power than men. How do you think these two factors will work together or against one another in forming social change in our future aging society?
3. As older people have demanded more autonomy concerning their physical beings, the medical community has begun to change. How do you think the social circumstances surrounding death and dying will change over the next fifty years?

SOURCE Matilda White Riley and John W. Riley, Jr. 1986. "Longevity and social structure: The potential of the added years," in *Our Aging Society: Paradox and Promise*, Alan Pifer and Lydia Bronte, eds, New York: W.W. Norton and Company, pp. 53–78.

1967, and amended it in 1987 to eliminate mandatory retirement. In 1975, they passed the Age Discrimination Act to prohibit discrimination on the basis of age in any federally assisted program (Kart, 1985). Research by the House Committee on Aging shows that formal charges of such discrimination filed with the Equal Employment Opportunity Commission rose to nearly 9,500 during 1981, an increase of 75 percent over the total in 1979 (Weaver, 1982). Obviously, increasing numbers of people believe they have been discriminated against because of their age. Legislation, combined with more realistic knowledge of the aging process and the abilities of the aged, should combat ageism in the United States of the future.

What Myths Are Used to Justify Ageism?

With industrialization, the belief often grows that middle age, also known as "the working years," should be the most privileged time in a person's life. Added to this is the idea that younger and older persons should be afforded less respect and receive fewer of society's rewards. This attitude assumes that personality, character, behavior, and social traits are determined not by individual differences or social situations but by chronological age (Neuhaus and Neuhaus, 1982, p. 16).

Ageism can be seen readily in television. Older people are greatly underrepresented on television, and when they are shown they are seen through negative stereotypes (Gerbner, 1980; R. Davis, 1984; Buchholz and Bynum, 1982). Television elders are often difficult to get along with, silly, or impulsive. Older women, who are even more rare on television, are shown as stubborn, eccentric, and foolish (Elliott, 1984). Advertising directed toward the aged urges them to cover up the natural signs of their age status, offering dye for gray hair, cream for wrinkles, and lotion to avoid baldness (Barrow, 1986). Commercials that feature the elderly picture them plagued by headaches, irregularity, constipation, backaches, and loose dentures while they wait at home for their children and grandchildren to call via AT&T.

TABLE 12.1 Images of the Aged

	Self-Image of Persons over 65	Public Image of Persons over 65	Difference
Very friendly and warm	72%	74%	+2%
Very wise from experience	69	64	−5
Very bright and alert	68	29	−39
Very open-minded and adaptable	63	21	−42
Very good at getting things done	55	35	−20
Very physically active	48	41	−7
Very sexually active	11	5	−6

SOURCE *The Myth and Reality of Aging in America*, a study prepared by Louis Harris and Associates, Inc., for the National Council on the Aging, Inc., Washington, D.C., 1975, p. 53. Reprinted by permission of The National Council on the Aging, Inc.

IMAGES OF THE ELDERLY

Partly as the result of television, and related to the fact that older persons are often devalued in an industrialized society, members of society hold images of the elderly that do not match those of the elderly themselves. Table 12.1 shows the extent of difference between these images, as determined through the Harris Poll for the National Council on Aging.

Such mythical images of the elderly are often used to justify their differential treatment. One myth, for instance, is that old people can't think clearly anymore. If this is true, other members of society can justify taking over positions of authority from the elderly. Extensive research has been conducted in this field, with interesting results.

Researchers make a distinction between fluid intelligence, or the ability to think and reason abstractly, and crystallized intelligence, or the ability to use an accumulated body of information to make judgments and solve problems. Some studies show that the elderly are somewhat less able in the use of fluid intelligence (Foner, 1986), whereas others show only minor or no age differences on verbal tests of either type of intelligence, especially when speed is controlled (Baltes and Schaie, 1974). Most researchers agree that crystallized intelligence continues to rise over the life span in active people with no brain disease, such as stroke victims. Intellectual deficits that have been found are minor and not usually demonstrable at all until the eighties (Goleman, 1984; Foner, 1986).

Ann Foner emphasizes that many intellectual abilities not measured by intelligence tests may actually grow during old age—for instance, practical intelligence, social intelligence, or wisdom. Foner asserts that the only time that intellectual functioning systematically declines demonstrably is when the old person is near death. It appears that as part of the process of shutting down the body's functions, the brain activity may significantly decrease immediately before dying (Foner, 1986).

John Horn, researcher in intelligence and aging, suggests that three things can aid people in maintaining their mental capabilities through old age (Horn, in Goleman, 1984):

1. Staying socially involved. Deterioration is most often found in old people who withdraw from life.
2. Being mentally active. People should continue their intellectual interests, including such mental exercises as reading, doing crossword puzzles, and playing word games to stimulate inductive reasoning. Such activity will actually tend to increase verbal intelligence through old age.
3. Having a flexible personality. Those people most able to live with ambiguity and enjoy new experiences in middle age will probably maintain their mental alertness through old age.

Robert Butler emphasizes that the loss of mental capabilities due to aging, which is commonly labeled senility, is a disease, not a natural part of growing older: "The belief that if you live long enough you will become senile is just wrong" (Butler, in Goleman, 1984). Butler and others believe that this stereotype is especially dangerous, because it can lead to family and health care personnel assuming that any confusion in old age is the beginning of irreversible senility. An older person might become temporarily confused as a side effect of drugs, or because of being in a strange environment like a hospital. Dr. Jerry Avorn of the Division on Aging at Harvard Medical School describes the situation:

> The condition is reversible, but the family, or even the physician, doesn't recognize that fact. They assume this is the beginning of senile dementia, and pack the person off to a nursing home. No one knows what exact proportion of people in nursing homes needn't be there, but we have ample clinical evidence that the numbers are large. (Avorn, in Goleman, 1984).

Modern American society also perpetuates a myth that sexuality is the province of the young and is inappropriate behavior for older persons. Again, this relatively new social attitude can be harmful to the elderly. If they begin to believe the stereotype, the aged may curb their sexual desires due to fear of failure or guilt at feeling ways they "shouldn't" feel. Researchers have, in fact, discovered that some older people discontinue sexual relations because of societal pressure against the behavior, rather than because they lose interest in it (Percy, 1974).

Research unequivocally shows that individuals can enjoy sexual intercourse and orgasm up to and through the eighth decade of life, and perhaps longer, if they are healthy and have had a history of an enjoyable sexual life (Busse, 1977; Brecher, 1984). A survey of over 4,000 older Americans shows that two-thirds of the women and four-fifths of the men 70 or older are still sexually active and that half of these have sexual relations at least once a week (Brecher, 1984). Not surprisingly, good marital sex after age 50 is as strongly linked to marital happiness as it is at all ages.

Scholarly research contradicts contemporary stereotypes concerning these and other myths about the elderly, such as the idea that they are all ill or they make poor employees. Overwhelming evidence that the elderly are very much like everyone else, only older, may help dispel myths about the aged and bring about changes in the way the younger generation treats and views them. The younger generation is, after all, not getting any younger itself.

Why Does Ageism Exist? Sociological Theories of Aging

Although the changes involved in the transition from an agricultural to an industrial base may encourage ageism, it is certainly not a necessary ingredient for the change. Sociologists from the three major perspectives have endeavored to answer the question of why it exists.

STRUCTURAL-FUNCTIONAL EXPLANATIONS

As you will remember, functional explanations assume that social structures exist because they serve a function for the society. The two basic theories of ageism from this perspective, therefore, seek to explain why society functions best under the present system rather than to consider that the system itself might need to be changed.

Disengagement theory, an outgrowth of the structural-functionalist school, states that *an inevitable withdrawal from society accompanies aging.* Elaine Cumming and William Henry (1961) base their theory on the idea that human beings gradually decline toward death and that withdrawing from their social roles and settings helps them to accept this end to their life, beginning with retirement from "productive" work. Furthermore, society must learn to exist even with the continuous loss of its older members, and disengagement of the elderly helps the group to do this. Disengagement theory is an outgrowth of the functionalist point of view, emphasizing as it does the "benefits," or functions, of disengaging for both society and the individual and suggesting that the process creates a stable situation for all members of society.

Functionalists explain social norms, such as mandatory retirement, as developing in order to support the disengagement process. Having a rite-of-passage ceremony, like a retirement party, also aids the elder person in disengaging from the work which he or she is no longer able to do for the benefit of society.

Activity theory, also called the implicit theory of aging, states that *although aging persons must adapt to physiological changes, their psychological and social needs remain stable during the aging process.* Those who support this view of aging suggest that those who age successfully will not disengage from society but resist the attempts of society to withdraw from them because they are older (Havighurst, 1968). They will find other meaningful activities to substitute for employment and continue to make new friends at any age to counter the loss of friends and relatives who die. Activity theorists suggest that people of the United States value being active and productive and that Americans still subscribe to this value after age 65.

Structural-functionalist theory has also been applied to the status of youth in the United States. Functionalists believe, for example, that compulsory education through age 16 is useful to society. Our modern industrial societies need trained workers, so young people must be educated in order to function adequately. Coincidentally, education became compulsory, and child-labor laws severely restricted the number of young workers, so that people in this age category no longer compete with the persons in the middle-age categories for jobs. This education is seen

Although aging persons must adapt to physiological changes, their psychological and sociological needs remain. Often their talent remains or increases as this gray-haired artist demonstrates. (*Lynn McLaren/The Picture Cube*)

as useful in helping the young to find good work later in life and useful in assuring society a pool of educated workers for production. Structural-functionalists, then, see age stratification of both the young and the old as inherent in a smoothly working society.

CONFLICT EXPLANATIONS

The introduction of Matilda White Riley's age stratification theory in the 1970s marked the end of the automatic acceptance of structural-functional thinking about aging (Riley, 1971; Riley et al., 1972; N. Foner, 1982, 1984). As noted earlier, age-stratification theorists observe that societies are arranged into age strata, with differing obligations and rights for each, just as they are arranged into social classes with differing access to society's rewards and differing behavioral expectations. Riley argues that social class and social mobility are, in fact, analogous to age strata and the aging process. She further suggests that sociologists should ask the same questions about aging that they ask about class stratification:

1. How does an individual's location in the age structure of a society influence his or her behavior or attitudes?
2. How do individuals relate to one another within and between age strata?
3. What difficulties does the aging person encounter?
4. How do the answers to these first questions affect society as a whole? What pressures for change exist and are generated by differences and conflicts between age strata?

Because these age strata are seen as social classes, they can be ranked in a hierarchy of power, prestige, and wealth and be assumed to be in competition with other age strata for society's resources. For instance, the aged may believe that federal health insurance should be enacted by Congress, whereas young adults would rather see that money spent on schools for their children. Thus, rather than the static, stable structure which the functionalists envision, these theorists see constant sources of conflict between age strata.

Exchange theory suggests that *decreased social interaction of elders is explained by the fact that the power of elders relative to their social environment may diminish over time, until they become compliant to others.* James Dowd, for example, writes that elders will disengage from social relationships unless they have some form of power or knowledge to exchange with others in their relationships (Dowd, 1975).

Kart and Longino (1983) attempted to evaluate the assumptions of exchange theory. When they studied the amount of support given and received by elders in relationship to life satisfaction and feelings of obligation, they found that many elderly actually *contribute* as much to others as they accept *from* others, including younger family members, friends, and community members. Furthermore, the amount of support that the elders received did not affect their feelings of self-worth, but the amount of support that they *gave* to significant others correlated positively with life satisfaction. Kart and Longino concluded that exchange theory may be applicable to short-term trading situations among the elderly and others, but that in general older people are most satisfied being engaged and useful to others.

Other studies corroborate the idea that social supports, especially from family members, are very important for meeting the emotional and social needs of the elderly (Sussman, 1985; Shanas, 1979). Informal social networks, for example, have been shown to reduce the adverse effects of illness and other stresses in the lives of the aged, whereas loss of such support can increase physical problems (Asher, 1984). Those who age "successfully," then, are likely to be active, involved in the world, and helping others.

Conflict theorists also point out that age systems in themselves contribute to inequality in society because they unequally distribute opportunities to different age groups. Foner believes that one way to reduce the conflict caused by such inequality would be to remove old age from its artificial position as "the end" of the life cycle and treat the aging process as a natural flow of life (Foner, 1984). Under such a system, society would realize that social relationships, the division of labor, and the distribution of rights and responsibilities all shape the ability of persons at every age stratum to reap the rewards of society. This would lead to an opening of these areas to all age strata, based on agreed-upon criteria of competence rather than on generalizations about age groups.

Conflict theorists see the roles of the young and old in industrial society as restricted also by mandatory retirement and compulsory schooling. They say that the most powerful members of society, the middle-aged workers, use these two social inventions to rid their field of unwanted competition (Phillipson, 1982). In support of this view is the fact that organized labor was one driving force behind passing child labor laws and setting mandatory retirement ages.

Conflict theory predicts that changes in the present American capitalist system will occur only when the balance of power changes—for instance, as the number of aged grows to balance the number of workers, as it is presently doing. It will be interesting to discover in our lifetimes whether the aged and the young increase in wealth, power, and prestige as their numbers grow, as this theory might predict.

THE SYMBOLIC INTERACTIONIST VIEWPOINT

Symbolic interactionism may help us to understand how older people understand and experience "aging" in our society today. For example, Ward thinks that the loss of social roles, health problems, and economically forced mobility often experienced in old age may alienate the elderly from their past identities and create the potential for new identities (1979). Marshall describes this same process as "status passage," or going from one age-based status to another to the final passage of death (1979). Symbolic interactionists see the person's subjective experience of these passages as extremely important in determining his or her sense of control over life in the various statuses. For example, it can be very important for persons who know they are preparing for death to have the opportunity to share a life review with others, in some ways defining themselves and their contributions to the world before they leave it. Institutions or nonunderstanding family and friends can make this process difficult or impossible for some aged persons.

Labeling theory provides another application of symbolic interactionism to understanding aging and society. Because we tend to think of ourselves in terms of how other people define us and react to us, how the other age strata label older Americans can socially determine much of their behavior. Much as the behavior of young children often conforms to their parents' expectations, whether positive or negative, the behavior of elders often conforms to their childrens' expectations as well (Kuypers and Bengston, 1973). For instance, when it is assumed that an older parent can no longer prepare meals, an important social role, that of physical nurturant, is taken away. This, in turn, can make the parent feel less adequate in other areas. In contrast, assisting older persons to manage their own life can help them to feel more self-confident.

What Is the Socio-Economic Status of the Elderly in the United States Today?

Over the past several years, the economic status of most of the aged in the United States has remained stable or improved, depending on how you read the figures and which group you study. In 1960 thirty-three percent of all aged Americans had incomes below the official government poverty line. In 1985, the percentage had dropped to 12.6 percent, versus 18.7 percent for the population as a whole (Bureau of the Census, 1960, 1985). As the number of aged has increased, their economic position has risen.

The median income of the elderly has improved as compared to the general population, largely due to increases in Social Security benefits. (See Figure 12.2.) Between 1972 and 1982, the median incomes of the elderly grew at twice the rate of those of the general population (Bureau of the Census, 1985). If in-kind aid such as Medicare, food stamps, and the lack of tax on Social Security income are figured in, a few theorists suggest they actually have a higher per capita income than the nonelderly (Thurow, 1980). Seventy percent of the aged own their own homes, a much higher per-

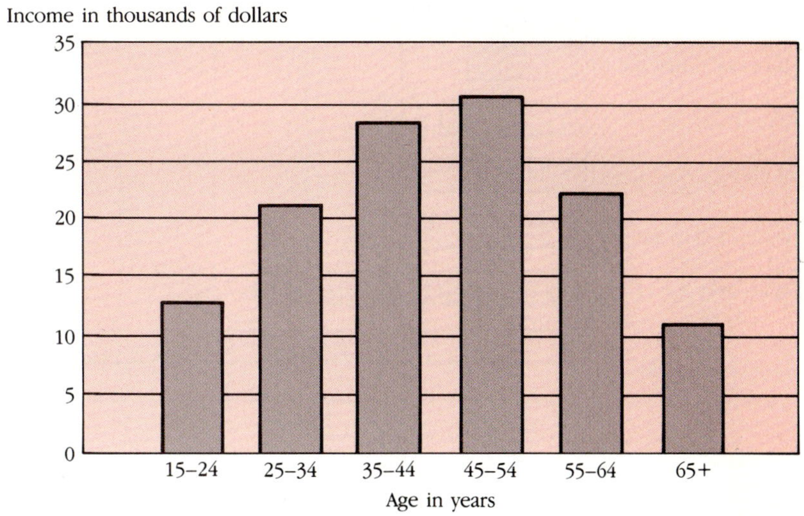

FIGURE 12.2 Median Income of Households by Age Groups. SOURCE U.S. Bureau of the Census, *Statistical Abstract of the United States, 1987* (107th ed.), Washington, D.C.: U.S. Government Printing Office, 1987.

centage than those in the lower age brackets, although rising energy and maintenance costs constantly threaten their ability to remain in them (Barrow, 1986). In terms of high income groups, 1.3 percent of Americans over 65 earn $50,000 or more, fairly close to the 2.3 percent of working age Americans with that level of income (James, 1985).

Caution must be taken when analyzing these gains, however. Per capita family income, for instance, can give an overly negative view of the financial situation of the elderly, because the families of older persons are usually smaller than younger families, making the per person income higher. Conversely, using per capita income to compare older families to younger may make the elderly's position seem better than it is, because young families have what economists term "economies of scale" in their favor. In other words, they pay a fixed amount for rent and utilities, which they spread over the number of people in their family, whereas older families must pay almost the same amounts for one or two persons. Furthermore, the medical expenses of the elderly are often much higher than those of younger families (Hendricks and Hendricks, 1986, p. 351.)

Although the overall economic position of the elderly in the United States has improved dramatically, old-age poverty is still a problem for minority groups such as women, blacks, and Hispanics. Seventy-two percent of all elderly poor are women, who earn less than men when they are employed and live longer than their husbands. Women's income has never reached more than two-thirds of men's, on the average, and they are often solely responsible for raising children on that lowered amount. Almost one in five women over 60 live in poverty (Barrow, 1986). The poverty rate among blacks is 35 percent, and the Hispanic rate is 24 percent, not substantially changed since 1970. Combining three minority statuses, a black woman who lives alone and is over 72 years old has a 70 percent chance of being poor (Barrow, 1986). (See Figure 12.3.) If you live most of your life in a group which is less economically advantaged, you will probably struggle to make ends meet in old age as well. On the other hand, if you were in the middle class and have a private pension as well as Social Security, you will probably be able to maintain a middle-class standard of living in retirement.

What Is the Situation Regarding the Elderly, Work, and Retirement?

The myth that old people are unproductive and can no longer create anything worthwhile grows directly from the investment that industrial society has in retirement. In a society with a surplus of workers, industry often believes it has much reason to replace older workers with younger, less-expensive employees (Spitzer, 1980; Phillipson, 1982; Atchley, 1985).

Although most people still retire around age 65, about 16 percent of men and 7 percent of women continue to work after that age (U.S. Bureau of Census, 1987). Older people *are* slightly slower at motor tasks, but they are also more productive than their younger counterparts. Additionally, they have 20 percent better absentee records, and fewer accidents (Neuhaus and Neuhaus, 1982). In short, most older people can do most jobs better or as well as most younger people, although they generally choose not to.

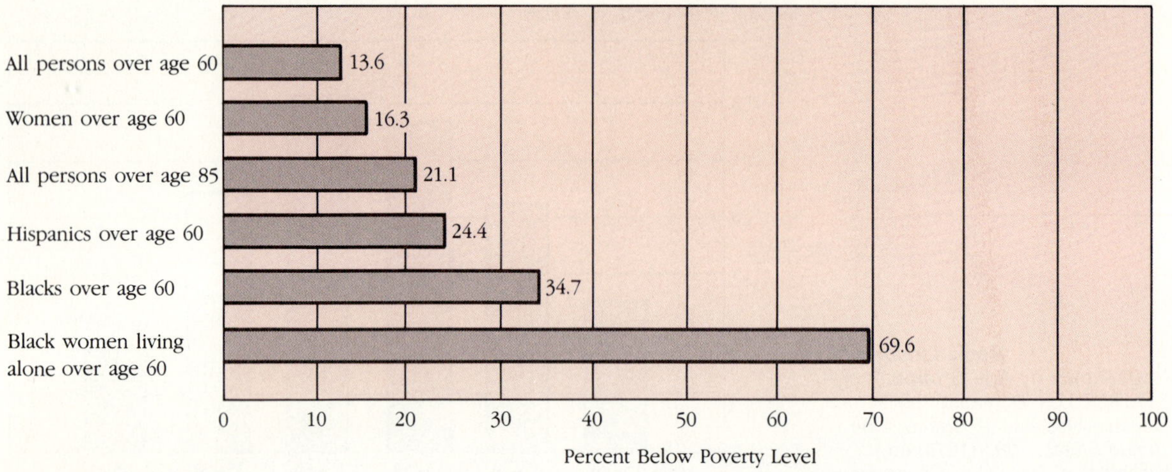

FIGURE 12.3 Who Are the Elderly Poor? As this chart clearly shows, being a member of a minority group or being one of the old-old (over age 85) significantly increases the possibility of being poor. SOURCE: U.S. Bureau of the Census, 1982.

The fact that today's elderly are generally no longer in the labor market sets them apart from previous generations. One hundred years ago, 75 percent of men over age 65 were still actively, full-time employed. Only fifty years ago, 50 percent of elderly American males were working (Kart, 1985).

Today fewer than one in five of this group are actively working, and many of them work part-time. By the year 2000, probably only one in ten will be employed. In 1983, only 8 percent of women over age 65 were employed. Earnings account for only 25 percent of the aggregate income of all the elderly (Atchley, 1985, p. 308).

How did this change come about? Some of the difference is accounted for by rapid industrialization. Traditionally, most elderly men worked in farming, an occupation from which they rarely retired. Instead, they might transfer the heavier tasks to others but continue in vital work for the farm themselves, planning, managing, and doing lighter physical tasks. As farming was replaced by industry as the predominant mode of work, fewer persons worked in this way throughout their lives.

Many of those over 65 today who *are* still employed are self-employed, as farmers were. These would include, for instance, physicians, lawyers, restaurant and store owners, and accountants. The amount and timing of the hours committed to these jobs can generally be controlled by the self-employed person and thus can be reduced to fit their desires and physical abilities.

Many elderly workers are in sales, clerical, and service occupations. Because sales and clerical work can often be done on a part-time basis, it attracts many elderly who do not wish to commit themselves to full-time work. Over 40 percent of elderly female workers worked in these categories in 1980 (Kart, 1985).

Lonely? Many older people continue to work to fend off feelings of uselessness and loneliness. (*Charles Kernaghan/FPG International*)

RETIREMENT

Sociologist Stephen Crystal points out that this is the first generation for whom retirement is the rule rather than the exception (1982). In fact, 69 percent of male and 21 percent of female workers are retiring *before* age 65. The average retirement age at General Motors, for instance, is 58 years (James, 1985).

What social forces have changed the United States in a little over fifty years from a nation in which no one retired to one in which people retire as early as possible? Many people believe the change began in the so-called "youth cult," which originated in the 1920s with emphasis on things young, fast, and progressive. It may have been encouraged by the fact that the nation was losing its frontiers, all of its territory having been explored, and that its people were living longer, due to less rigorous life-styles and improved medical techniques.

By the 1930s, marked prejudice against the old was evident. When combined with the Great Depression and the lack of jobs for persons of all ages, the social setting for a national retirement program was complete. William Graebner in *A History of Retirement* (1980) suggests that "Retirement was essentially a political device, imposed by one group (the young workers) upon another (the elderly workers)." Organized labor pushed hard for the passage of the Social Security Act, in order to ensure more jobs for its younger workers.

Some older workers welcomed it. Many of them felt more alienated from their factory jobs than they had from working their own land, so they were less invested in employment. Furthermore, society had begun to convince them that "leisure" was a thing to be desired, with the advent of such groups as the Golden Age Clubs and Senior Citizen Centers. The disengagement theory came into vogue. This "expert" advice began to convince senior citizens and their society that leaving paid work was an inevitable part of their life, which they should embrace as they made an "appropriate" transition toward death.

Atchley (1985) points out from a sociological viewpoint that the three conditions necessary for the emergence of retirement as a social institution were filled by the passage of the Social Security Act:

1. A number of people must live long enough to retire;
2. The economy must produce enough to have a surplus for those who are retired;
3. Some form of social insurance must support the retired.

Because of industry's inducements, the concept of early retirement has become increasingly attractive to workers. More companies are urging their employees to retire before age 65 with little loss of retirement benefits. Such policies are based on the assumptions that younger workers will have more up-to-date information and more energy to contribute than older ones and that beginning salaries are considerably lower, offsetting the need to pay retirement benefits. One study of 363 companies showed that over 60 percent of them had plans to encourage early retirement of their middle-managers and executives. Fifty percent of them had an average retirement age of 62 (D. White, 1985).

Ironically, this option that is being made attractive to today's elders may be unavailable to the next generation because of changes in the Social Security system. Fearful that the Social Security system will be overwhelmed by the year 2010 when the "baby boomers" retire, Congress has passed legislation to *raise* the age at which one might receive benefits, from 65 in 1987 to 70 by the year 2010. Whereas their parents will have been retiring with bonuses at ages from 55 to 65, this generation *must* work to age 70 in order to receive basic Social Security benefits.

AGE DISCRIMINATION

The current trend toward early retirement can lead to age discrimination. Companies unsuccessful in inducing voluntary retirement may lay off older workers, who have a difficult time finding other work, according to statistics.

In 1982, unemployment increased 24 percent for workers from ages 55 to 64, much higher than the 16 percent increase for other workers. Once unemployed, this group is three times more likely to become discouraged and stop looking for work (Select Committee on Aging, 1982). Their discouragement may be justified. Eighty-six percent of laid-off factory workers over age 45 do not find new jobs. Although one out of every six available workers is a man over forty-five, only one out of twenty-three jobs created in 1983 was filled by a man in that age group (Hendricks, 1984; *USA Today*, 1984).

Hendricks points out three other aspects of job experiences of older workers that point to discrimination. First, when they do find reemployment, it is often in a position of less authority than their previous job. Second, older workers have less upward job mobility and often stop progressing entirely by 50 to 59. Third, earnings profiles are lower for older workers (Hendricks and Hendricks, 1986, pp. 331–332).

Claude Pepper, congressman from Florida who is well respected as a spokesperson for the elderly, notes that the rationale used in their early retirement incentives may be faulty. He points out that it costs employers an average of $50,000 to replace a retired worker with a younger, supposedly "cheaper" one. He states vehemently that "if employers understood not only the virtues of older workers but also the costs of wasting their talents, we would see an end to age discrimination tomorrow" (Pepper in Barmash, 1982, p. 52).

Such actions as the 1985 Supreme Court ruling on mandatory retirement of pilots and flight engineers may help this group. In this decision, the Supreme Court stated that employers must prove either that anyone over a mandatory age presents a safety risk or that it is highly impractical to make individual judgments about his or her health. Such stringent requirements should make it more difficult for firms to strongly suggest retirement to workers who are not yet ready for it.

Retirement is a relatively new institution with many now retiring before age 65. This provides additional time for enjoying the fruits of one's labor such as sailboating. (*Photo courtesy the author*)

SOCIAL SECURITY AND PENSIONS

What supports this growing group of newly retired not-so-elders? Over 40 percent of Americans are now covered by private pension plans, but tax-based federal programs such as Social Security currently provide half of the income of the elderly. (See Figure 12.4.) For those living on $20,000 or more, Social Security is less than 16 percent of their income. However, without Social Security, 60 percent of the elderly would be poor (James, 1985).

Much has been written concerning the Social Security system's viability for the future, especially considering the increased number of retired persons anticipated in the next thirty to forty years. A number of social scientists feel this has been fed by a conservative bias against social programs during the Reagan Administration (Myles, 1985; Keyfitz, 1985; Atchley, 1985; Binstock, 1985). Nevertheless, the system will be severely taxed in its present form when 20 percent of the population reach the age at which they could receive its retirement benefits. It is important, therefore, to separate the myths about the system from the facts.

FIGURE 12.4 Sources of Income for Elderly Persons. SOURCE U.S. Bureau of the Census, *Statistical Abstract of the United States*, 1988 (108th ed.), Washington, D.C.: U.S. Government Printing Office, 1987.

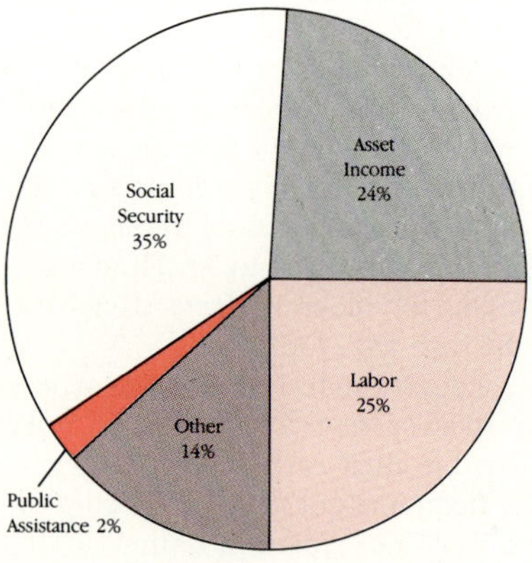

When the system was put into effect in 1939, the payroll tax deducted was 1 percent of the pay, and the average monthly check to a retiree was $22.60. The ratio of workers to retirees was nine to one. Today the tax is 6.7 percent (scheduled to rise to 7.65 by 1990), and the average payments are $650 for a couple and $400 for an individual. (See Figure 12.5.) The worker–retiree ratio is 3.3 to 1, heading for 2 to 1 about the year 2010 (Light, 1985).

It is not true that the Social Security system is "nearly bankrupt." This statement implies that the system is what it never was set up to be: a retirement *fund* that persons paid into and then received benefits from. Rather, it has always been a pay-as-you-go system,

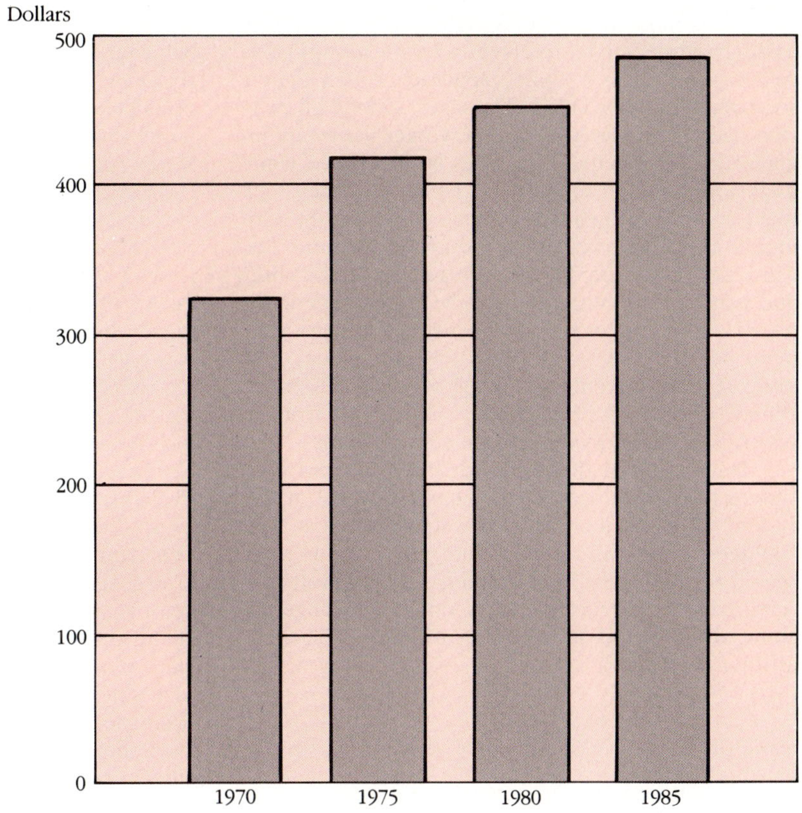

FIGURE 12.5 Average Monthly Benefit Payments to Retired Workers: 1970 to 1985 (in constant 1985 dollars). SOURCE U.S. Bureau of the Census, 1987, *Statistical Abstract of the United States, 1987* (107th ed.), Washington, D.C.: U.S. Government Printing Office, Figure 408, p. 337.

with benefits funded by current payroll taxes. The level of benefits and taxes required to finance them is a political choice of each group involved.

Critics point out that to suggest the Social Security system "won't have enough money by the time we retire" is similar to saying that the government won't have "enough" money to build the missiles, schools, or roads that are planned for the year 2010. As a society, we will choose our options and pay for them. Even Martin Feldstein, long-time critic of the Social Security system, admits, "as long as the voters support the Social Security system it will be able to pay the benefits that it promises" (Feldstein, 1977). Curiously, one of the suggested options for easing the projected crunch is to *slightly* increase the payroll tax of the "baby boomers" today, creating for the first time a "pool" of money to be saved toward the day that they descend upon the system as retirees (Myles, 1985).

The critical question to address, then, is how many baby boomers can the younger generation support and at what level will they support them? Although our social security tax is still at a moderate level compared to other Western industrialized nations (for instance Austria, West Germany, and Sweden), some think that increasing the tax would be detrimental to other areas of the economy. Several factors are encouraging in this regard, however. First, the extent to which the elderly population is a "burden" to the workers is determined not only by the size of the elderly population but by the relative ratio of the total nonworking population, children and young nonworkers included. Because we are having fewer children as a nation, we spend less in raising them. It has been estimated that raising a child costs 25 to 35 percent more than supporting someone over age 60 for the rest of his or her life (Schulz, 1980, p. 160). Second, labor force participation rates are already increasing, with more women employed and more women employed full-time. This increased rate of participation coupled with a relative increase in the amount of capital per worker should promote higher levels of production even with a smaller pool of workers. Third, because there will be fewer workers, their careers will progress more rapidly, and they will face less possibility of unemployment. This will produce higher per capita lifetime incomes with greater capacity to pay an increased tax (Myles, 1985).

A common criticism of Social Security is that it is a bad investment in terms of return for the money paid. Again, this implies a "fund" approach, rather than a social program provided for by taxes. Individual pension plans are often lost when a worker leaves an organization. Unless the worker has been with the company long enough to have his benefits "vested," or fixed, regardless of whether he stays with them, he may lose all the money he has contributed to the fund. Because Social Security benefits are adjusted to inflation and pensions are not, many people would experience a net loss of wealth if they invested only in pension plans for their retirement and inflation made their saved-up dollars worth continually less. Social Security benefits continue to be paid to the survivor of a worker, which is not true of most private pension plans.

Thus, we find that although the Social Security system has flaws many of the charges leveled at the system are founded on faulty reasoning, and that little has been offered in its place that is viable for most retired people. The crisis of confidence, however, that such charges have created may seriously challenge the ability of the Social Security system to do its job well, as it has in the past.

What Are the Challenges That the Elderly Face?

We have seen that the financial situation of the elderly in the United States has improved, and myths concerning old age are being corrected daily. Nevertheless, the elderly as a group do face certain problems. Most of these are not inherent in the fact that they are aging, and may be resolved in the coming decades as you approach old age.

DEBILITATING ILLNESS

One of the most frightening prospects for those growing older is debilitating illness. One writer notes that one-third of all suicides occur in the over-65 age group and believes that this reflects not the fear of death but the fear of becoming helpless, out of touch with reality, and totally dependent on others (Cowley, 1980).

This condition is termed organic brain syndrome (OBS). OBS problems most often begin between the seventh to ninth decade and occur more often in women (Fann, Wheless, and Richman, 1976). The most common OBS is primary degenerative dementia of the Alzheimer type, known as Alzheimer's disease. Alzheimer's disease follows a gradually progressive course, bringing loss of memory, judgment, and ability to think in abstract terms, as well as personality and behavior changes. For most victims, the decline takes six to eight years, but it may last for as long as twenty years before they lapse into coma and death. It is currently the fourth leading cause of death in the United States and affects an estimated 2.5 million Americans (Fischman, 1984).

Alzheimer's takes its name from Alois Alzheimer, a German neurologist who believed that the dementia (loss of reason) and brain lesions often found in autopsies of older, "senile" persons were linked to arteriosclerosis, or hardening of the arteries. His hypothesis was accepted as fact until the late 1960s, when researchers autopsied both demented and nondemented persons and found no relationship between arteriosclerosis and the dementia.

Research on the cause of Alzheimer's is inconclusive. Some observers believe that Alzheimer's is caused by a "slow virus," which can take years to exhibit effects. Another possibility is that Alzheimer's is linked to a genetic defect (Fischman, 1984). Most recently, neurologists have discovered that prolonged exposure of the respiratory system to aluminum may produce filamentary tangles that are similar to those found in Alzheimer patients' brains (Sullivan, 1987). Some physicians feel that a genetic component could be important: about 10 percent of those with the disease have others in their family history with the disorder (M. Clark, 1984).

Clinical descriptions of the illness, however, cannot begin to describe the tremendous social and psychological pressure that confronts the victims of this disease and their families. The disease involves a painfully slow loss of connection with the world. In the initial stages, the patient is aware of the fact that he or she sometimes does not make sense in terms of the rest of the world. One patient asks, "Can you imagine the embarrassment of an educated woman not knowing who the president is or having to ask where the bathroom is in your own house?" By the end, the family watches the patient lose all his or her former abilities, become increasingly confused, and eventually withdraw completely from social contact. In the words of one victim's wife, "It was devastating" (Clark, 1984).

As the proportion of elderly Americans rises, the number affected by this disease will also grow. Statistics suggest, however, that 95 percent of the young-old (below age 75) will not experience dementia, whereas 20 to 30 percent of those over age 85 will be at risk for Alzheimer's (Henig, 1981; Zarit et al., 1985). Now that scientists have discovered that it is not a "natural" result of the aging process, new focus is being placed on finding its origin and cure. Federal spending on Alzheimer's has increased tenfold since 1976, to $37 million dollars, and five major medical schools recently

Neither the young nor the old enjoy the status of those who are "not old" adults. This seems partly due to the fact that they often do not work in the paid labor force. This in turn gives them something in common. (*Photo courtesy Michigan Daily*)

have been designated Alzheimer's research centers (Clark, 1984). Alzheimer support groups offer invaluable help to families and sufferers. Perhaps someday soon it will not be the disease that is almost too frightening to discuss.

THE COSTS OF HEALTH CARE FOR THE AGED

Fifty percent of people over 65 have no detectable deterioration in their physical condition, and only 16 percent regard their health as poor (Neuhaus and Neuhaus, 1982, p. 17). Furthermore, much of the decline that *is* experienced may be due to inactivity and the feeling that physical deterioration is unavoidable, thus creating a self-fulfilling prophecy for the elderly.

Nevertheless, most of the elderly do consult medical practitioners at some point, and the cost of such care can be a burden on them. The United States is one of the few Western industrialized countries that has no national health program. Increases in physician's fees, inflation, and the fee-for-service system that has encouraged the use of expensive technologies have spurred tremendous growth in the cost of caring for the elderly. The United States has experienced what has been termed "runaway inflation in medical prices" in recent years and dramatic increases in the percentage of Gross National Product (GNP) devoted to health care (Myles, 1984). Health care costs over the past decade have been inflating at *double* the rate of the Consumer Price Index (CPI), from 5 percent of the GNP in 1970 to 11 percent in 1983 (K. Davis, 1986). In contrast, countries that have a national health insurance program, such as Canada, have stopped this growth in prices and actually brought health care expenditures *down* relative to the GNP.

The cost of research in diseases that threaten the elderly is incredibly high and shows no sign of slowing its growth. Most of us support such research in principle, and may even contribute to such organizations as the American Cancer Society. Those who are cured of acute illnesses and live longest are most likely to suffer chronic disease. As one writer reminds us "a cure for cancer increases our chance of dying from stroke or heart disease, just as a cure for all of these enhances the likelihood of living out our days with dementia" (Callahan, 1986).

When Clark and Menefee projected the proportion of the GNP required to maintain current Social Security benefits, taking into account the present rate of inflation of *health care costs* rather than a rate tied to the CPI, they found that twice as much of the GNP would have to be expended by the year 2025 to receive the same health care (1981). The problem of the future, then, may be deciding to maintain *health care costs* at an affordable level for all age groups, rather than of

SECRETS OF LONG LIFE

Morton Rothstein, a biochemist studying the aging process, suggests that the medical "ideal" in modern society is "to reach a very old age in excellent health and then die quickly" (Rothstein, 1986). Gerontologists call this "squaring off the age curve." What makes for this kind of longevity? Several researchers have approached the question, primarily though studying populations that have an unusual number of healthy old-old persons. Research indicates that some claims about large groups of the elderly were made by people interested in selling propaganda about their country, books, or yogurt (Georgakas, 1980; Palmore, 1984). For instance, research concerning large numbers of people reaching great ages in Abkhasia, U.S.S.R., has shown the claims to be largely false (Barrow and Smith, 1986). Furthermore, observers have discovered that the elderly in such places often exaggerate their years after age 70, a practice aided by the fact that most of these places have no birth records available.

Nevertheless, such places as Vilcabamba, a small village in the mountains of Ecuador, do have a higher percentage than would be expected of very old persons. The villagers live by crude farming, with a diet consisting of very little meat or milk, and subsistence amounts of lettuce, carrots, turnips, potatoes, yams, corn, and barley. They eat no butter or sugar, and use local fruits as desserts. All ages work in their culture, and work is valued as a pursuit. One old man stated, "To work is the best thing in life, even above sleeping with your woman." (Halsell, 1986, p. 397).

They have no modern medicine and use herbs and teas to cure their ailments. One visiting physician found their bones incredibly strong, and discovered no prostate trouble, cancer, heart attacks, or ulcers. Their life-style is devoid of the type of stress and anxiety that members of industrialized societies experience. Their strong Roman Catholic faith is credited for having taught them to accept life as it comes and enjoy the beauty around them. In contrast to modern North American society, aging in Vilcabamba brings distinction and respect.

One researcher has analyzed several population groups with large numbers of old-old members and finds that generally they spend hours every day in vigorous physical exertion, primarily farming, and that they eat fewer calories and less fats, cholesterol, and salt than the typical North American (Elrick, 1976). Perhaps because of these habits they share the following characteristics:

1. They are slender, young-looking, and strong.
2. Their cholesterol and triglyceride levels are lower than those of North Americans.
3. They show virtually no high blood pressure or heart disease. Recent advances in knowledge about the relationships between diet, stress, and the "typical" diseases of old age in the United States today may help to bring about the seeming fantasy of long and healthy life that these elderly of different cultures live out.

deciding whether or not to fund basic social security benefits.

Several plans to contain the cost of health care for the elderly specifically have been suggested. The most significant step in this direction is the implementation of the Diagnosis Related Group (DRG) system, in which Medicare pays hospitals a fixed amount per patient based on the diagnosis (Davis, 1986).

The DRG system is aimed at reducing the number of unnecessary tests and rewarding hospitals for efficient care. Another cost-containing suggestion is raising the age of initial Medicare eligibility to 68 or 70, which would be today's equivalent in mortality expectation of age 65 when Social Security was introduced in 1935 (Callahan, 1986). Also being considered is reducing the disproportionately high costs of care to maintain the last year of life. In the United States, 1 percent of the GNP is spent on health care for elderly persons who are in their last year of life (Fuchs, 1984). The obvious problem here is that, traditionally, medical personnel have committed themselves to the preservation of life, regardless of its quality, and that families have great difficulty in knowing when to let nature decide when a person's life will end, as we saw clearly in the story of Oliver Shay.

Perhaps the most feasible system would be to shift from an age-based Medicare system to one that is need-based. As we have seen earlier in this chapter, the elderly as a group have made economic gains since 1965 when Medicare was introduced to help them make ends meet, but many of them still depend upon government funds for survival. Two arguments are put forth against this plan: Medicare was designed to provide a base for a national health insurance policy for all ages, and Medicaid, the need-based program developed at the same time, has consistently failed to provide good care for the poor (Callahan, 1986).

The problem of paying for good medical care for the elderly is complicated. Although on the surface it would seem to involve simple economics, we can now see that moral issues of "need," decisions about quality of life, and the traditional American ideals of independence and resistance to any limitations on the free market system all will play a part in determining the future of health care in the United States.

NURSING HOMES

Only about 5 percent of the elderly over 65 are confined to their own homes, and fewer than 4 percent live in institutions at any point in their lives. In other words, 89 percent of those over 65 are self-sufficient and physically active. Among the old-old (those 85 years and over), chronic conditions are more prevalent and may prevent full activity, but even in this group 80 percent live independently (Neuhaus and Neuhaus, 1982).

Extension of life expectancy has meant that more "elderly" adults are caring for their "elderly" parents than ever before. The prevailing myth that in the "good old days" families took care of their own elderly ignores the fact that in the past few people lived to their 80s and required such long-term care. Today, for every elderly person living in a nursing home, two others who are equally impaired are living with family (E. M. Brody, 1985).

Most Americans of all ages view nursing homes with fear. Their opinions are, unfortunately, often grounded in fact. In 1986, the Institute of Medicine and the Senate's Special Subcommittee on Aging condemned most of the nation's nursing homes for substandard facilities and treatment. With the shortage of nursing-home beds, even badly run homes often can charge high prices. To make matters worse, the 1986 Senate committee estimates that 600,000 more beds will be needed by 1990 (Nyman, 1987).

The U. S. Senate Special Committee on Aging (1985) confirmed that hospitals are now discharging older patients "sicker and quicker" since the advent of DRGs, and many of these patients need at least some nursing home care. Furthermore, because most nursing homes have a guaranteed base of publicly supported Medicaid patients who comprise over 60 percent of all nursing home occupants, they have little financial incentive to upgrade their services in order to attract more private patients.

Demographically, seven out of ten nursing home residents are widows, 92 percent are white, 12 percent are married, and many are without family or other social supports (Kart, 1985). Logically, the older you are, the greater your chance of living in a nursing home. Most of us will spend most of our days in independent living circumstances, probably until shortly before death, when we may enter a hospital or nursing home. Over all, about 5 percent of all older persons in the United States are nursing home residents (Hendricks and Hendricks, 1986).

About 80 percent of the 25,000 nursing homes in the United States today are commercial operations with sizable profits. Although the federal government oversees enforcement of regulations, some unscrupulous owners have found ways to curtail services in order to increase their profits (Butler and Lewis, 1982). Nyman believes that the only long-term solution to the problem is for states to encourage new private construction and allow nursing homes to operate competitively, as restaurants and hotels do, with enough government controls to prevent major problems (1987).

ELDER ABUSE

When the police found Vera Dixon in August, 1985, she was lying in the kitchen with only a shirt on and a vacuum cleaner bag wrapped about her buttocks. She had starved to death within a few feet of the only food in the house: two containers of ice cream in the freezer and an almost empty jar of peanut butter placed on top of a kitchen cabinet, out of her reach. The apartment was filthy, with the exception of her son's bedroom and bath, which were clean and neat. However, due to a lack of laws addressing elder neglect and abuse, charges against her son were dropped (Bruno, Burgowere, and Miller, 1985).

The family is the primary social relationship for most older people, and the idea of abusing one of our parents or grandparents is anathema to most of us. Yet 1.1 million persons over the age of 65, nearly 4 percent of all elderly Americans, are abused, neglected, or exploited each year (Bruno, Burgowere, and Miller, 1985). This figure represents an increase of 100,000 cases since 1981, when the first Congressional report on the subject was released. ***Elder abuse*** can include *physical mistreatment, exploitation* (for instance, confiscating a parent's savings), *neglect* (failing to give food or medicine), *or psychological maltreatment* (calling names and degrading them) (Eastman, 1984).

Although some elderly are abused in nursing home settings, most are abused or neglected by members of their family who are their caretakers, as Vera was (Steinmetz, 1981). The most likely abuser is the son of an elderly person, followed by the daughter and the victim's spouse (Robinson, 1985). The average abused elder is 75 or older, a woman, and dependent on others (Keebler, 1985).

What inherent in the situation might lead to abuse? Stress from a long-term committment of care to a very physically or mentally impaired parent can lead to depression, hostility, and anger in the caretaker (Bruno, Burgowere, and Miller, 1985). If the caretaker has few coping skills and little social support in his or her own life, the setting is ripe for abuse. The situation worsens when the caretaker has no periods of relief from the burden of the elder (Douglass, 1983).

Recently passed laws aim at reducing elder abuse, with stiffer penalties and more power given to state agencies to investigate possible abuse situations. Neighbors and caseworkers are encouraged to report abuse when they see such signs as abrupt negative changes in appearance, bad attitude on the part of the caregiver, and deteriorated or isolated living quarters for the older person (Jensen, 1982). Clearly, as the number of old-old persons grows in the United States, society must develop ways to reduce the pressure on their caregivers in order to minimize the potential for abuse. The following "Close-Up on Research" summarizes the major work in the field done by sociologists in the early 1980s, when elder abuse was first being identified as a social problem.

CLOSE-UP on • *RESEARCH* •

Claire Pedrick-Cornell and Richard Gelles on Elder Abuse

The Researchers and the Setting

In this article, Claire Pedrick-Cornell and Richard Gelles, researchers at the Family Violence Research Program of the University of Rhode Island, summarize current research on the extent, patterns, and causes of elderly abuse. They were aware that elder abuse had gained great social, scientific, and media attention in a very short time, and attributed this to two factors:

1. "The discovery of a significant number of elderly victims of family violence was a natural outgrowth of research on family violence" (p. 457), which had begun in the 1960s and 1970s, and
2. The dramatic increase in the number of elderly, coupled with an average family of fewer children to care for them, may have led to an increase in the problem of elder abuse.

Pedrick-Cornell and Gelles were concerned that growing interest in this topic by the media had sometimes caused inaccurate information to be accepted as fact by both the public and otherwise uninformed social scientists.

The Researcher's Goal

Pedrick-Cornell and Gelles attempt to "examine the scientific status of knowledge about elderly abuse" (p. 458). Specifically, they (1) review problems of definition, (2) examine data and research on rates of elderly abuse, and (3) critique theories that try to explain the abuse of the elderly.

Theory and Concepts

The researchers suggest three propositions:

1. "The most significant impediment in the development of an adequate knowledge base on intrafamily violence and abuse has been the problem of developing a satisfactory and acceptable definition of violence and abuse" (p. 458).
2. "Despite the data presented in available reports, the extent and incidence of the abuse of the elderly is still unknown" (p. 460).
3. "Despite the consistency of factors reportedly associated with elderly abuse in the variety of articles and reports written on this subject, it is clear that the support for these claims is intuitive, speculative, and/or based only on findings from studies of other forms of family violence" (p. 462).

Research Design

The goal of this research was to summarize the work done thus far in this area, in order to give social scientists a clear view of its limitations and strengths. Pedrick-Cornell and Gelles did this by reviewing all scholarly articles in the field and analyzing them in light of their own experience and research.

Findings

The researchers discovered that the definition of abuse varied widely, making it difficult to measure quantitatively. Many articles use an "operational definition" of elderly abuse, which relies exclusively on cases that have come to professional attention, to make generalizations. Research on child and wife abuse, which has been studied much longer than elderly abuse, demonstrates that "those cases which come to public attention represent a skewed and biased portion of the entire population of victims of abuse" (p. 459). Therefore, to rely on this type of definition for the study of elderly abuse is to restrict the study of such abuse to reported cases.

Again, in terms of the extent and incidence of abuse, current estimates are based on cases reported to social service agencies. The researchers point out four problems with accuracy related to this approach:

1. The number of reported cases is only a fraction of the total number.
2. Because reporting elderly abuse is not mandatory, as is reporting child abuse, the number of reported cases of this type is probably an even smaller proportion than the fraction of child abuse cases that are reported.
3. The fact that this problem has only recently been uncovered means that many persons will not be alert to it.
4. The number of cases reported to agencies varies by type of agency, title, location, and other variables.

Based on these inherent problems, they suggest "extreme caution" in generalizing data from the current studies.

Pedrick-Cornell and Gelles state that the current research offers "some tentative insights into the profile of the abuse, abused, and abusive situation" (461). Although researchers have made claims about who is likely to be abused and to abuse, they used no comparison groups in their research designs as control groups. Therefore, they "cannot report whether the factors they found present in their cases of abuse were distinctive of abuse cases, compared to other clients where no abuse was present, or compared to the general population of the elderly" (p. 462). Corresponding to this lack of good empirical evidence on the abusing situation is a lack of "empirically tested propositions on the generative causes of the abuse of older persons" (p. 462). Thus far theories have consisted of conventional wisdom applied to abuse in general, borrowed ideas from research on spouse and child abuse, or assumptions about the status of the elderly within the family in society. None of these meet the standard of being able to be tested with quality empirical data.

Implications

Pedrick-Cornell and Gelles bluntly state that when faced with the basic questions about elderly abuse, based on current research we should answer "We do not really know" (p. 463). They prefer that programs and policies for the aged be built on good research and offer five steps toward that end:

1. Researchers should carefully construct a precise and measurable definition of elder abuse, as distinct from neglect.
2. Research must study more than public cases by using self-reports from subjects in nonclinical settings.
3. In order to determine the extent of elder abuse, researchers must draw a representative sample of subjects.
4. To identify factors associated with elder abuse, studies must include a comparison group.
5. Theories must be built of testable propositions.

This comprehensive study of the state of knowledge of elder abuse should be useful to us in evaluating the "facts" that we read about any current social problem in the mass media. As persons with a basic understanding of the processes of research and theory building, students could begin to ask themselves the kinds of questions Pedrick-Cornell and Gelles asked of their fellow social scientists and media personnel: Is it generalizable? Can it be tested? Was a control group used? Where did the data come from? Does the group tested represent the entire population? Asking such questions will help you to refrain from accepting everything you read as being "true."

Questions

1. How might researchers gain a more complete picture of the problem of elder abuse? If you were designing a study that would be generalizable, where would you begin?
2. Dozens of popular articles were written on the topic of elder abuse based on the limited studies that these researchers evaluate, many of which made claims that are not really substantiated upon close review. How might social scientists keep information that is limited in scope from being used by journalists in ways that could mislead the American public?
3. Based on our limited knowledge, what solutions do you see to the problem of elderly abuse? Where would you begin to attack the situation?
4. Pedrick-Cornell and Gelles suggest that the problem of elderly abuse came to national attention quickly because it grew on the coattails of the child-and spouse-abuse research of the 1960s and 1970s. Does this make sense to you? How might it be true or not true?

SOURCE Claire Pedrick-Cornell and Richard J. Gelles. 1982. "Elder Abuse: The Status of Current Knowledge," *Family Relations* 31, July, 1982, pp. 457–465.

What Are Social Reactions to Death and Dying?

A major social change has occurred due to the aging of our population through modern medical care: We have begun to artificially separate the dying process from the living process. At the beginning of this century, one-third of all children died before age 5, and another third of all persons died before they were 55. Most families had experienced death firsthand, at home, rather than receiving a phone call from the hospital where they have been visiting their aged parent for an hour a day during their last weeks (Atchley, 1983). Children learned as a part of growing up how to prepare a body for burial, and funerals routinely took place in their own parlors or churches, rather than in professional funeral parlors.

In modern societies, death has become bureaucratized. One of the functions of a bureaucracy, as we have discussed, is to maintain smooth functioning of the persons involved in the bureaucratic activity. For instance, most elderly express a desire to die at home, but most of them actually die in hospitals and nursing homes under supervision of professionals rather than family members (Cox, 1984). Upon death, they are taken away by another group of professionals, the morticians, and prepared for a secularized service at the funeral home rather than at their own home or church. The traditional gathering of family and friends at the home is increasingly bypassed.

Several researchers suggest that these new rituals make death less disruptive to the social group than the treating of the dying person within the home community, the preparation of his or her body by friends and relatives, and the community mourning led by the group spiritual leader. However, this bureaucratized death may be more disruptive for the individual who is dying and his or her family (Marshall, 1980; Kalish, 1981). Rituals have long been known to maintain group solidarity and to assist individuals during times of transition. Rituals surrounding death are thought to lessen the effects of severe grief. One gerontologist notes: "The deritualization of death means that individuals are left on their own to handle breavement and grief" (Ward, 1984, p. 322). This lack of a socially acceptable forum in which to work out grief within a supportive group setting may add to the stress of the modern mourner (Charmaz, 1980).

THE FEAR OF DEATH

The bureaucratization of death may reflect the fear of dying which has emerged more strongly in modern society, because most of us have little experience with the dying process. Research indicates that children are *taught* to fear death, most likely through their parents' being so secretive and fearful about it themselves (Kalish, 1981). For obvious reasons, older people are more likely than the young to think and talk about death and to be unafraid of it (Kalish, 1981; Marshall, 1980).

This fear of death is also reflected in the health care that the dying receive in hospitals and nursing homes. The dying are often placed in rooms farthest from nursing stations, and research shows that nurses answer call buttons from terminal patients more slowly than they do those from patients who may someday recover (Cox, 1984, p. 265). Similarly, physicians teaching medical students tend to avoid the terminally ill on their teaching rounds (Kubler-Ross, 1981). The dying person may even be ignored if he or she wants to discuss their impending fate: one writer suggests that a "code" exists that says such things won't be talked about in polite company (Shneidman, 1980). The sense of being powerless to help a dying person is uncomfortable for family and professionals alike and may be alleviated when they are "tucked away" safely in a quiet, out-of-the-way hospital room. In contrast, some family members may feel guilty at not being able to physically or emotionally handle the burden of an extremely ill elder, even though under different circumstances they would like to have done so.

One of the first researchers in the field of death and dying is Elisabeth Kubler-Ross, whose five stages of dying have become the cornerstone for much of the later research in the field (Kubler-Ross, 1969, 1981). The first stage she defines as *denial,* in which patients ignore the truth of the impending death. When the truth can no longer be hidden, they experience *anger* at their fate. In the third stage, they may attempt to *bargain* for an extension of their life, often with promises being made for their hoped-for future. In the fourth stage, *depression,* the patients feel hopeless about the future. Kubler-Ross implies that this sorrow is necessary to prepare patients for the final stage, *acceptance,* in which the struggle to continue life ends.

Although Kubler-Ross's work was the first to suggest different ways of dealing with the adjustment of dying persons, it is based on anecdotes and interviews from her own experience, rather than on more "scientific" evidence. Other researchers since have questioned her techniques and wonder if her work is really generalizable to the population as a whole (Shneidman, 1980; Kastenbaum, 1981). Some question the idea that everyone must pass through every stage in exactly this order (Cox, 1984). Of the five stages that she found, only depression has been universally found in subsequent research. Thus, several gerontologists today believe that her work should not be considered a

Sociologists at Work •

CARY S. KART
RESEARCHES WHAT WILLS REVEAL ABOUT FAMILIES
Department of Sociology
University of Toledo
Toledo, Ohio

Cary S. Kart is Professor of Sociology at The University of Toledo. His work has appeared in many scholarly journals. He is the author of *The Realities of Aging* 3rd Edition (Allyn and Bacon, 1989) and co-author of *Aging, Health and Society* (Jones and Bartlett Publishers, 1988). He shared with us some recent research carried out with Carol A. Engler, that examined family relationships from the perspective of aged people.

What Was Your Goal in This Research?

We examined inheritance practices from 1820 to almost 1970, dividing the 150 years into five 30-year segments. The wills we studied had been probated in Wood County, a rural area south of Toledo, Ohio. (Probate records in rural areas are often more neatly organized and accessible than those in larger, urban areas.) We drew samples of wills recorded during each of the five time segments were drawn and reviewed them with an eye toward understanding the nature of relationships between older testators (will writers) and their family members. Our goal was to identify changes in inheritance practices that reflected social changes across a 150-year period in family relationships between the testators and their family members.

What Did You Discover?

From 1820 to 1910, virtually all the wills were written by men. These men not only controlled the family assets when they were alive, but through the use of the will they also controlled these assets from the grave. They frequently used an inheritance practice that is called *life estate,* a condition of a will in which a testator leaves everything to his or her spouse until that spouse remarries or dies. At the time the husband or wife remarries or dies, the original testator through provisions in the will distributes the assets of the estate again.

The life estate was a device that some men used to maintain control for an extended duration over their children as well as their wives. A man would specify in his will, for example, that if, after his death, the children took care of their mother during her natural life, then she could share with them material goods and money or assets out of the estate; when she died, the property would then be divided among the children. Also specified in such a will was that if the adult children failed to provide support to their mother, disinheritance could result.

Thus it was a rare will that provided one-half the estate to my spouse and the other one-half to be distributed to my children. Rather, as I described above, testators used the life estate to say: "Everything for my spouse now. If the children do as I say, then they get the land and whatever else is available upon mother's remarriage or death." An interesting aspect of this practice is that children (including adult children) really were tied to the family land. If they did not have the land to work, they were in trouble. For the most part, they did have to take care of their mother until her death or remarriage to get the land. However, some of the children lacked the necessary patience or wanted to get out from under parental control, and they headed west!

After 1910, more women wrote wills than during the 1800s. Twentieth-century wills of both men and women were written in *fee simple*, a practice in which testators leave the bulk of the estate to a spouse who retains full control without any conditions. Under the terms of fee simple, will writers gave up the control from the grave which is inherent in the life estate wills.

What we found reflected in these wills, supported by other researchers, was that the twentieth-century brought a modest weakening of family obligations. Certainly people today have strong family obligations, but they have other obligations as well—to religious institutions or to friends or other kinds of voluntary associations in which they have participated. In our nineteenth-century wills, we did not observe these competing obligations; family obligation was the whole story with marital relationships reflecting the strongest responsibility.

What Other Changes Did You Note in the Writing of Wills?

Nineteenth-century wills were often lengthy documents, hand-written with a moral message. In effect, some testators left *values* to family members in addition to material assets. Survivors read not only of which horse was left to them but also of the importance of religious institutions, values and attendance at the local church. It is an interesting commentary that, with time, it became increasingly common for wills to deal only with the distribution of material assets. Moralizing and distributing values from the grave essentially disappeared. In the twentieth-century, wills have become *rational* documents. Today, you can buy a book with a form in it, fill in the blanks, and you have a will. It is structured as if the material goods are all we have of importance today to pass on to our heirs.

"theory of the dying process," but rather an "insightful discussion of some of the attitudes that are often displayed by people who are dying" (Schaie and Willis, 1986, p. 473).

Edwin Shneidman offers a more scientifically grounded stage theory of dying (1980). He suggests that the dying face two challenges: to prepare for their own death and to help prepare their loved ones to be survivors. In the process of doing these two tasks, they alternately show anger, grief, anxiety, denial, and anguish. This accounts for the fact that many dying people will straightforwardly confront their imminent death one day and talk of cure the next, which can be confusing for those loved ones who are trying to comfort them in their last days.

THE HOSPICE MOVEMENT

Negative reactions to dying within the bureaucratized atmosphere of the hospital and nursing home, coupled with a realistic appraisal of the difficulties of home nursing today's old-old, with their multiple medical problems, has led to the development of the *hospice* model of caring for the terminally ill (Holden, 1980). The ***hospice movement*** *endeavors to provide home or homelike care for terminally ill persons and to support their loved ones.* The first hospice facility, St. Christopher's, opened in Great Britain in 1967. The concept was transplanted to the United States in New Haven, Connecticut in 1974, and today over 200 hospice facilities exist throughout the United States. Some hospitals are even developing hospice units within their walls (Bayer and Feldman, 1982). The growth of the hospice movement was given a significant boost in 1983 when the Department of Health and Human Services agreed to provide Medicare benefits for hospice care. Although the payments provided are not considered adequate for the kind of personal care that the patients receive in hospice facilities or with home nursing care, they represent a commitment on the part of Congress to fostering home-based care programs for terminally ill persons.

Hospice emphasizes relieving the pain and maintaining the dignity of the dying person, rather than using technology to prolong life (Hamilton and Reid, 1980). In addition, the hospice staff offers supportive services to the family of the dying person, primarily through trained volunteers who support the family throughout the dying and grieving process. In a sense, the hospice organization replaces the traditional tight-knit community response to the dying of a member, providing counsel and care to both the dying one and the survivors. Hospice research has added much valuable knowledge to the study of death and dying (Greer, 1983; Kastenbaum, 1985).

The emphasis within the hospice system is on reduction of anxiety and control of pain. Patients control their own medication whenever possible, and family members are trained in whatever medical techniques they need in order to keep their loved one at home, an option that is frequently chosen by the patient and family (Buckingham, 1982).

Although the number of hospices has grown, they are still not available to most dying persons. Simply by existing, however, the hospice movement has sensitized medical personnel to the social and emotional needs of the dying and their families. Some gerontologists are hopeful that hospice principles could help to humanize nursing home care (Munley, Powers, and Williamson, 1983). Others believe that hospices may actually reverse the trend toward giving second-rate care to the dying elderly (Hamilton and Reid, 1980).

Conclusion

The field of gerontology in Western societies is growing as rapidly as the population of elderly persons. Gerontologists will continue to address such topics as ageism, the social and economic status of the aged, and the problems that the society as a whole faces when its population grows grayer. Many answers to the questions raised in this chapter will undoubtedly be forthcoming from research. One would hope that we might learn to avoid lingering deaths like that of Oliver Shay. Although we do not know what the future holds, we can safely assume that the family will continue to be the dominant institution affected by and affecting the aging process and that social relationships will change as we adapt to an increasingly older population base.

REVIEW

Summary Questions

1. How is the demographic picture of the United States different today from that at the turn of the century?
2. How is status accorded in different cultures?
3. What are the major determinants of the status of different age groups?

4. What is ageism, and why does it exist?
5. What myths are generated about the elderly, and what facts refute them?
6. What is the socioeconomic status of the elderly in the United States today?
7. How has the situation of the elderly changed in terms of work and retirement?
8. What other challenges do the elderly face?
9. What does research say about "long life"?
10. What is the current state of knowledge about elder abuse?
11. How has the social reaction to death and dying changed?
12. What are the positive aspects of increased longevity for society?

Summary Answers

1. In 1900 the median age was 24, and the average life expectancy 47 years. Only 4 percent of the population was over 65. Today, the median age is 33 years, the average life expectancy 74 years, and 12 percent of the population is over 65 years of age. This has occurred due to changes in birth, death, and migration rates as well as gains in food, clothing, housing, and medical care.
2. The status of older people varies from society to society. Sometimes they are treated as elder statespersons, and sometimes as drudges required to do all the work the younger members do not want to do. Primitive societies that have been the most respectful of the aged are those that are prosperous and have no written language, thus making the elders the only repository of tribal tradition. Research suggests that perhaps the status of the elderly drops as societies stabilize and move into the advanced stages of modernization.
3. Gender and age are the two most common characteristics used to divide people into status groups. Age roles are often determined by one's own age. Seven other determinants of status, which are unequally distributed over the age groups, are (1) property ownership, (2) strategic knowledge, (3) productivity, (4) mutual dependence, (5) tradition and religion, (6) kinship and family, and (7) community life. This unequal distribution leads industrial societies to value the middle-aged groups more highly than the lower- and upper-aged groups.
4. Ageism is having prejudiced attitudes and behavior toward the elderly. The structural–functionalist-based disengagement theory states that an inevitable withdrawal from society accompanies aging. Conflict theorists see ageism as reflecting the existing hierarchy of power, prestige, and wealth: Middle-aged persons have the power to keep other groups below them, and they use it. Symbolic interactionists address the subjective experience of aging in our society today; for instance, they study the loss of social roles, health problems, and economically forced mobility.
5. One of the major sources for myths that assume that older persons should be afforded less respect is television. Some of the myths they perpetuate are:

   As you grow older, your body deteriorates: Fifty percent of people over 65 have no detectable deterioration in their physical condition, and fewer than 4 percent live in institutions at any point in their lives.

   Old people can't think clearly any more: Although the elderly *may* be somewhat less able in the use of fluid intelligence, crystalized intelligence continues to rise over the life span. This is especially true when people stay socially involved, are mentally active, and have a flexible personality.

   Old people are not good workers: Although older people are slightly slower at motor tasks, they are also more productive and have better absentee records and fewer accidents than younger workers.

   Old people lose their interest and ability in sex: Individuals can enjoy sexual intercourse and orgasm up to and through the eighth decade of life, and longer, if they are healthy and have had a history of an enjoyable sexual life, especially linked with a happy marriage.

6. Over the past several years, the economic status of most of the aged in the United States has remained stable or improved. Nevertheless, certain target groups, such as women, blacks, and Hispanics, are still highly at risk for poverty in their later years.
7. At the turn of the century, 75 percent of men over 65 were still actively employed full-time. Today 20 percent are employed, many of them part-time.
8. Debilitating illness, especially Alzheimer's disease, which strikes 20 to 30 percent of those over age 85, can be devastating on the elderly and their families. The cost of health care in the United States has inflated at double the rate of the Con-

sumer Price Index, and will probably be a more important problem for the elderly of the future than continuing Social Security support. The problem of elder abuse, including physical mistreatment, exploitation, neglect, or psychological maltreatment, affects an estimated 4 percent of all elderly Americans.

9. Although many claims about large groups of golden-agers in exotic places like Abkhasia, U.S.S.R. have been discredited, some basic principles appear to those who study people who are healthy to old age. They spend hours every day in vigorous physical exertion, eat fewer calories, fats, cholesterol, and salt, are slender, young-looking, and strong, have low cholesterol and triglyceride levels, and show no high blood pressure or heart disease.
10. Pedrick-Cornell and Gelles, summarizing the state of scientific rather than journalistic knowledge of elder abuse, conclude that significant problems in the present "research" exist: problems of definition, significant reporting errors, and a skewed sample from which generalizations have been drawn.
11. Modern medical care has allowed society to begin separating the dying process from the living process. Many traditional rituals are increasingly replaced by bureaucratic structures, making it more difficult for survivors to handle their grief. The hospice movement, which endeavors to make home or homelike care available for the terminally ill and to support their loved ones, appears to be helping the process of dying become more "human" again.
12. The Rileys review literature indicating strongly that longevity has many positive effects on an individual's life, and that the capacity for the elderly to participate fully and usefully in our society is high. In order for this to happen, however, the life stages that have been previously agreed upon by members of society must be revised, creating strong positive changes in our society.

Glossary

activity theory states that although aging persons must adapt to physiological changes, their psychological and social needs remain stable during the process

age cohort a group of people who were born during a particular period of time

ageism prejudiced attitudes and behavior toward any age group

age stratum a group of people who are experiencing a certain stage in life at a certain time

disengagement theory states that an inevitable withdrawal from society accompanies aging

elder abuse physical maltreatment, exploitation, neglect, or psychological mistreatment of an elderly person by that person's caretaker

exchange theory states that decreased social interaction of elders is explained by the fact that the power of elders relative to their social environment is diminished over time until they become compliant to others

hospice movement endeavors to provide home or homelike care for terminally ill persons and to support their loved ones

rites of passage clearly recognizable signs and ceremonies surrounding the passage of persons from one age boundary to the next

Suggested Readings

Georgia M. Barrow. 1986. *Aging, the Individual, and Society,* 3d Edition. St. Paul, Minnesota: West Publishing.

An exceptionally clear text that comprehensively addresses all the major issues in the field of aging, from the stages in the life cycle to the problems inherent in stereotypes and images. Interesting and well-founded in research.

Cary S. Kart. 1985. *The Realities of Aging.* Boston: Allyn and Bacon.

An excellent introduction to the field of gerontology, covering all the major topics clearly and thoroughly. Very good at presenting complicated topics in a simpler format.

Alan Pifer and Lydia Bronte. 1986. *Our Aging Society: Paradox and Promise.* New York: W. W. Norton.

A truly representative sampling of articles by experts in the field, growing out of the Carnegie Corporation's Aging Society Project. Very well done, and fascinating reading.

K. Warner Schaie and Sherry L. Willis. 1986. *Adult Development and Aging,* 2d Edition. Boston: Little Brown.

A well-researched work by a well-known gerontology team that takes a broad approach to aging by including the entire life span from primary relationships in the family through the process of physical degeneration and death.

CHAPTER 13

MARRIAGE and FAMILY

- What Is a Family?
- What Changes Have Occurred in Family Structure?
- What Are the Functions and Dysfunctions of the Family?: Conflict and Functionalist Views
- Close-Up on Research: Carol Stack on the Black Urban Family in Poverty
- How Are Love and Marriage Related?
- How Do Societies Control Love and Marriage?
- What Are the Social Influences on the Choice of Marriage Partners?
- Close-Up on Theory: Bert Adams on Mate Selection
- What Are the Characteristics of Marriages That Succeed?
- What Kinds of Violence Are Found in the Family?
- What Is the Situation Regarding Divorce in the United States?
- What New Options Exist for the American Family?
- Sociologists at Work: Robert Ackerman Profiles Adult Children of Alcoholics

How's Your Sociological Intuition?

1. What is the likelihood that a person will remain unmarried throughout his or her life in the United States?
   a. 20 percent
   b. 10 percent
   c. 5 percent
   d. 1 percent
2. What proportion of all U.S. marriages are likely to end in divorce?
   a. One-twelfth
   b. One-fourth
   c. Two-fifths
   d. Two-thirds
3. Which of these was a family matter for nineteenth-century rural families?
   a. Care of aged family members
   b. Teaching occupational skills
   c. Producing most of the goods consumed by the family
   d. All of the above
4. Traditionally, the typical American family consisted of a working husband, a housewife, and their children. What proportion of American households now fit this description?
   a. 7 percent
   b. 50 percent
   c. 75 percent
   d. 83 percent

Answers

1. c. The great majority of Americans will marry at some time in their lives, as we will see in this chapter.
2. a. This is the best estimate based on present experience, though divorce rates are fluctuating. In this chapter we will consider why marriages succeed as well as factors influencing divorce.
3. d. A century ago the family was much more influential in the average person's life, as we will see in the section, "Changes in Family Structure."
4. a. Because people are exercising various other optional forms of the family, the traditional American family as portrayed by television programs in the 1960s has become the exception rather than the rule. We will look at some popular varieties of the contemporary American family in our section, "Options."

WHEN YOU HAVE FINISHED STUDYING THIS CHAPTER, YOU SHOULD KNOW:

- What the family is and what nuclear and extended families are
- How the American family changed as other institutions grew
- What the functions and dysfunctions of the family are
- The form and function of black urban families in poverty
- How love and marriage relate
- How societies control love and marriage
- What the social influences on choice of marriage partner are
- What the characteristics of successful marriages are
- The kinds of violence found in the family
- The profile of adult children of alcoholics
- What the situation is regarding divorce in the United States in terms of rates and effect on family members and the family
- What new options exist for the American family

Two anthropologists tried to explain to a group of teenage girls in India how young people date and marry in the United States, thinking to themselves how restricted these girls must feel in their system of arranged marriage and how unprepared for the questions that faced them:

"Doesn't it put the girl in a very humiliating position?" asked one of them. "She has to try to look pretty, and call attention to herself, and attract a boy, to be sure she'll get married. And if she doesn't want to do that, or if she feels it's undignified, wouldn't that mean she mightn't get a husband?"

"So a girl who is shy and doesn't push herself forward might not be able to get married," suggested another. "It makes getting married a sort of competition in which the girls are fighting each other for the boys. A girl can't relax and be herself. She has to make a good impression to get a boy, and then she has to go on making a good impression to get him to marry her."

"In our system," explained another, "we girls don't have to worry at all. We *know* we'll get married. We don't have to go into competition with each other."

"Besides," said a third girl, "how would we be able to judge the character of a boy we met and got friendly with? We are young and inexperienced. Our parents aren't as easily deceived as we would be."

Another girl shared eagerly, "But *does* the girl really have any choice in the West? It seems the boy does all the choosing. All the girl can do is to say yes or no." (Excerpt from *Marriage East and West* by Mace and Mace, 1960.)

Although arranged marriages are no longer the norm in India, they still exist and are honored. Contemporary young women in the United States would be outraged at the idea of having their marriage and family life "arranged" for them by their parents. Yet these young Indian women were equally stunned at the marriage and family arrangements considered "natural" today in Western countries.

What Is a Family?

Most marriages form the basis of a ***family***, or *two or more people related by marriage, blood, or adoption, who live together and share economic resources for an extended period of time.* The family is a universal institution, found in all societies, but in radically different forms, as this opening example indicates. In this chapter you will study the family in different cultures and different times; how and why certain persons get married and form families; what changes have occurred in the American family; what problems dissolved families face; and what new options are being considered for the contemporary Western family structure.

What Changes Have Occurred in Family Structure?

Family structure and other aspects of social organization are closely linked to technology and economic activities. For 99 percent of human history, hunting and gathering has been the major form of work. Most scholars agree that the agricultural revolution was a turning point in human history. As we have discussed in Chapter 3, this change in work style brought about the idea of personal property and its concomitant subjugation of women and unequal stratification system (Skolnick, 1973; Winch, 1971).

A century ago, most Americans lived in what sociologists termed an ***extended family*** *in which three or more generations live in close proximity.* Today, most Americans live in a ***nuclear family*** *consisting of two adults of opposite sex, sharing a socially approved sexual union, and living with their children.*

The ensuing shift from an agrarian to industrial base brings about a reemphasis on the nuclear family, with the separation of home and work and the household consuming goods rather than producing them.

Extended family ties are still of primary importance to most Americans, despite the mobility of modern society. Research shows strong ties of both obligation and affection between the generations, and much "helping out" both up and down the age structure. (*Photo courtesy the author*)

The shift also brings a more intense involvement between marriage partners and their children, which can be either positive or negative. In industrial societies the home is thought of as private space in which the society does not interfere unless invited.

It is difficult to separate the effects of industrialization and modernization from those of the shift from extended to nuclear families. Goode denies the myth that in modern societies all families are nuclear, and in agrarian times they were all extended goups of relatives living together (1963). In reality, many people live in extended family situations today, and nuclear families existed in earlier times.

Nuclear families have existed in Europe since the fifteenth century, well before industrialization. The reconstructive work of Demos, using records of births, deaths, marriages, land transfers, and wills, shows that the nuclear family flourished in United States colonies as well (Lasch, 1977; Demos, 1970).

Murdock found evidence of nuclear families existing in many of the 250 societies he studied, most often arising with an emphasis on the individual over the group (1949). Skolnick echoes his finding with her definition that "the nuclear family emerges whenever the individual is set off from the large family group" (1973, p. 108).

In an analysis of 549 cultures, Nimkoff and Middleton discovered a significant relationship between form of family and certain economic factors (1960). Important factors were the type of subsistence pattern in the culture and the amount of property a family owns. For instance, nomadic hunting and gathering cultures, which have little property to pass through the generations, tend to have independent (nuclear) families. Cultures in which people grow crops, stay in one place, and accumulate land rights tend to have extended families. Nimkoff and Middleton think that nomadic families must be small because they depend on changing food supplies, whereas agricultural families can be larger because they have a stable food source.

They further believe that the nuclear family dominates modern industrial society because of industry's small demand for whole-family labor and a larger emphasis on the breadwinner's role in providing for the family. Furthermore, modern breadwinners often must be mobile in order to provide more adequately for their dependents. In our society, consequently, property is often acquired in the form of money rather than land and can be handed down to future generations regardless of their locations.

Winch and Blumberg believe the extended family is "associated with a reliable food supply, a demand for the family as a unit of labor, little geographic mobility in subsistence activities, and the collective [familial] ownership of land" (1963, p. 92). They find parallels between these variables and extended families in contemporary American society, with groups that showed these characteristics more often living in extended family situations. When looking at 933 other societies in order of their complexity, they found that the nuclear family begins to appear before industrialism but after the society begins to grow more complex (1972). They conclude there are actually three family types in the United States: (1) the *isolated nuclear family*, which has been criticized for the pressures it places on its members, (2) the *nonisolated nuclear family*, in which there is much contact with the independent households of extended-family members living in the same metropolitan area, and (3) the *mother–child incomplete nuclear family*.

William Goode suggests other reasons for the isolated nuclear family's dominance in modern Western culture (1963). Because an industrial society is open class, workers in the system are geographically and socially mobile. They rise or fall on their work alone, instead of on family ties, social position, or accumulation of land, which might be the criteria for advancement in different societies. The very fact that the isolated nuclear family is more mobile and neolocal helps the worker advance in an industrial society.

Further, several observers believe that modern industrial society tends to treat its workers like objects rather than people, giving them only small jobs in large operations, thus reducing their feelings of self-worth about having done good work (Goode, 1963; Lasch; 1977). Goode believes that the small nuclear family can give more positive feedback and emotional support to its members, in compensation for the depersonalization of the modern industrial society.

THE AMERICAN FAMILY AND THE GROWTH OF OTHER INSTITUTIONS

The family in America has changed rapidly. In the process, other institutions have greatly expanded their influence, whereas the influence of the family has diminished in some areas. For example, as we have just seen, industrialization moved production off the farm, away from the family, and into the factory. In the past 150 years, the family began to share the function of being a unit of economic production with increasingly large commercial firms.

Industrialization also brought factory-style schooling in the form of mandatory mass education. Before industrialization the family was the major agent of career socialization. Working skills were learned from parents or from serving as apprentices in other families' businesses. One learned farming from farmers, blacksmithing from blacksmiths, and milling from mill operators. A high school or college education as a means of acquiring job skills was very unusual. Now the function of providing career socialization has almost been entirely adopted by formal education in schools and on-the-job training programs in industrialized settings.

In agrarian times social control depended almost entirely upon the family, with the father having nearly total power over, and responsibility for, other members of the household. With industrialization the father was gone most of the day, and with children in school for much of the day, social control became a function of schools and mothers. The state introduced public police forces to help serve a social control function which had previously been largely handled by the adult males of the community. Schools also took over much of the family's earlier role in conferring status and providing cultural socialization. Although the family retains a strong influence on social placement, status is increasingly dependent on how much schooling a person obtains, a practice that continues into the present. For the waves of immigrants from non-English-speaking nations schools provide important culture socialization.

When most Americans were involved in farming, children were an economic asset, because they could contribute to the family's economic productivity. When the nation industrialized and passed laws prohibiting child labor, chidren became primarily consumers rather than producers. In economical terms, they took on the nature of a liability rather than an asset. Therefore, with industrialization came a decline in family size. In less than a century, the average population per household in the United States dropped from 4.9 in 1890 to 3.7 in 1940 and to 2.7 in 1986 (U.S. Bureau of the Census, 1987).

Following World War II, the United States moved into the postindustrial era. This brought about further loss of functions once filled by the family. As Figure 13.1 shows, women began to enter the full-time work force, and families increasingly relied on other institutions to do what mothers had previously done. Children started attending schools at a younger age and went to school for more years. Schools therefore continued to increase in importance as agents of social control and cultural socialization. Members of the family who once would have lived out their less-active years with their grown children increasingly cared for themselves or were placed in nursing homes, a new form of dependent care. Postindustrial society brought the rapid growth and development of new social structures such as pensions, Social Security, retirement communities, and nursing homes.

The postindustrial family also increasingly surrenders its role as producer of the goods and services it consumes. Commercial firms now accomplish much of what the family once did for itself. Contractors like lawn services or cleaning firms do more and more household chores that were traditionally the domain

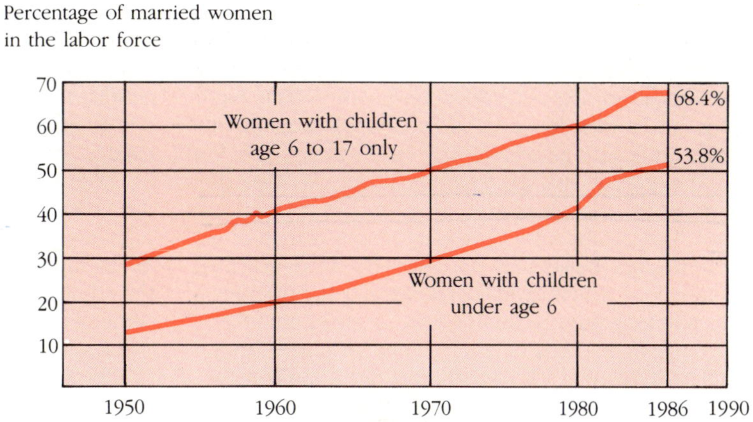

FIGURE 13.1 One of the major changes in the family structure in the past thirty years is the proportion of mothers in the work force. The two-paycheck family is now the norm rather than the exception, and 1987 marks the first year that over 50 percent of women with infants (under age 1) returned to work immediately after the birth of the child.

of the family. The traditional gathering for a family meal is frequently replaced by eating out. A convenience food industry has grown to reduce food-preparation chores at home.

Even in its leisure hours, the family relies increasingly on outside sources for entertainment. After-dinner conversations, games, and music making have been replaced by radio, television, videogames, and movies. The sandlot ball game once played with siblings and neighbors has been largely replaced by the mini-bureaucracy of Little League baseball and Pee Wee football. Age restrictions prevent other family members from joining in, except as members of the audience or chauffeurs for the carpool.

What Are the Functions and Dysfunctions of the Family? Conflict and Functionalist Views

Functionalists point out that families in all their diverse forms fill several functions for their societies. These include providing for human reproduction, caring for and socializing the young and other dependents, allowing the growth of enduring and intimate relations, and passing on social status from generation to generation. Functionalists see these as important both to the individual family members and to the societies in which they live (Parsons, 1965).

Conflict theorists point out that human reproduction often takes place outside the family structure and that families are not always pleasant places for dependents or for fostering the growth of intimate relationships. They point out that the family is a hotbed of internal conflicts of interests and is upheld by "unequal resources for domination" (R. Collins, 1985). Transcripts of family court hearings testify to the inherent inequalities in many family structures and to the pain that many people experience from their families, for instance, through incest, beatings, and psychological maltreatment. Conflict theorists suggest that we may continue to choose to live under such an unequal system from force of habit rather than out of choice of the better alternative.

The family is also important in determining a person's adult social status. As we found in Chapter 8, children take on the status of their parents and generally retain a similar status in their adult years. This happens for various reasons. The child is socialized to have a sense of self, which has similar status to his or her parents, regardless of whether that status is one of a prince, pauper, plumber, or pediatrician. Being raised in a family of a given status affects both the aspirations and the opportunities of the child. For instance, a child raised in a family in which both parents have advanced degrees will probably be expected to attend college. In partial pursuit of that goal, the parents will probably buy an encyclopedia, spend time reading with the child, and take trips to museums.

Functionalists tend to view this conferring of status as a function of the family. The family engages in anticipatory socialization, so the children become accustomed to status that is by and large appropriate to their future status in the society. The fact that they transmit this status minimizes conflict for prized positions. The family acclimates individuals to social differences that functionalists believe are needed for the smooth functioning of society.

Conflict theorists, in sharp contrast, see the family as an agent of inequality and an impediment to reform. The family perpetuates inequality in several ways (Engels, 1884). Wealthy persons often enjoy their high status because they inherited wealth from their parents. Those raised by the middle and upper classes benefit from the advantages money can buy, including private schools, or public schools in "better" neighborhoods, more books, more creative toys, private lessons, a college education, exposure to others with similar high status, and a broader range of experiences such as vacations to distant places.

The family also gives its members class-specific mannerisms that constitute a distinctive "touch of class." The genius who expresses himself or herself in working-class dialect may not always be recognized as a genius, nor may the fool surrounded by the trappings of wealth look quite so foolish as he or she might otherwise appear. Perhaps of more significance, the family shapes the sense of self so that individuals can come to accept themselves as working class, servants, slaves, or even untouchables. Because the family often transmits undeserved inferior status or unmerited advantage, conflict theorists tend to see the family as an institution of power, domination, and conflict (R. Collins, 1985; Chafetz, 1984).

The following "Close-Up on Research" discusses the contemporary black family. In it Carol Stack researches how some families reach out to extended family members and enlarge their families by redefining their boundaries. In this way families may surmount some of the problems they face due to their lower-class status, thereby transmitting a more positive sense of self to the next generation.

CLOSE-UP on • *RESEARCH* •

Carol Stack on the Black Urban Family in Poverty

The Researcher and the Setting

Carol B. Stack spent three years living in a poor black community and studying its family structure. Her book, *All Our Kin* (1974), is still one of the most comprehensive descriptions of black family structure in the United States. Stack has produced an important baseline for other researchers as well as a fascinating opportunity for "outsiders" to understand this subculture.

Theory and Concepts

Stack disagrees with scholars who have studied the black family and have "tended to reinforce popular stereotypes of the lower-class or black family—particularly the black family in poverty—as deviant, matriarchal, and broken" (p. 22). Stack does not formally introduce a theory or hypothesis but appears to view the black family as a healthy, creative adaptation to unhealthy environmental conditions. She is interested in "how black people organize and interpret their own cultural experience" (p. 26).

Research Design

Stack's research design is termed participant-observation and is similar to anthropological field work. Instead of starting with a preconceived image of the subject matter and a set of tools to take measurements (such as a survey), those who use the participant-observation approach often formulate their generalizations and methodology while collecting data. They rely on their subjects' interpretation of their culture.

The Researcher's Goal

In participant-observation, the researcher begins with questions to take to the field in search of *theoretical answers* as well as data. Specifically, Stack sought to answer these questions: What role do the ties of kinship or friendship play in the black community? Who socializes the children born in the ghetto? What folk criteria quality a woman to give birth or to raise a child? and What may be the adaptive functions of sexual unions and multiple household kin networks? (p. 24).

Stack lived and studied in an area she refers to as: "The Flats, . . . the poorest section of a black community in the Midwestern city of Jackson Harbor (these names are fictitious)" (p. 1). Stack explains:

> I spent almost three years in The Flats attempting to understand the complexities of their exchange system. I tried to learn how participants in domestic exchanges were defined by one another, what performances and behavior they expected of one another, who was eligible to become a part of the cooperative networks, how they were recruited, and what kept participants actively involved in these exchanges. If someone asked a favor of me, later I asked a favor of him. If I gave a scarf, a skirt, or a cooking utensil to a woman who admired it, later on when she had something I liked she would usually give it to me. Little by little as I learned the rules of giving and reciprocity, I tried them out. Eventually the children of those I was closest to would stay overnight or several days at my apartment, and my son stayed at their homes.
>
> . . . In time I knew enough people well who were closely related so that after any family scene, gathering, or fight, I could put together interpretations of the events from the viewpoints of different individuals. . . . I eventually asked others to assist me in the study. . . .

> I selected individuals from the families I knew who were interested in the study and who were imaginative and critical thinkers. At times these assistants became "informants," in the language of anthropology, that is, they provided me with data. Together we worked out questions on various topics to ask the families studied. . . . We selected questions in the general areas of social and domestic relations, kinship and residence, and childkeeping; these questions provided a starting point for a long discussion on a single issue. At no time did I formally interview anyone (pp. 28; xi–xii).

Findings

Stack's definition of family differs from the conventional sociological definition, and we should remain aware of this in reviewing her findings. "Ultimately I defined 'family' as the smallest, organized, durable network of kin and non-kin who interact daily, providing domestic needs of children and assuring their survival" (p. 31).

The black families Stack describes are not the "Mom, Dad, and the kids" type that is the stereotype of the American family. Stack's families are arrangements of relatives and intimate friends who share their meager resources to provide for the day-to-day living needs of themselves and their children. This often involves people who live in various houses or apartments in one "family." As Stack points out, it is not unusual for a man to sleep in one residence, take meals in another, and spend much of his time at a third.

Stack concludes that "distinctively negative features attributed to poor families; that they are fatherless, matrifocal, unstable, and disorganized, are not general characteristics of black families living substantially below economic subsistence in urban America. The black urban family, embedded in cooperative domestic exchange, proves to be an organized, tenacious, active, lifelong network" (p. 124).

"The structural adaptations of poverty described in this study do not lock people into a cycle of poverty preventing the poor from marrying, removing themselves from their kin network, or leaving town. But if such opportunities arise (and they rarely do), these chances only are taken after careful evaluation based on both middle-class standards and the experience of poverty" (p. 126).

"Mainstream values have failed many residents of The Flats. Nevertheless, the present study shows that the life ways of the poor present a powerful challenge to the notion of a self-perpetuating culture of poverty. The strategies that the poor have evolved to cope with poverty do not compensate for poverty in themselves, nor do they perpetuate the poverty cycle. But when mainstream values fail the poor, as they have failed most Flats' residents, the harsh economic conditions of poverty force people to return to proven strategies for survival" (pp. 128–129).

Implications

Because Stack used a long-term participant-observation design, her study was necessarily limited to one locality. Her claim that the poor black family is not broken, but different, deserves further research. If researchers in several localities reach similar conclusions, this would suggest that Stack's findings really do generalize most black families in poverty. Because many institutions, including the government, church, and businesses, view the poor black family as broken, they could benefit from an awareness that this family is different, not necessarily inferior.

Questions

1. Poor and unemployed black males sometimes do not reside with their wives and children because it would make the family ineligible for welfare benefits. In light of this fact, would Stack have been likely to arrive at the same image of the poor black family as together rather than as broken if she had relied on conventional definitions and on the survey research method?
2. By the dominant culture's definition of family, many poor black families *are* broken, because the father frequently does not reside with the mother. Stack redefines the family and is thus assured that the poor black family is intact. Is this making excuses? Is one definition of the family better than the other?
3. Was Stack's selection of the participant-observation research technique a good one for this study? Would a different research design be better?
4. Has Stack's research convinced you that the poor black family is a creative adaptation to difficult conditions? Why or why not?

SOURCE Carol B. Stack. 1974. *All Our Kin: Strategies for Survival in a Black Community.* New York: Harper & Row.

How Are Love and Marriage Related?

In modern Western societies, most families are begun within marriages. ***Marriage*** *is a long-term, socially approved sexual union between two people*. At some point in their lives, 94 percent of adult Americans form a marriage. Not surprisingly, Gallup consistently reports that a happy marriage is very highly valued by the majority of the population of the United States (Gallup, 1987).

Today, most people marry because they "fall in love." Romantic love, as is defined by our culture, is an irresistible attraction to another who is perceived as nearly perfect and one's life-long true love. The ro-

AN ABYSSINIAN WEDDING.—THE BRIDEGROOM CARRYING THE BRIDE TO HIS HOUSE.

Roots of our wedding traditions of honking the horns of the cars in the wedding procession and carrying the bride over the threshold are evident in this print of an Abyssinian wedding procession. Trumpets sound, the groom demonstrates gallantry or dominance by carrying the bride, and bystanders watch. (*Bettmann Archive*)

mantic love they desire lasts until death. Although they may never have seen such a love relationship in real life, they believe in it. They feel complete, immersed in the other person, sure of the rightness of the relationship, in agony when separated from their loved one. Based on these feelings, they marry.

This attitude toward romantic love is not universal. In truth, romantic love is not a biological reaction of two young people toward their sexual urges but is, rather, a cultural pattern into which people are socialized (F. Merrill, 1959). In other societies, and in previous times in our society, marriage has been based on other considerations, primarily the man's ability to support and protect his family or the woman's ability to bear children and run a household (Russell, 1929; Burgess and Locke, 1953).

The ancient Greeks, for example, believed that romantic love was only one of many types of love people could experience. They described romantic love as a "madness by which a person was afflicted through the caprice or malevolence of some god or goddess" (Sumner, 1906, p. 362).

The modern concept of romantic love originated in Europe in the eleventh century. At that time, it clearly was separated from the concept of marriage. One married to find a spouse who would provide for the social and economic needs of the family, and one fell in love—often with someone else—for the excitement. Romantic love began as an aristocratic phenomenon and was nearly always unconsummated; part of the ideal of romantic love required that the love object be unattainable.

PROBLEMS WITH ROMANTIC LOVE

Many sociologists question the usefulness of romantic love in developing lasting marriage relationships (Kephart, 1972; Kemper, 1982). Ironically, the idealization of romantic love may actually make lasting love more difficult for two people to experience (Winter and McAuliffe, 1984). For one thing, an essential ingredient in the Western ideal of romantic love is the chase: the element of the unknown and the constant pursuit of the mysterious loved one. In sharp contrast, the development of lasting love requires a commitment on the parts of both parties to work things out between them. This means, to some extent, that a couple gives up some of the excitement of an uncommitted relationship in order to achieve the security of a committed one. Commitment creates an environment that makes growth possible, but may limit the excitement that results from not having ties.

Most young Americans meet, fall in love, marry, and expect to live happily ever after. For many of them, the desired happiness is not automatic, and they end the relationship, seeking another. But romantic love can be the basis of a good relationship. Lasting love occurs when the parties who "fall in love" also bring a commitment to expand the concept of romantic love beyond the chase to a comfortable commitment.

This kind of love keeps spouses, parents, children, and siblings together and is different from that which is the basis of sexual attraction. Research indicates that passionate love does not last as long as a love that is based on many favorable interactions between two people, and that love which originally brings two people together must develop into the less-exciting but more stable type if the relationship is to last (Berscheid and Walster, 1976; R. Turner, 1970). This type of love, or "continuing positive affection," contributes to family stability (Rausch, Hertel, and Swain, 1974, p. 106). We will explore it more fully in the section on Marriages that Succeed.

How Do Societies Control Love and Marriage?

The vast differences in how mates are selected within the human population powerfully indicate the flexibility of human social behavior and pose one of the most fascinating puzzles of sociology. The form and quality of married life and families is of great consequence to a society. In most societies the decision of who will marry whom has been simply too important to the group to be left up to individual emotional attachments developed in late adolescence (Haviland, 1985).

For example, in societies where families are more dependent than ours on each other for economic support, it is important for families to be sure that a prospective member will be able to carry his or her load in terms of economic production. Males may be required to enter the family business and females to run the household efficiently. This is symbolized in such traditions as the Hopi custom of the prospective bride grinding corn and baking cornbread as a present for her future mother-in-law. If the bread, a staple food for the Hopi, is considered good, the bride is accepted.

The family also has a greater stake in the selection of new family members in societies where social hierarchies are highly structured. Here they develop controls to regulate romance and marriage, such as child marriage, kinship and locality rules, and isolation of adolescents (L. Freeman, 1958; W. Goode, 1959).

In these societies, if adolescents were allowed to fall in love with and marry anyone they chose, the stratification system would become less well defined, as upper-, middle-, and lower-class families became linked. Upper-class families with newly acquired links to lower classes, for instance, would be less socially prominent, and lower-class families with members newly married into upper-class families would gain status. Previous rules governing behavior of the groups would not apply to the newly merged levels, and the entire stratification system would need to be redefined continuously.

CHILD MARRIAGE

Child marriage, or marrying of children to other children whom the parents have selected as appropriate in economic potential and social class, has also been used to control spouse choice. Though the practice has declined, in some parts of India, for example, boys and girls are married in a ceremony called *shadi,* between ages 11 and 14. After *shadi,* they wait from three to four years to consummate the marriage, an event labeled *guana* (Collver, 1963; W. Goode, 1963). Because most 11- to 14-year-olds have not yet thought of choosing a mate for themselves, early marriage effectively eliminates a potential source of disruption in the stratification system.

Many such marriages end in divorce, most even before the marriage is consummated, while the children are still between ages 10 and 15. For instance, in Jakarta, Indonesia, at least half of the child marriages were legally dissolved before they truly began (Hutter, 1981).

KINSHIP RULES

Rules that specifically define those people who are eligible to become spouses at a child's birth provide another social-control mechanism to regulate the selection of marriage partners. It is almost impossible for us to imagine knowing the identity of our future bride or groom from birth, but in some societies it is decreed, for instance, that first cousins must marry each other, or that a woman must marry her mother's brother's son. Society's rules determine the spouses' identity, and parents must decide only when the marriage will occur (Malinowski, 1943; Murdock, 1949).

LOCALITY RULES

In some tribes, such as the Kurnai of Australia, strict locality rules govern the choice of a mate, with only certain groups available to each other. The list of "relatives," or people who live within the restricted territory, whom one may not marry, is very long. Also, the old men are a privileged group, able to select any young and attractive girl they wish before the young men choose. Due to these restrictive norms, there are often no "eligible" young women for a young man to marry (Goode, 1963).

TABLE 13.1 Forms of Marriage

Divided by Whom You May Choose to Marry:	Divided by How Many You May Choose to Marry:
Exogamy: *Marriage form in which your spouse comes from outside your social group*	**Monogamy:** *Marriage form in which one person marries one spouse*
Endogamy: *Marriage form in which your spouse comes from inside your social group*	**Polygamy:** *Marriage form in which there are multiple spouses*
	Polygyny: *Marriage form in which one man marries more than one woman*
	Polyandry: *Marriage form in which one woman marries more than one man*

In general, the more family members depend on one another economically, the less a person will be left on his or her own to choose a mate. Particular mating patterns such as endogamy or polygamy also usually fit well with other important social patterns such as the way the society organizes to produce its food.

ISOLATION

Some societies isolate adolescents in order to prevent inappropriate love relationships. This is done, for example, on the island of Manus, where a girl is removed from society and is closely supervised by her family when she begins to menstruate (Mead, 1939). Other societies segregate adolescents from the rest of the tribe and assign them permanent supervisors or decree that individuals may not marry others from their own village (Levy, 1949; Kingsley Davis, 1951).

Traditional rules can constrain who can marry whom, as well as how many spouses one can have. Table 13.1 describes five forms of marriage.

How Do Societies Control Love and Marriage?

All these forms of control are more overt than those used in the United States today, where most people believe romantic love should be the most important element in courtship and young people are given freedom to interact with each other and engage in premarital love play (Roper, 1974). Under this system, young people are considered able to choose their own mates. As we will see, however, their choice is carefully guided by their cultural backgrounds.

One important reason Americans are likely to use love as a reason for marriage is that economic production in our culture is less family-centered than it was in previous times, and modern conveniences have changed the face of homemaking. These considerations have consequently become secondary to the idea of "loving" your partner. Modern medical advances have also made it possible for potentially infertile women to bear children and for children with genetic "defects" to live, thus making genetic ability to produce less crucial.

Goode suggests several additional reasons why Americans have placed such a premium on romantic love as the basis of their families (1963). Goode notes that present-day American families generally live independently of the extended family system, forming instead their own nuclear family, creating a stronger tie to the spouse than to the parents and siblings. One's ***family of orientation*** *is the family in which one is socialized, generally including parents and siblings.* In the United States the bond between parents and children is especially strong. "Falling in love" gives young adult children a legitimate reason to break that bond by leaving their parents' home to form their own family unit elsewhere. *The family we create by marrying and becoming parents is called a* ***family of procreation.***

Goode also notes that adolescents in the United States are given much freedom, which increases the possibilities of them falling in love. For instance, most teenagers have access to an automobile, which can take them beyond the reach of their family and its social constraints. This gives rise to more intense love relationships than could occur before the advent of the automobile, because it allows young couples both privacy and the illusion of being in control of their own lives rather than still being dependent on their parents.

Some sociologists argue that the romantic ideal may arise in part because our society officially forbids sex before marriage. The resulting sexual tension that arises between two persons of marriageable age creates a good atmosphere for the growth of romantic love (Young, 1943). In societies where premarital sex is permitted or even encouraged, people choose marriage partners based more on friendship and shared ideas and less on romantic considerations (Gorer, 1938; Stephens, 1963). In other words, where romantic love is not idealized, young people choose friends and companions rather than sexually attractive partners to be their spouses.

What Are the Social Influences on the Choice of Marriage Partner?

Modern Americans are not only socialized to fall in love with their prospective mates, they are also social-

Marry you? Who marries whom and why depends on many factors. The issue has received much attention from sociologists as well as young men and women. (*Courtesy the Michigan Daily*)

ized to choose them from certain groups within the society. Although most Americans believe they choose their mates freely, several studies have shown that their choices are greatly influenced by social factors. August Hollingshead, in a now classic article, discusses how society effectively restricts the choice of spouse. He finds "strong association between several cultural factors and who marries whom," allowing for "individual choice within limits of cultural determinism" (Hollingshead, 1950, p. 620). These cultural factors include race, age, religion, social class, education, socialization, and family pressures (Carter and Glick, 1980; R. Johnson, 1980).

The factors that exerted the strongest influence in Hollingshead's study were race and age. These factors are still important, with relatively little interracial marriage and a strong association between ages of husbands and wives, especially when both partners are less than 20 years old (Heer, 1965; Morgan, 1981).

Hollingshead's study also showed that individuals tend to marry those of the same religion and ethnic background. Ethnic lines were, in his study, crossed within the Catholic and Protestant faith more frequently than in the past, but even people marrying outside their own ethnic group tended to marry *within* their religious groups. Intermarriages between religious groups are still less stable, and the tendency to marry within one's religious group remains (Bumpass and Sweet, 1972; Johnson, 1980).

Hollingshead also discovered that "the class of residential area in which a man's or woman's family home is located has a very marked influence on his or her marital opportunities (1950, p. 622). This was reconfirmed by Katz and Hill (Katz and Hill, 1958). Education, a strong indicator of social class, also sorts out potential marriage mates into "horizontal status group within the confines of religion" (Hollingshead, 1950, p. 625).

Closely related is the theory of *propinquity,* which simply states that people will choose partners from among those people with whom they live, work, and go to school, or from among those people with whom they are physically close during the time they are of a marriageable age. The choice of location for the family homestead, then, may affect the future of the children's families, as might the choice of college. Although the influence of propinquity is somewhat weaker today due to greater mobility in today's society, it still has an effect on partner choice (Morgan, 1981).

HOMOGAMY

Hollingshead's work supports the theory of *homogamy,* or the idea that people marry similar people. This continues to be true today, with similar social pressures working in mate choice. One factor not discussed by Hollingshead is previous marital status, sign of the rising rate of dissolved marriages. Robert Winch finds that marital status is also a homogamous factor; a person marrying for the first time is more likely to choose a mate who is also marrying for the first time (Winch, 1973).

Some studies indicate that homogamous marriages tend to be more stable marriages (Murstein, 1980). This suggests that the recent tendency of people to cross cultural and class lines in choosing marriage partners may be the cause of some of the strain on the American family that is evident today.

FAMILY INFLUENCE

Families greatly influence the choice of a marriage partner. Parents are the adults closest to children, and a child's image of what it is to be a married adult usually closely parallels the parental image. Also, everything the family does seems to the child at some level to be "the right way" for things to be done. Thus, if a person's family, say, always took vacations in the Caribbean during Christmas break, he or she will likely assume that is the right thing to do. A person who learns to sail boats at a young age, belongs to a yacht club, and has friends who sail may assume that most people, or "good" people, or "many" people, also see sailing as an enjoyable, positive recreational activity. A person who has always celebrated Christmas or Hanukkah with gifts for friends and family members will probably assume that others do the same. By example, and sometimes more overtly through suggestions that a friend "isn't like us" or "is a very nice person," families teach young adults what to value and what not to value in potential husbands and wives.

The following "Close-Up on Theory" incorporates the concepts of homogamy and family influence along with several new factors to build a comprehensive theory of how contemporary American marriages are formed.

CLOSE-UP on • *THEORY* •

Bert Adams on Mate Selection

The Theorist and the Setting

Bert N. Adams wrote his theory as part of an exciting project to link the world of sociological theory to that of sociological research. Harold Christensen and K. Barber (1967) note that until 1950 scholars usually produced either grand theories or narrow research studies of the family. In 1972 the four editors of the book in which Adams's theory is presented set out to change this. They began to build a systematic *theory of the family based on accumulated research* and chose Bert Adams as the person best suited to write the theory of mate selection.

The Theorist's Goal

In this theory Adams addresses the issue: Who marries whom and why? in the United States.

Concepts, Propositions, and Interpretation

A good social theory tells the general story of humanity, so Adams's theory of mate selection should closely parallel the way people actually pick their mates. To help you understand the nineteen propositions of Adams's theory, we consider it in light of the story of an actual courtship.

In high school Rick dated several girls on a rather steady basis. He found Pat and Janet appealing both physically and in terms of personality. They shared similar social backgrounds, but after graduation they went in different directions. Pat died of a rare blood disease in her freshman year. Janet went to Central and they lost touch.

So far, the case study fits Adams's propositions:

Proposition 1: Proximity facilitates contact, and this is a precondition for marriage.

Proposition 2: Marriage is increasingly more likely, as time passes, to be with someone currently propinquitous (close by physically) than with someone formerly propinquitous.

Proposition 3: One effect of propinquity is to increase the likelihood that one will meet, be attracted to, and marry someone of the same social categories as himself or herself.

Proposition 4: Immediate stimuli such as physical attractiveness, valued surface behaviors, and similar interests result in early attraction.

With the pressure of studies at the University, dating was a part-time affair for Rick. Amidst the superficiality of Friday afternoon mixers and loud Saturday night parties, he seldom talked much with the girls he took out. In dating, they played roles: Joe College and Sally Coed.

Along came Wendy. She had dated a couple of Rick's older fraternity brothers and had almost become a fixture around the house—one of the guys. You could expect to see her at dinner or studying at the fraternity house two or three times a week. One evening he noticed her typing in the living room. Stepping up behind her he put his hands on her shoulders. "Wendy, I want to ravish you."

"Let's go," she replied, only half in jest because she had long thought him attractive, and she rose and faced him.

"O.K., come on down to my room," he said, taking her hand.

"But I have to type Craig's paper."

"Craig's paper can wait. Come on."

Wendy managed to find a few minutes free from the typing for a visit to Rick's room, where she and Rick talked and engaged in some mock ravishing. A week later final exams were over, and it was time to head home. Wendy happened to be at the fraternity, and Rick offered her a ride to her home, which was close to his.

Wendy's family and friends liked Rick, and Wendy quickly won Rick's friends' approval. Perhaps because it had started as something other than formal dating, the relationship seemed comfortable from the start. The two talked openly, and as they did so, they discovered more common interests and values. The more they talked about themselves, their likes, dislikes, dreams and fears, the more comfortable it seemed. What had begun as a lark became a deepening relationship. This pattern is consistent with Adams's propositions 5 through 7, as charted in Figure 13.2.

Proposition 5: The more favorable the reactions of significant others to an early relationship, the more likely the rela-

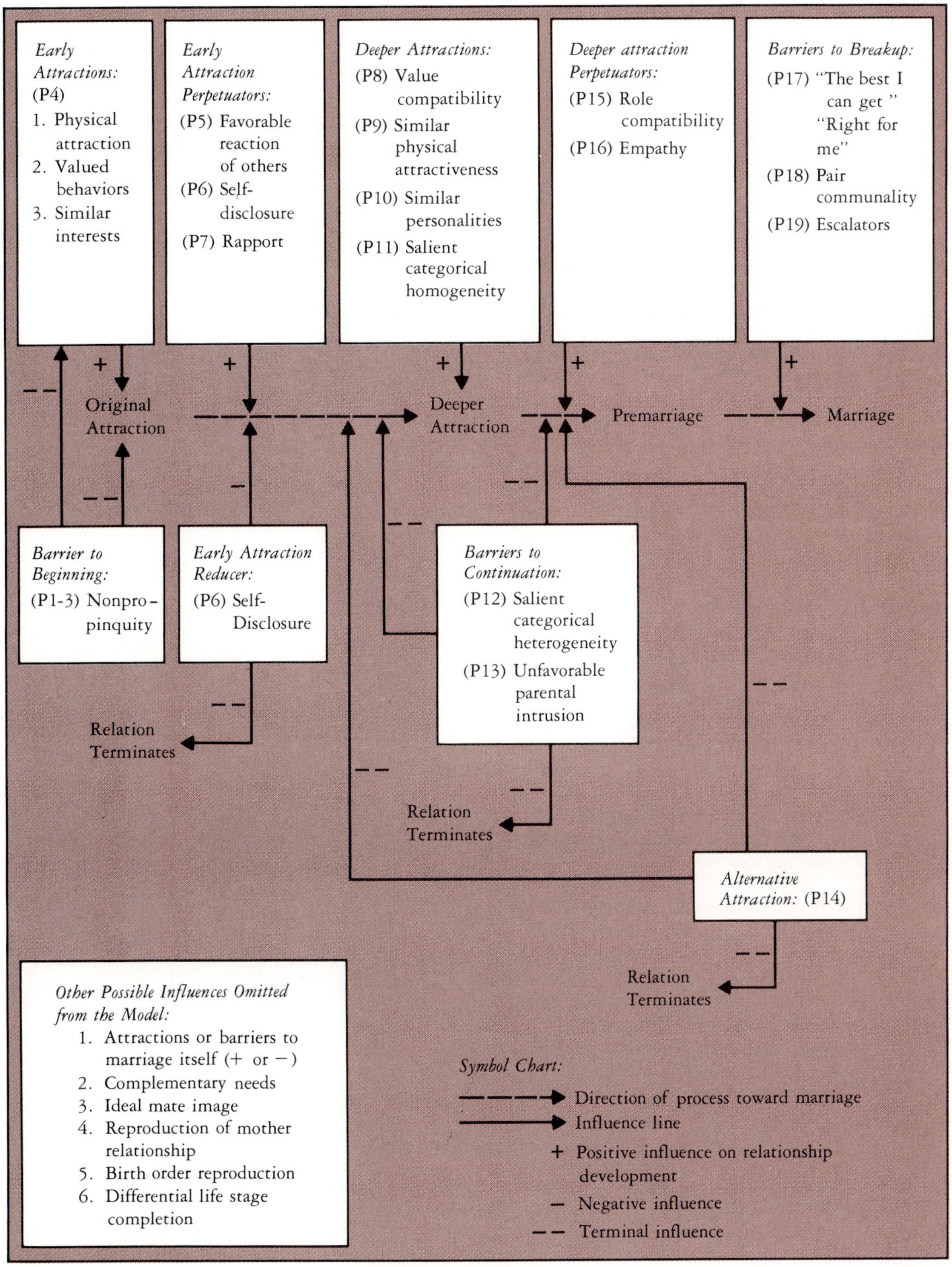

FIGURE 13.2 The Mate Selection Process. SOURCE Adams, 1979.

tionship will be perpetuated beyond the early-attraction stage.

Proposition 6: The more positive the reaction of the couple members to further disclosure, the better will be the pair's rapport.

Proposition 7: The better the couple's rapport, the more likely the relationship will be perpetuated beyond early attraction.

As the summer went on, Rick and Wendy discovered they had a lot in common. They both liked excitement, but they were moderate in its pursuit. Rick had a motorcycle, but he was no gang member. They both loved music. Both in their own way were more religious than most of their peers, although they did not speak much of religion. Physically, both were attractive, with neither outshining the other. Their personalities were also similar. Both were optimistic, gentle, bright, but sometimes impulsive. Each was popular and a person frequently looked to for leadership. They were also closely matched on important social dimensions: raised in the Midwest by middle-class Protestant parents of English and Western European ancestry. Again they fit Adams's propositions:

Proposition 8: The greater the value compatibility–consensus between couple members, the more likely it is that the relationship will move to the level of deeper attraction.

Proposition 9: The greater the similarity in physical attractiveness between couple members, the more likely it is that the relationship will move to the level of deeper attraction.

Proposition 10: The greater the personality similarity of the couple members, the more likely it is that the relationship will move to the level of deeper attraction.

Proposition 11: The more salient the categorical homogeneity of the members of a couple, the more likely it is that the relationship will move to the level of deeper attraction.

Rick and Wendy's scene was quite different from that of their friends Stan and Margie, who had also fallen passionately in love. When Margie's wealthy parents learned about her new middle-class black boyfriend they forced her to choose between him and her family. The relationship soon ended, illustrating Adams's next two propositions:

Proposition 12: The more salient the categorical heterogeneity of couple members, the more likely it is that a relationship will be terminated either before or after reaching the stage of deeper attraction.

Proposition 13: The greater the unfavorable parental intrusion, the more likely it is that relationship will be terminated either before or after reaching the stage of deeper attraction.

Once that summer Wendy went out with someone else and Rick looked up one of his earlier girlfriends. All that resulted from these excursions was a deeper appreciation of what Rick and Wendy had already found together. As Adams predicts:

Proposition 14: An alternative attraction may arise at any stage. The stronger the alternative attraction on the part of either couple member, the greater the likelihood that the original couple's relationship will be terminated.

The two seemed to fit together very well. Wendy was more outgoing and talkative. Rick was an appreciative listener. But in other areas where Wendy held back, Rick was strong and assertive. Both shared enough common traits and experiences that they could identify with the other and offer important emotional support. In an important sense Wendy was what Rick wanted in a woman, while Rick was what Wendy looked for in a man. Adams states this concept in Propositions 15 and 16:

Proposition 15: The greater the role compatibility on the part of couple members, the more likely the relationship will be perpetuated.

Proposition 16: The greater the empathy on the part of couple members, the more likely the relationship will be perpetuated.

By summer's end the relationship had moved from one of casual acquaintance to one of deep intimacy. Rick and Wendy were sure they had found their "one true love." Their friends saw them progress from boyfriend and girlfriend, to a couple "going steady," to an engaged couple. In the minds of their friends and relatives they were no longer just Rick and Wendy; they had become a pair. Though neither thought of breaking up, this growing reputation as a couple would itself have made a breakup difficult, since important expectations had been raised. The expectation of marriage was fulfilled in the early autumn when Rick and Wendy cut a week's classes and eloped. Again the pattern conforms to Adams's propositions:

Proposition 17: The more two individuals define each other as "right" or "the best I can get," the less likely it is that the relationship will break up short of marriage.

Proposition 18: The more a relationship moves to the level of pair communality [i.e., the more others see them as a pair] the less likely it is that the relationship will break up short of marriage.

Proposition 19: The more a relationship moves through a series of formal and informal escalators, the less likely it is that the relationship will break up short of marriage.

Questions

1. Consider a marriage you know well. Does it seem to conform to Adams's theory? If not, why do you think it does not?
2. Do you think you will conform (or did conform) to the process Adams describes in selecting a marriage partner?
3. Adams's theory is based on previous research. If the researchers overlook an important factor, the theory does too. What influences on mate selection appear to be missing?

SOURCE Bert N. Adams. 1979. "Mate selection in the United States: A theoretical summarization." In Wesley R. Burr, Reuben Hill, F. Ivan Nye, and Ira L. Reiss (eds.), *Contemporary Theories About the Family*, Vol. 1. New York: Free Press, pp. 259–267.

What Are the Characteristics of Marriages that Succeed?

Why are some marriages a haven from the world while others are a world from which people want to escape? Why do some marriages endure whereas others disintegrate? Many factors contribute to stability in marriage. Because the factors that lead to dissatisfaction and divorce tend to be the opposite of those that lead to satisfaction and stability, we will consider these topics together.

A THEORY OF MARITAL STABILITY AND QUALITY

Robert Lewis and Graham Spanier have developed a social exchange theory of marital satisfaction that deals with most of the major variables discussed by other researchers and theorists (1979). Their model indicates that high-quality marriages endure, whereas those with problems tend to come apart, with two notable exceptions. First, external pressures to remain married may keep even unhappy marriages together. These pressures can take the form of religious beliefs, restrictive divorce laws, economic dependency, or the expectations of friends or family members, especially the couple's own parents and children. This is borne out, for instance, by data that show that having one or more children reduces the short-term probability of divorce from .20 to .05 (Waite, Haggstrom, and Karouse, 1985).

Second, alternative attractions may draw one or both partners away from what otherwise might be a satisfying and lasting marriage. The alternative attractions could take the form of substance abuse, a hobby, a more satisfying partner, a career, a child, or a parent who draws attention away from the marriage partner.

Lewis and Spanier classify the factors influencing marital quality and stability into three major categories. The first category, *social and personal resources,* includes factors such as the couple's degree of homogamy (how much alike they are), their psychological health and social skills, the quality of their parents' marriage as a role model, the degree of support from significant others, and the absence of problems such as premarital pregnancy or personal difficulties that might cause one to marry as an escape.

The second major category is termed *satisfaction with life-style* and it generally refers to the degree to which the spouses are pleased with the social arrange-

Racial differences lessen the probability that two people will marry and stay married, but some racially mixed couples "beat the odds." (*Photo courtesy the author*)

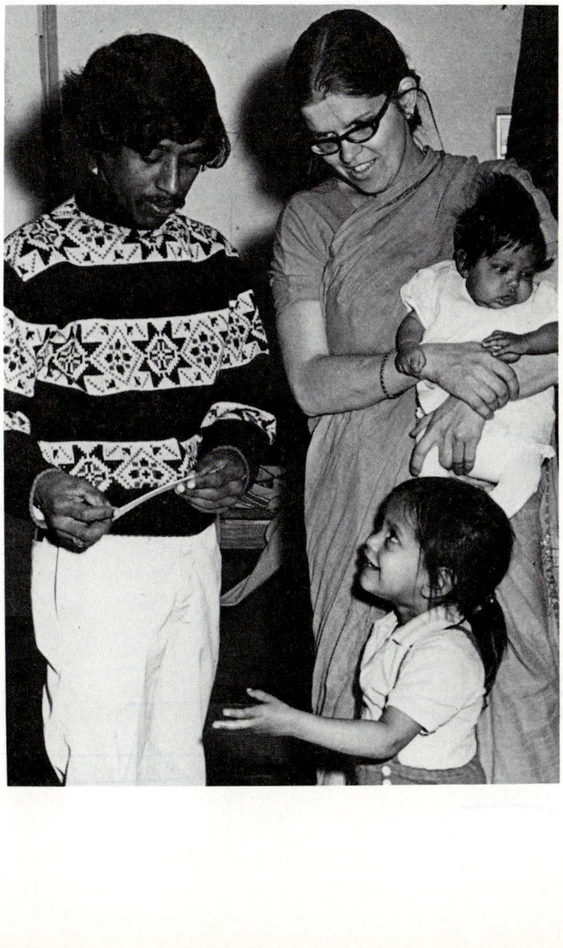

ments of the marriage. These include satisfaction with the number of children, with the wife's employment, with the degree of supportive interaction the couple has in the community, and their socioeconomic level.

The third major concept, *reward from spousal interaction*, refers to the quality of interaction between husband and wife. It includes the amount of mutual positive regard, the amount of emotional gratification between them, their effectiveness in communication, the degree to which their roles fit well together, and the amount of their interaction.

RESEARCH ON MARITAL QUALITY AND STABILITY

Several social factors have been identified that correlate with divorce rate. Breault and Kposowa have found that social integration indicators, including church membership, degree of population change in an area, and the urbanity of the social group studied, are factors in determining the divorce rate of the group. Higher rates of church membership and lower rates of population change and urbanity were correlated positively to lower rates of divorce. These factors explain much more of the variance in divorce rates than any of the socioeconomic variables studied, including income and unemployment, which were significantly correlated with divorce (Breault and Kposowa, 1987). Other studies corroborate the idea that social integration variables are important in determining stability of marriages (Shelton, 1987). The steady rise in divorce during the history of the United States is also partly because people in industrial and postindustrial settings are much more frequently away from their spouses in settings where attractive alternative partners can become significant liaisons (Feldburg and Kohan, 1976).

Lewis and Spanier's typology generally referred to factors affecting stability in individual marriages rather than probabilities within populations. In general, when an important factor enhances a marriage, its absence lowers the couple's satisfaction and decreases the stability of the marriage.

The lack of factors that contribute to good marital quality is likely to lead to dissatisfaction and divorce. Following the Lewis and Spanier typology, we will consider three of them: social and personal resources, spouses' satisfaction with marital life-style, and spouses' rewards from marital interaction.

SOCIAL AND PERSONAL RESOURCES. Several studies demonstrate the importance of social and personal resources to marital success. Having a sound economic base increases the probability that the marriage will last (Bumpass and Sweet, 1972). More specifically, the higher the male's income, the lower the probability of divorce (Glick and Norton, 1971; Bumpass and Sweet, 1972; Bernard, 1977). Marital satisfaction is also higher when the husband is moving up in his occupation (Scanzoni, 1972). The husband's job success correlates highly with the degree of satisfaction he feels with his marriage, and his marital satisfaction strongly affects his wife's marital satisfaction (Otto and Featherman, 1972). Age is a significant social resource because the younger a couple is when they marry, the higher the probability of divorce. Since the median age at first marriage is rising, the divorce rate may slow. (See Figure 13.3.) Education has a positive effect on marital stability; high school and college graduates have a lower probability of divorce than do high school and college dropouts (Glick and Norton, 1971).

Homogamy is a significant social resource for marriages. Several researchers have demonstrated that differences in religion, age, and education are all related to higher divorce rates. Conversely, similarity in these dimensions enhances the chance of success of the marriage. Strong support of the marriage by friends and family members helps ensure that the marriage continues, as does stability in the couple's parents' marriages. Finally, the absence of premarital pregnancy and previous marriages raises the chance of success of a marriage (Ackerman, 1963; Christensen and Barber, 1967; Furstenberg, 1967; Coombs and Zumeta, 1970; Bumpass and Sweet, 1972; R. Lewis, 1973; Glenn and Weaver, 1977).

SPOUSES' SATISFACTION WITH MARITAL LIFE-STYLE. The couple's satisfaction with their life-style also influences marital success and failure. Several important studies have investigated the extent to which becoming a parent affects one's marital satisfaction (Spanier, Lewis, and Cole, 1975; Dumon, 1978; Rollins and Galligan, 1978). For example, the early stages of parenting are stressful on a marriage (Burr, 1970; Rollins and Feldman, 1970). However, having children at a young age does not significantly raise the probability of divorce except in black marriages (Moore and Waite, 1981). A detailed study of those who *think* about divorce found that having children under 6 years old tends to increase women's thinking about divorce, whereas having children ages 6 to 11 tends to decrease men's thinking about divorce (Huber and Spitze, 1980). Present knowledge shows that although changes in family life-cycle stages, such as beginning or ending of parenting, do create stress, other factors are more important in changing marital satisfaction (Harry, 1976; Schram, 1979). For instance, both men and women are more likely to contemplate divorce the more the woman works outside the home and the more she believes that housework must be evenly shared (Huber and Spitze, 1980).

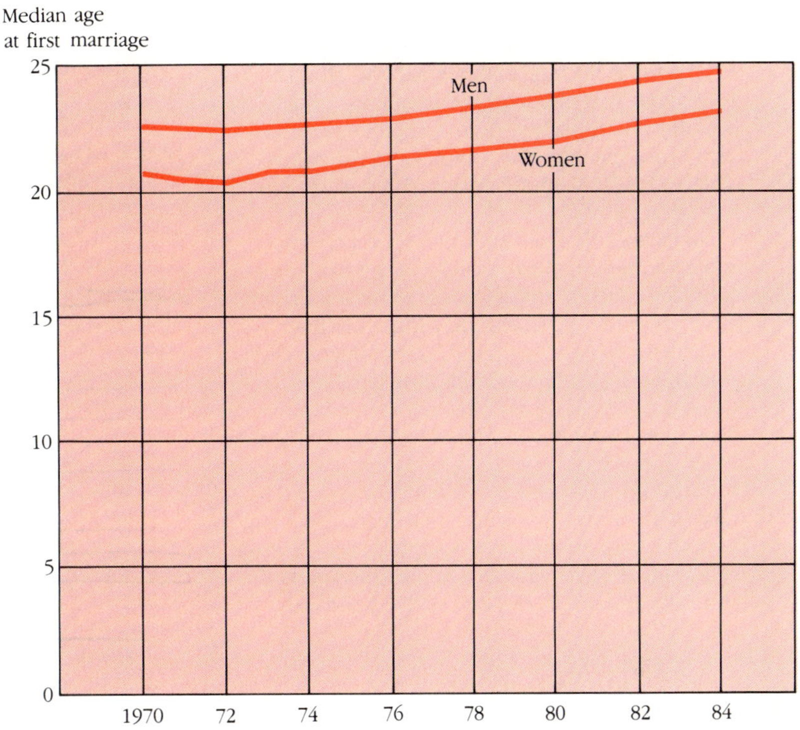

FIGURE 13.3 Median Age at First Marriage Is Rising. Because younger marriages tend to be less stable, this trend may help to decrease the number of dissolved marriages. SOURCE U.S. National Center for Health Statistics, 1986.

SPOUSES' REWARDS FROM MARITAL INTERACTION. The rewards the spouses get from their interaction are very important in producing stability. For instance, role strain, or potential conflict between roles within the marriage relationship, creates as much or more stress on the marriage as parenting strain (Rollins and Cannon, 1974). Also, the quantity of marital interaction is related to the quality, because the longer a couple stays married the less likely they are to consider divorce (Huber and Spitze, 1980). The positive affection that most persons seek when marrying can obviously be strong "cement" to marriages.

In sum, the factors that are associated with lower probability of divorce are:

- having children over age 6
- adequate income
- high homogamy
- positive parental marriage
- support from others
- no premarital pregnancy
- upward mobility of husband
- older age at marriage
- higher level of education
- no previous marriages

WHAT THE "EXPERTS" SAY ABOUT MARRIAGE

A number of "experts" from unmarried clerics to talk-show hosts and journalists have been consulted on the topic of what makes a good marriage. Sociologists who study the family present their views also, but no coherent and unified theory exists that consistently defines happiness for couples. Nevertheless, what is known thus far is interesting and can be useful. In this spirit, we present an anthology of the wisdom of these family sociology experts:

IT'S LIKE SEX . . .

> It is the style of interaction that determines whether a marriage will be good or bad. In a bad marriage, the partners get locked into a power struggle, their interactions become more and more negative. . . . Marriage should be something where both win. It's like sex; the better it is for one, the better it is for both. (Carlfred Broderick, Ph.D., Professor of Sociology and Director of the Marriage and Family Counseling Training Program, University of Southern California, quoted in Keen, 1976, p. 28)

SECURITY AND INTIMACY . . .

Few general maxims apply equally to all marriages, but two elements seem to apply widely; security and intimacy. Security can be described as a protective impulse; intimacy as the abandonment of this impulse—a freedom to explore new things. . . .

Marriages that endure probably represent a strong commitment to security at the expense of intimacy. Such marriages seem to have a brittle strength, and if untested, may last a lifetime. Their failure is epitomized by the moment when one or both partners ask the now familiar question: When did we become strangers? Marriages strongly committed to intimacy are the kinds about which novels are written: they are tumultuous, dramatic and often short-lived. The ideal is to learn how to live with both. (William Simon, Ph.D., Professor of Sociology and Director of the Institute for Urban Studies, University of Houston, quoted in *Redbook,* 1977, p. 264)

FEELINGS FLUCTUATE AND ARE INCONSISTENT . . .

People who love each other don't always like each other all the time. In a marital relationship, feelings fluctuate and are inconsistent. One marries a projection, an image, and part of the adventure is finding out who the person really is that you have married. The best single prediction of how a marriage is going to turn out depends on the quality of the family you came from and the kind of marriage your parents had. It is possible to have a better marriage than your parents, but not easy. Qualities that help make a marriage good include the ability to give and take, the capacity to communicate honestly, and the overflow of love to the children—all embedded in the context of real bonds of affection. Another condition is to fight fair—to deal with issues together (James L. Framo, Ph.D., Professor of Psychology, Temple University; editor, *Family Interaction,* quoted in *Redbook,* 1977, p. 115)

What Kinds of Violence Are Found in the Family?

Until recently violence in a family context received little scholarly attention. Now, however, family violence—including wife-beating, child abuse, and other violence between family members—has become a major public and sociological concern.

Murray Strauss, director of the University of New Hampshire's Family Violence Research Program, and two colleagues, Richard Gelles of the University of Rhode Island and Susanne Steinmetz of the University of Delaware, published the results of the first national survey dealing with family violence (Strauss, Gelles, and Steinmetz, 1979). Using a national sample of over 2,000 family members, they estimate that 8 million Americans are assaulted each year by a family member. This figure is sixteen times greater than the number of arrests for all assaults, within or outside of the family. Sixteen percent of married couples have violent confrontations of some sort. Although most abusers are men, researchers estimate that as many as 300,000 husbands a year are being beaten by their wives (O'Reilly, 1983).

Two million reports of child abuse and neglect were made in 1986, a number which has risen 15 percent a year since 1981 (Beissert, 1987). The National Committee for Prevention of Child Abuse estimates that each year 2,000 children die as a result of abuse (S. Wilson, 1986). Three percent of children are assaulted by their parents, and over a third of all children are severely beaten by a brother or sister during the course of a year.

In spite of the difficulties in measuring family violence, it is still easier to measure it than to explain it. No systematic theory of family violence exists, though Strauss, Gelles, and Steinmetz put forth several descriptions based on the social identity of their subjects. Family violence is more common among the urban poor, among blue-collar workers, among people under 30, among people without religious affiliation, in families with a jobless husband, and in families with four to six children. Child abusers are more often former victims of child abuse.

It is important to note that violence is found in virtually all types of families. The recent killing of 6-year-old Lisa Steinberg by her mother and father is a case in point. Lisa's ribs, nose, and jaw were broken and she was unconscious when police found her in the filthy New York apartment where she lived with her mother, a children's book writer, and her father, a lawyer. Heroin and $25,000 cash were found in the apartment as well (Beissert, 1987).

Public awareness of wife abuse and child abuse is increasing, and several measures have been proposed for reform. Most states have passed laws making the reporting of child abuse or neglect mandatory for child-care professionals. The federal government has established a National Center for Child Abuse and Neglect. Such moves challenge the once popular conception that what goes on inside the family is the family's business by proposing that "the legal response to family violence must be guided by the nature of the abusive act, not the relationship between the victim and the abuser" (Attorney General's Task Force on Family Violence, 1984). The criminal justice system is recognizing that it must provide adequate legal remedies in domestic violence cases.

In response to grass-roots movements, the community is responding differently to domestic violence issues (Goolkasian, 1986). Civic organizations have opened shelters for battered wives. Social services agencies are operating drop-off centers for parents who feel overpressured and liable to abuse their children.

Research has shown us that families, which we have thought of as the source of positive emotional support for its members, can be a primary source of pain and disillusionment. Some feel the solution must involve more fundamental changes in society, such as decreasing the amount of violence portrayed in the media, reducing unemployment, and working to make women's position in society less subservient to men. Better information about family violence will lead to more intelligent approaches to the problem.

What Is the Situation Regarding Divorce in the United States?

When a marriage does not have a sufficient base upon which to survive, it may end in divorce. In this section we look at divorce rates and how a divorce affects the family and its members.

DIVORCE RATES

The divorce rate in the United States in 1986 was 4.9 divorces per 1,000 population, over seven times as great as the rate of 0.7 in 1900. This is the lowest rate since 1975, however, down from 1981 when 5.3 per 1,000 divorced, the highest rate in the history of the United States (U.S. Bureau of Census, 1983, p. 63).

The United States has the highest divorce rate in the world, with as many marriages ending through divorce as through the death of a spouse (Cherlin, 1981; Weitzman, 1985). Family demographers expect that about 50 percent of all first marriages will end in divorce. Of those Americans between 35 and 39 in 1985 who had ever married, 32 percent had experienced a divorce. The Census Bureau projects that 55.5 percent of this group will experience at least one divorce before they die (Norton and Moorman, 1987). This means that half of all today's children will live in single-parent families, at least for a time, before they reach age 18. Seventy-five percent of all divorced people will remarry, however, and form new families.

The acceleration in divorce appears to have passed. The divorce rate, which doubled in the decade from 1970 to 1980, has leveled off at a record high level. (See Figure 13.4a.)

Several factors influence this leveling off of the rate of increase in divorce. Age at first marriage is rising, and those who wait longer to marry have a greater chance of having a lasting marriage. (See Figure 13.4b.) Second, as sociologist Andrew Cherlin states, "I don't think people think marriage is more fun than it used to be or somehow see a more ideal form, but the alternatives to marriage look less promising" (1987).

Several factors are working toward increasing stability in marriages. Most people have seen close up the emotional pain that a divorce has brought to themselves or a loved one. Casual sexual relations are less attractive with the increasing threat of AIDS and other sexually transmitted diseases. In an age of inflated prices and small paychecks, both men and women are aware of how difficult it is to viably maintain two households and of how many divorced women live in poverty. For these and other reasons, more young people are choosing the "old fashioned" route of committing to a relationship for life, regardless of its rough spots. A growing number of people who were previously married to one another are remarrying, as well.

HOW DIVORCE AFFECTS FAMILY MEMBERS

Partly as a result of worrying about making ends meet, and partly as a result of the loss of the emotional support of the marriage, divorced men and women have higher rates of mental health symptoms and admission rates to psychiatric hospitals and outpatient clinics than those in stable marriages (Bloom, 1978; Riessman, 1985; Warheit, 1979; Weiss, 1979). Recent research suggests that this may be due more to loss of material resources for women and to loss of the social support of the marriage relationship for men (Gerstl, Riessman, and Rosenfield, 1985).

Divorced persons have higher rates of suicide and death than married persons (S. Stack, 1985; Trovato, 1986). Divorced men are more likely to be fired from their jobs after divorce. Divorced women have more difficulty finding employment (Weiss, 1975; Emery, 1984). Both men and women experience negative changes in their self-concepts (Bloom, White, and Asler, 1979). Most researchers would agree with Spanier and Castro's assertion that "separation and divorce are disruptive and traumatic for the adults involved" (1979). These and other social facts indicate what a crushing blow the disintegration of a marriage usually is, even when it does not involve helping children live

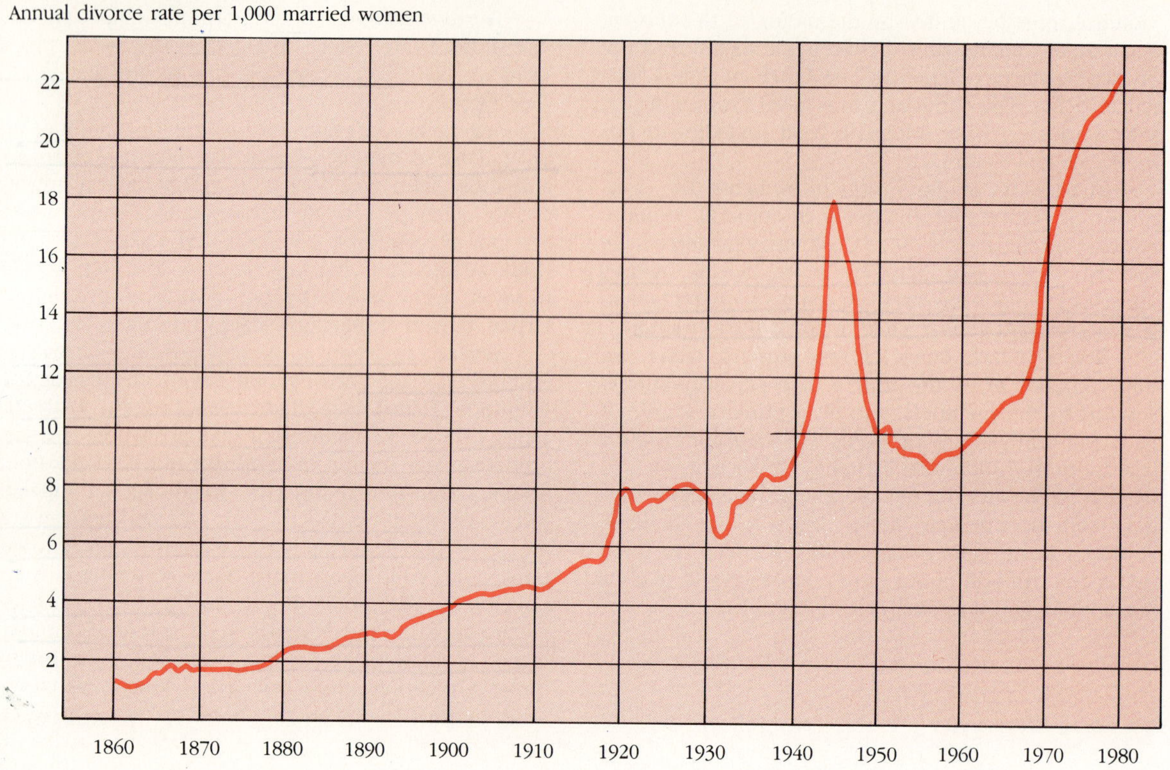

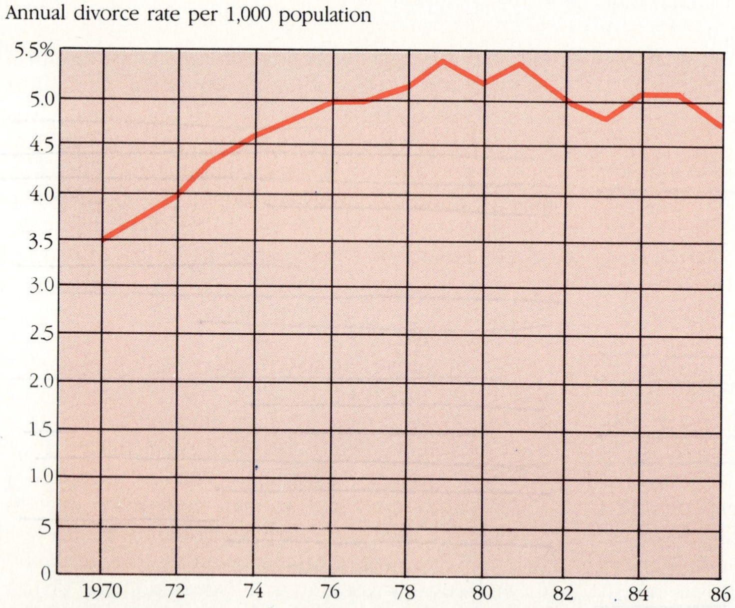

FIGURE 13.4 The divorce rate in the United States has been steadily rising over the past century. In the graph at the top, two peaks are evident: one following World War II and one after the relaxing of divorce laws in the 1970s. The graph at the bottom shows that growth in divorce has slowed during the past decade.

with a split world. Adding parenthood to the equation adds burdens to the divorced adults.

More women are leaving their families today (Fisler, 1983), leaving some fathers to bring up children by themselves. The predominant pattern still, however, is for the mother to be given custody of the children five days a week and the divorced father to see his children on weekends (Rosenthal & Keshet, 1980; Bowman and Ahrons, 1985).

DIVORCED MOTHERS. The material conditions under which she and her children live may provide a major stress on the divorced mother (Gerstl, Reissman, and Rosenfield, 1985). In the year after a divorce, the average woman's standard of living is reduced by 73 percent whereas the average man's standard increases by 42 percent (Weitzman, 1985). This leads to what we called in Chapter 8 "the feminization of poverty," or the disproportionate increase in the number of poor households headed by women. In 1984, the median annual income for husband-wife families was $29,686; for single parent families headed by males, it was $24,551. The same year, the median income for female-headed families was $13,473 (Statistical Abstract, 1987, p. 433).

One reason for this situation is that long-term alimony is often replaced by short-term maintenance support, designed only to help former wives to retrain and enter the work force to support themselves. Another is that only about one-half of all fathers pay child support, even when they are ordered to pay by the court (Lacayo, 1986). Many divorced fathers earn wages that will hardly support one household, and their contributions to the mothers are negligible, even when paid faithfully.

The pressures on most divorced mothers are obvious. They not only must earn a living but must attend to all the details of running a home. The demands placed on them by job, children, and home eradicate any time for themselves. They cannot physically do everything they would like to do and often feel guilty about not being a better worker, mother, and homemaker all at the same time. This overwhelming task is hardly conducive to happiness or serenity (Le Masters, 1970). Yet many women still choose this option instead of living in a marriage they feel has failed.

DIVORCED FATHERS. Whereas women become depressed after divorce due to the physical realities of taking care of their children, their home, and their job with limited resources, men become depressed due to the loneliness and lack of support in their single state (Wilcox, 1981; Gerstl, 1985). In fact, being divorced increases the possibility of psychiatric hospitalization for men considerably more than it does for women (Bernard, 1979). Perhaps because of the realization of the social loss they experience when they lose their wife and children, more men are asking for and winning custody of their children (Gersick, 1979).

Much recent attention has been focused on the phenomenon of part-time fathering. Researchers have discovered an almost universal fear in these fathers that their children will reject them, as well as feelings of guilt about being inadequate parents. The fathers studied said they had trouble learning to cope with everyday arrangements their wives had always made for their children, such as what food and clothes to pack for an afternoon picnic. On the other hand, the fathers had also grown more sensitive to their children's emotional needs and understood their own responses to those needs more clearly. They often learn to take more responsibility for their children and their relationships with their children than they did when their marriage was intact (Kashet, 1978).

DIVORCED CHILDREN. More than a million children experience divorce every year. A crucial question to the future of our society is, "What effects does divorce have on these children?" Thus far, research has produced varied results. There is no question that divorce is an extremely traumatic event for children. Some evidence suggests that it affects them for the rest of their lives, although the worst period for children is the first year or two after the divorce, a time during which they will cry, whine, ask for attention, and rebel against authority more than they ever have or ever will again (Heatherington, Cox, and Cox, 1978).

Longfellow suggests that the absence of the father may have its greatest impact on the economic and social position of the family (1979). When the family is disrupted, the children's entire standard of living may change drastically, as well as the location of home and schooling opportunities. The stress of worrying about paying for the basics of life added to the stress of losing one of their parents' attention may create the most important factors in the behavioral change often seen in children immediately after divorce.

Closely related to this is that the behavior, outlook, and mental health of the mother is crucial to the child's reaction (Longfellow, 1979). If the mother's energy is sapped by depression and anxiety, the children will not receive the attention and love they require so much in order to heal from their hurts. Although she may wish that she could treat them differently, she feels unable to break through the depressive inertia she experiences.

The age of the children at the time of the divorce can be important in determining their adjustment. Wallerstein's ten year study shows that preschool children most often deny the reality and continue to expect their father to come back. They tend to heal more quickly than older children, however. Children ages six to ten when their parents separate do not recover as quickly, and show feelings of sadness and powerlessness about the divorce for as long as ten years afterward. During the divorce, their school performance falls off and relations with their peers suffer. Teenagers may be the group most affected. They often take sides in the conflict and withdraw from the parent they feel is to blame. Sixty-eight percent of those who were in their teens during the breakup of their families evidenced behavior problems, from alcohol and drug abuse to theft and drug peddling. A college career can also be severely and negatively affected by the parents' separation (Wallerstein and Kelly, 1979, 1976, 1975, 1974). Rather than a single reaction to divorce being universal, however, research shows at least three distinct groups, from those children who are happy and thriving to those who are unhappy and lonely for extended periods (Wallerstein and Kelly, 1980).

Two basic differences in later life are found in children of divorce and those of intact families. Those from divorced homes have a greater tendency to identify their childhoods as the most unhappy times in their lives. Second, they evidence more anxiety as adults than those who grew up in intact homes (Kulka and Weingarter, 1979; Kalter, 1977). Persons whose parental homes were disrupted by divorce have higher rates of divorce in their own first marriages (Pope and Mueller, 1976).

Several factors can make the divorce less painful. The most important is continuing close contact with the missing parent, who is usually the father (Suransky, 1982). Another is having the parents develop a relationship good enough to enable them to handle questions about the children in a nonemotional and cooperative way (Ahrons, 1986).

Although divorce is traumatic for children, living in a home with constant conflict may be just as difficult for them (Raschke and Raschke, 1979). In some cases children who experience family breakup fare as well or better than those who remain in a family where conflict and violence is the rule (Zill, 1984). Family structure, social class, physical location, children's welfare, and the chance of change in the relationship are all variables that go into the complicated equations that those living in painful marriages must try to balance. Most child counselors, however, would agree with Wertlieb's observation that "the period of creative divorce we went through is going out of style, (because we have found that) the suffering for grown-ups and children is phenomenal" (1987).

HOW DIVORCE AFFECTS THE ENTIRE FAMILY

The rising divorce rate has several effects on the family as a whole. First, there are more female-headed families now than ever before. Fifteen million children—more than one in five in the country—live with only one parent, usually the mother. This is twice the number of children who lived with one parent in 1960 (Mead, 1977; U.S. Bureau of the Census, 1983, p. 53). Research reveals that in a majority of families, divorce effectively destroys the relationship between children and the parent living outside the home, with nearly half of those children studied not having seen their nonresident fathers in over a year (Fustenberg and Nord, 1985).

Eighty percent of formerly married persons and children will eventually become part of a "blended" family, consisting of parts of other families; children with a natural father blended with a new stepmother and her children, children with a natural mother blended with a new stepfather and his children, and the like. The special problems of blending families in these ways are only recently receiving attention. Several structural elements that distinguish blended families from first families have been identified (Visher and Visher, 1978):

1. One biological parent does not live in the household.
2. The members of a stepfamily have lost a primary relationship (parent, child, spouse).
3. The relationship between parent and child existed before the new relationship between the married couple.
4. The children consider themselves members of more than one household.
5. No legal relationship exists between stepparent and stepchild.

These structural differences between blended families and first families create potential conflicts and create an atmosphere of constant questioning as the family is defined and redefined. Where does the sympathy of the natural parent lie in conflicts between natural children and the stepparent? What role does the stepparent play in the childrearing? How does it affect the child's socialization to belong to two family groups?

Thus far, research suggests three problem areas for parents in blended families: discipline of the children, adjusting to the children's personalities, and becoming accepted by the children (Kompara, 1980). It appears that stepmothers in particular have a difficult time accepting the constraints in a blended family, including the difficulty and time commitment involved in beginning a new relationship with children and the monetary problems inherent when fathers support their children in new blended families (Duberman, 1975b). The stepparenting experience in general is more positive with live-in stepchildren (Amberg, 1986). As this form of family becomes more prevalent, norms will develop

New option? Being married to two or more women at the same time is legally not an option in the United States, though polygamy has been practiced frequently in other cultures and at other times. (*Photo courtesy the author*)

to cover the situations such families are facing for the first time.

The high divorce rate may also be a factor in the strong trend toward smaller families. Research on family size indicates that large families put more stress on parents' relationships than do small families (Nye, 1970). This trend, therefore, may enhance the quality of life for the average American family.

What New Options Exist for the American Family?

The traditional American family, some argue, is falling apart. Divorce rates are high. Millions of children live with only one parent. Families are sending elderly relatives to nursing homes and relegating young children to day-care centers, schools, camps, and babysitters. The number of children attending preschool has increased from 32 percent of the 3-to-5-year-olds in 1967 to 55 percent in 1986 (U.S. Bureau of the Census, 1987, p. 123).

Yet historically the family has been a persistent, resilient institution. As we have seen, nearly everyone marries and has children. Perhaps the traditional family should be seen as more in a state of flux than of decay. In the final section of this chapter, we consider several variations on the traditional American family today.

OPTION: REMAINING SINGLE OR DELAYING MARRIAGE

Some young people have decided to stay single rather than enter marriage as it is presently defined. The percentage of women between ages 25 and 29 who have never married rose from 10.5 percent in 1960 to 26 percent in 1985 (U.S. Bureau of Census, 1987, p. 38). New career options for women and pressure toward zero population growth have made producing children, one of the traditional functions of marriage, less immediate an issue (Poston and Gotard, 1977). Further, because sex outside of marriage has become more common, marriage is no longer the only outlet for sexual satisfaction.

Added to this group are those who are simply waiting longer to get married. In 1987, the median age for first marriage for men rose to 25.8 years, up two years from the 1975 age. Women married at age 23.6, up more than a year since 1980 (U.S. Bureau of the Census, 1987). These young people are looking for a stable, long-term relationship, and feel that waiting until they are older and have had more experience in the world may help them find what they seek (Clancy, 1987).

OPTION: SINGLE PARENTHOOD

The number of single-parent families in the United States increased 27 percent between 1980 and 1985 (U.S. Bureau of the Census, 1987). This means that single parents now head 26 percent of all families with children and 51 percent of all black families, as shown in Figure 13.5. The overwhelming number of these family heads are women, some divorced and some never married. Over half of them are living in poverty.

Single motherhood is a self-perpetuating phenomenon: single mothers are often the children of single mothers. White daughters of single parents, for instance, are 53 percent more likely than daughters of two-parent families to marry as teenagers, 164 percent more likely to have an illegitimate child, and 92 percent more likely to divorce (Garfinkel and McLanahan, 1987).

Called "children having children," these young mothers have little chance in today's world (Wallis, 1985). They have grown up during a time when unwed motherhood is losing its stigma and premarital sex has become more accepted. When both of these social pressures combine with the "chemistry" of adolescence, pregnancy often results.

The United States leads all other developed nations in the incidence of teenage pregnancy (Wallis, 1985). These young mothers become and stay poor for three reasons: (1) they earn less than men, partly due to lack of education and partly due to sexism, (2) they receive base benefits from welfare, and (3) only 40 percent of white fathers and 19 percent of black fathers pay any child support (Garfinkel and McLanahan, 1987). We have discussed this phenomenon elsewhere in this

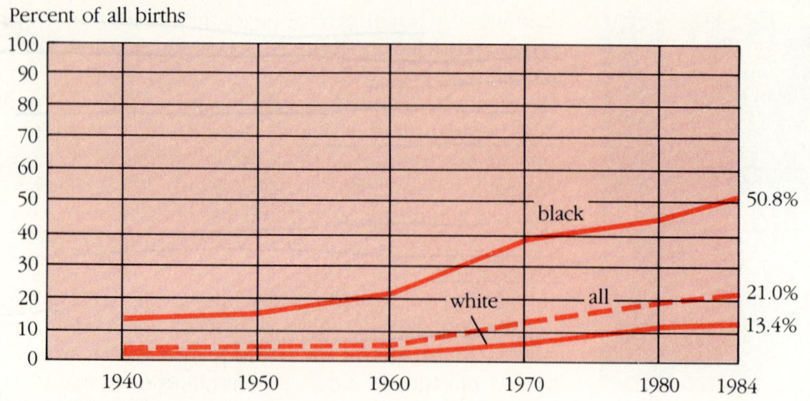

FIGURE 13.5 The Rising Proportion of Births to Unmarried Women, 1940–1980. In the past 45 years, the number of illegitimate births has risen phenomenally in both the black and white communities. The number of teenage black mothers today is partially responsible for the continuation of poverty in the black community; their children are born poor and rarely leave that condition. SOURCE Data from the U.S. Bureau of the Census, 1940–1986.

chapter, as well as in Chapter 8, but emphasize it here because it is such a rapidly increasing form of the family.

OPTION: CHILDLESS MARRIAGES

Married women have been choosing childless lifestyles more frequently, although 95 percent of all married women do still have children (Houseknecht, 1982). Some of them initially plan to have children, but become infertile because of a series of postponements for various reasons, such as career commitment. (Yorburg, 1983).

It is difficult to generalize about this group because it is very small and has not been studied in depth, but some social factors have been identified that correlate with childlessness. These include being only or firstborn children, white, middle class, and upwardly mobile, having no religious beliefs, and being more educated than the general population (Veevers, 1973).

To be childless is still an unpopular stance in today's society, and such couples often face sanctions especially from their own parents who desire grandchildren. Most childless women report that they are indifferent to the negative responses they often receive from their social world, knowing that their decision is correct for them.

OPTION: COHABITATION

A compromise between marrying and remaining single is *cohabiting*, or *living together without being married*. For some this is a kind of practice session for marriage; for others it may be a permanent alternative to marriage (Clayton and Voss, 1977). Interestingly, cohabitants who later marry have the same likelihood of divorce as those who marry without living together first (Blumstein and Schwartz, 1983). From 1970 to 1982 the number of cohabitants in the United States nearly quadrupled from 530,000 to 1.9 million people (*Time*, July 9, 1979; U.S. Bureau of the Census, 1983, p. 47). Cohabitation is still illegal in twenty states, and penalties can be as high as three years in jail (T. Schwartz, 1977), but few of these 1.9 million persons expect to be arrested.

So many of these unmarried couples are seeking help from counselors that the American Association of Marriage and Family Counselors (AAMFC) is considering changing the name of its members to "relationship counselors." Frederick Humphrey, president of the AAMFC, believes cohabitants have essentially the same problems that married couples have: "sex, money, power, and the need for space." He also believes that the bonds that they form are difficult to break. Humphrey's experience is that "the emotional pain and trauma of separation is often virtually identical to married couples getting a divorce." (Schwartz, 1977, p. 49).

Many different kinds of people cohabit. Social Security laws, which force one member of a retired couple to give up his or her Social Security income when marrying, are thought to invite this type of coupling rather than marriage. People who grew up in a metropolitan area are more likely to cohabit, as are those who have less than a high school education or who have dropped out of college. Blacks have a slightly higher incidence of cohabitation than whites. Cohabitants tend to be slightly more unconventional than those who marry. Finally, the earlier a person has sexual intercourse, the more likely he or she is to live with someone rather than marry (Clayton and Voss, 1977). Most people still choose marriage, with all its weaknesses as the way they relate in couples, and cohabitation is far from becoming the dominant form of family life.

OPTION: DUAL-CAREER MARRIAGE

The typical American family now includes two paychecks (Pepitone-Rockwell, 1980; Bergman, 1986). The term "dual-career marriage" was coined by Rhona and Robert Rapoport in 1969 to describe a new lifestyle in which both marriage partners have a high level of commitment to their work and expect it will be carried out in a continuous developmental sequence (Rapoport and Rapoport, 1971). This differentiates the dual-career couple from the couple in which the man "pursues a career" and the woman "has a job."

The stresses on dual-career families are many. The Rapoports identify five dilemmas they face: (1) overload of tasks traditionally done by the wife, (2) environmental sanctions, or societal pressures, on the women who choose to follow a career, (3) problems with personal identity and self-esteem caused by being socialized during a period in which their chosen lifestyle was considered deviant, (4) social-network dilemmas involving relationships with friends, colleagues, and institutions with which they come into contact, and (5) dilemmas of multiple-role cycling, or coordinating the demands of marriage, work, children, and so forth with the life-cycle stages (Rapoport and Rapoport, 1971).

Essentially, these stresses stem from the fact that the traditional male career is what has been termed a "two-person career" (Papaneck, 1973). In other words, men who are the primary breadwinners depend on their wives for support in the form of childcare, homemaking, entertaining, emotional backing in difficult business situations, and emergency assistance if any of their systems falter, including nursing care when they are ill. Because of this backup, men can commit themselves more fully to pursuing their careers. When both partners pursue such a career, *neither* of them has a backup to perform these functions. Nevertheless, they participate in occupations that assume they have this type of support, and they expect high levels of commitment. At the same time, they must cope with all the pressures of family and home life that others in those occupations who have a full-time housekeeper supporting their activities do not have to face (Ferber and Huber, 1979). Ordinary household chores may become a burden, and organization of all activities—from mundane to extraordinary—becomes extremely important (Holmstrom, 1972). Numerous researchers point to this as a source of role strain for both men and women (Poloma and Garland, 1978).

The lives of dual-career couples, therefore, are much less easygoing by definition. They must be extremely organized in order to survive with their daily pressures. They often struggle with issues of power, dependency, self-esteem, and trust. Many have difficulty resolving their desire to be successful both at work and at home (Toufexis, 1985).

Why do people still choose this lifestyle? Not only are they competing in the marketplace with one hand tied behind their back, but they have no letup of pressure once at home either, since they share the tasks there, as well. One obvious incentive is monetary. Two-career marriages generally earn more money than one. More often cited by such couples, however, is what the Rapoports term "self-expression," a category that includes the pleasure of creating something, being recognized as a worthwhile contributor in the outside world, using energies in areas not considered "homemaking," and enriching the marriage through contact with outside ideas and people (Rapoport and Rapoport, 1971). In spite of the pressures of dual-career couples, this life-style is growing, especially among educated groups. As more men and women pursue higher education leading toward professional positions, they will redefine the dual-career lifestyle and develop more ways to reduce the pressures on its participants.

OPTION: OPTIMISTIC GROWTH IN THE STATUS QUO

The family has become less important to society in terms of providing socialization, social control, and support for dependent people. But it is easy to mistake change for decline. Most authorities believe that, in spite of the pressures the family undergoes, it will survive in the United States (Keller, 1971; Glenn and Weaver, 1977; Mead, 1977a).

The overwhelming majority of people still get married. Of those who were 40 or older in 1984, only 4.9 percent of the women and 5.4 percent of the men had never married, and this proportion of single people had declined by about 25 percent during the previous decade. This indicates that marriage actually grew in popularity during the 1970s, a growth that occurred despite the fact that during this period the median age at first marriage rose by 1.5 years for both men and women (U.S. Bureau of the Census, 1986). The divorce rate, at 4.8 per 1,000 population, is the highest since 1950—with the exception of 1972, when it reached 10.9 per 1,000 population (U.S. Bureau of the Census, 1987). In spite of high divorce rates, Americans are more likely to marry than at virtually any other time in the last three decades.

Furthermore, the vast majority of those who marry

Sociologists at Work •

ROBERT ACKERMAN
PROFILES ADULT CHILDREN OF ALCOHOLICS
Indiana University
Indiana, Pennsylvania

Family sociologist Bob Ackerman is a nationally known expert on adult children of alcoholics. He has been able to share the knowledge gained from his ground-breaking research on adult children of alcoholics through his voluminous writing and public speaking, including through such avenues as "The Today Show" and *Newsweek Magazine.*

What Area of Sociology Is Your Primary Focus?
My training in sociological practice has allowed me to assess from a developmental point of view the impact on children who are raised in problem families, especially alcoholic families, by tracking them and finding out what has happened to them as adults. Addiction is not only an individual problem but a family, community, and national one. I honestly believe that my training as a sociologist was probably the best academic training I could get for being able to work at all of those different levels with addiction.

What Is Your Most Current Research?
I have just completed work on "The National Adult Children of Alcoholics Research Study" in which I examined approximately 1,000 adults in the United States from 38 states, half of whom were raised in alcoholic families. By applying research principles and theories from sociology of the family, I was able to determine what kinds of different environments they were raised in, the impact of their background on their adult lives, and their levels of emotional satisfaction as adults. One thing that we know from this work is that many people raised in such dysfunctional families or alcoholic families are more likely to become alcoholics themselves. Much of my work looks at these contributing factors and what we know about what happens to families in distress, especially to the development of children.

Is There a Typical Profile of an Adult Child of an Alcoholic Family?
Many of them are adults who are disproportionately more likely to have primary relationship problems in their adult lives. Second, they are highly concerned about their own ability to be healthy parents, not wanting to pass these problems on to another generation. Many of them wish to improve the relationships between themselves and their own parents. They are concerned with their own possible alcohol and drug addiction, much more than the general population. Daughters of male alcoholics are much more likely to marry a man who becomes alcoholic and thus to find herself in a position very similar to that of her mother. We still find a lot of concern among adult children of alcoholics about how to intervene to get their parents sober.

What Kinds of Things Are You Discovering That Are Useful to Counselors or Teachers Who Would Come into Contact with Children of Alcoholics?
We are finding to a great extent that when an adult child comes in for help, he or she may have relationship problems, stress problems, parenting problems, or some immediate crisis. We are able to tell counselors and clinicians, "If you see these particular kinds of problems, there is a high probability that the person you are working with may have been raised in an alcoholic family, and thus will have more issues than the one they are currently presenting." We are developing profiles and helping people in the mental health profession to be able to ask the right kinds of questions and get a better picture of family background.

What Would Be Your Advice to a Student Taking This Course Who Has an Alcoholic in the Family?
They should realize that their parent's alcoholism is not their responsibility at two levels: they are not responsible for the creation of the alcoholism, and they are not responsible for getting the alcoholic into treatment. It *is* their responsibility, however, to seek help for themselves. They should work through any kinds of issues they might have about being in a family with an alcoholic and the kind of parenting they received. Being in an alcoholic family makes a person feel very unique and isolated. We advise him or her to break down this barrier of isolation by seeking help, through counseling and joining a support group, such as Al-Anon or Adult Children of Alcoholic Support Groups. ●

still choose to have children. During the decade of the 1970s the average family size fell from 3.6 members to 3.3 members (U.S. Bureau of the Census, 1982). Still, only 5.6 percent of marriages are child-free. Families are getting smaller, but the proportion of families having children has not declined significantly. Birth control has made extramarital sex without pregnancy possible, but young men and women still opt to get married. Even in the *kibbutz*, where the economic ties of the family have been severed for two or more generations, people seek the emotional bonds that are found between long-term lovers and between parents and children. Finally, research continues to show that "married persons, as a whole, report substantially greater global happiness than any category of unmarried persons" (Glenn, 1975, p. 598).

Conclusion

The family has changed and will continue to change, largely due to changes in economic production. For example, the trend toward more women in the labor market brings increased economic independence for women and the use of more professional childrearing. Economics and social pressures often correlate with increases in family violence and high divorce rates. New forms of the family are being developed in response to new societal directions. Perhaps as a result of these changes, individuals are beginning to accept the idea that successful marriages do not just happen, but are the result of work, compromise, understanding, and mutual growth, and can provide a strong base for building a happy, satisfying life.

REVIEW

Summary Questions

1. What are the sociological definitions of marriage and the family?
2. How is romantic love historically and currently related to marriage?
3. How do societies control love and marriage?
4. What social influences are there on the choice of a mate in the United States?
5. What factors did Bert Adams suggest are likely to bring mates together?
6. What are the functions of the family as a social institution?
7. What changes have occurred in family structure worldwide and in the United States?
8. Can the family be replaced?
9. What are the conflict and functionalist views of families and social stratification?
10. What are some of the major disadvantages of the nuclear family?
11. How is violence seen in the family context?
12. What is the divorce situation in the United States today?
13. How does divorce affect the family members?
14. What is Carol Stack's view of the black urban family in poverty?
15. What social factors help marriages to succeed?
16. What new options are open for marriage in contemporary United States?

Summary Answers

1. Marriage is a long-term, socially approved sexual union between two people. Marriages usually form the basis of a family: two or more generations of people related by marriage, birth, or adoption, who live together and share economic resources.
2. Until recently, romantic love was not thought of as a viable reason for marriage. Marriages were arranged according to more socially important variables, such as family importance and genetic traits. In contemporary Western societies, most people marry for "love," although this love must mature into stable caring if the relationship will continue.
3. Societies control love and marriage through child marriage and rules about marriage partners, including kinship ties, locality, and isolation of pubescents.
4. Marriages in the United States show strong association between several cultural factors and who marries whom. These include race, age, religion, social class, education, socialization, and family pressures.
5. Adams suggests the following factors will help bring potential mates together: proximity, propinquity, physical attractiveness, valued surface behaviors, similar interests, favorable reactions of

significant others, rapport, positive response from the other person, value compatability, similarity in physical attractiveness, personality similarity, homogeneity, role compatability, empathy, and lack of stronger alternative attraction.

6. The family controls human reproduction, caring for dependents, socialization of children, and intimate relationships.
7. The shift from an agrarian to industrial base brings about a reemphasis on the nuclear family, with the separation of home and work and the household consuming goods rather than producing them. In the United States, many functions are now taken care of by other institutions, such as mass education, outside social control agents, and institutions for dependent care.
8. Although the Soviet Union, Israel, and the People's Republic of China have all made efforts to reduce the influence of the family, it still persists in all those countries, testifying to its resilience and dominance.
9. Functionalists see the family's role in transmitting social status as natural and valuable. Conflict theorists see it as an agent of inequality and an impediment to reform.
10. The nuclear family has an inherent lack of extended support system, an instability, and a vulnerability to economic stress.
11. Although families are usually considered positive social groups, recent research has uncovered rampant violence in the family, from spouse abuse to sexual and physical assault of children. This violence crosses class boundaries and is found in virtually all types of families.
12. The divorce rate in the United States has grown twenty-twofold in the past century but has begun to slow in the past decade. The United States has the highest divorce rate in the world, and if present trends continue, about 50 percent of marriages beginning in the 1980s will end in divorce.
13. Divorced men and women show great signs of emotional distress: higher suicide rates, loss of jobs, and admission to psychiatric treatment, for example. Divorced mothers will likely struggle against poverty, whereas divorced fathers struggle against loneliness. Children of divorce show symptoms from anxiety to drug abuse and poor school performance. Although these symptoms are greatest during the first two years, some effects of divorce continue into adulthood. In some cases, children who experience family breakup fare as well or better than those who remain in a family where conflict and violence is the rule.
14. Stack defines the black urban family in poverty to include neighbors and part-time fathers. She believes that such families use a system of cooperative domestic exchange that allows them to be active and adapt well to their environment.
15. Marriages have greater chances of succeeding if they score high marks in social and personal resources, satisfaction with life-style, and reward from spousal interaction, including having children over age 6, adequate income, high homogamy, positive parental marriage, support from others, no premarital pregnancy, upward mobility of husband, older age at marriage, higher level of education, and no previous marriages.
16. The options currently being pursued include remaining single or delaying marriage, single parenthood, childless marriages, cohabitation, and dual-career marriages.

Glossary

cohabitation living together without being married

endogamy marriage form in which spouses must come from inside the social group

exogamy marriage form in which spouses must come from outside the social group

extended family a family that includes three or more generations living in close proximity

family two or more people related by marriage, blood, or adoption, who live together and share economic resources for an extended period of time

family of orientation the nuclear family we are born into, our parents and siblings

family of procreation the family we create by marrying and becoming parents

nuclear family a group of at least two adults of opposite sex, sharing a socially approved sexual union and living with their children

marriage a socially approved long-term sexual union

monogamy marriage form in which one person marries one spouse

polyandry marriage form in which one woman marries more than one man

polygamy marriage form in which there are multiple spouses

polygyny marriage form in which one man marries more than one woman

romantic love an irresistible attraction to another who is perceived as nearly perfect and one's lifelong true love

Suggested Readings

Philip Blumstein and Pepper Schwartz. 1983. *American Couples.* New York: William Morrow.

This is an interesting study of the varieties of experience of a sample of 6,000 American relationships, showing the diversity of forms that we might call "couples."

Irwin Garfinkel and Sara McLanahan. 1987. *Single Mothers and Their Children: A New American Dilemma.* Washington, D.C.: The Urban Institute Press.

This book clearly addresses an issue of growing importance in our society and suggests possible solutions that we as a society must consider.

Mark Hutter. 1981. *The Changing Family: Comparative Perspectives.* New York: John Wiley.

Hutter presents families in a cross-cultural perspective. His vignettes of real family life in other societies are fascinating and well worth reading.

Lenore Weitzman. 1985. *The Divorce Revolution: The Unexpected Social Economic Consequences for Women and Children in America.* New York: Free Press.

Weitzman shows the inherent inequalities in the current divorce system, and how it has led to the current "feminization of poverty."

CHAPTER 14

RELIGION

- What Is Religion?
- How Does Religion Affect Society and the Individual?
- How Do Sociologists Classify Religions?
- Close-Up on Theory: Robert Bellah on Religion and Government in the United States
- What Are the Major Religious Faiths?
- What Is Happening in Religion Today?
- Close-Up on Research: Eileen Barker on Cults and Anticults Since Jonestown
- Sociologists at Work: Andrew Greeley Charts Religious Imagery and Social Behavior

How's Your Sociological Intuition?

1. Which of the following properly ranks the groups starting with those Americans *most* objected to as neighbors?
   a. members of religious sects, cults; blacks; religious fundamentalists; unmarried couples
   b. blacks; unmarried couples; members of religious sects, cults; fundamentalists
   c. unmarried couples; blacks; members of religious sects, cults; fundamentalists
   d. fundamentalists; members of religious sects, cults; unmarried couples; blacks
2. Which religion has the most adherents worldwide?
   a. Buddhist
   b. Hindu
   c. Muslim
   d. Christian
3. During the 1970s, church attendance in the United States:
   a. increased about 20 percent
   b. increased about 10 percent
   c. decreased about 10 percent
   d. decreased about 20 percent
4. Which of the following religious preference has grown as a proportion of the United States population during the past forty years?
   a. Jewish
   b. Catholic
   c. Protestant
   d. all the above

Answers

1. a. Cults and sects lead the "most unpopular neighbors" list by a large and widening margin. Some 44 percent of the population would object to having them in the neighborhood, compared to 13 percent for blacks or fundamentalists and 12 percent for unmarried couples.
2. d. Christianity has nearly twice as many adherents as the next largest faith, Islam (Muslims).
3. d. For explanation of this trend, see the "Church Attendance" section of this chapter.
4. b. Catholics grew from 20 to 28 percent of the population from 1947 to 1986, while Protestants dropped 14 points to 57 percent and Jews fell from 5% to 2%. Those reporting some other faith quadrupled from 1 percent in 1947 to 4 percent in 1986.

When You Have Finished Studying This Chapter, You Should Know:

- What is religion?
- According to Durkheim, what are the elements of religion?
- How has religion affected society and the individual?
- What are the functions of religion?
- How is religion related to social conflict?
- How do sociologists classify religions in terms of their beliefs?
- How do sociologists classify religions in terms of their organization?
- What has Robert Bellah to say regarding religion and government in the U.S.?
- What are the major religious faiths in the world, and how are they organized?
- What is happening in religion today?
- What are the trends in religiosity in the United States?
- What sorts of people are more likely to be religious?
- What sort of revival is going on in the United States?
- How is secularization part of the religious scene in the United States?
- In what way is religion becoming polarized in the United States?
- What have sociologists learned about cults?
- How has religion become politicized?
- What is the electronic church and what is its impact?
- How is Andrew Greeley involved in the sociology of religion?

A student relates his experience of participating in a recent occult ritual. The participants, members of a motorcycle club and their friends, locked arms together and circled around a pentagram illuminated only by colored candles. "The guy who was running it wasn't that experienced, and it got out of control. There was an icy cold feeling in the whole room. It wasn't like there was a draft. It was very weird. The cold feeling didn't hit every part of your leg; it felt like it was running through the veins. One of the guys screamed all of a sudden. Somebody panicked and turned on the lights. The guy had had one of those little ankle bracelets made out of a leather strap. It was torn off his leg, and there were scratch marks around his ankle. They weren't deep and yet there was blood. It was black magic witchcraft, and all these people told me they sold their souls to the devil."

In Calcutta, a woman walking past an open drain catches a glimpse of something moving. She finds a man dying and she takes him home to die in peace.

"I live like an animal in the streets, now I will die like an angel," he says.

"How wonderful to see a person die in love with the joy of love, the perfect peace of Christ on his face!" she exclaims.

Agenes Boyaxhi, or Mother Theresa, "heard the call to give up all and to follow him into the slums and to serve among the poorest of the poor." Since 1952 she and her "sisters" have brought love and comfort to 40,000 people abandoned to die in the streets. Mother Theresa has also won the hearts of the American public, who ranked her as the "most admired woman" in 1987 (Gallup, 1987).

These divergent images demonstrate the breadth

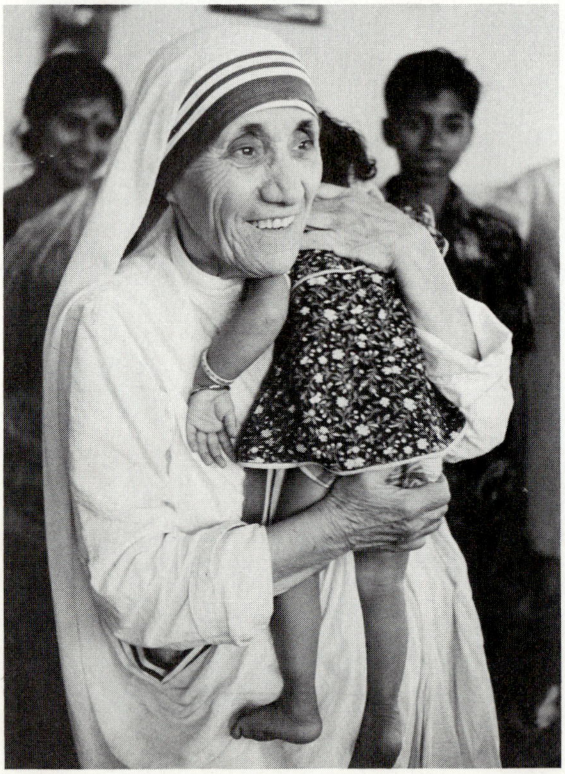

Hope for the hopeless. Answering the call to "follow Him (Christ) to the slums and serve among the poorest of the poor" brought love and comfort to some 40,000 abandoned street people. It also earned Agenes Boyaxhi (Mother Theresa) a Nobel Peace Prize in 1979 and a place in Americans' hearts as the most admired woman of 1987. Here she holds an abandoned handicapped child. *(Jean-Claude Francolon/Gamma Liaison)*

of our current topic: religion. In this chapter we consider massive organizational religions, such as the Roman Catholic Church, and the increasingly popular and controversial sects and cults, which usually involve small numbers of people. We consider the role of religion in the lives of societies and individuals, examine the major types of religions, look at various types of religious activities, and study emerging trends in religions and religiosity.

What Is Religion?

Just what is it that all religions have in common? Although we all sense that religions deal with ultimate realities and often supernatural forces of awesome power, even the experts have trouble agreeing on just what is and what is not religion! One sociology of religion text (McGuire, 1987) approaches the problem by listing ten different definitions created by ten well-known authorities.

Some definitions of religion are substantive, focusing on what religion *is*—for instance, a set of beliefs, particularly beliefs in sacred and supernatural things. Other definitions are functional and focus on what religions *do* in terms of providing a sense of ultimate meaning and a set of values for life. Neither definition is without problems. The substantive approach will sometimes seem too narrow. If, for instance, we define religion as dealing with God or supernatural matters, we leave some "religions" out, such as Confucianism, which does not involve God or the supernatural. But to define religion functionally, for instance, by defining religion as the basis of ultimate meaning, leaves us open to including those things that take the place of conventional religion, such as socialism in states that are explicitly atheistic. Many scholars conclude that religion defies definition; and consequently, some encyclopedias no longer carry articles on religion, opting instead for individual articles on Christianity, Judaism, Islam, and so forth. Because we will be considering both what religion is and what religion does, our broad definition encompasses aspects of substantive and the functional approach. We define ***religion*** *as a system of symbols, beliefs, values, and practices focused on questions of ultimate meaning* (Roberts, 1984; McGuire, 1987; Johnstone, 1983).

DURKHEIM'S CONCEPTS OF THE SACRED AND THE PROFANE

The ***sacred*** *consists of those aspects of culture that are respected by society as ideal and above daily living.* The ***profane*** *consists of those aspects of culture that are part of everyday life or routine experience* (Durkheim, 1912).

Different societies set aside different objects as sacred. For example, cows are highly regarded in India, yet are considered commonplace in the United States. Whatever is labeled by a society as sacred is from then on regarded with awe and respect. To violate a sacred value is to go against a strong, although perhaps unspoken, norm. For example, most people would protest using an abandoned church as a videogame center. Similarly, they would consider leftover pews as unsuitable seating for a disco. Emotional and possibly violent sanctions could follow such a violation. Consider, for example, how people might respond if they saw the country's flag being used as a car-wash rag.

Durkheim suggested that sacred things have seven observable characteristics. First, sacred things are believed to have power or force. Second, this force is ambiguous, being both physical and moral, human and above humanity, positive and negative, and so forth. Third, the sacred is nonutilitarian, which means it is not to be used for ordinary purposes. For instance, many Americans teach their children that it is inappropriate to pray for a new bike. Fourth, the sacred cannot be reduced to numbers; fifth, it does not involve knowledge gained through the senses, but is rather a kind of faith without "knowing" as other things are "known." Sixth, the sacred gives strength and support to its worshipers. Finally, Durkheim stated that the sacred in some way demands moral action from the believer. For example, in a courtroom a witness is told, "Place your hand on the Bible," and is then asked, "Do you solemnly swear to tell the truth, the whole truth, and nothing but the truth, so help you God?" This ritual is based on the assumption that the Bible somehow demands extraordinary moral action, in this case honesty, from the one who touches the sacred book.

RELIGIOUS BELIEFS AND RITUALS. Durkheim believes that there are three elements of every religion: beliefs, rituals, and symbols. *Religious* ***beliefs*** *are shared ideas that explain the sacred objects. Religious* ***rituals*** *are sacred acts that represent the religious beliefs. Religious* ***symbols*** *are objects, images, and words that take meaning from the sacred things that they represent, and that may become sacred themselves after repeated association with the sacred.* For example, Orthodox Jews *believe* that God commanded that they rest on the seventh day of the week—Saturday. They observe *rituals* to show that they are acting on that belief: going to temple for prayer and meditation, lighting the Sabbath candles on Friday at sundown, and cutting the challah bread. The *symbols* of this belief—the yarmulke that is worn by males at the Sabbath meal, the candles that are lit, and the bread that is cut—all hold special meaning for religious Jews who have for centuries practiced their ritual observance of the Sabbath.

Religions have different beliefs, rituals, and symbols, and believers assume that elements of their particular religion are the "right" ones. Muslims believe that there is only one God; Hindus are positive that there are many. Most Christians "keep the Sabbath" on Sunday; Jews observe it on Saturday. New Guinea natives worship the cargo that airplanes bring them as a gift from their ancestors, and it is no less rational to them than the reverence for holy water is to Catholics. Beliefs, rituals, and symbols vary with culture.

How Does Religion Affect Society and the Individual?

MAX WEBER

Max Weber agrees with Marx that religion influences the ways people think and even the course of history (Weber, 1904, 1958). Marx thought capitalism employed religions to support and justify its existence. Weber saw religion as an initiating power that helped shape capitalistic thought in the first place. In his important book, *The Protestant Ethic and the Spirit of Capitalism* (1904), Weber suggested that the values emphasized in the Protestant Reformation helped lead to the development of capitalism. Our "Close-Up on Theory" in Chapter 1 focused on this work.

The Calvinists, an influential early Protestant group, believes that people were predestined (were determined at birth) to be of the Elect, who were destined for heaven, or to be of the damned, who were destined for hell. Calvinists believed that financial and social well-being were indications of being among the Elect. This gave people an extremely strong impetus to succeed in their endeavors. The predominant values of the time grew to be hard work, responsible behavior, and moral living.

Weber contended that this religious emphasis on success encouraged the competition necessary for the growth of the capitalistic system. Furthermore, Protestant believers spent their money carefully, partly because frugality was considered evidence of virtue. When they produced profits, they reinvested in their businesses, again supporting the capitalistic system. The Protestant work ethic fit very well with the spirit of capitalism. In fact, Weber argues that these religious beliefs motivated people to act in a way that transformed the economy. The Protestant ethic contributed strongly to the rise of capitalism, though Weber did not say it was the sole cause.

RELIGION FROM THE FUNCTIONALIST PERSPECTIVE

The fact that religion is a universal institution suggests that it may serve functions that address basic human needs. Although they differ in form and content, the religions of the world do have several characteristics in common which point to their social functions.

ESTABLISHING NORMS AND RITUALS. Religious beliefs tend to reinforce the normative structure of the social community, thereby strengthening the community itself. Religion does this by spelling out what behavior is expected of a believer and by providing negative sanctions to be applied when the norms are violated. Most religions even provide rituals to allow transgressors to express distress at having violated a norm and to atone for this violation. The fact that the community holds common religious beliefs and accepts the religion's sanctions makes it an effective social control mechanism. Furthermore, as the society gathers to perform rites of atonement and other religious rituals, members affirm to themselves and each other their belief in the religion and their continuing sense of community in this belief.

MARKING LIFE EVENTS. Religion also marks major life events of the society's members and reduces the difficulties that surround these events. Most religions have ceremonies which mark a person's birth, coming of age, marriage, and death. These rituals have a dual function. Once again, they bring the society together in recognition of a life change of a member, and they provide definite activities in which the individuals concerned can engage while undergoing the life change. In this way, the rituals alleviate the anxiety surrounding important life events.

For example, in many simple societies the rights and responsibilities of a boy are distinct from those of a man. Often a religious ritual marks the passage from boyhood to manhood. Similarly, when a girl begins to menstruate, she becomes a woman, is often given new clothing or a new hairdo, and assumes new duties. The closest approximations of puberty rituals found in the United States are the reading of the Torah by Jewish boys and girls at age 13 and high school graduation ceremony at approximately age 18, marking the "commencement" of the adult life.

It has been suggested that the *lack* of a puberty rite in the dominant American culture today leads to confusion during the teen years, when youngsters are uncertain whether their rights and responsibilities are those of children or adults. The American emphasis on advanced education—once high school, and now college—leads to delayed adulthood. As a result, young people have the sexual and social desires of adults long before they have a socially approved way of expressing them. It is possible that this extended period of adolescence increases the natural difficulties that surround becoming an adult in any society.

EXPLAINING LIFE'S UNCERTAINTIES. Religion can also serve to reduce anxiety in several other significant areas. A universal attribute of religion is the attempt to define the meaning of existence. People's anxiety about their purpose on earth and their existence after death have spawned many explanations. Although religious stories about the origin of humankind vary from creation by a loving father figure to springing full-grown from the sea, each story is accepted as fact by those whose societies claim them.

Religions also often address themselves to the meaning of the seemingly senseless unhappiness involved in daily living. The hardships and inequities of social life are easier to bear if they appear to have meaning and if there is belief in a better life free of such problems beyond the earthly world. In present-day America, even nonreligious persons partake in religious ceremonies during situations of uncertainty. For example, some people who never enter a church or synagogue at any other time will arrange to be married by clergy, have their baby christened in a church, or have their loved ones buried under the care of some religious group. The ritual nature of these ceremonies is comforting to persons facing a great change with so much uncertainty attached to it. The fact that most religions attempt some explanations of future and present hardships and that they provide rituals to help during transitions may be helpful both in maintaining social order and nurturing individual contentment.

If religion does effectively reduce life's uncertainties, we might expect religious people to exhibit fewer emotional disorders. Recent research confirms that people who are religious have lower rates of psychiatric disorders and lower suicide rates than those who are not (Pope, 1976). We may recall from the "Close-Up on Theory" in Chapter 1, that Durkheim reported finding lower suicide rates for religious people and especially low rates for Catholics. Recent researchers confirm that suicide rates are lower for church members, but they find no Protestant–Catholic difference in suicide rates (Stark et al., 1983; Stack, 1983).

DURKHEIM'S EXPLANATION OF RELIGION. Durkheim believes that the most important function of religion is to make a group more cohesive or tightly knit, to serve as a kind of social glue. Shared religious beliefs and rituals help make the members of a society feel more a part of each other's lives. The rules about behavior that derive from religious beliefs also help keep a society together by limiting the amount of deviance. If, for example, everyone agrees that life is sacred, fewer people will murder someone. Religion also aids people by helping them define a common understanding of why they are here and what their lives mean.

Durkheim was primarily interested in religion as a force that binds people together, but in studying religion he arrived at a controversial explanation for it. Durkheim was convinced there was more to religion than there initially appears to be. On the surface people worship external things, often in the form of superhuman gods. They search for the meaning of life and the answer to questions about right and wrong. In many religions the worshiper seeks immortality. Durkheim observed that worship of the sacred was universal, whereas the form of the sacred varies from society to society. This can be viewed as a clue that these sacred objects—whether gods, animals, plants, or statues—are all actually symbolic representations of something else. Durkheim was convinced that the "something else" that is universally worshiped is society itself: "[R]eligion is . . . a system of ideas with which the individuals represent to themselves the society of which they are members" (Durkheim, 1912, p. 225).

One might argue in the same way that Santa Claus is an idealized symbol of the parents' love, or that God is an idealized representation of society. We can see similarities between God and society: Both offer answers to questions of what is right and wrong, both include superhuman force, and both offer the individual a chance for immortality. (A person like Abraham Lincoln who has been socially influential continues to have influence and be remembered after physical death.)

On the surface Durkheim seems to solve the riddle of why there are so many different forms of religion: Different societies have simply selected different symbols of themselves. All societies need a social glue or solidarity, so all employ religion toward these ends. However, viewing religion as a *purely* social creation leaves some other significant riddles to be answered, such as how was the universe created? What is the meaning of life? What is right and wrong? and What happens to our conscious self after death?

RELIGION FROM THE CONFLICT PERSPECTIVE

From the functionalist perspective, religion serves to create order in society and to help the individual deal with life's uncertainties. From the conflict perspective, religion supports unjust social orders and distracts people from the real problems at hand. Far from an agency of harmony, religion is often the arena of conflict. As Martin Marty observes:

> Every year I write the *Britannica* and *World Book* yearbook stories on world religion. Look up the *World Book* one on religion for the last twenty years and every year there is Marty there saying that this year the Sikhs killed the Hindus, and the Hindus killed the Muslims, and the

> Muslims killed the Buddhists, and the Jews and the Muslims are fighting, and in Northern Ireland the Catholics and the Protestants are fighting, and some editor sends back the first draft and says, "Are you sure you want to file this under religion? It looks more like war!" That's what's happening around the world. People . . . don't become religious in order to kill other people. They come for opposite reasons, for solace, comfort and belonging to something. That's why you're religious. But when there is conflict, religion often heats it up (Marty, 1987).

KARL MARX. Karl Marx saw religion in industrial society as a force standing in the way of social change. He believed that the function of religion in his time was to make the stratification system of the society sacred, and that religion was a tool used by the dominant class to keep the lower classes in line. As he expressed it, "Religion is the sigh of the oppressed creature, the sentiment of a heartless world, and the soul of soulless conditions. It is the opium of the people" (Marx, 1848).

Marx observed that a society's dominant religion is usually that of the society's economically dominant members. Often this religion emphasizes that hard work leads to success, and that earthly pleasures are not as important as salvation in the afterlife. These doctrines reinforce the belief that if an individual's life circumstances are not pleasant, he or she should work harder. Furthermore, people should not really be concerned about earthly riches, because they will be rewarded for hard work in heaven. To Marx, these ideas were beneficial to the ruling and managing classes, because they served to keep downtrodden people satisfied with their life situation by urging them to accept inequality in this world. When Marx called religion the opiate of the masses, he meant that, like the drug opium, religion distracts people from reality—in this case their oppression.

Marx called for the abolition of religion. He thought that without religious beliefs the masses could understand more easily that they were being oppressed and would unite to overcome their oppressors. Obviously, Marx's revolution has not become a worldwide reality, nor has religion been abolished, although Marxist states, like the Soviet Union, do officially discourage the practice of religion.

Religion often serves as a tool of the elites in their exploitation of the masses. In virtually all stratified societies, the priesthood and the military are ranked at the top of the social order. This is no mere coincidence. This partnership poses awesome potential to dominate society. The military leaders contribute brute strength, and the religious leaders shape the people's thoughts and feelings: The military can enforce the will of the religious leaders and the religious leaders can legitimate the conduct of the military. What we find in many societies, except the most primitive, is rather extreme inequality, which is fostered by religious doctrine and enforced by military means (Roberts, 1984).

Karl Marx and Frederich Engels were the first to reveal how religion often sustains the social-class inequality that occasionally breaks forth into open-class conflict. Religion serves to legitimate other forms of oppression as well. Racism and slavery have often been justified in religious terms. Similarly, most of the major religions of the world strongly support patriarchy, or sexism (Marx and Engels, 1848).

Religion is at least a contributor, if not the direct cause, of some of the most bitter conflicts in the world. For decades Protestants and Catholics in Northern Ireland have battled each other in a protracted form of guerrilla warfare. In the Middle East, Israel and neighboring Arab States contend over land, particularly Jerusalem, which has profound religious significance to Jews, Muslims, and Christians.

Nor is life always harmonious within religions. Shortly after its founding, the Christian Church split

The start of capitalism? Early Protestants such as Martin Luther and John Calvin protested Roman Catholic doctrine with no explicit intention of changing the entire social economic order of society. Yet Max Weber asserts that the Protestant ethic provided fertile soil in which the spirit of capitalism grew. Here Martin Luther nails fundamental Protestant claims to the door of a Catholic church. (*Bettmann Archive*)

between the Roman Catholic Church and the Eastern Orthodox Church. Later, in the seventeenth century, Protestants split Roman Catholicism. The division continues even into the present, with disputes among the various Baptist conventions and even within the largest, the Southern Baptist convention.

Religion has often served as a tool of liberation. Great Britain abolished slavery before the United States did, partly through the efforts of Wilberforce, the captain of a slave ship, who "came to Christ" in the midst of a voyage in which he was carrying slaves from Africa to the Americas. He wrote the familiar song *Amazing Grace* about this experience and became the champion of antislavery forces in England. Similarly, the abolitionist movement in the United States was fostered through the militancy of Quakers, who established the illegal underground railway as a means of escape for slaves.

The Civil Rights Movement in the United States was a movement founded by a group of ministers, including Martin Luther King, Jr., Ralph David Abernathy, Andrew Young, and Jesse Jackson. The U.S. clergy was influential in exposing atrocities in Vietnam. Quakers risked imprisonment by sending aid to both sides in the Vietnam War.

In present times, religious activists are highly visible—calling for an end to apartheid in South Africa, endorsing nuclear disarmament, and offering asylum to those who have escaped from the oppressive conditions and conflict of El Salvador. Although religion has often played a role in terrible exploitation, it has also often been the inspiration of great acts of courage. Many conservative Americans cheered Alexander Solzhenitsyn's heroic portrayal of life in a Soviet concentration camp. And the same religiosity that moved him to endure these hardships and risk exposing them, also moved him to condemn his haven in the West: "The entire twentieth century is being sucked into the vortex of atheism and self-destruction" (quoted in *Time;* May 23, 1983).

RELIGION FROM THE SYMBOLIC INTERACTIONIST PERSPECTIVE

Religion has not been a cultural issue with sociologists of the symbolic interactionist perspective, but it is an important aspect in the symbolic life of society. We may recall in Chapter 1 the symbolic interactionists' focus on how social settings are defined. Symbolic interactionists point out that he who defines a situation controls it.

In his classic work, Max Weber, the pioneering German sociologist, discussed how Protestantism redefined reality and created massive social change. In spite of Marx's classical observations on religion and the rather obvious links between religion, oppression, and conflict, most of the work in the sociology of religion avoids dealing with these issues, choosing instead to focus on the functions of society, the classification of types of religions and religious organizations, and religious movements, as well as religious participation (Johnstone, 1983; Stark and Bainbridge, 1985; McGuire, 1987; K. Roberts, 1984).

How Do Sociologists Classify Religions?

TYPES OF RELIGIOUS BELIEF SYSTEMS

Every religion, as Durkheim noted, holds something to be sacred, yet there the similarity seems to end. In parts of India holy rats still are worshiped in the temples. The Dayaks of Borneo took it for granted that rice has a soul that needs to be honored in order to prevent crop failures. The ancient Greeks had a pantheon of sacred gods and goddesses to be worshiped, though most people today believe there is just one God. Traditionally the Japanese worshiped ancestral spirits. In much of the Orient sacredness is vested in certain ethical principles. Many primitive people believe nature to be animated by spirits such as the bear spirit or the wolf spirit. The Melanesians believe in none of these manifestations of the sacred; they believe that sacredness resides in an impersonal force.

One way to organize the wide variety of religions in the world is to classify them according to what they hold sacred. The following typology defines five major types of religion according to that idea (McGee, 1975).

Simple supernaturalism *or* ***animatism*** *is a form of religion found in many simple societies that emphasizes a belief in an impersonal supernatural force but does not specifically define certain gods or spirits.* Instead, participants believe that there is a force one must worship in order to be successful in battle and to secure good crops.

The Melanesians call this force *mana.* A hunter's success is influenced by whether he can attract the mana to his weapon. Although not at all personal, the force does respond to the adherent's worship, which often takes place at altars built for this purpose.

Animism *is the belief that the sacred resides in spirits found in people or other natural phenomena, such as the wind and the rain.* These spirits are sometimes appeased through ritual or thwarted through magic. The spirits may also carry good or bad messages.

Traditional Shintoism of Japan is an example of animism in which the spirits of one's ancestors are the object of worship. The Penobscot Indians of New England also practiced ancestor worship. Other religions that believe in spirits or ghosts hold that they may be found in nonhuman forms.

Totemism *is a form of animism in which an animal or plant is worshiped as a god and ancestor.* Durkheim believed that totemism was the first form of religion (Durkheim, 1912). The totem is usually an object of supreme importance to the tribe, often a major food source or the most dangerous animal in the environment.

The Dayaks of India practiced totemism in their belief that rice has a soul. The Koryaks of Asia believed bears to have a sacred quality.

Theism *is a form of religion involving belief in god.* ***Polytheism,*** *belief in many gods,* usually involves one central god and several gods of lesser influence. For example, Hindus worship five gods, whom they revere as reflections of the sacred principle of *Brahman,* or "oneness." The ancient Greeks, Romans, and Aztecs practiced polytheism. Only three modern religions—Judaism, Christianity, and Islam—adhere to ***monotheism,*** *or belief in one God.* In terms of numbers, however, these three religions encompass the largest number of worshipers. (See Table 14.1.)

TABLE 14.1 Selected Principal Religions of the World

Religions	Membership
Total Christian	1,644,396,500
Roman Catholic	926,194,600
Protestant	372,016,400
Eastern Orthodox	160,063,500
Anglicans	69,971,500
Other	156,150,500
Muslim	860,388,300
Hindu	655,695,200
Buddhist	309,626,100
Confucian	5,914,400
Jewish	18,075,400
Total Membership	3,494,095,900
Total Population	4,997,609,000

SOURCE Reprinted with permission from the 1988 *Britannica Book of the Year,* copyright 1988, Encyclopedia Britannica Inc., Chicago, Illinois, p. 303

Over one-half the world's people are members of the nine largest religions of the world. Christianity, the largest, is almost twice as large as the Islam (Muslim) faith. Christianity is also the most evenly distributed over the continents, with no continent having more than 32 percent of the world population of Christians. Judaism, like Christianity, has spread around the world, with the largest concentration (45 percent) of Jews in North America. The other religions are based primarily in Asia: 69 percent of all Muslims and 99 percent of all Hindus, Buddhists, and Confucians are found in Asia.

Ethical religions *are those that do not worship a god as such, but rather promote a moral code or belief.* For example, a Buddhist's ideal is to achieve a kind of perfect moral state by following the "way" of Buddha, which involves study and meditation as well as acting in morally right ways. Similarly, the religions of Taoism and Confucianism stress the sacredness of certain ethical principles rather than spirits or forces.

TYPES OF ORGANIZATION WITH RESPECT TO SOCIETY AND OTHER RELIGIONS

We have just considered five types of religions based on differences in beliefs. We can also distinguish religions in terms of how the religious groups or organizations relate to the broader society and other religious groups.

Those religious organizations that are most thoroughly integrated are the ecclesia. An ***ecclesia*** *is a religious organization that is connected to and supported by the government and includes most of the members of the society.* In short, the ecclesia represents a virtual religious monopoly wherein the state recognizes one official religion, supports it by force and taxation, and requires citizens to participate at least to the extent of public funding. Understandably the ecclesia often suppresses the expression of other religious faiths. Through much of its history Christianity has taken this form. Ethiopia became the first Christian ecclesia when the Queen was converted to Christianity in the first century B.C., but in earlier times there were ecclesia as well. In Judaism, Moses was both the religious leader and the military leader. In current times ecclesia-like relations are still common. Tax dollars support the Lutheran Church, and only the Lutheran Church, in Norway. The Queen of England is the nominal head of state and highest official in the Anglican Church, while members of the House of Lords are also bishops in that church.

We are perhaps more familiar with **denominations,** which are religious organizations that compete for members within a society and are not directly connected to or supported by the government. As Table 14.1 indicates, Roman Catholicism is the largest single denomination in the United States today. Whereas none of the denominations enjoys a political monopoly, all operate on the shelter of tax exemptions, which is an indication that though we have, to some extent, separated church and state, our government still indirectly supports religious organizations.

As we move further from the mainstream experience, we encounter the sect. ***Sects*** *are small religious groups, usually marginal to society, in which lay members often replace a full-time professional pastorate.* Sects usually split off from denominations because they feel the

Sects such as the ultraorthodox Jews of the Lubavitcher sect shown at a 1987 gathering in Brooklyn, N.Y., emphasize a return to a more authentic version of their faith. Such authenticity often translates into plain clothes and facial hair, which we see in abundance in the photograph. (*AP/Wide World Photos*)

denomination has strayed too far from the original teachings of the religion. Members tend to see themselves as a fellowship of the elect—as true believers. Sects tend to emphasize spontaneity in religious expression; they deemphasize organizational authority and instead stress democracy. They often deliberately remain small and employ lay leaders. Outwardly they tend toward purity of doctrine, traditional ethics, and otherworldly issues such as, for Christian sects, heaven and hell. Usually the sect draws its members through conversion rather than birth, and often, though not always, from among those with less education and income than average.

The Puritans who left England seeking a truer expression of Christianity are an example of a sect, though they, like many sects, have grown into the denomination known today as the Congregational Church. Early Quakers would fit this category as well. Their uncompromising reading of the Bible caused many of them to be imprisoned for refusing to join the military or swear oaths. The Amish, most of whom live in parts of Pennsylvania, Ohio, Michigan, and Indiana, seek to live according to the Bible, which they believe calls for them to wear simple clothing, and, among some Amish, retain horse-and-buggy technology rather than tractors and cars. The part of New York City where diamonds are traded and several Brooklyn neighborhoods feature Hasidic Jews, the male members noticeable in their beards and side curls, plain black suits, and broad-brimmed hats. They believe they are being more nearly true to Judaism than other branches, such as Reformed congregations that have relaxed some of the more stringent requirements of the Old Testament. By their nature, sects are marginal groups, and we often find them in out-of-the-way places, sometimes meeting in temporary quarters and often not particularly visible to the community around them, unless, like the Amish and Hasidim, their faith leads them to reject conventional styles of clothing (Roberts, 1984).

Cults are a much more widely discussed phenomenon, and in a sense they are a recent addition to our set of types. Organizationally, cults are often similar to sects, but where sects typically center around a movement back toward religious origins, cults build on a new claim of revelation. For the sake of definition, we will define a ***cult*** *as a religious organization which claims a unique new revelation.* Cults usually arise around a dynamic leader who claims special spiritual knowledge. Mormonism, which describes itself as Christian (the Church of Jesus Christ of Latter-Day Saints) fits the definition because founder Joseph Smith claimed to have discovered and translated new scripture. Sometimes a cult leader directly or indirectly claims to be God. Jim Jones, founder of the People's Temple and leader of the mass suicide/homocide of about 1,000 followers, claimed greater spiritual authority than the Bible. Sun Myung Moon, leader of the Unification Church, encourages members to see him as the Christ (Roberts, 1984).

Whereas cults have often claimed to bring believers closer to God, we see in recent times a rapid growth of cults that explicitly reject not only conventional religion but God, as God is commonly understood. Melton's exhaustive tracking of some 484 cults during this century reveals that the most common focus of cults that emerged in the most recent period studied is Satan, Witches, and Magic. The distinction here is that instead of claiming a truer path to God, these cults are actively seeking to serve Satan, God's archenemy. This change in the complexion of cults combined with the notorious mass suicide/homocides within the Jim Jones cult helps to explain the public's growing distrust of them. In Gallup surveys the public has voiced a strong and growing objection to having cults and sects as neighbors. Some 44 percent said they would not like cults or sects as neighbors in 1987, compared to 30 percent as recently as 1981 (Gallup, March 1987b; Melton, 1978).

Classification of religious groups can help us to realize the variety of religious practices and experiences by understanding the organizational context in which they take place. We can expect members of ecclesias to act and be treated quite differently from members of sects or cults regardless of the personality traits of the members and leaders or the content of the religion. Members of ecclesias tend to be well-accepted conformists, whereas members of sects and cults are likely to be rejected nonconformists. But the typology also lets us understand the development of large-scale religious phenomena in general. Sects tend to grow toward denominations and eventually ecclesias; cults tend to grow toward entirely new religions (Nelson, 1968).

Let us consider religion in the United States in light of these concepts about organization. Quite clearly, we have a wide variety of denominations, sects, and cults. Our government does not formally endorse or support any one of these as the "official" religion. Instead, Americans often point with pride to their Constitutional-given right to freedom of religion and their formal separation of church from state. The United States is not an ecclesia. But in the following "Close-Up on Theory," Robert Bellah suggests that though we may have formally separated the organized church from our organized government or state, we have actually embedded religious ideas and beliefs in our government.

CLOSE-UP on • *THEORY* •

Robert Bellah on Religion and Government in the United States

The Theorist and the Setting

Unlike his predecessors Karl Marx and Emile Durkheim, who stressed the mythical nature of religion, Robert Bellah takes religion as a genuine encounter between individuals in society and a transcendent God. Bellah studied at the graduate level at Harvard and is on the faculty of the University of California at Berkeley, widely regarded as one of the finest sociology departments in the United States.

Bellah differs from many contemporary sociologists in assuming a literal interpretation of religion and in researching without complicated mathematical techniques. This has left Bellah open to attack by those who do not take religion seriously and who believe in a quantitative approach to understanding the human situation.

In 1974 Bellah received the honor of being appointed head of a new school of social science at the prestigious Institute for Advanced Study at Princeton University, once Albert Einstein's academic home.

The Theorist's Goal

In this essay Bellah raises the issue of how the state and religion are related in the United States.

Concepts and Propositions

Bellah presents two major propositions.

Proposition 1: "There exists alongside of and . . . different . . . from the churches an elaborate and well-institutionalized civil religion in America" (1967, p. 1).

Bellah uses the word *church* in the conventional sense to refer to religious organizations like the Roman Catholic Church. He acknowledges that in the United States there is a real separation of church and state, insofar as there is no official denomination and citizens have a right to choose their own religious affiliation. However, he contends that there is a clear "religion—or perhaps . . . religious dimension" to the state, which "has its own seriousness and integrity and requires the same care in understanding that any other religion does. . . . This public religious dimension is expressed in a set of beliefs, symbols and rituals that I am calling the American civil religion" (p. 1).

In Bellah's view the central belief of the civil religion is belief in God. In spite of the separation of church and state, this belief recurs with regularity and prominence throughout U.S. history. The Declaration of Independence mentions God in four places. Virtually all the presidents in major addresses refer to God. Currency carries the phrase "In God We Trust." The pledge of allegiance includes the phrase "under God." Presidents swear an oath of office before the people and God.

This clear and central belief in God within the ideology of the state is not a simple reflection of Christianity that dominates organized religion in this country. Indeed, Christ is not mentioned in any of these contexts. There is apparently a civil God of the civil religion, who is not in conflict with the God of the noncivil religions. As President Eisenhower rather bluntly put it: "Our government makes no sense unless it is founded in a deeply felt religious faith—and I don't care what it is."

Like all religions, the American civil religion has its own rituals, among them the holiday of Thanksgiving, which was proclaimed by Congress to be a "day of public thanksgiving and prayer" and official holidays like Memorial Day, Independence Day, Veterans' Day and the birthdays of George Washington and Abraham Lincoln. Another ritual is the inauguration of a president. In Bellah's opinion "it reaffirms, among other things, the religious legitimation of the highest political authority" (p. 4). Bellah suggests that when such civil observances are associated so strongly with God, they become quasi-religious observances with sacred values built in and revered.

In his second major proposition, Bellah rejects the idea that this civil religion might be just the rhetoric of political speechwriters. On the contrary, he argues that the civil religion provides the basis for the political structure.

Proposition 2: "the religious dimension in political life . . . not only provides a grounding for the rights of man, which makes any form of political absolutism illegitimate, it also provides a transcendent goal for the political process" (p. 4).

The ways in which great political figures in U.S. history have mentioned God support Bellah's claim. The Declaration of Independence states that the "laws of Nature and of Nature's God" decree that "all men are endowed by their Creator with certain unalienable rights" and suggests that the act of revolution is subject to the judgment of the "Supreme Judge of the world." In his first inaugural address President Washington stated: "Of all the dispositions and habits that lead to political prosperity, religion and morality are indispensable supports." President Lincoln related the Civil War to the will of God: "American slavery is one of those offenses which, in the providence of God, must needs come, but which, having continued through His appointed time, He now wills to remove, and He gives to both North and South this terrible war as the woe due to those by whom the offense came."

President John Kennedy clearly stated in his inaugural address the dependence of the political order on the religious order: "The rights of man come not from the generosity of the state but from the hand of God." President Lyndon Johnson spoke for a strong voting-rights bill by arguing that it was consistent with the will of God. "Above the pyramid on the great seal of the United States it says in Latin, 'God has favored our undertaking.' God will not favor everything that we do. It is rather our duty to divine his will. I cannot help but believe that He truly understands and that He really favors the undertaking that we begin here tonight."

Interpretation

Bellah's views are profoundly different from those of most sociologists of religion, and a close examination of them helps to explain why his views have been controversial among his colleagues and scientists from other disciplines. Both the structural-functionalists and the conflict theorists have dealt with religion as though it were manmade myth. Bellah takes the more theological position that religion is man's search for God and God's search for man. He takes seriously the idea that God acts in the lives of human beings, and that even modern states like the United States, which at times appear very secular, are actually firmly committed to an attempt to comply with the will of God.

This view implies there are important limits to the powers of science, especially to the ability of social science to predict behavior. A view of reality that assumes an active God is inconsistent with the scientific notion that all things including human beings have a fundamentally predictable nature. Because science cannot predict that which is unpredictable, many scientists would rather not believe in unpredictable gods or humans. To those who believe that science is the one true way to knowledge, people like Bellah are a nuisance or an embarrassment.

But Bellah performs a valuable service by redirecting attention to the issue of God. Durkheim relegates the idea of God to the status of being just one local form of religion, and Marx for different reasons suggests that God is myth. Much of contemporary science and sociology rules out the idea of a real God, but this leaves some questions about the meaning of existence. Bellah has reintroduced a traditional and still plausible answer to those issues.

Questions

1. Is the civil religion a serious religion or simply rhetoric? What evidence is there that the rhetoric is backed up by observable behavior?
2. Does the nondenominational nature of the civil religion make it more meaningful or more meaningless? Why?
3. Political leaders have often invoked God's will to justify political action. Do you think such justifications are sincere? Give examples to support your position.

SOURCE Robert N. Bellah. 1967. "Civil religion in America." *Daedalus,* 96 (Winter): 1–21.

What Are the Major Religious Faiths?

We can better understand the major religions of the world and the way sociologists approach them by considering five of the major religions of the world, their types of belief systems, and their organization (Johnstone, 1983; Roberts, 1984).

CHRISTIANITY

As Table 14.1 shows, Christianity is nearly twice as large as the next largest religion, which is Islam, the faith of Muslims. Christianity centers around Jesus of Nazareth whose birthdate marks the beginning of the calendar used in much of the world. Jesus, who lived until his mid-30s, claimed to be the only begotten Son of God. He taught that anyone who believed in him would gain everlasting life. He also taught that the greatest obligations are to love God and love one's neighbor, even to the point of dying for them.

Christianity is distinctly monotheistic in type, but organizationally it has taken and takes several forms. The Christian religion has repeatedly broken into denominations, the largest and oldest of which are the Roman Catholic and Eastern Orthodox, which trace their histories to Biblical times. Protestantism diverged from Catholicism in the sixteenth century. Throughout its history Christianity often has taken the form of an ecclesia. Ethiopia was the first nation to adopt Christianity as the official religion. Rome later became "Christian" by governmental decree. Most of Europe during the Middle Ages involved official religions or ecclesias. The United States was an innovator in separating organized religion from organized government. Yet the separation is far from complete. The state, for instance routinely grants clergy the right to make legally binding marriage contracts between citizens. In some nations, such as England and Norway, Christianity is still the official religion. However, in many parts of the world it is one religion among others.

ISLAM

Islam, the religion of Muslims, is the second largest faith in the world. Islam began with the teachings of Mohammed, who lived in the Arabian peninsula in the sixth century. Mohammed's religious authority rested on his visions, which included visitation by the angel Gabriel, who delivered the words of God now recorded in the Koran, the Islamic holy book. Islam, like Christianity, is a monotheistic faith; but Muslims view Jesus as a prophet of lesser stature than Mohammed. Whereas they honor Jesus as a great teacher, Muslims reject the claims that he rose from the dead and that he is the only begotten son of God and savior of sinful mankind. Islam teaches that people should follow the guidance of the Koran to become sinless and thus go to Paradise rather than Hell after death.

In principle, Islam holds that the state and religion should be one, which is, of course, an ecclesia. In practice, Islam divides into two major denominations within which congregations are very egalitarian. In this regard Islam takes on one of the major features of a sect, the rejection of central organizational authority figures.

HINDUISM

Hinduism, the third largest religious faith, is polytheistic in type. Hinduism seems to be a blend of the Vedic religion of Aryan invaders of India in 1500 B.C. and the beliefs and practices of natives. The holy works include stories about various gods. Although Hinduism is found nearly exclusively in India, it is not an official religion or ecclesia. In fact, it is organized only in the loosest sense of the word. Some rituals require the supervision of a special religious caste, the Brahmins. Hinduism has virtually no common set of beliefs but, instead, a vast array of sects. What they have in common is a shared belief that there is one divine principle and that the many gods are only aspects of that unity. Although life forms may appear as separation from the divine, they are various aspects of the divine. Unless one is pure in acts and thought, one will be repeatedly reborn into different life forms.

BUDDHISM

Founded in 525 B.C. by Gautama Siddhartha, Buddhism, the fourth largest religion in the world, represents the ethical or abstract ideal type of religion. As such, it has no belief in the supernatural. Siddhartha's religious authority rests on his achievement of enlightenment through intense meditation. His teachings are written in the Tripitaka, and followers believe that life is misery and decay, with no ultimate reality. Like Hinduism, Buddhism teaches that people are reincarnated in various lifetimes and varying life-forms. One escapes the cycle through right meditation and deeds. Organizationally, Buddhism exhibits lay-oriented, democratic sects as opposed to ecclesia or authoritarian denominations.

CONFUCIANISM

Born in 551 B.C. in China during a period of social upheaval, Confucius became China's most influential

Intense meditation, but not belief in a god, characterizes the Buddhist faith, which is the fourth largest religion in the world. These monks and nuns are about to begin a pilgrimage to raise money to finance a lamasery. (*Reuters/Bettmann Newsphotos*)

historical figure. His teachings shaped Chinese thought and daily action for the following 2,500 years. Three hundred years after Confucius' death, Confucianism became the official state religion, and until early this century one had to demonstrate proficiency in Confucian literature to work for the Chinese government.

Confucian morality emphasizes the perfectability of all persons and the desirability of jen, variously interpreted as love, human-heartedness, and virtue. Throughout its history various other sages have elaborated on Confucianism. Beginning about 100 A.D. Buddhists began to convert some Chinese, but a neo-Confucian movement around 960 A.D. effectively re-established the supremacy of Confucianism.

Confucianism does not teach of a god or gods, or of a creation or afterlife. Instead the religion emphasizes right social conduct and especially prizes practicing it through virtuous political leadership.

Confucianism influenced the cultures of Korea, Japan, and Vietnam, but it has declined somewhat following China's confrontation with the West. In 1911, with the establishment of the Republic of China, the state no longer officially embraced Confucianism, though its long-standing cultural influence continues even under the present Marxist-socialist regime.

JUDAISM

Although small when compared to other major world religions, Judaism, the religion of the Hebrews, has perhaps the clearest origins of all. Judaism as a religion begins with God contacting a man named Abram, whom God renames Abraham. God tells Abraham, "I am establishing my covenant between myself and you and your descendants after you throughout their generations as a perpetual covenant, to be God to you and your descendants." God promises the land of Canaan for all time, enters into dialogue with Abraham, and tests his loyalty by demanding that Abraham sacrifice his son Isaac. When Abraham prepares to follow the command God interrupts him, saying "Now I know you fear God." God also contacts Abraham's grandson, Jacob, telling him he shall be called Israel, the name to which Israelis trace their nationality. God honors his promise of land to Abraham by leading Moses, Abraham's descendant, and the Israelites out of Egyptian bondage and into the promised land. Later the Israelites build a massive temple and select a king, but they begin to allow their religious beliefs to be corrupted by outside beliefs.

About 2,800 years ago, Jewish prophets begin to predict that a messiah, or great leader, would arise to establish a holy community. About 200 years ago, Jews largely abandoned their belief that a messiah was coming to seek personal and national fulfillment on Earth during their own lifetimes. One Jewish movement, the Zionists, established the contemporary state of Israel in 1948, mainly to restore a Jewish homeland to survivors of the Holocaust of World War II. Few Jews presently live in Europe; most of the world's Jewish population lives in Israel, the Soviet Union, and the United States.

Judaism teaches about a single true god, creator of the universe, who comes looking for humanity. Contemporary Jews' view of themselves as God's chosen people often is described as the idea that God chose them to follow his commandments and to act as witness for all the peoples of the world. For Jews God's commandments have come in various forms. Some were delivered to Moses on stone tablets. Other rules governing obligations to God and fellow humans are included in the Old Testament and traditional Jewish laws and the commentaries on those laws: the Talmud.

Some religions have focused on other-worldly concerns, but Judaism emphasizes the here and now. Even during the 2,000-year period during which Jews awaited a savior they conceived of that figure as one who would establish an ideal society through a political kingdom. The notion of an afterlife per se plays no role in the beliefs of Judaism.

Judaism has proven to have enormous durability. For most of their history the Jews have not freely held a territory. For only relatively short periods has Judaism been the dominant faith of a society. One of those periods has been the past few decades since the establishment of modern Israel in 1948.

From the root of Judaism grew the two largest religions in the world. Both Jesus of Nazareth, the central figure in Christianity, and Mohammed, the central figure of Islam, trace their heritage to Abraham.

INTERPRETATION

We might note that none of the large world religions take the form of simple supernaturalism, animism, or totemism. These beliefs are found primarily in the relatively smaller and less technologically advanced societies which typically practice hunting and gathering, as opposed to agriculture or industrialism (Johnstone, 1983; Roberts, 1984). Also, none of these large religions appears from the inside to be a cult, but here there is an important lesson. A cult is a religious organization at odds with the dominant religion, and we have here discussed the most dominant religions of the world. The concept of cult takes on meaning only in relation to another religion. Thus in considering a society where Christianity is the dominant faith, a religion like Mormonism is a cult. The claim that Mormonism offers a unique new revelation in the form of tablets from God received and translated by Joseph Smith places believers at odds with Christians. Similarly, from the perspective of Orthodox Judaism, Christianity would itself fit the definition of a cult, since believers in Christianity take the books of the New Testament to be new and unique revelation from God. Or, for another example, when the Krishna Consciousness society seeks to operate in the U.S. culture, it can properly be regarded as a cult, though they are the dominant religion when practiced in India. From the perspective of a believer, a cult represents a false religion. From the sociological perspective, a cult is a dissonant belief system within a particular cultural setting. Sociology usually does not judge the truth of religious beliefs.

What Is Happening in Religion Today?

RELIGIOSITY IN THE UNITED STATES TODAY

How religious are you? Are Americans more religious than Europeans? Are the rich more religious than the poor? Is the United States growing more or less religious?

MEASURING RELIGIOSITY. All these questions presume that we can measure ***religiosity,*** or *the importance of religion to the life of a group or individual.* Sociologists have for decades been debating how best to do this. Roberts (1984) suggests that religious commitment is best measured in terms of two components: religious consciousness and religious participation. Religious consciousness refers to the importance an individual places on religion in his or her life. How important is religion to the person's sense of identity—intellectually, effectively, and behaviorally? He suggests that religious consciousness can be measured through three questions:

1. According to whatever standards are important to you personally, how religious would you say you are?
2. Overall, would you say religion is a positive or a negative force in making your life worthwhile?
3. To what extent would you say religious faith helps you in making daily decisions you have to make in life?

Religious participation refers to the respondent's involvement in explicitly religious behavior: ritual attendance, participation in other group-sponsored activities, and devotional behavior. Again, it is measured through responses to three questions:

1. How many worship activities do you attend in a typical month?
2. How many church organizations or activities do you participate in regularly?
3. Do you ever do any of the following:
   - **a.** pray privately outside church?
   - **b.** say grace before meals?
   - **c.** read the Bible outside of church?

Most sociologists studying religiosity have focused on the United States; consequently, their measures have sometimes taken into account the dominance of Christianity. While we could use most of the above questions in other cultural settings, the last question assumes a Christian setting. More general measures of religiosity must be developed and employed to make comparisons between religions.

RELIGIOUS CONSCIOUSNESS. For over half a century, the Gallup organization has polled public opinion and often included questions like these that can help us to discern trends and identify which sorts of people are more religious.

Americans typically define religion as important in their lives. (See Figure 14.1) As of 1986, 55 percent said religion is very important, compared with 30 percent who said it is fairly important and 14 percent saying religion is not very important. The latter proportion has nearly tripled from its 5 percent level in 1952. The proportion of those saying religion is very important has fallen from 75 percent in 1952 to 55 percent in 1986. As Table 14.2 indicates, it fell faster for Catholics than for Protestants. Women are more religious in this regard than men, though both are growing less so. These drops in religiosity tended to occur in the 1950s through the mid-1970s and then level off (Gallup, 1987).

Do Americans believe religion can answer today's problems? Again we see a drop from the 1950s, when 81 percent thought so, to 1986, when only 57 percent thought so. At the present women find religion more effective in solving problems than men did, and older people found religion more helpful than younger ones. The South was the most religious region in this regard, whereas the East was least. Blacks are more religious than whites; the less educated more so than the more educated. Republicans lead Democrats, and the poor

TABLE 14.2 Comparative Religiosity of Various Segments of the Public

Percent Saying Religion Is Very Important in My Life

Sex					
Men	1986	45%	Women	1986	64%
	1952	68%		1952	79%
Denomination					
Protestants	1986	61%	Catholics	1986	52%
	1952	76%		1952	83%

Percent Saying Religion Can Answer Today's Problems

Sex			
Men	50%	Women	65%
Age			
18-29	54%	50+	61%
30-49	56%		
Region			
East	49%	South	73%
Midwest	52%	West	51%
Race			
Whites	55%	Blacks	77%
Non-whites	72%		
Education			
College Graduates	47%	High School Graduates	61%
College Incomplete	61%	Not High School Graduates	59%
Politics			
Republicans	60%	Independents	56%
Democrats	58%		
Household Income			
$40,000+	48%	$15,000-24,999	57%
$25,000-39,999	59%	Under $15,000	65%
Denomination			
Protestants	65%	Catholics	50%

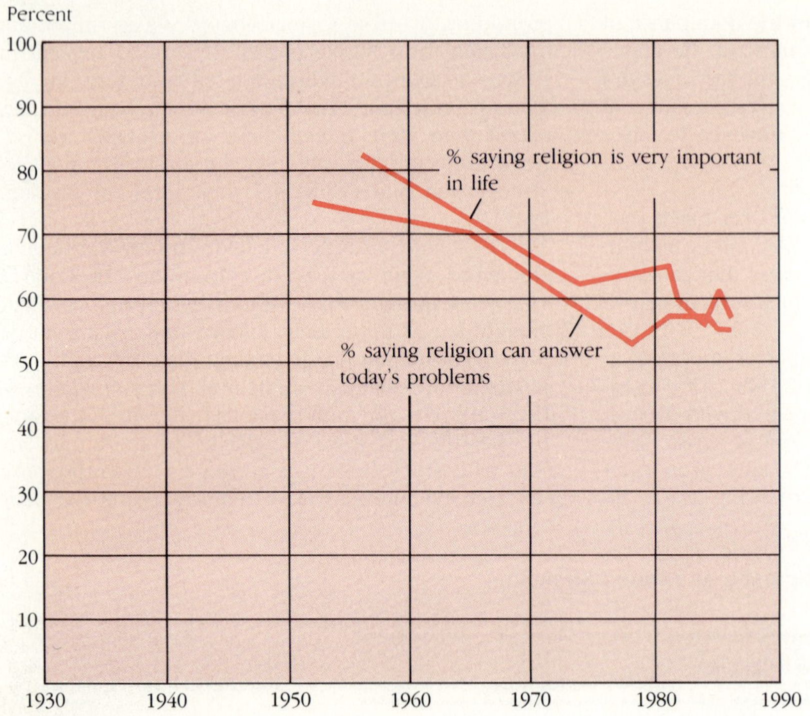

FIGURE 14.1 Religious Consciousness in the United States. Religious consciousness, as measured by the proportion of the population saying "religion is very important in life" or agreeing that "religion can answer today's problems," declined in the 1950s and 1960s. During the 1970s and 1980s, this sort of religious consciousness remained relatively constant.

lead the rich. Again, Protestants measure higher than Catholics. In Roberts' terms, religious consciousness has declined.

RELIGIOUS PARTICIPATION. Let's look at the other form of religiosity—religious participation. As Figure 14.2 indicates, the majority of Americans belong to a church or synagogue, and this proportion held relatively constant from its 1937 level of 73 percent to the 1986 level of 69 percent. Similarly, the proportion who reported they have attended church or synagogue in the last seven days has fluctuated by about ten points but stands at present at 40.5 percent, only a point away from the 1939 level of 41 percent (Gallup, 1987).

What about more private observations such as prayer and Bible study? A large majority of Americans respond positively to the question, "Do you ever pray?" (See Figure 14.2) In 1985, this proportion was 87 percent, which is quite close to the 1948 level of 90 percent. If we look more closely, we see another decline in religiosity here with some 31 percent saying they pray twice a day or more compared to 42 percent in 1952. Bible reading, on the other hand, has remained very constant, with 33 percent reporting they read the Bible once a week, and 10 percent reporting once a day. Women, blacks, older people, the less educated, Protestants, and Southerners are more inclined to read the Bible. Whereas religious consciousness distinctly declined in the past half-century, religious participation has held relatively constant (Gallup, 1987).

THEORETICAL INTERPRETATIONS. Our theoretical perspectives help to explain these patterns, and the patterns can help us to evaluate the perspectives. Conflict theory accuses religion of being an "opiate," or drug, which clouds the consciousness of oppressed peoples, making them less aware of their oppression and more willing to go along with it. Because women and racial and ethnic minorities are among the more oppressed, we should not be surprised that they turn more frequently to religion. Similarly, the less educated and lower-income people are typically exploited in menial occupations. They, too, would be expected to tend toward religion as an escape. The functionalist perspective mentions religion as a way of explaining life's uncertainties; and if we assume that women, racial and ethnic minorities, older people, the less educated, and the poorer people have more uncertainty in their lives, we would also expect them to display more religiosity from this perspective as well.

Sociologists are using Gallup's data from other surveys to try to develop better measures of religiosity. The trend is toward recognizing there are various dimensions of religiosity, such as Roberts' consciousness vs.

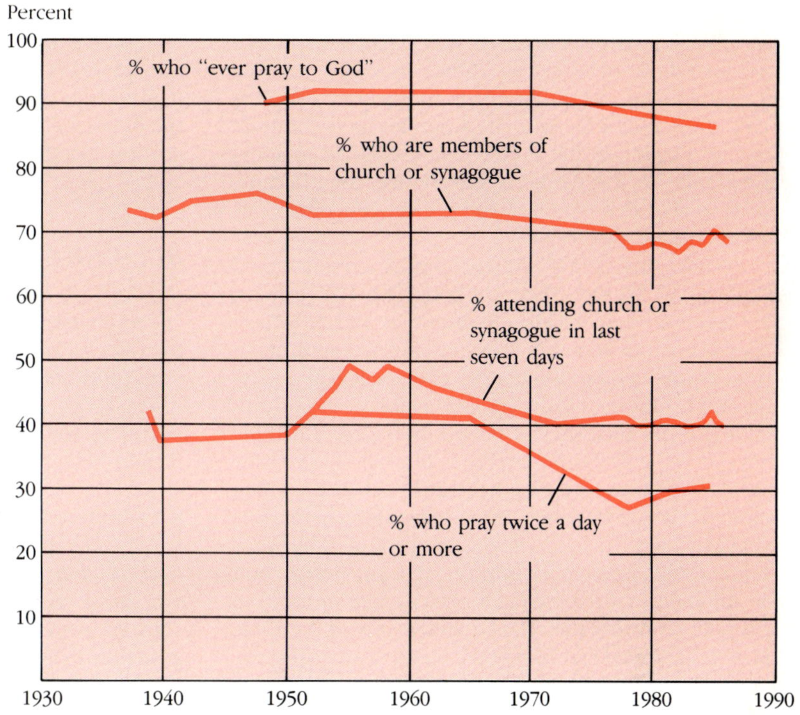

FIGURE 14.2 Religious Participation in the United States. Religious participation has held relatively constant over the past three or four decades. Church attendance rose during the 1950s and returned to its 1940s level for the 1970s and 1980s. The proportion of people praying twice a day fell during the late 1960s and early 1970s but has risen since.

participation idea. These tools will help us to better understand the role of religion in society (Hilty and Stockman, 1986; DeJong, Faulkner, and Warland, 1976).

EVANGELICAL REVIVAL

Over the past century the growth and spread of scientific thinking has challenged Christian claims. When nineteenth-century scholars examined various existing early versions of the Bible, many lost confidence that these documents could represent the literal word of God. Almost none of the original manuscripts are still in existence, and there are discrepancies between early versions. Early copies of the Bible agree virtually verbatim for most of the book, but there are enough discrepancies to suggest that in some passages material was added or deleted. This makes it harder to know which version is correct, and therefore it is harder to believe that the Bible represents an explicitly dictated infallible document from God. Along with this has come the acceptance of Darwin's evolutionary theory, which many see as refuting the Biblical account of the creation of the world and its life-forms.

In response to the challenge, some scholars of the late nineteenth century sought to restate Christianity in such a way that modern man could believe it without the sacrifice of his science, intellect, or scholarship. Christian theologians call this a liberal approach in contrast to a conservative one that holds to a literal interpretation of the Bible. Liberals began to reinterpret the Bible in figurative terms. Thus they reconciled the scientific claim that humans emerged through millions of years of evolution with the Biblical claim that God created humanity in one day, by taking the creation account of Bible as a figure of speech. Some reinterpreted the accounts of miracles as fictions, used to emphasize a point. Thus Jesus was increasingly defined, not as the unique son of God, but one in a series of great religious leaders. In short, liberals began to doubt and challenge many of the beliefs traditionally held by Christians.

A fundamentalist countermovement arose to oppose this theological liberalism. Fundamentalists insisted on several articles of faith: (1) the verbal inspiration of the Bible, (2) the virgin birth of Christ, (3) his substitutionary atonement, (4) his bodily resurrection, and (5) his imminent and visible second coming. These fundamentalists also emphasized godly living, prohibition of alcohol, and the rejection of science.

Evangelicals arose from the fight between liberals and fundamentalists. They found several faults with fundamentalists. First, they rejected the mood of fundamentalism, which they felt was harsh and lacked love for fellow believers in Christ. They also rejected the antieducational program of fundamentalists. Instead, they sought the best education for their children. They also believed that fundamentalists failed to apply Christianity to the whole of life. Hence, they became active in the area of social and ethical concerns (Patterson, 1983).

Many mistakenly equate fundamentalists and evangelicals. Though they are both Christian groups, they have different beliefs and priorities, and they have formed separate denominations or branches within denominations. Public awareness of evangelical beliefs and organizations is growing. For instance, in contrast to some other measures of religiosity we see a distinct increase in the proportion of the public who report they are "born again"—that is, that they reached a turning point in their lives when they committed themselves to Jesus Christ. In 1963 only 20 percent of Americans claimed this experience, but by 1984 the proportion had doubled to 40 percent. In contrast, the proportion of people reporting they hold a literal view of the Bible has not increased but remained constant over the period 1976–1984. Also, if we look more closely at growth in the denominations, we find that mainline denominations like the Methodists, Presbyterians, and Episcopalians lost membership of 5 to 15 percent during the period 1973 to 1983, the same period in which the evangelical churches, such as the Southern Baptist Convention, Assemblies of God, and Church of the Nazarene, grew at rates of 15 to 71 percent (Wills, 1978; Gallup, 1985; 1987).

TELEVISION EVANGELISM. Part of this dramatic growth illustrates the impact of technology on social structure. Early ministers were limited to addressing groups within the sound of their voices. Potential audience size grew as technology advanced from public address systems and radio toward television networks. Now a preacher can address millions and raise millions! Billy Graham, a pioneer among this new breed of mass media ministers, is a central figure in American evangelicalism.

Though television evangelists may be helping to fuel the evangelical revival, they may also be turning many people off. The intense media coverage to Oral Roberts' "hostage" plea to give him money or see God abduct him, the Bakkers' sexual and financial excesses, Pat Robertson's admission that his child was conceived prior to wedlock, and Jimmy Swaggart's confession of his "sinful pornographic" encounters with a prostitute all have contributed to declining confidence in especially the recent televangelists. Public confidence in organized religion has dropped from 66 percent in 1973 to just 54 percent in 1987. The public increasingly sees television evangelists as uncaring, dishonest, insincere, not having a special relationship with God, and untrustworthy with money. In 1980, about one-fourth of the public held such negative images; by 1987 the proportion rose to about one-half (Gallup, 1987b).

RELIGIOUS TRENDS

We might well be skeptical of a meteorologist who said the forecast is for simultaneously rising and falling temperatures. Yet societies are not bound by quite the same rules of logic that apply to the weather, and as we have begun to see, we are living among seemingly contradictory religious trends. In some ways religion seems clearly on the decline, in other ways it is stable, and in yet still other ways, it is growing increasingly stronger. Let us look first at what sociologists term ***secularization,*** *the transfer of influence in society from religious institutions to worldly, or secular, institutions.* We will then consider some dynamic religious movements that suggest that in many places and in many persons' lives, religion has profound growing significance.

SECULARIZATION. The idea that modern societies move steadily from the sacred to the secular has been a dominant theme in the social-scientific study of religion (Hammond, 1985; Wilson, 1985). Modern societies are much more secular than traditional ones, but the assumption that religiosity would soon dwindle down to nothingness is not born out by current observations. The best of contemporary research evidence indicates a persistence of the sacred in contemporary societies.

Sociologists like Talcott Parsons (1963) and Robert Bellah (1970) have portrayed secularization as a step in religious evolution. They see religion as becoming an increasingly private affair. Bellah describes five stages to religious evolution. These steps carry us through increasingly sophisticated distinctions and diferentiations between the sacred or supernatural and the secular. In the fifth stage, the modern period, the dualistic distinction between sacred and secular breaks down to be replaced by a multidimensional view of life and reality (Bellah, 1954). Everything, including religion, is seen as revisable. The old hard-and-fast distinctions between this world and the other world, sacred and profane, good and evil, and salvation and damnation, are removed or are in the process of being removed. Relativity replaces absolutism.

Norval Glenn (1987) reviewed data from 110 U.S. national surveys that indicated the proportion of the public indicating they have "no religion." Public opin-

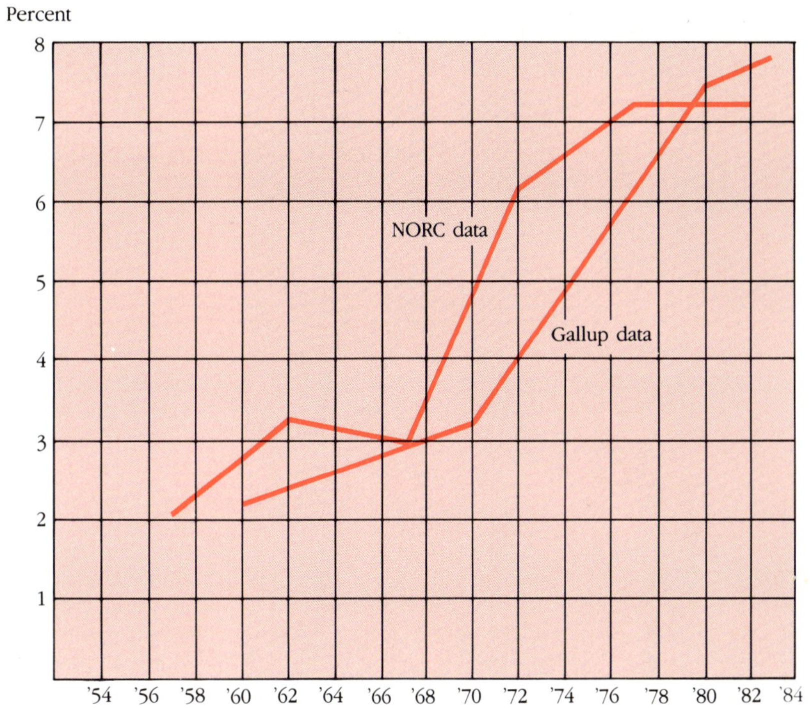

FIGURE 14.3 Percentage of Respondents to U.S. National Surveys Who Said They Had No Religion—Late 1950s to Early 1980s. Based on Glenn Norval, "The Trend in "No Religion" Respondents to U.S. National Survey's Late 1950s to Early 1980s," *Public Opinion Quarterly*, Vol. 51, No. 3 (1987), pp. 293–314. Used by permission.

ion pollsters have measured this nonreligious portion of the public for nearly forty years. During that time the proportion more than tripled from 2.1 percent in the 1955–1959 period to 7.3 percent in the 1980–1984 period. But as Figure 14.3 shows, the steadily growing trend seems to level off in the 1980s.

Other signs, too, point out that secularization is not a steady trend. During the period 1957–1970 the proportion of Americans who agreed that "religion is increasing its influence on American life" plummeted from 69 percent to 14 percent, but in the past fifteen years that figure has rebounded to 48 percent! Similarly, those reporting that religion is "very important in my life" dropped from a high of 75 percent in 1952 to a 1978 low of 52 percent, but that indicator, too, has risen to 56 percent in 1980, where it has remained stable. Both church membership and church attendance declined somewhat during the 1950–1970 period and then leveled off in the 1970s and 1980s. In 1952, 73 percent of the public said they were church members versus 69 percent in 1986. Also, in 1954, 49 percent of the public reported they had been to church within the past week, as compared with 40 percent in 1986 (Gallup, 1985, 1987).

Recently Stark and Bainbridge (1985) have shown that secularization actually stimulates religious innovation. They suggest that the decline of conventional religiosity promotes the growth of both sectarian revivals and cults. In the following section, we see that this idea describes much of what is going on in religion today.

POLARIZATION: MOVING AWAY FROM CONVENTIONAL RELIGION

During the past forty years the proportion of Protestants has dropped from 69 percent in 1947 to 59 percent in 1986. Over the same time period the Jewish proportion also dropped, from 5 percent to 2 percent. Catholics increased in proportion from 20 to 27 percent, as did two other categories. We have already discussed the increase in those persons who say they have no religion, but there is another interesting increase. The proportion who say it has some "other," that is, not Protestant, Catholic, or Jewish faith, has quadrupled from 1 to 4 percent. Several factors help explain these changes. During the years immigrants to the United States have often come from regions where other religious faiths are practiced. Within the growing "other" category are those who belong to cults (Gallup, 1985).

In a sense, religion is becoming somewhat polarized. Whereas at one end of the religious spectrum

The world's largest religion focuses on Jesus of Nazareth. Followers believe the unique works he performed, including healings and rising from his own death, were "signs and wonders" which validate his claim to be the only begotten son of God. (*Photo courtesy the author*)

some people and denominations seem to be clamoring to prove themselves the most authentically Christian, at the other end we see considerable activity in fundamentally new religious movements. Cults, as we learned earlier, draw their inspiration from other than the primary religion of the culture and are different from sects that break off from the traditional church to preserve or return to a purer form of the traditional faith (Glock and Stark, 1965).

Many people tend to associate the term *cult* with the dramatic mass suicide/murder of Jim Jones' People's Temple. The Unification Church provides another example of a cult. Members of this group believe that Sun Myung Moon is the true messiah—Moon teaches that Jesus was supposed to have established God's kingdom on earth but failed and was instead killed. But the term *cult* applies to other significant groups as well, some of which are often confused with traditional Christianity. As Roberts points out, the Church of Jesus Christ of Latter-Day Saints (Mormons) is one such example. "Although they believe that Jesus was the messiah and they believe in the Bible, they also have a second book that they hold as sacred scriptures. The new scripture (The Book of Mormon) came from Joseph Smith's 'translation' of some golden plates that he found in Upstate New York" (Roberts, 1984, p. 243). Mormonism is among the fastest growing religious groups in the United States, adding over 1,000,000 new members from 1973 to 1983 (Gallup, 1985). Armand Mauss, after reviewing the sociological literature on the Mormon subculture, concludes that "Mormonism may be on the verge of mushrooming into the first new world religion since Islam" (Mauss, 1984; p. 438).

What have sociologists learned about these cults that sometimes self-destruct and sometimes mushroom into world religions? Who joins them and why? We consider these questions now in our "Close-Up on Research."

CLOSE-UP on • *RESEARCH* •

Eileen Barker on Cults and Anticults Since Jonestown

The Researcher and the Setting

As Eileen Barker points out, anyone not familiar with the "cult problem" was awakened to it in November 1978. News spread around the world that hours after Congressman Leo Ryan was shot by members of the People's Temple, some 900 members of this cult enacted a suicidal ritual, rehearsed repeatedly, in which "babies had cyanide squirted down their throats by syringe, and then the older children, followed by adults, lined up to drink from cups of Kool-Aid laced with cyanide" (p. 330). By early December 1978, "a Gallup Poll found that 98 percent of the U.S. public had heard or read about the People's Temple and the Guyana massacre—a level of awareness matched in the pollsters' experience only by the attack on Pearl Harbor and the explosion of the atom bomb."

This tragedy influenced sociological research on new religious movements in two ways. First, it became obvious that much more had to be learned about the movements and their consequences for the involved individuals as well as society. Second, new religions would not be regarded in quite the same light or treated the same way after Jonestown.

The Researcher's Goal

Barker, who at the time of writing this article was dean of undergraduate studies at the London School of Economics and Political Science, sets out to summarize the sociological research on cult and anticult movements since Jonestown.

Theory and Concepts

Barker is seeking to report on the state of knowledge about cults rather than test a particular theory. We might note that *cult* is a relative term, which we have defined as a religious organization that claims a unique new revelation. As such, we define cults with respect to some preexisting dominant religion to which the cult places itself at odds. Barker is focusing on these cults as social movements of the sort we discussed in Chapter 7.

Research Design

The research design here is a review of the literature that exemplifies the research method we called "analysis of existing sources" in Chapter 1. Scholars like Barker, who write literature reviews, provide an important service to the discipline by summarizing and evaluating research and theories and suggesting directions for further study.

Findings

What are the aftereffects of the mass suicide/murder of followers of Jim Jones in Guyana? Barker reports that the People's Temple was "not to be found featured in the anticult literature" before 1978, but "for the rest of the 1970s and well into the 1980s it was difficult to find a page . . . published by the anticult lobby that did not contain at least one reference to the mass suicide/murder" (p. 330). Following the Jonestown event the media devoted more attention to cults, but in contrast to their pre-Jonestown coverage, "they tended to be all lumped together under the now highly derogatory label 'cult.' " Ironically, this was true in spite of the fact that J. Richardson (1980) had demonstrated that "the People's Temple was, in a number of important respects, markedly different from other new religions."

Increasing numbers of sociologists turned their attention to new religions, especially the Unification Church and the International Society of Krishna Consciousness.

What are the different theories for why people join the movement? Following Jonestown the public became more suspicious of all cults, and people increasingly believed cult leaders practiced mind control to which deprogramming, or the forcible kidnaping of members and holding them against their will until they renounce their faith, was a legitimate response. Governments commissioned reports, and legislators debated the respective rights of cults and the family members who were concerned for relatives who were in them. Even scholars debated whether they or their colleagues should accept invitations from cults, like the Unification Church, ISKCON, Sekai Kyusei Kyo, and the Church of Scientology, to attend their conferences.

Are all members brainwashed? Many sociologists have studied the anticult movements that have arisen in opposition to the cults. They note that "anticultists throughout the world are, however, well-nigh unanimous in their opinion that the new religions procure their membership through the employment of techniques of mind control or brainwashing. Sometimes anticultists suggest that people who join the new religions are abnormally pathetic or weak. Researchers who employ psychological testing to compare cult members to the general population find little evidence in this direction" (Galanter, 1980, 1983; Galanter, et al., 1979; Kilbourne, 1983; Kuner, 1984; Ungerleider & Wellisch, 1983). But clinical psychologists report a recognizable "cult-induced psychopathology" (Ash, 1983; 1985). Barker reports that "those who . . . interpret cult membership as the result of something being done to a helpless victim have tended to be psychologists or psychiatrists" (Clark, 1979; Clark et al., 1981; Conway and Siegelman, 1978, 1982; Singer, 1979; Verdier, 1980; West, 1982). Sociologists have tended to dismiss the brainwashing thesis, including Barker (1981, 1984a) herself, who studied the Unification Church and "found that 90 percent of those attending the Unification workshop did not join, and that the majority of those who did join left within two years" (p. 335). J. Richardson (1985a, b) insists that "the convert ought to be seen as an active agent who chooses, not a passive subject who responds to external powers" (p. 336). Barker has tried to bridge the gap between those who look inside the person and those who look to their surroundings by constructing a model that makes use of control groups to empirically test the effects of internal and external variables (1984a).

"Research on defectors has repeatedly shown, however, that there is a significant difference between the accounts of the movements given by those who have been "deprogrammed" and those who left of their own accord, the latter tending to be considerably less condemnatory (Barker, 1984a; Beckford, 1985; Solomon, 1981; Skonovd, 1981, 1983; Wright, 1983, 1984)" (p. 336).

Several sociologists have focused on the influence of the larger society, some saying that movements reflect the society while others say movements react to it. Although the People's Temple drew its membership mostly from the materially oppressed, this seems to be the exception rather than the rule. These movements usually recruit from those who are deprived of community, "real relationships," and spiritual stimulation rather than those who are materially deprived (Barker, 1979, 1984a; Wilson, 1981b, 1982a, b). Stark suggests that cults flourish better in the more secularized climate of western Europe than the United States because people there lack what they would be getting from the churches here which are stronger (Stark, 1985b). While those who have not read the sociological accounts may wonder why anyone joins these movements, those who have read the literature might, as Barker suggests, wonder "why all young adults are not members!" (p. 337). Consider all the possible reasons listed by Doress & Porter (1981): to find a family, as a spiritual search, for security, to differentiate themselves from their parents, as adolescent rebellion, seeking adventure, for attention, because of their idealism, because of underemployment and dead-end jobs.

From her study of the recent literature, Barker notes that increasingly sociologists have been drawn across the line from observers to participants in two ways. They have served as "expert witnesses" for one side or the other in court, and some have also accepted invitations to conferences sponsored by some of the movements such as the Unification Church and ISKCON. Sociologists now debate whether they or their colleagues should accept such hospitality.

Barker believes we now have enough detailed accounts of individual cults to allow for comparative analyses from various perspectives. She also suggests that we need more empirical studies that make use of control groups for comparison and recommends that scholars focus on the question: What challenges do the movements face after the death of their charismatic leaders?

Finally, Barker cautions: "there is no evidence that the new religions are continuing to grow—or indeed, that their numerical significance has been as great as their social and sociological interest" (p. 339). She hopes "sociologists will chart the failures as assiduously as they chart the successes" (p. 340).

Interpretation

"Differences between the movements are considerably greater than is often recognized and . . . there is a need for further comparative research and more refined classificatory systems before our theoretical knowledge can develop and be tested satisfactorily" (p. 340).

Questions

1. How might we use the information that Barker has developed here?
2. Eileen Barker has some of her articles published in books printed by the Unification Church. What are the pros and cons of researchers accepting invitations to conferences and publications from cult groups?
3. What kind of research projects might help us to fill in the gaps in our knowledge about cult and anticult movements?

SOURCE Eileen Barker. 1986. "Religious Movements: Cult and Anticult Since Jonestown." Reprinted with permission from the *Annual Review of Sociology*, Volume 12, © 1986 by Annual Reviews, Inc., pp. 329–46. J. T. Richardson, 1980. "People's Temple and Jonestown: A Corrective Comparison and Critique." *Journal of the Scientific Study of Religion*. 19:239–55.

POLITICALIZATION AND THE ELECTRONIC CHURCH

For a time religion and revolution seemed to be at opposite ends of the philosophical perspective. In 1971, for instance, Rodney Stark and his colleagues found that Protestant ministers in California gave little attention to political issues. Although it was the hottest social issue of the day, over one-third of those studied had never mentioned the Vietnam War from the pulpit. Further, only one-fourth reported they had delivered any sermon that year with a primary focus on a controversial social or political topic. The Stark study labeled America's ministers "wayward shepherds" and chided them for their lack of leadership in attacking social problems.

Indeed, in the United States we have sought to institutionalize a separation of religion and the state. Yet, religion increasingly crops up in political settings both at home and abroad. Here in the United States we have a long list of "church–state issues" which we heatedly debate. Not only are there the conservative favorites: abortion, prayer in schools, evolution versus creation, pornography, and sex education, but there is much church involvement among the liberals, especially surrounding nuclear disarmament, protest of U.S involvement in Nicaragua, and sex education in light of the AIDS epidemic. In the underdeveloped world, liberation theologians are blending Christianity and Marxism to build an ideology of revolution. The Pope personally involved himself in the recent Soviet struggle with the Solidarity Workers Movement in his native Poland. Perhaps it is naive to expect that politics and religion, which both so often deal in the realm of moral conduct, can keep out of each other's hair!

The so-called electronic church, led by television evangelists like Billy Graham, Oral Roberts, Jim Bakker, Jerry Falwell, Jimmy Swaggart, Pat Robertson, Robert Schuller, and Rex Humbard, has aggressively promoted social movements of a political as well as social nature. For the most part this loose coalition has taken political positions that are distinctly conservative politically. This tie to their evangelical nature, which is in contrast to the even more conservative fundamentalists, calls for them to get involved in transforming society.

Although the un-Godly revelations of misdeeds by some of these leaders have lessened confidence in them as individuals, we would be mistaken not to note the strength the movement has built and the political positions it promotes. Even in 1987, the year "televangelists" seemed to be doing their best to self-destruct, the electronic church was large and growing larger. Some 1,370 radio stations and 221 television stations

Even in 1987, a year when televangelists seemed to compete in a race toward self-destruction, the electronic ministry continued to grow rapidly. *(AP/Wide World Photos)*

carried full or substantial religious content. Each week twenty new radio and two new television stations joined the flock.

Interestingly, George Gallup and the Annenberg School of Communication's study showed that the electronic ministries typically did not compete with local congregations for money or commitment. Whereas in 1983, only about one-fifth regularly watched religious television programs, by 1987 the proportion had risen to one-fourth. During the same period the proportion of these who occasionally watched rose from 42 percent to 49 percent. Compared with other churchgoers, those who watch electronic church are much more likely to be poor, black, uneducated, and Protestant (Hadden and Swann, 1981; Associated Press, 1987).

The electronic church is big business and involves big clout. Jerry Falwell's ministry must raise $100 million a year to stay afloat. Schuller's Crystal Cathedral cost $18 million, and his television shows cost $8 million annually. Schuller takes no salary, and instead he lives off royalties from his books and his $15,000-per-appearance lecture fees (Ajemian, 1985; Stengel, 1985).

With rare exception, the electronic church, as a key element in the "New Christian Right," has taken opposing positions to those championed by liberals in earlier decades. They have condemned pornography, homosexuality, abortion, and, to a lesser extent, feminism. They have also promoted Christian schools, fought "secular humanism" as a false religion, and occasionally involved themselves in foreign policy debates as well. One of the most visible and politically influential among the television preachers is Jerry Falwell, who founded the religious–political movement called the Moral Majority. Falwell, who would rightly be called a television fundamentalist rather than evangelist, has been especially vehement in his attacks on homosexuality. Falwell and others involved in the electronic church have developed sophisticated fundraising techniques including computer-generated mass direct mailing campaigns, which arouse their followers to contribute, protest, and vote in ways recommended by the leaders.

INTERPRETATION

The popular and scholarly assumptions that in modern times religion would steadily die out are being challenged by new data to the contrary, at least in the United States. In response, sociologists are revising their interpretation of the scene. Recently Rodney Stark and William Bainbridge (1985) have suggested that secularization may itself stimulate religious innovation. Recent trends indeed support their contention that as we become more secular, we tend towards revival and cult formation. As they put it, "trying to drive out religion is like driving a nail—the harder you hit, the deeper it goes" (p. 17). In the instance of the United States, we have seen evidence of secularization, the decline of some previously strong denominations, but also vigorous growth in cults and evangelicalism especially through television.

Conclusion

Sociologists studying religion have a diverse and changing subject matter. Religions, which appear in all societies, take on differing beliefs and organizational forms. Paradoxically religion both unifies and divides societies.

Modern societies tend away from religion, but religion changes form more than it completely disappears. During the past half-century the United States has become somewhat more secular and religiously diverse. Mainstream Protestant denominations and Judaism have declined in terms of the proportion of the population following these faiths. Catholicism has grown, as have some of the more extreme religious groups called sects and cults.

Sociologists at Work

ANDREW GREELEY
CHARTS RELIGIOUS IMAGERY AND SOCIAL BEHAVIOR
University of Chicago
Chicago, Illinois

Andrew Greeley fills three interesting roles that on the surface seem to have little in common: sociologist, Catholic priest, and novelist. His several novels have sold very well. He teaches in one of the country's most highly respected sociology departments. One colleague spotted the connection. Though the average reader would not recognize this, his novels actually incorporate the findings published in his research monographs. As the colleague put it, "Now that I know your secret, I'll never read the research monographs again; I'll go directly to the novels, which are easier and more interesting reading."

Can You Tell Us About Some of the Work You Are Currently Doing Which Might Interest a New Student of Sociology?
My basic sociological concern for the last ten to twelve years has been the religious imagination. I became persuaded some time ago that religion takes its origins, both in the individual and in the species, in that dimension of the personality that we sometimes call the imagination or the creative intuition or the subconscious, and that experiences that renew human hopefulness are the basis of religion. Therefore, if one wants to know empirically and practically what a person's religion is, then one tries to get at the religious images that result in the experiences. I began with the idea of religion as a hope renewal experience and symbols or images as preserving that experience of individual faiths through stories one tells to share the experience with others. Religion is experiencing the stories, and maybe the storytelling community, that group of people who are understanding the symbols together. On the imaginative level, that is what a church is.

How Do You Implement This Theory?
I tried to find measures that we could administer in surveys that would get at the religious imagination. We have developed a sort of forced-choices-of-images-of-God 7-point scale, by asking, for instance, "Where do you picture God as being between father and mother; between friend and master; between spouse and lover?" Not unsurprisingly, perhaps, these factors have a very powerful predictive value on people's political and social attitudes. If you are on the end of the continuum that has one particular divine image of God, then you are about 15 percentage points more likely to have voted for Walter Mondale regardless of your political affiliation or your identification as conservative or liberal, for example.

How Do You Interpret These Findings?
It would seem that religion is the sort of underlying theme story of your life and that theme story predicts other stories. Interestingly, things like prayer or church attendance don't correlate nearly as well with other things as these religious images do.

How Does a Priest Relate That Image of Religion to the More Traditional Image That God Exists and Tries to Relate to Man?
I use this image in my class every year. I tell them "I wouldn't be a priest unless I believed in God. But we are not going to talk about that now. We are going to talk about how images of God affect society." Students can make that distinction and accept it very easily. As sociologists we don't know whether there is a God out there to correspond to our images. We are just saying these are the kinds of experiences that people have of God, which they code in their own image. This approach complements my faith by helping me to understand its nature.

Francesco Scavullo

Why Did You Start Writing Novels?
One of the powerful motivations I had when I decided I would start trying to write fiction is that I have become convinced that storytelling is the most effective way to talk about religion. Indeed, for most of human history, it has been the only way: stories around the fire at night, stories told to people's children. The stories are the best part of the Christian tradition: the story of David, Moses, and Joseph, for example. The best part of the Christian scriptures is the parables of Jesus. Thus, I am a sociological novelist, telling stories for today's audience.

Summary Questions

1. What is religion?
2. According to Durkheim, what are the elements of religion?
3. What are the functions of religion?
4. How is religion related to social conflict?
5. What are the types of religion?
6. What are the types of religious organizations?
7. What are the major religious faiths in the world, and how are they organized?
8. How are religion and government related in the United States today?
9. What are the trends in religiosity in the United States?
10. What sorts of people are more likely to be religious?
11. How is secularization part of the religious scene in the United States?
12. In what way is religion becoming polarized in the United States?
13. What have sociologists learned about cults?
14. How has religion become politicized?
15. What is the electronic church, and what is its impact?
16. How is Andrew Greeley involved in the sociology of religion?

Summary Answers

1. We define religion as a system of symbols, beliefs, values, and practices focused on questions of ultimate meaning.
2. Durkheim observed that all religions divide the world into a sacred and special realm and a profane or ordinary realm. He suggested that society itself is the true object of worship and that various cultures develop various symbolic representations of society.
3. Religion functions to promote social solidarity, strengthen the normative structure of the community, mark life events, and explain life's uncertainties.
4. Religion is also a contributor to bitter and often bloody conflict and a tool of exploitation. Elites use religion to justify their exploitation of the masses and to distract the masses from awareness of this exploitation. As Marx and Engels showed, religion often helps sustain social class inequality, which eventually leads to revolution. Religious groups often fight and divide. Religious figures are frequently found at the front of social movements such as those for civil rights, peace, nuclear disarmament, and liberation of third-world countries.
5. The various types of religions hold various objects to be sacred and or supernatural. In simple supernaturalism an impersonal force of nature is regarded as sacred, whereas in animism, the sacred resides in spirits of the animals and natural phenomena. Totemism is a form of animism in which an animal or plant is worshiped as a god and ancestor. Theistic religions focus attention on a sacred god or gods. Ethical religions focus on principles held to be sacred.
6. Religious organizations tend to fall into four types. Ecclesias are state supported, whereas denominations are not and must compete with other religious organizations for members within a society. Sects are usually small religious organizations emphasizing lay leadership and a return to the "true" beliefs of the dominant religion. Cults are often small, but they are distinguished primarily with a claim to new revelation often made by a charismatic leader.
7. Christianity, a theistic faith, is by far the world's largest religion. Islam, the second most popular religion, builds on Judeo-Christianity while denying the divinity of Jesus. Hinduism is a polytheistic religion involving many sects and found primarily in India. Buddhism is an ethical religion, which does not teach that there is a god or gods, but does teach reincarnation. None of the major religions is animistic or simple supernaturalistic in form.
8. In the United States church and state have been organizationally separated, but as Bellah points out, they overlap in their belief systems. The state is conceived of as "under God," and this provides the foundation for a civil religion of nondenominational form, but one that is distinctly theistic.
9. In terms of outward practices, the United States has been remarkably stable in church membership (70 percent) and weekly church attendance (40 percent) for the past forty years. However, public opinion pollsters report a steady decline in the number of people reporting that religion is very important and a source of help with everyday problems.
10. Women, the aged, minorities, those with less income, and those with less education are all more likely to be religious. The growth of science promoted a liberal form of Christianity that compromised on fundamental traditional beliefs such as

the literal accuracy of the Bible. This lead to a polarization between liberal and fundamentalist Christians. Evangelicalism emerged as an alternative stressing the authority of scripture but the need for loving attitudes and social change. The proportion of Americans holding evangelical beliefs including the importance of the "born again" experience is increasing.

11. At the same time that there is much dramatic religious activity in the United States, the proportion of people reporting that they have no religious belief has increased from about 2 percent to about 8 percent over the past three decades. This is evidence of a secularization that has been predicted by sociologists for the past century.
12. In an important sense religion is becoming polarized, with mainline Protestant denominations losing membership as evangelical and fundamentalist denominations grow. Similarly, we are seeing considerable cult growth, with the Mormons growing very rapidly in size and satanic cults growing in number faster than other cults.
13. Cults, typically, have not become large denominations. The public is extremely wary of them following the Jonestown tragedy and because of accusations of brainwashing by some cults. Barker suggests we need to look beyond brainwashing to the culture and the needs of people who join cults.
14. Religious leaders increasingly take political positions.
15. The television evangelists of the "electronic church" have been active in leading conservative social movements opposing abortion, homosexuality, pornography, and, to some extent, feminism. Recent scandals within the electronic church have at least temporarily roused public suspicion.
16. Greeley focuses on the images the believer holds of God, such as father or mother, friend and master, spouse and lover.

Glossary

animatism see *simple supernaturalism.*

animism the belief that the sacred resides in spirits found in people and other natural phenomena, such as the wind and the rain.

cult a religious organization the claims a unique new revelation.

denomination a religious organization that competes for members within a society and is not directly connected to or supported by the government.

ecclesia a religious organization that is connected to and supported by the government and includes most of the members of the society.

ethical religions religions that do not worship a god as such, but rather promote a moral code or belief.

monotheism form of religion involving belief in one god.

polytheism form of religion involving belief in many gods.

profane those aspects of culture that are part of everyday life or routine experience.

religion a system of symbols, beliefs, values, and practices focused on questions of ultimate meaning.

religiosity the importance of religion to the life of a group or individual.

religious beliefs shared ideas that explain the sacred objects.

religious rituals sacred acts that represent religious beliefs.

religious symbols objects, images, and words that take meaning from sacred things that they represent and that may become sacred themselves after repeated association with the sacred.

sacred those aspects of culture that are respected by society as ideal and above daily living.

sect small group that is not well integrated into society, in which members rather than a pastorate accomplish the work of the religious organization.

secularization the transfer of influence in society from religious institutions to worldly, or secular, institutions.

simple supernaturalism a form of religion found in many simple societies that emphasizes a belief in an impersonal supernatural force but does not specifically define certain gods or spirits; also called *animatism.*

theism a form of religion involving belief in god.

totemism a form of animism in which an animal or plant is worshiped as a god and ancestor.

Suggested Readings

Ronald L. Johnstone. 1983. *Religion in Society: A Sociology of Religion.* Englewood Cliffs, NJ: Prentice-Hall.

This book provides a valuable overview of the sociology of religion field. Johnstone illuminates the relation of religion to other major features of society.

C. S. Lewis. 1977. *The Case for Christianity.* New York: Macmillan.

A carefully reasoned explanation of and argument for the dominant religion in the world.

Meredith B. McGuire. 1987. *Religion: The Social Context.* Belmont, Calif.: Wadsworth.

This book surveys the sociological thinking on religion and reports on recent trends and research.

Keith A. Roberts. 1984. *Religion in Sociological Perspective.* Chicago: Dorsey Press.

Roberts offers a comprehensive overview of theory and research in the field of sociology. His discussion of religiosity and religious commitment are especially good.

Rodney Stark and William Sims Bainbridge. 1985. *The Future of Religion: Secularization, Revival and Cult Formation.* Berkeley: University of California Press.

This book provides an analytical explanation for the trends in contemporary religion that may sometimes seem contradictory. The authors suggest that secularization, the absence of religiosity, actually fosters revival and cult formation.

CHAPTER 15

WORK and the ECONOMY

- How Does Society Organize for Work and Exchange?
- How Do Economies Differ?
- How Do Economies Become Centralized Under Socialism?
- How Do Economies Become Centralized Under Capitalism?
- Why Do Economies Develop?
- Close-Up on Theory: Paul Harrison on the Causes of Economic Underdevelopment
- What Are the Major U.S. Economic Trends?
- How Is Work Organized in the United States?
- What Does Work Mean to Us?
- How Can the Work Setting Be Improved?
- Close-Up on Research: Rothschild and Russell on Democratic Participation in Work
- Sociologists at Work: Rosabeth Moss Kanter Offers Insights to Corporations About Entrepreneurship

How's Your Sociological Intuition?

1. When did the United States' standard of living peak?

a. 1962
b. 1973
c. 1982
d. it has never peaked

2. Which best describes our labor force trends?

a. men and women are working in increasing proportions
b. while an increasing proportion of women are joining the labor force, the proportion of men working has remained stable
c. as the proportion of women in the labor force has increased dramatically, the proportion of men in the labor force has decreased slightly
d. the proportion of both men and women working is declining gradually

3. What was the first year in which the majority of mothers with children under 1 year old were also in the paid labor force?

a. 1969
b. 1978
c. 1987
d. they never have been, and likely never will be

4. What proportion of the public reports that it is satisfied to very satisfied with its work?

a. 20%
b. 40%
c. 60%
d. 80%

Answers

1. b. Until 1973, the buying power of the average American rose relatively steadily for nearly three decades. Since then we have been losing ground.
2. c. The increased participation of women in the labor force is well noted, but fewer people are aware of the declining proportion of men working.
3. d. Whereas mothers of infants have traditionally stayed out of the work force, a majority of mothers first broke this tradition in 1987.
4. c. Most Americans report favorable attitudes toward their work, but a significant minority are apathetic or actively dissatisfied.

WHEN YOU HAVE FINISHED STUDYING THIS CHAPTER, YOU SHOULD KNOW:

- How work is important to society and the individual
- How society organizes work and exchange
- How economies differ
- How economies become centralized under socialism
- How economies become centralized under capitalism
- How multinational corporations affect world social order
- Why economies develop
- How sociologists, including Harrison, explain socio-economic development
- What the major economic trends are
- How work is organized in the U.S.
- Who is working
- How occupations are organized
- Who is unemployed, why, and with what effect
- What work means to us
- How and why democracy is coming into the work-place
- How Rosabeth Moss Kanter helps business firms

The students are on time, but the professor appears to be late for the first day of a class called "The World of Work." In one corner a maintenance man stands working on an electrical panel. He turns, approaches the students, and asks:

"Where's the professor?"

"That's what we'd like to know!" one of them responds.

He walks to the podium and unzips his coveralls, revealing that underneath he is wearing a tie, dress shirt, blue blazer, and gray slacks. Shedding the overalls, the maintenance man is transformed into the professor—not just in terms of wardrobe, but in the minds of the students. That anonymous blue collar worker who moments ago could be safely ignored is now someone of significance.

This charade gave our students a firsthand experience of how easily they could revise their estimate of a fellow human being when just one change was made—the person's occupation.

Work is of enormous significance to each individual. Where we fit into the world of work relates to virtually every aspect of our lives: our standard of living, our health, our life expectancy, our political affiliation, religious beliefs, even our self-esteem. Work provides us with a master status, one that dominates our social lives. It is central to our sense of meaning in life, and our self-concept. The doctor may be delighted to mention his or her status, but a janitor working for the postal service may mask his or her occupational identity by simply saying "I'm with the Postal Service." Virtually no one wants to admit that he or she is "out of work," or worse yet, has been "fired."

How we work in society largely determines the type of society we can have. Therefore, one of the best ways to classify societies is according to the dominant form of work they do—hunting and gathering, herding, horticultural, agricultural, industrial, or postindustrial. Because the way we work is so much of the way we live, we should expect that as the nature of work changes we will see repercussions throughout the rest of our social strucures.

How Does Society Organize for Work and Exchange?

All societies develop institutional arrangements that determine what is produced and consumed, how goods will be produced, who will own the means of production, and how goods and services will be exchanged. The ***economic institution*** is *the social structure that organizes the production and exchange of goods and services. Goods* refers to material products such as fruit, televisions, cars, and houses, and *services* refers to intangible products such as a haircut, legal advice, or an education.

In modern industrialized countries the economy includes an elaborate set of norms, roles, status positions, and organizations on which people rely to bring them products and services from around the globe. Our economic norms include laws that protect consumers from misrepresentation in the market place, laws that regulate child labor practices, as well as customs such as the eight-hour workday and the forty-hour work week. The economic institution involves a vast number of roles we call jobs or occupations. These occupations, as we saw in Chapter 8, classify people into status positions and strata, or classes, that influence the amount of wealth, power, and prestige they are afforded. Finally, the economic institutions also include thousands of organizations, in this case called businesses or firms, some of which, like IBM and General Motors, are among the largest and most powerful in the world, having revenues that exceed those of many small and even medium-sized countries.

No secondary sector work here. Produce passes from the primary sector work of agriculture to the tertiary sector work of merchant without having to pass through the secondary sector work of manufacturing. Oil and iron, in contrast, have little or no marketability in their raw form. They must pass through manufacturing before being sold. *(Jim Cesta/FPG International)*

ECONOMIC SECTORS

Sociologists consider economies to be made up of three major sectors. The ***primary sector*** *includes the work of securing raw materials directly from nature.* Mining, forestry, agriculture, fishing, and oil production are clear examples of primary sector activities. The ***secondary sector*** *involves the work of turning raw materials into manufactured goods.* Secondary sector industries include automotive production, construction, clothing, food processing, such as canning or freezing, and all other manufacturing. The ***tertiary sector*** *is the part of the economy which includes producing services.* Law, medicine, accounting, teaching, social work, as well as waitressing, cleaning, and entertainment, are all examples of work in the tertiary sector.

FUNCTIONS OF THE ECONOMIC INSTITUTION

The economic institution is crucial to society. Its major functions are revealed by its definition. The economy organizes production of goods and services and arranges for their distribution. Disruptions in the economy affect the entire society. Depressions, recessions, and inflation can lead to the collapse of nations. On the other hand, growing international trade and the interdependence it fosters may bring more international unity, despite previous failures of societies to organize through political and diplomatic means. Many theorists believe that changes in the economic institution are major determinants of changes in social life (Marx, 1904; Ogburn, 1936; Lenski, 1966).

CONFLICT IN THE ECONOMIC INSTITUTION

Perhaps no other institution generates as much cause for bitter disputes and conflict as the economic institution. Karl Marx identifies the conflicting interests of workers and business owners as the root of the class conflict that has characterized so much of history. The goal of virtually all revolutions is to establish a more just economic institution, not merely better government. Short of full-scale revolution, conflict arises from economic disputes in many places. As we learned in Chapter 10, "Race and Ethnic Relations," split labor markets, in which an ethnic minority works for substandard wages, are a major cause of ethnic antagonism. Our own society has a history of bloody and bitter struggles over the right of workers to form unions. Hostility between management and labor is still routine, frequently erupting in strikes. Finally, radical differences in economic philosophy between the communist and capitalist world contribute significantly to the hostility between nations.

How Do Economies Differ?

By developing a clear understanding of how economies differ, we will be better able to understand the differences between the developed and less developed nations as well as the differences between socialism and capitalism. In pre-agrarian societies, economic life is usually blended into the kinship structure, with people working and sharing mostly with their relatives. In modern societies with more sophisticated technology, the economic social structure employed in production and exchange becomes progressively more complicated, organized, centralized, and distinct from other institutions.

Economies differ in several important ways. One of the most important differences is in the dominant technology employed that divides the developed from the less-developed nations. Another important difference is the degree to which work has become specialized or labor has become divided. Some economies are more centralized, dominated by either the state or large corporations, whereas other economies are decentralized, with production and distribution spread broadly throughout the society. Economies also differ in the way exchange is organized, with some using barter and others employing sophisticated monetary arrangements. Let's consider these differences more closely.

ORGANIZATION FOR PRODUCTION

Scholars of economic institutions have divided economies into three classifications based on their means of production: ***less developed,*** *meaning an economy dominated by the primary sector;* ***developing,*** *meaning an economy dominated by the second sector;* and ***developed,*** *meaning an economy dominated by the tertiary sector.*

Developed economies and societies are not necessarily better than less developed economies or societies. Furthermore, their economies do not necessarily develop through a particular sequence of stages.

DIVISION OF LABOR

In the film classic *Modern Times,* Charlie Chaplin plays a factory worker whose sole job is to tighten two bolts on each part that passes on a conveyer belt by using the wrenches he holds, one in each hand. ***Division of labor,*** the *specialization of work roles,* characterizes developed economies, and as *Modern Times* illustrates, the division of labor in modern factories is sometimes carried to the extreme. As we saw in Chapter 5, "Groups and Organizations," division of labor is a major characteristic of bureaucracies. Developed economies divide labor according to occupations within the economy as well as tasks within the bureaucracy. The U.S. Department of Labor's Dictionary of Occupational Terms (U.S. Dept. of Labor, 1987), lists some 20,000 different occupations. Such specialization greatly improves productivity, so that developed economies far exceed the production of goods in undeveloped ones.

CENTRALIZATION

Centralization *refers to the degree to which the economy is dominated by a relatively small segment of the population.* Contemporary societies are sometimes centrally organized by the state. In socialist nations the economy is centralized and "planned" to the degree that the government owns at least certain key industries. Capitalist nations are highly centralized as well, in that many of the productive resources become concentrated within a small number of giant firms. In simple societies, the family is the major unit of production and consumption. Seldom does a single family or other small group influence the overall economy.

MEANS OF EXCHANGE

As economies become more developed and complex, the nature of exchange and the institutions devoted to trade change radically. The simplest societies have little need for trade, although individuals may occasionally barter goods, such as exchanging tools for food. Because most families produce the same things, preagricultural economies generally have no system of money. Developing a monetary system becomes necessary only when people become more specialized in their occupations. For example, when a potter must exchange pots for essentials like clothes and food, money facilitates this exchange.

Money is a social creation that grows progressively more abstract as the economic institution becomes more complex. Initially money has intrinsic value of its own, as in the case of gold and silver coins. Precious metals are logical materials of which to make coins, because they are both widely recognized to be valuable and are easy to carry, but many other valuables (such as furs, jewels, and tobacco) are sometimes used as a means of exchange.

Currency, or paper money, is not usually introduced into a society unless a strong and stable state has emerged. Paper money has no intrinsic value, but in its early history is exchangeable for its stated value in gold or silver. Today currency derives its value from the fact that it is widely accepted as a medium for exchange.

Within this century, currency has been replaced by an even newer form of money: credit. Most money in the United States no longer exists in the form of gold, silver, or even paper money, but rather as credits in bank accounts. Most major purchases are paid for by check, and workers are usually paid with checks, the most common means of exchange in the United States today. In fact, fewer than one-fifth of the amount of money on which the economy runs actually exists in negotiable currency or coin.

To summarize, economies differ in their organization for production, their degree of specialization or division of labor, their centralization, and their means of exchange. We now turn to a consideration of two major types of economy; socialistic and capitalistic.

How Do Economies Become Centralized Under Socialism?

States vary in their attempts to regulate the economy. No modern government leaves its country's economy completely alone, but even socialist countries do not try to control production and exchange totally. Choice of occupation and freedom of choice in purchasing goods and services are usually maintained.

Perhaps the most significant form of state control is ownership of the productive resources, such as key industries. Under ***socialism,*** *the state owns major industries* in order to ensure equality in the society. Socialism may take various forms in actual practice. In the Soviet Union and China, most industries are state controlled, whereas in Great Britain fewer of them are. ***Communism*** *is a type of socialism in which the state owns most or all of the industry,* and is usually established and maintained by a dictatorship.

Regulation of the ownership of the means of production and of profit making are among the important sorts of control. States attempt to regulate the economic institution in many other ways as well. Sometimes select industries, such as communications, are regarded important enough to socialize. In most industrialized nations, medical care has been socialized so that the state operates hospitals and pays physicians from public funds. Even in the United States, primary and secondary education are mostly owned and operated by governmental units, and thus can be considered to be socialized.

In contrast, under ***capitalism,*** as in the United States, *the means of production are generally privately held.* However, techniques such as wage and price controls tend to centralize the economic order by interceding in market forces that would otherwise serve to determine what goods and services would be produced, and at what prices they would be sold.

Intermediate between capitalism and communism is a compromise position: ***democratic socialism,*** which is *a political and economic system in which a republican form of representation,* as opposed to a dictatorship, *is coupled with state ownership of the "key" industries.* Most of the democratic socialist countries, like England, Norway, and Sweden, provide higher education for the intellectually able, and health care for those in need, independent of one's ability to pay. Such countries also have more income redistribution through taxes in order to minimize differences between the wealthy and the poor.

How Do Economies Become Centralized Under Capitalism?

In principle, capitalism involves a ***laissez-faire economy,*** *one which the state does not restrict.* In practice, even under capitalism most states exercise a variety of controls over the economy short of outright ownership of industry. These economies are not centrally organized by the state as socialist economies are. When the state exercises minimal control over modern economic institutions, economic power tends to become concentrated in the hands of a relatively small number of large firms. In the United States, for example, the 100 largest corporations constitute 0.0005 percent of all business firms, but they control over 50 percent of the industrial corporate assets (Dye, 1979). Capitalism concentrates wealth to this degree even in the presence of measures such as the Sherman Anti-Trust Act, which was designed to limit economic concentration.

When a corporation becomes very large, it may be able to afford to sell goods and services to consumers at lower prices than its competitors can. Sometimes large corporations can drive smaller competitors out of business this way. When a corporation successfully outlives its competitors, it may then be able to raise prices and earn abnormally high profits. *A corporation that controls a market has a* ***monopoly*** *on that market.*

Control by one or several firms conspiring to hold prices higher than they would be under fair competition is ***oligopoly or trust.*** Trusts rob the public of vast sums by causing them to pay higher prices than would prevail under fair competition. For instance, Texaco recently admitted cheating the public out of $1.25 billion dollars or more than 10 percent of all the money criminals steal in the U.S. in a typical year. Many governments attempt to limit trusts harmful to the society. For example, several of the largest firms in the United States, incuding Exxon, Standard Oil of California, Standard Oil (Indiana), and Standard Oil (Ohio) were once part of the original and enormous Standard Oil Corporation. The government forced Standard Oil to break into smaller separate units, although strong ties still exist among them. More recently AT&T was divided into smaller units because the government believed its enormous size was interfering with competition.

The original trust buster. "Teddy" Roosevelt's anti-trust posture was ridiculed by business interests, who depicted him as opposed to the railroad trust, the oil trust, the beer trust, Belamy stores, and *everything in general!* (Bettmann Archive)

Although no single corporation in the United States controls more than 2 percent of the gross national product, the giant corporations have tremendous monetary power. This can be converted into political power if corporations support politicians who are friendly to their points of view. Conflict theorists suggest that such informal arrangements between major owners of the giant corporations and politicians form part of the power elite in the United States (Mills, 1956; Domhoff, 1983; 1983). Even some functionalists have noted the potential influence that could be exerted by entities as large as the major oil, aircraft, automotive, and electronics producers (Dahl, 1973).

THE RISE AND DEVELOPMENT OF THE CORPORATION

General Motors, despite recent layoffs, still employs several times as many people as lived in classical Rome during the time of Julius Caesar. We have come to accept as natural the fact that most of us work in corporations where many of the other employees are strangers. Yet corporations that employ tens of thousands of people, making a highly diversified set of products and selling them around the world, are really a very recent social development—not more than 100 years old.

How did we arrive at contemporary corporations, many of which are larger in economic productivity than whole nations of people? The modern corporation grows from three roots: bureaucracy, mechanization, and capitalism. The technology of the modern factory and the modern corporation are actually very similar. Both factories and bureaucracies function by dividing labor into specialized jobs and coordinating the specialists involved.

The automobile factories of the early 1900s fabricated machines from basic materials, initially mostly steel, with some rubber, glass, and fabrics. Early factories also pioneered the specialization of the assembly line, using unskilled labor to replace skilled craftsmen of the earlier carriage trade. Even the office work was specialized, routinized, and organized by sets of rules. In short, bureaucracy was applied to production. The consequences for productivity were great and obvious, and the prime benefactors were those who ventured their capital to create even larger corporations. As you learned in Chapter 1, great thinkers like Max Weber attributed the rise of capitalism (and its partner, industrialization) to the rise of the Protestant ethic. Weber argued that the Calvinistic notions of working hard and living frugally naturally left people with *surplus resources, or* ***capital,*** and this in combination with the relaxing of the former taboo on making money through loans, led to the rapid and enormous growth of capitalism in Europe and the United States (Weber, 1904).

As corporations grew, their owners realized that by diversifying into various product lines they could gain additional control over suppliers and protect themselves against the whims of particular markets. Steel companies, for instance, decreased their reliance on outside suppliers like coal and iron mines by buying them out. Sears and Roebuck diversified in the products they marketed through mail order catalogs, thus assuring they could thrive even when some of the major manufacturers whose products they sold went out of business.

The largest corporations at the turn of the last century operated primarily in one nation; they were not yet international. Yet Karl Marx had predicted that the capitalists' relentless pursuit of profit would drive them around the globe in search of new markets (Marx, 1848). We now witness the validity of this prediction, for our world of work is becoming increasingly dominated by multinational corporations.

THE MULTINATIONAL CORPORATION AND ITS IMPACT

The third largest "economy" in the world, that of the multinational corporation, is growing at an annual rate of 10 percent, outpacing the growth rates of the economies of the United States and the U.S.S.R., which are the first and second largest, respectively. This rapidly growing economy is potentially the most influential and controversial economic unit in the world today. A ***multinational corporation*** *is a corporation that owns or manages businesses in two or more countries.* In purest form, multinationals manufacture in many countries, sell to world markets, draw management from several nations, and are owned by stockholders around the world. Examples of such "pure" multinationals are Shell, Unilever, and IBM, all among the thirty largest corporations in the world. At present, a multinational is likely to be centered in one home country, and often that country is the United States.

Though some multinationals began operations as long ago as seventy-five years, multinational corporations have only recently attained enormous size. In 1972, the Senate Foreign Relations Committee formed a new subcommittee to investigate multinational corporations, following revelations that International Telephone and Telegraph attempted to sabotage the 1970 Chilean presidential election to protect its $160 million investment in that country. Opponents of multinational corporations cite this case as an indication of the threat such corporations pose to national political independence.

Multinational corporations pose several threats. When they operate in a nation, they are actually likely to retard economic growth because rates of economic growth tend to decline as foreign investment increases (Evans, 1981). When multinational corporations move into a nation, they also tend to increase social inequality in the nation. Multinational corporations can promote increased inequality several ways. For instance, when they buy oil rights they can make some people enormously wealthy. At the same time, by hiring large numbers of local workers, they may disrupt the existing economy so that earlier means of production collapse, leaving some who had previously been able to earn a modest living totally out of work. Other critics point out that multinationals' abruptly moving out of a labor market, such as the case of several American firms that left France in 1963, can cause major disruptions in the country. Some multinational corporations have been accused of speculating in the international money market, thereby taking advantage of countries with unstable currencies by weakening the currencies with massive transfers, which drives the price lower.

Multinationals constitute a major new and independent force in the world political and economic scene. By straddling national boundaries, multinational corporations gain independence. Nestlé of Switzerland, one of the world's thirty largest corporations, does 98 percent of its business outside of Switzerland. This puts Nestlé into a position where it is hardly dependent on the authority of its native government.

Because of their size, multinationals often gain power over foreign economies. More than half of Canada's industrial capital is owned by United States or British multinational firms, raising the question of who really owns Canada. In a very real sense, a relatively small number of foreign corporations literally and legitimately own most of Canada's economy. In recognition of this, the Canadian government has begun to discourage foreign involvement in its economy.

In short, multinational corporations are relatively free of the influence of national governments, especially among the lesser developed nations whose labor they often exploit. The multinationals are able to destabilize economies by sudden departures. By contributing to the increased wealth of the rich nations by distorting the economic growth of the poor nations, they drive wedges between them. Ironically, some of the products multinationals make and sell, such as televisions, contribute to the poor nations' awareness of their poverty. This leads some experts to caution that the unrestrained profit-seeking of multinational corporations threatens world society (Bornschier and Hoby, 1981; Frank, 1984; Rubinson, 1981; Timberlake, 1985; Wallerstein, 1980; K. Ward, 1984).

Why Do Economies Develop?

Understanding the nature of changes in the economic order is central to understanding changes in society in general. Differences between living in a modern developed economy and living in an underdeveloped one are extreme. Vast differences in living also separate societies where the economy is centralized by the state, such as the Soviet Union, and those where it is not, like the United States.

Economic development also has great impact on all forms of social inequality. The nature of stratification and mobility changes as the economy becomes more developed (Lenski, 1966). Races and ethnic groups relate partly according to differences in their levels of economic development and the intensity of economic competition for scarce resources. The changing status of women is due, at least in part, to their changing relationship to the economic institution, with highly industrialized settings drawing them into the paid labor force. Even the "inferior" status of the young and old can be explained in terms of their lack of utility to the present economic order. Because the economic order is of such central importance, it is important to understand various factors that are involved in economic change, including technology, capital, colonization, availability of natural resources, societal values, and the contributions of other social institutions.

Different sociological perspectives offer differing interpretations of our economic institutions. Functionalists see capital as central to the stability and maintenance of society; conflict theorists see capital as a potential source of resentment, imbalance, and social change.

ACCELERATING INFLUENCES TO ECONOMIC DEVELOPMENT

TECHNOLOGY. One of the great engines of economic productivity is ***technology,*** *the tools and techniques used in producing goods and services.* The more economically advanced societies are generally those that have more sophisticated technology. By pioneering in the introduction of various technologies including steam engines, automobiles and trucks, telecommunications, and computers, the United States has generally led the world in economic development.

Improved mechanical and social technology dramatically alters the society and particularly the economic institution. Many social theorists see technological change in the means of production as the key to understanding all social change and social differences (Marx, 1904; Ogburn, 1936; Lenski, 1966). The introduction of key technological advances—such as the plow, sailing vessels, the steam engine, automobiles, and computers—has obvious as well as less apparent impact on societies and their economies. Clearly, advances in technology are necessary for economic development, but they are probably not enough to explain all of the differences in development between the economic orders of societies through history. Simple societies, for example, may borrow technology from more developed nations, rather than developing it themselves. Sheer knowledge of agricultural or industrial means of production is not sufficient to transform a hunting society into an agrarian one or an agrarian society into an industrial one.

The transformation from small, simply organized work groups to large, complex ones is one of many important factors in the development from a simple to a complex economy. Bureaucracy, as a social innovation, may be as important as key mechanical advances in explaining economic development. In the simplest societies, work groups are small, and workers perform similar or identical tasks. They share approximately equally in the productivity, and they are governed by custom and informal leadership. In industrialized economies, work groups are often large corporations in which workers perform highly specialized tasks within vast hierarchies where one executive's earnings often equal several times those of a laborer, and where company policy has replaced custom and informal leaders in governing the work activities.

Capitalism in action. Each day millions of shares of stock are traded here on the floor of the New York Stock Exchange as investors seek to maximize their profits. Interestingly, though billions of dollars of property is exchanged daily, transactions are purely verbal. No money, stock certificates, or even receipts change hands on the floor where a member's word constitutes a binding agreement. (*Photo courtesy the author*)

Economic development may bring the rewards of material well-being and relative freedom from hard, dangerous, or tedious labor. It also tends to disrupt much of the traditional culture, giving rise to the specialized institutions of the state, formal education, and science, and sometimes undermining the traditional institutions of kinship and religion.

The structural-functional perspective views technological innovation as a natural part of social life that results in functional adaptations for the improvement of society. Many conflict theorists see technology as destabilizing the rather precarious social order and releasing the pent-up social strain arising from latent class conflict. Marx believed that technological advances and the changes in social relations they bring carry us further toward the revolutionary transition into a classless socialistic society (Marx, 1848).

CAPITAL. ***Capital*** or *surplus resources that can be applied to creating new means of production,* is a key ingredient in economic development. Thousands of dollars in capital may be needed, for example, to buy a power boat equipped with modern fishing equipment to replace the traditional nets and rowboats used by fishing communities in Brazil. A farmer who spends some of his earnings to buy an irrigation system that will pay for itself several times over in increased productivity makes a capital investment. If capital is unavailable, growth may be impossible; if it is scarce, growth may be slow; and if it is abundant, growth can be very rapid.

Capital involves both a ***surplus,*** *more resources than are needed for bare subsistence,* and the willingness to use this surplus to improve production. Surplus resources such as labor, goods, land, or money may not always be used as capital. Surplus time can be used for leisure, surplus food for excessive consumption, and surplus land or money can be left idle. The idea of investing surplus in a productive way is relatively new, and the strength of the idea, and hence the availability of capital, depends on a society's values and beliefs.

Weber argued persuasively that Protestantism was an important though unrecognized ideology that gave rise to capitalism and the rapid economic development of the West. Functionalists are inclined to see capital as an organizing influence, tending to give powerful, progressive impetus to stable societal growth. Marx and many contemporary conflict theorists, on the other hand, point to the inherent inequality and instability of a small band of elites controlling the society's wealth. They argue that capitalism will constantly need to find new workers and markets to exploit to satisfy the capitalists' quest for more capital. This, they contend, inevitably leads to inequality, resentment, and an eventual collapse or overthrow of the prevailing capitalist hierarchy (Weber, 1904; Marx, 1867).

NATURAL RESOURCES. The availability of useful natural resources, such as land, oil, and minerals, also influences economic development. A society with an abundance of natural resources has an advantage in its potential for economic development. However, the rapid development and growth of Japan's economy in a densely populated territory demonstrates that economies can thrive even when the territory has few natural resources, provided certain crucial resources can be imported.

The value of natural resources sometimes depends on the level of technological sophistication. The oil-rich, less developed societies of the Middle East, for example, are industrializing rapidly because their oil is of great value to more developed nations. If the industrialized nations did not need oil to run engines, Middle Eastern economies would not be expanding so rapidly. Whereas functionalists would view natural resources as one of many societal resources, conflict theorists see them primarily as a means of production, through which owners can dominate workers (Fusfeld, 1985).

SOCIETAL VALUES. Differing definitions of the value of wealth, work, and material well-being affect the growth of the economic institution in the cultures in which they arise. During the seventeenth and eighteenth centuries, European economic thought was dominated by the doctrine of ***mercantilism,*** *the idea that the wealth of a nation was measured by the amount of gold and silver it held.* Adam Smith, an early proponent of capitalism, criticized mercantilism in his famous *Inquiry into the Nature and Causes of the Wealth of Nations,* published in 1776. Smith argued that wealth should be measured by a nation's ***productive base,*** *or its ability to produce things of value to that society.* He suggested that nations accumulating large quantities of gold and silver actually restricted their economic growth and wealth because valuable surplus resources were sitting idle and not being used productively.

On the other hand, if a culture trusts banks to hold money, the rich may keep their surplus in a bank, which will loan out much of it for productive use. The person who takes out the loan may benefit by being able to start a business in which to earn money. The bank earns interest on the loan and pays interest to those whose wealth is stored in the bank. This definition of wealth is more productive for society and allows the wealthy not only to have their accumulated wealth but to gain additional income through investment (Smelser, 1976).

Ideas about work and material well-being are also important in explaining why some economies have grown faster than others. The American culture generally regards work as desirable, and Americans who do not work are often treated as deviant and seen as lazy or irresponsible.

Not all cultures share this attitude. In some societies the culture encourages people not to seek more than a modest living standard. Introducing new technology into these cultures may merely mean that people choose to work less and enjoy more leisure time. Such societies are handicapped in terms of economic growth.

Functionalists are likely to reason that ideas are important constraints and causes of social change. Conflict theorists generally adopt the perspective that the

If I got that jacket, I'd be happy. Western cultures tend to identify well-being with material prosperity, and even these seemingly counter-cultural young men value expensive clothes. Materialism appears to be quite strongly associated with industrial societies. *(Reuters/Bettmann Newsphotos)*

ruling elites of an era determine the prevailing ideas. They tend to discount the impact of ideas on the political and economic structure, because they see ideas and attitudes as being force-fed to the exploited groups by the elites. For them, the material conditions of society, including technology, largely determine the social structure.

Western cultures tend to identify well-being with material prosperity. Industrialization raises most people's material standard of living considerably. However, as we explore more thoroughly in the chapter on population and the environment, industrialism places heavy loads on the environment and creates heavy reliance on high energy consumption, especially on limited fossil fuels. Whereas industrial and postindustrial social orders may seem advanced in the material sense, they are precariously dependent on limited supplies of energy. They also tend to stress materialism as the path to satisfaction. Simpler forms of society, which use less energy and define well-being in more spiritual terms, might ultimately prove to be more functional forms of society.

IMPEDIMENTS TO ECONOMIC DEVELOPMENT

COLONIALISM. The growth of some economies has been stunted by their colonization by more powerful nations who control their development in such a way that their economies are unevenly developed. Secondary sector work, such as the manufacturing and sale of diamonds from South Africa, was kept in the imperial power's homeland, providing rich resources to the imperial power while not allowing the colonial society to develop into a whole and independent economy. By not developing the refining and manufacturing sectors, the imperialists protect their own economies from competition and keep the colonies dependent on them for finished products like machines. Thus while functionalists would argue that colonialism is one path to reducing the differences in development between nations, the conflict theorists call attention to the often one-sided development of the economic sectors in the colonies (Frank, 1984; Rubinson, 1981; Timberlake, 1985; I. Wallerstein, 1980).

THE INFLUENCE OF OTHER SOCIAL INSTITUTIONS. A modern economy depends in part on certain institutions and organizations that are not always available in traditional societies. For example, developed economies are characterized by a high degree of division of labor, or specialization. This requires relatively highly developed institutions of formal education for workers.

In traditional societies, community pressure and long-standing relationships tend to discourage fraud in exchanges. In contrast, total strangers frequently exchange goods and services in modern societies, and the state establishes legal procedures to minimize fraud or other similar abuses. Thus, a well-developed political institution may benefit the development of the economic institution. Similarly, the introduction of state-sponsored money as a medium of exchange must precede rapid economic growth.

The question Why do economic institutions develop? is a complicated one. Many factors are important, including technological innovation; abundance of capital; degree of colonization; availability of natural resources; appropriate societal values concerning wealth, working, and material well-being; and supportive social institutions such as a well-developed state, a monetary system of exchange, and the availability of specialized training in the form of formal education.

Most Americans are familiar with great differences of wealth and poverty within their own nation. Culture shock still hits many Americans when they first experience the squalor of shanty towns and beggars in many of the major cities of the underdeveloped world. Why have some parts of the world developed so plentifully whereas others seem hopelessly poor? The following "Close-Up on Theory" explores the forces that keep much of the world's population living in poverty.

CLOSE-UP on • *THEORY* •

Paul Harrison on the Causes of Economic Underdevelopment

The Theorist and the Setting

Harrison devoted more than a decade to shuttling between those who study international poverty and those who live in it. He based *Inside the Third World: The Anatomy of Poverty* on five years of research and travel in eleven countries including Sri Lanka, Upper Volta, the Ivory Coast, Colombia, Peru, Brazil, Indonesia, Singapore, India, Bangladesh, and Kenya.

The Theorist's Goal

Harrison provides a "general survey of the entire field of development problems" (p. 9). He believes "underdevelopment of countries and of human beings cannot be compartmentalized if it is to be fully grasped. It is a total situation in which every element plays a part" (p. 9).

He addresses two central questions: (1) Why have some nations developed economically while others remain poor? and (2) why do the poor, or Third World, nations have difficulty becoming wealthy?

Concepts and Propositions

Proposition 1: Third World nations are typically handicapped by severe environments.

Authorities rarely mention environment as a primary cause of poverty. Harrison suggests, "Perhaps the idea conflicts with our constitutional optimism that wealth can be created solely by human endeavor" (p. 21). Yet, "the problem of underdevelopment appears to be confined to the tropics, between about 30 degrees north and south of the equator" (p. 21). "All but a tiny handful of developing countries lie inside . . . zones where average annual temperatures exceed 20 degrees centigrade [68 degrees Fahrenheit] (p. 22). Harrison points out that whereas the lush tropical rain forests have adapted to such climate, these nations actually have a very superficial soil, which is quite poor for agriculture when deforested. To complicate matters, the warm temperatures provide a favorable environment for insects and other parasites that attack crops. The tsetse fly, for instance, carries sleeping sickness to people and livestock. Furthermore, the people in these climates often face 95 degree Fahrenheit temperatures in which to work. Studies in the United States have shown productivity falls to about 50 percent its normal level when the temperature rises to 95 degrees.

Rain also poses problems. Close to the equator (0–20 degrees of latitude), regions like the Amazon and Congo and the islands of Southeast Asia get too much rain. A little further from the equator (between 20 and 30 degrees north or south), the problem is one of either too little rain, or drenching rains such as eight-inches-per-hour cloudbursts that erode the land. Growing seasons are much shorter and more susceptible to being ruined by a late start, and when the growing season fails, famine comes and with it disease.

In many ways the environment of the Third World is disastrous. Climate impedes food production and kills people outright. More than nine out of ten disaster-related deaths occur in the developing countries, largely from droughts, floods, cyclones, and earthquakes. Not only do these forces kill, they also destroy housing, leaving survivors homeless. In some locations, such as the southern edge of the Sahara Desert, overworking the soil has caused a steady southward creeping of the desert.

We should not be surprised that industrialism did not spring forth in such a hostile environment, but why did it start in Europe, as opposed to India, Asia, or the Arab world, all of which produced significant civilizations?

Proposition 2: Third World nations lack the crucial technologies that allowed Europe to establish economic development.

Specifically, Harrison points to Europe's early superiority in "the technology of war and sea travel, which were the basis of her military conquests" (p. 33). Harrison notes that Europe also had "evolved industrial capitalism, with its peculiar contempt for and exploitation of human beings and nature" (p. 33). One of the primary reasons for this technological gap relates back to proposition 1: the underdeveloped world lacks a significant agricultural surplus, so there is little left over to devote to developing new ways of doing things. But Harrison points to political impediments as well.

Proposition 3: Political despotism impedes development, whereas free cities and merchants facilitate development.

Harrison suggests that both China and India might have produced industrialization (the mechanization of production), had their political structures not been characterized by the absolute rule of despots who hoarded virtually all surplus wealth. Instead of investing their fortunes in enterprises that would increase the output of their societies, they tended to squander them on wars and conspicuous consumption. In India, for instance, the monarch had a throne worth $24 million and a residence worth $70 million. Europe, on the other hand, had "a healthy agricultural surplus; a class of entrepreneurs free to pursue wealth independently of the state and motivated to do so; the accumulation by them of enough capital to finance investment; the development of a practical science based on mathematics and mechanics; and the availability of expanding markets to encourage the rapid development of machine production" (pp. 38–39).

Proposition 4: Colonialization impedes the economic development of the colony as it accelerates the development of the imperial power.

European nations subdued and dominated most of the rest of the world as the result of superior military might and shipping technology. They plundered the colonies, destroying their governments and seizing the valuables, much as Cortez seized the gold and silver from the Inca temples. Typically the imperial power destroyed local industry, creating two markets—one a source of labor to work in the industrial facilities introduced by the imperial power, the other a market for goods and services that the natives must now buy from the outsiders or industries controlled by outsiders. The imperialist then exploited the colonies, drawing goods and services from them at the same time they developed the colonies as captive markets for European products.

Proposition 5: The extreme inequality of wealth in developing nations tends to slow their rate of development.

Developing nations often exhibit extreme inequality between the masses of poor people and the tiny minority of wealthy ones. Because new technologies like tractors are affordable only to the wealthy, the situation worsens as small landholders lose their plots to larger concerns. Similarly, new breeds of plants may be much more productive per acre, but they often require special attention such as very regular irrigation, which small farmers have difficulty providing. Also poor people frequently go into debt to wealthier ones and lose everything when they are unable to pay the high interest rates.

Proposition 6: Rapidly growing populations overload the ability of underdeveloped economies to grow.

This, according to Harrison, is the crucial variable. In 1900 developing nations included about 1 billion people. By 1960 the population had reached 2 billion, and in 1977 they passed the 3 billion mark.

Third World people tend to see large families as beneficial because extra children provide extra labor and some assurance of care for the parents in their old age. But when the family's small plot has to be divided among several sons, each ends up with even less chance of success than the father had.

Proposition 7: Through their contact with wealthy nations, poor nations' economies become distorted in ways that destabilize their societies.

Harrison says:

> These are the five fundamental imbalances of the typical developing economy: industrial development without adequate agricultural development, large-scale industry without the prior development of small-scale, urbanization outpacing industrialization, services growing too fast for the productive base for agriculture and industry, and population growth racing ahead of employment growth (p. 208).

Interpretation

According to Harrison's theory, circumstances such as climate, technological sophistication, and freedom from political despots gave European nations a head start in development. Once they took the lead they frequently exploited other nations in ways that advanced themselves as they distorted and destabilized the societies in the underdeveloped world.

Obviously the problems go beyond the willingness of the people in these countries to work hard, though this too may contribute. As a solution, Harrison suggests, "the balance has to be shifted toward developing agriculture and increasing the incomes of rural and urban poor" (p. 208).

Harrison's work provides a quick overview of the dynamics of economic development. He blends functionalist modernization theory, which focuses on development as a natural process through which societies grow, with the rival conflict, or world systems theory, which stresses the role of the powerful core nations who dominate and exploit the economies of the weaker "peripheral" nations. We explore this topic and these theories in more depth in Chapter 19, "Social Change: Urbanization and Modernization."

Questions

1. Has Harrison suggested anything that seems untrue?
2. Has Harrison omitted anything? How do his ideas compare with Weber's assertion that ideas were of central significance to European economic development?
3. If Harrison is right, is there any hope that the Third World can overcome all the handicaps it now has? If so, how?

SOURCE Paul Harrison. 1982. *Inside the Third World: The Anatomy of Poverty.* New York, Penguin Books.

What Are the Major Economic Trends?

For the past one-half century the United States has enjoyed a position of economic strength that has led to economic and political dominance in the world. As World War II began, the United States produced one-third of the world's manufactured goods. At the close of the war this proportion was close to one-half. No other nation ever commanded such a share of world production. By 1987, the U.S. share of world production had dropped to 20 percent (Kennedy, 1987). This suggests why the United States is in a weaker position to dominate other nations economically.

Average income figures also show decline. During the postwar years, the average American family increased its income substantially. As Figure 15.1 indicates, average family income, even when adjusted for inflation, doubled from $8,800 in 1947 to $17,600 in 1978. It peaked in 1973, wavering below that level and not reaching it again in more than a decade. Family income in constant dollars (these adjusted for inflation) is now no higher than about fifteen years ago.

FIGURE 15.1 Average Family Income in Constant 1986 Dollars SOURCE United States Department of Commerce, *Statistical Abstract of the United States, 1988* (108th ed.), p. 427.

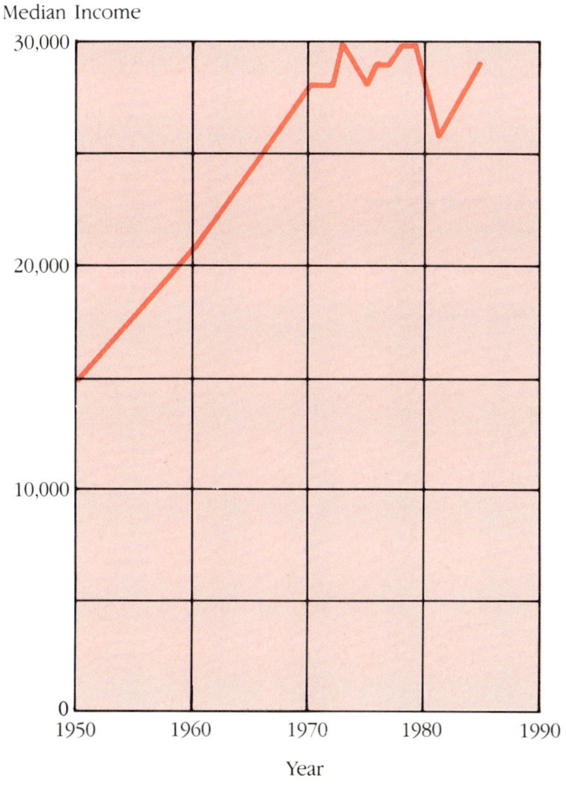

Are Americans working less effectively? Part of the cause of these trends actually lies with what is happening outside the U.S. workplace. As Figure 15.2 indicates, over the past decades other nations' economies have grown productive at faster rates than ours.

During the 1970s several nations approached and then exceeded United States productivity levels. As the United States became less competitive, family incomes stopped growing. Ironically part of the reason the United States is less competitive is the relatively high income enjoyed by its workers. Figure 15.3 shows that United States' labor costs are relatively high and rising rapidly. Since productivity decreases as wages increase, this trend helps explain our productivity difficulties.

Thus, even as the U.S. economy was growing, it was growing less rapidly than that of Japan and several other nations. Simultaneously, U.S. labor was getting expensive faster than that of several nations, notably Japan, where labor costs fell. Though the United States is actually more productive than two decades ago, it is far less competitive; as a result, the United States routinely imports more than it exports, which tends to strengthen foreign industry as it erodes its own.

When the United States tries to maintain military dominance, it spends large shares of what is produced on weapons, which further taxes productivity. Both the United States and the Soviet Union spend large proportions of their Gross National Product on defense. Japan, which has been prohibited from rearming, spends very little.

Debt also threatens the U.S. economy. Increasingly the United States has failed to balance its budget, and as the national debt increases, the interest on this debt rises to unprecedented amounts. Families in the future will have to pay even more of their earnings in taxes to cover the interest on this debt.

On the surface the United States appears simply to be losing ground because we do not compete well in world markets. However, being competitive depends both on the worker and the capital with which American firms work. In their search for profits, many U.S. firms have moved manufacturing and engineering out of the United States to cheap labor markets. At the same time they have often taken short-range profits on old technologies instead of investing in new, more productive technologies.

Frequently, Japan is praised as a success story based on hard work and smart management. As Mamouru Iga shows, Japanese growth rates are deceptively high, however, while real benefits to the Japanese worker are remarkably low. Workers may retire at 55, but they often retire to poverty given their very poor or nonexistent pension plans and Social Security benefits. Japanese workers also work within a feudal-

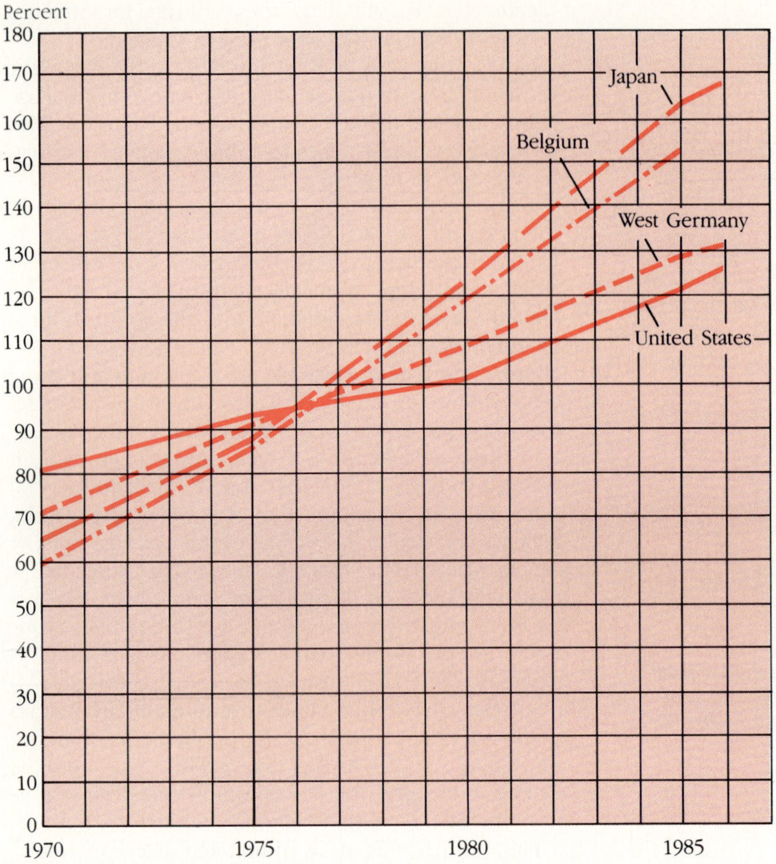

FIGURE 15.2 Growth in Manufacturing Productivity of Selected Countries, 1970–1986. Although United States' productivity is rising, other nations' productivity has risen faster and exceeded that of the United States. SOURCE U.S. Department of Commerce, *Statistical Abstract of the United States, 1988* (108th ed.), Washington, D.C., 1987, p. 813.

TABLE 15.1 Occupations and Median Weekly Earnings of Full-Time Workers, 1982

	Men	Women	All Full-Time Workers
Professional & technical	$489	$338	$411
Managers & officials	520	310	436
Clerical workers	337	236	247
Sales workers	397	222	326
Forepersons & skilled workers	380	232	370
Semiskilled workers	315	201	325
Laborers	256	208	250
Service workers	247	174	201
Farm workers	191	160	189
All occupations:	$370	$240	$308
Women's earnings as percent of men's:		65%	

Note: The earnings do not include fringe benefits, which may equal 20 to 30 percent of income.
SOURCE U.S. Department of Labor, Bureau of Labor Statistics, *News*, August 12, 1982, Tables 4 and 5.

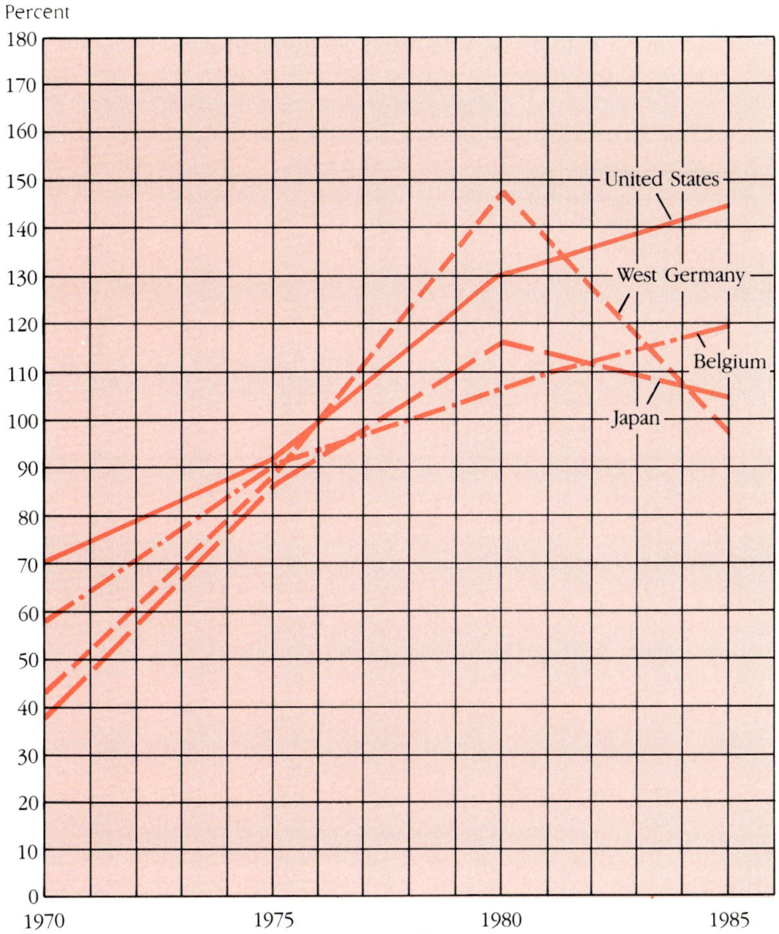

FIGURE 15.3 Growth in Unit Labor Costs for Selected Countries, 1970–1985. High and rapidly rising labor costs partly explain why the United States frequently loses the "productivity race" depicted in Figure 14.2. SOURCE U.S. Department of Commerce, *Statistical Abstract of the United States, 1988* (108th ed.), Washington, D.C., 1987, p. 813.

istic industrial organization that requires a marked degree of blind obedience and respect for the organization (Iga, 1986).

How Is Work Organized in the United States?

WHERE WE WORK

The question "What do you want to be when you grow up?" represents one way of thinking about where we will work. Most of us end up for a time in one of some 20,000 officially recognized occupations. But many, if not most people in this diverse set of occupations have little knowledge of the workplace they will work in until shortly before they enter it. Occupations represent a major way of classifying the world of work.

WORK AND CLASS. Another way to conceptualize the diversity of work in the United States is to think of work in terms of class stratification. In our earlier discussion of stratification we saw that functionalists describe occupations as varying in terms of their importance to society and the consequent prestige, power, and income associated with them. Table 15.1 displays this occupational grouping as well as the associated earnings.

GOODS AND SERVICES. This representation of the occupational structure is consistent with the status attainment models discussed in Chapter 8. Work and the economy may also be categorized into the primary, secondary, and tertiary sectors discussed earlier or into either service or goods-producing industries. Table 15.2 lists some of the major industrial groupings and shows how the nature of work has changed during the past

TABLE 15.2 Employment in Goods-Producing and Service-Producing Industries, 1890–1982 (in percent)

	1890	1950	1970	1982
SERVICE-PRODUCING INDUSTRIES	26	51	65	71
Finance, insurance, real estate	1	4	5	6
Business, personal, professional services	8	10	19	20
Trade: wholesale and retail	9	18	20	22
Transportation, utilities, communications	6	8	6	6
Government: federal, state, and local	2	11	15	17
GOODS-PRODUCING INDUSTRIES	74	49	35	29
Manufacturing	20	29	25	21
Construction	6	4	5	4
Agriculture, forestry, mining, fishing	48	16	5	4
Total employed labor force (in millions)	23.3	58.9	78.6	98.9

Note: Business, personal, and professional services include, for example, consulting and legal services, health services, private education, repair, cleaning and gardening services, entertainment, hotels and motels, barbershops and beautyshops, private household services. The military services are here excluded from federal government employment. In 1982 the armed forces employed about 2 million uniformed persons.

SOURCE 1890 and 1970 distributions are calculated from labor force data in Delbert C. Miller and William H. Form, *Industrial Sociology* (New York: Harper & Row, 1980), pp. 66, 68–69. 1950 data are drawn from *Statistical Abstract of the U.S., 1974*, p. 228; 1982, U.S. Department of Labor, Bureau of Labor Statistics, *Employment and Earnings*, 29 (May 1982): 25 and 56.

century. These data show that service-producing industries have grown steadily from 26 percent of the economy in 1890 to 71 percent in 1982. Over the same period goods-producing industries dropped from 74 percent to 29 percent. Whereas some people speak of the deindustrialization of the United States, the proportion of the labor force in manufacturing has remained relatively constant over the century at 20 to 30 percent. The big changes have come in agriculture. Once accounting for nearly half the jobs, it now includes fewer than 5 percent. During this same period, government employment grew nearly tenfold, from 2 percent in 1890 to 17 percent in 1982. Only the transportation, utilities, communication, and construction categories (along with manufacturing) have not dramatically increased or decreased.

Behind these statistics lie some very tough transitions. The family on a small farm which has been displaced by agribusiness leaves the work they have known all their lives to seek new work only with great difficulty. Similarly, even the most diligent of steel workers can find themselves unemployed because of plant closings. Economic change often brings with it traumatic experiences for individuals. The boundaries between sectors and industries are not easily crossed by individuals, and in fact they may be more aptly described as barriers.

TWO LABOR MARKETS. Social scientists now realize that in many important ways the economy divides into two distinct labor markets. The ***primary labor market*** *contains relatively well-paid blue- and white-collar jobs.* In contrast, the ***secondary labor market*** *contains jobs with relatively lower wages and high rates of turnover.* Primary labor market jobs are typically found within big businesses and in areas involving heavy investments in advanced technology; for example, being a management trainee for IBM, working on the Ford Motor Company assembly line, or repairing Xerox machines. Compared with secondary labor market jobs, they are more likely to be unionized and stable. They typically offer more job security, require more education, offer more opportunity for advancement, and require positive work habits and attitudes.

In contrast, the secondary labor market involves smaller businesses that are labor intensive, nonunionized, and offer lower wages and salaries. Here we often find high rates of turnover from people quitting and being let go. Little skill or education is required, the work may be boring, and the employers often tolerate casual attitudes and work styles in part because they have invested little in training and are investing little in wages and salaries. Secondary sector jobs usually offer almost no opportunity for advancement. Examples of these jobs would include foreman in a small manufacturing plant, secretary in a small law firm, and manager of a small discount clothing store.

Clearly these different labor markets offer distinctly different work experiences, and people tend to be channeled toward one or the other on the basis of social status. The primary labor market is dominated by white males aged 25–45. Women, blacks, Hispanics, and the young and old are in the secondary labor market.

Some economists believe that the split labor market emerged largely since World War II, perhaps as the result of such factors as the migration of blacks from southern to northern cities, the migration of Puerto Ricans to the United States, the influx of women into the paid labor force, the baby boom, the crowding of women and minorities into low-wage occupations, automation, and the moving of manufacturing overseas.

For several reasons the future looks bleak for those working in the secondary labor market. Even when economic times are good and unemployment drops, for instance to 2 percent for the primary labor market, unemployment rates in the secondary market usually remain very high, as much as 40 percent for young black females. The wage and salary gap between the sectors appears to be getting bigger rather than diminishing. One finds very few ladders by which to climb out of the secondary market. Finally, working under conditions in which the job is boring, the pay is low, and little is expected from one by co-workers and supervisors, fosters cynical attitudes and casual work habits that leave one poorly equipped to compete in the primary labor market.

The implications are not good for society either. As we see in Chapter 10, labor markets split along racial lines are a major source of racial antagonism. The secondary labor market is neither an attractive nor a particularly reliable means of support. Consequently we have implemented welfare programs that generally do not address the basic problem or even relieve the symptoms. Labor market segmentation poses a major challenge to us (Kalleberg, Wallace, and Althauser, 1981).

We have considered work as taking place in occupations, industries, and labor market sectors, but in another sense most of us work in a particular corporate setting. Only about one in ten people today are self-employed, a rate that has remained constant for nearly a century. Those of us who work for others change employers frequently. Men average only five years in a specific job whereas women average only two and one-half years (Tausky, 1984). Corporations represent the dominant link between the economy and the individual. We discuss the idea of corporate cultures in chapter 5. Later in this chapter we will discuss worker satisfaction as related to the culture of the corporation and the amount of control the worker has over his or her work (Bowditch and Buono, 1982).

Not just men! Increasingly we are a society of "people" working, including, in growing numbers, women and children. (*Photo courtesy the author*)

WHO WORKS

A century ago, in 1880, just 15 percent of women were in the labor force, and about one-half century ago, in 1940, the proportion of women working had risen to 25 percent. Since 1940 the proportion of women employed has more than doubled to a level of 55 percent in 1986. For most of the past 100 years, male labor-force participation hovered at about 80 percent, reaching 83 percent in 1960. Since then the proportion of employed males declined to 76 percent in 1986. (U.S. Bureau of the Census, 1970; U.S. Bureau of the Census, 1987, p. 366).

During the past decade, the proportion of working mothers has increased dramatically, moving from a minority of 45 percent of those with children under 18 in 1975 to a majority of 61 percent in 1986. In 1987 for the first time a majority of women with children less than a year old (51 percent) also worked in the paid labor force. (See Figure 15.4) Marital status also influences the proportion of women working. In 1986, the labor force participation rates for women of various marital statuses were: married 55 percent, separated 62 percent, divorced 76 percent (U.S. Bureau of the Census, 1986, p. 383).

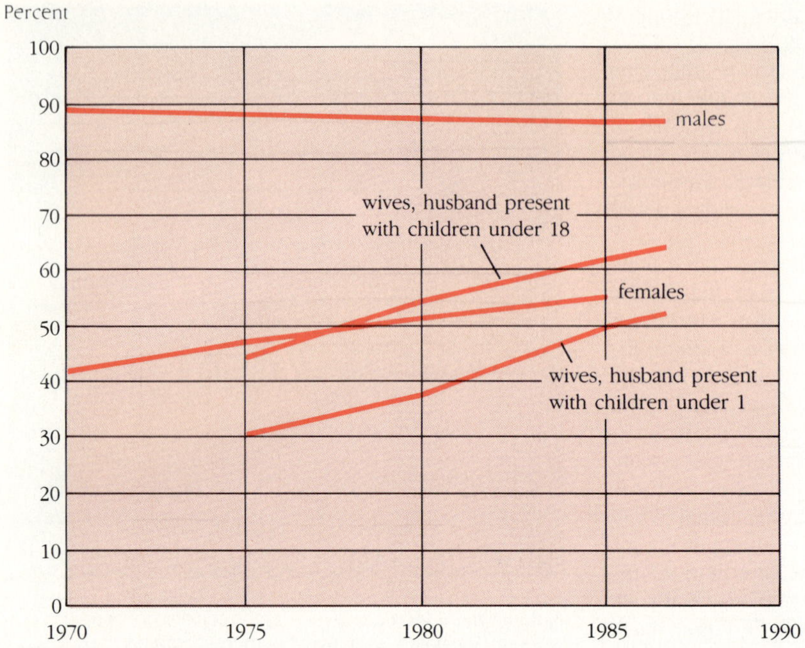

FIGURE 15.4 Males, Females, and Mothers in the Paid Labor Force: 1970–1987. With steadily rising female participation in the work force, we have reached the point where most women work for pay outside the home, even if they are married with a child less than 1 year old. SOURCE U.S. Bureau of the Census, *Statistical Abstract of the United States, 1988* (108th ed.), Washington, D.C. pp. 366–374.

Many factors help to explain why increasing numbers of women choose to be employed. Many women work for the psychic gratification. Although sexism is still common in our society, prejudice and discrimination have declined somewhat, and approval for women working has increased. Postindustrial society requires more of the less physical occupations that have traditionally been filled by females, so women have more opportunities to work. As a group, women have become more career oriented and assertive of their rights to equal opportunity. For many families, women entering the paid labor force have helped to lessen the effects of the leveling of the average American family's buying power.

Increasing numbers of teen-agers who are still in school have entered the paid labor force during the past decades. In 1947 only about one in four (27 percent) school-going boys worked, but by 1980 the proportion had come close to one in two (44 percent). Over the same time period, female students entered the work force even faster than males, from 17 percent in 1947 to 41 percent in 1980. Although the American culture has long prized hard work, several social scientists are documenting some of the adverse consequences of this trend. Ellen Greenberger and Laurence Steinberg point out that the vast majority of these after-school jobs offer little opportunity to build job skills for later life or to have meaningful contact with adults. About one-half of teen workers are either food service workers or store clerks. Such work is often related to weaker academic performance, increasingly cynical attitudes toward work, and higher rates of certain kinds of delinquency, including substance abuse (Greenberger and Steinberg, 1986).

ORGANIZED OCCUPATIONS

Does the "boss" always define the job? In many occupations the employees have formed unions or professional organizations to assist in defining their roles. Workers and employers struggle, sometimes bitterly and even violently, to arrive at a definition of who will do what work, under what terms, and how much they will be paid.

LABOR UNIONS. The strike by air traffic controllers a few years ago provided a dramatic example of employees battling their employer with both the employees' jobs and their union at stake. In that confrontation, members of the Professional Air Traffic Controllers Organization (PATCO) wanted their employer, the Federal Aviation Agency (FAA), to shorten their work week, make them eligible for retirement sooner, and pay higher wages. Though PATCO leaders and the FAA had reached a tentative agreement, the membership of PATCO soundly rejected it and walked off their jobs. While strikes are relatively common and legal in private businesses, they are illegal for government employees. In the past public workers have struck illegally, and sometimes won the battles rather than being penalized. In this case, President Reagan threatened to

President Reagan did not help the cause of unionism when he decertified PATCO, the air traffic controllers union. PATCO had engaged in an illegal strike against the Federal Aviation Administration while seeking a shorter work week, higher pay, and earlier retirement. Here the controllers and their families demonstrate in violation of a "back to work" order. *(UPI/Bettmann Newsphotos)*

decertify the union and fire the 12,000 air traffic controllers if they did not return to work. When they refused to return to their jobs, President Reagan carried out his threat.

A ***labor union*** is an *association of workers to promote and protect the welfare and rights of the members.* Labor unions have arisen primarily in this century and have grown mostly in working-class occupations. In 1900 only 3 percent of the U.S. labor force belonged to labor unions. Membership peaked after World War II at 23 percent, but by 1984 it had declined to 19 percent.

Unions have generally drawn their membership from blue-collar occupations. As white-collar jobs have become increasingly prevalent, unions have had fewer prospective members. Many of the new white-collar workers are women, who as a group are only about one-third as likely to join a union as men. Many white-collar workers think of unions as being for blue-collar workers rather than people of higher status. Some white-collar workers, like engineers and teachers, prefer to seek professional, rather than union, status. When unions do begin to organize white-collar workers, management often grants concessions that lessen the workers' interest in paying the cost of having a union. The fact that unions tend to win benefits even for nonunion workers is part of the reason they have not grown to a larger proportion of the labor force.

Other factors contribute to union decline as well. In the early days of unions, the two largest, the UAW and the CIO, competed with one another. In the 1950s they merged, thus removing a competitive incentive to do the best for their members. Also, during the 1950s, several major union officials were involved in union corruption. Finally, watching PATCO workers lose their jobs and members of the UAW–CIO accept major pay cuts has probably dulled the enthusiasm of some who might otherwise consider unions as a solution to problems in the workplace.

Despite the fact that unions involve a declining minority of the work force, they wield a great deal of power. Particularly in industries and occupations where unions have operated, such as manufacturing and construction trades, employers of nonunion labor are likely to watch the outcome of struggles between unions and management. They may seek to meet or come close to similar terms with their own employees in order to prevent their forming or joining unions. Conversely, where there is a substantial pool of nonunion labor, unions may have difficulty organizing, because they would have difficulty competing with cheaper nonunionized labor (Latta, 1981; Ritzer and Walczak, 1985).

PROFESSIONS. While some workers, mostly those in blue-collar occupations, were forming unions to gain control of their work, others, mostly in white-collar occupations, have been evolving into professions to gain almost total control of their occupations. Professions represent a second major attempt by workers to control the definition of their occupations, and they are often even more successful at securing benefits than are unions. The term ***profession*** describes *an occupation that has been able to establish exclusive jurisdiction over certain kinds of services and to negotiate freedom from external intervention and control over the conditions and contexts of their work.* A medical doctor is a prime example of a professional; but lawyers, dentists, pharmacists and even insurance brokers also fit the definition (Friedson, 1977). In practice, professions often succeed in establishing a legal monopoly on their work, giving them exclusive rights to do certain work. Only a medical doctor, for instance, can remove tonsils, and only a lawyer can practice law. Professions also establish ***autonomy,*** or *freedom from external social control* over their work. Physicians, for example, rather than some outside authority like the state, determine who will be allowed to practice medicine and under what circumstances.

The medical and legal professions are so strong today that we might mistakenly assume they are naturally so. But two hundred years ago, physicians were as likely to be quacks as not, and lawyers were distrusted for encouraging and profiting from disputes. As John Quincy Adams put it in 1787:

The mere title of lawyer is sufficient to deprive a man of public confidence . . . (and) prevails to so great a degree that the most innocent and irreproachable life cannot guard a lawyer against the hatred of his fellow citizens (quoted in Lieberman, 1979:47).

How do some occupations come to rate the privilege of professional status? For an occupation to rise to professional status, four things usually happen. First, the occupation must exclusively control a body of expert knowledge. Professions do this by creating their own exclusive training schools. Second, members of the occupation must form a professional association, much as physicians formed the American Medical Association. These professional associations lobby for laws that will allow the profession to regulate itself. They also try to promote the profession's schools as the only way to learn the skills of the occupation, seek to keep similar occupations from straying into areas of work they claim, and try to create a favorable public image of the profession (Rothman, 1987). The third major step toward professionalization is to persuade the state to require licensing of the occupation. The professional organization argue that it is in the public's best interest to license doctors, lawyers, or whatever, but the members of the occupation are also major winners. The fourth and final step toward professionalization is the establishment of a code of ethics. Again, the professional association portrays the code as protecting the public, yet it also significantly protects the profession by building public trust and solidarity within the profession. Often the code severely restrains competition and forbids advertising, frequently pushing the cost of professional services higher due to a lack of competition.

Several occupations, including law, medicine, dentistry, pharmacy, and nursing have cleared these hurdles and established themselves as professions (See Table 15.3). However, many of the professions fight ongoing battles with competing occupations.

As was the case with unions, some of the established professional strength is eroding. Sociologists refer to *the process of lessening monopoly and autonomy of a profession* as ***deprofessionalization.***

Several factors can induce deprofessionalization. Professions have traditionally been able to hoard their special knowledge, but as the general public becomes more educated, professions may experience difficulty keeping the professional "secrets" away from other educated people. With growing educational levels comes increased skepticism from the public regarding any questionable professional practices. The courts have also forced more involvement of the client in key decisions, for instance, by requiring patients to make an "informed consent" in the case of dangerous procedures. This means the physician must explain procedures and describe risks. Only when the informed patient consents can certain procedures like surgery be carried out. Clients are also seeking second opinions from professionals. As the public becomes better educated they become less convinced of the need for professionals to monopolize the work they do.

For several reasons lay people now perform tasks once reserved for professionals. Professional work, like most work, has grown bureaucratic. Individual tasks of a job can be done by lay people; one need not be a doctor or nurse to take information about a person's medical history, for instance. New occupations like medical technician and paralegal reduce the task ter-

TABLE 15.3 The Process of Professionalization in the United States

	Became Full-Time Occupation	First Training School	First University School	First Local Professional Association	First National Association	First State Licensing Requirement	Code of Ethics
Law	17th century	1784	1817	1802	1878	1732	1908
Medicine (M.D.)	17th century	1765	1779	1735	1847	1780	1912
Dentistry	17th century	1840	1867	1844	1840	1868	1866
Pharmacy	1646	1821	1868	1821	1852	1808	1850
Insurance brokerage	1750s	1927	—	1869	1890	1911	1929
Accounting	1718	1853	1882	1882	1886	1896	1917
Nursing	1790s	1839	1909	1886	1897	1903	1893
Funeral directing	1860s	1874	1914	1864	1882	1894	1884
Psychology	1880s	1888	1888	1892	1925	1945	1952
Optometry	1880s	1892	1910	1896	1897	1901	1935
Chiropractic	1895	1898	—	—	1926	1913	1966

SOURCE Harold L. Wilensky. "The Professionalization of Everyone?" *American Journal of Sociology*, 70 (Sept. 1964): 143. © 1964 by the University of Chicago Press. All rights reserved.

ritory that the profession can claim as its own. Increasingly, professionals find themselves competing with their former assistants. As professionals develop increasingly sophisticated techniques, such as laboratory tests, X-rays, braces, and artificial limbs or teeth, they have to rely on technicians to produce the devices. Occasionally these technicians become skilled enough to challenge the exclusive right of the professionals to market the devices. For instance, in Oregon, the dental technicians who had made dentures to the specifications of dentists won the right to organize as denturists who would, after special training, be able to service the public directly (Rothman, 1987).

Competition contributes to this trend toward bureaucracy in the professions, which in turn contributes to deprofessionalization. Typically, professionals must compete more than they previously did. Medical insurance companies contribute to this pressure by sometimes requiring second opinions. In the law profession, no-fault divorce laws and no-fault car insurance have eliminated much of the demand that once existed for lawyers. For decades the American Bar Associates' ethical code forbade advertising. Consumer groups challenged the legality of this code and the case went to the Supreme Court in 1977. The court outlawed the ban on advertising as a violation of federal antitrust laws.

Though professionals are more frequently practicing in bureaucratic settings like large law firms or group medical practices, these occupations still proved unusually high in power, prestige, and wealth. The professional who opts to practice in a large professional association will usually find his or her work more specialized and more subject to the authority of senior professionals in the firm than does the free professional. The free professional in a solo practice will have more discretion over his or her work, and the range of work will usually be more general.

UNEMPLOYMENT

At 11 P.M. financial analyst Brent Watson is diligently preparing an annual report. He has been working overtime, and he plans to be in on Saturday to wrap it up. Watson's boss calls him in. Though he had earlier told Watson that he was in line for a promotion, the boss now tells him that the firm no longer requires his services. "You may want to clean out your desk during the lunch hour to save yourself later embarrassment," he counsels. Brent has just joined the ranks of the unemployed. Later he will describe this loss of employment as "the most humiliating experience in my life," worse than being "drafted, divorced, or having a vasectomy."

Being involuntarily out of work in a society that is increasingly at work can be humiliating. As the case study suggests, the "unemployed" do not necessarily fit the popular stereotype. Brent was one of 1,100 people who were given the same "clean out the desk now" treatment in his firm on that day. ***Unemployment*** refers to *the situation in which one is seeking employment but unable to find it. Frictional unemployment* refers to short-term lack of work while changing to another job or seeking a new job. Economists tell us that an unemployment rate of about 3 percent is normal and unavoidable, even in good times, because it reflects frictional unemployment. *Structural unemployment* refers to long-term or permanent unemployment, often brought about when new machines replace workers, when an industry declines, or when people's skills are not needed (Raines and Day-Lower, 1986).

Who are the unemployed? Nearly anyone can occasionally be found among the frictionally unemployed, but certain social characteristics substantially raise one's chance of becoming part of the long-term unemployed. The high school dropout is four times as likely to be unemployed as the college graduate. Blue-collar work carries three times the risk of unemployment as white-collar work. Workers under 20 have three times the unemployment rate as those over 20. Not surprisingly, unemployment is twice as high in goods-producing as in service-producing industries. Blacks have twice the unemployment of whites, and women who head families are twice as likely to be unemployed as are married men with spouse present. However, in general, women are slightly less likely to be unemployed than men (Tausky, 1984).

What causes unemployment? Although the unemployed are likely to doubt their worth to the economy, they are often the victims rather than the causes of their unemployment. Much unemployment is structural. During the past century unemployment rates varied from a 1933 high of 24.9 percent to a 1943 low of 1.9 percent. The fact that the highest rate of the century came just ten years before the lowest rate illustrates that changes in the health of the economy are a major cause of unemployment. Unemployment rises dramatically during economic hard times and falls during good times.

Structural unemployment can also eliminate whole categories of jobs even during prosperous times. From 1975–1985, the U.S. auto industry lost some 200,000 jobs, partly due to foreign competition and partly due to automation (Devens et al., 1985). Mechanization has long been a source of structural unemployment. General Electric recently automated a plant in which seventy skilled machinists took sixteen days to make each locomotive frame. Robots and computers now produce one frame a day untouched by human hands (Rothman, 1987).

What are the consequences of unemployment? Perhaps the most obvious is financial hardship. Although various government, employer, and union programs seek to cushion the effect of sudden unemployment on income, most (nearly three-quarters) of the unemployed do not qualify (Guy, 1985).

Unemployment can also be a profound challenge to one's self-esteem. Even where the job loss was clearly a case of structural unemployment, the workers may feel that if they had worked harder they could have kept the job. Unfortunately, the loss of self-confidence resulting from unemployment typically remains, even after the person finds a new job (Perfetti and Bingham, 1983).

Unemployment also tends to impair both physical and mental health. On the physical dimension, unemployment is linked to high blood pressure, elevated cholesterol, and increased risk of heart disease (Kasl et al., 1975). On the emotional dimension, unemployment appears linked to psychiatric disorders and an increased tendency to drink alcohol. Researchers find a definite relationship between unemployment and distress, though the effect is mediated by the degree of social and economic support (Gore, 1978). For instance, unemployment is more devastating to the

TABLE 15.4 Unemployment and Social Stress: Cumulative Impact of a 1.4 Percent Increase in Unemployment on Selected Health Indicators, United States, 1970–1975

Health Indicators	Percent Increase in Incidence	Numerical Increase in Incidence	Economic Costs
Suicide	5.7%	1,540	$63 million
Admissions: State psychiatric hospitals	4.7	5,520	82 million
Admissions: State prisons	5.6	7,660	210 million
Homicides	8.0	1,740	434 million
Mortality: Cirrhosis of the liver	2.7	870	n/a
Mortality: Cardiovascular disease	2.7	26,440	1,372 million
Total Mortality	2.7	51,570	6,615 million

SOURCE M. Harvey Brenner, *Estimating the Social Costs of National Economic Policy.* Washington, DC: Joint Economic Committee of the Congress, 1976, pp. vii–viii.

formerly employed single parent than to the parent in a dual-career marriage. The married person has both social and economic support from his or her spouse, whereas the single parent may be left with little or no social or economic support (Warr and Payne, 1983, Warr, 1984; Gore, 1978).

Finally, as we see in Table 15.4, seemingly small rises in unemployment rates appear to have sizable social costs in terms of suicides, psychiatric hospital admissions, crime rates, and disease rates (Brenner, 1980; 1984; Rothman, 1987).

What Does Work Mean to Us?

Our popular music often reveals how we feel. Let's consider the underlying message of a few recent hits.

In Dolly Parton's "9 to 5" we hear:

It's a rich man's game,
No matter what they call it,
They spend their time,
Takin' money from your wallet.

Here the clear implication is that work is a "rip-off"—the exploitation of working-class women by rich men.

Sheana Easton's "Mornin' Train" has a less radical message:

My baby takes the mornin' train,
He works from 9 til 5 and then,
He takes another home again,
To find me waitin' for him.

Works all day,
To earn his pay,
So we can play
All night.

Here work is described neither as a rip-off nor anything intrinsically satisfying, but just as a means to an end—what one goes through to get to play.

Dire Straits implies something else about work:

Look at them yo-yos.
That's the way you do it.
You play the guitar on the MTV.
That ain't workin.
That's the way you do it.
Money for nothin' and your chicks for free.

The implication seems to be that if what you are doing is profitable and enjoyable, it is not work! So, work must be not profitable and not enjoyable.

In these three instances we see work variously portrayed as exploitative, a means to earn leisure, and intrinsically unrewarding, either financially or emotionally. Over a century ago Karl Marx predicted that as capitalists and machines become more prominent in the economy, people would find their work less meaningful and more frustrating—in short, they would become alienated from it.

ALIENATION FROM WORK

Karl Marx predicted that capitalism would eventually drive wedges between the worker and his work and between one worker and another. He called this coming separation *alienation* (Marx, 1864). Contemporary American sociologists have modified the concept, focusing more on the psychological effects of alienation than the causes Marx identified. In his now classic study, Blauner identified four components of alienation. *Powerlessness* refers to the feeling of domination by other people or objects and the feeling of being unable to reduce or eliminate that control. *Meaninglessness* refers to the inability to see one's work role in relation to others' roles and their purpose in the organization. *Isolation* means the lack of a sense of belonging to the work situation and identification with the workplace. *Self-estrangement* involves feeling unable to express one's unique abilities, potentialities, or personalities in one's work. ***Alienation***, then, refers to *the destruction of the meaningful relation of the individual workers to their work and each other and the resultant sense of powerlessness, meaninglessness, isolation, and self-estrangement* (Blauner, 1964).

Though Marx theorized that alienation would grow as technology became more sophisticated, Blauner, and later, Shepard, find that alienation reaches a peak with assembly-line work. They compared three types of work: (1) craft occupations, such as printing, which involve skilled work and the worker pacing himself or herself; (2) assembly-line work, which involves virtually no skill and forces the worker to keep pace with the line; and (3) work in continuous-process industries such as chemical plants, which involve tending highly automated production processes through which raw materials flow in at one end and finished products come out the other. These workers maintain the equipment and stand by to diagnose and repair the machinery when it malfunctions. Their work offers a combination of freedom and challenge. In independent studies of different occupations, both Blauner and Shepard found that the very "low-technology" craft jobs and the very "high-technology" jobs working with automated production facilities had lower levels of alienation than the "intermediate technology" assembly-line work (Blauner, 1964; Shepard, 1971).

SATISFACTION WITH WORK

Whereas some sociologists have concentrated on the specific discontent, alienation, others have studied satisfaction with work in a more global sense. Several public opinion research organizations, especially the National Opinion Research Center, have monitored worker satisfaction for nearly one-half century. On the surface the scene may look deceptively calm, with relatively high proportions (about 80 percent) of workers responding that they are satisfied or very satisfied with their work during the past half-century. Viewed from a different perspective, this suggests that about one in five workers are *dissatisfied* with their work (Glenn and Weaver, 1982).

When we begin to look behind the scenes, we see some disturbing signs, especially over the past fifteen years. By the late 1970s and early 1980s, the previously high and stable proportion of people who said their work was satisfying began to erode (Glenn and Weaver, 1982). Increasingly we are a society at work, and when we dislike our work or feel cheated by it, we are troubled in a major area of our day-to-day lives. Problems in the workplace spill over into leisure and family. Dissatisfied workers are not likely to put forth their best efforts, and as already discussed, we are heavily dependent on work to support our societies. What then is behind these changes in attitudes toward work?

Jeylan T. Mortimer's (1979) review of the literature on job satisfaction led her to two conclusions: (1) a pervasive decline took place in job satisfaction in the 1970s, and (2) this trend could best be addressed by improving the work setting, including increasing worker control over scheduling and safety decisions, choice of benefit programs, and protection from further income erosion.

People are more likely to be dissatisfied with their work when it is organized in such a way that they have little power over it and the work lacks meaning to them (Kohn, 1977). Mottaz (1981) studied 1,313 workers in seven occupational groups and found satisfaction most strongly linked to job conditions. Satisfaction also increases with age, although researchers are still trying to determine whether this is because of the jobs or dispositions of older workers. There certainly will be limits as to how far management is willing to alter the work scene, because the most satisfying work arrangements are not always the most profitable, and in a capitalistic economy, profits may take priority over worker satisfaction (Kalleberg, 1977; Kalleberg and Loscocco, 1983).

How Can the Work Setting Be Improved?

In our "Close-Up on Research" we look at a promising set of alternatives that directly involve workers in management and ownership of the enterprises in which they work (Whyte et al., 1983).

CLOSE-UP on • *RESEARCH* •

Rothschild and Russell on Democratic Participation in Work

The Researchers and the Setting

For most of the history of industrialization, decisions in the workplace have been a one-way street: Management decides and the workers carry out orders. Increasingly, managers are challenging this older style of bureaucracy and experimenting with more democratic ways of organizing. Joyce Rothschild and Raymond Russell are interested in what happens when workers are given more voice and power in the firms which employ them.

The Researchers' Goals

What social forces and public attitudes support worker ownership and worker control of the workplace? How is the state involved in such reforms? How do size, technology, and specialization affect an organization's ability to maintain active participation and democracy? How does employing democracy in work organizations affect worker satisfaction? How does democratization of work processes affect the economic performance of such firms? What blocks further democratic participation in the workplace? These are the specific questions Rothschild and Russell seek to answer.

Theory and Concepts

Many of the best known theorists have suggested that society drifts inevitably toward more bureaucracy and that control of big pervasive democracies tends to rest increasingly with small sets of people. However, many scholars hold that we can, and should, pursue more democratic forms of organizations.

Research Design

Rothschild and Russell use an important technique called the *literature review*, an example of the *analysis of existing sources* technique mentioned in Chapter 1. They compiled a bibliography of 147 relevant books and articles, predominantly from the 1980s and 1970s, and assessed the state of knowledge in this area.

Findings

What social forces and public attitudes support worker ownership and worker control of the workplace? The researchers found democracy in the workplace in three major forms: cooperatives, in which workers own and manage a firm; Employee Stock Ownership Plans (ESOP), in which the workers buy shares in the firm but have no special influence in the management of the firm; and Quality of Work Life (QWL) plans in which workers have increased control over the work setting through problem-solving groups, though they are not owners. These forms are very different, but they share a common spirit: "Although there are three separate movements struggling to create functioning alternatives to bureaucracy within the economy, they are perhaps united by the same *zeitgeist* that would recreate modern organization on a human scale, giving people at all ranks greater power over the organization's process and product" (p. 308).

Why should management be interested in democracy? Some experts argue that this sort of democracy is more efficient or that it ultimately gives management even more control over the worker. Others point out that democracy in the workplace may improve the motivation of workers and may provide tax advantages.

At least one study shows that workers prefer to work for employee-owned firms rather than those owned by outside investors or the government. Support for workplace democracy is stronger among blue-collar and professional/technical workers than managers, stronger among women than men, and stronger among younger rather than older workers.

How is the state involved in such reforms? "In the United States and even more in Europe, efforts to promote more democratic forms of work organization have also been actively encouraged by the state" (p. 312). The constitution of Yugoslavia grants workers the right to manage their workplaces. In the United States, the federal government has passed "sixteen laws since 1974 that grant a number of tax advantages both to employee-owned companies and to the banks that are willing to make loans to such companies" (p. 312). Interestingly, this legislation has been backed by both the most liberal and the most conservative law makers.

How do size, technology, and specialization affect an organization's ability to maintain active participation and democracy? Democracy in the workplace seems to work best in relatively small firms. For instance, the average size of a cooperative is 6.5 employees. Furthermore, "alternative organizations are most likely to arise and to succeed in industries and occupations in which skills and responsibilities can be widely shared" (p. 315). That is, democracy works better among people of similar skills.

How does employing democracy in work organizations affect worker satisfaction? Several studies reviewed by Rothschild and Russell showed that "alternative work organization generally has a positive effect upon workers' satisfaction with their jobs and identification with their firms" (p. 316). Yet workplace democracy is related to higher absenteeism, perhaps because it can lead to additional worry and strain.

How does democratization of work processes affect the economic performance of such firms? When workers buy out a firm in distress, the economic productivity frequently improves, but often not enough to save the firm. Studies of the more common ESOP approach bring mixed findings, perhaps due to difficulties in research design. Similarly, in the case of QWL programs, supporters have claimed they improve economic performance, but "hard-nosed critiques of these studies have often faulted many aspects of their designs and concluded that the economic merits of these QWL innovations remain unproved" (p. 321).

What blocks further democratic participation in the workplace? One potential problem in this type of reform is the much-noted tendency of democracies to degenerate into oligarchy. In his classic work on organizations, Michels (1915) described this tendency as an "iron law." Several theorists say the worker owners will eventually give in to the pressures of hiring cheap labor from outside the firm. Others say worker owners will lose their unique consciousness as division of labor and other bureaucratic features gradually creep in.

These problems are sometimes overcome. For example, cooperatives do better where they enjoy state support. In the United States, government helps ensure their stability by refusing to grant tax advantages if they dilute their democratic nature by employing outside, nonmember labor.

Implications

The results of this literature review can help us better understand our world. They suggest that workplace democracy could succeed in small, carefully financed, well-supported cooperatives. We may also have less intense democracy through QWL programs with no apparent detriment to profits.

Finally, literature reviews help to highlight what we do not know as well as what we do know. In this case we still do not know the effect ESOPs and QWL programs have on the profitability of firms. This is an important function, for it helps other theorists and researchers to know the issues still to be addressed.

Questions

1. Which type of workplace democracy appeals the most to you?
2. Based on this research how would you argue the case if you had to support or oppose a particular innovation such as worker cooperatives, Quality of Work Life plans, or Employee Stock Ownership Plans?
3. Where do you think the next generation of researchers should focus their attention in order to improve our understanding of workplace democracy?

SOURCE Joyce Rothschild and Raymond Russell. 1986. Alternatives to Bureaucracy: Democratic Participation in the Economy. *Annual Review of Sociology* 12: 307–28.

Sociologists at Work •

ROSABETH MOSS KANTER
OFFERS INSIGHTS TO CORPORATIONS ABOUT ENTREPRENEURSHIP
Professor, Harvard Business School
Harvard University
Cambridge, Massachusetts

Dr. Kanter's work centers around the study of organizational change and corporate entrepreneurship. She is the author of nine books including *The Change Masters: Innovation and Entrepreneurship in the American Corporation* and over 100 articles in books and scholarly journals. Dr. Kanter serves as Chairman of the Board of Goodmeasure, Inc., a management consulting firm she cofounded and helped to grow at an annual rate of 45 percent a year before coming to Harvard. She has advised such blue chip corporations as Procter and Gamble, BellSouth, Honeywell, General Electric, Apple Computer, Simon and Schuster, and Xerox.

How Did an Academically Trained Sociologist Become Interested in Business?
I switched my major to sociology in college during the activist 1960s, because I wanted to use the discipline to help me understand the forces that were propelling change in the society, making us aware of a number of problems, and perhaps offering solutions to those problems. I was particularly interested in the issues of complex social systems. American society was changing dramatically and experimenting with a number of new organizational forms. Among those forms were new organizations that challenged our ways of thinking about organizing work to not only produce maximum economic value but also to create value for the people who were doing the work. This sparked my interest in alternative institutions, such as collectives, but I also became fascinated by the large business corporation and its responsiveness, or lack of responsiveness, to those changes.

What Sociological Skills Led to Your Work in Organizations?
After settling down in an academic teaching position in 1967, I sought not only to become involved in activist causes but to see how I could apply the research techniques and theoretical insights of sociology to the problems of organizations. I found that my skills in survey research and in the use of simulation games for teaching made it possible for me to connect with a management consultant and get some assignments in business. I used those skills in the narrow sense to address immediate problems and used the broader training I had in field work to examine the corporations I was working in as social systems. I was thus able to offer insights to business people and government managers that went far beyond the narrower technical skills I was using in survey analysis and training/teaching of concepts.

Most valuable was a habit of mind developed by my sociological training—that of perceiving the essential issues involved in the functioning of major organizations. In addition, I have found that the issues on which I have been working are of vital importance not only to corporate leaders but also to government leaders, as we struggle with creating the best possible conditions in America to continue healthy economic growth while maintaining a good quality of work life for our citizens. ●

Conclusion

Work is a matter of profound importance to us as members of society, and we are rapidly changing the way we work. These changes are important because of what work means, but they are even more important because the way societies work impacts directly on the way we live. In this chapter we have begun to probe changes in our work life, their causes, and the implications for the future. As we have seen before, understanding social change is important to understanding society, being able to react to what is happening, and guiding social change in the directions we seek.

Summary Questions

1. How is work vital to society and the individual?
2. How does the economy organize work and exchange?
3. What are the features of contemporary developed economies?
4. Why do some economies develop?
5. What inhibits economic development?
6. What is in the future for the United States economy?
7. Where are we working as a society?
8. Who works?
9. How are occupations organized?
10. Who are the unemployed, why are they unemployed, and what are the consequences?
11. What does work mean to us?

Summary Answers

1. Most people spend much of their lives working; and their work provides them a master status influencing their living standard, health, life chances, beliefs, and social and self-esteem. The way a society works, such as hunting and gathering versus industrial production, profoundly influences the rest of the social structure.
2. The economy is the structure in which we produce and exchange goods and services. It functions as a means of material support and social order, but great conflicts arise within and around it.
3. Modern developed economies include high forms of technology and high degrees of specialization and centralization. Centralization usually involves socialism or capitalism. In the case of capitalism, these economies increasingly feature enormous multinational corporations that, though they may often provide low-priced products, threaten the economic well-being of people in the poorer nations. Developed economies employ money and credit as a major means of exchange.
4. Economic development involves a host of social variables. Technology is a major driving force toward development, but capital is also a key ingredient. Other important contributing factors are the presence of natural resources, colonialization, and appropriate social values such as those embedded in the Protestant ethic.
5. Those societies that do not immediately develop risk being dominated and colonized by the developing nations. Also, development comes slower when societies lack supportive institutions such as schools and a developed government. Harrison stresses the inhibiting effect of harsh climate, lack of key technologies including war-making and sea travel, the presence of a despotic regime that hoards all surplus wealth, the presence of an imperial power seeking to colonize the society in question, extreme inequality of wealth, which tends to breed even worse inequality, and finally, the problem of spiraling poverty with the disease and malnutrition it brings.
6. The United States' economy prospered for nearly three decades after World War II. However, due largely to the regeneration of other nations' economies, the United States has declined in terms of its relative share of world production. As other nations have become more developed, median family income in the United States has leveled off and begun to decline. Faced with declining ability to compete with other nations and rapidly growing debt, the implications for the future of the U.S. economy are ominous.
7. We can locate our work in terms of occupations, which are stratified in terms of income, power, and prestige. We also can consider industries. In this sense goods-producing industries, especially agriculture, have declined sharply during the past century as the proportion of people working in service-producing industries, especially government, has risen. The labor market is increasingly split between a primary sector with high-paying, stable, and interesting work, and a secondary sector of lower paid, mostly dead-end, temporary jobs. Minority group members are overrepresented in the secondary sector. Most people work for corporations that have their own subcultures.
8. The vast majority of both men and women now work in the U.S. economy. Women's participation, especially that of mothers, has risen dramatically in the past half-century. Teen-age students are also working in increasing proportions.
9. Aside from being structured by the corporations that employ them, many occupations are either unionized or professionalized. The union movement, though still very significant, has been declining in terms of membership since World War II. Professions are more common among white-collar occupations and involve a legal monopoly on the delivery of certain services claimed by the occupational group as their unique area of expertise. Some professions are losing power as our government limits practices that had restricted competition within the profession.

10. The uneducated, those in blue-collar occupations, younger workers, those in goods-producing industries, blacks, and divorced women have more difficulty finding and retaining jobs. Much unemployment is socially induced by foreign competition and technological innovations. Being unemployed is hazardous to one's physical and emotional well-being.

11. People find various meanings in their work, from a source of satisfaction through a means toward material ends, and including something they hate but are coerced into doing. A majority of workers report being satisfied with their work, but a significant proportion indicates signs of alienation, largely as a result of the product of the work rather than the worker. This suggests there are ways to improve the situation by improving the nature of jobs. Three trends in the workplace point toward increased workplace democracy: cooperatives in which workers own the firm, Employee Stock Ownership Plans where workers have a share in the ownership, though not necessarily the management, of the firm, and Quality of Work Life plans in which workers are given increased control over the work setting. Workers tend to like these programs, which may even improve economic productivity. Cooperatives often degenerate into oligarchies where the worker owners eventually exploit outside laborers.

Glossary

alienation the destruction of the meaningful relation of the individual workers to their work and to each other and the resultant sense of powerlessness, meaninglessness, isolation, and self-estrangement

autonomy freedom from external social control

capital surplus resources that can be applied to creating new means of production

capitalism political and economic system in which the means of production are generally privately held

centralization the degree to which economic institutions are dominated by a relatively small segment of the population

communism a type of socialism in which the government owns all or most of the industry.

democratic socialism political and economic system in which a republican form of representation, as opposed to a dictatorship, is coupled with state ownership of the "key" industries

deprofessionalization the process of lessening monopoly and autonomy of a profession

developed economy an economy which is largely already mechanized

developing economy an economy which has introduced industry or mechanized techniques

economic institution the social structure that organizes the production and exchange of goods and services

function the consequences of an institution which contribute to the stability and perpetuation of society and its members

labor union association of workers to promote and protect the welfare and rights of the members

laissez-faire economy the situation in which the state does not restrict the economy

mercantilism the idea that the wealth of a nation should be measured by the amount of gold and silver it holds

monopoly the situation in which one corporation controls a market

multinational corporation a corporation which owns or manages businesses in two or more nations

oligarchy dictatorial rule by the small upper stratum

oligopoly control by a small, powerful group which uses the authority vested in them to maintain their power

per capital gross national product GNP: or national income, divided by the population of the nation; also termed *average income*

productive base the ability of a state to produce things of value to that society

productive power the ability to offer valuables contingent upon compliance with commands or norms

profession an occupation that has been able to establish exclusive jurisdiction over certain kinds of services and to negotiate freedom from external intervention and control over the conditions and contexts of their work

surplus more resources than are needed for bare subsistence

technology the tools and techniques used in producing goods and services

trust control by one or several firms conspiring to hold prices higher than they would be under fair competition, also known as *oligopoly*

underdeveloped economy an economy which has a predominantly agricultural mode of production

unemployment the situation in which one is seeking employment but unable to find it

Suggested Readings

Richard H. Hall. 1986. *Dimensions of Work.* Beverly Hills, Calif.: Sage Publications.

Discusses work in terms of individual, horizontal, vertical, gender, age, racial and ethnic, organizational, power, and institutional dimensions.

George Ritzer, and David Walczak. 1985. *Working: Conflict and Change.* Englewood Cliffs, N.J.: Prentice-Hall.

Ritzer and Walczak focus on conflict in the world of work, a topic not often discussed in other works.

Robert A. Rothman. 1987. *Working: Sociological Perspectives.* Englewood Cliffs, N.J.: Prentice-Hall.

This up-to-date work discusses occupational and work subcultures, job dissatisfaction and work reform, and occupational careers, as well as many topics common to sociology of work texts.

Curt Tausky. 1984. *Work and Society: An Introduction to Industrial Sociology.* Itasca, Ill.: F. E. Peacock.

This succinct work contains a good summary of the historical events leading to the industrial revolution. Tausky also offers a clear discussion of who is working and what they gain from working.

PART 6

Social Change

CHAPTER 16

THE POLITICAL INSTITUTION

- What Is the State?
- What Is the Conflict View of the State?
- What Are the Functions of the State?
- What Are the Origins of the State?
- Close-Up on Theory: George Thomas and John Meyer on How the State Emerges, Grows, and Becomes Bureaucratic
- What Are the Bases of Power?
- What Are the Various Types of Authority?
- What Are Weber's Three Forms of Authority?
- How Is Power Formally and Informally Distributed in the United States?
- How Is Political Power Exercised in the United States?
- What Are Nonroutine Political Activities?
- Close-Up on Research: William Gamson on When Is Political Protest Successful?
- How Is the United States Losing Its Hegemony?
- Sociologists at Work: George Gallup Forecasts Elections and Charts Social Change

How's Your Sociological Intuition?

1. In the 1972 presidential election, Richard Nixon won by a record margin. What proportion of eligible voters voted for Nixon?
   - **a.** 74 percent
   - **b.** 33 percent
   - **c.** 51 percent
   - **d.** 67 percent
2. Which of the following are provided for by the Constitution of the United States?
   - **a.** Political parties
   - **b.** Congressional committees
   - **c.** Lobbyists
   - **d.** None of the above
3. What proportion of eligible voters actually vote in a typical United States presidential election?
   - **a.** 95%
   - **b.** 75%
   - **c.** 55%
   - **d.** 35%
4. Which of the following was found to be an important factor in explaining successful social protest movements?
   - **a.** The protest group used violence
   - **b.** The protest group addressed a single issue rather than several
   - **c.** The protest group did not seek to displace its opponent
   - **d.** All of the above

Answers

1. b. See the section "How Is Political Power Exercised?" to see why 33 percent is a landslide in the United States.
2. d. Informal arrangements over time have become formal, even though they were not included in the initial plan for government.
3. c. Although we tend to boast about our democracy, nearly half of the eligible voters do not even show up for presidential elections, which come once in four years. Voting is even lighter in off-year elections. Many of those who do not vote are poor or near poor, which suggests they may be alienated from the government that claims to rule in the best interest of all.
4. d. As we shall see in the Close-Up on Research, Gamson's study of fifty-three protest movements found that all these factors were among those contributing to success.

When You Have Finished Studying This Chapter, You Should Know:

- What the state is and what its major features are
- What the conflict view of the state is
- The functions of the modern state
- The origins of the state, how it emerges, and grows bureaucratic
- The bases of power and various types of authority
- The major ways in which states differ
- The major ideas and research findings about why states differ
- How power is formally and informally distributed in the U.S.
- Some United States institutions that exercise power outside the constitutionally provided structure
- The level of political participation and the influences of groups in the politics of the contemporary United States
- The major theories and research dealing with the distribution of political power in the United States
- The major forms of nonroutine political participation
- When protest groups are most likely to succeed
- What terrorism is, how it is growing, and who the terrorists are
- What hegemony is, why is the United States losing it, and what effect will this have on the world
- Who George Gallup is and what he does

The Organization is involved in gambling and operating a "protection scheme" for liquor producers. Producers who refuse to cooperate may be violently forced out of business. A well-trained civilian army holds entire communities accountable to the Organization, taking their money by force and seizing persons when they dare to refuse to comply. Occasionally there are violent confrontations between the Organization and its competitors. At these times, members of the community may be called upon to kill or die in the name of the Organization.

This is not a description of organized crime, but rather of the current United States government! Many state governments do organize gambling with lotteries and daily number schemes. Liquor production is controlled and taxed by the federal government, which coerces "independents" out of business, sometimes with raids on their operations. The public is held accountable by armed police agencies whenever it breaks rules established by the state and is expected to pay taxes with the threat of imprisonment for failure to do so. In times of war, the United States employs conscription to bring nonvolunteers into the military service.

Most potentially criminal behaviors can be defined as one kind of behavior when performed by a citizen or corporation and as another kind when performed by the state. The state is in the unique position of regularly engaging in behavior that it prohibits for all other institutions, groups, and individuals. Consider Table 16.1.

Few Americans equate their government with organized crime. Most people living under the influence of a particular state accept it as ***benign,*** or *generally operating in the public interest,* even in countries whose governments might seem criminal to us (Hyman, 1969). Our point is that most of us have come to accept as normal the rather remarkable fact that we are ruled by a political institution that violates the very standards of conduct it self-righteously and violently imposes on the citizenry.

Americans are not alone in this matter. In fact, we enjoy more "freedom" to participate in elections and manage our own economic affairs than people in most of the world. All states, by their nature, dominate individuals, often in brutish, exploitative ways. As we see in this chapter, the political institutions in virtually all societies and all times take liberties they routinely deny their citizenry. This "might-makes-right" mentality of the state is no minor matter, for this institution regulates much of our daily lives while linking us together in a vast network of life-and-death proportions. Of all institutions, the state is by far the most likely to demand that we kill or die in its name. Whereas differences in religious outlook may sometimes contribute to bloodshed, and economic competition may cause severe material deprivation, it is political differences that currently threaten the very survival of life on planet earth.

Why does the state arise as a prominent institution in the present, when in the most primitive societies it does not exist? What are the varieties of form that the state takes between cultures and across time? Why are they different? Whose interests do they serve? What are the forms and major processes of the state in our society and in our time? These are the major questions we seek to answer in this chapter.

What Is the State?

The concept of ***state*** has a special meaning in the social sciences. It is *the institution that monopolizes legitimate power in a territory through the establishment of courts, official leaders, written laws, and taxation* (Robin Williams, 1970, p. 233). By this definition the American

TABLE 16.1 Definitions of Behavior as Practiced by the State and Private Citizens

The Behavior	When Private Citizens Do It, It Is Called	When the State Does It, It Is Called
Organizing a game in which valuables are risked on a chance outcome	Illegal gambling	Lottery
Obtaining money by force or threat	Extortion	Taxation
Depriving someone of property	Robbery	Expropriation
Carrying a person off against his or her will	Kidnaping	Arresting
Artificially influencing prices	Price fixing	Introducing price controls
Gaining exclusive control of a market that makes price manipulation possible	Monopolizing	Creating a public utility
Excluding on the basis of race or ethnicity	Racial or ethnic discrimination	Maintaining immigration quotas

federal government would properly be called a state, as would various nations in the world, like the Union of Soviet Socialist Republics, Japan, and South Africa. Governmental units like Pennsylvania, Alabama, and North Dakota are not states in the sociological sense of the word, because their exercise of power is subject to the authority of the federal government.

The state is distinguished from an administration, or regime in that the state is an impersonal institution, whereas the ***administration,*** or ***regime*** consists of *those particular persons who happen to hold office in a state at one point in time.*

FEATURES OF THE STATE

Several features characterize the state. One is the presence of a *court system,* through which disputes between individuals or groups are settled by the intervention of a third-party agent of the state. The courts may use the resources of the society to enforce compliance with their decisions if necessary.

A state also involves the *organization of leadership into authority positions,* which are or could be filled by various incumbents. A state usually has ***codified norms,*** which are *rules that have been written and published.* Finally, most states exercise the power to raise revenue through *taxation.*

Many modern states have various levels of government, such as the local, state, and national governments in the United States. In such nestings of authority, only the highest level can properly be called a state. Because states are so important in today's societies, it is difficult to realize that for most of human history, societies functioned without them.

What Is the Conflict View of the State?

Conflict permeates the state more than any other institution. In conflict two parties struggle against one another for a commonly prized object. Closely aligned with conflict are the processes of coercion, being forced to act against one's will, and exploitation, the process in which one is deprived of things one is rightfully due.

Regardless of sociological perspective, we see conflict when we look at the state. Political institutions declare war, conduct war, gain and lose territory and subjects, and eventually negotiate or dictate settlements. The political institution also routinely coerces its citizens. Few of us would voluntarily support our state to the level at which we presently pay taxes if taxes were not extracted by threat of force. Often the state is called upon to settle conflicts between parties, for instance, through lawsuits.

But conflict theorists look deeper and see more than the other perspectives with regards to conflict and the state. As Karl Marx observed: "The history of all hitherto existing society is the history of class struggles" (Marx, 1888, originally 1848). Through most periods of history and in most cultures the state has been the tool of the elites.

A court system is a vital feature of the state as we use the term in sociology. States employ courts to resolve disputes. (*Photo courtesy the Michigan Daily*)

Often the upper classes have established governments that were subsequently displaced by revolutions of the lower classes. The United States itself was formed through a bloody and violent revolution. Today most of the monarchies in the world have been displaced by democracies.

Because of the frequently exploitative nature of the state we are wise to examine closely any state's claims of legitimacy. All governments, from contemporary United States to the repressive regimes of Nazi Germany and Stalinist Russia, claim their rule is legitimate, though we can clearly see this is not always the case. Indeed, conflict theorists have produced considerable evidence to suggest that even or perhaps especially in the United States, the state remains the tool of a small number of capitalists, who rule through what Mills termed the *power elite* (Mills, 1966). We may have moved only from obvious to less obvious exploitation of the masses by the elites.

All political observers concede that the state involves struggles. Those aligned with the state hold that the state minimizes conflict by establishing legitimate channels, such as courts and elections, by which disputes can be resolved. Conflict theorists suggest that we question the authority of any state. They assert that where people are exploited they may rightfully consider taking extraordinary actions, such as demonstrations, violent strikes, guerrilla warfare, and outright revolution (Wasburn, 1982).

What Are the Functions of the State?

Early theorists speculated about the origin of the state. The English philosopher Thomas Hobbes, for example, could be identified as a structural-functionalist, in that he conceived of the state as an institution designed to serve society by replacing chaos and injustice with order. Hobbes described life in society without the state as "solitary, poor, nasty, brutish, and short" (Hobbes, 1651).

Structural-functionalists, as we learn in Chapter 1, believe social structure exists to fulfill functions for society. They analyze an institution by looking for the functions or consequences by an institution that contribute to the stability and perpetuation of society and its members. Functionalists view the state as having an increasing number of specific functions in modern societies.

Perhaps the oldest function of the political institution is *to serve the community as arbiter in disputes* which might otherwise threaten both individuals and the community. In societies where no third party resolves disputes, bitter fighting and feuds are a menace to the individual and the society. When the state is accepted as the rightful arbiter of disputes and has the power to enforce its decisions, the destructive potential of such disagreements is limited. Prior to the development of the state, people sometimes resorted to custom and sometimes to feuding as the final means of settling disputes. When the state comes on the scene, it regulates or eliminates such feuding. During the Samurai era in Japan, vendetta feud justice had to be authorized by the shogun (a military governor) before revenge could be taken. In most modern states feuding has virtually disappeared.

A second major function of the state is *to contribute to social control* by providing specific norms, developing new norms for new situations, and enforcing traditional norms. Even the earliest states, which were organized as cities rather than as nations, soon developed specific norms called laws, which the states enforced. Early laws probably grew out of early court decisions that clarified customs of the time. Most modern states have a legislative body that creates law, but court decisions still serve as precedents or case law, which often have as much binding force as legislative law.

The state also serves as the *society's agent in relations with other societies.* These relations may consist of policies of isolation, mutual exchange, or conflict. For example, the United States and China were in many ways isolated from each other for several decades preceding their 1972 exchange of diplomats and reestablishment of trade. In an earlier era, the thirteen colonies vastly improved their ability to conduct foreign relations when they formed into a federation. The United States and most other nations carry out relations of *mutual exchange.* Conflict relations can range from a "cold" war embargo, such as that against Cuba during the early 1960s, to "hot" wars, such as those between Israel and its Arab neighbors. Although conflict between nations is sometimes based on what form the state should take, the presence of the institution of the state usually facilitates relations between nations or societies.

One state function that has grown more important as societies have become more complex is *to provide planning and direction for the society.* Some activities may be accomplished more efficiently if they are centrally organized. For example, the Cheyenne Indians of the mid-nineteenth century were periodically centrally organized by a political institution. During the season when buffalo were scarce, they would hunt only in groups in a manner that assured the tribe of a higher probability of obtaining game. A strict prohibition against individual hunting prevented frightening the herd out of range and interfering with the opportunity of other members of the tribe to obtain food. During this period a temporary police force was instituted to maintain surveillance and to apprehend and punish violators (Hoebel, 1960).

Modern states provide varying degrees of centralized organization for societies, but like the Navajo, modern states use such regulation most frequently when no viable alternative exists. Services such as planning a network of interstate highways are organized by the state in part to avoid the disorganization that might result if these services were left to be provided by competing private enterprises.

The most recently developed function of the state is *to provide for the welfare of those who are unable to care for themselves.* Until the last century, our state played little role in attempting to aid the handicapped and the victims of disease and poverty. Now it is common among industrialized nations for the state to provide financing of health care and other social services. Since 1935 the United States has had a Social Security system that provides income to the aged, the blind, and other physically disabled persons. The various state governments in the United States have departments of social services and employment security bureaus to provide income and other services to the poor and unemployed (Orum, 1983).

This relatively new function of the state is a controversial one, which some argue will ultimately prove to be dysfunctional rather than functional. Providing for those who do not or cannot provide for themselves may deplete personal initiative and allow nonproductive situations to grow rather than to end naturally. Conversely, providing help through a temporarily difficult period may enable a citizen to become once again a contributing member of society.

What Are the Origins of the State?

Most simple societies that subsist through hunting and gathering are governed through custom and lack a state, as we use the term. Societies that employ more productive techniques, such as agriculture, produce more food or goods and develop surpluses. These surpluses can be owned, as can agricultural tools and land.

When humans develop the concept of ownership to this level, they set the stage for disputes over private property. The state develops to serve as an arbitrator in these disputes in agrarian and industrial societies that are virtually absent in the more primitive ones.

Cities and city-states are usually the first governmental units that develop in agricultural societies. This is probably because traditional social relationships work best in small, intimate settings. Large, impersonal cities are more likely to require the central organization of a state and external forms of social control.

The state gains influence when the technology of a society becomes more sophisticated and the society becomes more complex. With industrialization the state grows, and the first nation-states come into being. As industrialism replaces agriculture, nation-states become the dominant institutions of legitimate authority. Once the state exists, it tends to grow in the amount of territory it successfully claims, in the size of the population it governs, and in the realms of social life that it enters.

But the state does not arise solely to satisfy the peoples' desire for "law and order." As societies develop technologically, control of the state becomes very attractive to those who would like to acquire property and extract the labor of others. Some theorists suggest that the state is the ultimate prize the capitalists seek in the class struggle, for it allows them to accomplish through force what they otherwise would not be able to accomplish in the marketplace. Early states, as well as many modern ones, gave the government the right to exploit. Massive projects such as the Egyptian pyramids are tributes to the power of the state to extract labor from which enormous wealth could be accumulated. Both early and modern states gain influence as much through violence and conquest as through appealing to a peoples' hearts and minds.

As symbolic interactionists point out, a new institution requires an ideology to provide its reason for being. This is especially true of the state, which must tax the population to survive and which employs violence while denying the population the use of violence. Technological change may be a prime mover, but changes in a culture must have meaning to the participants, as political sociologist Robert MacIver suggests (1965).

Social authority existed before the development of the state, but in order for the state to emerge, a new rationalization, ideology, or myth had to be created (MacIver, 1965, p. 37):

> So the myth-makers, inspired and sustained by the movements of their time, restated the myth of authority. They were for the centralization of authority. They were for public order against the private rights of feudalism, for public peace against the anarchy of private wars, now grossly accentuated by religious division. Sovereignty is one, indivisible, inalienable. Sovereignty is supreme, final, absolute.
>
> We cannot determine precisely how the first states came into being, and all states have been shaped either by their contact with other states or in reacting to an earlier political order (Fried, 1967). A society's means of production has a strong influence on the emergence and development of the state. The myths or ideology that are developed are also significant.

In the following "Close-Up on Theory" we see how contemporary sociologists are grappling with a closely related issue: How states emerge, grow, and become bureaucratic.

CLOSE-UP on • *THEORY* •

George Thomas and John Meyer on How the State Emerges, Grows, and Becomes Bureaucratic

The Theorists and the Setting

Some of the earliest theories ever written deal with the form and function of the state. Arisstotle is said to have commented that "The state is man's greatest creation." George Homans, looking back at the previous fifty years of sociology, observed that we have made more progress developing research tools and facts than we have in writing theories (Homans, 1986). The great classical theorists of the nineteenth century, such as Marx, Durkheim, and Weber, grappled with broad issues, such as why societies have states and what form they take. However, Thomas and Meyer suggest that "American sociologists have ignored the state, concentrating on voters, interest groups, power arrangements, and so on. . . . They tend to assume that the constitution of humans, society, and nature generated by the modern state system is natural, and therefore do not recognize the state as an object of analysis. . . . We have much better studies of why people vote the way they do than of why there are elections. . . ." (pp. 461–462)

The Theorists' Goals

Thomas and Meyer seek to address some very broad issues: How and why do states emerge? How and why do they expand? To what degree do they become bureaucratic, and why?

Concepts and Propositions

As Thomas and Meyer point out, "Most theorizing about the state takes on a functionalist form and is based on the conception that states arise from the internal evolution of societies" (p. 463). That is, states arise to meet the needs of society. Parson says that as technology becomes more sophisticated and the economy more specialized, the state is needed to coordinate the functions of society (1966). In a somewhat similar way, Marx thought that technological development leads to the formation of increasingly distinct classes. In this situation, the elites need political power to control the masses and extract surplus income from them. Both schools of thinkers agree that as societies evolve they develop states.

Our best research shows, however, that the emergence of states is not merely caused by internal technological development. So, instead of looking primarily at what is going on inside societies, sociologists have turned their attention to what is going on outside or around the societies that contributes to the birth of a state.

Earlier theorists tended to depict states as emerging out of anarchy or an absence of other political or cultural forces. Some theorists believed that states evolved to protect their society's self-interests. Other theorists saw the state as growing out of military conflict within stateless societies. More recently, Immanuel Wallerstein has stated that a highly organized world economy triggers the growth of new states (1980).

But Thomas and Meyer promote an even more recent theory advanced by political scientists who explain the emergence of states in terms of a wider political system. They argue that "there are rules of the game, called international regimes, that structure the balance of power, economic competition, and the goals of states—for example, rules defining how exchange is conducted, the permissible spheres of military action, the allocation of such shared goods as the sea or the air, and state obligation" (pp. 466–67). Thomas and Meyer point the way to a new theory based on one major proposition:

Proposition: Cultural conditions create broad political environments that trigger the emergence of states and influence their size and form.

Traditional theory taught that states arose out of a political void and took on form to suit either the local society or its elites. Thomas and Meyer believe that states emerge as part of a broader set of processes. The fact that European states generally have similar histories, functions, and growth patterns is consistent with their common cultural heritage. Specifically, they share a common religious heritage. In the words of Thomas and Meyer: "To an astonishing extent, at any given time different Western societies share very similar cultural frames, with, for example, common definitions of both justice and progress" (p. 470). Specifically, "the Western state . . . developed in part as a project . . . of the . . . Western Church . . ." (p. 470).

Interpretation

When Thomas and Meyer point out that the Western state has grown amidst a culture strongly influenced by the Church, they are also saying that under other cultural conditions, other forms of states might emerge. Even more broadly, they suggest that some cultural conditions might not trigger the emergence of states. Or, conversely, some cultural circumstances might be even more conducive to the emergence of states.

Contemporary theorists operate in different cultural climates than earlier theorists did. A nineteenth-century theory might "succeed" if it were plausible and appealing. Part of the joy and agony of contemporary sociology is seeing that very appealing theories sometimes lose their charm in the cold light of data. Contemporary research calls into question some of the simple formulations of the early masters, but it also confirms the insights of those theorists whose ideas have become classics.

Thomas and Meyer are taking the best of the discipline's ideas and carrying them a step further. Their theory is intended as another logical step in coming to understand the state. The theory may seem vague and tentative for two reasons. First, we are dealing with processes that began centuries ago, so our knowledge about how the first states emerged is very limited. Second, we are still exploring the various theoretical possibilities.

We are moving toward more sophisticated and valid theories. Especially in contemporary times, we should realize that new states do not emerge in vacuums. We can find obvious similarities between states in the West and among those in the East at the same time that those in the West are different from those in the East. In seeking to understand how states emerge, grow, and become bureaucratic, Thomas and Meyers alert us to look for explanations in the cultural environment both within and around the society in question.

Questions

1. Besides plausibility, what has the Thomas and Meyer proposition to offer? Is it consistent with the facts as we know them? Can you think of states that seem to be an exception to their rule?
2. What if they are right? What implication does this have for understanding and controlling the development of states?
3. What type of methodology could be used to test Thomas and Meyer's proposition to the test?

SOURCE George M. Thomas, and John W. Meyer. 1984. "The Expansion of the State." *Annual Review of Sociology* 10:461–82.

What Are the Bases of Power?

Max Weber developed a well-accepted definition of **power:** *"the ability of a person or a group of people to realize their own will in a communal action even against the resistance of others who are participating in the action"* (Weber, 1946, p. 180). Other forms of interpersonal influence, like emotional support, peer pressure, and role modeling, may alter individual behavior and could be considered forms of power, but this discussion focuses on the tangible and intentional forms of power that are exercised by governments. Power is capable of altering the behavior of others through the promise of punishments and rewards: coercive power and productive power.

COERCIVE POWER. ***Coercive power*** *refers to the ability to gain compliance over others through the threat or application of physical force.* In most states, the government has a virtual monopoly on the use of coercive power. In very small groups, an exceptionally strong individual may exercise coercive power through physical domination. Where weapons exist, they neutralize or override sheer physical strength. Weapons are a major source of coercive power, and the more destructive and reliable the weapons, the more coercive power available.

Social factors also influence coercive power. For instance, assuming similar weapons, larger groups usually, but not always, prevail over smaller groups. The smaller group may comply because it knows that it is outnumbered.

Social organization is another source of coercive power. When coercive power is tested, as in war, the outcome depends not only on the relative sizes of the two sides and the sophistication of the weaponry, but also on how well the group is organized and how tightly it is integrated. The ability to organize and manage an effective fighting force has often determined the outcome of battles, in spite of differences in size and weapons. Similarly, soldiers who are fiercely loyal to their groups have often performed surprisingly well. For example, the fact that such a small country as Norway could frustrate the German occupying forces into abandoning their Norwegian posts during World War II demonstrates the effectiveness of group solidarity against coercive power.

Dictators such as Colonel Khadafi establish and maintain their states largely through the threat and application of physical force. *(Daniel Simon/Gamma Liaison)*

PRODUCTIVE POWER. ***Productive power*** *refers to the ability to offer valuables contingent upon compliance with commands or norms.* Governments and other institutions, including businesses, religious organizations, schools, families, and individuals hold productive power (Dahl, 1973). Money, jobs, land, and other valuables may be incentives for people to change their attitudes or behavior. For example, employers have productive power because they can offer paid employment and can terminate such employment. Employers may fire anyone who deviates from their wishes.

The federal government is the largest employer and the largest consumer in the United States, and it exercises enormous productive power. For example, the current volunteer U.S. Army was created partly by offering higher financial inducements than had been offered previously, when the draft was the principal method of recruitment for the armed forces. Businesses that sell goods and services to the government are also subject to its productive power. An avowedly communist organization, for instance, would never receive purchase orders from a capitalist state.

Consumers have sometimes used productive power in organized boycotts against particular producers. One example of this is the lettuce boycott in support of the United Farm Workers in the early 1970s. Another is the attempt by institutions that are traditionally concerned about human rights, such as universities, to influence large firms that operate in South Africa because of that country's policy of *apartheid.* Such groups have sometimes divested themselves of stock in corporations that continue to do business with South Africa.

Access to land or water is also often controlled by the state and is sometimes a factor in productive power. Many manufacturing, agricultural, personal, and recreational activities depend on securing land or water. Governments also sometimes control access to business markets. Productive power can rest on control of these variables and on control of money or jobs. (Dye, 1987).

What Are the Various Types of Authority?

People may attain power as a result of the social status they occupy. Hence *Judge* Sanderson can cause a person to spend time in jail as a consequence of Mr. Sanderson's social status (judge) rather than his personal characteristics. *Officer* Watts can handcuff and forcibly take a suspect to police headquarters largely because Mr. Watts has the status of police officer.

When this type of power is legitimized by society it is called ***authority.*** Thus, Ms. Adams, legislative program review director, has the authority to subpoena records from state agencies because of her status; *Reverend* Jensen has the authority to perform certain sacred rituals because of his status in the church. *Professor* Bell has the authority to make assignments, administer examinations, and issue student evaluations as a result of having the status of professor.

Authority, like power, is a phenomenon of government but is also found elsewhere. Traditionally children have learned to accept the authority of their parents. Even in the simplest societies, elders usually have some degree of authority over younger members of the community.

In modern society authority is frequently visible and formal. Relationships of subordination and superordination are common and accepted. They are a defining feature of bureaucracy. People are familiar with and have come to accept the authority of the dean, the librarian, the Pope, the choir director, the Supreme Court Justice, and the meter person.

WHAT ARE THE BASES OF AUTHORITY?

Although actual and threatened rewards and punishments may underlie both power and authority, the exercise of power and authority often occurs smoothly even in the absence of direct exchange of rewards and punishments. People often comply with the demands of authority and power because they accept their legitimacy, rather than because they are sure of the consequences of noncompliance. Sociologists have explored how societies and social groups store power in particular status positions, thus creating this type of legitimized authority.

What Are Weber's Three Forms of Authority?

Max Weber theorized that authority is usually based on one or more of the following pure forms, or "ideal types," of authority: (1) traditional, (2) charismatic, or (3) rational–legal. Rather than studying the rewards and penalties that often back up authority, he chose to study why some persons are allowed to occupy such positions or, more precisely, how positions of authority are justified. Weber concludes that power comes to be vested in a status or social position because it is viewed as legitimate by the community.

Weber suggests that subordinates usually believe in the legitimacy of those who hold social power over them, even if outsiders view the authority as illegitimate. In other words, once authority is established, it continues to hold its position simply by virtue of having been there. Weber calls this phenomenon *traditional authority* (1946, p. 296, italics added):

> Traditionalism in the following discussions shall refer to the psychic attitude-set for the habitual workday and to the belief in the everyday routine as an inviolable norm of conduct. *Domination that rests* upon this basis, that is, *upon piety for what actually, allegedly, or presumably has always existed, will be called traditional authority.*

One type of traditional authority Weber discusses is ***patriarchalism,*** *the authority of the father, the husband, or the senior of the house over the household.* Weber suggests that patriarchalism is the most important type of domination. This traditional form of authority pervades today's societies and is still highly important. In the Tiwi culture of North Australia, for example, where one man may have several wives, the eldest wife has traditional authority over younger wives and directs both their work and their social behavior. For example, the eldest wife reports to the husband when one of the younger wives wanders off into the bushes with another man.

Weber says that a second basis for authority is ***charisma,*** *"an extraordinary quality of a person, regardless of whether this quality is actual, alleged, or presumed"* (Weber, 1946, p. 295). ***Charismatic authority*** *refers to "rule over men, whether predominantly external or predominantly internal, to which the governed submit because of their belief in the extraordinary quality of the specific person. . . .* The legitimacy of charismatic rule thus rests upon the belief in magical powers, revelations and hero worship" (Weber, 1946, p. 295). Examples of individuals who have had this kind of authority include Jesus Christ, Mohandas Gandhi, and many military and political figures. Much of Martin Luther King, Jr.'s influence was based on charismatic authority, as was that of John F. Kennedy, Winston Churchill, and Mao Tse-Tung.

Weber termed the third foundation of authority "legal authority," now known as rational–legal authority, common among modern societies and bureaucracies. ***Rational–legal authority*** *"rests upon rules that are rationally established by enactment, by agreement, or by imposition.* The legitimacy for establishing these rules rests, in turn, upon a rationally enacted or interpreted 'constitution' " (Weber, 1946, p. 294).

In rational–legal authority, an official holds powers as a trustee; the power does not belong to the person but to the position. This authority is more clearly defined than traditional and more limited than charismatic authority. Most of the authority figures in modern public life possess rational–legal authority-conferring status. This is true, for instance, of teachers, rabbis, business managers, and mayors.

HOW STATES DIFFER

We live in a world where over 200 nations claim to be sovereign authorities ruling over the people within their boundaries. We can come to better understand these important social units by looking systematically at their differences. The two most important differences involve the degree to which power is shared and the span of control the state seeks to influence.

AUTHORITY VERSUS DEMOCRACY

One of the most significant differences among political systems is their distribution of political resources, like authority. In some systems people are more politically equal than others. This inequality–equality runs from the extreme of total dictatorship, in which the entire power of the state is available to only one individual, to the opposite extreme of perfect democracy, in which all subjects share the state's power equally.

People assess political power and measure its distribution in various ways. The right to vote is one important form of political power that is extended differently from state to state. The United States, for instance, originally allowed only landholding males the right to vote. Later, all adult male white citizens were allowed to vote. With Emancipation, black adult males were given the vote. Still later, adult females were included in the population of eligible voters, and recently persons between the ages of 18 and 21 have been added. Measured by this indicator, the United States has moved progressively toward greater political equality.

Another political resource is knowledge that can contribute to political skills and depends to some degree on access to educational institutions. Some countries provide more equal access to education than others. In the United States, about 2,000 of every 100,000 people study in institutions of higher learning, whereas in some African countries not more than five people per 100,000 have this opportunity. Rates of literacy vary from 5 percent of the adult population for countries at the low end of the distribution to more than 95 percent within the most literate societies.

Wealth is another political resource that is unequally distributed. Whether measured by these variables or others, political equality is an important dimension along which states vary.

THE REALM OF POWER

States differ in the range of human conduct they try to control. At one extreme are societies where the state does not control anything, or, stated another way, there is no state. This is called ***anarchy****—the situation in which the state has no power.* Primitive societies frequently practiced anarchy, living without political offices, taxation, or courts.

At the opposite extreme from anarchy are states that control virtually all conduct. No state has ever truly attained total control over every aspect of every citizen's life, but some like Stalin's Russia, Hitler's Germany, and Mussolini's Italy have come close enough to be called *totalitarian*—seeking total control of the populace. ***Totalitarian*** *governments are characterized by six features: (1) an official ideology, (2) a single disciplined party, (3) terroristic police control, (4) a party monopoly of the mass media, (5) party control of the armed forces, and (6) central direction of the economy.* More recently political scientists have tended away from this rather restrictive term in favor of the concept of an authoritarian regime. An ***authoritarian*** *regime is one with little input from the masses.*

Authoritarian regimes are often looser and less permanent than totalitarian states. Jeane J. Kirkpatrick, the United States ambassador to the United Nations, thinks we should be less critical of an authoritarian regime, such as Argentina, which appears open to change, than we are of a totalitarian state, like the Soviet Union, which appears not to be open to change. Her critics fail to appreciate the distinction, because both totalitarian and authoritarian states often unfairly

TABLE 16.2 Central Government Revenue as a Percent of Gross National Product (GNP)

As Societies Become More Developed, the State Becomes More Dominant.

Type of Society	Mean (%)	Range (%)	Number of Societies
Traditional primitive societies	17	7–26	11
Traditional civilizations	13	9–23	15
Transitional societies	22	9–37	31
Industrial Revolution societies	25	10–40	36
High mass consumption societies	27	17–40	14

SOURCE Adapted from Dahl, 1970, p. 51.

imprison people, torture them, and deny them human rights. The critics see the distinction as an excuse to justify U.S. aid to authoritarian anti-Communist regimes regardless of their often deplorable human rights records (Roskin, 1982). Furthermore the Soviets' more recent adoption of their policy of glasnost, and Reagan's pronouncement that the days of the Soviet Union as an evil empire have passed, suggest that some totalitarian regimes change signfiicantly.

Without getting entangled in these somewhat parochial battles over terminology we should note two things. First, as we saw earlier, the state appears to arise with the dawn of agriculture as technology begins to develop. Second, the more the development grows, the larger the influence of state becomes. The data displayed in Table 16.2 confirm this.

Even within states we face major decisions about how power should be distributed. We face a dilemma: When we establish freedom of business enterprise, for instance, we leave the door open to the growth of interest groups such as large businesses that may exploit people. On the other hand, placing industry under government control opens the door to abuse by corrupt regimes. Recently Robert Dahl, a major political theorist, has suggested that where economic decisions affect employees' lives, we should include them in a democratic decision-making process if we are to get the most benefits from democracy (Dahl, 1982). As we saw in Chapter 5, American management styles have begun to shift toward more concern for workplace democracy. When the state limits its control within a society, the issues of democracy versus authority simply shift into a different arena. In the case of the United States, the state has left most businesses in private hands and relatively free of regulation. In earlier times owners ran businesses in a highly authoritarian fashion. We see now a call for, and some indication of, increased workplace democracy.

DIFFERENCES IN VALUE SYSTEMS

States also differ in their fundamental values. Such value differences may stimulate societies to create, maintain, and contemplate the use of world-destroying forces. For example, nearly every person in the United States and the Soviet Union lives near the target of an intercontinental ballistic missile from the other state and could be fatally incinerated or irradiated should one state decide that the other sufficiently threatens its existence to warrant nuclear attack.

Americans do not fear Russians as people who are naturally different or personally dangerous—in fact, Russian immigrants to the United States are generally treated much better than native citizens of minority racial status. The conflict between the two countries concerns, instead, social structure and values. Both nations spend billions annually to protect their way of life. Each state has sanctified its own ideology and portrays the alternative order as unacceptable under any terms.

The motto for the French Revolution advocated the pursuit of three values: liberty, equality, and fraternity. The government of the United States tends to stress liberty above equality and fraternity, emphasizing the rights to freedom of the press, assembly, and religion, and freedom to engage in economic enterprise for profit.

In socialist countries, the dominant value is equality at the expense of liberty. Inequalities of wealth and income are less extreme in the Soviet Union than in the United States, but the state does not allow freedom of the press or freedom to engage in entrepreneurial economic pursuits for profit.

Perhaps, in the simplest societies, fraternity, or feeling at one with one's people, is the dominant value. Issues of freedom and equality are not important in hunting and gathering societies, but these societies maintain many rituals that bind people together through mutual identification, or mechanical solidarity, rather than independence, or organic solidarity (see Chapter 2). Obviously, the values of liberty, equality, and fraternity are found to some degree in all societies and cultures.

DIFFERENCES IN IDEOLOGY

Because all states are caught in the contradiction of engaging in behavior they deny to the citizenry, all states need an ideology to explain the contradiction. Different states use varying ideologies. We earlier saw how essential ideology is in supporting stratification structures. Political ideology involves not only values but also a general world view and strategy for proceeding toward the ideal society. During the feudal era, for example, the monarchy was supported by promoting the idea of the divine right of monarchs to rule.

Presently many of the world's states employ one of two competing ideologies: capitalism or socialism. The United States epitomizes the capitalist ideal of private ownership and representative democracy. As we saw in Chapter 15, the United States can be viewed as having a civil religion through which the legitimacy of the state is traced to a belief in a god that transcends mortal authority. We also saw that the beliefs of Protestantism provide fertile ground for capitalism to grow.

The Soviet Union represents the alternative socialist ideology. Socialist ideology denies the reality of a god, focuses on the observable material present, and sees a major task to be collective ownership and development of the society's productive resources. The ideology is based on the assumption that the masses in nonsocialist societies will revolt when their society develops to a point where mass production is combined with very narrow ownership of industry. After the revolution, a dictatorship of the working class will develop to manage the transformation from a capitalist society to a truly democratic communistic one.

Although the two ideologies are quite different, they both justify the institution of the state. In doing so, capitalism justifies enormous inequality of wealth in the name of freedom, whereas socialism justifies enormous "temporary" differences in political power in the interest of eventual material equality. Both claim to be operating a democracy and each says the other's is a sham. We have abbreviated these ideologies; many variations of them exist among modern states that use them to maintain their legitimacy.

BUREAUCRACY AND THE STATE

As states develop they seem inevitably to become more bureaucratic. In totalitarian societies we would expect this because a central power is trying to strictly regulate the citizens. Even in democratic states like our own government bureaucracy has grown to enormous scale. In the past century and one-half the ratio of central government employees to population has grown to twenty times its original size. (See Figure 16.1.)

In principle, government workers are under the direct supervision of our obviously partisan political leaders. Yet we simultaneously insist that the workers are nonpartisan public servants. This contradiction creates tension and dysfunctions. For example, when President Carter took office, he created a cabinet and high-level administrative team of a few hundred people who would lead the nearly 3 million civil service workers working in the federal bureaucracy. Carter's administration naturally recruited and promoted bureaucrats who shared similar visions of how the United States should operate. When President Reagan took over, he, like other incoming Presidents, confronted an enormous federal bureaucracy composed of career civil servants who did not always agree with his visions. Understandably, those working in areas like the Departments of Education and Human Services frequently disagreed with Reagan's intention to severely cut budgets. While they are technically responsible to the administration, many of these workers resisted such "leadership" with techniques ranging from verbal protest through lack of cooperation and in some cases organizational sabotage. Because as a society we are committed to a democratic state, and because we have developed no better ways to administer most programs than bureaucracy, we must live with these tensions and conflicts that are built into the social structure (Etzioni-Halevy, 1983).

WHY DO STATES DIFFER?

In some sense, each of the 157 different nation-states in the world is unique, but we know that they share important similarities. Sociologists try to understand why some states tend toward democracy and relatively broad freedoms whereas others tend toward dictatorships and repression. The various theoretical perspectives offer differing insights into these matters, as they have on earlier issues.

Until recently there has been little information about different countries that could be used to test our theories. Since the 1960s, however, new data have become available that may open up "new and barely exploited opportunities for increasing our understanding of the similarities and differences among political systems" (Dahl, 1970, p. 48). The research, as we shall see, is provocative and useful, although still at a preliminary stage.

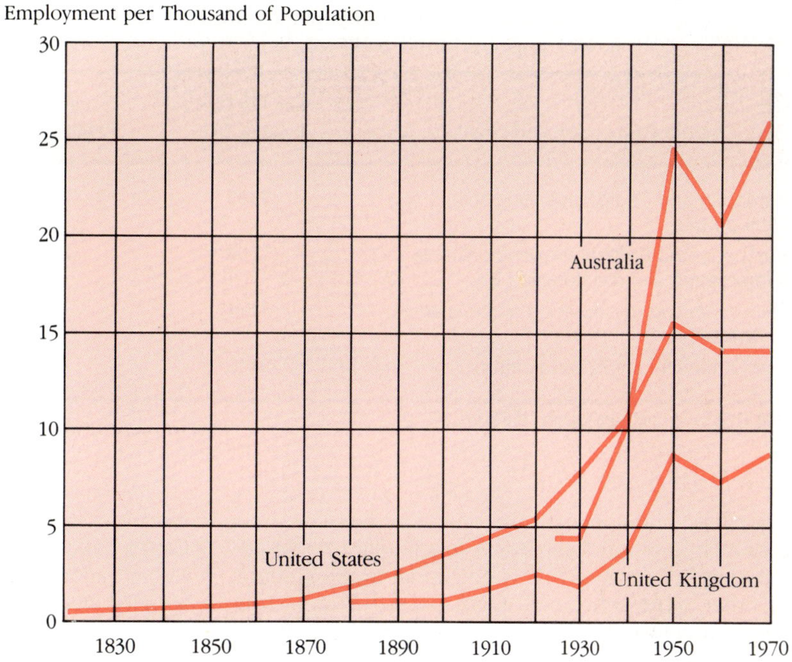

FIGURE 16.1 Growth in Central Government Employment per Thousand of Population. The twentieth century brought a rapid growth in the proportion of the population employed by the government. The United States' rate grew sixfold from 1910 to 1970. Australia's central government employs a proportion of its population almost twice that of the U.S. SOURCE Data presented in Eva Etzion-Holevy, *Bureaucracy and Democracy: A Political Dilemma.* London: Routledge and Kegan Paul (1983).

DEMOCRACY OR DICTATORSHIP?

Structural-functionalists explain the existence of democracies and dictatorships according to features of the societies and their people. For instance, Seymour Martin Lipset suggests that democracy is better suited to developed or industrialized nations with high literacy rates, an idea he attributes to Aristotle. As early as 1963 Lipset tested this theory against available data from fifty-four nations and finds strong support (1963, p. 31, italics added):

> The average wealth, degree of industrialization and urbanization, and level of education is much higher for the more democratic countries. . . . Only in a wealthy society in which relatively few citizens lived at the level of real poverty could there be a situation in which the mass of the population intelligently participates in politics and develops the self-restraint necessary to avoid succumbing to the appeals of irresponsible demagogues. A society divided between a large impoverished mass and a small favored elite results either in ***oligarchy*** [*dictatorial rule of the small upper stratum*], or in ***tyranny*** [*popularly based dictatorship*].

Democracy, then, seems more likely to emerge in relatively wealthy industrialized or industrializing societies, in which much of the population is educated (see Table 16.3).

At about the same time Harry Eckstein advanced the theory that for a government to be stable the type of authority exercised by that government must be similar to that exercised by its other major institutions (1966). If people are accustomed to authoritarian family, religion, and economic institutions, they may be poorly equipped to appreciate and understand democracy in the state. Conversely, in a society where egalitarianism prevails in the family, religion, and business, there may be serious trouble if the state takes an authoritarian stance.

More recent research reveals some important things about why states do or do not become democratic. For instance, Protestant cultures favor democratic states. This is consistent with Eckstein's idea that states must fit their cultures. Protestantism is generally less authoritarian than Catholicism, so we would expect it to fit better with democracy. Earlier ideas that dictatorships were particularly prone to emerge with rapid development are not born out by research, which is focusing on recently emerging states, but the research indicates that democracy is distinctly more likely to arise in developed countries. So-called peripheral societies, those that are poor, weak, overspecialized, and have been subject to manipulation or control by other nations, are especially prone to forming authoritarian states (Bollen, 1979; Bollen and Jackman, 1985). Un-

Democracy Is More Likely Where the Population Is Not Impoverished or Illiterate

Type of Government and Location	Mean Per Capita Income, 1949	Literate Population (%)
European and English-speaking stable democracies	$695	96
European and English-speaking unstable democracies and dictatorships	$308	85
Latin-American democracies and unstable dictatorships	$171	74
Latin-American stable dictatorships	$119	46

SOURCE Adapted from Lipset, 1963, pp. 35–37.

der what conditions will the state take the form of a dictatorship or an oligarchy? A functionalist might argue that this form of rule is functional in the absence of other more functional alternative structures. This interpretation is consistent with some major research findings. Dictatorships often arise with rapid industrialization during an unstable period when the traditional authority is rapidly crumbling but when the basis for rational–legal authority, including a minimally educated population, is not yet established. Russia offers a clear illustration of rapid industrialization leading to a dictatorial regime. From 1897 to 1913, the period just preceding the revolution in Russia, the population grew from 16 million to 26 million amidst very rapid industrialization (Lipset, 1963).

The conflict perspective offers a very different view on democracy and dictatorship. In classical Marxian thought dictatorship is a necessary step toward a truly equal society, one in which the state eventually withers because it is no longer needed to suppress the class conflict. From this perspective we would look below surface definitions of the situation to consider whether the dictatorship was socialistic and in the interests of the people, or capitalistic and therefore exploitive of the people. We might also want to examine the quality of the democracy to see whether it was really serving the workers' interest or a sham diversion constructed by the capitalists to divert workers' attention from their exploitation.

Symbolic interactionists look not only at the social structures we create but also at their symbolic meanings. Ideology itself may help explain the form of state a people adopt. Various sociologists have studied the importance of ideas in the formation of new states.

Off the southeastern coast of the United States are several island states. When they gained their independence from imperial powers, many participated in what sociologists have called the democratic revolution and formed states similar in structure to Western democracies (Bell, 1967). Cuba is a notable exception. Castro, once hailed as the "George Washington of Cuba," adopted a communist ideology and formed a socialist dictatorship in the United States' "backyard." This is dramatic witness to the power of ideas to shape social structure.

THE REALM OF POWER OF THE STATE: DEVELOPMENT AND IDEOLOGY

Why do some states involve themselves in a wide range of affairs whereas others limit themselves to relatively few matters? If we examine Table 16.2, "Central Government Revenue as a Percent of Gross National Product," we see some interesting findings and an interesting puzzle. First, it is clear from considering the "mean" column that as societies become more developed, the government becomes relatively larger in terms of the proportion of the societies' total production (GNP) which becomes government revenue. However, the mean column gives us averages; the range column to its right gives us the range of scores that produced the averages. Here we see that at every stage considerable differences exist in this measure of the breadth of government. Why? Again, our three perspectives help us understand this important aspect of political institutions.

Recall that the major functions of the state are dispute resolution, social control, intersocietal relations, planning and direction, and social services for dependents. In general, development tends to disturb traditional social organization and increase the power of the state in these areas.

Developed societies, for example, often have higher overall living standards and larger differences between the richest and poorest segments of the society. Development brings more disputes, especially over matters of private property, and offers fewer traditional resources for dealing with them, creating more need for the state to resolve disputes.

Similarly, development bring geographic mobility and higher average population density. Many informal methods of community control weaken under the strains of larger, more mobile communities, creating an increased need for governmental social control.

Two important aspects of development increase the potential for conflict between societies, and the accompanying need for a state to conduct intersocietal relations. First, as societies develop, they discover or invent means of transportation, such as the horse, sailing ships, trains, motor vehicles, and planes, which make contact between societies more frequent. Second, as we see in Chapter 3, advanced societies are more dependent on land and therefore more likely to fight for it. As the likelihood of conflict between societies rises, so does the apparent need for a state to conduct relations between societies.

Development also means complexity. As the society becomes more complex, one central authority grows to plan and direct activities. In a rural agrarian society, road construction can be left to local parties with little adverse consequence. In highly industrialized societies that rely heavily on highways it may be more functional to have a central public authority for planning interstate networks of roads.

Finally, as development continues and the family begins to shed the function of caring for dependents, governmental institutions provide this care. With development, also, the poor become more aware of their situation, more articulate in their arguments for a share of the socially produced resources, and more organized as a political group.

In general, development heightens certain societal needs, while disrupting earlier methods of meeting those needs. Thus large-scale government appears to be more functional as societies become more developed.

The conflict perspective offers alternative interpretations of why some states have large rather than small realms. In the postrevolutionary stages of socialism, leaders are setting up the apparatus to care for people who had previously been neglected, and they see a need to reshape the culture to make it more compatible with the new era of communism.

For instance, after Mao Tse-Tung successfully led a military revolution in China in 1949, he engaged in an ongoing "cultural revolution" to rid the society of its old ways. Such redesigning of a culture often involves the state in a wide range of matters. The state becomes much more involved in industry, since private property is expropriated in the name of the people. Of course, conflict theorists realize the state is often the pawn of the ruling elite. As class conflict increases and the oppressed become more aware of their oppression, elites need a stronger state to suppress the class conflict, often combined with more programs to appease the oppressed masses.

The state is now a major caretaker for older people. This woman, like half of Miami Beach's elderly, has no source of income other than Social Security. *(AP/Wide World Photos)*

Symbolic interactionists would point to the importance of the meanings we vest in our social structures. Capitalism as an ideology justifies a powerful militaristic state as a means of securing freedom. Communism justifies an expansive and intrusive state as a means of eliminating exploitation and creating equality. In countries where the dominant value is equality, the state must create systems to bring about at least the appearance of equality, thus broadening the domain of government. For example, in most developed socialistic countries, the population is provided with health care, and physicians are paid by the state. This means that all physicians' incomes are collected from the general population in taxes, which of course raises the level of government revenue.

Because the state owns and operates certain industries in socialist countries, much of what would be private income under a capitalist system becomes state revenue. Furthermore, when services are provided through bureaucracies rather than through free enterprise, more bureaucrats are employed and expenses may rise.

In a state in which the dominant ideology is freedom, some of the functions that are assumed by socialist states are taken over by free enterprise. Because health care in the United States is allocated by a relatively free market, less of the money spent and earned in this field has been government revenue. For similar reasons the state's portion of the Gross National Product is usually smaller under capitalism's "freedom" than socialism's equality. In this situation, a smaller proportion of the GNP becomes government revenue.

Interestingly, the very absence or weakness of ideology may set the stage for broader government. A regime that rules largely through force rather than through legitimacy and effectiveness will probably have to consume more of the society's resources to maintain its position of dominance.

Just as societies differ in their resources and power, so do their states. The state as an instrument of international relations may or may not be interested in maintaining friendly relations with its neighbors. Particularly in the past three centuries, the developing state has been an instrument of imperialism, preying on less developed and weaker societies. During this century many former colonies have demanded and/or been granted their independence, but the United States and the Soviet Union frequently play direct or indirect roles in trying to influence, dominate, or exploit their less developed neighbors.

In seeking to understand the varieties of political institutions, we should consider the balance among several sociological factors. For example, the fit between the state as an institution and the society as a culture, the relationships among levels of technology employed by the society, the level and awareness of class conflict, and the atmosphere of ideas surrounding the society are all important in assessing the specific functions of a state. We would also want to consider influences exerted on one state by another state.

How Is Power Formally and Informally Distributed in the United States?

The Constitution of the United States forms the basis of a highly stable political system that has survived two centuries that included major wars and violent internal upheavals. However, some important features of the political institutions of the United States were not planned by Jefferson, Paine, Franklin, and the other political architects who helped to formulate this particular state. In this section we consider some of these features.

CONGRESSIONAL COMMITTEES

The houses of Congress are defined by the U.S. Constitution, but their extensive array of committees and subcommittees are not. All bills are considered first by subcommittees, and informal congressional norms state that differences should be worked out within these subcommittees. Because the subcommittees are seen as experts, bills drafted there are often left unaltered when they come to the floor of the House or Senate. Subcommittees are important power centers, unanticipated by the authors of the Constitution.

CONGRESSIONAL STAFF

Staff personnel handle much work for which the legislator takes credit. Some handle correspondence with constituents, usually in the name of the legislator, often helping cut red tape for constituents who have written their legislators for assistance. Others become specialists, studying particular areas, helping draft legislation, and writing position papers or speeches for the legislator. Those assigned to a particular area of legislation are sometimes wined and dined by lobbyists who are rarely able to talk directly with the busy legislator.

Lobbying, which involves being paid by someone to try to influence a legislator, was a criminal offense 100 years ago. Now lobbying is legal, and lobbyists represent a vast array of interest groups that seek the attention of legislators and their staffs. Their means of influence ranges from legitimate transmission of facts and voter opinions to explicitly illegal actions, such as making sizable unrecorded campaign contributions.

Staff persons develop expertise in special areas and brief the legislator on what they believe to be the best course of action, sometimes sitting in on committee hearings so they will be immediately available for consultation. They may actually draft bills and ghost-write the legislator's speeches and articles.

The legislator and the staff endeavor to create the illusion that the legislator is actually doing all things being done in the legislator's name. The legislative staff is a sizable organization masquerading as an individual. No human being could possibly read, deliberate, consult, write, and attend functions to the extent that is expected of a senator or representative. Therefore, rather than a single legislator wielding much legislative power, dozens of staff people actually make decisions on priorities of legislation.

EXECUTIVE AGENCIES

The federal bureaucracies, known as executive agencies, also have legislative power not defined by the Constitution. Some of these agencies have staffs many times larger than those of Congress. Although most executive agencies are charged with facilitating the programs developed by Congress, a significant number of the higher administrators and their staffs take a direct hand in lawmaking.

Often the administrators testify on legislation being considered by Congress. Even more important, the agencies write the regulations or guidelines for carrying out legislation passed by Congress. These guidelines, which have the force of law, are often 10 to 100 times as long as the legislation they "clarify." In this way, through the executive agencies people who have not been elected by the population are acting as lawmakers, beyond the scope of the Constitution.

How Is Political Power Exercised in the United States?

We are taught as children that in a democracy the majority rules. A close look at our electoral process reveals that in our democracy a minority actually rules. If we study the 1984 presidential election, we find that Ronald Reagan was elected by only 33 per cent of the eligible voters. How is this possible? First, only 53 percent of those eligible to vote actually voted! Reagan carried 59 percent of the vote, so the proportion of the electorate that placed him in office was just 33 percent. Members of the House of Representatives stand for reelection every two years, and in nonpresidential-election years, voter turnout is even lighter, ranging in recent times from 35 to 55 percent. Hence one needs only about 23 percent of the eligible voters' votes to win a seat in Congress, and in some years like 1978 a candidate needed less than one in five (18 percent) of the eligible voters' votes to win the election.

Whereas the proportion of the people voting has stayed within the 50 to 65 percent range for at least one-half century, we are living in an age where the trend has been rather steadily downward from a high turnout of 63 per cent in 1960 to the 53 percent turnout for the 1984 election (see Figure 16.2). If the present twenty-five-year trend continues, then the election of 1992 will be the first in which the majority of American voters do not bother to cast a ballot in the presidential elections. Whereas the trend signals growing disinterest in the election, voter turnout has gotten smaller for other reasons, too. Those who compile statistics on eligible voters currently count even illegal aliens as part of the voting age population, though they

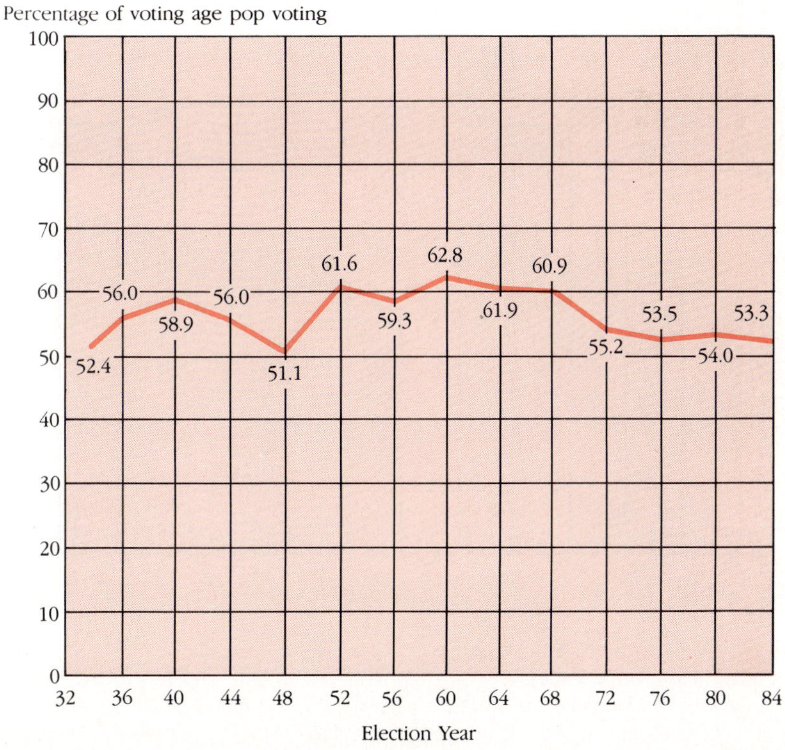

FIGURE 16.2 Voter Participation in Recent Elections. A large proportion of those old enough to vote do not. If the downward trend of the past twenty-five years continues, we will have a *majority* of eligible voters *not* voting in the early 1990s. SOURCE *The World Almanac and Book of Facts*, 1986. New York: Newspaper Enterprises Association.

cannot legally vote. Because this portion of our population grew rapidly since the 1960s, they have inadvertently exaggerated the trend. Also, during this time we have extended the right to vote to 18- to 21-year-olds who are especially unlikely to vote. The United States has the distinction of having the worst voter turnout of major democracies around the world. (U.S. Bureau of the Census, 1985; Edwards, 1985; Burnham, 1983; Hilsman, 1985)

WHO VOTES?

Figure 16.3 indicates that social status has a major effect on voting behavior. Education, a strong indicator of social class, is also a strong predictor of whether someone will vote. Those with four years of college or more are almost twice as likely (79 percent) to vote as those with less than an eighth-grade education (43 percent). Age has a pronounced effect as well, with only about one-third (37 percent) of 18- to 20-year-olds voting compared to nearly twice that many (70 percent) in the 45- to 64-year-old category. Ethnic origin also strongly predicts voting habits. In the 1984 presidential election, 33 percent of those of Spanish origin, 56 percent of blacks, and 61 percent of whites voted. Gender has a very weak ability to predict whether someone votes. Women with a rate of 61 percent slightly surpass the 59 percent participation rate of men (U.S. Bureau of the Census, 1985).

WHY PEOPLE DO NOT VOTE

The low voter turnout clearly signals that a large portion of Americans who are eligible to vote do not think it is worth the trouble. They apparently believe that the election is either of no significance or that they have no power. Given the high level of taxation and federal government involvement in our lives it seems unlikely that these nonvoters think the matter unimportant.

FIGURE 16.3 Social Status and Voting Behavior SOURCE U.S. Bureau of the Census, 1985.

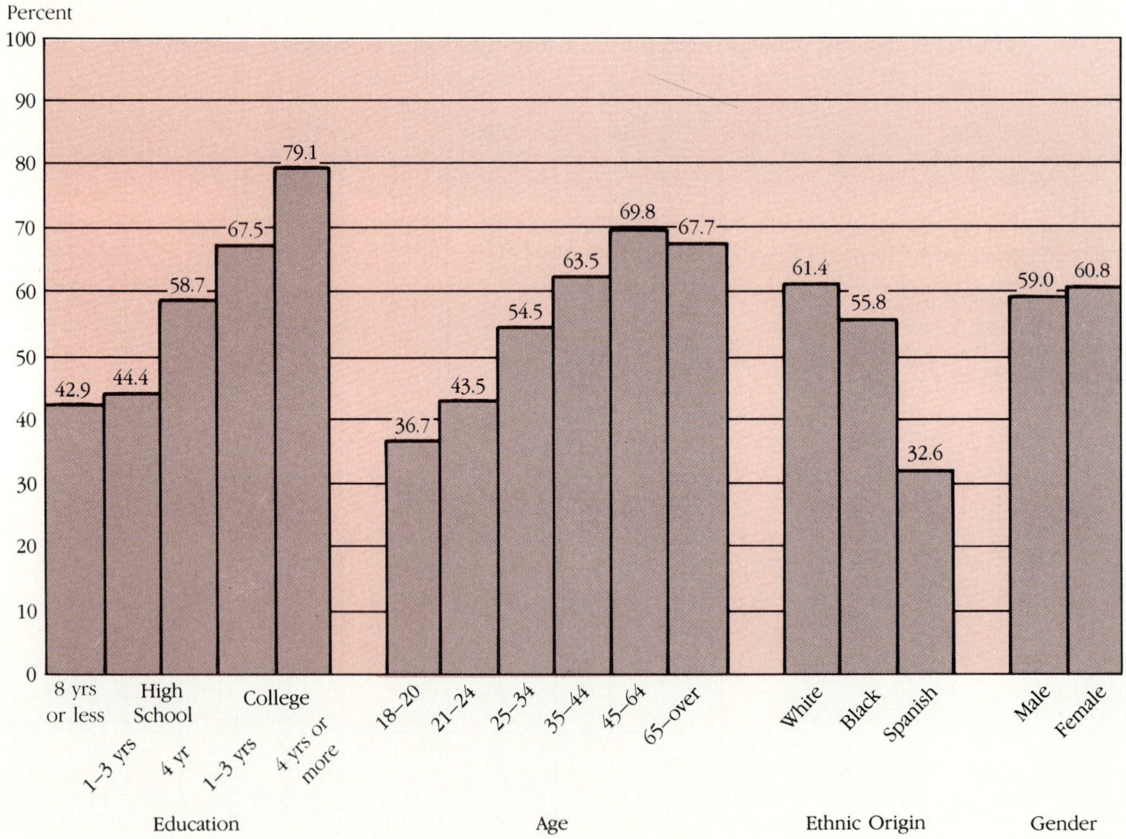

More likely, they feel powerless. They may feel that neither party will really improve their lot.

Almost two decades ago Rosalio Wences (1969) theorized that our election system, which differs considerably from that of most European nations, may be a major cause of the low voter turnout. The European system involves proportional representation by party. A party that attracts 20 percent of the vote is assured 20 percent of the seats in the legislative body. In the United States, if all the candidates from one party attracted 20 percent of the votes, they would all lose and the party would get 0 percent of the seats. Wences believes that the proportional representation by party contributes to higher voter turnout, because each vote actually counts toward a seat. Wences found, for instance, that under proportional representation, more people were likely to vote, and the working class parties typically gained a higher proportion of seats in cabinets and parliaments than when voter turnout was lower.

That those in the lower classes and among minority populations are especially unlikely to vote indicates their even greater alienation, as predicted by conflict theory. They indicate by their unwillingness to vote that they believe they cannot really win—and by not voting they help to fulfill their own prophecy (Burnham, 1983).

PARTY AFFILIATION. Over the past one-half century political party affiliation has declined, as indicated by the fact that the proportion of the public that labels itself as independent has nearly doubled from 16 percent in 1937 to 31 percent in 1985. Over this time period the Republicans have maintained about one-third of the population, though they temporarily became weaker in the 1960s and 1970s. The Democratic Party has steadily lost support from its high of 50 percent in 1937 to the present low of 37 percent. We are headed toward an interesting point where the proportion of Democrats, Republicans, and independents will all be about equal at one-third of the population each.

At the present we find that social status factors such as ethnicity, education, age, income, occupation, and labor-union membership are distinctly related to party affiliation. (See Figure 16.4) Blacks are over twice as likely (74 percent) to be Democrats as whites are (32 percent), and those of Spanish origin are half again as likely (47 percent) to be Democrats as whites are. Those with less than a complete high school education are half again as likely (47 percent) to identify with the Democratic Party as are college graduates (33 percent). Age has a pronounced effect as well. Those 50 or over are half again as likely (43 percent) as those in the 18- to 29-year age bracket (31 percent) to be Democrats.

Three different indices of social class show a relationship between status and party. Those with incomes less than $15,000 are roughly half again as likely (49 percent) as those with incomes over $35,000 (32 percent) to be Democrats. Similarly, 48 percent of unskilled workers identify themselves as Democrats compared to only 30 percent of professonal and business persons. The relation between labor-union membership and party affiliation is not as strong, with 48 percent of union members claiming to be Democrats compared to 38 percent of nonunion members. Finally, gender has little impact on party affiliation. Women are somewhat more likely (44 percent) than men (35 percent) to identify with the Democratic party. To summarize, the Democratic Party is stronger among blacks, voters without a high school education, voters over 50 years of age, voters with incomes of less than $15,000, unskilled workers, voters belonging to labor unions, and voters who are female. Note that we have ranked these groups from voters among whom the inclination toward the Democratic party is highest to those among whom the Democratic edge is the slightest (Gallup, 1986).

Of course, to not be a Democrat does not mean one automatically becomes a Republican. One could be an Independent. The Democratic Party has over the past one-half century lost part of its membership not to the Republicans so much as to the growing number of Independents.

WHO PAYS?

When the founders of our country drafted the Constitution, they probably had little idea how large government would grow and how expensive elections would become. Today's president works with secretaries of Defense, Transportation, Education, Human Services, and so on. Each of these secretaries administers budgets in billions of dollars and staffs of thousands of people. In Thomas Jefferson's presidency the entire executive branch consisted of Jefferson and a part-time private secretary paid by Jefferson himself.

As government has grown, so has the cost of waging an election campaign. The Constitution makes no provision for public funding of elections, but various social structures have been devised to meet these costs. During the latter half of the nineteenth century and for much of the twentieth century, political parties provided the major means of selecting candidates and funding their campaigns, and they still do. Some office seekers have developed individual campaign organizations to finance and manage their campaigns independent of the major political parties; John Anderson's candidacy in 1984 provides an example of a campaign financed through an independent candidate organiza-

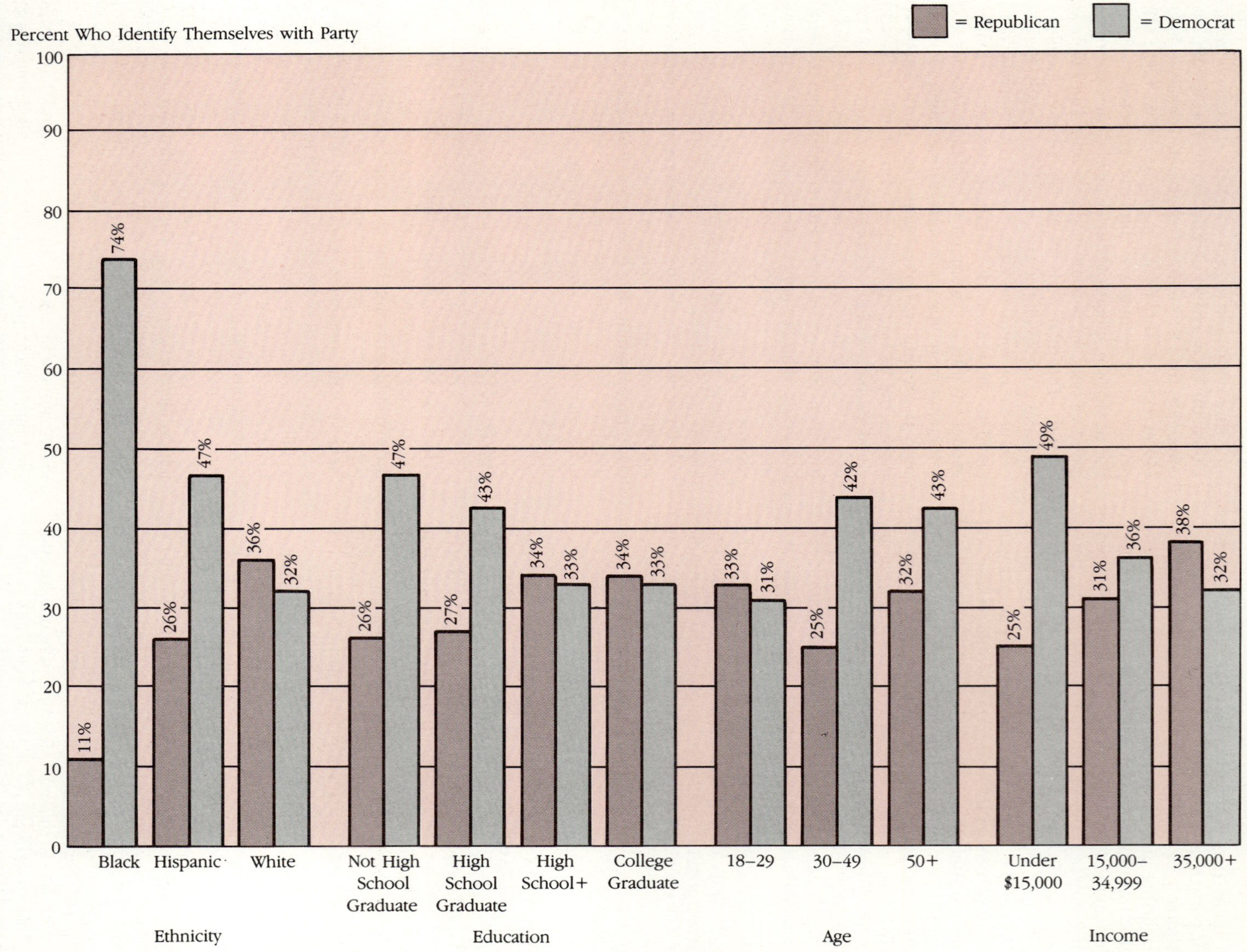

FIGURE 16.4 Social Status and Party Affiliation SOURCE George Gallup, *The Gallup Report*, No. 255, December 1986, p. 27.

tion. Even incumbent Republican President Richard Nixon in 1972 created an independent candidate campaign organization called the Committee to Reelect the President. One of the reasons this form of organization arose was because of the high and rising cost of participating in primary elections, which take place before one can be designated the candidate and therefore become eligible for party funds. In fact, presidential candidates actually spent more ($105 million) on the primary campaign in 1983–1984 than they did on the general election ($81 million) (U.S. Bureau of the Census, 1985).

The rising cost of elections gradually made it increasingly difficult for people of ordinary means to conduct a campaign. The high cost of campaigning also made candidates increasingly dependent on the support of large donors. These donors generally used their wealth to buy political power to represent their own special interests. This type of funding offers clear evidence of the operation of a power elite acting on its own behalf. Such large donors had no incentive to make donations except that they were receiving special benefits from them.

Congress became concerned with these abuses and passed the Federal Election Campaign Act in 1971 to limit to $1,000 the amount individuals could contribute per campaign per year. Under the Act candidates could receive $1 of federal matching funds for every $2 they raised on their own. These funds came from a voluntary "check-off" contribution made when taxpayers checked a box on their federal tax returns indicating they wanted $1 of their taxes to be spent for this purpose. In spite of the fact that this check-off does not alter an individual's federal tax, only 32 percent of Americans contribute to campaigns this way.

As one might expect, those wealthy people and organizations with a desire to influence elections sought new ways to buy political power. In 1975 when the Federal Election Commission ruled that Sun Oil Company could use general corporate funds to create, administer, and solicit voluntary contributions to establish a political program, many special-interest groups found what they had been looking for. Sun Oil had created what we now call a ***Political Action Committee (PAC)*** or *an organization that creates, administers, and solicits voluntary contributions to establish a political program.* Following the Sun Oil ruling, PACs exploded onto the election scene in the United States. In 1974 there were fewer than 500 PACs, but in one decade 3,500 had registered with the Federal Election Commission. In the four years between the elections of 1979–1980 and 1983–1984, contributions to congressional campaigns by PACs more than doubled, from $37.9 million to $77.4 million.

Whom do the PACs represent and what do they do? Three major interest groups account for most PACs: corporations, trade associations, and labor unions. Corporations such as Sun Oil form PACs that target especially influential candidates such as those who sit on key committees in the House or Senate. Depending on the situation, they may spend money to elect friendly candidates or to defeat unfriendly officeholders. A corporate PAC will be seeking special advantages such as favorable trade agreements, tax advantages, or even business with the government. Trade associations represent broader interests such as realtors, machinists, bankers, or automobile dealers. Like corporate PACs, they raise funds to influence elections to their own benefit. Labor unions, the smallest category of the three—for example, the United Auto Workers and the AFL–CIO—have launched their own PACs to protect the interests of their workers. Finally other special interest groups such as conservative and liberal groups, religious organizations, pro gun legislation and anti gun legislation groups, and organizations opposing or supporting abortion, sometimes form PACs to gain electoral power. Neither party has a monopoly on PAC contributions. Typically, the Democrats have received more funds in elections to the House whereas Republicans have benefited more from PAC contributions in elections to the Senate (U.S. Bureau of the Census, 1985, p. 258). Numerically, most contributors to PACs come from the middle class; most of the dollars come from elites who make much larger contributions. Although the typical PAC contributor comes from the middle class, the typical middle class person does not contribute to PACs; in fact, only 7 percent of the public contributes to PACs (Jones and Miller, 1985). Table 16.4 lists the PACs that have recently raised and donated the most money.

Whereas the framers of the Constitution intended senators and members of Congress to represent states and congressional districts respectively, PACs have a tendency to "nationalize" these elections. For instance, a representative from a district in Iowa who sits on the Armed Services Committee may have a vote that is important to a defense contractor in Burbank, California. What was once a decision left largely to the member of Congress and the local constituency now often becomes a contest between interest groups around the nation.

PACs and individual candidate campaign organizations have substantially reduced the influence of political parties. This concerns experts because parties represent a unifying influence in the political process in which large segments of the electorate are brought together. As Walter Burnham puts it:

> Our parties, even the Republicans, are weak and appear to be growing weaker. Interest groups occupy the political terrain that the parties have abandoned. As a result, our political system is

TABLE 16.4 Ten PACs That Raise and Spend the Most Money

Top Fundraisers	PAC Category	Total Money Raised
1. National Conservative Political Action Committee (NCPAC)	Nonconnected	$10.0
2. National Congressional Club	Nonconnected	9.7
3. Realtors Political Action Committee (R-PAC)	Trade	3.0
4. Fund for a Conservative Majority	Nonconnected	2.9
5. American Medical Association Political Action Committee (AMPAC)	Trade	2.5
6. National Committee for an Effective Congress (NCEC)	Nonconnected	2.4
7. Citizens for the Republic (CFTR)	Nonconnected	2.4
8. Committee for the Survival of a Free Congress (CSFC)	Nonconnected	2.4
9. Fund for a Democratic Majority	Nonconnected	2.3
10. Committee for the Future of America, Inc.	Nonconnected	2.2
Top Contributors to Federal Candidates	**PAC Category**	**Total Money Contributed[a]**
1. Realtors Political Action Committee (R-PAC)	Trade	$ 2.1
2. American Medical Association Political Action Committee (AMPAC)	Trade	1.7
3. UAW-V-CAP (United Auto Workers)	Labor	1.6
4. Machinists Non-Partisan Political League (MNPL)	Labor	1.4
5. National Education Association PAC (NEA–PAC)	Labor	1.2
6. Build Political Action Committee of the National Association of Home Builders (Build PAC)	Trade	1.0
7. Committee for Thorough Agricultural Political Education of the Associated Milk Producers (C-TAPE)	Cooperative	1.0
8. American Bankers Association BANKPAC	Trade	0.9
9. Automobile and Truck Dealers Election Action Committee	Trade	0.9
10. AFL–CIO COPE Political Contributions Committee	Labor	0.9

SOURCE Sabato, Larry J. (1984) *PAC Power: Inside the World of Political Action Committees*, by permission of W. W. Norton & Company, Inc., pp. 16–17. Copyright © 1985, 1984 by Larry J. Sabato.

> less able to contain the jungle of private and selfish interests, and our country is less governable. This road has led us to disaster in the past, and it may do so again (Burnham, 1983, p. 260).

The Federal Election Act of 1971 sought to limit the influence of special interests groups by limiting individual contributions and creating federal funding for campaigns for federal office. But big donors still buy influence through large contributions to elected officials, they simply have to put out a little extra effort. Technically, no individual can contribute more than $1,000 to a candidate and a PAC cannot contribute more than $5,000. But individuals can make multiple contributions to PACs and PACs can make contributions of up to $5,000 to as many other PACs as they chose. Someone seeking to channel $1 million to a candidate need only use or set up enough PACs to do the job. Many observers say that legislators' concern for contributions has grown in recent years and with it the potential for, and reality of, abuse. As one former Capitol Hill aide, says: "Now the politicians need more and more money; therefore, their threshold of principle is lower, and their willingness to compromise is greater. Everyone has learned that this is the way to do business" (anonymous source in Drew, 1983, p. 3).

The solution according to Elizabeth Drew is simple: finish off what Congress began! If the campaigns were completely, rather than partially, publicly financed, and candidates were limited in how much they could spend, the candidates would not need contributions from special interest groups and the public would be better served. Drew suggests the additional cost could be easily raised by increasing the voluntary tax check-off from $1 to $2 per year (Drew, 1983).

To summarize, the high and rising cost of political campaigns is being partly underwritten by the federal government. Political parties have lost ground to both independent candidate campaign organizations and PACs. PACs are a major new development in the electoral process and represent a means by which wealthy individuals and organizations still buy influence in the political process (Sabato, 1984).

PLURALISM VERSUS ELITISM

It is clear that power in the United States flows in patterns unforeseen by the drafters of the Constitution and not acknowledged in the simplistic view of formal government often taught in high school American Government courses. Many power brokers at the national level are not elected officials but hired assistants of the officials or lobbyists sent to Washington to influence the officials. Many citizens opt out of their role as voters, whereas the wealthy are heavily overrepresented in influence, partly through campaign contributions. Behind the curtain of staged committee hearings, convention theatrics, and press conferences, the public rarely catches a glimpse of the real backstage workings in Washington. Occasionally the media offers up a sniff of scandal and duplicity such as Watergate or Iranscam. This leaves many wondering how much else goes on behind the scenes.

Who really controls the political process? Sociologists are divided on the issue. Most agree that power is considerably concentrated and is exercised primarily by interest groups rather than by the broad electorate. Functionalists tend to take a ***pluralistic*** view *which holds that many relatively small groups have political power and that none dominates in general.* Most conflict theorists subscribe to an ***elitist*** view *which holds that a small virtually invisible set of elites holds the ultimate power of the state and uses it to maintain and advance their positions of privilege.*

Robert Michels advanced what he calls the "iron law of oligarchy," which states that bureaucratic organizations and governments naturally drift to a situation of ***oligarchy,*** *or control by a small, powerful group that uses the authority vested in it to maintain its power* (1915). Michels believes that even in representative democracies incumbent legislators and executives have such an advantage because of the authority they wield that outsiders have a difficult time trying to replace them. Once in office, a senator, a representative, or a president can take advantage of that position to further his or her reelection through such methods as press conferences and letters to constituents. Thus, politicians in the United States tend to be reelected many times.

Italian sociologist Vilfredo Pareto also believes power tends to become concentrated in the hands of an elite group (1950). Pareto contends that the elites often abuse their power, causing an uprising to replace that regime with another, which would again eventually become abusive. Pareto called this repeating cycle the "circulation of elites."

C. Wright Mills claimed that a power elite exists in the United States (1956). Although Mills believed there was an extreme concentration of power in the hands of a tiny minority, he did not portray this group as a ruling class. Instead, Mills's power elite is composed of high-level government officials, corporate elites from business, and the highest ranking military personnel. This group of enormously powerful individuals is not a tight conspiracy. As Mills put it, "The power elite is composed of political, economic, and military men, but this instituted elite is frequently in some tension: it comes together only on certain coinciding points and only on certain occasions of 'crisis' " (Mills, 1956, p. 276).

G. William Domhoff is one of the few researchers who has attempted to demonstrate empirically the existence of a power elite in the United States at the national level. Specifically, through systematic observation Domhoff attempts to define a ruling class, a concept that Mills rejected in describing the power distribution in the United States. Domhoff (1983) produces evidence that there is a national upper class, made up of rich businessmen and their descendants, who interact at private schools, exclusive social clubs, exclusive summer resorts, and similar institutions, and he claims that this upper class is also a ruling class. Domhoff suggests that this class has a disproportionate influence in the controlling institutions and the decision-making groups in the country, and he documents the idea that the upper class is numerically overrepresented in the federal government, the military, and the CIA. Domhoff acknowledges the problem of defining what constitutes a disproportionate number of members but does not resolve the conflict.

After two decades of studying who rules in America, Domhoff concludes:

> On the basis of available evidence the best answer still seems to be that dominant power in the United States is exercised by a power elite that is the leadership group of a property-based ruling class. Despite all the turmoil of the 1960s and 1970s, and the constant chatter about economic crisis that is ever with us, there

Nonroutine political activity includes demonstrating, violent strikes, and even terrorism. These youthful "nonroutine political activists" are hardly terroristic. (*Photo courtesy the Michigan Daily*)

> continues to be a small upper class that owns 20 to 25 percent of all privately held wealth and 45 to 50 percent of all privately held corporate stock, sits in seats of formal power from the corporate community to the federal government, and wins much more often than it loses on issues ranging from the nature of the tax structure to the stifling of reform in such vital areas as consumer protection, environmental protection, and labor law (Domhoff, 1983, pp. 222–223).

Thomas Dye (1986), having studied the issue for almost as long as Domhoff, comes to very similar conclusions. Dye notes that the elites include about 6,500 people who are overwhelmingly white, male, and drawn from the upper- or upper-middle class. However, many are upwardly mobile, as indicated by the fact that fewer than 10 percent of the top corporate elites he studied inherited their position. Similarly, most government elites rose from relatively obscure positions. Most of these climbers come from a remarkably small social stratum. Some 54 percent of top corporate leaders and 42 percent of top governmental leaders are alumni of just 12 well-known private universities. Elites tend to agree on the values of private enterprise, limited government, and due process of law. They even support liberal social welfare programs including social security, fair labor standards, unemployment compensation, a graduated income tax, and a federally aided welfare system. However they do disagree on important issues, such as how to achieve their ends. Issues like federal versus state-and-local control of social programs, tax reform, specific energy and environmental protection proposals, and specific measures for dealing with inflation and recession, often divide the elites (Dye, 1986).

Several studies of political organizations at the municipal level lend support to the idea of the power elite. Sociologists who have studied the power structure of Atlanta, Georgia, and Muncie, Indiana, are able to identify the elite groups who dominated the local governments in these communities at the times of their studies (Lynd and Lynd, 1929; and Hunter, 1953).

Although acknowledging that relatively small groups often acquire great political power, pluralists argue that many of these groups exist and tend to balance each other. As a result, policymaking is functional for the entire society or community, even if it is not arrived at through the traditional democratic method. For example, pluralists would say that the efforts of organized labor offset the power of big business. They also see groups like the American Civil Liberties Union as blocking government actions destructive to individual rights.

As Lipset points out, people affiliate with multiple interest groups that are sometimes politically inconsistent. For instance, a black businessman's affiliation with poorer blacks may offset his affiliation with his white business colleagues. A woman may be both a Roman Catholic and a member of the National Organization for Women, suffering politically inconsistent pressures both to support and to oppose legalization of abortion. Such joint memberships in different interest groups reduce the likelihood of any single elite group dominating the political system as a whole.

Pluralists have also amassed evidence to support

their claims. For example, Talcott Parsons demonstrates that the decisions on a particular issue are a compromise between interest groups, rather than the heavy-handed dominance of a monolithic power (1957). Robert Dahl studied political power in New Haven, Connecticut, and concludes that certain groups dominated specific realms, but no group, including the aristocrats, dictated policy in all or even most areas (1961).

Arnold Rose and William Domhoff claim that power is distributed through *both* pluralism and elitism. Rose claims that although the general public appears apathetic on the surface, it expresses itself on domestic issues through interest groups and voluntary associations. Rose believes that foreign policy, in contrast, is largely controlled by a group resembling Mills's power elite (Rose, 1967). Domhoff suggests that local government operates on a pluralistic basis, whereas the federal government is basically dominated by the upper classes (Domhoff, 1967).

The complexity of the processes involved in political institutions and the difficulties involved in making accurate measurements often impede the ability of social scientists to make definite interpretations about exactly who governs whom.

What Are Nonroutine Political Activities?

Most states provide for at least some of a variety of routine political activities that include campaigning for office and voting. In authoritarian or totalitarian regimes the participation may be no more than a sham election in which the citizen is given the honor of voting for the only party's only candidate. But political activity sometimes takes place outside the sphere that a particular state would define as legitimate. ***Nonroutine political activity*** *includes activities ranging from demonstrations, violent strikes, terrorism, revolution, and guerrilla warfare.* We focus on protest movements, which can involve demonstrations, violent strikes, terrorism, and torture as important types of nonroutine political activity (Wasburn, 1982).

In our "Close-Up on Research" we encounter William Gamson's ambitious attempt to test one version of the pluralist hypothesis by examining what happened in a random sample of 467 social movements that challenged established authority in the United States. His findings provide a rather provocative image of the American political process.

CLOSE-UP on • *RESEARCH* •

William Gamson on When Is Political Protest Successful?

The Researcher and the Setting

William Gamson is a political sociologist concerned with the application and impact of sociological ideas and findings in the world of politics. The research discussed here was begun in 1966 at a time of considerable unrest associated with urban riots and the Vietnam War. Although most political theorists at this time were describing American politics as pluralistic, Gamson was impressed by an article entitled, "Is There A Military–Industrial Complex Which Prevents Peace?" written by two of his friends, Marc Pilisuk and Tom Hayden (1965).

Gamson's work is motivated by his distrust of the dominant view of American politics as pluralistic. He seeks to answer the question: What are the levers of change in American society? As Gamson puts it, "Understanding the operation of power in American society seemed necessary for the agenda of peace research" (1975, p. *x*).

Gamson began pursuing such an understanding in an informal seminar during 1966 and 1967. He later secured two National Science Foundation grants and involved other faculty members and students in this research project. He published the results in book form nearly a decade after he began the research.

The Researcher's Goal

Although motivated by the broad issues mentioned above, Gamson focuses his research on *challenging groups*, or "voluntary groups [which] have challenged some aspect of the status quo" (p. *ix*). These groups would qualify as social movements, as we defined them in Chapter 7. They involved a wide variety of causes, including attempts to organize labor unions. We discuss them here to assess their impact on the American political process.

Gamson seeks to answer several questions, including: "What strategies work under what circumstances? What organizational characteristics influence the success of the challenge?" (p. 5).

Theory and Concepts

Gamson deals with the theory on two levels. His opening chapter, "The Pluralist Image of American Politics," discusses the global image or theory of pluralism, the central axiom of which is: "Instead of a single center of sovereign power there must be multiple centers of power, none of which is or can be wholly sovereign" (p. 6). From this definition of pluralism Gamson derives two hypotheses dealing with challenging groups (p. 12):

TABLE 16.5 How Often Challenge Groups Accomplished at Least One-Half Their Goals

	Percent of Groups Accomplishing One-Half or More of Goals
Size of challenge	
Sought to displace antagonist	
Yes	6
No	68
Multiple issues	
Yes	0
No	59
Solidarity	
Goals are universally beneficial	
Yes	40
No	51
Special incentives for membership	
Yes	82
No	40
Success of unruly behavior	
Use of violence	
Used violence	75
Received violence	0
Neither used nor received violence	53
Use of nonviolent constraints such as strikes or boycotts	
Yes	80
No	43
Combat readiness	
Bureaucratically organized	
Yes	62
No	38
Power centralized	
Yes	64
No	32
Factions	
Yes	22
No	70
Historical context	
Wartime	
Yes	64
No	39
Depression	
Yes	89
No	30
Historical era	
1800–1860	30
1861–1913	59
1914–1945	39

SOURCE Based on Gamson, 1975.

1. Only those groups whose objectives leave intact pluralist social structure and values will be 'successful.' Participation and success is denied to those who attack and try to change the pluralist order itself.

2. Only those groups which use institutionally provided means will be successful—in particular, the electoral system and the political pressure or lobbying system. Those who resort to the tactics of the streets will be unsuccessful.

Gamson does not test his two hypotheses directly, and returns to an explicit discussion of pluralism only in his last chapter, "The Limits of Pluralism."

The research described in the intervening chapters is guided by a less-abstract level of ideas. The discussion concerns the impact of various factors on challenging groups, including size or ambitiousness of the challenge, motivation of the participants, use of violence, type of organization, and prevailing social climate.

Research Design

First, the Gamson team searched historical sources to locate challenging groups active between 1800 and 1945. Of the more than 4,000 they could identify, they randomly selected 11 percent as a representative sample. Of these 467 potential subjects only 64 were found to fit the precise working definition of a challenging group: a group that seeks to mobilize an unmobilized population in order to challenge an antagonist outside its constituency. Eleven of the sixty-four finalists had to be deleted due to insufficient information. Because no apparent systematic bias was used in selecting the subjects, they should be representative of all challenging groups during the period.

The research team defined its concepts by specifying observable variables that could be measured by referring to historical accounts. The concept of *success* was divided into two variables; (1) *acceptance,* wherein the challenging group came to be accepted as at least a consultant to the antagonist in future decision making; and (2) *accomplishment,* in which the challenging group is considered by historians, by its antagonists, and by the challenging group itself to have accomplished more than one-half its goals.

To organize the information Gamson's team created a 100-item questionnaire used by the researchers to "interview" the historical literature used in their research. Over eighty hours were spent on each subject, and two separate researchers reviewed the accumulated information for each subject to ensure accuracy in interpreting the historical accounts.

Findings

Gamson's research design allowed him to investigate how various circumstances and characteristics of these challenge groups affected their success. For the sake of brevity we use goal accomplishment as the measure of success. He considered a wide variety of variables, and the results are summarized in Table 16.5, which indicates the percentage of groups which accomplished at least one-half their goals under a variety of conditions. For instance, we can see at the top of Table 16.5 that those who sought to displace their antagonist succeeded in accomplishing half or more of their goals in only 6 percent of the cases, whereas those who were satisfied to leave the antagonist in place recognized their goals in 68 percent of the cases.

Which factor had the most influence on success? Table 16.6 helps to answer this question. Here we have ranked the variables according to how large a percent difference they make to the outcome. For instance, we can find from Table 16.6 that groups that employed violence succeeded 75 percent of the time, whereas those who received violence never succeeded. This factor makes a 75 percent difference in success rate for the groups in the study. It turns out to be the most influential variable of those studied. In a similar manner we can get an estimate of the importance of the other variables by referring to Table 16.6.

Implications

In his final chapter Gamson relates his findings to the validity of the pluralist image. He is critical of that image, although the failure rate of groups that sought to displace antagonists could be taken as support of the first hypothesis—that efforts to replace pluralism fail. Gamson argues that the success of the unruly tends to invalidate the second hypothesis—that only institutionalized techniques work. So he has found some evidence that is consistent with pluralism and some that runs counter to it.

Gamson provides us with provocative findings about strategies for challenging groups, and perhaps about counterstrategies for antagonists. His testing of the minor theories seems considerably more effective than his test of pluralism.

TABLE 16.6 Relative Strength of Factors That Affected Challenge-Group Success

	Difference in Percent that Accomplished Goals
Used violence as opposed to receiving it	75*
Did not seek to displace antagonist	62
Country was in depression	59
Pursued a single issue	59
Neither used nor received violence	53
Experienced no factions	48
Offered special incentives for membership	42
Used nonviolent constraints such as strikes and boycotts	37
Had centralized power	32
Challenge occurred during wartime	25
Challenge group bureaucratically organized	24
Goals were not universally beneficial	11

*As can be seen from Table 16.5, groups that used violence succeeded in 75 percent of the cases, whereas those that received violence succeeded 0 percent of the time. The other figures in this table were computed in a similar manner (75% − 0% = 75%) from those that appear in Table 16.5.

SOURCE Based on data from Gamson, 1975.

Dying for peace. Demonstrators seek to win support for their peace movement by a dramatic "die-in." How would Gamson assess the likelihood their movement will succeed? (*Photo courtesy the Michigan Daily*)

Questions

1. Using Table 16.6, discuss the ideal setting and structure for a challenging group that seeks to achieve its objectives.
2. Are Gamson's findings more useful to the establishment or to those who would change it? Why?
3. Gamson's challenge movements are between 40 and 185 years old. Has the shift from agriculture to postindustrialism altered the political process enough to call into question Gamson's findings? Why or why not?

SOURCE William A. Gamson. 1975. *The Strategy of Social Protest.* Homewood, Ill.: Dorsey Press. Used with permission.

Several researchers have reanalyzed Gamson's data, and most confirm his basic findings. Jack Goldstone, however, challenges Gamson's conclusions, claiming Gamson's results are based on a series of very weak assumptions. Goldstone's reanalysis suggests that the organization and tactics of protest groups have no general effect on their success. Instead, Goldstone believes the challenge group is more likely to succeed if it does not seek to displace the antagonist and makes its challenge during a crisis. We might note that Gamson and Goldstone at least agree on these last two points. Why can't the experts agree on the other important issues here? Part of the difficulty is that the sample is rather small (53 protest groups) compared to what we would prefer in order for us to be sure our statistical tools are working. Also there is an element of judgment in selecting and interpreting statistical tools. For the time being we should regard Gamson's findings as highly suggestive, realizing that later and larger studies can clear up some of these issues (Goldstone, 1980a, 1980b; Gamson, 1980; Foley and Steedly, 1979, 1980; Weisburd, 1979; Mirowsky and Ross, 1979).

TERRORISM

> Any prediction ten years ago that terrorists would seize fifty embassies and consulates, take over the headquarters of the Organization of Petroleum Exporting Countries (OPEC) in Vienna, and hold the oil ministers of eleven nations hostage, kidnap hundreds of diplomats and businessmen and collect hundreds of millions of dollars in ransom, kidnap and murder the former premier of Italy, assassinate Lord Mountbatten and President Sadat, and try to assassinate the President of France, the commander of the North Atlantic Treaty Organization (NATO), and even the Pope, would have been regarded as the stuff of novels, not headlines (Jenkins, 1982).

Yet terrorists committed all of these acts in the preceding ten years.

As Lenin said, "the purpose of terrorism is to terrify." We define ***terrorism*** as *the blatant, spectacular use of violence to intimidate people either to support or bring* *about the collapse of a regime.* As the opening quotation suggests, terrorism, though by no means new, has mushroomed in recent years—by some estimates terrorism has increased tenfold in the past decade. Research indicates a rise in the severity of incidents as well as an increase in their frequency. Yet at this point terrorism, viewed socially, is primarily symbolic. Terrorists have not typically engaged in mass murder nor disrupted entire societies. The potential to harm society is much greater than has been presently realized. So far terrorists engage primarily in six basic tactics: bombings, assassinations, armed assaults, kidnapings, barricade and hostage situations, and skyjackings. Terrorists only recently invented skyjackings and seizing embassies. Unfortunately terrorists tend to imitate one another.

The typical international terrorist is single, middle or upper class, well-educated, urban, and male. He is an absolutist, seeing things only in black and white, is action prone, and is willing or eager to take risks. He did not become a terrorist overnight, and the process likely began with alienation, then proceeded to protest, and eventually led to his "going underground" as a member of a terrorist group. The terrorist frequently overestimates the strength of his movement and the imminence of victory. Typically he fails to develop a viable plan for taking power. Thus he fails to develop a viable plan for taking power. Thus he is primarily a kidnaper, bomber, or shooter, rather than a viable revolutionary leader. (Jenkins, 1982; Netanyahu, 1981)

Thus far we have looked at terrorism primarily in the international realm, but terrorists operate within nations both before and after revolutions. During the Reign of Terror of the French Revolution tens of thousands of "enemies of the revolution" received cursory trials and execution by the guillotine. Among the first was King Louis XVI, whose beheading was witnessed by an enormous crowd that included entire families. Once the blade had fallen the executioner held Louis' head up to the crowd and then auctioned off his hair ribbon and even some of his hair. The crowd dipped handkerchiefs and paper into his blood for souvenirs, and many danced around the guillotine singing the *Marseillaise.* But we can find more recent and widespread examples of terrorism in the name of the people. Revolution involves more than the military victory, and following his rise to power in 1949 Mao Tse Tung lead a cultural revolution to transform the Chinese society. During his lifetime he acknowledged that some 25 million enemies of the people were put to death for their alleged opposition to Mao's brand of communism (Goldstone, 1986).

Edward Muller (1985) has studied political violence within nations. He focuses on deaths that occur from domestic political conflict, because we have such limited data on other domestic political violence such as armed attacks and assassinations. Muller finds two major causes of violence. First, the more unequally a nation's income is divided the more political violence it has. Second, political violence is related to the repressiveness of the regime. Muller used several indicators developed by Raymond Gastil (1987) to measure repressiveness, including having no elections, having elections without allowing the citizenry to choose candidates for the ballot, not allowing groups to organize voluntarily, not allowing media criticism of the government, and denying citizens any rights or making rights minimal compared to those of government officials. Repressiveness is even more strongly linked to political violence than is income inequality, but the relationship is not as simple. Societies with medium levels of regime repressiveness had the highest rates of political violence. Those with the highest levels of repressiveness seemed to be able to hold levels of domestic political violence to levels as low as those with the least repressiveness. Thus, a high level of inequality of income combined with a regime that is neither democratic nor totalitarian seems to be the fatal combination. As Muller observes, "there seems to be truth in Machiavelli's dictum that a leader should either embrace or crush his opposition" (Muller, 1985, p. 60).

Alfred McLung Lee (1983), after years of studying terrorism in Ireland, offers these suggestions toward solving the problem. They apply not just to Ireland but to terrorism in general. First we should aim reform at basic socioeconomic and political changes. We need more of this preventive therapy in place of the crisis therapy we often apply. We should not despair, because the fabric of society under stress and apparently at the brink of chaos and disintegration manifests great resilience. Often crucial social groups emerge at this stage to create better organizations. Also, he advocates improved education of the masses and points out that the end to terrorism cannot by its nature be as dramatic as its beginning. This ending is likely to come from growing social consciousness and more adequate organization.

TORTURE

Sometimes the state itself uses terrorist techniques, including kidnaping and, especially, torture. Torture is terrorism institutionalized. The aim is still to terrify the opponent into compliance, but the means used by the state are often more calculated and cruel than those that are used against the state. ***Torture*** refers to *a public official inflicting, or causing someone else to inflict, severe pain on a person to extract information, a confession, or intimidation of him or others.* Methods vary widely, but the general intention is to create in the victim's mind a sense of total helplessness. Often the torturers isolate the victim for long periods of time. One prisoner at Evin Jail, the Revolutionary Court headquarters in Tehran, was held blindfolded for twenty-seven months. A torture victim in Turkey witnessed a married couple being tortured together, the wife being threatened with rape unless the husband would admit to the accusations made against him. In the Soviet Union prisoners have sometimes been kept in psychiatric hospitals and given debilitating drugs in an effort to compel them to renounce their religious or political beliefs.

Certain conditions are likely to give rise to torture. Special legislation that allows wide powers of arrest and detention facilitates torture. Also trial procedures that do not exclude from evidence statements extracted under torture encourage the growth of torture. Reports of victims give researchers an increasingly clear picture of torture. Although world opinion strongly condemns torture, people from many countries and almost all social backgrounds are still tortured (Amnesty International, 1984). The fact that totalitarian and authoritarian regimes are much more likely to practice torture than are democracies highlights the importance of understanding where these different social structures arise.

How Is the United States Losing Its Hegemony?

Part of the reason a state emerges is to manage relations between societies. In contemporary times societies interact more frequently than ever before. Increasingly often we live in a world in which goods are traded in an international market, and consequently we live in a world where states must and do interact with one another.

Many experts contend that this emerging world system is in a state of crisis. Following World War II much of the world experienced an economic boom that now seems to be followed by an economic contraction. Politically, we seem to be in transition as well. World history over the past five centuries is largely a history of hegemonies. ***Hegemony*** *is a situation in which one nation maintains a position of leadership or dominance over other nations.* Most observers agree that there was a Spanish hegemony in the sixteenth century, a British one from the mid-seventeenth century to the mid-nineteenth century, and a U.S. hegemony in the mid-twentieth century. Political dominance often rests on economic dominance. Great Britain's dominance eventually succumbed to economic competition from Germany and the United States. The United States hegemony was based in part on the fact that we emerged from World War II with our industrial base intact while that of most of the developed world lay in ruins. But just as competitors arose to challenge Britain's dominance, Japan and some European and newly industrialized nations now seem to challenge the United States hegemony (Bergeson, 1983).

During its period of economic dominance the United States made political and military commitments around the world. By 1970 the United States had 1,000,000 soldiers in thirty countries, was a member of four regional defense alliances and was an active participant in a fifth. The United States also had mutual defense treaties with forty-two nations, was a member of fifty-three international organizations, and furnished

Terrifying? In Belfast some residents have become relatively numb to terrorist tactics. In this photo the two people in the background evidence no alarm that someone's van has been torched. (*Reuters/Bettmann Newsphotos*)

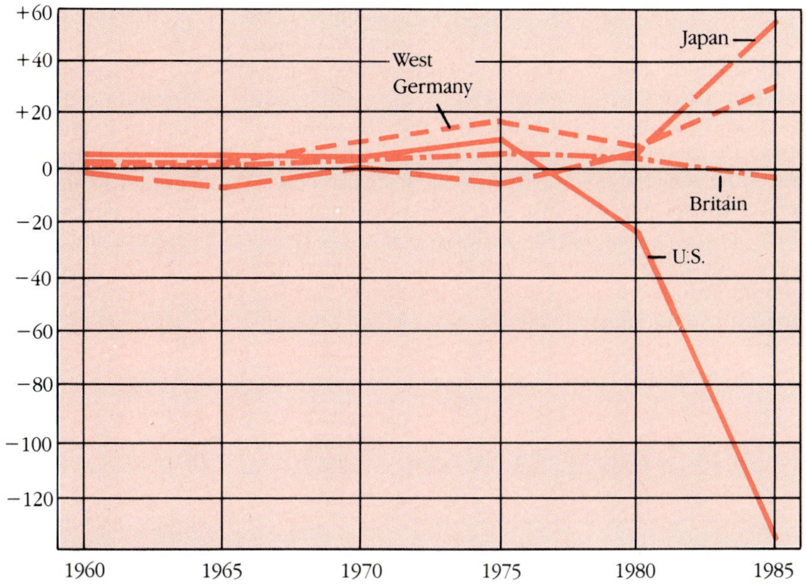

*In billions of current U.S. dollars.

FIGURE 16.5 United States Merchandise Balance of Trade, 1960–1985.* SOURCE © 1986 Institute for International Economics, Washington, D.C. Reprinted by permission from *American Trade Politics: System under Stress* by I. M. Destler.

FIGURE 16.6 Federal Budget Receipts and Outlays: 1975–1985. SOURCE United States Bureau of the Census. *Statistical Abstract of the United States, 1986* (106th ed.), Washington, D.C. (1985), p. 304.

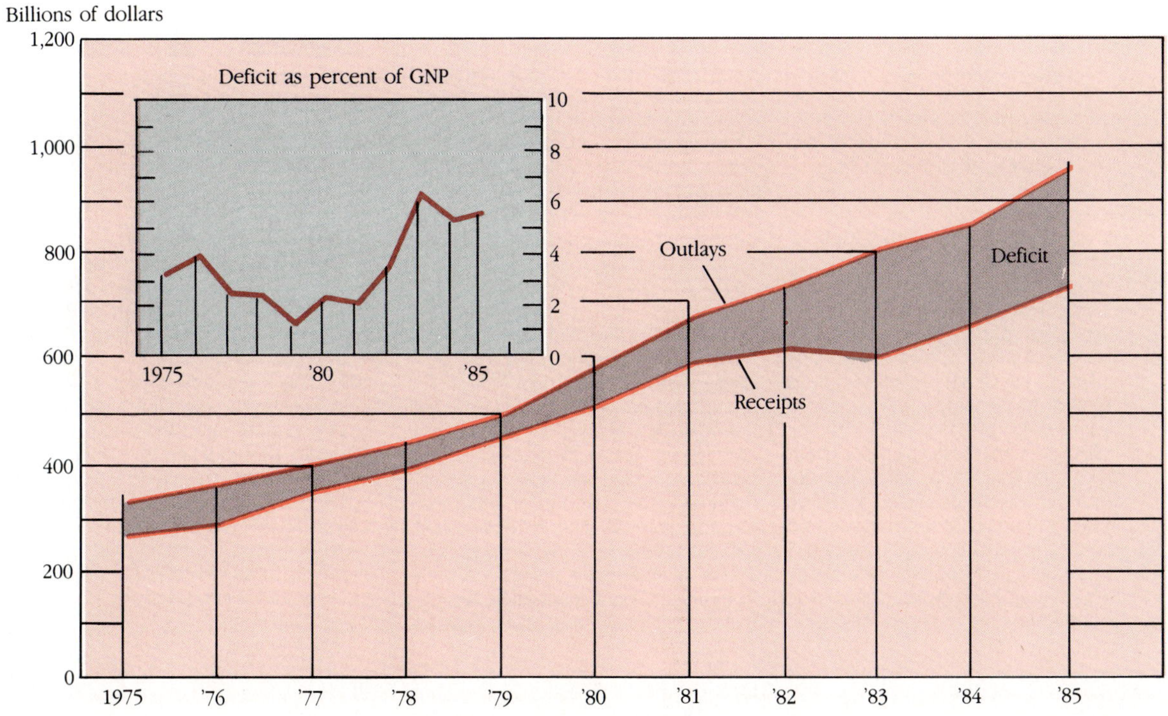

military or economic aid to about 100 nations around the world. But as Americans were expanding political commitments, we were also gradually losing our industrial dominance—first in textiles, iron, steel, shipbuilding, and basic chemicals, and now, to some extent, in robotics, aerospace technology, automobiles, machine tools, and computers. Also, to many observers' surprise, we have lost our dominance in agriculture, because scientists have discovered ways to improve food production that lessen other nations' need to import food from the United States. Figure 16.5 dramatically depicts the rapid erosion of relative economic strength by showing the balance of trade, the difference between what we buy from and sell to other nations.

These economic woes have created a variety of strains. The United States, for instance, imported $160 million in goods more than it exported in the year preceding April 1986. Our attempts to maintain military commitments around the world are partly responsible for our enormous defense budget, which in turn causes unprecedented federal deficits, as illustrated in Figure 16.6 (Kennedy, 1987).

Both the United States and world nations in general face a challenge in managing this transition. In

Sociologists at Work •

GEORGE GALLUP, JR.
FORECASTS ELECTIONS AND CHARTS SOCIAL CHANGE
The Gallup Poll
Princeton, New Jersey

George Gallup, Jr., uses his sociological training in charting social trends in the United States. George and his brother, Alec, took over the chairmanship of the Gallup organization at the death of their father, George Gallup, Sr., the man who laid the foundation for much of modern polling technique. Although the Gallup Poll addresses many social issues, it finds its most avid audience in election years. Here we discussed with George Gallup preparations for the 1988 presidential election.

What Methodology Do You Use in Your National Polling?

We are doing some new things this election year in that we are analyzing survey results by groups, based on clusters of values. Using these value clusters, we have defined various groups—for example, the "disenchanted," or the "moralists," or the "1960s liberals." This gives us a richer look at the electorate, because in today's social setting, it is too simplistic to study them as conservatives and liberals, Republicans, or Democrats.

Basically, however, we will stay with the methodology that has held us in good standing in recent elections. The outcome of every election depends on four major factors: personalities of the candidates, the issues, party affiliation, and voter turnout. In order to chart these, we will be using, for example, the turnout scale that we have refined over fifty-three years in polling, which was originally developed by Mr. Paul Perry. The turnout scale is very important, because in the United States, unlike most of the democracies in the world, only about one-half of the populace votes.

How Does the Turnout Scale Work?

We ask a series of questions to determine whether respondents are likely to vote; Are they registered? Are they interested in the campaign? Do they know where to go to vote? Did they vote before? We combine the results of all of those questions, and arrive at our turnout figure, which has actually been within a point or so in virtually all national elections over the last half-century.

What Other Polling Techniques Did the Gallup Organization Develop?

My father was the first to develop trial heats or test elections in the 1930s and 1940s. This is where we pit one candidate against another in a sort of mock election based on a sample of the populace. Testing the nomination choices is another early development; that is, giving people a list of persons from which they choose their favorite candidate. The Gallup Poll initiated

presidential popularity ratings in the 1930s. We will be continuing all of these techniques.

Are You Confident That You Will Be Able to Call the Election Before It Happens?

No. We were never confident before, although we have been very close to the actual election results again and again. The three factors that usually throw a survey organization off are: (1) not polling right up to the end of the campaign, (2) not being able to properly allocate the undecided vote, and (3) not being able to determine accurately who actually shows up at the polling booths. Fortunately, we have historically been very close to the actual results in calling elections. ●

economic terms, the United States struggles to remain competitive in the world market and to maintain the high standard of living established in the post World War II years. Whereas the relative decline of the United States' economy causes internal problems, these cause problems around the world. With the United States in a situation of economic decline, at least relative to the rest of the world, we must make decisions that balance the nation's international commitments with its power. When we begin to consider the implications of the United States' cutting back on military commitments and economic aid as well, we realize that the United States' economic problems will result in worldwide power shifts. As United States' international influence declines, other powers will naturally emerge. Perhaps Japan, the Soviet Union, or some other nation will assume hegemonic power. Perhaps nations will each gain more control over their own affairs when United States' influence declines. The transition could lead to crises or war, or it might lead to the strengthening of international political systems such as the United Nations and the World Court (Burnham, 1983).

Conclusion

States exercise enormous and growing power over their subjects. Conflict among modern nation-states poses a real threat to the survival of our species. We live in a world of many societies dominated by states of radically different form and content. Yet this world is shrinking as international trade grows. States arise and take their form as the result of particular cultural circumstances, including a degree of technological sophistication, mass literacy, and relatively high income. But fundamental ideas such as those promoted by the Western church or those of Karl Marx influence the form of states as well. Experts continue to debate who governs the United States and why a large portion of the electorate does not vote. Meanwhile, on the international scene, terrorists menace much of the world, and the United States faces the problem of managing military and political commitments abroad in the face of an eroding economic status in the world.

REVIEW

Summary Questions

1. What is the state, and what are its features?
2. What is the conflict view of the state?
3. What are the functions of the state?
4. What are the origins of the state?
5. What are the bases of power?
6. What are the types of authority?
7. How do states differ?
8. Why do states differ?
9. How is power institutionally distributed in the United States?
10. What is the level of political participation of citizens and the influence of groups in the United States' political process?
11. What are nonroutine political activities?
12. What influences success of protest groups?
13. What is terrorism, and who are the terrorists?
14. What is hegemony, why is the United States losing it, and what effect will this have on the world?

Summary Answers

1. The state is the institution that monopolizes legitimate power in a territory through the establishment of its major features: courts, official leaders, written laws, and taxation.
2. Conflict permeates the state, which exists in part to regulate it. But conflict theory shows the state to be a tool of the elites in the class struggle. This justifies sometimes resorting to nonroutine or extra-legal means of remedying this exploitation, such as demonstrations, violent strikes, terrorism, revolution, and guerrilla warfare.
3. The major functions of the state are to arbitrate disputes between private parties, to contribute to social control of the society, to serve as the agent of intersocietal relations, to provide planning and direction for the society, and, increasingly in recent times, to provide for the welfare of those unable to care for themselves.
4. The origins of the state are partly hidden, because many of the first states emerged in prehistoric times. Simple societies exist without states. City states emerged with the invention of agriculture. As technology expands, so does the state. New ideas, such as sovereignty, had to be invented for the state to be accepted. Thomas and Meyers point out that contemporary states emerge not in a vacuum, but out of cultural conditions that influence their size and form.
5. Power, the ability to realize one's will in a communal action even against the resistance of others,

rests either on the threat of physical force or the ability to offer valuables contingent upon compliance with commands.

6. Authority is power legitimized by tradition, charisma, or rational–legal institutions.
7. States differ primarily in how equally they distribute political power and how much of the societies' affairs they try to control. They also have important differences in ideology.
8. Democracy, one of the most important differences between states, is more likely to appear in developed or industrialized societies. Cultures whose other institutions operate democratically are more likely to have democratic states. Protestantism is associated with democratic states, but states that are weak and have a history of overspecialization of the economy and dominance by an outside political power are unlikely to become democracies.
9. A host of institutionalized structures not planned for in the Constitution channel power in the United States. They include: Congressional committees, Congressional staff, executive agencies, political parties, individual candidate campaign organizations, and political action committees.
10. Little more than one-half the eligible voters in the United States vote, with those who are uneducated, younger, and ethnic minorities, especially, likely not to vote. This signals significant alienation from the political process.

    Political party affiliation has declined, especially for the Democrats, who are more heavily represented among blacks, the less educated, the young, the poor, and those with low-status occupations.

    Individual candidate campaign organizations and political action committees are eroding the power of the political parties by becoming major channels of contributions. Federal funding of campaigns does not curtail influence buying through campaign contributions by those who can afford it.
11. Nonroutine political activities, such as protest movements and terrorism, are common, and terrorism is on the rapid increase.
12. Protest movements are more successful when they do not seek to displace the antagonist and if they act during a time of social crisis. Sticking to single issues, offering clear incentives for membership, and employing violence also seem to contribute to success.
13. Terrorism, the blatant spectacular use of violence to intimidate people, though on the rise, is largely symbolic and primarily the activity of young, educated males operating out of underground networks, who generally lack viable revolutionary plans. Political violence is more common in moderately repressive societies with high income inequality. Torture, the officially sanctioned use of severe pain, is quite common and arises particularly where wide powers of arrest and detention are present.
14. Hegemony, the situation in which one nation maintains a position of leadership or dominance over other nations, is being lost by the United States as our position of relative economic superiority fades. Because of our heavy international political commitments, this poses major challenges and could result in major shifts within the international political system.

Glossary

administration those particular persons who happen to hold office in a state at one point in time

anarchy the situation in which the state has no power

authoritarian regime one with little input from the masses

authority power that is legitimized by society

benign state one that generally operates in the public interest

charisma an extraordinary quality of a person, regardless of whether this quality is actual, alleged, or presumed

charismatic authority rule over men, whether predominantly external or predominantly internal, to which the governed submit because of their belief in the extraordinary quality of the specific person

codified norms rules that have been written and published

coercive power the ability to gain compliance over others through the threat or application of physical force

elitism the view that a small and virtually invisible set of elites holds the ultimate power of the state and uses it to maintain and advance their positions of privilege

hegemony a situation in which one nation maintains a position of leadership or dominance over other nations

nonroutine political activity an activity ranging from demonstrations, violent strikes, terrorism, revolution, and guerrilla warfare

oligarchy dictatorial rule of the small, upper stratum

pluralism the view that many relatively small groups have political power and that none dominates in general

Political Action Committees (PACs) organizations which create, administer and solicit voluntary contributions to establish a political program

power the ability of a person or a group of people to realize their own will in a communal action even against the resistance of others who are participating in the action

productive power the ability to offer valuables contingent upon compliance with commands or norms

rational–legal authority authority that rests upon rules that are rationally established by enactment, by agreement, or by imposition

regime see *administration*

state the institution which monopolizes legitimate power in a territory through the establishment of courts, official leaders, written laws, and taxation

terrorism the blatant, spectacular use of violence to intimidate people to either support or bring about the collapse of a regime

totalitarian government seeking total control of a populace

torture a public official inflicting, or causing someone else to inflict, severe pain on a person to extract information, a confession, or intimidation of him or others

tyranny a popularly based dictatorship

Suggested Readings

G. William Domhoff. (1983). *Who Rules America Now?: A View for the '80s.* Englewood Cliffs, N.J.: Prentice-Hall.

Domhoff's clearly written, clearly reasoned, well-documented case for the existence of a small powerful ruling class in the United States.

David V. Edwards. (1985). *The American Political Experience: An Introduction to Government.* Englewood Cliffs, N.J.: Prentice-Hall.

A comprehensive text on how the American government developed, who cares about politics, who decides in government, what rights and liberties American government provides, and what policies and programs our government produces.

Raymond D. Gastil. (1984). *Freedom in the World: Political Rights and Civil Liberties, 1983–1984.* New York: The Freedom House.

This is an interesting book to browse in as well as to read. Each year Gastil and his associates take stock of political and civil liberties in each nation around the world and issue a report and series of essays.

Michael G. Roskin. (1982). *Countries and Concepts: An Introduction to Comparative Politics.* Englewood Cliffs, N.J.: Prentice-Hall.

For those wanting to look at politics beyond the United States and our present time, this book provides a good starting place. Roskin provides a nice blend of ideas and research.

CHAPTER 17

EDUCATION

- How Have Schools Developed in the United States?
- What Is the Structural-Functional Theory of Education?
- Close-Up on Theory: Talcott Parsons on How Schools Shape and Channel People
- What Is the Conflict Theory of Education?
- How Equal Is the Opportunity for Education in the United States?
- What Is the Social Structure Within the Schools?
- What Are the Current Issues in American Education?
- Close-Up on Research: Sadker and Sadker on Sexism in the Classroom
- Why Is the United States a Nation at Risk?
- Sociologists at Work: Nathan Glazer Analyzes the Shortage of Minority Faculty

How's Your Sociological Intuition?

1. The proportion of 19- and 20-year-olds in the United States who are full-time students is:
   - **a.** considerably smaller than in other industrialized nations
   - **b.** considerably greater than in most other industrialized nations
   - **c.** just about average for industrialized nations
   - **d.** the lowest of all industrialized nations
2. Regarding the apparent quality of students in American secondary schools:
   - **a.** both grades and aptitude test scores have risen since 1960
   - **b.** both grades and aptitude test scores have fallen since 1960
   - **c.** grades have fallen while aptitude test scores have risen since 1960
   - **d.** grades have risen while aptitude test scores have fallen since 1960
3. The International Association for the Evaluation of Educational Attainment tested students from twenty-one countries on nineteen subjects and found that students in the United States rated:
   - **a.** first overall, including developed countries
   - **b.** last in seven of nineteen subjects
   - **c.** first in seven of nineteen subjects
   - **d.** higher than all the undeveloped countries, but lower than some developed countries

Answers

1. b. The emphasis on advanced education in the United States keeps most students in school longer than they would be in other industrialized nations.
2. d. The inflation of grades while scores on standardized tests have fallen is a primary concern of present-day educators and is addressed in the subsection entitled, "Declining Standards for Academic Achievement."
3. b. American schools lag behind other developed *and* undeveloped nations in performance on standardized tests, in spite of the fact that we spend more of our gross national product on education than any other country, as you will see in the section on "What Are the Current Issues in American Education?"

When You Have Finished Studying This Chapter, You Should Know:

- How schools developed in the United States
- How education is viewed by structural-functionalists
- How education is viewed by conflict theorists
- How the British, American, and Japanese educational systems compare
- How equal the opportunity for education is in the U.S.
- The scope of violence in today's schools
- How and why student achievement is declining
- How unconscious teacher bias can aid sexism
- Why America can be called "illiterate"
- What suggestions are being made for improving the United States' educational system
- How today's teachers differ from yesterday's
- Why a growing number of families are teaching their children at home

In 1940, the California Department of Education asked teachers at selected schools what they considered to be their top seven discipline problems. The answers were: talking in class, chewing gum, making noise, running in the halls, getting out of turn in line, wearing improper clothing, and not putting paper in the trash cans provided. In 1986, an enterprising educator decided to replicate this study in the same schools that had been studied forty-six years earlier, and received the following answers: drug abuse, alcohol use, teen pregnancy, suicide, rape, robbery, and assault.

This dramatic example of the changes in our society as reflected in our schools tells only a part of the story of education in the United States during this century. Schooling has gone from being based in homes to being based in institutions, from being literacy-oriented to being vocationally oriented, and from being a privilege for which youngsters would sacrifice to a requirement that some of them would and do skip if possible.

Until industrialization in the nineteenth century and the accompanying growth of specialized new jobs, it was naturally assumed that, after learning to read and write, young people would learn from their parents and other elders what they needed to know to survive and flourish. In preliterate societies, young people don't even take time away from learning how to live to learn how to read and write.

With the creation of schools, education and socialization became separate entities. Schools became charged with the responsibility of teaching the technical details of modern life, and families began to believe that they were somehow inadequate to handle the concepts their younger members were learning in school. This separation of "education" from learning about life is now being questioned, and many educators are striving to coordinate real-world activities and school activities. Presently, however, in industrialized societies schools are a major educational instrument.

Although schools have become synonymous with education in this context, true education begins at birth and continues until death. Children learn more about survival during their first five years than they could ever learn during twelve years of school, and some researchers now believe that the amount learned by babies in their first year of life is as great as that learned in the rest of their lives. During that twelve months, for example, babies learn to roll over, sit up, walk, use their hands together, follow light and sound with their eyes, communicate verbally, and feed themselves. A comparable curriculum guide for any school grade level would be overwhelming to the average teacher!

Some critics believe the entire society has become too dependent on the institution of education through public schools. These revolutionaries believe that the only solution is to "de-school" society by replacing schools with informal, noncompulsory educational resources that people would consult at will (Illich, 1971). Most members of society continue to accept the process as inevitable if not always enjoyable. Every person reading this book, for example, has gone through some sort of educational process to achieve this level and is therefore committed to the system in one way or another. This chapter will attempt to help you explore the basis of that system and to discover some of its covert functions in our society.

How Have Schools Developed in the United States?

We have come a long way from the unrealized dream of Thomas Jefferson of establishing a public school that would educate all children for three years and a few gifted boys for several years more. At the time of the founding of our country, education was accomplished by children sitting at the feet of their parents, usually through learning to read the Bible. Most college graduates of the time became ministers or professors. A few lucky individuals were tutored by clergy who regarded it as one of their appointed tasks to educate the intellectual elite in order that they might become leaders in the continuing battle between right and wrong.

The "little red school house" is becoming a rare reminder of the origins of public education in the United States. Although education has been compulsory only since the early 1900s, most school systems have grown into large bureaucracies. (*Photo courtesy the author*)

In the 1880s education in the United States made a change of direction from moral teaching and preparation for the professions to an emphasis on teaching basic skills to workers. After the War Between the States, much of the technology developed during wartime went toward developing the United States as an industrial nation. From 1880 to 1988 our society became increasingly urban and industrialized. Many workers switched from agriculture to industry and moved from rural areas to cities. In 1840, only 10 percent of the population lived in urban areas. By 1900 this had jumped to 40 percent, and in 1985 it was 77 percent (Silberman, 1970, 1971; U.S. Bureau of Census, 1987).

The initial expansion of schooling during this time was the result of competition for new positions. Research shows that technological change has been one important factor in expanding primary and secondary school enrollments. Rubison and Ralph studied the effects of technological change on school expansion for the United States from 1890 to 1970 (1984). They found that without technological changes at critical periods of the nation's development, the continued expansion of schools could not have been sustained.

The new industries needed workers who could not only read and write, but could also organize information, use labor efficiently, and adjust to new circumstances should any arise during work. An emphasis grew on developing these skills through extended education. In 1870 only 2 percent of all young people graduated from high school. In 1985 that number was 74 percent. The growing number of high school graduates was thought to provide a population more broadly able to deal with the complexities of modern life. Whether this has proven true in the present, postindustrial society will be discussed further in the section, "Why Is the United States a Nation at Risk?"

What Is the Structural-Functional Theory of Education?

Structural-functionalists, as you will recall from the discussion of their view in Chapter 1, do not speak in causal statements, because they focus on effects rather than causes, beginning with an existing structure and seeking to explain its presence by finding its function in society. This contrasts sharply with considering a behavior and seeking its cause, as is often done in theory construction. On the other hand, the work of the structural-functionalists can be especially useful in prodding us to view existing structures from a new perspective.

Functionalists suggest that the American educational system grew in direct proportion to the need for increasingly specialized workers for industry. The structure of the society changed from agrarian to industrial, and a new institution was needed to support the transition. Burton Clark, a sociologist who studies education, writes (1960, p. 570):

> Work itself became complicated and specialized under the advancing techniques of production and distribution, and with this the educational "threshold" of employment was progressively raised. The worker needed longer systematic instruction, although at first this amounted for most only to reading, writing, and arithmetic of the simplest kind.

Furthermore, functionalists believe that, as education becomes readily available to the masses, people may use it as a steppingstone up the stratification ladder. They see a close alliance between economic and educational systems, believing those with additional education more easily achieve economic success. This should, and indeed does, lead to an expansion of the middle and upper-middle classes in the United States.

Functionalists see mass education as beneficial to all members of society, because it brings rewards to workers and managers alike. Workers who have been through the required number of years in a bureaucratic school system should be literate and should have developed docile work habits. (We discuss this further in the section, "What Is the Social Structure Within the

Schools?") Furthermore, workers have been filtered out for the managers by passing the various hurdles in the educational system, proving along the way that they can learn a certain amount, be consistent enough in attendance to complete a task, and sociable enough not to have been excluded from the educational process. Thus, the workers who have diplomas are seen as possessing certain traits, making it easier for them to obtain work and for the managers to choose workers who will work well with the group. From this point of view, education fills many functions for an industrialized United States.

HOW IS FORMAL EDUCATION A MECHANISM OF CULTURAL TRANSMISSION?

One important function of formal education is the *transmission of culture* of the society. People must learn certain basic facts to exist in society: how to add and subtract, what red and green streetlights mean, how heavy a pound of meat or potatoes is. Much of this is taught by family and friends, with the details filled in by teachers at school. In addition to facts, many values are transmitted through schools. For example, the idea that all people deserve an education is taught simply by having everyone attend school. Obviously, this lesson would be different in Great Britain.

When the brightest students and the students with the most athletic ability receive awards at the end of the year, students learn that academic and physical abilities are highly revered in the schools. Music and art awards may be given also, but they are usually not those most remembered by students or faculty. In Italy, where artists are respected, this situation might be different.

POLITICAL SOCIALIZATION. The idea that the American flag—and consequently the country it stands for—deserves respect is taught when students face it every morning and "pledge allegiance" to the flag. This is an example of the form of cultural transmission called ***political socialization,*** *which teaches people what they may expect from their country and what their country expects from them.*

Most people believe their own country is the best place in the world, and they feel lucky to have such a great heritage and good opportunities. Coming from such diverse backgrounds as democratic or autocratic governments, capitalist or socialist economies, permissive or strict socialization, elite or mass education, urban or rural countrysides, people accept what they are born into. Very few give up citizenship in their country of birth for that of another country. This is partly due to being politically socialized to believe in one's country and its value systems.

People are also taught to read and write in order that they may participate in government. Especially in a participatory democracy like the United States, is is important that everyone be able to communicate in written words so they can understand issues and candidates and vote wisely. In fact, another reason for the introduction of mass education was so that the ***electorate,*** *the people who vote in elections,* would be educated.

One class required of high school graduates is civics or government, wherein students are directly taught how their government works and what role they can play in its workings. Another wisely taught class is history, in which students learn about the mistakes and triumphs of past governments, theoretically in order to avoid them in future governments. Political education may at least raise political awareness, as evidenced by studies that show that a higher percentage of college graduates than high school graduates usually vote in national elections (Orum, 1983).

ASSIMILATION. The United States is a country made up of immigrants, and its educational system plays an important role in their assimilation into society. ***Assimilation*** *is the process of learning the norms of a new group.* Between 1860 and 1910, sixty million immigrants settled in the United States (Morison, 1965). It was very important that these new citizens learn to read and write in English so that they could become productive members of society and educated citizens. Naturally, the schools became the centers for assimilation activities. Students were punished for speaking in their native languages. It was assumed to be useful to them and the rest of society for them to forget about their previous homeland.

Much has recently been written about the difficulties the immigrants and their children encountered during this period. The adults became ashamed of their home countries where they usually still had families. Most adults began working immediately upon arrival in America and did not have the benefit of learning at an early age how to fit into this new place. Children grew away from parents who were not "Americanized" enough.

Today different ethnic backgrounds are studied from the viewpoint of how they enrich, rather than detract from, American society. Classes in black history, Italian history, Polish history, and the like, and elementary schools that are bilingual (taught both in English and the recent immigrant's language) have changed the entire flavor of assimilation into American society (*Time,* 1978).

HOW IS FORMAL EDUCATION A WAY OF STIMULATING INNOVATION?

The story is told that in the medieval University of Paris the professors were disputing about the number of teeth in a horse's mouth. They agreed that the number could not be a multiple of three, for that would be an offense to the Trinity; nor could it be a multiple of seven, for God created the world in six days and rested on the seventh. Neither the records of Aristotle nor the arguments of St. Thomas enabled them to solve the problem. Then a shocking thing happened. A student who had been listening to the discussion went out, opened a horse's mouth, and counted the teeth. . . . Our present perplexities about universities derive from the act of this medieval student. He symbolizes the beginning of objective inquiry, the revolt against authority, the empirical attitude, the linking of academic study with the facts of life. His act introduced research into the university. After the horse's mouth was opened, knowledge became an open system (Ashby, 1978).

Another function of education is stimulating innovation. ***Innovation*** is *the process of developing new methods and concepts for society.* In today's rapidly changing world, anything that stays the same becomes obsolete. People must change in order to grow, and if they grow too slowly, they run the risk of being eliminated from the race altogether. The study of new areas has led to many great discoveries. Most of the new things learned, of course, come from research. Everyone reaps the benefits of pure research that goes on in colleges and laboratories.

Whether they agree with the educational philosophies of the universities or not, people are influenced by them in their daily lives. University research applied in business becomes the "space-age" technology in digital watches, video recorders, and automatic ice makers. Research initiates innovation and aids scientific development in many areas. Christopher Jencks suggests that "the men who teach in America's leading graduate schools determine for the rest of us not only what is true and what is false, but, in large measure, what is 'done' and 'not done' " (Jencks, 1972, p. 150).

Some people worry about the potential power of universities, because they control much of the education of national leaders, but because the universities are themselves dependent on government for financial support, the cycle tends to keep itself in balance. If anything, institutions of higher education are more conservative than radical, being necessarily made up of people who have succeeded within the system.

CLOSE-UP on • *THEORY* •

Talcott Parsons on How Schools Shape and Channel People

The Theorist and the Setting

Talcott Parsons was, until his death in 1982, a major figure in American sociology and a central proponent of the structural-functional approach. He was also a prolific writer. In the early 1940s Parsons founded the Department of Human Relations at Harvard University, which included the disciplines of sociology, psychology, and anthropology. The scope of the department reflects Parsons's breadth of view in studying human social behavior, and indicates why his influence is still strong in the field.

Typically Parsons speaks in generalities and seldom states explicit propositions. His rambling, conversational style sometimes makes it difficult to locate his central thesis. Furthermore, although Parsons refers to this twenty-page article as "the merest outline" of the subject, his depth and breadth of knowledge is considerable.

The Theorist's Goal

Parsons states his issues as follows: "Our main interest, then, is in a dual problem: First, of how the school class functions to internalize in its pupils both the commitments and capacities for successful performance of their future adult roles, and second, of how it functions to allocate these human resources within the role structure of the adult society" (1959, p. 130).

Concepts and Propositions

Parsons's statement of purpose reveals two of his major assumptions: (1) that schools or classes teach people certain values and techniques, and (2) that they channel people toward particular roles or occupations. The bulk of his essay explains in more detail how various aspects of the structure of American school classes determine the specific functions they serve.

Parsons portrays American school classes as being structures to sort pupils according to achievement. Four structural features ensure that the classes will serve this function:

> The first is the initial equalization of the "contestants" status by age and by "family background," the neighborhood being typically much more homogeneous than is the whole society. The second circumstance is the imposition of a common set of tasks which is compared to most other task-areas strikingly undifferentiated. We can more easily compare achievement in school classes where tasks are similar than elsewhere, for instance, in a small business where different people work at different tasks. Third, there is a sharp polarization between the pupils in their initial equality and the single teacher who is an adult and "represents" the adult world. And fourth, there is a relatively systematic process of evaluation. . . . Thus classes are generally structured to facilitate the sorting of students by achievement (Parsons, p. 134).

In high school, "the main dividing line is between those who are and are not enrolled in the college preparatory course." Separate classes are usually created for the two categories, and this structure clearly steers people toward or away from entering college. Parsons argued that assignment of students to one or the other of these categories is based primarily on achievement as measured by "the record of performance in elementary school." According to Parsons, then, several aspects of the structure of school classes serve to sort students by achievement and to send the more capable on to higher status positions in society.

Besides sorting students, school classes also serve to socialize pupils in several ways. First, schools tend to "emancipate the individual from the family" by bringing students away from the family into the formal classroom and by facilitating peer association outside of school. Schools also socialize pupils to accept universalistic values: "There is thus a basic sense in which the elementary school class is an embodiment of the fundamental American value of equality of opportunity, in that it places value both on initial equality and on differential achievement" (p. 144).

The pupil also learns about modern universalistic social patterns, in which people relate to others according to roles rather than as unique personalities, as discussed in the chapter on society. The elementary teacher's role may bear some resemblance to the mother's, but the pupil usually has a new teacher each year. Parsons explains (p. 143):

> The school year is long enough to form an important relationship to a particular teacher, but not long enough for a highly particularistic attachment to crystallize. More than in the parent–child relationship, in school the child must internalize his relation to the teacher's role rather than her particular personality; this is a major step in the internalization of universalistic patterns.

The school class also teaches students to perform both basic and specialized skills. For those not in the college preparatory course, the high school may be the major agent of career socialization. Similarly, extracurricular activities in high school may socialize some individuals toward "socially" or "humanly" oriented roles, such as salesperson or executive, whereas the standard curriculum might socialize the pupil toward more technical occupations, such as accounting or engineer.

Parsons thus indicates how the various structural features of American school classes help to determine what functions these classes serve for the individual and the society:

1. sort students according to achievement
2. emancipate the individual from the family
3. facilitate acceptance of cultural values
4. introduce relating to others through roles
5. teach basic and specialized skills

Interpretation

This article exemplifies the structural-functional approach. It is difficult to reduce this type of theory or analysis to operationalized propositions, because the concepts are not usually explicitly defined, and the major ideas are seldom identified as such. It does, however, clearly show the functional approach to the institution of education. Parsons seeks to explain the presence of an existing structure by finding its function in society.

Questions

1. Parsons is sometimes accused of making the obvious obscure. Has he said anything important and new about American school classes?
2. Reducing Parsons's writing to a set of explicit propositions and succinct definitions is difficult. Is the weakness in Parsons's thought or in the idea that all important things can be stated simply?
3. Which of Parsons's ideas could be tested through research? How might one proceed?

SOURCE Talcott Parsons. 1959. "The school class as a social system: Some of its functions in American society." *Harvard Educational Review,* vol. 29, no. 4, pp. 297–318.

What Is the Conflict Theory of Education?

Both functionalists and conflict theorists agree that a major function of modern schools is to determine who gets what kind of job. Because education is used as a basic criterion for certain prestigious jobs, it becomes very important to society which persons receive that education.

HOW DOES FORMAL EDUCATION SORT AND CHANNEL MEMBERS OF SOCIETY?

As early as kindergarten, children are tested to determine their ability to learn, or IQ (for Intelligence Quotient). Most elementary school classes are of mixed ability, but by the time many students enter middle school (or junior high school), they are "tracked" into high-, medium-, or low-ability classes. Sometimes the tracking is subtle—all students who take physics are in the same English class, for example, whereas all those who choose Machine Shop are in different English classes. In other systems, numerals are assigned to the groupings, or tracks, and students very quickly know by looking at their peers in relation to other groups how smart their group is thought to be (Oakes, 1985).

Students in slower tracks usually understand early on that they are being trained to be factory workers and waiters rather than doctors and lawyers. Few of them ever challenge the school's authority to make this life career decision for them. Many, indeed, may be grateful if their particular school has vocational education available for them as an alternative to the college preparatory courses of the faster tracks (Davis and Haller, 1981).

Sometimes, however, noncollege preparatory track students receive poor guidance counseling and actually misperceive their opportunities after graduation (Rosenbaum, 1980). These students do not understand that the courses they take will not be regarded as sufficient for college entrance, and, further, that any good grades they receive in those classes may be weighted by colleges such that they cannot gain entrance even with a high grade-point average in the "wrong" classes. This use of student tracking without sufficient counseling about its implications has important impact in frustrating students' educational plans.

Thus, conflict theorists point out that instead of reflecting a changing society, our growing educational system preserves inequities inherent in the society. Very few lowerclass young people enter college or graduate from it. This fact along may keep them, no matter how bright or ambitious, from ever obtaining most high-paying jobs or advancing to significant positions in business. Thus, the educational system reinforces stratification inequalities while it appears to encourage upward movement through education (Blumberg, 1980; Burris, 1983; Bowles and Gintis, 1977).

CONTRASTING CHANNELING IN BRITAIN AND THE UNITED STATES

England was one of the earliest industrialized countries to be aided by a large group of willing workers and a flourishing international market for industrial goods. During this time, the class structure in Britain became strengthened and was reflected in the educational system. The expansion of schooling for the peasantry resulted in the educated masses needed for the expansion of capitalism. At the same time, the continuation of the English "public school" (actually private), which was much too expensive for common people, ensured that the upper class would retain this distinction from others (Ballantine, 1983). When more educated middle-level management persons were needed, England provided access to higher education for more of its nonelite but intelligent students (Williamson, 1979).

Thus the British do not surreptitiously "track" people in higher and lower levels, or make it easy for them to ease out of difficulty by changing their major. Instead, they carefully select and train only those whom they believe will benefit from further training. Those the government deems will do better in vocational training than in academic training get rigorous vocational work.

Ralph Turner describes the American system as one of "contest mobility," in which "elite status is the prize in an open contest, with every effort made to keep lagging contestants in the race until the climax" (1960, p. 855). This system reflects the American ideal of all persons being able, through effort, to better their position in society. Fifty-four percent of high school graduates in the United States go on to at least begin college training, although only 31 percent graduate (Bureau of the Census, 1987, p. 137).

The British system, on the other hand, Turner labels "sponsored mobility", in which members of the elite "choose recruits early and carefully induct them into elite status" (Turner, 1962, p. 855). Rather than spend time and effort trying to ensure that every child reads at a specified level, including those for whom reading is extremely difficult, the British single out the best readers and mark them for further training in disciplines that might require excellent readers. As a result, only 30 percent of British students do advanced work (*London Times Sunday Magazine,* 1980). An even smaller percentage do advanced work at the most prestigious schools, Oxford and Cambridge, and thus qualify for the highest status positions in the outside world. Many Americans think of this as unfair. Most British believe it is the only logical way to proceed.

At least one researcher in the field believes that the American system could more usefully be termed "tournament mobility" (Rosenbaum, 1976). His suggestion is that our tracking system is a tournament in which the rule is "when you win, you only win the right to go on to the next round; but when you lose, you lose forever" (p. 74). Each year a few more students are dropped from the group that aspires to go on to higher education, and for those students the tournament is over. Although this terminology has not been widely adopted, it allows us to look at this phenomenon in a new light.

The fact that the American system of education is based on contest, or tournament, mobility affects it in many ways—from encouraging such programs as special education for the retarded or otherwise handicapped to emphasizing "practical" education rather than pure research or more highly refined intellectual pursuits. In Britain, to be a student is a profession, so students are generally subsidized if they cannot afford to pay for school themselves. In the United States some prestige is attached to saying that you worked your way through college. In Britain making money to live on would be seen as a frightful waste of studying time.

Most Americans believe that the schools' primary function is preparation for work, with 82 percent agreeing that schools are extremely important to future success (Gallup, 1980). This is not always the case, however, as students well know. What practical application does astronomy have, for instance? How many times a day do you use your background in diagramming sentences? Proponents of a strong liberal arts curriculum, as well as those who back the British system, argue that all knowledge is enlightening, that rapidly changing job conditions make it impossible for us to know what knowledge we may need, and that the primary function of any type of education is to open the mind to different ways of learning throughout life.

Which system is better? The American emphasis on mass education is for the purpose of building a "good" society and giving everyone a chance at success. This system is modified somewhat by the tracking systems that predominate in most schools. The British system is likewise aimed at a "good" society, but it concentrates on educating the academic elite for the intellectual pursuits of society and the rest of the students for the remaining jobs in society. Each system is deeply embedded in its own national thinking and reflects cultural biases. It is improbable that either society could embrace the other's system happily without other broad changes in the culture.

JAPANESE EDUCATION: QUALITY AND QUANTITY

Many educational observers have recently noted that Japanese schools currently enjoy what U.S. schools lost long ago: strict discipline, moral education, demanding classes and textbooks, and strong parental involvement in education (August et al., 1987). In Japan, only 7 percent of high school students dropped out of school, compared to 27 percent in the United States (Marquand, 1987). This rate is even more impressive when you recognize that Japanese students are required to work a great deal harder than American students are.

Japanese education is based on the idea of talent development, in that the excellence of the system is "defined by its ability to develop the talents of all its citizens. According to this conception, the education of those students who perform best on admission tests is not necessarily more important than the education of students at other levels of performance" (Astin, 1985). In many ways, the Japanese system appears to combine the best of the British and American systems. Japan has a strong commitment to educate all citizens to the level of high school completion, and has done it without lowering their standards of work (Walzer, 1983). Willie observes that "in the world of education, the illusion often is that quality is the opposite of quantity and that a society with an excellent system of higher education cannot have both quality and quantity. The Japanese experience contradicts this illusion" (1982, p. 20).

Several differences are apparent immediately. The first is the Japanese system of centralized control and conformity. The Ministry of Education, or Monbusho, selects textbooks, sets national education standards and curricula, and administers the teacher colleges. In all Japanese towns and cities, the educational regime is nearly identical, with even such decisions as the number of hours devoted to certain studies being decided centrally (August et al., 1987). This is in sharp contrast to the United States' system in which schools are under local community control and highly dependent on local funding. In the United States, all major educational standards come from local or state regulations rather than federal laws.

Japanese education also endeavors to be egalitarian. Students wear uniforms to diminish economic differences, teachers transfer from school to school frequently to keep the talent uniformly distributed, and every school district has the same per capita money to spend on education (Marquand, 1987).

Another difference is that the Japanese do not eliminate the fine arts in order to concentrate on "basics." Art, music, art history, and music history are incorporated into the basic program. In commenting on his department's recent report on Japanese education, Education Secretary William Bennett said, "I was very taken with the large amount of time Japanese children spend not just learning about and listening to great music, but learning to play" (Bennett, 1987).

For many Japanese, this education is their passport to a higher social and economic class. Because they know this, the pressure on them to succeed, even at an early age, is great. Because Japanese mothers are judged in some part by their ability to produce good students, they work hard to encourage their children. Such pressure is one of the drawbacks of the system. Another is the fact that attending the elite universities is closely linked to class divisions, with the upper classes being represented in much higher proportions despite the supposed egalitarian direction of the school system (Iga, 1986). We can expect that as Japan continues to outproduce both the United States and England, those countries may attend more carefully to the Japanese educational system.

CREDENTIALIZATION

Conflict theorists point out that mass education does not always precede industrialization. In Western Europe, for instance, the educational institution developed *after* the Industrial Revolution. Furthermore, they assert, many of the jobs that require college training in the United States are held by people with no college training in other countries (Lipset and Bendix, 1967). It is becoming clear that few of the jobs that "require" a higher education background actually use that education on the job (R. Collins, 1979). Instead, the "educational threshold" is rising (Clogg and Shockey, 1984; Rumberger, 1981). Jobs that required no high school years ago now require a high school diploma; those that previously required a high school diploma now require a college degree, and so forth. *The process of requiring a credential that is not immediately necessary for the work is called* ***credentialization.*** When factories originally began to spread over the United States, they were staffed by persons with an eighth-grade education. Now few factories will hire non-high school graduates. Similarly, someone with a flair for fashion in days past could probably obtain a position as a buyer of fashionable clothing for a department store by simply demonstrating that he or she knew the marketplace well enough to choose clothes. Today, that position requires a college degree, preferably in marketing or fashion design, and a training program that begins with a clerkship in a ready-to-wear department.

Similarly, years ago a man who aspired to a business career presented himself, eager and personable, to an established person in business for training. When he felt comfortable with his knowledge, he struck out by forming his own business. Today, most graduates with business degrees will never work outside of a large bureaucracy that they could ever have entered without their degree. Collins has even suggested that a college diploma be likened to a union card, necessary for employment but not indicative of any special skill (1979).

Some observers believe this emphasis on credentials rather than performance in the field was the cause of the lag in America's industries during the 1970s. They point out that a natural tension exists between the "professionalized" world and the entrepreneurial spirit needed to develop the ideas and designs for industrial growth. James Fallows notes (1985, p. 50):

> At just the time when American business is said to need the flexibility and the lack of hierarchy that an entrepreneurial climate can create, more and more businessmen seem to feel that their chances for personal success will be greatest if they become not entrepreneurs but professionals, with advanced educational degrees.

Other research shows, however, that although many college grads since the 1970s have been "overeducated" for their positions, this has not affected them financially. Smith argues that college graduates are often overcredentialed, but that their relative incomes continue to be high (1986). As more college graduates take positions requiring less training, they squeeze out high school graduates from their traditional jobs, who then squeeze out non-high school graduates from theirs. The situation for these groups is obviously more critical than that of the college graduates (H. Smith, 1986). It has not been shown that the additional schooling now required for certain jobs actually contributes to success in those jobs, but requiring higher levels of education does almost ensure that lower-class people will not reach upper levels of business.

How Equal Is the Opportunity for Education in the United States?

Equality of opportunity in the educational system has been a major issue for the last thirty years. As we have just seen, children in the American system are apparently tracked by socioeconomic status as well as by academic ability. This leads to the conclusion that the great American dream of advancement may not be possible through the public education system.

Conflict theorists raise an important question: Is there, indeed, equal access to education in the United States, where the ideal is equality of opportunity for all? Evidence seems to suggest, instead, that access is limited for a number of reasons, including varying family expectations, lack of money to pay for advanced schooling, and subcultural emphasis on education as a respected resource.

ACCESS TO EDUCATION

Obviously, there are many reasons an individual might value formal education: family expectations, feelings of wanting to contribute to society or work with people or ideas that are attractive, or just desire for the prestige in having a degree. Although there is some dissension by writers who believe that entrance into a highly paid trade will offset the difference in earning power and the high cost of a college education today, most people agree that a degree will generally increase lifelong earnings. With economic achievement a paramount virtue in the United States, this fact alone would assure that many people will aspire to higher education.

DIFFERENCES IN FAMILY EXPECTATIONS. When you answer honestly the question, "Why am I in college?" there is an excellent chance that your family's expectations of you and aspirations for you have played some part in your decision. Ability continues to be the best predictor of educational performance at all levels. Some students do not have the mental capacity to attend high school or college, and some do not have the finances to go on. However, one obstacle to lower-class students' access to college appears to be difference in parental attitudes toward the need for a college education.

Relatives outside the immediate family can also exert strong influence over educational and vocational plans and their fulfillment (Scritchfield and Picou, 1982). Relatives can do this in several ways, from providing role models in certain professions to specifically urging an individual to pursue an educational goal. If neither of your parents ever attended college, but you have an aunt who is an optometrist and who believes you could go into optometry, for instance, you might achieve this or a related goal because of her influence. Without such encouragement, you will more likely stop your education at high school if your parents expect you will.

Concern about the effects of the expectations of nonfamily significant others has prompted research in this area (Reitzes and Mutran, 1980). As suspected, the influence of close friends aids in the socialization process, exerting an effect on both academic performance and educational plans. Significant others help an individual to establish a self-concept that influences his or her educational and vocational plans (Sewell, Haller, and Ohlendorf, 1970; Sewell, Haller, and Alejandro, 1969). In other words, if you grow up in a working-class neighborhood and your friends see you as about as capable as they, you will be socialized by them to become a worker. To violate this by aspiring to go to college, for instance, would be to reject their interpretation of who you are.

One working-class neighborhood childhood friend of a Ph.D. candidate once asked him what it was he still had to learn about in school; he could imagine enough to learn about beyond high school to fill four years of college, but beyond that he could not understand what was left to study. To resist this kind of interpretation of education, the potential Ph.D. had to rely on his family and new friends' image of him as academically oriented and capable of contributing to higher education.

The expectations and aspirations of families and significant others, as we have seen, appear to influence access to formal education. From our earliest socialization experiences to the stated goals our parents express as we grow older, we are all somewhat products of our family and friendship experiences in terms of access to education.

Equal opportunity? Women attend college in increasing numbers, but find few women professors as role models. The Sadkers find sexism prominent in American classroom discussions. (*Photo courtesy the Michigan Daily*)

DIFFERENCES BETWEEN SOCIO-ECONOMIC AND GENDER GROUPS. Because there has been such a differential between the earning power of college and non–college educated individuals, some researchers have suggested that the idea of the American educational system as being the great equalizer and giving everyone a chance at the American Dream is false.

One study indicated that, of those in the top 25 percent of their high school class, fewer than 50 percent of the lowest income attend college, whereas close to 90 percent of those from the highest income group go to college. Similarly, of those in the bottom 25 percent of their high school group, 26 percent from high-income families still receive a college education, compared to 6 percent of those from low-income groups (Bowles and Gintis, 1977). (See Figure 17.1.)

Research shows, however, that the federally sponsored efforts to improve the educational achievement of economically disadvantaged students, from Head Start to Pell Grants, have produced significant change in the past twenty years (Stickney and Marcus, 1985). In 1984, 25 percent of children from families with incomes of less than $10,000 attended college, whereas 56 percent of those children with family incomes over $35,000 attended (Bureau of the Census, 1985). This two-to-one ratio is much more favorable than the four-to-one ratio found in 1974 (Sewell and Hauser, 1974).

Women are often denied a full range of courses, seeing female role models in high-ranking positions, and the high expectations and support for their academic performance that men enjoy from family and friends (Finn, Duiberg, and Reis, 1979). As we see in Chapter 11, this situation has improved dramatically over the past decade, but men and women do not yet have equal opportunity in education.

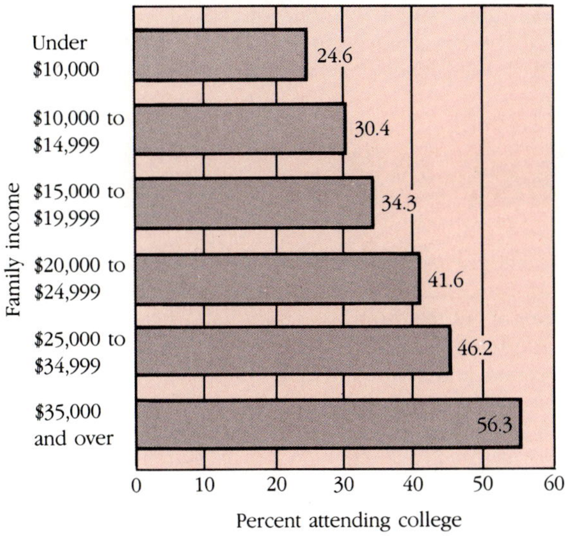

FIGURE 17.1 College Attendance and Family Income as of 1984. Although opportunity for higher education has equalized somewhat over the past twenty years, college students still come disproportionately from the upper income brackets. SOURCE U.S. Bureau of the Census. 1985.

Differences in access to formal education strongly affect a person's lifetime chances in terms of status, because education is an increasingly important factor in determining jobs and socioeconomic class. In 1985, the median income for a non-high school graduate was $12,757, a graduate $17,779, and a college graduate $32,270 (U.S. Bureau of the Census, 1987, p. 438). Beyond the monetary advantages of a college education, chances of job satisfaction, sense of meaning in work, and changes in outlook on life as a result of the experience of a liberal arts education are other strong reasons that such education is still sought after by persons from various socioeconomic levels and by men and women alike.

EFFORTS TO INCREASE EQUALITY OF OPPORTUNITY

Concern that the United States is creating a system that educates the lower classes to remain in the lower class spurred government interest in increasing opportunity for education. Several programs show promise for the future.

THE COLEMAN REPORT. James Coleman's controversial report to the United States Congress in 1966 marked one of the first occasions on which a sociologist had an impact on society's handling of an important issue—in this case, busing students for educational equality. Data from Coleman's massive sample of 4,000 American schools showed very unequal racial distributions and educational achievement levels.

Coleman reported that black students at predominantly white schools did better academically, whereas white students did no worse when blacks attended their schools than when they did not. Proponents of busing used this finding to argue for integration through busing. Coleman, however, noted that "differences between schools account for only 10 percent of differences in pupil achievement" (p. 22). Instead, Coleman believes that the quality of teachers shows a stronger relationship to pupil achievement, as do the educational background and aspirations of the other students in the school.

THE RUTTER REPORT. A longitudinal study by Michael Rutter and his associates challenged many of Coleman's conclusions (Rutter et al., 1979). Rutter's team believed it more carefully assessed the abilities of ten-year-old students in their study and the quality of the schools they attended, than did Coleman's study. Rutter's group used survey data, classroom observations, and interviews. The team repeated its assessment four years after the original study in order to determine what changes occurred in the students and how much of the change could be accounted for in terms of the school atmosphere.

Rutter found significant differences among schools in attendance, behavior, and academic performance. Some schools were clearly better at producing good behavior and good learning than others, even with matched samples of students in terms of behavior and learning potential. The Rutter report reinforces the traditional viewpoint that going to a "good" school will enhance your chances of doing well, and attending a "bad" school will be an academic liability. It is also a good example of how the methodology of a study can affect the outcome drastically. The Rutter report is accepted as methodologically sound and therefore as a good source on which to base future policy decisions.

COMPENSATORY EDUCATION. One form of help for students who begin school with a deficit in terms of socioeconomic class, skin color, or other social characteristic is compensatory education through such programs as Head Start and Upward Bound. ***Compensatory education*** is *education designed to give the lower-class students an extra boost to begin on an even level with the middle-class and upper-class student.*

Studies which evaluate compensatory education have produced mixed results (Stickney and Marcus, 1985). Some research shows that such preschool programs temporarily lessen the gap between lower-class and middle-class students, but the progress is often eradicated by the end of grade school. Those people involved in the programs, however, believe that many real gains are hard to measure, such as social competence and involvement of parents in the educational processes of their children, and that the new programs only need time to grow. Evidence does indicate that early compensatory programs do improve IQ and school performance (Ziglar, 1976).

In order to continue the gains made in preschool programs, the federal government designed Project Follow-Through to give lower-class schools more resources with which to increase their students' levels of learning. Some government programs have now been abandoned, but the influence of parents who are pleased with the results has kept many of them alive.

Another force for social change through preschool education are the popular "Sesame Street," "Electric Company," and "Villa Allegro" preschool TV programs. Children who watch these programs regularly learn signficantly more than children who watch them occasionally, and the gains they make in such areas as naming letters and numbers are matched by changes in attitudes. One study found that students who regularly watch "Sesame Street" are less racist and have more positive attitudes toward school than do children who do not watch the program (Tavris, 1976). Obviously, not all "Sesame Street" viewers are underprivileged children. Preschool education is becoming more popular in all socioeconomic levels.

Perhaps the best summary of the confusing literature surrounding compensatory education programs comes from Ed Ziglar, an educational psychologist who headed the Office of Child Development at HEW for two years (1976, p. 74):

> I've looked at all this stuff, and contrary to the view that nothing works, my own reading is that everything works. It's the commitment to something that makes the difference. Once a kid sees that you're doing something—and you *feel* like you're doing something—things happen. What will do kids in is the attitude that nothing works.

Through the combination of compensatory programs, federally funded higher education, and local school district efforts, nonwhite students have more educational opportunity today. The percentage of nonwhite students in American colleges and universities doubled between 1960 and 1977, but remained relatively stable during the Reagan administration's austere education budget program (Ford, 1983). This recent lack of federal aid has caused more low-income students to attend two-year institutions and public, rather than private, four-year institutions, as well. Although minorities now have more access to education, the level of education continues to be lower than that which the higher class students can afford.

What Is the Social Structure Within the Schools?

Sociologists have recently begun to explore the institution of education as a social structure, asking questions about the formal and informal structure of schools and touching upon relationships between students and teachers and among members of peer-groups. They are also studying what schools and teachers teach besides subject matter. As this research continues, a more accurate picture of the school as a social system is emerging.

FORMAL VERSUS INFORMAL STRUCTURE

On paper, the school is a rigidly defined bureaucracy. Grade schools and high schools all over the United States have many of the same characteristics: large groups of children, usually close in age, being lectured to by one teacher; classrooms designed to hold twenty or thirty students at a time; an unbroken day with one teacher for elementary students, and forty-five minute periods for high school; a principal in charge of the teachers' work and the students' discipline; a library; art, gym, and music in grade schools once or twice a week; a school year from September to mid-June; a school day from 8 or 9 A.M. to 2 or 3 P.M.; and so on.

Strangely enough, much of what is done with children in schools is based not on scientific theory or recent research but on tradition. "We've never done it that way before," is a common cry from the faculty room, which temporarily or permanently blocks much innovation in the formal structure of schooling. An excellent example of this is the following true story: A well-educated couple requested of a private school principal that provision be made for their daughter to finish her schoolwork in the first half of the day, so that she could be taught at home by her parents in the second half. The child, who was very bright and creative, had been extremely bored at school and most often finished her work in less than half the time allotted. The parents did not suggest they take over major responsibility for her curriculum, but that she be required to complete the entire amount of work for a child in her grade level during half the time, bringing home any left undone. At home, her parents would seek to expand her outward rather than push her upwards, bringing art history, music theory, computer operation and programming, and creative writing to her through their attentions. Whereas this program should have been seen as just the right combination for the child, with same-age peer contact during half the day and individually expanding work during the other half, the school administrators chose to deny the request. The stated reason: "We have our program, and you may either accept it as it is or reject it."

Because the formal school structure is so rigid, it requires that children learn early to be good members of the bureaucracy and fulfill their function in the system. Basically, this means that they become passive receptors of information rather than the actively seeking individuals that most 5-year-olds are by nature (Boocock, 1972). They learn to stand in lines, to listen to long lectures that may not interest them, and to wait to ask questions they *really* want answered until the teacher decides it is time. They must also learn to ignore their friends, with whom they have always been able to play and talk before, and to time their bodily needs to the teacher's schedule: nap time, bathroom time, snack time.

Two respected and progressive educators, Neil Postman and Charles Weingartner, explain this controlling function of the school (1973, p. 82):

> One characteristic of institutional essentials is that they are most clearly observable in the breach. That being so, the essential functions of school are often more visible when they are not being served than when they are. This is especially true of the school's supervisory function. Few teachers would list "to supervise and control the young" among the important functions of school, but you have only to imagine the consequences of failure in this function to see at once that supervision is essential. So essential, in fact, that it is one of the few requirements every state government specifies in its definition of school.

Thus, the formal structure of the school supports society by teaching its future members how to follow orders and be members of a formal group, beginning in kindergarten, as the following excerpt shows.

KINDERGARTEN AS ACADEMIC BOOT CAMP

In this excerpt, Harry Gracey defines the implicit function of kindergarten, which is to teach children how to be students rather than to teach them subject matter.

> Kindergarten is generally conceived by educators as a year in which small children, 5 or 6 years old, are prepared socially and emotionally for the academic learning which will take place over the next twelve years. . . .
>
> [However] Observations of kindergartens and interviews with the teachers both pointed to the teaching and learning of classroom routines as the main element of the student role. The teachers expended most of their efforts, for the first half of the year at least, in training the children to follow the routines teachers created. The children were, in a very real sense, drilled in tasks and activities created by the teachers for their own purposes and beginning and ending quite arbitrarily (from the child's point of view) at the command of the teacher. . . . By the end of the school year, the successful kindergarten teacher has a well-organized group of children. They follow classroom routines automatically, having learned all the command signals and the expected responses to them. They have, in our terms, learned the student role. The following observations show one such classroom operating at optimum organization on an afternoon late in May.
>
> . . . At 12:25 Edith [the teacher] opens the outside door and admits the waiting children. They hang their sweaters on hooks outside the door and they go to the center of the room and arrange themselves in a semicircle on the floor, facing the teacher's chair which she has placed in the center of the floor. Edith follows them and waits for the bell to ring. When she has finished attendance, which she takes by sight, she asks the children what the date is, what day and month it is, how many children are enrolled in the class, how many are present, and how many are absent.
>
> . . . The bell rings at 12:30 and the teacher puts away her attendance book. She then goes to the back of the room and takes down a large chart labeled "Helping Hands." Bringing it to the center of the room, she tells the children it is time to change jobs. Each child is assigned to some task on the chart by placing his name, lettered on a paper "hand," next to a picture signifying the task—e.g., a broom, a blackboard, a milk bottle, a flag, and a Bible. She asks the children who wants each of the jobs and rearranges their "hands" accordingly. Everyone stands and faces the American flag hung to the right of the door. Edith leads the pledge to the flag, with the children following again the familiar sounds as far as they remember them. Edith then asks the girl in charge what song she wants and the child replies, "My Country." Edith goes to the piano and plays

"America," singing as the children follow her words. . . .

The day in kindergarten at Wright School illustrates both the content of the student role as it has been learned by these children and the processes by which the teacher has brought about this learning, or, "taught" them the student role. The children have learned to go through routines and to follow orders with unquestioning obedience, even when these make no sense to them. They have been disciplined to do as they are told by an authoritative person without significant protest. Edith has developed this discipline in the children by creating and enforcing a rigid social structure in the classroom through which she effectively controls the behavior of most of the children for most of the school day. The most important thing the children will learn in kindergarten can be seen now in its operational meaning, which is learning to live by the routines imposed by the school. This learning appears to be the principal content of the student role (Gracey, 1972).

What Are the Current Issues in American Education?

Several areas in American education are of current interest. Changes in teacher–student relationships, including a rise in violence within the schools, research concerning self-concept, sexism, and teacher behavior, the high percentage of adult American illiterates, and the home-schooling movement have all received attention from sociologists interested in the field of education.

TEACHER–STUDENT RELATIONSHIPS

The major dynamic between students and teachers concerns power and its use (Dreeben, 1968). Teachers are by definition the more powerful of the two, and a large part of mastering the student role is learning to live in an environment in which one is constantly "one down" (Bloom, 1980). Most of us learned to live within the system very well by the time we reached first grade and were experts at it by high school graduation.

Another study in this area, R. Dreeben's *On What Is Learned in School* (1968), concentrates on the "between the lines" teaching of norms that he sees as most important to education as an institution: independence, achievement, universalism, and specificity. Dreeben also sees power as a major issue in the classroom and discusses the uses of praise and judgment.

Emile Durkheim believed teachers dominate students through their "moral authority," which comes from the fact that teachers are more experienced and more cultured than students and that they "represent" the society at large (Durkheim, 1977). Today's society does not bear out his assertion. Many adults are now more respected and are thought to have more knowledge of the world than teachers, especially public school teachers. Rather than seeing teachers as moral authorities who share some of their wisdom to help students become educated, today students see teachers as "the enemy," the one who decides whether they pass or fail (and, therefore, whether they get good jobs or bad ones) and the one who decides how pleasant or unpleasant their enforced hours in the schoolroom will be.

VIOLENCE IN EDUCATION

Traditionally, teachers maintained their power position through controlling the amounts of praise and punishment their students received. Students revered their teachers, or at least feared them. Today it appears this is no longer true. Teachers have fallen off their pedestals, and, with corporal punishment usually outlawed, they no longer wield the "hickory stick" that once gave them the upper hand (Rubel, 1980).

Some educators believe that the hickory stick should return, this time as a weapon of self-defense. The National Institute of Justice reports that 22 percent of teachers and 16 percent of students have been victims of violence inside their schools at some point (Toby, 1983). Three out of four National Education Association members state that discipline is a major problem in their classrooms (McGrath, 1984). Some of this increase in school violence simply reflects the increase in violence in society as a whole. For example, 11 students were killed and 105 wounded by gunfire in Detroit schools in six months, suggesting the special volatility of the large cities (Eisenstein, 1987). Nevertheless, measures must be taken to protect students from their violent classmates.

One researcher notes that unwilling students more often show violent behavior, and suggests that we lower the compulsory attendance age to 15, thereby eliminating some of those who may be violent because they are forced to be in school when they don't want to be (Toby, 1983). Other suggestions include stepping up vigilance toward internal indications of violence and external intruders.

Some schools now employ full-time private police to patrol the halls, and they have eliminated student privileges such as permission to leave the school grounds. Many schools have abolished lunch periods, dismissing the students for the day at 1:00 or 1:30, because much school violence occurs in or near the lunchroom. In some cases, as Haney and Zimbardo point out, "It's tough to tell a high school from a prison" (1975). Whatever the source of school violence, it is now a fact of life for many American students and will continue to be a topic of concern in education.

THE PYGMALION EFFECT

> You see, really and truly, apart from the things anyone can pick up [the dressing and the proper way of speaking, and so on], the difference between a lady and a flower girl is not how she behaves, but how she's treated. I shall always be a flower girl to Professor Higgins, because he always treats me as a flower girl, and always will; but I know I can be a lady to you, because you always treat me as a lady, and always will (Liza Dolittle, in George Bernard Shaw's *Pygmalion*).

This quotation, which is from Shaw's play about a professor of linguistics who passes off a flower girl as a duchess after training her in upper-class speech and manners, ends the book *Pygmalion in the Classroom* (Rosenthal and Jacobson, 1968). Their "Pygmalion" experiment touched off much research into the student–teacher relationship. Robert Rosenthal and Lenore Jacobson randomly selected a group of elementary school students and told the students' teachers that these individuals had been tested and should be expected to exhibit unusually high academic progress that year. The teachers apparently believed the researchers; the identified students, who in reality were no different than those they studied with, *did* make unusual strides during that year. Rosenthal and Jacobson conclude that "how they are treated" is indeed a key variable in students' progress.

Other researchers have attempted to replicate the Rosenthal and Jacobson studies, with mixed results (Rubovits and Maher, 1971, 1973; D. Williams, 1981a). None of the studies done, however, replicated all of the original circumstances. For instance, one did not identify the supposed spurters until the second semester, when the teachers already had had time to form strong opinions about the students' abilities. Another provided false information about IQ scores rather than suggesting that certain students were ready to come into their own academically. Several studies replicated the original intent, but did not follow the students and teacher for the entire eight months as did the original study. Finally, the publicity that the original study received may have made it impossible to replicate the study, since teachers were now aware of the previous studies.

A related study found a strong relationship between race and the perceived socioeconomic status teachers assign to students when shown pictures of randomly chosen children (Harvey and Slatin, 1975). It also appears that if children are physically attractive, teachers will think them more intelligent, and will perhaps treat them differently enough to help them receive better grades (Clifford and Walster, 1973).

Another study followed a group of black children and black teachers from kindergarten through second grade (Rist, 1970). As soon as children were separated into three kindergarten reading groups, based on the teacher's evaluation of how quickly they might learn, they grew further apart in test scores. Lower-class children were more often placed in the lower-level group, even when their test scores disagreed with the placement. The lower-level students were usually farthest away from the teacher and received less attention, which led to the lower-level students' actually becoming less able to perform than the other children in the class.

Another study showed that teachers gave low achievers more criticism and high achievers more praise (Brophy and Good, 1974). Furthermore, teachers worked harder at getting an answer from a "good" student than they did from a poor one. This has been witnessed by all of us. A teacher says to pretty little Mary, struggling at the board to add the column of numbers. "Come on, Mary, we know you can do it. We'll just give you a few more minutes." Moments later, she derides sloppy, unattractive Ruth with "Well, just put the chalk down and go back to your seat, then, if you can't do it." Although we have all witnessed such scenes, at the time we probably did not think of them as helping to determine those students' academic futures.

Research with a slightly different slant found that if children were encouraged to believe that they could perform well in some area they would, and their high expectations in that area often also raised their expectations of how well they could do in other areas (Entwisle and Hayduk, 1981). Again, this should not be surprising because we have all had the experience of feeling good about ourselves in general because of one particular accomplishment.

Modern public schools may be turning duchesses into flower girls and flower girls into duchesses every day, at least to some extent. By giving certain groups more attention and encouragement and labeling other groups as "slow," teachers may affect the ultimate outcome of their students' lives more than they realize. Our "Close-Up on Research" highlights recent research on teacher behavior and gender.

CLOSE-UP on • *RESEARCH* •

Sadker and Sadker on Sexism in the Classroom

The Researchers and the Setting

Myra and David Sadker teach at the American University in Washington, D. C. Their informal observations convinced them that classrooms at all levels were characterized by a general environment of inequity and that bias in classroom interaction inhibited student achievement. With funding from the National Institute of Education, they attempted to observe and measure inequity in the classroom, from grade school through graduate school.

The Researchers' Goals

The Sadkers were attuned to sexism in the classroom setting and wished to help teachers avoid it and nurture all their students equally. The first step in this process was to make scientific observations of teaching behavior that demonstrated sexist bias in teaching methods. Second, they designed and evaluated intensive training programs for teachers who wanted to eliminate bias and improve their teaching. From the grade school to graduate lectures, their program has met with success. As they describe their mission: "What other group starts out ahead—in reading, in writing, and even in math—and twelve years later finds itself behind? We have compensatory education for those who enter school at a disadvantage; it is time that we recognize the problems of those who lose ground as a result of their years of schooling" (p. 515).

Theory and Concepts

The Sadkers attempted to prove their theory that

Proposition 1: Male students receive more attention from teachers and are given more time to talk in classrooms.

Proposition 2: Educators are generally unaware of the presence or the impact of this bias.

Proposition 3: Brief but focused training can reduce or eliminate sex bias from classroom interaction.

Proposition 4: Increasing equity in classroom interaction increases the effectiveness of the teacher as well (p. 512).

Research Design

In the first phase of their study, researchers trained in the INTERSECT Observation System collected data in more than 100 fourth-, sixth-, and eighth-grade classrooms in four states and Washington, D. C. The sample was balanced so that urban, suburban, and rural populations were represented, as well as black, white, and integrated classrooms, male and female teachers, and varying teaching areas.

Their second phase trained college faculty members in equity and excellence in classroom instruction. Again field researchers collected data in forty-six classes in a wide range of academic and professional disciplines at American University.

Classes in both studies were videotaped to be used later in training sessons. Many teachers were initially sceptical of the Sadkers' finding any support for their thesis that bias existed, but most were convinced, and even appalled, at the video evidence of their own unconsciously biased teaching patterns.

Findings

At all three grade levels and in all subjects, the Sadkers found that "male students were involved in more interactions than female students" (p. 512). Regardless of the sex or race of the teacher, males received more attention. About one-fourth of the students never interacted with the teacher during class, 65 percent of them interacted once per class session, and 10 percent, "the stars," used more than three times their fair share of interactions with the teacher.

The Sadkers found differences in the quality of interaction as well. Teachers gave more precise feedback to males than females. This included: "praise (positive reactions to a student's comment or work), and criticism (explicit statements that an answer is incorrect), and remediation (helping students to correct or improve their responses)" (p. 513). More than one-half of the teacher responses fit into a fourth category of simple acceptance of student comments.

In the college classrooms, the overall amount of interaction decreased and the number of silent students increased to 50 percent. Again, women received less precise feedback than men, and accepting comments prevailed over praise, criticism, and remediation.

Implications

The Sadkers believe that their research gives a possible answer to why college women experience a decline in self-esteem as they progress through college and why girls, who begin grammar school academically ahead of boys, end high school behind them (Astin, 1977). They feel that the systematic ignoring of women's input in the classroom affects not only the amount they learn but their self-concept as well.

Their hypothesis is born out in findings concerning women in the world of work. Here, too, men talk more than 50 percent of the time. Men tend to dominate professional meetings through interrupting and answering questions that are not addressed to them. Furthermore, over 40 percent of professional women report that their own failure to speak up in groups of men and women is their greatest professional problem (Eakins and Eakins, 1978; Shockley and Staley, 1980). Sadker and Sadker suggest that this is due to the socialization of twelve or more years of schooling in which the females' input was not sought.

Sadker and Sadker believe that classroom teachers at all levels must be made aware of their potential bias and be trained out of the behavior. Such training, in their opinion, leads to excellence in teaching because it emphasizes "higher rates of interaction, more precise reactions, more academic contacts, and a greater number of student-initiated comments" (p. 515).

Rather than trying to reach all teachers, the Sadkers have developed a training program for principals. Those involved in the Principal Effectiveness–Pupil Achievement Project (PEPA) will "acquire the skills to analyze both classroom interaction and professional communication" (p. 515). They will then be able to lead their teachers toward more effective and equitable interactions with their students and away from systematically ignoring the young women in their care.

Questions

1. Has your experience in school thus far corroborated the Sadkers' data? Were you ever aware of sex bias in the classroom?
2. Much discrimination occurs unconsciously. Most of the teachers who exhibited bias were surprised and unhappy about it. Should the Sadkers' training be made mandatory for teachers, in order that they become aware of their bias and able to change it?
3. What other reasons might you think of to explain why girls start out ahead and end up behind twelve years later?

SOURCES Myra Sadker and David Sadker. 1986. "Sexism in the Classroom: From Grade School to Graduate School", *Phi Delta Kappan*, (March), pp. 512–515. Alexander Astin. 1977. *Four Critical Years: Effects of College on Beliefs, Attitudes, and Knowledge.* San Francisco: Jossey-Bass. Barbara Eakins and Gene Eakins. 1978. *Sex Differences in Human Communications*, Boston: Houghton Mifflin. Shockley, P. and Constance Staley. 1980. "Women in Management Training Programs: What They Think About Key Issues", *Public Personnel Management*, Vol. 9, pp. 214–224.

THE HOME SCHOOL MOVEMENT

Frustrated after years of working within the educational system, even at its highest level in the Department of Education, John Holt began a new approach. In his book, *Teach Your Own* (1981), he describes his decision: "While the question 'Can the schools be reformed?' kept turning up 'No' for an answer, I found myself asking a much deeper question. . . . Were schools the best place for learning? . . . I began to doubt that they were."

Increasing numbers of parents have taken Holt's advice and begun to teach their children at home (Moore; 1982; Wallace, 1985; Helwig, 1986). Estimates suggest that upwards of 1 million children are now taught at home (King, 1983). Child psychologist James Dobson (1986) describes home schools as "the wave of the future."

Home-schooling requirements vary by state. Most home schoolers are required to submit a curriculum guide to the local school district, keep attendance, take standardized tests at periodic intervals, and perhaps have a certified teacher supervise the parent (Helwig, 1986).

Parents choose to teach their own children for a variety of reasons. Some fear the present social situations in the public schools, from the emphasis on competition with others rather than doing one's individual best, to the rates of violence, pregnancy, and drug use. Other home-schooling parents are bright and well-educated, and think they can do a better job of teaching their bright children than school systems that turn out large numbers of illiterates. Still others operate home schools in an effort to reinforce religious values in the home and keep their children from what they perceive could be harmful effects of those with different value structures. These social, academic, and religious reasons generally underlie home schooling.

The most often-asked question of home-schooling parents is: "What about socialization?" Universally, such parents agree that it is not an issue. Community sports and classes, church groups, music groups, and home-schooling groups that plan field trips and other large-group activities give ample opportunity for home-schoolers to meet and interact with other children. In such activities, they often have a more natural setting to develop social skills than they do in classrooms, where they are required to sit individually and be quiet most of the six-hour day. Most home schoolers also have siblings with whom they interact (Helwig, 1986).

Some home-schooling advocates believe that the socialization that occurs in schools is not merely inadequate, but harmful. Dobson thinks that the feelings of inferiority and inadequacy that are seen in teenagers today are rooted in the ridicule, rejection, and social competition experienced by children when they are young. He states: "I have seen kids dismantle one another, while parents and teachers passively stood by and observed the 'socialization' process" (1986).

Raymond Moore, president of Hewitt Research

This child is going to school—at home. The homeschooling movement has grown rapidly, partly as a result of increased violence and lowered academic standards in public school systems, as well as concern for the lack of spiritual education. (*Photo courtesy the author*)

Foundation, agrees: "The pervasive idea that children are better socialized and adjusted if they are constantly surrounded by their peers is an extravagant myth. The example set before a child of loving, mature parents is very different from the example he may get from his peers, who teach him obscenities, ridicule, bullying, snobbishness, and conformity" (1986).

While growing quickly, home schooling will never address the serious questions this chapter has raised concerning the education of the general populace. In many ways, it is a return to the elite system of home tutoring that was in place before the idea of universal education came about at the beginning of this century.

ILLITERATE AMERICA

Twenty-five million adult Americans cannot read even the most basic words in English. Thirty-five million more cannot read at the "functional" level, or enough to survive fully in our industrialized society. One-third of our adult population, these 60 millions, are "functionally illiterate" (Kozol, 1985). Most of them have spent at least ten years in our school systems. Most of them regularly "bluff" their way through life, trying to hide the fact that they cannot read. All of them are handicapped in trying to lead a normal life in our complex society.

In raw numbers, most of these adults are white and born in the United States. However, the percentages for minorities are higher. Sixteen percent of white adults, 44 percent of blacks, and 56 percent of Hispanics fall into this category.

Fifteen percent of recent graduates of large-city high schools cannot read beyond the sixth-grade level. Eighty-five percent of juvenile delinquents and 75 percent of prison inmates are functionally illiterate (Stechert, 1985). Half of the heads of households receiving welfare payments are illiterate. Illiteracy costs the United States about $225 billion annually in lost productivity, welfare and unemployment benefits, lowered tax base, and the cost of crime (Cultural Information Service, 1987). The United States ranks forty-ninth out of 158 countries in literacy level.

When literacy expert Thomas Sticht was asked why so many Americans cannot read, he responded, "Many people have not received good education in schools" (1987). Sticht developed job-related literacy programs for the Army and Navy, and he encourages American businesses to attack the problem of illiterate workers. He estimates that $200 million a day is lost in business in this country, because an illiterate worker is 10 to 15 percent less productive than one who can read. Currently 9 percent of Fortune 500 companies offer basic education training.

What else can be done? The 50 percent of Americans over age 18 who are truly proficient in reading and writing can volunteer to teach those who are not. Literacy programs are growing in every state, and most of them survive on volunteer labor.

Federal and state funds must be made available to attack illiteracy. In 1982, the Executive Director of the National Advisory Council on Adult Education estimated that we would need to spend about $5 billion to eradicate the problem. The Reagan administration reduced the $100 million spent in 1984 to $50 million. Federal funding now amounts to $1.65 per year per illiterate. Current programs reach a maximum of 4 percent of the illiterate population (Kozol, 1985).

The obvious final solution is to improve the system of education such that it does not promote students on the basis of good behavior or because they are getting too old for elementary school. Students should be taught and retaught until they have learned the basic lessons necessary for them to survive in today's world.

Why Is the United States a Nation at Risk?

Because the Commission on Excellence in Education noted that we were a "nation at risk" because of our rising illiteracy rate and falling standardized test scores, many educators have suggested paths for reform (Commission on Excellence, 1983; Fantini, 1986; Goodlad, 1984; Sizer, 1984). Although they differ in many respects, certain reform themes are universal: (1) adopt more rigorous standards for pupil performance, (2) teach thinking skills rather than memorization, (3) increase the time spent on learning basic skills, (4) require more homework, (5) increase the amount of time in the classroom, and (6) improve teacher quality.

MORE RIGOROUS STANDARDS FOR PUPIL PERFORMANCE

During the same period that the cost of public schooling has risen 40 percent, high school SAT scores have dropped 25 to 40 points. (See Figure 17.2.) Nearly everyone has an opinion as to why students are not doing as well on standardized tests. The person-in-the-street interview yields such diverse interpretations as "They're all on drugs, you know," and "The teachers don't maintain discipline, so the kids can't learn."

One interesting suggestion grows from a recent study of college athletes and academics. Adler and Adler followed athletes through four years of college and found that due to inadequate academic ability, a negative peer-group image of studying, and the intensity of the athletic realm of their college life, many college athletes gradually withdraw from their initial committment to academics in college, ultimately often not graduating (1985). The researchers suggest that similar factors could affect nonathlete students as well. If these students are not well-grounded academically, distracted by an outside interest such as a job or avocation, and belong to a peer group that deemphasizes the role of academics, they are likely to be unsuccessful as well.

More students are graduating from high school. In 1985 the dropout rate was 27 percent as opposed to 48 percent in 1950. Also, a higher percentage of graduates attend college—33 percent, up from 23 percent in 1960. Only 19 percent graduate from college, however. In spite of these facts, most people do not believe the youth of today are really better educated (U.S. Bureau of Census, 1987, p. 159). Rather, the proliferation of junior colleges and small four-year colleges competing for students has changed the value of the high school and college degrees. Many students who receive college degrees today would not have received them a decade or two ago, and the value of education is decreasing as the average level of education increases (Milner, 1972).

GRADE INFLATION. A contributing factor to the decreasing value of a formal education is grade inflation. Standard curved grading, in which a few students fail, a few receive "A"s, and "C" is an average grade, has been abandoned by most schools in favor of an unspoken system in which "C" is regarded as all but failing and "B" is the average grade. In spite of the fact that standardized tests indicate that students know less, their grades are higher than ever before. In the late

1960s, twice as many college freshmen entered with "C" averages from high school as with "A" averages. Fifty-eight percent of freshmen in 1984 acknowledged openly that "grading in the high schools was too easy" (Astin, 1985, p. 212).

Some people blame grade inflation on the generally permissive attitude toward youth that has prevailed since the 60s. Others believe it began when grades were used as a way of choosing those college students who would be drafted to fight in Vietnam. Professors who did not want to be responsible for anyone's death in Vietnam gave blanket "A"s and "B"s to thwart the draft requirement. Another possibility is that for the first time there is an overabundance of Ph.D.s who want to teach in college, coupled with a reduction in the number of available college teaching positions. Pro-

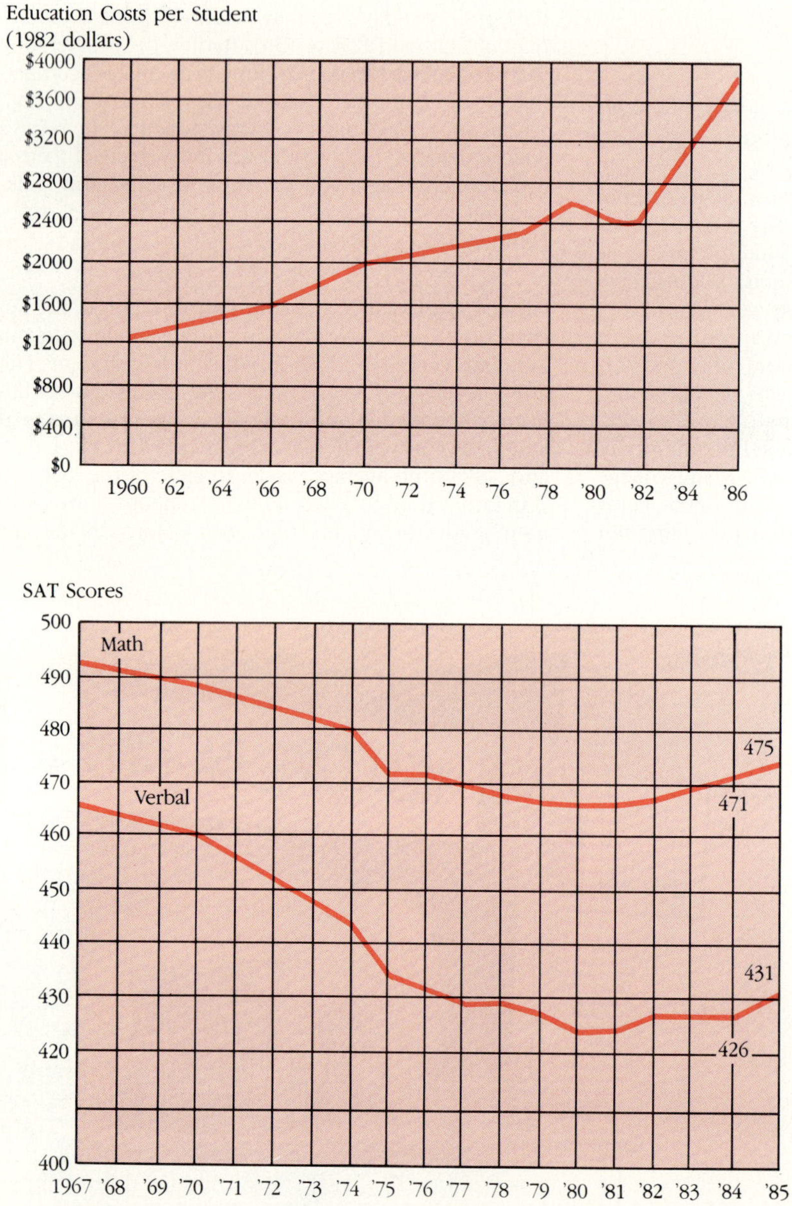

FIGURE 17.2 Cost of Education in Comparison with Test Scores. Whereas the cost of education has risen since 1962, the scores of students on SAT exams have dropped. SOURCE U.S. Bureau of the Census, 1987, pp. 150, 152, 158.

A nation at risk? Are students not working hard enough? Socializing with peers has long been a latent function of education, but in other nations, students do more homework. *(Photo courtesy the Michigan Daily)*

fessors who are popular with their students keep their jobs (or so the logic goes), and one way to be popular is to give good grades.

TEACHING THINKING SKILLS

In part to meet the needs of minority students who are increasingly often continuing their education past age 16, the curriculum of the public schools has been watered down. High school textbooks, for example, are written at the sixth-grade level (Hechinger, 1979). This, coupled with a failure to teach complex thinking skills and a bureaucratic emphasis on passive student behavior, may account for falling test scores (Dollar, 1983; Karp, 1985; Goodlad, 1984; Sizer, 1984). The proliferation of non–college-track courses in high schools has set the stage for graduating students who lack what was once thought of as a "basic" education.

Students are rarely challenged to think in today's schools, but only invited to memorize facts. Goodlad found that almost all teacher-made tests were based on short answers and recall of information (1984). Not even 1 percent of instructional time was devoted to discussions that "required some kind of open response involving reasoning or perhaps an opinion from students." The fact that stood out most clearly in his observations of over 1,000 classrooms was the passivity of the students, who have learned their role as receivers well by the time they reach high school. The fact that 63 percent of American high school students are in huge institutions of education reinforces this behavior, because large schools tend to create passive and compliant students (Karp, 1985). Only in classes labeled "gifted" are students allowed or encouraged to think for themselves.

Such classrooms are described by Goodlad as "flat" and by Sizer as "bland," hardly adjectives to describe an exciting learning situation. Sadker and Sadker observed that teacher responses that were noncommittal and "flat" encouraged the development of such an atmosphere (1985). When trying to observe instances of sexist interactions between teachers and students, the Sadkers noted that most of the time they were unable to record *anything.* The response of the teachers was acceptance, but not encouragement or clarification.

Research shows that students learn best when they know specifically what is expected of them, when they learn quickly about their errors, and when they receive precise guidance toward improving their work (Berliner, 1984). The fact that over one-half of classroom

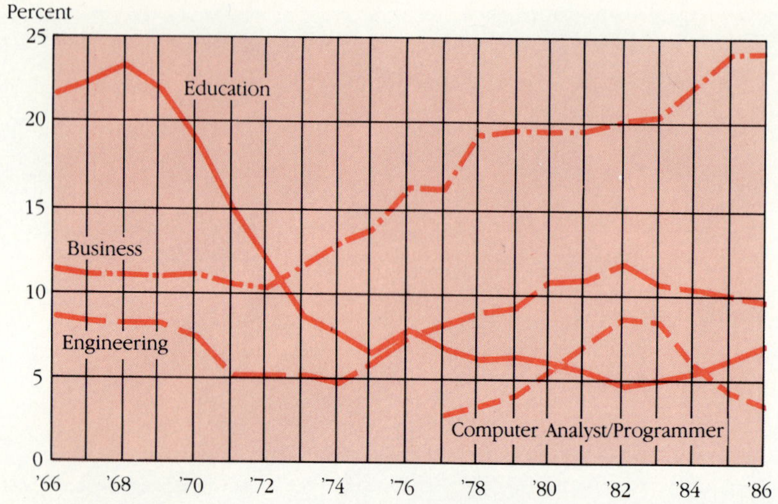

FIGURE 17.3 Freshman Career Preferences, 1966–1986. In this line graph, freshmen choosing education as their career are declining, whereas business-related occupations are growing. SOURCE *The American Freshman National Norms for Fall 1986* (Los Angeles: Higher Education Research Institute, UCLA, December 1986). Author: Alexander W. Astin et al.

interactions consist of bland, accepting statements must negatively affect the learning environment for all the children. This combination of passive learning, watered-down courses, and memorization rather than thinking has created a system of schools that encourage minimal learning.

LEARNING BASIC SKILLS

Growing cuts in public school budgets for such "frills" as music and art has accompanied an emphasis on teaching more basic subjects. Even at Harvard, distribution requirements have been reenacted in order to assure that every Harvard graduate will have read and absorbed those materials which their professors believe are required for truly educated men and women (Schiefelbein, 1978).

The National Commission on Excellence in Education has recommended a compulsory high school curriculum in the "new basics," including four years of English; three years of math, science, and social studies; and one-half year of computer science for all students, plus two years of a foreign language for the college bound. (National Commission on Excellence in Education, 1983). They cite excessive student choice in "cafeteria-style" curricula as the cause of a migration away from academic courses to less demanding general-track courses. Since 1969, one-quarter fewer graduating seniors are following the college-preparatory track.

REQUIRING MORE HOMEWORK AND CLASSROOM TIME

A report by the International Association for the Evaluation of Educational Achievement (IEA) shows that on nineteen tests covering subjects such as reading comprehension and chemistry, American students as a group *never* took first or second place in a comparison of students in twenty-one countries, both developed and undeveloped (Lerner, 1982). When the scores of undeveloped nations are excluded, the United States scores at the bottom in seven of the nineteen areas. This occurs despite the fact that the United States spends more money on education than any of the other countries and has the world's highest student retention rate: three-quarters of our children finish twelfth grade (see Figure 17.3).

The only factor the IEA could correlate with high achievement was the size of homework assignments to be completed by students. The larger the assignment, the higher achievement tended to be. Because studies show homework levels steadily declining in the United States since the 1960s, educators may begin to work toward excellence by increasing the amount of homework given the average student.

Several reports have also suggested that more days be spent in school and that the school day itself be lengthened (National Commission on Excellence, 1983). Although a few districts have begun to follow this suggestion, most school systems still conform to the 180-day, six-hour-per-day schedule (Bowen, 1985c).

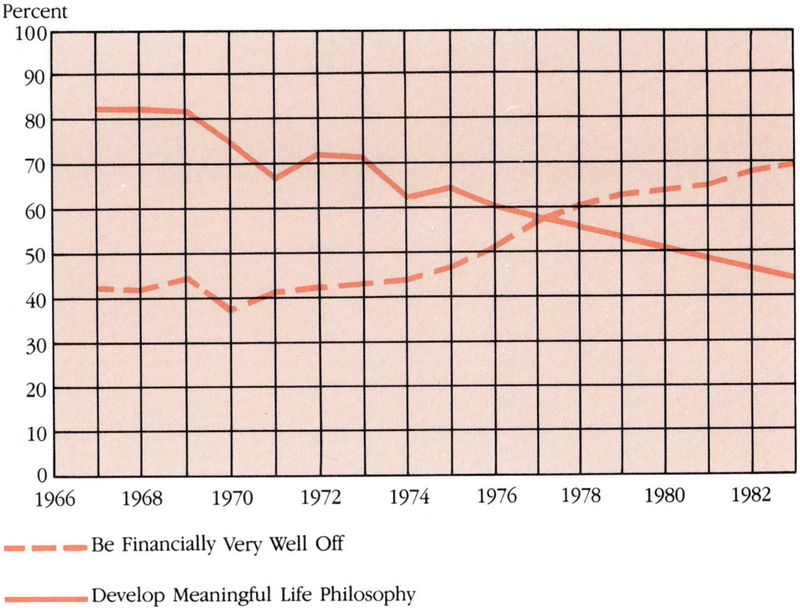

FIGURE 17.4 Student Life Goals. Reflecting changes in society as a whole, more students are interested in making money and fewer are interested in developing a meaningful philosophy of life. SOURCE Cooperative Institutional Research Program.

Gatekeeper. High performance on tests, especially the Scholastic Aptitude Test, helps open doors to "better schools" and "better jobs." *(Michael Hayman/Black Star)*

IMPROVING TEACHER QUALITY

Closely related to quality of student learning is quality of instruction. Ironically, the equalizing of gender roles that has created many positive benefits for society has given bright women, who in years past would become teachers, other options. Many of them are now becoming lawyers, doctors, researchers, and business executives, and our traditional talent pool for teaching has been depleted (McGrath, 1983; Wagenaar, 1985). Ernest Boyer of the Carnegie Foundation for the Advancement of Teaching summarizes present thinking by saying, "Whether we can start drawing in excellent people is the Number One question" (1983). Toward this end, many suggestions have been made.

Teaching as a field does not attract as many people as it did twenty years ago, perhaps as a general trend away from human service occupations and toward business. Astin's research shows that many more entering college freshmen are interested in financial gain over and above "meaningful" experiences today (Astin, 1985). (See Figures 17.3 and 17.4.)

Many educational observors note that potential teachers these days are likely to be "education" majors, taking the majority of their classes in methods of teaching. As a result, many of them are inadequately prepared in the basic subject areas that were once mastered by all teachers (Astin, 1985). Some educators suggest that certification should require fewer educa-

Sociologists at Work •

NATHAN GLAZER
ANALYZES THE SHORTAGE OF MINORITY FACULTY
Harvard University
Cambridge, Massachusetts

Sociologist Nathan Glazer serves on the faculty of the education school at Harvard University. Much of his recent work considers how ethnic minorities achieve in schools. He especially studies the effects of policies aimed at improving the performance of low achieving minorities, especially blacks.

Tell Us About Minorities in Higher Education

There has been great concern over the very small number of minority faculty in higher education. On the whole, while the black minority makes up something like 11 or 12 percent of the population, they make up only about 2 percent of faculty in colleges and universities and probably even smaller percentages in higher status colleges and universities.

We have had policies since the early 70s whereby colleges and universities are required to report to the Federal government the numbers of minorities in faculty positions. They are also required to develop and report on programs to improve the numbers of minority faculty. We call these affirmative action programs, and I have pointed out that whatever the efforts we attempt in this field, we are going to be frustrated by the fact that the numbers of blacks getting doctoral degrees is very small, about 4 per cent. Most of these are in just a very few fields, particularly education and social work. So much of the excitement and conflict around affirmative action in colleges and universities has really been fighting over a solution which is impossible—impossible as long as the number of blacks who are interested in going in for doctoral programs is so small.

Now the percentage of blacks in higher education has increased greatly since the late 60s, but when you come to doctoral programs, which are the requirements for teaching jobs in universities and colleges, the percentages are very small, and the increase of blacks has not been evident because more blacks have gone into professional school programs such as law and medicine.

I think any analysis of the problem points to the fact that the solution is not to be found in stronger affirmative action, in seeking for faculty at the college and university level, but has to be found down below in increasing the numbers who apply to doctoral programs and even below that, to increasing the percentages that take the kind of work in college that might encourage them to or prepare them for entering the doctoral program.

Are There Programs That Encourage Blacks to Enter Graduate Programs?

There are programs of that sort. But there is good evidence that the problem lies in a lower level. The fact is that when you go to that lower level, you find the problem pushes you back to an even lower level. So, for example, if you look at those prepared to go to college or prepared to go to colleges with a strong emphasis on academic skills, you will find a higher drop out rate among blacks. So we move on to an even lower level until we have to do work at the high schools, but even there we think of the kinds of preparations that occur in junior high schools and the elementary schools. I have reviewed in my own work the entire range of academic and education programs from pre-school up through college and beyond which are addressed to low income minorities, and in all of them, there are great difficulties and no easy solutions.

What Have You Found That Helps?

The most promising kinds of programs, and I am not saying that they show tremendous success, are really almost beginning programs such as pre-school programs. Even at the level of entering first grade, there are already very substantial differences by ethnic group and by class. Pre-school programs which involve exposure to more talk and more varied talk and talk which consists of more than commands, such as "do this and don't do that" kind of interactional talk, seem to be very useful. Studies have shown that exposure to such programs will help students up to the high school level, in terms of such matters as reducing the numbers who have to repeat classes, reducing the numbers who get into trouble with juvenile delinquency and so on. So that is one area where there has been some promise. •

tion classes and more liberal arts classes and should mandate a certain level of proficiency in them.

Others note that education majors are often from the "bottom of the barrel," and suggest that we offer incentives to bright students who might be talented teachers (Boyer, 1983; Fantini, 1986). For instance, high school seniors who planned to become teachers scored in the bottom half of their classes for the amount of homework they completed, and had taken fewer math, foreign language, and science courses than their counterparts who were thinking of other fields (Wagenaar, 1985). Toward this end, several Ivy League colleges have recently modified their teacher-training programs, offering such things as tuition-free semesters toward certification and placement services that guarantee good job placements (Schacter, 1987).

The recent increase in teacher-qualification examinations also speaks to the growing interest in upgrading teacher qualifications. Almost half of the states now have competency exams (Bowen, 1985a). The failure rates range from 60 percent of Houston public school teachers in 1983 to 2 percent in the state of Georgia (Mayfield, 1987). Three states, Texas, Arkansas, and Georgia, have decided to fire all teachers who fail the exams.

From a positive perspective, several studies have recommended that merit pay be given for excellent teaching, and that the status of master teacher be institutionalized. This person would be a role model for others, and would spend some part of each day actively teaching others to teach better (Shanker, 1987; McGrath, 1983).

Whether improving minimal education, giving more homework, emphasizing basic skills, and upgrading teachers will produce changes in the achievement of our students remains to be seen. Perhaps the students' lax attitudes toward studying and low motivation to do their best will subvert these and other suggested measures because the American educational system simply reflects a social problem with motivation.

Conclusion

Schools reflect their societies. As we have seen, a society based on the idea of participatory democracy often seeks to educate the masses. Similarly, in a society where racism is institutionalized, schools are apt to perpetuate a racist system.

Public education has undergone very little substantive change in its lifetime. Changes in such an influential institution are likely to occur slowly, because change in that area would mean change in many others as well.

REVIEW

Summary Questions

1. What is the history of the development of schools in the United States?
2. How do functionalists and conflict theorists view education?
3. What factors affect access to formal education in the United States?
4. How does Parsons believe schools shape and channel people?
5. How does formal education serve as the career-sorting and channeling mechanism of society?
6. Contrast the British, American, and Japanese educational institutions.
7. How does formal education transmit culture and stimulate innovation?
8. How is the formal social structure in the schools different from the informal?
9. According to Harry Gracey, what is the implicit function of kindergarten?
10. What is the situation with violence in schools?
11. Discuss the "Pygmalion" effect.
12. What did the Sadkers' research show about sexism in the classroom?
13. What are the factors determining equality in education?
14. How are declining standards and grade inflation related?
15. What is minimal education?
16. Why can America be called illiterate?
17. What suggestions for reform of the schools have been offered?
18. What is the basis of the growth of the home-school movement?

Summary Answers

1. Schooling is not synonymous with education. Until the beginning of the twentieth century, most literate education consisted of children learning to read from their parents. Schools began to expand when the society became increasingly urban and industrialized.
2. Functionalists suggest that the American educational system grew in direct proportion to the need for increasingly specialized workers for industry and that people use it as a steppingstone up the stratification ladder. They see mass education as beneficial to all members of society. Conflict theorists point out that mass education does not always precede industrialization, and that requiring educational credentials actually keeps people in their places in the stratification system. They see the system as another battlefield between the classes.
3. Several factors that affect access to formal education are differences in family expectations, differences in gender, and differences in socioeconomic group. Some inequality in economic group and gender has been reduced through federal programs, but much still exists.
4. Parsons believes that schools sort students according to achievement, emancipate the individual from the family, facilitate acceptance of cultural values, introduce relating to others through roles, and teach basic and specialized skills.
5. Education sorts and channels students by systematically separating those who appear to have the intellectual capability to do further academic work and those who do not, what Clark calls the "cooling out" function.
6. The British system educates the elites for academic pursuits and the rest of the students for meaningful vocational work, with all schooling paid for by the government. In the United States, the emphasis is on mass education, with all students supposedly having an equal chance to get ahead academically and little real vocational training. Most higher education is paid for by the student. The Japanese talent-development system is defined by its ability to develop the talents of all its citizens. Japan has a strong commitment to educate all citizens to the level of high school completion, and has done it without lowering standards of work or eliminating the arts as a subject. Japan offers higher education funded by the government.
7. Formal education transmits culture through political socialization and assimilation of new groups. It stimulates innovation by supporting the research of our intellectual elite.
8. The formal purpose of the school is to teach, but much of its real reason for being is to control young people during the day while adults work.
9. Gracey believes that the implicit function of kindergarten is to teach children how to be passive students.
10. Traditionally teachers controlled students through praise and punishment. Today's teachers and students are often the victim of in-school violence, from assault to murder, implying another difference between the real and ideal structure of the schools.
11. Several research studies show that teachers' expectations of students will greatly affect their performance. This is dubbed the "Pygmalion" effect.
12. The Sadkers found that at all levels, from grade school to graduate school, males received more attention and more of the precise feedback valuable to learning than females.
13. Factors determining equality in education include: the growth of private schools and cutting of public school budgets, busing for racial equality, compensatory education, and federal efforts toward educational opportunity.
14. Standards for students are declining at the same time that grades are inflating and costs of education are climbing.
15. Minimal education is the watered-down curriculum, presented with flat affect by teachers, emphasizing memorization rather than thinking, and directed toward passive rather than active students.
16. One-third of our adult population is "functionally illiterate," unable to lead a normal life due to a reading deficit.
17. Among the proposals for reform of the educational system are increasing the amount of time spent learning basic skills, requiring more homework, increasing the amount of time in class, teaching thinking skills, improving teacher quality, and adopting more rigorous standards for pupil performance.
18. Some parents choose to teach their own children due to fear of the present social situations in the public schools, from the emphasis on competition rather than doing one's individual best, to the rates of violence, pregnancy, and drug use. Other reasons are that bright, well-educated parents believe they can do a better job of teaching their bright children than schools can. Other parents keep their children home to reinforce religious values and protect the children from exposure to different value structures.

Glossary

assimilation the process of learning the norms of a new group

compensatory education education designed to give the lower-class student an extra boost in order that he or she might begin school on an even level with the middle-class and upper-class student

credentialization the process of requiring a credential that is not immediately necessary for the work

electorate the people who vote in elections

innovation the process of developing new methods and concepts for society

peer group group of friends

political socialization teaching people what they may expect from their country and what their country expects from them

Suggested Readings

Alexander Astin. 1985. *Achieving Educational Excellence.* San Francisco: Jossey-Bass.

In academic, but readable, style, Astin dispassionately paints a picture of the depths to which American education has sunk and suggests some positive responses to the current situations.

John Goodlad. 1984. *A Place Called School.* New York: McGraw-Hill.

Based on observations of over 1,000 classrooms throughout the United States, Goodlad's study reports an atmosphere of blandness and lack of excitement that today characterizes the places we call schools.

Jonathan Kozol. 1985. *Illiterate America.* Garden City, N.Y.: Anchor Press.

Although somewhat painful to read, Kozol's book accurately and clearly presents this major problem that affects all aspects of society.

Theodore Sizer. 1984. *Horace's Compromise: The Dilemma of the American High School.* Boston: Houghton Mifflin.

Sizer describes minimal education as being practiced in American high schools today: A setting in which a silent bargain is struck between teachers and students to expect very little from one another.

CHAPTER 18

POPULATION and the ENVIRONMENT

How's Your Sociological Intuition?

1. The most significant change in population trends during the 1980s was:
   - a. The population grew more than expected
   - b. The world became divided between those nations whose growth had stabilized and those that were still growing very quickly
   - c. Males were being born less frequently than females
   - d. Longevity rates fell
2. The major reason for rapid population growth in the United States in this century has been:
   - a. More babies being born
   - b. More children growing into adulthood
   - c. Immigration
   - d. Emigration
3. Some researchers have predicted famine as a result of explosive population growth. Famine:
   - a. Has not occurred anywhere recently
   - b. Has occurred in some regions recently
   - c. Will inevitably occur by the end of the 1980s
   - d. Is only a myth propagated by the American Grain Association
4. At present growth rates, the world population will double in:
   - a. 2,000 years
   - b. 180 years
   - c. 41 years
   - d. 12 years

Answers

1. b. Although most industrialized countries are reaching zero population growth (ZPG), Third World countries face an "ecological trap," as their populations outstrip their ability to grow food.
2. a. Most of the change in U.S. population growth rate was due to changes in the number of babies born, as we see in the section, "What Are the Basic Population Processes?"
3. b. Famine is a fact of life in some parts of the world, as we learn in the "Close-Up on Research."
4. c. A decade ago demographers expected the world population would double in thirty-five years. Now it appears it will take forty-one years or longer if population growth rates slow further. We look more closely at population growth dynamics in "How Is the Population Exploding?"

When You Have Finished Studying This Chapter, You Should Know:

- What demography is and what the elements of population are
- The major tools that demographers use
- How fertility, mortality, and migration affect populations
- How a census is used
- Why gender and age are the two most important composition variables
- What a dependency ratio is
- How to read a population pyramid
- How fertility and fecundity differ
- How life expectancy and infant mortality vary from country to country
- The importance of Malthusian theory
- What a demographic transition is
- Today's population growth experiences around the world
- How population growth in the United States differs from world population growth
- The social differences between modern and previous birth control methods
- How the ecosystem of Third World nations is being affected by rapid population growth
- How crowding affects our health
- What present rates of consumption mean in terms of the world's resources
- How the "green revolution" addresses world food problems
- How nuclear energy affects society

How will the world change within our lifetime? Perhaps the future holds technological wonders that will amaze us as much as automobiles, supersonic air travel, television, and computers amazed those who lived before their introduction. We might make as much progress in conquering chronic diseases, such as cancer and heart disease, as we have in defeating dread killers of the past, such as diphtheria and smallpox. As we delegate much of our tedious work to computers and robots, we may have ever-increasing amounts of consumer goods and leisure time. A breakthrough in energy production, such as the development of a controlled fusion reactor, could make the cost of energy trivial.

Where some see a future boom, others see gloom. They worry that our civilization has already peaked and is in a state of decline. Perhaps the human race is already hopelessly dependent on fossil fuels, which will run out in the next century and will simultaneously render the earth uninhabitable through pollution. Down the road may lay shortages of food, energy, and water, which will cause starvation, disease, drought, famine, and war.

Those with the gloomier perspective see booby traps hidden within technological advance. They point to the fact that scientific developments have brought curses as well as blessings. With automobiles and factories came air pollution and heavy reliance on nonrenewable fossil fuels. Air travel threatens to burn away the ozone layer that shields life on this planet from deadly doses of ultraviolet radiation. Even medical cures have sometimes backfired. With anesthesia came drug addiction, and "conquering" infectious diseases has led to overpopulation in the less developed world. The discovery of nuclear fission has failed to deliver the cheap energy it once promised, but it has placed most of the earth on a nuclear powder keg that could momentarily wipe out most life on earth.

Whose vision of the future is the most valid? One thing seems certain: barring a major calamity, the earth's population will double in our lifetime. This means roughly twice the problems and half the resources now available. To maintain our present living standard, humanity will need to double all existing resources in thirty-five years, creating twice the jobs, twice the food, twice the amount of housing, schools, roads, and other public facilities. We also will have to cope with twice the potential for pollution, putting twice the strain on our environment. Can we make it?

The outcome depends on our ability to face several challenges. Can the economic productivity of the world double to provide for this doubling of population? Can we develop new technologies to produce the energy, food, housing, and transport needed without exhausting crucial resources or polluting to hazardous levels? Can we slow the population growth rate enough to avoid disasters that would accompany massive shortages? Can we get along with one another well enough to avoid unleashing the weapons of mass destruction we have stockpiled?

Population growth is a dominant force driving us toward our destiny. The clock is running, and during the three minutes it took to read this introduction, planet earth's human population grew by 495 people. In the time it takes to complete an average fifteen-week college course, the population will grow by 25 million persons—more than the combined populations of New York City and San Francisco.

In this chapter we consider how populations grow and the effects they have on their environment. We explore how the distribution of characteristics such as age and sex influences the behavior of societies. We explore the forces governing how populations are distributed. We create an image of the world population and circumstances, and develop some understanding of the dynamics of human populations.

In order successfully to cope with these challenges of population growth, we need to understand the information provided by the social scientists who study population. We also need to learn, and to communicate to others, the vision of one humanity, living on a solitary and fragile planet. Viewed from the broad perspective, our long-range best interests are one and the same as those of our neighbors.

What Is Demography?

Demography *is the study of the size, composition, and distribution of society as it is affected by three major population processes: fertility, mortality, and migration.* Demographers study how many people exist in a territory, where they live, what groups they belong to, and how they are distributed in terms of traits such as sex and age. Although you may not personally know any demographers, their work affects most people's daily lives. Demographic questions enter the headlines often. Will people soon be starving because the population has grown too fast? Are less intelligent people reproducing faster than the more intelligent people, and does that mean that the general level of intelligence is decreasing? What does the increase in the number of aged mean in terms of Social Security income, retirement age, low-cost housing for the elderly, and the like? Such questions rely on demographic data for answers.

What Are the Elements of Population?

Demographers divide people into many categories. The first, and probably most often quoted demographic variable, is size of the population. The second variable is the composition of the population, or how it breaks down into categories like sex and age. Finally, demographers estimate present and future social situations by studying the distribution of the population, or how the composition covaries.

SIZE

Population size is the basic measurement of demography. All demographic projections about the future are based on estimates of the size of a population at a certain time. Demographers have tried to estimate the population of humankind ever since they have had tools for such estimates.

Historians usually date the beginning of the modern age at 1650. At that time the earth's population was about 500 million. By 1985 that figure had grown to 4.8 billion.

Note that these numbers are estimates. Many factors could cause the estimate to be faulty. For example, China has about 20 percent of the world's population, and even the Chinese government is not sure how large the population is or how fast it is growing. Because China has such a large proportion of the earth's population, an error in estimating China's population means an error in estimating world population.

WHAT IS A CENSUS? Governments have long understood the importance of knowing how many people they control and where they are located in order to plan services, assess taxes, and predict future needs. A ***census*** *is an official count of people and their relevant characteristics such as age, sex, and occupation.* Demographers use a census to measure the size, distribution, and composition of a population. The Roman Empire took the census mentioned in the story of the birth of Jesus, and William the Conqueror took the first census in England in 1086.

A census is taken by a government and is intended to include every person within a certain specified territory. It should ideally be done simultaneously all over the territory, on a single day. In the United States a census is usually completed in three to four weeks, but in some countries it may last as long as several years. To facilitate comparisons, the census should contain the same information every time it is collected (Nam and Philliber, 1984). Sometimes questions on a census are changed, however, in order to provide more meaningful current information.

The United States census began in 1790 and has been repeated every ten years. When a full census is taken, data are published for "Urbanized Areas (UA)," cities and the area around them that is continuously built-up. In the intervening years, county data is used to watch change in urban areas. A county may qualify as a "Metropolitan Statistical Area (MSA)" if it contains a city of 50,000 or more population, or an Urbanized Area of 50,000 or more population surrounded by a total metro bringing the total population to 100,000 or more. MSAs are classed from Level A, having a population over 1 million, to Level D, having less than 100,000.

A county or group of counties may qualify as a "Primary Metropolitan Statistical Area (PMSA)" if local opinion supports separate recognition for this, which demonstrates relative independence within the

Despite a slowing of population growth, the United States continues to grow at about 1 percent per year, as the constant turning of this Population Clock graphically illustrates. (*Photo courtesy the author*)

metro complex. A metro area may qualify as a "Consolidated Metropolitan Statistical Area (CMSA)" if it contains 1 million or more population and has a qualifying PMSA within it (Haub, 1985). Within any of these metropolitan areas, census tracts are units of 3,000 to 6,000 people who live in the same "neighborhood" of an urban area.

Even in industrialized countries there are errors in the census. For instance, it is estimated that almost 8 percent of the black population was left out of the 1970 United States census, because census workers did not find their places of residence or refused to go to their neighborhoods, or because the people themselves did not cooperate with the census takers (Reinhold, 1979).

In less developed countries a census has even greater problems. The population can be nomadic, for instance, and thus difficult to count because people are not in one place long enough. A chiefly agricultural population also poses some difficulties for a census, because the people are more spread out than an urban population and more difficult to find.

After World War II most countries tried to begin a regular census, and the United Nations sponsored much census activity in order to help plan the future of the world. Even with this effort, some populations of the world still have never been officially counted.

COMPOSITION

Composition *refers to the distribution of a population in various categories like age and sex.* The only categories that have been counted in every United States census since 1790 are address, name, sex, and age (Yaukey, 1985). Sex and age are very important variables, because only women between about age 14 and age 49 can bear children. In order to make an accurate judgment about future population size, demographers must know how many women are in that age group at present, and how many will enter and leave that age group soon. Furthermore, more infants and old people die than do children and adults, so the size of each age group is also important to know to predict future population. The three major measures of composition of a population are the sex ratio, the median age, and the dependency ratio of that population.

SEX RATIO. *The number of males per 100 females in a population is known as the* ***sex ratio.*** More boy babies are born, but fewer boys reach adulthood than girls. Knowing the sex ratio of a population allows demographers to estimate how difficult or easy it will be for the marriage structure of a society to continue as it has in the past. For example, during the 1960s there was a ratio of four males to every five females, resulting in a shortage of single men of marriageable age in the American population. Because of this, a higher percentage of men and a lower percentage of women than usual were getting married (Akers, 1967). Even if there had been an unusually high number of women between ages 14 and 49 during this period, it is possible that no more than the usual number of children would be produced.

Sex ratios also vary according to region of the country. In Alaska, where the weather makes life somewhat more difficult than elsewhere in the United States, the male-to-female sex ratio is 122—or 122 men for every 100 women. Most American cities, in contrast, have a lower male-to-female sex ratio, because cities support industries that often employ many women.

MEDIAN AGE. *The* ***median age*** *is that age which is the middle figure of all of the ages of the population, with half of the population older than that age and half of it younger.* The United States has had a steadily rising median age, except during the 1950s baby boom, which will be discussed later. In the first United States census in 1790, the median age was 16 years. By 1960 it had risen to 23 years, and in 1985 it was 30 years (Yaukey, 1985; U.S. Bureau of Census, 1987). The median age helps demographers estimate whether the population is predominantly old or young.

DEPENDENCY RATIO. The other important composition measure is the division of the population into three major age groups: children, the aged, and active persons. These groupings are important in assessing the state of the group being studied, because having a high proportion of economically dependent people (conventionally those over 65 or under 15) creates a strain on the economy of the society. *The number of economically dependent people per 100 people who are economically productive (conventionally between ages 15 and 64) is the* ***dependency ratio*** of a society.

In 1980, 44 percent of the population of the United States were dependents, a proportion not presently considered detrimental to economic growth. Twenty-three percent of the population was under age 15, a figure that corresponds with that of most other industrialized countries (United Nations 1982).

In less developed countries a much higher proportion of the population is under 14. For instance, 41 percent of the population of Brazil is under 15. Underdeveloped countries face a high infant and child mortality rate, however, and the chance that those children will live long enough to be productive members of society is much lower than that in the United States. Ironically, if there were fewer children in the underdeveloped countries, the chances would be better that they would be cared for adequately, and a higher proportion of them would survive into adulthood. Many poor people, however, regard children as potential workers and consider large families necessary to ensure survival of a medium-sized group (United Nations, 1982).

In addition to sex and age, several other elements of population composition that are important to the demographer include marital status, national origin, economic activity, literacy and education, and place of residence. All of these are useful in determining the nature of a population and what it can be expected to achieve in the future (Matras, 1973).

THE POPULATION PYRAMID

A pictoral representation of the age and sex distribution of the population of an area is termed a ***population pyramid.*** A population pyramid can give a clearer demographic picture of a particular territory. Consider, for example, the population pyramids of the United States and Mexico in Figure 18.1. The difference in age structure of the two countries is striking. In Mexico high birth rates combined with moderate death rates produce the rapidly thinning shape at the top of the pyramid. In contrast, more children in the United States live to middle age, and a higher proportion of its population is aged. Population pyramids are useful in showing the major differences graphically.

Population pyramids can also show past, present, and future populations of a society. If we consider population pyramids for the United States over this century, for instance, we learn several things (see Figure 18.2). In 1910 there were fewer people in all categories than in 1960. Looking at the 1940 pyramid, we note a shortage of those under age 14 resulting from lowered fertility and higher infant mortality rates during the Great Depression. The broad base of the 1960 pyramid is formed by those persons born during a period of high fertility immediately after World War II. Fertility was high during this period because many couples had delayed having children during the war. The year 2000 pyramid suggests the future effects of this increase in fertility in a large number of 10- to 19-year-olds. We can also see the beginnings of a society that has a disproportionate number of elderly people, as discussed in Chapter 12, "Aging in Industrial Society."

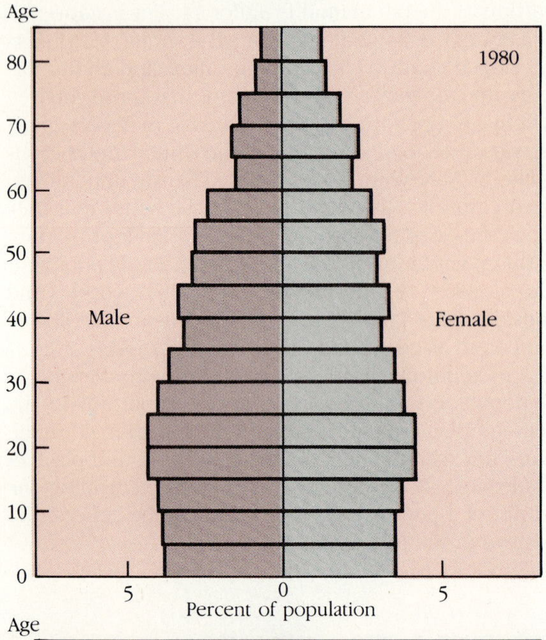

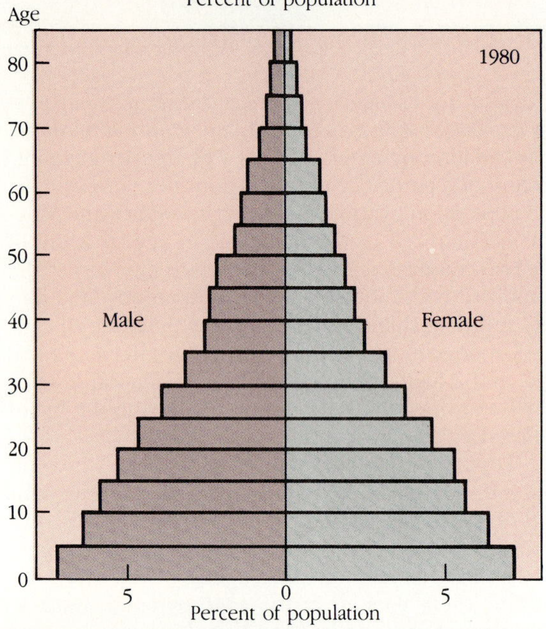

FIGURE 18.1 Population, by Sex and Age, of the More Developed Regions and the Less Developed Regions, 1980. Population pyramids can portray the character of societies. The broad base of the pyramids of the less developed regions reflects high fertility, whereas the narrow top indicates high mortality. The more developed regions show much more equal distribution in age, having a columnar shape rather than a pyramidal one. The more developed regions also have a predominance of females in the older age categories, unlike the less developed regions. SOURCE *World Population Trends and Policies: 1981 Monitoring Report.* Vol. I: *Population Trends* (United Nations publication, Sales No. E.82.XIII.2), p. 135, Fig. 17.

TERRITORIAL DISTRIBUTION

The world's population is distributed according to where the environment is amenable to human life. Factors that determine this include climate; location of water, soil, energy, and minerals; and the ability to reach and be reached by the outside world (Heer, 1975). The world is becoming urbanized, and many people fear the crowding they see in the future of an urban society. Some have believed that enough land exists for everyone and that new territories must simply be settled. Unfortunately, however, the environmental factors that have led people to choose the land they presently inhabit would probably make it difficult to live on previously rejected land. Much work is being done, however, to determine the possibilities of settling new areas.

What Are the Basic Population Processes?

Three processes affect population size: fertility, mortality, and migration. These are the three major areas of study for demographers.

Demographers predict fertility, in part, by counting the number of women between 14 and 49 years of age in a society at a given time. ***Fertility*** *refers to the frequency of births in a population.* Fertility is distinguished from the crude birth rate, which is derived by dividing the number of live births in a population during a given year by the total population at the midpoint of the year and multiplying by 1,000. The ***crude birth rate*** *is the number of live births per 1,000 persons in a population during one year.*

Fertility is also distinguished from fecundity. ***Fecundity*** *is the potential number of children that the women in a population could produce.* Most demographers suggest twelve as an individual fecundity limit, allowing time for the mother to be pregnant and to nurse her children. One of the few known societies in which fertility approached fecundity is that of the Hutterite communities in the United States and Canada. In the 1950 census the average number of children reported born to married Hutterite women between ages 45 to 54 (the end of their childbearing years) was 10.6 (Eaton and Mayer, 1953). Fertility never equals fecundity because almost every society voluntarily uses social controls to limit the number of children it produces.

AGE AT MARRIAGE. The age at which young couples are allowed to marry or have intercourse is one social control on the number of children. If people were free to have sex as soon as they were biologically capable of producing children and were encouraged to

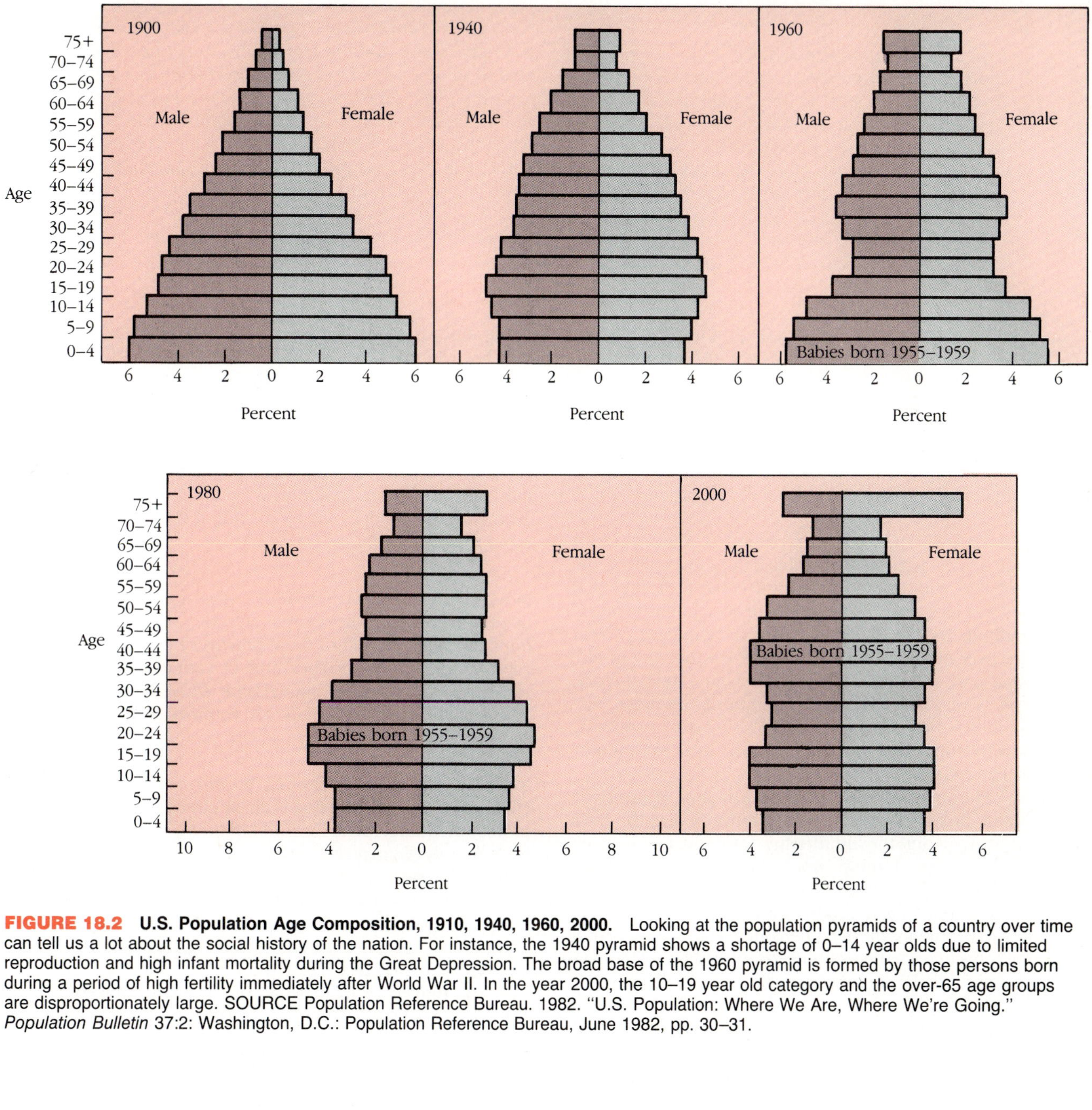

FIGURE 18.2 U.S. Population Age Composition, 1910, 1940, 1960, 2000. Looking at the population pyramids of a country over time can tell us a lot about the social history of the nation. For instance, the 1940 pyramid shows a shortage of 0–14 year olds due to limited reproduction and high infant mortality during the Great Depression. The broad base of the 1960 pyramid is formed by those persons born during a period of high fertility immediately after World War II. In the year 2000, the 10–19 year old category and the over-65 age groups are disproportionately large. SOURCE Population Reference Bureau. 1982. "U.S. Population: Where We Are, Where We're Going." *Population Bulletin* 37:2: Washington, D.C.: Population Reference Bureau, June 1982, pp. 30–31.

MARGARET SANGER: CONTRACEPTIVE CRUSADER

Incredible as it may now seem, only seventy-five years ago a brave woman spent time in prison so that it would be legal to limit family size. Margaret Sanger was a nurse working in a slum section of New York City. Recognizing the need for birth control information to be dispensed to the people she worked with, she searched in vain for physicians who would teach her about contraception so that she could teach her patients.

Contraception and any written words concerning the subject were against the law. The Puritan forefathers apparently had the same attitude toward limiting families as Thomas Malthus: the only acceptable method of not having children was not having sex. Sanger was willing to say that this did not make sense in the world she lived in. She traveled to Europe to learn about contraception and returned knowing more about it than most physicians in the United States, because they by law could not study the subject. When she opened a birth control clinic, she was promptly arrested and jailed. The government continued to harass her, but she prevailed against them and ultimately saw birth control information become legal through her efforts.

continue until death, they would produce many more children. Most societies have some form of marriage, however, and restrict the time of marriage (see Chapter 13). For instance, in Europe during the last century, a gentleman would not think of marrying until he had "prospects"—a good job or an inheritance with which he could support a family. In New Guinea a productive manioc garden often served the same purpose.

CONTRACEPTION. Contraception is another factor that affects fertility. The Bible refers to "spilling the seed," or withdrawal, as a contraceptive technique that has had long use. In one survey of ancient birth control methods the Greek writer Aetius recommends, "Wear the liver of a cat in a tube on the left foot . . . or else wear part of the womb of a lionness in a tube of ivory. This is very effective." A later authority, Soranus, recommends holding one's breath during sex or sneezing and having a cold drink immediately after sex (quoted in Petersen, 1974).

The most commonly used birth control measures today, besides sterilization and abortion, are the birth control pill and the intrauterine device (IUD) (Watson, 1982). Both of these innovations differ from other methods in that they require no special preparation when intercourse is desired. Condoms (sheaths used to cover the penis during intercourse) are an older but still effective method of birth control; they were originally made of animal skins or fine linen and were one of the first products made of latex rubber when it was invented in the 1800s. Concern about the side effects of birth control pills and IUDs, coupled with the fear of AIDS and the refinement of condoms, has recently led to their increasing use as a birth control method.

SOCIETAL ATTITUDES TOWARD FAMILY SIZE. Some societies encourage large families and discourage contraception, whereas others value small families. These attitudes change over time within one society, too. For example, in the United States until fairly recently a large family was thought to be a happy, well-adjusted one. Today, small families are the rule and large families are often looked upon with disdain. Some societies have institutionalized these beliefs concerning family size—for example, by offering money to individuals who are voluntarily sterilized, as the government of India does, or by making it illegal to have more than one child, as China has.

INFANTICIDE AND ABORTION. Abortion and infanticide, the killing of newborns, are other social limitations on fertility. Both of these practices have been accepted in different societies and at various times. In some primitive societies infants born while the mother is still nursing another infant are routinely left to die. Most of these societies have severe protein shortages, and the mother's protein intake would not allow her to be able to produce enough nourishment for both children; rather than having both children face a severe protein deficiency, which could kill them or leave both permanently damaged, the family decides to nourish only one. One tribe in Kenya, which depends upon camel hide for sustenance and can only support a fixed number of members, routinely kills all boys born on Wednesdays as one method of keeping their population size stable (Petersen, 1974).

Abortion is an increasingly used means of social control, in such diverse nations as Japan and Hungary, where it is readily available and subsidized by the government. Japan's population was growing so fast after World War II that the government made abortion legal to reduce certain birth defects, to safeguard the life of the mother, and for families suffering economic hardship. By 1958 there were 682 abortions per 1,000 live births in Japan. The birth rate fell from 34.3 in 1947

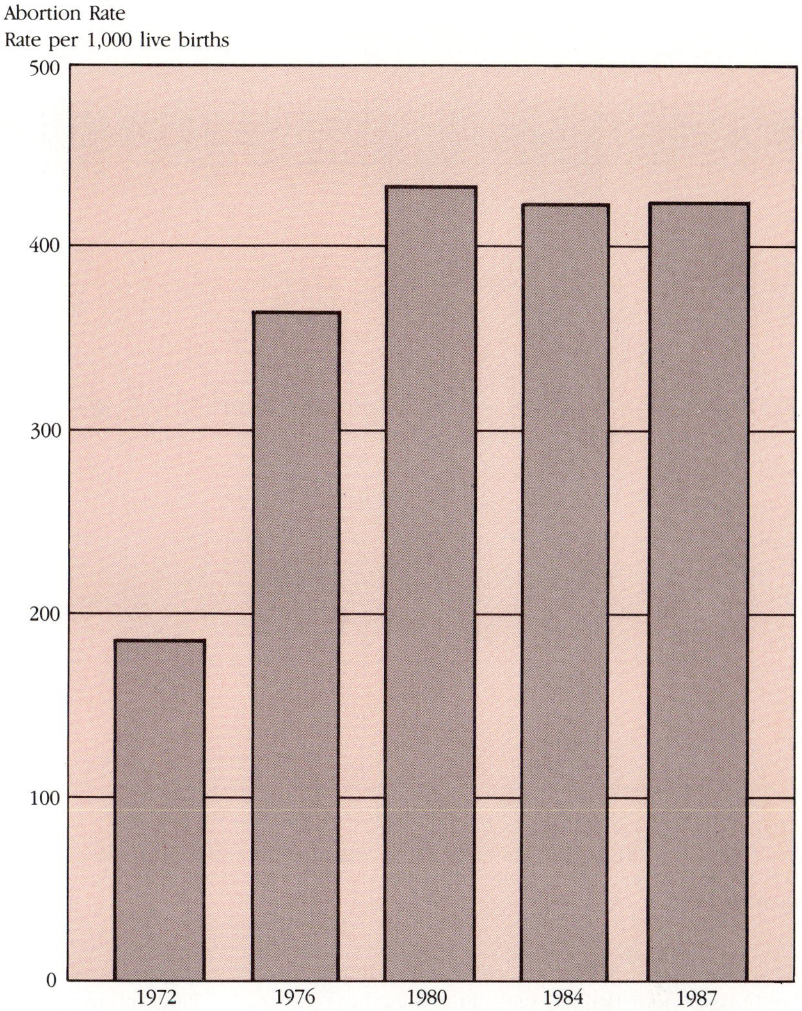

FIGURE 18.3 The legalization of abortions greatly increased the rate of abortions in the United States during the 1970s and 1980s, and consequently reduced the overall fertility and population growth. SOURCE U.S. Bureau of the Census, 1987. *Statistical Abstract of the United States, 1987*, 107th ed. Washington, D.C.: Government Printing Office.

to 17.2 in 1957, an unprecedented 50 percent drop in only ten years (Muramatsu, 1960). In Hungary the number of abortions in 1969 exceeded the number of live births (Heer, 1975). In the United States, the number of abortions has risen steadily since the procedure was legalized in 1972 (see Figure 18.3). Physicians now abort 1.5 million pregnancies per year, meaning that about 30 percent of all pregnancies terminate by abortion (U.S. Bureau of the Census, 1987).

MORTALITY

The ***crude mortality rate*** *is the number of deaths per 1,000 people in one year.* The crude mortality rate is the most common measure of mortality, but demographers also measure other mortality rates important to understanding population change. The age-specific mortality rate, for instance, gives a much clearer picture of exactly who dies when. The ***age-specific mortality rate*** *measures the number of deaths per 1,000 people in certain age groups.* If much of a population's mortality takes place between ages 40 and 45, the society is probably a primitive one that has a low life expectancy at birth. ***Life expectancy at birth*** *refers to the number of years a child can expect to live, on the average, when he or she is born.*

The ***infant mortality rate*** *is the ratio of deaths of children under 1 year of age in a given year to the total number of live births in that year.* Americans think of the United States as the most advanced country in the world in terms of medical care, but its infant mortality rate is only seventh highest in the world (see Figure 18.4). In most other developed nations the state controls and finances medical care regardless of the patient's ability to pay. American poor people have less access to quality medical care because medical care is still largely part of the private sector. As we saw in

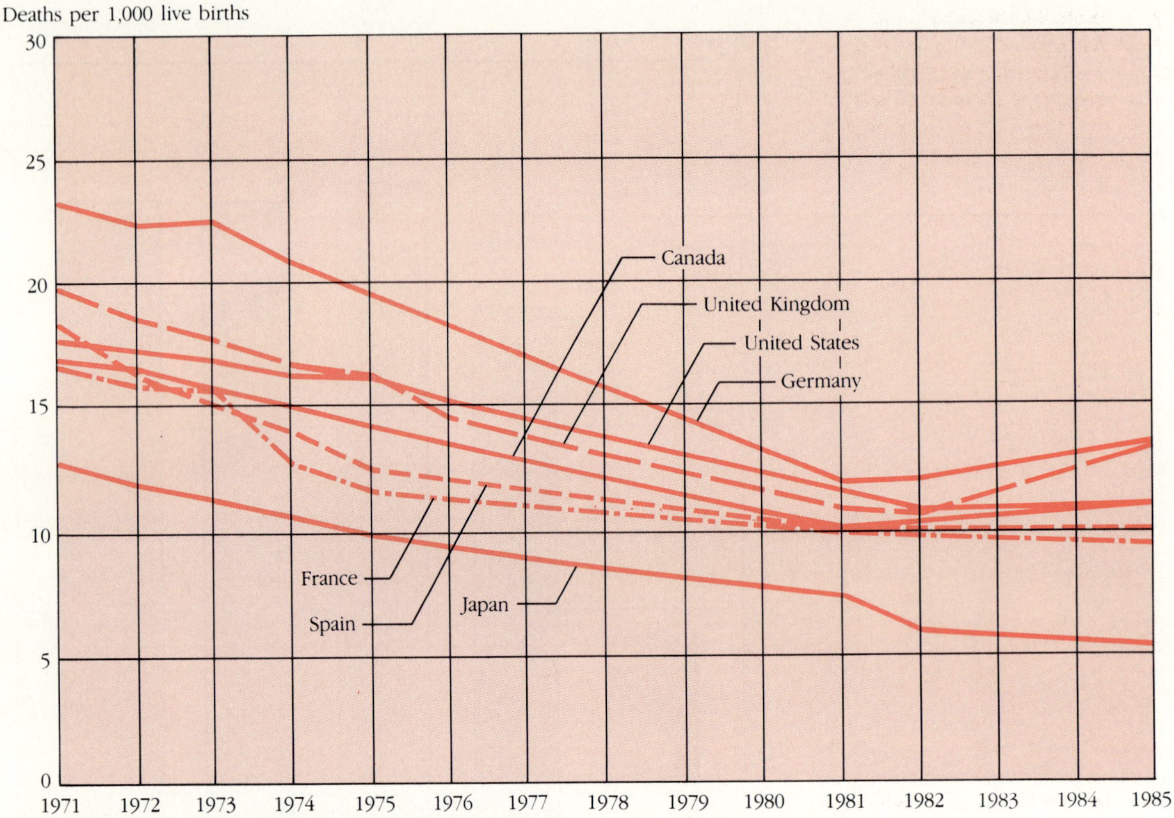

FIGURE 18.4 The Infant Mortality Rates, Selected Countries: 1971–1985. SOURCE U.S. Bureau of the Census. 1980. *Social Indicators III.* Washington, D.C.: Government Printing Office, p. 89; U.S. Bureau of the Census, 1987, p. 57.

Chapter 8, most babies who die in the United States are born to poor families with limited medical care.

The average life expectancy in the United States in 1900 was 47 years. In 1985 it was 75 years. More people live through their 60s today, and the proportion of people who reach age 80 has risen. Life expectancy has risen because more people are living through their 60s (Statistical Abstract, 1987).

War may have a great, although temporary, effect on the mortality of a nation. For instance, Russia had a mortality rate of 53 per 1,000 in 1942, compared to a rate of 18 per 1,000 normally (Biraben, 1958). During the siege of Leningrad, 1 million of the 3 million residents of the city died of starvation and disease. Twenty-five million Russian adults died between 1941 and 1945. Russian women rose to positions of importance after World War II partly because so many Russian men had died during the two world wars that there were not enough men to fill the usually male-dominated positions.

Social class is a variable that also affects mortality. Lower classes have a shorter life expectancy than higher classes due to a combination of factors that include poorer food and shelter and inadequate medical care.

MIGRATION

Migration, *the relatively permanent movement of persons over a significant distance,* can be an important factor in the population growth or decline of an area. Americans tend to think of migration chiefly as a way of adding to a nation's population, because the United States from 1880 to today has been the destination for one of the largest mass immigrations ever recorded. *The people who leave an area are* ***emigrants*** *from the area. The people who enter an area are* ***immigrants*** *to the area. The* ***crude migration rate*** *is expressed as the number of emigrants or immigrants per 1,000 people in an area.*

Two factors influence migration: push, or reasons for people to leave an area; and pull, or reasons for people to come to a new area. Europe in the nineteenth century was experiencing food shortages and the beginnings of crowding, both push factors. The United States offered unclaimed land, a democratic government, and freedom of opportunity, strong pull factors.

TYPES OF MIGRATION. William Petersen has described several types of migration, divided according to reasons for changing residence. The first is *primitive migration,* including tribes that move when they cannot cope with a change in their environment, such as drought or hurricanes. This category also includes hunting and gathering and herding tribes that must remain on the move to secure food for themselves and their livestock. These types of migration can be thought of as "flights from the land" (Petersen, 1974).

Migration can also be *impelled,* or strongly suggested, by means of penalties for nonconformance, or it can be forced, when no choice is offered. People who left Germany when the anti-Jewish laws were passed there in 1938 were impelled migrants. African slaves were brought to the United States through forced migration. These types of migration can be thought of as flights from the state or displacement by the state.

The United States was populated largely through *free migration.* Free migrants usually move in order to better themselves or their families. They are not restricted as to where or when they can go in search of a better life. Most free migrants are teenagers or young adults who stand to benefit from changing their environment because they have many years before them (Petersen, 1974).

After a few people leave one country for another through free migration, their friends and families may want to follow them. When this becomes an accepted practice, and many people are immigrating, *mass migration* occurs (Yaukey, 1985). Mass immigration occurred from Sweden to the United States between 1860 and 1870. Many Swedes had come to the United States and settled in the rich farmlands of the northern Plains, especially Minnesota. They formed American–Swedish communities, and wrote home to friends about their new lives. The people remaining in Sweden gradually learned the customs of the new country, so that when they finally emigrated from Sweden, they already felt somewhat at home in their new environment.

The years between the world wars represent a transition from premodern to modern migration (Yaukey, 1985). During this time, massive free migration declined to almost nothing and the beginnings of large forced migrations were apparent. For example, millions of Jews fled Germany during Hitler's rise to power in the 1930s (Weller and Bouvier, 1981).

Since the war, free migration has not stopped altogether, but has been supplanted for the most part by forced migration. For example, the partition of India and Pakistan in 1947 caused 14 million Hindus and Moslems to leave their countries. Millions of Chinese left their homeland after the Communist revolution there in 1949. The founding of Bangladesh in 1971 forced many migrations, again into India and Pakistan. The Cuban revolution brought thousands of migrants to the United States (United Nations, 1979).

The major effect of this shift in migration patterns in modern times has been the increase of the pace of migration from the less developed regions to the more developed regions (Yaukey, 1985). Today, for instance, Europe has become a net importer of migrants, primarily from less developed regions, whereas Latin America has become a net exporter of people, primarily to the more developed regions. Observors note also that temporary migration, refugee migration, and illegal migration are increasing at least as rapidly as traditional migration, which assumes a permanent move from one country to another (Kritz and Keely, 1981). These changes make for an entirely different migration picture for modern society than existed in premodern times.

Population control? Widespread adoption of abortion has significantly reduced population growth, but opponents liken this practice to the Holocaust. *(Photo courtesy the Michigan Daily)*

THE FUNDAMENTAL SCIENTIFIC LAWS OF DEMOGRAPHY

Political scientist Ross Baker has recently attempted what every sensible demographer knows is impossible: creation of infallible scientific laws for demography to provide a framework for predicting current population trends. The laws he has formulated must be taken with a grain of salt:

1. *The First Law of Thermo-Demographics:* Bodies are attracted by hot places and repelled by cold ones.
2. *The Second Law of Demographic Directionality:* A body that has headed West tends to remain at West.
3. *The Law of Supply-Side Senility:* The elderly population grows in direct proportion to increases in Social Security benefits.
4. *The First Law of Bio-Demographics:* Bodies tend to reproduce themselves in direct proportion to the availability of two-bedroom town houses.
5. *The Coyote State Corollary:* All things being equal, South Dakota will always lose population.

SOURCE Ross Baker. 1982. *American Demographics*. vol. 4, no. 1.

IMMIGRATION AND THE UNITED STATES

Immigration into the United States was virtually unlimited until after World War I, with the peak years being between 1900 and 1920. During these first two decades of this century, many Americans wished to impose severe limitations on the number of southern and eastern Europeans who could enter this country. Several bills were passed, but vetoed by presidents, which would have required, for immigrant status, literacy tests designed to keep out those whom this group considered "undesirable" (Glazer, 1985).

In 1917, Congress passed a law that excluded or deported aliens holding certain political beliefs and stopped all immigration from China and Japan. In 1921, Congress limited immigration from Europe to an annual total of 3 percent of the number of people already here from each European country. (See Figure 18.5.)

The immigration law was updated several times until 1965, when a new act was passed that abandoned the quota system entirely. This new law brought the largest wave of immigration since the turn of the century, with most of the new citizens from Third World countries, especially Asia and Latin America, rather than from Europe (Adams, 1983). (See Figure 18.6). The diversity of backgrounds of the newcomers has and undoubtedly will continue to enrich and expand the culture of the United States (Morrow, 1985).

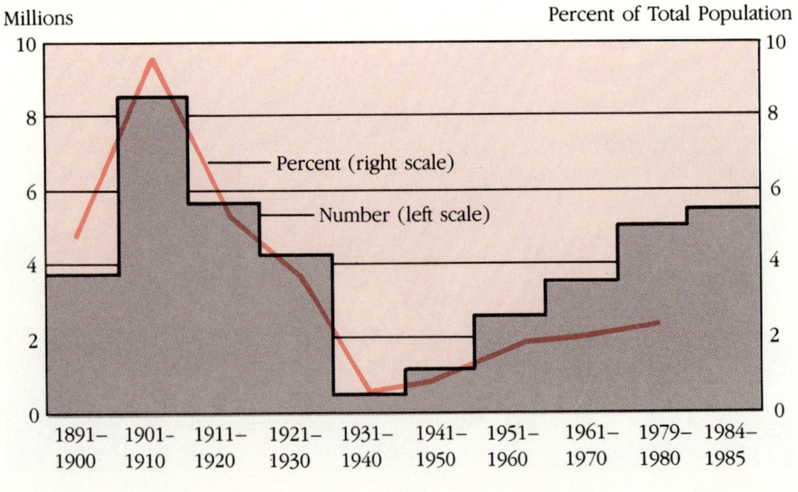

FIGURE 18.5 Immigrants Admitted 1891–1985 to the United States. This chart shows the drop in immigration after Congress limited immigration in 1921. SOURCE U.S. Bureau of the Census. 1976, 1987; *Social Indicators II.* Washington, D.C.: Government Printing Office, U.S. Bureau of the Census 1983, p. 88.

FIGURE 18.6 Change in Composition of the Immigrant Population to the United States by Country of Origin. At the turn of the century, the overwhelming majority was from Europe. Today, the majority is from either Mexico or Canada, with Asia a close second. SOURCE Adams, 1983.

Reactions to the new group are mixed. Recent surveys show that 66 percent of Americans believe that the present number of legal immigrants is too high and should be more strictly limited. The same percentage, however, agreed that the United States should take in people who are being persecuted in their homelands (Friedrich, 1985). Whatever the reactions, however, the growth in Third World migration has permanently changed the face of America.

What Is the Malthusian Theory of Population?

One of the first social scientific attempts to explain population trends such as those Baker is satirizing was by Thomas Malthus, born into a rich English family in 1766. Malthus became a minister and later in his life returned to the seminary where he had done his undergraduate work to teach there until his death. He was the first professor of political economy in England, and he made a great contribution to understanding economics and population.

Malthus' most important work was really seven books. He published the first, *Essay on the Principle of Population,* in 1798, when he was 32, and spent the rest of his life studying and refining the theories it presented. Each time he felt it to be substantially changed he produced a new edition. Seven editions of the essay were published, the last after he died in 1872.

Malthus' basic thesis was relatively simple. He suggested that population, without any external controls, would double once every generation, thus increasing geometrically as 2, 4, 8, 16, 32, 64, and so forth.

Malthus suggested the existence of "preventive checks" on population, which could occur before overpopulation occurred. These include postponing marriage or sexual intercourse and practicing "moral restraint" (abstinence in sexual relations). Because Malthus was a devoutly religious man, he believed birth control and abortion were abominations before God. He therefore called on people threatened with overpopulation to abstain from sexual relations in order to save the society.

Malthus believed that postponing sexual gratification could be useful to society in another way, also. If a man had to wait for sexual gratification until he could own land, have a bride price, or support a family, his sexual energy would drive him to work especially hard to reach that goal.

FIGURE 18.7 Components of Population Change. Selected Years: 1930–2000. The similarity between the curves for "births" and "net change" reveals the fact that fertility rates explain population change better than changes in death or migration rates during this era. SOURCE U.S. Bureau of the Census. 1980. *Social Indicators III.* Washington, D.C.: Government Printing Office.

Malthus noted that food supply increased only arithmetically, as 1, 2, 3, 4, 5, and so on. Therefore, "in two centuries the population would be to the means of subsistence as 256 to 9; in three centuries as 4,096 to 13, and in two thousand years the difference would be almost incalculable" (Malthus, 1872). This lack of subsistence is the last of what Malthus called *positive checks* on population, the others being such factors as war, disease, and "excesses."

Malthus saw a connection between the uppermost level of subsistence and population size. When a primitive population grows to the limit that the land can support, the group may face famine and disease and may war over scarce resources. Malthus explained that positive checks lowered the size of the population until the land could again accommodate the number. (See Figure 18.8.)

The case of Ireland and the potato is a good example of Malthusian theory. Potatoes were introduced into Ireland from the New World in 1785; by 1800 they were the country's basic food. At least partly because people were fed well, Ireland gradually became overpopulated. In 1846 the growing environment in Ireland was poor for potatoes and was especially good for certain potato pests. Thus, the famous Irish Potato Famine began, in which thousands died of starvation

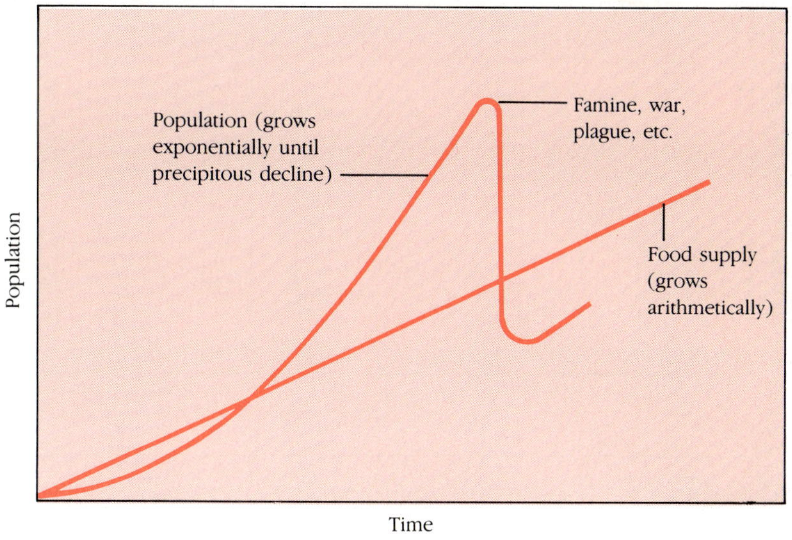

FIGURE 18.8 **Changes That Occur in Populations According to Malthus's Theory of Positive Checks on Population Growth.**

and disease and hundreds migrated to other countries before the population stabilized again at a number the island could manage to support.

Eighteenth-century England provides another example. Here, the price of wheat was strongly correlated to the marriage rate. When wheat was scarce, the price was driven up and the poor had little food. With little food and no jobs, few people chose to marry and have children. The population would therefore level off, and the price of wheat would drop as demand lowered. This encouraged farmers to plant more land and hire more workers. When the poor were given these farm jobs, they would marry and produce children until the population grew to the point where wheat was again scarce and the price again was high. This circular chain could be affected by voluntary sexual abstinence, according to Malthus.

Some researchers have respected and refined Malthus' ideas, and some challenge their validity for modern societies. Marx, for example, stated that there was no universal law of population, but that population was related to social and economic conditions in the society: Overpopulation existed only in capitalist society, because in a socialistic one, the economy would always have room for more workers (Nam and Philliber, 1984). Other researchers point out cases in which Malthus' theory appears not to explain population change—for instance, in slowing growth in developed countries (Piotrow, 1980). Nevertheless, Malthus is the forerunner of serious consideration of the cause-and-effect relationships between population and the food source. His work laid the foundation for the scientific analysis of demographic change in the demographic transition theory.

What Is the Demographic Transition Theory?

The demographic transition theory presents another, more modern, view of population growth. *As nations develop from an agricultural base to an industrial base, their populations appear to follow a somewhat predictable pattern known as the* ***demographic transition.*** This pattern of development from an agricultural to an industrial base consists of three basic stages, correlating with the level of economic development: primitive, developing, and industrial.

Stage one, the primitive society, is characterized by high birth rates and high death rates. Many children die in infancy, and few people reach old age. A high birth rate is needed to replace the dying.

Stage two, where many of the underdeveloped countries are found, has a high birth rate and low death rate. Modern advances in medical treatment and food production allow many people to survive, but custom and cultural pressures maintain a high birth rate. The population in stage two grows very rapidly.

By state three, industrialization has begun, more people live in cities, and children are no longer an economic asset to most families. On farms every child is a potential worker, but in cities children contribute little to the economic well-being of the family until they are out of school. Furthermore, there are more opportunities for women to work in jobs outside the home in an industrial society, which may decrease women's desire to have more children. The birth rate falls and meets the mortality rate, bringing about a stable population size again. This stable population is character-

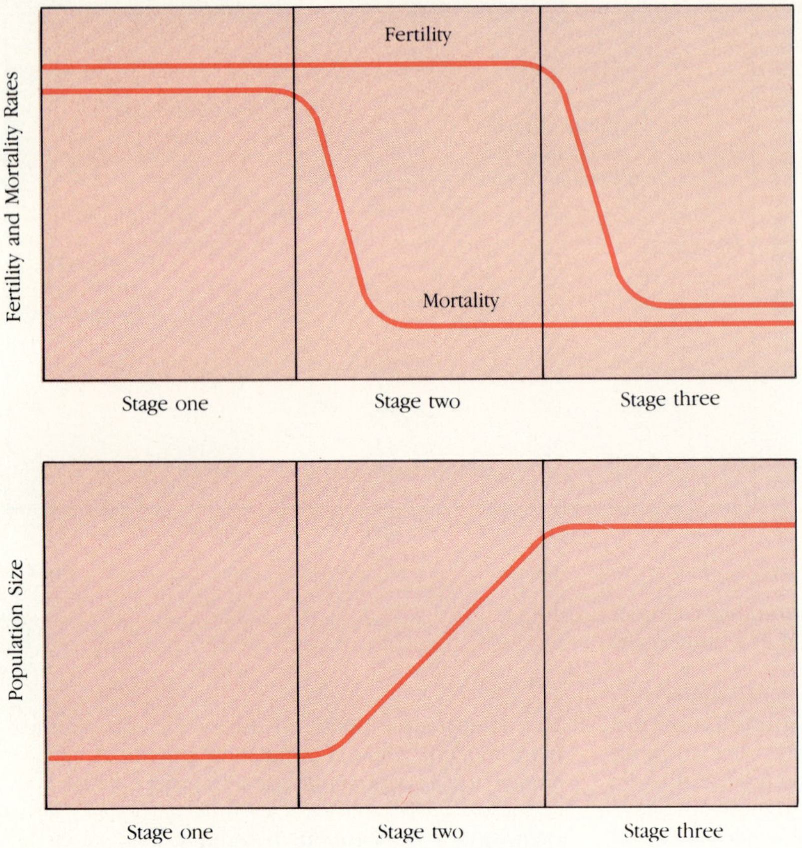

FIGURE 18.9 Population Growth during the Demographic Transition Stages. Note that in Stage 2, when fertility is still high but mortality is declining, population growth leaps.

ized by low fertility and low mortality, instead of the high fertility and high mortality found in stage one. (See Figure 18.9.)

The populations of Europe and the United States appear to have closely followed the predicted pattern of the demographic transition. Some developing nations, however, are not quite so predictable in their growth. Some researchers have even hypothesized a "new" demographic transition that fits today's picture more closely (Kirk, 1971). One variable that can change the pattern is economic growth of a country. With high fertility and low mortality, the population has a high proportion of children. Children contribute essentially nothing to the economy, but they use disproportionately high amounts of resources in food, clothing, and time. It may be difficult, therefore, for a country to go from stage two to stage three, because so many resources are supporting children rather than increasing industrialization and producing more jobs. In this cycle, less industrialization forces the population to rely upon agriculture, again making it desirable to have more children to work in the fields. Some countries have broken the cycle at some point and risen into relative affluence through industrialization, but others have not.

How Is the Population Exploding?

In this century the world population picture has changed dramatically from one that encourages reproduction to one in which governments reward people for nonreproduction or sterilization. In the seventeenth century, plagues and famines regularly decimated populations, and governments encouraged people to reproduce as protection against extinction. Colonies needed to be populated by the imperial powers, in order to keep them under control of the mother country. To this end, shiploads of women, often from correctional facilities, were sent to marry soldiers stationed in the colonies. Soldiers who would not marry were punished by their officers. In England, when the lacemaking industry began, so many workers were needed to produce enough lace to meet the large demand that virtually all children were forced to work, and parents were fined for keeping their children out of factories. Obviously, people were at a premium.

Today, most governments spend time and money trying to decide how best to stabilize their populations at optimal levels. India, for example, doubles its population about every thirty years. The average family has 5.2 children, and the birth rate has not slowed significantly, in spite of government efforts in this direction. Because improved medical care has cut mortality rates, the overall population growth is up slightly to 2.23 percent annually. Although sterilization is suggested after a family has three children, the popular saying "one son is no sons" still has force in the culture. Most couples rely on their sons to take care of them in their old age, because they have no social security or other pension plans. They therefore delay birth control until they have enough sons. Observors feel that even implementing a government social security program would not change this practice, because Indians do not trust that their government would take care of them as their own sons would (Freed and Freed, 1985).

Why has the world moved so quickly from being short of people to being threatened with a surplus? Many factors account for the difference, including disease and pest control, the end of large-scale infanticide, and perhaps surprisingly, the growing use of the potato as a staple food.

Inoculation against diseases that had formerly killed large numbers of people and the availability of modern medical techniques for treating infants and children have added millions to the populations of many countries. Developed countries have given underdeveloped countries drugs and other means of extending their people's lifespan without at the same time giving them the means to produce more food or the conviction that small families are optimal. For example, the widespread use of DDT to kill the mosquitoes that transmit malaria saved millions of lives in tropical countries. The resulting increase in population without greater food production, however, has resulted in food shortages.

One researcher thinks that the end of large-scale infanticide may be another reason for population increase (McKeown, 1977). Thomas McKeown points out that the Greeks and Romans often destroyed unwanted female children as a way to keep the population within a manageable size; they would later adopt a son if they needed heirs. In the Far East peasants eliminated children who would place a burden on the family, terming it "thinning the rows," as they thinned rows of vegetables. Even in England a much higher proportion of babies than would be expected were reported dead by being "laid over," or smothered, while the mother was asleep. In the ninteenth century the church began to pay attention to infanticide as a major social issue, and it became a serious crime, often punishable by death. Laws and church policies, coupled with a change in public opinion, may have had major consequences on population size.

Another factor McKeown emphasizes is the use of the potato as a staple food (1977). Until the potato was brought from the Americas, Europeans depended on grains for their staple food: bread. Grains are highly susceptible to drought, rain, cold, and heat. A poor harvest brought starvation and malnutrition. The potato is a hardy, easily stored vegetable that can weather severe conditions and still remain a good source of food. With the introduction of the potato, Europe became less dependent on grain, and the number of deaths from famine and disease declined.

THE WORLD SITUATION

Many people believe Malthus' theory is about to be proven true again, but with new and more complicated factors involved than the simple relationship between food and population size. Modern demographers measure change in population through ***growth rate,*** which is *the number of people both added to and subtracted from a population through birth, migration, and death, expressed as a percentage of the total population.* Growth rates can appear small and still have a tremendous effect on a population. For instance, a population growing at only 1 percent per year will double in size in only 70 years.

Because of its obvious implications for societies, demographers often use this ***doubling time,*** or *number of years for a group to double in size,* as a basic measure of population growth. For instance, we know that every day 200,000 new babies are born, but this fact does not describe the entire world picture to us. When demographers tell us, however, that in 1985 the population of the earth totaled over 4.8 billion and was doubling every 35 years, we have a stronger sense of what we as a world society are facing (Eberstadt, 1976; U.S. Bureau of Census, 1987, p. 813).

The history of world population is summarized by Paul Ehrlich in his famous book, *The Population Bomb* (1968, p. 18):

> It has been estimated that the human population of 6000 B.C. was about 5 million people, taking perhaps 1 million years to get there from 2.5 million. The population did not reach 500 million until almost 8,000 years later—about 1650 A.D. This means it doubled roughly once every 1,000 years or so. It reached 1 billion people about 1850, doubling in some 200 years.

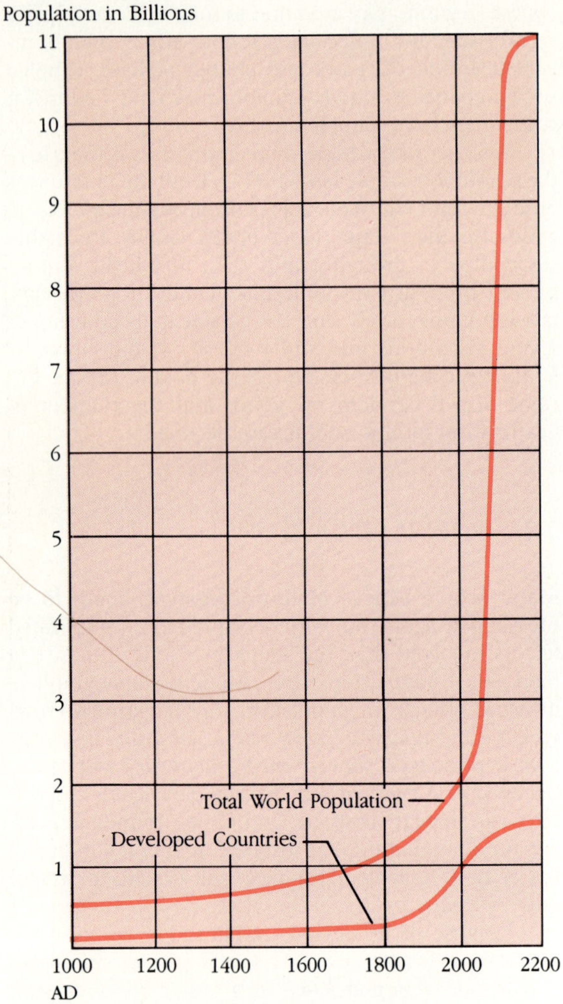

FIGURE 18.10 The difference in population growth of developed countries that have stabilized and that of the world as a whole. SOURCE Adapted from Thomas W. Merrick, "World Population in Transition," *Population Bulletin*, 41:2. Washington, D.C.: Population Reference Bureau, January 1988 reprint, p. 4.

> It took only eighty years or so for the next doubling, as the population reached 2 billion around 1930.

As Ehrlich prophesied, world population reached 4 billion in 1975, this time taking only 45 years to double rather than eighty. By 1990, it will be 5 billion (Brown and Jacobson, 1986). This rapid modern growth is shown graphically in Figure 8.10.

The rapid growth rates that now account for the biggest gains in population occur in the less developed countries in the world, which make up more than 75 percent of the world's population. (See Figure 18.11.) The population doubling time in the less developed countries averages thirty-three years, as opposed to ninety-six years for the United States at the 1980 rate. Nearly 40 percent of the people of the less developed countries are under 15 years old, a fact that suggests even more future growth. This means that, in order to avoid Malthus' "positive checks," these countries should produce at least twice as much food, shelter, and clothing in the coming thirty-three years, a challenging goal for countries that even today are facing shortages.

Fortunately, population growth in the less developed countries slowed down in the 1970s, in spite of new medical techniques and new pesticides (Brown, 1976). Between 1970 and 1986 the annual rate of world population growth fell from 2.0 percent to 1.7 percent. This drop means that the population is gaining 5 million fewer people each year, and the world population will double in forty years instead of in thirty-three years.

One major factor in reduced population growth is starvation. The price of wheat has doubled since the 1960s, and many of the poorer people of the world can no longer afford to eat. It appears that mortality rates among the very young and the very old are increasing, a consequence to be expected, because their lives are more easily affected by improper nourishment. People who own some land and can produce their own food suffer less from food shortages than do those who are dependent on others for their source of food. However, in most Third World countries, the number of rural families who are landless is growing (Brown and Jacobson, 1986).

Governments have also effectively slowed the growth rates of their populations; China is an example. In 1983, the population of China was estimated as 1,023,300,000, having grown by 15 million people since the 1982 census. This puts it well ahead of the second-largest nation numerically, India, with a population of "only" 730 million, and the third and fourth—the Soviet Union with 272 million and the United States with 234 million (Population Reference Bureau, 1983).

Presently one of every five persons on the earth is Chinese, and although China's population is growing at an annual rate of 1.4 percent, well below the 1.7 world average, the Chinese government has instituted strong measures to slow growth even farther (United Nations, 1973; Population Reference Bureau, 1983). These include providing social services and fulfilling people's basic needs, implementing an authoritarian family planning program, and at times forcing abortion for families that already have two children (Brown, 1976; Population Reference Bureau, 1983).

Fifteen million couples in China have pledged to have only one child, a fact that is all the more remarkable considering the strong cultural bias against female children. In return for this pledge, however, couples

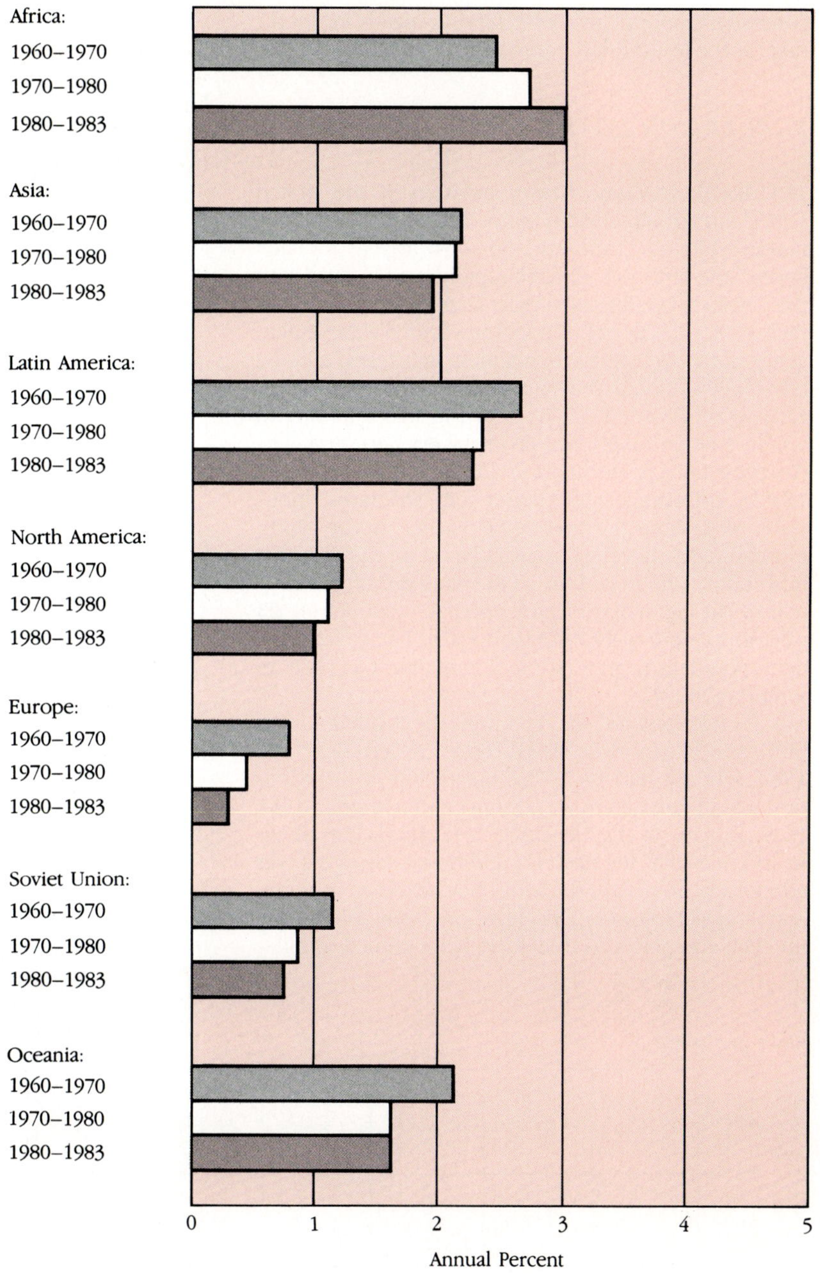

FIGURE 18.11 Annual Growth Rate of the World Population, by Continent, 1960–1983. Because of differences in population growth rates, the world is becoming more African, Asian, and Latin, as it becomes less American, Oceanian, European, and Russian. SOURCE U.S. Bureau of the Census, 1983, p. 852.

receive "only-child glory certificates" which entitle them to such benefits as free medical care and school tuition for their child, monthly cash bonuses or work points, preferential treatment in housing, and extra old-age pensions. In addition, their only child will receive preferential job treatment when he or she is grown. In contrast, families who have a third child have their monthly wages reduced by 10 percent, must remain in housing meant for a two-child family, and are charged for the extra child's rations.

Brown (1986) suggests that other countries concerned about their population size could follow China's example, providing family planning in cooperation with satisfying basic needs, educating the populace, offering career choices for women, and creating economic incentives for small families. Unless they do, he concludes, more people will starve to death in the future, as the Malthusian positive check remains in force.

POPULATION IN THE UNITED STATES

THE BABY BOOM. The population of the United States has grown steadily since the beginning of the nation's history. During the post-World War II "baby boom" the birth rate climbed rapidly, and in the 1950s the country experienced a great leap in population (see Figure 18.12). The baby boom represented a movement away from "spinsterhood, childless marriages, and the one-child family, and a bunching together of births at early ages" (Westoff, 1976, p. 55). It caused a flurry of building new schools, training new teachers, and constructing new living quarters for families (see Figure 18.13). Encouraged by government programs, thousands of students prepared to be teachers in the 1960s, estimating the need for teachers based on the idea that birth rates would continue as they had during the baby boom. The elementary school population grew from 23 million in 1950 to 37 million in 1970. The college student population grew from 3.2 million in 1960 to 9 million in 1975.

Fortunately for the country, the United States' birth rate fell by over 40 percent between 1957 and 1984, when it was 14.7. This means that the elementary school population was just over 30 million in 1984 (U.S. Bureau of the Census, 1987). Hindsight allows us to know that the need for additional educators was temporary, an insight that does not help the education majors and professors who have not been able to find the teaching positions they have been trained to fill.

Because the baby boom's female children are now old enough to be mothers, and there are thus more women in the 14- to 49-years age group than there have been in decades, the United States may still have more population growth, even at the current average of 1.8 children per family. Annual birth rates have turned up slightly, from 3.1 million in 1973 to 3.9 million in 1987, and are expected to continue to rise sharply for some time. This should result in an increase in the school-age group and again create more jobs for teachers.

ZERO POPULATION GROWTH. If the present trend continues, the population of the United States should become stabilized at about 270 million in the middle of the next century. This stable state was labeled ***zero population growth (ZPG)*** by Kingsley Davis (Davis, 1967). *If two old people died for every two babies born, the population would remain the same.* Even with controlled fertility and no further decreases in mortality, the United States will not reach ZPG for at least sixty years, primarily because it has a young population. However, the United States has many more young, reproducing people than old, nonreproducing people. When the present reproducing generation becomes the old generation, if the birth rate remains stable at around 1.8 children per family, the population will be at the point of simply replacing itself. Once again, however, this prediction is based on current trends.

FACTORS IN STABILIZATION. Why has the birth rate in the United States fallen? One reason for the trend toward smaller families is the availability of in-

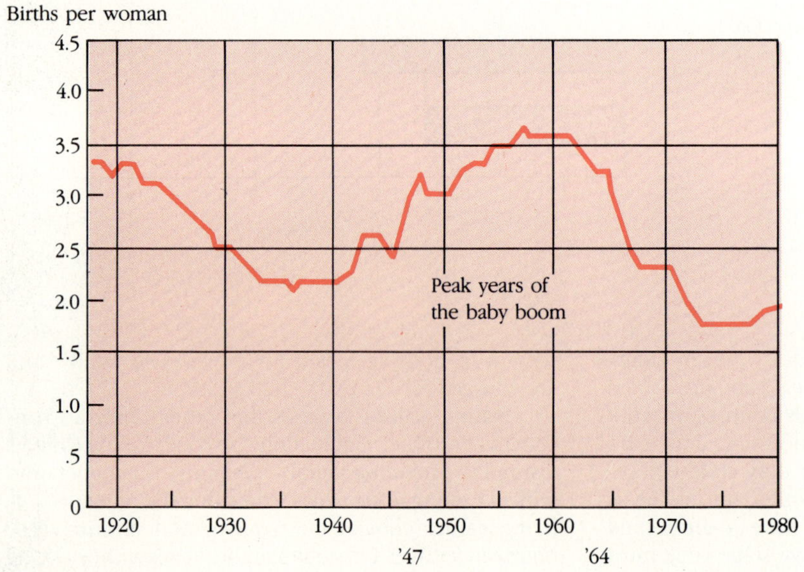

FIGURE 18.12 Total Fertility Rates for U.S. Women: 1917–1980. The well-known baby boom is clearly visible in this fertility graph. The boom appears between periods of reduced fertility during the Depression–World War II era and during the 1970s. SOURCE Population Reference Bureau Staff and Guest Experts [1982]. "U.S. population: Where We Are: Where We Are Going." *Population Bulletin*, vol. 37, no. 2.

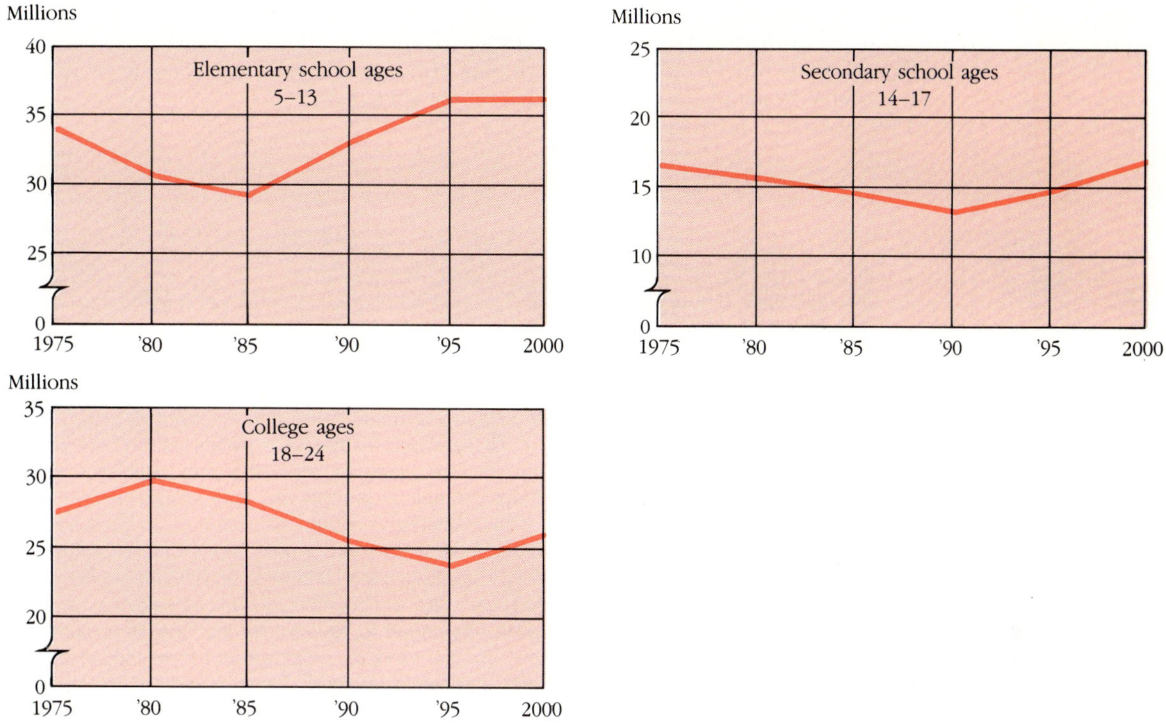

FIGURE 18.13 Projected U.S. School-Age Population: 1975–2000. The baby boom has dramatically affected the need for schools. The bottom chart reveals the decline in college youth following the 1970s peak resulting from the boom. A second "echo" boom results as the baby boom generation enters the traditional childrearing years, creating increased demand for elementary education beginning around 1985. SOURCE U.S. House of Representatives, Select Committee on Population. *Domestic Consequences of United States Population Change.* 95th Cong., 2d sess., 1978. Figure 11, p. 45.

expensive and effective birth control. Birth control devices have been known since before the existence of the written word, but only recently have they become so easy to use and so effective against pregnancy. In terms of fertility, they have another important characteristic: they must be stopped in order to conceive a child. Until now, something had to be done in order to *keep* from having a child. Today, in many cases something has to be done in order to *have* one. This transmits a strong sense of responsibility to the prospective parent. Most children of the future will be born because they were planned. Conversely, many people who would probably have raised and loved a child they did not plan to have now never have the child at all. The world may be about to accept contraception rather than conception as the normal state of being, a complete turnaround from the past (Westoff, 1976).

A second reason for the lower birth rate is that many people now have fewer children in order to maintain their economic status (Westoff, 1976). Most new parents today were raised in comparative prosperity. Their parents' standard of living rose as they grew, and they became used to having most material wants fulfilled. Their lives would change drastically if they had large families. The high and rising costs of raising a child make it difficult for most people to have a large family and continue to raise or even to maintain their standards of living. Most couples apparently choose to keep a house in the suburbs and to have only two children rather than move into a flat in the city and have four.

Another factor limiting population size has certainly been government and private encouragement to do so. Private and public groups such as ZPG, a national group whose purpose is to promote awareness of population problems, have sponsored ads, promotions, and television programs to make people aware of the world's future with and without population control. Many people who could afford more children are choosing not to have them because of their awareness of the issue.

Gains in women's rights may also be a factor. More women today have careers rather than "jobs," and they hesitate to interrupt their careers to raise children. The growing use of abortion and its legalization in most states is also associated with women's rights.

Approximately 1.5 million births are avoided through abortion every year (U.S. Bureau of Census, 1987).

The United States, then, is on its way toward zero population growth. Birth control is becoming more sophisticated and more easily available, and people are voluntarily limiting their families. The self-imposed limits have come about due to a combination of factors, including concern over loss of economic status and gains in women's rights.

CLOSE-UP on • *RESEARCH* •

Lester Brown and Jodi Jacobson on Our Demographically Divided World

The Researcher and the Setting

Lester Brown has devoted his career to bringing social scientific research findings to the attention of policymakers and the public. His intent is to alleviate worldwide social problems through the Worldwatch Institute, an independent nonprofit research organization created to identify and focus attention on global problems.

His study is an example of the *review essay,* in which the researcher gathers a set of related scientific works either to trace progress, to clarify findings, or to help guide future research or policy. In this case Brown attempts to summarize the major trends in world population growth as a guide to policymakers.

Brown's research is well-respected by both factions in the world population discussion, those who feel the world is doomed to destruction and those who are optimistic about its future. Because of Brown's dispassionate but thorough investigation of all the available research, Worldwatch Papers are almost universally accepted as truth in these issues.

The Researcher's Goal

Brown's goal in this work is to review the available data concerning population growth and potential ecological disaster in what he sees as the two halves of the world: that that has completed or nearly completed the demographic transition and that where rapid population growth is "beginning to overwhelm local life-support systems, leading to ecological deterioration and declining living standards" (p. 5). Brown organizes his study around the concepts of carrying capacity, food and income trends, rural landlessness, and conflict.

Theory and Concepts

Brown persuasively argues that the world is effectively divided in half. Forty years ago, countries were classified as developed (one-fifth) or developing (four-fifths). Brown suggests that today we should instead classify them according to whether their incomes are rising or falling and which direction they are likely to take in the future. As Brown theorizes (p. 7), "By this measure, polarized population growth rates are driving roughly half the world toward a better future and half toward ecological deterioration and economic decline."

Those countries that have completed the demographic transition are close to achieving zero population growth (.8 percent annual growth) and face a better future. Those that have failed to complete the transition still have high birth rates (2.5 percent annual growth) coupled with lowering death rates. They have been "unable to achieve the economic and social gains that are counted upon to reduce births," and their growth has begun to "overwhelm the local life-support systems" (p. 6). Although projections of their populations can reach astronomical heights, Brown points out that such projections "are unrealistic for the simple reason that life-support systems will begin to collapse before they materialize" (p. 9). In other words, both the researchers who see imminent disaster in terms of soaring population and those who are more optimistic are partially right, in Brown's view.

Research Design

Fewer rules guide the conduct of review-article research than exist to govern survey or experimental research. A scholar generally begins with a question and seeks all material relevant to the question through library searches. A good reviewer gives accurate summaries, significant criticism, and occasional new insights. Although the author of a review article seldom gathers data in the sense of making direct observations, many scientists see reviews as the most important forms of research and publication.

Findings

Brown finds divergent patterns in the four major variables he studied: carrying capacity, food and income trends, rural landlessness, and conflict.

Carrying capacity "focuses on interactions between a population, its activities, and the surrounding environment and highlights natural thresholds that might otherwise remain obscure" (p.11), from the viewpoint that the various support systems cannot readily be separated. For instance, "once the demand for fuelwood exceeds the sustainable yield of local forests, it not only reduces tree cover but also leads to soil erosion and land degradation. When grasslands deteriorate to where they can no longer support cattle, livestock herders often take to lopping foliage from trees, thus putting even more pressure on remaining tree cover. Both contribute to a loss of protective vegetation, without which both wind and water erosion of soil accelerates, leading to desertification—a sustained decline in the biological productivity of land" (p. 15).

Desertification is occurring in almost all of the overpopulated countries that Brown has studied, causing an "ecological transition" that is almost the reverse of the demographic transition and is virtually irreversible: (p. 16):

> In the first stage, expanding human demands are well within the sustainable yield of the biological support system. In the second, they are in excess of the sustainable yield but still expanding as the biological resource itself is being consumed. . . . In the final stage . . . the biological system collapses.

When nations reach the third stage, mass starvation occurs, the population size drops, and the process begins again.

Next Brown addresses the topic of food supply and income. He notes that between 1950 and 1973, the world economy was expanding everywhere, and grain production was growing over 3 percent per year. Since the 1973 oil price hike, coupled with soil erosion and desertification, Third World nations have been having difficulty feeding their own people, and much of their export earnings pays interest on external debts, causing a general lowering of average income. In the past, when populations grew, more land was cleared or found to feed them. By the middle of this century, the amount of new land for agriculture was diminished just as the population growth was accelerating due to lowered death rates. Especially in the Third World rural areas, people are facing landlessness, or the inability to own or rent land for growing their own food, and most of the land is concentrated in the hands of a few. "In Latin America, the most extreme case, it is not uncommon for 5 percent of the populace to own four-fifths of the farmland" (p. 23). The largest landless populations, however, are concentrated in South Asia, especially in India, where 44 million households will not have any land on which to grow their own sustenance by the year 2000.

Brown summarizes several recent efforts to study the relationship between population growth and social conflict. First, he notes that rapid population growth adds pressure to already saturated labor markets, while taxing the government's ability to provide services. Because rapidly growing populations are dominated by young people, educational systems are overburdened and competition between young workers for jobs is stiff. Conflict over land and water access is intense, because the competitors' lives may hang in the balance.

Political conflict may grow simply due to the decline in living standards and growing social unrest. As Brown summarizes the situation in Mexico, for instance (p. 28):

> An economic slowdown induced by rising external debt, rising numbers of unemployed youth, and a highly skewed income distribution seem certain to breed social tensions and increasing unrest. The wealthiest 10 percent of Mexicans receive 41 percent of total income; the poorest one-fifth, less than 3 percent. Real wages have declined at least one-fifth during the 1980s. Fiscal stringencies have forced the elimination of subsidies on tortillas, the cornmeal food staple.

Implications

Brown sees most Third World countries as caught in a demographic trap: returning to the first stage of the transition after their economies and environments deteriorate. The doubling of death rates in Africa since 1970 is a perfect example of this trap in action. If governments are to avoid this regression they must "forge ahead with all the energies at their disposal to slow and halt population growth" (p. 34).

Brown suggests imitating such nations as China, Thailand, and Cuba in lowering birth rate. The programs of these nations have in common "a committed leadership and locally designed programs," including such incentives as subsidies for small families and tremendous mass education efforts. Brown points out, however, that nations that are already facing possible decimation do not have the financial resources to mount such campaigns and suggests that nations like the United States, which has achieved slowed population growth and should stabilize soon, must support effective family-planning programs in the half of the world currently at risk.

Questions

1. Contributions of the United States toward lowering of birth rates in Third World countries have recently declined rather than increased. React to this situation.
2. Brown sees only one solution to the demographic trap: lowering the birth rate. Do you see any alternatives?
3. How might the concept of carrying capacity affect industrialized nations such as the United States?

SOURCE Lester R. Brown and Jodi L. Jacobson, 1986. "Our Demographically Divided World: Worldwatch Paper 74." Washington, D.C.: Worldwatch Institute.

What Are the Implications of Today's Population Trends?

ECOLOGY

With the world population doubling every forty years, people are using up more of the earth's resources and polluting more of its surface than ever before. The obvious question is: How long can this go on? What are the limits of population on this earth? How long can people ignore the other elements of the ecosystem without destroying it? These are questions that must be answered within a few decades.

*An **ecosystem** is a system of living organisms and their environment.* Any change in one organism of an ecosystem will involve the other organisms of that system as well. ***Ecology** is the study of ecosystems.* The study of interrelationships in ecological systems was originally done by biologists and zoologists. As it became apparent that human beings are affected by where they live and the conditions in their environment, and that human beings affect their environment by the ways they live, sociologists have become involved in the study of human ecology. ***Human ecology** is the study of the relationships of people to their ecosystem.* Decisions soon to be made concerning our ecosystem will depend on the knowledge and skills of both biological and social scientists.

Majesty? Junk cars mar the beauty of this view of a majestic mountain peak. Ecology addresses the relation of living organisms to their environment. (*EPA Documerica*)

POLLUTION

Every day the air receives over 200 million tons of gasses from factories, automobiles, smoking, and furnaces (Crandall, 1987). Cars, because they are the most numerous, are the biggest offenders. Toxic lead, primarily from automobile exhaust, has been released into the air in such quantities that it is being found in increasing amounts as far from population centers as the Greenland ice cap. Rates of respiratory disease are climbing steadily, especially in urban areas.

Between 1972 and 1985, industry, government, and consumers spent $632 billion to clean up America's air and water (Crandall, 1987). Even this amount of effort, however, has had limited effect, partly due to the fact that air monitors were often installed incorrectly or positioned improperly (Stanfield, 1985). Nationwide, the average airborne concentration of particulate matter, sulfur dioxide, and carbon monoxide fell by about one-third between 1976 and 1985. Nevertheless, smog is almost as bad most places as it was when the Clean Air Act was passed in 1970 (Crandall, 1987; Mosher, 1981).

In many areas, today's major air pollutant is a new one: ozone. Ozone smog is formed when pollutants such as auto emissions and house paint interact with heat and sunlight. Major cities across the country are afflicted with ozone pollution, and it is the only pollutant that still exceeds EPA standards in some areas (Knobelsdorff, 1986).

This ozone pollution is not to be confused with the earth's ozone layer, the layer of protective gas that surrounds the earth and protects its inhabitants from the sun's damaging ultraviolet rays, and which is also under attack by humans (Rheem, 1986).

Ozone is a form of oxygen with three atoms per molecule rather than two. It is formed through the action of sunshine on the upper atmosphere, and is routinely destroyed by natural chemical processes. Chemical pollution from the earth is in danger of changing the balance of the atmosphere such that more is destroyed than is naturally replaced (Cowen, 1986). Fluorocarbons, primarily from air conditioners, refrigerators, rigid and flexible foams, solvents, and aerosol propellants destroy ozone and may have created "holes" in the ozone layer.

Scientific monitoring shows a 3 percent drop in the ozone layer since 1975. A continuation of this trend would result in large numbers of additional skin cancer cases and other damage to plants, animals, and marine ecosystems (Rheem, 1986). Scientists have recently agreed to a new set of international standards for fluorocarbon use that should forestall such an occurrence.

Many lakes and streams no longer support fish or other wildlife. This break in the food chain affects the tiniest organisms as well as large animals that drink the water. In 1972 the Public Health Service cited over sixty American cities in which the water was not safe to drink (Ehrlich and Ehrlich, 1972).

Results of water-pollution controls are mixed. Only 11 percent of U.S. streams and 2 percent of lakes evaluated in 1982 were cleaner than they were in 1972. The amounts of bacteria borne by sewage have been cut almost in half since then, due primarily to 10,000 federally subsidized water-treatment plants. But industrial polluters and farm and city runoffs, which account for more than one-half of all water pollution, are still largely uncontrolled (Crandall, 1987).

Acid rain, caused by coal combustion in the industrial Midwest states, has left hundreds of lakes devoid of fish life. High-sulfur coal is plentiful in Illinois, Indiana, and Ohio, and factories and power plants that use it spew 28 million tons of sulfur oxides into the atmosphere every year (Krohe, 1984). Weather patterns cause the acid to be dropped primarily in the Northeast and Canada, producing acid lakes and damaging forests (Postel, 1984). Canada's former environment minister warned the United States concerning the situation, "You can't continue to dump on us the garbage that you are producing on your own property" (Vogel, 1987, p. 66).

Low-sulfur coals are more expensive, and thus undesirable from industry's point of view. The only other current alternative is to require the use of smokestack "scrubbers" to remove sulfur oxides from existing plants, as federal law now requires for new large plants. At a cost of $200 million per scrubber, however, the cost of reducing emissions by 8 million tons a year would be $40 billion by 1995 (Krohe, 1984). In spite of the cost, ten major Western nations have pledged themselves to reduce their sulfur dioxide output by almost one-third from 1985 to 1995. Thus far the United States has not joined their cause, but observers believe this must happen soon if the damage presently being done is to ever be reversed (Vogel, 1987).

The oceans are becoming polluted with the same metals and insecticides that affect the air and lakes, as well as with oil from offshore oil rigs, from tanker spills, and from refueling operations at sea. The oil may destroy entire populations of sea birds, fish, shellfish, and other sea animals. Oil has been found in shellfish months after they were exposed to spills. Because fish are often at the bottom of a food chain, the harmful effects of spilled oil could still be reaching human beings years after an accident. (Vogel, 1987).

Every year, 26,000 pounds of garbage per person is dumped on refuse heaps in the United States. The trash includes 7 million cars and one-half billion dollars' worth of package materials (Crandall, 1987). Burning this amount of trash would produce even more air pollution, but leaving it intact pollutes water supplies and attracts dangerous rats, roaches, and disease-carrying insects. HEW has labeled 94 percent of the nation's 12,000 dumps as "unacceptable."

Pesticides are another pollution concern. The uproar over mother's milk containing more DDT than cows' milk is allowed to contain has caused some women to reconsider nursing their children. We had been subjected to a constant bombardment of DDT from the environment—finding it on our fruits and vegetables and breathing it in the air. It is estimated that the United States sprayed more than 1 billion pounds of DDT into the air (Goldsmith, 1972).

Newer synthetic pesticides have proved almost as bad for human beings and the environment as DDT, and have created their own problems. For instance, pesticide sprayings often create vermin troubles where none existed before. Wiping out certain predators often allows others to grow in prominence. Natural methods of pest control, in a system of integrated pest management (IPW) devised by agricultural scientists, may be the least expensive and most viable alternative on the horizon. Such a plan would require massive education efforts, but would save acreage and lives (Dover, 1985).

Another environmental concern is the heat produced by using fossil fuels like oil and coal. Primitive societies used natural energy from the sun to grow their crops and to nourish their animals and fish. They used none of the earth's nonrenewable fossil fuels and produced only the amount of heat necessary to obtain food. Today, people burn more fuel and create more heat than ever before. Most people do not make, gather, or hunt their own food, so they use energy in other pursuits.

The accumulation of carbon dioxide in Earth's atmosphere that occurs as the result of burning these fossil fuels has caused what is termed a "greenhouse effect" (Schelling, 1984). This not only means a gradual raising of the earth's temperatures, but also a drop in rain and snowfall. The global warming trend coupled with thawing of polar ice caps could raise sea levels by 16 to 20 feet, with resultant loss of coastal regions. Because other air pollutants are currently blocking the sun's rays and making the Earth cooler than it would normally be, thermal pollution and air pollution seem to balance each other and create an equilibrium. However, the disruption of our thermal equilibrium is such an important change in the ecosystem that scientists are watching developments here very closely (Cowen, 1986).

RESOURCE DEPLETION

The United States has only 6 percent of the world's population, but it uses 33 percent of the world's oil and a disproportionately high share of other nonrenewable resources (Meadows, 1985). A person in India uses six times less energy than a person in the United States. In other words, it would be better in terms of world energy crisis if six Indian babies were born than if one American baby is born.

United States citizens have only recently admitted that energy sources are limited. In 1972, when the Oil Producing and Exporting Countries (OPEC) boycotted the United States and reduced oil supply to a trickle. Americans began to panic. There was much talk about becoming independent, about rationing, and about returning to coal and wood as sources of fuel. Although OPEC countries raised their oil prices dramatically after the boycott, Americans continued living much as before, and the "energy crisis" became less of a concern to the media and the average person. It seems that as long as their daily lives are not threatened, most Americans would rather not face the issue of long-term resource depletion.

How long the United States will be able to continue this high consumption of the world's resources is unknown. Estimates of the world's reserves of oil and coal run from fifty to several hundred years (Meadows, 1985; Hayes, 1979).

Two hundred times our weight in garbage? Every year 26,000 pounds of garbage per person is dumped on refuse heaps in the United States. Much of it is industrial and not "set out at the curb." *(Therese Frare/The Picture Cube)*

RECYCLING

In the early 1970s concern with environmental issues was high, and recycling centers sprang up around the United States, encouraging people to save and recycle their paper, glass, and metal. Some of the spirit of the World War II era existed, when a "victory garden" planted in the backyard was a symbol of wanting to help in the effort to subdue the enemy. The common enemy now was waste, and people banded together against it. The goal was eminently sensible, because it saved new materials and conserved space in overcrowded dumps. Today, however, many recycling centers have closed due to lack of interest. The United States has returned to its "throw-it-away" mentality.

HUNGER

Another resource Americans presently overconsume is food. The United States' calorie intake is the highest in the world, closely followed by Western Europe. When most people in the world do not have enough to eat, Americans spend millions of dollars a year on diet books, pills, foods, and exercisers. It has been estimated that one-half of the earth's population is chronically undernourished, suffering from malnutrition and disease (Scrimshaw and Taylor, 1980). More than 10 million people die of starvation every year (Hanlon, 1983).

In 1972 and 1973 bad weather caused a significant drop in the amount of wheat and rice produced in the world. The United States that year contracted to sell large quantities of wheat to the Soviet Union, and the price of bread and other wheat-based products in the United States skyrocketed. Most Americans still had enough to eat. For the first time, however, the United States had little surplus to send to countries in need. Millions of people in the underdeveloped countries died, because their crops were also bad and they had no reserves from richer nations (Douglas, 1976).

Severe drought in Africa produced a famine which captured the attention of the American people in 1985 and 1986 (Hanlon, 1985). The plight of starving Africans was seen on television daily, and such diverse groups as the Baptist Convention and a British and

Irish rock 'n roll band came together for a concert called *Band Aid* to raise funds to help. Although much money was donated and food distributed, the basic problems of inadequate farming methods, drought, and/or rapidly growing population still combine to produce famine and hunger in much of Africa and in other Third World countries, also.

EFFECTS OF POPULATION DENSITY

Sociologists also study crowding and the accompanying psychological and physical stress caused by rapid population growth. For example, in large cities like Manhattan the population density is 67,000 people per square mile (U.S. Bureau of Census, 1987). Anyone who commutes from the suburbs to the city or who visits cities knows that one "feels different" in the noisy, crowded, fast-paced city than in suburbs or rural areas. Some sociological researchers have recently tried to isolate the effects of living in large groups, as people increasingly are doing.

Some evidence has been found to suggest that high population density may be associated with "pathological" behaviors like juvenile delinquency and mental illness (Galle et al., 1972). Researchers have also studied the physical and emotional effects of noise pollution in cities (Glass, Cohen, and Singer, 1973). Because this issue will affect large portions of our population, work continues in this area, perhaps along the interdisciplinary lines of our next "Close-Up on Theory."

CLOSE-UP on • *THEORY* •

John Cassel on Is Crowding Hazardous to Health?

The Theorist and the Setting

The boundaries between academic disciplines are artificial constructions rather than descriptions of natural territories. John Cassel is professor and chairman of the Department of Epidemiology in the School of Public Health, University of North Carolina. Epidemiologists and medical sociologists are concerned with the relationships between disease and social factors such as population characteristics. In this article, Cassel (1972) challenges an idea that had been generally accepted by scientists in all these disciplines.

Cassel's article defies categorization as simply "theory" or "research." This work is an especially strong blending of the two, as Cassel reviews earlier research to arrive at a theoretical understanding.

The Theorist's Goal

In Cassel's words (pp. 462–467):

> The view that crowding and increasing population density are deleterious to health is so widespread and generally accepted as to have become almost a medical axiom. . . . A careful review of recent data, however, indicates some important inconsistencies in the relationship between crowding and health that throws some doubt on this generally accepted formulation, particularly on the processes through which crowding may influence health. . . . This paper will examine some of the reasons that may account for the conflicting data and suggest the need to reformulate some of our conceptual models if the effects of such phenomena are to be better understood.

Concepts and Propositions

Cassel begins with a brief review of the types of evidence that have been introduced to support the proposition that "crowded communities provide a more fertile ground for the spread of infection than more scattered communities" and that "the deleterious effects of crowding are . . . also seen in increased mortality from all causes, both infectious and non-infectious" (p. 462). As Cassel indicates, other researchers have noted higher death and illness rates in densely populated urban centers and dramatic increases in death rates following industrialization and urbanization. Researchers have also reported higher rates of disease under other types of crowded conditions, such as in military training camps and nurseries. Finally, studies of crowding among animals suggest that crowding brings about a rise in maternal and infant mortality, and that it lowers resistance to drugs, microorganisms, and x-rays.

Cassel then introduces findings that appear to support his propositions and to refute the traditional view of the effects of crowding. For instance, although urban areas had higher mortality rates than rural areas in the 1940s, urban mortality rates have fallen and rural rates have risen, so that by the 1960s rural areas had significantly higher mortality rates, even though cities were generally becoming more crowded. Cassel acknowledges that part of the difference may be due to cities having generally younger populations than rural areas, and cities may have better medical care and sanitation. However, rural mortality rates are higher even when people of similar ages are compared and when diseases (like scarlet fever), which are not usually preventable or curable, are considered.

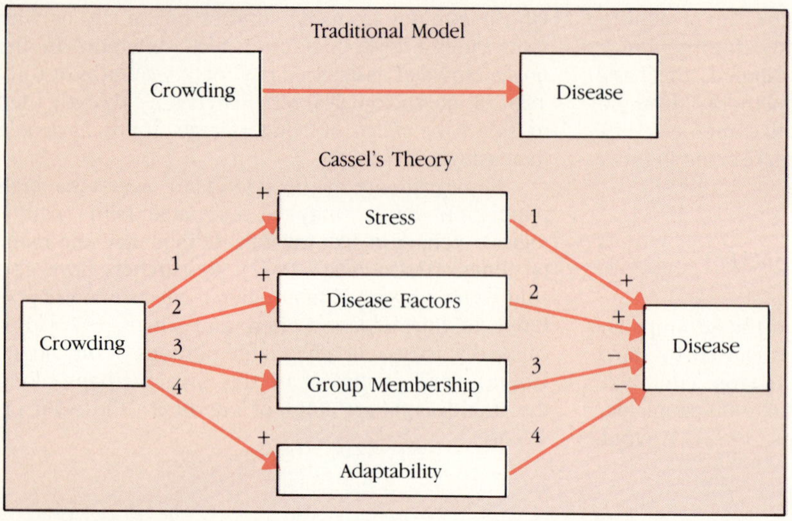

FIGURE 18.14 Comparison of the Traditional Theory of the Effects of Crowding with Cassel's Theory. Numbers indicate the specific proposition: + indicates a positive effect, − a negative one.

Cassel offers some working hypotheses as an alternative to the simple crowding-threatens-health thesis. Although he does not try to present a formal theory, his central ideas are stated here as propositions to make them easier to understand.

Proposition 1: Crowding may cause stressful disturbances that convert latent infections into overt symptoms.

One puzzling finding in previous research involves outbreaks of upper respiratory infection due to a virus among recruits in crowded military training camps. These outbreaks do not occur in crowded colleges or schools. This seems to indicate that simple crowding is not the deciding factor in these outbreaks. Both students and recruits may be carrying the virus, but the recruits succumb to it because they are under more physical—and sometimes more social—stress.

Proposition 2: Increased population density may cause an indirect rise in disease by bringing about increases in factors that are more directly related to health, such as poverty, malnutrition, poor sanitation, and social and physical stress.

Cassel focuses not on population density but on the consequences of crowding experienced by some urban areas and not by others. Here Cassel cites a 1968 study by Rene DuBois which indicates that "despite the fact that Hong Kong and Holland are among the most crowded areas in the world, they enjoy one of the highest levels of physical and mental health in the world" (p. 464). Furthermore, the crowding-threatens-health axiom has difficulty explaining why some diseases such as tuberculosis "rose for 75 to 100 years following industrialization, then started to fall spontaneously, and have continued to fall in the face of ever-increasing population density. . . . The diminishing rates in Britain and the United States started in 1850 and 1900, respectively, 50 to 100 years before any useful antituberculosis drugs were discovered and several decades before any organized antituberculosis programs were started" (pp. 465–466).

Proposition 3: "Group membership can exert a protective influence on the individual" (p. 472).

This suggests that high-density population could even have a benign effect, if it meant more opportunity to find a support group. For instance, tuberculosis is more likely to occur in marginal people—those deprived of meaningful social contact. Rates of this disease are higher for isolated ethnic minorities, people living alone in one room, those who have experienced multiple occupational and residential moves, and those who are single or divorced. Similarly, schizophrenia, accidents, and suicides are also more common among socially marginal people.

Proposition 4: Groups and individuals adapt to adverse environments.

Cassel supports this proposition by citing the fact that some diseases, such as tuberculosis, become less common as time passes and as population size rises. Other studies have also found that individuals who are the first from their families to leave the rural life-style and work in factories have higher rates of disease than those who grew up as children of previous factory workers. This proposition may help explain why some very densely populated territories like Hong Kong and Holland have normal or above average health.

Extreme crowding has sometimes also resulted in disease rates similar to the noncrowded situation. Alexander Kessler (1966) found that for populations of mice, disease rates tended to increase as crowding increased. However, when the level of crowding became extreme, the disease rates dropped to a normal level.

Interpretation

Cassel criticizes traditional crowding-threatens-health propositions. He suggests too little attention has been paid to the specific mechanism by which crowding promotes disease, the traditional explanation being that "crowding increases the risk of disease mainly through an increased opportunity for the spread of infection" (p. 468). Cassel reminds us that most diseases are caused by organisms that are virtually everywhere but that exert pathological effects "only when the infected person is under conditions of physiological stress" (p. 468). He also points out that the traditional interpretation does not explain higher rates of noninfectious diseases that sometimes occur under crowded conditions.

As Cassel points out, the term *crowding* is not well defined. If it simply means "high-density," it may fail to distinguish precise factors that might be related to disease, like poverty, poor nutrition, inadequate sanitation, and changes in the quantity and quality of social interactions. This simplistic high-density definition of crowding also fails to explain why the mice in Kessler's experiments and the human beings in Hong Kong and Holland do not have high rates of illness.

Questions

1. Could Cassel's ideas be used in predicting disease rates? How much use would they be in controlling disease?
2. Is this theory sociological? Why?
3. How might a research team proceed to test Cassel's working hypothesis systematically?

SOURCE John Cassel. 1972. "Health Consequences of Population Density and Crowding." In Office of the Foreign Secretary, National Academy of Sciences (ed.), *Rapid Population Growth*, vol. 2. Baltimore: Johns Hopkins University Press.

What New Resources Are Available for Maintaining an Ecological Balance with a Growing Population?

THE GREEN REVOLUTION

Much faith has been put in the "green revolution" as a solution to the world's food shortage and increasing population. *The* ***green revolution*** *refers to the development of new strains of grains and other plants that produce food faster and may be less dependent upon good weather conditions to grow.*

Global food production has more than doubled in the past thirty years, and per capita food production is up by more than 25 percent, despite a global population increase. In the most needy Third World countries, output grew by 33 percent between 1972 and 1982. At the same time, real food prices in the world market are declining and the percentage of the world's income spent on food has shrunk (O'Brien, 1985).

Advances in agricultural technology account for much of the increased output. Third World farmers are being taught to reclaim land that was thought untillable, new bacteria are being used to fertilize the soil, and vaccines against hoof–and–mouth disease are being perfected. Observers believe that Third World countries should concentrate on teaching their people to support themselves through new agricultural techniques rather than to quickly industrialize without a sufficient agricultural base to support the population (Avery, 1985). Although the goal of feeding the world is a viable one today, its realization will require the commitment of the industrialized world toward further research and development in agriculture (Scrimshaw and Taylor, 1980).

SOLAR POWER

Coal, because it creates thermal pollution and gives off noxious gases, could produce irreversible changes in climate and air. Nuclear energy is not proving cheap or reliable enough to gain public acceptance as an alternative. The Three Mile Island accident in 1979 and the Chernobyl explosion in 1986 dampened hopes of nuclear power advocates for expansion of this type of power (Marples, 1986; Norman, 1985; Lanouette, 1985). Although no one yet knows the long-term effects of these accidents, evidence is great that much human and ecological damage has been done, and citizens are eager to avoid more of the same.

Denis Hayes and Christopher Flavin of Worldwatch Institute suggest that solar energy may outpace coal and nuclear power as the alternative for the future (1976; 1983). Introduced by the General Electric Company at the 1939 New York World's Fair, solar energy's major drawback thus far has been cost: approximately $15,000 per peak kilowatt of electrical energy. To be practical for most use, the price needs to be reduced to $500 per peak kilowatt (Wheeler, 1977). Recent technological progress brings this goal closer. Hayes suggests that as much as 75 percent of the world's energy may come from the sun by the year 2025, because the sun as a form of energy is more sound in ecologic terms.

Sociologists at Work •

WILLIAM FREUDENBERG ESTIMATES SOCIAL IMPACT OF NUCLEAR WASTE DUMPS
University of Wisconsin
Madison, Wisconsin

William Freudenberg is a sociologist who brings his rigorous empirical focus to bear on current social issues. As do increasing numbers of sociologists, Freudenberg shares his insights by consulting with both private and governmental agencies.

What Is the Current Focus of Your Work?

I have been looking at the socioeconomic impacts of potential high-level nuclear waste repositories. Currently, nuclear waste is either stored at defense installations or in swimming pools at the nuclear power plants that produce the waste. But, the swimming pools are filling up. Several states, including California, have passed laws that no more nuclear power plants will be built until the nuclear waste problem is solved. Physical scientists have looked at the issues and considered options ranging from burying the waste in the ocean, to shooting it into space, to melting it into the polar icecap. They have decided that the responsible thing to do is to bury it far below the surface of the earth. The U.S. Department of Energy started looking at three sites, Washington State, Nevada, and Texas, although they're now looking just at the Nevada site. All of these sites are west of the Mississippi, even though 85 percent of the commercial waste is produced in the East.

What Is Your Part in the Process?

I'm working with the state of Nevada in helping to design and oversee the studies. The Department of Energy is planning to spend $1 billion studying the site in Nevada; they'll spend billions more in putting the waste into the ground if they ever manage to get a site approved. They received 50,000 to 60,000 letters of protest on an obscure document called the Draft Area Recommendation Report a few years ago. If a sociological study points to the conclusion that place A would be bad for some reason, people at location B may not only disagree, but be spending thousands of dollars of their own to show that conclusion is wrong. The politics here make the scientific quality most important. I believe it is possible to deal dispassionately with issues that people care passionately about to produce the best, clearest, most balanced, most comprehensive answers.

What Specific Questions Are You Looking At?

I am studying the socioeconomic impact a repository would have on the people who live nearby. Economic questions include economic and demographic changes. For example, if you built a dump, new workers will be coming to town who will require housing, schooling, perhaps new sewer systems, and so on. Social and cultural questions include: What will happen to the communities nearby? Will there be an increase in tension and conflict? Will people be hostile toward it or greet it?

The effect can also be studied from the point of view of standard and special impact. Standard impacts are the kinds of changes that would be created by any large-scale facility in a rural area. Nuclear waste, however, creates special impact. The official federal standards specify that this facility must be built in such a way that the waste won't get out for 10,000 years. Most of the nuclear waste will have decayed to be harmless well before that 10,000-year point, but a very small minority will remain dangerous for about a quarter of a million years. Partly because the waste has such a long life, and partly because the nuclear industry in the past has made some mistakes and promised things it couldn't deliver, people have special reactions to anything with "nuclear" in its title. One concern is what we informally call the "Dan Rather Scenario." Imagine a train carrying nuclear waste fell off the track, landed on top of a gasoline truck, and erupted into flames. Coast to coast that night people would hear: "Dan Rather, good evening. Just outside of Las Vegas earlier today, a train carrying highly toxic nuclear waste crashed. We don't know yet whether any of the waste actually got out." Within thirty seconds, the switchboards could start lighting up all over Las Vegas as people cancelled their vacation plans—even if no waste actually got out of the special casks that carry it.

There is also the problem of credibility. DOE has been assuring everyone that the repository will be safe, but given the number of times in the past when government agencies have been wrong in making such claims, the public may not believe them.

As you can see, predicting the impacts of these repositories is a terribly complicated process, combining psychology, sociology, economics, and my knowledge of what's physically possible. Having people stake millions of dollars on the outcome puts me into a highly politicized situation that I never really expected to be in when I was studying sociology in graduate school. ●

NUCLEAR ENERGY

Nuclear power was once heralded as the cure to the future's energy problems: It would be plentiful and "too cheap to meter" (Council on Economic Priorities, 1979). Proponents of nuclear energy still see it as the best alternative to fossil fuels such as oil and coal, in spite of the accidents mentioned earlier. However, Pennsylvania residents near the Three Mile Island disaster mobilized quickly and effectively to block restarting of the reactor adjacent to the one that was damaged (Walsh, 1981; Walsh and Warland, 1983; Walsh, 1984). The Chernobyl meltdown has caused over 30 deaths thus far, and the long-range effects of the radiation which it quickly spread across Europe are unknown, although herds of livestock have already been affected. The fears spurred by these situations, coupled with massive cost overruns on existing facilities, have caused the canceling or postponing of future nuclear plants in the United States (Lanouette, 1985).

A second problem associated with nuclear reactors is how to dispose of the radioactive waste they produce. It has been termed an "acute embarrassment" that the waste problem has not yet been solved (Carter, 1983). Until disposal is safe and swift, and plants are made considerably more "fail-safe," opposition to nuclear power as an alternative energy source will continue (Stoler, 1984). William Freudenberg, this chapter's "Sociologist At Work," has spent a number of years studying the physical and social impact of the disposal of nuclear waste.

Cursed blessing. Nuclear power advocates promised electricity "too cheap to meter." Concern for accidents and waste storage has halted construction but not operation of these plants. *(Photo courtesy the Michigan Daily)*

Conclusion

When Donella Meadows' *The Limits of Growth* was published in 1972, it set off a public furor. The dire predictions of the Dartmouth computer model of the world's environment regarding overpopulation, resource depletion, and the destruction of the ecosystem were difficult reading at best. Since that time, critics have supported both this pessimistic view of the future and more optimistic ones (Ophuls, 1977; Simon, 1981; Schell, 1982). As this chapter has suggested, the picture is mixed. Some impressive gains have been made in controlling pollution, creating new resource alternatives, and producing food, but the population is still growing at what has been termed an "alarming rate," and people are still starving (Russell, 1984).

The equation that is Earth is simply too complicated for any one system of thought to accurately predict change. Much has happened in the years since the Dartmouth study that would have been totally unpredictable then. Even Meadows has written more recently that the present problems center on inequities, wastefulness, and mismanagement rather than on actual scarcity (Meadows, 1985).

Summary Questions

REVIEW

1. What is demography?
2. What are the elements of population, and how are they measured?
3. What are the three processes that affect population size?
4. What is the history of immigration in the United States?
5. What is the Malthusian theory?
6. What is the demographic transition?
7. Describe the present world population explosion.
8. What is the population picture in the United States?
9. What does Lester Brown see as the current world demographic structure, and why?
10. What are the implications of today's population trends?
11. What are Cassel's findings on the relationships between crowding and health?
12. What new resources are available for maintaining an ecological balance with a growing population?

Summary Answers

1. Demography is the study of the size, composition, and distribution of society as it is affected by three major population processes: fertility, mortality, and migration.
2. The elements of population are size, composition, and distribution. Size is measured through a census, or official count of people and their relevant characteristics such as age, sex, and occupation. Composition refers to the distribution of a population in various categories like age or sex. Composition can be measured by such terms as the sex ratio, the median age, the dependency ratio, and the population pyramid, a pictoral representation of the age and sex distribution of the population of an area.
3. Three processes that affect population size are fertility, mortality, and migration. Fertility refers to the frequency of births in a population, and its study includes crude birth rate, age at marriage, use of contraception, societal attitudes toward family size, infanticide, and abortion, but fertility is distinguished from fecundity, or the potential number of children that the women of a population could produce. Mortality is measured in a crude mortality rate, an age-specific mortality rate, a life-expectancy-at-birth rate, and an infant mortality rate. Studying migration includes counting the emigrants and immigrants in order to find a crude migration rate.
4. Immigration into the United States was virtually unlimited until after World War I, when Congress passed a law that excluded or deported aliens holding certain political beliefs, stopped all immigration from China and Japan, and limited immigration from Europe to an annual total of 3 percent of the number of people already here from each European country. In 1965, the United States abandoned the quota system, and today's immigrants come primarily from the Western Hemisphere and Asia.
5. Malthus believed that population, without any external controls, will double once every generation until the uppermost level of subsistence will not support the population size, at which time preventive checks will come into play.
6. The demographic transition is the pattern populations follow as their nations develop from an agricultural base to an industrial one. Stage one has high birth and death rates. Stage two has a high birth rate and lower death rate. In stage three, the birth rate falls, bringing about a stable population size again.
7. Although population growth has slowed somewhat, mostly due to stabilization in nations that have completed the demographic transition, the world population is still doubling every 35 or 40 years, and now totals 4.8 billion.
8. The population of the United States has grown steadily since the beginning of the nation's history, with a peak in the 1950s labeled the "baby boom." If present trends continue, the U.S. population should become stabilized at about 270 million in the middle of the next century.
9. Brown sees the world divided demographically between those nations that have completed the demographic transition and have no or low growth rates (.8 percent) and those that are still in stage two of the transition and have high growth rates (2.5 percent per year). Barring a drastic lowering of the birth rates in these countries, Brown sees death rates climbing in these countries as the ecology of the nation deteriorates in trying to accommodate too many people.
10. Our ecosystem is currently under attack in many areas: air and water pollution, overproduction of nonrecyclible garbage, resource depletion, overconsumption of food by the developed countries, and crowding.
11. Cassel criticizes traditional crowding-threatens-health propositions and suggests we should research the specific mechanism by which crowding promotes disease—for instance, physiological stress.
12. The green revolution, making it possible for Third World countries to produce more food on their available territory, and solar energy, a pollution-free alternative energy source, are two promising alternatives for today's growing and polluting world population.

Glossary

age-specific mortality rate a measure of the number of deaths per 1,000 people in certain age groups

census an official count of people and their relevant statistics, such as age, sex, and occupation

composition the distribution of a population in various categories like age and sex

crude birth rate a mathematical measure of the number of live births per 1,000 persons in a population during one calendar year

crude migration rate the number of emigrants or immigrants per 1,000 people in the area

crude mortality rate the number of deaths per 1,000 people in one year

demographic transition a somewhat predictable pattern the populations of many nations follow as they develop from an agricultural base to an industrial base

demography the study of the size, composition, and distribution of society as it is affected by three major population processes: fertility, mortality, and migration

dependency ratio the number of economically dependent people per 100 people who are economically productive (conventionally between ages 15 and 64)

doubling time the number of years for a group to double in size

ecology the study of ecosystems

ecosystem a system of living organisms and their environment

emigrants people who leave an area

fecundity the potential number of children that the women in a population could produce

fertility the frequency of births in a population

green revolution the development of new strains of grains and other plants that produce food faster and may be less dependent upon good weather conditions to grow

growth rate the number of people both added to and subtracted from a population through birth, migration, and death, expressed as a percentage of the total population

human ecology the study of the relationships of people to their ecosystem

immigrants people who enter an area

infant mortality rate the ratio of deaths of children under 1 year of age in a given year to the total number of live births in that year

life expectancy at birth the number of years a child can expect to live on the average, when he or she is born

median age that age which is exactly the middle figure of all the ages of the population, with half of the population older than that age and half of it younger

migration the relatively permanent movement of persons over a significant distance. Types of migration are forced migration, free migration, impelled migration, mass migration, and primitive migration

population pyramid a bar graph that represents the age and sex characteristics of a population

sex ratio the number of males per 100 females in a population

zero population growth (ZPG) the situation in which the population of a country is stabilized at one level

Suggested Readings

Lester Brown and Jodi Jacobson. 1986. "Our Demographically Divided World: Worldwatch Paper 74." Washington, D.C.: Worldwatch Institute.

Once again, Brown has created order out of chaos, bringing to light the salient studies on the current population/ecological-disaster situation in the world.

Nathan Glazer. 1985. *Clamor at the Gates.* San Francisco, Calif.: Institute for Contemporary Studies.

Glazer has compiled a fascinating set of articles addressing the history/analysis of immigration to the United States from its earliest years to date.

Gupte Pranay. 1984. *The Crowded Earth: People and the Politics of Population.* New York: Norton Press.

An interesting text that discusses the effects of overpopulation on the political process.

World Bank. 1984. *World Development Report, 1984.* New York: Oxford University Press.

This report details the situations of the various Third World countries with regard to population processes and economic growth.

CHAPTER 19

SOCIAL CHANGE: URBANIZATION and MODERNIZATION

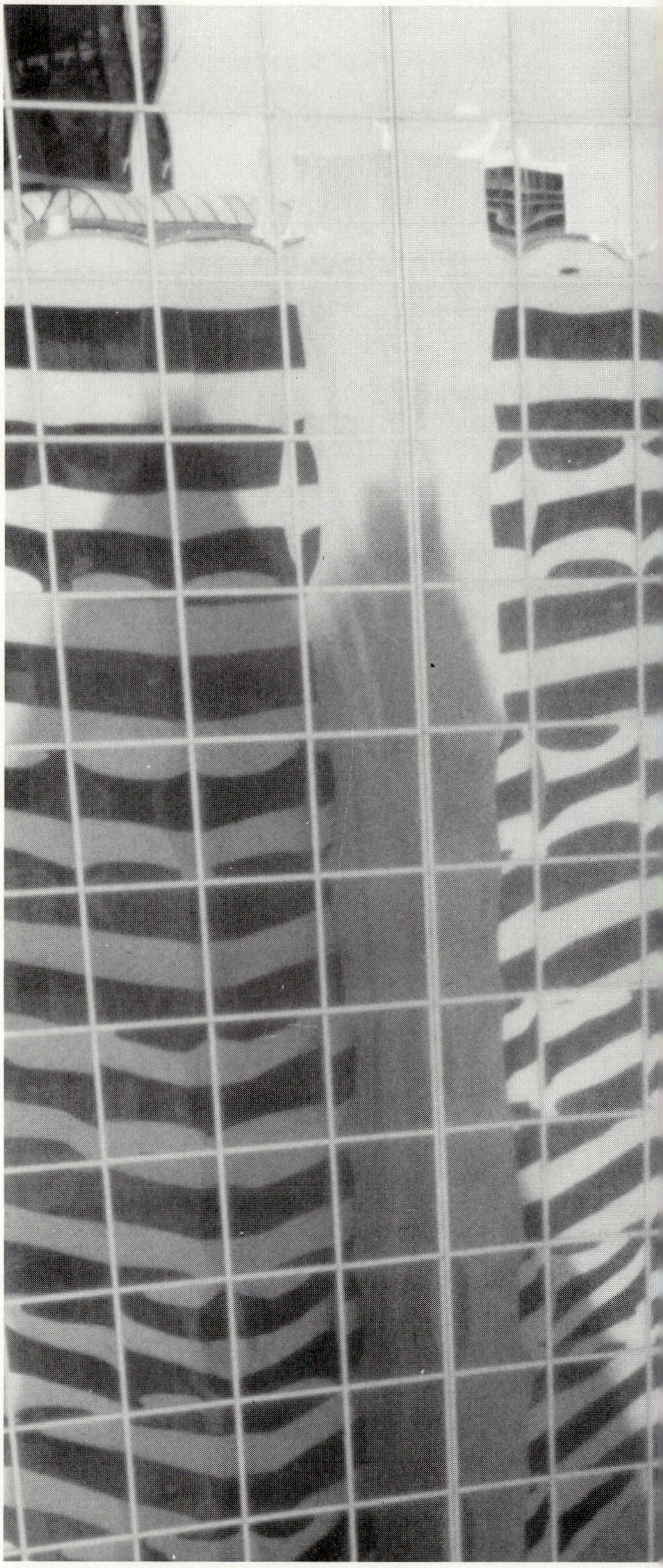

- What Are the Major Theories of Social Change?
- What Are the Causes of Social Change?
- How Do Sociologists Explain Urbanization?
- Close-Up on Theory: Kingsley Davis on Recent and Rapid World Urbanization
- How Has Urbanization Proceeded in the United States?
- How Are Cities Socially Structured?
- How Can World Development Be Seen as Social Change?
- Close-Up on Research: Alex Inkeles on Making Men Modern
- World Systems Theory: The Conflict Perspective
- How Can We Predict Social Change?
- Sociologists at Work: William Foote Whyte Advocates New Levels of Cooperation in the Workplace

How's Your Sociological Intuition?

1. When we compare cities of antiquity to modern cities, we discover that:

a. Few cities of antiquity could claim a population as large as that of Tampa, Florida, which has roughly one-quarter million people
b. Even in the Greek and Roman empires, cities accounted for about 2 percent of the population, whereas the United States is presently over 70 percent urbanized
c. Early cities were troubled by plagues and diseases, partly as a result of poor sanitary facilities
d. All of the above

2. Cities are:

a. Like the family and religion—as old as societies are
b. A quite recent development in the history of humankind
c. Actually less common in the United States than they were in Aztec society
d. Only found in industrial societies

3. In the United States:

a. Center-city populations are declining
b. Metropolitan population is increasing
c. Suburban populations are growing
d. All of the above

4. Which has the largest proportion of people living in cities?

a. the United States
b. China
c. Spain
d. the Soviet Union

Answers

1. d. Each of these dramatic statements is true, and we discuss each fact in more detail in this chapter.
2. b. The city is by no means a universal social structure like the family, but cities did exist in preindustrial times.
3. d. All of these facts are true. People are leaving the center cities for the suburbs; but metropolitan areas still grow, because they include the suburbs and because population continues to rise in general in the United States.
4. c. Spain has 91 percent of its population living in cities, whereas the United States has 74 percent, the Soviet Union 65 percent, and China only 21 percent.

When You Have Finished Studying This Chapter, You Should Know:

- What social change is and how the evolutionary, cyclical, functional, and conflict theories explain it
- How technology, demographic processes, ideological factors, and outstanding individuals affect the processes of social change
- How cities originally grew
- How cities developed in the United States
- The differences between Gemeinschaft and Gesellschaft
- How Simmel viewed urbanization in social terms
- The major ideas of the Chicago School
- Gan's assessment of social relationships in the city
- What urban ecology is
- The bases of three classic theories of urban spatial structure: concentric zone theory, sector model, and multiple nuclei model
- What a megalopolis is and how its growth may affect the future
- The basis of the urban–suburban crisis
- Proposed solutions to the "problem of the cities"
- What city planning involves
- How urban renewal has addressed the problem of urban blight
- What "new towns" are, and what promise they hold for urbanization
- How modernization theory explains world development
- How men become "modern"
- How world systems theory explains world development
- How extrapolation and analysis help us to predict social change
- What sort of social change Whyte studies and advocates

Our social world has changed and continues to change. Throughout this text we have repeatedly dealt with social change in our discussions of specific areas such as race relations, gender roles, the family, work, religion, government, education, and population. In comparing our world to that of a few decades ago we found that race relations had become significantly more equal and harmonious, gender roles are being redefined as somewhat more equal, men and women marry later, have fewer children, and are more divorce-prone, though the soaring divorce rate has leveled off. As a society we are working more in offices and factories and less in agriculture. Women work in the paid labor force in unprecedented numbers. Though we enjoyed a period of relative prosperity during the post–World War II era, our income, corrected for inflation, is falling. Religion, once thought to be dying out, persists, but new sects and cults are displacing established groups. Our government has grown to enormous proportion, but recent economic competition threatens our ability to sustain international commitments. Though we send our children to day-care centers or nursery schools at increasingly early ages, our schools seem to be in a state of decline. Whereas our population growth has almost stopped, that of many poor nations soars. Many of these changes are part of even broader transitions such as industrialization, which we considered both in Chapters 3 and 15.

In this chapter we look at the process of social change in general and the theories advanced to explain it. We focus on two massive social transitions: urbanization and modernization. We will explore both their causes and their widespread consequences. Urbanization and modernization trigger changes throughout our culture, but this happens so slowly that these two massive transitions are not "newsworthy" and may be relatively unnoticed. Yet these trends eventually change the social landscape so drastically that we may have difficulty recognizing and adjusting to the new world that almost imperceptibly overtakes us.

We will also look at how sociology can help predict social change. Here we will find we need both the tools of the researcher, who charts trends, and the theorist, who explains them, if we are to understand and predict social change.

What Are the Major Theories of Social Change?

Social change *is change in social structure or organization.* In one sense, the study of social change is the essence of sociology. August Comte, the man who gave sociology its name, believed that when sociologists determined the roots of social change, they would be able to help plan for a better future society (1896). Sociologists are still working toward this goal, and have come a long way toward being able to predict changes and help us plan for the future.

Comte stated that social change is (1) inevitable, (2) follows one line of development (is unilinear), and (3) progresses naturally toward a better world. Comte

Equality? Among the major recent social changes is increasing equality between the genders. Here a girl "tackles" her male opponent in a soccer match. *(Photo courtesy the Michigan Daily)*

believed that through social change humans changed from ignorant savages to educated beings, and that those things that we learned or developed along the way were part of God's plan for the progress of humankind.

EVOLUTIONARY THEORISTS

Herbert Spencer (1898) developed an evolutionary theory of social change based on the premise that society functions like a biological organism. Spencer viewed the relation of various institutions to society as similar to the relation of the various organs to a living organism. From this perspective, for instance, the postal system can be likened to an organism's nervous system: both transmit information.

Spencer also saw the relationship between society and the environment as determining the structure of society, much as the environments of biological organisms often influence their physical structures. Spencer believed that those people and social structures that best fit their environment would be the ones to survive. In fact, Spencer coined the phrase "survival of the fittest," which is often associated with Charles Darwin. Ironically, Spencer's work stimulated Darwin's, but because Darwin became better known, Spencer's ideas are sometimes called "Social Darwinism."

Gerhard Lenski, a later evolutionary theorist, believed that evolution toward complex forms of society is not necessarily universal and that change is not necessarily always toward progress for the society (Lenski, 1966). Lenski believe in ***multilinear change,*** *change that occurs in different directions through various means depending on the conditions in the society undergoing the change.*

Evolutionary theory provides the basis for some of our contemporary thinking about economic development. Later we will look more closely at modernization theory, which holds that the less developed nations are simply at earlier stages and can eventually become modern like the economically developed world.

CYCLICAL THEORISTS

In contrast to the evolutionary theorists, who see change as continuous progress, are the cyclical theorists, who view change as an enormous circle. Oswald Spengler was the first in a long line of social scientists who have predicted the fall of Western civilization based on a cyclical perspective.

Spengler's major work, *The Decline of the West* (1918), defines five stages in the lives of civilizations: birth, childhood, maturity (the Golden Age), decline into old age, and death. The early stages are creative and rapidly developing times, whereas the later stages lack originality and overemphasize material goods. From his in-depth study of eight previous civilizations, Spengler concludes that Western civilization is inevitably declining and will die out, to be replaced by a new society (Spengler, 1918).

Arnold Toynbee offered another macro theory (1962). He studied the progression of twenty-one societies through similar cycles, beginning with a *challenge* offered to the society and ending with the society's *response* to the challenge. The first challenges are from the environment. Can the tribe find enough food and water to survive? Later challenges arise within the society itself or come from enemies of the society: Will the city wall keep out the invaders from the next province? If the society's response is successful, the society flourishes until the next challenge. If its response is unsuccessful, the society dies out, and another one takes its place.

The major difference between Toynbee and Spengler is that Toynbee saw hope for the long-range survival of some societies. He believed that some societies continue to meet challenges and rise to new levels, rather than inevitably winding down. Although Toynbee's twelve volumes hold an impressive number of examples of his hypothesis, he does not explain why some societies meet challenges and others do not, or why a society successfully responds to one challenge and not to another. His writing remains a picture of how some societies work instead of a general explanation of how societies change.

Pitirim Sorokin is the third well-known cyclical theorist. He describes two basic types of societies: *those that emphasize things that can be sensed, called* ***sensate societies,*** *and those that emphasize things that can be thought about but not necessarily felt through the senses—the* ***ideational societies*** (1941). Sensate societies are practical, scientific, and materialistic. Ideational societies tend to be abstract, religious, and concerned with "higher" things than the material culture. Sorokin's ideal culture is a blending of these two.

According to Sorokin, societies tend to follow one or the other of these philosophies until the society's members think it has gone too far in that direction and reverse philosophies. Traditional India, with its religious focus on spiritual matters, exemplifies the ideational society; the early twentieth-century United States, with its emphasis on material things, typifies the sensate society. Sorokin believes this cycle of changes is irregular and that societies repeat the alternations on different schedules.

Sorokin's theory does not explain why societies shift from one phase to another; it states only that shifting is a "natural" occurrence. His writing also treats today's materialistic, sensate society harshly and tends to eulogize the "old days" when ideational cultures were more common. Still, his theory is insightful and has influenced many sociologists, including his pupil at Harvard, Talcott Parsons.

Contemporary cyclical theories hold the advantage over evolutionary theories of being able to explain reversals. Such theories are particularly popular in dealing with the economy. Economist Ravi Batra, for instance, bases his prediction of a great depression between 1990 and 1996 on what he calls the law of social cycles. Batra draws many parallels between the 1920s and the 1980s. In his book, written before the October, 1987 stock market crash, he predicted that such a crash would precede this worldwide depression (Batra, 1987).

In the remaining sections of this chapter we will use these theoretical concepts to better understand some of the massive social changes that have spread around the world during the past two centuries. We begin by considering urbanization, move on to the even broader concept of modernization, and close with a discussion of how sociologists use theories and research techniques to forecast the future.

FUNCTIONAL THEORISTS

Whereas the cyclical theorists see change as the natural state of society, functional theorists believe society tends toward a condition of equilibrium. Structural-functionalists use their stance to explain both how society will change and how it will remain the same.

The central proposition of functionalism is that the features of a society persist because they contribute to the endurance of that society. From this perspective, for instance, religion is considered functional because it binds the worshipers together and promotes solidarity in society. The violent puberty rites of many native American tribes are seen as helping those societies by preparing men for life in physically torturous environments. Similarly, the persistence of the family is explained in terms of the functions it fulfills for society and the individuals living in it.

Talcott Parsons, a modern functionalist, believed a society provides for its own stability, or equilibrium, to ensure its survival. The interaction between social innovations and their environment serves as a filter, incorporating positive changes into the society and eliminating those that could be fatal to the society.

Many examples can be found to support Parsons' conception. As industrial societies develop, the simple, undifferentiated kinship structure is replaced by the institutions of the modern state and economy, each highly differentiated and integrated. When changes in technology, such as computerized banking, create undesirable new social structures, such as organized computer fraud, the society develops other new structures to meet the threat, such as detective squads specializing in computerized crime. If the change is dysfunctional, such as the introduction of drugs for recreation, the society acts to stabilize culture by labeling the new behavior as deviant. When a society fails to resist a dysfunctional innovation, the society itself may collapse, but this, of course, means dysfunctional innovations will not last long. In these ways, a society's cultural features can be seen as functional and change can be seen as proceeding toward new functional forms.

Parsons suggests change is introduced from two major sources: the environment and internal strains of the society. An innovation might be introduced to cope with a change in physical environment or to cope with a change due to contact with another culture. For example, the elevator was invented when space within cities was becoming very expensive. The elevator made it possible to create multistoried buildings and use the city space efficiently. This innovation, in turn, caused further social change, as it paved the way for skyscrapers and increased concentrations of people in cities.

Change may also come about to reduce strain built up in a society. For instance, labor unions can be viewed as a response to strain introduced by people striving for higher living standards, which often accompanies the introduction of industrialization. Functionalists argue that, whatever their source, only those changes that contribute to the maintenance of society will become a lasting part of that society.

CONFLICT THEORISTS

Functionalists and conflict theorists agree that internal tensions in a society can lead to social change. Conflict theorists from the time of Karl Marx have focused on tensions within society as the driving force toward social change, viewing society as primarily conflicting rather than consensual. Conflict theorists claim that apparent stability in a society merely reflects a temporary standoff between two sides in the conflict; change happens when one side gains ground in the battle. Conflict theorists view the social order as serving the elites at the expense of the nonelites, whereas functionalists view the social order as serving the interests of society as a whole.

Marx believed social change occurs largely with changes in the means of production or with technological change that challenges the existing order. He believed that as the world became industrialized and workers' conditions worsened, workers would develop a "class consciousness," recognize the seriousness of the situation and their common plight, and organize to overthrow their oppressors in a violent revolution. They would then form a new state to monopolize the productive resources of the society in the name of, and for the sake of, the masses. This socialist dictatorship would eventually lead the way to a harmonious society of equals.

Ralf Dahrendorf has attempted to revise some of Marx's ideas to explain modern situations not accounted for by traditional Marxian theory (1959). For example, contrary to Marx's theory, no strong lower-class consciousness emerged among industrialized nations like the United States and Japan. The communist ideology has been adopted, however, by some of the more primitive nations, a situation Marx did not predict.

Dahrendorf agrees with Marx that social life is more often characterized by conflict and change than by consensus and stability. Dahrendorf claims that conflict arises whenever individuals engage in authority relations, and not just between economic classes. According to Dahrendorf, modern organizations continually place people in positions of authority and subservience. Even church, union, and school members must deal with differences in authority. The conflict generated by authority serves to divide people into enemy camps and to heighten solidarity among those of similar status. Modern societies have so many different dimensions, however, that few people are consistently at the bottom or top of the authority hierarchy. Most people have several reference groups, and the class consciousness Marx predicted does not necessarily occur.

No single theory has thus far been able to account for the many differences in social structure that occur over time, which we label social change. From Comte's simplified unilinear theory of good emanating from God to Dahrendorf's explanation of our varying group allegiances, each theory helps us see a part of the puzzle.

What Are the Causes of Social Change?

How can we synthesize the broad array of theories of social change into a coherent understanding of the dynamics of social change? Some theories seem more like descriptions than explanations. For instance, the cyclical theories of Spengler, Toynbee, and Sorokin attribute social change to "natural" cycles. This seems to leave little room for causes, human intervention, or control. The evolutionary, functional, and conflict approaches appear somewhat better at explaining what has happened than at predicting what will happen. Yet there are some recurring themes. Several of the theorists, including Spencer, Lenski, Parsons, and Marx, recognize the fundamental importance of technology to understanding social change. In this section we try to identify the major causal agents that bring forth social change.

TECHNOLOGY

Human beings are unique among all of the animal species in that they are constantly developing new technology, including knowledge as well as tools. ***Technology*** *refers to ways of manipulating the environment to achieve desired practical ends.* William F. Ogburn believed

Culture lag? The introduction of new technology may trigger social changes. Here, for example, a personal computer has allowed the office to be moved into the home. Generally, however, culture lags behind technology. (*Dick Luria/FPG International*)

technological change was the primary source of social change, and changes in the material realm are generally followed by changes in the social and cultural realm (1922). Often changes in technology precede changes in the rest of the society, producing culture lag. ***Culture lag*** *occurs when some parts of a culture change at a faster rate than other related parts, resulting in disruption of the integration and equilibrium of the culture.*

Ogburn applied the concept of culture lag to modern society and suggested that modern material culture has developed through technology much faster than the other parts of the culture have developed. Societies have not always been able to adjust easily to the technological changes of recent years, because corresponding social changes have lagged behind. Ogburn cites the invention of the automobile as a technological advance that greatly altered living patterns, making it possible to live outside cities while continuing to work in them. The automobile also gave rise to secondary industries such as petroleum and road construction. Clearly, most of these could not have been anticipated at the time cars were introduced. There was a lag of decades between the time the automobile was introduced and the time these cultural adjustments took place.

Ogburn's theory suggests that a period of rapid social change lies ahead due to rapid technological changes. For example, development of computers and microcircuitry may eventually result in even more social change than the automobile caused. Computers could result in the work setting returning to the home. With the increasing cost of transportation and office space and the decreasing cost of communication, workers who previously used offices may work from their homes, linked together through communication networks that provide the same functions presently provided by close physical proximity.

It is interesting to note that Alvin Toffler's best sellers *Future Shock* (1970) and *The Third Wave* (1980) are based on the idea that changes in a society's core technology result in massive changes in social structure and ideas. The major premise of *The Third Wave* is that the rapid social change we now experience is the result of the third great transformation in technology. The first major technological innovation is agriculture, which transforms society as we saw in Chapter 3. The second major breakthrough is powered machines and industrialization, which again restructured the social landscape. The third advance is the computer and the postindustrial, or information, society. Daniel Bell (1973), who first wrote of postindustrial society more than a decade before Toffler, is apparently not flattered by his imitators, for he has referred to some of their work as "future schlock."

DEMOGRAPHIC INFLUENCES

Ongoing demographic processes, too, sometimes bring social change. For instance, when the crime rate increased during the late 1960s and early 1970s, the United States had a surplus of young adult males born during the postwar baby boom; because most crime is committed by young adult males, more crime was committed during this period. College enrollment during this period was also near an all-time high. Enrollment has leveled off as the baby-boom bulge passes through these age brackets. What may seem to be a permanent social trend, then, such as more crime or increasing college enrollment, may actually be due to a passing change in the population structure of the society.

IDEOLOGIES

Material change is not the only source of social change. Social ideas and ideals also have consequences. Some sociologists suggest that competing ideologies may result in social change. ***Ideologies*** *are explanations of the social, moral, religious, political, and economic institutions of a group.*

For example, as we saw in the chapter on religion, Max Weber believed Protestantism was a major cause of the development of capitalist economics. Similarly, a democratic revolution or a communist revolution may make converts to its ideology, resulting in either violent conflict or peaceful but dramatic social change.

INDIVIDUALS

Individual human beings may be significant agents of social change. George Homans, in his 1964 presidential address to the American Sociological Association, urged sociologists to "bring men back in" to their considerations of social phenomena.

Weber noted the significance of the charismatic personality as a source of authority. (See Chapter 16, "The Political Institution.") Many historical figures have had profound influence on societies, including Jesus of Nazareth, Mohandas Gandhi, Eli Whitney, Karl Marx, Benjamin Franklin, and Thomas Edison. Often special individuals combine with particular social circumstance to create social change. Henry Ford, for example, could not have developed assembly-line production in a hunting and gathering society.

How Do Sociologists Explain Urbanization?

It is 6:30 A.M., and we're half an hour from our Hillsdale home, cruising through the rolling Irish Hills of Michigan on our way to a flight for Boston to see our friends. The land is a quilt of wheat fields and cornfields with an occasional cluster of farm buildings.

Hillsdale, with a population of 10,000, is small-town American, with one high school, one movie theater, one taxi, and one restaurant that aspires toward formal dining. On Saturdays farmers drive their pickup trucks into town to trade at the farmer's market at the fairgrounds and shop at local stores. Most people buy such things as clothing and Christmas presents from the three national catalog stores in town.

Hillsdale lacks many attractions of contemporary metropolitan living, as well as some of its problems. Traffic never jams. There are only six traffic lights. A significant number of people walk to work. Burglar alarms are practically nonexistent. No one worries about walking outside after dark. Noise, congestion, pollution, and crime, which plague many cities and suburbs, are absent. Present are trees and birds, small shops where people learn your name, a slower pace of life, lakes, and a small college. The signs of unemployment and poverty may be harder to find than in the city. The community of people is so small that newcomers must accustom themselves to having others know about them before they have even met. It is generally a safe assumption that if you tell one person about your daughter's illness or your trip to Boston, others will soon know.

Eventually, the same highway winds its way through Saline, a town not much bigger than Hillsdale, but an hour closer to Detroit. On the east edge, an enormous Ford Motor Company plastics plant thrusts its smokestacks into the sky adjacent to a large white farmhouse with a big red barn, a woodpile, and grazing cattle. The contrast is almost too stark to adequately symbolize the agrarian-to-industrial revolution.

Near Ann Arbor we join the four-lane interstate, one of several that feed tractor trailers and commuters into Detroit. We exit at Detroit Metropolitan Airport, still some twenty miles from the center city. Only when we reach Boston do we directly encounter a major city. The air is laden with the smell of exhaust fumes. Dilapidated housing, street people, and trash litter the scene. The noise and congestion offend our senses, and a ride through a "rough" neighborhood, with a cab driver who has mastered neither the English language nor the streets of Boston, reminds us that racial tensions and violent crime are an all-too-familiar part of this environment.

The meetings go well with our friends. We are reminded of the great benefits of large cities: the diversity of people, universities, symphony orchestras, museums, fine restaurants, specialty stores, and (especially) publishers. In the evening we dine out with a long-time friend who produces television documentaries. Different though our environments are, it is clear each is "home" to those who live there. In this day we have made a rural-to-urban transition reminiscent of the one that has preoccupied the country and the world for much of this century. Gradually the population has moved in from the countryside to the Hillsdales, Salines, Detroits, and Bostons of America.

The great rural-to-urban transition that parallels the industrial revolution is a major phase of social change in our society. This dramatic social change has greatly affected the quality of social life in our world. Yet urbanization is only one of several great changes of the twentieth century. As we have seen throughout this text, our culture and social structure are in a state of flux. During this century our society has grown larger, generally more equal (though this trend has recently reversed with regards to the distribution of wealth and income), more bureaucratic, and more centralized. Meanwhile, deviance has become more visible; schools, businesses, and government have become more prominent; families have become smaller, and marriages shorter. To help integrate and understand these changes, we directly address the urbanization process as an example of social change, discussing its causes as well as its directions.

CITIES IN HISTORICAL PERSPECTIVE

Eight thousand to 10,000 years ago, agriculture developed and people began to build permanent dwellings. Animals were tamed for milk and meat, and pottery was developed, providing storage for surplus food. These advances made it possible for as many as 200 people to live together in a group. Because no mechanism existed to carry food any distance, growing fields surrounded the villagers' houses. The villages were naturally spaced, because each had enough land around it to feed its population. Thus began ***urbanization,*** *the movement of population from rural areas to cities.*

THE FIRST CITIES

*A **city** is a densely populated, permanent settlement of people engaged in nonagricultural pursuits.* The first real cities began 6,000 to 8,000 years ago along the large rivers in Asia and the Middle East. The riverbanks were especially fertile and could produce more food than most other farmland. People invented the plow for cultivation and irrigation for using the river's water for producing crops farther inland, and they learned to store grain for long periods of time. These developments allowed the growth of cities with 10,000 to 20,000 inhabitants.

Even with these new agricultural techniques, seventy-five farmers were required to support one nonfarmer in the city (K. Davis, 1965). The non-farmers began to specialize in other trades, and division of labor developed.

Early cities had many problems. Because of a lack of sanitation and sewage treatment, plagues and disease often destroyed entire city populations. Until the development of reading, writing, and arithmetic, it was difficult to bring the people of the city together in order to develop a sense of community or to work at creating better living conditions. Also, no large business existed that could employ many workers. Only a few craftspeople could really make a living in a city. Family ties were strong, and because most families still lived in the

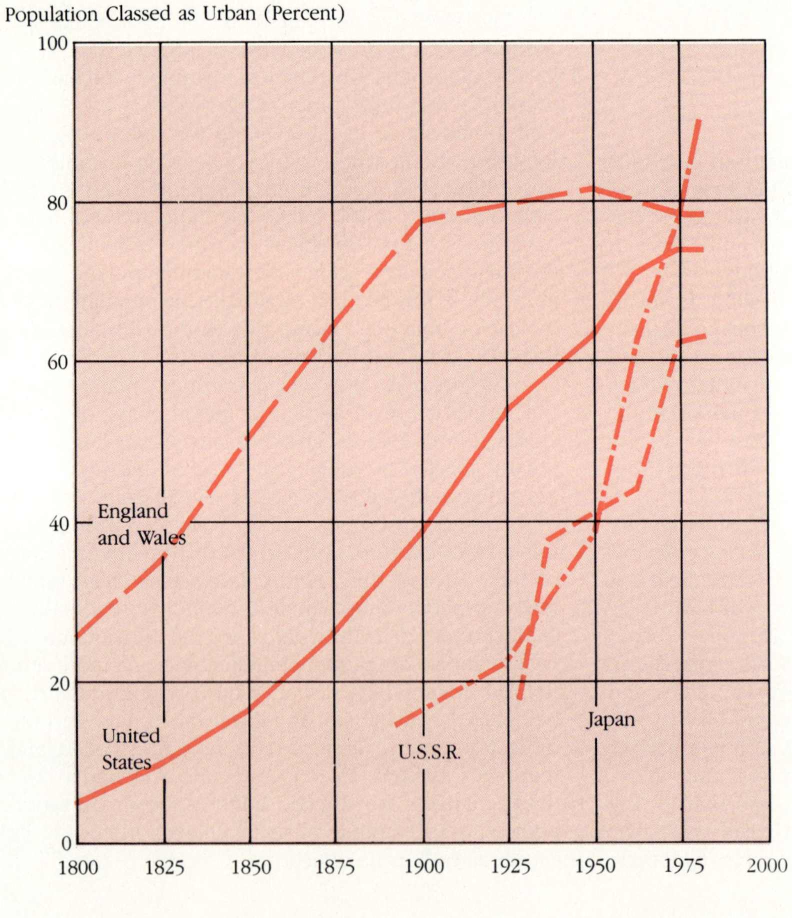

FIGURE 19.1 Urbanization Rates for Various Nations. As these data indicate, urbanization is rapid, but not complete even among the earliest and most urban societies. In fact, both the United States and the Soviet Union have recently become somewhat less urban, as did England and Wales for a time. SOURCE United Nations. 1985. *The Prospects of World Urbanization.* New York: United Nations.

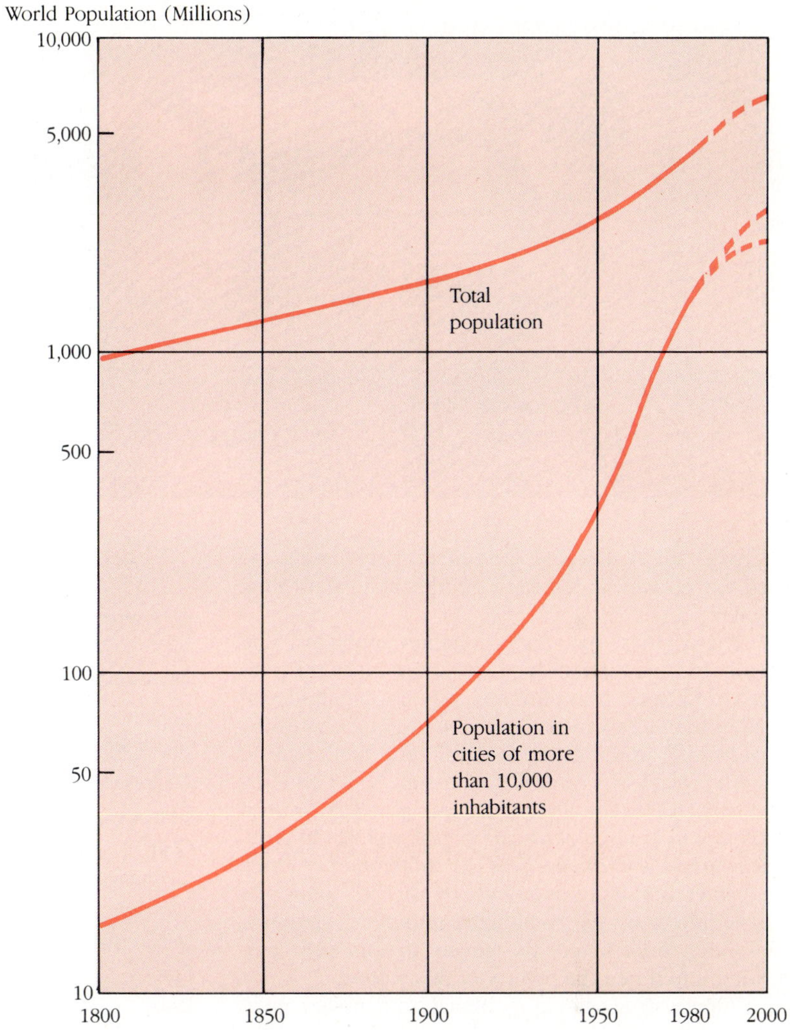

FIGURE 19.2 Urbanization of the World's Population. This graph shows how rapid the urbanization of the world's population has been over the past 200 years, from fewer than 20 million in 1800 to near 4,400 million projected by the year 2000. SOURCE Scientific American. 1969. *Cities.* New York: Knopf. Data for 1980 from Thomas Kane and Paul Myers. *1980 World Population Data Sheet.* Washington, D.C.: Population Reference Bureau.

countryside, most people avoided the risky business of living in the city.

The growth of cities slowed for a few thousand years, until the Romans and Greeks solved several urban problems. The Romans, for instance, used water pipes and sewer systems, as well as metal money for commerce and taxes for city maintenance. Record-keeping techniques were perfected, enabling the government to take a census of the cities' inhabitants and to tax them. Large cities taxed outlying districts in return for protection against attackers.

It has been estimated that 1 million people lived in Rome under Augustus Caesar. Life in Rome was categorically different from life as it had ever been elsewhere. The people lived in publicly built apartments, attended inexpensive schools open to all, read books from twenty-eight public libraries, and received free grain from the city supplies during shortages. Even Rome, however, finally fell to the barbarians, and cities once again waned in influence (Coe, 1980).

PREINDUSTRIAL TO INDUSTRIAL CITIES

Preindustrial cities *differed from modern cities in that they were smaller and their social organization was based on family ties.* In the twelfth century, cities began to grow again, and they have dominated the developed world since that time. Workers were typically members of guilds that controlled the politics of the city, set the price of goods and wages, and decided who would receive training in the trades. ***Guilds*** *were strong fraternities through which working skills were taught.* Membership in the guilds was almost always hereditary

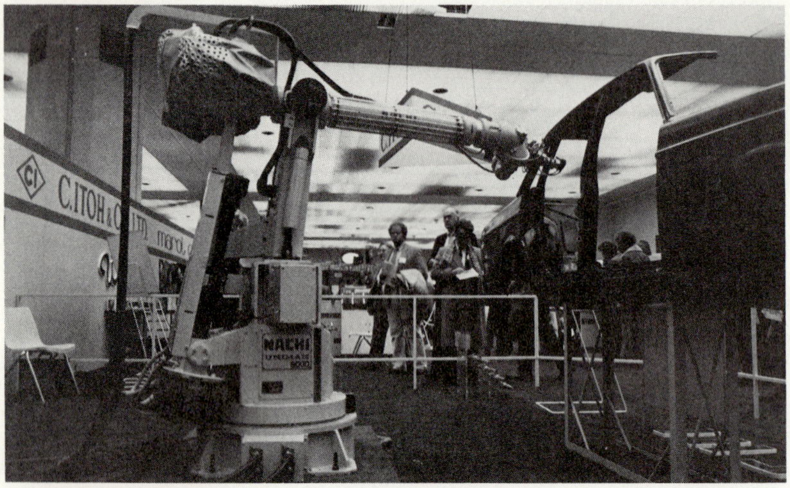

High technology, such as this robot, causes social change in the way we work. As robots and other automation replace factory workers, the white collar workforce grows to absorb them. (*Photo courtesy the Michigan Daily*)

(Sjoberg, 1960). Because little or no government existed, norms were enforced by families and fellow guild members.

These cities, too, had sanitation problems, and plagues frequently destroyed great portions of the population. Because transportation was not highly developed, bringing raw materials to the cities for processing was difficult, and industry was still on a small scale.

The social structures were different, too. Preindustrial cities were typically divided into ***quarters,*** *or areas of the city in which a particular type of craftsperson or religious group worked and lived.* In contemporary cities, the center is usually populated by the very poor and the periphery by the wealthier commuters. Preindustrial cities, built before the advent of cars and commuting, often had the reverse of this pattern.

Preindustrial cities also differed from modern cities in the physical placement of the social classes. In the United States today, the so-called inner city often houses the major businesses and the poorest residents of the city, as well as a few very rich families. The suburbs, in contrast, house the upper-middle and middle classes. In the preindustrial city, no "downtown" area existed. Separate residential and business sections did not exist.

The eighteenth century brought the industrial revolution and, with it, changes in cities. Advances in agriculture produced increases in food and animal products, so that fewer farmers were needed to support the urban population. Advances in transportation, including canals and railroads, meant that raw materials could be shipped to large industrial centers and finished goods could be distributed for sale. Many farmers who were displaced in the fields by technology moved to the city and became industrial workers. With technological developments like elevators, which made skyscrapers possible, even greater concentrations of people

TABLE 19.1 Urban Population of Selected Nations

	Percent Urban
Spain	91
United Kingdom	90
Australia	86
Germany, West	85
Chile	81
Germany, East	77
Canada	76
United States	74
France	73
Brazil	68
Italy	67
Mexico	66
Soviet Union	65
Iraq	64
Poland	60
Iran	47
Yugoslavia	47
Egypt	44
Algeria	41
India	23
China, People's Republic of	21
Nigeria	16
Nepal	4

Sources: U.S. Bureau of the Census, 1987. *Statistical Abstract of the United States: 1988* (107th edition) Washington D.C., p. 800.

Though many nations have become highly urbanized, others, including China, the most populous, have not.

and businesses were possible. Figure 19.1 shows how particular nations have become urbanized during the past two centuries. Figure 19.2 shows the rapid urbanization of the world's population, in general, over the past 200 years (Light, 1983).

WORLD WIDE URBANIZATION

The movement of people from rural areas into cities has been one of the most rapid, steady, and dramatic social changes in the history of man. As Figure 19.2 shows, the vast majority of the world's people lived in rural settings in 1800, but in fewer than 200 years this situation has been reversed. Now much of the world lives in cities. As Figure 19.1 indicates, the urbanization process has been nearly complete for many of the industrialized nations.

Although urbanization is a worldwide trend, many nations, including some of the largest such as China (21 percent urban) and India (23 percent urban), are predominantly rural. (See Table 19.1, "Urban Population of Selected Nations.") Also as Table 19.1 shows, urbanization even among the highly urban societies, has not reached 100 percent. A close look at Figure 19.1 indicates that England and Wales, the United States, and the Soviet Union have all experienced some reversals in their urbanization levels.

We can expect this worldwide trend toward urban residential patterns to continue. What accounts for the recent and rapid urbanization of the world? In the following "Close-Up on Theory," Kingsley Davis offers a general explanation for this phenomenon.

CLOSE-UP on • *THEORY* •

Kingsley Davis on Recent and Rapid World Urbanization

The Theorist and the Setting

Kingsley Davis is one of the United States' foremost sociologists and an internationally recognized expert on population policy. This classic article originally appeared in an edition of the *American Journal of Sociology* devoted to world urbanization. As Davis points out, "compared to most other aspects of society—for example, language, religion, stratification, or the family—cities appeared only yesterday, and urbanization . . . has developed only in the last few moments of man's existence (1955, p. 429).

Davis cites three major reasons sociologists should be concerned with urbanization: First "Urbanism represents a revolutionary change in the whole pattern of social life." . . . Second cities "tend to be centers of power and influence throughout the whole society." . . . Third, "the process of urbanization is still occurring" (p. 429).

The Theorist's Goal

This article describes and explains the initially sporadic growth of cities, which eventually led to the modern urbanization revolution. Davis's question is: "Why was there so little urbanization in ancient times, and why did it proceed so slowly from that point?" (p. 430).

Concepts and Propositions

Davis's explanation of urbanization is both historical and sociological. He goes beyond merely reciting the historical list of events leading to modern urbanization, but he falls short of constructing a formal theory with explicitly defined concepts and propositions.

Davis defines urbanization as the situation in which "a sizable proportion of the population lives in cities" (p. 429). He first seeks to explain the origin of the earliest cities, which typically had populations of 5,000 to 25,000 persons living in an area of a few square miles or less.

Proposition 1: "The diverse technological innovations constituting neolithic culture were necessary for the existence of settled communities" (pp. 429–30).

The major characteristics of neolithic culture include stone tools, domestication of plants and animals, weaving, and pottery. Probably the domestication of plants or animals is the key ingredient *necessary* for settled communities, but, as Davis points out, "one should not infer that these innovations, which began some 8,000 to 10,000 years ago, were sufficient to give rise to towns as distinct from villages" (pp. 429–430; italics ours).

Proposition 2: "Certain inventions—such as the ox-drawn plow and wheeled cart, the sailboat, metallurgy, irrigation, and the domestication of new plants facilitated . . . a more intensive and more productive use of the neolithic elements themselves. When this enriched technology was utilized in certain unusual regions where climate, soil, water, and topography were most favorable . . . the result was a sufficiently productive economy to make possible . . . urban existence" (p. 430).

These early cities were small, containing only a fraction of the population of their societies. They were also unstable, often collapsing under attack from neighboring towns and the less urbanized population.

Davis explains why these cities were so slow to grow and spread. Fifty to ninety farmers were apparently required to support one person in a city. This is true, Davis argues, because the early instruments of production—the ox-drawn plow, stone hoe, and ax—were clumsy ones. Hence agriculture remained static instead of growing.

Proposition 3: "The static character of agriculture and of the economy generally was fostered perhaps by the insulation of the religio-political officials from the practical arts and the reduction of the peasant to virtually the status of a beast of burden. The technology of transport was as labor-intensive as that of agriculture. . . . The size of the early cities was therefore limited by the amount of food, fibers, and other bulky materials that could be obtained from the immediate hinterland by labor-intensive methods" (p. 431).

Proposition 4: "The difficulty of communication and transport and the existence of multifarious local tribal cultures made the formation of large national units virtually impossible" (p. 431).

Because of poor communication, primitive transportation, and diverse cultures in the surrounding areas, early cities could not usually exert power over larger territories as modern cities do.

Proposition 5: "Other limiting factors were the lack of scientific medicine (which made urban living deadly), the fixity of the peasant on the land (which minimized rural–urban migration), the absence of large-scale manufacturing (which would have derived more advantage from urban concentration than did handicraft), the bureaucratic control of the peasantry (which stifled free trade in the hinterland), and the traditionalism and religiosity of all classes (which hampered technological and economic advance)" (pp. 431–32).

As a result of these limitations, even the largest of early cities scarcely exceeded 200,000 inhabitants by Davis's estimate, and these represented only 1 to 2 percent of the total population of their host societies.

In Western Europe, the appropriate conditions arose to permit the urbanization that is spreading throughout the world. Davis identifies the bases for such growth:

Proposition 6: "It (the development of cities) kept going on the basis of improvements in agriculture and transport, the opening of new lands and new trade routes, and above all, the rise in productive activity, first in highly organized handicraft and eventually in a revolutionary new form of production—the factory run by machinery and fossil fuel" (pp. 432–33).

Advances in transport have enabled urban populations to draw their support from increasingly distant areas. "The same forces which have made extreme urbanization possible have also made metropolitan dispersion possible" (p. 436).

Proposition 7: "Almost any technological advance from now on is likely to contribute more to the centrifugal [moving outward] than the centripetal [moving inward] tendency" (p. 437).

The nature of urban areas is indeed changing, with people in metropolitan areas living farther from the centers of the cities, and businesses moving outward as well.

Interpretation

Although Davis is seen as a leading functionalist, in this urbanization article, Davis does not employ the rhetoric often associated with functionalism. The article is both theoretical and general. Davis has identified important factors leading to urbanization in Europe and later in much of the rest of the world, which understanding should be useful in studying the growth of urbanization.

Davis lists two sets of factors: those that contribute to urbanization and those that inhibit urbanization. (See Figure 19.3) The absence of important contributing factors must be expected to have an inhibiting effect, although the absence of inhibiting factors is not necessarily sufficient to cause urbanization. Contributing factors can be grouped into four broad sets: (1) *food production technology,* including domestication of plants and animals, invention of the plow, and eventually, mechanized agriculture; (2) *transportation technology,* including sailboats, ox-carts, and, eventually, motorized transport; (3) *benign geography,* including fertile soil, adequate water, and appropriate climate; and (4) *social technology,* including writing, accounting, science, bureaucracy, freedom of migration and trade, large-scale manufacturing, and modern values (such as belief in progress). Among the inhibiting factors Davis mentions are a lack of contributing factors, isolation of leaders, and conflict within a population that might otherwise become urbanized.

Questions

1. Would Davis's ideas be useful in predicting the rates of industrialization for various territories in a less industrialized continent such as Africa or South America? Would his ideas allow policy planners to gain control of industrialization? How and why?
2. This article was written three decades ago. Is it out of date? Why?
3. Are there some other important explanations of urbanization which Davis has missed? Has he included any that you believe are unimportant?

SOURCE Kingsley Davis. 1955. "The Origin and Growth of Urbanization in the World." *American Journal of Sociology* 60, no. 5, pp. 429–37.

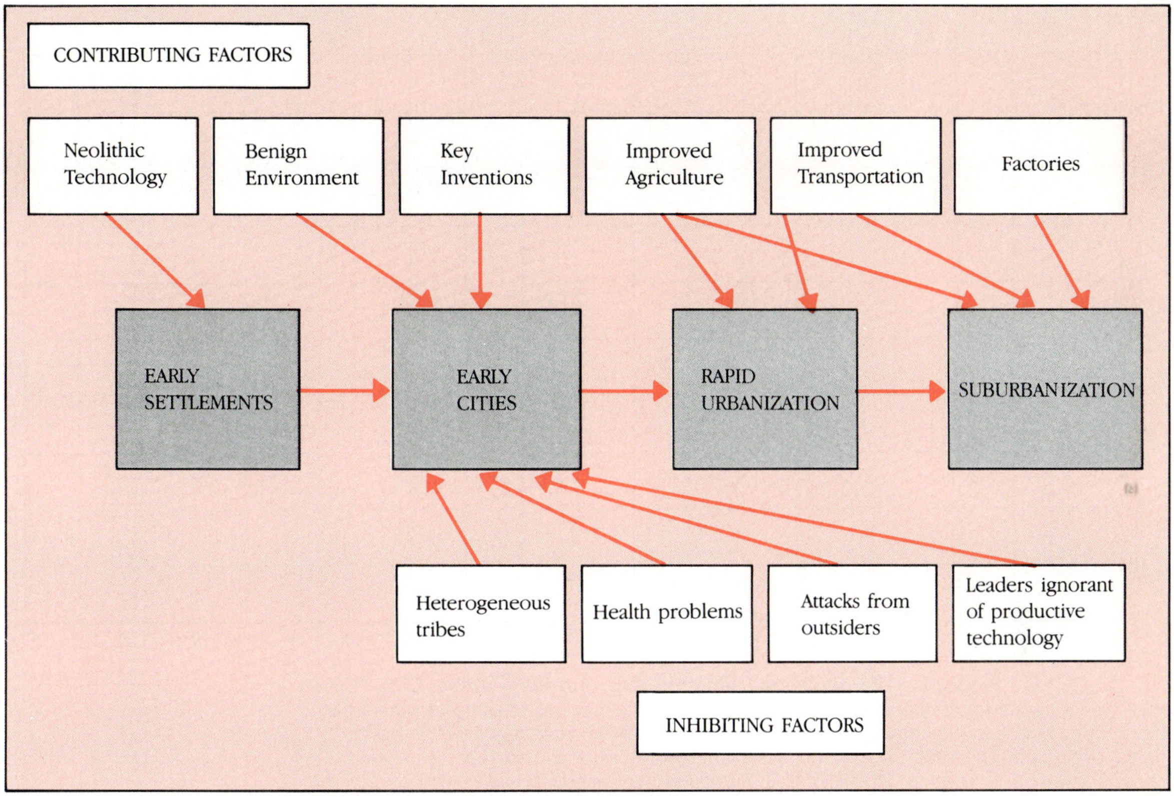

FIGURE 19.3 Factors Contributing to, or Inhibiting, Urbanization. The progression from small early settlements, through early cities, rapid urbanization, and on to suburbanization has been propelled by innovations but slowed by conflict, ignorance, and disease.

How Have Cities and Suburbs Grown in the United States?

As Figure 19.4 indicates, the United States has been on a steady march from rural areas towards cities throughout its history. This trend nearly parallels the exodus of the work force from agriculture into industrial and postindustrial occupations that we studied in Chapter 15. However, more people remain in rural areas than remain in agriculture at the present time. Over the first half-century of our history, the proportion of people living in cities increased only 5 percent, but beginning with 1840 the proportion of the population living in urban areas grew about 5 percent per decade until 1960, pausing only once during the Great Depression. (People seem to have sat out the 1930s where they were.) Then, during the 1960s, growth of the urban proportion of our population lowered and, during the 1970s, it stopped.

Is the United States becoming more or less urbanized? The 1980 census surprised many by revealing that major cities including New York, Boston, Philadelphia, Detroit, and Chicago had for the first time in history lost population! Some mayors reacted with shock, disbelief, and even anger. The mayors had more than an academic interest, because many forms of federal aid as well as representation in Congress are determined by these population statistics. Some mayors charged that census takers had undercounted the population, perhaps because they did not want to make calls in certain neighborhoods or because some people living in the city are hard to reach. Though these arguments may have an element of truth, they probably do not explain the change in the count. One would

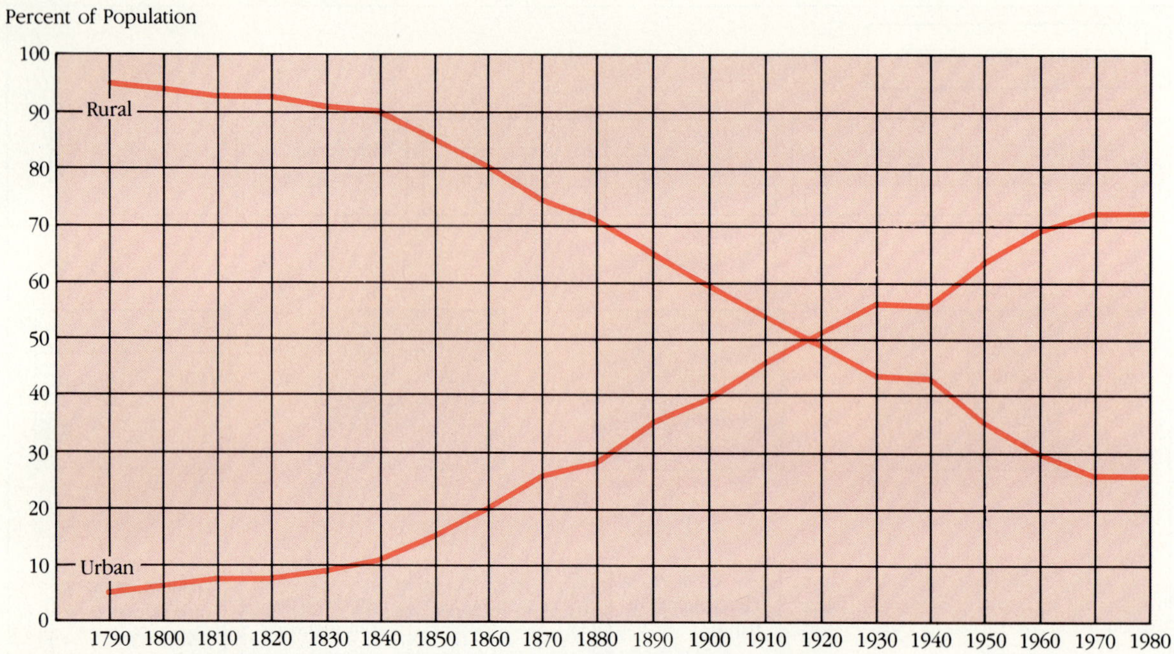

FIGURE 19.4 Proportion of Population Living in Urban and Rural Areas, 1790–1980. With only a pause for the depression of the 1930s, the United States became progressively more urban and less rural throughout its history until the 1970s. At that point urbanization again leveled off. The 1990 Census will reveal whether the two-hundred year trend will resume, level off, or reverse. SOURCE U.S. Bureau of the Census, *Statistical Abstract of the United States, 1988* (106th ed.), Washington, D.C., 1987, p. 16.

have to believe that there has been a major change in the reliability of census takers for this to be the case.

The fact of the matter seems quite clearly to be that most of the population of the United States, although not rural, is not urban in the sense of large cities of a million or more people. Figure 19.5 shows that small cities and towns are the most popular settings and they are growing fastest in population. Frequently these are *small cities and towns that are adjacent to large cities* and are properly called ***suburbs.*** Of course, people tend to move where they can find employment, but nearly half (48 percent) of the people in the United States indicated they would live in a rural area or small town if they were given the choice (Gallup, 1987).

As Davis's theory predicts, rapid urbanization is followed by suburbanization. However, there may be limits to the trend toward suburbanization. The United States is the most suburbanized country in the world in part because Americans have been prosperous enough to afford the relatively high cost of suburban living. Suburbs are costly in two ways that cities are not. First, heating costs are higher for single-family homes typically found in the suburbs than they are for the multiple-family homes typical of the cities. Second, suburbanites are much more reliant on automobiles for commuting to work and for shopping. Many experts expect a long-term economic decline combined with rising oil prices. These trends could pressure people into living in urban rather than suburban settings (Jackson, 1985; Muller, 1981).

We now consider the social structure of cities, some of the problems of cities, and some of the solutions offered. As Davis has suggested, and as recent trends confirm, the "solution" to urban problems for many people is to move further from them into the suburbs and rural areas.

HOW ARE CITIES SOCIALLY STRUCTURED?

Sociologists are concerned about the effects of concentration of people on human groups. They have studied various aspects of urbanization, including social relationships, ecology, spatial development, and social problems of cities. Early sociologists, confronted with

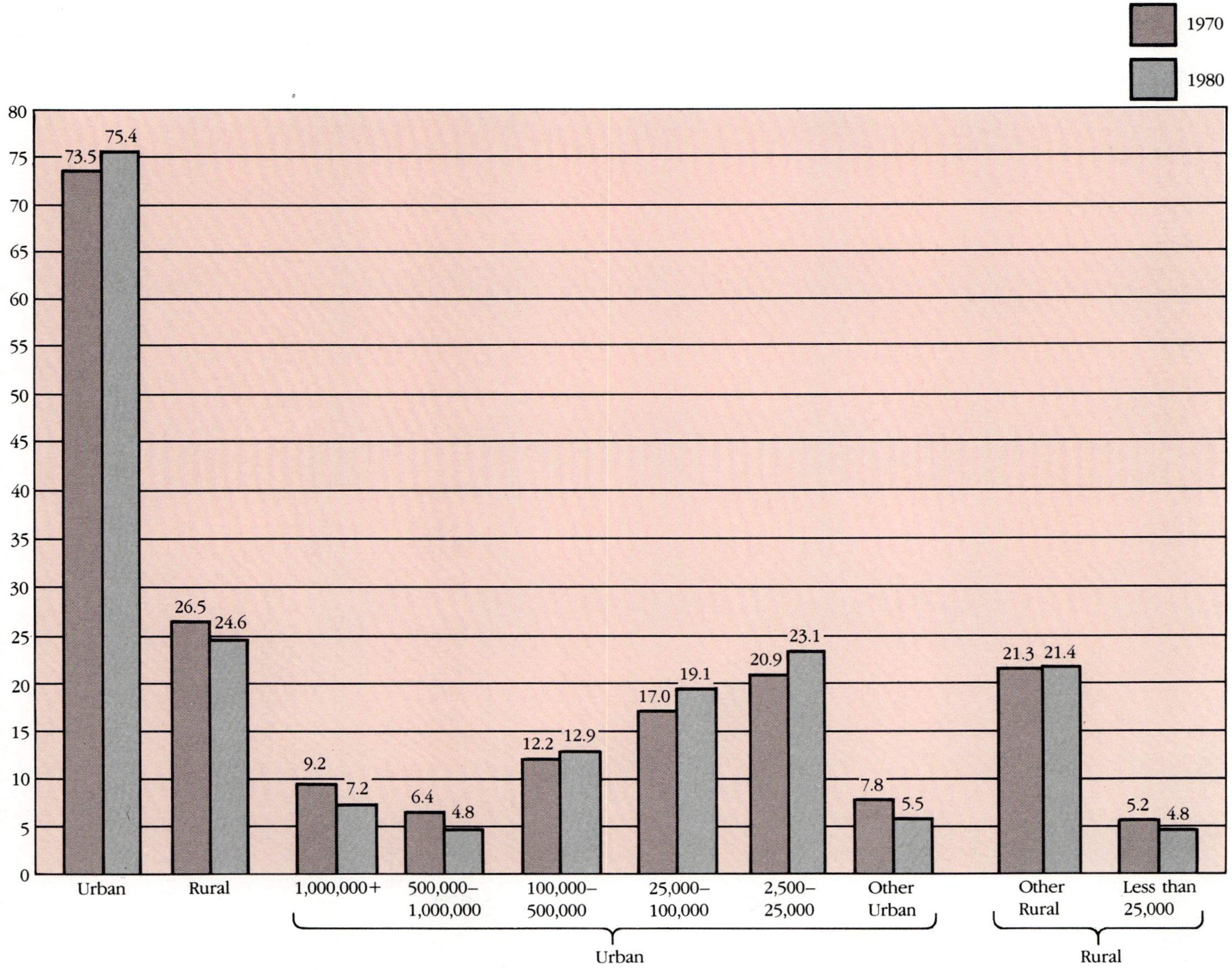

FIGURE 19.5 By studying this chart we can see that, though some large cities did lose population between 1970 and 1980, the overall population became a bit more urban and a bit less rural. Large cities of 500,000 or more typically lost population while smaller ones grew. Very small towns or villages also lost population.

cities that were small by today's standards, first studied the effect of urbanization on social relationships.

TÖNNIES: GEMEINSCHAFT AND GESELLSCHAFT

Ferdinand Tönnies (Tone-ee-ez) was the first sociologist to suggest that a qualitative difference exists between the social relationships in a small town and those in a large city (Tönnies, 1887). He termed these differences ***Gemeinschaft*** (Guh-mine-shoft), *the primary community in which relationships are based on intimacy, and* ***Gesellschaft*** (Guh-zell-shoft), *the voluntary society in which relationships are based on business or self-interest.*

Gemeinschaft refers to a small-town atmosphere, in which the people of a group consider each other friends. Because the entire community is aware when a norm is broken, and the breaking of norms intimately affects other members of the group, the group informally punishes offenders through criticism and exclusion from normal group activities. The social group also works together in positive directions. If a school is needed, the group builds it. If a member is sick or temporarily needs food or shelter, the group works together to fill these needs. Many people in small towns are related, through the intermarriage that is more likely in a small group. The group has a strong sense of history, and many families have lived in the same area for generations. In short, *Gemeinschaft* is a family-type atmosphere of caring for and taking responsibility for the group's well-being.

Gesellschaft, in contrast, is the atmosphere Tönnies found prevalent in a large city, where most people do not know each other or take responsibility for each other. Because social pressure is only a strong force in groups where members value each other's opinions, rule breakers in cities are dealt with through institutions such as laws and police departments. Joint projects are chosen by officials of the group, not the members, and the group members rarely work together on any project. Few people are related, and family ties are not as likely to be important to work or social relationships. Because people know little about each other's backgrounds, the present plays a larger role in their lives than does the past. Also, because large cities experience more migration than do smaller urban areas, there is a sense of transience rather than permanence.

Since Tönnies introduced the concepts of *Gemeinschaft* and *Gesellschaft,* many other sociologists have compared urban and rural life. Tönnies's explanations of these two types of social organization have been the basis for theories of deviance, family stability, and job performance in cities and urban areas.

SIMMEL: PEOPLE AS NUMBERS

Georg Simmel died in 1918, but even in that less urbanized era he was convinced that people who lived in what he thought of as "modern" cities were overstimulated by the constant barrage of information, people, and situations they encountered (Simmel, [1902] 1950). Simmel believed that people in urban settings cannot process all of the information they receive, and therefore they learn to screen it. City dwellers also learn to filter out some of the people they meet and become involved with only a few. He suggested further that the cities' emphasis on commerce teaches city dwellers to constantly evaluate everything, including friendships and other social relationships, in terms of cost. Simmel believed that in such settings people are treated like numbers, a complaint frequently heard today in the United States. His ideas are frequently used by present-day theorists and researchers because of their relevance to problems of modern urban societies.

THE CHICAGO SCHOOL

Building on Simmel's ideas, three sociologists from the University of Chicago—Robert Park and his students Ernest Burgess and Louis Wirth—furthered the study of urbanism. ***Urbanism*** *is the study of the social structure of cities.* Beginning in the 1930s these three developed what is known as the "Chicago School" perspective on the social effects of urbanization. Wirth's article "Urbanism as a Way of Life" in many ways summarizes these views (Wirth, 1938). Wirth notes three aspects of urban life that are categorically different from rural life: size, density of population, and heterogeneity. Together they create an environment that fosters impersonal relationships.

The large size of Chicago, the city Wirth studied, made it impossible for small-town-style personal relationships to develop there. City dwellers know many more people, and their social interactions are much more varied than those in rural areas. Urban residents often know each other, however, only in specialized roles. The urban grocer is simply the grocer, not also Tom who bowls with Dad. This separating of social roles makes it more difficult for people to view others as whole beings and encourages categorizing others by role or status rather than as persons.

Wirth suggests that the population density of the city leads to segregation. When many people live in close proximity, they separate themselves into like groups in order to feel more at home within the traditions and norms of their own group. These smaller groups tend to segregate themselves from the larger group, leading to less integration in the community as a whole. This heterogeneous nature of urban areas makes it difficult for cities to act as units unto themselves.

Wirth also believes it is more difficult for people from greatly varied backgrounds, such as those found in cities, to form long-term, intimate relationships. The impersonal relationships that characterize social life in the city, however, may allow more individual freedom. Urban relationships, because they tend to be transitory and shallow, exert less social pressure on an individual's behavior than do small-town relationships, which are more intimate. This frees urban people to be different from those around them. The city's vastness adds to this permission to be different. One man wearing an ostrich-plume hat and pink-striped knickers may be viewed as mildly amusing in New York City, whereas in Hillsdale, Michigan such a costume would rate much comment and immediate negative social sanctions.

The work of Park, Burgess, and Wirth shows obvious bias against large cities. All three were raised in small towns and lived in Chicago at the time of their research. Perhaps their positive feelings toward their own small-town origins affected their theoretical judgments. Also, in the 1920s and 1930s, when this work was being completed, large numbers of immigrants in Chicago were causing some social disorganization and reevaluation of the existing social structure in the city.

PRESENT-DAY THEORISTS

Is it true that people cannot or do not form intimate social relationships while living in large cities? This question has been studied by many sociologists since Wirth. Today's researchers may be as eager to discover positive aspects of urbanization as the Chicago School seemed to be to find negative ones. At any rate, present research indicates that people can and do find satisfying social relationships in urban settings.

Herbert Gans was one of the first sociologists to suggest that Wirth's assessment of cities was somewhat harsh (1962). Gans believes the type of social relationships that Wirth discussed are more common among poor and otherwise unstable residents of cities than among working-class and middle-class residents who feel part of some ethnic or social community. Gans (1970) names such residents the "urban villagers" and suggests that members of these groups do maintain strong social ties and provide each other with the sense of community Wirth found lacking. Finally, Gans distinguishes among living in the inner city, in the suburbs of a city, and in the satellite towns of a metropolitan area.

Gerard Suttles lived for several years in the Chicago slums, and his participant-observation research questions both Wirth's and Gans's conclusions (Suttles, 1972). He found an intricate order, even in the poor neighborhoods he studied. Allied neighborhood members supported each other and clearly defined the boundaries between neighborhods, usually based on ethnicity. In contrast to Wirth's suggestion that many people are lost in a large city, Suttles found that people created a small-town atmosphere in their own section of a large city. In their own section, most people know their neighbors well and are involved in their neighbors' lives.

Scott Greer (1962) suggests that extended family ties, like those Wirth finds in rural areas, can flourish in the city also. Greer found that over half the people he studied visited family members at least once a week. This contradicts Wirth's assertion that city living greatly weakens family ties.

More recent research by Claude Fischer (1981) agrees that a large city does not weaken ties among people but encourages them to form strong cohesive groups within their particular subcultures, groups based on occupation, ethnicity, or personal interests. Fischer notes that large cities may in fact foster more intimacy than do rural areas, because in a larger group it is more likely that nonmainstream people can seek out others like themselves in order to form cohesive interest or ethnic groups.

THE SPATIAL STRUCTURE OF CITIES

Some theorists study the social relationships within cities; others have developed theories to account for *the spatial structure of cities, or* ***urban ecology***. The study of urban ecology began at the University of Chicago. Burgess (1925) and his colleagues Park and McKenzie approached the study of urban populations and their environment much the way biologists study the relationships between life forms and their environments. The Chicago group suggested that urban land use and population distribution be studied as if the city were a "social organism" (Park, 1916). Park focused on the processes of concentration and dispersion, centralization, segregation, invasion and succession.

Invasion and succession, the most widely studied processes, change the nature of city areas by "invasion" from the outside. For example, homes near the center of a small but growing town, which probably once housed the upper classes, may lose value as light industry or business moves in nearby. A mansion may be converted to a funeral parlor. Before the remaining residents mobilize, other businesses may begin to buy properties, attracted by land near the center of town.

"THIRTY-EIGHT WHO SAW MURDER DIDN'T CALL THE POLICE" NEW YORK TIMES, MARCH 27, 1964

The Kitty Genovese story is one of the most dramatic examples of distant and impersonal urban relationships. Although the incident may be used to oversimplify the urban–rural controversy, its existence was the impetus for research in the area of prosocial behavior.

For more than half an hour thirty-eight respectable, law-abiding citizens in Queens watched a killer stalk and stab a woman in three separate attacks in Kew Gardens.

Twice their chatter and the sudden glow of their bedroom lights interrupted him and frightened him off. Each time he returned, sought her out, and stabbed her again. Not one person telephoned the police during the assault; one witness called after the woman was dead.

That was two weeks ago today.

Still shocked is Assistant Chief Inspector Frederick M. Lussen, in charge of the borough's detectives and a veteran of twenty-five years of homicide investigations. He can give a matter-of-fact recitation of many murders. But the Kew Gardens slaying baffles him—not because it is a murder, but because the "good people" failed to call the police.

"As we have reconstructed the crime," he said, "the assailant had three chances to kill this woman during a thirty-five-minute period. He returned twice to complete the job. If we had been called when he first attacked, the woman might not be dead now."

This is what the police say happened beginning at 3:20 A.M. in the staid, middle-class, tree-lined Austin Street area:

Twenty-eight-year-old Catherine Genovese, who was called Kitty by almost everyone in the neighborhood, was returning home from her job as manager of a bar in Hollis. She parked her red Fiat in a lot adjacent to the Kew Gardens Long Island Railroad Station, facing Mowbray Place. Like many residents of the neighborhood, she had parked there day after day since her arrival from Connecticut a year ago, although the railroad frowns on the practice.

She turned off the lights of her car, locked the door, and started to walk the 100 feet to the entrance of her apartment at 82–70 Austin Street, which is in a Tudor building, with stores on the first floor and apartments on the second.

The entrance to the apartment is in the rear of the building because the front is rented to retail stores. At night the quiet neighborhood is shrouded

Unless the residents are able to stop the process, the downtown neighborhoods eventually consist of beauty salons, interior decorating storefronts, and antique shops, and the original residents move farther out of the city to whatever housing they can afford. The invasion is complete. Residents have been replaced by businesses, through succession.

Three major theories of spatial structure have been developed, following Park's initiative (see Figure 19.6). First is the ***concentric zone theory,*** *which describes the expansion and internal development of cities in terms of a series of concentric zones that center on a central business district.* Second, the ***sector model,*** which suggests that *specialized areas of a city develop in regions based around lines of transportation rather than in concentric circles.* Third, the ***multiple nuclei model*** hypothesizes *a pattern of city growth in which several business centers or districts develop, each having its own special activities based on separate communities or ethnic and class differences, rather than having an entire city develop around one central business district.*

CONCENTRIC ZONE MODEL

Burgess was the first urban ecologist to develop a model to describe the growth of cities: the concentric zone model. Burgess suggests that economic factors are a prime determinant of the growth patterns of cities, and his spatial zones have economic bases.

Zone 1, the central business district, is an expensive place to locate and contains the most successful enterprises. Zone 2 is the transition zone, originally a rural area that housed the lower classes. When absorbed by the city, it becomes the home of prostitution, in the slumbering darkness that marks most residential areas.

Miss Genovese noticed a man at the far end of the lot, near a seven-story apartment house at 82–40 Austin Street. She halted. Then, nervously, she headed up Austin Street toward Lefferts Boulevard, where there is a call box to the 102nd Police Precinct in nearby Richmond Hill.

She got as far as a streetlight in front of a bookstore before the man grabbed her. She screamed. Lights went on in the ten-story apartment house at 82–67 Austin Street, which faces the bookstore. Windows slid open and voices punctuated the early-morning stillness.

Miss Genovese screamed: "Oh, my God, he stabbed me! Please help me! Please help me!"

From one of the upper windows in the apartment house, a man called down: "Let that girl alone!"

The assailant looked up at him, shrugged, and walked down Austin Street toward a white sedan parked a short distance away. Miss Genovese struggled to her feet.

Lights went out. The killer returned to Miss Genovese, now trying to make her way around the side of the building by the parking lot to get to her apartment. The assailant stabbed her again.

"I'm dying!" she shrieked. "I'm dying!"

Windows were opened again, and lights went on in many apartments. The assailant got into his car and drove away. Miss Genovese staggered to her feet. A city bus, 0-10, the Lefferts Boulevard line to Kennedy International Airport, passed. It was 3:35 A.M.

The assailant returned. By then, Miss Genovese had crawled to the back of the building, where the freshly painted brown doors to the apartment house held out hope for safety. The killer tried the first door; she wasn't there. At the second door, 82–62 Austin Street, he saw her slumped on the floor at the foot of the stairs. He stabbed her a third time—fatally.

It was 3:50 by the time the police received their first call, from a man who was a neighbor of Miss Genovese. In two minutes they were at the scene. A neighbor, a seventy-year-old woman, and another woman were the only persons on the street. Nobody else came forward.

The man explained that he had called the police after much deliberation. He had phoned a friend in Nassau County for advice and then he had crossed the roof of the building of the apartment of the elderly woman to get her to make the call.

"I didn't want to get involved," he sheepishly told the police.

SOURCE Martin Gensberger, 1964. "Thirty-eight who saw murder didn't call the police." *The New York Times*, March 27, 1964, pp. 2, 38.

bars, and similar activities. The two inner zones have a higher crime rate than the outer ones.

Zone 3 is close enough to the city center so that workers who live there can use public transportation or walk to work, but it consists of individual homes. Zone 4 contains expensive apartments and better-built single homes for the upper-middle classes. Commuters live in Zone 5, the suburbs, in larger, more expensive homes.

Burgess believed that as cities grow new outer zones are added, and the status of the inner zones drops whenever a new zone appears on the outside of the circle. Generally, the status of the city residents rises as one moves outward from the center. More people in the outer circles own their own homes, for instance, and are paid salaries rather than hourly wages. Immigrants often settle first in the middle zones and later move outward.

Burgess thought his theory was applicable to all city growth. It appears now, however, that although it fairly accurately describes the growth patterns of Chicago and other larger cities during the large immigration period before the 1920s, many modern developing cities do not follow this pattern.

THE SECTOR MODEL

Fourteen years later, when automobiles had become widely used, Homer Hoyt developed the *sector model* to explain the growth of urban areas (1939). In studying how the automobile changed the structure of urban living areas, Hoyt suggested that cities are divided into pie-shaped sectors rather than concentric circles. Hoyt's housing, business, and industrial districts expanded

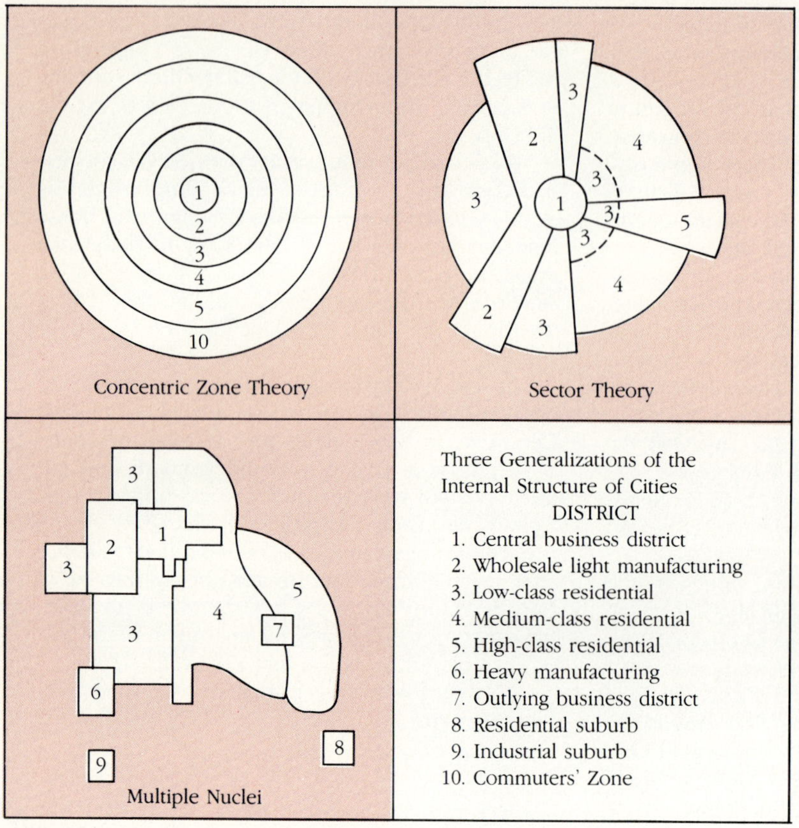

FIGURE 19.6 Generalizations of Internal Structure of Cities. The concentric zone theory is a generalization for all cities. The arrangement of the sectors in the sector theory varies from city to city. The diagram for multiple nuclei represents one possible pattern among innumerable variations. SOURCE Chauncy D. Harris and Edward L. Ullman. 1945. "The Nature of Cities." *Annals of the American Academy of Political and Social Science*, vol. 242 (November), pp. 7–17. With permission of the American Academy of Political and Social Science and Chauncy D. Harris.

outward from the center of the city following major highways or railways of the time.

In contrast to Burgess, who described Chicago in the 1920s, Hoyt's model was hypothetical. He knew the geography of each city would modify its sectors. For example, a city like Montreal built on a cliff would have different lines of transportation than a city built on the plains, like St. Louis. Many cities have grown along the lines Hoyt suggested, with various districts following existing or new transportation lines.

THE MULTIPLE NUCLEI MODEL

By the 1940s more was known about the growth of cities, and an extensive model was proposed by Chauncy Harris and Edward Ullman, the multiple nuclei model (1945). They proposed that early in a city's development, centers of business, industry, and living are established outside of the original center of town. In other words, the city does not grow from one center but rather from many centers, concentrically or in sectors.

Harris and Ullman identified four variables affecting the development of these centers. First, different activities require different facilities. For instance, a company needing raw materials from distant states and cities requires access to the railroad. Second, some businesses may locate close together for their mutual benefit. For example, several retail shops may jointly build a shopping center to maximize their access to customers and to share expenses for facilities and advertising. Third, some types of centers naturally avoid each other. For example, it is highly unlikely that an expensive apartment building would locate near a stockyard. Fourth, some enterprises may be unable to afford a location that would otherwise be of benefit. For example, a small, inner-city tailor might prosper at a shopping center farther out of town, but the monthly rent and deposit required there may prohibit him from moving.

Each of these models provide some insights into urban growth, but the multiple nuclei model appears best able to explain the shape of today's cities. No model has yet been developed to accurately predict how cities of the future will grow (Macionis and Spates, 1987).

THE MEGALOPOLIS

Perhaps one reason city growth appears so unpredictable is that the actual forms of cities are changing. Sociologist Jean Gottmann describes a new form of urban area developing, which she terms the megalopolis, or "great city" (1964). *A **megalopolis** is a group of cities, each more or less continuous with the last.* Gottmann uses the Eastern Seaboard from Maine to Virginia, encompassing Boston, New Haven, New York, Philadelphia, and Washington, D.C., as an example of this new form. She calls this megalopolis the "Boswash Corridor." Over 40 million people live in this string of end-to-end communities, with more than 100 people per square mile. "Every city in this region spreads out far and wide around its original nucleus; it grows amidst an irregularly colloidal mixture of rural and suburban landscapes; it melts on broad fronts with other mixtures, of somewhat similar though different texture, belonging to the suburban neighborhoods of other cities" (Gottmann, 1964, p. 1).

The U.S. Bureau of the Census describes a megalopolis as a *Standard Consolidated Area (SCA)* and defines thirteen such areas in the United States today. Besides the Eastern Seaboard, these include San Francisco–Los Angeles–San Diego, Dallas–San Antonio–Houston, and Chicago–Detroit–Pittsburgh. Demographers predict that more of these areas will grow in the future, and that eventually a large proportion of the American population will live in these very large urban areas.

Some Americans are apparently resisting this push to larger cities and moving to small towns. In the 1970s rural areas grew faster than urban ones. Small towns may, of course, eventually become incorporated into an SCA as the latter moves outward from a large city.

THE URBAN–SUBURBAN CRISIS

Center cities house a very diverse group of people. Because the city is often a center for the arts, business, theater, public relations, and banking, it is an attractive home to professional, upper-middle-class people who are interested in and involved in these activities. The center city also has a greater proportion of poor and unemployed persons than the suburbs. In 1975, 10 percent of the people in small towns and suburban areas had incomes below the poverty line, as opposed to 30 percent of center-city populations (U.S. Bureau of the Census, 1976). Unemployment in inner-city areas remains twice the national average.

CENTER-CITY DWELLERS

Gans (1965) describes five types of people who live in center cities. His descriptions illuminate some of the problems faced by cities. The *cosmopolites* are well-educated professionals who live in the city to be near its cultural opportunities and business contacts. They are not linked to one particular neighborhood by ethnic ties but enjoy the atmosphere of the city as a whole. Cosmopolites are often artists, writers, advertising persons, or members of other professions.

Unmarried or childless people often live in the city because it is advantageous for work and social activity. They are not committed to life in the city, however, and often move to the suburbs when they marry or have children.

In contrast to these two voluntary groups, three other groups live in the city for other reasons. The *ethnic villagers* are people who have immigrated to the United States and form a small community within a city with others from their homelands. They isolate themselves from the larger city and maintain a strong commitment to their community. The ethnic villagers remain in the city from tradition and lack of enough money to find the same community atmosphere in the suburbs. The *deprived* are the poor, nonwhite, handicapped, or otherwise economically disadvantaged people. They live in the city because housing is cheap and jobs may be more available for them, as well as because of family ties. The *trapped* are generally older people who have lived in the city all their lives and cannot afford or do not wish to move.

Only two of Gan's categories, the unmarried and childless and the cosmopolites, live in the city by free choice. This lack of commitment to the city has caused central-city deterioration and booming suburb populations (C. Fischer, 1984).

THE FLIGHT TO THE SUBURBS

The flight to the suburbs began when the automobile made it possible for middle-class people to commute to work. With fewer working people, the cities' tax bases eroded and cities began to lack money for necessary services. Because many inner-city residents are poor, they use more city services than the middle class, while paying little or no tax. Raising taxes might provide temporary relief, but it is also likely to force even more upper-class and middle-class residents to the suburbs. Many businesses have also moved out of cities, taking with them the unskilled and semiskilled jobs many people from the inner cities could fill.

One cause of the flight to the suburbs that compounds the city's problems is that so many things are

Modernization brings forth urbanization which in recent times seems inevitably to call forth glass buildings that simultaneously reflect and distort society. (*Photo courtesy the author*)

more expensive in the city. Buildings are generally older than those in suburbs and thus require more maintenance and more fire protection. The crime rate is higher in more densely populated areas, and thus police protection is more expensive. Often cities cannot pay for all the added services they need, so they deteriorate. Schools are not maintained, and school districts often cannot pay enough to attract the best teachers and administrators. Police patrols are cut back rather than augmented. Public transportation gradually becomes less reliable and safe. People who live in cities, then, often pay more taxes and receive fewer services than people who live in the suburbs. The next step is the first step again: more upper-class and middle-class people move to the suburbs, and the cycle repeats itself.

Those who remain in cities are often the very rich and the very poor. The rich enjoy the advantages of the city and compensate for its disadvantages by buying services, such as sending their children to private schools, driving their own cars rather than using public transportation, and hiring private police to guard their houses. The poor cannot afford to buy or rent a house

PROBLEMS OF THE CITIES REVISITED

Two historians, Charles Adrian and Ernest Griffith, say that the problems cities are facing today are far from new. After carefully studying town records, newspaper files, and personal recollections of senior citizens, they concluded that much of what is described today as "urban crisis" is old hat.

Pollution, for instance, is not a modern malady. The pollution by horses on the streets caused much concern before acceptable measures were found to control the problem. Polluted water was such a problem in the nineteenth century that cities were frequently destroyed by disease carried in the water supply. Public transportation was also a problem. The horsecar was too expensive for the common man and could only be used by the middle classes. Even ghetto riots during the summer are not a new invention. According to Adrian and Griffith, they began in the 1820s and peaked in the 1860s.

Apparently, when a large number of people live together in a small space, some problems are inherent. Sociologists continue to believe, however, that understanding the problems is the first step toward solving them.

in the suburbs or to own a car to commute; in fact, most people would not have enough cash to move their belongings from city to suburb.

The differences between inner cities and suburbs are becoming more distinct. The suburbs are growing steadily more white and middle-class, and the inner city more black or Hispanic and lower- or working-class. Ninety-one percent of the suburban population in 1980 was white while in that year the proportion of whites in central cities dropped to 25 percent, 2 percentage points lower than it had been in 1970. During the same period the proportion of blacks grew from 53 percent to 58 percent of the central-city populations and declined from 35 percent to 32 percent in noncity areas (U.S. Bureau of the Census, 1970; 1980). It has been suggested that the suburbs are a fortress to which the middle classes have fled in an effort to avoid the city's problems while still being able to reap its benefits (Peterson, 1985).

PROPOSED SOLUTIONS

Some cities now tax suburbanites who work in the city in order to support city services they use: lights, streets, sidewalks, trash removal, police and fire protection, public transportation. For example, New York City collects a tax from commuters who live in New Jersey or Connecticut. The major risk of this, of course, is that if the tax becomes burdensome the businesses will be pressured by employees to move out, again decreasing the tax base.

Perhaps suburbs should provide some low-income housing in an effort to spread the cost of services for the poor more uniformly across an area. Resistance to this idea has been great. Those who moved to the suburbs did so partly to get away from the problems of the city and do not want those problems to follow them (Williams, 1978). Also, low-income housing strains suburban school systems, because the tax base is essentially unchanged and more students exist to be educated.

The problems of the cities remain, but the awareness grows that cities perform many valuable functions even for those who do not live or work in them. Cities must be protected to maintain today's way of life. In many ways, cities are the "Main Streets" of the United States. Few people aspire to live on Main Street, but everyone trades there occasionally. The United States needs centers of business like Wall Street, centers of food processing like Chicago, and distribution centers for imported goods, such as oil, like Houston and Norfolk. Because the countryside cannot thrive without cities, it is important to continue to learn to live with them.

CITY PLANNING

City planning *refers to proposing and regulating all aspects of a city's growth.* Urban planning has been known in some form since ancient times, when the city leaders of Rome and Athens planned to achieve the stated goals of their city-states. However, the particular "problems of the cities" we have been discussing have given rise to a new profession: city planning. The professional city planner addresses all problems involved in the growth of urban areas, including zoning, sanitation, health, communications, and transportation.

URBAN RENEWAL

Urban renewal *is a form of urban development that stresses prevention of the spread of urban blight into good areas, rehabitation and conservation of areas that can be economically restored, and clearance and redevelopment of areas that cannot be saved* (Cole, 1958). Urban renewal was widely practiced for a number of years but has recently lost favor among city planners. The major problem of urban renewal programs was that they failed to provide adequately for the people they displaced in their clearance and redevelopment phases, making the poor unable to find new low-rent housing. The result was homelessness or increased rents for the poor, who already spend a higher percentage of their income for housing than the middle or upper classes.

Another problem is that the projects city governments choose to support are not always useful or necessary to the community and therefore sometimes remain unused; for example, parks which are never walked in because the surrounding area is too dangerous, or expensive apartments that remain unrented due to lack of sufficient interest by high-income persons living in that area.

NEW TOWNS

City planners have also been experimenting with new towns, such as Columbia, Maryland. ***New towns*** *are cities which are designed to contain a balance of socioeconomic status groups, age groups, and working groups, and to carefully monitor the placement of industry, park land, business, and residences.* Only a few such communities exist, and many of them are having financial difficulties. A stated goal of the new towns is to encourage a sense of community. There is some evidence that this has been successful in Columbia, in that new residents have become more involved in community affairs there than they had been in their old home communities (Eichler and Kaplan, 1967).

CONSOLIDATED AREAS

Some cities are consolidating with suburbs in order to plan for the future more effectively. Neighboring communities share such concerns as highways, pollution control, utilities, and schooling, and combining communities and commissions facilitates progress in these areas. The area surrounding Minneapolis and St. Paul is a community that is pioneering in establishing joint metropolitan government agencies to solve problems. As the megalopolis becomes predominant, this solution may gain more adherents, though it typically faces opposition from suburbanites.

OBSOLESCENCE

Another possibility is that cities will become obsolete. At least a few sociologists have suggested that the world may eventually enter a "posturban" age, in which communications and transportation will have improved so much that people no longer need to live together in large groups in order to transact business. Advances in telephone and television technology move us in this direction.

As in many social problem areas, these proposed solutions to urban problems are sometimes antithetical and depend to a great extent on the often unpredictable actions of human beings. There is no doubt, however, that the complexity and size of modern cities requires city planning rather than unmonitored urban growth or decline (Peterson, 1985; Macionis and Spates, 1987).

Decline of tradition marks the transition to modernization. Here a father carries his child on his back in a manner similar to the way mothers in traditional societies carry their young. (*Photo courtesy the Michigan Daily*)

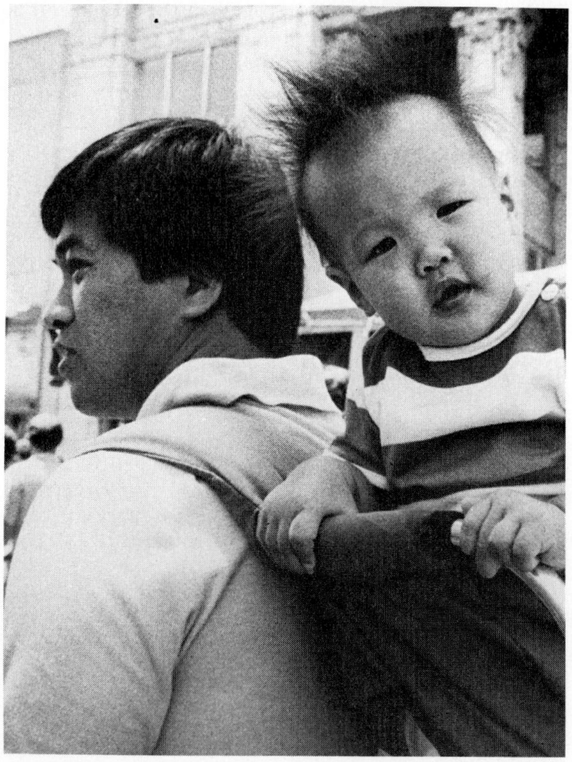

How Can World Development Be Seen as Social Change?

Urbanization, as Davis explained, is one major social change sweeping the world. As such it brings with it many other changes and problems. But urbanization is itself a part of an even broader process of social change that we call ***modernization***—*the process by which a society becomes industrialized, urbanized, and nontraditional.*

MODERNIZATION THEORY: THE FUNCTIONALIST PERSPECTIVE

Modernization theory portrays economic and cultural development as a natural step in the evolution of societies. Modernization theorists emphasize the impact of industrialization on urbanization, and they point out how the culture and therefore the beliefs and attitudes of people change as a result of this process.

United States' foreign aid policy has been based in part on the theory that we can help underdeveloped nations become modernized by contributing to their industrial and economic growth. In fact the assumption that people could create relative prosperity where it has not existed has been widely shared by the United States, the Soviet Union, and the United Nations, among others. Following World War II, the American and Soviet governments tried to outdo one another, offering dams, roads, fertilizer plants, and irrigation systems to the poorer nations. The results have sometimes been disasters, as in Uruguay, Argentina, Brazil, Mexico, and much of Africa. Elsewhere they have been disappointing, as in southern Italy, Yugoslavia, Cuba, and India. China has launched various schemes in an effort to make the "Great Leap," but all so far have fizzled. China, the world's largest, and one of its most underdeveloped, nations adopted a tough one-child-per-family policy in 1979 in an effort to spur modernization. We will soon be able to tell whether this radical policy will succeed, fail, or make the situation worse (Lauer, 1982; Chen, 1985). Jane Jacobs concludes that authorities have often made things worse rather than better in efforts to develop nations and in efforts to save cities which have become stagnant or declined economically (Jacobs, 1984).

Modernization, by its definition, involves a dramatic change in the culture. As a result, people view their world differently. Here, in our "Close-Up on Research," we present Alex Inkeles' fascinating and thorough cross-cultural research on how modernization changes the way we look at reality, or as he puts it: how people are made to be "modern."

CLOSE-UP on • *RESEARCH* •

Alex Inkeles on Making Men Modern

Modernization changes both social structures and human beings. Social scientists have suggested that "modern man" is different from "traditional man" in socially significant ways. Only a few had tested this concept, however. Alex Inkeles and his colleagues set out to understand and measure the impact of participation in the process of modernization on the individual.

Inkeles began this ambitious survey research project at Harvard's Center for International Affairs in 1962. The project involved eight major collaborators who directed a survey of 6,000 adult males in six developing countries.

The Researcher's Goal

Inkeles seeks to answer four questions:

1. "Is there an empirically identifiable modern man, and what are his outstanding characteristics?" (1973, p. 344).
2. "What are the influences that make a man modern? Can any significant changes be brought about in men who are already past the formative early years and have already reached adulthood as relatively traditional men?" (p. 347).
3. "Are there any behavioral consequences arising from the attitudinal modernizations of the individual? Do modern men act differently from the traditional man?" (p. 352).
4. "Is the consequence of the individual modernization inevitably personal disorganization and psychic strain; or can men go through this process of rapid sociocultural change without deleterious consequences?" (p. 358).

Theory and Concepts

Inkeles does not state what theory guides this research, but this is not uncommon for large survey studies, which often contain concepts and variables borrowed from many theories. This "shotgun" approach to conceptualization and measurement is economical. The additional cost of adding items to a survey is small compared to the cost of conducting a second survey. Therefore it makes sense to get as much information as possible at one time. Before the introduction of the computer, however, sociologists ran statistical calculations on mechanical calculators and could not have handled the amount of data they now use. This itself is an example of a change in technology bringing about a change in technique.

Research Design

Inkeles addresses the general topic of modernization. He drew subjects from Argentina, Chile, India, Israel, Nigeria, and East Pakistan (now Bangladesh). The 6,000-person sample covers the range from young to old, from tribal lifestyles to ancient high cultures, and from those closely related to European culture to those distant from it. Some of the young adult male subjects cultivate land in rural communities, whereas others work in relatively modern factories. The group also included a subsample of students in secondary schools and universities.

The measuring instrument was an elaborate interview form. By Inkeles's description (p. 344):

> Our interview included almost 300 entries. Some 160 of these elicited attitudes, values, opinions, and reports on the behavior of others and oneself, touching on almost every major aspect of daily life. The questionnaire included various tests of verbal ability, literacy, political information, intelligence, and psychic adjustment. In some cases it took four hours of interviewing to complete—a demanding experience for both interviewer and interviewee.

Findings

Inkeles found the "empirically identifiable modern man" in substantial numbers in all of the nations studied. The personal qualities that distinguish the "modern man" from the "traditional man" include (p. 345):

1. Openness to new experience
2. The assertion of increasing independence from the authority of traditional figures like parents and priests
3. A belief in the efficacy of science and medicine, and a general abandonment of passivity and fatalism in the face of life's difficulties
4. Ambition for oneself and one's children to achieve high occupational and educational goals
5. A desire that others be on time and show an interest in carefully planning their affairs in advance
6. A strong interest and tendency to participate in community affairs and local politics
7. A tendency to strive energetically to keep up with the news, and within this effort to prefer news of national and international import over items dealing with sports, religion, or purely local affairs

Not all "modern men" exhibit all of these qualities, but the characteristics form a distinct scale; item 1 is the most commonly reported quality and item 7 the least commonly reported. The items represent increasing degrees of modernity, and there is a high probability that the individual exhibiting quality 7 will also exhibit qualities 1 through 6. Similarly, if item 4 is the highest quality exhibited by a subject, there is a high probability that that subject will exhibit items 1 through 3 as well. Thus, the scale allows Inkeles to measure the degree of "modernity" of an individual, ranking people as more or less modern.

Inkeles next turns to the question: "What makes men modern?" The fact that Inkeles calls these personal traits "modern" indicates his assumption that the traits are associated with modern social settings. He tests this assumption by looking for statistical association between the degree of exposure to modernity and one's score on the modernity scale. Inkeles finds that two aspects of modern social life—schools and factories—have the strongest relationship with modernity as he measures it:

"On the average, for every additional year a man spent in school he gains somewhere between two and three additional points on a scale of modernity scored from zero to 100" (p. 347). The effect of years spent in factories was about two-thirds as great as that of years spent in schools.

Inkeles finds that exposure to modern socialization factors explains about one-third of the differences in modernity among his subjects. These factors have about the same influence when they occur during adulthood as when they occur during childhood:

"Our results indicate that substantial changes can be made in a man's personality or character, at least in the sense of attitudes, values, and basic orientations, long after what are usually considered the most formative years" (p. 350). Furthermore, Inkeles found that modern attitudes are associated with modern behavior (p. 353):

> In all six countries we found action intimately related to attitude. At any given educational level, the man who was rated as modern on the attitudinal measure was also more likely to have joined voluntary organizations, to receive news from newspapers every day, to have talked to or written to an official about some public issue, and to have discussed politics with his wife. In many cases the proportion who claimed to have taken those actions was twice and even three times greater among those at the top as compared with those at the bottom of the scale of attitudinal modernity.

Finally, Inkeles attempts to measure the degree to which becoming modern results in personal disorganization and psychic strain. To measure the subject's personal adjustment, Inkeles' interviewers administered the Psychomatic Symptoms Test as part of the regular questionnaire. This test indicates the presence or absence of some seventy-four symptoms. In all but two of the symptoms, no statistically significant association was found. Apparently modernity had little impact on the psychological adjustment of Inkeles' subjects. However, as he points out, the sample is slightly biased toward the better adjusted, because it considers only those who are employed or in school.

Implications

Inkeles' research clearly shows the impact of social setting on personality traits. He also demonstrates that attitude and behavior are sometimes strongly related. Finally, he challenges a conventional belief of social scientists that personality is formed early in life and is subsequently resistant to change.

Although he did not set out to test an explicit theory or set of hypotheses, his findings make several important theoretical statements. They confirm the idea that modern people differ from traditional people. They also strongly support socialization theory but challenge the theory of early and final formation of personality.

Questions

1. Inkeles finds that modernity influences personality. Merton suggests that bureaucracy also influences personality. What other social structure might affect personality?
2. How might a different research method be employed to test the findings of this project?
3. How might Inkeles' work be of use to governments or businesses dealing with the less developed nations?

SOURCE Alex Inkeles, 1973. "Making Men Modern: On the Causes and Consequences of Individual Change in Six Developing Countries." In Eva Etzioni-Halevy and Amitai Etzioni, eds. *Social Change: Sources, Patterns, and Consequences*, 2d ed. New York: Basic Books, pp. 342–61. Reprinted by permission of the publisher.

WORLD SYSTEMS THEORY: THE CONFLICT PERSPECTIVE

World systems theory is a variant of the conflict perspective. Proponents of this perspective, especially Immanuel Wallerstein (1980), point out that powerful, or core nations, often deliberately or inadvertently block the development of the weaker, or peripheral, nations. This theory calls our attention to important dynamics that modernization theory tended to overlook, such as the importance of exploitative political and economic powers.

World systems theory grew out of the theories of Karl Marx and V.I. Lenin, but it has grown into a distinct perspective. This theory states that the nations of the world fall into one of three categories: Core, periphery, or semiperiphery. The core nations are like a world capitalist class whereas the periphery nations are similar to the proletariat.

Core nations keep periphery nations from developing through several forms of dependence including: debt, military, trade, foreign ownership, and low wages. For example, many of the nations of Central America owe great debts to the United States. This leaves the United States in a position to manipulate the recipient nation by either offering to delay repayment or insist on prompt payment. Many core nations including the United States and the Soviet Union foster dependence by offering military aid to weaker states. Later the core nation can exert tremendous influence over the peripheral nation by threatening not to support it militaristically in times of crisis. Often peripheral nations become overly dependent on a particular core nation because of trade. When, for instance, the United States is a major consumer of the raw materials produced in a South American nation, that nation will seek to maintain good will with the United States, even at the expense of its own long-term interests. Similarly, small nations in which major shares of the industry are owned by foreign firms must take into account these owners as they map out their own policies. These owners may be able to exploit their economic clout by threatening to close down or move plants that are important to the economy of the periphery nations. Finally, when these companies pay low wages, they provide workers in the periphery nation with little surplus to save. A shortage of savings means less capital for local business to borrow and less hope for internal economic growth (Delacroix and Ragin, 1981; Bornshier, Chase-Dunn, and Rubinson, 1978).

COLONIALISM

As we discussed in Chapter 16, the world system is often dominated by a particular nation. In earlier times, such dominance was established and maintained by brute force. The Spanish fleet sailed into parts of this hemisphere that had been populated by people of simpler cultures, and through military conquest Spaniards rendered it Latin America. Great Britain, during its era of dominance, colonized much of the world including Canada, Australia, Bermuda, much of the Caribbean, and, for a time, what is now the United States. For most of the nineteenth century, most of the Southern Hemisphere was dominated by European powers, but during the twentieth century most of these nations have become politically independent.

NEOCOLONIALISM

For those nations that once were colonies, economic dependency did not end with political independence. Much of the underdeveloped world is characterized by largely rural-agricultural societies combined with labor-intensive factories or other labor-intensive industry such as mining. Often these industries are owned by outside interests, especially multinational corporations in this era.

In the 1970s, some world systems theorists predicted that capitalism would soon collapse under pressure from socialism and the peripheral powers. More recently they have decided this demise is not likely to come soon (Chirot, 1986).

SOCIAL REVOLUTION

Societies seem to brew development and rebellion in the same pot, leading many theorists to the conclusion that we can best understand social change in terms of social revolution. A ***social revolution*** encompasses *a rapid, fundamental, and violent domestic change in the dominant values and myths of a society.* Social revolutions transform the political institution, the social structure, the leadership, and government activities and policies. By this definition only a small number of successful revolutions has ever happened, but they have left the societies not only changed but very powerful. Examples include England in the seventeenth century, France in the eighteenth century, and the Soviet Union and the Peoples' Republic of China in this century. The fact that this sort of revolution leaves a society powerful, rather than devastated, suggests that revolution is often a sudden transformation to a superior social arrangement.

SYNTHESIS

Societies develop both evenly and unevenly. In isolation or relative isolation, economic growth and development may progress, as modernization theorists suggest, in a relatively orderly way. As new technologies emerge, collectively called *industrialization,* society adjusts. People begin to migrate to cities, government becomes predominant, and religion loses influence. But as Marx suggested, and contemporary researchers and theorists reiterate, these changes bring strain to the societies. The strains sometimes cause the society to explode in a revolution that demolishes old political structures, usually replacing them with new ones that are more democratic.

To more completely understand these processes and our present situation, we need to bear in mind the global environment in which various societies function. World systems theory helps us to understand that dominant societies seek to block the development of weaker societies. But as history teaches, societies seldom can maintain their dominant position for more than a century. As the dominant nations begin to exploit cheap labor from other countries, they unconsciously contribute to their development. As people seek inexpensive foreign goods, they undercut the jobs in their own countries. Power eventually moves away from those who were in control to those who were not. Thus, Great Britain once sought to exploit the labor of the American colonies, only to be eventually displaced by their descendent, United States. Similarly the United States, the undeniable military–political victor in World War II, now after a few decades of temporary prosperity, finds itself losing business to Japan. Apparently, a society can temporarily exploit the labor of a neighbor; but in the presence of relatively free trade, the exploited develops strength as the exploiter loses it.

None of the theories tell the whole story. World development is a combination of gradual change and revolutionary transformations; it is regulated partly through political hierarchies, but largely by international economic forces that elude the control of even totalitarian states. In this chapter we have focused mostly on massive social change affecting most of society and involving hundreds of years. As we have seen throughout this text, sociologists often make predictions about stratification, race and ethnic relations, gender roles, the family, the economy, the state, religion, and many other social patterns. In the following section, we consider the two major techniques for trying to predict the course of future social change (Chirot, 1986).

How Can We Predict Social Change?

The promise of any scientific enterprise is that it will lead to forecasting of, and perhaps control over, the subject matter. Sociology is a developing science operating in a complex subject area. As time passes, and increasingly clear and valid theories are developed, the predictive power of sociology grows. Popular works like *Future Shock, The Third Wave,* and *Megatrends* (Naisbitt, 1982) borrow from major sociological theorists and researchers.

Sociologists are not prophets, and the uniqueness and freedom of individual human beings limits our ability to generalize. Yet important and solid predictions can be made about future social life, using two basic strategies: extrapolation and analysis.

EXTRAPOLATION

Knowledge of the past is often the best available guide to what will happen in the future. For instance, past growth of an organization is generally the best known predictor of future growth (Wallace, 1976). Similarly, past behavior patterns of an individual often foreshadow future behavior patterns. Those who have had criminal careers are the most likely to engage in more crime.

Extrapolation is the major technique employed by John Naisbitt in his popular work, *Megatrends* (1982). ***Extrapolation*** *involves studying a social phenomenon with the assumption that present trends will continue.* Naisbitt used content analysis of newspaper topics to chart ongoing social change in the United States. His work hangs on the assumption that massive trends will spread and continue rather than diminish. This assumption is often well-founded.

Naisbitt suggests that we are in the midst of ten "megatrends." Some of these are familiar, whereas others are less obvious. They include: (1) the transition from an industrial to an information society, (2) a transition from a forced or industrial technology to high technology such as computers, (3) a trend from a national economy to a world economy, (4) a tendency away from short-term to long-term business planning, (5) a trend away from centralization of government to decentralization, (6) a trend away from institutional help toward self-help, (7) a trend from representative democracy toward participatory democracy, (8) a trend away from hierarchies toward networking, (9) a population shift from the North to the South, and (10) a turning away from forced either/or options toward multiple choices, for instance, in options to work other than a nine-to-five schedule.

Using extrapolation we can often make important and accurate predictions. As we have seen, some trends such as the increase in the urban population of the United States are very steady over long periods of time. Hence, we may be able to predict future needs for housing, transportation, and education. Even steady trends like urbanization sometimes level off or reverse. If we had predicted the 1990 divorce rate based on the trend of the 1960s and 1970s, we would have concluded that the divorce rate would have reached the marriage rate. This would mean the probability of divorce would be virtually 100 percent. However, in the 1980s the rapidly rising divorce rate slowed and even declined slightly. As these examples suggest, extrapolation is not enough. We need another tool if we are to deal with trends that level off, reverse, or oscillate.

ANALYSIS

Analysis is *the use of theory to interpret the past or present and to predict the futre.* We can use analysis along with extrapolation to predict, or understand, social change. For example, in predicting population growth we would be interested in the present growth rate of a nation because we could extrapolate from that rate to arrive at estimates of future population size. However, we would also want to analyze the situation in the light of demographic transition theory. As we recall from the population chapter, rapid population growth rates tend to fall as the society develops economically. Similarly, in forecasting divorce rates, we would want to look at present rates and then apply our best theoretical understanding. Thus the person forecasting divorce in the 1970s would want to consider the factors that might affect the divorce rate, such as the liberalization of divorce laws. These laws made it easier for couples to divorce, and we might expect their introduction to temporarily increase the divorce rate while people who had been earlier restrained from divorce took advantage of the new laws.

Social forecasting through extrapolation and studying the future through theoretical analysis can serve several purposes. These techniques can be useful in helping us understand what is going on in our social world. They can often help us predict what will happen next, so that we can better respond to the change. Also, when our analyses are valid, they can provide a basis for social planning to help determine the course of social change.

Conclusion

Urbanization and the attendant making of "modern man" is a central aspect of the great social changes of the twentieth century. As we have seen throughout this text, our culture and social structure are in a state of flux. As we enter the postindustrial, or information, stage, our society continues to change. It has grown larger, somewhat more equal, more bureaucratic, and more centralized. Meanwhile, deviance has increased; schools, businesses, and government have become more prominent; families have become smaller; and marriages, shorter.

Social change provides an appropriate closing topic for us, because it highlights the flexible nature of social structure. The study of sociology arouses our awareness and heightens our understanding of our social world. Using this knowledge, our wisdom, and our love for our neighbors, we should be able to build a better social world for the future.

Sociologists at Work •

WILLIAM FOOTE WHYTE ADVOCATES NEW LEVELS OF COOPERATION IN THE WORKPLACE
New York State School of Industrial and Labor Relations
Cornell University
Ithaca, New York

William Foote Whyte, past president of the American Sociological Association, has been creatively contributing to the fields of sociology and anthropology since the 1930s. Educated at Harvard and the University of Chicago, both leaders in the field, Whyte has spent most of his teaching and researching career at Cornell University. His classic, *Streetcorner Society*, (1955) is widely used and is recently in a third edition. He has recently been involved in consulting, finding ways to avoid plant closings and massive layoffs through increased efficiency. Bill Whyte is an outstanding human being as well as an outstanding sociologist.

What Is Your Most Recent Publishing Effort?
This year my wife, Kathleen Whyte, and I are completing our book *The Making of Mondragón.* Since my first visit to Mondragón in the Basque country of Spain in 1975, I've been fascinated by the Mondragón cooperatives, because up until they were discovered it was almost universally assumed that worker cooperatives were not a viable form of business or sociological organization but a Utopian notion.

How Is Mondragón Different from Other Cooperatives?
Here we have a whole complex of industrial worker cooperatives linked together with a cooperative bank, a research and development cooperative, a very impressive educational system, and a number of other units that are mutually supporting. The cooperative complex has grown from zero in 1956 to 21,000 members today, with over 100 worker cooperatives and associated cooperatives. The organization has been extraordinarily efficient, has withstood a very severe recession, and continues to gain ground.

How Did This Cooperative Begin?
The initial firm was started by five young men under the leadership of Father José María Arizmendi, a Catholic priest who settled the Mondragón in 1943 and developed a number of community organizations including the technical school, which began in 1943. Five of the first graduates of the two-year program there then went to work in private industry and later managed to work out an arrangement with The University of Zaragoza to get engineering degrees without being on campus, that is, to go there for the examination. After they had their degrees, they got together with the priest to form a cooperative firm, pooling their own savings and calling on the community to chip in. They raised a substantial sum of money, particularly for that time when the Basque country was quite poor.

Then in 1959 the cooperative bank was created. Its capital was used not primarily for individual consumer loans, as is usually the case in credit unions, but to provide capital to finance the creation of new worker cooperatives. It now ranks twenty-fourth or twenty-fifth in Spain in terms of its resources, and is the most prosperous and rapidly growing bank in the Basque country. The first worker cooperative there, Ulgor, founded in 1956, started making an oil-burning heater, which is primitive by today's standards; Ulgor is now the largest producer of stoves and refrigerators in Spain.

How Have You and Kathleen Contributed to This Growth?
Kathleen and I have been working with the personnel department of Fagor, helping them to develop methods to do their own social research. The Mondragón system has very highly developed technological and economic research, but they haven't had until now any social research going on in which they themselves are taking the leading role. This project grew out of our original personal research project into participatory action research. Under the leadership of Ouvydd Greenwood, the Director of our Center for International Studies and an expert in the Basque country, we guide them to do the research on their own organization.

How Could This Experience Be Transferred to the United States?
I think there are important possibilities for the Mondragón environment to be translated into parallel developments in our culture. A single worker cooperative in a private enterprise does not have very good prospects for long-run survival: some kind of network of supporting relations must be developed. Some university and private organization people are trying to help in this networking, and we're hopeful that as they develop more strongly here, they will find ways of bringing themselves together as has been done in Mondragón so they can gain economies of scale without sacrificing their independence. The possibilities for the future are exciting! •

Summary Questions

1. How do evolutionary, cyclical, functional, and conflict theorists explain social change?
2. How do technology, demographic processes, ideological factors, and outstanding individuals affect social change?
3. How did cities initially grow?
4. How have cities and suburbs developed in the United States?
5. What is the social structure of cities?
6. How are cities and suburbs interacting?
7. How do sociologists explain world development?
8. How are "modern" people different from "traditional" ones?
9. How can we use sociology to predict social change?

Summary Answers

1. Evolutionary theorists say that societies change by developing into more complex forms in response to their environments. Cyclical theorists say that societies pass through stages involving rises and declines. Some, like Sorokin, see social change as a process of long-term oscillation between ideational and sensate culture. Functional theorists emphasize that social change usually moves the society toward equilibrium. Conflict theorists emphasize the importance of class conflict, the dominance of elite owners, and the eventual likelihood of revolutionary change.
2. Social change is also clearly linked to technological developments, though the culture often lags behind these changes. Demographic processes, such as the baby boom, can generate social change, such as rises in crime rates, as the baby boomers reach ages at which crime is most common. Ideas, such as liberty, have major consequences on social structures when they are embraced by the people of a society. Individuals, especially charismatic ones, can have a major impact toward social change.
3. Cities arose in geographically favorable settings like fertile river banks and became more common as people adopted agriculture. Early cities were small and plagued with health problems, attacks from outsiders, conflict, and fires. Gradually improvements in agriculture and transportation have led to a worldwide trend toward urbanization, but significant populations, especially including China, remain rural.
4. The United States became steadily more urban from its creation through 1970. Still, nearly half of Americans live in either rural areas or cities of fewer than 25,000. Large cities lost population during the 1970s but are growing again in the 1980s. The United States, the most suburbanized nation in the world, may be forced to give up this expensive residential pattern in the face of a declining economy and rising fuel costs.
5. Tönnies characterizes urban relations as *Gesellschaft*, or voluntary relationships based on business or self-interests, in contrast to the *Gemeinschaft*, a primary community in which relationships are based on intimacy, more commonly found in small towns. Simmel observed that city dwellers, bombarded by information, people, and possibilities, learn to evaluate everything and everybody in terms of costs. Urbanism is the study of the social structure of cities. Early scholars viewed the city as made up of impersonal relationships. More recent scholarship identifies considerable community within even large cities. Several models of spatial structures of cities have been developed, including the concentric zone model, the sector model, and the multiple nuclei model. As cities grow, they sometimes overlap to form a megalopolis. Gans has typified city dwellers as cosmopolites, unmarried or childless people, ethnic villagers, the deprived, and the trapped.
6. Problems of cities, including declining economies and racial and ethnic prejudice, combined with the attractiveness of suburban settings, have produced a flight to the suburbs. Possible solutions include taxing the commuters or having suburbs provide low-income housing to help share the cost of the cities' poor. City planning involves urban renewal, new towns, and consolidated areas.
7. Two schools of thought address the issue of how the world is becoming economically developed. Modernization theory is functional and evolutionary in many regards. It depicts development as an orderly evolution through stages. World systems theory works from the conflict perspective and focuses on powerful core nations that develop rapidly at the expense of weaker peripheral nations whose economies they exploit.

8. After extensively interviewing 6,000 adults in six developing countries, Inkeles identified the following traits as distinguishing "modern man" from "traditional man": (1) openness to new experience, (2) asserting independence from traditional authority figures, (3) belief in science and medicine and abandonment of passivity fatalism, (4) ambition toward high occupational and educational goals, (5) a desire for others to be on time and plan affairs in advance, (6) a strong interest in politics, and (7) a tendency to keep up with the news, especially national and international affairs.
9. Sociology can help predict social change by extrapolating existing trends in research data and by applying theories to analyze social settings.

Glossary

analysis the use of theory to interpret the past and present and to predict the future

city a densely populated, permanent settlement of people engaged in nonagricultural pursuits

city planning proposing and regulating all aspects of a city's growth

concentric zone theory describes the expansion and internal development of cities in terms of a series of concentric zones which center on a central business district

culture lag occurs when some parts of a culture change at a faster rate than other related parts, resulting in disruption of the integration and equilibrium of the culture

extrapolation studying a social phenomenon with the assumption that present trends will continue

Gemeinschaft primary community, in which relations are based on intimacy

Gesellschaft voluntary society, in which relations are based on business or self-interest

guilds strong fraternities through which skills were taught

ideational society one that emphasizes things that can be thought about but not necessarily felt through the senses

ideologies explanations of the social, moral, religious, political, and economic institutions of a group

megalopolis a group of cities, each more or less continuous with the last, also known as the Standard Consolidated Area (SCA)

modernization the process by which a society becomes industrialized, urbanized, and nontraditional

multiple nuclei model a pattern of city growth in which several business centers or districts develop, each having its own special activities based on separate communities or ethnic and class differences, rather than the entire city being developed around one central business district

multilinear change change that occurs in different directions through different means, depending upon the conditions in the society undergoing the change

new towns cities that are designed from the beginning to contain a balance of socioeconomic status groups, age groups, and working groups, and to carefully monitor the placement of industry, park land, business, and residences

preindustrial cities cities that were smaller than modern cities and whose social organization was based on family ties

quarter an area of a preindustrial city in which a particular type of craftsperson or religious group worked and lived

sector model specialized areas of a city develop in the form of sectors rather than concentric zones based on lines of transportation

sensate society one that emphasizes things that can be sensed

social change change in social structure or organization

social revolution a rapid, fundamental, and violent domestic change in the dominant values and myths of a society

suburbs small cities and towns that are adjacent to large cities

technology ways of manipulating the environment to achieve desired practical ends

urban ecology the study of the social and spatial structure of cities

urban renewal a form of urban development that stresses prevention of the spread of urban blight into good areas, rehabilitation and conservation of areas that can be economically restored, and clearance and redevelopment of areas that cannot be saved

urbanism the study of the social structure of cities

urbanization the movement of population from rural areas to cities

Suggested Readings

Claude Fischer. 1984. *The Urban Experience.* San Diego: Harcourt Brace Jovanovich.

Fischer discusses cities, the characteristic life within them, and their future.

Kenneth T. Jackson. 1985. *Crabgrass Frontier: The Suburbanization of the United States.* New York: Oxford University Press.

Jackson skillfully and engagingly portrays the past, present, and future of American suburbanization.

Jane Jacobs. 1984. *Cities and the Wealth of Nations: Principles of Economic Life.* New York: Random House.

Jacobs makes an impressive case for letting cities and nations go their own way economically. She argues that the modernization model is inadequate, but that we presently have nothing better. In fact, she contends, efforts to save cities and promote development usually only increase the problems.

Richard H. Lauer. 1982. *Perspectives on Social Change.* Boston: Allyn and Bacon.

Lauer guides the reader through the wide variety of theories of social change and then applies them to the contemporary scene with an eye toward developing strategies for social change.

Paul E. Peterson, ed. 1985. *The New Urban Reality.* Washington, D.C.: The Brookings Institute.

The various experts who contribute to this collection present a clear, contemporary, and candid appraisal of the difficult reality of large cities.

REFERENCES

Abel, Theodore. (1937). "The Pattern of a Successful Political Movement." *American Sociological Review,* 2, 347–352.

Aberle, David. (1966). *The Peyote Religion Among the Navaho.* Chicago: Aldine.

Abrahamson, Mark. (1973). "Functionalism and the Functional Theory of Stratification: An Empirical Assessment." *American Journal of Sociology,* 78, 1236–1246.

———. (1976). "A Functional Theory of Organizational Stratification." *Social Forces,* 58, 128–145.

Ackerman, Charles. (1963). "Affiliations: Structural Determinants of Differential Divorce Rates." *American Journal of Sociology,* 69, 13–21.

Adams, Bert. (1973). *The American Family: A Sociological Interpretation.* Chicago: Rand McNally.

———. (1979). "Mate Selection in the United States: A Theoretical Summarization." In Wesley R. Burr et al. (eds.), *Contemporary Theories About the Family* (Vol. 1). New York: Free Press, 259–267.

Adams, James Truslow. (1931). *The Epic of America.* Boston: Little, Brown.

Adams, Virginia. (1979). "Studies Relate Physical Causes to Delinquency." *New York Times* (June 26), C1, C3.

Adams, Willi Paul. (1983). "A Dubious Host." *Wilson Quarterly,* New Year's, 100–131.

Adler, Peter, and Patricia Adler. (1985). "From Idealism to Pragmatic Detachment: The Academic Performance of College Athletes." *Sociology of Education,* 58 (October), 241–250.

Adorno, Theodore W., et al. (1950). *The Authoritarian Personality.* New York: W. W. Norton.

Ahrons, Constance. (1986). "Divorces Seen Hurting Children." *Rome* (GA) *News Tribune* (October 23), 1.

Ajemian, Robert. (1985). "Jerry Falwell Spreads the Word." *Time* (September 2), 58–61.

Akers, Donald S. (1967). "On Measuring the Marriage Squeeze." *Demography,* 4, 907–924.

Albrecht, William P. (1986). *Economics* (4th ed.). Englewood Cliffs, NJ: Prentice-Hall.

Alford, Robert, and Roger Freidland. (1975). "Political Participation." In Alex Inkeles, et al. (eds.), *Annual Review of Sociology.* Palo Alto, CA: Annual Reviews.

Allegier, Elizabeth, and Naomi McCormick (eds.). (1983). *Changing Boundaries: Gender Roles and Sexual Behavior.* Palo Alto, CA: Mayfield.

Allen, John. (1977). *Assault with a Deadly Weapon: The Autobiography of a Street Criminal.* New York: Pantheon.

Allport, Gordon W. (1954). *The Nature of Prejudice.* Reading, MA: Addison-Wesley.

Allport, Gordon W., and Leo J. Postman. (1947). *The Psychology of Rumor.* New York: Holt, Rinehart & Winston.

Altman, Dennis. (1986). *AIDS in the Mind of America.* Garden City, NY: Anchor Books/Doubleday.

Ambet, Anne-Marie. (1986). "Being a Stepparent: Live-in and Visiting Stepchildren." *Journal of Marriage and the Family,* 48 (November), 795–804.

American Psychiatric Association (APA). (1980). *Diagnostic and Statistical Manual of Disorders.* (3d ed., DSM-III), Washington, D.C.: American Psychiatric Association.

Amir, Menachem, and Titzchank Berman. (1970). "Chromosomal Deviation and Crime." *Federal Probation,* 34, 55–62.

Amnesty International. (1984). *Torture in the Eighties.* London: Amnesty International Publications.

Anderson, Daniel, and Elizabeth Pugzles Lorch. (1983). "Look at Television: Action or Reaction?" In Jennings Bryant and Daniel Anderson, (eds.), *Children's Understanding of Television: Research on Attention and Comprehension.* New York: Academic Press, 1–33.

Anderson, Kurt. (1982). "What Are Prisons For?". *Time Magazine* (September 13), 38–40.

Anderson, L. S. (1979). "The Deterrent Effect of Criminal Sanctions: Reviewing the Evidence." In P. J. Brantingham, and J. M. Kress, (eds.). *Structure, Law and Power: Essays in the Sociology of Law,* Beverly Hills, CA: Russell Sage, 123–134.

Arens, Richard (ed.). (1976). *Genocide in Paraguay.* Philadelphia: Temple University Press.

Asch, Solomon E. (1951). "Effects of Group Pressure upon the Modification and Distortion of Judgments." In T. Guetzkow (ed.), *Groups, Leadership, and Men.* Pittsburgh: Carnegie Press.

———. (1956). "Studies of Independence and Conformity: A Minority of One Against a Unanimous Majority." *Psychology Monographs,* 70 (9), No. 416.

Ash, Roberta T. (1977). *Social Movements in America* (2d ed.). Chicago: Markham.

Ash, S. M. (1983). *Cult-Induced Psychopathology: A Critical Review of Presuppositions, Conversion, Clinical Picture, and Treatment.* Ph.D. thesis. Rosemead School of Psychology, Biola University.

———. (1985). "Cult-Induced Psychopathology, Part I: Clinical Picture." *Cultic Studies,* 2, 31–90.

Ashby, Eric. (1978). "Any Person, Any Study: An Essay on Higher Education in the United States." Ann Arbor, MI: Books on Demand, Division of University Microfilms.

Ashenfelter, Orley, and Albert Reiss (eds.). (1973). *Discrimination in Labor Markets.* Princeton: Princeton University Press.

Asher, C. C. (1984). "The Impact of Social Support Networks on Adult Health." *Medical Care,* 22, 349–359.

Ashton, Heather, and Rub Stepney. (1982). *Smoking: Psychology and Pharmacology.* New York: Tavistock.

Associated Press. (1987). "Electronic Church Booming." *Rome News Tribune* (January 30), 6a.

Astin, Alexander. (1977). *Four Critical Years: Effects of College on Beliefs, Attitudes, and Knowledge.* San Francisco: Jossey-Bass.

Astin, Alexander. (1985). *Achieving Educational Excellence,* San Francisco: Jossey-Bass.

Atchley, Robert C. (1972). *The Social Forces in Later Life.* Belmont, CA: Wadsworth.

———. (1983). *Aging: Continuity and Change.* Belmont, CA: Wadsworth.

———. (1985). *Social Forces and Aging* (4th ed.) Belmont, CA: Wadsworth.

Attorney General's Task Force on Family Violence. (1984). *Final Report.* Washington, DC: U.S. Government Printing Office, September.

August, Robert, et al. (1987). *Japanese Education Today.* Washington, DC: U.S. Government Printing Office.

Avery, Dennis. (1985). "U.S. Farm Dilemma: The Global Bad News Is Wrong." *Science* (October 25), 408–412.

Avorn, Jerome. (1986). "Medicine: The Life and Death of Oliver Shay." In Alan Pifer and Lydia Bronte (eds.), *Our Aging Society.* New York: W. W. Norton.

Bach, George R., and Ronald M. Deutsch. (1973). "Intimacy." In Laswell (ed.). *Love, Marriage, and the Family.* Chicago: Scott, Foresman.

Bach, Robert L. (1980). "The New Cuban Emigrants: Their Background and Prospects," *Monthly Labor Review,* 103 (10), 39–46.

Bailey, Kenneth D. (1978). *Methods of Social Research.* New York: Free Press.

Bailey, William. (1980). "Deterrence and the Celerity of the Death Penalty: A Neglected Question in Deterrence Research." *Social Forces,* 58, 4 (June), 1308–1332.

Baird, Leonard L., Mary Jo Clark, and Rodney T. Harnett. (1973). *The Graduates.* Princeton: Educational Testing Service.

Baker, Mary Anne, et al. (1980). *Women Today: A Multidisciplinary Approach to Women's Studies.* Monterey, CA: Brooks/Cole.

Baker, Ross. (1982). "The Fundamental Scientific Laws of Demography," *American Demographics,* 4 (1).

Bales, Robert F., and Fred L. Strodtbeck. (1951). "Phases in Group Problem Solving." *Journal of Abnormal and Social Psychology,* 46, 485–495.

Bales, Robert F., et al. (1951). "Channels of Communication in Small Groups." *American Sociological Review,* 16, 461–468.

Bales, Robert F. (1953). "The Equilibrium Problem in Small Groups." In Talcott Parsons, Robert F. Bales, and E. A. Shils (eds.), *Working Papers In the Theory of Action.* New York: Free Press, 111–161.

Ball, Leslie D. (1982). "Computer Crime." *Technology Review* (April), 21–30.

Ballantine, Jeanne. (1983). *The Sociology of Education.* Englewood Cliffs, NJ: Prentice-Hall.

Baltes, Paul B., and Warner K. Schaie. (1974). "The Myth of the Twilight Years." *Psychology Today* (May), pp. 35–38.

Bandura, Albert. (1963). "Imitation of Film-Mediated Aggressive Models." In Albert Bandura and R. H. Walters (eds.), *Social Learning and Personality Development.* New York: Holt, Rinehart & Winston, 47–60.

———. (1977). *Social Learning Theory.* Englewood Cliffs, NJ: Prentice-Hall.

Bandura, Albert, D. Ross, and S. Ross. (1961). "Transmission of Aggression Through Imitation of Aggressive Models." *Journal of Abnormal Social Psychology,* 63, 575–582.

Bandura, Albert, and Richard H. Walters. (1963). *Social Learning and Personality Development.* New York: Holt, Rinehart & Winston.

Bane, Mary Jo. (1976). *Here to Stay: American Families in the Twentieth Century.* New York, Basic Books.

Banner, Lois. (1983). *American Beauty.* New York: Knopf.

Bardo, John W., and John J. Hartman. (1982). *Urban Sociology.* Itasca, IL: F. E. Peacock Publishers, Inc.

Bardwick, Judith M., and Elizabeth Douvan. (1971). "Ambivalence: The Socialization of Women." In Vivian Gornick and Barbara K. Moran (eds.), *Women in Sexist Society.* New York: Basic Books.

Barker, Eileen. (1986). "Religious Movements: Cult and Anticult Since Jonestown." *Annual Review of Sociology,* 12, 329–346.

———. (1979). "Whose Service Is Perfect Freedom: The Concept of Spiritual Well-being in Relation to the Reverend Sun Myung Moon's Unification Church in Britain." In D. Moberg (ed.), *Spiritual Well-Being.* Washington, DC: University Press of America.

———. (1981). "Who'd Be a Moonie? A Comparative Study of Those Who Join the Unification Church in Britain." In B. R. Wilson. (ed.), *The Social Impact of New Religious Movements,* Barrytown, NY: Unification Theological Seminary, pp. 59–96.

Barker, E. V. (1984). *The Making of a Moonie: Brainwashing or Choice?* Oxford: Blackwell.

Barmash, Isadore. (1982). "Older Managers Fighting Dismissal." *New York Times.* January 10, Section 12, p. 52.

Barrow, Georgia, and Patricia Smith. (1986). *Aging, the Individual, and Society* (3d ed.). St. Paul, MN: West Publishing Co.

Barry, H., III, M. K. Bacon, and I. L. Child. (1957). "A Cross-cultural Survey of Some Sex Differences in Socialization." *Journal of Abnormal and Social Psychology,* 55, 237–332.

Barthel, Joan. (1985). "No Place to Call Home." *Family Circle* (November 11), 32, 46, and 48.

Bassuk, Ellen, Lenore Rubin, and Alison Lauriat. (1986). "Characteristics of Sheltered Homeless Families." *American Journal of Public Health* (September) 76(9), 1097–1101.

Batra, Ravi. (1987). *The Great Depression of 1990.* New York: Simon and Schuster.

Baumgartel, H., and R. Sobol. (1959). "Background and Organizational Factors in Absenteeism." *Personnel Psychology,* 12, 431–443.

Bayer, R., and E. Feldman. (1982). "Hospice Under the Medicare Wing." *Hastings Center Report,* 12(6), 5–6.

Beals, Alan R. (1962). *Gopalpur: A South Indian Village.* New York: Holt, Rinehart & Winston.

Becker, Howard S. (1963). *Outsiders: Studies in the Sociology of Deviance* (2d ed.). New York: Free Press.

———. (1964). *The Other Side: Perspectives on Deviance.* New York: Free Press.

———. (1967). "Whose Side Are We On?" *Journal of Social Problems,* 14, 239–247.

Becker, Howard S., et al. (1961). *Boys in White.* Chicago: University of Chicago Press.

Beckford, J. A. (1985). *Cult Controversies: The Societal Response to the New Religious Movements.* London: Tavistock.

Beckhouse, L., et al. (1975). "And Some Men Have Leadership Thrust Upon Them." *Journal of Personality and Social Psychology,* 31, 557–566.

Beissert, Wayne. (1987). "N.Y. Death Dramatizes U.S.A. Child Abuse Problem." *USA Today* (November 6), 8A.

Bell, Alan P., and Martin S. Weinberg. (1978). *Homosexualities: A Study of Diversity Among Men and Women.* New York: Simon and Schuster.

Bell, Alan P., Martin S. Weinberg, and Sue Keifer Hammersmith. (1981). *Sexual Preference: Its Development in Men and Women.* Bloomington, IN: Indiana University Press.

Bell, Daniel. (1973). *The Coming of Postindustrial Society: A Venture in Social Forecasting.* New York: Basic Books.

Bell, Wendell. (1967). *The Democratic Revolution in the West Indies: Studies in Nationalism, Leadership, and the Belief in Progress.* Cambridge, MA: Schenkman.

Bell, Wendell, and James Mau. (1971). *The Sociology of the Future.* New York: Russell Sage.

Bellah, Robert N. (1954). "Religious Evolution." *American Sociological Review,* 29(3), 358–374.

———. (1967). "Civil Religion in America." *Daedalus,* 96, 1–21.

———. (1970). "Religious Evolution." In *Beyond Belief: Essays on Religion in a Postindustrial World.* New York: Harper and Row, 20–50.

———. (1981). "The Ethical Aims of Social Inquiry." *Teacher's College Record.* Fall. New York: Columbia University Press.

Bem, Sandra Lipsitz. (1981). "Gender Schema Theory: A Cognitive Account of Sex-Typing." *Psychological Review,* 88(4), 354–364.

———. (1983). "Gender Schema Theory and Its Implications for Child Development: Raising Gender—A Schematic Children in a Gender-Schematic Society." *Journal of Woman in Culture and Society,* 8, 4 (Summer), 598–616.

Benanti, Mary. (1987). "Hispanic Officeholders 'Barometer' of Progress." *USA Today* (September 18), 1.

Bendix, Reinhard B. (1961). *Max Weber: An Intellectual Portrait.* Garden City, NY: Doubleday.

Bendix, Reinhard B., and Seymour Martin Lipset (eds.). (1966). *Class, Status, and Power: Social Stratification in Comparative Perspective* (2d ed.). New York: Free Press.

Benedict, Ruth. (1934). *Patterns of Culture.* Boston: Houghton Mifflin.

Bennett, Ruth, and Judith Eckman. (1973). "Attitudes Toward Aging: A Critical Examination of Recent Literature and Implications for Future Research."

In Carol Eisdorfer and M. Powell Lawton (eds.), *The Psychology of Adult Development and Aging.* Washington, DC: American Psychological Association, pp. 575–597.

Bennett, William. (1987). Interviewed by Robert Marquand. "U.S. Study Looks at Japan's Successful School System." *Christian Science Monitor* (January 5), 3–4.

Berger, Peter. (1963). *Invitation to Sociology.* Garden City, NY: Doubleday.

———. (1967). "Religious Institutions." In Neil J. Smelser (ed.), *Sociology: An Introduction.* New York: John Wiley.

———. (1969). *A Rumor of Angels: Modern Society and the Rediscovery of the Supernatural.* New York: Doubleday.

Bergesen, Albert, ed. (1983). *Crises in the World-System* (Vol. 6: Political Economy of the World-Systems Annuals). Beverly Hills: Sage Publications.

Bergman, Barbara. (1986). *The Economic Emergence of Women.* New York: Basic Books.

Berk, Richard A. (1974). *Collective Behavior.* Dubuque, IA: William C. Brown.

Berkowitz, Leonard. (1962). *Aggression: A Social Psychological Analysis.* New York: McGraw-Hill.

Berliner, David. (1984). "The Half-Full Glass: A Review of Research on Teaching." In Philip Hosford (ed.), *Using What We Know About Teaching.* Alexandria, VA: Association for Supervision and Curriculum Development.

Bernard, Jessie. (1966). "Marital Stability and Patterns of Status Variables." *Journal of Marriage and the Family,* 28, 421–439.

———. (1971). "The Adjustment of Married Mates." In T. Christensen (ed.). *Handbook of Marriage and the Family.* Chicago: Rand McNally.

———. (1977). "Jealousy and Marriage." In Gordon Clanton and Lynn Smith (eds.), *Jealousy.* Englewood Cliffs, NJ: Prentice-Hall, 141–150.

———. (1979). "Foreword." In George Levinger and Oliver Moles (eds.), *Divorce and Separation.* New York: Basic Books, ix–xvi.

———. (1981). *The Female World.* New York: Free Press.

Berne, Eric. (1972). *What Do You Say After You Say Hello?* New York: Grove.

Berscheid, E., and J. Fei. (1977). "Romantic Love and Sexual Jealousy." In G. Clanton and L. G. Smith (eds.), *Jealousy.* Englewood Cliffs, NJ: Prentice-Hall, pp. 101–110.

Berscheid, E., and Walster. (1976). "Physical Attractiveness." In L. Berkowitz (ed.), *Advances in Experimental Social Psychology* (Vol. 7). New York: Academic Press.

Best, Raphaela. (1983). *We've All Got Scars: What Boys and Girls Learn in Elementary School:* Bloomington: University of Indiana Press.

Bettelheim, Bruno. (1976). "Untying the Family." *Center Magazine* (September), pp. 5–9.

Bianchi, Suzanne, and Daphne Spain. (1986). *American Women in Transition.* New York: Russell Sage Foundation.

Biaraben, Jean Noel. (1960). "The Age Structure of the Population of the Soviet Union." *Population,* 15, 894–898.

Binstock, Robert H. (1985). "The Aged as Scapegoat." In *Growing Old in America* (3d ed.). New Brunswick, NJ: Transaction Books, 489–505.

Blake, Judith. (1979). "Is Zero Preferred? American Attitudes Toward Childlessness in the 1970s." *Journal of Marriage and the Family,* 41, 245–257.

Blau, Judith R., and Peter M. Blau. (1982). "The Cost of Inequality: Metropolitan Structure and Violent Crime." *American Sociological Review,* 47, 114–129.

Blau, Peter M. (1973). *The Dynamics of Bureaucracy* (rev. ed.). Chicago: University of Chicago Press.

Blau, Peter M., and Otis Dudley Duncan. (1967). *The American Occupational Structure.* New York: John Wiley.

Blau, Peter M., and Marshall W. Meyer. (1971). *Bureaucracy in Modern Society* (2d ed.). New York: Random House.

Blauner, Robert. (1964). *Alienation and Freedom: The Factory Worker and His Industry.* Chicago: University of Chicago Press.

Blood, Robert O., Jr., and Donald M. Wolfe. (1960). *Husbands and Wives: The Dynamics of Married Living.* New York: Free Press.

Bloom, Benjamin. (1980). *All Our Children Learning.* Washington, DC: McGraw-Hill.

Bloom, B. L., S. J. Asher, and S. W. White. (1978). "Marital Disruption as a Stressor." *Psychological Bulletin,* 85, 867–894.

Bloom, Bernard, Stephen White, and Shirley Asher. (1979). "Marital Disruption as a Stressful Life Event." In George Levinger and Oliver Moles, (eds.), *Divorce and Separation.* New York: Basic Books.

Blumberg, Paul. (1980). *Inequality in an Age of Decline.* New York: Oxford University Press.

Blumberg, Rae Lesser. (1973). "Women of the Kibbutz: Retreat from Sexual Equality." Paper presented at meetings of the Society for Applied Anthropology, Tucson, AR.

Blumer, Herbert. (1948). "Public Opinion and Public Opinion Polling." *American Sociological Review,* 13, 542–549.

———. (1951). "Collective Behavior." In Alfred McClung Lee (ed.), *Principles of Sociology.* New York: Barnes & Noble.

Blumstein, A. (1982). "On the Racial Disproportionality of United States Prison Population." *Journal of Criminal Law and Criminology,* 73, 1259–1281.

Blumstein, Philip, and Pepper Schwartz. (1983). *American Couples.* New York: Morrow.

Blusciewicz, Catherine. (1984). "What Price Day Care?" In Russell Watson, et al. (eds.), *Newsweek* (September 10), 14–17, 19–21.

Boas, Franz. (1965). *The Mind of Primitive Man* (rev. ed.). New York: Free Press.

Bogue, Donald. (1949). *Population of the United States.* Glencoe, IL: Free Press.

Bollen, K. A., and D. P. Phillips. (1981). "Suicidal Motor Vehicle Fatalities in Detroit: A Replication." *American Journal of Sociology,* 87, 404–412.

Bollen, Kenneth. (1979). "Political Democracy and the Timing of Development." *American Sociological Review* (August), 572–587.

Bollen, Kenneth, and Robert Jackman. (1985). "Political Democracy." *American Sociological Review* (August), 438–458.

Bolman, L. (1970). "Laboratory Versus Lecture in Training Executives." *Journal of Applied Behavioral Science,* 6, 323–335.

Bonacich, Edna. "Abolition, the Extension of Slavery, and the Position of Free Blacks: A Study of Split Labor Markets in the U.S., 1830–1863." In *American Journal of Sociology,* 81, 601–628.

Bonacich, Edna. (1972). "A Theory of Ethnic Antagonism: The Split Labor Market." *American Sociological Review,* 37, 547–559.

Bonn, Robert. (1984). *Criminology.* New York: McGraw-Hill.

Boocock, Sarah Spence. (1972). *An Introduction to the Sociology of Learning.* Boston: Houghton Mifflin.

Booth, Alan. (1977). "Wife's Employment and Husband's Stress: A Replication and Refutation." *Journal of Marriage and the Family* (November), 647–651.

Bornschier, Volker, Chris Chase-Dunn, and Richard Rubinson. (1978). "Cross-National Evidence of the Effects of Foreign Investment and Aid on Economic Growth and Inequality: A Survey of Findings and Reanalysis." *American Journal of Sociology,* 84 (November), 651–683.

Bornschier, Volker, and Jean-Pierre Hoby. (1981). "Economic Policy and Multinational Corporation in Development: The Measurable Impacts in Cross-National Perspective." *Social Problems,* 28, 363–377.

Botwinick, Jack. (1973). *Aging and Behavior.* New York: Springer.

Bowditch, James L., and Anthony F. Buono. (1982). *Quality of Work Life Assessment: A Survey-Based Approach.* Boston: Auburn House Publishing Company.

Bowen, Ezra. (1985a). "And Now, A Teacher Shortage." *Time Magazine* (July 22), 63.

———. (1985b). "Schools for All Seasons." *Time Magazine* (August 12), 48.

———. (1985c). "Dramatic Drops for Minorities." *Time Magazine* (November 11), 84.

Bowen, Murray, (1978). *Family Therapy in Clinical Practice.* New York: Jason Aronson.

Bowers, William, and Glenn Pierce. (1980). "Deterrence of Brutalization: What Is the Effect of Executions?" *Crime and Delinquency,* 26, 453–484.

Bowles, Samuel, and Herbert Gintis. (1977). *Schooling in Capitalist America.* New York: Basic Books.

Bowles, Samuel, and Henry M. Levin. (1968). "The Determinants of Scholastic Achievement—An Appraisal of Some Recent Evidence." *Journal of Human Resources* (Winter).

Bowman, Madonna, and Constance Ahrens. (1985). "Impact of Legal Custody Status on Father's Parenting Postdivorce." *Journal of Marriage and the Family,* 47 (May), 481–488.

Boyer, Ernest. (1983a). "Attracting Good Teachers." *Newsweek* (May 9).

———. (1983b). *High School.* New York: Harper and Row.

Bracey, G. W. (1985). "Youth Suicide." *Phi Delta Kappan,* 66, (March) 509.

Bracy, James H. (1976). "The Quality of Life Experience of Black People." In Angus Campbell, Philip E. Converse, and Willard Rodgers (eds.), *The Quality of American Life: Perceptions, Evaluations, and Satisfactions.* New York: Russell Sage Foundation.

Braithwaite, John. (1979). *Inequality, Crime, and Public Policy.* London: Routledge and Kegan Paul.

———. (1984). *Corporate Crime in the Pharmaceutical Industry.* London: Routledge and Kegan Paul.

———. (1985a). "White Collar Crime," *Annual Review of Sociology,* 11, 1–25.

———. (1985b). *To Punish or Persuade: Enforcement of Coal Mine Safety.* Albany: State University of New York Press.

Braudel, Fernand. (1985). *Civilization and Capitalism: 15th–18th Century: Vol. 1, The Structures of Everyday Life: The Limits of the Possible.* (translated by Sian Reynolds). New York: Harper and Row.

Brazelton, T. Berry, and David Elkind. (1984). In Glenn Collins, "Experts Debate Impact of Day Care." *New York Times* (September 4), 311ff.

Breault, K. D., and Augustine Kposowa. (1987). "Explaining Divorce in the United States: A Study of 3111 Counties, 1980." *Journal of Marriage and the Family,* 49 (August), 549–558.

Brecher, Edward. (1984). *Love, Sex, and Aging.* Boston: Little, Brown, and Co.

Brenner, M. Harvey. (1976). "Estimating the Social

Costs of National Economic Policy." Joint Economic Committee of the Congress. Washington, DC: U.S. Government Printing Office.

———. (1980). "Industrialization and Economic Growth: Estimates of Their Effects on the Health of Populations." In M. H. Brenner, et al. (eds.), *Assessing the Contributions of the Social Sciences to Health.* Washington, DC: American Academy for the Advancement of Science.

———. (1984). "Estimating the Effects of Economic Change on National Health and Social Well-Being." Joint Economic Committee. Washington, DC: U.S. Government Printing Office.

Brewer, Earl D. C. (1962). "Religion and the Churches." In Thomas R. Ford (ed.), *The Southern Appalachian Region: A Survey.* Lexington: University of Kentucky Press.

Briggs, Kenneth. (1981). "Religion Has Found a Strong Face in City's Life." *New York Times* (December 25).

Britannica Book of the Year, 1988. Encyclopaedia Britannica, Inc. Chicago.

Brody, Jacob. (1985). "Prospects for an Aging Population." *Nature* (June 6), 463–466.

Brody, Jane E. (1979). "Marriage Is Good for Health and Longevity, Studies Say." *New York Times* (May 8), 1–2.

Bronfenbrenner, Urie. (1970). *Two Worlds of Childhood.* New York: Russell Sage.

Brophy, Jere, and Thomas Good. (1974). *Teacher–Student Relations.* New York: Holt, Rinehart & Winston.

Brown, Dee. (1970). *Bury My Heart at Wounded Knee.* New York: Holt, Rinehart & Winston.

Brown, Lester. (1976). *World Population Trends: Signs of Hope, Signs of Stress.* Washington, DC: Worldwatch Institute.

Brown, Lester, and Lenore Jacobson. (1986). *Our Demographically Divided World.* Washington, DC: Worldwatch Institute.

Brown, Robert. (1965). *Social Psychology.* New York: Free Press.

Bruck, David. (1983). "Decisions of Death." *The New Republic* (December 12), 18–25.

Bruno, Mary. (1985). "Campus Sex: New Fears." *Newsweek* (October 28), 81–82.

Bruno, Mary, Barbara Burgowere, and Mark Miller. (1985). "Abusing the Elderly." *Newsweek Magazine* (September 23), 75–76.

Brunvard, Jan Harold. (1985). *The Vanishing Hitchhiker: American Urban Legends and Their Meanings.* New York: W. W. Norton.

Buchholz, Michael, and Jack Bynum. (1982). "Newspaper Presentation of America's Aged: A Content Analysis of Image and Role." *Gerontologist,* 22(1), 83–87.

Buckingham, R. W. (1982). "Hospice Care in the United States: The Process Begins." *Omega,* 13, 159–171.

Bumpass, Larry L., and James A. Sweet. (1972). "Differentials in Marital Instability." *American Sociological Review,* 37, 754–767.

Burchinal, Lee G. (1964). "Characteristics of Adolescents From Unbroken, Broken, and Reconstituted Families." *Journal of Marriage and the Family,* 26, 44–51.

Burgess, Ernest W. (1984). "The Growth of the City." In Robert E. Park and Ernest W. Burgess (eds.) *The City.* Chicago: University of Chicago Press, 47–62.

Burgess, Ernest W., and Harvey J. Locke. (1953). *The Family.* New York: American Books.

Burgess, Ernest W., and Paul W. Wallin. (1953). *Engagement and Marriage.* New York: Lippincott.

Burke, Ronald J., and Tamara Weir. (1976). "Relationship of Wives' Employment Status to Husband, Wife, and Pair Satisfaction and Performance." *Journal of Marriage and the Family,* 38, 279–287.

Burnette, Robert. (1971). *The Tortured Americans.* Englewood Cliffs, NJ: Prentice-Hall.

Burnette, Robert, and John Koster. (1974). *The Road to Wounded Knee.* New York: Bantam.

Burnham, Walter Dean. (1983). *Democracy in the Making: American Government and Politics.* Englewood Cliffs, NJ: Prentice-Hall.

Burr, Wesley. (1970). "Satisfaction with Various Aspects of Marriage over the Life Cycle." *Journal of Marriage and the Family,* 32, 29–37.

Burris, Val. (1983). "The Social and Political Consequences of Overeducation." *American Sociological Review,* 48, 454–467.

Busby, Linda. (1975). "Sex-Role Research on the Mass Media." *Journal of Communications,* 25 (Autumn), 107–131.

Buskirk, E. R. (1985). "Health Maintenance and Longevity: Exercise." In C. E. Finch and E. L. Schneider (eds.), *Handbook of the Biology of Aging* (2d ed.). New York: Van Nostrand Reinhold.

Busse, E. (1977). "Theories of Aging." In C. Busse and E. Pfeiffer (eds.). *Behavior and Adaptation in Later Life.* Boston, MA: Little, Brown, and Co.

Butler, R. N., and M. I. Lewis. (1982). *Aging and Mental Health.* St. Louis: The C. V. Mosby Company.

Butler, Robert N. (1980). "Ageism: A Foreword." *Journal of Social Issues,* 36(2), 8–11.

Butterfield, Fox. (1977). "Family Ties in Rural China Seem More Binding than Party's Rule." *New York Times* (December 19).

Cain, Glen C., and Harold W. Watts. (1970). "Problems in Making Policy Inferences from the Coleman Report." *American Sociological Review* (April).

Callahan, Daniel. (1986). "Health Care in the Aging

Society: A Moral Dilemma." In Alan Pifer and Lydia Bronte (eds.), *Our Aging Society: Paradox and Promise.* New York: W. W. Norton.

Cameron, Juan. (1979). "The Shadow Congress the Public Doesn't Know." *Fortune* (January 15).

Campbell, Angus, et al. (1976). *Quality of American Life.* New York: Russell Sage.

Campbell, Ernest. (1961). "On Desegregation and Matters Sociological." *Phylon* (Summer), 140–142.

Cantril, Hadley. (1963). "A Study of Aspirations." *Scientific American,* 208, 42ff.

"Capital Punishment in the United States." (1980). *Crime and Delinquency,* 26 (October), 441–635.

Caplow, Theodore. (1969). *Two Against One: Coalition in Triads.* Englewood Cliffs, NJ: Prentice-Hall.

———. (1954). *The Sociology of Work.* Minneapolis: University of Minnesota Press.

Carniero, Robert L. (1968). "Culture: Cultural Adaptation." In David L. Sills (ed.), *International Encyclopedia of the Social Sciences.* New York: Macmillan and Free Press, 551–554.

Carroll, John B. (1956). *Language, Thought, and Reality: Selected Writings of Benjamin Lee Whorf.* Cambridge: MIT Press.

Carter, Douglass, and Stephen Strickland. (1975). *TV Violence and the Child: The Evolution and Fate of the Surgeon General's Report.* New York: Russell Sage.

Carter, Hugh, and Paul Glick. (1980). *Marriage and Divorce: A Social and Economic Study.* Cambridge, MA: Harvard University Press.

Carter, J. Luther. (1983). "The Radwaste Paradox." *Science,* 219 (January 1), 33–36.

Carter, Malcom N. (1979). "The Bizarre Case of Rebecca Holmes." *Saturday Review* (August).

Carter, V. G., and T. Dale. (1974). *Topsoil and Civilization* (rev. ed.). Norman, OK: University of Oklahoma Press.

Cartwright, D., and A. F. Zander (eds.). (1960). *Group Dynamics: Research and Theory.* Evanston, IL: Row, Peterson.

Castro, Janice. (1985). "More and More, She's the Boss." *Time Magazine* (December 2), 64–66.

Catalano, Ralph A., David Dooley, and Robert L. Jackson. (1985). "Economic Antecedents of Help Seeking: Reformulation of Time-Series Tests." *Journal of Health and Social Behavior,* 26, 141–152.

Centers, Richard. (1949). *The Psychology of Social Classes.* Princeton: Princeton University Press.

Chafetz, Janet Saltzman. (1984). *Sex and Advantage: A Comparative, Macro-Structural Theory of Sex Stratification.* Totowa, NJ: Rowman and Allanheld.

Chambliss, W. J. (1967). "Types of Deviance and the Effectiveness of Legal Sanctions." *Wisconsin Law Review* (Summer), 703–719.

Chambliss, William J. (1973). "The Saints and the Roughnecks." *Society,* 11, 24–31.

Chambliss, William J., and Robert B. Seidman. (1982). *Law, Order, and Power.* 2d ed. Reading, MA: Addison-Wesley.

Charmaz, Kathy. (1980). *The Social Reality of Death: Death in Contemporary America.* Reading, MA: Addison-Wesley.

Chase, Ivan D. (1980). "Social Process and Hierarchy Formation in Small Groups." *American Sociological Review,* 45 (6), 905–924.

Chemers, M. M., et al. (1975). "Leader Esteem for the Least Preferred Co-worker Score, Training, and Effectiveness: An Experimental Examination." *Journal of Personality and Social Psychology,* 31, 401, 409.

Chen, Xiangming. (1985). "The One-Child Population Policy, Modernization, and the Extended Chinese Family." *Journal of Marriage and the Family,* 47 (1), 93–202.

Cherlin, Andrew J. (1981). *Marriage, Divorce, and Remarriage.* Cambridge, MA: Harvard University Press.

Cherlin, Andrew. (1987). In Barbara Kantrowitz, "How To Stay Married." *Newsweek* (August 24).

Cherlin, Andrew, and Frank Furstenberg. (1983). "The American Family in the Year 2000." *The Futurist* (June), Bethesda, MA: World Future Society.

Chirot, Daniel. (1986). *Social Change in the Modern Era.* New York: Harcourt Brace Jovanovich.

Christensen, H. T., and Barber K. (1967). "Interfaith Versus Intrafaith Marriage in Indiana." *Marriage and Family Living,* 29, 461–469.

Clancy, Paul. (1987). "Waiting to Wed Is on the Rise." *USA Today* (September 10).

Clark, Burton. (1960). *The Open-Door College.* New York: McGraw-Hill.

Clark, J. G. (1979). "Cults." *Journal of American Medical Association,* 281–299.

Clark, J. G., et al. (1981). *Destructive Cult Conversion: Theory, Research and Treatment.* Weston, MA: American Family Foundation.

Clark, Joseph S. (1971). "Starvation in the Affluent Society." In B. Ficker and Herbert S. Graves (eds.). *Deprivation in America.* Beverly Hills, CA: Glencoe Press.

Clark, Joseph. (1984). "American Blacks: A Passion for Politics." *Dissent* (Summer), 261–264.

Clark, Kenneth B., and Mamie P. Clark. (1947). "Racial Identification and Preference in Negro Children." In T. M. Newcomb and E. L. Hartley (eds.), *Readings in Social Psychology.* New York: Holt, Rinehart & Winston.

Clark, Matt. (1984). "A Slow Death of the Mind." *Newsweek* (December 3), 56–62.

Clark, Robert, and John Menefee. (1981). "Federal Expenditures for the Elderly: Past and Future." *Gerontologist,* 21, 132–137.

Clarke-Stewart, Alison. (1984). In Glenn Collins, "Experts Debate Impact of Day Care." *New York Times* (September 4), B311ff.

Clausen, J. A. (1972). "The Life Course of Individuals." In Matilda White Riley, M. Johnson, and Anne Foner (eds.), *Aging and Society (Vol. 3): A Sociology of Age Stratification.* New York: Russell Sage, 475–514.

Clayton, Richard R., and Harwin L. Voss. (1977): "Shacking-Up: Cohabitation in the 1970s." *Journal of Marriage and the Family* (May), 273–283.

Clemente, Frank, and William J. Sauer. (1976). "Life Satisfaction in the United States." *Social Forces,* 54, 621–631.

Clifford, Margaret M., and Elaine Walster. (1973). "Effect of Physical Attractiveness on Teacher Expectations." *Sociology of Education,* 46 (Spring), 248–258.

Clinard, Marshall B. (1974). *The Sociology of Deviant Behavior* (4th ed.). New York: Holt, Rinehart & Winston.

Clinard, Marshall B., and Richard Quinney. (1973). *Criminal Behavior Systems.* New York: Holt, Rinehart & Winston.

Clogg, Clifford, and James Shockey. (1984). "Mismatch Between Occupation and Schooling: A Prevalence Measure, Recent Trends and Demographic Analysis." *Demography,* 21, 235–257.

Coe, Michael D., and Richard A. Diehl. (1980). *In the Land of the Olmec (Vol. 1): The Archaeology of San Lorenzo Tenochtitlan.* Austin, TX: University of Texas Press.

———. (1980). *In the Land of the Olmec (Vol. 2): The People of the River.* Austin, TX: University of Texas Press.

Cohen, Albert K., and Harold Hodges. (1963). "Characteristics of the Lower Blue-Collar Classes." *Social Problems,* 10.

Cohen, Lawrence E. (1981). "Residential Burglary in the United States: Life-Style and Demographic Factors Associated with the Probability of Victimization." *Journal of Crime and Delinquency,* 18, 113–127.

Cohen, Lawrence E., and Marcus Felson. (1979). "Social Change and Crime-Rate Trends: A Routine Activity Approach." *American Sociological Review,* 44, 588–608.

Cohen, Lawrence E., Marcus Felson, and Kenneth C. Land. (1980). "Property Crime Rates in the United States: A Macrodynamic Analysis, 1947–1977; with Ex-Ante Forecasts for the Mid-1980s." *American Journal of Sociology,* 86(1), 90–118.

Coleman, James S. (1961). *The Adolescent Society.* New York: Free Press.

Coleman, James S., et al. (1966). *Equality of Educational Opportunity.* Washington, DC: Office of Education.

———. (1974). *Youth: Transition to Adulthood.* Chicago: University of Chicago Press.

Coles, Robert, and Jane Hallowell Coles. (1978). *Women in Crisis.* New York: Delacorte Press/Seymour Lawrence.

Collins, Glenn. (1981). "The Childhood Industry: Conflicting Advice." *New York Times* (March 16), 17–18.

———. (1984). "Experts Debate Impact of Day Care on Children and Society." *New York Times* (September 4), 311ff.

Collins, Randall. (1971). "Functional and Conflict Theories of Educational Stratification." *American Sociological Review,* 36, 1002–1018.

———. (1974). *Conflict Sociology: Toward an Explanatory Science.* New York: Academic Press.

———. (1979). *The Credential Society.* New York: Academic Press.

———. (1985). *Sociology of Marriage and the Family.* Chicago: Nelson-Hall.

Collver, Andrew. (1963). "The Family Cycle in India and the U.S." *American Sociological Review,* 28, 86–96.

"Comes the Revolution." (1978). *Time Magazine* (June 26), 54–59.

Comptroller General of the United States. (1979). *Resources Devoted by the Department of Justice to Combat White-Collar Crime and Public Corruption.* Washington, DC: Government Printing Office.

Comte, Auguste. (1868). *The Positive Philosophy of Auguste Comte.* Translated by and condensed by H. Martineau. London: Chapman.

Comte, Auguste. (1915). *The Positive Philosophy.* Translated and edited by Harriet Martineau. London: Bell.

Conklin, John E. (1986). *Criminology* (2d ed.). New York: Macmillan.

Conway, F., and J. Siegelman. (1982). "Information Disease: Have the Cults Created a New Mental Illness?" *Science Digest,* 90, 86–92.

———. (1978). *Snapping: America's Epidemic of Sudden Personality Change.* Philadelphia: Lippincott.

Cooley, Charles Horton. (1909). *Social Organization: A Study of the Larger Mind.*

———. (1902). *Human Nature and the Social Order.* New York: Scribner's.

Coombs, L. D., and A. Zumeta. (1970). "Correlates of Marital Dissolution in a Prospective Fertility Study: A Research Note." *Social Problems,* 18, 92–102.

Cooper, D. (1970). *The Death of the Family.* New York: Pantheon.

Corcoran, Mary, and Greg Duncan. (1979). "Work History, Labor Force Attachment, and Earnings

Differences Between the Races and Sexes." *Journal of Human Resources,* 14 (Winter), 3–12.

Cornish, Edward. (1986). "Farewell, Sexual Revolution. Hello, New Victorianism." *The Futurist* (January–February), 48–49.

Cosell, Hilary. (1985). "Did We Have the Wrong Dreams?" *Ladies' Home Journal* (April), 168–171.

Coser, Lewis A. (1956). *The Functions of Social Conflict.* Glencoe, IL: Free Press.

Coser, Rose Laub, and Lewis Coser. (1974). "Jonestown as a Perverse Utopia." *Dissent* (Spring), 158–163.

Council on Economic Priorities. (1979). *Jobs and Energy.* New York: Council on Economic Priorities.

Courtney, Alice and Thomas Whipple. (1983). *Sex Stereotyping in Advertising.* San Diego: Lexington Books.

Cowen, Robert. (1986). "Experts Debate Just What Is the Source of Global Warming Trend." *Christian Science Monitor* (November 5).

Cowen, Robert. (1986). "'Greenhouse Effect' on Climate Is a Cloudy Issue." *Christian Science Monitor* (December 23), 19.

Cowgill, Donald O. (1972). *Aging and Modernization.* New York: Meredith.

Cowley, Malcolm. (1982). *The View from 80.* New York: Penguin Books.

Cox, Harold. (1984). *Later Life: The Realities of Aging.* Englewood Cliffs, NJ: Prentice-Hall.

Cox, Harvey. (1977). "Eastern Cults and Western Cultures: Why Young Americans Are Buying Oriental Religions." *Psychology Today* (July), 36–42.

Cox, Oliver C. (1948). *Caste, Class and Race: A Study in Social Dynamics.* New York: Modern Reader.

Crandall, Robert. (1987). "Learning the Lessons: The Environment." *Wilson Quarterly* (Autumn), 69–80.

Cratsley, John. (1972). "The Crime of the Courts." In Bruce Wasserstein and Mark Green (eds.), *With Justice for Some.* Boston: Beacon Press.

Cressey, Donald R. (1955). "Changing Criminals: The Application of the Theory of Differential Association." *American Journal of Sociology,* 61(2), 116–120.

Cressy, Earl Herbert. (1955). *Daughters of Changing Japan.* New York: Farrar, Straus, and Giroux.

Crosbie, Paul V. (1975). *Interaction in Small Groups.* New York: Macmillan.

"Cross-National Evidence of the Effects of Foreign Investment and Aid on Economic Growth and Inequality: A Survey of Findings and Reanalysis." (1978) *American Journal of Sociology,* 84 (November), 651–683.

Crystal, Stephen. (1982). *America's Old-Age Crisis.* New York: Penguin Books.

Cullen, F. T., et al. (1983). "Public Support for Punishing White-Collar Crime: Blaming the Victim Revisited?" *Journal of Criminal Justice,* 11, 481–493.

Cullen, F. T., B. G. Link, and C. W. Polanzi. (1982). "The Seriousness of Crime Revisited." *Criminology,* 20, 83–102.

Cultural Information Service. (1987). "We All Pay the Heavy Costs of Illiteracy," *USA Today* (September 10), 9A.

Cumming, Elaine, and William H. Henry. (1961). *Growing Old.* New York: Basic Books.

Currie, Elliott P. (1982). "Crime and Ideology." *Working Papers* Part 1 (May–June), 26–35; Part 2 (July–August), 17–25.

Curtiss, Susan R. (1977). *Genie: A Psycholinguistic Study of a Modern-Day 'Wild Child'.* New York: Academic Press.

Dahl, Robert A. (1958). "A Critique of the Power Elite Method." *American Political Science Review,* 52, 463–469.

———. (1961). *Who Governs? Democracy and Power in an American City.* New Haven: Yale University Press.

———. (1970). *Modern Political Analysis* (2d ed.). Englewood Cliffs, NJ: Prentice-Hall.

———. (1973). "Governing the Giant Corporation." In Ralph Nader and Mark Green (eds.), *Corporate Power in America.* New York: Grossman.

———. (1976). *Modern Political Analysis* (3d ed.). Englewood Cliffs, NJ: Prentice-Hall.

———. (1982). *Dilemmas of Pluralist Democracy: Autonomy Versus Control.* New Haven: Yale University Press.

Dahrendorf, Ralf. (1959). *Class and Class Conflict in Industrial Society.* Palo Alto, CA: Stanford University Press.

D'Andrade, Roy G. (1966). "Sex Differences and Cultural Institutions." In Eleanor E. Maccoby (ed.), *The Development of Sex Differences.* Palo Alto, CA: Stanford University Press.

Dank, Barry M. (1971). "Coming Out in the Gay World." *Psychiatry,* 34, 180–197.

Dannefer, Dale. (1984). "Adult Development and Social Theory: A Reappraisal." *American Sociological Review,* 49(1), 100–116.

Das, Frieda M. (1932). *Purdah.* New York: Vanguard.

Davis, Cary, Carl Haub, and JoAnne Willette. (1983). "U.S. Hispanics: Changing the Face of America." *Population Bulletin,* 38(3), 1–43.

Davis, James H., and F. Restle. (1963). "The Analysis of Problems and Prediction and Group Problem Solving." *Journal of Abnormal Social Psychology,* 66, 103–116.

Davis, Karen. (1986). "Paying the Health-Care Bills of

an Aging Population." In Alan Pifer and Lydia Bronte (eds.), *Our Aging Society: Paradox and Promise.* New York: W. W. Norton.

Davis, Kingsley. (1940). "Extreme Social Isolation of a Child." *American Journal of Sociology,* 45, 554–564.

———. (1951). *The Population of India and Pakistan.* Princeton: Princeton University Press.

———. (1955). "The Origin and Growth of Urbanization in the World." *American Journal of Sociology,* 60(5), 429–437.

———. (1965). "The Urbanization of the Human Population." *Scientific American,* 213(3), 41–53.

———. (1976). "Sexual Behavior." In Robert K. Merton and Robert Nisbet (eds.), *Contemporary Social Problems.* New York: Harcourt Brace Jovanovich.

Davis, Kingsley, and Wilbert Moore. (1945). "Some Principles of Stratification." *American Sociological Review,* 10, 242–249.

Davis, Richard. (1984). "TV's Boycott of Old Age." *Aging* (August–September), 12–19.

Davis, Sharon, and Emil Haller. (1981). "Tracking, Ability, and SES: Further Evidence on the Revisionist–Meritocratic Debate." *American Journal of Education,* 89 (May), 283–304.

DeBeauvoir, Simone. (1972). *The Coming of Age.* New York: Putnam.

DeJong, Gordon F., Joseph E. Faulkner, and Rex H. Warland. (1976). "Dimensions of Religiosity Reconsidered: Evidence From a Cross-Cultural Study." *Social Forces,* 54(4), 866–889.

Delacroix, Jacques, and Charles Ragin. (1981). "Structural Blockage: A Cross-National Study of Economic Dependency, State Efficacy, and Underdevelopment." *American Journal of Sociology,* 86 (May), 1311–1347.

Della Fave, L. Richard. (1980). "The Meek Shall Not Inherit the Earth: Self-Evaluation and the Legitimacy of Stratification." *American Sociological Review,* 45, 955–971.

DeLoria, Vine, Jr. (1969). *Custer Died for Your Sins: An Indian Manifesto.* New York: Macmillan.

———. (1981). "Native Americans: The American Indian Today." *Annals of the American Academy of Political and Social Science,* 454 (March), 139–149.

Demos, John. (1970). *A Little Commonwealth.* New York: Oxford University Press.

Destler, I. M. (1986). *American Trade Politics: System Under Stress.* New York: Twentieth-Century Fund.

de Tocqueville, Alexis. (1856, 1955). *The Old Regime and the French Revolution.* Garden City, NY: Doubleday.

Devens, Richard M., Jr., et al. (1985). "Employment and Unemployment in 1984." *Monthly Labor Review,* 108, 3–15.

DeVos, George, and Hiroshi Wagatsuma. (1970). "Status and Role Behavior in Changing Japan." In Georgene H. Seward and Robert C. Williamson (eds.), *Sex Roles in Changing Society.* New York: Random House.

DeVries, Hilary. (1983). "Physiology of Exercise and Aging." In D. W. Woodruff and J. E. Birren (eds.), *Aging: Scientific Perspectives and Social Issues.* Monterey, CA: Brooks/Cole.

———. (1986). "A Warm Van and a Helping Hand." *Christian Science Monitor,* (November 26), 3, 8.

Diagnostic and Statistical Manual of Mental Disorders (2d ed.) (DSM II). Washington, DC: American Psychiatric Association.

Dickson, Paul. (1975). *The Future of the Workplace.* New York: Weybright and Talley.

Diener, Edward and Crandell, Rick. (1979). *Ethics in Social Behavioral Research.* Chicago: University of Chicago Press.

Diener, E. (1980). "Deindividuation: The Absence of Self-Awareness and Self-Regulation in Group Members." In P. B. Paulus (ed.), *The Psychology of Group Influence.* Hillsdale, NJ: Lawrence Erlbaum Associates.

Dobell, Elizabeth Rodgers. (1978). "God and Woman: The Hidden History." *Redbook,* (March).

Dobson, James C. (1985). "The Greatest Gift You Can Give Your Child." *Reader's Digest,* 127 (December), 125–130.

Doering, C. H., et al. (1975). "A Cycle of Plasma Testosterone in the Human Male." *Journal of Clinical Endocrinology and Metabolism,* 40.

Dohrenwend, Bruce. (1982). "Perspectives on the Past and Future of Psychiatric Epidemiology." *American Journal of Public Health,* 72 (November), 1271–1279.

Dolan, Jay P. (1978). *Catholic Revivalism: The American Experience, 1830–1900.* South Bend, IN: University of Notre Dame Press.

Doleschal, Eugene, and Norah Klapmuts. (1973). *Toward a New Criminology.* Hackensack, NJ: National Council on Crime and Delinquency.

Dollar, Bruce. (1983). "What Is Really Going on in Schools," *Social Policy* (Fall), 7–19.

Domhoff, G. William. (1967). *Who Rules America?* Englewood Cliffs, NJ: Prentice-Hall.

———. (1970). *The Higher Circles.* New York: Random House.

———. (1974). *The Bohemian Grove and Other Retreats.* New York: Harper.

———. (1975). "Social Clubs, Policy-Planning Groups, and Corporations: A Network Study of Ruling-Class Cohesiveness." *Insurgent Sociologist,* 5, 173–184.

———. (1983). *Who Rules America Now?: A View For the 80s.* Englewood Cliffs, NJ: Prentice-Hall.

Domhoff, G. William, and Beverly Duncan. (1968). "Socioeconomic Background and Occupational Achievement: Extensions of a Basic Model." Ann

Arbor: University of Michigan, Population Studies Center.

Doress, I., and J. N. Porter. (1981). "Kids in Cults." In T. Robbins and D. Anthony (eds.), *In Gods We Trust: New Patterns of Religious Pluralism in America.* New Brunswick, NJ: Transaction.

Dorfman, D. D. (1978). "The Cyril Burt Question: New Findings." *Science,* 201 (29), 1177–1186.

Dorris, Michael A. (1981). "The Grass Still Grows, the Rivers Still Flow: Contemporary Native Americans." *Daedalus,* 11, 43–69.

Douglas, J. H. (1975). "Invisible Famine." *Science News,* 108, 381.

Douglass, Richard L. (1983). "Domestic Neglect and Abuse of the Elderly: Implications for Research and Service." *Family Relations,* 32 (July), 395–402.

Dove, Adrian. (1968). "The Dove Counterbalance Intelligence Test." *Denver Post,* (July 8), 6.

Dover, Michael. (1985). "Getting off the Pesticide Treadmill." *Technology Review* (November–December), 52–63.

Dowd, James J. (1975). "Aging as Exchange: A Preface to Theory." *Journal of Gerontology,* 30, 584–594.

Doyle, James A. (1983). *The Male Experience.* Dubuque, IA: Wm. C. Brown and Company.

Dreeben, Robert. (1968). *On What Is Learned in School.* Reading, MA: Addison-Wesley.

Drew, Elizabeth. (1983). *Politics and Money: The New Road to Corruption.* New York: Macmillan.

Duberman, Lucile. (ed.) (1975a). *Gender and Sex in Society.* New York: Praeger.

———. (1975b). *The Reconstituted Family: A Study of Remarried Couples and Their Children.* Chicago: Nelson-Hall.

Dubos, Rene Jules. (1968). *So Human an Animal.* New York: Scribner.

Dumon, Wilfried A. (1978). "When Two Become Three." Paper presented to the International Union of Family Organizations, Vienna (June).

Durkheim, Emile. (1893, 1964). *The Division of Labor in Society.* (Translated by Sarah Solovay and John Muleer, edited by George Catlin.) New York: Macmillan.

———. (1895a, 1950). *The Rules of the Sociological Method.* New York: Free Press.

———. (1895b, 1964). *The Rules of the Sociological Method.* (Translated by Sarah Solovay and John Muleer, edited by George Catlin.) New York: Macmillan.

———. (1897, 1951). *Suicide: A Study of Sociology.* Translated by John A. Spaulding and George Simpson. New York: Free Press.

———. (1912, 1947). *The Elementary Forms of the Religious Life.* New York: Free Press.

———. (1977). *The Evolution of Educational Thought.* London: Routledge and Kegan Paul.

Duverger, Maurice. (1954). *Political Parties.* New York: John Wiley.

Dye, Thomas R. (1979). *Who's Running America?* Englewood Cliffs, NJ: Prentice-Hall.

———. (1986). *Who's Running America? The Conservative Years* (4th ed.). Englewood Cliffs, NJ: Prentice-Hall.

———. (1987). *Power and Society: An Introduction to the Social Sciences* (4th ed.). Monterey, CA: Brooks/Cole.

Eakins, Barbara, and Gene Eakins. (1978). *Sex Differences in Human Communications.* Boston: Houghton Mifflin.

Eastman, Peggy. (1964). "Elders Under Siege." *Psychology Today,* 18 (January), 30.

Eaton, Joseph W., and Albert J. Mayer. (1954). *Man's Capacity to Reproduce: The Demography of a Unique Population.* Glencoe, IL: The Free Press.

Eberstadt, Nick. (1978). "World Population Figures Are Misleading." *New York Times* (March 26), 18.

Eckholm, Erik. (1985). "Malnutrition in Elderly: Widespread Health Threat." *New York Times' Science Times* (August 13), C1.

Eckstein, Harry. (1966). *Division and Cohesion in Democracy: A Study of Norway.* Princeton: Princeton University Press.

Economic Report to the President. (1974). Washington, DC: U.S. Government Printing Office.

Edwards, David V. (1985). *The American Political Experience: An Introduction to Government* (3d ed.). Englewood Cliffs, NJ: Prentice-Hall.

Edwards, Lonnie. (1985). "AIDS Fear Is Leading to Safer Sex." *Jet,* 68 (September 2), 5.

Egan, Jack. (1982). "Hollywood's Hysterical Summer." *New York* (July 26), 33–35.

Ehrlich, Paul, and Ann Ehrlich. (1972). *Population, Resources, and Environment.* San Francisco: W. H. Freeman.

Eichler, Edward P., and Marshall Kaplan. (1967). *The Community Builders.* Berkeley: University of California Press.

Eisenstadt, S. H. (1956). *From Generation to Generation: Age Groups and the Social Structure.* New York: Free Press.

Eisenstein, Paul. (1987). "Detroit Works to Break Cycle of School Shootings." *Christian Science Monitor* (May 1), 1.

Eitzen, D. Stanley. (1974). *Social Structure and Social Problems in America.* Boston: Allyn and Bacon.

Elkins, Stanley M. (1975). "The Slavery Debate." *Commentary,* 60 (6), 40–61.

Elliott, J. (1984). "The Daytime Television Drama Portrayal of Older Adults." *Gerontologist,* 24 (6), 628–633.

Ellis, Dean. (1967). "Speech and Social Status in America." *Social Forces,* 45, 431–437.

Elrick, Harold. (1976). Quoted in Richard Keelor, "Physical Fitness and Health: Part II." *Aging* (May/June), 8–9.

Emery, Robert. (1984). "Divorce, Children, and Social Policy." In Harold Stevenson and Alberta Siegal (eds.), *Child Development Research and Social Policy.* Chicago: University of Chicago Press.

Employment and Training Report of the President. (1978). Washington, DC: U.S. Government Printing Office.

Engels, Friederich. (1884). *The Early Development of the Family.*

———. (1972). *The Origins of the Family, Private Property, and the State, in Light of the Researches of Lewis H. Morgan.* New York: International.

Ennis, Phillip H. (1967). "Crimes, Victims, and the Police." *Transaction,* 4, 36–44.

Entwhistle, Doris, and Leslie Hayduk. (1981). "Academic Expectations and the School Attainment of Young Children." *Sociology of Education,* 54 (January), 34–50.

Epstein, Edward J. (1974). "The Strange, Tilted World of TV Network News." *Reader's Digest* (February), 142–146.

Erikson, Erik H. (1964). *Childhood and Society.* New York: Norton.

———. (1965). "Inner and Outer Space: Reflections on Womanhood." In Robert Jay Lifton (ed.), *The Woman in America.* Boston: Houghton Mifflin.

Erikson, Kai T. (1962). "Notes on the Sociology of Deviance." *Social Problems,* 9, 307–314.

———. (1978). *Everything in Its Path.* Simon and Schuster, Touchstone Books.

Erlanger, Howard S. (1974). "Social Class and Corporal Punishment in Childrearing: A Reassessment." *American Sociological Review,* 39, 68–85.

Etzioni, Amitai. (1961). *A Comparative Analysis of Complex Organizations.* Glencoe, IL: Free Press.

———. (1969). *A Sociological Reader on Complex Organizations.* New York: Holt, Rinehart & Winston.

Etzioni-Halevy, Eva. (1983). *Bureaucracy and Democracy: A Political Dilemma.* Boston: Routledge and Kegan Paul.

Evans, Gaynelle. (1985). "Gains by Blacks in Education Found Eroding." *Chronicle of Higher Education* (April 17), 30, (7), 1, 14.

Evans, Peter B. (1981). "Recent Research on Multinational Corporations." *Annual Reviews of Sociology.* Palo Alto, CA: Annual Reviews, Inc., 7, 199–233.

Fallows, James. (1985). "The Case Against Credentialism." *Atlantic Monthly* (December), 49–67.

Fann, W., J. C. Wheless, and B. W. Richman. (1976). "Treating the Aged with Psychotropic Drugs." *Gerontologist,* 16, 322–328.

Fantini, Mario D. (1986). *Regaining Excellence in Education.* Columbus, OH: Merrill Publishing.

Farley, Reynolds. (1984). *Blacks and Whites: Narrowing the Gap?* Cambridge: Harvard University Press.

Featherman, David L., F. Lancaster Jones, and Robert M. Hauser. (1975). "Assumptions of Mobility Research in the United States: The Case of Occupational Status." *Social Science Research,* 4, 329–360.

Federal Offenders in the United States District Courts. (1970). Washington, DC: Administrative Office of the U.S. Courts.

Feldstein, Martin. (1977). "Facing the Crisis in Social Security." *Public Interest,* 47 (Spring), 90.

Felson, Marcus, and David Knoke. (1974). "Social Status and the Married Woman." *Journal of Marriage and the Family* (August), 516–521.

Ferber, Marianne, and Joan Huber. (1979). "Husbands, Wives, and Careers." *Journal of Marriage and the Family,* 41, 315–325.

Ferree, Myra Marx. (1976). "The Confused American Housewife." *Psychology Today* (September), 76–80.

Ferree, Myra Marx, and Beth Hess. (1985). *Controversy and Coalition: The New Feminist Movement.* Boston: Twayne Press.

Ficker, Victor B., and Herbert S. Graves. (1978). *Social Science and Urban Crisis: Introductory Readings* (2d ed.). New York: Macmillan.

Fielder, Fred E., and M. M. Chemers. (1975). *Leadership and Effective Management.* Glenview, IL: Scott, Foresman.

Field, Mark G., and Karin I. Flynn. (1979). "Worker, Mother, Housewife: Soviet Women Today." In Georgene H. Seward and Robert C. Williamson (eds.), *Sex Roles in Changing Society.* New York: Random House, 257–284.

Fine, Gary Alan. (1979). "Cokelore and Coke Law: Urban Belief Tales and the Problem of Multiple Origins." *Journal of American Folklore,* 92, 478–482.

———. (1980). "The Kentucky Fried Rat: Legends and Modern Society." *Journal of the Folklore Institute,* 17, 222–243.

———. (1987). *With the Boys: Sport and Culture in Little League Baseball.* Chicago: University of Chicago Press.

Finn, Jeremy, et al. (1979). "Sex Differences in Educational Attainment: A Cross-National Perspective." *Harvard Educational Review,* 49 (November), 447–503.

Fischer, Arlene. (1986). "I Want To Stay Home—Where I Belong." *Redbook* (April), 96–97, 157.

Fischer, Claude S. (1981). "The Public and Private Worlds of City Life." *American Sociological Review,* 46, 306–316.

———. (1984). *The Urban Experience* (2d ed.). New York: Harcourt Brace Jovanovich.

Fischer, David. (1977). *Growing Old in America.* New York: Oxford University Press.

Fischer, Pamela J., et al. (1986). "Mental Health and Social Characteristics of the Homeless: A Survey of Mission Users." *American Journal of Public Health,* 76(5), 519–524.

Fischman, Joshua. (1984). "The Mystery of Alzheimer's." *Psychology Today* (January), 27.

Fisher, Judith L. (1983). "Mothers Living Apart from Their Children." *Family Relations,* 32, 351–357.

Fisse, B., and J. Braithwaite. (1983). *The Impact of Publicity on Corporate Offenders.* Albany, NY: State University of New York Press.

Flavin, Christopher. (1983). *Nuclear Power: The Market Test.* Washington, DC: Worldwatch Institute.

Fodor, E. M. (1978). "Simulated Work Climate as an Influence on Choice of Leadership Style." *Personality and Social Psychology Bulletin,* 4, 111–114.

Fogel, Robert W., and Stanley L. Engerman. (1974). *Time on the Cross.* Boston: Little, Brown.

Foley, John W., and Homer R. Steedly, Jr. (1980). "The Strategy of Social Protest: A Comment on a Growth Industry." *American Journal of Sociology,* 85 (6), 1426–1427.

Foner, Anne. (1986). *Aging and Old Age: New Perspectives.* Englewood Cliffs, NJ: Prentice-Hall.

Foner, Nancy. (1982). "Some Consequences of Age Inequality in Nonindustrial Societies." In M. W. Riley, R. P. Ables, and M. S. Teltelbaum (eds.), *Aging From Birth to Death, (vol. 2), Sociotemporal Perspectives.* Boulder, CO: Westview Press, 71–86.

———. (1984). *Ages in Conflict: A Cross-Cultural Perspective on Inequality Between Old and Young.* New York: Columbia University Press.

Ford, Clellan S. (1940). "Society." In *Papers Presented Before the Monday Night Group, 1939–1940.* New Haven: Institute for Human Relations, Yale University.

Ford, Clellan S., and Frank A. Beach. (1951). *Patterns of Sexual Behavior.* New York: Harper and Row.

Ford, William D. (1983). "Education and America's Future," *USA Today Magazine* (September), 27–29.

Forman, Maxine. (1984). "Social Security Is a Women's Issue." In *Growing Old in America* (3d edition). New Brunswick, NJ: Transaction Books, 537–562.

Forst, Brian. (1983). "Capital Punishment and Deterrence: Conflicting Evidence." *Journal of Criminal Law and Criminology,* 74 (Autumn), 927–943.

Fox, James Alan. (1978). *Forecasting Crime Data.* Lexington, MA: Lexington Books.

Fox, D. J., and I. Lorge, (1962). "The Relative Quality of Decisions Written by Individuals and Groups as the Available Time for Problem Solving Is Increased." *Journal of Social Psychology,* 57, 227–242.

Fraiberg, Selma H. (1977). *Every Child's Birthright.* New York: Basic Books.

Frank, Andre Gunder. (1984). *Critique and Anti-Critique: Essays on Dependence and Reformism.* New York, NY: Praeger Publishers.

Freed, Stanley, and Ruth Freed. (1985). "One Son Is No Sons." *Natural History* (January).

Freedman, Robert. (1986). *The Mind of Karl Marx: Economic, Political, and Social Perspectives.* Chatham, NJ: Chatham House Publishers.

Freeman, Jo. (1974). "The Origins of the Women's Liberation Movement." *American Journal of Sociology,* 78 (4), 792–811.

———. (1983). *Social Movements of the Sixties and Seventies.* New York: Longman Press.

Freeman, Linton C. (1958). "Marriage Without Love: Mate-Selection in Nonwestern Societies." In Robert F. Winch (ed.), *Mate Selection.* New York: Harper and Row.

Freeman, Richard B. (1976). *The Overeducated American.* New York: Academic Press.

Freitag, Peter. (1975). "The Cabinet and Big Business: A Study of Interlocks." *Social Problems,* 23, 137–152.

French, Marilyn. (1985). *Beyond Power: On Women, Men, and Morals.* New York: Summit Books.

Freud, Sigmund. (1938). *Basic Writings.* Translated and edited by A. A. Brill. New York: Modern Library.

Fried, Morton H. (1967). *The Evolution of Political Society.* New York: Random House.

Friedan, Betty. (1963). *The Feminine Mystique.* New York: Dell.

———. (1981). *The Second State.* New York: Summit.

Friedrich, Otto. (1985). "The Changing Face of America." *Time Magazine* (July 8), 26–35.

Friedson, Eliot. (1977). "The Futures of Professionalization." In M. Stacey, et al. (eds.), *Health and the Division of Labor.* London: Croom Helm, 14–38.

Fries, J. F. (1980). "Aging, Natural Death, and the Compression of Morbidity." *New England Journal of Medicine,* 300, 130–135.

———. (1985). "Separating Death from Disease." *New York Times* (February 17), E5.

Fuchs, Victor. (1984). "Though Much Is Taken: Reflections on Aging, Health, and Medical Care." *Milbank Memorial Quarterly/Health and Society* (Spring), 164–165.

Furstenberg, F. F., Jr. (1967). "Premarital Pregnancy and Marital Instability." *Journal of Social Issues,* 32 (1), 67–86.

Furstenber, Frank F., Jr., and Christine Winquist Nord. (1985). "Parenting Apart: Patterns of Childrearing After Marital Disruption." *Journal of Marriage and the Family,* 47 (November), 893–904.

Fusfeld, Daniel R. (1985). *Economics: Principles of Political Economy* (2d ed.). Glenview, IL: Scott, Foresman.

Galanter, M. (1980). "Psychological Induction into the

Large-Group: Findings from a Modern Religious Sect." *American Journal of Psychiatry*, 137, 1574–1579.

———. (1983). "Unification Church ("Moonie") Dropouts: Psychological Readjustment After Leaving Charismatic Religious Groups." *American Journal of Psychiatry*, 140, 984–989.

Galanter, M., R. Rabkin, J. Rabkin, and A. Deutsch. (1979). "The 'Moonies': A Psychological Study of Conversion and Membership in a Contemporary Religious Sect." *American Journal of Psychiatry*, 136, 165–179.

Gallagher, Bernard J. (1980). *The Sociology of Mental Illness*. Englewood Cliffs, NJ: Prentice-Hall.

Galle, O., and W. Gove. (1978). "Overcrowding, Isolation, and Human Behavior." In Karl Tauber and James Sweet, (eds.), *Social Demography*. New York: Academic Press.

Gallup, George H. (1972). *The Gallup Poll: Public Opinion, 1935–1971*. New York: Random House.

———. (1976). *The Gallup Poll: Public Opinion, 1972–1977*. 2 vols. Wilmington, DE: Scholarly Resources, 627–629.

———. (1980). *The Gallup Poll*. Wilmington, DE: Scholarly Resources.

Gallup, Jr., George. (1985). "Religion in America: 50 Years: 1935–1985." *The Gallup Report*, 236 (May).

———. (1987a). *The Gallup Report*, 256–257.

———. (1987b). *The Gallup Report*, 259 (April).

———. (1987c). *Emerging Trends*. Princeton: Princeton Religion Research Center.

Gallup Graphics. (1987). Los Angeles: *Los Angeles Times Syndicate*. October 28.

Gallup Opinion Index. (1975). *Religion in America*. Report No. 114.

———. (1978a). *Religion in America: 1977–1978*. Report No. 145.

———. (1978b). *How Americans View the Public Schools*. Report No. 151.

———. (1982). *Religion in America: 1981–1982*. Report No. 201–202.

Gamson, William. (1968). *Power and Discontent*. Homewood, IL: Dorsey Press.

———. (1975). *The Strategy of Social Protest*. Homewood, IL: Dorsey Press.

———. (1980). "Understanding the Careers of Challenging Groups: A Commentary on Goldstone." *American Journal of Sociology*, 85(5), 1043–1060.

Gamson, William, Bruce Fireman, and Steven Rytina. (1982). *Encounters with Unjust Authority*. Homewood, IL: Dorsey Press.

Gans, Herbert J. (1962). *The Urban Villagers*. New York: Free Press.

———. (1970). "Urbanism and Suburbanism as Ways of Life." In Robert Guttman and David Popenoe (eds.), *Neighborhood, City, and Metropolis*. New York: Random House.

———. (1972). "Vance Packard Misperceives the Way Most American Movers Live." *Psychology Today* (September), pp. 20f.

Gansberg, Martin. (1964). "Thirty-eight Who Saw Murder Didn't Call Police." *New York Times* (March 27), 1, 38.

Garbarino, Joseph W. (1984). "Unionism Without Unions: The New Industrial Relations." *Industrial Relations*, 23, 41.

Garey, Ellen. (1986). "How I Rediscovered My Kids." *Parents Magazine* (April), 89–92.

Gardner, Marilyn. (1987). "Younger Women Sidestep Politics." *Christian Science Monitor* (September 4), 21.

Garfinkel, Harold. (1949). "Research Note on Inter- and Intra-Racial Homicides," *Social Forces*, 27 (May), 369–381.

———. (1956). "Conditions of Successful Degradation Ceremonies." *American Journal of Sociology*, 61, 420–424.

Garfinkel, Irwin, and Sara McLanahan. (1987). *Single Mothers and Their Children: A New American Dilemma*. Washington, DC: The Urban Institute Press.

Gastil, Raymond, ed. (1987). *Freedom in the World: Political Rights and Civil Liberties: 1986–1987*. Westport, CT: Greenwood Press.

Geerken, Michael, and Walter Gove. (1977). "Deterrence, Overload, and Incapacitation: An Empirical Evaluation." *Social Forces*, 56, 424–447.

———. (1983). *At Home and at Work: The Family's Allocation of Labor*. Beverly Hills, CA: Sage Press.

Geertz, Clifford. (1968). *Islam Observed: Religious Development in Morocco and Indonesia*. Chicago: University of Chicago Press.

Geis, Gilbert. (1978). In M. David Ermann and Richard J. Lundman, (eds.), *White-Collar Crime: The Heavy Electrical Equipment Antitrust Cases of 1961 in Corporate and Government Deviance*. New York: Oxford University Press.

Geist, William. (1985). *Toward a Safe and Sane Halloween and Other Tales of Suburbia*. New York: Times Books.

Georgakas, D. (1980). *The Methuselah Factors: Strategies for a Long and Vigorous Life*. New York: Simon and Schuster.

Gerbner, G., et al. (1980). "Aging with Television: Images in Television Drama and Conceptions of Social Reality." *Journal of Communications*, 30, 37–47.

Gerson, Menachem. (1978). *Family, Women, and Socialization in the Kibbutz*. Lexington, MA: D. C. Heath.

Gerstl, Naomi, Catherine Kohler Riessman, and Sarah Rosenfield. (1985). "Explaining the Symptomatology of Separated and Divorced Women and Men: The Role of Material Conditions and Social Networks." *Social Forces*, 64(1), 84–101.

Gerth, H. H., and C. Wright Mills (eds.). (1959). *From Max Weber: Essays in Sociology*. New York: Oxford University Press.

Gesell, Arnold. (1940). *The First Five Years of Life: A Guide to the Study of the Preschool Child*. New York: Harper and Row.

Gibbs, Jack. (1975). *Crime, Punishment, and Deterrence*. New York: Elsevier Press.

Gilligan, Carol. (1982). *In a Different Voice: Psychological Theory and Women's Development*. Cambridge: Harvard University Press.

Gintis, Herbert. (1971). "Education, Technology, and the Characteristics of Worker Productivity." *American Economic Review*, 61.

Glascock, Anthony, and Susan Feinman. (1981). "Social Asset or Social Burden: An Analysis of the Treatment of the Aged in Nonindustrial Societies." In Christine Fry (ed.), *Dimensions: Aging, Culture, and Health*. New York: Praeger.

Glass, David C., and Jerome E. Singer. (1972). *Urban Stress: Experiments on Noise and Social Stressors*. Orlando, FL: Academic Press.

Glazer, Nathan. (1985). *Clamor at the Gates*. San Francisco: Institute for Contemporary Studies.

Glazer, Nathan, and Daniel Patrick Moynihan. (1963). *Beyond the Melting Pot*. Cambridge: MIT Press.

Glenn, Norval D. (1975). "The Contribution of Marriage to the Psychological Well-Being of Males and Females." *Journal of Marriage and the Family*, 37, 594–600.

———. (1987). "The Trend in 'No Religion' Respondents to U.S. National Surveys, Late 1950s to Early 1980s." *Public Opinion Quarterly*, 51, 293–312.

Glenn, Norval D., and Ruth Hyland. (1967). "Religious Preference and Worldly Success: Some Evidence from National Surveys." *American Sociological Review*, 32, 43–75.

Glenn, Norval D., and Charles N. Weaver. (1977). "The Marital Happiness of Remarried Divorced Persons." *Journal of Marriage and the Family* (May), 331–337.

Glenn, Norval D., and Charles N. Weaver. (1982). "Enjoyment of Work by Full-Time Workers in the U.S., 1955 and 1980." *Public Opinion Quarterly*, 46, 459–470.

Glick, Paul C. (1947). "The Family Cycles." *American Sociological Review*, 12, 164–174.

Glick, Paul C., and Arthur J. Norton. (1971). "Frequency, Duration, and Probability of Marriage and Divorce." *Journal of Marriage and the Family* (May).

Glock, Charles Y., and Rodney Stark. (1965). *Religion and Society in Tension*. Chicago: Rand McNally.

———. (1966). *Christian Beliefs and Anti-Semitism*. New York: Harper and Row.

———. (1968). *American Piety: The Nature of Religious Commitment*. Berkeley: University of California Press.

Glueck, Sheldon, and Eleanor Glueck. (1950). *Unraveling Juvenile Delinquency*. Cambridge: Harvard University Press.

———. (1956). *Physique and Delinquency*. New York: Harper and Row.

Goffman, Erving. (1956, 1959). *The Presentation of Self in Everyday Life*. Social Science Research Center, University of Edinburgh. Reprint Garden City, NY: Doubleday.

———. (1961). *Encounters*. Indianapolis, IN: Bobbs Merrill.

———. (1963a). *Asylums: Essays on the Social Situation of Mental Patients and Other Inmates*. Garden City, NY: Doubleday.

———. (1963b). *Stigma: Notes on the Management of Spoiled Identity*. Englewood Cliffs, NJ: Prentice-Hall.

———. (1966). *Encounters: Two Studies in the Sociology of Interaction*. Indianapolis: Bobbs Merrill.

———. (1967). *Interaction Ritual: Essays on Face-to-Face Behavior*. Garden City, NY: Doubleday.

———. (1971). *Relations in Public*. New York: Basic Books.

———. (1977). "Genderisms: An Admittedly Malicious Look at How Advertising Reinforces Sexual Role Stereotypes." *Psychology Today* (August), 60–63.

———. (1979). *Gender Advertisements*. New York: Harper and Row.

Goldberg, Steven. (1973). *The Inevitability of Patriarchy*. New York: William Morrow.

Goldfarb, Ronald L. (1974). "American Prisons: Self-Defeating Concrete." *Psychology Today* (January), p. 204.

Goldman, Daniel. (1977). "Don't Be Adultish: An Interview with Ashley Montagu." *Psychology Today* (August), 45–46.

Goldsmith, Edward, et al. (1972). "Blueprint for Survival." *The Ecologist*, 2, 2–6.

Goldstine, Daniel, Shirley Zuckerman, and Hilary Goldstine. (1977). "The Three Stages of Marriage." *The Dance-Away Lover*. New York: William Morrow.

Goldstone, Jack A. (1980a). "The Weakness of Organization: A New Look at Gamson's *The Strategy of Social Protest*." *American Journal of Sociology*, 85 (5), 1017–1042.

———. (1980b). "Mobilization and Organization: Reply to Foley and Steedly and to Gamson." *American Journal of Sociology,* 85 (6), 1428–1432.

———. (ed.). (1986). *Revolutions: Theoretical, Comparative, and Historical Studies.* New York: Harcourt Brace Jovanovich.

Goleman, Daniel. (1984). "The Aging Mind Proves Capable of Lifelong Growth," *New York Times: Science Times* (February 21), c1, c5.

Goodall, Jane. (1971). *In the Shadow of Man.* London: Collins.

Goode, Erich. (1966). "Social Class and Church Participation." *American Journal of Sociology,* 72, 102–111.

Goode, William J. (1959). "The Theoretical Importance of Love." *American Sociological Review,* 24, 38–47.

———. (1963). "World Revolution and Family Patterns." *World Revolution and Family Patterns.* New York: Free Press.

Goodlad, John. (1984). *A Place Called School.* New York: McGraw-Hill.

Goody, Jack. (1976). "Aging in Nonindustrial Societies." In Robert Binstick and Ethel Shanas, eds., *Handbook of Aging and the Social Sciences.* New York: Van Nostrand Reinhold.

Goolkasian, Gail A. (1986). *Confronting Domestic Violence: A Guide for Criminal Justice Agencies.* Washington, DC: U.S. Department of Justice (May).

Gordon, Milton. (1964). *Assimilation in America.* New York: Oxford University Press.

Gore, Susan. (1978). "Effect of Social Support in Moderating the Health Consequences of Unemployment." *Journal of Health and Social Behavior,* 19, 157–165.

Gorer, Geoffrey. (1938). *Himalayan Village.* London: Michael Joseph.

Gornick, Vivian, and Barbara K. Moran (eds.). (1971). *Women in Sexist Society.* New York: Basic Books.

Gortmaker, Steven L. (1979). "Poverty and Infant Mortality in the United States." *American Sociological Review,* 44, 280–297.

Gottman, Jean. (1984). *Megalopolis: The Urbanized Northeastern Seaboard of the United States.* Cambridge: MIT Press.

Gough, Kathleen. (1971). "The Origin of the Family." *Journal of Marriage and the Family,* 33, 760–771.

Gracey, Harry. (1972). "Learning the Student Role: Kindergarten as Academic Boot Camp." In Dennis Wrong and Harry Gracey (eds.), *Readings in Introductory Sociology.* New York: Macmillan.

Graebner, William. (1980). *A History of Retirement: The Meaning and Function of an American Institution: 1885–1978.* New Haven: Yale University Press.

Greeley, Andrew. (1976). "Council or Encyclical?" *Review of Religious Research,* 18 (1), 3–24.

Greeley, Andrew M., and William C. McCready. (1974). *Ethnicity in the United States.* New York: John Wiley.

Greenberg, David F. (ed.). (1981). *Crime and Capitalism: Readings in Marxist Criminology.* Palo Alto, CA: Mayfield.

Greenberger, Ellen, and Laurence Steinberg. (1986). *When Teenagers Work: The Psychological and Social Costs of Adolescent Employment.* New York: Basic Books.

Greenfield, Lawrence A. (1985). "Examining Recidivism: A Bureau of Justice Statistics Special Report." Washington, DC: U.S. Department of Justice, Bureau of Justice Statistics, February.

Greenhouse, Linda. (1983). "As Appeals Hit Final Stage, Life on Death Row Runs out," *New York Times* (December 19), E5.

Greenwald, John. (1986). "Deadly Meltdown," *Time Magazine* May 12, 38–44, 49–50, 52.

Greer, D. S. (1983). "Hospice: Lessons for Geriatrics," *Journal of the American Geriatrics Society,* 31, 67–70.

Greer, S. (1962). *The Emerging City: Myth and Reality.* New York: Free Press.

Griffith, Thomas. (1977). "The Do's and Don'ts of Television News." *Time Magazine* (December 5).

Gross, Samuel and Robert Mauro. (1984). "Patterns of Death: An Analysis of Racial Disparities in Capital Sentencing and Homicide Victimization." *Stanford Law Review,* 37 (November).

Gruenberg, Barry. (1980). "The Happy Worker: An Analysis of Educational and Occupational Differences in Determinants of Job Satisfaction." *American Journal of Sociology,* 86, 247–271.

Guetzkow, Harold S. (1951). *Groups, Leadership, and Men: Research in Human Relations.* Pittsburgh: Carnegie Press.

Gusfield, Joseph R. (1963). *Symbolic Crusade.* Urbana: University of Illinois Press.

Guy, Pat. (1985). "Unemployed Benefits Hit Fewer Hands." *USA Today* (Nov 6), 1B.

Hacker, Helen Mayer. (1975). "Gender Roles from a Cross-Cultural Perspective." In Lucile Duberman (ed.), *Gender and Sex in Society.* New York: Praeger.

Hadaway, Christopher. (1978). "Life Satisfaction and Religion: A Reanalysis." *Social Forces,* 57 (2), 636–643.

Hadden, Jeffrey K., and Charles E. Swann. (1981). *Prime-Time Preachers: The Rising Power of Televangelism.* Reading, MA: Addison-Wesley.

Hagestad, G. O., and Bernice Neugarten. (1985). "Age and the Life Course." In R. Binstock and E. Shanas (eds.), *Handbook of Aging and the Social Sciences.* New York: Van Nostrand Reinhold, 35–61.

Haley, Alex. (1976). *Roots.* Garden City, NY: Doubleday.

Haley, Jay. (1971). "A Review of the Family Therapy Fields." In *Changing Families: A Family Therapy Reader.* New York: Grune & Stratten.

Hall, Edward T. (1959). *The Silent Language.* New York: Doubleday.

———. (1983). *The Dance of Life: The Other Dimension of Time.* Garden City, NY: Anchor Books.

Hall, Richard H. (1986). *Dimensions of Work.* Beverly Hills: Sage Publications.

Hallowell, Christopher. (1985). "New Focus on the Old." *The New York Times Magazine* (December 15), 42, 44, 48, 50, 109–11.

Halsell, Grace. (1986). *Los Viegos—Secrets of Long Life from the Sacred Valley.* Emmaus, PA: Rodale Press.

Hamilton, M., and H. Reid (eds.). (1980). *A Hospice Handbook.* Grand Rapids, MI: Eerdmans.

Hamilton, Richard. (1972). *Class and Politics in the United States.* New York: John Wiley.

Hammett, Theodore. (1986). "AIDS in Prisons and Jails: Issues and Options." *National Institute of Justice Research in Brief.* U.S. Department of Justice, Washington, DC (February).

Hammond, Phillip E. (ed.). (1985). *The Sacred in a Secular Age.* Berkeley: University of California Press.

Haney, Craig, and Phillip Zimbardo. (1975). "Blackboard Penitentiary: It's Touch to Tell a High School from a Prison." *Psychology Today,* 9 (June), 26.

Hanlon, Michael. (1985). "Famine: A Race Against Time." *World Press Review* (February), 37–42.

Harder, Mary White, James T. Richardson, and Robert B. Simmonds. (1972). "Jesus People." *Psychology Today,* 6, 45–113.

Hare, A. Paul (1964). "Interpersonal Relations in the Small Group." In Robert E. L. Faris (ed.), *Handbook of Modern Sociology.* Chicago: Rand McNally.

———. (1976). *Handbook of Small Group Research* (2d ed.). New York: Free Press.

Hareven, Tamara. (1982). "The Life Course and Aging in Historical Perspective." In Tamara Hareven and Kathleen Adams (eds.), *Aging and Life-Course Transitions: An Interdisciplinary Perspective.* New York: Guilford Press, 1–26.

Harlow, Harry F., and Margaret K. Harlow. (1962). "Social Deprivation in Monkeys." *Scientific American,* 297, 137–147.

Harper's Magazine. (1984). "Mistakes and the Death Penalty." 269 (July), 18–19.

Harrington, Michael. (1984). *The New American Poverty.* New York: Holt, Rinehart & Winston.

Harris, Chauncy D., and Edward L. Ullman. (1945). "The Nature of Cities." *Annals of the American Academy of Political and Social Science.* 242 (November), 7–17.

Harris, Louis. (1981). *The Harris Survey.* New York: Louis Harris and Associates.

Harris, Marvin. (1964). *Patterns of Race in the Americas.* New York: Walker.

———. (1974). *Cows, Pigs, Wars, and Witches: The Riddles of Culture.* New York: Random House.

———. (1975). "Male Supremacy Was Just a Phase in the Evolution of Culture." *Psychology Today* (January), 66ff.

———. (1986). *Good To Eat: Riddles of Food and Culture.* New York: Simon and Schuster.

Harrison, Paul. (1981). *Inside the Third World: The Anatomy of Poverty.* New York: Penguin Books.

Harrison, R. V. (1978). "Person–Environment Fit and Job Stress." In C. L. Cooper and R. Payne (eds.), *Stress at Work.* New York: John Wiley.

Harry, Joseph. (1976). "Evolving Sources of Happiness for Men over the Life Cycle: A Structural Analysis." *Journal of Marriage and the Family,* 38, 289–296.

Hartley, Eugene L. (1946). *Problems in Prejudice.* New York: King's Crown Press.

Hartley, Ruth. (1966). "A Developmental View of Sex-Role Identifications." In Bruce J. Biddle and E. J. Thomas (eds.), *Role Theory: Concepts and Research.* New York: John Wiley.

Harvey, Dale, and Gerald Slatin. (1975). "The Relationship Between Child's SES and Teacher Expectations: A Test of the Middle-Class Bias Hypothesis." *Social Forces,* 54 (September), 40–59.

Haub, Carl. (1985). "The Last Metro Definition." *Population Today* (November), 6–8.

Haviland, William A. (1985). *Anthropology* (4th ed). New York: Holt, Rinehart, & Winston.

Havighurst, Robert. (1968). "Personality and Patterns of Aging." *Gerontologist,* 8, 20–23.

Hayes, Cheryl, and Sheila Kamerman eds. (1981). *Children of Working Parents: Experiences and Outcomes.* Washington, DC: National Academy Press.

Hayes, Denis. (1976). *The Solar Energy Timetable.* Washington, DC: Worldwatch Institute.

Hazelrigg, Lawrence, and Maurice Garnier. (1976). "Occupational Mobility in Industrial Societies: A Comparative Analysis of Differential Access to Occupational Ranks in Seventeen Countries." *American Sociological Review,* 498–510.

Heatherington, M., M. Cox, and R. Cox. (1978). "The Aftermath of Divorce." In J. Stevens and M. Matthews (eds.), *Mother–Child, Father–Child Relations.* Washington, DC: National Association for the Education of Young Children.

Hechinger, Fred M. (1979). "Schoolyard Blues: The Decline of Public Education." *Saturday Review,* 6 (January 20), 20–22.

Hedges, J. N., and J. K. Barnett. (1972). "Working Women and the Division of Household Tasks." *Monthly Labor Review,* 95, 9–14.

Heer, David M. (1965). "Negro–White Marriage in the United States." *New Society* (August 26), 7–9.

Heer, David M. (1975). *Society and Population* (2d ed.). Englewood Cliffs, NJ: Prentice-Hall.

Heilman, Samuel. (1982). "The Sociology of American Jewry: The Last Ten Years." *American Review of Sociology,* 8, 135–160.

Heiskanen, Veronica Stolte. (1971). "The Myth of the Middle-Class Family in American Family Sociology." *American Sociologist* (February), 14–18.

Helwig, Terry. (1986). "How Will We Educate Our Children?: Teaching the Kids at Home." *Today's Christian Woman* (March).

Hemphill, J. K. (1950). "Relations Between the Size of the Group and the Behavior of 'Superior' Leaders." *Journal of Social Psychology,* 32, 11–22.

Hendricks, Jon. (1984). "Impact of Technological Change on Older Workers," in P. K. Robinson, J. Livingston, and J. E. Birren (eds.), *Aging and Technological Advances.* New York: Plenum Press–NATO Scientific Affairs Division, 113–124.

Hendricks, Jon, and C. Davis Hendricks. (1986). *Aging in Mass Society: Myths and Realities* (3d ed.). Boston: Little, Brown.

Henig, Jeffrey. (1981). "Gentrification and Displacement of the Elderly: An Empirical Analysis." *The Gerontologist,* 21, 67–75.

Henslin, James M. (1975). *Introducing Sociology.* New York: Free Press.

Hersey, R. B. (1931). "Emotional Cycles in Man." *Journal of Mental Sciences,* 77.

Hess, Beth B. (1983). "New Faces of Poverty." *American Demographics,* 5 (May), 26–31.

Hewitt, Christopher. (1977). "The Effect of Political Democracy and Social Democracy on Equality in Industrial Societies: A Cross-National Comparison." *American Sociological Review,* 32, 562–578.

Hill, Robert B. (1986). "The Black Middle Class: Past, Present, and Future." *The State of Black America.* New York: National Urban League.

Hilsman, Roger. (1985). *The Politics of Governing America.* Englewood Cliffs, NJ: Prentice-Hall.

Hilty, Dale M., and Sue J. Stockman. (1986). "A Covariance Structure Analysis of the DeJong, Faulkner, and Warland Religious Involvement Model." *Journal for the Scientific Study of Religion,* 25 (4), 483–493.

Hindman, M. (1975–1976). "Children of Alcoholic Parents." *Alcohol World Health and Research* (Winter).

Hirschi, Travis. (1969). *Causes of Delinquency.* Berkeley: University of California Press.

Hirshey, Gerri. (1977). "When Mommy Leaves Home." *Family Circle* (August 23), 70–76.

Hite, Shere. (1976). "Older Women." *The Hite Report: A Nationwide Study of Female Sexuality.* New York: Macmillan, 369–383.

Hitt, C. (1982). "Risk Reduction: A Community Strategy." *Community Nutritionist* (January–February), 12–17.

Hobart, C. W. (1958). "Disillusionment in Marriage and Romanticism." *Marriage and Family Living,* 20, 156–162.

Hobbes, Thomas. (1651, 1958). *Leviathan.* New York: Liberal Arts Press.

Hodge, Robert, Paul Siegel, and Peter Rossi. (1966). "Occupational Prestige in the United States 1925–1963." In R. Bendix and S. M. Lipset (eds.), *Class, Status, and Power.* New York: Free Press.

Hoebel, E. Adamson. (1960). *The Cheyenne: Indians of the Great Plains.* New York: Holt, Rinehart & Winston.

Hoffman, Louis W. (1974). "The Effects of Maternal Employment on the Child: A Review of the Research." *Developmental Psychology,* 10, 204–228.

Holden, Constance. (1980). "The Hospice Movement and Its Implications." In Renee Fox (ed.), *The Social Meaning of Death: Annals of the American Academy of Political and Social Science,* 447, 59–63.

———. (1986). "Youth Suicide: New Research Focuses on a Growing Social Problem." *Science* (August 22), 839–841.

Holland, P. A. (1982). "The Effectiveness of Prosecutions Under the Environment Protection Act." *Environmental Paper No. 2.* Melbourne: Graduate School of Environmental Science, Monash University.

Hollander, Edwin P., and J. W. Julian. (1970). "Studies In Leader Legitimacy, Influence, and Innovation." In L. Berkowitz (ed.), *Advances in Experimental Social Psychology,* 5, New York: Academic Press.

Hollingshead, August B. (1950). "Cultural Factors in the Selection of Marriage Mates." *American Sociological Review,* 15, 619–627.

Hollingshead, August B., and Frederick Redlich. (1958). *Social Class and Mental Illness.* New York: John Wiley.

Holmstrom, Lynda L. (1972). *The Two-Career Family.* Cambridge, MA: Schenkman.

Holt, John. (1981). *Teach Your Own.* Dell Publishing.

Homans, George C. (1950). *The Human Group.* New York: Harcourt Brace.

———. (1958). "Social Behavior as Exchange." *American Journal of Sociology,* 62, 597–606.

———. (1974). *Social Behavior: Its Elementary Forms* (rev. ed.). New York: Harcourt Brace Jovanovich.

———. (1975). "What Do We Mean by Social Structure?" In Peter M. Blau, *Approaches to the Study of Social Structure.* New York: Free Press.

———. (1986). "Fifty Years of Sociology." *Annual Review of Sociology,* 12, xiii–xxx.

Horner, Matina. (1969). "Fail: Bright Women." *Psychology Today,* 3(6), 36ff.

Hornung, Carl, and B. Clair McCullough. (1981). "Status Relationships in Dual-Employment Marriages." *Journal of Marriage and the Family,* 43 (February), 25–41.

House, James S. (1985). "Social Support: An Important Factor in the Quality and Span of Life." *LSA Magazine* (Winter). Ann Arbor, MI: University of Michigan.

———. (1987). "Social Support and Social Structure." *Sociological Forum,* 2 (1), 135–146.

Houseknecht, Sharon. (1982). "Voluntary Childlessness." *Alternative Lifestyles,* 1 (August), 379–402.

Houseknecht, Sharon, and Ann Macke. (1981). "Combining Marriage and Career: The Marital Adjustment of Professional Women." *Journal of Marriage and the Family,* 43 (August), 651–662.

"How Gay Is Gay?" (1979). *Time Magazine* (April 23), 68, 72–77.

Hoyt, Homer. (1939). *The Structure and Growth of Residential Neighborhoods in American Cities.* U.S. Federal Housing Administration: Washington, DC: U.S. Government Printing Office.

Huber, Joan, and Glenna Spitze. (1980). "Considering Divorce: An Expansion of Becker's Theory of Marital Instability." *American Journal of Sociology,* 86 (1), 75–81.

Humphreys, Laud. (1970). *Tearoom Trade: Impersonal Sex in Public Places.* Chicago: Aldine.

———. (1975). *Tearoom Trade: Impersonal Sex in Public Places* (rev. ed.). Chicago: Aldine de Gruyter.

Hunt, Chester L., and Lewis Walker. (1979). *Ethnic Dynamics: Patterns of Intergroup Relations in Various Societies.* Holmes Beach, FL: Learning Publications.

Hunter, Floyd. (1953). *Community Power Structure.* Chapel Hill: University of North Carolina Press.

Hutter, Mark. (1981). *The Changing Family: Comparative Perspectives.* New York: John Wiley.

Hyman, Herbert. (1969). *Political Socialization: A Study of the Psychology of Political Behavior.* New York: Free Press.

Hyman, Herbert, and Charles R. Wright. (1971). "Trends in Voluntary Association Memberships of American Adults: Replication Based on Secondary Analysis of National Sample Surveys." *American Sociology Review,* 36, 191–206.

Iga, Mamouru. (1986). *The Thorn in the Chrysanthemum: Suicide and Economic Success in Modern Japan.* Berkeley: University of California Press.

Illich, Ivan. (1971). *De-schooling Society.* New York: Harper and Row.

Inkeles, Alex. (1964). *What Is Sociology? An Introduction to the Discipline and Profession.* Englewood Cliffs, NJ: Prentice-Hall.

———. (1973). "Making Men Modern: On the Causes and Consequences of Individual Change in Six Developing Countries." In Eva Etzioni-Halevy and Amitai Etzioni (eds.), *Social Change: Sources, Patterns, and Consequences* (2d ed.). New York: Basic Books, 342–361.

Inkeles, Alex, and David H. Smith. (1974). *Becoming Modern: Individual Change in Six Developing Countries.* Cambridge: Harvard University Press.

Internal Revenue Service Report. (1985). "Millionaires Doubled." Reported in *The Hillsdale Daily News* (March 7), 3.

Irish, Marian, et al. (1981). *The Politics of American Democracy* (7th ed.). Englewood Cliffs, NJ: Prentice-Hall.

Irvin, Victoria. (1986). "Counting America's Homeless." *Christian Science Monitor* (October 20), 3–4.

Isaac, Larry, and William R. Kelley. (1981). "Racial Insurgency and the State, and Welfare Expansion." *American Journal of Sociology* (May), 1348–1386.

"It's Your Turn in the Sun." (1978). *Time Magazine* (October 16), 48–61.

Jackson, Kenneth T. (1985). *Crabgrass Frontier—The Suburbanization of the United States.* New York: Oxford University Press.

Jacob, John. (1986). "An Overview of Black America in 1985." *The State of Black America.* New York: National Urban League.

Jacobs, Jane. (1984). *Cities and the Wealth of Nations: Principles of Economic Life.* New York: Random House.

Jacoby, Neil H. (1970). "The Multinational Corporation." *Center Magazine,* 3, 37–55.

Jacques, Jefrey M., and Karen J. Chason. (1979). "Cohabitation: Its Impact on Marital Success." *Family Coordinator* (January), 35–39.

Jaeger, Gertrude, and Philip Selznick. (1964). "A Normative Theory of Culture." *American Sociological Review,* 29 (5), 653–659.

Jaffee, David, and Randall Stokes. (1982). "Another Look at the Export of Raw Materials and Economic Growth." *American Sociological Review* (June), 402–407.

Jain, Shail. (1975). *Size Distribution of Income: A Compilation of Data.* Washington, DC: World Bank.

James, Timothy. (1985). "The Trade." *Wilson Quarterly,* 9, 107–125.

Janis, Irving L. (1971). "Groupthink." *Psychology Today* (November), 43.

———. (1982). *Groupthink: Psychology Studies of Policy Decisions and Fiascoes.* Boston: Houghton Mifflin.

Janowitz, Morris. (1978). *The Last Half.* Chicago: University of Chicago Press.

"Japanese Managers in America." (1984). *Wilson Quarterly* (Winter).

Jefferson, Thomas. (1782, 1972). *Notes on the State of Virginia.* New York: W. W. Norton.

Jencks, Christopher, et al. (1972). *Inequality: A Reas-*

sessment of the Effect of Family and Schooling in America. New York: Harper.

Jenkins, Brian M. (1982). "Statements About Terrorism." *Annals of the American Academy of Political Science,* 463, 11–23.

Jensen, Arthur. (1969). "How Much Can We Boost IQ and Scholastic Achievement?" *Harvard Educational Review,* 39, 273–274.

———. (1973). "The Differences Are Real." *Psychology Today* (December), 80–86.

Jensen, C. (1982). "Recent Law Aims to Reduce Abuse of the Elderly." *Cleveland Plain Dealer* (July 25), 16.

Johnson, David L. (1983). "A Significant Socialization Experience." Unpublished manuscript.

Johnson, Lyndon B. (1964). "Address at Howard University Announcing the Signing of Executive Order 71246."

Johnson, Richard Tanner, and William G. Ouchi. (1974). "Made in America (Under Japanese Management)." *Research Paper 201.* Stanford University Graduate School of Business Research Paper Series.

Johnson, Rita V., and Donald R. Cressey. (1963). "Differential Association and the Rehabilitation of Drug Addicts." *American Journal of Sociology,* 69 (2), 129–142.

Johnson, Robert. (1980). *Religious Assortative Mating in the United States.* New York: Academic Press.

Johnson, Trebbe. (1986). "Indian Wars in the Nuclear Age." *Amicus Journal* (Summer), 14–25.

Johnstone, Ronald. (1975). *Religion and Society in Interaction: The Sociology of Religion.* Englewood Cliffs, NJ: Prentice-Hall.

———. (1983). *Religion in Society: A Sociology of Religion.* Englewood Cliffs, NJ: Prentice-Hall.

Jonas, Steven. (1986). "On Homelessness and the American Way." *American Journal of Public Health* (September), 76 (9), 1084–1086.

Jones, Ruth S., and Warren E. Miller. (1985). "Financing Campaigns: Macro-Level Innovations and Micro-Level Response." *Western Political Quarterly,* 38, 187–210.

Josephy, Alvin M., Jr. (1982). *Now That the Buffalo's Gone.* New York: Alfred Knopf.

Kagan, Jerome, Richard B. Kearsley, and Philip R. Zelazo. (1978). *Infancy: Its Place in Human Development.* Cambridge: Harvard University Press.

Kalish, Richard. (1981). *Death, Grief, and Caring Relationships.* Monterey, CA: Brooks/Cole.

Kalleberg Arne L. (1977). "Work Values and Job Rewards: A Theory of Job Satisfaction. *American Sociological Review,* 42, 124–143.

Kalleberg, Arne L., and Larry Griffin. (1980). "Class, Occupation, and Inequality in Job Rewards." *American Journal of Sociology,* 85, 731–768.

Kalleberg, Arne L., and Karyn A. Loscocco. (1983). "Aging, Values, and Rewards: Explaining Age Differences in Job Satisfaction." *American Sociological Review,* 48, 78–90.

Kalleberg, Arne L., Michael Wallace, and Robert Althuser. (1981). "Economic Segmentation, Worker Power, and Income Inequality." *American Journal of Sociology,* 87, 651–683.

Kalleberg, Arne L., et al. (1975). "The Experience of Losing a Job." *Psychosomatic Medicine,* 37, 106–122.

Kallen, Horace M. (1958). "On Americanizing the American Indian." *Social Research,* 25, 470.

Kalter, N. (1977). "Children of Divorce in an Outpatient Psychiatric Population." *American Journal of Orthopsychiatry,* 47, 50–51.

Kamerman, Sheila. (1983). "Child Care Services: A National Picture." *Monthly Labor Review,* 106 (December), 35–39.

Kane, Thomas, and Paul Myers. (1980). *World Population Data Sheet.* Washington, DC: Population Reference Bureau.

Kanter, Rosabeth Moss. (1972). "Getting It All Together: Some Group Issues in Communes." *American Journal of Orthopsychiatry,* 42(4).

———. (1983). *The Change Masters.* New York: Simon and Schuster.

———. (1986). *Men and Women of the Corporation.* New York: Basic Books.

Kanter, Rosabeth Moss, and Barry A. Stein (eds.). (1979). *Life in Organizations.* New York: Basic Books.

Kantrowitz, Barbara. (1986). "The Grim ABCs of AIDS." *Newsweek* (November 3), 66–67.

Karlins, Marvin, Thomas Goffman, and Gary Walters. (1969). "On the Finding of Social Stereotypes: Studies in Three Generations of College Students." *Journal of Personality and Social Psychology* (September), 4–50.

Karmel, Carey Adina. (1984). "Why Blacks Still Haven't Made It." *The American Lawyer* (March), 121–127.

Karp, Walter. (1985). "Why Johnny Can't Think." *Harper's Magazine* (June), 69–73.

Kart, Cary S. (1985). *The Realities of Aging* (2d edition). Boston: Allyn and Bacon.

Kart, Cary S., and C. F. Longino. (1983). "The Support Systems of Older People: A Testing of the Exchange Paradigm." Paper presented at the 36th Annual Scientific Meeting of the Gerontological Society of America, San Francisco.

Kashet, S. V., et al. (1975). "The Experience of Losing a Job." *Psychosomatic Medicine,* 37, 106–122.

Kastenbaum, R. (1981). *Death, Society, and Human Experience* (2d ed.). St. Louis: Mosby.

———. (1985). "Dying and Death: A Lifespan Approach." In J. E. Birren and K. W. Schaie (eds.), *Handbook of the Psychology of Aging* (2d ed). New York: Van Nostrand Reinhold.

Katz, Alvin M., and Reuben Hill. (1958). "Residential Propinquity and Marital Selection: A Review of Theory, Method, and Fact." *Journal of Marriage and the Family,* 20, 27–35.

Katz, Ellis. (1980). "States Rediscovered: Education Policymaking in the 1970's." *State Government,* 53 (Winter), 31–35.

Kaye, Evelyn. (1974). *The Family Guide to Children's Television.* New York: Pantheon.

Keebler, N. (1985). "Abuse of the Aged Probed but Not Prosecuted." *Sacramento Bee* (March 8), B3.

Keen, Sam. (1976). "An Interview with Dr. Carlfred Broderick: How Both Partners Can 'Win' at Marriage." *Family Circle* (May), 25–32.

Keene, Karlyn. (1984). "American Values: Change and Stability: A Conversation with Daniel Yankelovich." *Public Opinion,* 6 (December–January), 2–8.

Keller, Suzanne. (1971). "Does the Family Have a Future?" *Journal of Comparative Family Studies,* 2, 1–14.

Kelly, Dean M. (1972). *Why the Conservative Churches Are Growing: A Study in the Sociology of Religion.* New York: Harper and Row.

Kemper, Theodore. (1982). "Love and Like and Love and *Love.*" Paper presented at Annual Meeting of American Sociological Association, San Francisco.

Kennedy, Paul. (1987). "The (Relative) Decline of America." *The Atlantic Monthly* (August) 29–38.

Kephart, William M. (1972). *The Family, Society, and the Individual.* Boston: Houghton Mifflin.

———. (1982). *Extraordinary Groups: The Sociology of Unconventional Life Styles* (2d ed.). New York: St. Martin's Press.

Kerbo, Harold R. (1983). *Social Stratification and Inequality.* New York: McGraw-Hill.

Kerckhoff, Alan C., and Kurt Back. (1968). *The June Bug.* New York: Appleton–Century–Crofts.

Keshet, Harry Finkelstein, and Kristine M. Rosenthal. (1978). "Fathering After Marital Separation." *Social Work,* 23(1), 11–18.

Kessler, Alexander. (1966). "Interplay Between Social Ecology and Physiology, Genetics and Population Dynamics." Unpublished doctoral thesis, Rockefeller University.

Kessler, Ronald C. (1982). "A Disaggregation of the Relationship Between Socioeconomic Status and Psychological Distress." *American Sociological Review,* 47 (December), 752–764.

Kessler, Ronald C., and Paul D. Cleary. (1980). "Social Class and Psychological Distress." *American Sociological Review,* 45, 463–478.

Kessler, Ronald C., James S. House, and J. Blake Turner. (1987). "Unemployment and Health in a Community Sample." *Journal of Health and Social Behavior,* 28(1), 51–59.

Kessler, Ron, and James McRae, Jr. (1982). "The Effect of Wives' Employment on the Mental Health of Married Men and Women." *American Sociological Review,* 47 (April), 216–227.

Keyfitz, Nathan. (1985). "Age, Work, and Social Security." In *Growing Old in America* (3d edition), ed. by Beth B. Hess and Elizabeth W. Markson. New Brunswick, NJ: Transaction Books, 524–536.

Kilbourne, B. K. (1983). "The Conway and Siegelman Claims Against Religious Cults: An Assessment of Their Data." *Journal for the Scientific Study of Religion,* 22, 380–385.

Kilson, Martin. (1981). "Black Social Classes and Intergenerational Policy." *The Public Interest* (Summer), 63.

King, David R. (1978). "The Brutalization Effect: Execution Publicity and the Incidence of Homicide in South Carolina." *Social Forces,* 57(2), 683–687.

King, Gerald. (1983). "Home Schooling: Up from Underground." *Reason* (April), 21–29.

Kinsey, Alfred C., et al. (1948). *Sexual Behavior in the Human Male.* Philadelphia: W. B. Saunders.

Kirk, Dudley. (1971). "A New Demographic Transition." In Study Commission of the National Academy of Sciences, *Rapid Population Growth: Consequences and Policy Implications.* Baltimore: Johns Hopkins Press.

Kitsuse, J. I. (1962). "Societal Reaction to Deviant Behavior: Problems of Theory and Methods." *Social Problems,* 9, 247–256.

Klandermans, Bert. (1984). "Mobilization and Participation: Social-Psychology Expansions of Resource Mobilization Theory." *American Sociological Review,* 49, 583–600.

Kleck, Gary. (1981). "Racial Discrimination in Criminal Sentencing: A Critical Evaluation of the Evidence with Additional Evidence on the Death Penalty." *American Sociological Review,* 46 (December), 783–805.

Klein, Susan Shurberg. (1984). "Education." In Sarah Pritchard (ed.), *The Women's Annual, No. 4: 1983–1984.* Boston: G. K. Hall and Company, 9–30.

Klineberg, Otto (ed.). (1944). *Characteristics of the American Negro.* New York: Harper and Row.

Kluckhohn, Claude. (1948). "As an Anthropologist Views It." In Albert Duetch (ed.), *Sex Habits of American Men.* New York: Prentice-Hall Press.

Kluckhohn, Clyde. (1985). *Mirror for Man: The Relation of Anthropology to Modern Life.* Tucson: University of Arizona Press.

Knobelsdorff, Kerry. (1986). "Failure to Control Ozone Pollution Prompts East Coast Lawsuit." *Christian Science Monitor* (December 16).

Knopf, Terry Ann. (1975). *Rumors, Race, and Riots.* New Brunswick, NJ: Transaction Books.

Knowles, Louis L., and Kenneth Prewitt. (1969). *Institutional Racism in America.* Englewood Cliffs, NJ: Prentice-Hall.

Knudsen, Dean D. (1969). "The Declining Status of Women: Popular Myths and the Failure of Functionalist Thought." *Social Forces,* 48, 183–193.

Koenig, Frederick. (1985). *Rumor in the Marketplace: The Social Psychology of Commerical Hearsay.* Dover, MA: Auburn House.

Kohlberg, Lawrence. (1981). *Essays on Moral Development.* San Francisco: Harper and Row.

Kohlberg, Lawrence, and Carl Gilligan. (1971). "The Adolescent as a Philosopher: The Discovery of the Self in a Postconventional World." *Daedalus,* 100, 1051–1086.

Kohn, Melvin L. (1974). "Social Class and Parent-Child Relationships: An Interpretation." *American Journal of Sociology,* 68, 471–480.

———. (1977). *Class and Conformity: A Study in Values* (2d ed.). Homewood, IL: Dorsey Press.

Kohn, Melvin L., and Carmi Schooler. (1982). "Job Conditions and Personality: A Longitudinal Assessment of Their Reciprocal Effects." *American Journal of Sociology,* 87(6), 1257–1286.

Kolko, Gabriel. (1962). *Wealth and Power in America.* New York: Praeger.

Komisar, Lucille. (1971). "The Image of Women in Advertising." In Vivian Gornick and Barbara Moran (eds.), *Women in Sexist Society.* New York: Basic Books.

Kompara, Diane Reinhart. (1980). "Difficulties in the Socialization Process of Stepparenting." *Family Relations,* 29, 69–73.

Kosa, John, Aaron Antonovsky, and Irving K. Zola (eds.). (1969). *Poverty and Health: A Sociological Analysis.* Cambridge: Harvard University Press.

Kozol, Jonathan. (1985). *Illiterate America.* Garden City, NY: Anchor Press.

Krahn, Harvey, Timothy F. Hartnagel, and John W. Gartrell. (1986). "Rates: Cross-National Data and Criminological Theories." *Criminology,* 24(2), 269–295.

Krauss, Irving. (1976). *Stratification, Class, and Conflict.* New York: Free Press.

Kraut, Robert E. (1976). "Deterrent and Definitional Influences on Shoplifting." *Social Problems,* 23 (February), 358–368.

Kritz, Mary, Charles Keely, and Silvani Tomasi (eds.). (1981). *Global Trends in Migration: Theory and Research on Internation Population Movements.* Staten Island, NY: Center for Migration Studies of New York.

Krohe, James. (1984). "Can We Stop Acid Rain? And Who Should Pay the Bill?" *Across the Board,* 21 (2), 14–25.

Kubler-Ross, Elisabeth. (1969). *On Death and Dying.* New York: Macmillan.

———. (1981). *Living with Death and Dying.* New York: Macmillan.

Kuhn, Mantora H., and Thomas S. McPartland. (1954). "An Empirical Investigation of Self-Attitudes." *American Sociological Review,* 19, 68–76.

Kulka, R., and H. Weingarter. (1979). "The Long-Term Effects of Parental Divorce in Childhood on Adult Adjustment." *Journal of Social Issues,* 35, 50–78.

Kuner, W. (1984). "New Religious Movements and Mental Health." In E. V. Barker (ed.), *Of Gods and Men: New Religious Movements in the West.* Macon, GA: Mercer University Press.

Kuypers, Joseph A., and Vern L. Bengston. (1973). "Competence and Social Breakdown: A Social-Psychological View of Aging." *Human Development,* 16(2), 37–49.

Lacavo, Richard. (1986). "Second Thoughts About No-Fault." *Time Magazine* (January 13), 55.

LaFranchi, Howard. (1986). "Immigration." *Christian Science Monitor* (October 30), 16–17.

Laing, R. D. (1971). *The Politics of the Family and Other Essays.* New York: Pantheon.

Lakin, M. (1972). *Experimental Groups: The Use of Interpersonal Encounter, Psychotherapy Groups, and Sensitivity Training.* Morristown, NJ: General Learning Press.

Landis, Judson, and Mary Landis. (1958). *Building a Successful Marriage.* Englewood Cliffs, NJ: Prentice-Hall.

Landis, Paul H. (1953). "The Broken Home in Teenage Adjustments." *Rural Sociology Series on the Family* (No. 4). Pullman, WA: Institute of Agricultural Science, State College of Washington.

Lanouette, William. (1985a). "Nuclear Power in America." *Wilson Quarterly,* 9 (Winter), 33.

Lanouette, William. (1985b). "Atomic Energy—1945–1985." *Wilson Quarterly* (Winter), 21–37.

Lapiere, Richard. (1976). "Attitudes and Actions." *Social Forces,* 13 (December), 230–237.

LaRocco, James M., James S. House, and John R. P. Finch. (1980). "Social Support, Occupational Stress, and Health." *Journal of Health and Social Behavior,* 21(3), 202–218.

Lasch, Christopher. (1977). *Haven in a Heartless World: The Family Besieged.* New York: Basic Books.

Latta, Geoffrey W. (1981). "Union Organization Among Engineers: A Current Assessment." *Industrial and Labor Relations Review,* 35, 29–42.

Lauer, Richard H. (1982). *Perspectives on Social Changes.* Boston: Allyn and Bacon.

Lauer, Robert H. (ed.). (1976). *Social Movements and*

Social Change. Carbondale: Southern Illinois University Press.

Leavitt, Ruby R. (1970). "Women in Other Cultures." In Georgene H. Seward and Robert C. Williamson (eds.), *Sex Roles in Changing Society.* New York: Random House.

LeBon, Gustave. (1895, 1946). *The Mind of the Crowd: A Study of the Popular Mind.* New York: Macmillan.

Lee, Alfred McClung. (1978). *Sociology for Whom?* New York: Oxford University Press.

———. (1983). *Terrorism in Northern Ireland.* Dix Hills, NY: General Hall, Inc.

Lee, Alfred McClung, and Elizabeth Briant Lee. (1939). *The Fine Art of Propaganda.* New York: Farrar, Strauss.

Lee, Richard. (1979). *The !Kung San: Men, Women, and Work in a Foraging Society.* New York: Cambridge University Press.

LeMasters, E. E. (1970). "Parents Without Partners." In *Parents in Modern America.* Homewood, IL: Dorsey Press.

Lemert, Edwin M. (1951). *Social Pathology.* New York: McGraw-Hill.

———. (1972). *Human Deviance, Social Problems, and Social Control* (2d ed.). Englewood Cliffs, NJ: Prentice-Hall.

Lengermann, Patricia, and Ruth Wallace. (1985). *Gender in America: Social Control and Social Change.* Englewood Cliffs, NJ: Prentice-Hall.

Lenski, Gerhard E. (1961). *The Religious Factor: A Sociological Study of Religion's Impact on Politics, Economics, and Family Life.* Garden City, NY: Doubleday.

———. (1966). *Power and Privilege: A Theory of Social Stratification.* New York: McGraw-Hill.

———. (1971). "The Religious Factor in Detroit: Revisited." *American Sociological Review,* 36, 49–50.

Lenski, Gerhard E., and Jean Lenski. (1987). *Human Societies* (5th ed.). New York: McGraw-Hill.

Leo, John. (1988). "A Chilling Wave of Racism: From L. A. to Boston, the Skinheads Are on the March." *Time Magazine* (January 25), 57.

Lerner, Barbara. (1982). "American Education: How Are We Doing?" *The Public Interest* (Fall), 14–18.

Lerner, Monroe. (1969). "Social Differences in Physical Health." In Kosa, et al. (eds.), *Poverty and Health.* Cambridge: Harvard University Press.

Lever, Janet. (1978). "Sex Differences in the Complexity of Children's Plays and Games." *American Sociological Review,* 43, 471–483.

Levi, M. (1981). *The Phantom Capitalists: The Organization and Control of Long-Firm Fraud.* London: Heinemann.

Levinson, Andrew. (1975). *The Working-Class Majority.* New York: Penguin Books.

Levinson, Daniel J. (1978). *The Seasons of a Man's Life.* New York: Knopf.

Levitan, Sar and Belous. (1981). "Working Wives and Mothers: What Happens to Family Life?" *Monthly Labor Review,* 104 (September), 26–30.

Levy, Martin J. (1949). *The Family Revolution in Modern China.* Cambridge: Harvard University Press.

Lewis, Jerry M. (1972). "A Study of the Kent State Incident Using Smelser's Theory of Collective Behavior." *Sociological Inquiry,* 42(2), 87–96.

Lewis, Michael. (1972). "Culture and Gender Roles: There's No Unisex in the Nursery." *Psychology Today,* 5, 54–57.

Lewis, Oscar. (1966). "The Culture of Poverty." *Scientific American* (October), 19–25.

Lewis, Robert A. (1973). "Social Reaction and the Formation of Dyads: An Interactional Approach to Mate Selection." *Sociometry,* 36, 409–419.

Lewis, Robert A., and Graham B. Spanier. (1979). "Theorizing About the Quality and Stability of Marriage." In W. R. Burr, et al. (eds.), *Contemporary Theories About the Family* (Vol. 1). New York: Free Press, pp. 268–294.

Lieberman, Jethro K. (1979). *Crisis at the Bar.* New York: Norton.

Lieberson, Stanley. (1985). "A New Ethnic Group in the United States." In Norman Yetman (ed.), *The Dynamics of Race and Ethnicity in American Life* (4th ed.). Boston: Allyn and Bacon.

"Life At the Edge." (1987). *Consumer Reports* (June), 375–376.

Light, Paul. (1985). *Artful Work: Building a Social Security Compromise.* New York: Random House.

Light, Ivan. (1983). *Cities in World Perspective.* New York: Macmillan.

———. (1970). "The Swedish Model." In Georgene H. Seward and Robert C. Williamson (eds.), *Sex Roles in Changing Society.* New York: Random House.

Linton, Ralph. (1936). *The Study of Man: An Introduction.* New York: Appleton–Century.

———. (1940). "Culture Change." *Papers Presented Before the Monday Night Group: 1939–1940.* New Haven: Yale University Institute of Human Relations.

Lipman-Blumen, Jean. (1984). *Gender Roles and Power.* Englewood Cliffs, NJ: Prentice-Hall.

Lipset, Seymour Martin. (1960). *Political Man: The Social Bases of Politics.* Garden City, NY: Doubleday.

———. (1963). "The Value Patterns of Democracy: A Case Study on Comparative Analysis." *American Sociological Review,* 28(4), 515–531.

———. (1967). *Social Mobility in Industrial Society.* Berkeley: University of California Press.

Lipset, Seymour Martin, and Earl Raab. (1970). *The Politics of Unreason.* New York: Harper and Row.

Loehlin, John, Gardner Lindzey, and J. M. Spuhler.

(1975). *Race Differences in Intelligence.* San Francisco: W. H. Freeman.
Lombroso, Cesare. (1911a). *Crime: Its Causes and Remedies.* Boston: Little, Brown.
———. (1911b). In G. L. Ferrero, *Criminal Man.* New York: Putnam.
Editorial. *The London Guardian* (1985). (February 19).
Longfellow, Cynthia. (1979). "Divorce in Context: Its Impact on Children." In George Levinger and Oliver C. Moles (eds.), *Divorce and Separation: Context, Causes, and Consequences.* New York: Basic Books.
Lopata, H. Z. (1973). *Widowhood in an American City.* Cambridge, MA: Schenkman.
Lorenz, Konrad. (1966). *On Aggression.* New York: Harcourt, Brace and World.
Loy, Pamela Hewitt, and Lea P. Stewart. (1984). "The Extent and Effects of Sexual Harassment of Working Women." *Sociological Focus,* 17(1), 31–43.
Luce, Gay G. (1973). *Body Time.* New York: Bantam.
Luce, Terrence S. (1974). "They All Look Alike to Me." *Psychology Today* (November), 105–108.
Luft, Harold S. (1978). *Poverty and Health: Economic Causes and Consequences of Health Problems.* Cambridge, MA: Ballinger.
Lurie, Nancy Oestreich. (1970). *The American Indian Today* (rev. ed.). Baltimore: Penguin Books.
Lynd, Robert S., and Helen M. Lynd. (1929). *Middletown: A Study in American Culture.* New York: Harcourt Brace.
Lynn, David B. (1974). *The Father: His Role in Child Development.* Belmont, CA: Wadsworth.
Lyons, Nona Plessner. (1983). "Two Perspectives: On Self, Relationships, and Morality." *Harvard Educational Review,* 53, 125–145.
Mace, David, and Vera Mace. (1960). *Marriage: East and West.* Garden City, NY: Doubleday.
Macionis, John J., and James L. Spates. (1987). *The Sociology of Cities* (2d ed.). Belmont, CA: Wadsworth.
MacIver, Robert M. (1965). *The Web of Government.* New York: Free Press.
Magnet, Myron, (1983). "What Mass-Produced Child Care Is Producing." *Fortune* (November 28), 157–174.
Magnuson, Ed. (1985). "A Problem That Cannot Be Buried." *Time Magazine,* 126(15), 76–78, 83–84.
Malinowski, Bronislaw. (1943). *The Family Among the Australian Aborigines.* London: University of London Press.
———. (1948). *Magic, Science, and Religion and Other Essays.* Boston: Beacon Press.
Malthus, Thomas R. (1776, 1972). *An Essay on the Principle of Population* (7th ed.). London: Reeves and Turner.
Mankiewicz, Frank, and Joe Swerdlow. (1978). *Remote Control: Television and the Manipulation of American Life.* New York: New York Times Books.
Markovsky, Barry, LeRoy Smith, and Joseph Berger. (1984). "Do Status Interventions Persist?" *American Sociological Review,* 49 (June), 373–382.
Marples, David. (1986). "Chernobyl and Ukraine." *Problems of Communism.* U.S. Information Service, Washington, DC: (November–December).
Marquand, Robert. (1987). "U.S. Study Looks at Japan's Successful School System." *Christian Science Monitor* (January 5), 3–4.
Marris, Peter. (1960). *Family and Social Change in an African City.* Evanston, IL: Northwestern University Press.
Marshall, V. (1979). "No Exit: A Symbolic Interactionist Perspective on Aging." *International Journal of Aging and Human Development,* 9, 345–358.
Marshall, Victor. (1980). *Last Chapters: A Sociology of Aging and Dying.* Monterey, CA: Brooks/Cole.
Marty, Martin. (1987). "Address at Berry College." Rome, GA (January 8).
Martin, Wendy. (1971). "Seduced and Abandoned in the New World: The Image of Woman in American Fiction." In Vivian Gornick and Barbara K. Moran (eds.), *Women in Sexist Society.* New York: Basic Books.
———. (1964). *Early Writings.* Edited by T. B. Bottomore. New York. McGraw-Hill.
———. (1867, 1967). *Das Kapital.* New York: International Publishers.
———. (1904). *A Contribution to the Critique of Political Economy.* New York: International Library.
———. (1848, 1888). *Manifesto of the Communist Party.* Chicago: Charles H. Kerr.
Matras, Judah. (1973). *Population and Societies.* Englewood Cliffs, NJ: Prentice-Hall.
Matthiessen, Peter. (1984). *Indian Country.* New York: Viking Press.
Mauss, Armand L. (1975). *Social Problems of Social Movements.* Philadelphia: Lippincott.
———. (1984). "Sociological Perspectives on the Mormon Subculture." *Annual Review of Sociology,* 10. Palo Alto: Annual Reviews, Inc., 437–60.
Mayfield, Mark. (1987). "Teachers Who Failed, Fired." *USA Today* (August 31), 1.
McCarthy, John D., and Mayer N. Zald. (1973). *The Trend of Social Movements in America: Professionalization and Resource Mobilization.* Morristown, NJ: General Learning Press.
———. (1977). "Resource Mobilization and Social Movements: A Partial Theory." *American Sociological Review,* 82(6), 1212–1241.
McDonald, Laughlin. (1978). "Jim Crow Is Alive and Well in the Old South." *Saturday Review* (April 1), 22–26.
McGahey, Richard M. (1980). "Dr. Ehrlich's Magic

Bullet: Econometric Theory, Econometrics, and the Death Penalty." *Crime and Delinquency,* 26, 485–502.

McGee, Reece. (1975). *Points of Departure.* Hinsdale, IL: Dryden Press.

McGrath, Ellie. (1983). "The Bold Quest for Quality." *Time Magazine* (October 10), 58–66.

———. (1984). "Preparing to Wield the Rod." *Time Magazine,* 121(4), 57.

McGuire, Meredith B. (1987). *Religion: The Social Context.* Belmont, CA: Wadsworth.

McGurk, Frank C. J. (1956). "A Scientist's Report on Race Differences." In *U.S. News and World Report* (September 21), 92–96.

McKeown, Thomas. (1976). *The Modern Rise of Population.* New York: Academic Press.

McLuhan, Marshall. (1970). *Understanding Media.* New York: New American Library.

Mead, George Herbert. (1934). *Mind, Self, and Society: From the Standpoint of a Behaviorist.* Edited by Charles W. Morris. Chicago: University of Chicago Press.

Mead, Margaret. (1935). *Sex and Temperament in Three Primitive Societies.* New York: Morrow.

———. (1939). "Growing Up in New Guinea." Pages 163–166 in *From the South Seas.* New York: Morrow.

———. (1966). "Marriage in Two Steps." *Redbook,* 127 (July), 48–49.

———. (1977a). "Can the American Family Survive?" *Redbook* (February).

———. (1977b). "Redbook's Young Mothers in a Changing World." *Redbook* (September), 33–34, 169.

Meadows, Donella H. (1985). *The Electronic Oracle Computer Models and Social Decisions.* New York: John Wiley and Sons.

Means, Gardiner S. (1970). "Economic Concentration." In Maurice Zeitlin (ed.), *American Society, Inc.* Chicago: Markham.

Meese, R. F., and J. F. Short, Jr. (1984). "White-Collar Crime as Hazard: Perceptions of Risk and Seriousness." Unpublished paper, Washington State University.

Melnick, N. (1976). "The Back Door into Davis." *New Physician* (November), 33.

Melton, J. Gordon. (1978). *Encyclopedia of American Religions* (2 vols.). Wilmington, NC: McGrath (A Consortium Book).

Mendel, Perry. (1984). In Russell Watson, et al., "What Price Day Care?" *Newsweek,* 104 (September 10), 14–17, 19–21.

Merrill, Francis E. (1959). *Courtship and Marriage.* New York: Holt, Rinehart & Winston.

Merton, Robert K. (1941). "Intermarriage and the Social Structure: Fact and Theory." *Psychiatry,* 4, 361–374.

———. (1948). "The Self-Fulfilling Prophecy." *Antioch Review,* 8, 192–210.

———. (1949). "Discrimination and the American Creed." In Robert M. MacIver (ed.), *Discrimination and the National Welfare.* New York: Harper and Row.

———. (1976). "Discrimination and the American Creed." Pages 189–216 in *Sociological Ambivalence and Other Essays.* New York: Free Press.

———. (1957, 1968). *Social Theory and Social Structure* (2d ed.). New York: Free Press.

Meyersohn, Rolf, and Elihu Katz. (1957). "Notes on a Natural History of Fads." *American Journal of Sociology,* 62, 594–601.

Michels, Robert. (1915). *Political Parties.* Translated by E. and C. Paul. Glencoe, IL: Free Press.

Middleton, Russell. (1973). "Do Christian Beliefs Cause Anti-Semitism?" *American Sociological Review,* 38, 33–52.

Milgram, Stanley. (1964). "Group Pressure and Action Against a Person." *Journal of Abnormal and Social Psychology,* 69, 137–143.

———. (1965). "Liberating Effects of Group Pressure." *Journal of Personality and Social Psychology,* 1, 127–134.

Mills, C. Wright. (1956). *The Power Elite.* New York: Oxford University Press.

———. (1959). *The Sociological Imagination.* New York: Oxford University Press.

Milner, H. Stuart. (1973). "Is It Further Education?" *Forum,* 15 (Spring), 49–51.

Mincer, Jacob, and Haim Ofek. (1982). "Interrupted Work Careers: Depreciation and Restoration of Human Capital." *Journal of Human Resources,* 17 (Winter), 3–24.

Mintz, Beth. (1975). "The President's Cabinet, 1897–1972: A Contribution to the Power Structure Debate." *Insurgent Sociologist,* 5, 131–148.

Mirowsky, John, II, and Catherine E. Ross. (1979). "Protest Group Success: The Impact of Group Characteristics, Social Control, and the Situation." Mimeographed. New Haven: Yale University, Department of Sociology.

Model, Suzanne. (1981). "Housework by Husbands: Determinants and Implications." *Journal of Family Issues,* 2 (June), 225–227.

Modleski, Rania. (1980). "The Disappearing Act: A Study of Harlequin Romances." *Signs: Journal of Women in Culture and Society,* 5(3), 435–448.

Money, John, and Anke Ehrhardt. (1972). *Man and Woman, Boy and Girl.* Baltimore: Johns Hopkins University Press.

Moody, Charles D., Sr. (1986). "Equity and Excellence: An Educational Imperative." *The State of Black America.* New York: National Urban League.

Moon, Marilyn, and Eugene Smolensky. (1977). *Improving Measures of Economic Well-Being.* New York: Academic Press.

Moore, Gaylen. (1983). "The Beast in the Jungle." *Psychology Today* (November), 38–45.

Moore, Joan, and Harry Pachon. (1985). *Hispanics in the United States,* Englewood Cliffs, NJ: Prentice-Hall.

Moore, Kristen, Daphne Spain, and Suzanne Bianchi. (1984). "The Working Wife and Mother." *Marriage and Family Review,* 7 (Fall–Winter), 77–98.

Moore, Kristen A., and Linda J. Waite. (1981). "Marital Dissolution, Early Motherhood, and Early Marriage." *Social Forces,* 60(1), 20–40.

Moore, Raymond, (1982). *Home-Grown Kids.* Waco, TX: Word Book Publishers.

———. (1986). *Homespun Schools.* Waco, TX: Word Book Publishers.

Moore, Sally Falk. "The Chagga of Kilimanjaro." In Sally Falk Moore and Paul Pruitt (eds.), *The Chagga and Meru of Tanzania.* Ethnographic Survey of Africa. London: International African Institute.

Moore, Wilbert E. (1964). "Social Aspects of Economic Development." In Robert E. L. Faris (ed.), *Handbook of Modern Sociology.* Chicago: Rand McNally, 882–911.

———. (1966). "Global Sociology: The World as a Singular System." *American Journal of Sociology,* 71(5), 475ff.

"More Blacks Win Elections." (1987). *USA Today* (August 8), 1.

Morgan, Barrie. (1981). "A Contribution to the Debate on Homogamy, Propinquity, and Segregation." *Journal of Marriage and the Family,* 43, 909–921.

Morison, Samuel Eliott. (1965). *Oxford History of the American People.* Oxford University Press.

Morris, Desmond. (1978). "Understanding the Beast in All of Us: An Interview with Desmond Morris by Gerald Clarke." *Family Circle* (May 19), 68–77.

Morrow, Lance. (1985). "Immigrants." *Time Magazine* (July 8), 24–25.

Mortimer, Jeylan T. (1979). *Changing Attitudes Toward Work.* New York: Work in America Institute, Inc.

Mosher, Lawrence. (1981). "The Clean Air That You're Breathing May Cost Hundreds of Billions of Dollars." *National Journal* (October 10).

Moss, Howard. (1976). "Are We Born into Our Sex Roles or Programmed into Them?" *Woman's Day* (January).

Moteki, Robert. (1985). "WW II Ordeal Haunts Japanese Americans." *NASW News,* 30(2), 3–4.

Mother Theresa. (1983). *Words to Love By. . . .* South Bend, IN: Ave Maria Press.

Mottaz, Clifford J. (1981). "Some Determinants of Work Alienation." *The Sociological Quarterly,* 22, 515–529.

Moynihan, Daniel Patrick. (1981). *The Negro Family: The Case for National Action.* Washington, DC: Office of Policy Planning and Research, U.S. Department of Labor.

———. (ed.). (1968). *On Understanding Poverty.* New York: Basic Books.

Mulder, John M., and John F. Wilson. (1978). *Religion in American History.* Englewood Cliffs, NJ: Prentice-Hall.

Muller, Edward N. (1985). "Income Inequality, Regime Repressiveness, and Political Violence." *American Sociological Review,* 50, 47–61.

Muller, Peter. (1981). *Contemporary Suburban America.* Englewood Cliffs, NJ: Prentice-Hall.

Mullins, Nicholas C., with Carolyn J. Mumns. (1973). *Theories and Theory Groups in Contemporary American Sociology.* New York: Harper and Row.

Munley, Ann, Cynthia Powers, and John Williamson. (1983). "Humanizing Nursing Home Environments: The Relevance of Hospice Principles." *International Journal of Aging and Human Development,* 15(4), 263–284.

Muramatsu, Minori. (1960). "Effect of Induced Abortion on the Reduction of Births in Japan." *Milbank Memorial Fund Quarterly,* 38, 153–166.

Murdock, George P. (1945). "The Common Denominator of Cultures." In Ralph Linton (ed.), *The Science of Man in the World Crisis.* New York: Columbia University Press.

———. (1949). *Social Structure.* New York: Macmillan.

Murstein, Bernard. (1980). "Mate Selection in the 1970s." *Journal of Marriage and the Family,* 42, 777–792.

Myers, Jerome. (1974). "Classroom Discussion of Deviant Socialization Processes." Yale University (Spring Quarter).

Myles, John. (1985). "The Trillion-Dollar Misunderstanding." In Beth Hess and Elizabeth Markson (eds.), *Growing Old in America.* New Brunswick, NJ: Transaction Books, 507–523.

Myrdal, Gunnar, with Richard Steiner and Arnold Rose. (1944). *An American Dilemma: The Negro Problem and Modern Democracy.* New York: Harper and Row.

Nagel, Joane. (1982). "The Political Mobilization of Native Americans." *Social Science Journal,* 19(3), 457–463.

Naisbitt, John. (1982). *Megatrends.* New York: Warner Books.

Nakell, Barry. (1978). "The Cost of the Death Penalty." *Criminal Law Bulletin,* 14 (January–February), 69–80.

Nam, Charles, and Susan Gustavus Philliber. (1984). *Population: A Basic Orientation* (2d ed.). Englewood Cliffs, NJ: Prentice-Hall.

Nash, Dennison. (1968). "A Little Child Shall Lead Them: A Statistical Test of an Hypothesis That Children Were the Source of American Religious Revival." *Journal for the Scientific Study of Religion,* 7(2), 238–240.

National Center for Educational Statistics. (1978). *Digest of Educational Statistics: 1978.* Washington, DC: U.S. Government Printing Office.

National Commission on Excellence in Education. (1983). *A Nation at Risk: The Imperative for Educational Reform.* Washington, DC: U.S. Government Printing Office.

National Institute of Mental Health. (1982). *Television and Behavior: Ten Years of Scientific Progress and Implications for the Eighties* (2 vols.). Washington DC: U.S. Government Printing Office.

National Opinion Research Center. (1983). *General Social Surveys: 1972–1983: Cumulative Codebook.* Chicago: National Opinion Research Center.

National Lampoon. (1979). "Parents' Pages." (Kids' Issue, June).

Nelson, Geoffrey. (1968). "The Concept of Cult." *Sociological Review* (November), 351–363.

Netanyahu, Benjamin. (1981). *International Terrorism: Challenge and Response; Proceedings of the Jerusalem Conference on International Terrorism.* Jerusalem: The Jonathan Institute.

Neugarten, Bernice L. (1971). "Grow Old Along with Me! The Best Is Yet to Be." *Psychology Today,* 5 (December), 45–48, 79–81.

Neugarten, Bernice L. (ed.). (1968). *Middle Age and Aging: A Reader in Social Psychology.* Chicago: University of Chicago Press.

Neuhaus, Ruby Hart, and Robert Henry Heuhaus. (1982). *Successful Aging.* New York: John Wiley.

New Haven Register. (1977). "The Average Child Has Seen 15,000 Hours of Television." (April 17), 1.

"The New Morality." (1977). *Time Magazine* (November 21), 111–115.

The New Republic. (1985). "America Becomes Less Equal." (February 18), 7–8.

New York Times, [*The*]. (1987a). "Youth Suicide Rate Is Rising." (February 22), 28.

———. (1987b). "Family in AIDS Case Quits Town After House Fire." (August 30), 1.

———. (1987c). "Boys with AIDS Virus Get Mixed Welcome at School." (September 24), 14.

Newman, Philip. (1965). *Knowing the Gururumba.* New York: Holt, Rinehart & Winston.

Newsweek on Campus. (1984). (May), 9.

Nickols, Sharon, and Edward Metzen. (1982). "Impact of Wife's Employment upon Husband's Housework." *Journal of Family Issues,* 3 (June), 199–216.

Niebuhr, Reinhold. (1929, 1968). *The Religious Situation.* Edited by Donald R. Culter. Boston: Beacon Press.

Nie, Norman H., Sidney Verba, and John R. Petrocik. (1976). *The Changing American Voter.* Cambridge: Harvard University Press.

Nimkoff, M. F., and Russell Middleton. (1960). "Types of Family and Types of Economy." *American Sociological Review,* 65(3), 215–225.

Nisbet, Robert A. (1970). *The Social Bond.* New York: Alfred A. Knopf.

———. (1982). "Genius." *The Wilson Quarterly* (Special Issue), 98–107.

Nörma, Colin. (1985). "Assessing the Effects of a Nuclear Accident." *Science* (April 5).

Norton, Arthur, and Jeanne Moorman. (1987). "Current Trends in Marriage and Divorce Among American Women." *Journal of Marriage and the Family,* 49 (February), 3–14.

Nottingham, Elizabeth L. (1971). *Religion: A Sociological View.* New York: Random House.

Nydegger, R. F. (1957). "Information Processing Complexity and Leadership Status." *Journal of Experimental Social Psychology,* 11, 317–328.

Nye, F. Ivan. (1970). "Family Size, Interaction, Affect, and Stress." *Journal of Marriage and the Family,* 32(2), 216–226.

Nyman, John A. (1987). "Improving the Quality of Nursing Homes: Regulation or Competition?" *Journal of Policy Analysis and Management* (Winter).

Oakes, Jeannie. (1985). *Keeping Track: How High Schools Structure Inequality.* New Haven: Yale University Press.

O'Brien, Patrick. (1985). "Agricultural Productivity and the World Food Market." *Environment* (November).

O'Connell, Martin, and Carolyn Rogers. (1983). "Child-Care Arrangements of Working Mothers." *Current Population Reports,* Series P-23, No. 129. Washington, DC: U.S. Government Printing Office.

O'Dea, Thomas, (1966). *The Sociology of Religion.* Englewood Cliffs, NJ: Prentice-Hall.

Official Report to the United Nations on the Status of Women in Sweden. (1968). Swedish Government.

Ogburn, William F. (1922, 1936). *Social Change.* New York: Viking Press.

"Older Men Left in Job Squeeze." (1984). *USA Today* (November 28).

Olmstead, Michael S., and Paul A. Hare. (1978). *The Small Group* (2d ed.). New York: Random House.

Olson, Mancur. (1977). *The Logic of Collective Action: Public Goods and the Theory of Groups.* Cambridge, MA: Harvard University Press.

Ophuls, William. (1977). *Ecology and the Policy of Scarcity.* San Francisco: W. H. Freeman.

O'Reilly, Jane. (1983). "Wife Beating: The Silent Crime." *Time Magazine,* 122, 10 (September 5), 22–24.

Orum, Anthony M. (1983). *Introduction to Political Sociology: The Social Anatomy of the Human Body Politic* (2d ed.). Englewood Cliffs, NJ: Prentice-Hall.

Ossorio, Elizabeth. (1986). "Homelessness and Community Mental Health." *American Journal of Public Health,* 76(4), 464.

Otto, Luther, and David L. Featherman. (1972). "On the Measurement of Marital Adjustment Among Spouses." Unpublished Working Paper, Center for Demography and Ecology, University of Wisconsin.

Ouchi, William. (1981). *Theory Z: How American Business Can Meet the Japanese Challenge.* Reading, MA: Addison-Wesley.

Owen, D. R. (1972). "The 47 XYY Male: A Review." *Psychological Bulletin,* 78, 209–233.

Page, Benjamin I. (1983). *Who Gets What from Government.* Berkeley: University of California Press.

Palmore, Erdman. (1984). "Longevity in Abkhazia: A Reevaluation." *Gerontologist,* 24(1), 95.

Palmore, Erdman B., and Kenneth Manton. (1974). "Modernization and Status of the Aged: International Correlations." *Journal of Gerontology,* 29(2), 205–210.

Papanek, Hanna. (1973). "Men, Women, and Work: Reflections on the Two-person Career." *American Journal of Sociology,* 78, 852–872.

Pareto, Vilfredo. (1950). *The Ruling Class in Italy Before 1900.* New York: Vanni.

Park, Robert. (1916). "The City: Suggestions for the Investigation of Human Behavior in the Urban Environment." *American Sociological Review,* 20 (March), 577–612.

Park, Robert E. (1950). *Race and Culture.* New York: Free Press.

Parker, Barbara. (1976). "Physical Problems as Mental Illness in the Elderly." *Geriatrics* (June).

Parlee, Mary Brown. (1978). "The Rhythms in Men's Lives." *Psychology Today* (April), 82–91.

Parsons, Talcott. (1931). *The Structure of Social Action.* New York: McGraw-Hill.

———. (1951). *The Social System.* Glencoe, IL: Free Press.

———. (ed.). (1954). *Essays in Sociological Theory Pure and Applied.* Glencoe, IL: Free Press.

———. (1957). "The Distribution of Power in American Society." *World Politics,* 10, 123–43.

———. (1959). "The School Class as a Social System." *Harvard Educational Review,* 19(4), 297–318.

Parsons, Talcott, et al. (1961). *Theories of Society.* New York: Free Press.

———. (1964a). "A Revised Analytical Approach to the Theory of Social Stratification." In *Essays in Sociological Theory.* New York: Free Press.

———. (1964b). "Christianity in Modern Industrial Society." In Edward Tiryakian (ed.), *Sociological Theory, Values, and Sociocultural Change.* Glencoe, IL: Free Press.

———. (1965). "The Normal American Family." In S. M. Farber, P. Mustacchi, and R. H. L. Wilson (eds.), *Man and Civilization: The Family's Search for Survival.* New York: McGraw-Hill.

———. (1966). *Societies: Evolutionary and Comparative Perspectives.* Englewood Cliffs, NJ: Prentice-Hall.

Parsons, Talcott, and Robert Bales. (1955). *Family Socialization and Interaction Process.* Glencoe: Free Press.

Pascale, Richard Tanner, and Anthony G. Athos. (1981). *The Art of Japanese Management.* New York: Simon and Schuster.

Pastore, Paul A. (1979). *Decriminalization of a Victimless Crime: A Preliminary Look at the Impact of Drunkenness Decriminalization, Contemporary Drug Problems.* 585–606.

Patterson, Bob E. (1983). *Carl F. H. Henry.* Waco, TX: Word Books.

Pear, Robert. (1986). "Poverty Rate down Slightly in 1985, to Level of '81." *New York Times* (August 27), A17.

Pedrick, Cornell, Claire Gelles, and Richard Gelles. (1982). "Elder Abuse: The Status of Current Knowledge." *Family Relations* (July), 457–465.

Pelletier, K. R. (1979). *Holistic Medicine: From Stress to Optimum Health.* New York: Descorte Press/Seymour Lawrence.

Pepitone-Rockwell, Fran. (ed.). (1980). *Dual Career Couples.* Beverly Hills, CA: Sage.

Percy, Charles. (1974). *Growing Old in the Country of the Young.* New York: McGraw-Hill.

Perfetti, Lawrence J., and William C. Bingham. (1983). "Unemployment and Self-Esteem in Metal Refinery Workers." *Vocational Guidance Quarterly,* 195–201.

Perkins, John S. (1987). "Living the Hope." Address to the NACSW Convention, Nashville, TN (October 8).

Perlman, Richard. (1976). *The Economics of Poverty.* New York: McGraw-Hill.

Perrow, Charles. (1986). *Complex Organizations* (3d ed.). New York: Random House.

Peter, Laurence J., and Raymond Hull. (1969). *The Peter Principle.* New York: William Morrow.

Petersen, Paul E. (1985). *The New Urban Reality.* Washington, DC: Brookings Institute.

Petersen, William. (1974). *Population* (3d ed.). New York: Macmillan.

Peterson, Donald W., and Armand L. Mauss. (1973).

"The Cross and the Commune: An Interpretation of the Jesus People." In Charles Y. Glock (ed.), *Religion in Sociological Perspective: Essays in the Empirical Study of Religion.* Belmont, CA: Wadsworth, 261–279.

Phillips, David P. (1977). "Motor Vehicle Fatalities Increase Just After Publicized Suicide Stories." *Science,* 196, 1464–1465.

———. (1980). "The Deterrent Effect of Capital Punishment: New Evidence on an Old Controversy." *American Journal of Sociology,* 86, 139–148.

———. (1982). "The Impact of Fictional Television Stories on U.S. Adult Fatalities: New Evidence on the Effect of Mass Media on Violence." *American Journal of Sociology,* 87(4), 1340–1359.

Phillips, David P., and Lundie Carstensen. (1986). "Clustering of Teenage Suicides After Television News Stories About Suicide." *New England Journal of Medicine,* 315(11), 685–689.

Phillipson, Chris. (1982). *Capitalism and the Construction of Old Age.* London: Macmillan Press Ltd.

Piaget, Jean, and Barbel Inhelder. (1969). *The Psychology of the Child.* New York: Basic Books.

Pilisuk, Marc, and Thomas Hayden. (1965). "Is There a Military Industrial Complex Which Prevents Peace?" *Journal of Social Issues,* 21, 67–117.

Pilisuk, Marc, and Phyllis Pilisuk (eds.). (1971). *How the White Poor Live.* New Brunswick, NJ: Transaction Books.

Piotrow, Phyllis. (1980). *World Population: The Present and Future Crisis.* Washington, DC: The Foreign Policy Association.

Polanyi, Karl. (1957). *The Great Transformation.* Boston: Beacon Press.

Poloma, Margaret, and Neal Garland. (1978). "Two Sides of the Coin: An Investigation of the Dual-Career Family." In J. Ross Eshleman and Juanne Clarke, *Intimacy, Commitments, and Marriage.* Boston: Allyn and Bacon.

Pomper, Gerald M. (1971). *Elections in America: Control and Influence in Democratic Politics.* New York: Dodd, Mead.

Pope, Whitney. (1976). *Durkheim's Suicide: A Classic Analyzed.* Chicago: University of Chicago Press.

Pope, Hollowell, and Charles W. Mueller. (1976). "The Intergenerational Transmission of Marital Instability: Comparisons by Race and Sex." *Journal of Social Issues,* 32, 49–65.

Popenoe, Paul. (1950). *Marriage Is What You Make It.* New York: Macmillan.

Population Reference Bureau. (1983). "The Population of China." *Interchange: Population Newsletter* (May).

Postel, Sandra. (1984). "Air Pollution, Acid Rain, and the Future of Forest." *Worldwatch Paper 58,* Worldwatch Institute.

Postman, Neil, and Charles Weingartner. (1973). *Teaching as a Subversive Activity.* New York: Dell.

Poston, Dudley L., and E. Gotard. (1977). "Trends in Childlessness in the United States: 1910–1975." *Social Biology,* 24(3), 212–224.

Poussaint, Alvin F. (1974). "Minority Group Psychology: Implications for Social Action." In Rudolph Gomez (ed.), *The Social Reality of Ethnic America.* Lexington, MA: D. C. Heath.

Princeton Religious Research Center. (1987). "Cults Lead List of Groups 'Not Wanted as Neighbors'." 9, 3 (March).

President's Commission on Law Enforcement and Administration of Justice. (1967). *The Challenge of Crime in a Free Society.* Washington, DC: U.S. Government Printing Office.

Prudenski, G., and B. Kolpakov. (1962). "Questions Concerning the Calculations of Nonworking Time in Budget Statistics." *Problems of Economics,* 12, 31.

Queen, Stuart A., and Robert W. Haberstein. (1974). *The Family in Various Cultures* (4th ed.). New York: J. B. Lippincott.

Quinney, Richard. (1970). *The Social Reality of Crime.* Boston: Little, Brown.

Rabkin, Leslie Y. (1976). "The Institution of the Family Is Alive and Well." *Psychology Today* (February), 66–73.

Radway, Janice. (1983). "Women Read the Romance." *Feminist Studies,* 9(1), 53–79.

Raines, John C., and Donna C. Day-Lower. (1986). *Modern Work and Human Meaning.* Philadelphia: The Westminster Press.

Rainwater, Lee. (1966). "Marital Stability and Patterns of Status Variables: A Comment." *Journal of Marriage and the Family,* 28, 442–446.

———. (1968). "The Problem of Lower-Class Culture and Poverty–War Strategy." In Daniel Moynihan (ed.), *On Understanding Poverty.* New York: Basic Books.

Rallings, E. M., and F. Ivan Nye. (1979). "Wife–Mother Employment, Family, and Society." In Wesley Burr, et al. (eds.), *Contemporary Theories About the Family.* New York: Free Press, 203–226.

Ramey, James W. "Emerging Patterns of Behavior in Marriage." *Journal of Sex Research,* 8, 6–30.

Rangel, Jesus. (1984). "Survey Finds Hispanic Groups More Unified." *New York Times* (September 8), 22.

Rapoport, Rhona, and Robert N. Rapoport. (1971). *Dual-Career Families.* Harmondsworth, Middlesex, Eng.: Penguin.

Raschke, Helen, and Vern Raschke. (1979). "Family Conflict and Children's Self-Concept: A Comparison of Intact and Single-Parent Families." *Journal of Marriage and the Family,* 41, 367–375.

Raush, H. L., et al. (1974). *Communication, Conflict, and Marriage.* San Francisco: Jossey-Bass.

Reckless, Walter C., Simon Dinitz, and Ellen Murray. (1956). "Self-Concept as an Insulator Against Delinquency." *American Sociological Review,* 21, 744–746.

Reckman, Richard F., and George R. Goethals. (1973). "Deviance and Group Orientation as Determinants of Group Composition Preferences." *Sociometry,* 36(3), 419–423.

Redfield, Robert. (1941). *The Folk Culture of the Yucatan.* Chicago: University of Chicago Press.

Reid, Ksue Situs. (1976). *Crime and Criminology.* Hinsdale, IL: Dryden Press.

Reinhold, Robert. (1979). "Census Finds Unmarried Couples Have Doubled from 1970 to 1978." *New York Times* (June 27), A1, B5.

Reiss, Albert J. (1971). *The Police and the Public.* New Haven: Yale University Press.

———. (1976). *Studies in Crime and Law Enforcement in Major Metropolitan Areas.* Washington, DC, U.S. Government Printing Office.

Reisman, David, et al. (1961). *The Lonely Crowd.* New Haven: Yale University Press.

Reitzes, Donald C., and Elizabeth Mutran. (1980). "Significant Others and Self-Conceptions: Factors Influencing Educational Expectations and Academic Performance." *Sociology of Education,* 53 (January), 21–32.

Renne, K. S. (1970). "Correlates of Dissatisfaction in Marriage." *Journal of Marriage and the Family,* 32, 54–66.

"Return to God: Solzhenitsyn Speaks out." (1983). *Time Magazine* (May 23).

Rheem, Donald. (1986). "Scientists Moving Closer to Global Consensus on Ozone." *Christian Science Monitor* (October 24).

Rice, Berkeley. (1976). "Honor Thy Father Moon." *Psychology Today* (January), 36–47.

Richardson, J. T. (1980). "People's Temple and Jonestown: A Corrective Comparison and Critique." *Journal of the Scientific Study of Religion,* 19, 239–255.

———. (1985a). "The Active Versus Passive Convert: Paradigm Conflict in Conversion/Recruitment Research." *Journal for the Scientific Study of Religion,* 21, 255–268.

———. (1985b). "Studies of Conversion: Secularization or Reenchantment?" In P. Hammond (ed.) *The Sacred in a Secular Age.* Berkeley: University of California Press, 104–121.

Richmond, J. B. (1979). *Healthy People: The Surgeon General's Report on Health Promotion and Disease Prevention.* Washington, DC: DHEW Publication No. 79–55071, U.S. Government Printing Office.

Riegel, K. F., and R. M. Riegel. (1972). "Development, Drop, and Death." *Development Psychology,* 6(2), 306–319.

Riessman, C., and N. Gerstl. (1985). "Marital Dissolution and Health: Do Males or Females Have Greater Risk?" *Social Science and Medicine,* 20, (6), 627–635.

Riley, Matilda White. (1971). "Social Gerontology and the Age Stratification of Society." *The Gerontologist,* 11(1), 79–87.

Riley, Matilda White, Marilyn Johnson, and Anne Foner. (1972). *Aging and Society: Vol. 3: A Sociology of Age Stratification.* New York: Russell Sage Foundation.

Rist, Ray. (1970). "Social Class and Teacher Expectations: The Self-Fulfilling Prophecy in Ghetto Education." *Harvard Educational Review,* 40, 411–451.

Ritzer, George, and David Walczak. (1985). *Working: Conflict and Change.* Englewood Cliffs, NJ: Prentice-Hall.

Roberts, Keith A. (1984). *Religion in Sociological Perspective.* Chicago: The Dorsey Press.

Robinson, D. (1985). "How Can We Protect Our Elderly?" *Parade Magazine* (February 17), 4–8.

Robinson, Robert V., and Jonathan Kelley. (1979). "Class as Conceived by Marx and Dahrendorf: Effects on Income Inequality and Politics in the United States and Great Britain." *American Sociological Review,* 44, 38–58.

Roby, Pamela (ed.). (1974). *The Poverty Establishment.* Englewood Cliffs, NJ: Prentice-Hall.

Rockmore, Milton. (1978). "Age 65 and Kicking Even Higher." *American Way* (July), 25–59.

Roethlisberger, F. J., and W. J. Dickson (1939). *Management and the Worker.* Cambridge: Harvard University Press.

Rollins, Boyd C., and Kenneth L. Cannon. (1974). "Marital Satisfaction over the Family Life Cycle: A Reevaluation." *Journal of Marriage and the Family,* 35, 271–284.

Rollins, Boyd C., and Harold Feldman. (1970). "Marital Satisfaction over the Family Life Cycle." *Journal of Marriage and the Family,* 32, 20–28.

Rollins, Boyd C., and R. Galligan. (1978). "The Developing Child and Marital Satisfaction of Parents." In R. M. Lerner and G. B. Spanier (eds.), *Child Influence on Marital and Family Interaction.* New York: Academic Press.

The Roper Organization. (1980). *The 1980 Virginia Slims American Women's Opinion Poll.*

Rose, Arnold. (1967). *The Power Structure: Political Process in American Society.* New York: Oxford University Press.

Rose, Jerry. (1982). *Outbreaks: The Sociology of Collective Behavior.* New York: Free Press.

Rose, Peter I. (1974). *They and We.* New York: Random House.

———. (ed.). (1979). *Socialization and the Life Cycle.* New York: St. Martin's Press.

Rose, Stephen J. (1986). *The American Profile Poster.* Random House.

Rosenbaum, James E. (1976). *Making Inequality.* New York: Wiley.

———. (1980). "Track Misperceptions and Frustrated College Plans: An Analysis of the Effects of Tracks and Track Perceptions in the National Longitudinal Survey." *Sociology of Education,* 53(2), 74–88.

Rosenblatt, Paul C., and Michael R. Cunningham. (1976). "Sex Differences in Cross-Cultural Perspective." In Barbara Lloyd and John Archer (eds.), *Exploring Sex Differences.* London: Academic Press.

Rosenthal, Kristine, and Harry Keshet. (1980). *Fathers Without Partners.* New York: Rowman and Littlefield.

Rosenthal, M. (1971). "Where Rumor Raged." *Transaction,* 8, 34–43.

Rosenthal, Robert, and Lenore Jacobson. (1968). *Pygmalion in the Classroom: Teacher Expectations and Pupils' Intellectual Development.* New York: Holt, Rinehart & Winston.

Roskin, Michael G. (1982). *Countries and Concepts: An Introduction to Comparative Politics.* Englewood Cliffs, NJ: Prentice-Hall.

Rosow, Irving. ((1974). *Socialization to Old Age.* Berkeley: University of California Press.

Ross, Catherine, John Mirowsky, and Joan Juber. (1983). "Dividing Work, Sharing Work, and In-Between: Marriage Patterns and Depression." *American Sociological Review,* 48 (December), 809–823.

Ross, Ellen, and Rayna Rapp. (1981). "Sex and Society: A Research Note from Social History and Anthropology." *Society for Comparative Study of Society and History,* 23, 51–72.

Ross, Hugh Allen. (1959). "Commitment of the Mentally Ill: Problems of Law and Policy." *Michigan Law Review,* 57, 945–1018.

Rossi, P. H., R. A. Berk, and K. Lenihan. (1980). *Money, Work, and Crime.* New York: Academic Press.

Rossi, Alice. (1972). "Sisterhood Is Beautiful: A Conversation with Gordon Bermant." *Psychology Today* (August), 40–46, 72–75.

Rossides, Daniel W. (1976). *The American Class System.* Boston: Houghton Mifflin.

Roszak, Theodore. (1969). *The Making of a Counter Culture.* New York: Doubleday.

Rothman, Robert A. (1987). *Working: Sociological Perspectives.* Englewood Cliffs, NJ: Prentice-Hall.

Rothschild, Joyce and Raymond Russell. (1986). "Alternatives to Bureaucracy: Democratic Participation in the Economy." In *Annual Review of Sociology.* Palo Alto, CA: Annual Reviews Inc. 307–328.

Rothstein, Lawrence E. (1986). *Plant Closings: Power, Politics, and Workers.* Dover, MA: Auburn House.

Rothstein, Morton. (1986). "Biochemical Studies of Aging." *Chemical and Engineering News,* 64 (August), 26–39.

Rowe, David, and Wayne Osgood. (1984). "Heredity and Sociological Theories of Delinquency: A Reconsideration." *American Sociological Review,* 49(4), 526–540.

Rubel, Robert J. (1980). *School Crime and Violence.* Lexington, MA: D. C. Heath.

Rubin, Lillian. (1979). *Women of a Certain Age: The Midlife Search for Self.* New York: Harper and Row.

Rubin, Jeffrey Z., F. J. Provenza, and A. Luria. (1974). "Eye of the Beholder: Parents' Views on Sex of Newborns." *American Journal of Orthopsychiatry,* 44(4), 512–519.

———. (1976). "Are We Born into Our Sex Roles or Programmed into Them?" *Woman's Day* (January).

Rubington, Earl, and Martin S. Weinber. (1978). *Deviance: The Interactionalist Perspective* (3d ed.). New York: Macmillan.

Rubinson, Richard. (1981). *Dynamics of World Development:* Vol. 4: *Political Economy of the World-Systems Annuals.* Beverly Hills, CA: Sage Publications.

Rubison, Richard, and John Ralph. (1984). "Technical Changes and the Expansion of Schooling in the United States, 1890–1970." *Sociology of Education,* 57 (July), 134–152.

Rubovits, P. C., and A. L. Maher. (1971). "Pygmalion Analyzed: Toward an Explanation of the Rosenthal–Jacobson Findings." *Journal of Personality and Social Psychology,* 19, 197–203.

———. (1973). "Pygmalion Black and White." *Journal of Personality and Social Psychology,* 25, 210–218.

Rudé, George. (1964). *The Crowd in History: 1730–1848.* New York: John Wiley.

Rumberger, Russell. (1981). *Overeducation in the U.S. Labor Market.* New York: Praeger Press.

Russell, Bertrand. (1929). "Marriage." In *Marriage and Morals.* New York: Garden City Publishing Co.

Russell, Louise. (1984). *The Baby-Boom Generation and the Economy.* Washington, DC: Brookings Institute.

Rutter, Michael. (1974). *The Qualities of Mothering: Maternal Deprivation Reassessed.* New York: Aronson.

———. (1980). *Changing Youth in a Changing Society: Patterns of Adolescent Development and Disorder.* Cambridge, Harvard University Press.

Ryan, William. (1971). *Blaming the Victim.* New York: Pantheon.

———. (1982). *Equality.* New York: Vintage Press.

Rytina, Nancy. (1982). "Earnings of Men and Women." *Monthly Labor Review* (April), 26–29.

Sabato, Larry J. (1984). *PAC Power: Inside the World of Political Action Committees.* New York: W. W. Norton.

Sadker, David, and Myra Sadker. (1985a). "Is the OK Classroom OK?" *Phi Delta Kappan* (January), 358–361.

———. (1985b). "Sexism in the Schoolroom of the '80s." *Psychology Today,* 19 (March), 54–57.

Safran, Claire. (1976). "How TV Changes Children." *Redbook* (November).

Saint-Simon, Henri. (1964). *Social Organization: The Science of Man.* Translated and edited by Felix Markham. New York: Harper and Row.

Salzman, Philip. (1967). "Political Organization Among Nomadic Peoples." *Proceedings of the American Philosophical Society,* 111(2), 115–131.

Sandeen, Ernest R. (1967). "The Origins of Fundamentalism." *Church History,* 36, 66–83. Also in John Muldern and John F. Wilson, *Religion in American History.* Englewood Cliffs, NJ: Prentice-Hall, 1978.

Sapir, Edward. (1928). "The Meaning of Religion." *American Mercury,* 16, 72–79.

———. (1962). *Culture, Language, and Personality,* Berkeley: University of California Press.

Sapiro, Virginia. (1986). *Women in American Society.* Palo Alto, CA: Mayfield Press.

Scanzoni, John. (1972). *Sexual Bargaining.* Englewood Cliffs, NJ: Prentice-Hall.

Scarr-Salaptek, Sandra, and Richard A. Weinberg. (1975). "When Black Children Grow up in White Homes." *Psychology Today,* 9 (December), 80–82.

Schachter, Stanley. (1959). *The Psychology of Affiliation: Experimental Studies of the Sources of Gregariousness.* Palo Alto, CA: Stanford University Press.

Schacter, Ronald. (1987). "Attracting the 'Best and Brightest' to Teaching." *Christian Science Monitor* (January 5), 23.

Schaefer, Richard T. (1984). *Racial and Ethnic Groups* (2d ed.). Boston: Little, Brown and Co.

Schafly, Phyllis. (1977). *The Power of the Positive Woman.* New York: Arlington House.

Schaie, K. W. (1984). "Midlife Influences upon Intellectual Functioning in Old Age." *International Journal of Behavioral Development,* 7, 463–478.

Schaie, K. Warner, and Sherry Willis. (1986). *Adult Development and Aging* (2d ed.). Boston: Little, Brown.

Scheff, Thomas J. (1963). "The Role of the Mentally Ill and the Dynamics of Mental Disorder: Research Framework." *Sociometry,* 26, 436–473.

———. (1964). "Screening Mental Patients." *Social Problems,* 11(4), 401–413.

———. (1984). *Being Mentally Ill: A Sociological Theory* (2d ed.). Hawthorne, NY: Aldine.

Schell, Thomas. (1982). *The Fate of the Earth.* New York: Knopf.

Schelling, Thomas. (1984). "Anticipating Climate Change." *Environment* (October).

Schiefelbein, Susan. (1978). "Confusion at Harvard: What Makes an Educated Man?" *Saturday Review,* 5 (April 1), 12–20.

Schlesinger, Yaffa. (1977). "Sex Roles and Social Change in the Kibbutz." *Journal of Marriage and the Family,* 39 (November), 771–779.

Schoen, R., H. N. Greenblatt, and R. B. Mielke. (1975). "California's Experience with Nonadversary Divorce." *Demography,* 12(2), 223–243.

Schooler, Carmi, et al. (1984). "Work for the Household: Its Nature and Consequences for Husbands and Wives." *American Journal of Sociology,* 90(1), 97–124.

Schram, Rosalyn W. (1979). "Marital Satisfaction over the Family Life Cycle: A Critique and Proposal." *Journal of Marriage and the Family,* 41, 7–12.

Schramm, Wilbur, and Donald F. Roberts (eds.). (1971). *The Process and Effects of Mass Communications* (rev. ed.). Urbana: University of Illinois Press.

Schulz, James. (1980). *The Economics of Aging.* Belmont, CA: Wadsworth.

Schuman, Howard. (1971). "The Religious Factor in Detroit: Review, Replication, and Reanalysis." *American Sociological Review,* 36, 30–48.

———. (1987). *Racial Attitudes in America: Trends and Interpretations.* Cambridge, MA: Harvard University Press.

Schwartz, Richard D., and Jerome H. (1963). "Two Studies of Legal Stigma." In Becker (ed.), *The Other Side.* New York: Free Press.

Schwartz, Toney, et al. (1977). "Living Together." *Newsweek,* 1 (August 1), 56–59.

Scientific American. (1969). E. Stull & C. Greenfield (ed.) *Cities.* New York: Knopf.

Scott, Ann Crittenden. (1972). "The Value of Housework: For Love or Money?" *MS* (July).

Scrimshaw, Nevin, and Lance Taylor. (1980). "Food." *V 243/3* (September).

Scritchfield, Shirley, and J. Steven Picou. (1982). "Structure of Significant Other Influence on Status Aspirations: Black–White Variations." *Sociology of Education,* 55 (January), 22–30.

Selden, (1983). In Laurel Richardson and Verta Taylor, *Feminist Frontiers: Rethinking Sex, Gender, and Society.* Reading, MA: Addison-Wesley.

Self, Patricia, and Nacy Datan. (1976). In "Are We Born into Our Sex Roles or Programmed into Them?" *Woman's Day,* (January).

Seligman, Daniel. (1984). "Why Are People Poor?" *Fortune,* (October 1), 189–191.

Sewell, William, and Robert Hauser. (1976). "Causes and Consequences of Higher Education: Modes of the Status Attainment Process." In William Sewell, Robert Hauser, and David Featherman (eds.), *Schooling and Achievement in American Society.* New York: Academic Press, 9–28.

Sewell, William H., Archibald O. Haller, and George W. Ohlendorf. (1970). "The Educational and Early Occupational Status Attainment Process: A Replication and Revision." *American Sociological Review*, 35, 1014–1027.

Sewell, William H., Archibald O. Haller, and Alejandro Portes. (1969). "The Educational and Early Occupational Attainment Process." *American Sociological Review*, 34, 82–92.

Shanas, Ethel, (1979). "Social Myth as Hypothesis: The Case of the Family Relations of Old People." *The Gerontologist*, 19, 1 (February), 3–9.

Shanker, Albert. (1987). "On the Education of a Teacher." *The Innovator*. Ann Arbor: University of Michigan School of Education.

Shaw, Clifford R., and Henry D. McKay. (1929). *Delinquency Areas*. Chicago: University of Chicago Press.

Shaw, Marvin E. (1981a). *Group Dynamics* (3d ed.). New York: McGraw-Hill.

———. (1981b). *Group Dynamics: The Psychology of Small Group Behavior* (3d ed.). New York: McGraw-Hill.

Shaw, Marvin E. and J. C. Gilchrist. (1966). "Intragroup Communication and Leader Choice." *Journal of Social Psychology*, 43, 133–138.

Sheehy, Gail. (1972). "Divorced Mothers as a Political Force." In Louise Kapp Howe (ed.), *The Future of the Family*. New York: Simon and Schuster.

Sheldon, William H. (1940). *The Varieties of Human Physique*. New York: Harper.

———. (1949). *Varieties of Delinquent Youth*. New York: Harper and Row.

Shelton, Beth. (1987). "Social Integration, Community Size, and Divorce Rate." *Journal of Marriage and the Family*, 49 (November), 827–832.

Shepard, Jon M. (1971). *Automation and Alienation: A Study of Office and Factory Workers*. Cambridge, MA: The MIT Press.

Sherman, Julia. (1980). "Mathematics, Spatial Visualization, and Related Factors: Changes in Boys and Girls, Grades 8–11." *Journal of Education*, 72 (August), 476–482.

Sheuey, Audrey M. (1958). *The Testing of Negro Intelligence*. Little Rock: J. W. Bell.

Shibutani, Tomotsu. (1966). *Improvised News: A Sociological Study of Rumor*. Indianapolis: Bobbs-Merrill.

Shneidman, E. D. (1980). *Voices of Death*. New York: Harper and Row.

Shockley, P., and Constance Staley. (1980). "Women in Management Training Programs: What They Think About Key Issues." *Public Personnel Management*, 9, 214–224.

Shulman, Alex. (1971). "Organs and Orgasms." In Vivian Gornick and Barbara K. Moran (eds.), *Women in Sexist Society*. New York: Basic Books.

Silberman, Charles. (1970). "Murder in the Classroom: How the Public Schools Kill Dreams and Mutilate Minds." *The Atlantic*, 225, 82–94.

———. (1971). *Crisis in the Classroom: The Remaking of American Education*. New York: Random House.

Silverman, Dr. Mervyn. (1984). *San Francisco Chronicle*, (July 18).

Simmel, Georg. (1902, 1950). *The Sociology of Georg Simmel*. Translated by Kurt Wolff. Glencoe, IL: The Free Press.

Simon, Julian L. (1981). *The Ultimate Resource*. Princeton: Princeton University Press.

Simpson, George Eaton, and Milton J. Yinger. (1972). *Racial and Cultural Minorities: An Analysis of Prejudice and Discrimination* (4th ed.). New York: Harper and Row.

"Sinfully Together." (1979). *Time Magazine* (July 9), 55.

Singer, Jerome, and Dorothy Singer. (1973). "Psychologists Look at Television: Cognitive Developmental, Personality, and Social Policy Implication." *American Psychologist*, 75(1), 64–86.

Singer, M.T. (1979). "Coming out of the Cults." *Psychology Today*, 8, 72–82.

Sizer, Theodore, (1984). *Horace's Compromise: The Dilemma of the American High School*. Boston: Houghton Mifflin.

Sjoberg, Gideon. (1965). *The Preindustrial City*. New York: Free Press.

Skillen, B. F. (1971). *Beyond Freedom and Dignity*. New York: Knopf.

Skolnick, Arlene. (1973). *The Intimate Environment: Exploring Marriage and the Family*. Boston: Little, Brown.

Skonovd, L. N. (1981). *Apostasy: The Process of Defection from Religious Totalism*. Ph.D. thesis. Davis, CA: University of California.

———. (1983). "Leaving the 'Cultic' Religious Milieu." In D. G. Bromley and J. T. Richardson, *The Brainwashing/Deprogramming Controversy: Sociological, Psychological, Legal, and Historical Perspectives*. New York: Edwin Mellen.

Slater, Philip. (1961). "Parental Role Differentiation." *American Journal of Sociology*, 67(3), 296–311.

———. (1970). *The Pursuit of Loneliness: American Culture at the Breaking Point*. Boston: Beacon Press.

Smelser, Neil J. (1963). *The Theory of Collective Behavior*. New York: Free Press.

———. (1976). *The Sociology of Economic Life* (2d ed.). Englewood Cliffs, NJ: Prentice-Hall.

Smith, Adam. (1776, 1976). *Inquiry into the Nature and*

Causes of the Wealth of Nations. Edited by R. H. Campbell and A. S. Skinner. Oxford: Clarendon.

Smith, Hendrick. (1976). *The Russians.* New York: Quadrangle.

Smith, Herbert. (1986). "Overeducation and Underemployment: An Agnostic Review." *Sociology of Education,* 59 (April), 85–99.

Smith, Ralph E. (1979a). *The Subtle Revolution.* Washington, DC: Urban Institute.

———. (1979b). *Women in the Labor Force in 1990.* Washington, DC: Urban Institute.

Smith, Ralph R. (1978). "Bakke's Case Versus the Case for Affirmative Action." *New York University Education Quarterly,* 9(2), 2–8.

Solomon, T. (1981). "Integrating the 'Moonie' Experience: A Survey of Ex-members of the Unification Church." *In Gods We Trust: New Patterns of Religious Pluralism in America.* Transaction Books, 275–294.

Sorenson, E. Richard. (1971). *The Evolving Force: A Study of Socialization and Cultural Change in the New Guinea Highlands.* Palo Alto, CA: Stanford University Press.

Sorokin, Pitirim A. (1937). *Social and Cultural Dynamics.* New York: American Books.

———. (1941). *The Crisis of Our Age.* New York: E. P. Dutton.

Sowell, Thomas. (1981a). "A Dissenting Opinion About Affirmative Action." *Across the Board* (January), 64–72.

———. (1981b). *Ethnic America: A History.* New York: Basic Books.

———. (1983). *The Economics and Politics of Race.* New York: Morrow.

Spanier, G. B., Robert A. Lewis, and Charles L. Cole. (1975). "Marital Adjustment over the Family Life Cycle: The Issue of Curvilinearity." *Journal of Marriage and the Family,* 37, 263–277.

Spanier, Graham, and R. Castro. (1979). "Adjustment to Separation and Divorce: An Analysis of 50 Case Studies." *Journal of Divorce,* 2 (Spring), 241–253.

Spates, James L., and John J. Macionis. (1986). *The Sociology of Cities* (2d ed.). Belmont, CA: Wadsworth.

Special Committee on Aging (U.S. Senate). (1985). "Heinz Says First DRG Study Flags Potential Hazards for Older Americans." *Newsweek.* (February 25).

Spector, Malcolm, and John I. Kitsuse. (1973). "Social Problems: A Reformulation." *Social Problems,* 21, 145–159.

Spencer, Herbert. (1898). *The Principles of Sociology.* New York: Appleton.

Spender, Dale. (1982). *Women of Ideas.* London: Routledge and Kegan Paul.

Spengler, Oswald. (1918). *The Decline of the West.* New York: Knopf.

Spitz, Rene A. (1945). "Hospitalism: An Inquiry into the Genesis of Psychiatric Conditions in Early Childhood." In Anna Freud, et al., (eds.), *The Psychoanalytic Study of the Child.* New York: International University Press.

Spitzer, Steven. (1980). "Toward a Marxian Theory of Deviance." In Delos H. Kelly (ed.), *Criminal Behavior: Readings in Criminology.* New York: St. Martin's Press, 175–191.

Stack, Carol B. (1974). *All Our Kin: Strategies for Survival in a Black Community.* New York: Harper and Row.

Stack, Steven. (1979). "The Effects of Political Participation and Socialist Party Strength on the Degree of Income Inequality." *American Sociological Review,* 44, 168–171.

———. (1983). "The Effect of Religious Commitment on Suicide: A Cross-National Analysis." *Journal of Health and Social Behavior,* 24 (December), 362–374.

———. (1985a). "A Comparative Analysis of Durkheim's Theory of Egoistic Suicide: A Comment." *The Sociological Quarterly,* 24 (Autumn), 625–627.

———. (1985b). "The Effect of Domestic/Religious Individualism in Suicide: 1954–1978." *Journal of Marriage and the Family,* 47 (May), 431–447.

———. (1987). "Publicized Executions and Homicide: 1950–1980." *American Sociological Review,* 52 (August), 532–540.

Staines, Graham, Tobey Epstein Jayaratne, and Carol Tarvis. (1974). "The Queen Bee Syndrome." *Psychology Today,* 7(8), 55–60.

Stanard, Una. (1971). "The Mask of Beauty." In Vivian Gornick and Barbara K. Moran (eds.), *Women in Sexist Society.* New York: Basic Books.

Stanfield, Rochelle. (1985). "No One Knows for Sure if Pollution Control Programs Are Really Working." *National Journal* (March 23).

Staples, Robert. (1971). "Toward a Sociology of the Black Family: A Theoretical and Methodological Assessment." *Journal of Marriage and the Family* (February), 119–135.

Stark, Rodney, and William Sims Bainbridge. (1985). *The Future of Religion: Secularization, Revival, and Cult Formation.* Berkeley: University of California Press.

Stark, Rodney, Daniel Doyle, and Jesse Rushing. (1983). "Beyond Durkheim: Religions and Suicide." *Journal for the Scientific Study of Religion,* 22(2), 120–131.

Stark, Rodney, et al. (1971). *Wayward Shepherds.* New York: Harper and Row.

Stechert, Kathryn. (1985). "Illiteracy in America: The Shocking, Silent Crisis." *Better Homes and Gardens* (November), 27–28.

Steedly, Homer R., Jr., and John W. Foley. (1979).

"The Success of Protest Groups: Multivariate Analyses." *Social Science Quarterly,* 8, 1–15.

Steele, William. (1985). "Preventing the Spread of Suicide Among Adolescents." *USA Today Magazine* (November), 58–61.

Stein, Timothy R. et al. (1980). "Leadership Valence: Modeling and Measuring the Process of Emergent Leadership." In J. G. Hunt and L. L. Larson (eds.), *Crosscurrents in Leadership.* Carbondale: Southern Illinois University Press, 126–147.

Steinmetz, Suzanne. (1981). "Elder Abuse." *Aging,* 315–316 (January–February), 6–10.

Stengel, Richard. (1985). "Apostle of Sunny Thoughts." *Time Magazine* (March 18).

Stephens, William N. (1963). *The Family in Cross-Cultural Perspective.* New York: Holt, Rinehart & Winston.

Sticht, Thomas. (1987). "What USA Business Can Do to Education Workers." *USA Today* (October 29), 4b.

Stickney, Benjamin, and Laurence Marcus. (1985). "Education and the Disadvantaged 20 Years Later." *Phi Delta Kappan* (April), 559–564.

Stoler, Peter. (1984). "Pulling the Nuclear Plug." *Time Magazine* (February 13), 34–40.

Stoller, E. P., and L. L. Earl. (1983). "Help with Activities of Everyday Life: Sources of Support for the Noninstitutionalized Elderly." *Gerontologist,* 23(1), 64–70.

Stoner, J. A. F. (1965). "A Comparison of Individual and Group Decisions Involving Risk." Unpublished master's thesis, Massachusetts Institute of Technology. Reported in Robert Brown, *Social Psychology.* New York: Free Press.

Storr, Catherine. (1967). "Freud and the Concept of Parental Guilt." In Jonathan Miller (ed.), *Freud: The Man, His World, His Influence.* Boston: Little, Brown.

Strauss, Murray A., Richard Gelles, and Suzanne Steinmetz. (1979). *Behind Closed Doors: A Survey of Family Violence in America.* New York: Doubleday.

Strohmeyer, John. (1986). *Crisis in Bethlehem: Big Steel's Battle to Survive.* Bethesda, MD: Adler.

Strother, Deborah Burnett. (1986). "Suicide Among the Young." *Phi Delta Kappan,* June, 756–759.

Stubbing, Richard A., with Richard A. Mendel. (1986). *The Defense Game: An Insider Explores the Astonishing Realities of America's Defense Establishment.* New York: Harper and Row.

Sullerot, Evelyn. (1971). *Women, Society, and Change.* New York: McGraw-Hill.

Sullivan, Cheryl. (1986). "Women Established New Political Beachheads in '86 Election." *Christian Science Monitor* (October 15), 1.

Sullivan, Walter, (1987). "Metal's Link to Alzheimer's Studied." *New York Times* (May 5).

Sumner, William Graham. (1883). *What the Social Classes Owe Each Other.* New York: Harper.

———. (1906, 1959). *Folkways: A Study of the Sociological Importance of Usages, Manners, Customs, Mores, and Morals.* New York: Dover.

Summers, Harry G., Jr. (1983). "Lessons: A Soldier's View." *Wilson Quarterly* (Summer), 125–135.

Sunday Times Magazine. (1980). London. December 14, 94.

Suransky, Valerie Palokow. (1982). "A Tyranny of Experts." *Wilson Quarterly* (Autumn), 53–85.

Sussman, Marvin B. (1985). "The Family Life of Old People." In R. Binstock and E. Shanas, (eds.), *Handbook of Aging and the Social Sciences.* New York: Van Nostrand Reinhold, 415–419.

Suter, Larry E., and Herman P. Miller. (1973). "Income Differentials Between Men and Career Women." *American Journal of Sociology,* 78, 962–974.

Sutherland, Edwin H. (1939). *Principles of Criminology.* Philadelphia: Lippincott.

———. (1949). *White Collar Crime.* New York: Holt, Rinehart & Winston.

———. (1983). *White Collar Crime: The Uncut Version.* New Haven: Yale University Press.

Suttles, Gerald. (1972). *The Social Construction of Communities.* Chicago: University of Chicago Press.

Swafford, Michael. (1978). "Sex Differences in Soviet Earnings." *American Sociological Review,* 43(5), 657–673.

Sweet, Ellen. (1985). "Date Rape: The Story of an Epidemic and Those Who Deny It." *Ms./Campus Times* (October), 56–69, 84–85.

Sweet, James. (1977). "Demography and the Family." *Annual Review of Sociology,* 3, 363–405.

Swensen, C. H. (1972). In H. Otto (ed.), *Love Today.* New York: Association Press.

Swinton, David. (1986). "The Economic Status of Blacks, 1985." *The State of Black America.* New York: National Urban League.

Szasz, Thomas S. (1960). "The Myth of Mental Illness." *American Psychologist,* 15, 113–118.

———. (1961, 1974). *The Myth of Mental Illness.* New York: Harper and Row.

———. (1986). *Insanity: The Ideal and Its Consequences.* New York: Wiley.

Szcepanski, Jan. (1970). *Polish Society.* New York: Random House.

Szymanski, Albert. (1983). *Class Structure: A Critical Perspective.* New York: Praeger.

Tannenbaum, Arnold S., et al. (1974). *Hierarchy in Organization: An International Comparison.* San Francisco: Jossey-Bass.

Tavris, Carol. (1974). "Field Report: Women in China, the Speak-Bitterness Revolution." *Psychology Today,* 7(12), 43–98.

———. (1975). "Male Supremacy Is on the Way out:

It Was Just a Phase in the Evolution of Culture. A Conversation with Marvin Harris." *Psychology Today* (January), 61ff.

Tausky, Curt. (1984). *Work and Society.* Itasca, IL: F. E. Peacock.

Taylor, Frederick W. (1911). *Principles of Scientific Management.* New York: Harper and Row.

Taylor, Verta. (1983). "The Future of Feminism in the 1980s: A Social Movement Analysis." In Verta Taylor (ed.), *Feminist Frontiers: Rethinking Sex, Gender, and Society.* Reading, MA: Addison-Wesley.

Technical Committee for an Age-Integrated Society: Implications for the Economy. (1981). *Economic Policy in an Aging Society.* Washington, DC: White House Conference on Aging.

Terry, Sara. (1986). "Welfare Reform—1987 May Be the Year It Happens." *Christian Science Monitor* (October 21), 3.

Thomas, George M., and John W. Meyer. (1984). "The Expansion of the State." *Annual Review of Sociology,* 10, 461–82.

Thomas, Melvin, and Michael Hughes. (1986). "The Counting Significance of Race: A Study of Race, Class, and Quality of Life in America, 1972–1985." *American Sociological Review,* 51 (December), 830–841.

Thomas, W. I. (1923). *The Unadjusted Girl.* Boston: Little, Brown.

———. (1937). *Primitive Behavior: An Introduction to the Social Sciences.* New York: Irrington Publishers.

Thomas, W. I., and Forian Znaniecki. (1918). *The Polish Peasant in Europe and America.* New York: Alfred A. Knopf.

Thurow, Lester. (1980). *The Zero-Sum Society.* New York: Basic Books.

Thurow, Lester C. (1984). "The Leverage of Our Wealthiest 400." *The New York Times,* October 11, pp. 27.

Tienda, Marta, Vilma Ortiz, and Shelley Smith. "Industrial Restructuring, Gender Segregation, and Sex Differences in Earnings." *American Sociological Review,* 52 (April), pp. 195–210.

Tiger, Lionel. (1970). "The Possible Biological Origins of Sexual Discrimination." *Impact of Science on Sociology,* 20(1), pp. 29–44.

Timberlake, Michael. (1985). *Urbanization in the World Economy.* Orlando, FL: Academic Press.

Tittle, Charles T., Mary Jean Burke, and Elton F. Jackson. (1986). "Modeling Sutherland's Theory of Differential Association: Toward an Empirical Clarification." *Social Forces,* 65 (2), 405–432.

Tobias, Sheila, and Carol Weissbrod. (1980). "Anxiety and Mathematics: An Update." *Harvard Educational Review,* 50, 63–70.

Toby, Jackson. (1983). "Violence in Schools." *National Institute of Justice: Research in Brief.* U.S. Department of Justice (December).

Toffler, Alvin. (1970). *Future Shock.* New York: Random House.

———. (1980). *The Third Wave.* New York: William Morrow.

Tönnies, Ferdinand. (1887, 1963). *Community and Society.* Translated and edited by C. P. Loomis. New York: Harper and Row.

Toufexis, Anastasia. (1985). "The Perils of Dual Careers." *Time Magazine,* (May 13), 67.

Townsend, Robert. (1970). *Up the Organization.* Greenwich, CT: Fawcett.

"Tragic Princess: Love, Death, and Fleet Street." (1978). *Time Magazine* (February 18), 46.

Treiman, Donald J. (1970). *Occupational Prestige in Comparative Perspective.* New York: Academic Press.

Treiman, Donald. (1970). "Industrialization and Social Stratification." In E. O. Laumann (ed.), *Social Stratification Research and Theory for the 1970s.* New York: Bobbs-Merrill, 207–234.

Troeltsch, Ernst. (1957). "Church and Section." In Milton J. Yinger (ed.), *Religion, Society, and the Individual: An Introduction to the Sociology of Religion.* New York: Macmillan.

Troll, Lillian, and Vern Bengston. (1983). "Time, Aging, and the Continuity of Social Structure: Themes and Issues in Generation Analysis." *Journal of Social Issues,* 39 (Winter), 45–71.

Trovato, Frank. (1987). "A Longitudinal Analysis of Divorce and Suicide in Canada." *Journal of Marriage and the Family,* 49 (February), 193–203.

Tsuchigane, Robert, and Norton Dodge. (1974). *Economic Discrimination Against Women in the United States.* Lexington, MA: Lexington Books.

Tuchman, Gaye. (1979). "Women's Depiction by the Mass Media." *Journal of Women in Culture and Society,* 4, 528–542.

Tumin, Melvin M. (1953). "Some Principles of Stratification: A Critical Analysis." *American Sociological Review,* 18, 387–394.

———. (1963). "On Inequality." *American Sociological Review,* 29, 19–26.

Turner, Ralph H. (1962). In A. M. Rose (ed.), *Human Behavior and Social Process.* Boston: Houghton Mifflin.

———. (1970). *Family Interaction.* New York: John Wiley.

Turner, Ralph, and Lewis Killian. (1972). *Collective Behavior* (2d ed.). Englewood Cliffs, NJ: Prentice-Hall.

Tyler, T. R., and R. Weber. (1982). "Support for the Death Penalty: Instrumental Response to Crime or Symbolic Attitude?" *Law and Society Review,* 17(1), 21–45.

Udry, Richard. (1971). *Social Context of Marriage.* Philadelphia: Lippincott.

Uhlenberg, Peter. (1980). "Death and the Family." *Journal of Family History,* 5 (3), 313–320.

United Nations. (1982). *Population Trends. Vol. I.* Population Studies No. 79. New York: United Nations.

U.S. Bureau of the Census. (1973a). *Estimates of the Population of States, by Age: July 1, 1971 and 1982.* Series P-25 (500). Washington, DC: U.S. Government Printing Office.

———. (1973b). *Our Cities and Suburbs: We the Americans.* Report No. 7. Washington, DC: U.S. Government Printing Office.

———. (1975). *Historical Statistics of the United States, Colonial Times to 1970.* Washington, DC: US Government Printing Office.

———. (1976). *Some Demographic Aspects of Aging in the United States.* Series P-23 (43). Washington, DC: U.S. Government Printing Office.

———. (1977). *Social Indicators.* Washington, DC: U.S. Government Printing Office.

———. (1979). *The Social and Economic Status of the Black Population in the United States: An Historical View, 1790–1978.* Special Studies Series P-23 (890), Washington, DC: U.S. Government Printing Office.

———. (1980a). *Money Income and Poverty Status of Families and Persons in the United States, 1978.* Series P-60. Washington, DC: U.S. Government Printing Office.

———. (1980b). *Social Indicators III.* Washington, DC: U.S. Government Printing Office.

———. (1978, 1981a). *Current Population Reports.* (For years 1977 and 1981). Washington, DC: Government Printing Office.

———. (1981b). *Money Income and Poverty Status of Families and Persons in the United States: 1980.* Series P-60. Washington, DC: U.S. Government Printing Office.

———. (1982a). *Current Population Reports: Households and Families, by Type, March, 1981.* Series P-20 (367). Washington, DC: U.S. Government Printing Office.

———. (1982b). *Current Population Reports: Marital Status and Living Arrangements, March, 1981.* Series P-20 (372). Washington, DC: U.S. Government Printing Office.

———. (1983a). *Statistical Abstract of the United States. 1982–* Washington, DC: U.S. Government Printing Office.

———. (1983b). *Statistical Abstract of the United States, 1984* (104th ed.). Washington, D.C.: U.S. Government Printing Office.

———. (1984). *Statistical Abstract of the U.S.* (105th ed.). Washington, DC: U.S. Government Printing Office.

———. (1985). *Statistical Abstract of the United States* (106th ed.). Washington, DC: U.S. Government Printing Office.

———. (1986). *Statistical Abstract of the United States* (107th ed.). Washington, DC: U.S. Government Printing Office.

———. (1987). *Statistical Abstract of the United States: 1987.* (108th ed.). Washington, DC: U.S. Government Printing Office.

U.S. Department of Justice. (1970). *Uniform Crime Reports.* Washington, DC: U.S. Government Printing Office.

U.S. Department of Justice, Federal Bureau of Investigation. (1986a). *Uniform Crime Reports: Crime in the United States.* Washington, DC: U.S. Government Printing Office.

———. (1986b). *Uniform Crime Reports: Crime in the United States.* Washington, DC: U.S. Government Printing Office.

U.S. Department of Labor. (1984). *Dictionary of Occupational Titles.* Washington, DC: U.S. Government Printing Office.

U.S. Department of Labor, Bureau of Labor Statistics. (1982). *Employment and Earnings.* Washington, DC: U.S. Government Printing Office.

———. (1983). *Productivity and the Economy: Chartbook.* Bulletin 2171. Washington, DC: U.S. Government Printing Office.

U.S. Department of Labor, Women's Bureau. (1969a). *Fact Sheet on the Earnings Gap.* Washington, DC: U.S. Government Printing Office.

———. (1969b). *Handbook on Women Workers.* Washington, DC: U.S. Government Printing Office.

U.S. National Center for Health Statistics. (1984 and earlier annual editions). *Vital Statistics of the United States.* Washington, DC: U.S. Government Printing Office.

———. *U.S. Public Health Survey.* (1970). Washington, DC: Government Printing Office.

———. (1986). *Public Health Reports,* Vol. 101 (1, January–February).

———. (1979). *Vital Statistics of the United States: Life Tables* (Vol. 2). Washington, DC: U.S. Government Printing Office.

U.S. Office of Management and the Budget. (1973). *Social Indicators.* Washington, DC: U.S. Government Printing Office.

U.S. Senate Select Committee on Aging. (1982). *The Early-Retirement Myth: Why Men Retire Before Age 62.* Washington, DC: U.S. Government Printing Office.

U.S. Senate Special Committee on Aging. (1985). *Developments in Aging: 1984.* Washington, DC: U.S. Government Printing Office.

Ungerleider, J. Thomas, and David K. Wellisch. (1979). "Coercive Persuasion (Brainwashing), Religious

Cults, and Deprogramming." *American Journal of Psychiatry* (March 1979), 279–282.

Ungerleider, J. T., and D. K. Wellisch. (1983). "The Programming (Brainwashing)/Deprogramming Religious Controversy." In D. G. Bromley and J. T. Richardson (eds.), *The Brainwashing/Deprogramming Controversy: Sociological, Psychological, Legal, and Historical Perspectives.* New York: Edwin Mellen.

United Nations. (1979). *Trends and Characteristics of International Migration Since 1950.* New York: United Nations.

———. (1982). *Vol. I: Population Trends.* Population Studies No. 79, New York: United Nations.

———. (1985). *The Prospects of World Urbanization.* New York: United Nations.

U'Ren, Marjorie B. (1971). "The Image of Women in Textbooks." In Vivian Gornick and Barbara K. Moran (eds.), *Women in Sexist Society.* New York: Basic Books.

Vander Zanden, James W. (1972). *American Minority Relations: The Sociology of Racial and Ethnic Groups* (3d ed.). New York: Ronald Press.

———. (1981). *Human Development* (2d ed.). New York: Alfred Knopf.

———. (1983). *American Minority Relations* (4th ed.). New York: Alfred Knopf.

Vecsey, George. (1979). "Approval Given for Homosexual to Adopt a Boy." *New York Times* (June 21).

Veevers, J. E. (1972). "Factors in the Incidence of Childlessness in Canada: An Analysis of Census Data." *Social Biology,* 19.

———. (1973). "Voluntary Childless Wives." *Sociology and Social Research,* 57, 356–366.

Verba, Sidney, and Nie, Norman H. (1972). *Participation in America: Political Democracy and Social Equality.* New York: Harper and Row.

Verbrugge, Lois M., and Jennifer Madans. (1985). "Women's Roles and Health." *American Demographics,* 7 (March), 36–39.

Verdier, P. A. (1980). *Brainwashing and the Cults: An Exposé on Capturing the Human Mind.* North Hollywood, CA: Wilshire.

"Violent Families." (1979). *Time Magazine* (July 9), 55.

Visher, Emily B., and John S. Visher. (1978). "Major Areas of Difficulty for Stepparent Couples." *International Journal of Family Counseling,* 6, 71–72.

Vogel, David. (1987). "A Big Agenda: The Politics of the Environment, 1970–1987." *Wilson Quarterly* (Autumn), 51–68.

Vold, George, and Thomas Bernard. (1986). *Theoretical Criminology* (3d ed.). New York: Oxford University Press.

Wagenaar, Theodore C. (1985). "Education in Trouble." *Hillsdale* (MI) *Daily News* (August 13), 13B.

Waite, Linda, Gus Haggstrom, and David Kanouse. (1985). "The Consequences of Parenthood for the Marital Stability of Young Adults." *American Sociological Review,* 50(6), 850–857.

"Waiting to Wed." (1979). *Time Magazine* (July 16), 59.

Walker, Samuel. (1985). *Sense and Nonsense About Crime: A Policy Guide.* Monterey, CA: Brooks/Cole.

Wallace, Nancy. (1985). "Homeschooling's Unique Structure." *Mothering* (Summer), 77–81.

Wallace, Richard. (1978). *Growth of Organizations.* Ann Arbor: University Microfilms.

Wallach, M. A., N. Kogan, and D. J. Bem. (1962). "Group Influence on Individual Risk Taking." *Journal of Abnormal Social Psychology,* 65, 75–86.

Wallerstein, Immanuel. (1980). *The Modern World System II: Mercantilism and the Consolidation of the European World Economy, 1600–1750.* New York: Academic Press, Inc.

———. (1986). "Marxisms as Utopias: Evolving Ideologies." *American Journal of Sociology,* 91(6), 1295–1308.

Wallerstein, James S., and Clement J. Wyle. (1947). "Our Law-Abiding Law Breakers." *Federal Probation,* 24, 107–112.

Wallerstein, Judith, and Joan B. Kelly. (1974). "The Effects of Parental Divorce: The Adolescent Experience." In J. Anthony and C. Koupernik (eds.), *The Child and His Family: Children at Psychiatric Risk.* New York: John Wiley, 479–505.

———. (1975). "The Effects of Parental Divorce: Experience of the Preschool Child." *Journal of Child Psychiatry,* 14, 600–616.

———. (1976). "The Effects of Parental Divorce: Experiences of the Child in Early Latency." *American Journal of Orthopsychiatry,* 46, 20–32.

———. (1979). "Children and Divorce: A Review." *Social Work* (November), pp. 468–475.

———. (1980). "California's Children of Divorce." *Psychology Today,* 13, 67–76.

Wallis, Claudia. (1985). "Children Having Children." *Time Magazine,* 126 (23) (December 9), 78–90.

Walsh, Edward. (1981). "Resource Mobilization and Citizen Protest in Communities Around Three Mile Island." *Social Problems,* 29(1), 1–21.

———. (1984). "Local Community Versus National Industry: The TMI and Santa Barbara Protests Compared," *International Journal of Mass Emergencies and Disasters,* 147–163.

Walsh, Edward J., and Rex H. Warland. (1983). "Social Movement Involvement in the Wake of a Nuclear Accident; Activists and Free Riders in the Three Mile Island Area." *American Sociological Review,* 48, 764–781.

Walum-Richardson, Laurel. (1981). *The Dynamics of Sex and Gender.* Boston: Houghton Mifflin.

Walzer, M. (1983). *Spheres of Justice: A Defense of Pluralism and Equality.* New York: Basic Books.

Ward, Kathryn B. (1984). *Women in the World-System: Its Impact on Status and Fertility.* New York: Praeger Publishers.

Ward, R. A. (1979). *The Aging Experience.* New York: J. B. Lippincott.

Ward, Russell. (1984). *The Aging Experience, An Introduction to Social Gerontology.* New York: Harper and Row.

Warheit, G. J. (1979). "Life Events, Coping, Stress, and Depressive Symptomatology." *American Journal of Psychiatry* 136, 502–507.

Warner, W. Lloyd. (1937). *Black Civilization.* New York: Harper.

Warner, W. Lloyd, and Paul S. Lunt. (1941). *The Social Life of a Modern Community.* Yankee City Series (Vol. 1). New Haven: Yale University Press.

Warr, Peter. (1984). "Work and Unemployment." In P. J. D. Drenth, et al. (eds.), *Handbook of Work and Organizational Psychology.* London: Wiley.

Warr, Peter, and Roy Payne. (1983). "Social Class and Reported Changes in Behavior After Job Loss." *Journal of Applied Social Psychology.* London: Wiley.

Warren, W. Lloyd, and Leo Srole. (1945). *The Social Systems of American Ethnic Groups.* New Haven: Yale University Press.

Wasburn, Philo C. (1982). *Political Sociology: Approaches, Concepts, Hypotheses.* Englewood Cliffs, NJ: Prentice-Hall.

Watson, Russell, et al. (1984). "What Price Day Care?" *Newsweek* (104, September 10), 14–17, 19–21.

Watson, Walter N. (1982). "Family Planning Programs: Developing Countries." In John Ross (ed.), *International Encyclopedia of Population.* New York: The Free Press.

Wattenberg, Ben J. (1976). *The Real America.* New York: Capricorn.

Wax, S. L. (1948). "A Survey of the Restrictive Advertising and Discrimination by Consumer Reports in the Province of Ontario." *Canadian Jewish Congress: Information and Comment,* 7, 10–13.

Weaver, Warren, Jr. (1982). "Age Discrimination Charges Found in Sharp Rise in U.S." *New York Times* (February 22), A12.

Weber, Max. (1904, 1958). *The Protestant Ethic and the Spirit of Capitalism.* Translated by Talcott Parsons. New York: Charles Scribner's Sons.

———. (1922, 1963). *The Sociology of Religion.* Translated by Ephraim Fischoff. Boston: Beacon Press.

———. (1925, 1947). *The Theory of Social and Economic Organization.* Translated and edited by A. M. Henderson and Talcott Parsons. Glencoe, IL: Free Press.

———. (1946). *From Max Weber: Essays in Sociology.* Translated and edited by H. H. Gerth and C. Wright Mills. New York: Oxford University Press.

Weede, Erich. (1980). "Beyond Misspecification in Sociological Analysis of Income Inequality." *American Sociological Review,* 45, 497–501.

Weeks, Jeffrey. (1985). *Sexuality and Its Discontents.* London: Routledge and Kegan Paul.

Weg, R. B. (1983). "Changing Physiology of Aging: Normal and Pathological." In D. W. Woodruff and J. E. Birren (eds.), *Aging Scientific Perspectives and Social Issues* (2d ed.). Monterey, CA: Brooks/Cole.

Weisburd, David. (1979). "Unity, Conflict, and the Necessity of Reciprocal Causation in Conflict Theory." Mimeographed. New Haven: Yale University, Department of Sociology.

Weiss, Jane A., Francisco O. Ramirez, and Terry Tracy. (1976). "Female Participation in the Occupational System: A Comparative Institutional Analysis." *Social Problems,* 23, 593–608.

Weiss, Robert S. (1970). "Marriage and the Family in the Near Future." In Katherine Elliott (ed.), *The Family and Its Future.* London: Ciba Foundation.

Weiss, Robert. (1975). *Marital Separation.* New York: Basic Books.

———. (1979). "The Emotional Impact of Marital Separation." In George Levinger and Oliver Moles (eds.), *Divorce and Separation.* New York: Basic Books.

Weitzman, Lenore. (1979). *Sex Role Socialization.* Palo Alto, CA: Mayfield Press.

———. (1985). *The Divorce Revolution: The Unexpected Social and Economic Consequences for Women and Children in America.* New York: Free Press.

Weitzman, Lenore, J., and Eifler, Deborah. (1972). "Sex Role Socialization in Picture Books for Preschool Children." *American Journal of Sociology,* 77, 1125–1144.

Welch, Finis. (1981). "Economics of Affirmative Action." *The American Economic Review* (May), 132.

Welch, Susan, and John R. Hibbing. (1984). "Hispanic Representation in the U.S. Congress." *Social Science Quarterly,* 65(2), 328–335.

Weller, Robert H., and Leon Bouvier. (1981). *Population: Demography and Policy.* New York: St. Martin's Press.

Wells, Alan. (1975). *Mass Media and Society* (2d ed.). Palo Alto, CA: Mayfield Press.

Wells, H. G. (1971). *Outline of History.* New York: Doubleday.

Wences, Rosalio (1969). "Electoral Participation and the Occupational Composition of Cabinets and Parliaments." *American Journal of Sociology,* 75 (September), 181–192.

Wertlieb, Donald. (1987). Quoted in Jennet Conant, "You'd Better Sit Down, Kids." *Newsweek* (August 24), 58.

West, L. J. (1982). "Contemporary Cults: Utopian Image, Infernal Reality." *Contemporary Magazine,* 15, 10–13.

"What Makes a Good Marriage?" (1977). *Redbook,* 115, 254–262.

White, Burton. (1980). *The First Three Years of Life.* Englewood Cliffs, NJ: Prentice-Hall.

———. (1984). In Glenn Collins, "Experts Debate Impact of Day Care." *New York Times* (September 4), 311ff.

White, D. (1985). "Sixty-Five Is No Longer 'the' Retirement Age." *San Francisco Chronicle* (January 23), 30.

White, Leslie A. (1949). *The Science of Culture.* New York: Farrar, Strauss.

Whorf, Benjamin Lee. (1956). *Language, Thought, and Reality.* New York: John Wiley.

Whyte, William Foote. (1955). *Streetcorner Society.* Chicago: University of Chicago Press.

Whyte, William F., et al. (1983). *Worker Participation and Ownership: Cooperative Strategies for Strengthening Local Economies.* Ithaca, NY: ILR Press.

Wicker, Tom. (1985). "A Bloodbath Deepens." *New York Times* (January 11), 25.

———. (1975). *A Time to Die.* New York: Quadrangle.

Wilcox, B. L (1981). "Social Support in Adjusting to Marital Disruption: A Network Analysis." In B. H. Gottlieb (ed.), *Social Networks and Social Support.* New York: Russell Sage Foundation.

Wilkinson, Karen. (1974). "The Broken Family and Juvenile Delinquency: Scientific Explanations or Ideology?" *Social Problems,* 21, 726–739.

Willerman, B., and L. Swanson. (1953). "Group Prestige in Voluntary Organizations." *Human Relations,* 6, 67–77.

Williams, Dennis. (1981a). "Why Public Schools Fail." *Newsweek,* 97 (April 20), 62–65.

———. (1981b). "Grownups on Campus." *Newsweek,* 98 (December 21), 72–74.

Williams, M. J. (1985). "The Baby Bust Hits the Job Market." *Fortune* (May 27), 122–126, 135.

Williams, Robert L. (1974). "The Silent Mugging of the Black Community." *Psychology Today* (May), 32–41.

Williams, Robin M., Jr. (1960). *American Society.* New York: Random House.

———. (1970). *American Society: A Sociological Interpretation* (3d ed.). New York: Alfred A. Knopf.

———. (1983). "Values, Conflict, and Conflict Resolution." *Man, Environment, Space, and Time,* 3(2), 83–128.

Williamson, William. (1979). *Education, Social Structure, and Development.* London: Macmillan.

Willie, D. V. (1982). "Educating Students Who Are Good Enough: Is Excellence an Excuse to Exlude?" *Change* (March), 16–20.

Wills, Gary. (1978). "What Religious Revival?" *Psychology Today* (April), 74–80.

Wilson, B. R. (1981). "Time, Generations, and Sectarianism." In B. R. Wilson (ed.), *The Social Impact of New Religious Movements,* Barryton, NY: Unification Theological Seminary.

———. (1982a). *Religion in Sociological Perspective.* Oxford: Oxford University Press.

———. (1982b). "The New Religions: Some Preliminary Considerations." In E. V. Barker (ed.), *New Religious Movements: A Perspective for Understanding Society.* New York: Edwin Mellen.

———. (1985). "Secularization: The Inherited Model." In Phillip E. Hammond (ed.), *The Sacred in a Secular Age.* Berkeley: University of California Press, 9–20.

Wilson, Edward O. (1975). *Sociobiology: The New Synthesis.* Cambridge: Harvard University Press.

———. (1978). *On Human Nature.* Cambridge: Harvard University Press.

Wilson, James, and Richard Herrnstein. (1985). *Crime and Human Nature.* New York: Simon and Schuster.

Wilson, John. (1973). *Introduction to Social Movements.* New York: Basic Books.

Wilson, Stephen. (1976). *Informal Groups: An Introduction.* Englewood Cliffs, NJ: Prentice-Hall.

Wilson, Suzanne. (1986). "Child Abuse: A Critical Issue in Our Society." *Scouting* (September), 36–37, 66–68.

Wilson, William J. (1984). "The Black Underclass." *Wilson Quarterly* (Spring), 88–89.

Wilson, William Julius. (1980). *The Declining Significance of Race: Blacks and Changing American Institutions* (2d ed.). Chicago: University of Chicago Press.

Winch, Robert F. (1963). *The Modern Family.* New York: Holt, Rinehart & Winston.

———. (1973). "Courtship and Mate Selection." In Ellis and Arabel (eds.), *Encyclopedia of Sexual Behavior,* New York: Hawthorn Books.

Winch, Robert F., and Rae Lesser Blumberg. (1963). "Societal Complexity and Familial Organization." In Robert F. Winch and Louis Wolf Goodman (eds.), *Selected Studies in Marriage and the Family* (3d ed.). New York: Holt, Rinehart & Winston.

Winch, Robert F., and Rae Blumberg. (1972). "Societal Complexity and Familial Complexity." *American Journal of Sociology,* 77 (March), 898–920.

Winch, Robert F., Thomas Ktsanes, and Virginia Ktsanes. (1954). "The Theory of Complementary Needs in Mate Selection: An Analytic and Descriptive Study." *American Sociological Review* 19(3), 241–249.

Winn, Marie. (1983). *Children Without Childhood.* New York: Pantheon Books.

Winick, Myron. (1976). *Malnutrition and Brain Development.* New York: Oxford University Press.

———. (1980). "Nutrition and Brain Development." *Natural History,* 89(12), 6–13.

Winter, David, Abigail Steward, and David McClelland. (1977). *Journal of Personality and Social Psychology,* 35(3), "Husband's motives and wife's career level," p. 159–166.

Wirth, Louis. (1938). "Urbanism as a Way of Life." *American Journal of Sociology,* 44.

Wirth, Louis. (1945). "The Problem of Minority Groups." In Ralph Linton (ed.), *The Science of Man in the World Crisis.* New York: Columbia University Press.

Wolfinger, Raymond E., and Steven J. Rosenstone. (1980). *Who Votes?* New Haven: Yale University Press.

Womack, John, Jr. (1972). "The Chicanos." *New York Review of Books,* 19(3), 12–18.

"Women March on Houston." (1977). *Time Magazine* (November 27).

World Almanac and Book of Facts. (1980). New York: Newspaper Enterprise Association.

Wright, Erik Olin. (1983). "Is Marxism Really Functionalist, Class Reductionist, and Teleologist?" *American Journal of Sociology,* 89, 452–457.

———. (1984). "A General Framework for the Analysis of Class Structure." *Politics and Society,* 13(4), 383–423.

Wright, Erik Olin, and Bill Martin. (1987). "The Transformation of the American Class Structure: 1960–1980." *American Journal of Sociology,* 93, 1–29.

Wright, James. (1978). "Are Working Women Really More Satisfied? Evidence from Several National Surveys." *Journal of Marriage and the Family,* 40 (May), 301–313.

Wright, S. A. (1983). *A Sociological Study of Defection from Controversial New Religious Movements.* Ph.D. thesis, Storrs, CT: University of Connecticut.

———. (1984). "Postinvolvement Attitudes of Voluntary Defectors from Controversial New Religious Movements." *Journal for the Scientific Study of Religion,* 23, 172–182.

Wuthnow, Robert. (1976). "The New Religions in Social Context." In Charles Glock and Robert Bellah (eds.), *The New Religious Consciousness.* Berkeley: University of California Press.

Wuthnow, Robert, and Charles Y. Glock. (1974). "God in the Gut." *Psychology Today,* 8, 131–136.

Yamaguchi, Kazuo. (1987). "Models for Comparing Mobility Tables: Toward Parsimony and Substance." *American Sociological Review,* 52, 482–494.

Yankelovich, Daniel. (1981). *New Rules.* New York: Random House.

Yarrow, Marian Radke, et al. (1955). "The Psychological Meaning of Mental Illness in the Family." *Journal of Social Issues,* 11(4), 12–24.

Yaukey, David. (1985). *Demography: The Study of Human Population.* New York: St. Martin's Press.

Yetman, Norman. (1985). *Majority and Minority: The Dynamics of Race and Ethnicity in American Life* (4th ed.). Boston: Allyn and Bacon.

Yinger, J. Milton. (1960). "Contraculture and Subculture." *American Sociological Review,* 25(5), 625–635.

Yorburg, Betty. (1983). *Families and Societies: Survival or Extinction.* New York: Columbia University Press.

———. (1974). *Sexual Identity: Sex Roles.* Melbourne, FL: Kreiger.

Young, Paul Thomas. (1943). *Emotion in Man and Animal.* New York: John Wiley.

Yunker, James A. (1982). "The Relevance of the Identification Problem to Statistical Research on Capital Punishment." *Crime and Delinquency,* 28, 96–124.

Zarit. S. H., N. K. Orr, and J. M. Zarit. (1985). *Caring for the Patients with Alzheimer's Disease: Families Under Stress.* New York: New York University Press.

Zeitlin, Maurice, Kenneth Lutterman, and James Russell. (1973). "Death in Vietnam: Class, Poverty, and the Risks of War." *Politics and Society,* 3 (Spring), 313–328.

Zigler, Edward. (1976). "Project Head Start: Success or Failure?" *Children Today* November–December, 2–7, 36.

———. (1984). In Glenn Collins, "Experts Debate Impact of Day Care." *New York Times* (September 4), 311ff.

Zill, Nicholas. (1984). Data from Child Trends, Inc., national survey, reported in "Kids Aren't Broken by the Breakup," *USA Today* (December 20), 5D.

Zimbardo, Philip Y. (1972). "Pathology of Imprisonment." *Society,* 9, 4–8.

Zimmerman, Carle C., and Lucius F. Cervates. (1960). *Successful American Families.* New York: Pageant Press.

INDEX

About the Authors

Richard and Wendy Wallace began their collaborative work twenty-three years ago while undergraduates at the University of Michigan. After brief careers in other disciplines, both focused their talents on sociology with an eye toward improving our social world. Richard earned his doctorate at Yale University and Wendy pursued her Masters of Social Work from the University of Connecticut. They have taught at various colleges and universities in the east, midwest, and south, including Yale University, Temple University, University of Hartford, Hillsdale College, and Berry College. Presently Wendy teaches at Spring Arbor College, Richard teaches at the University of Michigan, and they reside outside of Ann Arbor, Michigan.

Richard and Wendy have studied a variety of interesting and important issues including why organizations grow, how judges sentence felons from various social backgrounds, the social profile of drunk-driving fatalities, and how to apply sociology to areas as diverse as housing problems, marriage, and parenting. Their works appear in many publications, including American Sociological Association journals, major newspapers, and popular magazines such as *Redbook*.

From the start, the Wallaces have been most interested in teaching and promoting the teaching of introductory sociology. Generalists at heart, they enjoy the challenge of presenting this multifaceted field to students in an interesting, memorable, and scholastically solid format. They have learned a great deal from their students while pursuing this goal over the years, and many of the examples that they use in this and the first edition of their book are drawn directly from their students' lives. They look forward to many more years of such contact with the future generation of sociologists.